the AMERICANA ANNUAL

1988

AN ENCYCLOPEDIA OF THE EVENTS OF 1987

YEARBOOK OF THE ENCYCLOPEDIA AMERICANA

This annual has been prepared as a yearbook for general encyclopedias. It is also published as *Encyclopedia Year Book*.

Library of Congress Catalog Card Number: 23-10041

ISBN: 0-7172-0219-4
ISSN: 0196-0180

Printed and manufactured in the United States of America

Contents

Feature Articles of the Year

The Alphabetical Section

Entries on the continents, major nations of the world, U.S. states, Canadian provinces, and chief cities will be found under their own alphabetical headings.

© Owen Franken/Picture Group

The Year in Review

Shouts of "Sell! Sell! Sell!" broke out on the floor of the New York Stock Exchange on what would become known as "Black Monday," October 19. By the closing bell, the Dow Jones industrial average had plummeted a record 508.32 points—22.6%.

In the kaleidoscope of events and people—of weapons and treaties, of scandals and celebrations, of world leaders and victims of war, disaster, and plague—1987 may well be remembered as a year of altered perceptions, perhaps of turning tides. Almost everywhere, it seemed, there were shifts in policy, changes in goals and expectations, and some rude awakenings that brought new perspectives, if not promise, to longstanding problems and conflicts.

At a December summit in Washington, U.S. President Ronald Reagan and Soviet General Secretary Mikhail Gorbachev signed a treaty on the elimination of intermediate-range nuclear forces. The signing came 14 months after the stalemate at Reykjavik.

The fighting continued in Central America, but the presidents of five nations gathered in Guatemala City to sign a breakthrough regional peace agreement. President Oscar Arias Sánchez of Costa Rica, the main architect of the plan, was awarded the 1987 Nobel Peace Prize.

In its seventh year, the Iran-Iraq war entered a new phase, as foreign vessels in the Persian Gulf were repeatedly attacked or struck by mines. American warships began escorting reflagged Kuwaiti tankers; one U.S. vessel, the Navy frigate *Stark,* was "accidentally" attacked by an Iraqi plane. The key diplomatic change was a new Arab unity in support of Iraq.

Higher levels of tension and shifting political climates were witnessed in a number of other nations. The war in Afghanistan dragged on, but speculation of a Soviet pullout increased. In South Korea, escalating public protests forced the nation's first presidential election, but the outcome little assuaged the opposition. Haiti's first free elections in 30 years were called off at the last minute amid a wave of violence. Voters in the Philippines approved a new constitution, but the government of President Corazon Aquino remained fragile. In Israel, the long-festering issue of Palestinian autonomy erupted in the West Bank and Gaza late in the year. Libya and Chad agreed to a cease-fire in their border conflict, but a peace agreement in Sri Lanka's bitter civil war had little effect.

It was an historic year in Canada, highlighted by an agreement to bring Quebec into the nation's constitution and by the conclusion of a free-trade pact with the United States.

Prime Minister Margaret Thatcher won reelection in Britain, as did Chancellor Helmut Kohl in West Germany. Japan got a new premier, Noboru Takeshita, and China's Prime Minister Zhao Ziyang was elevated to party general secretary.

It was a year of transition in the United States as well. On October 19, dubbed "Black Monday," the New York Stock Exchange (*photo, opposite page*) suffered the worst day in its history, as the Dow Jones plunged 508.32 points. *Newsweek* called it the "final collapse of the money culture . . . , the death knell of the '80s." Meanwhile, the federal budget exceeded $1 trillion for the first time, the trade deficit soared ever higher, and the value of the dollar plummeted.

The bicentennial of the U.S. Constitution served as a backdrop to pitched battles between the legislative and executive branches. Congress held televised hearings on secret White House arms sales to Iran and the diversion of funds to "contra" rebels in Nicaragua; Marine Lt. Col. Oliver North admitted to having lied to Congress but emerged, for a time, as a national hero. Later, the Senate rejected the nomination of Judge Robert Bork to the Supreme Court on the grounds of his judicial philosophy. Reagan's next nominee, Judge Douglas Ginsburg, withdrew from consideration after admitting to past marijuana use.

As the Reagan era entered its twilight—an impression reinforced by the departure of several high officials—six Republicans and eight Democrats were campaigning for their party's nominations in 1988. Democrats Joseph Biden and Gary Hart had quit the race amid scandal; Hart later returned.

Other highlights: The Soviets set a space endurance record. Pope John Paul II made a nine-city U.S. tour. *Platoon* won the Oscar for best picture; *Les Misérables* was the big hit on Broadway. Dennis Conner won back the America's Cup; football fans endured another strike. Hemlines were up, and a Van Gogh sold for $53.9 million.

THE EDITORS

January

2 Penn State upsets Miami, 14–10, in the Fiesta Bowl to win the unofficial national championship of college football.

4 In an upsurge of fighting between Libya and Chad—and rebel forces on both sides—Libyan jets bomb targets in southern Chad.

An Amtrak train collides with three diesel engines north of Baltimore, MD, leaving 16 people dead and dozens injured.

5 U.S. President Reagan submits to Congress a $1.024 trillion federal budget for fiscal 1988.

President Reagan undergoes "routine" prostate surgery.

6 The 100th U.S. Congress convenes, with the Democrats controlling both the House of Representatives and the Senate.

8 The Dow Jones average of industrial stocks surpasses the 2,000 mark.

9 Iran launches a major offensive in its war against Iraq.

10 Japan's Yasuhiro Nakasone begins an official seven-day visit to Eastern Europe, the first ever by a Japanese prime minister.

13 Mohammed Ali Hamadei, a Lebanese suspect in the June 1985 hijacking of a TWA jet to Beirut, is arrested in West Germany.

France's state-owned rail and electric companies restore full service after workers end four weeks of strikes.

14 Austria's two largest political parties form a "Grand Coalition" government. Socialist Franz Vranitzky remains chancellor.

15 The Soviet-backed government of Afghanistan begins a cease-fire, announced January 1, in its war against Muslim rebels. Resistance leaders, however, have rejected the plan as a "trap."

The seventh round of U.S.-Soviet arms talks opens in Geneva. Yuli Vorontsov takes over as the Soviet chief negotiator.

16 In the wake of widespread student demonstrations for democratic reform, Hu Yaobang is ousted as general secretary of the Chinese Communist Party. Premier Zhao Ziyang takes over temporarily.

Ecuador's President León Febres-Cordero is kidnapped by renegade air force troops. He is released after 12 hours in exchange for a general who had been arrested for rebellion.

20 Anglican church envoy Terry Waite disappears during a mission to Lebanon to seek the release of Western hostages.

In his ongoing efforts to gain the release of Western hostages in Lebanon, Anglican church envoy Terry Waite (right, with Druse guard) *returned to Beirut on January 12. Eight days later he disappeared.*

AP/Wide World

21 Japan's Finance Minister Kiichi Miyazawa holds an emergency meeting in Washington with U.S. Secretary of the Treasury James Baker on the declining value of the dollar. No intervention is planned.

22 The U.S. Commerce Department reports that the gross national product grew 2.5% in 1986, the lowest rate since 1982.

24 Three U.S. teachers and an Indian professor are taken hostage in Lebanon.

25 West German Chancellor Helmut Kohl and his center-right coalition are returned to power in general elections.

The New York Giants defeat Denver, 39–20, in Super Bowl XXI.

27 In a speech to the Communist Party Central Committee, Soviet leader Mikhail Gorbachev calls for major political reforms.

President Reagan gives his sixth State of the Union address.

The United States and Mongolia establish diplomatic relations.

28 Former Philippine President Ferdinand Marcos is foiled in a plan to return from exile. One day earlier, a coup attempt by dissident soldiers also was foiled.

U.S. Secretary of State George Shultz holds talks in Washington with African National Congress (ANC) President Oliver Tambo.

29 After winning trade concessions from the European Community, the Reagan administration cancels plans to impose 200% duties on agricultural products from EC countries.

The Organization of the Islamic Conference concludes a three-day summit in Kuwait. Iran boycotted the meeting.

© Markel/Gamma-Liaison

Politically weakened by the Iran-contra scandal, President Reagan delivered his sixth State of the Union message on January 27. He called the failure of his Iran initiative the "one major regret" of his presidency, but he added, "The goals were worthy."

February

2 Voters in the Philippines overwhelmingly approve a draft constitution, confirming the government of President Corazon Aquino.

William J. Casey, recovering from the removal of a cancerous brain tumor, resigns as head of the U.S. Central Intelligence Agency.

4 The U.S. Congress overrides President Reagan's veto of the $20 billion Clean Water Bill, making it law.

The U.S. yacht *Stars & Stripes*, skippered by Dennis Conner, wins the America's Cup by completing a four-race sweep of Australia's *Kookaburra III* off Fremantle, Australia.

In a national referendum on February 2, the Philippines' 25 million registered voters turned out in heavy numbers and gave overwhelming support for the draft constitution of the fledgling Aquino government. Strong pro-constitution majorities were registered in nearly every region of the country.

AP/Wide World

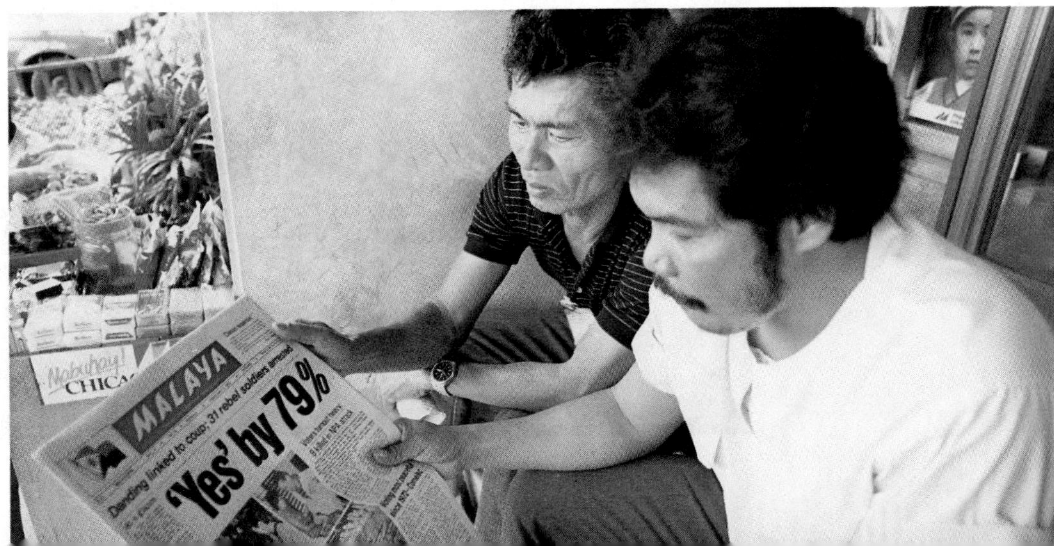

5 The Soviet Union announces the end of its moratorium on nuclear testing. The move comes, as threatened, after the first U.S. underground nuclear test of 1987, held two days earlier.

9 Former U.S. National Security Adviser Robert McFarlane, a key figure in the Iran-contra arms affair, is hospitalized after an apparent suicide attempt.

10 Moscow announces that 140 political dissidents have been officially pardoned and released from prisons and labor camps.

13 Martin A. Siegel, a 38-year-old investment banker, pleads guilty to criminal charges involving insider trading. On February 12, three other investment bankers were charged with insider-trading violations as a result of evidence supplied by Siegel.

15 Major new fighting breaks out in West Beirut, Lebanon, between Shiite Amal militiamen and Druse-led leftist factions.

17 James H. Webb is named to succeed John F. Lehman as U.S. secretary of the Navy. Lehman's resignation was announced on February 12.

19 In the first of a series of planned pullbacks, India and Pakistan complete the withdrawal of 150,000 troops from their border.

20 The government of Brazil announces that it is suspending interest payments on debts to foreign commercial banks.

The Soviet Union frees noted Jewish dissident Iosif Begun.

22 In Paris, finance ministers of the United States and five major allies announce an agreement to stabilize their currencies.

26 A presidential commission appointed to study the U.S. National Security Council issues its report. The commission, headed by former Sen. John Tower, concludes that the "chaos" of the Iran-contra dealings resulted from President Reagan's detached "management style" and the dishonesty of some staff members.

27 Donald T. Regan resigns as White House chief of staff. President Reagan names former Sen. Howard H. Baker as his replacement.

28 Soviet leader Mikhail Gorbachev calls for an agreement with the United States, not linked to any other arms-control issue, on the elimination of medium-range nuclear missiles from Europe.

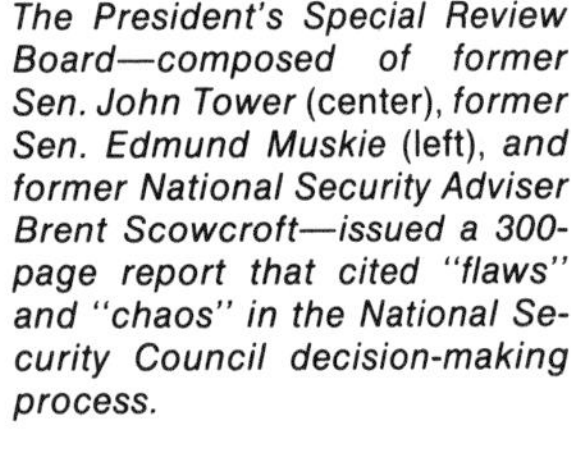

The President's Special Review Board—composed of former Sen. John Tower (center), *former Sen. Edmund Muskie* (left), *and former National Security Adviser Brent Scowcroft—issued a 300-page report that cited "flaws" and "chaos" in the National Security Council decision-making process.*

March

3 President Reagan withdraws his nomination of Robert M. Gates as director of the Central Intelligence Agency and names FBI director William H. Webster to head the agency.

6 A British ferryboat capsizes in the English Channel off the coast of Belgium. Of 543 people aboard, 188 are believed dead.

A two-day series of earthquakes in northeastern Ecuador leaves at least 300 people dead and 4,000 missing.

9 Chrysler Corporation announces that it has agreed to acquire American Motors Corporation for some $1.5 billion.

10 Following general elections February 17, Ireland's parliament elects Charles Haughey of Fianna Fail as prime minister.

The Vatican issues a statement condemning artificial fertilization and calling on governments to outlaw surrogate motherhood.

13 Reputed Mafia boss John Gotti is acquitted of federal racketeering and conspiracy charges in New York City.

17 At the 40-nation Geneva Committee disarmament talks, the USSR proposes an international agency to bar deployment of space weapons.

18 The U.S. Senate votes against a measure to block payment to Nicaraguan contras of $40 million in aid remaining from a package approved in 1986. The House had passed a similar resolution.

Former Reagan aide Michael Deaver is indicted for perjury in testimony to a grand jury and Congress regarding his lobbying activities after leaving the White House in May 1985.

19 Television evangelist Jim Bakker resigns his PTL Club ministry after admitting to an extramarital sexual encounter in 1980.

23 A faction of the Red Brigades terrorist organization claims responsibility for the March 20 shooting and death of an Italian general in Rome.

25 In his keynote address at the 16-day annual session of China's National People's Congress, Premier Zhao Ziyang backs economic reform but assails "bourgeois liberalization."

The U.S. Supreme Court upholds, 6–3, a voluntary affirmative action plan for public employees to correct sex discrimination.

26 A month-long series of strikes by workers in Yugoslavia, in protest of emergency wage controls, comes to an end.

Chinese and Portuguese officials initial a joint declaration to return Macao to mainland rule on Dec. 20, 1999.

27 President Reagan announces retaliatory duties of 100% on a variety of Japanese consumer electronic goods.

U.S. military prosecutors charge that two Marine guards at the American embassy in Moscow, Sgt. Clayton Lonetree and Cpl. Arnold Bracy, had given Soviet agents access to sensitive areas.

Chad announces that it has retaken the town of Faya-Largeau, the last major stronghold of the Libyan army in northern Chad.

28 Britain's Margaret Thatcher arrives in the USSR for a four-day visit, the first by a British prime minister in 12 years.

Turkey and Greece take steps to avoid open conflict in a new dispute over oil rights in the Aegean Sea.

29 Voters in Haiti overwhelmingly approve a new constitution, providing for a return to democratic civilian government.

30 The Indiana Hoosiers defeat the Syracuse Orangemen, 74–73, to win the NCAA Division I men's college basketball championship.

At the 59th Academy Awards ceremony in Los Angeles, *Platoon* wins the Oscar for best picture.

© J.L. Atlan/Sygma

William H. Webster, serving as director of the FBI since 1978, was nominated by President Reagan on March 3 to become head of the Central Intelligence Agency. The 62-year-old Missourian, a former federal judge, would succeed the late William J. Casey.

Marlee Matlin (center) *shares the joy of winning an Oscar with her parents. She was named best actress for her first screen performance, as a deaf woman in "Children of a Lesser God." Matlin, who is deaf, signed her acceptance speech.*

Photos AP/Wide World

31 A New Jersey state judge rules that a surrogate motherhood contract is "constitutionally protected" and awards custody of the child—known as "Baby M"—to the biological father. All parental rights of the surrogate are terminated.

The National Assembly of Suriname approves a draft constitution that opens the way for elections later in the year.

April

2 The U.S. Congress overrides President Reagan's veto of an $87.5 billion highway and mass-transit bill, making it law.

6 President Reagan and Canada's Prime Minister Brian Mulroney conclude their third annual summit in Ottawa. Free trade and acid rain dominated the two days of talks.

The National Democratic Party of President Hosni Mubarak retains a commanding majority in Egypt's parliamentary elections.

7 Chicago Mayor Harold Washington wins reelection.

9 Amid strained relations over his reform initiatives, Soviet leader Mikhail Gorbachev begins a two-day visit to Czechoslovakia.

12 Texaco Inc. files for bankruptcy after failing to settle a $12 billion legal dispute with Pennzoil Co.

13 Pope John Paul II concludes a 13-day trip to South America.

14 Turkey applies for membership in the European Community.

15 U.S. Secretary of State George Shultz ends a three-day visit to Moscow, during which General Secretary Gorbachev offered to eliminate shorter-range intermediate nuclear missiles from Europe.

20 The United States deports accused Nazi war criminal Karl Linnas to the USSR, where he has already been sentenced to death.

21 In Sri Lanka, a terrorist bombing and an armed attack by Tamil rebels four days earlier leaves hundreds of people dead.

For the second time in two days, a rebellion in the Argentine military is peacefully suppressed.

22 A strike by black South African railway workers erupts in violence as police in Johannesburg open fire and kill at least six.

The U.S. Supreme Court rejects, 5–4, a challenge to the death penalty on the grounds of racially biased sentencing procedures.

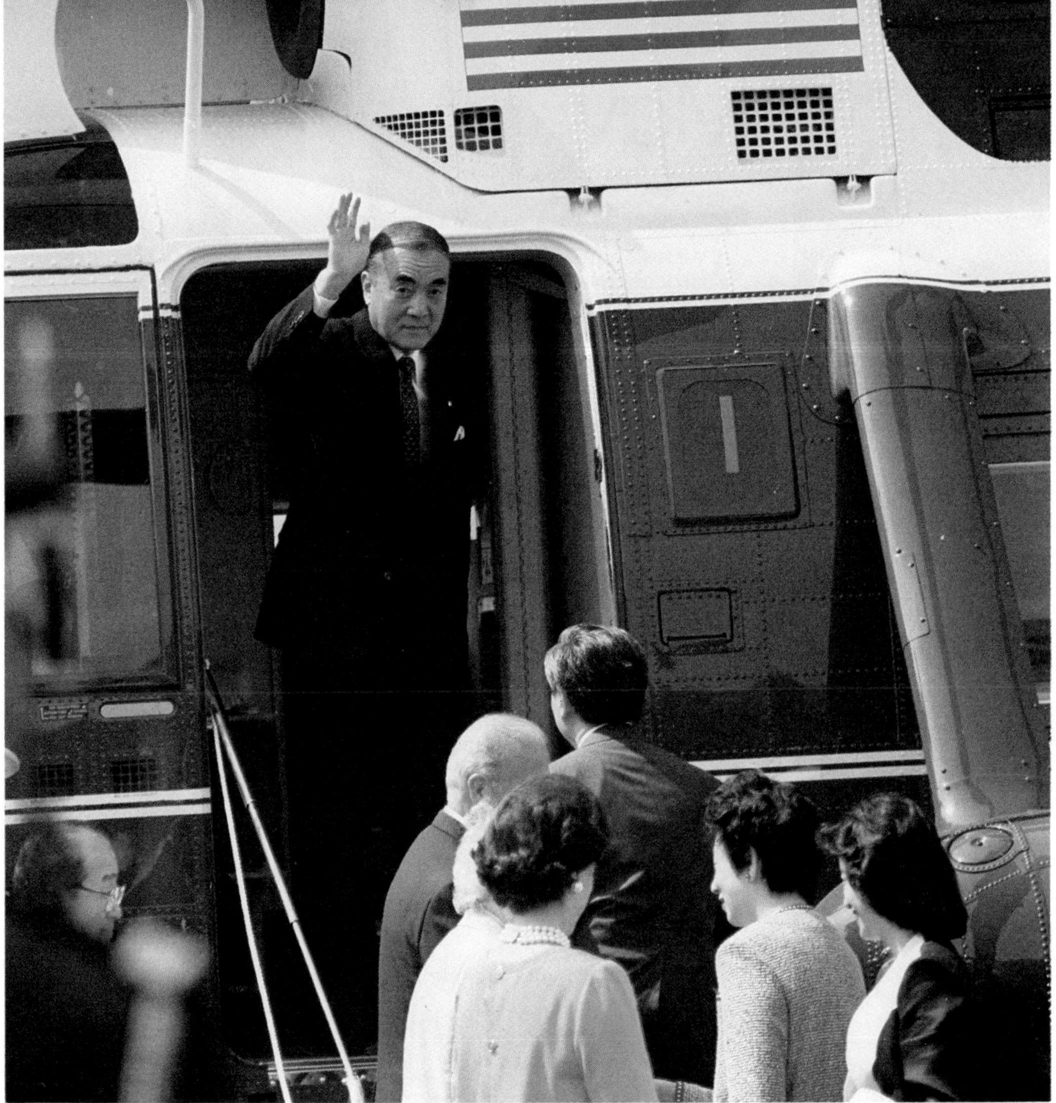

Japan's Prime Minister Yasuhiro Nakasone leaves Washington May 2, after two days of talks with President Reagan. The leaders issued a statement calling for a reduction of the "politically unsustainable" trade imbalance between their countries.

23 Golkar, Indonesia's ruling political organization, wins a record 73% majority in national elections.

25 South African troops raid southern Zambia and kill five alleged ANC terrorists; Zambia claims the victims were civilians.

26 Feuding factions of the Palestine Liberation Organization end talks in Algeria with a reconciliation under the leadership of Yasir Arafat.

27 The United States bars entry to Austria's President Kurt Waldheim on the grounds of his suspected participation in Nazi war crimes during World War II.

28 Italy's ten-day-old government of Christian Democratic Prime Minister Amintore Fanfani loses a vote of confidence, and parliament is dissolved. The government crisis began with the March 3 resignation of Socialist Prime Minister Bettino Craxi.

29 Amid growing trade tensions, Japan's Prime Minister Yasuhiro Nakasone arrives in Washington for talks with President Reagan.

30 In Finland, a four-party coalition, led by new Prime Minister Harri Holkeri and his conservative Kokoomus Party, is sworn in. General elections concluded March 16.

Agriculture Secretary Richard E. Lyng announces that the USSR has agreed to buy 4 million metric tons of subsidized American wheat.

© Ron Dirito/Sygma

Gary Hart ended his campaign for the Democratic presidential nomination after newspaper reports of an extramarital tryst. "We're all going to have to seriously question the system for selecting our national leaders," he said, "for it reduces the press of this nation to hunters. . . ."

May

2 Alysheba wins the 113th running of the Kentucky Derby.

4 President Chadli Benjedid of Algeria and King Hassan II of Morocco hold talks on the 11-year-old war in the Western Sahara.

5 U.S. Senate and House committees investigating the Iran-contra affair open joint public hearings on Capitol Hill.

Some 50,000 illegal aliens turn out at special offices of the U.S. Immigration and Naturalization Service to take advantage of the amnesty program established under 1986 legislation.

6 In whites-only parliamentary elections, South Africa's President Pieter W. Botha and his Nationalist Party are returned to power.

8 Democratic presidential candidate Gary Hart withdraws from the race. The move comes five days after a newspaper report that a young woman apparently had stayed with him overnight in his Washington home.

The United States offers the Soviet Union a draft treaty on the reduction of strategic offensive nuclear weapons, calling for 50% cuts over seven years.

11 U.S. Attorney General Edwin Meese asks for an independent criminal investigation of his ties with Wedtech Corporation, a New York defense contractor that is already the subject of several probes.

Supporters of President Aquino do well in national legislative elections in the Philippines.

12 Guatemala's President Marco Vinicio Cerezo begins a three-day visit to the United States, the first by a Guatemalan leader in nearly 100 years.

Eddie Fenech Adami of the Nationalist Party is sworn in as prime minister of Malta. General elections were held May 9.

14 One month after being installed, Fiji's Prime Minister Timoci Bavadra and his cabinet are ousted in a coup. Lt. Col. Sitiveni Rabuka names a new government, with himself as chief executive.

17 The U.S.S. *Stark,* a Navy frigate on patrol in the Persian Gulf, is struck by missiles fired from an Iraqi warplane, killing 37 U.S. sailors. Iraq apologizes and calls the attack an accident.

19 Citicorp, the largest bank in the United States, puts $3 billion in reserve to cover expected losses from Third World loans.

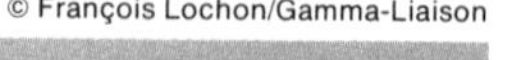

© François Lochon/Gamma-Liaison

In an apparently accidental attack on May 17, the U.S.S. "Stark" was struck by missiles from an Iraqi jet while on patrol in the Persian Gulf. The damaged frigate had to be towed to Bahrain for repairs.

© J.L. Atlan/Sygma

The bodies of the 37 U.S. sailors killed in the attack on the "Stark" arrived at Dover (DE) Air Force Base on May 26. In a memorial service four days earlier, President Reagan hailed the victims as "ordinary men who did extraordinary things."

24 Al Unser wins his fourth Indianapolis 500 auto race.

25 Former U.S. Secretary of Labor Raymond J. Donovan is acquitted of larceny and fraud charges by a jury in New York City.

At the start of a five-day visit to Canada, France's President François Mitterrand addresses a joint session of Parliament.

26 The U.S. Supreme Court upholds, 6–3, the "preventive detention" of dangerous suspects prior to trial.

28 A top Cuban military officer, Brig. Gen. Rafael del Piño Diaz, defects to the United States.

29 At the close of a two-day summit in East Berlin, leaders of the Warsaw Pact call for direct talks with NATO.

30 The Soviet Politburo dismisses Defense Minister Sergei Sokolov. The action comes one day after a young West German pilot flew unimpeded over Soviet airspace and landed his private plane in Moscow's Red Square.

31 The Edmonton Oilers win hockey's Stanley Cup championship.

Alan Greenspan, 61, who had served as chairman of the Council of Economic Advisers under President Ford, was named to succeed Paul Volcker as chairman of the Federal Reserve Board. Volcker's retirement and Greenspan's nomination were announced on June 2.

© Ted Thai/Sygma

June

1 Lebanon's Prime Minister Rashid Karami, who tendered his resignation May 4, is killed in a bomb explosion aboard a military helicopter.

West Germany announces qualified acceptance of a Soviet proposal, called the "double-zero option," to rid Europe of shorter- and longer-range intermediate nuclear missiles.

3 U.S. Rep. Mario Biaggi (D-NY) is indicted on federal racketeering charges for his alleged dealings with the Wedtech Corporation.

Prime Minister Brian Mulroney and the premiers of Canada's ten provinces sign the final version of an agreement to bring Quebec into the 1982 federal constitution.

4 India airlifts food and medicine to besieged Tamil rebels in neighboring Sri Lanka.

© Cavendish-Reflex/Picture Group

Margaret Thatcher of Great Britain became that nation's first prime minister since 1827 to be elected to a third consecutive term, as her Conservative Party won a strong victory in June 11 elections. Meanwhile in South Korea, below, a three-week surge of rioting and demonstrations in June finally forced the military regime of President Chun Doo Hwan to promise election of the next president by direct popular vote.

5 The Third International Conference on Acquired Immune Deficiency Syndrome (AIDS) concludes after four days in Washington, DC. Some 6,000 scientists and health professionals from 50 nations attended the meeting.

8 Pope John Paul II begins a seven-day visit to his native Poland.

After a ten-day investigation, a special U.S. State Department panel calls for an overhaul of the chancery building of the new U.S. Embassy in Moscow to rid it of Soviet bugging devices.

10 Leaders of the seven major industrial democracies conclude their three-day, 13th annual economic summit in Venice, Italy.

East Germany and China restore formal diplomatic relations.

11 Britain's Prime Minister Margaret Thatcher is elected to a third consecutive term, as her Conservative Party wins 375 of 650 seats in Parliament.

12 Speaking at the Brandenburg Gate in West Berlin, President Reagan calls on the Soviet Union to "tear down" the Berlin Wall.

In the Central African Republic, former Emperor Jean Bedel Bokassa is convicted and sentenced to death for ordering the murder of at least 20 political opponents during his rule.

14 The Los Angeles Lakers defeat the Boston Celtics in the sixth game of the best-of-seven final play-off series to win their tenth National Basketball Association championship.

16 U.S. arms negotiators in Geneva propose the complete global elimination of U.S. and Soviet intermediate nuclear forces.

New York subway gunman Bernhard Goetz is acquitted of attempted murder in the December 1984 shooting of four black youths.

17 U.S. journalist Charles Glass is taken hostage in Lebanon.

18 After a week of nationwide antigovernment protests, rioting students battle police in the streets of Seoul, South Korea.

19 The U.S. Supreme Court strikes down, 7–2, a Louisiana law requiring public schools that teach evolution to teach "creation science" as well.

© Charlie Cole/Picture Group

A car bombing in Barcelona, Spain, leaves 17 persons dead. The Basque separatist organization ETA claims responsibility.

Prime Minister Lynden Pindling of the Bahamas wins a sixth term, as his Progressive Liberal Party scores an easy election victory.

24 West Germany announces that it will try suspected Lebanese terrorist Mohammed Ali Hamadei on charges of murder and air piracy, rather than extradite him to the United States.

25 Amid criticism from the international Jewish community, Pope John Paul II gives an audience to Austria's President Kurt Waldheim, suspected of participating in Nazi war crimes.

After a two-day plenum of the Communist Party Central Committee, Soviet General Secretary Gorbachev calls for a "radical reorganization of economic management."

28 The Organization of the Petroleum Exporting Countries (OPEC) concludes a three-day meeting in Vienna, Austria, after agreeing to limit combined oil production to 16.6 million barrels per day.

July

1 After weeks of growing political violence, South Korea's President Chun Doo Hwan gives in to opposition demands and promises direct popular election of the next president.

President Reagan nominates U.S. Appeals Court Judge Robert H. Bork to replace Lewis F. Powell, Jr., as an associate justice of the U.S. Supreme Court. Justice Powell announced his retirement June 26.

4 Former Nazi Klaus Barbie is convicted by a French court of crimes against humanity and is sentenced to life in prison.

5 Australia's Pat Cash upsets Ivan Lendl to win the men's singles tennis title at Wimbledon. Martina Navratilova defeated Steffi Graf the day before for her sixth straight women's crown at Wimbledon.

7 Lt. Col. Oliver North begins testimony before the U.S. House and Senate committees investigating the Iran-contra scandal.

A total of 72 Indian Hindus are dead after two days of bus attacks by radical Sikh separatists.

11 The Australian Labor Party, led by Prime Minister Bob Hawke, wins national general elections for the third straight time.

12 White South African dissidents and exiled black leaders of the African National Congress (ANC) conclude three days of talks in Dakar, Senegal.

13 Backed by Prime Minister Rajiv Gandhi, Ramaswami Venkataraman is elected president of India.

14 In the worst terrorist incident in the modern history of Pakistan, two car-bomb explosions in Karachi leave at least 72 people dead.

16 Lyn Nofziger, a longtime political adviser to President Reagan, is indicted by a federal grand jury for his alleged lobbying activities on behalf of the Wedtech Corporation.

17 France breaks off diplomatic relations with Iran in a dispute over an Iranian national, wanted by France for questioning, who took refuge in the Iranian embassy in Paris.

Brazil's President José Sarney and Argentina's President Raúl Alfonsín sign ten accords stemming from the mutual integration and development pact reached in 1986.

19 Portugal's Social Democratic Party wins an absolute majority in national parliamentary elections. Prime Minister Aníbal Cavaco Silva is returned to office.

Australia's Pat Cash, the 11th seed, won the men's singles tennis title at Wimbledon. In the finals July 5, he defeated top-seeded Ivan Lendl in straight sets, 7-6, 6-2, 7-5.

AP/Wide World

21 The government of Mozambique reports that rightist rebels have massacred 386 civilians in the southern town of Homoine.

22 Soviet leader Gorbachev discloses that the Kremlin is willing to accept global elimination of intermediate nuclear weapons.

U.S. Navy warships begin escorting Kuwaiti oil tankers, sailing under American flags, into the Persian Gulf.

24 Crew members of an Air Afrique jetliner overpower a Lebanese hijacker during a refueling stop at the Geneva airport.

President Reagan names U.S. District Judge William S. Sessions as director of the Federal Bureau of Investigation (FBI).

25 U.S. Secretary of Commerce Malcolm Baldrige is killed in a freak rodeo accident in Walnut Creek, CA.

29 India and Sri Lanka sign an agreement to end the four-year-old rebellion of Sri Lanka's Tamil minority. However, the chief rebel group and many of the Sinhalese majority reject the accord, and violence continues.

Giovanni Goria, a Christian Democrat, is sworn in as premier of Italy, ending a political crisis that began with the March 3 resignation of Socialist Prime Minister Bettino Craxi.

31 Thousands of protesting Iranians clash with Saudi police during the Muslim *hajj,* or annual pilgrimage, near the Grand Mosque in Mecca. Some 400 people die in the rioting.

August

AP/Wide World

Prime Minister David Lange of New Zealand was reelected August 15, as his Labour Party won a 15-seat majority in the new 97-seat Parliament.

1 Mike Tyson unifies the world heavyweight boxing title with a unanimous 12-round decision over Tony Tucker.

7 The presidents of five Central American nations sign a preliminary agreement calling for a regional cease-fire and other steps toward lasting peace.

8 In their first major fighting in nearly five months, Chadian forces overrun the last strip of border territory occupied by Libya.

10 C. William Verity, Jr., is nominated to succeed the late Malcolm Baldrige as U.S. secretary of commerce.

12 In a televised speech about the Iran-contra scandal, President Reagan asserts, "I was stubborn in pursuit of a policy that went astray." The speech comes nine days after the conclusion of public hearings by the joint House and Senate committees investigating the scandal.

15 The Labour Party government of New Zealand's Prime Minister David Lange is easily reelected to a second term.

16 At least 156 people are killed in the crash of a Northwest Airlines passenger jet after takeoff from Detroit Metropolitan Airport.

18 U.S. journalist Charles Glass, held hostage in Lebanon for two months, escapes to freedom.

21 Meeting in Los Angeles, President Reagan assures Nicaraguan contra leaders of continuing U.S. backing.

The Zimbabwe House of Assembly votes to abolish the 20 seats reserved for whites.

23 The X Pan American Games, held in Indianapolis, IN, end after 15 days of athletic competition and several political incidents pertaining to the participation of Cuba.

24 U.S. Marine Sgt. Clayton Lonetree, a former guard at the American embassy in Moscow, is sentenced to 30 years in prison for spying for the Soviet Union.

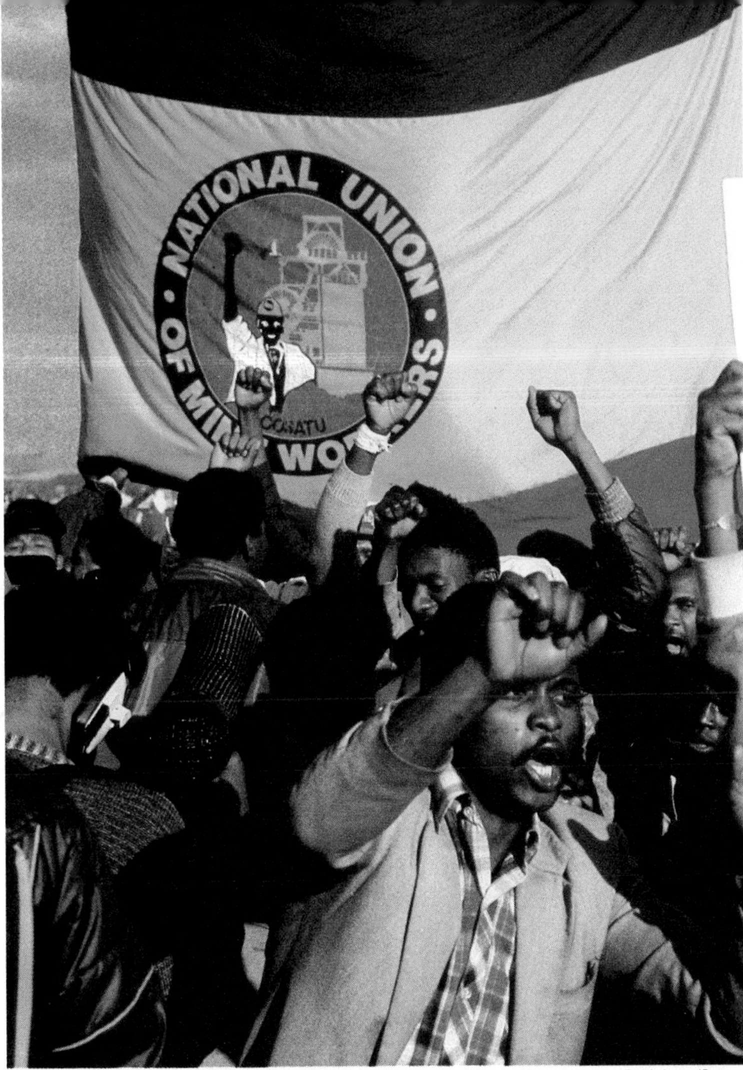

© P. Littleton/Sygma

More than 250,000 black miners in South Africa's gold and coal industries went on strike August 9, demanding higher pay and improved benefits. Three weeks later, amid mass firings and staunch resistance by mine owners, the strikers went back to work without the gains they had sought.

29 Loyalist government troops in the Philippines put down an armed uprising, the worst since the installation of the Corazon Aquino government in 1986, by a mutinous faction in the military.

Breaking an informal 45-day cease-fire, Iraqi warplanes bomb Iranian offshore oil installations.

30 After a three-week nationwide strike, the largest and costliest in South African history, some 250,000 black mine workers return to their jobs with minimal wage increases.

31 Amid ongoing labor unrest and political agitation, the ruling and opposition parties in South Korea agree on a draft constitution paving the way for direct presidential elections.

September

3 President Jean-Baptiste Bagaza of Burundi is overthrown in a bloodless military coup while he is away at a summit in Canada.

4 Mathias Rust, the young West German who landed a small plane in Moscow in May, is sentenced to four years in a Soviet labor camp.

In Bangladesh, weeks of flooding have left a reported 24 million people homeless or without food.

AP/Wide World

Pope John Paul II took in some of the sights during a visit to San Francisco on his nine-city U.S. tour in mid-September. The 20-hour stopover was highlighted by a Mass at Candlestick Park and a confrontation with a large crowd of protestors.

6 In escalating conflict, Chadian troops cross into Libyan territory for the first time and destroy a key air base.

Voters in Turkey call for the lifting of a ban against political activities by hundreds of opposition figures.

7 Erich Honecker arrives in West Germany for a five-day visit, the first to that country by an East German head of state.

South Africa frees 133 Angolan prisoners and two Europeans in exchange for a South African soldier captured by Angola.

8 Denmark's Conservative Prime Minister Poul Schlüter is returned to power despite election losses for his four-party coalition.

9 Twenty-five British soccer fans are extradited to Belgium on charges relating to 1985 riots at a soccer match in Brussels.

Sweden's Prime Minister Ingvar Carlsson meets in Washington with President Reagan.

10 Pope John Paul II begins a ten-day, nine-city U.S. visit.

12 Yugoslavia's Vice-President Hamdija Pozderac, who was to have become president in 1988, resigns in a financial scandal.

14 Ivan Lendl wins the U.S. Open men's singles tennis title. Martina Navratilova took the women's crown two days earlier.

15 The 42d session of the UN General Assembly opens in New York City. UN Secretary-General Javier Pérez de Cuéllar ends an unsuccessful four-day peace mission to Iran and Iraq.

16 In Montreal, Canada, representatives of 24 nations sign a treaty reducing production of ozone-destroying chemicals.

17 The Ford Motor Company and United Auto Workers union reach tentative agreement on a new three-year contract.

18 President Reagan announces a tentative agreement with the Soviet Union on the global elimination of intermediate-range nuclear missiles. The final treaty is expected to be signed during a U.S. visit by Soviet leader Gorbachev before year's end.

21 A U.S. helicopter attacks and disables an Iranian ship seen laying mines in the Persian Gulf.

West Germany and France begin four days of joint war games.

22 U.S. Rep. Mario Biaggi (D-NY) is found guilty of accepting illegal gratuities but is acquitted on bribery and conspiracy charges.

23 Sen. Joseph Biden, Jr., (D-DE) quits the race for president amid widening publicity of apparently plagiarized speeches and inaccurate claims regarding his educational achievements.

30 Voters in Suriname overwhelmingly approve a new constitution.

October

1 In Lhasa, Tibet, up to 19 people are killed as Chinese police move in to break up pro-independence demonstrations.

The Los Angeles area is rocked by a severe earthquake, causing six deaths, dozens of injuries, and widespread damage.

The International Monetary Fund and World Bank end their annual joint session in Washington, DC, after three days of talks but no major action on currency stabilization or Third World debt.

3 Canada and the United States reach a comprehensive trade pact on the elimination of all bilateral tariffs over ten years.

U.S. Vice-President George Bush concludes a high-profile visit to Poland and five members of the North Atlantic Treaty Organization (NATO).

4 Mexico's ruling Institutional Revolutionary Party names Carlos Salinas de Gortari as its candidate in 1988 presidential balloting. The nomination virtually assures his election.

5 Egypt's President Hosni Mubarak is reelected to a six-year term.

6 Army chief Lt. Col. Sitiveni Rabuka, who seized power 11 days earlier in his second coup of the year, formally proclaims Fiji a republic and promises a new constitution.

7 In a speech to the Organization of American States, President Reagan faults the Central American peace plan and renews his commitment to seek $270 million in aid for Nicaraguan contras.

8 The U.S. Senate and President Reagan reach a compromise agreement on a $1 billion arms sale to Saudi Arabia.

President Reagan names James Burnley to succeed Elizabeth Dole as secretary of transportation; Dole resigned as of October 1.

11 Libya and Chad agree to a cease-fire in their border war.

13 President Oscar Arias Sánchez of Costa Rica, the architect of the Central American peace plan signed in August, is named the winner of the 1987 Nobel Peace Prize.

15 The Soviet Union announces that it will pay all outstanding debts to the United Nations, amounting to about $245 million.

The National Football League Players Association ends a 24-day strike against team owners after failing to win a new collective bargaining agreement.

The leader of Burkina Faso, Capt. Thomas Sankara, is overthrown in a military coup led by former adviser Capt. Blaise Compaore.

17 The annual Commonwealth Heads of Government Conference concludes in Vancouver, B.C., after bitter debate over Great Britain's opposition to tougher economic sanctions against South Africa.

U.S. First Lady Nancy Reagan undergoes a single mastectomy after a biopsy revealed cancerous cells.

18 The governing centrist coalition of Switzerland is returned to power in general elections.

U.S. Supreme Court nominee Judge Robert H. Bork testified for an unprecedented five days before the Senate Judiciary Committee in September. On October 23, the Senate voted, 58-42, to reject the nomination.

© Terry Ashe/Gamma-Liaison

Federico Mayor Zaragoza of Spain is chosen to succeed the controversial Amadou-Mahtar M'Bow as director general of UNESCO.

19 On what is to become known as "Black Monday" for the U.S. stock market, the Dow Jones industrial average plunges 508.32 points, by far the largest one-day loss ever.

U.S. warships destroy an Iranian offshore oil rig used as a base for gunboats. The bombardment comes in retaliation for an Iranian missile attack against a U.S.-flagged oil tanker in Kuwaiti waters three days earlier.

20 Japan's Prime Minister Yasuhiro Nakasone names former Finance Minister Noboru Takeshita to succeed him as president of the ruling Liberal Democratic Party. The appointment virtually assures Takeshita of becoming the nation's next prime minister.

India's Prime Minister Rajiv Gandhi and President Reagan hold talks in Washington on ways to improve bilateral relations.

23 The U.S. Senate votes, 58–42, to reject President Reagan's nomination of Judge Robert H. Bork to the Supreme Court.

25 The Minnesota Twins win baseball's World Series with a 4–2 defeat of the St. Louis Cardinals in the seventh and deciding game.

26 President Reagan declares a complete ban on imports from Iran.

November

2 Zhao Ziyang is officially elected general secretary of China's Communist Party. Deng Xiaoping had resigned his top posts at the end of the 13th national party congress on November 1.

In a major speech marking the 70th anniversary of the Bolshevik Revolution, Soviet leader Mikhail Gorbachev denounces the late Joseph Stalin for "enormous and unforgivable" crimes.

5 U.S. Secretary of Defense Caspar Weinberger announces his resignation; President Reagan names National Security Adviser

The 70th anniversary of the Bolshevik Revolution was marked by a weeklong celebration that culminated on November 7 with the traditional parade in Red Square. The parade, this time, was expanded to offer a recapitulation of Soviet history.

© Bisson-Orban/Sygma

Vincent Van Gogh's "Irises" (1889), which he painted only days after entering a mental asylum in St. Remy, France, was auctioned for a record $53.9 million at Sotheby's in New York City, November 11.

© R. Maiman/Sygma

Frank Carlucci to succeed him. Two days earlier, Reagan named Ann Dore McLaughlin to succeed William Brock as secretary of labor; Brock announced his resignation October 15.

The Central American peace plan signed in August in Guatemala officially takes effect.

The government of South Africa frees the 77-year-old former chairman of the African National Congress, Govan Mbeki, who had been held in prison since 1964.

7 Tunisia's President Habib Bourguiba, who had led the country since independence in 1956, is overthrown by Prime Minister Zine al-Abidine Ben Ali on the grounds of "senility." Bourguiba, 84, had appointed Ben Ali prime minister on October 2.

8 In Enniskillen, Northern Ireland, a bomb explosion kills 11 persons and injures more than 60 others. The Provisional Irish Republican Army claims responsibility.

10 President Seyni Kountche of Niger dies in Paris. Hours earlier, Col. Ali Seybou, the army chief of staff, was named acting president.

11 President Reagan announces that he will nominate U.S. Appeals Court Judge Anthony M. Kennedy of California to the Supreme Court. The announcement comes four days after his second nominee for the high-court vacancy, Judge Douglas H. Ginsburg, withdrew from consideration amid disclosures of past marijuana use.

At the conclusion of a four-day emergency Arab League summit in Amman, Jordan, the participants issue a final communiqué condemning Iran and supporting Iraq in the Persian Gulf war.

The South African government acknowledges for the first time that its troops had fought Soviet and Cuban forces in Angola.

Boris N. Yeltsin, the Soviet Communist Party chief of the city of Moscow and a reformist protégé of General Secretary Mikhail Gorbachev, is ousted by the party's Central Committee.

13 After meeting in Washington with U.S. House Speaker Jim Wright (D-TX), Nicaragua's President Daniel Ortega presents an 11-point cease-fire proposal that includes direct negotiations, to be held in the United States, with contra rebels. The White House criticizes Wright for interfering in its foreign policy.

18 A rush-hour fire in central London's busiest subway and train depot, King's Cross Station, leaves 30 persons dead.

AP/Wide World

The sudden death of Chicago Mayor Harold Washington on November 25 unleashed a power struggle in the city council that culminated in the December 2 election of Democratic Alderman Eugene Sawyer, above, *as acting mayor. Sawyer, 53, was the longest-serving black member of the city council.*

18 The U.S. House and Senate committees investigating the Iran-contra affair issue their final report, blaming the scandal on White House "secrecy, deception, and disdain for the law." A minority report rejects the panels' "hysterical conclusions."

To preserve the nation's foreign currency reserves, the Mexican government halts support of the peso against the U.S. dollar on the open market. The value of the peso plummets.

23 The second exiled left-wing rebel leader in three days returns to El Salvador in a political opening provided by the Central American peace agreement signed in August.

24 At the conclusion of three days of meetings in Geneva, U.S. Secretary of State George Shultz and Soviet Foreign Minister Eduard Shevardnadze announce resolution of the final obstacle to a treaty eliminating intermediate-range nuclear forces.

Li Peng, 59, is named acting premier of China, succeeding Zhao Ziyang, the new general secretary of the Communist Party.

25 Mayor Harold Washington of Chicago dies suddenly of a heart attack. The 65-year-old second-term Democrat was Chicago's first black mayor.

29 Haiti's first free elections in 30 years are called off at the last minute amid widespread violence by supporters of exiled President Jean-Claude Duvalier. Thirty-four persons are reported killed and 70 injured.

In Poland's first national referendum in 40 years, voters reject economic and political reforms proposed by the government.

Turkey's Prime Minister Turgut Ozal easily wins reelection.

In a three-day series of moves, two French hostages in Lebanon are set free, and France and Iran release diplomats being held in their respective Tehran and Paris embassies.

Leaders of eight Latin American nations conclude a four-day summit in Acapulco, Mexico. The area's foreign debt of almost $400 billion, peace in Central America, and regional economic integration were topics of discussion.

December

3 The central banks of seven West European nations, including West Germany, lower key interest rates to help stem the declining value of the U.S. dollar.

After reaching an agreement with U.S. officials, Cuban inmates end their 11-day siege at a federal penitentiary in Atlanta. A similar eight-day siege in Oakdale, LA, ended November 29. The takeovers were precipitated by the revival of a U.S.-Cuban pact under which thousands of Cubans who had come to the United States in 1980 would be deported.

4 After three days of talks in France, former Cambodian leader Prince Norodom Sihanouk and Prime Minister Hun Sen of the current Vietnamese-backed regime announce an agreement to work toward peaceful resolution of the nation's political conflict.

5 Leaders of the 12 European Community (EC) nations conclude a two-day meeting in Copenhagen without agreement on key issues.

8 On the first day of a three-day summit meeting in Washington, President Reagan and Soviet leader Gorbachev sign a treaty on the global elimination of intermediate-range nuclear forces.

9 A wave of Palestinian unrest breaks out in the Israeli-occupied Gaza Strip and West Bank. The violence reaches unprecedented levels, as Israeli forces respond to rioting with gunfire.

13 Elections in Belgium fail to resolve a two-month-old government crisis. Caretaker Prime Minister Wilfried Martens and other party leaders continue efforts to form a majority coalition.

14 Meeting in Vienna, the Organization of the Petroleum Exporting Countries (OPEC) extends its benchmark price of $18 per barrel and its production quota of 16.6 million barrels per day.

In an effort to boost its struggling economy, Mexico devalues the peso by 22% against the U.S. dollar.

15 Former Sen. Gary Hart, who ended his Democratic presidential campaign in May amid scandal, reenters the race.

16 Roh Tae Woo, the candidate of the ruling Democratic Justice Party, defeats four opposition candidates in South Korea's long-awaited presidential election. The opposition charges vote fraud.

Former White House aide Michael Deaver is convicted on three counts of perjury for lying about his lobbying activities.

17 Gustav Husak, 74, steps down as head of the Czechoslovakian Communist Party. Miloš Jakeš, 65, is elevated to the post.

18 Gary Kasparov of the Soviet Union retains his world chess championship with a final-game victory and a 12-12 tie in his match with challenger Anatoly Karpov in Seville, Spain.

20 A passenger ferry and an oil tanker collide and sink off the Philippines' Mindoro island, killing some 1,500.

U.S. congressional leaders and the White House agree to provide $8.1 million in nonmilitary aid to Nicaragua. The same day, contra forces attack three towns in northern Nicaragua in one of their largest and most successful campaigns to date.

22 The U.S. Congress adjourns after passing a $604 billion omnibus spending bill and a separate bill to hold down the federal budget deficit. President Reagan signs both bills into law.

Two associates of U.S. Attorney General Edwin Meese 3rd and a third man are indicted on charges of obtaining payments from Wedtech Corporation, a Bronx, NY, military contractor, to influence Meese (who is not charged).

29 Soviet astronaut Col. Yuri V. Romanenko returns to earth from the space station Mir after a record 326 days in orbit.

31 Robert Mugabe is sworn in as the first executive president (head of state and government) in Zimbabwe, marking the nation's transition from a constitutional democracy to a one-party state.

Israeli security forces were deployed in mass after an outbreak of Palestinian unrest in the occupied Gaza Strip, below, and West Bank. As the violence escalated, scores of Palestinians were killed by Israeli gunfire.

AP/Wide World

THE IRAN-CONTRA AFFAIR

© J. L. Atlan/Sygma

Sygma

The joint public hearings of the U.S. House and Senate committees investigating the Iran-contra affair were held from May 5 to August 3, alternating between the Senate Caucus Room (left) *and the Rayburn House Office Building. Key figures on the panel included* (above, at front, left to right): *Arthur Liman, chief counsel for the Senate; John Nields, Jr., chief counsel for the House; Sen. Daniel Inouye (D-HI), chairman of the Senate Committee; and Rep. Lee Hamilton (D-IN), chairman of the House committee.*

By Robert Shogan

Mindful of the failings of humankind, the Founding Fathers of the United States designed a constitution intended to assure future generations a government of laws, not men. But for all the genius that went into creating the U.S. constitutional system, history has shown the difficulty of shielding it from human fallibility. This lesson again was driven home to Americans with disturbing force by the public reconstruction of the bizarre events that constituted the Iran-contra affair.

The revelations, laid out principally in televised joint hearings conducted by select committees of both houses of Congress, shook the nation's confidence in President Ronald Reagan, who until the scandal broke late in 1986 had been riding a crest of popularity and approbation. The revelations also tarnished U.S. prestige abroad. Above all, as the select committees argued in their report, the episode served as a

About the Author: Robert Shogan has been national political correspondent in the Washington Bureau of the *Los Angeles Times* since 1973. Previously he was an assistant editor of *The Wall Street Journal* and a correspondent for *Newsweek* magazine. Mr. Shogan's books include *None of the Above: Why Presidents Fail & What Can Be Done about It,* a study of the American presidency.

vivid reminder of the need to maintain vigilant guardianship over the guardians of public trust.

"The problem at the heart was one of people, not process," declared Gen. Brent Scowcroft, one of three members of the special review board appointed by the president, when that panel issued its report Feb. 26, 1987. "It was not that the structure was faulty. It was that the structure was not used."

Strikingly similar language was used by the select committees in their majority report, which concluded that "the Iran-contra affair resulted from the failures of individuals to observe the law, not from deficiencies in existing law or in our system of governance." The report contended that this judgment "pointed to the fundamental soundness of our constitutional process." But this diagnosis of systemic good health left no room for broad structural reforms to cure the malady that manifested itself in the Iran-contra affair. Instead it seemed that hopes of preventing a repetition required an understanding of events that could be gained only from an exhaustive study of the behavior and motivations of those involved.

AP/Wide World

Despite gavel-to-gavel coverage on television, the congressional hearings attracted daily throngs of spectators. On some mornings, the lines outside the hearing room began forming at 5 A.M.

Fortunately there was no dearth of such information. Not since the Watergate scandal forced the resignation of President Richard Nixon in 1974 had the misadventures of any administration produced such a plethora of inquiries. Even before the year began there had been a flurry of congressional hearings. Then in January the Senate Intelligence Committee released a report which challenged President Reagan's assertion that his administration's main reason for selling arms to Iran was to establish ties to so-called moderate elements in that country.

Already under way as the Senate panel reported was the inquiry conducted by the special review board made up of, in addition to General Scowcroft, former Republican Sen. John G. Tower of Texas, who served as chairman, and former Democratic senator from Maine and secretary of state, Edmund S. Muskie. Also beginning work was the independent counsel whom the president had appointed to probe for evidence of criminal violations of the law, former Federal Judge Lawrence E. Walsh.

And finally there was the investigation conducted in partnership by the select committees of the Senate (11 members), chaired by Democrat Daniel K. Inouye of Hawaii, and the House of Representatives (15 members), headed by another Democrat, Lee Hamilton of Indiana. The committees collected more than 300,000 documents, conducted more than 500 interviews and depositions, and ultimately heard from 28 witnesses in 40 days of public hearings from May to August.

AP/Wide World

Lawrence E. Walsh, a former federal prosecutor, judge, and U.S. deputy attorney general, was named by a three-judge panel in December 1986 as the independent counsel—or special prosecutor—in the Iran-contra affair. He was given a broad investigative mandate and the authority to issue criminal indictments. The outcome of his probe was keenly anticipated as 1987 ended.

The Background and the Revelations. It was the committees' 690-page report released in November that provided the clearest narrative of the tangle of events lumped together under the rubric of Iran-contra. In broad outline the story that emerged was rooted, the report pointed out, in two revolutions in distant parts of the world. In 1979 longtime U.S. ally Shah Mohammed Reza Pahlavi of Iran was overthrown by Muslim extremists led by the Ayatollah Khomeini. And that same year another ruler close to the United States for many years, President Anastasio Somoza Debayle of Nicaragua, was supplanted by a regime controlled by Marxist Sandinistas, eventually headed by President Daniel Ortega.

Concerned that the Sandinista regime and its Soviet and Cuban allies threatened hemispheric security and the United States itself, the Reagan administration began supporting the so-called contras, a guerrilla force waging war against the government in Managua. When Congress balked at continued support for these insurgents, the administration sought funds from other nations and from private parties. The funds were used to finance a private organization called "the Enterprise," established under the aegis of the National Security Council and the leadership of NSC staff member Lt. Col. Oliver North. Its mission was to provide covert aid to the contras, help which, as the report pointed out, Congress believed it had prohibited.

While these clandestine and illegal activities were going forward, the National Security Council staff became involved

AP/Wide World

The final report of the so-called Tower Commission—a special presidential panel, headed by former Sen. John Tower (R-TX), to review the activities of the National Security Council—was issued February 26, blaming the president and his aides for the "chaos" of the Iran-contra dealings. The report appeared in book form within two days and quickly became a best-seller.

in another secret and dubious operation—the sale of arms to Iran. This activity had begun at the suggestion of the Israeli government with the hopes of gaining the release of American hostages held in Lebanon and of improving relations with Iran. Ultimately, the two operations became linked when the NSC staff, with considerable spare cash on hand from the arms deals, determined to use those funds to help support the contras. Just as the support for the contras undercut the intent of Congress, the transactions with Iran, notorious for its support of terrorism, contradicted the stated public policy of the United States to refuse to negotiate with terrorists. The transactions also violated the Arms Export Act and the U.S. Arms Embargo against Iran.

"The common ingredients of the Iran and contra policies were secrecy, deception, and disdain for the law," said the report of the select committees. "The administration's departure from democratic process created the conditions for policy failure and led to contradictions which undermined the credibility of the United States."

But the report's sweeping condemnation of the entire affair, a judgment shared by many other national leaders, still left open important questions of individual responsibility. The first individual about whom that question had to be asked was, of course, the chief executive himself. Recalling the Watergate scandal, a compelling memory throughout the public debate on Iran-contra, many looked for a facsimile of the "smoking gun" that had forced Richard Nixon from office. But no such damning evidence came to light. Even most of Reagan's critics conceded that his greatest sin had been ineptitude, combined with self-deception.

In rendering the first objective judgment on the president's behavior, the Tower commission report in February, referring to what critics have described as his disengagement from certain aspects of his job, declared: ''President Reagan's personal management style places an especially heavy responsibility on his key advisers.'' More broadly, the commission said: ''The NSC system will not work unless the president makes it work.'' Noting that Reagan had not met that responsibility, the commission said: ''At no time did he insist upon accountability and performance review.''

In a nationally televised address on March 4, President Reagan accepted the report's judgment without serious disagreement and also accepted responsibility for the actions of his subordinates: ''As the Navy would say, this happened on my watch.'' On the critical point of the real motivation for the transaction, he said: ''A few months ago I told the American people I did not trade arms for hostages. My heart and my best intentions still tell me that is true, but the facts and the evidence tell me it is not.'' Having acknowledged error, the president told the nation it was time to move on to other concerns.

President Reagan acknowledged the error of the Iranian arms sales and took responsibility for the actions of his subordinates, but insisted he had no knowledge of the diversion of profits to the contras. Former National Security Adviser Adm. John Poindexter (in cartoon) *testified that information on the diversion was withheld from the president.*

AP/Wide World

But concern over the Iran-contra revelations persisted. On March 19, in Reagan's first full-dress press conference since the scandal broke, he was peppered with questions about it. The president once again acknowledged error. ''I would not go down that same road again,'' he said. But he continued to insist that the arms sales to Iran developed into a swap for hostages only inadvertently, not through his original design, and that he had no knowledge of the diversion of funds to the contras. Asked if he might have been told of this and forgotten it, he said: ''Oh no. You would have heard me without opening the door to the office if I had been told that at any time.''

For many Americans, whether or not Reagan knew of the fund diversions became the key determinant of the president's culpability in the entire affair. Thus his supporters breathed a sigh of relief when Rear Adm. John M. Poindexter, Jr., formerly national security adviser, testified on July 15 before the select committees that he had personally authorized the use of profits from the Iran sales to help the contras and had withheld

© 1987 Bill Day/''Detroit Free Press''

that information from Reagan. "I made a very deliberate decision not to ask the president so that I could insulate him from the decision and provide some future deniability," Poindexter said. "The buck stops here with me," he added. But on that point the president himself felt obliged to disagree with his former national security chief. "The buck does not stop with Admiral Poindexter," the president said in a televised address August 12. "I had the right, the obligation to make my own decision."

But the fact that he had not been told produced an excoriating judgment from the select committees. "This kind of thinking is inconsistent with democratic governance," their report said of Poindexter's behavior. "The ultimate responsibility for the events in the Iran-contra affair must rest with the president," the joint committees concluded. "If the president did not know what his national security advisers were doing, he should have."

Photos AP/Wide World

The Principals. If President Reagan, as he himself acknowledged, had to bear the main responsibility for the Iran-contra affair, he was only the highest ranking member of a cast of public servants who one way or another played a part in the drama. Most of their roles became known through their testimony during the hearings conducted by the select committees. Here are some of the significant players, in their order of appearance:

FAWN HALL. Col. Oliver North's secretary, an attractive part-time model, Fawn Hall became the first of the committee witnesses to command heavy media and public attention. Testifying under a limited grant of immunity on June 8 and 9, she said that she shredded so many documents when the affair became public in November 1986 that the office shredding machine broke. And she testified that she smuggled other documents out in her boots and clothing. Hall's testimony was most memorable for her defense of her efforts to foil the investigations of North's activities. "Sometimes you have to go above written law," she said.

OLIVER NORTH. Described by the report of the select committees as "the central figure" in the scandal, "who coordinated all of the activities and was involved in all aspects of the secret operations," Oliver North, a decorated Marine, provided the most forceful defense yet heard of the Iran-contra affair. He did so in six days of compelling testimony beginning July 7. His rugged good looks and evocation of patriotic values touched off a new wave of national sympathy and support called "Olliemania."

"I came here to tell the truth—the good, the bad, and the ugly," North declared at the outset. He said he had believed his superiors had chosen him as the scapegoat to "take the spears in his own chest" if his undercover actions ever became, as they had become, a public scandal. Unwilling to accept this role with criminal charges threatening, North claimed he had done nothing that had not been approved by his superiors. He said he had always assumed that President Reagan knew of all his actions, including the diversion of

AP/Wide World

LT. COL. OLIVER L. NORTH

During six days of testimony before the House and Senate investigating committees in July 1987, Marine Lt. Col. and former National Security Council (NSC) aide Oliver L. North, the central figure in arranging the secret arms sales to Iran and diverting the proceeds to Nicaraguan contra rebels, captured the attention of the American public and generated controversy as few other figures in recent memory. Testifying in full uniform, the highly decorated 43-year-old Marine evoked powerfully ambivalent reactions with his passionate rhetoric of duty, honor, and service, and his unflinching admissions of lying to Congress and falsifying and shredding official documents. His defiant patriotism and can-do image brought an outpouring of support that became known as "Olliemania." Telegrams from admiring citizens poured in by the thousands; "Ollie for President" tee-shirts did a lively business. Nevertheless, Colonel North came under severe criticism in the majority report of the congressional committees and faced possible criminal charges by the special prosecutor.

Background. The eldest of four children, Oliver Laurence North was born in 1943 in San Antonio, TX, and was raised in the village of Philmont in upstate New York. After graduation from high school in 1961, he attended the State University College at Brockport but transferred to the U.S. Naval Academy. He was graduated from Annapolis in 1968.

With the rank of second lieutenant, North served as a platoon leader in Vietnam from December 1968 to November 1969, earning a Silver Star, Bronze Star, and two Purple Hearts. In 1981 he was hired by then National Security Adviser Richard Allen to work on the NSC staff in Washington. As deputy director for political-military affairs, he played a key role in planning the invasion of Grenada (1983), the capture of the *Achille Lauro* hijackers (1985), and the support of the contras. Despite serving in relative obscurity, he earned a reputation in the White House as a "man of action" and was said to "have the ear" of President Reagan.

After being fired from the NSC in November 1986, North was assigned a desk job in the Office of Manpower and Policy Planning at Marine headquarters in the Pentagon. He lives with his wife Betsy (*pictured above*) and three children on a two-acre farmstead in rural Virginia.

funds to the contras, though he had never "personally discussed" this with the president.

Despite acknowledging the massive shredding of documents and misleading Congress about his activities on the National Security Council, he denied that he had ever broken any laws. "It's a dangerous world," he said in defense of his actions.

Immediately after North was dismissed, Robert McFarlane, who had been national security adviser and North's supervisor (1983–85), denied authorizing many of North's secret activities.

JOHN M. POINDEXTER. Apart from seemingly clearing the president of the charge that he had known of the diversion of funds from the Iran arms sales to support the contras, the main import of John M. Poindexter's testimony was to provide rare insight into the ethics of intelligence as it was practiced in the Reagan White House. Poindexter testified on July 15 that the president had indeed signed a finding authorizing the sale of arms to Iran in exchange for hostages, as others had said but as the president himself claimed he could not remember. Poindexter, who had been Reagan's national security adviser from December 1985 until he was forced to resign by the Iran-contra scandal in November 1986, said he destroyed the document soon after the Iran deal became public knowledge.

"I think it's always the responsibility of a staff to protect their leader and certainly in this case where the leader is the commander-in-chief," he explained. "One has always to put things in the president's perspective and to make sure that he's not put in a position that can be politically embarrassing."

As to the diversion of funds, Poindexter said he regarded that transaction as just "a detail" in carrying out the president's overall policy of supporting the contras in the face of congressional opposition.

GEORGE SHULTZ. Although George Shultz had opposed the arms deal with Iran from the start, the secretary of state had been criticized along with Defense Secretary Caspar Weinberger for not being more vigorous in his objections. In his testimony on July 23, Shultz pictured himself as a victim of deceit and dissembling by other White House officials, specifically McFarlane, Poindexter, and Central Intelligence Director William Casey. These officials, he charged, also withheld information from the president in order to protect the Iran operation, which Shultz himself characterized as "pathetic."

Photos AP/Wide World

Because of his disapproval of the dealings with Iran, Shultz claimed he "felt a sense of estrangement" from the National Security Council staff and other White House officials. "I knew they were very uncomfortable with me," he said. "I had a terrible time. There was a kind of guerrilla warfare going on, on all kinds of little things," he added, contending that the White House staff had retaliated against him by restricting his travel on Air Force planes.

Rejecting the rationalizations that had been offered for the Iran arms deal, Shultz said: "I don't think desirable ends justify means of lying, deceiving, of doing things that are outside our constitutional processes."

EDWIN MEESE III. So far as anyone knew, President Reagan's longtime confidant and attorney general, Edwin Meese, had no direct role in the sale of arms to Iran or in the secret support provided to the contras. What Meese was open to questioning about was his handling of the investigation into the affair that President Reagan had ordered him to undertake in November of 1986.

Sen. George Mitchell (D-ME) pressed Meese during his appearances on July 28 and 29 to explain why he had conducted the early interviews in the inquiry in the presence of other witnesses and had carefully taken notes, while by contrast after disclosure of the diversion of funds to the contras, Meese interviewed five important officials and took no notes. The five were Vice-President George Bush, White House Chief of Staff Donald T. Regan, McFarlane, Poindexter, and Casey. Meese's answer—that these were "totally different types of conversations"—evidently did not satisfy most members of the joint committees. Their report pointedly made mention of the solo interviews as well as citing public statements Meese had made about his inquiry in a November 1986 press conference—statements which turned out to be incorrect.

DONALD T. REGAN. Though known as one of the most dominating personalities to hold the position of White House Chief of Staff, Donald Regan described himself as largely uninformed and uninvolved in the machinations that produced the Iran-contra scandal. Indeed, he testified on July 30 as the hearings drew to a close that he had complained to the president that "We'd been had," after a February 1986 arms shipment to Iran had not led to the freeing of hostages. "We'd been snookered again and how many times do we have to put up with this rug merchant type of stuff?", Regan said he told the president. Admitting that he himself had shifted back and forth in his view on the Iranian arms sales, Regan offered his own notion of why the transactions had continued. "A lot of it was plotting by arms dealers to involve the United States in massive arms transfers to Iran," he testified. Meanwhile, he said, "our own people had become so involved in trying to extricate the hostages . . . they were led down this garden path."

Photos AP/Wide World

One major figure in the affair, former CIA Director William J. Casey, who died May 6, 1987, from pneumonia five months after undergoing surgery for a brain tumor, was only a shadowy presence at the congressional hearings. Based on circumstantial evidence and the testimony of other witnesses, the members of the select committees said in their report that they believed that Casey had encouraged Oliver North, had "promoted the concept of an extra legal covert organization," and was involved in the diversion of funds to the Nicaraguan contras.

In its summation, the report quoted the late Supreme Court Justice Louis Brandeis' warning against government violating the law: "If the government becomes a law breaker, it breeds

The Supporting Cast

In addition to Lt. Col. Oliver North, Adm. John Poindexter, and other individuals who became household names during the Iran-contra hearings, the 40 days of public testimony brought to light the key roles played by some lesser-known figures. Nine of the most important are listed below.

Elliott Abrams: assistant secretary of state for inter-American affairs and coordinator of the administration's Central America policy. He testified that he was not involved in covert aid to the contras despite his frequent meetings with Colonel North and solicitation of a $10 million contribution from Brunei, which he had hidden from Congress.

Adolfo Calero: head of the largest contra faction and Colonel North's chief contact with the rebels during the two-year congressional ban on U.S. military aid. He was responsible for distributing private funding sent to the contras.

Manucher Ghorbanifar: Iranian-born arms dealer who arranged early U.S. arms sales to Iran and acted as a middleman. Colonel North testified that the idea of diverting the proceeds to the Nicaraguan contras had first come from Ghorbanifar.

Albert Hakim: an Iranian who later became an American, was a business partner of General Secord and financial coordinator of the Iranian arms sale and contra supply operations.

Adnan Khashoggi: Saudi Arabian arms dealer and business tycoon who provided financing for initial arms shipments to Iran.

David Kimche: former director general of the Israeli foreign ministry. He helped set up contacts between Washington and Tehran in 1985 that led to the sale of arms.

Amiram Nir: adviser on terrorism to former Israeli Prime Minister Shimon Peres. He took charge of Israel's arms deals with Iran from David Kimche in early 1986.

Robert Owen: nicknamed "the courier," he was Colonel North's personal representative in Central America. Under contract with U.S. State Department, he delivered money and intelligence materials to contra leaders.

Richard Secord: retired U.S. Air Force major general hired by Colonel North to direct Iran arms sales and the funneling of profits to the contras. Set up an elaborate network of individuals, companies, and bank accounts—called the "enterprise"—toward those ends. He denied any interest in profiting personally from the operation.

contempt for law, it invites every man to become a law unto himself, it invites anarchy." Said the report: "The Iran-contra affair resulted from a failure to heed this message."

Eight Republican members of the select committees filed a dissent from the majority report, challenging its findings as "hysterical." They acknowledged that the president and his aides had made mistakes, but they argued: "There was no constitutional crisis, no systematic disrespect for the rule of law."

As the year drew to a close, special prosecutor Lawrence E. Walsh was pushing ahead with his investigation. Without revealing his hand, Walsh said his work would not be affected by what the committee had done. "We have a large base for our own action," he said. Whatever the outcome of his investigations, the last word on the Iran-contra affair remained for the future. It would be up to historians to judge the total effects of the case and for future presidents and other government officials to decide what lessons it taught.

AP/Wide World

The Bicentennial of the U.S. Constitution

The year 1987 marked a most significant milestone in the history of the United States—the 200th anniversary of its Constitution. In addition to books, articles, seminars, debates, and colloquiums on the history and meaning of this great document, the event was marked by special ceremonies and celebrations throughout the year. On May 25 the opening of the Constitutional Convention of 1787 was reenacted in Philadelphia; on July 16 the U.S. Congress met in that historic city for the first time since 1800; on September 16, from the steps of the Capitol in Washington, DC, President Ronald Reagan led the nation's schoolchildren in reciting the Pledge of Allegiance; and on the following day, September 17, the actual anniversary of the signing of the Constitution, the president was at Independence Hall in Philadelphia for a Constitution Day gala.

Editor's Note: This article was prepared by the editors of the yearbook in consultation with George Anastaplo, a professor of law at Loyola University of Chicago and a lecturer in the liberal arts at the University of Chicago. An expert on the U.S. Constitution, Professor Anastaplo recently completed *A Commentary on the United States Constitution,* which is to be published by Johns Hopkins University Press in 1988.

On Sept, 15, 1787, after the precise wording had been worked out, the new U.S. Constitution was submitted for engrossing—the final handwritten preparation. A calligrapher named Jacob Shallus was paid $30 to copy it in his own handwriting. The document was penned on animal skin, but experts today do not know whether it was calf, goat, or sheep.

In his speech on September 17, President Reagan characterized the bicentennial observance as an act of renewal, a reaffirmation of "what will always be America's foremost duty—. . . to complete the work begun 200 years ago, that grand noble work that is America's particular calling—the triumph of human freedom—the triumph of human freedom under God." Although the birth of the United States is traditionally dated from the signing of the Declaration of Independence on July 4, 1776, the president also suggested that "it was with the writing of our Constitution, setting down the architecture of democratic government, that the noble sentiments and brave rhetoric of 1776 took on substance, that the hopes and dreams of the revolutionists could become a living, enduring reality."

Warren E. Burger, who resigned as chief justice of the U.S. Supreme Court in 1986 to serve full-time as chairman of

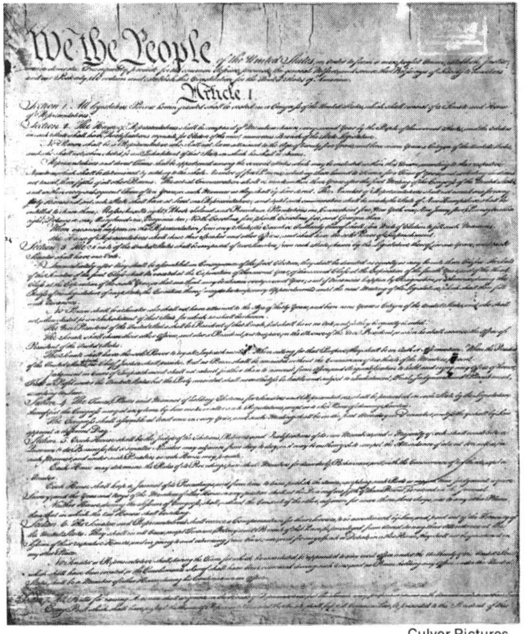
We the People
Article I

Culver Pictures

The U.S. Constitution—a Synopsis

Preamble: "We the People of the United States, in Order to form a more perfect Union, establish Justice, insure domestic Tranquility, provide for the common defence, promote the general Welfare, and secure the Blessings of Liberty to ourselves and our Posterity, do ordain and establish this Constitution for the United States of America."

Article I: invests legislative authority in a bicameral Congress, consisting of a Senate and House of Representatives; defines the terms of office, personal qualifications, and election procedures for senators and congressmen; establishes the procedure by which a bill becomes law; enumerates the powers of the legislative branch.

Article II: invests executive authority in a president; defines the term of office, personal qualifications, and election procedures for the presidency and vice-presidency; enumerates the duties and powers of the president; provides for the succession of presidential power; establishes the grounds for impeachment.

Article III: invests judicial authority in a Supreme Court; defines the jurisdiction of the federal judiciary.

Article IV: requires that "Full Faith and Credit" be given to the public acts and records of the separate states; entitles citizens of each state to "all Privileges and Immunities" of U.S. citizenship; provides for the admission of new states into the Union.

Article V: establishes the procedure for amending the Constitution.

Article VI: declares the Constitution, treaties, and all federal laws "made in Pursuance [of the Constitution] . . . the supreme Law of the Land."

Article VII: specified ratification by nine state conventions as sufficient for the Establishment of this Constitution.

The Bill of Rights (1791)

Amendment I: guarantees freedom of religion, speech, the press, assembly, and petition.

Amendment II: guarantees "the right of the people to keep and bear Arms."

Amendment III: prohibits the forcible quartering of soldiers in private homes.

Amendment IV: prohibits "unreasonable searches and seizures;" establishes the requirement of search and arrest warrants.

Amendment V: defines the rights of the accused in criminal cases.

the official bicentennial commission, echoed the theme of renewed dedication by calling for greater public understanding of the document. "The bicentennial of the Constitution," he wrote, "presents an ideal opportunity for 'We the people' to give ourselves a history lesson on our great charter."

Precursor—The Articles of Confederation. The American people were governing themselves before they had a national constitution, before they declared themselves independent, and indeed before the Revolutionary War. The Continental Congress met frequently beginning in September 1774, and the individual states, pursuant to recommendations by that body, had adopted constitutions of their own beginning in January 1776. But it was on June 7, 1776—the same day that a motion was introduced to declare the colonies independent—that the Second Continental Congress established a committee to draft

Since 1952, the original copy of the U.S. Constitution has been housed at the National Archives Building in Washington, DC. The parchment remains on display in the building's rotunda, contained in a brass case under a sheet of glass. Alongside it is the Declaration of Independence.

Amendment VI: establishes the right to a fair and speedy trial in criminal prosecutions.

Amendment VII: establishes the right to a jury trial in civil cases.

Amendment VIII: prohibits excessive bail and fines or other "cruel and unusual punishment."

Amendment IX: preserves all rights of the people not specifically enumerated in the Constitution (or its amendments).

Amendment X: preserves all powers of the states and the people not delegated to the national government.

Other Amendments (date of adoption)

Amendment XI (1798): bars lawsuits by citizens of one state against another state in federal court.

Amendment XII (1804): alters the Article II procedure for election of the president and vice-president.

Amendment XIII (1865): abolishes slavery.

Amendment XIV (1868): guarantees citizenship, "due process of law," "equal protection of the laws," and other civil rights to all persons born or naturalized in the United States.

Amendment XV (1870): grants voting rights to persons of any "race, color or previous condition of servitude."

Amendment XVI (1913): empowers Congress to levy a federal income tax.

Amendment XVII (1913): alters the Article I procedure for electing U.S. senators; calls for direct popular elections.

Amendment XVIII (1919): prohibits the manufacture, sale, or transport of liquor.

Amendment XIX (1920): grants voting rights to women.

Amendment XX (1933): changes the dates on which the president and vice-president and Congress take office, to January 20 and January 3, respectively.

Amendment XXI (1933): repeals Amendment XVIII prohibition against liquor.

Amendment XXII (1951): limits a president to two terms in office.

Amendment XXIII (1961): grants citizens of the District of Columbia the right to vote in presidential elections.

Amendment XXIV (1964): prohibits poll taxes in federal elections.

Amendment XXV (1967): establishes the chain of presidential succession and the procedure by which presidential disability is determined.

Amendment XXVI (1971): grants voting rights to all citizens age 18 or older.

Culver Pictures

The closing session of the Constitutional Convention—on Sept. 17, 1787, at Independence Hall in Philadelphia—was depicted in a painting by Junius Brutus Stearns. George Washington (on platform), *who presided over the body, wrote in his diary that the delegates then "dined together and took a cordial leave of each other."*

their first national constitution, the Articles of Confederation. John Dickinson of Pennsylvania headed the committee and was the principal author of the first draft. The Articles were completed in 1777 and then submitted to the states for ratification, a process which took until March 1781 to complete. The national and state governments, guided by the Articles of Confederation and state constitutions, conducted the affairs of the country during the Revolutionary War and for several years thereafter.

Under the Articles of Confederation, the 13 former colonies became a group of united states. The central government was embodied in a congress of delegates chosen annually by the states. The Continental Congress was empowered to conduct foreign affairs, declare war, negotiate treaties, raise armies, establish a navy, oversee Indian affairs, coin and borrow money, and establish a post office. Various powers, some of them shared with the central government, were retained by the states.

During the Revolutionary War it was generally understood that new constitutional arrangements would have to be made once independence had been secured. Among the questionable features of the Articles of Confederation were: the lack of a chief executive and of independent national courts; the limited legislative power of the Continental Congress and its complete lack of power to tax, with the Congress completely dependent on the states to provide the revenues necessary for the national government; and, of particular concern to the larger states, the fact that all states—regardless of size—had only one vote in Congress.

Most of all it was Congress' lack of authority to regulate commerce—and hence the inability of the national government to deal with national economic interests at home and abroad—that prompted efforts in various states to seek constitutional reform. In September 1786, representatives from five states met in Annapolis, MD, to discuss their commercial problems and disputes. The major result of that meeting was

UPI/Bettman Newsphotos

As part of the bicentennial commemorations of 1987, 50 members of the U.S. Congress—representing the original signers—gathered in Independence Hall. On July 16, the Congress met in Philadelphia for the first time since 1800.

a formal request to the Continental Congress to call a convention of the states the following spring "to devise such further provisions as shall appear to them necessary to render the constitution of the Federal Government adequate to the exigencies of the Union. . . ."

The Constitutional Convention. The Continental Congress responded favorably to the recommendation of the Annapolis convention, and in February 1787 it invited the 13 states to send delegates to a convention in Philadelphia "for the sole and express purpose of revising the Articles of Confederation." The Virginia legislature promoted interest in the convention by including George Washington, then the most influential public figure in the United States, in its delegation. When it became known that Washington was willing to serve, the other states were challenged to choose delegates of high caliber as well. The 12 states that participated (Rhode Island boycotted) chose a total of 73 delegates, 55 of whom attended the convention at one time or another; the average daily attendance was about 30 delegates. In addition to Washington, who presided over the convention, the delegates included such luminaries as James Madison, Alexander Hamilton, Benjamin Franklin, Gouverneur Morris, William Paterson, George Mason, and James Wilson. Upon seeing the list, Thomas Jefferson exclaimed in a letter to John Adams (they were serving as envoys in Europe), "It is really an assembly of demigods."

The convention was scheduled to begin on May 14, but it was not until May 25 that enough delegates had arrived to get the proceedings under way. Over the next 16 weeks, through the hot summer, the convention held sessions six days a week, except when it adjourned for committees to catch up on their work. At the beginning of its deliberations, the convention decided that it should conduct all its proceedings behind closed doors, thereby permitting completely frank discussion of issues. It would be many years before the public knew much about the debates that took place behind those doors.

A fundamental issue at the convention was how much power should be extended to the national government and how much reserved to the states. Indeed, there were other luminaries—such as Patrick Henry and Samuel Adams—who refused to attend the convention, fearing that it would create too strong a national government. Another major obstacle facing the convention was the conflicting interests of the larger and smaller states—whether all states, regardless of size, would continue to have equal votes in the national legislature. Among the other problems to resolve were how the national president should be elected and how to accommodate the strong pro-slavery interests.

One thing that the delegates quickly acknowledged was that the Articles of Confederation were beyond repair and that a completely new constitution would have to be prepared. This conclusion was reached during the opening days of the convention, during presentation of a plan by the Virginia delegation. The Virginia Plan, in which Edmund Randolph and James Madison played prominent roles, emphasized a strong national government and promoted the interests of the larger states. The plan included a legislature composed of two houses and a system of checks and balances that recognized a separate executive and judiciary. This was the general blueprint that the delegates ultimately would adopt, but not before weeks of debate and compromise.

Once the Virginia Plan was before the convention, each of its 15 propositions was considered individually to determine precisely what was wanted in the new constitution. This process (in which each delegation had one vote) was to continue for two months. The major sticking point—indeed a crisis that threatened to wreck the convention—was the issue of state representation according to population in the legislature. The Virginia Plan called for proportional representation in both houses. On June 15, William Paterson presented a "small-state" alternative which became known as the New Jersey Plan. This called for a unicameral legislature in which each state would be equally represented. The lines were drawn, and the convention was deadlocked.

© Danziger/"The Christian Science Monitor"

Through 200 years of often stormy social change and ever-shifting public values, the U.S. Constitution has pursued the course of democracy.

A breakthrough came on June 20, when Roger Sherman, a 66-year-old merchant and public official from Connecticut, revived an earlier proposal: a bicameral legislature with equal representation in the Senate and proportional representation in the House of Representatives. This arrangement, which the convention finally adopted on July 16, became known as the Connecticut Plan or Great Compromise. It rescued the convention from catastrophe.

By July 26 the convention had approved 33 resolutions that could serve as the basis for a first draft of the new constitution. The Committee of Detail, made up of five delegates headed by John Rutledge of South Carolina, took a week to do this work, while the convention stood in recess. On August 6 the committee presented its draft of 23 articles, which was the basis of the next month of debate. The convention reconsidered everything that it had already accepted, modifying and refining wherever it deemed necessary.

A major focus of debate during this period was the importation of slaves—an issue that evoked sometimes angry disagreement. The assertion in the Declaration of Independence that "all men are created equal" posed an inherent challenge to the institution of slavery, but several states were adamant in protecting their investment in the supply of slave labor. The compromise on this issue prohibited Congress from outlawing slave trade until 1808 but allowed it to levy limited taxes on the importation of slaves. Another accommodation to the slavery interests was the three-fifths formula for slave representation in the House. These were accommodations that many delegates were unhappy with, but they helped bring the final document to fruition.

On September 8 the convention assigned the five-member Committee of Stile (Style) and Arrangement the task of putting the constitution into final form. This was to be principally the work of Gouverneur Morris. The committee presented its draft on September 12, the convention made further adjustments over the next three days, and the official document was ready for signing on Monday, September 17.

Of the 41 delegates present for the signing, 38 put their signatures to the proposed new U.S. Constitution; the name of a 39th delegate was added by proxy. The three other delegates—two from Virginia and one from Massachusetts—refused to sign. Afterward, as Washington noted in his personal diary, the "delegates dined together and took a cordial leave of each other; after which I returned to my lodgings, did some business with, and received the papers from, the secretary of the convention, and retired to meditate on the momentous work which had been executed. . . . "

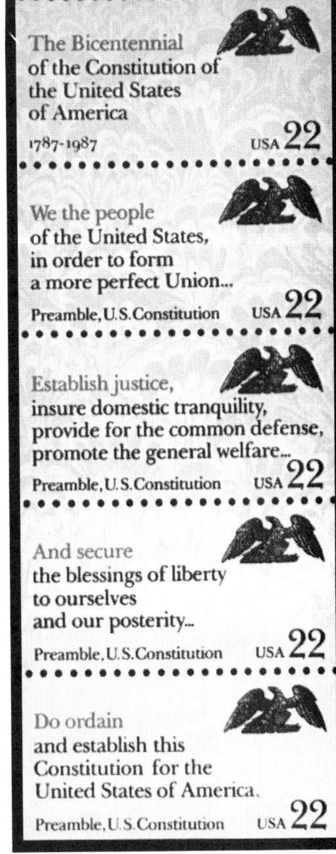

U.S. Postal Service

The U.S. Postal Service marked the bicentennial by issuing a series of five stamps that quote (sequentially) the Preamble to the Constitution.

Ratification. The Constitution was transmitted by the Convention to the Continental Congress, then sitting in New York, with the recommendations that it be submitted for ratification to popularly elected conventions in the individual states and that the document would take effect for those states ratifying it when nine of them agreed to it. The Continental Congress, impressed both by the caliber of the work done by the Constitutional Convention and by the political stature of the delegates, complied with these various requests.

Ratification was far from a foregone conclusion. Anti-federalist opponents were quick to point out the dangers of a powerful and remote central government. A major deficiency of the Constitution, they argued, was the lack of a bill of rights to protect their fundamental liberties against federal abuse. Three federalist defenders—Madison, Hamilton, and John Jay —wrote a series of 85 newspaper pieces called *The Federalist* papers to win support in the crucial state of New York. To meet the complaint of a lack of a bill of rights, Massachusetts federalists drafted a series of amendments that would also be proposed to other states.

Although the ratification process would not be fully completed until mid-1790, the required nine states had approved the document well within a year of its submission to the Continental Congress. The first of the nine, Delaware, voted to

The New York Historical Society

Virginia Museum

James Madison, top, *and John Marshall both had a major influence on the development of the Constitution and the constitutional process. Madison (1751–1836) played a key role at the Constitutional Convention. His notes on the delegates' debates are the only complete record of the convention's proceedings. Marshall (1755–1835) served as chief justice of the Supreme Court (1801–35) and was instrumental in establishing the principal of judicial review.*

ratify on Dec. 7, 1787; the decisive ninth state, New Hampshire, ratified on June 21, 1788. Rhode Island was the last state to endorse the document, on May 29, 1790. Half the state conventions gave their consent with the recommendation that a bill of rights be promptly considered in the first Congress under the Constitution. Although there was widespread concern over the expanded power of the proposed federal government and the much firmer Union provided by the new Constitution, by and large the people recognized the need for a strong central government to deal with pressing problems at home and abroad. Disturbances such as the Shays' Rebellion in Massachusetts—an armed insurrection by farmers against the state government—had convinced many people that the national government should be strengthened.

Upon ratification, the Continental Congress set up a schedule for the immediate implementation of the new U.S. Constitution. State selection of members of Congress and of presidential electors followed promptly. The first Congress under the Constitution assembled in New York on March 4, 1789, counted the votes for president, and arranged for Washington's inauguration on April 30. Congress then turned to the creation of the various executive departments, to the levying of necessary taxes, and to the establishment of a federal judiciary.

Bill of Rights and Judicial Review. One of the principal matters taken up by the first session of Congress was the consideration of constitutional amendments that would define and protect the fundamental rights and liberties of American citizens. The issue of a bill of rights was taken up in the House of Representatives at the urging of James Madison. On Aug. 21, 1791, the House sent to the Senate a bill containing 17 articles, which the Senate reduced to 12. The bill that emerged from the House-Senate committee and was submitted to the states for ratification included the first ten amendments as they exist today. They were preceded by two more of a technical nature, providing for changes in congressional apportionment and regulating congressional salaries, but these were not ratified by the states. The first ten amendments—the formal Bill of Rights—were ratified by the required three fourths of the states and became part of the Constitution on Dec. 15, 1791.

The 11th and 12th Amendments both addressed problems left by the Constitutional Convention. The 11th Amendment, adopted in 1798, barred the jurisdiction of federal courts in litigation by citizens of one state against the government of another state. The 12th Amendment, adopted in 1804, established separate voting for president and vice-president.

Another issue not clearly spelled out in the Constitution was who should have the ultimate authority to interpret the precise meaning of the document. The U.S. Supreme Court in an 1803 case called *Marbury v. Madison,* ruled that the federal judiciary has the power to interpret the Constitution and to nullify any laws passed by the federal or state legislatures that it deems unconstitutional. Chief Justice John Marshall argued that the Constitution requires the courts to enforce any law that complies with the Constitution. Thus, he reasoned, before the court is entitled to enforce a law, it first must determine whether the law is, in fact, in compliance with the Constitution.

This process, called "judicial review," has remained critical to constitutional interpretation to the present day. Over the decades, the U.S. Supreme Court has struck down as unconstitutional many acts of the federal and state legislatures. Such rulings have been guided by the changing judicial philosophies of the court members (who, according to Article II of the Constitution, are appointed by the president in collaboration with the Senate). An instrument of considerable flexibility, the Constitution requires continual interpretation and reinterpretation in its application to human affairs and the changing society. Its precise meanings are constantly being reconsidered.

A Living Document. The amendment process (established in Article V) and the practice of "judicial review" are two mechanisms by which the Constitution has been adapted to the changing needs and attitudes of American society. Among the fundamental alterations and additions effected through the amendment process were the abolition of slavery (13th Amendment, 1865), the guarantee of citizenship rights and "due process of law" for all persons born in the United States (14th Amendment, 1868), and the assurance of voting rights to women (19th Amendment, 1920). Under the process of judicial review—in the broadest sense of the term—the Supreme Court banned racial segregation (*Brown v. Board of Education,* 1954) and guaranteed the right to legal counsel in criminal proceedings (*Gideon v. Wainwright,* 1963). These are just two recent illustrations of the considerable influence of courts in American life.

Since ratification of the Bill of Rights in 1791, some 10,000 proposals for amending the Constitution have been introduced in Congress. Of that total, only 33 have been approved by Congress for submission to the states for ratification, and only 26 have been ratified and added to the Constitution. (*See* box, page 38). Indeed, new proposals are constantly being advanced. Since its founding in 1984, for example, the Committee on the

The United States has been generally reluctant to alter its Constitution. Only 26 amendments have been added during its 200-year history. During the 1970s and early 1980s, many women demonstrated their support for the Equal Rights Amendment (ERA), which Congress had approved in 1972. Although Congress extended the period for ratification by the states, the amendment was defeated in 1982.

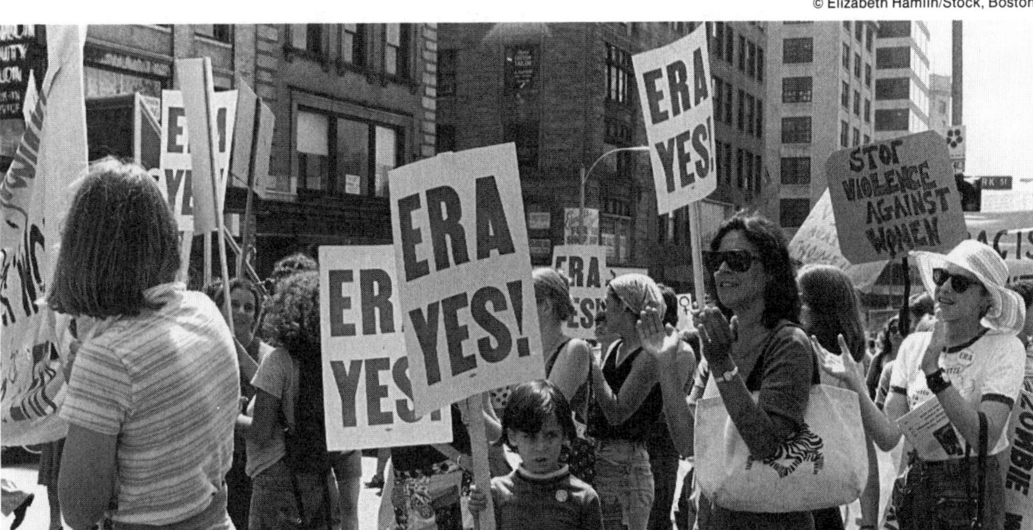

Constitutional System—headed by Washington lawyer Lloyd Cutler, U.S. Sen. Nancy Kassebaum (R-KS), and former U.S. Treasury Secretary C. Douglas Dillon—has sought to improve government performance through a variety of means, including several structural amendments to the Constitution. There has also been talk of lengthening congressional terms of office and coordinating them with the presidential term—proposals for which there appears to be little popular support. In recent years Congress has refused to adopt proposed amendments involving school prayer, abortion, and a balanced federal budget. In addition, the Equal Rights Amendment and an amendment granting the District of Columbia full congressional representation—both of which were approved by Congress—failed to win ratification by the states. The reluctance to adopt new amendments suggests that Americans are generally satisfied with the constitutional system they have, despite its apparent inefficiencies and the frustrations it sometimes causes.

The process of change, therefore, is left largely to the case-by-case deliberations of the Supreme Court. Yet even in that sphere, the way in which the Constitution is applied has been subject to debate. The conflict has to do with two distinct approaches to judicial intervention. In one tradition, known as "judicial activism," judges have taken considerable liberty in expanding the meaning and applying the "spirit" of Constitutional provisions. By contrast, the jurisprudence of "original intent" calls for restraint in extending the Constitution beyond the original intention of the Framers, as best determined. It was this approach—and its outcome on particular issues—that proved controversial in the Senate confirmation hearings of Supreme Court nominee Robert Bork during 1987.

Another major event of 1987 moved Americans to consider the meaning and limits of the Constitution. As a backdrop to the bicentennial celebrations, joint investigating committees of the U.S. House and Senate held public hearings on the sale of U.S. arms to Iran and the disbursement of proceeds to Nicaraguan contra rebels. The hearings focused on the relationship between Congress and the chief executive, and on the merits and limits of the rule of law in the conduct of foreign affairs. Sen. Daniel Inouye (D-HI), the chairman of the Senate committee, stated the basic issue: "Did this unseemly chapter in our history result from the disregard of our laws and Constitution . . . ? Or are we here today because of the inadequacy of our laws and Constitution?"

UPI/Bettmann Newsphotos

Warren E. Burger resigned in 1986 as chief justice of the United States to serve as head of the official Constitution bicentennial commission.

The first great celebration of the U.S. Constitution was a three-mile parade in Philadelphia on July 4, 1788. More than half the population of the city turned out as participants or spectators. For the Constitution's 100th birthday in September 1887, one and a half million people gathered in Philadelphia for a "moral and intellectual harvest" of speeches and parades. And the bicentennial of the Constitution in 1987 featured an even broader series of inspirational and educational events. As former Chief Justice Burger suggested, the ultimate aim of these celebrations was to encourage citizens to study and consider the meaning of their Constitution.

© Dick Durrence/Woodfin Camp & Assoc.

Industrial Competitiveness

The Challenge of the Global Marketplace

By Robert A. Senser

About the Author. During a writing career spanning 40 years, Robert A. Senser has specialized in labor and economic subjects. After an apprenticeship as a newspaper reporter in Illinois and Wisconsin, he served as editor of *Work,* published by the Catholic Council on Working Life, in Chicago, IL, in the 1950s and 1960s. He then was a labor and political officer in the U.S. Foreign Service for 22 years. His work as a free-lance writer includes the book *Primer on Interracial Justice* (1962), numerous pamphlets, and articles in various national publications. He is currently on the staff of the Asian-American Free Labor Institute in Washington, DC.

In 1956 a team of young engineers at Ampex Corporation, a small firm in Redwood City, CA, made a dramatic electronic breakthrough: they succeeded in recording a television picture on a reel of magnetic tape. After watching two minutes of the recorded tape, Ampex officials jumped to their feet, applauding and cheering. Here was another case of good old American know-how coming to the fore. Ampex had invented a new product, the videotape recorder, that would create another vast market for American industry—that is, if the usual scenario of 20th-century industrial innovation would prevail. But it did not.

Over the next two decades, some of the biggest names in U.S. industry—including the Radio Corporation of America (RCA), the Columbia Broadcasting System (CBS), and Music Corporation of America (MCA)—all plunged into the race to transform the videotape recorder, or VTR, into a machine for the home. But it turned out that Japanese companies, first Sony and then others, were the ones to perfect a marketable videocassette recorder, or VCR. In fact, it was so marketable that it became the most successful electronic appliance since

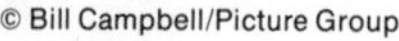
© Bill Campbell/Picture Group

© M. Setboum/JB Pictures

© Greg Davis/Sygma

South Korean autoworkers, above, *salute as their product, the Hyundai, is loaded for export. A worker at a Japanese electronics plant,* left, *does her part to make sure that her product is the best—a key feature of the Japanese work ethic. The United States faces strong competition from abroad on both the auto and the electronics fronts. By 1987, approximately 35% of new car sales in the United States were imports, and about 50% of the U.S. consumer electronics market had been taken by imports. Accordingly, many American retailers, including the car dealer,* above left, *advertise to discourage the buying of non-U.S. manufactured goods.*

the color television. Today nearly half the households in the United States have a VCR—none of them made in America.

The Japanese triumph over U.S. competitors in the VCR race has become a symbol of a growing challenge to the U.S. economy: How can American industry, long accustomed to competing almost alone in the huge U.S. market, cope in today's interdependent global market? The products of U.S. factories have lost ground among consumers both abroad and in the United States itself. Reversing that trend has become a major national concern. In the view of many experts from different ideological backgrounds, the problem has reached crisis proportions.

"Our ability to compete internationally faces unprecedented challenge from abroad," declared the 1985 report of the President's Commission on Industrial Competitiveness, a group of leaders from the public and private sectors. Not surprisingly, there is no national consensus on how to respond to that challenge, nor even a consensus on the precise nature of the challenge itself.

Defining the Goal. One way of looking at the challenge is that the United States, which has long been the strongest economic power in the world, must do its utmost to maintain that lead position. President Ronald Reagan reflected this view in his State of the Union Message of January 1987, when he stressed the urgency of pursuing "a national goal of assuring American competitive preeminence into the 21st century." The challenge, in this view, is simply to remain Number 1.

President Reagan's Commission on Industrial Competitiveness suggested a somewhat different approach. In its provocative two-volume study, "Global Competition: The New

Reality,'' the commission did not identify preeminence as the basic goal. ''Competitiveness,'' the commission states, ''does not require American leadership in all sectors.'' Nor is it ''a winner-take-all game, [since] all nations should benefit from the economic growth of their trading partners.'' Instead, in the commission definition, the competitive challenge is to ''produce goods and services that meet the test of international markets'' well enough to expand or at least maintain the nation's standard of living, specifically ''the real incomes of its citizens.''

In its own 1987 report on competitiveness, the National Association of Manufacturers (NAM) explicitly endorsed the approach of the President's Commission. ''While we could compete by lowering the American standard of living,'' the NAM said, ''that is a prescription for failure.''

A further distinction was made in the book *U.S. Competitiveness in the World Economy,* published by the Harvard Business School Press. The coauthor, Professor Bruce R. Scott, while agreeing that the ultimate measure of success in international competition is the effect on a nation's standard of living, argued that this ''means *earning* [it], not borrowing it.''

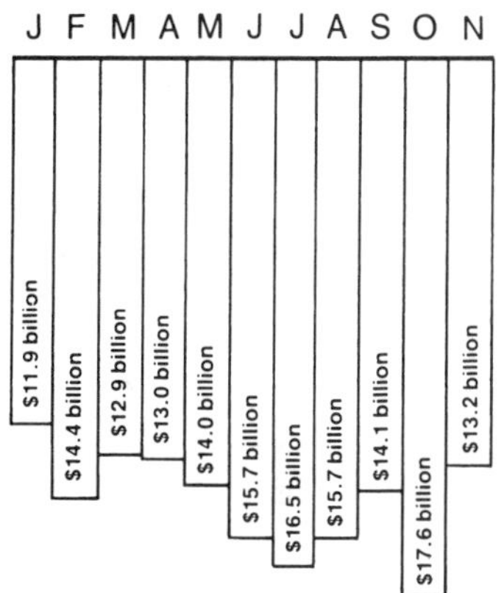

U.S. Department of Commerce

What's the Big Worry? However the challenge is defined, statistics on the U.S. position in world markets are not reassuring. Among the most worrisome are the following:

• Thanks to the nation's growing habit of buying more foreign goods (imports) than it sells abroad (exports), the U.S. international trade deficit is reaching a new record each year. The merchandise trade account for 1986 was in the red by almost $170 billion, a figure larger than the gross national product (GNP) of all but 20 countries in the world.

• In manufactured products alone, the U.S. trade deficit in 1986 came to a record $145 million, accounting for more than four fifths of the total merchandise trade deficit. Once the world leader in manufactured exports, the United States fell behind West Germany more than 15 years ago. Then in 1985 it came in third behind West Germany and Japan, both of which took full advantage of the freedom to ship to the U.S. market, the largest in the world and one of the most open to foreign business.

In monitoring the dark trade clouds, some economists have spotted what they think are silver linings. One of the positive forces they see is the U.S. capacity for the export of ''services''—a catch-all category of financial transactions, sometimes called ''invisibles,'' that includes such items as international travel, income on foreign investments, royalties, and sales of business services. The Council of Economic Advisers, for one, believes the U.S. competitive advantage in international services has the potential to offset the deficit in manufactured goods. After an exhaustive study, however, the Congressional Office of Technology Assessment (OTA) found that hope illusory. ''Trade in services [for the United States as well as other countries] will remain considerably smaller than trade in goods,'' wrote the OTA in its 1987 report.

Susan V. Steinkamp/Picture Group

In January 1987, a group of Americans concerned about the status of U.S. competitiveness held a rally near the Capitol to foster improved productivity.

High hopes also have been pinned on high technology. Although variously defined—but always including such areas as microelectronics, biotechnology, robotics, and lasers—high-tech industries are commonly recognized as the "sunrise industries," bound to replace "sunset industries"—such as steel and rubber—as the U.S. strength in international competition. But high tech's sun has risen in other countries, too. After surpluses in previous years, the United States ran a $2.6 billion deficit in high technology in 1986.

The Role of Manufacturing. "A strong manufacturing sector is not a requisite for a prosperous economy," said a 1984 report by the Office of Economic Research of the New York Stock Exchange. That conviction, held in various forms, has for many years influenced the policies and practices of the U.S. business community and government, with inevitable consequences for the nation's position in world trade. The Office of the U.S. Trade Representative once assured Congress that an evolution from manufacturing to a "post-industrial" service economy was a "natural change."

This view has its intellectual underpinnings in a much-quoted 1973 book by Daniel Bell, a professor of sociology at Harvard, *The Coming of Post-Industrial Society: A Venture in Social Forecasting*. A book published in 1987, however, titled *Manufacturing Matters: The Myth of the Post-Industrial Economy,* makes the first full-scale rebuttal to the popular scenario that minimizes the importance of manufacturing. The authors, Stephen S. Cohen and John Zysman, professors at the University of California at Berkeley and codirectors of the Berkeley Roundtable on International Economy, argue persuasively that a thriving manufacturing sector is vital to the health and wealth of a modern society.

The heart of their argument is as follows: The manufacturing industries create business and jobs—income of all kinds—not just within their own sector but throughout the economy. (Manufacturing and the services sold to manufacturing firms account for half the entire U.S. GNP.) Besides, they contend, manufacturing is the seedbed for expanding technological know-how and hence for advancing competitiveness across the whole range of the production process. "For example," Cohen and Zysman write, "by abandoning the production of televisions, the U.S. electronics industry quickly lost the know-how to design, develop, refine, and competitively produce the next generation of that product, the VCR." Similarly, the United States until not long ago was the major source of technological know-how for steel and automobile makers, but now it has to import such services. And the decline in hands-on production experience is threatening other areas of traditional U.S. expertise, such as petrochemical engineering and construction engineering.

"The transition we are experiencing is not out of industry into services," Cohen and Zysman maintain, "but from one kind of industrial society to another." It is one in which the competitive edge belongs to those who master and control modern manufacturing production processes, particularly through "mass application of microelectronic-based tech-

The cartoon below illustrates concern about the growing U.S. trade deficit and the United States' ability to compete successfully on the world scene. The one at right points out the extent to which Japan's exports exceed its imports. With Japan's trade surplus totaling $83 billion in 1986, its allies are pressuring the Asian nation to curb exports and open its markets to imports.

© Linda Boileau/Rothco Cartoons

David Langdon © Punch from Rothco Cartoons

Some 450,000 companies in West Germany participate in a program to help train the nation's teenagers for the labor force through vocational education ("voc ed") courses. Seventy-five percent of West German youth enter the job market directly after high school.

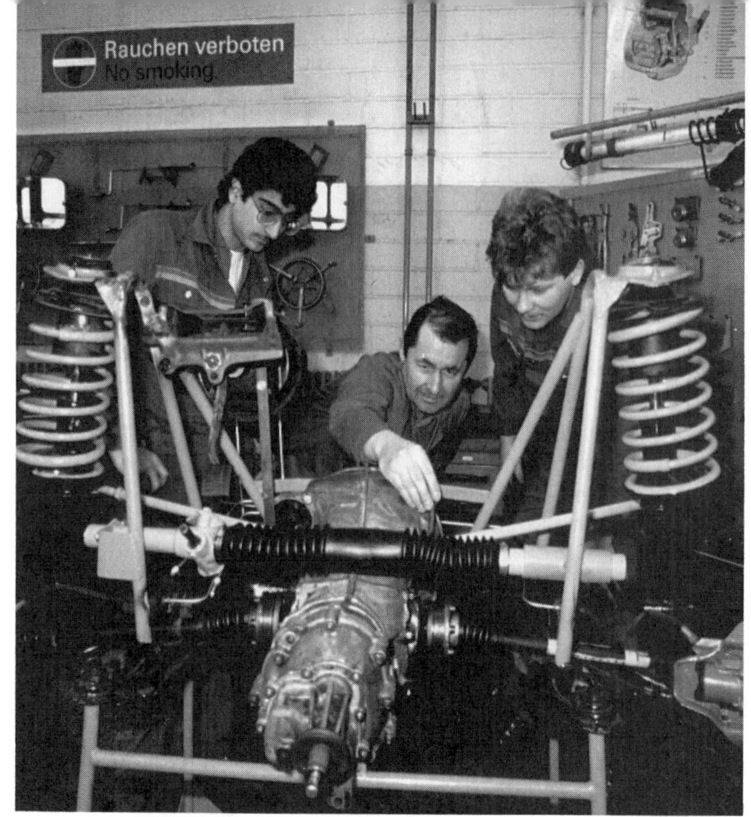

© Bossu/Sygma

niques." The movement of production outside the United States, therefore, is a "fast track to disaster," because the shift will carry even the growing service sector into decline.

In a similar vein, *Business Week* has decried the emergence of a new kind of U.S. corporation—"manufacturing companies that do little manufacturing [but] import components or products from low-wage countries, slap their own names on them, and sell them in America," thereby "retarding productivity, innovation, and the standard of living." Before his death in July 1987, U.S. Secretary of Commerce Malcolm Baldrige testified to a congressional committee that the United States, in order to reduce its mounting trade deficit, must depend on revitalizing its manufacturing industries.

Hard Choices. The U.S. competitive position in the world marketplace derives from a vast number of daily activities and decisions, ranging from how well people work in factories and offices to how well the officials of the Federal Reserve Board and the central banks of other nations mesh their policies.

Fortunately, labor productivity in the United States, sluggish for years, is picking up, especially in manufacturing. The turnaround came in 1986. For the first time in the 37 years that the Bureau of Labor Statistics has collected comparative data, manufacturing labor productivity rose faster in the United States than in nine other major industrial nations. The annual increase in U.S. output per work hour was 3.7%, compared with 2.9% in Great Britain, 2.8% in Japan, 1.9% in West Germany and France, and 1.2% in Italy. Along with this record performance in productivity came a decline in labor cost per unit of production. The United States posted a 0.4% decrease

Japan's educational system is given considerable credit for the nation's economic success. Some 90% of the populace graduate from high school, and those that do not go to college receive special job-oriented training.

© J.P. Laffont/Sygma

in 1986, while all major competitors showed heavy increases —an average of 22% in U.S. dollar terms.

A country's trade performance, however, also depends greatly on what happens outside the workplace. Of transcending importance is the huge arena of public policy—what governments do or do not do and how they interconnect their actions. In recent years, the United States has traveled an economic policy road different from that of its major foreign competitors. As pointed out in a report by the U.S. Commerce Department, the United States, unlike its competitors, adopted a series of "expansionary" policies in the early 1980s —e.g., deregulation, broad tax-rate reductions, and investment tax credits—which spurred huge inflows of foreign capital. These, in turn, "allowed the United States to consume more than it produced, simultaneously financing enlarged consumer spending, an investment boom, and a growing government deficit." One way out, concerted action on reducing the federal government's enormous budget deficit, has long been hampered by a sharp conflict over the best method: whether it should be achieved by increasing revenues (and, if so, whose taxes?) or by decreasing expenditures (and, if so, which ones?), or by both.

Controversy over public policy on competitiveness abounds, and that is quite natural given the powerful effect that government decisions have on different public and private interests. Prime examples are the impact of the federal government on two key areas of competitiveness: research and development, and the conditions of international trade.

The hottest controversy centers on what conditions, if any, Washington should place on U.S. trade with other nations. The free-trade policies that the United States has adopted—and, with some success, actively promoted to others—since World War II have remained largely intact despite the nation's burgeoning trade deficit. Under similar circumstances, "no other country in the world would have left its market as open as the U.S., and clearly this has been of enormous benefit to the rest of the world," says U.S. Trade Representative Clayton Yeuter.

In one classic case, the U.S. government gave foreign competitors free entry into the vast American telecommunications market, the largest in the world, when it broke up the AT&T monopoly in 1984. By not requesting any quid pro quo from other governments, it put U.S. firms at a competitive disadvantage in the international marketplace. Sen. John Danforth (R-MO) called the U.S. inaction "nothing less than the unilateral giveaway of the U.S. market" to Japanese and European manufacturers.

In the dispute over trade policy, one side, vigorously defended by many economists, advocates no conditions at all on trade (apart from those set by buyers and sellers themselves) and opposes all trade barriers and any form of "protectionism." The other side, with a growing following in the U.S. Congress and elsewhere, argues that other countries are not living up to the ideals of free trade and that the U.S. government should therefore intervene more actively to establish and enforce rules of trade. One such rule would be reciprocity backed up by retaliation if necessary: for example, your country cannot sell telephones in ours unless we can in yours.

Courtesy, Hewlett-Packard Company

John A. Young, 55-year-old president and chief executive officer of Hewlett-Packard, is the founder and head of the Council on Competitiveness.

Finding Solutions. On a variety of other issues, the United States has not pursued its national interest as single-mindedly as many of its competitors. Consequently, while some sectors may make gains, the overall outlook is not bright for a substantial improvement soon in the U.S. competitive position. Defying the odds, however, many groups both within and outside government are working as never before to make competitiveness a national priority. Some 200 members of Congress have joined a special caucus devoted to it. Universities and research organizations are funding special studies of it. And the mass media are raising public consciousness about it.

Perhaps the most ambitious effort is that by 24 leaders of U.S. business, labor, and academia. This group has launched a joint national initiative through its newly founded Council on Competitiveness, headquartered in Washington, DC, and headed by John A. Young, the president and chief executive officer of Hewlett-Packard Corporation. The council, an outgrowth of the President's Commission on Industrial Competitiveness (also headed by Young), is dedicated to making sure that competitiveness will be more than a buzzword that passes out of fashion. Its goal, according to Young, is to create a national consensus "about what's required to improve America's competitiveness and then to serve as a catalyst [for] solutions."

See also INTERNATIONAL TRADE AND FINANCE; UNITED STATES—The Economy.

© Grey Villet/Black Star

Baby Craving

New Alternatives for the Childless

By Jenny Tesar

Millions of couples today want a child but cannot have one in the normal manner. They are unable to conceive or the woman cannot carry a pregnancy to term. In the past, the only alternative for such couples was to adopt. In recent years, however, advances in medical science have given them several new options, such as artificial insemination, in vitro fertilization, and surrogate motherhood. The adoption field is changing, too, as would-be parents compete for the comparatively few children placed for adoption each year. Nor are married couples the only people eager to have children. Many unmarried couples and single people also are anxious to become parents, adding to the competition at adoption agencies and increasing the use of the new technologies.

The new alternatives available to the childless raise a number of difficult legal, social, and ethical questions. Who is the mother when a baby is the product of one woman's egg and another woman's womb? Do sperm and egg donors have parental rights? Should federal moneys be used to subsidize adoption by lower-income families? Does a woman have a right to make a profit for gestating a baby? How might a child

About the Author. Jenny Tesar, a free-lance writer, living in Connecticut's Fairfield County, specializes in the fields of science, medicine, and technology. She is the author of the *Introduction to Animals,* a part of the Wonders of Wildlife series, and *Parents as Teachers.* A computer enthusiast, Ms. Tesar has written a variety of educational programs.

be affected by the knowledge that he or she is the product of a surrogate womb or of an in vitro fertilization of an anonymous donor egg and donor sperm?

Another issue is cost. A couple can easily spend $30,000 or more to have a child via one of the new technologies. Adoption may cost upward of $10,000. Is it fair that such high costs restrict many options to the well-to-do?

And what laws, if any, are needed to regulate the business of artificially aided conception, surrogate motherhood, and adoption? How do we balance public policy with the rights of people who desperately want children?

Infertility—Causes. Approximately one out of every six American couples of childbearing age suffers from infertility, generally defined as the inability to conceive after a year or more of trying. Infertility has many causes, some still undefined, some affecting both sexes. Cigarette smoking may be a factor in both male and female infertility. So are sexually transmitted diseases (STDs), which affect some 30 million Americans and, if untreated, can cause not only impaired fertility but even sterility.

The chief cause of male infertility is faulty sperm—either a low sperm count, abnormally shaped sperm, or sperm with low motility. Some of these problems can be solved with hormone injections or steroids. Changes in life-style, such as improved nutrition and decreased intake of alcohol or nicotine, often can dramatically improve sperm count. Another common cause of infertility in men is varicoceles—varicose veins in the scrotum. This causes elevated temperature in the scrotum, which inhibits sperm production and motility. The problem can be corrected surgically, and almost half the men who undergo the operation later father a child.

Female infertility often results from malfunctioning Fallopian tubes, a pair of delicate ducts that extend from the ovaries to the uterus. Fertilization normally occurs in a Fallopian tube as a sperm traveling up from the uterus unites with an egg moving down from the ovary. If the tube is scarred, blocked, or missing, fertilization cannot take place. STDs may cause scarring of the tubes, and endometriosis—an abnormal growth of uterine tissue—may block the tubes. Surgery can sometimes correct these problems.

Other causes of female infertility include the failure of ovaries to release eggs, uterine scars and tumors, and abnormalities in the cervix. Again, many of these problems can be corrected with surgery and/or drugs. For example, 80% of the women who have difficulty ovulating (producing eggs) can be treated successfully with so-called fertility drugs.

Alternate Methods of Reproduction. Infertile people who cannot be helped by traditional treatments and who are either unable or unwilling to adopt can turn to one of several alternatives, including artificial insemination, in vitro fertilization, gamete intra-Fallopian transfer (GIFT), and embryo transfer.

In artificial insemination, the oldest of these techniques, a syringe is used to deposit semen either directly into the uterus

© Hank Morgan

AP/Wide World

In vitro fertilization is one of the new technologies developed to help infertile couples conceive. As part of the procedure, eggs, which have been removed from a woman, are placed in a glass laboratory dish (above) *and mixed with a man's sperm. The fertilized eggs are cultured and later placed in the woman's uterus. Lynda and Bruce Jacobssen* (left) *are the proud parents of five sons, the first all-male quintuplets conceived by the technique.*

or near the uterine entrance. This procedure can be used in cases where the woman's cervix is excessively acid or alkaline and therefore "hostile" to sperm. It also can be used when the man has a very low sperm count. In that case, the physician collects a number of ejaculates, separates out the sperm, and deposits the entire amount at once.

Artificial insemination can be used as well to deposit donor sperm. This procedure is employed when husbands are totally infertile or are known to suffer from genetic disorders such as Huntington's disease. Artificial insemination of donor sperm also is used by single women who wish to bear children. An estimated 8,000 American women annually give birth to babies conceived with donor sperm.

In vitro is Latin for "in glass." In vitro fertilization is the technique that produces so-called test-tube babies. The procedure is generally used to enable women with blocked or damaged Fallopian tubes to conceive a child. Typically, the woman is treated with hormones that stimulate the development and maturation of eggs. A small incision is made in the abdominal wall, and a fiberoptic instrument called a laparoscope is used to remove the eggs. The eggs are then placed in a glass laboratory dish and mixed with the sperm of the man. The fertilized eggs are cultured until cell division begins. Then, some 42 to 78 hours after the laparoscopy, several of the fertilized eggs are placed in the uterus of the woman, with the hope that some will attach to the uterine wall and develop into embryos.

The first baby born from in vitro fertilization was Louise Brown of Great Britain in 1978. Since then, some 2,000 babies have been born from this technique. The best success rate for in vitro fertilization has been obtained in Australia, where women undergoing the procedure have a 50% chance of having a baby after four in vitro treatments. In the United States, the success rate is about 20%. According to researchers, one reason for the discrepancy is the U.S. ban on federal funding of research on human embryos and on external fertilization of human eggs. Consequently, they maintain, many of the technical developments in this area have been achieved by researchers in other countries.

Joseph Cardinal Ratzinger, head of the Congregation for the Doctrine of the Faith, explains the March 1987 ruling by the Catholic Church, condemning all forms of artificial fertilization and generation of human life outside the body.

AP/Wide World

Meanwhile, however, Dr. Ricardo Asch of the University of Texas Health Center has developed a procedure somewhat similar to in vitro fertilization, called gamete (reproductive cell) intra-Fallopian transfer, or GIFT. Here, too, a laparoscope is used to remove mature eggs. The eggs are then mixed with sperm and immediately returned to the woman's body via the laparoscope. But instead of being placed in the uterus, they are deposited in the upper portion of the Fallopian tube, where conception normally occurs. The GIFT procedure can be used when there is cervical hostility, a low sperm count, or any of several other problems. It also can be used for women whose ovaries do not produce eggs or whose eggs are suspected of carrying genetic defects. The man's sperm is used to fertilize donor eggs, which are then deposited in one of the woman's Fallopian tubes.

Patients who undergo the GIFT procedure are reported to conceive 35% to 40% of the time. Dr. Elynne Margulis, director of the GIFT program at Columbia-Presbyterian Medical Center in New York City, says: "We believe that GIFT has a high rate of success because the fertilized eggs travel down the Fallopian tube, just as in natural conception. In addition, since we don't interfere with the uterus when placing the gamete into the body, the endometrial lining, which is crucial for embryonic development, is undisturbed."

Embryo transfer is another method used when a woman is sterile or concerned about genetic risks. This procedure involves a second, donor woman who is artificially inseminated with the husband's sperm. The fertilized egg is then removed from the donor and implanted in the wife's uterus.

© Paul L. Merideth/Click, Chicago

With the guidance of counsel, right, a couple interviews a possible surrogate mother. More than 500 babies have been born to surrogate mothers since the first such arrangement in 1976, 65 of them in 1986.

For women who are unable to carry a baby to term because of a defective uterus, a "surrogate womb" may represent a viable option. In this procedure, a wife's egg is fertilized with her husband's sperm in the laboratory and then implanted in the uterus (womb) of another woman, who gives birth to the child.

The techniques described above are not cure-alls. They may help some patients but not others. Nor are they universally accepted. In March 1987 the Congregation for the Doctrine of the Faith, the Vatican agency responsible for monitoring Catholic orthodoxy, released a report condemning all such methods, and the document was endorsed by Pope John Paul II. However, like the processes it condemned, the report itself caused some debate.

Surrogate Motherhood. This approach enables a man to have a genetically related child if his wife is unable to bear children. Through a specializing agency or a lawyer, an agreement is made between the couple and a "surrogate mother." The latter agrees to be artificially impregnated with the man's sperm and, if pregnancy results, to turn over the child to the couple at birth. Typically, the couple pays all medical, legal, and insurance costs and gives the woman $10,000—a total of $25,000 or more. Since the first such arrangement in 1976, more than 500 babies have been born to surrogate mothers. The great majority of cases have gone as planned.

Photos AP/Wide World

After surrogate mother Mary Beth Whitehead (right) *refused to turn over the child, "Baby M"* (above), *to her father, William Stern* (also above), *and his wife Elizabeth, the headline-making case landed in New Jersey Family Court. The judge ruled in favor of the Sterns.*

The most notable exception was the case of "Baby M." On Feb. 6, 1985, Mary Beth Whitehead, a young New Jersey mother of two, signed a surrogate agreement with William and Elizabeth Stern, also of New Jersey. On March 27, 1986, Whitehead gave birth to a baby girl but refused to relinquish her to the Sterns. Whitehead did not accept her fee or sign over custody, instead taking the child home with her. When the Sterns sued for custody, Whitehead and her husband fled with the baby to Florida. Detectives hired by the Sterns tracked down the Whiteheads, seized the baby, and took her to the Sterns. The case went before New Jersey Family Court Judge Harvey Sorkow, who on March 31, 1987, awarded custody of Baby M to William Stern. Sorkow held that the surrogate motherhood contract was legal and binding and that it was in the child's best interest to be with the Sterns.

In his ruling, Judge Sorkow pointed out that "there can be no solution satisfactory to all in this kind of case." He stressed that "it is necessary that laws be adopted to give our society a sense of definition and direction if the concept is to be allowed to further develop. . . . If there is no law then society will suffer the negative aspects of this alternative reproduction vehicle that appears to hold out so much hope to the childless who make up a substantial segment of our society."

Legislators in a number of states have since introduced legislation to regulate surrogate motherhood. Some groups, however, including Roman Catholics and orthodox Jews, condemn the practice and believe it should be banned. Some believe it violates laws against baby selling, although Sorkow rejected this argument, pointing out that Stern is Baby M's

© Arthur Grace/Stock, Boston

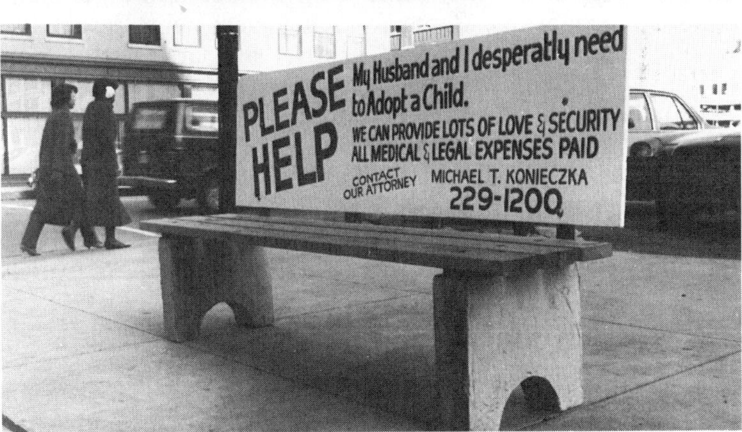

AP/Wide World

The number of adoptable white infants has declined in recent years. Consequently, many Americans wishing to adopt children are turning to new avenues. Some are resorting to clever advertising (left); others are delighted to welcome foreign-born children into their homes.

biological father. Other people support the practice but recognize the need for guidelines.

If surrogate motherhood is to be regulated by formal legislation, questions that need to be answered include: If a surrogate changes her mind, should she be allowed to keep the baby? If an abnormality in the fetus is detected during gestation, should abortion be an option? Who should decide? If the baby is born physically or mentally handicapped, who is responsible for the child? Should any couple be allowed to use surrogates, or only those who are infertile? Should single men be allowed to have surrogates bear their children?

New Doors to Adoption. While more Americans than ever before are seeking to adopt children, the pool of available children has been shrinking over the past two decades. At least three factors have been cited as responsible for the tight supply: more widespread use of contraceptives, greater availability and acceptability of abortions, and greater acceptance of unwed parenthood.

In particularly short supply are adoptable white infants. Adoption agencies often tell couples to expect a wait of eight years or more for a healthy white infant. As a result, many white couples are looking elsewhere. One trend is a growing interest among white couples in adopting black infants. Although the social stigma attached to such adoptions has decreased tremendously in recent decades, the trend is condemned by certain groups. The National Association of Black Social Workers, for example, opposes placement of minority children in white homes, considering interracial adoption an affront to black pride. Many blacks also feel that social service agency regulations discriminate against adoption by black adults. Requirements for relatively high income levels, stable employment, and two-parent families make many would-be parents ineligible, they say.

Another avenue being pursued by infertile couples is adoption of foreign-born children. The number of such children adopted by Americans rose from 4,868 in 1981 to 9,945 in 1986. The great majority of these adoptees came from South Korea; most of the rest came from Mexico and other Latin American countries. Some foreign governments resent this practice, however, and have set strict standards for adoption of native children by citizens of other nations.

Some couples wanting to adopt have found truth in the slogan, "It pays to advertise." In their effort to find unwed mothers who wish to surrender their babies, these couples may take out ads in newspapers and send mass mailings to doctors. They may even place notices in supermarkets, on bulletin boards in Laundromats, or on windows of parked cars.

At the same time, unfortunately, there has been an increase in the number of unscrupulous individuals and groups who prey on people eager to have children. Some lawyers and private agencies charge exorbitant fees to arrange adoptions. Although baby selling is illegal, there have been instances of payments to women in return for their giving up babies. Worst of all are the smugglers who bring babies, some of whom have been kidnapped, into the United States to sell to the highest bidders.

More subtle legal, ethical, and psychological issues also have arisen. Are open adoptions, in which children know their natural parents as well as their adoptive parents, wise? Should single adults be allowed to adopt? Should homosexual couples be allowed? Should federal funds be used to support adoption of handicapped children and older children? To support adoption by minority adults? Should private adoptions be prohibited throughout the country? (They already are in some states.)

The quest for a baby, whether by adoption or by one of the other means now available to infertile people, is not an easy undertaking. It can involve legal risks, frustration, and heartbreak. But for the couples who are successful, the joy of parenthood is worth every expense and every moment of anguish. For these lucky people, having a child of their own is a dream come true.

The Southland Corporation

The Convenience Boom

By Jeffrey H. Hacker

8:15 A.M. The programmable coffee maker is already brewing when the Jones family comes downstairs. Henry Jones grabs a cup and hurries off to work. On his way to the office he stops at the 7-Eleven store to fill up with gas, get some cash from the bank machine, and pick up the dry cleaning. While he's waiting in line, he scans the rack of videocassettes and takes one off. Back in the car, it finally occurs to him. "The 15th! Our anniversary!" He grabs the radio phone and orders a dozen roses.

Back at home, Mary Jones puts breakfast in the microwave and calls the Grocery Express. As she's giving her order, the microwave buzzes, and she gives Tommy his breakfast.

"And could you deliver that at 5:30?" she asks.

Before leaving the house, Mary writes a check for the Lawn Doctor and leaves a key for the Molly Maid. On the way to work, she drops off Tommy at the Kinder-Care and leaves a roll of film at the Fotomat. She's at her desk by 9:00.

About the Author. Jeffrey H. Hacker, editor of this annual, is the author of four books for young adults—*Government Subsidy to Industry* (1982), *Franklin D. Roosevelt* (1983), *Carl Sandburg* (1984), and *The New China* (1986). A free-lance writer and editor, Mr. Hacker has done extensive promotional writing for various consumer products.

Convenience car-care facilities represent one of the fastest and most competitive new industries in the United States today. Some 2,000 rapid oil-change and lubrication centers, many franchised, were operating by 1987.

Jiffy Lube International

Convenience. With the possible exceptions of exotic food, home-equity loans, and designer workout clothes, there is no commodity in greater demand among young working Americans today. Time savers. Work savers. Anything to help with the chores and unknot the tangle of career, family, home, and leisure. Faster than a ten-minute oil change, supply has met demand and the "convenience industry" is venturing into goods and services that make the rugged frontier spirit look like so much instant pudding. In major cities throughout the United States, personal convenience firms will pick up the kids, walk the family dog, or water the plants at the drop of a phone receiver. Pizza-delivery franchises are booming, microwave dinners are taking over the supermarket freezers, and new fast-food outlets continue to sprout up. Malls stay open late, but you can shop at home if you prefer. You have one machine to open your garage door and another one to answer your phone. Child care, pet care, lawn care: it is all right at your fingertips. The signs of the times read "fast," "easy," "convenient."

Time and Money There is nothing new about the convenience industry, of course. It is really as old as technology itself. What is new is the breadth of goods and services that have sprung up to meet the demands of a changing society. The new era in time-efficient consumerism can be traced to the first McDonald's restaurant and the birth of the fast-food industry in the 1950s. More recently, however, sweeping changes in the American way of life have opened up vastly greater market opportunities for the convenience trade.

The real commodity is time. The key demographic changes are sharp increases in the number of two-income families and households headed by singles. In the early 1960s, 26% of all U.S. families had two wage earners; today about 44% wield two paychecks, and the proportion is expected to exceed 50% by the early 1990s. Meanwhile, the number of persons living alone or with nonrelatives accounts for about 30% of U.S. households; such "nonfamily" residences have accounted for 48% of the households added since 1980. What this all amounts to is a radical decline in the proportion of traditional households with one wage earner and one full-time homemaker. Two-income families have more money to spend, but they have less time in which to spend it. Single-member households are even harder pressed. In short, time is becoming a scarce resource on the American landscape, and the demand for convenience is soaring.

Rothco

"She can't decide what to serve at her dinner party."

For the so-called "baby boomers," a generation that grew up on fast foods, TV dinners, and canned vegetables, convenience was already a way of life. Gratification, like oatmeal, was instant. Now, as that generation juggles parenthood and professional life, the demands are even greater. If "instant" used to mean 15 minutes, now it means five. What's more, instancy itself is not enough. Two-income affluence also has brought with it a demand for higher quality and broader variety. Canned franks and beans just does not cut the mustard anymore. Seafood Newburg and spinach soufflé are the orders of the day. Beef Wellington might be nice tomorrow. Whether it comes to food, clothes, household products, or entertainment, convenience today means superior quality and wide selection as well as fast, easy access.

All that carries a price, of course. Goods and services targeted at the time-pressed, upscale consumer typically carry a substantial price premium. Convenience stores, featuring a broad diversity of goods and late-night hours, might charge $1.45 for a loaf of bread that costs $1.20 in the supermarket. Some quality mail-order houses, which offer unconditional guarantees and one-day delivery, may charge more for a ski jacket, say, than do some department stores for a similar product. Convenience plus quality and selection equals cost.

Faster Food. The new emphasis on convenience perhaps is most evident in the $500 billion U.S. food and beverage industry. Both the retail-food industry and the restaurant trade are acutely aware of the ever-rising demand for fast, convenient fare. Changes in consumer behavior have opened whole new realms in product development and marketing.

In the grocery business, no development in the last decade has had a greater impact than the introduction and market penetration of microwave ovens. An estimated 60% of U.S. kitchens now are equipped with the device, with the proportion expected to reach 90% by the 1990s. The microwave boom has sent food packagers scrambling to come up with new concepts in home "cooking." Already it has given birth to such tasty time savers as gourmet frozen entrées, one-minute sauces, and microwave popcorn. One major food company is developing a line of microwave-only products that includes a ten-minute cake mix. A host of other companies are introducing new recipes or repackaging existing products for the microwave.

But the changes in the neighborhood supermarket extend well beyond the freezer case. The demand for convenience and quality also has given rise to a whole smorgasbord of

The convenience factor has always been a prime reason for the success of the fast-food restaurant. Recognizing this fact, McDonald's is trying to improve service by adding staff and a second drive-through window at its busier establishments, and Burger King, a chief competitor, has adopted a new ad slogan: "the best food for fast times."

© L.L.T. Rhodes/Taurus

alternatives—do-it-yourself salads and desserts, prepared foods, store-baked bread and pastry, specialty cheese and deli items, lobsters fresh from the tank, and just about anything else the stomach desires. Along with microwave items, carryout fresh foods are at the top of America's shopping list in the late 1980s.

With all the innovations in the grocery business, however, restaurants continue to gobble up an increasing share of the consumer-spending pie. In 1987, meals eaten away from home accounted for more than 40% of total U.S. spending on food; that represented an increase of more than 4% from 1983. The biggest rise continues to be seen in the franchise chains; food sales topped $52 billion in 1986, compared with only $15 billion a decade earlier. As McDonald's, Burger King, Wendy's, Kentucky Fried Chicken, Domino's Pizza, and all the others battle it out for market share, the public appetite seems to grow and grow. In 1972 there was a restaurant for every 845 people in the United States; by 1987 the figure had fallen to 685. Meanwhile, the microwave revolution and competition among the chains themselves have put a new emphasis on the *fast* in "fast foods." Burger King's new ad slogan is "the best food for fast times." McDonald's describes its Egg McMuffin as "breakfast by the hand."

Convenience Stores. That the convenience boom goes beyond food is perhaps best evidenced by the changes taking place in that American institution known as the convenience store. Once the place where you picked up a quart of milk on a Sunday night or a doughnut and coffee on the way to work, the convenience store today is a virtual one-stop shopping mall. Along with packaged food, beverages, candy, newspapers, and cigarettes, many convenience stores now offer everything from gasoline to pizza and hamburgers, videocassette rentals, automatic-teller machines, dry-cleaning services, and airplane-ticket dispensers. Southland Corporation, owner of the 7-Eleven chain, is even installing Hardee's fast-food outlets in several of its stores. The new ultraconvenience store has been one of the great successes in U.S. re-

New and larger malls, with longer and longer shopping hours, continue to sprout up across the United States. At such centers, consumers can purchase almost anything; be entertained by special performances or events; partake of a wide variety of food; as well as catch the most recent movie.

© Stephanie Silverman/Gamma-Liaison

tailing over the last decade. The number of stores increased from 30,200 in 1976 to 75,000 in 1986. Over the same ten-year period, sales skyrocketed from \$8.6 billion to \$65 billion.

At-Home Shopping. Mail order, television, and electronic shopping services represent another major part of the new convenience industry. The 1980s home-video revolution—which gave rise to cable television, videocassettes, on-line data bases, and various other home-communications systems—has not only given consumers a greater selection of (and easier access to) entertainment and information, but it also has opened up new outlets for at-home shopping. Meanwhile, mail-order trade continues to grow by leaps and bounds. Catalogue sales were expected to reach more than \$50 billion in 1987, compared with \$28.8 billion in 1980. All told, at-home shopping has been growing at a rapid annual rate of 12%, with purchases expected to total \$65 billion in 1987. Within a decade, say some experts, one third of all U.S. retail purchasing may be done from the home.

Lands' End, Inc.

More and more busy Americans are doing their buying through the catalog. Sales at Lands' End have increased sevenfold since 1981. Overall mail-order sales were expected to exceed \$50 billion in 1987.

Now That's Service! Beyond food and beyond retail trade, the new demand for convenience has given rise to an array of services never before available even to the most conspicuous of consumers. Major commercial enterprises have introduced special services that cater more to the customer, and, in the best tradition of free-market entrepreneurship, small businesses have sprouted up to fill almost any day-to-day consumer need. Several of these small start-up ventures have grown into national franchise chains; many others continue to do a lively business at the local level.

Among the many major industries in which consumers have benefited from basic service innovations are telephone communications, banking and finance, and travel. In communications, recent years have seen the introduction of so-called "smart" telephones, cellular radio car phones, automatic answering machines, and, since the divestiture of AT&T in 1984, a variety of service alternatives. In banking, the new conveniences include bill paying by telephone, banking from the

The videocassette recorder (VCR) has given rise to a vast new home-entertainment industry. As of 1987, videocassette rentals and sales had reached some \$7.2 billion annually.

© David Falconer/Black Star

© Billy E. Barnes/Click, Chicago

Electronic banking systems, introduced on a wide scale in the late 1970s, offer customers the luxury of 24-hours-a-day service.

home, and automatic-teller machines. In addition, changes in U.S. law have hastened the era of one-stop investment and finance by allowing banks to participate in the discount brokerage and insurance businesses, and by allowing other types of financial companies to enter traditional banking business. In the travel industry, the innovation of curb-side airport check-in has been supplemented by such services as computerized information and booking for flight connections, hotel rooms, car rentals, and the like. Indeed, technological advances—especially the ever-expanding use of the computer—have translated into greater convenience for consumers and workers alike in almost any area of trade and commerce. One need only look around to notice the changes.

Beyond that, the great American time shortage has given birth to a whole host of totally new service enterprises. One idea that really has caught on is convenience car care, especially the quickie oil change and lube job. In a vast, rapidly expanding, and increasingly competitive market, several major franchise chains are now fighting for the consumer dollar. Jiffy Lube, with 525 shops and nearly $40 million in sales, is the market leader. Quaker State's Minit-Lube, with 185 shops, ranks second and is enjoying strong growth. Other major competitors include the Grease Monkey Holding Company and Ashland Oil's Rapid Oil Change.

Child care is another area in which young professionals are getting new help. With demand far outstripping the availability of private sitter services, several franchise chains have had success in the business of child day-care. Kinder-Care and La Petite Academy, for example, two of the largest chains, both enjoyed 40% growth in 1986.

Success stories abound. The sky's the limit for *any* good idea. In just two years, the Molly Maid housework chain has sold 66 franchises in 25 states; business was expected to qua-

Kinder-Care Learning Centers, Inc.

Enterprising entrepreneurs are meeting the demand for convenience with innovative service franchises. Kinder-Care Learning Centers (right), *which enjoyed 40% growth in 1986, is a saving grace for many working couples with preschool children.*

Molly Maid, Inc.

Molly Maid offers its clientele in 25 states help with the house-cleaning chores. Sales at the privately owned company were expected to quadruple in 1987.

druple in 1987 to $12 million. The Tender Sender, a new package wrapping and mailing service, has grown to 72 outlets. Grocery Express, the $2.5 million San Francisco phone-order grocer, is expanding to the Bay Area suburbs—and perhaps beyond. The list goes on.

In short, whether it is plant care, pet care, at-home workout instruction, one-hour dry cleaning, one-hour photo finishing—almost anything at all—one is bound to find it. Whether it is a franchise outlet or a personal errand service, someone can be found to meet the needs. The new convenience industry is the commercial equivalent of a magic lantern. All one has to do is pay the genie.

6:15 P.M. Henry Jones pulls into the driveway, gets out of the car, and scans the lush, green lawn. Mary greets him at the door.

"Happy anniversary, darling. The flowers are beautiful. We'll eat shortly but first let's have a glass of champagne in honor of the occasion. There are a couple of individual splits in the refrigerator."

After supper—veal Parmesan for Henry, chicken Kiev for Mary, meatballs and spaghetti for Tommy—the Joneses move into the living room. Henry goes through the mail and orders three shirts from the Land's End catalogue. Mary thumbs through her photos, switches on the TV, and orders new dishes from the QVC home-shopping service. After putting Tommy to bed, Mary makes some microwave popcorn and Henry slips the tape into the VCR. They settle in for the movie. When it's over, Mary sets the coffee maker for 8:00 A.M. and Henry makes a mental note to return the tape in the morning.

"I don't know about you, dear," says Henry on the way upstairs, "but I'm exhausted."

"Me, too," says Mary. "I wish there were some way to make our lives a little simpler!"

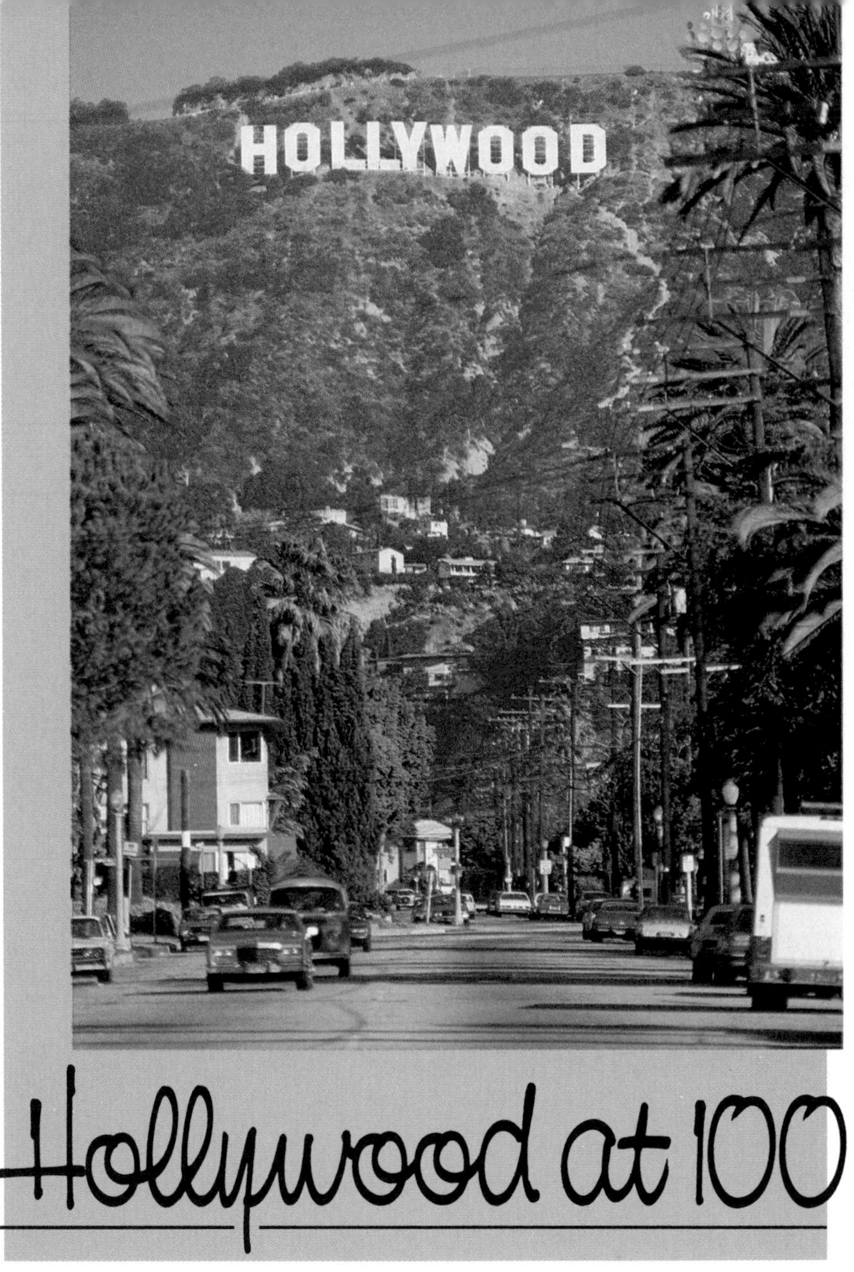

Hollywood at 100

By William Wolf

About the Author. William Wolf is a longtime movie critic and observer of the Hollywood scene. His film reviews have appeared in such magazines as *Cue* and *New York* and in various Gannett newspapers. A member of the National Society of Film Critics, Mr. Wolf is the author of *The Marx Brothers* (1976) and *The Landmark Films: The Cinema and Our Century* (1979). He also lectures on film at New York University and St. John's University.

A hundred years is not such a long time in the life of a community, but for Hollywood, CA, which celebrated its 100th birthday in 1987, a remarkable history has been crowded into that period. The rise of the motion-picture industry turned Hollywood into a legendary kingdom of entertainment, and although movies today are made the world over, Hollywood remains the symbolic film capital.

The economics and dynamics of Hollywood have changed drastically over the years, but the aura persists. Hollywood exists as a state of mind as well as a geographic entity. It represents the very evolution of movies, both as commerce and art, and in more recent years it also has become the hub of television production. People throughout the world are still dazzled by what pours out of Hollywood.

The 100th anniversary of Hollywood's founding was marked officially by a rush of activities beginning in February 1987. The motion-picture industry, never shy about self-promotion, pitched in to lend glamour and significance to the occasion. Before a throng of 3,500 at the Walk of Fame on Hollywood Boulevard, actor Robert Wagner dedicated a new star in the sidewalk in memory of his late wife, the actress Natalie Wood. Church bells throughout the city chimed, and a gala celebration was held at the newly renovated Hollywood Roosevelt Hotel. The activities continued in June with a series of celebrity luncheons, an automobile show, pro-celebrity polo and tennis exhibitions, and a ceremony honoring Bob Hope as Hollywood's "citizen of the century."

History. Hollywood was not founded as a movie enclave. The community was born as a real-estate project, and its nucleus was a citrus ranch of 120 acres (49 ha). In February 1887, the Los Angeles County recorder's office noted the registration of the land by one Harvey Wilcox, who named the property after a friend of his wife. In 1910, Hollywood officially became part of Los Angeles.

Economics always have played a key role in the upward and downward fortunes of what became known as Lotus Land. The movie industry began to take hold when filmmakers headed to California from the East, then the center of the new business, in the early years of the 20th century. The first Hollywood studio was set up in 1911 by the Nestor Film Company of Bayonne, NJ.

It was after World War I that Hollywood emerged as the international center of the motion-picture industry. Underlying its rise was the public's infatuation with movies and the eagerness of budding moguls to exploit that interest. A constellation of silent-screen stars—such as Charlie Chaplin, Theda Bara, Clara Bow, Gloria Swanson, Mary Pickford, Lillian Gish, and Douglas Fairbanks—soon held sway over a vast, adoring public. The birth of such celebrities in turn

Photos Culver Pictures

Photo opposite page, © Bill Nation/Picture Group

Beginning in 1912, the producer and director Mack Sennett made about 1,000 movies at his Hollywood studio, left. His best-known films featured the Keystone Kops. Other great stars of the Silent Screen era included Charlie Chaplin, top in "The Gold Rush"; Gloria Swanson, center in "Her Gilded Cage"; and Douglas Fairbanks, Sr., bottom in "Don Q, Son of Zorro."

spawned the publicity mills that created new stars. There was mystery and remoteness to these glamorous figures, who appeared larger than life on the screens of big cities and small towns throughout America. There were no television talk shows to spoil the mystique. Instead, the public eagerly read fan magazines and devoured news and gossip of the lives and loves of the stars.

The rush to sound movies, triggered by the impact of *The Jazz Singer* in 1927, further enhanced Hollywood's influence. The period from the 1930s to World War II proved to be Hollywood's "Golden Age." Millions thronged to the movies to escape the worries of the Depression, and an array of charismatic new talent captivated the public. Clark Gable, James Stewart, Cary Grant, Katharine Hepburn, Jean Harlow, Mae West, and Fred Astaire (*see* OBITUARIES) were but a few of the stars who brought unparalleled glamour and excitement to the world of cinema. More than any other movie, *Gone With the Wind* (1939) epitomized Hollywood at its peak as a manufacturer of mass entertainment. In 1941, Orson Welles' *Citizen Kane* took a leap forward in the realm of innovation and the growing recognition of cinema as a major art form.

After World War II—during which movies had played a vital morale-building role on the home front—Hollywood and the entire motion-picture industry were changed forever by a major economic development. Movie studios were barred from their monopolistic ownership of theater chains, thereby giving independent producers a better chance to exhibit their films. Meanwhile, rising costs—due to union-pay scales, executive extravagance, inflation, and a growing taste for realistic settings—resulted in more films being shot away from Hollywood.

"The Jazz Singer" (1927), below, *starring Al Jolson, was the first major motion picture with sound. It was only partly a "talkie," but it revolutionized the movie industry. "Gone With the Wind" (1939),* below right, *the Civil War saga starring Clark Gable and Vivian Leigh, epitomized Hollywood at its peak as a manufacturer of mass entertainment.*

Photos The Museum of Modern Art Film Stills Archive

The rise of television led to further upheaval and hastened the decline of Hollywood's dominance. The studios introduced wide-screen projection and other ploys to lure the public from their television sets, but the new medium was a powerful competitor. Eventually, Hollywood was to exploit the small screen as another outlet for its film product and also to become a production center for sitcoms, action shows, and made-for-TV movies.

Issues and Controversies. As a purveyor of popular culture and a center of wealth, fame, and power, Hollywood has faced a long series of public issues and controversies. It has had a nervous history in many respects. In the 1930s, responding to criticism that movies were becoming too racy and violent, the industry adopted a Production Code that set rigid taboos on content. A film would have to meet these standards in order to receive a formal seal of approval from the industry.

Welles' *Citizen Kane,* which suggested the life of newspaper tycoon William Randolph Hearst, generated controversy even before its 1941 release. A group of movie moguls offered to cover the costs of the film if the studio, RKO, would destroy all the prints and negatives. Fear of embarrassment might have led to the destruction of this landmark film had the offer not been rejected.

In the late 1940s, the rise of McCarthyism turned Hollywood into a place of anxiety and bitterness. Blacklisting of persons accused of being Communists or leftist sympathizers was a common practice. The noted Hollywood Ten went to prison for defying congressional inquisitors.

In 1968, after a rash of films that defied the old Production Code, the Motion Picture Association of America (MPAA)

"Adam's Rib" below left, *was one of nine comedies highlighting the special chemistry between two of Hollywood's biggest names, Katharine Hepburn and Spencer Tracy. The 1949 hit also featured Judy Holliday* (center). *"Citizen Kane" (1941),* below, *directed by and starring Orson Welles, is considered a classic for its brilliant and innovative cinematography.*

Photos The Museum of Modern Art Film Stills Archive

adopted a system of movie ratings. Such ratings, the MPAA reasoned, would be a responsible way to head off attacks by censor boards in various states against court rulings that outlawed censorship. (It had not been until 1952 that a Supreme Court decision gave movies the protection of the 1st Amendment.) However, some charged that the ratings themselves, which exist today in modified form, constituted censorship.

Tinseltown Today. The changes in the movie industry after the decline of the studio system turned Hollywood into a packaging center for agent-producer-star deals. Actors were now free agents, and the millions that top stars could earn for a few weeks of work made the old studio salaries, considered grandiose at the time, look paltry. A further development was the swallowing of production companies by huge conglomerates. Instead of the intuitive reactions and prejudices of the early moguls, the industry now was driven by bottom-line economics, market studies, and other tools of conventional corporate enterprise.

Movie companies today aspire to blockbusters like *Star Wars* and *E.T.*, and there is very little room for films that do

© Craig Aurness/West Light

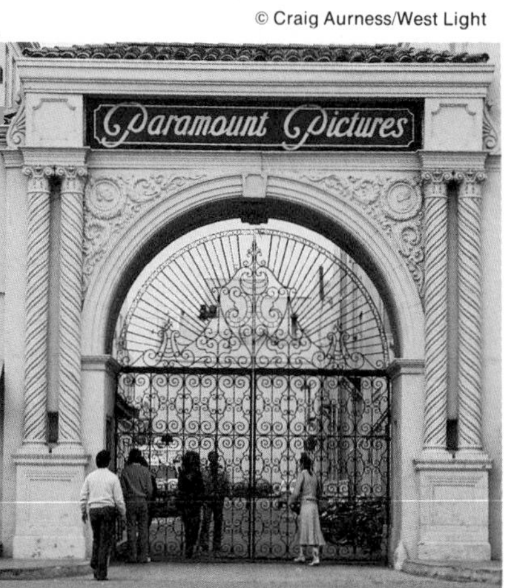

AP/Wide World

A dream factory for decades, Paramount Studios, above, *remains one of the most popular tourist attractions in Tinseltown. A galaxy of stars,* right, *showed up at the Shrine Auditorium in Los Angeles for the taping of "Happy Birthday, Hollywood," a TV special that aired in May.*

© Bill Nation/Picture Group

Visitors to Hollywood are surprised to find little of the glitz and glamor that its image suggests. Covering 14 sq mi (36 km²), Hollywood today is a rather ordinary residential neighborhood in northwest Los Angeles.

not strike it rich quickly. With the rising costs of production, advertising, and promotion, a movie is usually shelved if it does not show strong box office results in the first few weeks after release.

In the 1980s the burgeoning videocassette market, which now at least equals theatrical distribution as a source of profit, has further changed the economics of Hollywood. The question of residuals for actors, writers, and directors has become crucial in union bargaining over videocassette, pay-TV, and cable revenues. In 1987 it was precisely this issue that nearly led to a potentially costly strike by the Directors Guild of America.

As a geographic entity, Hollywood today is a somewhat tarnished, even seedy, memory of the past—a far cry from the glitzy image created in its heyday. There are still relics of the Golden Age, but the scene is very different. Even where there is new development, chic restaurants edge out the stomping grounds of the old stars, and multiplex theaters replace the grand movie palaces of the 1930s.

Yet despite the changes, the lore of Hollywood remains very much alive after 100 years. On Oscar night, millions of movie fans continue to tune in for the awards ceremony. New generations revel in movie classics on videocassette. And when a great star dies, the print and television reports are thick with nostalgia. The glory, the myth, and the enchantment of Hollywood live on. The tendency is still to think of American films, no matter where they are made, as synonymous with Hollywood. It's still America's Dream Factory, and there is no other place quite like it.

© Leo Mason/Photo Trends

America's Cup 1987

> ***About the Author.*** Jay Broze spent several weeks in Western Australia in 1986 and 1987, covering the America's Cup for *Sail* magazine. A contributing editor of that publication, Mr. Broze is the coauthor of such publications on past Cup competitions as *The Challenge* and *Newport to Perth*. He also is the author of *The Sailor's Edge*, which was published in 1986.

By Jay Broze

For the 136-year-old America's Cup yachting competition, 1987 was a year of firsts. It marked the first time that the races were held outside the United States, the result of Australia's historic 1983 victory over the previously unbeaten Americans. It marked the first time that U.S. corporations provided major financial backing, this due in part to the increased expense of campaigning large yachts and their support teams on the far side of the world. And, as one benefit of the distant time zone, it marked the first time that the America's Cup races were televised live, start to finish, in the United States. Millions of

Americans were exposed for the first time to match racing between 12-meter yachts, to the colorful and unique atmosphere of the America's Cup scene, and to a beautiful and largely unfamiliar corner of the world, Western Australia.

Setting Sights, Setting Sail. After the stunning defeat at the hands of *Australia II* in 1983, the United States was swept by a nationwide drive to recapture "our" Cup. The Australian victory had given every yacht club in America a chance to win back the coveted trophy, and indeed it inspired dreams of triumph among yachtsmen throughout the world. But from the moment *Australia* crossed the finish line in 1983, no one was more determined to win the next challenge series—and no one worked harder to achieve it—than Dennis Conner (*see* profile, page 79), the losing skipper aboard *Liberty*.

In October 1986, when the final deadlines passed, a total of 13 racing teams from six countries gathered in Fremantle, Western Australia, to compete for the right to challenge the Aussies. Together, the would-be challengers had built or redesigned 27 yachts, with their total investment conservatively estimated at more than $70 million. The Australians, meanwhile, were just as thorough and hardly less spendthrift in their preparations for the Cup's defense. Their largest syndicates for the defense were headed by two business rivals from Perth. Alan Bond, whose *Australia II* had won the Cup in 1983, built two new boats for the 1987 challenge. Kevin Parry financed the *Kookaburra* team, which had three boats. Two smaller teams from other regions filled out the Australian card.

In the end, however, the greatest Australian contribution to the 1987 America's Cup was not its fleet of yachts. It was the setting itself. Night after winter night, American television viewers were treated to hours of coverage from a hot, sunny, sea-swept corner of the world. In Fremantle, an entire harbor

AP/Wide World

In the best-of-seven-race finals in the Indian Ocean off Fremantle, Australia, the U.S. yacht "Stars & Stripes" (at left, photo page 76) *defeated the Australian entry "Kookaburra III"* (at right in photo) *four straight. Thus ended the Aussies' bid to keep the America's Cup. Iain Murray,* left, *the 28-year-old skipper of the "Kookaburra," commented that he "didn't see a foot put wrong in any one of the races by any one of their [the U.S.] team."*

AP/Wide World

The tactics of skipper Dennis Conner and the clockwork maneuvering of the crew contributed significantly to the "Stars & Stripes" victories. Conner considered the crew—11 on board and one alternating grinder—"by far the best and the most experienced in Freemantle."

had been built to accommodate the yachts, and most of the days were ideal for sailing. Onboard cameras brought the sport of sailing into the living rooms of America, zooming in on brawny, suntanned men struggling with highly complex racing machines, taming the wind, enduring the waves. The facilities, the conditions, and the intense competition combined to make the regatta off Fremantle nearly perfect.

Qualifying Matches. By New Year's Day 1987, after a series of elimination rounds, only four boats were left from the original fleet of challengers. These four boats would compete in a series of best-of-seven matches to decide the final challenger to Australia. Two of the four were American: Dennis Conner's *Stars & Stripes,* the product of a $10 million research and design effort; and Tom Blackaller's *USA,* featuring rudders at the stern and bow and an unconventional torpedo underbody. *New Zealand,* the world's first fiberglass 12-meter, skippered by Chris Dickson, was undefeated in the early elimination rounds. *French Kiss,* skippered by Marc Pajot, was considered the underdog.

In the semifinal qualifying matches, Conner's *Stars & Stripes* defeated Blackaller's *USA* in four straight races, while *New Zealand* also eliminated *French Kiss* in four straight. Thus, in the final qualifying round, *Stars & Stripes* faced the formidable *New Zealand* for the right to challenge the Australian entry. Both teams sailed out to the cheers of thousands of

The Skipper

AP/Wide World

Dennis Conner practices sailing the way a doctor practices medicine. He works hard, he minimizes mistakes, he internalizes the lessons of every day's efforts, and he constantly strives to increase the odds of success while reducing the chances for failure. He has always been a "professional" in the old-fashioned sense of the word. Now that he has won back the America's Cup, he may become a professional by the current sports definition as well. He is a celebrity, he is highly sought after for commercial endorsements, and he intends to compete for a long time to come.

When Dennis Conner led the *Stars & Stripes* invasion of Western Australia, the 44-year-old custom drapery manufacturer from San Diego, CA, had logged 30 years of sailing experience. He began as a junior member of the San Diego Yacht Club. ("I thought it was more fun than little league, and you didn't get dusty," he once told an interviewer.) He then went on to gain a reputation as one of the club pests, always asking questions, always looking for crew berths on bigger and better boats. He reached prominence within the yacht-racing community in the early 1970s and took part in his first America's Cup in 1974.

"The summer of 1974 taught us how not to sail for the Cup," Conner later said. He started out as a tactician for Ted Turner on a disastrously slow boat, then was part of an acrimonious syndicate reshuffle, and finally was recruited by another team to sail on the eventual winner, Ted Hood's *Courageous*. In 1977, Conner won the prestigious Star Class world championship—one of three such triumphs—and signed on for the 1980 America's Cup competition. As the skipper of *Freedom,* Conner successfully defended the Cup with a 4–1 win over *Australia*. His 1980 preparations also revolutionized Cup campaigns, making the process longer, more focused, more expensive, more team-oriented, and more certain of victory. Critics said he took the pure fun out of sailing, but his winning crew disagreed strongly.

In 1983, Conner was convinced that there was nothing new under the sun in terms of boat design, and was blindsided by the radical wing-keeled *Australia II*. After guiding *Liberty* to a 3–1 advantage, Conner lost three consecutive races—and the America's Cup—to the innovative Aussie challenger. And so, for the 1987 competition, Conner put his trust in a team of technicians, scientists, and designers headed by John Marshall—while concentrating his own efforts on training a crew and planning his tactics. It was one of the hardest decisions of his racing career, but the results bore out the wisdom of his choice.

It used to be said that if the America's Cup ever were lost, the New York Yacht Club (where it had been housed since 1851) would replace it with the head of the losing skipper. The Cup was lost in 1983, but Dennis Conner kept his head—and his racing organization—intact. More than three years later, with the Cup back in hand, he had become the best-known American sailor since John Paul Jones.

spectators who lined the breakwaters of Fremantle harbor each morning. Both boats suffered breakdowns during the best-of-seven match, but both crews managed to overcome their problems. In the end, after five very exciting races, it was the Americans who proved to have the better boat for the conditions. The Kiwi challengers had been lulled into complacency by their domination of the early rounds, and last-minute heroics were not enough to catch a team that had been on an upward performance curve all year. Dennis Conner, aboard *Stars & Stripes* and representing the San Diego Yacht Club, would finally have his chance to win back the America's Cup.

In the Aussie camp, meanwhile, *Australia IV* of the Bond syndicate suffered a surprising defeat at the hands of Parry's *Kookaburra III* in the final qualifying round. *Kookaburra III,* skippered by 28-year-old Iain Murray and representing the Royal Perth Yacht Club, thus won the right to defend the Cup.

The Finals. The match between *Stars & Stripes* and *Kookaburra III* was almost anticlimactic after the excitement of the qualifying rounds. Conner's boat was considered faster in heavy air, but proved faster in moderate and light winds, as well. Its size and sail power, along with Conner's tactics and the crew's clockwork maneuvering, made *Stars & Stripes* the superior vessel over the eight-leg, 24.3-mile (39.1-km) course.

In the first race, held in light winds on January 31, the American challengers cruised to an impressive victory margin

© Daniel Forster/Duomo

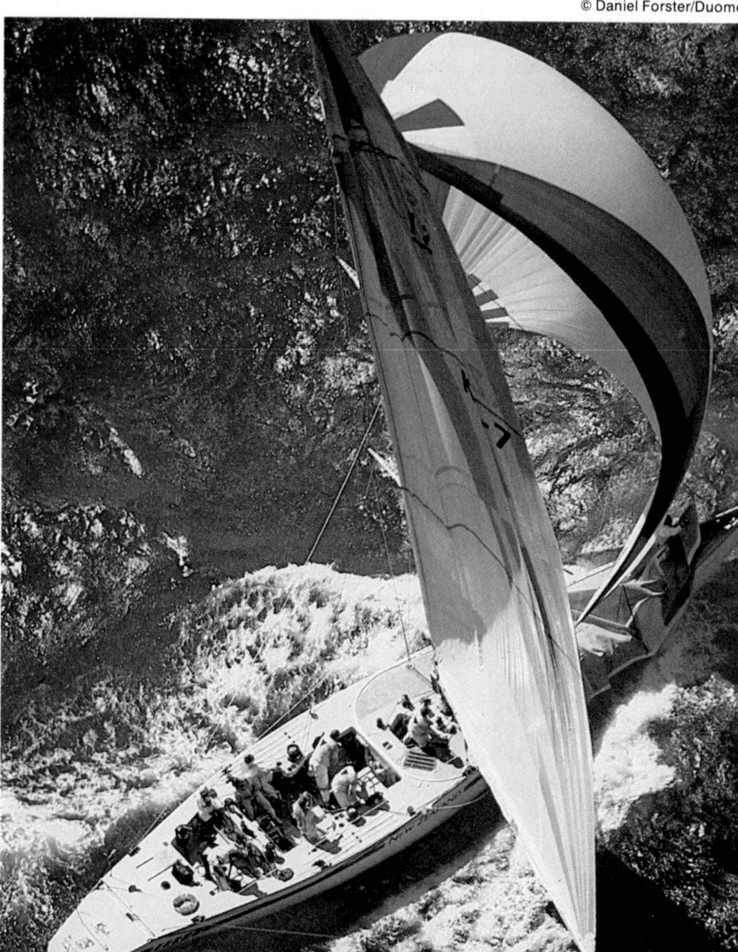

The "New Zealand," the world's first fiberglass 12-meter, was undefeated in the early elimination rounds and provided tough competition for the "Stars & Stripes" in the final qualifying round. Of the Kiwi challengers, U.S. skipper Dennis Conner said, "they pushed us to the limit and when they got behind they never quit. They fought to the end."

© Chiasson/Gamma-Liaison

After returning triumphantly to the United States with the America's Cup, the skipper and crew of the "Stars & Stripes" were received at the White House and honored in many cities. Along New York's Fifth Avenue, above, *real-estate developer Donald Trump staged a parade.*

of 1 minute, 41 seconds. The next day, in slightly heavier winds, *Kookaburra III* looked good early, but *Stars & Stripes* rushed back and won by 1 minute, 10 seconds. The Aussies managed another early lead in the third race, but Conner used some brilliant sailing to jump ahead and crossed the finish line 1 minute, 46 seconds ahead of the Cup defenders. Then, after a one-day layoff, the series resumed on February 4. With his back to the wall, Murray employed aggressive tactics from the very start. But Conner and the American crew sailed a nearly flawless race, and *Stars & Stripes* completed the 4–0 sweep with a 1 minute, 59 second victory.

As it proved in later competition under different conditions, *Kookaburra III* was indeed a fine 12-meter racing yacht. In the waters off Fremantle, however, nothing could stop *Stars & Stripes*. Iain Murray's feelings of despair were recorded in an exchange with race officials who zoomed alongside *Kooka* toward the end of the third race. As Murray reported the exchange, "The chap shouted over that there might be a bomb on board. The boat could blow up at any moment. I looked at the crew, we looked up ahead to *Stars & Stripes*. 'Okay,' we asked back, 'so what's the bad news?' "

After an absence of more than three years, the America's Cup came "home" to the United States in the clutches of Dennis Conner. It was paraded through midtown Manhattan, taken to the White House, feted at its new home in San Diego, and toured throughout the country.

Hardly had the fanfare subsided, however, before the next America's Cup competition appeared on the horizon. In early December, after a controversial court ruling, the San Diego Yacht Club accepted a challenge from a New Zealand syndicate for a best-of-three series using larger boats. The competition was set for September 1988—at least two years earlier than expected—at a location to be determined.

People, Places, and Things

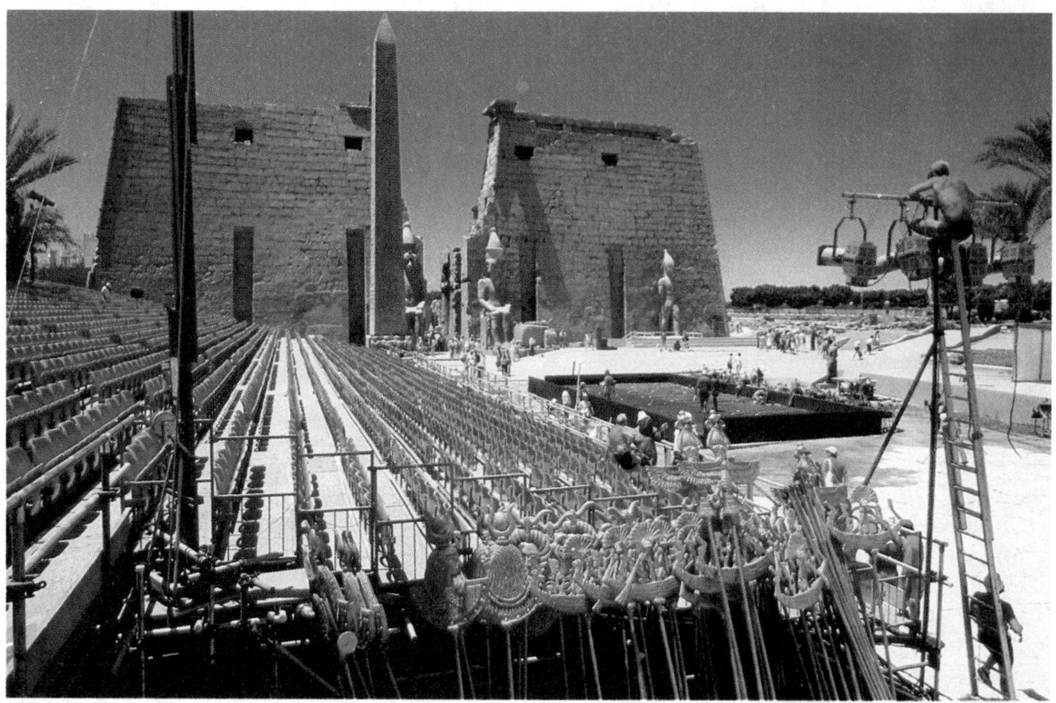

© Laurent Maous/Gamma-Liaison

© 1937 The Walt Disney Company

© P. Vauthey/Sygma

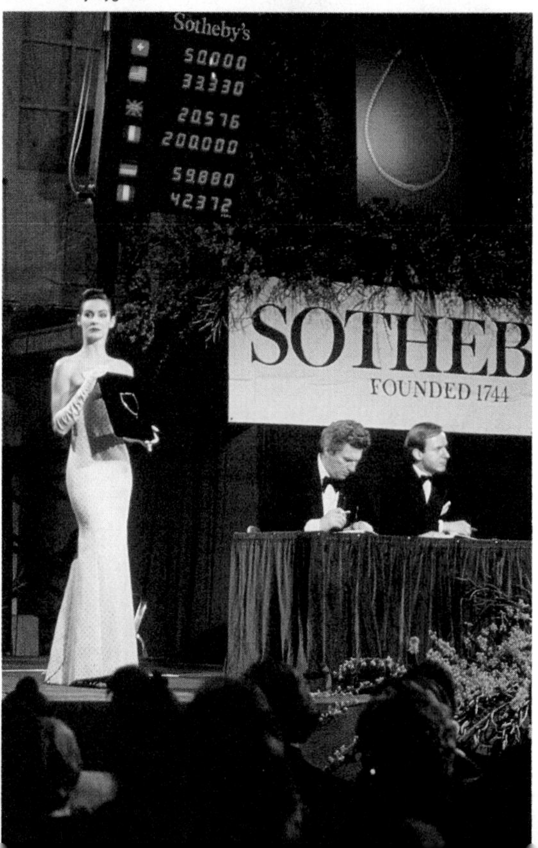

Gems: *Amid the 3,500-year-old ruins of the Temple of Luxor in Egypt,* top, *a $10 million staging of Giuseppe Verdi's classic opera "Aida" premiered May 2. The production featured Maria Chiara and Placido Domingo in starring roles. A more recent classic, Walt Disney's "Snow White and the Seven Dwarfs,"* above*—the first feature-length animated cartoon—was celebrated on the occasion of its 50th anniversary. The runaway princess and seven jewel miners came back to the screen in a Golden Jubilee reissue. Diamonds, rubies, sapphires, and other gems were in the spotlight in early April, as the jewelry collection of the late Duchess of Windsor (who died in 1986) went on auction,* right. *The two-day sale, conducted by Sotheby's in Geneva, fetched a glittering $50.3 million. In accordance with the duchess' will, the proceeds went to the Pasteur Institute in Paris.*

© Martin Klinek/Sygma

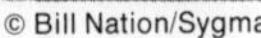

© Bill Nation/Sygma

© Ira Wyman/Sygma

Landmarks: *On the tenth anniversary of Elvis Presley's death—August 16—some 50,000 people visited his grave at Graceland,* top, *the singer's estate in Memphis, TN. A record 600,000 fans made the pilgrimage during 1987. An estimated 250,000 pedestrians jammed onto San Francisco's Golden Gate Bridge,* left, *on May 24, the 50th anniversary of its opening. The celebrations included a parade of ships and an airshow by vintage biplanes. An aerial event of a different kind—and a landmark in its own right—was the 37-hour voyage of the "Virgin Atlantic Flyer,"* right. *Pilots Richard Branson and Per Lindstrand lifted off in Maine on July 2, soared 3,400 mi (5 500 km) across the Atlantic, and went down in the Irish Sea—with their landing target literally in sight! Sympathetic followers gave Branson and Lindstrand credit for the first transatlantic crossing in a hot-air balloon.*

© Vandystadt/All Sport

© Jay Dickman/"Denver Post"

Fun, Fulfillment, and Cosmic Harmony: *The latest craze in winter recreation was "snowboarding,"* above, *which claimed 100,000 or more enthusiasts in the United States alone. The snowboard—a cross between a ski and a surfboard—is typically 5 ft (1.5 m) long and 10 inches (25 cm) wide, is made of laminated wood or fiberglass, and has a fixed binding that straps around an ordinary boot. No poles are needed—only courage. For Hoang Nhu Tran,* left, *courage and dedication brought a great personal honor: graduation from the U.S. Air Force Academy as class valedictorian. Tran, who fled Vietnam in 1975, planned to attend Oxford for two years on a Rhodes Scholarship. Meanwhile, for millions of "New Agers," Aug. 16–17, 1987, marked the beginning of a new age of world peace and harmony. At "power points" from Hawaii,* below, *to Mt. Olympus in Greece to Machu Picchu in Peru, the New Agers joined hands to sing, meditate, and do "vibrational intoning." The two-day event, called Harmonic Convergence, coincided with a rare astronomical event, the alignment of the nine planets in a configuration called a grand trine.*

© Bruce Asato/Gamma-Liaison

Girl Scouts of America

Courtesy of Hormel

© Lenore Weber/Taurus

American Institutions: *The year 1987 marked noteworthy anniversaries for other fixtures on the American scene. The game of softball,* left, *first played in Chicago, turned 100. The Girl Scouts of America,* above left, *marked their 75th birthday on March 12 with a worldwide simultaneous recitation of "The Girl Scout Promise." And the Hormel company honored Spam,* above*—that canned classic of inexpensive processed meat—on its 50th birthday. Also turning 50 were Superman, the Appalachian Trail, the Bonneville Dam, and the patent for nylon stockings.*

The Duke and Duchess: *Prince Andrew and Lady Sarah—the much-photographed duke and duchess of York—made a 25-day summer tour of Canada. In Medicine Hat, Alberta, their itinerary included a rodeo and an Indian celebration. The couple visited the United States in September.*

© T. Graham/Sygma

AP/Wide World

Soviet General Secretary Gorbachev and U.S. President Reagan sign treaty banning intermediate-range nuclear forces.

We make history. Changing its direction is within our power. However, such change is not easy and can be accomplished only when leaders of both sides have no illusions, talk with candor, and meet differences head on.

—U.S. President Ronald Reagan
The White House, Dec. 8, 1987.

It is our duty . . . to move together toward a nuclear-free world which holds out for our children and grandchildren, and for their children and grandchildren, the promise of a fulfilling and happy life without a senseless waste of resources on weapons of destruction. We can be proud of planting this sapling which may one day grow into a mighty tree of peace.

—Soviet General Secretary Mikhail Gorbachev
The White House, Dec. 8, 1987.

The Alphabetical Section

Peace is a never-ending process, the work of many decisions by many people in many countries. It is an attitude, a way of life, a way of solving problems and resolving conflicts. It cannot be forced on the smallest nations or enforced on the largest. It cannot ignore our differences or overlook our common interests. It requires us to work and live together.

—President Oscar Arias Sánchez of Costa Rica
Nobel Ceremony, Oslo, Norway, Dec. 10, 1987.

Costa Ricans congratulate their president, Oscar Arias Sánchez, after learning that he has won the 1987 Nobel Peace Prize.

ACCIDENTS AND DISASTERS

AVIATION

Jan. 3—In a forest outside of Abidjan, Ivory Coast, a Brazilian jetliner crashes, killing 49 of 51 persons aboard.

Jan. 13—In Asmara, Ethiopia, an Ethiopian Air Force plane crashes, killing all 54 passengers aboard.

March 4—A Northwest Airlines commuter plane crashes during landing at Detroit's Metropolitan Airport, killing nine passengers and injuring at least 14 others, including eight on the ground.

May 9—On the outskirts of Warsaw, Poland, a New York-bound Polish jetliner crashes; all 183 on board are killed.

June 25 (reported)—A Burma Airways plane crashes into a mountain in eastern Burma; all 45 persons on board lose their lives.

June 26—A Philippine Airlines plane crashes on Mount Ugu, killing all 50 persons on board.

July 30—A cargo plane crashes on a crowded highway in Mexico City, Mexico, killing 54.

Aug. 16—A Northwest Airlines jet crashes on takeoff at Detroit Metropolitan airport, killing 156.

Aug. 31—A Thai Airways plane crashes into the sea near Phuket Island, Thailand, killing all 83 aboard.

Oct. 11—A Burma Airways plane crashes southeast of Pagan, Burma, killing 49.

Oct. 15—An Italian passenger plane en route from Milan to West Germany crashes into the northern foothills of the Italian Alps. All 37 aboard the plane are feared dead.

Nov. 15—At least 19 are killed and more than 54 injured when a DC-9 jet crashes at Denver, CO, while attempting to take off during a snowstorm.

Nov. 28—A total of 160 passengers and crew are killed when a South African Airways Boeing 747 crashes into the Indian Ocean near Mauritius.

Nov. 29—Some 115 are feared dead when a South Korean airliner vanishes near the Thai-Burma border.

Dec. 7—A Pacific Southwest Airlines commuter jet crashes in central California, killing 44; the crash was preceded by gunfire aboard the plane, reportedly fired by a disgruntled former employee of the airline.

Dec. 8—A Peruvian navy plane carrying Peru's top soccer team crashes into the ocean near Lima; 42 persons are feared dead.

FIRES AND EXPLOSIONS

June 2—A huge forest fire in northeastern China, burning since May 6, has killed 193 persons; more than 50,000 are left homeless.

Nov. 18—A fire breaks out in the King's Cross subway station in London, killing 30 and injuring 53.

LAND AND SEA TRANSPORTATION

Jan 4—An Amtrak passenger train collides with three Conrail locomotives near Baltimore, MD, killing 16 and injuring more than 170 others.

Jan. 23—A ferry on the Sitalakhya River, near Rupganj, Bangladesh, sinks after colliding with a motor launch; at least 30 people are feared dead.

Feb. 17—Two commuter trains collide on the outskirts of São Paulo, Brazil; at least 41 are killed and 155 injured.

Feb. 20—In Saraburi, Thailand, a government-owned bus collides with a truck, killing 22 persons and injuring 35 others.

March 6—A British ferry carrying 543 persons capsizes in the English Channel off the Belgian coast soon after leaving Zeebrugge, Belgium, on a crossing to Dover, England; more than 180 are killed.

May 8—A ferry collides with a tugboat in the Yangtze River near Nantong, China; more than 90 people may have drowned.

July 2—At Kasumbalesa Shaba in southeastern Zaire, a trailer-truck crashes into a train, killing 128.

July 5—A barge sinks in the Luapula River between Zaire and Zambia, killing 51.

Aug. 7—One hundred persons are feared dead in Uttar Pradesh state, India, after a bus plunges into a canal.

Oct. 6—More than 50 persons are killed when a boat carrying them from the Dominican Republic to Puerto Rico sinks in the Mona Passage.

Oct. 12—At least 115 people are injured when an Amtrak passenger train crashes into a railroad crane in Russell, IA.

Oct. 19—A total of 102 are killed and about 300 are injured when a commuter train crashes into another near Jakarta, Indonesia.

Nov. 13—40 people are killed and five are injured when a city bus overturns into a lake in Mexico City.

Dec. 5—A Panamanian freighter catches fire near the coast of Spain, forcing the crew to abandon ship and killing at least 22.

Dec. 11—A bus carrying schoolchildren home from a holiday outing is struck by a train at an unmarked crossing outside Cairo, Egypt. Fifty-seven persons, including 50 children, are killed.

Dec. 20—A tanker and an overcrowded ferry collide off Mindoro, the Philippines. An estimated 1,500 persons are believed dead.

STORMS, FLOODS, AND EARTHQUAKES

Jan. 13 (reported)—In Europe, severely cold weather, avalanches, and other problems have caused the deaths of almost 100 people.

Jan. 24—Severe cold and snow across the eastern half of the United States are responsible for 37 deaths.

March 5–6 (reported)—Over the past week a series of earthquakes and flooding have struck northeastern Ecuador; 1,000 are reported dead, 4,000 others are missing, and the country's oil pipeline is damaged, forcing the suspension of vital oil exports.

May 22—A tornado strikes Saragosa, TX, killing 29 and injuring at least 120.

July 14—A flash flood sweeps through campgrounds crowded with vacationers in Le Grand-Bornand, France, killing at least 19.

July 22—Nearly 100 people are feared dead after floods, mudslides, and stormy seas are triggered by a typhoon in South Korea.

July 25—In northeastern Iran, 100 are killed and 36 injured when torrential rains cause the river Boojhan to overflow its banks.

July 31—Twenty-seven persons are killed and nearly 300 are injured when a tornado strikes Edmonton, Alta., and its suburbs.

Sept. 4—Some 1.5 million people are left homeless and at least 670 are dead after a month of flooding in Bangladesh.

Oct. 1—Six persons are killed and more than 100 are injured when an earthquake measuring 5.9 on the Richter scale strikes the Los Angeles, CA, area. This is the strongest quake to hit the area since 1971.

Oct. 3—Floods caused by a five-day rainstorm in Natal Province, South Africa, leave at least 174 dead and 86 missing.

Oct. 15—At least 18 are killed when a fierce storm with hurricane-force winds strikes southern England.

Nov. 26—Winds and giant waves caused by a typhoon kill at least 500 and injure more than 1,000 in the Philippines.

MISCELLANEOUS

April 2—More than 100 people are believed to be dead after mudslides bury three to five buses traveling a coastal highway near Cochancay, Ecuador.

April 5—The center of a 540-ft (165-m) bridge collapses near Amsterdam, NY, throwing at least two cars and a truck into the swollen Schoharie Creek; ten persons are killed.

April 9—Thirty-four miners are killed in a methane gas explosion in a coal mine in eastern Transvaal, South Africa.

April 23—An apartment building under construction in Bridgeport, CT, collapses, killing 28 workers.

July 28—A heat wave affecting Greece is responsible for the death of at least 700 people.

Aug. 4—A massive heat wave affecting much of the United States from the Midwest to the East Coast has left at least 80 dead.

Aug. 31—At least 50 people are killed when an elevator plunges to the bottom of a gold mine shaft near Welkom, South Africa.

Sept. 18—At least 175 people are killed in Medellin, Colombia, when an avalanche of mud tumbles down a mountainside.

ADVERTISING

The general business trend toward unfriendly takeovers finally caught up with large publicly owned advertising agencies in 1987. Among the acquisitions was that of J. Walter Thompson Company (JWT), one of the oldest and largest ad agencies in the United States, by the London-based WPP Group. In an unstable year for the industry, several major U.S. advertisers moved their accounts, the state of Florida passed an advertising tax, and there was controversy over condom advertising on television.

Takeovers and Restructuring. Turmoil at JWT became public late in January, when Joseph O'Donnell, the chairman and chief executive officer (CEO), was fired by his boss and predecessor, Don Johnston, the chairman and CEO of the JWT Group holding company. Other top management dismissals by Johnston, combined with poor financial results, left JWT vulnerable and led WPP Group to accumulate stock. In late June, WPP won the board's approval for a $566 million buyout.

After the sale, JWT suffered major account losses that were related more to its internal turmoil than to the acquisition itself. Ford Motor Company, its largest worldwide client, pulled out $100 million in overseas billings one week after the WPP buyout. And by early fall, JWT would lose the $200 million U.S. Burger King account to N W Ayer. That was the largest account ever to change from one agency to another, breaking the record set just a few months earlier when Nissan Motor Corporation moved its $150 million U.S. account from William Esty Company to Chiat/Day.

The sale of JWT to WPP was only the latest in a string of purchases of American agencies, many of them worldwide players, to British companies. And it was only one of several major developments during 1987 that significantly restructured the advertising industry. Ownership of six of the top ten worldwide agencies became concentrated among three holding companies as the result of consolidation moves. London-based Saatchi & Saatchi PLC, the world's largest agency as the result of a series of acquisitions in 1986, merged its Backer & Spielvogel and Ted Bates Worldwide agencies, as well as its Saatchi & Saatchi Compton and DFS-Dorland subsidiaries. The Interpublic Group of Companies, another of the supergroups, merged its SSC&B Lintas Worldwide and Campbell-Ewald subsidiaries to give it a second top-ten agency. These moves followed the creation of a third supergroup, Omnicom, in 1986.

In other deals that altered the structure of the industry, two publicly owned companies from outside the agency world, Mickelberry Corporation and Lorimar-Telepictures, shed their major agency holdings.

Ad Volume. Advertising expenditures in the United States were expected to rise 7.5% over 1986 to $109.8 billion in 1987, according to the McCann-Erickson ad agency. That breaks down into a 6.7% increase for national advertising, to $60.65 billion, and an 8.6% increase for local advertising, to $49.18 billion.

Florida Ad Tax. Agencies, advertisers, and the media all found themselves under the greatest legislative threat they had ever faced when Florida in the spring passed a 5% tax on most services, including advertising. But by pulling advertising from the media in the state and by canceling industry meetings and conventions, the ad industry put pressure on Florida to reverse itself and lead to the repeal of the tax late in the year. It also became apparent that other states that were considering their own service tax now would be reluctant to tackle advertising forces and would be hesitant to enact such a levy on advertising.

At the national level, however, other legal pressures were still looming on the horizon. Among these were proposals to reform airline advertising and advertising aimed at children, as well as to ban cigarette advertising and to limit the amount of advertising outlays that could be deducted as a business expense in corporate taxes.

Acceptability Standards. Health became the primary impetus behind the breaking of new ground in advertising acceptability standards. The AIDS (Acquired Immune Deficiency Syndrome) epidemic brought a new legitimacy to condom advertising both in broadcast and print. Early in the year, the NBC television station in San Francisco became one of the first major-market network affiliates to accept condom commercials. Time Inc., the leading U.S. magazine publisher, also began accepting condom ads. By October, Ansell Americas, the first condom maker to advertise on network television, also became the first to create a special marketing program aimed at gay men.

Prescription-drug advertising aimed directly at consumers rather than at physicians has been predicted as a major growth area, but pharmaceutical companies have been reluctant to do more than run what they call "health information ads," which do not name their specific products. But in September 1987, Sandoz Pharmaceuticals broke the taboo by running newspaper ads specifically for its Tavist-1 antihistamine product.

Safety and beauty were other forces working to expand the limits of acceptability in U.S. advertising. American Airlines in the summer became the first airline directly to address safety issues in its advertising. International Playtex, with commercials for its "Cross Your Heart Bra," became the first advertiser to run network TV commercials with live models wearing lingerie.

STEWART ALTER, *"Adweek"*

Novosti/Gamma-Liaison

The Afghan regime freed thousands of political and other prisoners as part of a national reconciliation campaign, but the resistance remained committed to total victory.

AFGHANISTAN

In its eighth year, thanks in part to new antiaircraft weapons, the war between Soviet troops and the Afghan resistance shifted in favor of the latter. U.S. aid to the Afghan *mujahidin* (''holy warriors'') increased. Government efforts to pacify the country by political means were ineffective. The economy continued to deteriorate. The Soviet commitment to prosecute the war appeared to be flagging.

Military Developments. Military activity in 1987 intensified. The Afghan resistance's procurement of effective antiaircraft missiles, including 600 U.S.-made Stingers and 300 British Blowpipes, changed the tide of battle. These sophisticated, hand-held weapons not only neutralized the Soviet MI-24 helicopter gunships and SU-25 ground-attack jets but also significantly affected both sides' morale, ground tactics, and politics. Soviet air losses climbed sharply to 1.2 per day for the period October 1986 through June 1987. To avoid the missiles, Soviet aircraft began flying either higher than 10,000 ft (3 048 m) or under 50 ft (15 m), thus reducing bombing accuracy and increasing accidents. Other U.S. aid near the year's end reportedly included 120-mm mortars, mine-clearing equipment, and even mules. U.S. aid in 1987 exceeded $600 million, up from $470 million in 1985.

The Soviet offensive strategy for 1987 involved decisive blows by ground forces against resistance strong points and supply lines from Pakistan. Defensively, the Soviets hoped to secure the main Afghan towns and main roads. Neither strategy succeeded. Largely free of harassment from the air, the resistance successfully massed its forces and fought pitched battles with Soviet and regular Afghan army troops. A three-week assault in May and June by 5,500 Communist troops, including a 2,500-man battalion of Soviet elite *spetsnaz* commandos, failed to dislodge 1,000 *mujahidin* protecting supply routes at Jaji in Paktia Province. The *mujahidin* controlled large parts of Kandahar and Herat for much of the year. Rocket attacks on Kabul intensified.

Defections from the Afghan army mounted, with more than 2,500 reported during the summer alone. Except in Kabul, the source of 92% of the recruits, the government could not enforce conscription. Both Soviet and Afghan losses climbed. According to one Moscow official, 25,000 Soviet servicemen had been killed in Afghanistan since 1979. The Soviet occupation strength remained at 115,000–120,000, with another 30,000 available from Soviet Central Asia. The Afghan government claimed its own security forces—including army, police, secret police, and militia—totaled 127,000, but this was probably an inflated figure.

Politics. Failing to advance militarily, General Secretary Najib of the ruling People's Democratic Party of Afghanistan (PDPA) tried to achieve victory by political means, intensifying his 1986 campaign for ''national reconciliation.'' On Jan. 2, 1987, he announced a unilateral six-month cease-fire to take effect on January 15, and in early July he extended it to Jan. 15, 1988. The seven-party resistance coalition in Pakistan unanimously rejected the cease-fire.

National reconciliation also included a stepped-up campaign to call refugees home, a proposal to rename the country the Republic of Afghanistan (RA), formation of a ''national unity coalition government'' that would allow 23 noncritical prestige posts to be held by non-

Communists, a general amnesty of prisoners, countrywide elections, a new law on political parties, and a new constitution. Three small rump parties, apparently created for propaganda purposes, joined the government, which proclaimed its devotion to Islam and insisted that it was neither socialist nor Communist but "national democratic" in nature. In an attempt to project piety, Najib changed his name back to its original form, Najibullah ("noble of God"). These moves seemed designed to legitimize the regime and disguise its Marxist-Leninist roots, but none succeeded in splitting the resistance or dampening its commitment to press on for total victory.

Meanwhile, factionalism within the PDPA intensified. The old split between the Parcham (urban, multiethnic, flexible, internationalistic) and Khalq (rural, Pashto-speaking, rigidly socialist, nationalistic) wings remained, and a new one within the Parchamis developed. In May, former party leader Babrak Karmal was sent to the USSR, allegedly for medical treatment but probably in involuntary exile, to remove a focus of intraparty opposition. In September, Najib became president of the Revolutionary Council, a post that gave him sweeping powers under the new constitution. In October he purged 15 known Babrakists from the Central Committee and named 13 of his own followers to replace them. At the Second Party Conference, also held in October, further purges were hinted.

Economy. The economy continued to spiral downward. Annual inflation was about 20 to 30%. In September total war damages were assessed at $50 billion, and the cost to the Soviet Union since 1979 was judged to have been $20 to $30 billion. The percentage of foreign trade with the USSR dropped significantly, from 80% in 1986 to 60% in 1987. The official silence concerning Soviet aid to Afghanistan may indicate that this figure also fell. Nevertheless, plans to tie the country into the Soviet Central Asian electric power grid remained in effect, as did pledges to increase direct transborder trade with Soviet Central Asia. To improve economic performance, the regime canceled its land-reform program and encouraged private enterprise, which continued to account for 80% of national income. Despite earlier efforts to establish state control, 99.9% of agriculture and 87% of commerce remained in private hands.

Diplomacy and Foreign Affairs. As with its internal affairs, the Kabul government was totally dependent on Moscow in foreign affairs. The thrust of the Democratic Republic of Afghanistan/USSR foreign strategy was to project the image of an earnest search for peace while prosecuting the war vigorously. To deter further Pakistani aid to the *mujahidin,* Kabul's transborder air attacks reached unprecedented levels, and Afghan secret police (*Wad*) agents planted bombs in cinemas and other civilian targets in northern Pakistan. Some 200 civilians died in air raids in four days at the end of March, but Pakistan's policies held firm.

To establish a better international image, Kabul sent emissaries to 53 countries in July and August. Several Third World states entered into diplomatic discussions, but the only nonsocialist country to establish diplomatic relations was Austria. Kabul claimed relations with "more than 80 states and national liberation movements," but it did not enjoy warm relations with any country outside the socialist bloc except India. It had no diplomatic relations with such leading Islamic states as Pakistan, Egypt, Saudi Arabia, or Iran.

Indirect talks between Pakistan and Afghanistan under United Nations auspices at Geneva were resumed from February 25 to March 9 and again from September 7 to 10. The main issue remained the time needed for withdrawal of Soviet forces, but the gap between the two sides' positions narrowed. At the last break the Afghans were insisting on 16 months and the Pakistanis on eight. The most active combatants—the Soviets and the *mujahidin*—were not, however, direct participants in the talks. In mid-November a Soviet spokesman said that a 7-to-12-month pullout could occur if "national reconciliation" (that is, an interim government) could be worked out.

The critical element for peace remained the Soviet commitment to prosecute the war. An unofficial poll of Moscow residents in August revealed 53% in favor of withdrawing the troops, and only 27% in favor of fighting on. In the fall, Soviet press coverage resumed its emphasis on combat drama (largely abandoned since early 1985) in an apparent effort to popularize the war.

International criticism of the Soviet role continued. The annual November UN General Assembly vote on a resolution calling for the withdrawal of foreign troops from Afghanistan was 123 in favor, 19 opposed, and 11 abstentions.

ANTHONY ARNOLD
Hoover Institution, Stanford

AFGHANISTAN • Information Highlights

Official Name: Democratic Republic of Afghanistan.
Location: Central Asia.
Area: 250,000 sq mi (647 500 km²).
Population: (mid-1987 est.): 14,200,000.
Chief Cities (March 1982): Kabul, the capital, 1,036,407; Kandahar, 191,345; Herat, 150,497.
Government: Najibullah, general secretary, People's Democratic Party (appointed May 1986) and president, Revolutionary Council (Sept. 1987); Soltan Ali Keshtmand, prime minister (named June 1981).
Monetary Unit: Afghani (50.6 afghanis equal U.S.$1, July 1987).
Gross National Product (1985): $3,520,000,000.
Foreign Trade (1985 U.S.$): *Imports,* $999,000,000; *exports,* $566,000,000.

© George Wirt

In the Macina region of Mali, above, as throughout much of the African continent, severe drought conditions left the weekly outdoor market with little food for sale.

AFRICA

For many of the estimated 600 million people living on the African continent during 1987—a figure that was growing at an alarming rate, according to a United Nations report—economic stagnation, political instability, ethnic and religious strife, a hostile environment, and a deadly epidemic combined to diminish any real hope for the foreseeable future.

Electoral and Constitutional Change. Local and national elections were held in East, West, and Southern Africa during 1987, although most served only to generate support for existing regimes without offering voters a meaningful choice. In June and July, elections took place for a new national assembly in Ethiopia, for provincial and municipal offices in Gabon, and, for the first time in 20 years, for parliament in the Central African Republic. Government nominees were either returned or elected in these highly controlled one-party elections.

The ruling National Party in South Africa reaffirmed its dominance in white electoral politics while the right-wing Conservative Party replaced the Progressive Federal Party as the official opposition in the May 6 election for the all-white parliament. In the one democratically contested election in Africa in 1987, Sir Dawda Jawara, president of The Gambia, was reelected with 59% of the vote, down from 73% in 1982. His minister of economic planning, however, lost his bid for reelection, necessitating a cabinet reshuffle.

Under the terms of Zimbabwe's 1980 constitution, the overrepresentation of whites in the national parliament was readjusted. Late in the year the nation's opposition parties agreed to merge with the ruling party, and the offices of president and prime minister were abolished in favor of an executive president elected for a six-year term.

Guerrilla leader Col. John Garang of the Sudan People's Liberation Movement (SPLM), in coalition with a number of southern Sudanese opposition parties, jointly called for peace talks with the government. By late in the year, Colonel Garang and Prime Minister Sadiq al-Mahdi were close to agreement on the formation of a national all-parties committee which would prepare the groundwork for a constitutional convention.

Economic Conditions. Faced with a mounting debt crisis (a continent-wide total of more than $100 billion in foreign loans) and generally deteriorating economic conditions, many governments throughout Africa implemented belt-tightening reforms to meet the requirements of international lending agencies and sought new financial assistance from the West. Late in the year, major aid donors reached agreement with the World Bank and International Monetary Fund (IMF) on an emergency financial assistance package that would provide Africa's poorest countries more than $1 billion per year in additional aid over the next three years. Targeting about 20 of the poorest countries in sub-Saharan Africa, the package would provide those countries with a total of up to $500 million in extra direct assistance from Western governments, new debt relief, and another $500 million in new IMF loans.

In February the U.S. General Accounting Office announced that $66.5 million in aid given to the Liberian government between 1980 and 1985 could not be accounted for. In addition, Liberia had defaulted on repaying its foreign debts in 1986 and, as a result, had been denied assistance from the World Bank, the IMF, and the African Development Bank. This mismanagement, the country's growing economic crisis, and the threatened cutoff of all U.S. aid forced Liberia to take the unusual and drastic step of inviting U.S. "operational experts" to take control of the government's finances beginning in 1988. The experts were asked to work with Liberian counterparts in preparing a realistic national budget and were promised cosigning authority in the ministries of finance, commerce, and planning, as well as in the Central Bank and the National Oil Company. While many Liberians welcomed these extreme measures because they thought that the economy was out of control, others saw the moves as a form of U.S. colonialism.

In Uganda, President Yoweri Museveni and his National Resistance Council introduced far-reaching measures to improve the country's economic prospects and to meet the requirements for World Bank and IMF loans. Among other things, the currency was devalued by 77% with the introduction of a new shilling (worth 100 old ones) and the levy of a 30% tax on all money converted from old to new. However, a $200 million debt repayment obligation for 1987 and reduced coffee earnings held back significant economic recovery.

Stringent economic reform measures instituted by the government of Gen. Ibrahim Babangida in Nigeria appeared to have positive results in 1987. Cuts in government spending, reductions in imports, the devaluation of the *naira,* the institution of a single foreign-exchange market, and efforts to reschedule repayments on the external debt, improved the nation's foreign-exchange situation.

Meanwhile a number of African leaders proposed measures to enhance cooperation and promote mutual economic growth on the continent. Among the issues they discussed were the establishment of an African Economic Community to spur trade, the development of "complementary" rather than "self-sufficient" industries, the scaling down of costly development projects, and the mobilization of internal African savings.

One trend that became increasingly evident across the continent was privatization, the transfer of government-owned companies to the private sector. Nigeria, for example, planned to sell its stake in more than 160 companies. In Togo, 18 companies were to be privatized by 1988. State-owned cocoa plantations were being sold in Ghana, and a privatization program focusing on the banking and financial sector was getting under way in Senegal. Even the Marxist governments in such countries as Angola, Benin, and the Congo planned to sell off money-losing state companies.

Drought and Famine. Although crop harvests and food production showed modest increases—with some countries even enjoying surpluses—rapid population growth, drought conditions, ongoing desertification in the Sahel, insects, and civil war conspired to create famine conditions in widespread areas. Africa remains a "continent in crisis," said Edouard Saouma, the director general of the UN Food and Agriculture Organization (FAO).

In Ethiopia, the lack of rainfall left river beds as dry and crops as withered as during the crisis of 1984–85. The UN Development Program estimated that more than one million Ethiopians faced starvation and, according to the World Food Program, an additional three million people in Eritrea and Tigre were in need of outside food aid.

Drought in southern Mozambique and civil strife throughout the country have left more than one million people in need of emergency food and supplies. Civil war in Angola has left some two million people in need of food assistance. Botswana suffered through its sixth straight year of drought, compounded by an infestation of crop-destroying insects. Zimbabwe was experiencing one of its driest periods in 40 years. The loss of arable land to desertification in the Sahel diminished that area's already meager agricultural resources. And food shortages were growing ever more serious in areas of the Sudan, Somalia, Uganda, and other countries.

AIDS. While many African governments were reluctant to discuss the problem of AIDS (Acquired Immune Deficiency Syndrome), it appeared in 1987 that the threat was even greater than that posed by famine and starvation. U.S. State Department officials considered the AIDS epidemic the most serious threat facing Africa. Although statistics on the spread of the disease remain unreliable, the World Health Organization (WHO) estimated in early 1987 that 2 million to 5 million Africans carried the AIDS virus—predominantly in central and eastern regions—and that at least 50,000 people had died from the disease. In Africa the epidemic affects heterosexuals, and men and women in equal numbers. Moreover, a greater percentage of Africa's population is in its sexually active years, and the continent's birthrate is higher than anywhere else in the world—leading to some alarming projections of increases in the mortality rate. The overall pessimism is compounded by the fact that, even if a cure is found soon, there are few diagnostic laboratories and inadequate medical services to cope with an epidemic of this magnitude.

Political Instability. The governments of Uganda and Sierra Leone announced in January and March, respectively, that they had thwarted coup attempts. In Uganda, eight supporters of former President Milton Obote were arrested for plotting to assassinate current government leaders. This was the second plot uncovered in Uganda in the same month. And in Sierra Leone, loyal members of the armed forces put down a coup attempt against President Joseph Momoh. A large cache of arms was seized, and more than 60 people, including former Vice-President Francis Minah, were arrested on suspicion of participating in the plot.

Antigovernment attacks by the South African-backed Mozambique Resistance Movement (RENAMO) guerrillas continued throughout the year in an effort to destabilize Mozambique and isolate Maputo, the capital.

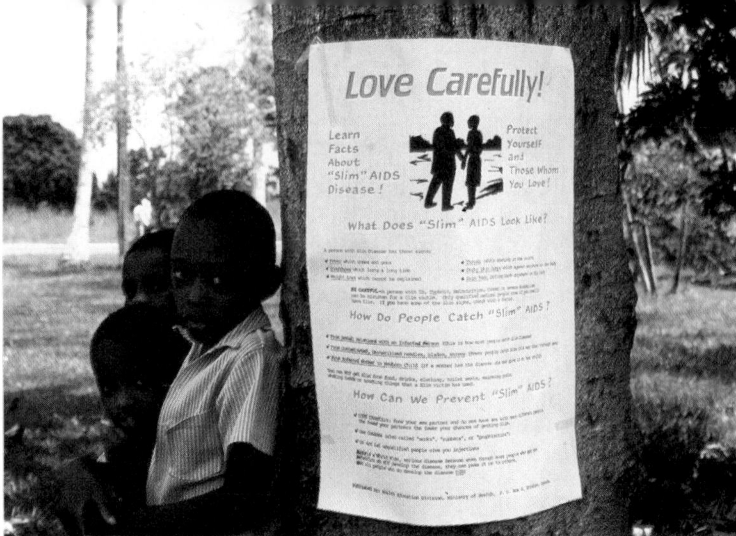

With an estimated 2–5 million Africans carrying the AIDS virus and at least 50,000 already having died from the disease, governments in 1987 finally began vigorous information and education campaigns.

© W. Campbell/Sygma

RENAMO massacres killed hundreds of civilians in July, October, and November.

In Burundi, 38-year-old Maj. Pierre Buyoya and "a military committee for national salvation" seized power early in September, while former President Jean-Baptiste Bagaza, who had ruled for 11 years, was attending a summit meeting in Canada. The coup was the direct result of a number of anti-Catholic decrees issued by Bagaza, including a shutdown of Catholic primary schools and a ban on Catholic church services. Bagaza, a member of the ruling Tutsi ethnic minority, saw the church as a stronghold of the Hutu majority. While Major Buyoya also is a Tutsi, and while he effected no change in the ethnic composition of the government or military, he made it clear that religious persecution would cease.

Capt. Blaise Campaoré, who had been chief adviser to the former leader of Burkina Faso, Capt. Thomas Sankara, led a military coup on October 15. On the following day, Sankara, who had seized power in 1983, along with 12 of his top officials, was executed and buried near the capital city of Ouagadougou. Sankara had made efforts to cut back the privileges of civil servants and had instituted a number of reforms—including bans on prostitution and begging—to instill a sense of national pride, but lack of economic development and widespread poverty appeared to have led to his downfall.

The transition was more orderly in Niger, where the ruling Supreme Military Council on November 10 appointed the army chief of staff, Col. Ali Seybou, as interim head of state in place of the seriously ill President Seyni Kountché. Only hours later, Kountché, who had taken power in a coup in 1974, died of a brain tumor in a Paris hospital. Colonel Seybou, his cousin and most trusted aide, was named full successor to the presidency.

Regional Conflicts. Throughout 1987, Zimbabwean troops actively assisted Mozambique in its military campaign against rebel RENAMO forces. The Zimbabwean troops were able to improve security in the 190-mi (300-km) Beira corridor, which is of vital economic importance for the region. For Zimbabwe it is the shortest transportation link to the sea, and for many of the landlocked countries of the region it is the only viable alternative to using the South African transportation network.

Allegations that Kenyan police were mistreating Ugandans residing in Kenya and that Kenyan security forces were harassing Ugandans at their common border in February and March led to increased tensions between the two countries. Diplomatic talks at the ministerial level in June and the subsequent release of Kenyan prisoners by Uganda and of Ugandan prisoners by Kenya served to reduce these new tensions.

Fighting between Libyan and Chadian forces continued in the contested Aouzou strip separating northern Chad and southern Libya. Control of the settlement of Aouzou changed hands several times during the summer.

Racial conflict continued in South Africa, but a secret four-day meeting between leaders of the banned African National Congress (ANC) and predominantly Afrikaner business leaders, academics, and politicians was held in Dakar, Senegal, in July. Organized by the Institute for a Democratic Alternative for South Africa (IDASA) and its director, former Progressive Federal Party (PFP) leader Frederik Van Zyl Slabbert, the meeting was an attempt to open a dialogue on the structure of the government and economy in a liberated South Africa and on the problems and strategies of transition. IDASA emphasized that its willingness to talk to the ANC did not indicate any support for the nationalist movement or its strategies. Pretoria was quick to criticize the meeting and questioned the loyalty of those who attended.

See also articles on individual countries in The Alphabetical Section and others in NATIONS OF THE WORLD, page 576.

PATRICK O'MEARA
N. BRIAN WINCHESTER
African Studies Program, Indiana University

AGRICULTURE

World agriculture experienced several "beginnings" in 1987, while at the same time coping with enduring surpluses in some countries and recurring food shortages in others.

A revolution in biogenetics was bursting from the wings, sooner and with greater promise than had been imagined. This new biotechnology made it possible, in the crossbreeding of farm animals, for example, to do in two years what previously had required 20 years. First to be affected by this emerging technology were the already prolific agricultural systems in the United States and Europe. Governments in these countries were harder-pressed than ever to control overproduction.

India, meanwhile, was accumulating large stocks of wheat and rice until severe drought conditions devastated crops and made substantial food imports once again seem imperative. The Soviet Union, one of several food-short socialist countries, was increasing its production using an "intensification" strategy which would more carefully manage inputs rather than simply add more fertilizer, land, and machinery. In some socialist countries, national policy encouraged private enterprise. In Europe and the United States, agricultural lobbies provided adequate support for large agricultural budgets. Their farm programs controlled domestic prices and had an impact on world prices of major commodities.

U.S. farmers, on the average, began to see a turnaround from the hard times of the previous five years. Land values moved upward slightly. Cash farm expenses projected for 1987 were down \$10-\$15 billion from 1986. Farm debt had dropped from \$200 billion to \$160 billion within three years. Farmers generally enjoyed an adequate cash flow like that of the good years. Canadian farmers, too, were experiencing some recovery, with relatively few bankruptcies occurring in 1987. However, the North American farm economy as a whole remained depressed. U.S. land values were still at less than half of earlier levels, and in Western Canada land values similarly remained one fourth lower than previously. Land ownership was slipping away from indebted farmers, many of whom had been part of a promising new generation. U.S. government-sponsored farm credit banks, saddled with bad loans and depreciated collateral, asked for a federal bailout which might cost taxpayers as much as \$6 billion. Surviving farmers sharply reduced their expenditures for fertilizer, equipment, and other inputs, thereby causing a second wave of agricultural distress in small towns and in the agribusiness economy.

U.S. Policy. U.S. agriculture received a generous share of the federal budget, which was used mainly for reducing crop surpluses and increasing farm income. The U.S. crop would have been much larger without these federal programs, given that weather was hot but on the whole favorable. The 1987 U.S. corn crop, for example, was expected to be smaller by 12% than that of 1986; and with increased utilization, reduced corn stocks were in prospect.

To reduce production, a U.S. federal conservation reserve program rented and retired marginal croplands under long-term lease—18 million acres (7.2 million ha) with a goal of 40 million acres (16.2 million ha) by 1990. In addition, producers of wheat, corn, and other crops were paid to idle a percentage of their allotted cropland. Producers and grain companies were also offered storage subsidies to stabilize existing stocks. To increase agricultural sales, prices were allowed to fall. Farmers' income was maintained through large cash payments from the federal government. The search continued for secondary uses of surpluses, such as the use of corn for gasohol.

U.S. Exports. The U.S. government expanded its export enhancement program (EEP), which gives exporters bonus commodities from the government's surplus stocks. The EEP subsidies facilitated grain sales particularly to countries in North Africa and Eastern Europe, and permitted increased cotton exports as well.

Despite these incentives, exports of surplus commodities declined both in volume and in value, and economic projections to 1990 suggested U.S. commodity exports would not soon regain the levels of earlier years. U.S. exporters faced not only increased productivity abroad but also reduced purchasing power among heavily indebted foreign customers. Major impediments to exports were the protectionist walls which many countries had busily reinforced in order to help their own producers and to improve their trade balance. Still, there were hopeful signs for increased U.S. export of processed grains, especially to Europe. Prepared foods familiar to U.S. customers were catching the fancy of foreign consumers.

Meanwhile the U.S. government took the lead in seeking to wind down a de facto trade war. At extended negotiations among 94-member nations under the 40-year-old General Agreement on Tariffs and Trade (GATT), U.S. delegates spoke optimistically of a "breakthrough" to abandon all farm subsidies by the year 2000. But European and Japanese farmers, who stood guard over two of the largest agricultural markets, would have been severely hurt by a reduction in import barriers; and consumers in those countries seemed ready to pay high food prices.

Other Exporters. Canada, Australia, and New Zealand, whose economies had depended on agricultural exports, became outspoken in support of freer trade. New Zealand's government offered itself as a model by repealing most subsidies and marketing controls. Australian agriculture, despite falling income, did not experience the high indebtedness evident in the United States. Australia and New Zealand sought to trim production costs so that they could offer commodities at attractive prices in nontraditional markets. Both of these Pacific nations were finding significant Asian customers; Australian beef, for example, was being processed for Japanese tastes.

Canada, too, sought new trading partners, looking elsewhere than the United States for its imports of fruits, nuts, and vegetables. Although Canada experienced a trade deficit, brisk export sales of Canada's grain and oil seeds offered the likelihood of a record marketing year for these products.

Europe. Europe's Community Agricultural Program, backed by farmers' groups throughout the Economic Community (EC), continued to stimulate domestic agricultural production and to exceed its budget for price subsidies and surplus removal. European crops were expected to be larger in 1987 than in 1986, including wheat, for which per-acre yields had been climbing for 25 years, and oil seeds, which were planted on larger acreages. Output of red meat and poultry also continued upward. Dairy production rose despite production quotas.

European farmers were improving their incomes also through employment in adjacent manufacturing, mining, and service industries. In Europe as in many other regions, farmers were playing important roles off the farm even as they maintained family units in agriculture.

Middle East. Winter rains in Iran, Jordan, Syria, and Israel were expected to improve grain yields in the Middle East, but U.S. exports to the region rose, due in large measure to the bonuses offered under the U.S. export enhancement program. The area experienced further diversification into fruit and vegetable production. In Saudi Arabia, intensive wheat production registered spectacular per-acre outputs, and success was reported also with horticulture crops and forage raised in greenhouses on newly irrigated land.

In Lebanon, agricultural capacity declined again, as many productive people emigrated because of the financial and civil disorder in that country. Turkey experienced rising agricultural production and exported much of it to its warring neighbors, Iran and Iraq. Turkey in turn increased imports from the United States.

Sub-Saharan Africa. Africa's food dilemmas persisted despite some improvements in weather. With Africa's population having more than doubled since 1975, its food needs were at the point of surpassing its enormous agricultural potential. A study by the UN's Food and Agriculture Organization (FAO) concluded that about 13 of 38 countries, with half of Africa's population, no longer had the resource potential to support their populations at a self-sufficiency level. The UN study lamented that governmental investment in food and agriculture showed a pattern of support for consumption rather than for production.

Food imports to the region were rising, with increasing reliance on food assistance from other countries' surpluses. Famine alarms were broadcast again for Ethiopia. Meanwhile, prices of several major African export crops—cotton, sugar, cocoa, and tea—were unstable and verging toward unprofitable levels.

Latin America. Food production in Latin America declined in 1986, both per capita and in total volume. Projections for 1987 indicated further decline.

In Mexico, production for domestic consumers was discouraged by low prices in the sluggish economy, by reduced government spending for producer and consumer subsidies, and by inflated production costs. Elsewhere in Central America, overall production showed little growth. For Costa Rica, Guatemala, and Honduras, a move continued to nontraditional exports—such as ornamental plants and winter vegetables—to supplement sugar, coffee, and bananas.

In Caribbean countries, the pace of development remained slow, as governments—including those of Haiti, the Dominican Republic, and Cuba—were unable either to offer farmers higher prices or to pay for increased imports. Haiti, however, continued to rely heavily on food aid.

Argentine agriculture actually experienced a decline in 1986-87 crop production, due to a smaller planted acreage and reduced per-acre yields.

Brazil's diverse agriculture experienced some successes, including record wheat and rice crops. The government's agricultural policies were intended to make the nation more self-sufficient, to generate export earnings, and to manufacture much of its motor fuel from agricultural commodities.

Brazil, Argentina, and Paraguay joined the United States as leading competitors in the world soybean market. The 1987 soybean output of these three countries was 26 million tons, compared with the U.S. output of 55 million tons.

Concern was expressed about the increasing debt handicap of Latin America, which included six of the world's most indebted nations: Brazil, Mexico, Argentina, Venezuela, Peru, and Colombia. These countries, all of them major agricultural trading partners of the United States, were being asked to undertake austerity programs under which imports would be curtailed.

Eastern Europe. Agricultural policies in Eastern Europe encouraged self-sufficiency, in which the region's northern countries would increase imports from the southern countries while maintaining a favorable balance of trade outside the region. Exports from the region

© David Hutson/NYT Pictures

LDC Inc., left, *is a unit of National Farms, which hopes to become the world's largest hog producer. Such "superfarms"—the 1,000 or so with annual sales of more than $5 million—are accounting for a rapidly expanding share of production, revenues, and profits in the U.S. agricultural sector.*

were expected to increase. Emphasis was placed on developing private agriculture and to using price incentives as a major planning tool. With pesticides and some other inputs in short supply, governments tried to use existing resources more efficiently. Yet agriculture's share of total national investment remained steady. Irrigated acreage was expanded in East Germany and Romania.

Grain output, which had been up in 1986, was expected to fall somewhat as the result of an extremely cold winter. Livestock exports, however, were expected to increase.

Soviet Union. The USSR vigorously pursued its "intensive growth strategy," emphasizing careful management of inputs rather than simply adding more land, fertilizer, and horsepower. The Soviet government concluded that this strategy had greatly increased production. As "intensive" acreage was rapidly expanded, however, management may have become less effective.

The Soviets also were developing industrial livestock complexes (evocative of "chicken factories" in the United States), which in 1987 already produced more than one half of all Soviet poultry, meat, and eggs. USSR feed grain and livestock production were expected to increase in 1987. Wheat production was expected to be down from 1986, suggesting that the Soviets would make substantial wheat purchases under the U.S. export subsidy program.

Asia. Several populous South Asian countries moved further toward food self-sufficiency. Larger cereal harvests were predicted in Bangladesh, Pakistan, and Afghanistan. Bangladesh, however, still relied heavily on food aid from other nations' surpluses. Vietnam, too, lacked the means either to produce adequate food or to pay for large food imports.

China's leaders increased agricultural prices and provided more inputs for agriculture, hoping to continue a trend toward increased production which had been interrupted by two years of reduced grain production in 1985 and 1986. Production increases were occurring for most major products—wheat, rice, corn, and pork. China's agricultural trade surplus of previous years was expected to decline in 1987. Farm exports were expected to increase but at a slower pace than in the previous year. Meanwhile, U.S. exports to China were on the increase, as China became a buyer under the U.S. export subsidy program.

Another goal of Chinese leaders was to improve the rural standard of living, still far behind the urban standard. Strong efforts were made to improve literacy and technical skills in rural areas, and to provide new services such as electrification. Additional measures to be carried out over the next ten years included faster adoption of new technology, improving marginal croplands, encouraging development of some large commercial family farms, and increasing the output of agricultural machinery. Output of China's rural economy grew by 11%, slightly more than overall national growth.

Robust growth characterized the national economies of South Korea, Taiwan, and Hong Kong. South Korea moved out of its status as a debtor nation; the South Korean government, facing a national presidential election, increased the budget for rural development by six times. South Korea increased its imports from the United States, mainly cotton and cattle hides for use in its booming textiles and leather industries. However, the U.S. share of total Korean imports fell.

Japan, with an enormous trade surplus and with the yen appreciating against the dollar, was still reluctant to permit large increases of American commodities and processed foods.

The Philippine economy ended years of agricultural backslide in 1986. The turnaround was mainly due to increased harvests of corn and a recovery of the coconut sector, which employs about one third of the Philippine population. The turnaround was expected to continue in 1987, though food production would not be quite so strong as in 1986.

DONALD F. HADWIGER
Iowa State University

ALABAMA

The change from a Democratic to a Republican governor was the biggest event in Alabama in 1987.

On January 19, Guy Hunt (R) was sworn in as the state's 58th governor. He is the first Republican to serve as governor of Alabama since David P. Lewis (1872-74). In his inaugural address, Hunt promised to work to reform Alabama's education, tax, and election systems and to reduce the burden of civil lawsuits borne by business and professional people in the state.

Legislative Actions. Alabama's overwhelmingly Democratic legislature—Senate (30D-5R) and House of Representatives (89D-16R)—assembled in regular session on April 21. The new lieutenant governor, Jim Folsom, Jr., encountered criticism, especially from black legislators, early in the session. Some changes in committee assignments were made in response to the criticisms of Folsom.

Major spending bills were not passed until August 3, the last night of the session. Budgets for education ($2.07 billion) and the general fund ($698 million) were approved at that time. On September 2, Governor Hunt was able to announce an end to proration of education funding. Proration, which had started on Oct. 1, 1986, the first day of the 1987 fiscal year, causes mandatory cuts in spending when revenue collections do not match legislative appropriations. Alabama statutes forbids deficit spending.

Other measures passed in 1987 included a package of tort-reform measures, a bill raising the speed limit on rural portions of interstate highways to 65 miles per hour (105 km/hr), a requirement that parents be notified prior to the performance of abortions on minor girls, and a constitutional amendment allowing many more officials, including legislators, to qualify for retirement pensions. (The latter required ratification by voter referendum, scheduled for early 1988.)

One of the civil-liability bills eliminated a 10% penalty defendants had to pay when they were unsuccessful in appealing lower-court decisions, and another permitted payments of damages to be spread out over a 15-year period. Governor Hunt signed the tort-reform package into law on June 11, saying that the measures would "tear away some of the shackles that have bound Alabama's economic vitality."

The Economy. The state's economy fared reasonably well in 1987. In August it was reported that the unemployment rate had declined to 7.2%, the lowest figure recorded in eight years. For the same period, the national unemployment rate was 5.9%.

Education Issues. Controversies related to education were debated heatedly in several arenas in 1987. On August 28, Charles Payne resigned as head of the state's two-year college system. This decision came after it was discovered that a number of claims Payne had stated on his résumé in applying for his position, including an earned doctorate and the publication of numerous articles in scholarly journals, were false.

On March 4, U.S. District Judge W. Brevard Hand, in response to a suit filed by 600 parents and teachers, ordered the state to remove 39 history and social-studies and five home-economics textbooks from school classrooms because, he said, they promoted the doctrines of secular humanism and thus violated the 1st Amendment's injunction against establishing a state religion. On March 27 a federal appeals court in Atlanta suspended enforcement of Judge Hand's ruling and allowed continued use of the banned textbooks. On August 26 the same court directed Judge Hand to rescind the book ban and throw out the lawsuit which had stimulated his original order.

In another important U.S. appellate court ruling, federal District Judge U. W. Clemon's directive to several Alabama colleges to produce a plan to get rid of any "vestiges" of segregation was overturned on October 6. The appellate panel said that the matter would have to be looked at fresh in new proceedings and Clemon, Alabama's first black federal judge and a former state legislator active in behalf of black educational concerns, would be disqualified from participating in them.

Horse Racing. The $84-million Birmingham Turf Club opened on March 3 with great fanfare as Alabama's first pari-mutuel horse track. However, horse racing in Alabama proved not to be the attraction its backers had hoped. During its first month in operation, nightly losses totaled approximately $100,000. Thus in July the legislature passed a bill allowing out-of-state residents to invest in the track.

WILLIAM H. STEWART
The University of Alabama

ALABAMA • Information Highlights

Area: 51,705 sq mi (133 915 km²).
Population (July 1, 1986): 4,053,000.
Chief Cities (July 1, 1986 est.): Montgomery, the capital, 194,290; Birmingham, 277,510; Mobile, 203,260; Huntsville, 163,420.
Government (1987–88): *Chief officers*—governor, Guy Hunt (R); lt. gov. Jim Folson, Jr. (D). *Legislature*—Senate, 35 members; House of Representatives, 105 members.
State Finances (fiscal year 1986): *Revenue,* $6,801,000,000; *expenditure,* $6,438,000,000.
Personal Income (1986): $45,939,000,000; per capita, $11,336.
Labor Force (June 1987): *Civilian labor force,* 1,889,900; *unemployed,* 145,800 (7.7% of total force).
Education: *Enrollment* (fall 1985)—public elementary schools, 517,361; public secondary, 213,099; colleges and universities (Fall, 1984), 179,343. *Public school expenditures* (1985–86), $1,723,-000,000 ($2,508 per pupil).

ALASKA

The depression in oil and related activities continued as the major problem confronting Alaska in 1987.

Government and Politics. Local governments in Alaska had, in varying degrees, become dependent upon state revenue sharing and municipal-assistance monies during the past decade, and cutbacks in these funds severely hurt some localities. In order to maintain services, many local governments were forced to reinstate sales taxes, as well as to raise existing sales and property taxes. In many cities and boroughs, tax issues were placed on the ballot, and many referenda failed for lack of voter support. The newly inaugurated governor, Steve Cowper, called upon public employees to accept wage cuts voluntarily; to set a good example, he cut the salaries of top elected and appointed officials—including his own—by 10%.

The governor made two appointments to the State Senate, due to the retirement or death of long-term political leaders from both the Democratic and Republican parties. While the appointment of Alaska Native leader Willie Hensley to the Democratic seat was well received both within the Senate and the legislative districts represented, the Republican vacancy became an issue for partisan conflict between the Democratic governor, the Republican majority in the Senate, and the leadership in the three legislative districts comprising the constituencies for the seat. The major actor in the confrontation proved to be the governor's opponent in the gubernatorial election—the erstwhile Libertarian turned Republican Dick Randolph, whose name was the only one submitted by the party leaders of the three legislative districts involved. The seat remained vacant in late 1987.

Economy. The economic downturn had a demonstrated impact on personal income in the state, as Alaska fell to the number three spot after 13 straight years at the top of the per-capita, personal-income rankings among the states. According to the Alaska Department of Labor, the state's unemployment rate in July fell below the double digit level for the first time in 1987, registering 9.7%. However, the change was attributed to a large exodus of unemployed people rather than to an improved employment picture. Employment gains in July were only 3.1%, the smallest seasonal gain in wage and salary employment since 1979. Among the few industries showing gains in 1987 was the fishing industry, with 300 additional jobs in the course of the year. The other area of gain, after large losses in employment and wages, was the oil industry. Higher and more stable prices have provided some boost in employment, and the November opening of the Endicott field, the first offshore arctic oil field to be developed, added about 100 more oil-industry positions.

The state has actively sought the opening of the Arctic National Wildlife Refuge to oil and natural gas exploration and development. In April, U.S. Interior Secretary Donald Hodel recommended that 1.5 million acres (607 287 ha) of the refuge and 750 million acres (304 million ha) of the offshore continental shelf be made available for this purpose. Some estimates indicated that these areas might yield as much as 26 billion barrels of oil, which would make them the richest untapped source of petroleum in the United States. Hearings by relevant congressional committees about the proposal were held in late summer, but no final action was taken in 1987.

Office of the Governor

Steve Cowper (D), 48-year-old attorney from Fairbanks, took the oath as governor of Alaska in December 1986. Economic matters were prime concerns during his first year in office.

ALASKA • Information Highlights

Area: 591,004 sq mi (1 530 700 km²).
Population (July 1, 1986): 534,000.
Chief Cities (1980 census): Juneau, the capital, 19,528; Anchorage (July 1, 1986 est.), 235,000; Fairbanks, 22,645; Sitka, 7,803.
Government (1987): *Chief Officers*—governor, Steve Cowper (D); lt. gov., Stephen McAlpine (D). *Legislature*—Senate, 20 members; House of Representatives, 40 members.
State Finances (fiscal year 1986): *Revenue,* $6,115,000,000; *expenditure,* $4,221,000,000.
Personal Income (1986): $9,495,000,000; per capita, $17,796.
Labor Force (June 1987): *Civilian labor force,* 260,400; *unemployed* 29,200 (11.2% of total force).
Education: *Enrollment* (fall 1985)—public elementary schools, 77,211; public secondary, 30,134; colleges and universities, 27,479. *Public school expenditures* (1985–86), $723,000,000 ($8,044 per pupil).

Other. Alaska played host to a delegation of Siberian medical researchers over a two-week period in October and November. The delegation represented the Siberian Branch of the Soviet Academy of Medical Sciences in Novosibirsk, the USSR emissary to the Alaska-Siberia Medical Exchange Agreement of April 1987. The delegation visited and met with community leaders in Anchorage, Fairbanks, Barrow, Kotzebue, Nome, and Buckland before returning to the USSR.

In September, Alaska filed suit to prevent the federal government from implementing a plan whereby planes carrying shipments of plutonium from Europe to Japan would make fuel stops in the state. Governor Cowper denounced the project, arguing that the radioactive material would pose a health hazard to Alaskans and a threat to the environment.

The Alaska Federation of Natives (AFN) continued its efforts to amend the Alaska Native Claims Settlement Act so as to safeguard 44 million acres (18 million ha) of land held by the Indian, Eskimo, and Aleut peoples.

CARL E. SHEPRO
University of Alaska

ALBANIA

In 1987, Albania took further steps to abandon its long, self-imposed isolation from the rest of the world.

Party Congress. In November 1986, about 1,500 delegates and guests from 20 other countries had attended the Ninth Congress of the Albanian Workers' (Communist) Party (AWP) in Tirana. It was presided over by Ramiz Alia, first secretary of the AWP and head of state. Alia pledged that Albania would continue to adhere to the policies of the deceased Enver Hoxha, including "pure" Marxism-Leninism, free of right and left-wing deviations; complete independence of all political and military alliances; and total economic self-reliance, refusing to accept foreign aid or grant access to foreign companies. He denounced U.S. and Soviet "imperialism" and Chinese and Yugoslav "revisionism." At the close of the congress, he was reelected first secretary.

Economy. Prime Minister Adil Carçani declared that the Seventh Five-Year Plan (1981–1985) had been fulfilled in all aspects except for a shortfall in the oil and gas industry. Housing and health care had been improved markedly and a number of major projects, such as the Enver Hoxha hydroelectric power station at Koman in northern Albania, completed. In the Eighth Five-Year Plan (1986–1990), 83% of all capital investment would go into heavy and light industry, agriculture, and the production of foodstuffs. Real per-capita income was to rise between 5.8 and 12.7%.

Elections. In February 1987, elections to the People's Assembly (legislature) reportedly produced a 100% turnout of the 1,830,653 registered voters. They voted unanimously for the slate of 250 party-approved candidates and for the reelection of Alia as chairman of the Presidium.

Foreign Affairs. Continuing the trend of the previous two years of improving its relations with a variety of other countries, Albania assumed a more hospitable attitude toward the importation of foreign ideas and settled some longstanding political disputes. In November 1986, Alia had called upon Albania's institutions of higher learning to acquire foreign research and expertise.

In March 1987, Greece announced that the official treaty ending the technical state of war with Albania which had existed since World War II would be signed by year's end. In July, Albania and West Germany concluded three years of difficult negotiations by agreeing to reestablish diplomatic relations and exchange ambassadors. Alia also called upon Great Britain to complete discussions leading to a resumption of diplomatic ties with Albania, severed in 1946. But Albania continued to rebuff overtures from both superpowers, the United States and the Soviet Union, for talks that might lead to an improvement in bilateral relations.

Relations with neighboring Yugoslavia continued to be strained over Yugoslav allegations that Albania was stirring up the ethnic Albanian majority in its autonomous province of Kosovo against the minority of Serbs and Montenegrins, perhaps with ultimate absorption of this area in mind. Albania denied that it entertained any claims to Yugoslav territory and that it was interfering in Yugoslav affairs. In October 1987, however, it did denounce the sending of Yugoslav federal police into the province. In September, Foreign Minister Reis Malile told the United Nations General Assembly that Albania intended to take an active part in the development of international relations.

JOSEPH FREDERICK ZACEK
State University of New York at Albany

ALBANIA • Information Highlights

Official Name: People's Socialist Republic of Albania.
Location: Southern Europe, Balkan peninsula.
Area: 11,100 sq mi (28 750 km²).
Population (mid-1987 est.): 3,100,000.
Chief City (mid-1983): Tiranë, the capital, 206,100.
Government: *Head of state,* Ramiz Alia, chairman of the Presidium (took office November 1982) and first secretary of the Albanian Workers' Party (April 1985). *Head of government,* Adil Carçani, chairman, Council of Ministers—premier (took office January 1982). *Legislature* (unicameral)—People's Assembly, 250 members.
Monetary Unit: Lek (7 leks equals U.S.$1, August 1987).
Gross National Product (1986 est. U.S.$): $2,700,000,000–$2,900,000,000.

ALBERTA

Key 1987 events in Alberta included increased activity in the oil and gas industry, devastating tornadoes in Edmonton, and preparations in Calgary for the 1988 Winter Olympics.

Business and Industry. After several years of declining activity, the oil and gas industry showed improvement in 1987, with consequent sales, exploration, and developmental drilling. Sales of government-owned gas and oil rights totalled more than C$300 million, the highest figure in more than five years. In June, Suncor Inc. announced plans for a $150 million project to increase production at its oil sands plant near Fort McMurray by 1,000 barrels per day. A serious fire at the Suncor plant cut synthetic oil production for several weeks.

Improved activity in gas and oil marketing favorably affected residential construction in Calgary and Edmonton. Both cities also experienced decided improvement in commercial construction, although office vacancy rates continued high, as did financial failures.

Increased activity in construction caused that industry's largely nonunion labor force to demand restoration of benefits surrendered in the slowdowns of the early 1980s. Alberta was also affected by brief national postal strikes, first by letter carriers and later by inside postal workers.

Weather. A late, heavy snowstorm hit central Alberta in May, causing substantial property loss and damage to foliage-laden trees, telephone and power lines, and some buildings. This precipitation, as well as almost daily rain in July and August, minimized forest fires, resulting in good but not record grain crops. A fine, warm fall facilitated harvesting, with no deterioration of grain quality.

On July 31, Edmonton, historically tornado-free, was hit by a series of twisters that devastated a residential section, an industrial area, and a mobile-home park. Some 27 lives were lost, and damage was estimated at $500 million. Relief workers and financial and material assistance immediately poured into the stricken areas from local and outside organizations and other sources.

Agriculture. Grain prices remained depressed, resulting in increased production of canola (rapeseed) and, because pork prices remained attractive, the diversion of large quantities of coarse grain into hog feed. Strikes in rail and Great Lakes transportation facilities briefly interrupted the movement of grain to markets.

Government. In spite of continuing if limited inflation, the provincial government decreased grants to educational, health, and social services. The move placed increased demands on private charities and led to calls for rollbacks on contracts of public employees.

ALBERTA • Information Highlights

Area: 255,286 sq mi (661 190 km²)
Population (1986 census): 2,375,278.
Chief Cities (1986 census): Edmonton, the capital, 573,982; Calgary, 636,104; Lethbridge, 58,841.
Government (1987): *Chief Officers*—lt. gov., Helen Hunley; premier, Don Getty (Progressive Conservative). *Legislature*—Legislative Assembly, 79 members.
Provincial Finances (1987–88 fiscal year budget): *Revenues,* $8,627,000,000; *expenditures,* $10,388,254,424.
Personal Income (average weekly earnings, July 1987): $453.28.
Labor Force (September 1987, seasonally adjusted): *Employed* workers, 15 years of age and over, 1,278,000: *Unemployed,* 124,000 (9.7%).
Education (1987–88): *Enrollment*—elementary and secondary schools, 475,300 pupils; postsecondary—universities, 45,130, community colleges, 25,700.
(All monetary figures are in Canadian dollars.)

Royal Visitors. England's Duke and Duchess of York celebrated their first wedding anniversary at Head-Crushe-In Buffalo Jump in Southern Alberta. They also attended a rodeo at Medicine Hat and paid a formal visit to the province's capital. (*See also* page 85.)

Professional Sports. In the National Hockey League the Edmonton Oilers won a second successive Stanley Cup, while a Lethbridge team captured the Memorial Cup to become Canada's junior hockey champions. The demise of the Montreal team of the Canadian Football League resulted in the transfer of Winnipeg to the eastern division, leaving Edmonton with only three opponents in the West. At midseason its Eskimos had a precarious hold on first place in their division. However they went on to capture the 75th Grey Cup championship on November 29. Before a crowd of 59,478 at B.C. Place Stadium in Vancouver, the Eskimos defeated the Toronto Argonauts, 38–36. Backup quarterback Damon Allen of Edmonton completed 15 of 20 passes for 255 yards, and was named the game's most valuable offensive player.

1988 Winter Olympics. Preparations for the 1988 Winter Olympic Games in Calgary were marked by a mix of politics, optimism, and controversy. Most problems were associated with ticket sales. Calgarians were outraged when they discovered that some 23% of all tickets—and nearly 50% of those for the most popular events—had been reserved for Olympic "insiders." This figure was ultimately reduced. The original director of ticket distribution was dismissed for irregularities in sales. Adding to the problems, some recruited volunteers were released to cut costs, while many of those remaining felt that the resulting increased demands on their time were unacceptable. (*See* page 102.)

JOHN W. CHALMERS
Historical Society of Alberta

Calgary Prepares for the Winter Games

Photos XV Olympic Winter Games Organizing Committee

Chosen to host the XV Olympic Winter Games for two weeks in February 1988, the city of Calgary, Alberta, completed six years of preparation in October 1987. The final major project was a $40-million speed skating oval, above, *on the campus of the University of Calgary —also the site of the Olympic Village. Canada Olympic Park, located just outside the city, features the new 70- and 90-meter ski jumps,* left, *as well as the bobsled and luge runs. Hidy and Howdy,* below, *the official mascots of the Calgary Games, will welcome some 2,600 athletes from 60 nations to Alberta's largest city. Behind the mascots stands the Saddledome (home of the NHL Flames), the hockey and figure skating venue. The cost of the Calgary Games is expected to be nearly $1 billion.*

ALGERIA

A flurry of rumors concerning a union with Libya highlighted Algeria's regional diplomacy during 1987. Relations with Libya proved to be the most controversial dimension of Algerian activities to reorganize the political map of North Africa. Extensive diplomatic consultations indicated that the Algerian leadership increasingly conceived the nation's future in terms of what it called the Greater Arab Maghreb (North Africa).

Greater Maghreb Policy. In the 2½ months from May to mid-July, President Chadli Benjedid met with the leaders of all the neighboring Maghreb states. His May meeting with Morocco's King Hassan II, prompted by the mediation efforts of King Fahd of Saudi Arabia, raised hopes of a diplomatic breakthrough on the long-standing dispute over Western Sahara. Algerian-backed Polisario Front guerrillas continued to fight Moroccan troops over control of the region. In July, Algeria cautiously took note of Hassan's statement that he would recognize an independent Sahrawi state if a referendum there should indicate such a preference. Yet despite these signs of interest in a political settlement, and despite a prisoner exchange, the war went on.

At the end of June, Libyan President Muammar el-Qaddafi arrived in Algiers on an impromptu visit and stayed for four days. The Central Committee of Algeria's ruling National Liberation Front (FLN) party subsequently announced that discussions of a working document proposing a union between Libya and Algeria had taken place. In the days following the extended Qaddafi visit, Benjedid traveled to Tunisia and sent his foreign minister to Morocco and his minister of state to Mauritania for consultations. This round of contacts and soundings led to a reaffirmation by the FLN Political Bureau of the importance of the four-year-old Friendship Treaty linking Algeria, Tunisia, and Mauritania. Algeria appeared to be seeking to amend the Libyan proposal along lines compatible with its standing commitments to Tunisia and Mauritania. In September, Qaddafi intimated that a union would be proclaimed on the first of November, Algeria's National Day. Algeria indicated in October that union was not imminent and could only occur after a national referendum, but the diplomatic maneuvering continued as Tunisia sought to organize a regional summit.

In other foreign-policy initiatives, Algeria undertook a sustained campaign to reconcile warring factions of the Palestine Liberation Organization (PLO). Benjedid traveled to Libya in December 1986 in an attempt to coordinate the two governments' postures toward the various Palestinian groups. He sponsored a series of informal meetings in Algiers between rival leaders preparatory to hosting the official session of the Palestine National Council in April. Algeria took in the Chadian rebel leader, Goukouni Oueddi, and became involved in mediations between Chadian adversaries and between warring Chad and Libya. (*See also* CHAD and LIBYA.)

Economic Policies. Shortly after the 25th anniversary of independence in July, Benjedid delivered a major speech to regional administrators that stressed his major economic goal for the future: "autonomy of enterprises." By this he meant his intention to give Algeria's public-sector managers a much freer hand in directing their firms. The National Assembly passed several bills designed to shift more managerial authority, including investment and marketing decisions, into the hands of company executives. The National Assembly also approved a deficit budget, reflecting the crunch of lower oil prices. Algeria helped to launch the African Petroleum Producers' Association in an effort to encourage producer unity and increase revenues.

Politics and Society. Elections took place in February for the National Assembly. Less than half the incumbent members (132 of 295) were renominated by the FLN, and of these only 62 actually won reelection. As the new national census conducted in April confirmed that about two thirds of Algeria's population has been born since independence in 1962, this turnover implemented the party's (and the voters') desire to see new, generally younger persons in positions of responsibility.

The new deputies liberalized the conditions under which voluntary associations may be formed. The liberalization measures were designed in part to open channels of expression other than fundamentalism. The violent Muslim activist "Bouiali Band" was largely dismantled after the death of its leader, Mustapha Bouiali, and six followers in a shoot-out with the security police in January.

ROBERT A. MORTIMER
Haverford College

ALGERIA • Information Highlights

Official Name: Democratic and Popular Republic of Algeria.
Location: North Africa.
Area: 919,591 sq mi (2 381 740 km²).
Population (April 1987 census): 22,971,558.
Chief Cities (Jan. 1, 1983): Algiers, the capital, 1,721,607; Oran, 663,504; Constantine, 448,578.
Government: *Head of state,* Chadli Benjedid, president (took office Feb. 1979). *Head of government,* Abdelhamid Brahimi, prime minister (appointed Jan. 22, 1984).
Monetary Unit: Dinar (4.976 dinars equal U.S.$1, July 1987).
Gross Domestic Product (1985 est. U.S.$): $57,000,000,000.
Economic Index (1984, Algiers): *Consumer Prices* (1980 = 100), all items, 138.7; food, 145.6.
Foreign Trade (1986 U.S.$): *Imports,* $10,162,000,000; *exports,* $7,876,000,000.

ANTHROPOLOGY

Fossil discoveries continued to offer new views on human evolution, anthropologists narrowed contending versions of the hominid family tree to two main alternatives, and a study of Tibetan nomads gave insight into cultural and physical adaptation to life at high altitudes.

Early Humans. Newly discovered limb bones and skull fragments from about 1.8 million years ago indicate that members of what is considered the first truly human species had unexpectedly small, ape-like bodies. The species in question, *Homo habilis*, appeared in Africa between 2 million and 1.6 million years ago, and is thought to be the earliest tool user. The partial skeleton, uncovered in Tanzania's Olduvai Gorge, is strikingly similar to "Lucy," the 3.3-million-year-old partial skeleton found in 1974. The latest fossils belong to an adult female who had long, heavily built arms and stood between 3 and 3.5 ft (90 and 110 cm) tall.

Investigators who found and analyzed the fossils, led by Donald C. Johanson of the Institute of Human Origins in Berkeley, CA, reported that the primitive body was attached to the more delicate face and larger brain case typical of species directly related to modern humans. They proposed that *H. habilis* was a "mosaic creature," with a facial anatomy evolving in the human direction and limb proportions like those of much earlier ancestors. This called into question the assumption of some scientists that, beginning about 4 million years ago, with the emergence of the first human-like species that eventually gave rise to *H. habilis*, body size increased gradually along with brain size.

Johanson and his colleagues also noted that there may have been an abrupt evolutionary transition between the primitively built *H. habilis* and the taller, more modern-looking *H. erectus*. Fossils from the latter species have been found in the same region of Africa and date to about 1.6 million years ago.

Hominid Family Tree. Several contending versions of the family tree of hominids, the human-like creatures that eventually evolved into modern humans, have been narrowed down to two main alternatives, according to Eric Delson of the City University of New York. The two versions of the evolutionary tree emerged from a recent meeting of scientists from around the world concerning the so-called "robust australopithecines"—a group of hominids that evolved at the same time as the lineage that gave rise to modern humans but became extinct about 1 million years ago.

At the base of both versions of the tree stands *Australopithecus afarensis*, a species which dates to between 3.5 million and 3.1 million years ago and was near in time to the common ancestor of all later hominids. The most widely held theory is that *A. afarensis* led in two directions: one to the species *A. aethiopicus*—which was related to the later robust australopithecines, *A. robustus* and *A. boisei* (which became extinct); and in the other direction to *A. Africanus*, a species that has been found only in southern Africa, and then to the genus Homo.

The second evolutionary hypothesis proposes that *A. boisei* includes fossils which have been incorrectly labeled *A. aethiopicus;* that *A. africanus* led only to *A. robustus;* and that the exact ancestry of the Homo line is unclear.

Whatever the actual relationships between groups of robust australopithecines, members of these species appear to have been smaller than often assumed. Yoel Rak of Tel Aviv University in Israel examined several *A. boisei* skulls and found massive teeth and jaws imposed on a relatively small creature, with delicate bone surrounding the brain and eyes.

Tibetan Nomads. The Phala nomads of Tibet live at the highest known altitude for a human population, ranging from 16,000 to 18,000 ft (4,900 to 5,500 m) above sea level. In the first investigation of the Phala by Western scientists, anthropologists from Case Western Reserve University in Cleveland found that these hardy wanderers are organized into families with four or five members that live in animal-skin tents. The families tend small herds of goat, sheep, and yak, and hunt wildlife along craggy mountainsides. Although the nearest village is three weeks away, Phala men engage in fairly consistent trade, mainly for barley flour. Surprisingly, the scientists found that a high consumption of salt and animal fat among the nomads does not translate into high blood pressure.

BRUCE BOWER, *"Science News"*

ARCHAEOLOGY

At sites in the Eastern and Western Hemispheres dating from the Stone Age to the 20th century, archaeologists in 1987 worked painstakingly to excavate, analyze, and sometimes simply preserve the remains of the past.

Eastern Hemisphere

Egyptian Tomb. An international team of restorers pasted 10,000 strips of gauze and rice paper on the painted murals lining the burial chambers of Queen Nefertari, the favorite wife of Pharoah Ramses II. This is expected to prevent further deterioration of the murals until full-scale restoration efforts begin. Salt in the rock behind the painted plaster has recrystallized, causing plaster to detach and paint to flake away. There are two levels of elaborate murals in the 3,200-year-old tomb, but about 20% of the painted surface has been lost.

© Eric Meyers/Joint Sepphoris Project

The ancient city of Sepphoris in Galilee (now northern Israel), where the book of rabbinical laws is believed to have been compiled, was one of several important archaeological sites under excavation in the Holy Land during 1987.

Minoan Disaster. Danish scientists said that an immense volcanic eruption destroyed the Mediterranean island of Thera, also known as Santorini, and its thriving Minoan civilization in 1645 B.C. This is 150 years earlier than the commonly accepted date of the disaster and throws the timetable of Minoan history into doubt. The new evidence comes from an ice core extracted in Greenland that contains layers of annual ice deposits. Chemical analyses revealed that a layer corresponding to 1645 B.C. contained remnants of a major eruption that spewed ash into the stratosphere. If this date is confirmed, it would squeeze into a relatively short span of a few centuries the construction of huge palaces and other complex structures by the Minoans on Crete and the Aegean Islands, including Thera.

Dog Burial. A mysterious 2,500-year-old dog cemetery, containing both adults and puppies, was uncovered by archaeologists excavating an ancient settlement on a seafront bluff in Israel. The carefully buried dogs are all of the same breed, which today is called a greyhound or a whippet. The cemetery contains hundreds of individual graves and appears to have been in use for about 50 years, at a time when the Persians were in overall control of Palestine and Phoenicians served as their local rulers in coastal harbors. Both the Persians and Phoenicians enjoyed hunting as a sport, and the site may have been a major kennel where prized hunting hounds were raised.

Stone Age Camp. A prehistoric campsite unearthed on a small knoll in the boggy coastal lowlands of Denmark may have been the Stone Age equivalent of a summer cottage. Investigators said the knoll was once a tiny island in a now-vanished arm of the Baltic Sea. Discarded fish bones indicate that foragers exploited an abundant marine life created 7,000 years ago by the retreating ice sheets of Europe. Numerous recovered artifacts, including flint axes, arrowheads, and scrapers, suggest that small groups of people also used the island as a base for repairing hunting equipment and as an isolated area to butcher and skin animals. The 40-ft- (12-m-) wide prehistoric island was only above sea level for about 400 years and was occupied by no more than ten people at a time. It should provide a unique glimpse of life during the Middle Stone Age, from 8000 B.C. to 3000 B.C.

First Polynesians. Preserved seed cases uncovered on an island just north of Papua New Guinea provided firm evidence that the Lapita people, prehistoric mariners whose descendants first settled Hawaii and the rest of the Polynesian islands, grew and harvested many edible tree crops, such as apples and coconuts. Some investigators previously suggested that the Lapita, who colonized the South Pacific from around 1600 B.C. to 500 B.C., engaged almost exclusively in fishing.

Archaeologists who found the buried seed cases also uncovered remnants of a stilt house that once stood in shallow water along a former shoreline. This is the first such structure linked to the Lapita culture.

Western Hemisphere

Titanic. Hundreds of artifacts—from china and a chandelier to a small safe and a leather bag containing jewelry, bank notes, and coins

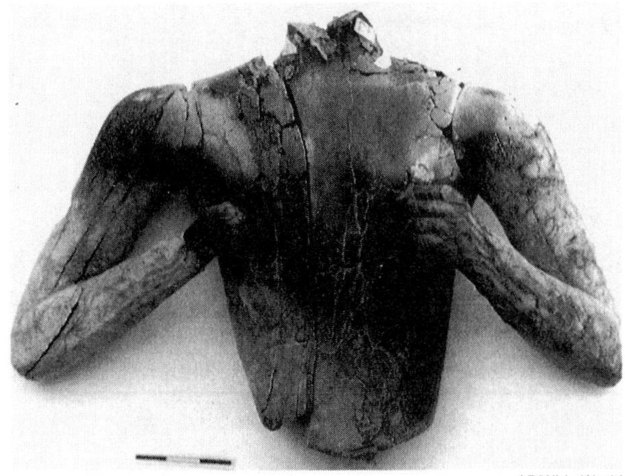

AP/Wide World

The torso and arms of a 3,500-year-old ivory figure were uncovered on the island of Crete in May. The figure dates from the artistic peak of the Minoan civilization.

—were recovered from the wreck of the luxury liner *Titanic* by members of a French salvage expedition. Divers in a minisubmarine 2.5 mi (4 km) below the ocean surface also conducted a photographic survey of the ship. Project leaders denied accusations that they were fortune hunters plundering the site of the 1912 disaster. They said the artifacts would first be shown on a television program and then put on permanent display after a worldwide tour. None of the recovered items would be sold.

Just before the salvage operation took place, the U.S. Senate passed a resolution barring the sale or profit-making display of *Titanic* artifacts in the United States.

Civil War Ship. The most detailed look yet at the Civil War ironclad *Monitor,* which rests upside down in 220 ft (67 m) of water 16 mi (26 km) off the coast of North Carolina, was obtained on an expedition conducted by the U.S. Navy and a branch of the U.S. Commerce Department. Using a remotely operated submersible vehicle attached to an ocean-going tug, researchers completed a corrosion study of the wreck, examined the hull and gun turret, and put together a photomosaic of the entire archaeological site.

The *Monitor* battled another ironclad warship, the *Merrimack,* on March 9, 1862. The *Monitor* sank in a storm later that year, and its site was discovered in 1974.

Early Americans. Studies of artifacts from two North American sites fueled a scientific debate over when the first Americans arrived. At the Calico Mountains site in California's Mojave Desert, scientists excavated flaked stones, some of which they said were human-produced tools, in a 200,000-year-old layer of earth. Along the Old Crow River in Canada's Yukon Territory, investigators found bones that appear to have been broken and flaked by stone hammers and scrapers. They estimated that the bones are at least 100,000 years old. Other archaeologists, however, questioned the accuracy of the age estimates for the two sites. For several decades, it has generally been agreed that the first people entered America around 12,000 years ago.

Ancient Maya. At the foot of a temple-pyramid in the ancient Honduran city of Copan, scientists uncovered a cache of jade and flint artifacts. They said it was a ceremonial offering made by a Maya king at the dedication of the temple-pyramid in A.D. 756. Included in the find were two jade figures that may have been heirlooms passed down by generations of Copan kings. The cache also contained several flint lance heads, stingray spines, and a spiny oyster shell containing a reddish-brown substance that is probably dried blood. According to the researchers, it is likely that these objects were used by the Maya king to draw his own blood for use in the offering. It is also possible that the lance heads were used to rip out the heart of a sacrificial victim, which was then placed in the shell.

Grave Robbers. Archaeologists and government officials in Peru reported that what was apparently the largest cache of ancient gold objects yet discovered in that country was unearthed by fortune hunters. Only a few of the 1,900-year-old artifacts, dug out of a burial ground beneath a pyramid of mud bricks, have been recovered. The rest will probably end up with private collectors or buyers in the international market for stolen archaeological treasures. The grave robbers uncovered what may have been the tomb of a Moche ruler, warrior, or priest. The Moche culture flourished along Peru's northern coastal plains from about A.D. 100 to A.D. 700. The Peruvian government is now financing a formal excavation at the site where the artifacts were taken. A deposit of more than 1,000 ceramic vessels and a ceremonial copper scepter have been found, but no other golden artifacts have emerged.

Custer Battlefield. The first thorough excavations at the site of Gen. George Armstrong Custer's "last stand" in southeastern Montana revealed that the Indians not only outmanned the soldiers, but they outgunned them as well. General Custer's men, about 260 strong, carried single-shot carbines and six-shot Colt revolvers, while about 2,000 Sioux and Cheyenne warriors had at least 41 different kinds of firearms, including 16-shot repeating rifles. The Indians also used arrows with iron arrowheads. Battlefield analyses showed that the soldiers were relatively stationary, while the Indians moved about freely and overran one position after another.

The famed Battle of Little Bighorn took place on June 25, 1876, but scientific work began only after a prairie fire cleared the site of tall grass and sagebrush in 1983.

BRUCE BOWER, *"Science News"*

ARCHITECTURE

The future of architecture, and indeed the world, was considered at the 16th triennial congress of the International Union of Architects in Brighton, England, in 1987. Despite much discussion of the needs for more humane environments and for quality living space for the economically disenfranchised, the trends of the future in the United States seemed inevitable. Larger and larger buildings were proposed for the suburbs—as evidenced by the design of architects Kohn Pedersen Fox Associates (KPF) for an enormous condominium and office complex in White Plains, NY, and for a similar project in Reston, VA, by RTKL Associates, which won a national competition. And taller and taller buildings were proposed for cities. On the list were a 50-story office building in Los Angeles by architects Albert C. Martin & Associates, which, by its design features, would overcome worries about earthquake damage; and a 71-story building in midtown Manhattan by KPF, which would allay concerns about adding to an already crowded area.

The growing popularity of large-scale, multipurpose, multiple-building projects was exemplified by the Fan Pier complex in Boston, which was proposed for a 19-acre (7.7-ha) landfill site. The project was to hold 1.4 million sq ft (130,000 m^2) of office space plus other buildings centered on a 50-story hotel. Another such massive, mixed-use project was proposed for outside Washington, DC, by architects Sasaki Associates to contain 2 million sq ft (186,000 m^2) of offices plus apartments, a hotel, and stores. And Battery Park City in Manhattan—designed by various architects, including Cesar Pelli, Davis Brody, and the team of Charles Moore/Rothzeid, Kaiserman Thomson and Bee —neared completion with its 6 million sq ft (557,000 m^2) of office space and 14,000 apartments. What sports fans had long awaited was finally announced in Toronto: the world's first stadium with a retractable dome, by architects Robbie/Adjeleian/Norr Consortium.

All of these buildings except the stadium were designed with some form of historic recall classified as Post-Modernism, a blanket term that could be applied to an ever-increasing number of buildings. Indeed, the design of Fan Pier was to be a collaboration of some of the country's leading architects in that style. The project's hotel, by Pelli (who developed the master plan and design guidelines for the whole site), was to recall architect Raymond Hood's Chicago Tribune Tower of the 1920s. An apartment house by Robert A.M. Stern, one of the founders of the style, was to recall turn-of-the-century design with a steep sloping roof and dormers. Another, by style-founders Venturi, Rauch and Scott Brown, would seem to take its cue more from the 1930s. One of the office buildings by Hammond, Beeby and Babka would seem to be a continuation of miles of sturdy 19th-century commercial buildings along the Boston Harbor.

© Osamu Murai/"Time" Magazine

Kenzo Tange, 74, designed Tokyo's new metropolitan government offices, Japan's biggest project to date. The Post-Modernist architect won the 1987 Pritzker Prize.

At West Virginia University, Michael Graves, a style founder whose built work had seemed to suffer from chronic underexposure, got a boost from the completion of an alumni center. But the leader in Post-Modern design, at least in quantity of buildings under way, might well have been KPF, which produced designs for buildings from the west coast to the east. And the winner of the Pritzker Architecture Prize in 1987 was Kenzo Tange, the father of postwar Modernism in Japan.

One debate that might best illustrate the division between laypersons' and critics' points of view on what should be built was that concerning Washington Harbour—another project containing offices, apartments, and shops—in the Georgetown section of the U.S. capital. While the project was disliked by many critics for what they described, in effect, as an overabundant use of discordant decorative motifs, the public flocked into its parks and promenades in obvious admiration. And architect Ar-

AMERICAN INSTITUTE OF ARCHITECTS

1987 Honor Award Winners

The Humana Building, Louisville, KY; Michael Graves, Architect; "is an important, full-blooded addition to the grand tradition of American office towers"

The Procter & Gamble General Offices Complex, Cincinnati, OH; Kohn Pedersen Fox Associates PC; modestly scaled twin octagonal towers that have a "distinctive profile"

National Commercial Bank, Jeddah, Saudi Arabia; Skidmore, Owings & Merrill; a "monumental" tower "projecting a powerful sculptural image for the bank"

House on Long Island Sound, Stony Creek, CT; Steve Izenour; an "engaging and idiosyncratic house"

Private Residence in Western Connecticut; Tigerman, Fugman, McCurry; an "interesting and creative interpretation of an English country villa"

House for Roy and Norma Reed, Hogeye, AR; Fay Jones & Associates; this "gentle" and "modest" house "is superbly responsive to its environment"

Fuller House, Scottsdale, AZ; Antoine Predock; "works well with the sun"

Norton Residence, Venice, CA; Frank O. Gehry & Associates; "the ultimate beach shack"

Middleton Inn, near Charleston, SC; Clark & Menefee; "sympathetic to its surroundings . . . but . . . not passive"

Lewis Thomas Laboratory, Princeton University; Payette Associates and Venturi, Rauch and Scott Brown Associated Architects; "a beautifully functioning object"

ICS/ERL, University of California at Irvine; Frank O. Gehry & Associates; a three-building "high-tech village" for computer science and engineering classrooms

Computer Science Building, Columbia University, New York City; R. M. Kliment & Frances Halsband Architects; "not only knits itself skillfully to existing buildings, but knits those buildings from different eras to each other"

Michael C. Carlos Hall, Emory University, Atlanta, GA; Michael Graves, Architect; "the gallery spaces enrich the experience of the objects on display through the architect's skillful use of color, form, ornament, and manipulation of space . . ."

Hood Museum of Art, Dartmouth College, Hanover, NH; Charles W. Moore and Chad Floyd; "connects two existing but stylistically different buildings, forming a series of courtyards, ramps, and gateways that allow people to walk through, under, and around this intricate and engaging structure"

Museum für Kunsthandwerk (Museum for Decorative Arts), Frankfurt, West Germany; Richard Meier & Partners; an expansion of the museum's riverside villa, which "deftly incorporates" the original but also is "a mature and poetic expression of the architect's . . . disciplined language"

Conrad Sulzer Regional Library, Chicago; Hammond Beeby and Babka Inc. and the City of Chicago Department of Public Works, Bureau of Architecture; "generously large, airy, high-ceilinged interior celebrates the public character of the building"

New York City Public Library Restoration; Davis, Brody & Associates; "almost magically revived the vibrancy and vitality" of three major spaces in the 75-year-old library

Restoration of the Frank Lloyd Wright Home and Studio in Oak Park, IL; The Restoration Committee of the Frank Lloyd Wright Home and Studio Foundation; "honors not only Wright but also the architects and craftspersons who brought this important part of American architectural history back to life"

O'Hare International Airport Rapid Transit Extension, Chicago; City of Chicago Department of Public Works, Bureau of Architecture; "uses light, color, and form to make the train rider's experience pleasant, interesting, and special"

Claudia's, San Diego, CA; Grondona/Architects; a cinnamon-roll bakery that is a "charming assault on the senses where even the air has calories"

thur Cotton Moore was prompted to defend himself in *The Washington Post* by saying that, while no one has ever been pilloried for producing a boring building, the most beloved buildings in Washington, DC—such as the Old Post Office, The Smithsonian, and the Library of Congress—were both idiosyncratic and roundly condemned by the critics at the times they were built.

Efforts to add onto rather than replace existing building stocks continued to grow. But so did the size of additions—to the point in the case of historic buildings, some argued, of overwhelming the existing structures. A project in Coral Gables, FL, proposed by architects Spillis Candela & Partners, would roughly quadruple the size of a local landmark, the Colonnade Building, built in the 1920s. So, too, would an award-winning design by architects James Stewart Polshek and Partners to add onto the Brooklyn Museum, an 1893 Beaux-Arts landmark designed by McKim, Mead and White.

Nevertheless, respect for past architectural achievements was shown by increasing interest in restoration techniques. Terra cotta, the fired-clay building cladding preferred by architects up to the 1920s for its ability to be molded into complex and often ornate decorative facade elements, enjoyed a revival as new manufacturers entered the field to satisfy the demand for both renovations and new designs. In a residential design that also paid tribute to past architectural achievement, the Tamarkin Techler Group produced a glass-roofed conservatory for an estate in Virginia that would rival the ambitious 19th-century glass-roofed pavilions of George Paxton at, for instance, Chatsworth in England.

While architects felt growing peer pressure to design their buildings on computers, there was much discussion of the ultimate usefulness of CAD (computer-aided design) systems: Are present systems useful for anything more than the production of repetitive plans on contractors' drawings? Do machines constrain the creative aspect of the design process or liberate it through such capabilities as three-dimensional modeling? A symposium of systems suppliers at the Massachusetts Institute of Technology concluded that design on computers was still in its infancy because of the complex creative process of building design, involving pluralistic, often indirect thoughts and images. Meanwhile, architects seized on computers to fulfill other needs—such as expansion into businesses traditonally engaged in by others, including facility and construction management.

CHARLES K. HOYT
"Architectural Record"

© Diego Goldberg/Sygma

With Argentina facing a possible military rebellion in April, the Alfonsín government called for popular support. In response, thousands of Argentines gathered in the streets of Buenos Aires to protest a mutiny in Córdoba.

ARGENTINA

Among the issues confronting Argentina in 1987 were the questions of continuing the trials of officers accused of crimes against civilians during the period of military rule; the increase of Peronist political power after the September elections; and the problems of a weakening economy and a growing foreign debt.

Government. National elections were held on September 6, for 21 provincial governorships, including Buenos Aires province. (The governorship of Buenos Aires, with more than one third of the 19.5 million registered voters, is considered a stepping stone to the presidency.) Also contested were one half of the 254 seats in the lower chamber of the bicameral legislature. Once the tallies were made, it was possible to ascertain the magnitude of the defeat suffered by the ruling Radical Civic Union (UCR). While the UCR received only 37.8% of the popular vote (as opposed to 43.2% in 1985), the Peronist Justicialista Party captured 41.5% (34% in 1985). The Justicialistas won 16 of the governorships, while the Radicals retained only two. Among the Peronists' biggest gains was wresting the leadership of Buenos Aires province from the UCR. By a landslide win in that province, Antonio Cafiero, 65, leader of a reform wing of the Peronists and a former economy minister, improved his chances of heading the divided Justicialista Party's ticket in the 1989 presidential race.

Although the Radicals, with 118 seats, remained the largest delegation in the chamber of deputies, the electoral reverse cost them 12 places and their majority. The Peronists gained four seats in that chamber, giving them 107, and continued to control the senate, where no positions were at stake.

Economic indicators worsened during the campaign, and the opposition accelerated its attacks on Radical policy. With the major setback suffered by his party, it was unlikely that President Alfonsín could count on the two-thirds majority in the national legislature needed to adopt the constitutional changes that he wanted, such as replacement of the presidential system with a parliamentary one.

Economy. A widely held perception was that the austerity plan introduced in 1985 was dead. Inflation had again reached triple-digit levels. Wage and price freezes were ignored by virtually everyone. Argentina was unable to service its foreign debt. Privatization and deregulation programs were stalled. Domestic oil production declined to the point that internal consumption was not being covered. Exports fell by 25% in the first half of the year, in comparison with the first semester of 1986. An average worker's real wage fell by 20% under the economic policy of Alfonsin's government.

During July and August, Argentina was given a new set of adjustment measures, in yet another attempt to cope with its economic situation. Export duties were removed from agricultural products in order to boost sales abroad. Rates were raised on public services provided by state-owned utilities. Controlled prices were allowed to increase by 5%

monthly. Interest rates were set at 3% above the rate of inflation. To cope with the debt-service burden, Argentina renegotiated payments on $34 billion of its $53 billion external debt. Those agreements made fresh loans of $1.95 billion available from private banks.

Argentina agreed in October to a drastic deregulation and de-monopolization of its huge, money-losing, state-run enterprises. The state petroleum monopoly, YPF, was split into four operational divisions, and the industry was opened in April to further foreign investment. There were mini-devaluations of the austral throughout the year, with larger devaluations of 6.7% in February, 10.2% in June, 9.6% in August, and 11.5% in October. Taxes announced on November 15 promised the government at least $3.5 billion in new revenues.

Labor Unrest. The Alfonsín administration sparred with the largely Peronist-dominated labor movement throughout the year. The eighth general strike since 1983 was called on January 26. Claiming that the government refused to talk about wage increases, strikers brought industrial and transportation activity to a standstill in and around Buenos Aires. Wage and price controls were imposed in February. In an apparent bid for control of the General Confederation of Labor (CGT), Carlos Alderete, of the Electrical Workers Union, was named labor minister on April 2. The union was one of a pro-government group of 15 powerful and moderate-to-conservative syndicates that favored a dialogue with the administration.

As national elections approached, the Alfonsín economic team offered labor a package intended to win its electoral support. Social security contributions by employers would be hiked, temporary workers would become permanent after three months on the job, more union representation within factories would be allowed, and strikes would be permitted under a wider range of circumstances. However, inflation worsened, and work stoppages became more frequent. On August 6, a 48-hour strike began among workers at 24 state hospitals. On August 12 that strike was followed by railroad workers, who were joined by 500 pilots from a state-owned airline.

At the end of August, wildcat strikes disrupted oil and gas distribution, and workers at the state-owned telephone company walked out, protesting the government's refusal to honor wage increases that had been negotiated previously. In order to avert the threat of another general strike, wage increases of 12% were authorized for public employees and the minimum wage was hiked by 75%.

Civil-Military Relations. The government's military professionalization campaign got underway when the UCR proposed in December 1986 that compulsory military service be replaced by a volunteer force. The administration also moved toward domination of military intelligence units by reviving a coordinating body for all intelligence work conducted by the separate branches. With support from the Peronists, the Alfonsín government issued a defense law on November 18 that prohibited the armed forces from intervening in domestic politics. The legislature approved a law in December 1986, setting a time limit on the filing of charges against military excesses during the "dirty war" (1976–1983).

Gen. Carlos Guillermo Suarez-Mason (ret.) a former junta member who had been in hiding since 1984 or 1985, was apprehended in California in January. The general, charged with 177 crimes, was alleged to have been responsible for thousands of deaths and incidents of torture. In February six admirals were placed on trial. A naval school under their jurisdiction had been a notorious detention center during the era of military rule.

After refusing to testify before a civil court on charges that he violated human rights while stationed in Cordoba, Maj. Ernesto Barreiro went into hiding, surfacing at a military post in Cordoba where he received the protection of the officers there. Two days later, Barriero fled, and the officers surrendered, except for a small group that occupied an army school at Camp de Mayo, 20 mi (32 km) west of Buenos Aires. President Alfonsín personally intervened at Camp de Mayo. His action in defense of civilian rule was hailed by opposition parties and by 400,000 residents of Buenos Aires.

In June an administration-sponsored bill granted amnesty to most military men accused of committing atrocities during the "dirty war." The armed forces had not been permitting accused officers on active duty to be tried in civilian courts.

Foreign Affairs. Regional integration was a major theme as Argentina signed additional accords with both Brazil and Uruguay in July and August. Brazil and Argentina agreed to increase bilateral trade, and created a common monetary unit for that purpose.

LARRY L. PIPPIN, *University of the Pacific*

ARGENTINA • Information Highlights

Official Name: Argentine Republic.
Location: Southern South America.
Area: 1,068,297 sq mi (2 766 890 km²).
Population (mid-1987 est.): 31,500,000.
Chief Cities (1980 census): Buenos Aires, the capital, 2,922,829; Cordoba, 983,960; Rosario, 957,301.
Government: *Head of state and government,* Raul Alfonsín, president (took office Dec. 10, 1983). *Legislature*—Senate and Chamber of Deputies.
Monetary Unit: Austral (3.1225 australs equals U.S.$1, Oct. 14, 1987).
Gross Domestic Product (1985 U.S.$): $63,300,-000,000.
Economic Indexes (1986): *Consumer Prices* (1980 = 100), all items, 256,314.1; food, 258,006.7. *Industrial Production* (1980 = 100), 94.
Foreign Trade (1986 U.S.$): *Imports,* $4,724,000,000; *exports,* $6,852,000,000.

Photos, AP/Wide World

In Arizona, Ed Buck, top left, *founded a movement to recall the state's newly inaugurated Gov. Evan Mecham,* above, *who had begun his gubernatorial term by rescinding a state holiday honoring the late civil-rights leader Martin Luther King.*

ARIZONA

Arizona celebrated its 75th year of statehood in the midst of political controversy. Gov. Evan Mecham found himself the object of a recall campaign shortly after he assumed office and followed through on a campaign promise to rescind the state's Martin Luther King holiday. Criticism of the governor mounted in the wake of a number of controversial appointments and pronouncements, and a boycott campaign by convention planners hurt the state's lucrative convention business. Mecham added to his difficulties when he appealed to conservatives across the country for support against the "militant liberals and homosexuals" he said were behind the recall movement. By the middle of December, validated recall signatures had far exceeded the 216,746 required for the election. The state's most widely respected conservative, former Sen. Barry Goldwater, was among a growing number of Republicans calling for the governor to resign.

New Legislation. A new law requiring unmarried girls under 18 to have parental consent in order to have an abortion was ruled unconstitutional by a federal judge. Under other legislation, divorced parents ordered to pay child support will have payments automatically withheld from their paychecks by employers.

Drug laws have been tightened to include punishment ranging from life sentences with no parole for drug crimes involving children to mandatory fines and community service for possession of even the smallest amount of a drug. Motorists who refuse to be tested for drugs may have their licenses revoked.

The Arizona Supreme Court unanimously ruled that patients have a legal right to refuse medical treatment, even if their decisions result in death.

Indian Affairs. After an extensive investigation of federal programs on the state's vast reservations, the *Arizona Republic* concluded that

ARIZONA • Information Highlights

Area: 114,000 sq mi (295 260 km²).
Population (July 1, 1986): 3,317,000.
Chief Cities (July 1, 1986 est.): Phoenix, the capital, 894,070; Tucson, 358,850; Mesa, 251,430; Tempe, 136,480; Glendale, 125,820.
Government (1987): *Chief Officers*—governor, Evan Mecham (R); secretary of state, Rose Mofford (D). *Legislature*—Senate, 30 members; House of Representatives, 60 members.
State Finances (fiscal year 1986): *Revenue,* \$6,038,000,000; *expenditure,* \$5,074,000,000.
Personal Income (1986): \$44,719,000,000; per capita, \$13,474.
Labor Force (June 1987): *Civilian labor force,* 1,602,200; *unemployed,* 111,800 (7.0% of total force).
Education: *Enrollment* (fall 1985)—public elementary schools, 386,057; public secondary, 162,195; colleges and universities, 216,854. *Public school expenditures* (1985–86), \$1,395,000,000 (\$2,829 per pupil).

no more than ten cents of every dollar actually reaches the Indian people. The Bureau of Indian Affairs was blamed for the "fraud, incompetence, deceit, and a morass of red tape" that has left the programs in "shambles."

Environment. The state's environmentalists welcomed the new federal law regulating flights over the Grand Canyon. Henceforth, flights below the rim are banned and flight-free zones have been established over portions of the canyon.

Work continued on the last leg of the Central Arizona Project, a canal extending east from the Colorado River almost to Tucson.

Science. Citing advantages of climate and geology, representatives of the state's scientific and business communities joined with politicians to lobby Congress for $4.4 billion in federal funds to build the world's first superconducting super collider in Arizona.

Population. To the delight of real-estate investors, Arizona continued to draw new residents in record numbers. According to the Census Bureau, Maricopa County (Phoenix) is the second fastest growing county in the nation.

JAMES W. CLARKE, *University of Arizona*

ARKANSAS

Arkansas' economy continued to struggle in 1987. Severe declines in tax collections caused state budget officials to reduce expenditures a record number of times. New standards in public education also went into effect, and a number of school districts were forced to consolidate due to their inability to offer the minimum number of courses.

On the political side, national attention was focused on the state for several weeks as first U.S. Sen. Dale Bumpers and then Gov. Bill Clinton toyed with the possibility of entering the Democratic presidential campaign. In the final analysis both men decided not to seek the nomination.

ARKANSAS • Information Highlights

Area: 53,187 sq mi (137 754 km²).
Population (July 1, 1986): 2,372,000.
Chief Cities (1980 census): Little Rock, the capital (July 1, 1986 est.), 181,030; Fort Smith, 71,626; North Little Rock, 64,288; Pine Bluff, 56,636.
Government (1987): *Chief Officers*—governor, Bill Clinton (D); lt. gov. Winston Bryant (D). *General Assembly*—Senate, 35 members; House of Representatives, 100 members.
State Finances (fiscal year 1986): *Revenue,* $3,623,000,000; *expenditure,* $3,355,000,000.
Personal Income (1986): $26,268,000,000; per capita, $11,073.
Labor Force (June 1987): *Civilian labor force,* 1,080,900; *unemployed,* 87,700 (8.1% of total force).
Education: *Enrollment* (fall 1985)—public elementary schools, 303,536; public secondary, 129,874; colleges and universities, 77,958. *Public school expenditures* (1985–86), $1,052,000,000 ($2,642 per pupil).

Politics. Despite some substantive legislation, including an early retirement plan for state employees and an emergency powers act to relieve prison overcrowding, the 1987 session of the General Assembly was remembered for more trivial actions. These included proposed legislation to require athletic contests between the state's two largest universities (which was defeated), adopting three different musical compositions as official state songs, and adopting English as the official state language.

In addition to the regular session, the governor also called two special sessions: one to raise more revenue for education, the prison system, and human services; and another to revise the fees paid by truckers for using the state highway system.

In other political matters, the state hosted the 41st Annual Southern Legislators Conference in August. Governor Clinton served as host of the conference and received national attention by being elected chairman of the National Governor's Association and chairman of the Education Commission of the States.

Economy. The economy opened the year struggling, stabilized by midyear, and saw a mild recovery in the last quarter. During the first quarter business failures in the state increased 164% over the previous year, and the state's business climate index, as rated by Grant Thorton, fell to 21st (compared with 15th in 1986) in the nation. Retail sales suffered the most in the economy followed by the service industry.

Certain segments of the agricultural economy, particularly the tomato industry, continued to be depressed and the number of farms declined to less than 50,000—the smallest number since 1870. However, a decision by a Japanese conglomerate, Yamato Kosyo Company, to build a $175 million steel plant at Blytheville opened the way for an upturn in the economy. Tourism increased by some 12% at state parks, and fall farm prices, particularly in rice and poultry, added to the growth. Arkansas again led the nation in rice and broiler production. The state's economy was relatively stable at year's end.

Other. In April an Arkansas grand jury indicted ten members of the Neo-Nazi Aryan Nations group for sedition; among the defendants were Aryan Nations Leader Richard Butler and Robert Miles, former Michigan chief of the Ku Klux Klan. At Christmastime, 16 persons were killed in or near Dover and Russellville in one of the worst mass murders in U.S. history.

Little Rock public schools were closed for six days in September and October by the first teachers' strike in the state's history.

C. FRED WILLIAMS
University of Arkansas at Little Rock

© Don Jones/Gamma-Liaison

Under the Intermediate-Range Nuclear Forces (INF) Treaty signed in December, the United States agreed to remove 108 Pershing-2 missiles, left, *and 256 Ground-Launched Cruise Missiles from Europe. The Soviets will destroy 441 SS-20s, 112 SS-4s, and about 120 SS-12s.*

ARMS CONTROL

On Dec. 8, 1987, the United States and the Soviet Union achieved two firsts in arms negotiations. One was agreement to eliminate an entire class of nuclear weapons known as intermediate nuclear forces (INF)—ballistic missiles and cruise missiles with ranges from 300 mi (480 km) to 3,500 mi (5,630 km). The other first-ever agreement was for both nations to permit the other's inspectors into their factories and military facilities in order to verify compliance with the disarmament accords. The treaty containing these agreements was signed in Washington during a summit meeting between U.S. President Ronald Reagan and Soviet General Secretary Mikhail Gorbachev. Coming about a year after the failure of the two leaders to work out an arms agreement at the Reykjavik, Iceland, meeting, the 1987 summit was hailed widely in the United States and abroad on its own merits, and as a possible point of departure for efforts to achieve substantial reductions in the numbers of long-range strategic offensive forces in the future.

The Weapons. The specific deployed weapons covered by the Intermediate Nuclear Forces Treaty include, for the United States: 108 Pershing-2 missiles based in West Germany; and 256 Ground-Launched Cruise Missiles (GLCMs) based in Britain, Belgium, Italy, and West Germany. Since the American missiles carry one warhead each, the total number of deployed U.S. warheads to be removed from inventory is 364.

The Soviets agreed to destroy 441 SS-20s, 112 SS-4s, and approximately 120 SS-12s. Because the SS-20s carry three warheads each the total number of Soviet warheads to be removed is about four times the American number. The weapons involved in the INF Treaty constitute approximately 4% of the U.S.-USSR nuclear arsenals. Previously the West German government had agreed to destroy its old U.S. Pershing IAs.

The INF Treaty calls for the weapons to be dismantled and destroyed in a three-year period, with inspections to ensure there is no cheating to extend for an additional ten years. Exactly how the weapons will be destroyed had not been fully worked out in 1987. The preferred means for the United States, however, appeared to involve removal of the fissionable material from the warhead for storage, with the missile, its fuel tank, and engine being cut in two and burned. The fuel would also be burned. In the United States, at least, there was concern that the burning would release toxic fumes into the atmosphere. Thus the final destruction process would have to be worked out in consultation with the Environmental Protection Agency.

Who Should Receive Credit? In the warm glow following the successful summit various persons and groups in the United States sought credit for the remarkable achievement. The many peace groups claimed that they, and members of Congress who were sympathetic, had maintained programs of public education and political pressure that led to the treaty. For their part, White House spokesmen pointed out that it was President Reagan's idea to seek complete elimination of INF weapons (the so-called zero-zero option) in 1981, backed by his firm insistence on building up American military strength, that led to the Soviets' agreeing to the treaty.

Others noted that President Reagan and General Secretary Gorbachev each needed to negotiate an agreement for domestic political reasons. For example, it was suggested that after the embarrassment of the Iran-contra affair the president needed to prove he was still effective in foreign-policy affairs. Some thought Nancy Reagan supported the treaty so that her husband would be regarded in the history books as an architect of peace. American observers noted that Gorbachev needed to demonstrate before the world that he stood on a par with the U.S. president, and that he required a respite in arms competition so that his plan for economic restructuring (*perestroika*) would have a greater chance of success.

Ratification. The U.S. Constitution requires that the treaty be sent to the Senate for ratification by a two-thirds vote. In the Soviet Union the treaty must be submitted for ratification to the 1,500 members of the Supreme Soviet, the Russian parliament, where it can be approved by a simple majority vote. Although he was denounced harshly by some conservative Republicans for negotiation with the "evil empire," Reagan ended the year by expressing confidence that the treaty would receive overwhelming support from the Senate.

On-Site Inspection. Many observers believed the most important feature of the treaty was its provisions for intrusive on-site inspection to provide guarantees against cheating. Heretofore, verification of arms agreements has been obtained by what is called NTM (national technical means). NTM include satellites and other externally located means of verification. It generally is believed that on-site inspection will be necessary if extensive additional arms reductions, particularly for mobile intercontinental ballistic missiles (ICBMs), are to be realistic.

The INF Treaty calls for a group of Soviets to live in the United States at such places as Magna, UT, where Hercules Aerospace Company produces the propulsion system for the Pershings. In a comparable encampment American inspectors will be quartered at Votkinsk, some 600 mi (965 km) from Moscow.

In addition, there will be a complicated arrangement for short-notice "challenge" inspections of facilities where INF missiles are located, or where they have been located in the past. The INF Treaty language detailing the inspection program is far more specific than that of any previous U.S.-USSR agreement.

The destruction and verification provisions constitute many of the treaty's 200 pages. For example, it is stated that 30 days after the treaty enters into effect each side must provide the other with updated information on missile numbers and location. The next step is for the two nations to exchange inspectors. With the inspectors in place the destruction of the missiles will occur over 29 months, after which time neither nation may have more than 200 nuclear warheads. These must be removed during the following seven months.

The short-notice "challenge" inspections are covered by precise rules. These specify that a short-notice inspection may begin with either nation's inspectors going to two designated cities in the other country, and giving four hours notification of where they want to make an inspection. The host nation then has nine hours to convey the inspection group to the chosen site. The kinds of inspection equipment that the inspection teams may use are set forth in great detail.

Nuclear Risk Reduction Centers, one each in Washington and Moscow, will transmit initial INF data to the other's staff. Disputes about the implementation of the INF Treaty will be handled by a new entity, the Special Verification Commission.

Reaction to the Treaty. Amidst the general climate of bipartisan political support for the treaty, as suggested by various polls, there remained those who were not enthusiastic. Gen. Bernard Rogers, recently retired North Atlantic Treaty Organization (NATO) commander, noted the treaty would create a "gap in the deterrent spectrum" because the United States was giving up the capability to hold Soviet territory at risk during a European war.

The Warsaw Pact nations, however, were supportive of Gorbachev. And NATO leaders such as Britain's Margaret Thatcher and West Germany's Helmut Kohl endorsed the treaty, followed by other West European leaders.

The Future. The INF Treaty, and the summit meeting of which it was the high point, were generally viewed as being a step toward much more important disarmament negotiations. Specifically, both President Reagan and General Secretary Gorbachev called for renewed discussions that could lead to a 50% reduction in long-range strategic forces such as ICBMs, submarine-launched ballistic missiles (SLBMs), and heavy bombers.

But looming as a shadow over these possibilities remained the president's Strategic Defense Initiative (SDI, or "Star Wars"). Whether the Soviets would be as opposed to the testing and deployment of SDI systems as previously, and whether Reagan would be as insistent in wanting to test and deploy parts of the SDI as previously, were questions left publicly unresolved at the INF summit's conclusion. Optimists noted, however, that both men seemed at times to suggest that some kind of a compromise might be worked out and codified in a 1988 Moscow summit meeting.

A Resignation. The director of the U.S. Arms Control and Disarmament Agency, Kenneth Adelman, announced his resignation in the summer and left office in December. Early in 1988, President Reagan named Army Maj. Gen. William Burns, one of the INF Treaty negotiators, as the new director.

ROBERT M. LAWRENCE
Colorado State University

© Christie's London

At Christie's London in March, van Gogh's "Sunflowers" (1889) was auctioned for $39.9 million, a record for a single painting. But at Sotheby's New York in November, van Gogh's "Irises" (1889) broke the mark, fetching $53.9 million.

ART

The year 1987 was an especially eventful one in the world of art, featuring a large number of works sold at auction—for remarkably high prices—as well as a variety of important exhibitions and the inauguration of several new museums and museum wings (*see* page 118).

Auctions. Throughout the year, sales records were set and quickly broken, both for works of art and for other precious objects that passed through salesrooms, such as a Mozart manuscript, which sold for $4.34 million, and the jewels of the Duchess of Windsor, which went for $50.3 million. But it was the record prices paid for two paintings by Vincent van Gogh—$39.9 million for *Sunflowers* (1889) in March and $53.9 million for *Irises* (1889) in November—that caused the greatest amazement. The winning bidder in the auction for *Sunflowers,* held at Christie's in London, was later revealed to be the Yasuda Fire and Marine Insurance Company of Tokyo. The canvas, the largest and best-known of seven versions of sunflowers that van Gogh painted in Arles, France, during the year before his death, was to become the centerpiece of the Yasuda Museum, which possesses about 450 works by Japanese, French, and other Western artists of the 19th and 20th centuries. The winning bid in the auction for *Irises,* held at Sotheby's in New York, was made by a European agent on behalf of an unidentified collector. The masterpiece was painted during van Gogh's first week at an insane asylum in Saint-Rémy, France.

The Yasuda purchase underscored the growing presence of Japanese buyers in the international art market in recent years. Encouraged by the yen's 50% increase in value over the U.S. dollar since the beginning of 1985, Japanese collectors are spending enormous sums for Western art, often bought as an investment or for prestige, and sending up prices. During the 1986–87 season, Japanese purchases at auction included two more for the Yasuda Museum, both by Auguste Renoir: *The Bather* for $1.5 million and *Young Woman With a Hat* for $792,000. Other Japanese collectors bought Piet Mondrian's *Composition in a Square with Red Corner* for $5.06 million, a record for that artist; Willem De Kooning's *Woman* for $2.3 million; and Gustav Klimt's 1914 portrait of Eugenia Primavesi for $3.85 million. The latter sale, made in May, broke the record of $2.8 million for a Klimt, set only two months earlier.

The spiraling prices themselves lured a number of works to the auction block, while U.S. collectors also were persuaded to sell by changes in federal tax law. The final months of 1986 saw the sale of several works that might otherwise have been donated to the museums in which they had been on extended loan. Rembrandt's *Portrait of a Young Girl Wearing a Gold-Trimmed Cloak,* for example, which had been on loan to the Boston Museum since 1930, was sold for a record $10.3 million. Van Gogh's *Sunflowers* had been on loan to the National Gallery in London, and his *Irises* had been housed in a small gallery at Westbrook College in Portland, ME. Concern was expressed by museum officials, who are no longer able to compete at sales and now also are losing gifts.

Other new records for works by individual artists included François Boucher's *Boy with Girl Blowing Bubbles* for $1.9 million; Jacques Louis David's *Farewell of Telemachus and Eucharis* for $4.07 million; Georges Braque's *Woman Reading* for $9.5 million (also a record for a 20th-century artist); and De Kooning's *Pink Lady* and Jaspar Johns' *Out the Window* for $3.63 million each (a record for a living artist). The English painter Francis Bacon saw his works set three records in quick succession, as *Seated Figure* sold for $935,000, *Portrait of George Dyer Talking* fetched $1.43 million, and *Study for Portrait II* went for $1.76 million. After the death in February of Andy Warhol (*see* page 121), the value of his paintings and prints increased rapidly; *White Car Crash 19 Times* set a record at $660,000.

Meanwhile, other types of art objects also were selling at record prices: for silver, an epergne by Paul de Lamerie at $1.1 million; in furniture, a porcelain-mounted Louis XVI desk at $2.09 million; a Ming plate at $1.46 million; a Greek neolithic sculpture at $1.32 million; a fragment of a Byzantine mosaic from Torcello at $427,152; and in sculpture, *Reclining Nude* by Henri Matisse at $1.43 million and *Large Female Standing* by Alberto Giacometti at $3.63 million.

Sotheby's set a record of $1.3 billion in worldwide sales for the season, an 85% increase over the preceding year. Sotheby's figures for single-session sales also continued to rise. Its record of $42.4 million in November 1986 was exceeded in the March session at Christie's, in which the sale of *Sunflowers* contributed to a single-session total of $61.1 million. Sotheby's upped the record to $63.6 million in May with a session that featured the Klimt portrait—and shattered it in November (the 1987–88 season) with a total of $110 million, including the *Irises* sale.

At Christie's International, worldwide sales totaled $900 million in 1986–87, a 50% increase over the previous season. Between them, Christie's houses in London and New York sold 40 paintings for $1 million or more. Christie's also handled two important collections: the holdings of Belgian banker Baron Lambert, whose modern and contemporary art sold for $26 million and 12 drawings from the famous collection of the Duke of Devonshire at Chatsworth, which sold for $10.1 million.

Exhibitions. The year saw a preponderance of shows featuring modern and contemporary artists. Vincent van Gogh dominated in the museum world as well as in the auction rooms. As a kind of sequel to the 1986 exhibition at New York's Metropolitan Museum, "Van Gogh in Arles," which showed his work from 15 months beginning in February 1888, "Van Gogh in Saint-Rémy and Auvers" showed his art of the period just following, the last 15 months of his life. During that time he spent more than a year at an insane asylum in Saint-Rémy and then left to live near his brother in Auvers, a small town 20 mi (32km) north of Paris. On July 27, 1890, he shot himself. Even in his depression, however, van Gogh was remarkably prolific. He did some portraits and self-portraits, but mainly painted from nature (the sunflower series belongs to this period) and many landscapes.

At the Museum of Modern Art (MoMA) in New York, the most popular show was devoted to the Swiss artist Paul Klée (1879–1940). The first exhibition to display the full range of his work, it included 300 paintings, watercolors, drawings, and prints—100 of them on loan from the Kunst-museum in Bern, Switzerland. The Cleveland Museum of Art also mounted the retrospective.

The Spanish modernist Joan Miró (1893–1983) was the subject of a major retrospective that originated in Zurich and Düsseldorf and then moved to New York's Solomon R. Guggenheim Museum. The show brought together 150 of Miró's works—paintings, drawings, graphics, and sculpture—from 1915 to 1977.

A Red Grooms retrospective at New York's Whitney Museum was highlighted by the return of two of his most famous and unusual works: the three-dimensional *City of Chicago* (1967) and *Ruckus Manhattan* (1976), which capture the life, movement, and color of the American urban environment. Another contemporary artist, Roy Lichtenstein, was represented at MoMA by 318 drawings, most of them working sketches and studies. The highly publicized, highly controversial series of paintings by Andrew Wyeth—the "Helga" series, discovered in 1986—began a six-stop U.S. tour in May 1987 at the National Gallery in Washington, DC. "The Helga Pictures" was a great success with the public, but less well received by many critics and even refused by a few museums, notably the Metropolitan. Meanwhile, a show called "An American Vision: Three Generations of Wyeth Art"—featuring the important works of N. C. Wyeth, his son Andrew, and grandson James—became the first international exhibition of American art in the Soviet

James Wyeth attends the "An American Vision: Three Generations of Wyeth Art" exhibit. The show was viewed in Leningrad and later began a four-city U.S. tour.

© Nan Coulter/courtesy, Dallas Museum of Art

© Shone/Gamma-Liaison

In honor of the 100th anniversary of the birth of Marc Chagall, an exhibit of some 300 of his paintings, drawings, and lithographs opened at Moscow's Pushkin Museum in September. The artist was born near the Russian city of Vitebsk, but fled his native land in 1922.

Union. The show then began a four-city U.S. tour in July, before moving on to Japan, Italy, and Britain in 1988.

One of America's foremost collectors was honored on the occasion of his 150th birthday by three separate exhibitions at the Morgan Library in New York. "J. Pierpont Morgan, Collector: European Decorative Arts from the Wadsworth Atheneum" brought to New York 80 pieces of decorative art, including Italian Renaissance majolica, 18th-century Meissen and Sèvres porcelain, German silver and ivory objects. The two other exhibitions, "Pierpont Morgan's Manuscripts and M. R. James" and "From Mr. Morgan's Library," brought together some of the rarely seen items kept at the Morgan Library itself.

The extraordinary art collection of the Queen of England has been exhibited with increasing frequency in recent years. In 1987 a group of 61 drawings traveled to the United States under the title "Italian Master Drawings from the Royal Collection: Leonardo to Canaletto." The works were exhibited at the National Gallery in Washington, DC, as well as in San Francisco and Chicago.

A royal collection from a totally different time and place, 16th-century Turkey, was exhibited at the National Gallery early in the year, before moving on to Chicago's Art Institute and New York's Metropolitan. Titled "The Age of Sultan Süleyman the Magnificent," the show included illuminated manuscripts, textiles, caftans, rugs, and a variety of other treasures.

From England, 48 of the paintings acquired by the art patron Samuel Courtauld between 1922 and 1937 toured the United States under the name "Impressionist and Post-Impressionist Masterpieces: The Courtauld Collection," with stops at the Metropolitan Museum in New York, the Kimbell Museum in Fort Worth, TX, the Art Institute of Chicago, and the Nelson-Atkins Museum of Art in Kansas City.

A more recent collector was remembered in a show at New York's Guggenheim Museum. The late Peggy Guggenheim, a niece of the museum's founder (Solomon R. Guggenheim) and a New York collector and gallery owner in her own right during the 1940s and 1950s, helped legitimize Abstract Expressionism and focused serious attention on such artists as Jackson Pollock, Robert Motherwell, and Mark Rothko. The 1987 show included a number of rarely seen works that Guggenheim had owned or donated to various institutions.

Changing political currents in the Soviet Union appear to have affected the official attitude toward art, as public exhibition of modern Russian artists was permitted for the first time in 50 years. The first beneficiary of the new attitude was Marc Chagall (1887–1985). To mark the 100th anniversary of his birth, a major exhibition was held at the Pushkin Museum in Moscow. The show featured 250 of his paintings, drawings, and prints borrowed from Soviet museums and private collections. Meanwhile, the long-hidden works of other Soviet avant-garde artists—including Kasmir Malevich and Wassily Kandinsky—were removed from the attic of the State Russian Museum in Leningrad for five foreign shows in 1987 and, in 1988, their first exhibition in the Soviet Union.

Restoration. Controversy over the restoration of Michelangelo's Sistine Chapel at the Vatican grew more heated in 1987. The project, begun in 1980, has uncovered the bright colors and details of Michelangelo's work but has come under criticism for endangering—and even altering—the fresco.

ISA RAGUSA, *Princeton University*

New Museums

© Arthur A. Murphy/The Metropolitan Museum of Art

As evidence of the increased public interest in art, several new museums opened their doors for the first time in 1986/1987, and major museums in the United States and Europe, including New York's Metropolitan Museum of Art and London's Tate Gallery, added new wings. As part of this activity in the museum world, three American private collections became available to the public.

New Buildings and Additions. The growing role of Los Angeles as a center for contemporary art was seen by two openings late in 1986. The $23-million Museum of Contemporary Art was constructed in the downtown business district with funds donated, in accordance with a local ordinance, by developers of the district. Designed by Arata Isozaki, it features curving lines, a reddish sandstone exterior, and a main exhibition space located under a courtyard and lit by skylights. Meanwhile, the Los Angeles County Museum of Art (LACMA) opened the $35.3-million Robert O. Anderson Building to house its collection of contemporary art. Hardy Holzman Pfeiffer Associates designed a massive, yellow limestone structure, marked with bands of green tile and glass, that screened the museum's original buildings and caused some controversy. The museum also was constructing a new pavilion for Japanese art.

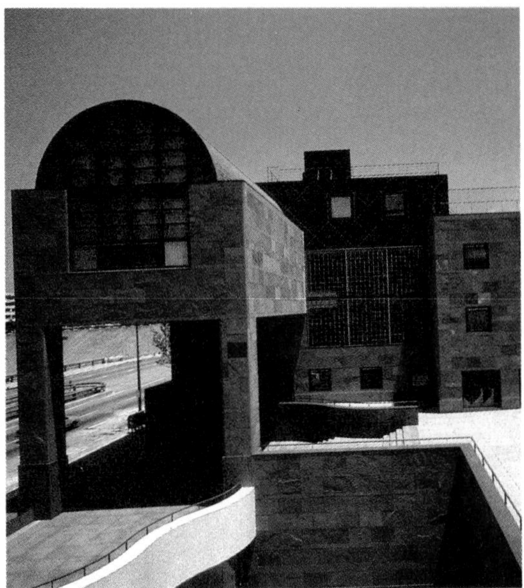

© Tim Street-Porter/The Museum of Contemporary Art

Light, air, and space are the dominant features of the sculpture gallery, top, *of the new Lila Acheson Wallace Wing at New York's Metropolitan Museum. The wing, named for the late cofounder of the "Reader's Digest" is devoted to 20th-century art. The main exhibit areas of Los Angeles' Museum of Contemporary Art,* above, *are below the courtyard level and lit by skylights.*

The principal hall of Paris' Musée d'Orsay—a sculpture-exhibit area—is 453 ft (138 m) long and 131 ft (40 m) wide.

Even more controversial than the LACMA wing was the new Musée d'Orsay in Paris, which likewise opened late in 1986. Housed in the former Gare D'Orsay, an elegant turn-of-the-century railway station on the Left Bank, the museum was designed to hold the Louvre's collections of 19-century art, including the Impressionist works formerly hung in the Jeu de Paume. ACT Architects renovated the exterior and the structure, while Italian architect and designer Gae Aulenti did the interior. She chose to contrast rather than harmonize with the existing building, constructing two massive marble and limestone structures beneath the station's central vault. Inside these buildings-within-the-building are galleries for paintings; between them and on their roofs, space for sculpture.

In late September 1987, two new galleries—one focusing on the art of Asia and the Near East and the other on African art—opened at the Smithsonian Institution complex in Washington, DC. The Asian art center was donated by the late Dr. Arthur M. Sackler and contains a core of 1,000 art pieces. Thomas Lawton is its director. The National Museum of African Art, which had been housed on Capitol Hill since its founding in 1964, is the first U.S. museum to be devoted entirely to African art, specifically art from south of the Sahara. It became part of the Smithsonian in 1979. Under the directorship of Sylvia H. Williams, the African art center opened with 6,000 art pieces, of which 600 would be displayed at a particular time. Both museums were built predominantly underground and designed by the architectural firm of Shepley, Bulfinch, Richardson & Abbott of Boston.

The Metropolitan Museum of Art in New York City opened its Lila Acheson Wallace Wing in February 1987 to house its growing collection of 20th-century art. The $26-million wing, which with 60,000 ft^2 (5 574 m^2) of exhibition space is large enough to be a museum within a museum, was the latest in a series of additions begun in 1970. It features high-ceilinged galleries flooded with natural light and was designed by Kevin Roche, John Dinkeloo & Associates. Its collection consists of some 8,000 objects and, while criticized as uneven, is expected to grow into its new space under curator William S. Lieberman, formerly of New York's Museum of Modern Art. A new exhibition area for the Metropolitan's holdings of some 15,000 pieces of Japanese art also opened at the museum later in the year.

When England's landscape and seascape painter J.M.W. Turner died in 1851, he left a

© Xavier Testelin/Gamma-Liaison

The new National Museum of Women in the Arts in Washington, DC, opened with the exhibition "American Women Artists: 1830-1930." The show, organized by Eleanor M. Tufts of Southern Methodist University, included works by Mary Cassatt, Constance Coleman Richardson, and Georgia O'Keeffe.

great body of his work to the British nation with instructions that it be displayed in its own gallery. That wish was finally met with the April 1, 1987, opening in London of the Clore Gallery for the Turner Collection. An L-shaped addition to the Tate Gallery and designed by James Stirling, the new gallery is within sight of the Thames River, often a subject of Turner's work. Some 300 of the painter's oils are on display; roughly 19,000 sketches and watercolors also are part of the collection.

Private Collections Become Public. A controversial new museum, the National Museum of Women in the Arts, opened in Washington in April. The core of its collection—some 500 works by women, dating from the 1500s to the present—was assembled by Wallace and Wilhelmina Holladay, who wanted to correct what they saw as the underrepresentation of women in public collections. The works are housed in a former Masonic temple that was restored in elegant style with crystal chandeliers and pink faux marbling. While some art lovers praised the museum's goal and its opening show, "American Women Artists: 1830–1930," others decried what they saw as a worrying trend toward the segregation of women artists. Mrs. Holladay, the museum's president, said that the gallery's "intent is not to separate art into male and female, but to uncover and celebrate the hidden contribution of women in the history of art."

As Chicago's Art Institute readied a series of renovated galleries and made plans for a $23-million addition, another new museum opened in the city. The Terra Museum of American Art began as the personal collection of Dan Terra, a 76-year-old industrialist, who originally put his works on public view in a former florist shop in nearby Evanston. In April 1987, the museum reopened in new quarters in two buildings on North Michigan Avenue that had been gutted and redesigned by architect Larry Booth. Four floors of galleries are available to show the collection's 800 works, most of which date from the 18th and 19th centuries. Plans include expansion into two adjacent properties.

A $25-million museum, built to house the 20th-century art collection of Dominique de Menil, opened in Houston in June. The De Menil collection, the third American private collection opened to the public in 1987, was considered one of the greatest private art assemblages in the United States. Primarily 20th-century art, it includes prime examples of School of Paris modernism, Cubism, and Surrealism. Mrs. de Menil expressed particular satisfaction with the two-story museum, which was designed by Italian architect Renzo Piano. Its spacious interior structure accomplished her objectives of giving "the art priority over the building" and of giving "the viewer time and space to look at art."

ELAINE PASCOE

SPECIAL REPORT/ART

Andy Warhol (1928?–87)

The acknowledged leader of the pop-art movement and a controversial figure in the art world, Andy Warhol died of a heart attack Feb. 22, 1987, following routine gallbladder surgery. With works that drew on the mass-produced images of popular cultures, the artist, who was believed to be 58 years old, had provoked a radical shift in the perception of what constitutes art.

Warhol was an enigmatic figure. Born Andrew Warhola, the son of a Pittsburgh coal miner, he began his career as a commercial artist specializing in magazine ads and window displays. In the early 1960s he began to produce works in the pop style that would soon become his trademark, and he displayed what were to rank among his most famous works—images of Campbell's soup cans—at his first one-man show, at a gallery near Hollywood, CA, in 1962.

These and other works, including silk-screen portraits of celebrities such as Marilyn Monroe and paintings that glorified such everyday objects as Brillo boxes, brought him to the notice of the New York art world. They also attracted the attention of collectors—the highest price ever paid for a Warhol work during his life was $385,000, for *200 One Dollar Bills.* Warhol quickly became one of the most widely known artists in the United States.

As his popularity grew, he broadened his creative approach to include photography and film. He produced some 60 underground movies, including *Empire* that presented eight straight hours of New York City's Empire State Building. He also produced the 1960s multimedia presentations of the rock group Velvet Underground, designed an album cover for the Rolling Stones, created several shows for cable television, and launched the magazine *Interview,* which focused on the rich and famous. He was the author of several books, including *The Philosophy of Andrew Warhol (From A to B and Back Again),* a collection of epigrams.

The artist himself was often seen rubbing shoulders with celebrities and was a fixture at New York's trendiest nightclubs. A pale figure dressed in black leather and wearing a white wig (a childhood illness had left him balding), he became something of a cult figure in the city. His studio, the Factory, was the center for his followers, who included artists, actors, celebrities, and hangers-on. In 1968 he was shot by one of them, Valerie Solanis, an actress, who claimed that he controlled her life.

© Hy Simon/Photo Trends

A toy company had commissioned Andy Warhol, the world's leading pop artist who died in 1987, to paint the Barbie Doll.

Perhaps the most controversial aspects of Warhol's career were his emphasis on "trashy" popular culture and the blatant commercialism of his work. He upset two key suppositions that underlay the art world of the early 1960s: that true art was somehow above popular taste, and that true artists were above commercial concerns. His work reflected what he saw as an insatiable public demand for new images; one of his most quoted remarks was that in the future, everyone would be famous for 15 minutes. He also saw no harm in making money—"Being good in business," he once said, "is the most fascinating kind of art." At his death he left an estate valued at between $10 and $15 million, the bulk of which was to be donated to the Andy Warhol foundation "for the advancement of visual arts."

ASIA

For much of Asia, the year 1987 marked a period of relative political stability and economic progress. But some Asian states appeared to be in a state of rapid evolution, and key regional conflicts remained unresolved.

The leaders of the six ASEAN states (Thailand, Malaysia, Singapore, Indonesia, Brunei, and the Philippines) held their third summit—and first in ten years—in Manila in November. They agreed to lower tariffs, increase regional trade, and begin more joint industrial ventures. They also signed a declaration reaffirming the association's political tenets.

Democracy: Promise and Perils. One of the most significant recent trends in Asia has been the rise of popular unrest against several authoritarian regimes. In 1987 the most dramatic events occurred in South Korea and the island of Taiwan (Republic of China), where the process of transition from dictatorship to democracy accelerated. In South Korea, massive street demonstrations protesting military dominance in political affairs led the ruling junta under President Chun Doo Hwan to agree to a significant liberalization of the political process. In mid-October the National Assembly overwhelmingly approved a new constitution calling for broader civil rights and the strengthening of the authority of the legislature. President Chun agreed to step down, and the nation's first direct presidential election in 16 years was held in mid-December.

A similar shift from authoritarian-style politics was taking place in Taiwan. There, on July 14, 1987, the government of President Chiang Ching-kuo officially lifted martial law, which had been in effect since 1949. While the move would not affect the political dominance of the ruling Kuomintang Party, it was a clear step toward legalizing opposition political activities.

There also was some movement toward democratization in Indonesia, which held elections in April, and in Pakistan, where President Zia ul-Haq has restored limited parliamentary powers. Other nations in the region were discovering, however, that democracy entails risk. In the Philippines, the government of President Corazon Aquino remained fragile. An attempted military coup to restore former President Ferdinand Marcos was suppressed in August, but the government faced a continuing challenge from Communist-led insurgents.

Democracy was also under fire in South Asia. In India, agitation by separatist Sikhs did not abate, while discontent with the government of Prime Minister Rajiv Gandhi was fueled by growing economic problems and charges of widespread corruption. In neighboring Sri Lanka, the civil war launched by dissident Tamils demanding independence for the northern regions escalated to new levels of violence, despite an agreement by President J. R. Jayewardene and the government of India to seek a political solution to the conflict.

Economic Developments. Asia in 1987 remained one of the most dynamic economic regions in the world, with several of its industrializing states displaying a vigorous level of growth despite the overall sluggishness of the global economy and growing signs of protectionism in the advanced nations of the West. Of course, the worldwide collapse of stock prices in October dramatically affected the markets in Tokyo and Hong Kong.

Behind the scenes, an intriguing economic trend was the growing tendency of socialist regimes to resort to capitalist techniques. The most publicized example is that of China, which has emphasized the importance of capitalist incentives to promote economic growth and technological modernization. Student protests in January aroused concern among conservative leaders and led to a brief purge of progressive intellectuals, but new Communist Party chief Zhao Ziyang asserted that economic reforms would remain in force.

To the south, Beijing's bitter rival Vietnam was also increasingly tempted to abandon the Communist model of central planning as a means of stimulating a lagging economy. The new party secretary general, Nguyen Van Linh, has vigorously advocated a new spirit of openness and economic innovation in Vietnamese society, leading to inevitable comparisons with the reformist policies of Mikhail Gorbachev in the USSR.

Regional Conflict and Diplomacy. In international affairs, the most significant development in Asia in 1987 was probably the diplomatic offensive launched by the Gorbachev leadership in the Soviet Union. Moscow called for arms reductions and a spirit of peaceful coexistence throughout the region.

On a bilateral basis, the USSR intensified efforts to improve relations with China. Moscow's initiative led to a perceptible warming in Sino-Soviet relations, marked by a rising level of commercial and cultural contacts. But key issues continued to prevent a comprehensive rapprochement between the two states. Although the USSR voiced a desire to remove troops from Afghanistan—one of the "three obstacles" that China views as preventing improved relations—there were no signs of a comprehensive agreement to end that conflict.

Nor was the civil war in Cambodia (Kampuchea) resolved, despite Vietnamese and Soviet efforts to obtain international acceptance of the status quo. In early December, former Cambodian leader Prince Norodom Sihanouk and Premier Hun Sen of the current Vietnamese-backed regime held talks in France and announced an agreement to work toward peaceful resolution of the nation's political problems.

WILLIAM J. DUIKER
The Pennsylvania State University

National Optical Astronomy Observatories

Supernova 1987A (at right) *appeared in the Large Magellanic Cloud, a galaxy about 160,000 light years away. The exploding star was the first visible to the naked eye (from the Southern Hemisphere only) in nearly four centuries.*

ASTRONOMY

The supernova that suddenly appeared on Feb. 24, 1987, was greeted by scientists as the astronomical event of the century. It was discovered nearly simultaneously by Oscar Duhalde and Ian Shelton, two astronomers working atop a Chilean mountain called Las Campanas.

A supernova is a star that explodes, and this one did so in the Large Magellanic Cloud, a companion galaxy to ours some 160,000 light-years away—in our backyard by astronomical standards. The supernova brightened to magnitude 2.9 in late May, when it shone as one of the 100 or so most conspicuous stars in the sky, and remained visible to the naked eye until the end of the year. Not since 1604 had a supernova been so evident to sky-watchers.

From a variety of observations with telescopes in the Southern Hemisphere, it is known that the supernova was born during the collapse of the core of a relatively young star. The star was about 15 times more massive than our Sun, and its diameter was about 50 times larger. The energy released during its collapse caused the star to brighten more than 5,000 times, while its atmosphere was blown away at a velocity up to 18 000 km per second (40 million mph). By June 1, at wavelengths visible to the eye, this shell had expanded to a diameter of some 135 billion km (84 billion mi), or about 900 times greater than the Earth's distance from the Sun.

Perhaps more amazing than the outburst of the star itself, which was officially named Supernova 1987A, was the detection of neutrinos spawned at the instant that the star's core collapsed. These elementary particles were registered during a 12-second interval by instruments in Japan and the United States. This marked the first time that neutrinos had been detected from an extraterrestrial source other than the Sun.

Neutrinos are litttle-known, ghost-like particles which presumably have no mass and travel at the speed of light. They also have virtually no interactions with matter. Thus, from the 20-odd neutrinos that were detected, physicists concluded that 10 billion or so of these supernova-induced particles passed through every square centimeter of the Earth's surface. Such a wave of neutrinos was exactly what theorists had predicted would result from the collapse of a stellar core having about 1½ times the Sun's mass. During such a catastrophic event, an enormous amount of energy is released—equivalent to all that the Sun would produce if it shone at its present brightness for 3 trillion years! Virtually all of this energy is carried away by the neutrinos.

The end product of this supernova explosion should be a neutron star, an object only about 10 km (6 miles) in diameter—about 7 million times smaller than the original star. It should contain 1.3 to 1.4 times the Sun's mass and spin some 200 times per second. As the supernova's debris cloud continues to expand into space, cool, and thin out, astronomers will try to glimpse this whirling cinder, the remains of a star that died.

Bombarded Earth. In 1978, Nobel laureate Luis Alvarez and colleagues announced that the impact of a giant meteorite some 65 million years ago caused the sudden extinction of about half of all life forms on Earth, including the dinosaurs. The main line of evidence was a widespread geologic layer of iridium, a chemical element rarely found on Earth but one that is common in meteorites.

In 1987 additional evidence for that ancient catastrophe came from the discovery of quartz crystals that had been crushed by pressures 90,000 to 300,000 times greater than we experience every day from the Earth's atmosphere. This so-called shocked quartz was found in New Zealand, Europe, and the north-central Pacific Ocean. Coupled with similar material found in 1984 in Montana, the wide distribution of this anomalous quartz suggests origination in an event—much greater than any volcano could produce—whose effects were felt around the globe.

The jury is still out as to whether the impacting bodies were meteorites, comets, or both. But in 1987 the evidence grew rapidly that the Earth has been and continues to be bombarded by large bodies from space. Excess iridium was found at Tunguska, Siberia, the site of an enormous explosion in 1908 that has been widely attributed to a cosmic impact, perhaps by a so-called stony meteorite. Going back much farther in time, the same element was found in Pacific Ocean sediments dating back 2.3 million years, an epoch in which ice suddenly covered much of the Earth's Northern Hemisphere. Finally, Canadian scientists announced the discovery of a 50-million-year-old crater on the floor of the Atlantic Ocean. This impact scar is enormous, being some 45 km (28 mi) in diameter and 2.7 km (1.7 mi) deep, and is the first such feature to be found on an ocean bed.

Pluto. For half a century after its discovery in 1930, our solar system's most distant planet remained a mystery world; not even its size or mass could be determined with any certainty. Perhaps the situation would be the same today, except for the discovery in 1978 of Pluto's only known moon, called Charon, which circles its neighbor every 6.4 days. Such a binary system allows, among other things, for an accurate assessment of Pluto's mass, which now appears to be only a few thousandths that of the Earth's.

Fortuitously, during the last several years, Pluto and Charon have been passing behind one another, a circumstance that permits a wide variety of studies. From observations of these eclipses, it is evident that Pluto and Charon are quite small, being only about 2 300 km and 1 300 km (1,400 mi and 800 mi) in diameter, respectively. Also, infrared measurements suggest that Pluto's rocky surface is covered by extensive polar caps of methane ice and perhaps a tenuous methane atmosphere as well. Charon, on the other hand, appears to be covered mainly by water ice, perhaps mixed with some kind of dark slag; in this respect its surface may be similar to Uranus' satellite Miranda.

The Sunspot Cycle. The abundance of dark spots on the Sun has been known to wax and wane in an approximately 11-year cycle since 1843. Yet evidence presented in 1987 confirmed that sunspots mark only the tail end of a much longer cycle of solar activity, one lasting 18 to 22 years. At any instant, therefore, two overlapping cycles must be operating in the Sun. The implication of this finding is profound, for traditional theoretical models used to describe how solar activity works can accommodate only one cycle at a time.

Giant Galactic Arcs. The most bizarre announcement in 1987 concerned enormous circular arcs nestled in three clusters of galaxies. The one in the cluster known as A370 has been the most studied. It is some 500,000 light-years long (but only 30,000 light-years wide) and could easily wrap around the circumference of our Milky Way galaxy. In fact, these arcs are the largest visible objects known in the universe, and their energy output is equivalent to that of the brightest galaxies.

Using the 3.6-meter telescope in Chile, French scientists determined that the arc around A370 results from the so-called gravitational lens effect. That is, the gravitational field of the cluster of galaxies has bent and "focused" the image of a more distant galaxy to form the arc that can be seen. In other words, the arc around A370 is merely a celestial optical illusion!

Younger Universe. Two studies reported during 1987 indicate that the universe may be only about 60% or so as old as generally supposed (16 to 18 billion years). Interestingly, the lines of evidence are quite diverse. One study was based on the radioactive decay of thorium-232, which has a half-life (the time required for its abundance to be halved) of 14 billion years. The observed abundance of thorium-232 suggests a universe younger than 10 billion years.

The other study involved calculating the age of the intrinsically faintest (and therefore the oldest) white-dwarf stars, taking into account the amount of time required for them to form and evolve into their present state. According to this reckoning, the universe is 10.3 billion years old, give or take a few billion years. Should these conclusions stand up, theories describing the evolution of the universe will need radical modification.

LEIF J. ROBINSON
"Sky & Telescope"

AUSTRALIA

Generally, the year in Australia ranked as one of deep-seated change behind a facade of continuity. Throughout, grave concerns had been expressed over economic trends, especially the rapid rise in foreign and domestic debt, but although the political agenda moved to the right, the Australian Labor Party (ALP) government of Prime Minister Robert J. Hawke was returned to office in July for its third term in an atmosphere of euphoria. In September, buoyed by hopes of an economic miracle, media commentators eagerly embraced a budget built around a highly optimistic evaluation of the economy by Treasurer Paul Keating. Meanwhile, underlying but less-publicized change was occurring.

The Political Round. In a year of heightened political sound and fury, minimal realignment occurred; Hawke increased Labor's House of Representatives majority from 16 to 24 but failed to gain control of the Senate. A major effort by the New Right had little success, returning only one senator (former Treasury Secretary John Stone). The overall ALP vote slipped slightly, but highly professional "targeting" gave Labor candidates a winning edge in key marginal seats, especially some in Queensland narrowly won in 1985 by non-Labor candidates.

Environmental issues continued to excite political activists. Two Nuclear Disarmament Party candidates were elected to the Senate. In October antinuclear demonstrators orchestrated their efforts to coincide with the tenth anniversary of the U.S.-operated Pine Gap satellite-monitoring facility in central Australia.

Labor. Union power remained a matter of central concern; sporadic strikes and highly disruptive "work bans" occurred. In a controversial move in Melbourne, the financial assets of an intransigent union—the Builders Laborers' Federation, stripped of official registration in the state of Victoria since early 1986—were seized in October under a special order by Victoria's Labor government.

The Confederation of Australian Industry moved to set up a defense fund to finance employers during conflicts with unions and governments. Voluntary contributions were drawn from industry bodies and thousands of companies in order that financial, legal, and public relations support could be given during disputes. The confederation said the Arbitration Commission system and industrial legislation were inadequate "to defend employers against recalcitrant union behavior."

With the unresolved high cost structure and inflation posing major difficulties, employers continued, without success, their efforts to halt the ongoing wage escalation. A new formula for wage increases linked claims to demonstrable gains in productivity; however, not all unions abided by this rule, and many wage-linked strikes occurred.

Australia's Prime Minister Robert Hawke and Mrs. Hawke celebrate the Labor Party's victory at the polls July 11. The win marked the first time in history that the ALP had won three consecutive general elections.
Australian Overseas Information Service

Economy. The year's most significant development came in mid-October with a 40% stock-market fall when, after marching in step with New York and world markets to record heights not long before, Australian share indices plummeted in line with Wall Street's great sell-off. In the collapse, many fortunes and the prevailing optimism were shattered, leaving investors extremely wary.

Australia's external debt rose to equal 32% of the gross domestic product (GDP). This foreign-debt crisis prompted assessments of the national future and studies on appropriate policy directions by both government and special-interest groups across the political spectrum. After reelection in July, the ALP government recognized that wage restraints and a tightening of fiscal policy were necessary.

The thrust of the budget presented by Treasurer Keating in September had been foreshadowed in May when cuts in expenditures were announced. For the first time in a decade, the budget offered hope that revenue (a gross A$78 billion, or U.S. $57 billion, to be offset by asset sales of A$1 billion) and the deficit (down to a nominal A$27 million) would decline as a proportion of GDP. By restraining growth in public-sector expenditures, budget outlays rose less (at 4.3%) than revenues (up 8%). After allowing for inflation, outlays were to fall by 2.4%, or 1.2% if asset sales were excluded. Repayment of $1 bilion of both domestic bonds and external debt was intended. A marked fall in public-sector borrowing was designed to relieve pressure on financial markets and help sustain the lowering of interest rates seen from midyear.

Forecasts were for a 2.75% lift in real GDP (with most of the slight gain from the previous year's 2% in nonfarm GDP); a mild rise in private consumption; an improvement (close to 5%) in business investment and buildings; a fall in inflation to 7%; a continuation of the 6.5% annual rise in average earnings; unchanged unemployment (at 8%); and a gradual lowering of the rate of the current-account overseas deficit.

Critics of the budget observed that it failed to hold down the rate of wage increases (widely reported to be close to 10%), and also doubted that hopes on the balance-of-payments outcome could be fulfilled. Nevertheless, immediate reaction was enthusiastic.

Foreign Policy. Developments in the South Pacific took center stage, notably an offer by Libya to back some ministates in the region and France's unwillingness to relinquish power in New Caledonia, where tensions arose from an independence movement sponsored by the territory's indigenous people. A military coup in Fiji generated special difficulties when, at the request of Fiji unions, Australian transport unions rebuffed Canberra and banned shipping and threatened air links.

Hawke fought Britain's opposition to having Fiji removed peremptorily from the Commonwealth and led opinion supporting acceptance by Queen Elizabeth II of the resignation of Fiji's governor-general, Ratu Sir Penaia Ganilau, thus ending Fiji's link with the Crown. (*See* FIJI.)

Hawke's ongoing foreign-policy aim centered on a desire for freer international trade, and he pressed internationally for the curbing of protectionism. In October he raised the issue in San Diego, CA, in an address to the Australian-American Chamber of Commerce. In San Francisco he pressed the same point with U.S. Secretary of State George Shultz, warning that U.S.-Australian relations could be under strain if the United States adopted legislation damaging to Australia's export trade or put pressure on Japan to buy American beef or coal on uncompetitive terms. Hawke took up the same theme when addressing representatives of the General Agreement on Tariffs and Trade (GATT) in Geneva.

Earlier, Hawke had reassured the United States that its defense bases would not be used as a lever in trade negotiation, but warned the United States should not take for granted any other element of the alliance.

Policy Developments. Hawke's greatest setback came in October, when he found it necessary to ditch legislation requiring universal use of an identity card in all financial and social-welfare matters. Commentators had pointed to the parliamentary, political, and administrative problems involved in pursuing the controversial "Australia Card" measure, to which public opposition was strong, but Labor persisted doggedly. A dramatic turnabout came when the opposition announced that it would use its Senate majority to disallow the legislation over a newly discovered technical flaw. Rather than persist with alternative means of implementing the proposal, the government retreated.

AUSTRALIA • Information Highlights

Official Name: Commonwealth of Australia.
Location: Southwestern Pacific Ocean.
Area: 2,967,896 sq mi (7 686 850 km^2).
Population (mid-1987 est.): 16,200,000.
Chief Cities (June 30, 1986, provisional): Canberra, the capital, 285,800; Sydney, 3,430,600; Melbourne, 2,942,000; Brisbane, 1,171,300.
Government: *Head of state,* Elizabeth II, queen; represented by Sir Ninian Martin Stephen, governor-general (took office July 1982). *Head of government,* Robert Hawke, prime minister (took office March 11, 1983). *Legislature*—Parliament: Senate and House of Representatives.
Monetary Unit: Australian dollar (1.4570 A$ equal U.S.$1, Nov. 16, 1987).
Gross Domestic Product (1985 U.S.$): $153,000,000,000.
Economic Indexes (1986): *Consumer Prices* (1980 = 100), all items, 162.4; food, 158.0. *Industrial Production* (June 1986, 1980 = 100), 106.
Foreign Trade (1986 U.S.$): *Imports,* $23,847,000,000; *exports,* $22,496,000,000.

Major restructuring of the nationally funded tertiary education system was initiated by Employment, Education, and Training Minister John Dawkins. The move affected all 19 universities and 46 colleges of the tertiary system, which have total expenditures of A$2.5 billion and some 68,000 employees. The Tertiary Education Commission was eliminated and its powers absorbed by Dawkins' department. Reforms were aligned to the urgent needs of the economy (including reintroduction of tertiary fees, dropped in 1973), greater emphasis on mathematics and science, and closer ties with industry on courses and finance allocation.

The government decided to break cross-media ownership ties. Melbourne-born media magnate Rupert Murdoch made a successful bid for the Herald and Weekly Tribune Ltd. newspaper and broadcasting group, forcing him to choose between print and electronic media. He retained and expanded print activities and by year's end was challenged almost solely by Sydney's John Fairfax organization. In the rearranged patterns of ownership, the former Herald and Fairfax television and radio networks went to new media tycoons.

Trends and Events. As Australia's population passed 16 million, the numbers of Australians over 65 years old showed steady gains, and women continued to outnumber men (by 18,000). Considerable media attention was given to the long-term decline in the birthrate, down to an average of 2.0 children per woman in 1984 from 3.5 in 1960. The sustained fall was reflected in fewer children under five and a rise in the median age to 31.1 years, compared with 29.6 in 1981 and 28.4 in 1976.

The recent census showed a sharp rise in those willing to identify themselves as Aboriginals. Increasing attention was given to proposals for an agreement between the national government and the Aboriginal community. The idea was mooted in a Senate committee's report in 1983 and then left unnoticed; Prime Minister Hawke revived it in mid-1987.

Preparations for national celebrations in the bicentennial year of 1988 were advanced. The First Fleet reenactment—a replay of the 1787-88 voyage from England of the original founding group—began in May, with the ships reaching Australian waters in December. In Canberra the massive, elaborately designed new Parliament House moved toward completion. In Brisbane, World Expo 88 was constructed. A A$70 million indoor tennis center was rushed to completion in Melbourne.

Work began on a A$400 million four-lane road tunnel under Sydney Harbor, to be completed by 1992, as an alternative crossing to the famed Harbor Bridge (opened in 1932). Such a tunnel had been under discussion for many decades.

R. M. YOUNGER
Author, "Australia and the Australians"

AUSTRIA

Formation of a coalition cabinet and the barring of President Kurt Waldheim from visiting the United States highlighted Austrian affairs in 1987.

Government. The parliamentary elections on Nov. 23, 1986, had given the Social Democrats 80 seats, the People's Party 77, the Freedom Party 18, and a new environmentalist group—the Green Alternative List, led by Freda Meissner-Blau—8. Franz Vranitzky, a Socialist, continued on as chancellor and immediately announced he would attempt to form a "grand coalition" government with the People's Party, similar to the ones that had governed Austria from 1945 to 1966.

Vranitzky was successful, and on Jan. 14, 1987, the new government was announced, consisting of eight ministers from each party and a nonparty minister of justice, Egmont Foregger. Alois Mock, chairman of the People's Party, became vice-chancellor and foreign minister. The surrender of the foreign ministry to the People's Party led Bruno Kreisky, former chancellor (1970–83), to resign in protest as honorary life chairman of the Social Democratic Party. The new cabinet was sworn in on January 21.

In presenting the government program, Chancellor Vranitzky stressed four policy areas: reduction of the budget deficit and modernization of the economy; improvement of the environment; electoral reform and enhancing direct democracy and civil rights; and the burnishing of Austria's image abroad.

On February 14-15 two of the three environmentalist groups that had jointly contested the November elections formally constituted themselves as the Green Alternatives (*Grüne Alternativen*). Seven of their elected deputies agreed to affiliate with the new party, but Josef Buchner, the more conservative leader of the United Greens of Austria, refused to join.

AUSTRIA • Information Highlights

Official Name: Republic of Austria.
Location: Central Europe.
Area: 32,375 sq mi (83 850 km²).
Population (mid-1987 est.): 7,600,000.
Chief Cities (1981 census): Vienna, the capital, 1,531,346; Graz, 243,166; Linz, 199,910; Salzburg, 139,426; Innsbruck, 117,287.
Government: *Head of state,* Kurt Waldheim, president (took office July 1986). *Head of government,* Franz Vranitzky, chancellor (took office June 16, 1986). *Legislature*—Federal Assembly: Federal Council and National Council.
Monetary Unit: Schilling (11.77 schillings equal U.S. $1, Nov. 10, 1987).
Gross National Product (1985 U.S.$): $66,260,-000,000.
Economic Indexes (1986): *Consumer Prices* (1980 = 100), all items, 129.0; food, 125.4. *Industrial Production* (1980 = 100), 110.
Foreign Trade (1986 U.S.$): *Imports,* $26,843,-000,000; *exports,* $22,522,000,000.

Foreign Affairs. Foreign Minister Mock visited Brussels March 17-18 seeking to integrate Austria more closely into the European Community. It was agreed that the existing European Commission to the United Nations in Vienna would also be accredited to the Austrian government and that a ministerial-level meeting would be held every year.

On April 27, President Waldheim was barred from entering the United States "as an individual" by the U.S. Justice Department because of his suspected participation in Nazi war crimes. The department had been investigating Waldheim for more than a year and, acting under a U.S. law of 1978, had placed Waldheim on a "watch list" of some 40,000 undesirables who are excluded from the United States as war criminals, Communists, common criminals, or carriers of dangerous contagious diseases. The action aroused consternation in Austria, and the government immediately issued a statement, approved later by the parliament, supporting Waldheim. Chancellor Vranitzky, in a U.S. visit May 19-24, was unsuccessful in getting Secretary of State George Shultz and President Ronald Reagan to stay the ban. Austrian Ambassador Thomas Klestil was withdrawn from Washington to become secretary-general for foreign affairs in Vienna. Canadian Prime Minister Brian Mulroney on April 28 issued a statement that Waldheim would not be welcome in Canada, but other countries took no steps to bar Waldheim.

On June 25, Pope John Paul II welcomed Kurt Waldheim to the Vatican. The Jewish community protested the meeting because of the Austrian president's alleged Nazi past.

© Felici/Gamma-Liaison

On June 25, President Waldheim paid an official visit to the Vatican, and Pope John Paul II praised him for his work as United Nations secretary-general and his services for peace. Jewish groups, particularly from the United States, bitterly opposed the visit. On March 24, King Hussein of Jordan had invited Waldheim to his country, and on July 1 the president and his wife made an official visit to Amman. Here he was cited for his work at the UN and for his general "patriotism, intregrity, and wisdom" and was awarded a high Jordanian decoration. Other countries extended invitations to Waldheim, and his diplomatic isolation, sought by the United States, was, in a measure at least, broken.

In mid-August the Austrian government published a "White Book" compiled by the foreign ministry refuting allegations that Waldheim was involved in Nazi war crimes. U.S. Ambassador Ronald S. Lauder resigned and in an October 9 interview alleged that the Austrian people harbored anti-Semitic feelings. This led to an Austrian protest to the State Department, which made no response. President Reagan subsequently nominated Henry Anatole Grunwald, former editor of *Time* magazine, to the Vienna post.

Economy. A revised budget submitted in February provided for revenues of 398,500 million schillings (about $31 billion) and expenditures of 509,600 million schillings (about $40 billion), with a reduced net budget deficit of 74,700 million schillings (about $6 billion) or 4.9% of the gross domestic product (GDP). Late in October there were street demonstrations in Vienna against the government's budget-reduction austerity program calling for cuts in state subsidies and social benefits. The GDP was expected to grow only at a rate of 1% in 1987. There was a reduction in the value-added tax on most luxury goods from a rate of 32% to the normal charge of 20%. While employment increased slightly in 1986 (0.8%), unemployment rose from 4.8% to 5.1% because of many young persons and women entering the job market. Inflation remained low.

ERNEST C. HELMREICH, *Professor of History Emeritus, Bowdoin College*

AUTOMOBILES

Rising demand for light trucks, including utility vehicles, offset a downswing in new-car sales in the United States during 1987 and inspired industry optimism for steady sales volumes in 1988. The bullish predictions from the Big Three domestic automakers—Chrysler, Ford, and General Motors (GM)—followed a historic three-year contract agreement reached in a marathon bargaining session in mid-September between Ford Motor Company and the United Auto Workers (UAW), in which "job security" was guaranteed for the first time by any auto manufacturer.

Upon peaceful resolution of the UAW's contract negotiations with GM early in October —also resulting in a three-year pact stressing job security—industry executives predicted 1988 sales in the United States of 10.2 million cars and a record 5 million trucks. The combined total would equal that of 1987, except that car sales fell to an estimated 10.3 million and truck volume rose to a peak 4.7 million. A further spurt in retail deliveries of trucks and their companion utility vehicles to the 5-million mark in 1988 would for the first time result in a sales mix of one truck for every two cars.

The job security clause in the new Ford contract, which GM embraced as a basis for a UAW settlement of its own, insured the jobs of all 104,000 Ford hourly workers in the United States except in industry-wide sales recessions. Although the contract led to moderate price increases on 1988 models, Ford and the UAW applauded the job-security breakthrough as a morale builder after a decade of extensive plant closings by all domestic automakers. The UAW was planning to pursue job security at Chrysler Corporation when the No. 3 automaker's contract comes up for renewal in September 1988.

Ford successfully was chosen by the UAW to be the "target" for the job-security issue after the second largest producer not only earned higher net profits than GM in the first half of 1987 but also raised its share of the U.S. car market to 20.3% in the first nine months of 1987 from 17.9% in the comparable period of 1986. GM's share plunged in the same periods from 42.8% to 37.4% and Chrysler's from 12.2% to 10.7%.

Joining Ford's penetration of the market on the upside was the share held by overseas-headquartered manufacturers through imported cars plus those assembled by a steadily increasing number of plants located in the United States. Sales of imported cars plus "transplant" domestic cars rose 5.3% to 2,751,000 units in the January–September period of 1987, amounting to 31.6% of the market. This compared with 2,619,000 cars in the comparable period of 1986, when the share stood at 27.1%.

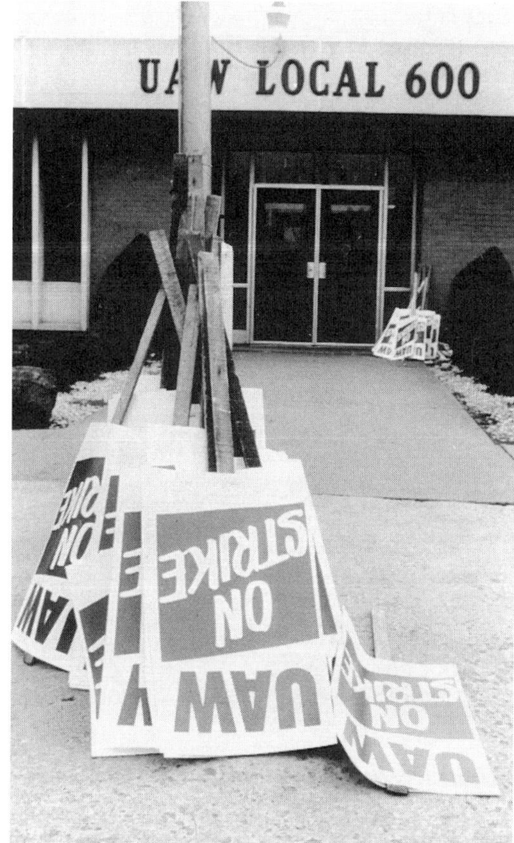

© Jerome Magid/"Time" Magazine

The picket signs were ready as the contract between the United Auto Workers and Ford expired on September 14. But the company's 104,000 union members did not strike, and a new contract agreement was reached three days later.

The changing lineup of the U.S. auto industry was demonstrated graphically as the 1987-model year drew to a close. The last remaining domestic independent, American Motors, was acquired by Chrysler Corporation on Aug. 5, 1987, after a 33-year history of building cars in Kenosha, WI, and the popular Jeep vehicles in Toledo, OH. Less than a month after Chrysler took over AMC and renamed it the Eagle-Jeep division of Chrysler Motors, a new assembly plant of Japan's Mazda Motor began production of Mazda MX-6 compact cars in Flat Rock, MI.

The momentum attained by Ford was illustrated in another feat—Ford Division outsold GM's Chevrolet Division in combined car and truck sales in the 1987-model year for the first time since 1956. Chevrolet, stung by the setback, launched a "beat Ford" sales drive for calendar 1987 in a move underscoring GM's concern over its loss of volume and market share.

With its luxury cars hardest hit by softening demand throughout the 1987-model year, GM was pinning its comeback hopes on a restyled series of front-wheel-drive midsize cars, the

Chrysler Corporation

AP/Wide World

Chrysler's 1988 New Yorker Landau, top, *was one of the new front-wheel-drive "luxosedans" aimed at the upscale market. Earlier in the year, Ford moved to expand its subcompact sales by putting its Festiva model,* above, *on the market in the western part of the United States.*

WORLD MOTOR VEHICLE DATA, 1986

Country	Passenger Car Production	Truck and Bus Production	Motor Vehicle Registrations
Argentina	137,889	32,609	5,260,000
Australia	337,206	25,041	8,974,300
Austria	6,801	4,906	3,153,135
Belgium	258,393	42,270	3,698,815
Brazil	829,477	227,030	11,483,608
Canada	1,061,365	792,760	14,266,599
China	5,500	409,500	2,887,126
Czechoslovakia	186,989	52,604	3,120,168
France	2,773,094	421,521	24,090,500
East Germany	218,256	45,300	3,963,053*
West Germany	4,310,828	286,135	27,821,940
Hungary	–	17,808	1,612,051
India	115,285	122,668	3,699,100
Italy	1,652,452	178,637	23,324,000
Japan	7,809,809	4,450,008	46,157,261
South Korea	457,383	144,163	1,113,430
Mexico	169,567	102,601	7,199,486
The Netherlands	118,976	23,378	5,329,354
Poland	289,665	55,240	4,534,207
Spain	1,281,899	250,724	10,883,973
Sweden	421,255	65,897	3,382,637
United Kingdom	1,018,962	228,685	19,303,045
United States	7,828,783	3,490,176	171,690,733**
USSR	1,320,000	950,000	21,350,700
Yugoslavia	239,841	41,940	3,516,684
Total	32,849,675	12,461,601	487,543,666***

* Includes East Berlin. ** U.S. total includes 132,108,164 cars and 39,582,569 trucks and buses. U.S. total does not include Puerto Rico, which has 1,299,167 vehicles. *** World total includes 374,727,233 cars and 112,816,433 trucks and buses. Other countries with more than one million vehicle registrations include: Bulgaria, 1,057,573; Colombia, 1,148,944; Denmark, 1,768,353; Egypt, 1,012,045; Finland, 1,746,615; Greece, 1,885,099; Indonesia, 2,036,697; Malaysia, 1,312,311; New Zealand, 1,797,231; Nigeria, 1,250,000; Norway, 1,763,627; Portugal, 1,541,000; Saudi Arabia, 4,131,847; South Africa, 4,172,279; Switzerland, 2,828,462; Taiwan, 1,344,969; Thailand, 1,201,819; Turkey, 1,536,862; and Venezuela, 1,692,911. Source: Motor Vehicle Manufacturers Association of the United States, Inc.

GM10 line. The Buick Regal was the first of the GM10 cars to go on sale. The GM10 family marked the end of a ten-year program in which each of the No. 1 automaker's major car platforms was converted from rear to front-wheel-drive.

In a major managerial change, GM installed Robert C. Stempel, 54, as its new president on September 1. Stempel, an engineer, previously led the Chevrolet and Pontiac Divisions, as well as the overseas group. On the day Ford planned to announce its 1988 models, September 29, former Ford Chairman Henry Ford II died at the age of 70 (see OBITUARIES).

The 1988 Models. Facing growing inroads from the imports in the upscale segments of the marketplace, the domestic Big Three each unveiled restyled luxury cars.

GM's Buick Division, first with the mid-size front-drive Regal, also scheduled an early 1988 debut of the Reatta two-seater sports coupe, priced at about $30,000. The Reatta would join Cadillac's year-old and slow-selling Allante twin-seater, which was priced at $57,000, in the "personal-car" arena. Cadillac also drastically redesigned its Eldorado coupe after only a year of development work, while Pontiac introduced a four-wheel-drive system for its 6000STE mid-range sedan.

Chrysler and Ford met GM's upmarket thrusts with new front-drive "luxosedans" of their own—the Chrysler New Yorker and Dodge Dynasty and the Lincoln Continental. Also in the Chrysler fold was the Eagle Premier mid-size sedan acquired with the purchase of AMC.

The Imports. Honda's Acura Division chalked up sales of 100,000 Legend and Integra cars in 1987, spurring Toyota and Nissan to undertake invasions of the higher-priced car arena with new Luxus and Infiniti divisions, respectively, in 1989 or 1990. Other luxury-car newcomers in 1987 included the Sterling sedan and Range Rover utility vehicle from Great Britain and the Scorpio sedan imported by Ford from West Germany.

Four new entry-level cars from South Korea quickly reached brisk volume goals in the United States. The Hyundai Excel subcompact reeled off an estimated 250,000 sales in its second year of U.S. marketing and reached fourth place among all imports. The other Korean cars were the Pontiac Le Mans, Ford Festiva, and Mitsubishi Precis (a derivative of the Excel). Ford's Mercury Tracer and Volkswagen's Fox, both subcompacts, were the first U.S. cars from Mexico and Brazil, respectively.

Due to open in 1988 were a new Toyota assembly plant in Georgetown, KY, and a Chrysler-Mitsubishi facility in Bloomington, IL.

MAYNARD M. GORDON
Editor, "Motor News Analysis"

AP/Wide World

Following widespread antigovernment demonstrations and strikes in Bangladesh during 1987, a state of emergency was declared November 27, and Parliament was dissolved nine days later. The extreme force used by the government against the demonstrators helped to bring together the divided opposition.

BANGLADESH

Opposition to Bangladesh's President H.M. Ershad mounted in 1987, and the economy was threatened by the worst flooding in 40 years.

Politics. Progress toward stable civilian politics was threatened with the declaration of a national emergency on November 27 and the dissolution of Parliament on December 6. All opposition strikes and demonstrations were banned, press censorship was imposed, and fundamental citizens' rights were suspended.

Leading to these events were demonstrations and strikes which virtually crippled the capital, Dhaka, and other major cities. The two main opposition groups to the Jaitya Party government of President Ershad remained the eight-party coalition headed by the Awami League (AL) and the seven-party coalition led by the Bangladesh Nationalist Party (BNP). Both of these were chaired by women: the AL by Sheikh Hasina Wajed, daughter of the late President Sheikh Mujibur Rahman, and the BNP by Begum Khaleda Zia, widow of the late President Zia. Both groups maintained that the president's rule is illegal because of the allegedly fraudulent parliamentary and presidential elections in 1986. Their main demands were that Ershad step down and that new, fair elections be held. The president refused to resign.

While the opposition groups were at odds with each other and fragmented internally, two main factors facilitated coordinated action between them. First, the government used heavy-handed tactics against demonstrators. At least 200 persons were killed in skirmishes with police and more than 2,300 people, including main opposition leaders, were jailed after the emergency declaration. Second, on July 2, legislation was enacted permitting military representation on all district councils, a move strongly resisted by the entire political opposition. President Ershad promised new elections within the constitutionally mandated 90 days after the emergency declaration and offered to discuss other issues with the opposition, but demonstrations continued.

Economy. Bangladesh hoped for a growth rate of 5.1% for 1987, with agriculture growing at 3.7% and industry at 8.7%. Foreign investment was solicited, and the World Bank and other donors committed $1.95 billion for fiscal 1987. However, with the strikes and floods, it appeared doubtful that targeted growth would be achieved. Heavy flooding in August and September left some 24 million people homeless or without food, destroyed more than 4 million acres (1.5 million ha) of cropland, and caused serious damage to the nation's infrastructure.

Foreign Affairs. To shore up deteriorating relations, Bangladesh and the Soviet Union signed a cultural exchange agreement in June. Washington supported economic assistance but showed signs of unease with political developments. Most problematic were relations with neighboring India. The key issues were the fate of Bangladesh refugees in India and what Bangladesh feels is Indian support for a continuing insurgency in the Chittagong Hills.

ARUNA NAYYAR MICHIE
Kansas State University

BANGLADESH • Information Highlights

Official Name: People's Republic of Bangladesh.
Location: South Asia.
Area: 55,598 sq mi (144 000 km^2).
Population (mid-1987 est.): 107,100,000.
Chief City (1981 census): Dhaka, the capital, 3,430,312.
Government: *Head of state,* Hussain Mohammad Ershad, chief executive (assumed power March 24, 1982) and president (Dec. 1983). *Head of government,* Mizanur Rahman Chowdhury, prime minister (took office July 1986). *Legislature*—Parliament.
Monetary Unit: Taka (31.0 taka equal U.S.$1, August 1987).
Economic Indexes: *Consumer Prices* (Dhaka, 1986, 1980 = 100), all items, 182.4; food, 193.9.
Foreign Trade (1986, U.S.$): *Imports,* $1,999,000,000; *exports,* $779,000,000.

BANKING AND FINANCE

Nineteen eighty-seven was a dramatic year in U.S. banking and finance. The long bull market in bonds that had started in 1982 and saw interest rates decline by more than 50% topped out—although interrupted in the aftermath of the October stock market drop—and rates began to increase again. By year's end, rates on long-term U.S. Treasury bonds stood at 9⅛%. This was 1.60 percentage points above their lowest level of nearly 7% but some 80 percentage points below the high for the year. Short-term rates responded similarly. The prime rate charged by banks to their best loan customers, which had declined from 20% in 1981 to 7½% in early 1987, increased to 8¾% by year's end. The prime rate had increased briefly to 9¼% before coming down again after the Wall Street crisis.

The sharp reversal in interest rates and bond prices could be attributed to a combination of at least five factors. One, continued strong demand for funds to finance the longest completely peacetime economic expansion in the post-World War II period. Two, increasing expectations of a resurgence of inflation as excess labor and capital capacity in the economy declined to low levels and commodity prices reversed their decline of the earlier 1980s. Three, fears of continued decline in the foreign exchange value of the U.S. dollar, which both increases the cost of imports and reduces the incentive for foreigners to invest in the United States. Four, a continuation, although at a somewhat slower rate, of very large deficits in the federal budget ($148 billion in fiscal 1987, compared with $221 billion in fiscal 1986), and a mounting federal debt. In mid-1987, the debt was $2.1 trillion, double the size of only six years earlier. And five, particularly before the October stock market decline, concern over monetary tightening by the Federal Reserve to head off overheating of the economy.

Bank Failures and Losses. Although not greatly affected by the sharp turnaround in interest rates, U.S. banking experienced a tumultuous year in 1987. Some 185 commercial banks failed during the year, the largest number since the creation of the Federal Deposit Insurance Corporation (FDIC) in 1934, and another 19 required financial assistance from the FDIC to remain open. A record 1,575 banks, or 10% of the approximately 15,000 commercial banks in the United States, were on the FDIC's list of problem banks. In the first half of the year, 2,250 banks, more than 15% of the U.S. total, experienced losses. This divergence in performance is typical of deregulated industries and, in part, reflected the ongoing deregulation of commercial banking.

Most of the banks experiencing difficulties were small and located west of the Mississippi, but several large ones also faced problems. The Bank of America, the second largest bank in the United States, continued to struggle, and the FDIC effectively closed and reorganized First City Bancorporation, which owned some 70 banks in Texas. For the most part, the problems reflected continuing economic difficulties in the agricultural and energy belts of the country.

The problems were not confined to commercial banks. Savings and loan associations (SLAs) experienced even more severe difficulties. Again the problems were primarily regional, most notably affecting associations in Texas and California. In addition to losses from the normal course of business, some SLAs had been purchased by unscrupulous investors who took advantage of federal deposit insurance to expand the size of their institutions greatly and then make highly risky and questionable loans to themselves and their friends, particularly to finance real-estate development. By year's end the losses in the SLA industry were estimated to total almost $50 billion. In addition, many healthy SLAs worried that the rise in interest rates threatened to increase their cost of deposits more than their interest income from long-term fixed rate mortgage loans.

A rush of savings deposits after the stock market collapse—an increase of $6.1 billion in October, the largest monthly rise in more than three years—was expected to help, but certainly not cure, the ailing SLA industry.

Legislation. The drain on the Federal Savings and Loan Insurance Corporation (FSLIC) from resolving the failures was so great that the corporation ran out of reserves and had to be recapitalized by Congress in order to remain in business. The Competitive Equality Banking Act of 1987 permitted the FSLIC to borrow $10.8 billion against its future premium income. The funds were to be used to resolve the worst of the insolvencies and impose more responsible management.

Besides providing for the recapitalization of FSLIC, the new legislation strengthened the responsibility of Congress for the FSLIC's insurance commitments to depositors and made it more difficult for regulators to close insufficiently capitalized SLAs to minimize perceived adverse impacts on their communities.

With respect to commercial banks, the Competitive Equality Banking Act slowed deregulation. It ended the "non-bank bank loophole," by which banks that either did not offer demand deposits or make business loans escaped the jurisdiction of the Bank Holding Company Act and thus could be affiliated with investment banks, mutual funds, and nonfinancial firms, which other banks cannot. The act prohibited the formation of new institutions of this type and limited the future asset growth of existing institutions. This prohibition reduces the probability of entry into banking of new, highly capitalized competitors.

The Home-Equity Loan

Considering the materialistic mood of the United States in 1987, it was no surprise that American consumers lined up to borrow against the equity in their homes without being asked. In fact, home-equity loans were so popular that their number was expected to double in 1987. Banks had to cancel promotional advertisements for the home-equity loan after being overwhelmed by applications.

The amounts of money obtainable through the home-equity loan were in multiples never before envisioned by people of ordinary means. On a house appraised at $120,000, for example, many lenders would allow more than $100,000—approximately 80% of the home's market value—to be borrowed. If the homeowner had an existing mortgage loan of $40,000, the home-equity loan could be for $60,000, minus any up-front charges or legal fees involved in obtaining the loan. True, in most instances, the homeowner was required to show the ability to handle monthly repayments, but doing so was not as difficult as it might have been a few years earlier. The reason: interest rates on such loans were sometimes only half those of credit-card loans (because the collateral was first rate), and maturities could be extended to 20 years, versus three to five years on many installment loans. In addition, borrowed money became available simply by writing a check or showing a credit card. Few lenders asked what the customer wanted the money for, as they did previously.

Much of the borrowed money went for education or repayment of bills, investments, or down payments on houses for children. A large part went for cars or home improvements. And some was used to pay for vacations, swimming pools, and second homes, which the borrowers otherwise could not afford on their incomes. In fact, with the savings rate slipping to all-time lows of under 2%, it was obvious that a good many households were living far beyond their two or more incomes, their life-style financed by the equity stored in their homes. The good life meant the biggest home loan you could get. The new debt probably was for life.

Viewed in a historical context, the home-equity loan seemed to be the climax of an omnivorous appetite for credit and leverage. In 1960, consumer credit totaled $65.1 billion. It exceeded $750 billion in 1987. In 1960, a total of $162.2 billion of residential property loans was on the books. In 1987, there was more than $2 trillion, or close to 14 times the earlier amount. And when figures eventually are broken down, they are likely to show that the trend for the year 1987 was accelerated sharply by the use of home-equity credit.

Pros and Cons. There are dangers but some advantages, especially tax benefits, in the new credit lines. In an effort to raise revenue and reduce perennial federal budget deficits, the U.S. Congress in 1986 voted to phase out the deductibility of interest on most consumer credit, such as car loans, credit-card borrowing, and department-store installment plans. But it dared not end the deduction on home-mortgage credit.

It did not take long for the increasingly deregulated, and therefore more highly competitive, financial institutions to spot their opportunity. If home-equity loans offered a tax deduction, and other loans did not, would not it be logical for homeowners to finance purchases by borrowing on their houses?

The benefits, however, were no more obvious than the dangers. Eager to cash in on the great new market, lenders offered loans to homeowners who never sought them and to people who could not afford the payments. Some lenders never bothered to appraise the properties on which they lent. Many failed to tell customers that up-front charges added to their real-interest rates. Too often, Congress feared, lenders failed to stress potential dangers, such as the chance of foreclosure.

Unlike other mortgage loans, most home-equity loans did not have interest-rate caps. While the monthly carrying costs of regular adjustable-rate mortgages could rise with interest rates in general, they could do so only to a certain level, where they became capped. But rates on the vast majority of home-equity loans could continue skyward, conceivably doubling or tripling. Incredibly, many lenders chose not to consider the repayment problems that might occur should rates rise that much. As Congress' concern grew, representatives of responsible lenders feared restrictive legislation and the possibility that their industry might face wholesale repossessions in the future, an action that might incur the wrath not just of Congress but of an entire society. Concerned by the criticisms and dangers, the American Bankers Association in July issued a brochure, "What You Should Know About Home Equity Loans," stressing that such loans "should not be used to cover current living expenses or to increase your standard of living beyond your means."

JOHN CUNNIFF

Structural Changes. The trend toward deregulation of financial services continued during the year, although it was slowed by the new legislation. Nineteen eighty-seven was the first full year since 1932 that banks were not subject to ceilings on the interest rates they could offer for time and savings deposits, although the prohibition on interest payments for demand deposits remained in force. As a result, banks could compete on an equal basis for funds. However, the increased cost of the time and savings deposit rates put pressure on the banks to raise their service charges to match the increase in their deposit costs.

The most visible change in banking during the year was the continued breaking down of geographical barriers. By year's end, only a handful of states had not enacted legislation permitting bank holding companies chartered in other states to acquire banks in their states. While some of the states restricted this authority only to holding companies in neighboring states, an increasing number permitted acquisitions by holding companies in any state on a reciprocal basis. In addition, the 1987 banking legislation made it somewhat easier for bank holding companies to acquire failing large banks and SLAs in other states.

Banks have increasingly taken advantage of the more liberal rules, resulting in the development of a number of large regional bank holding companies. At the same time, Citicorp (New York), by acquiring banks in a few smaller states and failing SLAs in California, Illinois, Florida, and Washington, DC, became both the largest commercial bank and largest SLA holding company in the United States.

Although there was no new legislation allowing banks to offer securities products per se, banks continued to expand their securities operations, in particular their discount brokerage services. In addition, federal regulatory agencies permitted U.S. banks for the first time to underwrite and deal as principals in almost all municipal revenue bonds, commercial paper, and asset-backed securities, such as mortgage-backed and consumer-loan-backed securities. However, implementation of this authority was suspended by a one-year moratorium (scheduled to expire in March 1988) included in the 1987 banking legislation and by a legal court challenge.

Market Index Deposits. The major new securities product introduced by banks in 1987 was the market index deposit (MID). The returns on these accounts are tied to the performance of the stock market index, gold, or other important assets. Depositors are given a choice of combinations of guaranteed minimum return and percent participation in the increase in the price of the particular asset; the higher the guaranteed minimum return, the lower the participation percentage. Some banks have even tied the increase in the return on their MIDs to declines in stock prices, effectively permitting depositors to sell stocks short. To generate income sufficient to pay these returns, the banks invest in futures contracts on the assets specified in the deposit accounts. As long as the futures contracts are for securities in which the banks are permitted to deal on the cash market (such as gold) or can be settled only in cash (as on the stock market), the transactions are not considered securities transactions in violation of the provisions of the 1933 Glass-Steagall Act (which separated commercial banking from investment banking). MIDs differ only slightly from shares in mutual funds, and, by being a deposit whose principal value cannot decline and is insured up to $100,000 by the FDIC, offer an advantage over mutual funds.

AP/Wide World-

Louisiana's Capital Bank went bankrupt and could not find a buyer. In November, under new federal legislation, the FDIC came in to run the bank until a buyer could be found.

Federal Appointments. New chairmen were appointed to two U.S. federal banking agencies. Alan Greenspan (*see* BIOGRAPHY) replaced Paul Volcker as chairman of the Board of Governors of the Federal Reserve System; and M. Danny Wall, former chief of staff of the U.S. Senate Banking Committee, replaced Edwin Gray as chairman of the Federal Home Loan Bank Board.

GEORGE G. KAUFMAN
Loyola University of Chicago

BELGIUM

In 1987 the central concerns of Prime Minister Wilfried Martens' Christian Democrat-Liberal coalition were the economy and the linguistic issues that brought the cabinet's fall in October.

Economy. The coalition's success at the polls in late 1985 was widely interpreted as a mandate to continue austerity programs for bringing the economy under control. Yet a growth rate of about 1% for 1987 meant that the domestic deficit could be reduced to only 8.5% of the gross national product (GNP) rather than the announced goal of 8%. The inflation rate did stay below 2%, held down by the decline of the U.S. dollar, reduced price controls, and increased price competition. The Belgian franc strengthened and no longer seemed so closely tied to the fortunes of the Franch franc. Unemployment, at a recent low in the beginning of the year, was expected to rise past the 12.25% level in the later months.

The low growth rate of the domestic economy required further budget cuts for 1988 of some 190 billion francs ($4.5 billion). Strikes the previous year indicated the difficulty of trimming social services; thus, the military took the brunt of the cuts. Steps were initiated to sell major government-owned firms (a gas utility, the government maritime transport company, and a housing-loan office). Revenues from these sales were expected to reduce the 1988 budget deficit to $9.6 million, or 7.5% of the gross domestic product (GDP).

Economies in the defense budget produced criticism. Belgium commits 2.3% of its GDP to defense (5.4% of the budget), well less than its neighbors. Amid reports that the 28,000 Belgian troops in West Germany did not have sufficient clothing or practice bullets, that the air force was short of fuel, and that Belgium would not buy Patriot missiles to replace its antiquated Nikes, the country's neighbors protested that they were being forced to take over some of Belgium's defense. Belgium was meeting about 38% of its force goals, compared with 70% for most NATO states.

The deficit problem was complicated by Martens' promise to reform the Belgian tax system before the 1989 elections. In August, it was proposed that the top personal rate would be dropped from 72% to 50%, although a special tax would be levied on annual incomes of more than $77,000. Child allowances would increase, and the double incomes of married couples would no longer be considered as one, a practice that had begun to discourage marriage. Once implemented over a four-year period, these changes may cost the government $1.7 billion per year. Some of this may be made up by cuts in business deductions and by indirect taxes. The reforms may also stimulate investment, slowing the $3 billion annual flow of capital outside Belgium. A new Dutch law requiring banks in the Netherlands to report interest earnings was already improving Belgian capital holdings, as Dutch investors crossed the border to make deposits.

BELGIUM • Information Highlights

Official Name: Kingdom of Belgium.
Location: Northwestern Europe.
Area: 11,780 sq mi (30 510 km²).
Population (mid-1987 est.): 9,900,000.
Chief Cities (Dec. 31, 1985): Brussels, the capital, 976,536; Antwerp (including suburbs), 483,199; Ghent, 234,251; Charleroi, 210,234; Liège, 201,749; Bruges, 117,799.
Government: *Head of state,* Baudouin I, king (acceded (1951). *Head of government,* Wilfried Martens, prime minister (formed new government Oct. 1985). *Legislature*—Parliament: Senate and Chamber of Representatives.
Monetary Unit: Franc (34.98 francs equal U.S.$1, Nov. 10, 1987).
Gross National Product (1985 U.S.$): $79,900,-000,000.
Economic Indexes (1986): *Consumer Prices* (1980 = 100), all items, 142.3; food, 143.3. *Industrial Production* (1980 = 100), 106.
Foreign Trade (1986 with Luxembourg, U.S.$): *Imports,* $68,663,000,000; *exports,* $68,874,000,000.

Politics. The issue that provoked an offer of resignation (rejected by King Baudouin) by Martens the previous fall never was resolved: the refusal of the mayor of Voeren (Fourons in French) in the Flemish region of Belgium to speak Flemish when conducting official business. The mayor, José Happart, was deposed by the Council of State, the nation's highest administrative court, but was promptly elected first alderman and thus acting mayor by the municipal council. Martens' Flemish Christian Democrat party would not accept this; the Walloon Christian Democrats insisted Happart not be permanently dismissed until Parliament resolved the status of officials in regions containing large contingents of both language groups.

On October 19, the king accepted Martens' resignation and then asked him to continue in a caretaker capacity while attempting to form a new government. Martens called an election, held December 13, which gave his coalition a bare majority in the Chamber of Representatives. But the Christian Democrats indicated that they preferred a coalition with the Socialist parties—primarily over the language issue—and the formation of a new government was expected to take several more weeks.

Other. Prime Minister Martens visited Washington in midsummer to discuss trade and missile issues. In the fall he endorsed the proposed Intermediate Nuclear Force (INF) treaty.

On March 6, a British ferry capsized off Zeebrugge. More than 175 of the 543 people aboard drowned. Twenty-five British soccer fans were extradited to Belgium for trial on manslaughter and assault charges connected with the 1985 World Cup soccer match riots.

J.E. HELMREICH, *Allegheny College*

BIOCHEMISTRY

Biochemists in 1986–87 made remarkable strides in elucidating the molecular basis of Alzheimer's disease, succeeded in creating antibodies that work like enzymes, and continued to seek out clues about cancer.

Alzheimer's Disease. Alzheimer's disease (AD) is a degenerative brain disorder afflicting more than 2 million elderly Americans. A few years ago, scientists reported that the autopsied brain samples of deceased AD patients contained abnormal amounts of plaques, consisting of a protein called amyloid and tangles of filaments which clogged the nerve cells: Interestingly, these pathological changes were similar to those observed in the brains of aged patients with Down's syndrome (DS).

Recently, scientists have begun to describe the biochemistry of AD and its relationship to that of DS. First, they reported that at least one form of AD is inherited and that the genetic defect is located on chromosome 21—the same chromosome of which there is an extra copy in DS. Meanwhile, another group of scientists identified and localized a gene that codes for a protein which apparently is a precursor of amyloid. This gene also is located on chromosome 21, and in the vicinity of the genetic defect for AD. Although this marked the first time that a gene had been associated with AD, it only implicated—but did not prove—that the amyloid gene is the cause of the disease.

The link between AD and DS was further strengthened when scientists found an extra copy of the amyloid gene in cells from both AD and DS patients. Presumably this would lead to excessive amyloid production and deposition in brain tissue characteristic of the two diseases. However, researchers also reported that the amyloid gene is expressed in many other human tissues in addition to the brain. This suggests that additional molecular factors may be involved in the pathologic accumulation of amyloid in AD and DS, and that amyloid protein or its precursor has some fundamental—but yet unknown—role in normal cell function.

In still other research, scientists reported finding abnormal amounts of a new protein, designated A68, in the brains of AD and DS patients but not in normal brains. This has provided the first definitive diagnostic test for AD and differentiates the disease process from normal changes that occur in aging. A68 is associated with neurofilaments but is distinct from amyloid and other known substances of the tangled filaments seen in AD brain samples. Importantly, A68 was found in nerve cells that had not yet been damaged, suggesting that it appears relatively early in the disease and may be the causative agent of the destructive process in the AD brain. Indeed, A68 turned out to be an enzyme—protein kinase—which regulates the activities of other cellular proteins and enzymes by the process of phosphorylation (the addition of phosphate groups). It is possible that abnormal phosphorylation may underlie the tangled filaments in AD.

Abzymes. Antibodies and enzymes both are proteins that bind their target molecules with exquisite specificity and affinity. Nevertheless, their biological functions are different. Antibodies advertise the presence of a foreign substance (antigen) in the blood so that the antigen-destroying immune system can respond. Enzymes, on the other hand, catalyze (speed up) specific chemical reactions within organisms. Over the years, biochemists have wondered if it is possible to design antibodies with the catalyst potential of enzymes—to create "abzymes." Now this has been accomplished.

Enzymes are believed to speed up chemical reactions by favoring the formation of mid-reaction structures—called "transition states" —from the reacting molecules, or substrates, during the conversion to products. A group of scientists reasoned that they could create antibodies that would bind specifically to molecules that resemble the transition state of an enzyme's particular substrate. With that aim in mind, they synthesized compounds called phosphonate esters, which resemble biologically important carboxylic esters in transition during hydrolysis (cleavage by water). The phosphonate esters were injected into mice to elicit antibodies, which were expected not only to bind the carboxylic esters but also to hydrolyze them. The purified antibodies were found to do exactly that. This technique represents a potentially powerful strategy for designing new tools for biochemical research and for biomedical applications that might one day include the dissolving of blood clots or the searching out and destroying of tumor cells.

Cancer Research. Cancers may result when certain kinds of genes—called oncogenes—are activated. Now, for the first time, scientists have identified a gene which acts to prevent cancer in humans. Retinoblastoma (RB) is a disease in which tumors grow in the eyes of young children. Previous research had traced these tumors to the absence of a section of chromosome 13. Recently, a group of Boston-area scientists isolated a piece of chromosome 13 DNA and, using it as a probe, showed that it matches the genetic material from normal retinal cells but not from tumor cells. Subsequently, a team in California cloned and sequenced the entire gene, and pinpointed the reasons why it fails to function in RB patients. Using the cloned gene, they found that the RB gene was not expressed, or its expression was prematurely terminated, in tumor cells from children with this cancer. The gene was predicted to code for a protein of 816 amino acids and the protein believed to check the activities of genes involved in cell growth.

PREM P. BATRA, *Wright State University*

BIOGRAPHY

A selection of profiles of persons prominent in the news during 1987 appears on pages 137–148. The affiliation of the contributor is listed on pages 591–94; biographies that do not include a contributor's name were prepared by the staff. Included are sketches of:

Arias Sánchez, Oscar
Assad, Hafiz al-
Baker, Howard Henry, Jr.
Bork, Robert Heron
Carlucci, Frank Charles, 3d
Falwell, Jerry L.
Giuliani, Rudolph W.
Goria, Giovanni
Greenspan, Alan
Inouye, Daniel Ken
Jones, James Earl
Jordan, Michael Jeffrey
Koop, Charles Everett
Koppel, Edward James (Ted)
Minnelli, Liza May
Newman, Paul Leonard
Sessions, William Steele
Takeshita, Noboru
Tyson, Mike
Upshaw, Eugene, Jr.
Winfrey, Oprah
Wright, James Claude, Jr.
Yard, Mary Alexander (Molly)

ARIAS SÁNCHEZ, Oscar

In October, Costa Rican President Oscar Arias Sánchez won the Nobel Peace Prize for his determined and continuing efforts to bring about a peace plan for Central America. The award surprised many people because the treaty was only partly in effect at the time of the award, and many of its terms faced opposition from Central-American factions as well as from Washington.

Shortly after his inauguration in May 1986, President Arias called upon Central American chief executives from El Salvador, Guatemala, Honduras, and Nicaragua to reinvigorate the so-called Contadora process which had bogged down because of differences between the United States and Nicaragua's Sandinista government. The key to Arias' plan was to seek peace through personal diplomacy of the Central-American leaders. Costa Rica's tradition of neutrality in isthmian affairs undoubtedly aided Arias, but he had to cope with the bitterness of long-standing civil wars in Guatemala and El Salvador as well as the pressure of the Reagan administration upon him to assist in the overthrow of the Sandinistas. But on August 7, the five presidents signed the treaty in Guatemala City, promising to carry out certain peace measures by Nov. 7, 1987. (*See* CENTRAL AMERICA.)

The Nobel award embarrassed the Reagan administration, which could scarcely announce opposition to any Central-American peace plan even though some of its terms could nullify Washington's aid to the contras. President Ronald Reagan called the treaty "fatally flawed," but warmly congratulated President Arias.

Background. Oscar Arias Sánchez was born in Heredia, Costa Rica, on Sept. 13, 1941, into one of Costa Rica's wealthiest coffee-producing families. He was educated in local schools before commencing a premedical program at Boston University. But the 1960 Kennedy-Nixon presidential-campaign debates intrigued him, and he returned home to study law and economic science. While a student at the University of Costa Rica he took an active role in the liberal National Liberation Party (PLN), led by former President José Figueres Ferrer. Arias' work as well as writings began to attract national attention. He next studied in England at the London School of Economics and obtained a doctorate at the University of Essex. Between 1969 and 1972 he taught political science at the University of Costa Rica, and then served as minister of planning in the cabinets of both Presidents Figueres and Daniel Oduber. In 1978 he was elected to represent Heredia in the national assembly; he became head of the PLN the next year. In 1986 he defeated Rafael Angel Calderón Fournier for the presidency of Costa Rica, becoming its 47th and youngest chief executive.

He is married to Margarita Peñón Góngora, a U.S.-educated biochemist. They have two children. Friends describe him as quiet and single-minded, but highly intelligent and determined to maintain Costa Rica's traditions of neutrality, peace, and stability.

THOMAS L. KARNES

ASSAD, Hafiz al-

A key player in the contemporary drama of the Middle East, President Hafiz al-Assad of Syria is one of the most enigmatic as well as one of the most powerful rulers in the region. Described by some as the greatest Arab leader to emerge since World War II, he also has been dubbed by the London *Economist* as "a man with ambitions too big for his country." These descriptions are not necessarily incompatible. President Assad does wield an influence in Middle Eastern affairs out of scale with his country's population (11 million) and its ailing economy. Syria has been implicated in various international terrorist attacks, it is the most tightly closed state in the Middle East, and Assad's real views and intentions remain inscrutable.

President Assad's positions on the two central conflicts in the Middle East—the Israeli-Arab confrontation and the Iraqi-Iranian war—have separated him from the rest of the Arab world and established major barriers to peace. As an adamant opponent of Israel whose sole declared policy on the issue is "liquidating the Zionist presence," Assad is now the only neighbor of Israel opposed to its very existence. As Iran's supporter in its war with Iraq, he is the odd man out in the Arab world. However, the year 1987 did provide some indications of changes in Syrian policies, or at least the tactics of its leader. The change began with a reconciliation with Jordan in December 1985. Then in early 1987, with Syria facing a boycott by Western European nations, President Assad closed the Damascus offices of the Abu Nidal terrorist group. In April he held a secret meeting with Iraq's President Saddam Hussein. In November he assented at the Arab summit in Amman, Jordan, to anti-Iranian resolutions and a general opening toward Egypt. During a visit to Moscow in April, he reportedly came under pressure to adopt more accommodating views, even toward Israel. (*See also* MIDDLE EAST; SYRIA.)

Background. Hafiz al-Assad was born in either 1928 or 1930 in the town of Qardaha, located in Syria's Latakia province. He was the eldest son of a small landowner; the family adhered to the small, secretive Alawi sect of Shia Islam.

Like many leaders in the Middle East, Assad rose to power through the commissioned ranks of the military. He attended the Homs Military College and then the Syrian Air Academy. He entered the air force in 1955 and advanced rapidly through the ranks, possibly aided by the disproportionate number of Alawis in the officer ranks of the army and in the Baath (Arab socialist) Party. A political activist from early in life, Assad joined the Baath Party in 1946, the year of Syria's independence from France. Already a squadron leader in the air force, he served briefly in Egypt during the short-lived United Arab Republic (UAR), or Egyptian-Syrian union (1958–61). Dismissed from the air force for his opposition to the ending of the UAR, he was reinstated in 1963 when the Baath Party took power in Syria. In 1966 he became commander of the air force, serving in subsequent years also as defense minister. In November 1970 he led a successful coup that put him in power as premier. The following year, under a new constitution, he was elected president. He has held that office ever since, making him one of the longest-ruling leaders in the Middle East.

President Assad reportedly has suffered from diabetes and heart disease since 1985. Observers at the 1987 Amman summit, however, noted that his health seemed to have improved. He is married and has four sons and one daughter.

ARTHUR CAMPBELL TURNER

BAKER, Howard Henry, Jr.

For Howard Baker, his appointment in February 1987 as White House chief of staff in the midst of the unfolding Iran-contra affair carried with it a considerable measure of irony. In accepting the assignment, Baker agreed to set aside his long cherished dream to win the presidency for himself. And he made that decision in order to help salvage the prestige of the incumbent chief executive, Ronald Reagan, who in winning the Republican presidential nomination in 1980 had crushed Howard Baker's own candidacy for the White House.

Nevertheless it was understandable that the 61-year-old former Tennessee senator accepted the call to duty. His long experience in Washington and the respect he enjoyed among politicians in both parties made him a logical choice for the task of helping put the Reagan presidency back on its feet. Many in Washington looked forward to his relaxed, soft-spoken manner as providing a pleasant contrast with the hard-driving style of his predecessor, Donald Regan. "He is a genius at finding the compromise point and pushing it through," said Democratic Sen. Jim Sasser from Baker's home state.

Given the difficulties of Baker's new job, it was inevitable that he encountered criticism. Some claimed that he had been overly optimistic in promising "significant accomplishments" for the economic summit in Venice, Italy, in June, thus causing public disappointment when the conference produced no great achievements. And conservatives remembering Senator Baker's advocacy of the Panama Canal Treaty, which many considered his most important legislative accomplishment, blamed him for a variety of administration misfortunes, including the Senate's rejection of the Supreme Court nomination of Robert Bork. But these were the sort of vicissitudes Baker had learned to accept in his long career.

Howard H. Baker, Jr.

AP/Wide World

Background. Born in Huntsville, TN, on Nov. 15, 1925, Howard Henry Baker, Jr., came by his interest in politics honestly. Both his father and stepmother had served in the U.S. House of Representatives. After World War II service in the Navy, he earned a law degree from the University of Tennessee. Defeated for the Senate in 1964, he ran again in 1966 and became the first popularly elected Republican senator from Tennessee.

An early effort at winning the Republican Senate leadership failed in 1969 as did one subsequent attempt, but he finally won the position in 1977, thus taking over a job once held by his late father-in-law, Sen. Everett Dirksen of Illinois.

Meanwhile Baker had compiled a legislative record as a moderate conservative, first winning national renown during the Senate investigation of Watergate, when his oft-repeated query—"What did the president know and when did he know it?"—became a hallmark of the televised hearings. With Reagan's landslide victory in 1980, which helped the GOP gain control of the Senate, Baker became majority leader. He held that post until 1984 when he concluded his Senate career to practice law in Washington and make plans for a possible second try for the presidency in 1988.

ROBERT SHOGAN

BORK, Robert Heron

When the U.S. Senate voted, 58–42, on Oct. 23, 1987, to kill the nomination of Judge Robert H. Bork to the Supreme Court, it ended one of the bitterest fights over a high-court nominee in history. Bork's defenders said he was the victim of a "lynch mob" that unfairly portrayed him as a threat to the civil-rights advances of the past 30 years. They also warned that political partisanship in the confirmation process would have repercussions for future Supreme Court nominations. But those who led the campaign that deprived Bork of a high-court seat said he was undone by his own career-long attacks on past Supreme Court rulings and his austere, scholarly demeanor during an unprecedented five days of questioning by the Senate Judiciary Committee. Judge Bork, a staunch conservative on the U.S. Circuit Court of Appeals for the District of Columbia, was nominated by President Reagan on July 1 to replace the retiring Justice Lewis F. Powell, a centrist and key swing vote on the Supreme Court. Bork became the 27th man in U.S. history to fail to win confirmation to the nation's highest court and only the sixth in the 20th century. Six Republicans and 52 Democrats opposed him, representing the highest negative total for any nominee to the court. Bork's defeat left the court temporarily with eight members and one vacancy. (*See* LAW.)

Background. Robert Heron Bork was born in Pittsburgh, PA, on March 1, 1927. His father, half German and half Irish, was a steel-mill employee; his mother was Pennsylvania Dutch. He received his bachelor's degree from the University of Chicago in 1948 and his law degree there in 1953. Bork served in the Marine Corps Reserve from 1945 to 1946 and from 1950 to 1952. His political views as a young man were a far cry from today's Reagan Republicanism. Bork worked for the Socialist ticket in Chicago in 1948 and for liberal Democrat Adlai Stevenson in the 1952 presidential race.

After practicing law in New York and Chicago during the mid-1950s and early 1960s, he became an associate law professor at Yale University in 1962, where his intellectual odyssey began in earnest. A full professor by 1965, he wrote extensively for law journals and magazines. He ultimately espoused a doctrine of "judicial restraint" that attracted the attention of President Richard Nixon in 1973, who named him solicitor general in the Justice Department. Bork achieved undesired notoriety that year, when, in the so-called Saturday Night Massacre, he carried out Nixon's order to fire Watergate Special Prosecutor Archibald Cox. Bork returned to Yale in 1975 and remained there until 1981, when he left for private law practice. President Reagan named him to the U.S. Court of Appeals in Washington in 1982.

Bork was married to the former Claire Davidson on June 15, 1952; they had two children. His wife died in 1980, and two years later he was married to the former Mary Ellen Pohl. He is the author of *The Antitrust Paradox: A Policy at War With Itself* (1980).

JIM RUBIN

CARLUCCI, Frank Charles, 3d

True to President Ronald Reagan's philosophical inclinations, his administration generally has looked for leadership in the ranks of successful business people rather than government officials. To this rule, Frank Charles Carlucci 3d has been a striking exception. The man President Reagan selected in November 1987 to succeed Caspar W. Weinberger as secretary of defense has spent nearly all of his working life toiling in the bureaucracy in a broad range of domestic and foreign posts. He has spent only brief and unremarkable periods in the private sector. Yet it was to Carlucci whom President Reagan turned twice during a turbulent 12-month period in his presidency to fill critical vacancies.

A year before being selected to head the Pentagon, Carlucci was picked to be the president's national security adviser, taking over from Rear Adm. John Poindexter, who had resigned because of his role in the Iran-contra affair. Carlucci's stint at the National Security Council was marked by the same conscientious pragmatism that has characterized his service elsewhere in the government. Mindful that the agency's involvement in the Iran-contra imbroglio had heightened its normal tensions with the State Department, Carlucci sought to avoid the center stage, particularly during his early months on the job. He also tried to avoid confrontations on Capitol Hill, being credited with helping to persuade the White House to delay seeking more aid for the contra rebels in Nicaragua on grounds that this request would likely be defeated while negotiations were going forward with the Sandinista regime.

Background. Born Oct. 18, 1930, in Scranton, PA, Frank Carlucci was raised in comfortable circumstances

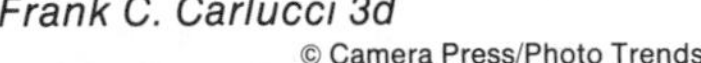

Frank C. Carlucci 3d

© Camera Press/Photo Trends

and was graduated from Princeton University in 1952. After two years as a Naval gunnery officer, he studied at the Harvard Business School. He then tried his hand at business—as a management trainee, rental agent, and salesman—before joining the U.S. Foreign Service in 1956. He served in such trouble spots as the Congo (now Zaire) and South Africa as well as in Washington.

When Richard Nixon took over the White House in 1969, a former Carlucci classmate at Princeton, Donald Rumsfeld, persuaded him to work under him at the Office of Economic Opportunity, an agency which Carlucci ultimately headed. He later became deputy director of the Office of Management and Budget and undersecretary of Health, Education, and Welfare, in both jobs working under Weinberger. President Ford brought Carlucci back to international affairs, naming him ambassador to Portugal, where he was credited with maintaining U.S. ties to that country during a period when Communism seemed on the rise there.

President Carter named Carlucci deputy director of the Central Intelligence Agency where he fought to narrow the Freedom of Information Act, arguing that it threatened necessary government secrecy. When Reagan won the presidency in 1980 and named Weinberger his defense secretary, Carlucci moved over to the Pentagon to serve once again as Weinberger's deputy. In this post he renewed his fight on behalf of secrecy, urging polygraph tests to find those responsible for leaking information to the press.

ROBERT SHOGAN

CONNER, Dennis, *see* page 79.

FALWELL, Jerry L.

The Rev. Jerry Falwell became head of the multimillion dollar PTL television ministry after founder Jim Bakker resigned in March, only to resign himself seven months later. Falwell claimed that a federal bankruptcy judge's ruling would make it impossible to salvage the scandal-plagued ministry. (*See* RELIGION.) No stranger to controversy in the worlds of politics and religion, the independent Baptist minister had tried to put PTL's house in order while satisfying both his own fundamentalist supporters and Bakker's Pentecostal followers.

Then, in November, Falwell announced his resignation as president of the conservative political group Moral Majority, saying that he wished to devote more time to his church and television ministry. The group's lobbying activities were credited as a key factor in the 1980 election victories of Ronald Reagan for the presidency and other conservative Republicans in various congressional races.

Falwell acknowledged that the fallout from the year's so-called "holy war" had reduced giving to his own Christian television program, *The Old Time Gospel Hour.* But he said that his main reason for withdrawing from political activism was a desire to return to his "first love," preaching and winning souls. He would remain on Moral Majority's board of directors but said, "I will never work for a candidate as I did for Ronald Reagan."

Meanwhile, Falwell completed his autobiography, due to be published in November, and the Supreme Court docketed his lawsuit against *Hustler* magazine for its 1987–88 term. Falwell was suing the magazine and its publisher for intentional infliction of emotional distress because of a parody published in 1983 and 1984.

Background. Born Aug. 11, 1933, in Lynchburg, VA, Jerry Falwell excelled academically and in athletics at Brookville High School. He planned a career in mechanical engineering when he enrolled in Lynchburg College in 1950, but in 1952 his life changed when he attended a service at Park Avenue Baptist Church and publicly declared his commitment to Jesus Christ.

Falwell transferred to the Baptist Bible College in Springfield, MO, where he graduated with a Th.D. degree in 1956 and was ordained by the Baptist Bible Fellowship. He returned to Lynchburg and founded a

Jerry L. Falwell

church, which held its first service in an abandoned building.

That was the start of Falwell's Thomas Road Baptist Church, which grew to 22,000 members. The church was six months old when he started his *Old Time Gospel Hour* television program, now aired by more than 300 stations.

Falwell founded Lynchburg Baptist College in 1971 without a campus or facilities. It subsequently developed into the 7,500-student Liberty University. With the help of several conservative political activists, Falwell organized Moral Majority, Inc., his first purely secular enterprise, in 1979.

Falwell's battles against abortion, gay rights, and pornography made him a subject of national controversy in the 1980s, as did his criticism of Archbishop Desmond Tutu of South Africa and his praise of former Philippines President Ferdinand Marcos. In 1986 he expanded Moral Majority into a larger movement called Liberty Federation, and resigned from both in 1987.

Falwell married the former Macel Pate in 1958. They have three children, Jerry Jr., Jeannie, and Jonathan.

DARRELL J. TURNER

GIULIANI, Rudolph W.

As U.S. attorney for the Southern District of New York, Rudolph Giuliani has emerged as perhaps the most aggressive and certainly the best-known criminal prosecutor in America. With a mission "to make the justice system a reality for the criminal," he has prosecuted many of the biggest organized-crime, political-corruption, and stock-fraud cases in recent history. Using the Racketeer-Influenced and Corrupt Organizations (RICO) Act, he won convictions against nine members of the Colombo organized-crime family (June 1986); 17 participants in the so-called Pizza Connection, a New York drug-distribution network alleged to be run by the Mafia (March 1987); and eight members of a national ruling "commission" of Mafia families (November 1986). Giuliani's office also investigated, prosecuted, and won convictions in the 1986 Parking Violations Bureau scandal in New York City. Its investigation of the Wedtech scandal, in which a Bronx military contractor was alleged to have paid public officials to help obtain federal contracts, led to indictments of U.S. Rep. Mario Biaggi and six others (June 1987); in December 1987, further indictments in the case were handed down against officials in the U.S. Justice Department. In conjunction with the Securities and Exchange Commission, his office unraveled the Wall Street insider-trading scandal in 1986, successfully prosecuting arbitrageur Ivan Boesky and other key figures.

For the grim-faced, 43-year-old prosecutor, June 1987 marked the end of a four-year appointment by President Ronald Reagan. As the year came to an end, he remained on holdover status, weighing his future. His high public profile and crime-busting image have generated speculation of national political office.

Background. Rudolph W. Giuliani was born on May 28, 1944, in Brooklyn, NY, where his father ran a small pizza parlor. He attended Bishop Laughlin High School in Brooklyn and, after graduation, planned to study for the priesthood. That summer, however, he changed his mind and enrolled in Manhattan College. It was there that he settled on a career in law. After graduating from New York University Law School in 1968, he clerked for two years under U.S. District Judge Lloyd MacMahon. In 1970 he went to work as an assistant U.S. attorney in the New York office he would later run. Over the next five years, he rose rapidly through the ranks, earning a reputation for his aggressive prosecutions.

From 1975 to 1977, Giuliani served in the Justice Department under President Gerald Ford, during which time he completed his transformation from a liberal Democrat to a registered Republican. In 1981, after four years in private practice, he was appointed associate attorney general in the Reagan administration; he was the number three man in the Justice Department, with responsibility for the entire criminal division. Two years later, however, to the surprise of Washington insiders, he gave up the position to return to New York as head of the U.S. attorney's office.

Giuliani lives in an Upper East Side Manhattan apartment with his wife, Donna Hanover, a local television news broadcaster. They have one child.

GORIA, Giovanni

On July 26, 1987, Giovanni Goria, a new face in Italy's well-worn pack of Christian Democratic prime ministerial hopefuls, became Italy's youngest head of government since World War II. He heads the same five-party coalition of Christian Democrats, Socialists, Social Democrats, Republicans, and Liberals that Bettino Craxi, his Socialist predecessor, led for 3½ years.

Goria's appointment came in the wake of early parliamentary elections on June 14. These were precipitated by Prime Minister Craxi's unwillingness to abide by his 1986 bargain with the Christian Democrats to allow them to take over the government in March 1987, pending the next regular elections. (*See* ITALY.)

Goria, who modestly describes himself as "the nation's accountant who became a politician," was asked by Italian President Francesco Cossiga to form a government because of the skills he had displayed as minister of the treasury in cutting inflation. But Goria knows well that he was chosen essentially because the leaders of the two big parties (the Christian Democrats' Ciriaco De Mita and the Socialists' Bettino Craxi) would not let each other have the post.

However Byzantine the reasons for his appointment, Goria's dark good looks (he wears a salt-and-pepper beard), soft-spoken style, and straightforward manner have made him a favorite on Italian television, where image is becoming increasingly important. An Italian newsmagazine proclaimed him a "superstar." When the new prime minister finished reading on television the list of his ministers, he added, under his breath, "Oh, Lord, wish us luck!" He would need all he could get in order for his government to survive for long.

Background. Giovanni Goria was born on July 30, 1943, in Asti, the Piedmont town best known for its sparkling *spumante* wine. The son of a civil servant and shopkeeper, he is married and has two children, ages 15 and 11.

Goria studied economics and worked at a savings bank. Local businessmen encouraged him to embark upon a career in the Christian Democratic Party. In 1975 he became secretary of its Asti branch. The following year he was elected to Parliament. A protégé of party leader De Mita, Goria soon was named undersecretary of the budget. Rapidly becoming his party's most authoritative voice on economic matters, he was appointed treasury minister in 1982. It was reported that this came as such a surprise that he had to borrow the blue suit in which to attend the swearing-in ceremony at the Quirinale Palace.

CHARLES F. DELZELL

GREENSPAN, Alan

"Consummate economic conservative, laissez-faire pragmatist, and avowed capitalist" are some of the descriptions offered for Alan Greenspan, the New York economic consultant that President Ronald Reagan chose in June 1987 to replace Paul A. Volcker as chairman of the Federal Reserve Board (the "Fed"). Since Greenspan has described himself as a "free enterpriser," those other terms are undoubtedly appropriate.

Greenspan has been in Washington before, serving President Gerald Ford as chairman of the Council of Economic Advisers (CEA) from September 1974 to January 1977. He also was chairman of President Reagan's National Commission on Social Security Reform.

The new Fed chairman acquired a firm reputation as a foe of inflation. As a result, the transition from Volcker to Greenspan went smoothly, despite a brief moment of panic in the bond, foreign exchange, and commodity markets right after the appointment. Indeed, the 61-year-old economist was expected, as *The Wall Street Journal* put it, "to generally pursue policies on inflation, interest rates, and economic growth that may appear almost indistinguishable from Mr. Volcker's."

Greenspan believes in as little government intervention in the free-market system as possible. He is considered the high priest of the "old time religion," the traditional Republican economic policy of budget balancing and fiscal restraint. At the Fed, however, he would have less to do with the budget and more to do with money. He is not considered a "monetarist," an economist calling for fixed, modest growth of the nation's money supply as the best way to tame the business cycle and lower the level of inflation. Nonetheless, Greenspan does regard money as important, and there is some suspicion that he may pay more attention to it than his predecessor.

Background. Alan Greenspan was born March 6, 1926, in New York City. Raised in a broken home in Manhattan's Washington Heights, Greenspan early developed a love of music. He studied at the Juilliard School of Music and toured the country for a time playing clarinet in a dance band. After a year, Greenspan decided he would rather go to college. He majored in economics at New York University, graduating summa cum laude in 1948. Two years later he received an M.A. degree in economics from the same school. Then he worked on a doctorate at Columbia University, studying under the late Arthur F. Burns, who was to become a chairman of the Fed during the Nixon presidency. Greenspan was not awarded a doctorate until 1977.

After a stint at the Conference Board, he joined bond trader William Townsend in 1954 in founding Townsend-Greenspan & Co., a leading economic consulting shop. Greenspan became in the 1950s a friend and follower of Ayn Rand, author of *Atlas Shrugged* and an advocate of the morality and ultimate desirability of complete laissez-faire capitalism and "rational selfishness." He remains an opponent of much government regulation—an attitude that may be reflected in his decisions at the Fed on bank regulation.

DAVID R. FRANCIS

Photos, AP/Wide World

Daniel K. Inouye

INOUYE, Daniel Ken

Daniel K. Inouye's experience as a junior U.S. senator on the Watergate Committee almost soured him on the biggest assignment of his life: chairman of the Select Committee on Secret Military Assistance to Iran and the Nicaraguan Opposition.

Inouye, a loyal Democrat from Hawaii, finally yielded to intense pressure from Majority Leader Robert Byrd and accepted the chairmanship of the special 11-member panel which looked into the Reagan administration's secret arms deal with Iran and the diversion of funds to the Nicaraguan contras. In an effort to avoid what he considered to be the mistakes of the Watergate hearing, Inouye asked New Hampshire Republican Warren Rudman to serve as vice-chairman. The Hawaii senator ruffled some feathers by choosing committee staff without regard to political party, unlike the procedure in the Watergate hearings of 1973, when there were two committee staffs, separate budgets, and even separate agendas. His efforts to streamline the investigation and avoid competing panels paid off during the 11 grueling weeks of the hearing. Nearly 30 witnesses testified and more than 250 hours of testimony were taken.

Inouye, who promised his constituents that he would conduct an "impartial and thorough investigation" of the controversy, had predicted that the sessions would be "challenging, controversial, and time-consuming." He received more than 150,000 telegrams, cards, and letters during the hearing—far more than he received at any one time during his 35 years in politics. Many of the messages dealt with the confrontation between Inouye and Marine Lt. Col. Oliver C. North, a key figure in the Iran-contra arms deal. When North began his testimony in July, the letters and telegrams ran five-to-one in the colonel's favor. But by the end of the hearing, more than two thirds of them praised the Hawaii Democrat for his handling of the investigation.

A World War II hero who won a battlefield commission, Inouye was unawed by North, who had a distinguished military career in Vietnam. Nor was Inouye awed by the eloquence of other witnesses. He had become well-known at home and in Congress for his ability to match rhetoric with all who dared challenge him from the time he served as an assistant city prosecutor in Honolulu in the early 1950s.

Background. Daniel Ken Inouye was born Sept. 7, 1924, in Honolulu, the son of immigrants from Japan. He wanted to be a surgeon but switched to a law career after losing his right arm in World War II. He was graduated from the University of Hawaii (A.B., 1950) and the George Washington University Law School (J.D., 1952) and was in private practice before entering politics. A member of the territorial House of Representatives and its majority floor leader (1954–58), he served in the territorial Senate (1958–59). When Hawaii won statehood in 1959, he won election to the U.S. House and was an easy winner in 1962 when he opted for the U.S. Senate. He has won reelection handily in every succeeding campaign.

Inouye is secretary of the Democratic Conference of the Senate and chairman of the Select Committee of Indian Affairs. He also serves on the committees on appropriations; commerce, science, and transportation; and rules and administration.

Senator Inouye is married to the former Margaret Shinobu Awamura. They are the parents of a son, Daniel K., Jr.

CHARLES H. TURNER

JONES, James Earl

In winning his second Tony Award—as the 1987 season's best actor for his performance in the Broadway play *Fences*—James Earl Jones confirmed his standing at the top of his profession. A tall, powerfully built man with a deep, resonant voice and a commanding stage presence, he reached that pinnacle after overcoming roadblocks that included abandonment by his father and a severe stutter.

Perhaps best known for his portrayal of Shakespeare's Othello, a role he has taken seven times, Jones has had a career that is both wide-ranging and unconventional. He has appeared in television commercials and soap operas, and as the voice of Darth Vader in the film *Star Wars* as well as in serious dramas. His first Tony came in 1969, for his role as the prizefighter Jack Jefferson in *The Great White Hope. Fences,* a powerful drama about a black family on the eve of the civil-rights era, picked up numerous other Tonys as well. Jones also was seen during the year in the films *Matewan,* about labor strife in West Virginia in 1920, and *Gardens of Stone,* directed by Francis Coppola.

Background. Jones was born in Arkabutla, MS, on Jan. 17, 1931. His father, Robert Earl Jones, left the family before he was born to become first a prizefighter and later an actor; Jones had no early contact with him. Jones was raised by his maternal grandparents and saw his mother, who worked in various jobs, only on weekends. The family moved to Michigan when he was five.

By the time he reached high school, Jones had developed a stutter. A teacher took an interest in him and, encouraging him to enter debates and public speaking contests, helped him overcome the handicap. He entered the University of Michigan on a scholarship, planning a career in medicine but later switching his focus to drama. After a stint in the Army, he went to New York City in 1955 to take up a stage career. There he joined his father, whom he had met for the first time a few years before.

After a number of small roles on and off Broadway, Jones won critical acclaim for his portrayal of Deodatus Village in Jean Genet's *The Blacks* in 1961. He also began to appear in productions of the New York Shakespeare Festival, and his various roles brought him a 1962 Obie Award as best off-Broadway actor. More accolades came in 1964, when he appeared in the Shakespeare Festival's production of *Othello*. But it was his role in *The Great White Hope* (a play based on the career of Jack Johnson, the first black to win the world heavyweight boxing championship) that first brought him widespread public attention.

He repeated his role in a film of the play in 1970. By that time he was no stranger to movies; he had already appeared in small roles in *Dr. Strangelove* (1964) and other films. While he continued to appear on stage in a wide range of productions (including *Master Harold and the Boys,* in 1982–83), he pursued a career both in films (including *Conan the Barbarian* in 1982) and on television. He won an Emmy in 1964 for his part in an episode of the television series *East Side, West Side* and later starred as a detective in his own series, *Paris* (1979–80). He married the actress Cecilia Hart in 1982; a previous marriage had ended in divorce.

ELAINE PASCOE

JORDAN, Michael Jeffrey

With the retirement of Julius Erving at the end of the 1986–87 National Basketball Association (NBA) season, Michael Jordan of the Chicago Bulls inherited the role as the league's consummate showman and gate attraction. In just his third professional season, Jordan led the NBA in scoring and emerged as its most popular player. His point total of 3,041 (37.1 per game) was the highest in league history for a guard, and he became only the second player (besides Wilt Chamberlain) to surpass the 3,000 mark in a single season. The 6′6″ (1.98 m) Jordan was elected to the all-NBA first team and finished second to Earvin "Magic" Johnson in the voting for the league's most valuable player award.

Jordan led the NBA in several offensive categories in 1986–87, including minutes played (3,281), field goals attempted (2,279), field goals made (1,098), free throws attempted (972), and free throws made (833). He also became the first player to have more than 100 blocked shots and 200 steals in one season. But his impact on the game cannot be measured entirely with statistics. He is basketball's premier dunk-shot artist, a high-leaping, acrobatic player who is among the most creative ever to play the game. With Jordan as their only star, the Bulls had the second-highest road attendance in the league, behind the Boston Celtics.

Background. Michael Jeffrey Jordan was born on Feb. 17, 1963, in Brooklyn, NY, and was raised in Wilmington, NC. One of five children, he was a latecomer to basketball and did not become a standout until his senior year at Laney High School in Wilmington. He attended the University of North Carolina on a basketball scholarship, and in his freshman year he made the winning shot in the 1982 NCAA championship game. Jordan led the Atlantic Coast Conference in scoring in both his sophomore and junior years, and in the latter season he was

Michael Jordan

named the college player of the year. He was also the leading scorer on the 1984 gold-medal-winning U.S. Olympic team. On the advice of his college coach, Dean Smith, Jordan passed up his senior year to enter the NBA. A first-round pick of the Bulls, he finished third in the league in scoring with 2,313 points and was named rookie of the year for 1984–85. Jordan hurt his foot in the third game of the 1985–86 season and missed 64 games. However, in a memorable play-off performance, he scored an NBA-record 63 points in a double-overtime loss to the Celtics.

Jordan has gained a reputation for being one of the most personable and outgoing players in the NBA. He is very active in charity work, especially causes that benefit children, and he may lead the league in endorsements. His line of basketball shoes, Nike's Air Jordan, have become the biggest-selling basketball footwear in history. While basketball is his first love, Jordan is also a golf fanatic. A bachelor, he lives in a townhouse in Chicago but spends much of the NBA's off-season in North Carolina.

PAUL ATTNER

KOOP, Charles Everett

After becoming surgeon general of the United States in 1982, Dr. C. Everett Koop was perhaps best known for his outspoken opposition to abortion and his aggressive campaign against cigarette smoking. In 1987, however, Surgeon General Koop came more fully into the spotlight for his controversial response to the AIDS (Acquired Immune Deficiency Syndrome) epidemic. He has pressed television stations to accept ads for condoms, which he believes are the best protection for sexually active individuals, and opposes mandatory AIDS testing. Believing that teaching children about sex is essential if society hopes to limit the AIDS epidemic, he has urged schools to start sex education "at the lowest grade possible."

Background. Charles Everett Koop was born in Brooklyn, NY, on Oct. 14, 1916. He was graduated from Dartmouth College in 1937 and obtained his M.D. degree from Cornell Medical College in 1941. In 1948 he was appointed surgeon-in-chief at Children's Hospital in Philadelphia, PA.

A pioneer in pediatric surgery, Dr. Koop developed dozens of new surgical and diagnostic procedures, such as correcting certain birth defects previously considered uncorrectable. He also established the first neonatal intensive surgical care unit in the United States and developed criteria for the safe use of anaesthesia on children. In the mid-1970s, Dr. Koop became a vociferous opponent of abortion and other practices that he called "antifamily trends," including homosexuality and some forms of contraception.

In 1981, President Ronald Reagan nominated Dr. Koop to the post of surgeon general. Significant opposition greeted the nomination. In the confirmation hearings, however, Dr. Koop pledged that he would not use the position to promote his opposition to abortion. The Senate confirmed the nomination, and Dr. Koop took office on Jan. 21, 1982.

Within a month of his taking office he made national headlines by announcing the strongest indictment of cigarette smoking ever issued by the Public Health Service. His report focused exclusively on the connection between cigarette smoking and cancer, which stated scientific evidence linking tobacco consumption to about 30% of all cancer deaths. Dr. Koop has urged a ban on all cigarette advertising and on smoking in the workplace. In early 1986, President Reagan asked Dr. Koop to prepare a report on AIDS, which was completed late in that year.

Dr. Koop was married in September 1938 to Elizabeth Flanagan. They are the parents of two sons and one daughter. A third son was killed by an avalanche while mountain climbing.

An evangelical Christian, Dr. Koop is the author of the book *The Right to Live: The Right to Die* as well as many articles and monographs on a variety of medical subjects. He also is a founder of the *Journal of Pediatric Surgery* and is the recipient of many awards and honorary degrees.

See also MEDICINE AND HEALTH.

JENNY TESAR

KOPPEL, Edward James (Ted)

The late-night news show *Nightline,* hosted by veteran television journalist Ted Koppel, seemed to make headlines as often as it reported them in 1987: Robert McFarlane and Richard Secord on the Iran arms deal, exclusive interviews with television evangelists Jim and Tammy Bakker, and an off-the-cuff racist remark by Los Angeles Dodgers vice-president Al Campanis that led to his resignation. With pointed interviews and debates between such controversial figures, ABC's entry often outscored such competing fixtures as Johnny Carson's *Tonight* show.

Nightline, which airs for a half hour each weeknight, began in 1979 as a special format for reporting news of the Americans held hostage in Iran. It became permanent in 1980, and since then Koppel has won both viewers and the respect of his colleagues with his ability to zero in, without the aid of a script, on just the right questions to ask. Yet in 1987, he was rumored to be considering leaving the show.

Background. Edward James Koppel was born on Feb. 8, 1940, in Lancashire, England, the son of German Jewish immigrants who had fled the Nazi regime two years before. The family moved to the United States when he was 13 and settled in New York City. By that time Koppel, inspired by the voice of Edward R. Murrow, had already decided to become a broadcast journalist. He majored in speech at Syracuse University and took a master's degree in journalism at Stanford University, finishing in 1962. He married Grace Anne Dorney, a Stanford classmate, the following year.

Too young-looking for a television news job, Koppel worked first in radio, as a newswriter for WMCA and WABC in New York and then as an ABC network correspondent. ABC News sent him to Vietnam in 1967, and it was there that he made the switch to television. He returned to the Far East in 1969 as Hong Kong bureau chief.

Ted Koppel

Photos, AP/Wide World

Koppel's next post, as the network's chief diplomatic correspondent in 1971, brought him in contact with Henry Kissinger, then secretary of state. The two developed a lasting rapport, and Koppel later anchored an ABC "Action Biography" on Kissinger. By this time a seasoned journalist, he produced a number of other specials but cut back his work in 1976, when he took a leave to care for his son and three daughters while his wife went to law school. He still appeared on television, anchoring the Saturday night news, and was back as diplomatic correspondent in 1977.

Koppel's special late-night reports on the hostage situation, beginning in 1979, boosted the network's ratings so much that ABC decided to keep the format alive. The show generally begins with a brief taped segment summarizing the night's topic—which may range from AIDS to arms control—and then moves to live, in-studio interviews. Among the more notable *Nightline* shows have been a week of programs from South Africa in 1985; one of those shows pitted Bishop Desmond Tutu with Foreign Minister R. F. (Pik) Botha in a direct debate, a first.

Koppel has received a number of journalism awards, and his salary is reported to be more than $1 million. In 1976 he cowrote (with then CBS news correspondent Marvin Kalb) a spy thriller, *In the National Interest.*

ELAINE PASCOE

MINNELLI, Liza May

With a three-week sellout booking at New York City's famous Carnegie Hall in June 1987, Liza Minnelli showed herself firmly in command of her career. As an actress and singer, Minnelli often has seemed haunted by the shadows of her illustrious show-business parents, the legendary Judy Garland and the renowned film director Vincente Minnelli. A spate of early successes—including Tony awards for the Broadway musicals *Flora, the Red Manace* (1965) and *The Act* (1977), an Oscar for the film *Cabaret* (1973), and an Emmy for the television special *Liza With a Z* (1978)—was followed by a bout with alcohol and drugs that threatened to ruin her career. But the program notes for her 1987 Carnegie Hall appearance announced firmly, "I don't drink anymore," and her performance showed new confidence and maturity.

Liza Minnelli

Background. Minnelli was born in Hollywood, CA, on March 12, 1946. Her parents divorced in 1951, and by all accounts her childhood was chaotic, marked by her mother's emotional and financial troubles and marital breakups. Despite her parents' involvement with show business, Minnelli showed little interest in the stage until she reached high school. At that point she was bitten by the bug. She apprenticed in summer stock on Cape Cod and won the lead in a high-school production of *The Diary of Anne Frank* that toured Israel, Greece, and Italy in the summer of 1961.

At 16, Minnelli quit school to pursue a career in the theater, moving to New York City and landing a part in a stock production of *Anne Frank.* Soon after, she was picked for the third lead in an off-Broadway revival of the musical *Best Foot Forward,* in which her expressive features, confident on-stage manner, and ability to belt out a song won critical acclaim. Television appearances and recording contracts followed, as did a televised appearance with her mother at the London Palladium in 1964. The next year she won the lead role in *Flora.* The show itself, a spoof of the American Communist movement in the 1930s, had only a brief run, but it marked Minnelli's Broadway debut and brought her a Tony at the age of 19.

From Broadway, Minnelli branched out to nightclubs and motion pictures, appearing in a supporting role in *Charlie Bubbles* (1967) and as a kooky collegiate misfit in *The Sterile Cuckoo* (1969). Her role in the latter film brought an Academy Award nomination, presaging the Oscar she would win for *Cabaret* three years later. In 1977 she returned to Broadway in *The Act,* winning a second Tony award. Minnelli's other films include *Tell Me That You Love Me, Junie Moon* (1970), *That's Entertainment* (1974), *Silent Movie* (1976), *New York, New York* (1977), and *Arthur* (1981). In addition to *Liza With a Z,* she has appeared in a number of television specials, among them *Goldie and Liza Together* and *Baryshnikov on Broadway* (both in 1980).

Two marriages, to Peter Allen and Jack Haley, ended in divorce; in 1979, she married Mark Gero.

ELAINE PASCOE

NEWMAN, Paul Leonard

It took seven nominations over a 30-year career, but in 1987 Paul Newman finally won an Oscar for best actor—playing the same character that won him his second nomination in 1961. Fast Eddie Nelson, the cocky small-time pool shark in *The Color of Money* (1986) and *The Hustler* (1961), was a quintessential Paul Newman part. But then, Newman's roles have always seemed to mirror his times. As one interviewer observed, he symbolized the "indifference" of the 50s, the "danger" of the 60s, the "mellowing" of the 70s, and the "individualism" of the 80s.

Background. Paul Leonard Newman was born on Jan. 26, 1925, in Cleveland, OH. He began acting in high school and, after graduation from Kenyon College with a B.A. in English, in summer-stock theater. He studied at the Yale School of Drama and the Actors Studio and made his Broadway debut in 1953 in William Inge's *Picnic.* Newman then signed a motion-picture contract with Warner Brothers, but his first film, *The Silver Chalice,* so embarrassed him that he went back to Broadway to play a psychotic killer in Joseph Hayes' *The Desperate Hours.* His next film, *Somebody Up There Likes Me,* a biography of boxer Rocky Graziano, was released to glowing reviews in 1956, and Newman went on to increasingly successful parts. Among these were Brick in *Cat on a Hot Tin Roof* (1958), his first Oscar-nominated role.

Many film critics regard his "H" movies of the 1960s—*The Hustler* (1961), *Hud* (1963), *Harper* (1966), *Hombre* (1967)), and *Cool Hand Luke* (1967)—as Newman's best work. Then, however, seeing his selection of suitable

Paul Newman

roles diminishing, Newman turned to directing, most notably of *Rachel, Rachel* (1968), starring his wife since 1958, the actress Joanne Woodward. Newman also formed a motion-picture production company whose most successful release was *Butch Cassidy and the Sundance Kid* (1969). Featuring Newman and Robert Redford in the title roles, *Butch Cassidy* was the highest-grossing Western in movie history. Newman and Redford teamed up again in *The Sting,* a Depression-era comedy which won the Oscar for best picture in 1973.

Roles of a different kind began turning up in the late 1970s, and Newman's career entered a new phase. Beginning with *Slap Shot* in 1977, he created a series of older characters as memorable as the young-men-on-the-make he had played early in his career. With *Absence of Malice* (1981) and *The Verdict* (1982), he finally seemed to triumph over his image as a "star" and began to be recognized by the public and critics alike as a "best actor."

Off the set, Newman's interests include car racing, which he has done professionally since 1977, and politics. An outspoken liberal, he served as a delegate to the 1968 Democratic National Convention and has lobbied for various causes, including civil rights, environmental protection, and a nuclear freeze. And in a venture that started as a joke in 1982, he began marketing his own recipe for salad dressing. The proceeds, which have mounted into the millions, go to a variety of charities. Among these are the Scott Newman Foundation, which he set up after his son died of a drug overdose in 1978, and a summer camp for terminally ill children, which was being built in Connecticut in 1987. Newman has two surviving children from his first marriage, to Jacqueline Witte, and three daughters with Joanne Woodward.

LINDA TRIEGEL

NORTH, Oliver L., *see* page 33.

SESSIONS, William Steele

On July 24, 1987, President Ronald Reagan named U.S. District Judge William S. Sessions of San Antonio, TX, as director of the U.S. Federal Bureau of Investigation (FBI); he would succeed William H. Webster, who became head of the Central Intelligence Agency. Judge Sessions, a 57-year-old moderate Republican, was unanimously confirmed by the Senate for a ten-year term on September 25. The swearing-in was postponed, however, when Sessions was hospitalized with a bleeding ulcer upon his arrival in Washington, October 1. He was released on October 3, only to suffer a relapse three days later. The swearing-in finally was held on November 2.

During his 12 years on the U.S. District Court for the Western District of Texas, including six years as chief judge, the tall, silver-haired jurist earned a reputation for tough but fair "law and order" justice. He drew national attention in 1982, when he handed down stiff sentences to five convicted conspirators in the 1979 murder of a colleague, John Wood, Jr., the only federal judge to be assassinated in modern U.S. history.

Background. A minister's son, William Steele Sessions was born on May 27, 1930, in Fort Smith, AR. He grew up mostly in Kansas City, where he attended high school. After graduation, he enlisted in the Air Force, where he served as a radar instructor and rose to the rank of captain. In 1952, while in the service, he was married to the former Alice June Lewis.

After he left the Air Force in 1955, the couple moved to Waco, TX, where Sessions completed B.A. (1956) and J.D. (1958) programs at Baylor University. For the next ten years he worked in private law practice in Waco. In 1969 he moved to Washington to serve as a senior criminal prosecutor in the U.S. Justice Department. During his two years in that position, he gained notice for his stiff prosecutions of Vietnam War draft evaders. In 1971, President Richard Nixon appointed him U.S. attorney for the Western District of Texas, and in December 1974, President Gerald Ford appointed him a district judge. In the latter capacity, he served first in El Paso and later, after becoming chief judge in 1980, in San Antonio. In addition to his rigorous but scrupulous enforcement of criminal law, Judge Sessions was known for his skills as a legal administrator.

William and Alice Sessions have four children; the two oldest sons are law partners in San Antonio. Judge Sessions is an avid mountaineer who twice climbed to the base of Mt. Everest in Nepal. Many quieter moments are spent reading, often about Winston Churchill, American history, and politics.

William S. Sessions

Photos, AP/Wide World

Noboru Takeshita

TAKESHITA, Noboru

On Oct. 20, 1987, Noboru Takeshita won nomination as president of Japan's ruling Liberal-Democratic Party (LDP). He was chosen by Prime Minister Yasuhiro Nakasone, only the second time in post-World War II history that an outgoing party chief had named his own successor. Nakasone took the unusual step to avoid a bruising party primary among the "three new leaders," LDP Secretary-General Takeshita; a former foreign minister, Shintaro Abe; and Finance Minister Kiichi Miyazawa.

At an extraordinary convention of the LDP on October 31, Takeshita was formally selected party president and then, as head of the majority party, was elected by the Diet (parliament) on November 6 to be Japan's 17th prime minister since the end of World War II. Prime Minister Takeshita promptly formed a new cabinet, to which he reappointed Miyazawa as finance minister (and concurrently, deputy prime minister) and named Abe to the sensitive post of party secretary-general.

Takeshita is a short, dapper man who, in contrast with his predecessor, has had relatively limited experience in international affairs. Within the perennially ruling LDP, Takeshita has a long-established reputation as an efficient fund-raiser and a man skilled in settling party disputes while characteristically building a consensus on delicate issues. He is said to have an astonishing memory for dates, places, and names related to party politics.

Background. Noboru Takeshita was born on Feb. 26, 1924, in rural Shimane, a poor rice-growing prefecture. His father, Yuzo Takeshita, was a successful sake brewer and a local politician. Young Takeshita's training at Waseda University, Tokyo, was interrupted by wartime service in the army air corps. He graduated from Waseda in 1947, taught school for four years, and then launched his political career.

In 1958, at the age of 34, he won the first of 11 consecutive terms in the lower house of the Diet. He served the LDP loyally, acting as chief cabinet secretary, construction minister, finance minister (twice), and, most recently, secretary-general of the party. Takeshita heads the largest faction, the Keiseikai, within the LDP.

In 1946 he was married to the former Naoko Endo; the Takeshitas have three daughters. For recreation, Takeshita plays golf—often with Nakasone, Abe, and Miyazawa—and displays an interest in fine arts. He holds a black belt in judo.

ARDATH W. BURKS

TYSON, Mike

Heavyweight boxing champion Mike Tyson is said to have the most powerful punch since Rocky Marciano and the fastest hands since Muhammed Ali. He has a place in the record books as the youngest heavyweight ever to win a world title. And in August 1987, the 5′11″ (1.80-m), 220-lb (100-kg) battler from Catskill, NY, became the first heavyweight in nearly ten years to reign as the division's *undisputed* champion.

Despite the reluctance of other fighters to take him on, "Iron" Mike Tyson has been one of the busiest boxers on the professional scene. On Nov. 22, 1986, in Las Vegas, NV, he scored a second-round technical knockout (TKO) over Trevor Berbick to capture the World Boxing Council (WBC) title. At the age of 20 years, 4 months, and 22 days, he thus became the youngest fighter ever to wear a heavyweight championship belt. (The previous record had been held by Floyd Patterson, who in 1956 won the title at the age of 21 years, 11 months.) On March 7, 1987, Tyson won the World Boxing Association (WBA) version of the title with a unanimous 12-round decision over James "Bonecrusher" Smith in Las Vegas. On May 30 he successfully defended his WBC and WBA crowns with a 6th-round TKO of Pinklon Thomas in Las Vegas. Then on August 1, again in Las Vegas, he unified the heavyweight title by wresting the International Boxing Federation (IBF) belt from Tony Tucker in a unanimous 12-round decision. And finally, to close out the year, he registered an impressive seventh-round TKO over Tyrell Biggs on October 16 in Atlantic City. The victory raised Tyson's professional record to 32-0, with 28 knockouts. And he was still only 21 years old.

Background. Mike Tyson's rise to success was as hard fought outside the ring as inside. He was born on June 30, 1966, and grew up in the streets of the Brownsville section of Brooklyn, NY. At the age of 13, after committing a series of burglaries and robberies, he was sent away to a juvenile detention facility called the Tryon School in Johnstown, NY. The staff at Tryon included a former pro boxer named Bobby Stewart, who got Tyson interested in the sport and began training him. A few months later, Stewart brought Tyson to a gym in nearby Catskill run by Cus D'Amato, a well-known trainer who had handled Floyd Patterson and other champions. D'Amato watched Tyson work out and told him, "If you stay with me, you'll be the youngest heavyweight champion in boxing history."

In September 1980, at age 14, Tyson was released to D'Amato's custody and lived with him in a large house overlooking the Hudson River. The elderly trainer took the boy close under his wing, providing him with an education and developing his boxing skills. By the time Tyson had his first professional fight in March 1985, D'Amato had become his legal guardian; Tyson regarded him as his father. D'Amato died in November 1985 at age 77, having seen his teenage protégé win his first 11 fights—all of them by knockout, nine of them in the first round. One year later, Tyson took the WBC crown.

UPSHAW, Eugene, Jr.

For Gene Upshaw, a former all-pro lineman for the Oakland (now Los Angeles) Raiders and the current executive director of the National Football League (NFL) Players Association, 1987 was a year of both enormous gratification and deep frustration. On January 27, five years after his retirement as a player, the 6′5″ (1.96-m), 255-lb (116-kg) Texas native was elected to the Pro Football Hall of Fame in Canton, OH. Along with six others, he was formally inducted into the Hall on August 8.

Even as he was relishing that honor, however, Upshaw was facing new pressures in his capacity as the head of the players' union. The collective-bargaining agreement reached with team owners in 1982 was due to expire in a matter of weeks, but the two sides had yet to sit down at the bargaining table. The standoff continued. Finally on September 22, accusing the owners of trying

Gene Upshaw

to "bust the union," Upshaw called a strike after the second week of regular-season games. Team owners responded by hiring "replacement players," and, after a one-week hiatus, games were played as scheduled. The Players Association clearly was in a precarious position, and the strike lasted only 24 days. On October 15 the union voted to end the strike despite having failed to win a new collective-bargaining contract or even a back-to-work agreement. Upshaw lodged an antitrust suit against the league, but he came under widespread criticism for underestimating the resolve of the owners and for the timing of the strike. (*See also* SPORTS—Football.)

Background. Eugene Upshaw, Jr., was born on Aug. 15, 1945, in the village of Robstown in southern Texas. He spent much of his boyhood in a four-room schoolhouse, playing sports (at which he did not excel) and picking cotton. He attended college at his father's insistence, traveling a few miles down the road to small, inexpensive Texas A&I. Having grown nearly to his adult size, he tried out for the football team and went on to star as a center, tackle, and end. After an impressive senior season, he was the first-round draft pick of the Oakland Raiders (then in the American Football League—AFL) and started his first game as a rookie guard in 1967. During his 15-year career with the Raiders, Upshaw was acknowledged as one of pro football's toughest and most durable linemen. He played in 207 consecutive regular-season games, ten AFL or AFC championship games, and three Super Bowls (winning two). He was elected to the Pro Bowl six times and voted the NFL's lineman of the year in 1977.

Active in civic, charitable, and labor activities throughout his playing career, the soft-spoken giant was elected to the first of two terms as president of the NFL Players Association in 1980. He played a prominent role in the contract negotiations (and strike) of 1982 and became the union's executive director upon the resignation of Ed Garvey in 1983. In that capacity, and as a member of the AFL-CIO executive council, Upshaw is the most conspicuous black labor official in the United States today.

He lives with his second wife, the former Terri Buich, in the Virginia suburbs of Washington, DC. He has two children, one from his previous marriage.

WINFREY, Oprah

Within a few months of its national syndication in the fall of 1986, Oprah Winfrey's daytime talk show ranked as the third most popular program on television after *Wheel of Fortune* and *Jeopardy*. The show's phenomenal popularity was not the only coup for its host, who also won two daytime Emmy awards in 1987.

Winfrey's success came after ten years of hosting local television talk shows in Baltimore and Chicago and after a movie role, as Sofia in *The Color Purple* (1985), that brought her an Academy award nomination as best supporting actress. Like her rival television host Phil Donahue, she engages her guests and audiences in frank discussions of controversial topics. Her on-screen personality—a blend of warmth, concern, spontaneity, and earthy humor—is credited for much of her popularity. On the air, she has discussed openly her own weight problem and the sexual abuse she suffered as a child.

Background. Oprah Winfrey was born in Kosciusko, MS, in 1954. (Her parents intended to name her Orpah, after a minor character in the Bible, but letters were transposed on the birth certificate.) Her parents were unmarried and separated soon after her birth, and she was reared to the age of six by her maternal grandmother, a strict disciplinarian. She then went to Milwaukee to join her mother, who worked as a domestic. Her mother's busy schedule left little time for close supervision, and Oprah experienced acts of sexual abuse by several trusted family friends. At 13, after a series of rebellious incidents (which included tossing her mother's jewelry out the window), she was sent to live with her father, a barber and shopkeeper in Nashville.

In the more structured environment of her father's home, Winfrey developed into an A student. She won a full scholarship to Tennessee State University and, before her high-school graduation, began to work as a newscaster for a local radio station. As a sophomore in college, she became the first black woman to co-anchor the evening news on the local Nashville television station. That experience brought her a job offer from WJZ-TV in Baltimore.

As a newscaster, however, Winfrey often found herself in conflict with station management. After several incidents (including a botched permanent wave, obtained at the management's insistence, that left her temporarily bald), she was switched to cohost (with Richard Sher) of a morning talk show. By the end of her first day

Oprah Winfrey

Photos, AP/Wide World

on that show, she later recalled, she had concluded that "this is what I was born to do." She stayed with the Baltimore show for seven years before accepting an offer from WLS-TV to take over its morning talk show, *A.M. Chicago.* Within a month, she had changed the show's format to cover more controversial subjects and had begun to beat *Donahue* in the ratings.

Winfrey won her role in *The Color Purple* after the composer and producer Quincy Jones saw her television show in Chicago. Following her success in *Purple,* she took a small role in *Native Son* (1986). She also began work as producer and costar of a television miniseries, *The Women of Brewster Place,* and a pilot for a situation comedy.

ELAINE PASCOE

WRIGHT, James Claude, Jr.

The speakership of the U.S. House of Representatives has long been associated with power, although most speakers have preferred to use their power behind the legislative scenes. That has not been the case with Speaker Jim Wright of Texas who in 1987, his first year as leader of the House, shook up Capitol Hill and the White House by boldly and prominently displaying his authority and influence.

Most notable was Wright's involvement in Central American affairs which began in August when the new speaker agreed to join with President Reagan in supporting a peace proposal to end the fighting in Nicaragua. That maneuver spurred Central American leaders to offer a plan of their own, which Wright promptly embraced. Moreover, in November, when Nicaraguan President Daniel Ortega came to Washington, he met with Wright to discuss his own peace proposal before unveiling it publicly. For this behavior, Wright was accused by the Reagan administration of undercutting U.S. policy in Central America. But Wright stood his ground, pointing out that it was the administration which had invited him to become involved in the first place.

Dealing with domestic issues Wright provoked controversy right after being selected for his new post in December 1986 by advocating a delay in the tax-rate reduction for upper-income taxpayers called for in the recently passed tax-reform bill. And Wright's ethical behavior also stirred controversy because of his intervention on behalf of several Texas businessmen facing problems with federal regulations of the savings and loan industry. Wright claimed he was only giving constituents normal help in dealing with the bureaucracy.

Background. Wright's personal outlook and political philosophy have been shaped over the years both by his ties to freewheeling Texas entrepreneurs and by his populist background as a young man coming of age in the depths of the Great Depression. James Claude Wright, Jr., who was born in Fort Worth on Dec. 22, 1922, spent much of his youth shifting with his family from one Texas Dust-Bowl community to another. Emerging from World War II as a decorated Air Force bomber pilot, Wright won election to the Texas legislature and then as mayor of Weatherford, TX.

Entering Congress in 1955, he concentrated on building his influence on the Public Works' Committee. He became known for his skill as an orator and his success in getting defense contracts for his district. In 1977 he won election as House majority leader and used that post during the early years of the Reagan presidency to battle the new chief executive's efforts to cut back the role of the federal government.

Wright began planning to run for the speakership immediately after his predecessor in that office, Thomas P. (Tip) O'Neill, announced early in 1984 that he planned to retire after the 1986 elections. By February 1985, Wright was able to publicly claim the backing of more than 75% of Democratic House members, thus effectively assuring himself of the prize that he officially won nearly two years later.

ROBERT SHOGAN

AP/Wide World

Molly Yard

YARD, Mary Alexander (Molly)

On July 18, 1987, the National Organization for Women (NOW) chose as its new president Molly Yard, a staunch feminist with 50 years' experience as a political activist. Yard's sweeping victory in the NOW vote was seen as a confirmation of the confrontational tactics of her predecessor, Eleanor C. Smeal.

Yard, who has described herself to the press as a spiritual descendant of Eleanor Roosevelt, has been a force in NOW's national activities for the past decade and is well known for her public speaking, organizational, and fund-raising abilities. Following her election, she set as immediate goals the defeat of Robert H. Bork's nomination to the U.S. Supreme Court, protests of the Vatican's position on abortion and birth control, and demonstrations in favor of lesbian and gay rights. But she also outlined a more subtle program of court, legislative, and political action aimed at advancing the position of women.

Background. Yard, who is in her 70s but declines to give her precise age, was born Mary Alexander Yard in Shanghai, China, the daughter of Methodist missionaries. She grew up in Chengdu, the capital of Sichuan Province, and moved to the United States with her family at the age of 13. She had her first taste of political activism as a student at Swarthmore College, where she worked to abolish campus fraternities and sororities because of their discrimination against Jews.

After graduation in 1933, Yard worked briefly as a social worker and then became involved in the American Student Union, a group that was highly critical of the New Deal. Her outspoken criticism brought her in contact with Eleanor Roosevelt, who became a friend. Over the following years, she also became active in trade-union and civil-rights causes and in Democratic politics.

Yard joined NOW at the local level in Pittsburgh in 1974 and soon became involved at the national level. In the late 1970s, she spearheaded the group's efforts to gain an extension for the ratification of the ill-fated Equal Rights Amendment, and she subsequently raised more than $1 million for an ERA media campaign. (Passage of an equal rights amendment remains one of her top concerns.) She was also a leader in lobbying efforts aimed at defeating four antiabortion bills.

Yard married labor arbitrator Sylvester Garrett in 1938 and has three children and four grandchildren. She and her husband live on a farm near Ligonier, PA.

ELAINE PASCOE

BIOTECHNOLOGY

Biotechnology is the science of applied biology. It is the field of study devoted to developing and improving industrial and agricultural processes that make use of biological systems. It has benefited such diverse areas as food production, food processing, waste disposal, mining, and medicine. Although biotechnology has existed since ancient times and has brought many improvements to the quality of human life, some of the most dramatic advances have come in recent years. Many of these are direct outgrowths of the ability to insert and delete specific genes in various organisms (recombinant DNA techniques) and then use these organisms for a variety of purposes. The ability to alter the genetic constitution of microorganisms has led to a serious public debate over the possible dangers resulting from the accidental or deliberate release of such organisms into the environment.

Food Production. With the rapid expansion of the world population—it reached 5 billion in 1987 and is expected to exceed 10 billion within 41 years—the need for greater food production is self-evident. For centuries, food production has been increased through the selective breeding of plants and animals. This approach often involves the hybridization of genetically diverse strains, followed by selective breeding of those offspring with the greatest number of desirable traits. One shortcoming of this approach is that the strains must be sexually compatible. In recent years, a series of discoveries by biotechnologists have provided a procedure for circumventing this problem.

One discovery was that individual cells from the leaf, stem, or root of a plant can be grown in tissue culture, which, under appropriate conditions, can regenerate entire plants. The regenerated plants are normal in every respect. A second discovery was that foreign genetic material can be introduced into the plant cells while the cells are growing in tissue culture. This can be done using viruses, bacteria, or even other plant cells. Through the use of viruses, for example, it has been possible to produce tomato plants which are resistant to a serious disease caused by the tobacco mosaic virus. Through cell fusion, it has been possible to cross potatoes and tomatoes, something which cannot be done through sexual reproduction. The aim of this procedure is to produce a potato strain that contains the tomato gene which confers resistance to "late blight disease" (the cause of the great Irish potato famine in the 1840s).

World food production also would be increased if the insect pests that destroy crops were eliminated. The method commonly used to achieve this is the spraying of plants with chemical insecticides. More recently, however, sprays have been developed that contain microbes known to kill insects. The best known example of a bacterial insecticide is *Bacillus thuringiensis*. This bacterium produces spores that contain an endotoxin which, upon ingestion, is released into the digestive tract of the insect and kills it.

There are a number of insects, however, whose larvae burrow into the soil and eat the roots of the plants. These pests are relatively safe from chemical sprays. Biotechnologists at the Monsanto Corporation have therefore used recombinant DNA techniques to develop an effective bacterial insecticide. The endotoxin-specifying gene from *B. thuringiensis* was transferred to another bacterium, *Pseudomonas fluorescens,* which typically lives on the roots of a number of crop plants. When root-eating insects ingest the genetically engineered *P. fluorescens,* the toxin produced by the transferred gene kills them. Scientists have also developed plans for transferring the insecticidal gene to bacterial species that live on other parts of plant crops, thus reducing the need for chemical spraying.

A third biotechnological approach to increasing world food production has been the development of methods to protect plants from sudden changes in weather. This effort has generated a good deal of opposition because it entails the release of genetically engineered microorganisms into the environment. In 1987, after four years of legal challenges, approval was given for a series of experiments involving the spraying of plants with genetically engineered bacteria to protect them from frost formation. The first such field test was conducted on April 24 by Advanced Genetic Sciences, Inc., on a plot of strawberry plants. Similar experiments on potatoes were subsequently conducted by scientists at the University of California, Berkeley.

The procedure involved genetic alteration of the bacterium *Pseudomonas syringae,* which normally lives on plants and secretes a protein that initiates the formation of ice crystals. Through recombinant DNA techniques, the gene that codes for this protein was deleted from the bacteria. When the modified *P. syringae* was sprayed on plants in carefully controlled greenhouse experiments, frost formation did not occur until temperatures fell well below the freezing point.

The objection raised to these experiments —and indeed any method of increasing food production through the release of genetically altered microbes—is that such organisms might, in some as yet unknown fashion, alter the world's ecosystems and cause serious damage. In the present instance, the U.S. Environmental Protection Agency determined that no such danger exists and gave its approval for the tests. More generally, however, there is still widespread concern about the possible adverse effects of inadvertent or deliberate release of

AP/Wide World

In April 1987, technicians at Advanced Genetic Sciences Inc. sprayed a genetically altered bacteria on a California strawberry field. The test was to prevent frost from forming.

genetically altered organisms into the environment. Since 1973, when the recombinant DNA technique was first performed, genetic material has been transferred thousands of times without any of the feared catastrophes. Nevertheless, the debate continues.

Food Processing. One of the oldest processed foods known to human beings is cheese. A critical step in its production is the coagulation of the milk protein casein by the enzyme rennin (chymosin) to form a curd. The curd is then treated in one of several ways, depending on the type of cheese being produced. For at least 4,000 years, rennin has been obtained from the tissue of calf stomachs when the calf is slaughtered for veal. Recently, however, scientists at the British biotechnology company Celltech succeeded in producing rennin through recombinant DNA. The calf gene for rennin production was placed in bacterial cells, and the rennin produced by the bacteria was found to be just as effective in coagulating milk as the natural enzyme obtained from calf stomachs.

Waste Disposal. In the processing of cheese, the formation of curd is accompanied by the draining off of a liquid called whey, which is usually just discarded. The whey contains the sugar lactose, which can be used for the production of alcohol. The organism of choice in the conversion of lactose to alcohol is the yeast *Saccharomyces cerevisiae. S. cerevisiae* has long been used by the brewery industry to convert the grain sugar maltose into alcohol, and procedures for its commercial-scale production are highly developed. Unfortunately, this yeast species lacks the enzyme systems necessary to perform the biochemical steps in the conversion of the milk sugar lactose into alcohol. Recently, however, scientists at the University of Kentucky were able to transfer the required genes from other yeast species to *S. cerevisiae.* Thus, biotechnology has developed the means for transforming a waste product of the cheese industry into a useful compound for use by breweries.

Microbiological Mining. In their natural states, such metals as copper, zinc, and lead are not found in pure form but rather in chemical combination with other elements, such as sulfur and oxygen. Such naturally occurring inorganic compounds are referred to as minerals. To obtain the pure form of a metal, the particular mineral must be subjected to a chemical process which separates the elements. These processes tend to be expensive, making mining economically feasible only where there are heavy deposits of the particular mineral. It has been found, however, that certain species of bacteria live in mineral deposits and, through their biochemical activities, can take the elements of a mineral and form compounds that are easily broken down. The most widely used bacterial species is *Thiobacillus ferrooxidans,* which acts on the copper-containing mineral chalcopyrite. This results in the formation of the compound copper sulfate, which can be easily and inexpensively treated to obtain pure copper. Currently, the use of bacteria accounts for more than 10% of copper production in the United States, and the percentage will rise as conventionally mined high-grade deposits are exhausted. Programs are also being developed for the use of bacteria in the mining of zinc, lead, and other minerals.

Vaccine Production. One way a person can develop immunity to a bacterial or viral disease is by being injected (vaccinated) with a substance (vaccine) that resembles the disease-causing organism. This substance can be a relatively harmless organism, such as the cowpox virus used by Edward Jenner in 1798 to create an immunity against smallpox. Research has shown that it is the protein coat of the virus that functions as the vaccine.

One of the more widespread disease-causing viruses among humans is the so-called hepatitis B virus. Some 200 million people suffer from liver disease caused by hepatitis B, which, research shows, also contributes to the production of liver cancer. Working to develop a vaccine against this virus, scientists at the National Institutes of Health (NIH) in Bethesda, MD, were able to transfer the protein coat gene of hepatitis B virus to the cowpox (vaccinia) virus. The genetically engineered vaccinia virus was then injected and found to stimulate production of antibodies against both the hepatitis B virus and the smallpox virus.

Using the same technique, scientists at the New York State Health Department inserted three different foreign genes—one from hepatitis B virus, one from herpes simplex, and one from influenza virus—into a single vaccinia virus. Injection of test animals with this multiple vaccine resulted in the production of antibodies against all three disease-causing viruses.

Similar efforts are currently under way to produce a vaccine against the AIDS (Acquired Immune Deficiency Syndrome) virus.

Human Growth Hormone. Growth in children is determined by a number of factors, including nutrition, genetic constitution, diseases, and the amount of growth hormone produced by the pituitary gland. A child with insufficient production of growth hormone cannot hope to grow taller than about 4 ft (1.21 m).This condition, known as hypopituitarism, affects up to 15,000 children in the United States. In the past, the missing hormone could be obtained only from cadavers. Unfortunately, a single cadaver produces only enough hormone for one week's injections for one child, and complete treatment requires an average of ten years of weekly injections. Under these conditions, there was not nearly enough hormone for all those who needed it.

Recently, however, scientists at the biotechnology company Genentech have been able to transfer the human gene for growth hormone into the *Escherichia coli* bacterium. When the bacterium replicates its own genes prior to cell division, it also replicates the transferred human gene. The rapid multiplication of the bacteria soon results in billions of cells. Although each cell produces only a tiny amount of the growth hormone, collectively they can produce enough for everyone who needs it.

The Future of Biotechnology. Biotechnology in the United States has become a thriving industry. There are currently at least 400 companies using modern biological techniques to develop new products. In 1986 sales of genetically engineered products totaled more than $350 million. In 1987 more than $3 billion was invested in biotechnology research.

It has been estimated that it takes an average of seven to nine years and an investment of about $55 million to develop, test, and market a new genetically engineered product. Amid ongoing debates over the ethical implications and unknown dangers of genetic engineering, the continued existence of the industry and the prospects for enormous financial returns have been given a strong boost. Rulings of the U.S. Supreme Court and the Commerce Department's Patent and Trademark Office have allowed the patenting of organisms with unique, man-made characteristics that do not occur in nature. The rulings have applied to viruses, bacteria, plants, and—in April 1987—animal life. In the future, biotechnology is sure to play an increasing role in many aspects of our lives, especially such areas as food production and medicine.

LOUIS LEVINE, *City College of New York*

© Bruce Hoertel

A human growth-hormone gene was transplanted into pig embryos so as to increase the size and value of the animal. Such procedures have led to much scientific and ethical debate.

BOLIVIA

In 1987 the government of Bolivia continued to pursue its economic stabilization plan, the New Economic Policy (NEP), launched in 1986. The NEP is designed to check Bolivia's runaway inflation, which reached an unprecedented 24,000% in 1985, and to carry on the privatization of the productive sector, particularly the mining industry, in the hope of revitalizing the Bolivian economy and reducing unemployment.

The stabilization plan has been successful in fighting inflation, which declined to 12% in 1987. Tax reform and tighter collection procedures reduced the federal budget deficit from 28% of the gross domestic product (GDP) in 1984 to 4% in 1986. Taxes now amount to 14% of GDP, an historic high for Bolivia. Other features of the NEP have proven unpopular, however. Reorganization of COMIBOL, the state mining company, brought about the closing of several uneconomic tin mines, throwing more than 20,000 miners out of work. At the same time, the fall in tin prices slashed Bolivia's foreign exchange earnings.

Overall, unemployment reached 18% in 1987. The GDP slumped by 2.9% in 1986 and continued to fall in 1987. As a result, the government of Victor Paz Estenssoro, who is serving his fourth term as president since leading the Bolivian revolution of 1952, came under increasing attack from labor and opposition political parties. In May, Juan Lechin, the head of COB (Bolivian Workers' Central), the largest union confederation in the country, called on Paz Estenssoro to resign. Strikes were frequent during the year. Constant walkouts by the nation's 50,000 teachers—who seek a tripling of their salaries, now ranging from $40 to $80 a month—paralyzed the public educational system.

Debt. Bolivia continued to struggle under a foreign debt load estimated at $3.3 billion. The International Monetary Fund (IMF), however, agreed to lend Bolivia $173.3 million over the next three years, opening the way to disbursement of $1.3 billion in new funds committed by foreign governments and multilateral institutions. In addition, the government signed an agreement with a consortium of commercial banks allowing it to repurchase as much as $660 million of its debt at discounts of up to 90%. Foreign governments will purchase Bolivian bonds to fund the operation.

The government also signed an agreement with a private U.S. conservation foundation, which would purchase and cancel $650,000 of Bolivian debt in return for Bolivia's commitment to set aside 3.7 million acres (1.5 million ha) of Amazonian tropical forest for a conservation preserve.

Drugs. In September 1987, a State Department spokesman said that Bolivia would lose $8.7 million in U.S. aid because the country had not done enough to eradicate the coca crop, used for making cocaine. Although Bolivia had "substantially improved its overall narcotics program," it had not met crop eradication requirements ordered by Congress in 1986 as a condition for American aid.

RICHARD SCHROEDER, *"Visión" Magazine*

BOLIVIA • Information Highlights

Official Name: Republic of Bolivia.
Location: West-central South America.
Area: 424,162 sq mi (1 098 580 km²).
Population (mid-1987 est.): 6,500,000.
Chief Cities (1982 est.): Sucre, the legal capital, 79,941; La Paz, the actual capital, 881,404; Santa Cruz de la Sierra, 376,912; Cochabamba, 281,962.
Government: *Head of state and government,* Victor Paz Estenssoro, president (took office Aug. 6, 1985). *Legislature*—Congress: Senate and Chamber of Deputies.
Monetary Unit: Bolivianos (2.070 bolivianos equal U.S.$1, June 1987).
Gross Domestic Product (1986 est. U.S.$): $3,790,-000,000.
Economic Index (April 1987): *Consumer Prices* (La Paz, 1980 = 100), all items, 7,781,109; food, 8,131,384.
Foreign Trade (1985 U.S.$): *Imports,* $765,000,000; *exports,* $673,000,000.

BRAZIL

Deteriorating economic conditions diminished the popularity of President José Sarney, leader of Brazil's first civilian government since the termination of 21 years of military rule in 1985.

Politics and Government. The erosion of support for Sarney was reflected in a proposed new constitution as well as in conflicts within the so-called "national unity" government composed of the huge but amorphous Brazilian Democratic Movement (PMDB) and the small, right-wing Liberal Front Party (PFL). The new constitution, scheduled for completion by the end of 1987, would replace the fundamental law imposed by the military regime 20 years before. The draft document proposed that the 559-member Congress adopt a parliamentary system, while abolishing many powers of Brazil's exceptionally strong presidency.

On May 11 the congressional subcommittee on executive powers urged that Brazil switch to a parliamentary regime by creating the office of prime minister to share leadership with the president. Although the draft constitution enjoys the backing of key elements within the PMDB, President Sarney—an advocate of a five-year presidential term—refused to endorse it, and political scientists voiced skepticism about the viability of parliamentarianism in an enormous nation renowned for relatively weak political parties. Yet, the chairman of the drafting committee declared that "Brazil seems on the verge of adopting the type of dualistic par-

© Manchete/Sygma

Riot police in Rio de Janeiro came out in full force during late June, when demonstrations against a 50% hike in bus fares turned violent. Scores of buses were damaged, and more than 100 protestors were arrested.

liamentary system my commission recommended. . . . We intend to do away with this lamentable Latin American tradition of unlimited presidential powers.'' In November the drafting committee voted to cut the presidential term from five to four years—with an election tentatively scheduled for 1988.

Sarney's PMDB held 22 of 23 stage governorships and a majority in both the Chamber of Deputies and the Senate. The initial honeymoon between pro- and anti-Sarney factions, nourished by improving economic conditions at the beginning of the Sarney administration, quickly degenerated with the return of triple-digit inflation and mounting unemployment. Internal struggles, which focused on the effort by Sarney's detractors to trim the presidential term, hampered the party's effectiveness in 1987. Sarney's inability to control the governing party prompted him to explore forming a center-right bloc composed of conservative elements in the PMDB and small conservative parties in the Assembly. Attempts to forge such a coalition were complicated when the PFL leader, Sen. Marco Maciel, urged that his party leave the government lest identification with the enfeebled Sarney regime prove disastrous in the 1988 municipal elections.

Economic hardships catalyzed social unrest. The loss of 1 million jobs from January to May, combined with sharply higher prices, triggered more than 750 strikes, including work stoppages by farmers, longshoremen, bank employees, hospital workers, university professors, and school teachers. The gravity of the situation prompted Sarney, himself the target of street demonstrations, to deploy the military both to safeguard port facilities and to prevent sabotage of oil refineries. Many politicians and union leaders decried what was deemed as the chief executive's ''heavy-handedness.''

On June 30 thousands of Rio de Janeiro residents took to the streets to burn buses and ransack stores in response to a 50% increase in bus fares. In this and other domestic flare-ups, the police used a relic of the old military regime —the National Security Law—to charge as leftist activists participants in disturbances. This law allows authorities to try prisoners, who may be held incommunicado, in military rather than civilian courts. Observers viewed the invocation of this statute as the government's attempt to placate military leaders alarmed at the erosion of central authority.

Economy. The February 5 termination of a 12-month price freeze and the attendant rise in living costs brought Sarney's popularity to an all-time low. The Cruzado Plan, a financial package instituted by the president and Finance Minister Dilson Funaro, had temporarily controlled inflation, spurred economic activity, and slashed unemployment. The program's

BRAZIL • Information Highlights

Official Name: Federative Republic of Brazil.
Location: Eastern South America.
Area: 3,286,475 sq mi (8 511 970 km^2).
Population (mid-1987 est.): 141,500,000.
Chief Cities (1985 est.): Brasília, the capital, 1,576,657; São Paulo, 10,059,086; Rio de Janeiro, 5,615,149; Belo Horizonte, 2,122,073.
Government: *Head of state and government,* José Sarney Costa, president (took office April 21, 1985). *Legislature*—National Congress: Senate and Chamber of Deputies.
Monetary Unit: Cruzado (59 cruzados equal U.S.$1, Nov. 17, 1987).
Gross National Product (1986 est. U.S.$): $250,000,-000,000.
Economic Indexes (1986): *Consumer Prices* (São Paulo, 1980 = 100), all items, 16,509; food, 20,007. *Industrial Production* (September 1986, 1980 = 100), 125.
Foreign Trade (1985 U.S.$): *Imports,* $13,168,-000,000; *exports,* $25,639,000,000.

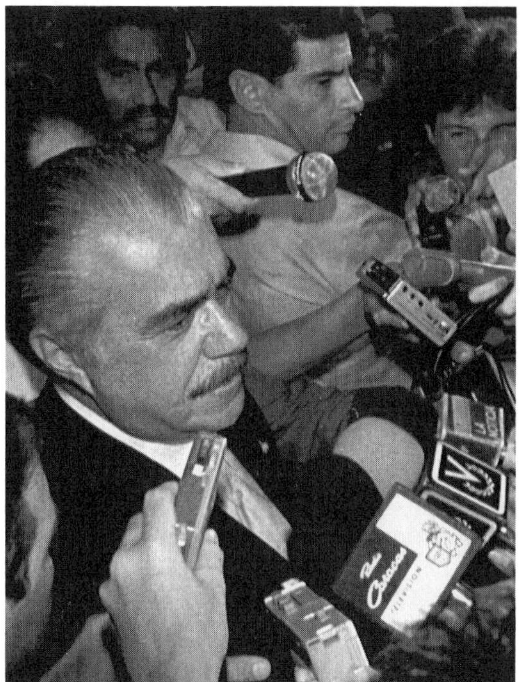

AP/Wide World

At an eight-nation Latin American summit in Mexico during November, Brazil's President José Sarney called for unity of action in dealing with common economic problems.

success proved short-lived as prices shot up 116% amid flagging growth and sluggish imports. Failure of the vaunted Cruzado Plan impelled Funaro's resignation on April 26, and Sarney replaced him with Luiz Carlos Bresser Pereira, a 53-year-old economist. A new economic package, the Bresser Plan, was unveiled on June 12. This scheme included a temporary wage and price freeze (after a raise in public sector prices), elimination of automatic wage adjustments, and a commitment to trim the public sector deficit. Designed to slow inflation, the plan specified the time and manner of the wage-price thaw, and differed from the Cruzado Plan in that no real salary increases were granted. During the year, there was a steady devaluation of the cruzado against the dollar in order to stimulate exports.

Brazil remained the Third World's most indebted nation with a $113 billion external debt. On February 20, Sarney, to the chagrin of the world financial community, suspended Brazil's interest payments on $68 billion of medium- and long-term commercial bank debts. The moratorium resulted in a tightening of the money supply, higher interest rates, and a chilling of the foreign investment climate. Brazil justified its actions as necessary to defend its remaining foreign reserves, which were severely depleted during 1986.

The moratorium was associated with a long list of unfavorable developments: the continued devaluation of the cruzado, high interest rates, shortages aggravated by price disputes, official curbs on imports, labor stoppages, and lack of external credit. Consequently, industrial sector growth rates plummeted in 1987. The outcome of the Bresser Plan was expected to influence not only the economic sectors of society, but to have severe ramifications on political and social affairs. Sarney's effectiveness and prospects were inextricably bound to economic recovery.

Foreign Affairs. Mixed reactions greeted Brazil's suspension of interest payments. While pledging rhetorical support for their Latin American brothers, other hemispheric countries responded in a generally low-key fashion, and none adopted the Brazilian policy as their own. The United States, whose banks hold 30% of the debt, and European countries criticized Brazil's unilateral move. Meanwhile, the Soviet Union said that the decision would not affect Soviet-Brazilian relations. Japan, which is Brazil's second largest trading partner after the United States, decided in September to downgrade Brazilian bank loans and to withhold extensions of new credits.

A November 5 agreement with international creditor banks stipulated that they would lend another $1 billion to enable Brazil to repay interest due them in the final quarter of the year. Consequently, Brazil—which had paid no interest on its medium- and long-term debt for more than eight months—would furnish only $500 million of the $1.5 billion that it was to pay. The banks and Brazil pledged to work out, by early 1988, a mechanism for payments of $3 billion in pending 1987 arrearage as part of a three-year rescheduling accord. At year's end, negotiations also were continuing between Brazil and its public creditors.

Brazil's aggressive debt strategy, coupled with formidable trade barriers, sharpened tensions with the United States. In the face of possible retaliation, Brazil reluctantly softened its policy on the importation of U.S.-produced computers. While many different reasons sparked frictions, one senior Brazilian official said, "The current difficulties . . . derive from an identity crisis that exists in Brazilian society and has little to do with the United States itself. The problems have to do with our soul-searching, our efforts to define such basic things as the role of the state in the economy, the future structure of our government, and the space for foreign investment."

In the political realm, U.S.-Brazilian relations were free of major disputes. Yet, Brazil's support for the Contadora peace initiative in Central America, its reluctance to press for democratic reform in Panama and Chile, its ties with Cuba and the USSR, and its proposal in the UN for a South Atlantic nuclear free zone were sources of irritation in bilateral affairs.

GEORGE W. GRAYSON
College of William and Mary

© Perspective 5, courtesy of Vancouver Trade & Convention Centre

Built for Expo 86, the C$144 million Canada Place pavilion on Burrard Inlet in Vancouver, B.C., was opened as a trade and convention center in 1987.

BRITISH COLUMBIA

Premier Bill Vander Zalm's first year in office was marked by widespread opposition to the government's labor policy and the resignation of several ministers under fire.

Politics. The spring 1987 session of the legislature was dominated by debate on a controversial overhaul of the province's labor law. Bill 19, the Industrial Relations Reform Act, increased the government's power to force settlement of labor disputes. Bill 20, the Teaching Profession Act, paved the way for full collective-bargaining rights for teachers, but also ended compulsory membership in the teachers' union. Protests against these bills included a work-to-rule slowdown by teachers and a one day province-wide general strike on June 1 by 300,000 workers. Implementation of the new administrative framework under an industrial-relations commissioner was boycotted by the B.C. Federation of Labour.

During the summer an agreement with the federal government provided for the creation of a 145,000-hectare (360,000-acre) national park in the South Moresby area of the Queen Charlotte Islands.

Prior to the opening of a fall sitting of the legislature, Premier Vander Zalm announced two radical initiatives for the restructuring of government. Eight ministers of state were appointed from the cabinet to coordinate regional economic-development initiatives as the first stage of what was announced as a decentralization of provincial public services. A review of all provincial government services and operations resulted in phase one of a privatization initiative which proposed the sale or transfer of 11 government operations, including all bridge and road maintenance and two Crown corporations.

BRITISH COLUMBIA • Information Highlights

Area: 365,946 sq mi (947 800 km²).
Population (1986 census): 2,889,207.
Chief Cities (1986 census): Victoria, the capital, 66,303; Vancouver, 431,147; Prince George, 67,621; Kamloops, 61,773; Kelowna, 61,213.
Government (1987): *Chief Officers*—lt. gov., Robert G. Rogers; premier, William Vander Zalm (Social Credit Party). *Legislature*—Legislative Assembly, 69 members.
Provincial Finances (1987–88 fiscal year budget): *Revenues,* $9,350,000,000; *expenditures,* $10,200,-000,000.
Personal Income (average weekly earnings, July 1987): $448.74.
Labor Force (September 1987, seasonally adjusted): *Employed* workers, 15 years of age and over, 1,477,000; *Unemployed,* 169,000 (11.4%).
Education (1987–88): *Enrollment*—elementary and secondary schools, 525,700 pupils; postsecondary—universities, 35,700; community colleges, 23,300.
(All monetary figures are in Canadian dollars.)

A number of changes were made in the provincial cabinet. In April, Minister of Forests and Lands Jack Kempf was replaced in the wake of an investigation into the financial administration of his office; allegations of conflicts of interest resulted in the transfer of Environment and Parks Minister Stephen Rogers, and also to a temporary resignation by Stan Hagen as advanced education minister. A further conflict-of-interest charge led to the resignation in November of Transportation Minister Cliff Michael.

Finances. Tax changes included a 1% reduction in sales tax to 6% and the elimination of personal income surtaxes. Personal income tax rates and small business tax rates increased, however, and a real property purchase tax was introduced. Medical-services premiums also increased by 10%.

Economy. Economic indicators were promising throughout 1987, and business confidence ran high. While the softwood lumber export tax made the outlook for lumber uncertain, non-United States destined exports continued to rise, and pulp, paper, and newspaper benefited from high prices and high levels of production. Growth in employment was led by increases in forest-related manufacturing and construction jobs, and, although high by national standards, the November unemployment rate of 10.4% was 3 percentage points below that for November 1986. In the mining sector, optimism in gold and copper remained overshadowed by the dramatic drop in Japanese demand for B.C. coal.

NORMAN J. RUFF, *University of Victoria*

BULGARIA

In 1987 Bulgaria initiated an extensive reform program similar to the *perestroika* (restructuring) mandated by Mikhail Gorbachev in the USSR. Internationally the country's reputation continued to suffer because of its repression of its Turkish minority.

BULGARIA • Information Highlights

Official Name: People's Republic of Bulgaria.
Location: Southeastern Europe.
Area: 42,823 sq mi (110 910 km²).
Population (mid-1987 est.): 9,000,000.
Chief Cities (Dec. 31, 1983): Sofia, the capital, 1,093,752; Plovdiv, 373,235; Varna, 295,218.
Government: *Head of state,* Todor Zhivkov, chairman of the State Council and general secretary of the Communist Party (took office July 1971). *Head of government,* Georgi Atanasov, chairman of the Council of Ministers (took office March 1986).
Monetary Unit: Lev (1.31 leva equal U.S.$1, August 1987).
Gross National Product (1985 U.S.$): $57,800,000,000.
Economic Index: *Industrial Production* (1986, 1980 = 100), 128.
Foreign Trade (1985 U.S.$): *Imports,* $13,656,000,000; *exports,* $13,348,000,000.

Domestic Affairs. In July head of state and Communist Party chief Todor Zhivkov proposed a series of major changes within the party and state structures. Their purpose was, ostensibly, to provide a significantly greater measure of economic and political independence for Bulgarians and to reduce the role of the party in running the country. The culmination of some 18 months of experiment and discussion, the wholesale reorganization was prompted by Bulgaria's persistent economic problems over the past several years and allegedly stimulated by the Gorbachev reforms.

Zhivkov proposed that the State Council and Council of Ministers be replaced by a single new administrative organ and that there be multi-candidate elections for representatives to the Bulgarian National Assembly. He called for "greater market influence" in economic affairs, seeming to endorse limited private enterprise. He also asked for a more realistic valuation of the lev, the national currency, and "democratization of foreign trade" by permitting Bulgarian companies to trade more freely with foreign companies.

In August the Bulgarian National Assembly translated many of Zhivkov's proposals into a wide-ranging program of changes scheduled to take effect on Jan. 1, 1988. The central and regional administrative systems were restructured and steps taken toward the devolution of economic management, with appropriate changes in the constitution planned.

A large number of key ministries and other important bodies, many of which had been newly established in 1986, were abolished or merged into new structures. Among the latter were a new Ministry for Economy and Planning, headed by Stojan Kostov Ovcharov, and ministries of Foreign Economic Relations, Agriculture and Forestry, Health and Social Welfare, and Culture, Science, and Education. The Assembly also adopted a law to set up tariff-free zones in Bulgaria to attract foreign business and capital.

Foreign Affairs. In November the Western media reported the breakup of a Bulgarian spy ring that had been smuggling Western high-technology equipment into the Eastern bloc. The country also continued to receive very unfavorable publicity for its unyielding campaign of "forced Bulgarianization" of its ethnic Turkish minority, estimated at about 1.5 million people. Traditionally subjected to discrimination in employment, the military, and the universities, since 1984 the Turks also have been deprived of their Muslim faith, language, culture, customs, traditional clothing, and even their very names, and refused permission to emigrate to Turkey. It is estimated that more than 1,000 ethnic Turks have died and some 40,000 have been imprisoned.

JOSEPH FREDERICK ZACEK
State University of New York at Albany

BURMA

A quarter century of ideological consistency and economic doldrums was suddenly under review in 1987 by the very political leadership that had guided Burma since seizing power in 1962.

Politics. At the age of 76 and in his 25th year in power, Gen. Ne Win called for a reappraisal of the country's political and economic policies at the August meeting of the Central Executive Committee of the ruling Burma Socialist Program Party. While the move took most Burmese by surprise, there had been indications over the previous year that the leadership recognized the nation's dire economic straits. In December 1986, Burma had applied to the United Nations for "least-developed nation" status, a move that would enable it to receive more aid and easier credit terms.

As it has for much of Burma's post-independence history, the army continued to be the base of political power. The year 1987 was unusual, however, in that the army was called out to control serious student riots in September after the government demonetized most large Burmese bank notes in an attempt to control black marketeering. The riots were Burma's first major campus protests since 1974.

Economy. Despite official statistics proclaiming modest growth, the Burmese economy in 1987 showed much evidence of deterioration. Government ministries were told to plan budgets that assumed no foreign exchange. Many factories were closed or subject to slowdowns as needed imports were canceled. The foreign debt of $4.7 billion has become crippling as Burma's exports have continued to decline; in 1987 debt servicing took up some 90% of Burma's export revenues. The revenue decline has been a product of many factors, including falling world prices for teak and pulses. Nearly 70% of Burma's rich natural resources are in areas held by insurgents. A severe drought has jeopardized Burmese self-sufficiency in rice, leaving no surplus for sale abroad. A nationalized economy with low official prices has led to shortages, an absence of export items, a thriving black market, and an unofficial inflation rate of more than 25% annually.

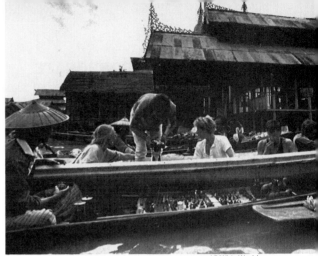

AP/Wide World

Tourists inspect merchandise at a floating market on Inle Lake. Burma's tourist industry is growing as more travelers are seeking a look at a vanishing traditional Asia.

Like other capital-intensive projects, major development of promising gas fields was postponed. In an effort to boost agricultural productivity, however, the government extended its agricultural modernization plan—called the Whole Township Extension Program—from rice to 20 other crops.

Insurgencies. More than a dozen ethnic-based insurgent groups have long controlled some 40% of Burma's northern territory. What is new about these insurgencies is their willingness to coordinate and collaborate on guerrilla objectives. In March the Burmese National Democratic Front (BNDF), an umbrella group of nine ethnic rebel armies, forged an alliance for military goals with the Communist Party of Burma. In July the BNDF elected Saw Maw Reh, 67, of the Karenni National Progressive Party as the leader of the coalition. The insurgents considered allowing some majority Burman representation into the BNDF to counter the organization's image as a separatist force. The BNDF seeks autonomous ethnic status within a Burmese Union, but the government continues to oppose the rebels with military force. More than 200 troops were involved in a bloody clash in June.

Foreign Relations. Burma has emerged somewhat in recent years from its radical isolationist stance, but it has retained its commitment to nonalignment. While it has actively sought more foreign aid, it has kept its sources of assistance as diversified as possible. Its principal donor is Japan, and it receives aid from both the United States and Soviet Union.

LINDA K. RICHTER
Kansas State University

BURMA • Information Highlights

Official Name: Socialist Republic of the Union of Burma.
Location: Southeast Asia.
Area: 261,216 sq mi (676 550 km²).
Population (mid-1987 est.): 38,800,000.
Chief City (1983 est.): Rangoon, the capital, 2,458,712; Mandalay, 532,895.
Government: U Ne Win, chairman, Burma Socialist Program Party. *Head of state,* U San Yu, president (took office Nov. 1981). *Head of government,* U Maung Maung Kha, prime minister (took office March 1977). *Legislature* (unicameral)—National Assembly.
Monetary Unit: Kyat (6.792 kyats equal U.S.$1, July 1987).
Gross Domestic Product (fiscal year 1986 U.S.$): $7,050,000,000.
Economic Index (Rangoon, 1985): *Consumer Prices* (1980 = 100), all items, 123.5; food, 120.8.
Foreign Trade (1986 U.S.$): *Imports,* $304,000,000; *exports,* $265,000,000.

BUSINESS AND CORPORATE AFFAIRS

What were to have been the major business stories of 1987—mergers, divestitures, takeovers, and the bull market—were quickly superseded by the "Stock Market Crash of '87." On "Black Monday," Oct. 19, 1987, the Dow Jones Industrial Average plummeted 508 points—the largest one-day drop in the history of the exchange; the 22.6% decline that day also was a record. The crash had serious implications for the business community, the U.S. economy, and world financial markets. (*See* STOCKS AND BONDS, page 501.)

The U.S. economy as a whole was experiencing its fifth straight year of stable growth. By the third quarter, gross national product was up strongly at an annual rate of 3.8%; inflation was tolerable at an annual rate of 4.3%; and unemployment was below 6.0% for the first time since 1979. Nevertheless, there were still serious pockets of economic recession, particularly in the "rust belt" (steel-producing areas), oil-producing areas (e.g., Texas), and the agricultural sector, where the federal government was pouring in more than $26 billion in support. Both consumer and business confidence was shaken by the stock-market crash, but in neither case did it appear that there would be major collapses in consumer or business spending.

Overall corporate profits during 1987 continued to run ahead of 1986. The Crash of '87 was in no way due to a weakness in corporate profits. LTV Corporation, the parent company of the nation's second-largest steelmaker, which had filed for bankruptcy in 1986, had third-quarter earnings in 1987 of more than $100 million. The major bankruptcy news of 1987 concerned Texaco, which filed for Chapter 11 protection from creditors on April 12. The move forestalled enforcement of a court judgment won by Pennzoil in 1985, in which Texaco was ordered to pay Pennzoil $10.3 billion for improperly interfering with a merger agreement between Pennzoil and Getty Oil Company.

Even Procter & Gamble Company had some financial problems during 1987, taking an $800 million pretax charge against earnings to cover the cost of closing factories and restructuring several key product lines. A sizable portion of the write-off came from the company's retreat from its costly battle to become a power in the ready-to-eat cookie business.

Chrysler had its share of problems during 1987. The company was indicted on charges that it had committed fraud by disconnecting the odometers on as many as 60,000 new cars that were driven by its executives and which were later sold as new; some of the cars had even been damaged in accidents. The company responded with double-page advertisements in major newspapers across the country expressing regret and promising to extend and expand the warranty for those who had purchased the "tested" cars; for those who had purchased cars that had been in accidents, new cars of like kind would be provided. By autumn, Chrysler sales were down and 3,000 employees had to be laid off.

A major piece of legislation being considered by the U.S. Congress—which aroused one of the most bitter labor-management disputes of the Reagan years—would require employers to notify employees at least 60 days in advance of permanent layoffs or plant closings. As the year drew to a close, the business community and labor unions continued to battle over the proposal.

Mergers and Divestitures. The year 1987 saw continuing activity in the area of corporate mergers and divestitures. Among the industries most seriously affected was air travel. The takeover of Piedmont by USAir was approved by the U.S. Department of Transportation late in 1987 despite the fact that an administrative law judge had ruled that the merger would have significant anticompetitive effects in certain markets. With the mergers of 1985–87, the large airlines have come to control pricing in

AP/Wide World

Alfred De Crane, Jr. (right), *Texaco's chairman of the board, joins James Kinnear, the company president and chief executive officer, in announcing that Texaco will continue to contest a $10.3 billion judgment won by Pennzoil for Texaco's improper interference in a merger agreement between Pennzoil and Getty. In mid-December, however, Texaco agreed in principle to a $3 billion settlement, with another $2.5 billion going to its creditors to bring the company out of bankruptcy.*

AP/Wide World

Chrysler Corp., the third largest U.S. automaker, acquired American Motors and its Jeep line of four-wheel vehicles in 1987. The new company became Jeep-Eagle.

major markets in a way that few foresaw. While 12 major carriers controlled 85.5% of air travel in 1986, eight accounted for 94% in 1987. The eight were Texas Air, which had taken over Continental, Eastern, PeopleExpress, New York Air, and Frontier; United; American; Delta; Northwest; USAir; Trans World Airlines; and Pan Am.

One result of airline deregulation and the approval of major airline mergers by the federal government has been a movement toward monopoly at many major and smaller airports where only one airline has been able to survive. As the "hub" system has developed, at 15 of the nation's top airports either half the business is already controlled by one carrier, or two airlines share more than 70% of the business. As of 1987, Northwest Airlines had 86.6% of the market at the Memphis Airport, 81.6% at Minneapolis-St. Paul, and 64.9% at Detroit; USAir had 82.8% at Pittsburgh; TWA had 82.3% at St. Louis; Continental had 71.5% at Houston; American had 63.4% at Dallas-Fort Worth; Delta had 52.5% at Atlanta; United had 49.2% at Chicago and 44.3% at Denver; and Eastern had 48.5% at Miami. At Atlanta, Delta and Eastern together accounted for 94.7% of the market; at Denver, United and Continental had a combined 85.2% share.

Other activity in the merger field included the approval by the U.S. Federal Trade Commission (FTC) of Chrysler's acquisition of American Motors, with the name changed to Jeep-Eagle. Ford Motor Company moved to preserve its biggest customer by purchasing Hertz from Allegis for $1.3 billion. Greyhound Lines acquired Trailways for $80 million, which left Greyhound as the only remaining national bus line in the United States. Earlier in the year, Greyhound Corporation had sold the bus line for $350 million to a privately held investor group.

An unusual change in corporate ownership was the takeover of the Avis car rental company for $1.75 billion by management in an employee stock ownership plan. This was the ninth time since 1954 that Avis has been sold. Other buy-outs during 1987 in which management took at least part ownership included those of Beatrice Companies (for $6.2 billion), Beatrice International Food ($985 million), Playtex ($1.3 billion), and Americold ($530 million).

Major mergers also continued in the advertising industry. The J. Walter Thompson agency, one of the largest advertising agencies in the world, was sold to WPP Group, a British marketing services and communications company.

The business community's most important divestitures were those of the General Electric Company and Allegis. General Electric sold its National Broadcasting Company (NBC) Radio Network to Westwood One, a California-based radio production and syndication company. Then it sold its huge consumer electronics business ($3.2 billion in sales in 1986) to Thomson, the Paris-based conglomerate owned by the French government. Allegis was in the process of divesting itself of Hertz, as well as its holdings in the Westin and Hilton hotel chains.

Executive Changes. Allegis Corporation had run into a variety of financial problems. Its chief executive officer (CEO), Richard J. Ferris, had had the master plan to bring under one corporate roof a full-service travel company including an airline, a rental car company, and hotels. The plan did not work and Ferris was replaced by Frank A. Olson. Among the year's new CEOs at major U.S. companies were William J. Alley at American Brands; Joseph E. Antonini at K Mart; John C. Marous at Westinghouse Electric; James J. Renier at Honeywell; Albert E. Suter at Firestone Tire and Rubber; Robert D. Krebs at Santa Fe Pacific; Ronald W. Allen at Delta Air Lines; Fernando R. Gumucio at Del Monte; and William G. Roth at Dravo. At U.S. Sprint Communications, CEO Charles M. Skibo resigned under pressure as the unprofitable long-distance telephone carrier announced second-quarter losses of $350 million; he was replaced by Robert H. Snedaker. Frank Lorenzo, CEO of Texas Air, the parent company of Continental Air, took over as CEO of Continental after forcing out Thomas G. Plaskett.

Corporate Name Changes. United Airlines, whose name had been changed to Allegis, was in the process of changing back to United Airlines as it proceeded to sell off its hotel and rental car business to become just an airline. This seemed to be in line with a poll showing that most Americans were unable to identify the new corporate names given to some of the nation's largest firms. Only 12% of those polled gave USX as the new name for U.S. Steel. Only 8% knew that Unisys was the name of the merger of Burroughs and Sperry Corporations. Only 6% knew that Navistar was the new name of International Harvester, and only 2% knew that Allegis was the parent company, at the time of the survey, of United Airlines, Westin Hotels, and Hertz.

In the first six months of 1987, 919 U.S. companies changed names, up 59% from 1986.

See also UNITED STATES—The Economy.

STEWART M. LEE, *Geneva College*

CALIFORNIA

A new, conservative state Supreme Court was appointed in 1987, and its influence was quickly felt. State taxpayers received a rare refund.

Budget and New Laws. The 1988 state budget of just under $41.0 billion was arrived at after many item vetoes by Gov. George Deukmejian. He also vetoed a record 183 other bills, more in five years than former Gov. Ronald Reagan had vetoed in eight years. Vetoes included those funding the Los Angeles County emergency trauma centers (the governor said they could be financed from state block grants), a plan to modify the organization of the Los Angeles public transportation system, and the extension of welfare benefits.

After four years of large increases for education at all levels, the governor made sharp cutbacks in 1987, resulting in a feud of nine months with William Honig, the state school superintendent. Deukmejian held his ground. Nearly 71% of the budget is for health, welfare, and education at all levels.

Perhaps the most controversial new law allows an abortion on an unwed minor only with her consent and that of one parent or legal guardian. An alternate approach allows a petition to juvenile court. The act passed narrowly and was the first in the state to restrict abortions since they were generally legalized.

Tax Rebate. The legislature, under considerable pressure from the governor, voted to rebate a tax surplus of $1.1 billion. Persons who filed returns but owed nothing will also receive a small payment. Another $87 million of the surplus went to extra school aid.

The tax code was overhauled to allow for more business write-offs and cut income taxes for 6.5 million individuals. It was also brought closer to conformity with the new federal code.

Courts. After voters refused to allow three members of the state Supreme Court to continue in office, Governor Deukmejian appointed their replacements and promoted Malcolm M. Lucas to chief justice. The new court promptly reversed the most controversial case of the previous Bird court, which stated that intent to kill had to be proved for the death penalty to apply when a murder was committed during a felony.

The long struggle between the governor and a Senate leader over where to locate a new prison in Los Angeles County was settled when it was agreed to build two, one in a poor section of the city and another in a suburb.

Former Assemblyman Bruce E. Young was convicted on five counts of mail fraud. It was the first conviction in a political corruption trial in California in thirty years.

Election Results in San Francisco. State Assemblyman Art Agnos and Supervisor John Molinari finished first and second in an 11-candidate field trying to succeed Dianne Feinstein as mayor. The 49-year-old Agnos was elected in a runoff December 8. Voters rejected a proposal to build an $80 million stadium to give the baseball Giants an alternative to windy Candlestick Park.

Water. Californians, always sensitive to water matters, were shocked when Secretary of the Interior Donald P. Hodel proposed in August that Hetch Hetchy dam and water system in Yosemite be dismantled to establish another valley for campsites. This system provides nearly all of the water for San Francisco. Mayor Feinstein said it would be a "very bad trade-off." The legislature authorized its own study.

Condors. A bit of California died on April 19 when the last condor known to be in the wild was captured southwest of Bakersfield. The seven-year-old male was taken to join 26 other California condors at the San Diego Wild Animal Park, where they are to be bred in captivity. (*See* ZOOS AND ZOOLOGY.)

Weather. After a very dry winter in most of the state, the southern portion had the coolest summer in over 20 years. An earthquake measuring 6.1 on the Richter scale struck on October 1, centered just north of Whittier, southeast of Los Angeles, where the most damage was done. (*See also* LOS ANGELES.)

AP/Wide World

Residents of Groveland, CA, publicly thanked members of the state's Department of Forestry for their efforts to control forest fires. Sections of California were struck by serious brush fires during September and October.

CALIFORNIA • Information Highlights

Area: 158,706 sq mi (411 049 km²).
Population (July 1, 1986): 26,981,000.
Chief Cities (July 1, 1986 est.): Sacramento, the capital, 323,550; Los Angeles, 3,259,000; San Diego, 1,015,000; San Francisco, 749,000; San Jose, 712,080; Long Beach, 396,280; Oakland, 356,960.
Government (1987): *Chief Officers*—governor, George Deukmejian (R); lt. gov., Leo McCarthy (D). *Legislature*—Senate, 40 members; Assembly, 80 members.
State Finances (fiscal year 1985): *Revenue,* $57,894,000,000; *expenditure,* $51,840,000,000.
Personal Income (1986): $456,098,000,000; per capita, $16,904.
Labor Force (June 1987): *Civilian labor force,* 13,830,100; *unemployed,* 750,600 (5.4% of total force).
Education: *Enrollment* (fall 1985)—public elementary schools, 2,926,705; public secondary, 1,328,849; colleges and universities, 1,650,439. *Public school expenditures* (1985–86), $15,132,000,000 ($3,573 per pupil).

Scientific Research. The first outdoor test of genetically engineered bacteria was conducted by scientists of the University of California, Davis on bacteria altered to eliminate a gene that normally promotes the formation of ice crystals on plant leaves. The goal is to reduce frost damage in commercial crops. Protesters argued that altered life forms may have harmful effects on the environment.

CHARLES R. ADRIAN
University of California, Riverside

CAMBODIA

During 1987, the only significant change in the Cambodian situation was some diplomatic probing aimed at ending the nine-year military struggle for control of the country.

Political and Military Developments. Vietnam continued to maintain an occupation force of about 140,000 men in Cambodia, while Communist and non-Communist resistance groups were backed by China, the United States, and the Association for Southeast Asian Nations (ASEAN). Although the Vietnamese had destroyed their bases in 1985, the resistance groups continued to carry out small acts of sabotage in many parts of Cambodia. Visiting newsmen reported signs that the non-Communist resistance led by Prince Norodom Sihanouk was gaining support among the Cambodian people, who have traditionally resented Vietnamese encroachment.

Economy. The collectivization of agriculture was proceeding slowly, because the Vietnamese-backed regime is wary of antagonizing the people. Annual rice production has not yet reached 2.5 million tons, the crop yield in the last prewar year, 1969. Although once a net exporter of grain, Cambodia has been unable to provide fully for domestic needs in recent years because of a lack of adequate fertilizer, seeds, and pesticides. Severe droughts and bureaucratic mismanagement also have taken a toll. Cambodia was forced to seek 152,000 tons of emergency rice aid in late 1986, and the outlook seemed even worse at the end of 1987.

Although a private sector is officially tolerated, only a small number of wealthy Cambodians can afford consumer goods smuggled in from Thailand. State-owned factories produce far below capacity for lack of raw materials and spare parts. The Soviet Union is Cambodia's leading trade partner.

Foreign Relations. In February, Prince Sihanouk announced that Vietnam had proposed talks between the three resistance groups and the Vietnamese-backed regime in Phnom Penh to establish a new coalition government. According to Sihanouk, Hanoi had indicated it would be willing to negotiate with such a government for a cease-fire and withdrawal of its troops from Cambodia. Hanoi promptly denied it had made such an offer. The Vietnamese have been unwilling to let the Khmer Rouge resistance group return to power, because it is closely linked to Vietnam's main enemy, China.

Whether or not Hanoi made an offer along the lines described by Sihanouk, their Soviet patrons have been urging them to reach some kind of understanding with China and with the ASEAN states. In March, Soviet Foreign Minister Eduard Shevardnadze made a brief stopover in Bangkok, Thailand, en route to Australia. He urged the ASEAN states to negotiate with the Phnom Penh regime, but they believe they must deal with Hanoi, which controls Cambodia.

In early December, Prince Sihanouk and Prime Minister Hun Sen held three days of talks in Fere-en-Tardenoi, France, at the end of which they announced an agreement to work toward a peaceful solution of Cambodia's political conflict. It was the first meeting between Sihanouk and the Cambodian regime since it came to power in 1979. Additional talks were scheduled for early 1988 in the same place and perhaps later that year in North Korea.

In 1987, the United Nations once again called for the withdrawal of all foreign forces from Cambodia.

PETER A. POOLE
Author, "Eight Presidents and Indochina"

CAMBODIA • Information Highlights

Official Name: People's Republic of Kampuchea.
Location: Southeast Asia.
Area: 69,900 sq mi (181 040 km²).
Population (mid-1987 est.): 6,500,000.
Chief City (1986 est.): Phnom Penh, the capital, 700,000.
Government: *Head of state,* Heng Samrin (took office 1979). *Head of government,* Hun Sen, prime minister (took office Jan. 1985).
Monetary Unit: Riel (4 riels equal U.S.$1, 1984).

© John Major

On June 3 at the old Union Station in Ottawa, Prime Minister Brian Mulroney and the ten provincial premiers signed the final version of an agreement which, in Mulroney's words, "welcomes Quebec back into the Canadian constitutional family."

CANADA

Nineteen eight-seven was a year that Canada's historians will always look back on. At Meech Lake, Quebec, on April 30, Prime Minister Brian Mulroney and the ten provincial premiers reached an agreement that completed the unfinished business of Canada's constitution. In Washington, DC, on October 3, desperate last-minute bargaining produced a comprehensive free-trade agreement that lowered the few remaining economic barriers between the two neighbors. In Ottawa, Parliament rejected a return to the death penalty but raised the barriers against immigrants claiming refugee status. The Mulroney government, despite its major achievements and a general climate of economic recovery, fell to new depths of unpopularity, while the left-wing New Democrats, led by Edward Broadbent, surged to unprecedented heights in the polls.

Constitution. Upon taking office in 1984, Conservative Prime Minister Mulroney had promised to complete the constitutional process his Liberal predecessor, Pierre Elliott Trudeau, had left unfinished. A constitutional conference on native self-government, held in Ottawa, March 26–27, failed to produce an agreement. Ottawa proposed that the principle of self-government be proclaimed in an amendment to the constitution, with specific aboriginal rights to be defined later, but provincial premiers balked.

The April 30 meeting at Meech Lake, site of a secluded government conference center, seemed equally ill-fated. Prime Minister Mulroney called the meeting to resolve the issue, deadlocked since 1982, of Quebec's inclusion in the constitution. The French-speaking province had demanded that certain conditions be met, while most of the other premiers resisted the granting of special privileges. But a sense of historic opportunity and Mulroney's bargaining skills led to an agreement that brought Quebec, in the prime minister's words, "back into the Canadian constitutional family." The price was high: recognition for Quebec as a "distinct society"; unanimity instead of a seven-province majority for future major amendments; a provincial voice in future Senate and Supreme Court appointments; and the right to financial compensation for provinces that opt out of federal programs in health, welfare, education, and other areas of provincial jurisdiction.

In the wake of public criticism, another meeting was held at Ottawa's Langevin Building, June 2–3. After an all-night marathon session, exhausted premiers emerged with further guarantees for linguistic minorities inside and outside Quebec and assurances that aboriginal and ethnic rights would be protected. The final version of the agreement was signed on June 3, but it would not be officially incorporated into the constitution until ratification by the provincial legislatures and Parliament. The latter gave its approval on October 26.

All three federal party leaders—Mulroney, Broadbent, and John Turner of the Liberals—endorsed the Meech Lake-Langevin compromise, but some of their followers and certain other groups were not content. Former Prime Minister Trudeau, who had refused any such concessions to the provinces during his tenure, twice emerged from retirement to denounce the prime minister as a coward. Feminist groups argued that women's rights had been overlooked. Native leaders protested that Quebec's demands had been met while theirs had been rejected. Many critics complained that Mulroney had sacrificed federal powers to the provinces and wondered what meaning judges would give to Quebec's new special status.

Free Trade. Eighteen months of negotiations ended in another history-making marathon on October 2–3, when Canada and the United States reached agreement on a comprehensive trade accord (*see* special report, page 165).

The free-trade agreement came after a year punctuated by examples of what U.S. protectionism could do. January 1987 revealed the details of a last-minute softwood lumber deal at the end of 1986: a 15% self-imposed tax that hurt the entire Canadian industry more than the intended U.S. target, British Columbia, where stumpage fees were abnormally low. Saskatchewan's potash industry was another well-publicized victim of a U.S. countervailing duty, urged by competitors in New Mexico. While resource-producing provinces hoped for an early deal that would save their markets in the United States, anxiety about free trade grew. This was particularly true in prosperous Ontario, where union leaders and academics feared the loss of jobs and spreading U.S. political and cultural influence. By August a majority of Canadians opposed a deal.

The opponents may have been relieved on September 23 when Canadian trade negotiator Simon Reisman left the table. He claimed that the United States had ignored Canadian determination to retain subsidies for its depressed regions and cultural industries and to get a binding disputes-settlement mechanism to prevent future U.S. countervailing duties. Top-level negotiations between Prime Minister Mulroney and President Ronald Reagan revived the talks, with both sides eager to avoid the political fallout that would result from failure. Trade Minister Pat Carney and Finance Minister Michael Wilson took over as the Canadian negotiators and met the U.S. deadline for a fast-track approval by Congress. The resulting agreement left a lot for future discussion. Both sides promised to eliminate tariffs (already at a minimal level) and to create continental free trade in energy, but Canada's demand for binding disputes-settlement had dwindled to a bilateral commission that would act only if either side broke its own trade laws.

While the Reagan administration prepared to defend its version of the deal before Congress, Prime Minister Mulroney wondered whether the unexpected agreement might prove popular enough to win him reelection.

Foreign Affairs. Although free trade dominated Canada's foreign policy in 1987, the government tried hard to demonstrate its strong links outside North America. In February, the prime minister visited front-line states in southern Africa to condemn apartheid, a message he repeated at the June summit of major industrial democracies in Venice. Leaders of 41 French-speaking nations and territories met at Quebec City in September. Canada marked the summit by forgiving $325 million in loans to the poorest participants and repeated the generosity when Commonwealth heads of state met in Vancouver in October.

THE CANADIAN MINISTRY

M. Brian Mulroney, prime minister
George H. Hees, minister of veterans affairs and minister of state for senior citizens
Joseph Clark, secretary of state for external affairs
Flora I. MacDonald, minister of communications
John C. Crosbie, minister of transport
Donald F. Mazankowski, deputy prime minister, president of the Treasury Board, president of the Queen's Privy Council for Canada, and government house leader
Elmer M. MacKay, minister of national revenue
Jake Epp, minister of national health and welfare
John Wise, minister of agriculture
Ramon J. Hnatyshyn, minister of justice and attorney general of Canada
David E. Crombie, secretary of state
Robert R. de Cotret, minister of regional industrial expansion and minister of state for science and technology
Henry Perrin Beatty, minister of defence
Michael H. Wilson, minister of finance
Harvie Andre, minister of consumer and corporate affairs
Otto J. Jelinek, minister of state for fitness and amateur sport
Thomas E. Siddon, minister of fisheries and oceans
Charles J. Mayer, minister of state for grains and oilseeds
William H. McKnight, minister of Indian affairs and northern development
Thomas M. McMillan, minister of environment
Patricia Carney, minister of international trade
Benoit Bouchard, minister of employment and immigration
Michel Côté, minister of supply and services
James F. Kelleher, solicitor general of Canada
Marcel Masse, minister of energy, mines and resources
Barbara J. McDougall, minister of state for privatization and minister responsible for the status of women
Gerald S. Merrithew, minister of state for forestry and mines
Monique Vézina, minister of state for transport
Stewart McInnes, minister of public works
Frank Oberle, minister of state for science and technology
Lowell Murray, leader of the government in the Senate and minister of state for federal-provincial relations
Paul W. Dick, associate minister of defence
Pierre Cadieux, minister of labour
Jean Charest, minister of state for youth
Thomas Hockin, minister of state for finance
Monique Landry, minister for external relations
Bernard Valcourt, minister of state for small business, tourism, and Indian Affairs and Northern Development
Gerry Weiner, minister of state for immigration
Douglas Lewis, minister of state for Treasury Board
Pierre Blais, minister of state for agriculture

Though it had taken three years and three defense ministers, the government delivered on its promise of a new defense-policy statement. The white paper issued in June reaffirmed Canada's commitment to NATO (North Atlantic Treaty Organization) and NORAD (North American Air Defense Command) but promised to end the 1964 commitment of troops and planes to NATO's northern flank in favor of sending the same reinforcement to Canada's existing contingent in West Germany. While regular forces would grow only slightly, Minister of Defence Perrin Beatty promised a big increase in the reserves. The Canadian Navy, neglected for a generation, was promised more frigates and up to 12 nuclear submarines to allow it to patrol all three of Canada's ocean frontiers. More northern bases also would allow Canada to use its CF-18 fighter planes to enforce its Arctic sovereignty.

Canada's military welcomed the proposals, but Washington discreetly disapproved of nuclear submarines as a diversion from Canada's more mundane military roles. Opposition parties also condemned the $12 billion submarine program as costly and unnecessary. The New Democratic Party (NDP) published its own defense policy, renewing old pledges to leave NATO and NORAD while worrying its own pacifist wing by promising a serious commitment to defense and frontier surveillance.

Politics. NDP defense policies were politically important because Liberals and Conservatives saw them as the most vulnerable feature of a party that had bypassed them both in the opinion polls. NDP support reached an all-time high of 40% in midsummer. On July 20, the NDP won by-election victories in Newfoundland, Ontario, and the Yukon, taking two solid Conservative seats.

NDP popularity was due partly to a respected leader, Ed Broadbent, but mainly to Conservative and Liberal disarray. The Conservatives began the year with a messy land scandal involving Junior Transportation Minister André Bissonnette. Minister of State Roch Lasalle resigned after it was revealed that he had hired aides with criminal records. And the prime minister himself was hurt by reports that he and his wife had spent close to $1 million (a third of it from a private party fund) to redecorate their official residences. Tighter management came in March with the appointment of Derek Burney, a career civil servant, to run the prime minister's office. In late spring, Mulroney took the offensive, scrapping existing Liberal-created regional development agencies in favor of a new Atlantic Provinces Opportunities Agency (APOA) for the East and a Western Economic Diversification Initiative (WEDI) for the West. The new agencies, each under a popular local ministry, were designed to harvest political gratitude as well as economic growth.

The short-term political effect was invisible. Nor did Meech Lake or the promise in June of sweeping tax reform by Finance Minister Michael Wilson improve Conservative fortunes. While taxpayers might welcome lower tax rates, they would not feel them until 1988—a likely election year—and they could look forward to a sweeping new national sales tax whose details had yet to be worked out. It was not a recipe for quick popularity.

Far from profiting from Tory troubles, the Liberals stumbled in the polls. The major opposition party found itself split on major issues ranging from free trade to the Meech Lake accord. Party leader Turner, despite a 76% vote of confidence from Liberal delegates at the end of 1986, became the target of criticism from party President Michel Robert and certain members of his own caucus. Trudeau loyalists blamed him for agreeing to Mulroney's consti-

Frank McKenna, a 39-year-old lawyer, was elected premier of New Brunswick on October 13, as his Liberal Party took all 58 ridings in the province's 30th general election. McKenna was sworn in two weeks later, ending the 17-year rule of Conservative Richard Hatfield.

Canada-U.S. Relations

"Good relations, super relations with the United States will be the cornerstone of our foreign policy" declared Canada's Conservative Prime Minister Brian Mulroney after his landslide election victory on Sept. 4, 1984. Three years later, some Canadians wondered what benefits they had reaped from Mulroney's efforts to win favor with the Ronald Reagan White House. Americans could reply that Canada had profited from a mounting trade surplus with the United States while doing little to share the U.S. military burden or to open barriers to U.S.-based cultural and financial service businesses. Two years of negotiations on an extensive bilateral trade agreement, which reached their climax in October 1987, focused attention, particularly in Canada, on relations between the two neighbors.

Similar but Separate. Except for French-speaking Quebec, outsiders find little difference between Canada and its southern neighbor. Most Canadians speak English, share American culture and life-style, and work in industries that compete with those in the adjoining tier of U.S. states—fishing, farming, mining, and manufacturing. In recent decades, both countries have experienced a boom in service and information industries. But with all their similarities, the two countries remain quite separate and distinct. Canada was created by people who chose not to be Americans. The War of 1812 confirmed the territorial boundaries established by the American Revolution. The Confederation that created Canada in 1867 was designed to protect British North Americans from U.S. visions of "manifest destiny."

Yet Canadians have always welcomed U.S. ideas, know-how, and investment. By 1919, American capital had supplanted British business influence. By the 1950s, U.S. branch plants dominated Canadian manufacturing and U.S. investors controlled most of Canada's major resource industries. The Ogdensburg agreement of 1940 integrated the defenses of the two countries. From 1947, Canadian armed forces adopted U.S. equipment and methods. At the same time, English-Canadian nationalists, who had chafed at the British connection, grew more critical of U.S. dominance of Canada's economy and culture. A Royal Commission report in 1957 warned that Canada's sovereignty might be endangered by foreign ownership. Since 1945, Canadian governments have sought to preserve the material benefits of the U.S. relationship while trying, usually with little effect, to establish countervailing economic and diplomatic linkages outside the Western Hemisphere.

A Cornerstone? By proclaiming good relations a "cornerstone," Prime Minister Mulroney went further than most postwar Canadian leaders, partly because he had claimed that his predecessor, Pierre Elliott Trudeau, had damaged Canada-U.S. relations during his 16 years in power. While nowhere near the nadir reached in 1962 by former Conservative Prime Minister John Diefenbaker in relations with the Kennedy administration, Trudeau and his Liberal government were out of tune with the Reagan administration. Under Trudeau, Canada cut military spending, protected Canadian mass media from American ownership, expanded regional economic subsidies, created a Foreign Investment Review Agency (FIRA) to screen foreign takeovers for their benefits to Canada, and, in 1981, proclaimed a National Energy Program (NEP) to make Canada self-sufficient in energy and to "Canadianize" the oil and gas industries. Nor did the Liberals follow the U.S. example of privatization, deregulation, and down-sizing government.

Those Canadians who advocated a Reagan-type conservative revolution felt vindicated by the early-1980s recession. Canada became more dependent on U.S. markets, the destination of 80% of exports. In tough times, annoying Washington seemed a luxury. Under Reagan, the United States did little to meet Canadian concerns about trans-border pollution or about trade disputes ranging from fish to softwood lumber. Canadians welcomed Mulroney's promise to improve U.S. relations as a way of getting outstanding problems solved. U.S. officials assumed it was a victory for rightist thinking.

To the pleasure of some Canadians as well as Americans, both the FIRA and NEP were gutted within weeks of the Conservative election victory in September 1984. At the "Shamrock Summit" at Quebec City in March 1985, Prime Minister Mulroney and President Reagan agreed that Canada would pay 60% of the cost of a rebuilt North Warning System, while Reagan agreed to study the acid-rain problem.

Free Trade? More spectacular was an agreement to negotiate a comprehensive U.S.-Canada free-trade agreement. Ever since the 1854 Reciprocity Agreement ended in 1868, such deals have been a staple of Canadian-American discussions, and both sides have always weighed economic benefits against polit-

© Dirck Halstead/"Time" Magazine

Free trade was a key issue when Prime Minister Mulroney and President Reagan held their third annual summit in Ottawa, April 5–6. An agreement was signed in October.

ical risks. Would the 1985–87 negotiations be different? Were they needed at all when GATT (General Agreement on Tariffs and Trade) and quiet diplomacy had eliminated most tariff walls?

For President Reagan, the 1985 initiative was a way to score against protectionist critics. Prime Minister Mulroney, hitherto an opponent of any major free-trade deal, wanted to seem positive. He was pushed by the report of a Trudeau-appointed Royal Commission, which warned that dire consequences would befall a Canada caught outside the rising walls of U.S. protectionism. The refrain was echoed by major business and industrial organizations and by academic economists. Few critics were heard when Mulroney chose Simon Reisman, negotiator of the 1965 Canada-U.S. Auto Pact, to meet with U.S. trade negotiator Peter Murphy.

A Millstone? Mulroney's "cornerstone" soon became a political millstone, helping to pull the prime minister to historic lows in the opinion polls. Friendship with President Reagan produced little American action on the acid-rain, trade, and fisheries disputes. Canadian sensitivity about its Arctic frontier was ignored in 1985, when Washington refused to seek permission for the U.S. Coast Guard vessel *Polar Sea* to pass through waters claimed by Canada. Nor could President Reagan discourage Congress from imposing countervailing duties on Canadian exports of lumber, fish, steel, and potash. Americans could point out that Canada enjoyed a $10 billion surplus on its $200 billion export business to the United States.

Eighteen months of negotiations raised fears and hopes on both sides of the border. While few Americans were even aware of the talks, Canadians were regularly reminded that their prosperity or their independence hung on the outcome. Americans wanted a "level playing field" for cross-border trade, cleared of tariffs and nontariff barriers that impeded U.S. investment, exports, and the sale of services in Canada. Canadians insisted on protecting existing industries, such as automobile manufacturing, on guarding so-called "cultural industries," and on protecting regional subsidies. A key Canadian demand, raised by the harsh experience with countervailing duties, was that trade disputes be referred to a special body for binding settlement. As the implications of free trade for Canada were spelled out, polls showed dwindling public support. Voter suspicions that Mulroney was glib and untrustworthy easily shifted to fears that he would sacrifice too much. At the same time, regions dependent on U.S. trade and indifferent to arguments about Canadian autonomy and culture showed support for almost any deal.

In a crisis atmosphere heightened by the walkout of negotiator Reisman, much tough talking on both sides, and high-level intervention by the prime minister and president, a comprehensive agreement on bilateral trade was reached within minutes of the U.S. bargaining deadline, midnight on October 3.

At the core of the agreement was a provision calling for the elimination of tariffs by both countries over a ten-year period beginning Jan. 1, 1989. In the area of energy—resources which Ottawa had worked hard to protect during the 1970s—all restrictions on imports and exports, including quotas, taxes, and minimum price requirements, would end. Controls on U.S. investment in Canada were abandoned. The 1965 U.S.-Canadian Auto Pact was formally preserved, but Canada surrendered tariff subsidies for car exports. Washington agreed to a binding-arbitration panel to resolve bilateral disputes, but only if a U.S. or a Canadian trade law had been broken.

The agreement was subject to the approval of the Canadian Parliament and U.S. Congress. For critics in Canada, the deal fulfilled their worst fears. But Conservatives, their backers in the business community, and most provincial premiers were ecstatic. Whether Canadians and Americans generally would share the rejoicing was a question only time would answer. What was certain was that a milestone in Canada-U.S. relations had been reached.

DESMOND MORTON

tutional changes. Image makers condemned his speaking style. Turner's greatest sin in the eyes of Liberals was allowing the party to slip behind the NDP in the polls. But Turner soldiered on, ignoring his critics and the calls for his resignation. He and the Liberal Party could only hope that Broadbent and the NDP would stumble and that the Liberals could capitalize nationally on their sweeping provincial victories in Ontario and New Brunswick.

Parliament. Prime Minister Mulroney had promised to make Parliament more effective, but the results were not always what he wished. A promised free vote on capital punishment, sought by Conservative backbenchers, seemed certain to restore the death penalty until a powerful campaign led by the Christian churches and an eloquent speech by the prime minister himself turned the scales. The vote, held on June 30, came out 148–127 against the motion, with a solid bloc of Quebec Conservatives making the difference.

Conservatives were more united on legislation to increase patent protection for large multinational pharmaceutical companies, a measure intended to pacify Washington. The Senate, dominated by Liberal appointees, blocked the legislation on the popular argument that it would send prescription drug prices soaring. Mulroney's angry threats to reform the Senate were made ironic by the fact that his own Meech Lake deal made substantial changes to the institution almost impossible.

Parliament won fresh headlines when it was summoned for a special summer session to pass a tougher version of laws to restrict immigrants claiming refugee status. The recall came after the July 12 boat landing of 173 Sikhs on the south shore of Nova Scotia—recalling the 155 Tamils found floating off Newfoundland in 1986. This time there was more anger than sympathy, and the government responded to the public outrage. The uproar seemed to fade once Parliament met, but stiff new legislation was passed.

CANADA • Information Highlights

Official Name: Canada.
Location: Northern North America.
Area: 3,849,656 sq mi (9 970 610 km^2).
Population (1986 census): 25,354,064.
Chief Cities (1986 census): Ottawa, the capital, 300,763; Montreal, 1,015,420; Toronto, 612,289.
Government: *Head of state,* Elizabeth II, queen; represented by Jeanne Sauvé, governor-general (took office May 14, 1984). *Head of government,* M. Brian Mulroney, prime minister (took office Sept. 17, 1984). *Legislature*—Parliament: Senate and House of Commons.
Monetary Unit: Canadian dollar (1.3172 dollars equal U.S.$1, Nov. 17, 1987).
Gross Domestic Product (1986 U.S.$): $360,000,000,000.
Economic Index: *Consumer Prices* (July 1987, 1981 = 100), all items, 139.2; food, 134.2.
Foreign Trade (1986 U.S.$): *Imports,* $81,099,000,000; *exports,* $86,725,000,000.

© Canapress Photo Service

The Letter Carriers Union conducted a three-week series of rotating walkouts beginning in mid-June. There were several clashes with nonunion replacements.

Labor. The year 1987 was a good one for Canadian workers, as unemployment fell and wage increases began to exceed inflation for the first time since 1977. But it was not a very good year for unions. The newly autonomous Canadian Auto Workers proved that it could win partially indexed pensions from the "big three" automakers (General Motors, Ford, and Chrysler), but Conservative federal and provincial governments made clear that they wrote the rules for collective bargaining. For the first time, a federal crown corporation, Canada Post, used strikebreakers during a legal strike. Although the tactic failed in the letter carriers' strike in June, it was more successful against the indoor postal workers in October.

A national railway strike in August ended, as expected, when Parliament ordered resumption of work. For the first time, the back-to-work legislation offered strikers no job security or interim wage increase. In British Columbia and Alberta, new labor codes were condemned by unions as cutting their bargaining power. Canadian Labour Congress President Shirley Carr led union resistance to the free-trade deal as a threat to Canadian jobs, particularly in unionized sectors. Meanwhile, the unionized share of the Canadian work force continued to slip from its 1982 high of 31.2%, to 29%.

Social Issues. In the International Year of the Homeless, experts claimed that a quarter-million Canadians were badly housed and that a few thousand each night had no homes at all. The paradox was that Canada probably built more and bigger houses in 1987 than ever before, but almost all of them were for middle-class couples with two incomes and few children. Such families mattered increasingly in a Canada with a reviving economy and a shrinking birthrate. Experts agreed that day care was a central issue, but they split on whether it should be run as a profitable business or, as the NDP insisted, as a nonprofit public service like schools.

Canadians wondered about crime and its victims, too. A Calgary jury acquitted a druggist who had shot down a fleeing robber. Three Toronto police went to jail on the testimony of a fourth, after one of them had beaten a witness and the other two had falsified their reports. In Sydney, N.S., a judicial inquiry exposed the police work that had sent a young Micmac Indian to jail for 11 years for a murder he had not committed.

People and Diversions. As usual, a few heroes lifted Canadians out of such sordid preoccupations. On May 22, Rick Hansen ended his two-year, round-the-world wheelchair run, bringing home to Vancouver an image of fortitude, a fiancée, and a few million dollars for spinal-cord research. At the World Track and Field Championships in August, a West Indies-born Toronto athlete, Ben Johnson, confirmed that he was the fastest man in the world by smashing the world record for the 100-meter dash. At the end of the 1986–87 season, the Edmonton Oilers were champions of the National Hockey League. Baseball's Toronto Blue Jays appeared to have won the American League Eastern Division race, but collapsed at season's end. In September, the two best teams in international hockey, the Soviet Union and Canada, met in the finals of the Canada Cup tournament. All three games in the series ended in a score of 6–5, with the home team emerging victorious. It was only one climax in a historic year.

DESMOND MORTON
Erindale College, University of Toronto

The Economy

During 1987 the Canadian economy gave a stellar performance. It grew during the first two quarters of the year at a sparkling annual rate of 6.1%, the highest among the industrialized countries. In August alone, the economy expanded in real terms by 0.8%, double the expansion recorded in July and the strongest monthly growth since February 1987. The growth in August was widespread in both the goods and services sectors. The only major decline was in transportation services because of the one-week nationwide railway strike.

The buoyancy of the economy was reflected by its trading, manufacturing, and housing sectors, In August housing starts climbed to a ten-year peak annual rate of 281,000 before leveling off to 222,000 in October. In the meantime the housing market, with the mortgage rates moving up, slackened. The retail-trade sector, on the other hand, continued to show strength due to increased consumer spending on durable goods. The seasonally adjusted monthly value of retail sales in August rose by 1.8%. However, the decline in households' saving rate from the first quarter's 9.9% of disposable income to 8.8% in the second quarter suggested that consumers might find it difficult to dig deeper into their pockets for sustaining demand for high-ticket items. This was especially true when one considers that over the previous two years, average weekly wages increased by 5%, compared with a 7% annual increase in the Consumer Price Index.

In the corporate sector, the level of business activity remained strong. During the first nine months of 1987, corporate profits for 213 reporting private companies rose 59% to C$8.2 billion. The gain was attributed to outstanding profit performance in key resource sectors. Plunging oil prices forced oil companies to drastically pare costs. These reductions were as lean as those undertaken by the mining and forest companies in 1986. Consequently, 19 oil and gas companies saw their profits soar by 121% to $147 billion over the first nine months of 1987. Seventeen companies in the forestry sector and 22 mining concerns found their profits increased by 100% and 267%, respectively, during the same time period.

Firms operating in the publishing, financial, industrial-products, and telecommunication sectors experienced a period of brisk activity. In September shipments for the manufacturing sector were up for the sixth consecutive month, while new orders increased for the fifth time in six months and the backlog of new unfilled orders hit a record high.

The growth in the foreign-trade sector, where Canada's trade surplus with the rest of the world grew to $8.6 billion during the first nine months of the year as compared with $7.9 billion for the same period in 1986, reflected buoyant economic activity. The surplus with the United States, which accounts for 80% of all Canadian trade, reached $12.5 billion during the first three quarters of the year.

Strong growth in employment was apparent from the beginning of the year. The September unemployment rate declined to 8.6%, the lowest level since January 1982.

R. P. SETH
Mount Saint Vincent University, Halifax

The Arts

In a move designed to cut costs, the Canadian Broadcasting Corporation (CBC), Canada's biggest employer of artists, augmented its fall prime-time schedule by broadcasting a series of reruns. During 1987, in another cost-cutting move, CBC eliminated 325 jobs. Unfortunately, these saving measures were more than wiped out by inflation, which meant that the C$881 million that the corporation received from the federal government for a year's operations would not suffice to maintain the previous year's standard of operations. However, Communications Minister Flora MacDonald still hoped that CBC would somehow be able to increase its Canadian programming content.

Visual Arts. In Ottawa, the National Gallery of Canada held an open house before closing for eight months while its contents were moved to a new C$132 million gallery. The new director of the National Gallery was Shirley Thomson, former secretary general of the Canadian Commission of UNESCO.

The Montreal Museum of Fine Arts mounted a large da Vinci exhibition, entitled "Leonardo da Vinci: Engineer and Architect," comprised of working models of his inventions, technical drawings, and three manuscripts. It was the first time since da Vinci died in 1519 that so many of his works had been shown in one location. The museum drew criticism for issuing some posters that gave the French version of the artist's name, "Leonard de Vinci," instead of the Italian, "Leonardo da Vinci." The Art Gallery of Ontario exhibited the works of Alexander Cozens and his son John Robert Cozens, English landscape water colorists of the 18th century. The Winnipeg Art Gallery celebrated its 75th birthday with exhibitions, notably "1912: Break Up of Tradition," a showing of European paintings of that era, organized by guest curator Louise d'Argencourt.

Willard Holmes, who had been head of exhibitions for the National Gallery of Canada, was appointed director of the Vancouver Art Gallery. He succeeded Jo-Anne Birney Danzker, who resigned for health reasons. The gallery's exhibition, "Recent Acquisitions," showed 190 paintings, sculptures, and photographs. During 1986 and 1987, the gallery spent C$1 million on acquisitions, half of this amount on local art. "Water, Pine and Stone Retreat" was an exhibition of Asian art collected by Hugh Moss of Hong Kong. The People's Republic of China sent an exhibition of the works of Li Kuchan, 1899–1983, a modern artist maintaining the Chinese artistic traditions.

Artist Paul Wong began a second legal action against the Vancouver Art Gallery, claiming that it again had promised to exhibit his work, "Confused: Sexual Views," but then had refused it. Wong lost his original suit in British Columbia Supreme Court in 1986. In his 1987 suit, also in Supreme Court, Wong claimed Scott Watson, former acting director of the gallery, had made a verbal agreement to show his work. His application for an injunction forcing the gallery to present the show was dismissed.

Performing Arts. At Stratford, Ont., the Stratford Festival celebrated its 35th anniversary. Richard Sheridan's *The School for Scandal* was presented; directed by Robin Phillips,

"Leonardo da Vinci: Engineer and Architect," a major exhibition at the Montreal Museum of Fine Arts, brought together the largest-ever collection of the inventions, technical drawings, and illustrated manuscripts by the Renaissance master.

© Bob Mahoney/Picture Group

© Barry Gray, courtesy of National Ballet of Canada

Kim Glasco and Kevin Pugh danced a pas de deux in "Don Quixote" as part of a gala celebration in Toronto marking the 35th anniversary of the National Ballet of Canada.

it starred Sheila McCarthy as Lady Teazle, Douglas Campbell as Sir Oliver Surface, and William Hutt as Sir Peter Teazle. Ralph Manheim's English translation of Bertolt Brecht's antiwar satire *Mother Courage* starred Susan Wright in the title role. The Broadway musical *Cabaret,* directed and choreographed by Brian Macdonald, featured Brent Carver as Master of Ceremonies, Sheila McCarthy as Sally Bowles, and Scott Wentworth as Clifford Bradshaw. Shakespeare's *Othello,* directed by John Neville, proved a personal triumph for Colm Feore as Iago. And Shakespeare's comedy, *Much Ado About Nothing,* was directed by Peter Moss, who chose a Victorian setting.

At Niagara-on-the-Lake, Ont., the Shaw Festival's 26th year scored a hit with *Marathon 33,* June Havoc's play about marathon dancers during the Depression. It starred Camille Mitchell as June and Dan Lett as Patsy. Shaw's *Major Barbara,* directed by Christopher Newton, saw Martha Burns as Barbara and Jim Mezon as Adolphus, with Douglas Rain as Andrew Undershaft. Noel Coward's 1924 play, *Hay Fever,* had Jennifer Phipps as a convincing Judith Bliss.

Richard Ouzounian staged his adaptation of Molière's *Tartuffe* at Halifax's Neptune Theatre, where he is artistic director. He offered it as a political satire on Canadian politics, with Rodger Barton playing Orgon as a cartoon of Prime Minister Brian Mulroney and Walter Borden offering a Tartuffe that suggested President Ronald Reagan.

The new artistic director of the Playhouse Theatre in Vancouver was Guy Sprung. The playhouse's previous director, Walter Learning, resigned to direct the Charlottetown Festival on Prince Edward Island.

At the Charlottetown Festival, Learning raised opposition by choosing as the opening work Alan Bleasdale's musical play *Are You Lonesome Tonight?*, about the life of Elvis Presley. Opponents felt the play had language that was at times obscene, and that it was too great a contrast to *Anne of Green Gables,* which the festival shows yearly. Learning won the day, however, for the expected furor over the language did not develop, and the play's first night earned a standing ovation.

In Halifax, the International Street Performers' Festival drew a large attendance and earned provincial sponsorship for the next festival. Prince Rupert, B.C., opened its new 700-seat Performing Arts Centre, built at a cost of C$4.2 million with almost no funding by the provincial or federal governments. The Festival by the Sea in Saint John, N.B., presented one or more groups from every province and territory in Canada.

The Vancouver Symphony Orchestra, which lost C$600,000 in the previous two seasons, ended its 1987 season with a small surplus, which was to be used to reduce its accumulated debt. The surplus was accomplished by cutting expenses, reducing the season by four weeks, and receiving a grant of C$180,000 from the Canada Council. Conductor Rudolph Barshai, whose contract is up at the end of the 1987–88 season, was opposed by some who felt a new leader was needed.

Celebrating its 35th year, the National Ballet of Canada, founded by Celia Franca, announced the first annual Erik Bruhn Prize for young dancers. Bruhn was artistic director of the National Ballet until his death in 1986.

Film. Canadian filmmaker Brigitte Berman's documentary, *Artie Shaw: Time Is All You've Got,* won an Oscar at the Academy Awards. Canada made a coproduction agreement with Czechoslovakia under which the two countries arranged to share the cost of 12 children's films being made by producer Rock Demers of Quebec. Demers also gained Chinese financial support for his children's film, *Tommy Tricker and the Stamp Traveller,* part of which is to be filmed in China. Montreal's 11th World Film Festival, under its founder, Serge Losique, had a record attendance and featured a tribute to Michael Caine. For the first time a Canadian film, *The Kid Brother,* directed by Claude Gagnon, won the festival's top prize. Toronto's ten-day Festival of Festivals opened with a showing of the Canadian film *I've Heard the Mermaids Singing*.

DAVID SAVAGE, *Free-lance Writer*

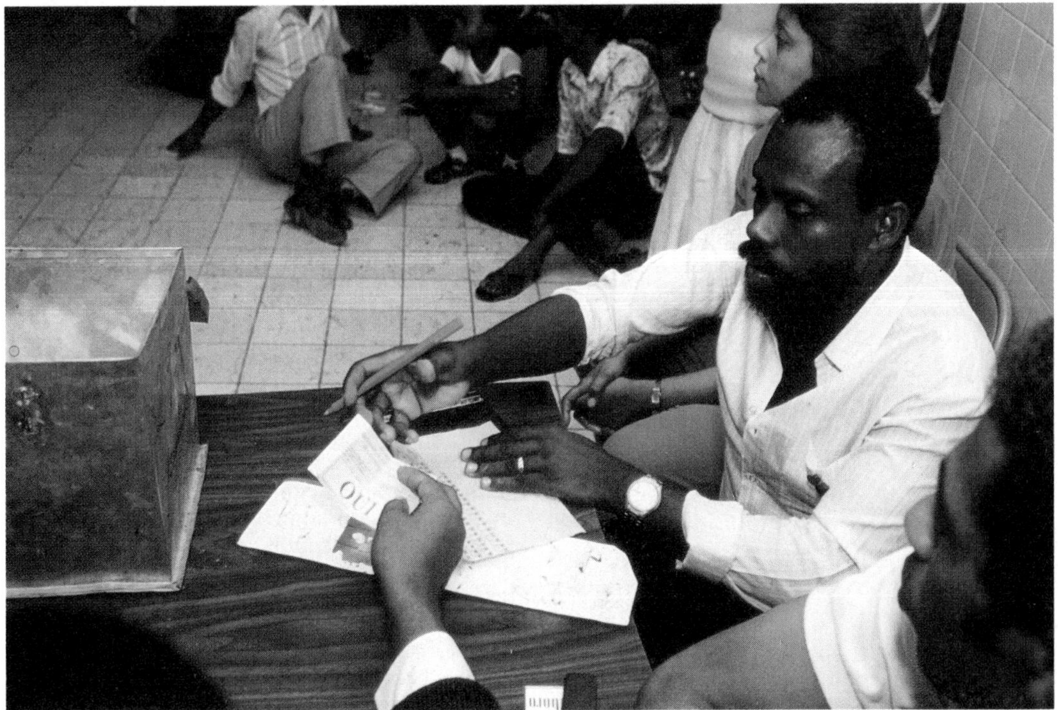

© Dominique Frank Simon/Sygma

In the Caribbean in 1987, the spotlight centered on Haiti. In March, Haitian voters, above, *overwhelmingly approved a new constitution; eight months later, an outbreak of violence led to the cancellation of presidential elections.*

CARIBBEAN

Fresh efforts from both within and outside the Caribbean sought in 1987 to break the grip of the recession that has held the region in thrall throughout the 1980s. In July the heads of government of the Caribbean Economic Community (CARICOM) agreed to create a Caribbean Export Bank to finance intra- and extra-regional trade. In the United States a group of U.S. congressmen, after a fact-finding tour of the Caribbean, introduced a bill to strengthen the Caribbean Basin Initiative (CBI), the Reagan administration's trade-preference plan that gives duty-free entry into the United States for a variety of Caribbean exports. Experts say trade improvements are critical because the Caribbean has been losing ground in its trade performance, despite the duty-free incentives of the CBI. In the first half of 1987, the U.S. Department of Commerce reported, U.S. imports from 22 countries eligible for CBI benefits (including some in Central America) fell by 6.2% from first-half 1986 levels, to $3.22 billion. At the same time, U.S. exports to Basin countries rose by 7%, reversing the worldwide pattern of widening U.S. trade deficits.

Tourism was virtually the only bright spot in an otherwise bleak Caribbean economic panorama in 1987. Tourist arrivals during the first half of the year rose by about 11% over 1986, making this period the "best ever" for the tourism industry, according to the newsletter, *Caribbean Update*. Tourism is second only to agricultural exports in the region and is the mainstay of several Caribbean economies.

Export Bank. The new Caribbean Export Bank will start up with equity capital of $16.7 million, to be provided by the Caribbean Development Bank, member governments of the Caribbean Community, and private sources. CARICOM officials say they will seek additional financing from outside the region.

The Export Bank will provide pre-shipment and post-shipment financing for goods exported from the community as well as for goods traded within the region. Creation of the Bank is expected to help reactivate intra-regional trade, which fell from $550 million in 1980 to $290 million in 1986.

In a further effort to boost trade within the community, the Caribbean leaders agreed to seek to remove trade barriers that have grown up among CARICOM members themselves in recent years. Also under consideration was a common tariff on goods imported into CARICOM from outside the region.

CBI. The proposed U.S. legislation to strengthen the CBI would extend duty-free and quota-free entry into the United States to textiles and apparel produced in CBI-eligible countries. Footwear from the Caribbean also would receive duty-free treatment. Textiles, apparel, and footwear are currently excluded from CBI coverage. The proposed legislation

AP/Wide World

Sir Lynden O. Pindling, prime minister of the Bahamas, dances with supporters during a preelection rally. Pindling's Progressive Liberal Party won a solid mandate June 19.

would also extend the life of the CBI to 2007, twelve years beyond the current expiration date of 1995.

A key provision of the bill would raise Caribbean Basin sugar quotas back up to 1982 levels. The global U.S. sugar quota was cut from more than 5 million tons in 1981 to less than 1 million tons in 1987. The cuts have severely affected Caribbean sugar producers. The quota for the Dominican Republic, for example, was slashed from 302,000 short tons in 1986 to 160,000 tons in 1987, representing a loss of more than $50 million in potential export earnings. To compensate for the loss, the Dominican Republic signed an agreement with the Soviet Union for the sale of up to 100,000 tons of Dominican sugar a year for three years at a guaranteed price of eight cents a pound.

In September a special trade committee of the Organization of American States condemned "the clear trend to cut back sugar import quotas of the region's countries to the United States market, a situation that could result in the collapse of the region's sugar-export industry, and do serious damage to those countries' economies and to the social peace of their peoples."

Unity Push. Members of the Organization of Eastern Caribbean States (OECS), a subregional English-speaking grouping, met in St. Lucia in July to explore the formation of a new unitary political federation. Five of the countries—Dominica, Grenada, St. Christopher and Nevis (St. Kitts), St. Lucia, and St. Vincent and the Grenadines—along with the British colony of Montserrat, agreed to the establishment of a single government for the 550,000 people of the six islands. A seventh OECS member, Antigua, has not committed itself to joining the federation.

The preliminary plan is to submit the federation to a referendum by June 1988, and to bring the new state into being in 1989. OECS officials say a unitary state would give the eastern Caribbean a stronger negotiating position on such matters as the CBI. The OECS is the group that asked U.S. intervention in Grenada in October 1983.

In other significant cooperative action, two treaties aimed at controlling oil spills and other marine and atmospheric pollution in the Caribbean entered into force in May. In addition to the Caribbean countries, signatories of the pact include Britain, France, and the Netherlands, which have dependent territories in the region. Studies show that 7% of the oil produced in the Caribbean area is spilled into the sea.

Politics. Prime Minister Lynden O. Pindling and his Progressive Liberal Party (PLP) won a solid victory in elections in the Bahamas in June. The PLP took 29 of 49 seats in the House of Assembly to extend Pindling's 20-year rule another five years. Pindling and some close associates survived a series of scandals involving drug corruption and trafficking that the opposition Free National Movement (FNM) was unable to exploit.

In St. Lucia, Prime Minister John Compton's ruling United Workers' Party staved off a strong challenge from the opposition St. Lucia Labor Party, winning 9 of the 17 seats in parliament in elections on April 6. In August, Chief Minister John Osborne was returned to power in Montserrat when his People's Liberation Movement captured 4 of 7 seats in the island's parliament. Meanwhile, campaigning began in Jamaica for parliamentary elections scheduled to be held early in 1988. The contest will match incumbent Prime Minister Edward Seaga of the Jamaica Labor Party (JLP) against opposition leader Michael Manley of the People's National Party (PNP). Manley is a former Jamaican prime minister.

Barbados—and the entire Caribbean—suffered a deep loss when Prime Minister Errol Barrow died suddenly on June 1 at the age of 67. Barrow was succeeded as prime minister by his deputy, Erskine Sandiford, 50. Barrow was the architect of Barbadian independence and an apostle of Caribbean unity. He had been reelected prime minister in 1986, after being out of power for ten years.

RICHARD C. SCHROEDER
"Visión" Magazine

Haiti

A crescendo of violence on Nov. 29, 1987, brought about the cancellation of Haiti's first free presidential elections in 30 years and cast a pall over plans to return the country to democratic rule on Feb. 7, 1988, the second anniversary of the overthrow of longtime dictator Jean-Claude Duvalier.

Under a constitution overwhelmingly approved by Haiti's voters on March 29, an independent Provisional Electoral Council (CEP) had been appointed to organize and supervise local and national elections, including the November balloting for a president. The preelectoral period was marked by frequent street demonstrations against the country's provisional ruling body, the National Council of Government (CNG), and by violent clashes between protestors and police and army troops.

In June, the CNG, headed by Lt. Gen. Henri Namphy, the army chief of staff under Duvalier, attempted to take control of the electoral process from the CEP but backed down under pressure from protest marches and prodding by the Catholic Church and foreign governments. At the time, Namphy said the CNG would support the organizing work of the CEP and the army would provide the security.

On November 2, the CEP rejected the presidential candidacies of 12 men who had been associated with the dictatorship of Jean-Claude Duvalier and his father, François. (One of the most discussed provisions of the constitution approved in March had been the article banning close associates of the Duvaliers and key members of their regime from participating in Haitian public life for ten years.) That night, arsonists burned down the CEP headquarters in Port-au-Prince, Haiti's capital. Later there were attacks on five other election facilities in the capital and six in the countryside and on the homes of election officials; candidates' homes were raked by gunfire and bombs. A leading presidential candidate, Yves Volel, already had been assassinated in October on the steps of the Port-au-Prince police headquarters. Police and soldiers stood by and watched as much of the violence took place.

When voters lined up to cast their ballots on the morning of November 29, many of them were attacked by roving bands of armed men, widely believed to be former members of the Tontons Macoute, the dreaded Duvalier paramilitary secret police, which was disbanded but not disarmed after the dictator's ouster. Newsmen and international observers of the election reported that the attackers were joined, in some cases, by soldiers and riot police in firing indiscriminately into the voting lines. At least 34 people were killed and 60 others wounded in the attacks.

Within a few hours, the CNG suspended the elections and later dissolved the CEP. Subsequently, the CNG set a new date for elections, Jan. 17, 1988, and appointed a new electoral commission composed of government employees, teachers, and lawyers, whose independence was challenged by opposition parties. Four of the front-running contenders in the aborted November elections, Marc Bazin, Sylvio Claude, Louis Dejoie, and Gerard Gourgue, immediately announced they would boycott the January balloting. Bazin, a former World Bank economist, had returned from exile to run for president. The other three had been prominent opponents of the Duvalier regime.

On December 19, the CNG issued a new decree tightening its control over the January elections. The law prohibits "unjustified" challenges to the qualifications of candidates, a move to prevent the disqualification of Duvalier-linked figures. The law also provides penalties for anyone who urges abstention from voting, bars independent observers from polling places, and allows the army to enter voting sites to scrutinize ballots.

Although an international observer group, several U.S. Congressmen, and leading U.S. newspapers urged outside intervention, such as an Inter-American Peace Force, in Haiti, to guarantee free elections, the international community was largely opposed to such action. The Permanent Council of the Organization of American States (OAS) urged the provisional government to respect the constitution and provide electoral security, but it stressed the principal of nonintervention and said no OAS member should interfere "directly or indirectly" in Haitian affairs. A group of "concerned Caribbean leaders," led by Jamaican Prime Minister Edward Seaga, met with Namphy in Port-au-Prince on December 10 and issued a joint statement supporting the revised electoral schedule and the formation of the new electoral council.

By the end of 1987, it seemed apparent that if elections were indeed held on Jan. 17, 1988, and a new government installed on February 7, Haiti would remain under the control of the army and former Duvalier associates, and violent manifestations of discontent would in all likelihood continue unabated.

RICHARD C. SCHROEDER

© A. Robles/JB Pictures

A breakthrough in the Central American peace process came on August 7, when five presidents—left to right, *Daniel Ortega of Nicaragua, José Napoleón Duarte of El Salvador, Marco Vinicio Cerezo of Guatemala, José Azcona of Honduras, and Oscar Arias of Costa Rica—signed a sweeping regional accord in Guatemala City. Arias was the plan's main architect.*

CENTRAL AMERICA

The most significant development in Central America during 1987 was the signing of a regional peace treaty in Guatemala City on August 7 by the presidents of Costa Rica, Guatemala, El Salvador, Honduras, and Nicaragua. The document was the consummation of months of discussion, often held amid bitter political feelings about some of the issues. The driving force was Costa Rica's President Oscar Arias Sánchez (*see* BIOGRAPHY), who sought to supplant the earlier negotiations of the so-called Contadora group (Colombia, Mexico, Panama, and Venezuela) with Central American efforts. In brief, the treaty called for: periodic free elections; an end to outside military aid to insurrectionary forces (including the Nicaraguan contras); cease-fire negotiations; amnesties; reductions in armed forces; and promotion of "pluralistic democracies." The treaty was given a boost in October, when President Arias was awarded the 1987 Nobel Peace Prize.

November 7 was set as the deadline for implementing the treaty, but that date proved too early, and the target was changed to January 1988. Some elements of the treaty stood in opposition to U.S. policy, and the Reagan administration faced the dilemma of supporting Central America or appearing to oppose peace. Compromise seemed likely, and in November, U.S. Secretary of State George Shultz announced that to give the treaty every chance the administration would not ask for additional military aid for the contras until 1988. The five regional presidents planned to put the enforcement procedures into the hands of a number of commissions. By the end of the year, a few steps toward implementation had been taken, but the contras were still active, and peace had not been secured.

A long and bitter investigation by the U.S. Congress revealed that much private aid had been illegally transferred to the contras. Former members of the National Security Council admitted lying to Congress and running what amounted to their own foreign policy. (*See* feature article, page 26.)

The Reagan war against Communism in the Caribbean brought unexpected results that could prove dangerous for Central America in the long term. While there were some fledgling civilian governments, they were all propped up with varying degrees of U.S. support. Reagan policy had brought a 15-fold increase in military aid to the region and a doubling of army size from 1981 to 1986. The question arose whether the United States can help the creation of democratic regimes by strengthening the armed forces of states in which the military has always meant the antithesis of democracy.

Belize

Fortunate to remain outside the strife of so much of Central America, Belize changed little in 1987. Prime Minister Manuel Esquivel and his United Democratic Party concentrated on developing the infant economy and reducing its dependency on Great Britain, the former mother country. Many Belizeans feared that the tiny republic might become just as dependent on the United States now that political freedom is a reality. In addition, Belize struggled to recover from the recession of the early 1980s, which damaged the price of several of its staple agricultural products, such as coffee, sugar, and bananas. Belize's reliance on sugar for more than one half of its foreign exchange became increasingly risky, as the United States reduced its purchase of that crop by about 40%.

Belize's gross domestic product (GDP) has remained static for nearly seven years, averaging about $850 per capita annually. The nation is very dependent on foreign trade, importing much expensive fuel and food and doing little manufacturing. To cut government expenses and raise revenue, the administration has sold a number of government enterprises to private interests.

The U.S. economic presence is substantial in Belize. The United States is the chief trading partner and provides more economic assistance per capita to Belize than to any other nation except Israel. Military aid for 1987 amounted to $600,000, and Great Britain still maintained some 1,800 troops in the republic.

The opposition United Democratic Party complained of the heavy influx of American diplomats, businessmen, and Peace Corps volunteers and may make it an issue in the next elections. But U.S. investment is sorely needed, and the opportunities remain very favorable, especially with the tax breaks provided by the Belize government. Among the major recent investors are Hershey Foods, which grows cacao for cocoa and chocolate; a new syndicate which bought 700,000 acres (283 280 ha) of land near the Guatemala border, probably for cattle raising; and the World Bank, which invested $12 million in an important power transmission project.

Costa Rica

Almost from the day of his inauguration in February 1986, Costa Rica's President Oscar Arias Sánchez has been leading Central American efforts to bring peace to the region. Traditionally Costa Rica has maintained a position of neutrality, or even isolationism, in Central American affairs to avoid the strife so common to its neighbors. Arias has preserved that neutrality but moved Costa Rica from isolationism to a leadership role in the region. Decrying military solutions, Arias refused to let the United States use airstrips in Costa Rica to supply the Nicaraguan contras, even though Costa Rica's own relations with the Sandinista regime remained cool.

At home some of Arias' political opponents found fault with his peace efforts on the grounds that he was ignoring more pressing domestic problems. Critics agreed that he was very popular but charged him with careless administration. The National Housing Institute fell far behind in its program and was alleged to be riddled with corruption; its director resigned. Also during the year, two foreign-service officers were caught smuggling gold and had to be dismissed.

Because Costa Rica relies heavily on foreign aid, mostly from the United States, Arias' neutrality in Central American affairs brought much pressure—though no less financial help—from Washington. The nation during 1987 continued to face a serious fiscal imbalance, which the government sought to reduce through ongoing stabilization efforts and the rescheduling of debts. But export declines threatened the debt repayment program; coffee prices were down again; the U.S. sugar quota was reduced; bananas lost some of their European market; and the regional strife meant a continuing decline in exports to the Central American Common Market.

The rate of population increase has slowed, but new difficulties were brought about by rapid urbanization. In 1987, the population of Costa Rica was nearly one half urban. Since there is little farmland left for expansion, the growing cities will have to be fed by increasing imports or more intensive agriculture. Either alternative is costly. To improve farm output, a number of major projects were under way during 1987. Experimental irrigation brought water to thousands of acres in Guanacaste province. Some 1,600 families were resettled on land near the Panama border. Combined Japanese and Inter-American Bank funds built a new geothermal power plant. The coast-to-coast highway neared completion, and hundreds of miles of farm road were being upgraded. But the per capita gross national product again was lower than in 1980. Many Costa Ricans placed their hopes for the country in a manufacturing boom, since the work force is more educated than in any other nation in the region.

El Salvador

Probably no nation faced the prospect of more damage from the U.S. Immigration Reform and Control Act of 1986 than El Salvador. According to President José Napoleón Duarte, between 400,000 and 600,000 Salvadorans had illegally entered the United States since January 1982 and would be subject to deportation under the terms of the legislation. Duarte asserted that the remigration of these people would add dangerously to the nation's unemployment rolls and, perhaps more critically, reduce significantly the estimated $500 million that the migrant workers send home each year. He asked the United States for an exemption from the law, but was denied.

Squeezed from both sides, President Duarte continued to pursue a middle road in domestic affairs during 1987. Early in the year Rightist businessmen called a general strike and pressured him to resign, and the right-wing National Conciliation Party refused to participate in legislative debates or votes for three months. In late March the left-wing national labor union joined the calls for Duarte's resignation.

Salvadoran troops continued to battle Leftist guerrilla rebels throughout the year. In an attack on a key army base in March, the guerrillas killed some 60 government soldiers and a U.S. adviser, the first to die in combat in El Salvador. By August the rebels had stepped up their urban campaign for the first time in several years.

To cope with the unrest, the government announced sweeping social and economic reforms for Duarte's final two years in office. His popularity had slipped to about 30% in the polls, but the measures were expected to be passed because of his party's majority in the legislative assembly. Duarte's party, the Christian Democrats, for the first time was charged with significant wrongdoing, including smuggling, the sale of government property on the black market, and easy tax evasion. However, the U.S. State Department reported that human-rights violations had been cut from more than 5,000 in 1981 to fewer than 300 in 1986.

Duarte clung to office in part because of U.S. sufferance. Economic aid from Washington amounted to about $1.3 million per day, an important reason why the Salvadoran military has remained loyal to the president. The military numbered 56,000 in 1987, four times its size in the early 1980s. The United States also gave some $50 million to relieve suffering from the severe earthquake of October 1986. That emergency was well handled, but little has been achieved in solving the fundamental problem of poverty. Some of the wealthy were seeking the president's removal because they were being taxed for the first time. The land-reform program remained alive but far from successful. The earthquake harmed some manufacturing and led to a greater trade deficit within the Central American Common Market. The per capita GDP declined in 1986–87.

During the last months of the year, in accordance with the proposed regional peace treaty, President Duarte let the state of siege lapse, and the National Assembly enacted a new amnesty law that absolved most groups of political crimes; about 700 political prisoners were released. However, the law prohibited the investigation or prosecution of government troops accused of killing civilians. Duarte then decreed a unilateral, limited cease-fire. The government met with the rebels several times, as required by the treaty, but little was accomplished. Ominously, the army declared its opposition to the peace treaty.

Guatemala

In January 1987, Marco Vinicio Cerezo Arévalo completed his first year as president of Guatemala. His surprising victory at the polls had been achieved in part because of the passive role of the army, weakened in the public's eye by the economic crisis of 1985. During his first year in office, Cerezo did little to antagonize the military. He supported better police work, abolished a security agency, and promised to end human-rights violations, but he kept the army quiet by ignoring the matter of the estimated 38,000 Guatemalans who had disappeared under previous regimes.

In other matters, the president was strongly on the side of social justice, encouraging labor movements and putting few restraints on public demonstrations. But, if anything, Cerezo has a narrower line to walk than does President Duarte of El Salvador. Guatemala gets much less help from the United States—only $2 million in military aid during 1987. The land distribution pattern is probably the worst in Latin America, with perhaps 3% of the farm families holding 80% of the arable land and 90% of the farmers having plots too small to support a family. Land reform is a major demand of Guatemalan peasants, but Cerezo's tenuous control over the army barred him from making any drastic changes. In October he pushed through a package of tax laws, and business responded with a three-day strike against government waste and corruption. Few groups supported his effort to have business begin paying its share of the social debt, but the taxes remained in effect, at least temporarily. Curiously, while Guatemala's first democratic government in a generation has been able to reduce political violence sharply, the decline in the military pres-

CENTRAL AMERICA • Information Highlights

Nation	Population (in Millions)	Area (sq mi)	Area (km^2)	Capital	Head of State and Government
Belize	0.2	8,865	22 960	Belmopan	Minita Gordon, governor-general Manuel Esquivel, prime minister
Costa Rica	2.8	19,575	50 700	San José	Oscar Arias Sánchez, president
El Salvador	5.3	8,124	21 040	San Salvador	José Napoleón Duarte, president
Guatemala	8.4	42,042	108 890	Guatemala City	Marco Vinicio Cerezo Arévalo, president
Honduras	4.7	43,278	112 090	Tegucigalpa	José Azcona Hoyo, president
Nicaragua	3.5	50,193	130 000	Managua	José Daniel Ortega Saavedra, president
Panama	2.3	29,760	77 080	Panama City	Eric Arturo Delvalle, president

ence has resulted in a great increase in random crime, such as theft and assault, and the murder rate has doubled since 1985.

One potentially overwhelming problem that arose late in 1987 had to do with the thousands of Guatemalan Indians who had gone to Mexico in the early 1980s to escape civil war, draft, or persecution for their presumed support of the guerrillas. As the prospects for peace in Guatemala became more likely, many of those still in Mexico—estimated by the Catholic Church at more than 150,000—wanted to return home. The first few hundred who repatriated were rumored to have been treated badly, while some were arrested on charges of having been guerrillas. The rate of return declined sharply, as the Indians wondered if it were safe to come out of asylum; many of them had no home left in Guatemala. At first the Guatemalan military wanted them to stay in Mexico but later agreed to let them return and stay in army-run "model villages." Often this left the Indians totally dependent on the army, which would not let them farm, move about, or even talk to UN representatives. The government program was less punitive than the army's but encountered many problems; little food was available, and few funds could be found to tide the refugees over until crops could be raised.

The Central American peace plan called for a cease-fire and talks with rebels in Guatemala as well as in Nicaragua and El Salvador. The Cerezo government met with the guerrillas in early October, but little progress was made. Later that month, also in compliance with the peace plan, the Congress passed an amnesty law, but the fighting continued.

Honduras

One unexpected consequence of the installation of a civilian government in Honduras in 1986 was the lack of experience of many officials. In the National Assembly, for example, it was discovered that two thirds of the delegates had no legislative experience. In an unusual assistance plan during 1987, a number of assemblymen were brought to Vermont to watch the state legislature in action. While the new Honduran government seemed reasonably free of corruption and violence, the nation generally expects the military to make the important decisions and see that they are executed.

Much of the power of the military is due to U.S. financial aid. Military assistance in 1987 was about ten times higher than in 1981, while the size of the army doubled during that same period. In spite of the many peace efforts, Honduras' role in the Nicaraguan civil war has remained unchanged, a factor which often determines domestic developments and deprives Honduras of much of its own decision-making power. In 1987, for example, the United States was building a road from Jocon to Tegucigalpa whose usefulness would be almost entirely military.

Large numbers of U.S. National Guardsmen served brief tours of duty in Honduras during 1987. About 700 paratroopers spent two weeks there in February, and in the spring operations "Pegasus" and "Solid Shield" brought thousands of Americans for maneuvers near Trujillo. These combined air and marine assaults were the largest ever held in Honduras; they included 15 ships and the 101st Airborne Division. All told, the United States has spent more than $4 million on base construction for its 1,100 troops regularly stationed in Honduras.

From the beginnings of the contra movement, Nicaraguan rebels and refugees have established themselves along the border in Honduran territory, reasonably safe from Sandinista attacks. Local Hondurans have become irritated by this growing presence, while the government has tolerated it as the price for U.S. aid. In August 1987, however, after a number of incidents in which the Nicaraguans were charged with stealing crops and firewood, the Honduran military placed troops around one camp, not permitting the 7,000 Nicaraguans to leave without permission. New camps have been added to accommodate the crowds of refugees, estimated at 50,000 (including Salvadorans and Guatemalans).

President José Azcona Hoyo was among the signers of the regional peace plan, one clause of which required a government pledge to prevent Nicaraguan contras from waging war from within Honduran borders. Under the agreement all Nicaraguans were to leave Honduras by January 1988, a development which grew increasingly unlikely as the date approached.

Meanwhile, Honduras continued to live on U.S. aid and the sale of bananas and coffee—all of which were shaky sources of revenue. The nation's overall economic outlook, according to the Inter-American Development Bank, was discouraging. The coffee market was shrinking, and fuel costs began rising again. The economy was growing, but not so fast as the population. Inflation, however, was under better control than in the rest of Central America.

Nicaragua

After two years of discussion, dozens of town meetings, and six months of drafting, Nicaragua adopted a new constitution in January 1987. Many of its most liberal elements, however, such as freedom of expression and assembly, were nullified by the continuing state of emergency, generally in effect since 1982. About 1,000 persons protested the continuance of martial law, but many more thousands

Despite the signing of the peace agreement, the bloody civil war in Nicaragua raged on. Right: *A funeral procession is held for a young Sandinista conscript killed in action. Family members refused to drape a flag over the coffin as an act of protest against his call-up.* Below: *Contra forces ferry military supplies in a chopper disguised with a Red Cross insignia.*

© Peter Jordan/"Time" Magazine

© Bill Gentile/Picture Group

cheered the promulgation of the new document.

The unity of the contra movement was strained by disputes among its leaders. Under U.S. pressure, a common front called the United Nicaraguan Opposition had been created in 1986, to be led by Adolfo Calero, Arturo Cruz, and Alfonso Robelo. Early in 1987, however, the latter two complained that Calero would not share power, and they forced his resignation. Then in March, Cruz also resigned, saying that he was being ignored. Thus for the opposition, agreeing on a representative to the four-member National Reconciliation Commission called for by the regional peace plan proved almost impossible. The only commission member actively opposing the Sandinistas was Miguel Cardinal Obando y Bravo.

The peace treaty created much uncertainty in Nicaragua. President Daniel Ortega insisted that his government would meet the terms of the agreement, but the opposition wanted quicker action. Although the government established unilateral cease-fire zones in small, isolated areas, hundreds of men were killed in combat after the August 7 treaty signing. The Catholic radio station was allowed to resume broadcasting, but it still could not report the news. Two priests were allowed to return from exile, but many others were not. Antigovernment demonstrations were the most numerous since 1979, but some were suppressed. Opposition political parties were allowed to hold rallies, and the U.S.-supported opposition newspaper *La Prensa* was permitted considerable freedom in criticizing the government. But the required amnesty for some 4,000 prisoners was not implemented, though the Sandinistas did promise amnesty to any rebels who would lay down their arms. All in all, the months after the treaty signing saw little change in political conditions in Nicaragua.

Carrying out the preliminary steps by the original November 7 deadline proved problematic in Nicaragua's case because of U.S. opposition to portions of the treaty. President Ortega wanted to talk with the United States; President Reagan wanted him to talk with the contras. Both positions had been firm for many years, but by late 1987 signs of softening appeared as each president sought outside support. The November 7 deadline passed with few consequences, and the Central American presidents spoke of January 1988 as the "true" deadline. In November, Ortega addressed the Organization of American States and, to the annoyance of the Reagan administration, met with some members of the U.S. Congress.

Nicaragua in 1987 moved to break its long-standing reliance on Pacific Coast ports for

© Murillo/Sygma

Panamanians took to the streets during the summer to protest alleged election fraud, murder, and other abuses by the nation's powerful military leadership. The regime responded by suspending constitutional guarantees.

receiving goods from Europe. With Communist-bloc financing, work was begun on a deepwater port at El Bluff on the Caribbean coast, ultimately to be linked with Managua by highway. At midyear, however, the Soviet Union significantly reduced its economic aid to Nicaragua, including a 40% cut in oil. President Ortega announced wage and price hikes to boost the economy, cut government oil consumption by 5%, and sought supplies of fuel from Eastern European countries and Mexico.

From 1984 to 1987, amid rampant speculation and black marketeering, Nicaragua's consumer price index rose 700%. By year's end 1987, it was expected to reach 800%. Salaries were raised 30%, but the cost of most basic foods rose more. The price of gasoline increased 400%.

Panama

While it has remained largely aloof from the civil struggles pervading the rest of Central America and was not party to the latest treaty discussions, Panama has its own problems. Throughout 1987 the very integrity of the tiny state was in jeopardy. In June retired Col. Roberto Diaz Herrera claimed to have proof that the nation's armed-forces chief and former de facto leader, Gen. Manuel Antonio Noriega, had rigged the 1984 presidential election, planned the murder of a political opponent, and been responsible for the death of Panamanian leader Gen. Omar Torrijos in 1981.

As a consequence of these charges, demonstrations and strikes occurred almost daily throughout much of the year. Noriega supporters in the legislature claimed that Panama's oligarchy promoted the unrest to provoke the United States into setting aside the treaty which turns the canal over to Panama in the year 2000. During the summer, after President Eric Arturo Delvalle suspended portions of the constitution and the U.S. embassy was attacked with rocks and paint, the U.S. Senate passed a resolution calling for Noriega's resignation, and the Reagan administration suspended military and economic aid. Other actions by the Panamanian regime included the temporary shutdown of opposition newspapers and the University of Panama. In August, Colonel Diaz and several of his associates were arrested; others fled the country. The turmoil caused foreign investors to withdraw some $1 billion from Panama banks. The archbishop, Marcos Gregorio McGrath, called the government corrupt, and U.S. officials linked Noriega with the international drug trade. Business stagnated, raising unemployment to 50% in the province of Colón.

Panama receives about $75 million in tolls from the 12,000 ships using the canal each year, but there has been increasing competition from containerized rail transit across the United States. During 1987 a joint U.S.-Japanese-Panamanian commission studied ways to improve the canal, build a new one, or find alternative ways of moving freight across the isthmus. Of Panama's $5 billion annual gross product, more than 10% comes from the expenditures of 10,000 military and civilian personnel residing in the Canal Zone. The living standard in Panama is higher than in most of Central America, but world lending agencies have asked for stricter austerity to help repay huge debts.

See also CARIBBEAN.

THOMAS L. KARNES
Arizona State University

CHAD

Military success against Libya and the collapse of opposition to President Hissein Habré's government in 1987 moved Chad closer to being a unified state than at any time in the two decades of civil war.

Domestic Developments. The main opposition to Habré's rule had been the Transitional Government of National Unity (GUNT), a coalition of various factions supported by Libya. Led by former President Goukouni Oueddi, GUNT forces at one time controlled a number of key points in northern Chad and posed a considerable threat to Habré.

Libya's role in GUNT provoked dissention in the organization. When Oueddi in late 1986 indicated his willingness to negotiate with Habré, Libyan President Muammar el-Qaddafi placed Oueddi under arrest in Tripoli. Qaddafi then supported Acheikh Ibn Omar of the Democratic Revolutionary Council (CDR) as the chief Chadian opponent to Habré. By mid-1987 the CDR military units within Chad were estimated at only 1,000 men; Habré's reconciliation policy was advanced by other GUNT leaders who had joined him.

Factionalism, which had all but destroyed Chad's economy, was thus brought under control. France guaranteed the security of the southern sections of Chad with 1,500 troops, missile battalions, and aircraft. Life for the average citizen in the more productive central and southern sections returned to normal. Cotton production, the mainstay export, exceeded 1975 levels.

Foreign Affairs. Crucial in 1987 was the escalation of the war with Libya, which for a decade played a dominant role in the civil war. Military and economic support for Habré's government from Zaire, the United States, and particularly France increased, enabling Habré to plan a major offensive. In January an outnumbered Chadian force overran the Fada Oasis in the Faya-Largeau region, killing more than 1,000 Libyans and capturing much equipment, especially tanks. In March, Chad ousted Libya from its main fortress at Wadi Doum in northern Chad. Habré's goal was to drive the estimated 10,000 foreign troops from the Aozou strip in northernmost Chad, which had been occupied and annexed by Libya in 1975.

Against French advice, Habré took the offensive once again in August. Trying to minimize their direct involvement, the French wanted Habré to concede the area above the 16th parallel. Chadian army units, however, routed a Libyan column headed toward Ounianga-Kebir and invaded Libya for the first time. After heavy fighting they took the air base of Matan at Sarra 60 mi (100 km) inside Libya on September 6. The Chadians claimed to have killed some 1,700 Libyans.

The invasion of Libya brought the conflict into the open on an international level. Habré, fortified with his successful reconciliation policy and the open backing of the United States and continued support from France, had upset the precarious balance in the north and was prepared to accept nothing but capitulation from Qaddafi. On October 11, however, both Chad and Libya accepted a cease-fire brokered by Zambia's President Kenneth Kaunda, the chairman of the Organization of African Unity.

HARRY A. GAILEY
San Jose State University

CHAD • Information Highlights

Official Name: Republic of Chad.
Location: North-Central Africa.
Area: 495,753 sq mi (1 284 000 km²).
Population: (mid-1987 est.): 4,600,000.
Chief City: Ndjamena, the capital.
Government: *Head of state and government,* Hissein Habré, president (seized control June 7, 1982).
Monetary Unit: CFA franc (308.55 CFA francs equal U.S.$1, July 1987).

Chadian troops returned victorious from major offensives against Libya in January, March, and August-September. In the latter confrontation, the Chadian forces repelled an advancing column and overran an air base inside Libyan territory.

CHEMISTRY

Developments in chemistry in 1987 included the creation of magnetic polymers, advances in cluster chemistry, and isotopic separation techniques. Excitement was generated by the discovery of higher-temperature superconducting materials (*see* special report, page 427).

Magnetic Polymers. Polymers are the so-called giant molecules upon which the plastics industry is based. Along with most common materials they do not normally exhibit ferromagnetism, the permanent magnetism associated with iron and a few other metals. Ferromagnetism depends on the mutual alignment of electron spins: most common materials have their spins paired up so that they cancel one another. Thus great interest was aroused in 1987 when research groups in the Soviet Union and the United States independently reported the creation of ferromagnetic organic polymers—in effect, "plastic magnets." The Soviet workers produced polymers from subunits containing carbon, nitrogen, oxygen, and hydrogen. The Americans, from the IBM Almaden Research Center in San Jose, CA, polymerized triaminobenzene and iodine. The ferromagnetism of both polymers persisted at temperatures well above room temperature. In both cases the yields of ferromagnetic materials were quite low and the products were difficult to characterize, but the hope exists that such materials may eventually replace metals in some applications.

Cluster Chemistry. Cluster compounds are aggregates of metals and other elements that often have useful properties. Developments in cluster chemistry were highlighted at an international conference on the subject held in West Germany. Much attention was focused on the catalytic properties of clusters, since catalysts can have great commercial value. Advanced cluster catalysts were described for the formation of aldehydes from olefins and for the production of polyethylene plastics. A new cluster catalyst also was described for the production of hydrocarbons from synthesis gas (carbon monoxide and hydrogen). Unlike earlier systems, the catalyst was not destroyed by the presence of sulfur in the gas, and the product contained a high proportion of useful two- and three-carbon compounds.

Chemists at the University of Illinois, Chicago, reported the synthesis of a new, large bimetallic cluster. Containing both gold and silver, it was the second-largest metal cluster to be characterized. Large clusters may help shed light on the transition from single-atom to bulk metallic behavior.

Isotopes. Isotopes are forms of the same element which have different masses. They are difficult to separate because their chemical properties are usually identical and their physical properties tend to be similar. Late in 1986 a research group at Illinois State University described a new and efficient method for separating isotopes. The method depends on the discovery that the abilities of certain compounds to attract electrons depend on the isotopes they contain. In liquid ammonia, for example, nitrobenzene molecules containing nitrogen-15 atoms attract electrons better than do those with nitrogen-14 atoms. Salts can be formed from the negative species (anions) generated, and these salts can be separated from the residual nitrobenzene. By repeating the process several times, a product highly enriched in nitrogen-15 can be produced. Suitable techniques for enriching carbon and hydrogen isotopes also have been discovered.

Isotopes provide a standard way to identify the influence of the phenomenon of tunneling on chemical reaction rates. Tunneling is a curious, quantum-mechanical effect, somewhat analogous to exiting a room by passing through a wall. According to quantum theory, a finite probability exists that a particle will pass *through* a potential energy barrier that, in terms of classical physics, it lacks the energy to pass over. Lighter particles penetrate barriers more readily than heavier particles, hence the isotope effect. A research group at the University of Illinois, Chicago, reported results on tunneling in the reaction of oxygen atoms with hydrogen molecules, comparing rates of product formation for the hydrogen isotopes H (protium) and D (deuterium). At lower temperatures fewer reactant atoms possess sufficient energy to pass over the barrier, so tunneling (which is insensitive to temperature) should become relatively more important. As expected, the Chicago workers observed that at lower temperatures the ratio of the H to D rates increased.

Other. Nuclear chemists at the Lawrence Berkeley Laboratories in California announced that they had succeeded in measuring some of the chemical properties of element 105, a transuranium element created by bombarding the element berkelium with oxygen ions. Measurements had to be made quickly since the element is unstable, decaying to half its original amount in just 35 seconds. The California workers concluded that the element's chemical behavior conforms to that expected from its position in the periodic table.

Chemists continued their efforts to duplicate the rate-enhancing properties and selectivities of nature's own catalysts, the enzymes. DuPont scientists reported partial success in employing iron and porous zeolite materials to catalyze the oxidation of alkanes. High selectivities for certain useful reactions were obtained with these completely inorganic enzyme mimics. The problem remains of how to extract the products, which tend to be trapped in the zeolite cavities.

PAUL G. SEYBOLD, *Wright State University*

© 1987 Wayne Cable/Cable Studios

The $35-million Terra Museum of American Art opened April 21 on Chicago's fashionable North Michigan Avenue. The outside design features a vertical glass and white marble facade. The museum's collection includes some 800 works valued at more than $250 million.

CHICAGO

Harold Washington, the first black to serve as mayor of Chicago, died Nov. 25, 1987, after suffering a heart attack at his desk in City Hall. The 65-year-old Democrat, who was elected Chicago's mayor in 1983, had served in the state legislature and the U.S. House of Representatives. More than 500,000 persons paid their respects as the mayor's body lay in state, and nearly 4,000 persons attended his funeral.

Earlier in the year, Mayor Washington had become Chicago's first mayor to win reelection since Richard J. Daley in 1973. Mayor Washington turned back strong challenges by former Mayor Jane Byrne in the February 24 Democratic primary and by his principal city council foe, Alderman Edward Vrdolyak, who ran as an independent in the April 7 general elections. Washington captured 53.3% of the vote in the general election, to 41.6% for Vrdolyak and 4.2% for Republican Donald Haider.

For the first time, Washington supporters also won control of the city council. The mayor's forces captured control of 27 of the city council seats, and many aldermen formerly loyal to Vrdolyak changed their allegiance to the mayor. In September, Vrdolyak joined the Republican Party amid speculation that he would seek countywide office under that banner. Vrdolyak had been chairman of the Democratic Party of Cook County.

On December 2, Alderman Eugene Sawyer, the longest-serving black member of the city council, was selected as the city's acting mayor. After much political infighting, he defeated Alderman Timothy Evans, Mayor Washington's floor leader in the city council. Although the 53-year-old Sawyer was an early Washington supporter, he also remained friendly with forces loyal to the late Mayor Daley. A special election for a full four-year term would be held in 1989.

Floods. Overnight rains of as much as 10 inches (25 cm) in parts of Cook County left Chicago and its suburbs in a sea of water on August 15. Thousands of homes were flooded, expressways were closed, and air travelers were left stranded at O'Hare International Airport when highway and rail arteries were covered by water. The flash flooding left an estimated $200 million in damage in Cook and DuPage counties, and President Ronald Reagan declared parts of those counties a federal disaster area. The 9.35 inches (24 cm) of rain recorded in Chicago proper on August 14 and 15 was an all-time record for the city in 24 hours.

Courts. Federal investigations continued to result in the indictment and conviction of political figures, including city officials, judges, and even a former Illinois governor. Dan Walker, a maverick Democrat who served as governor from 1973 to 1977 and had dreams of the White House, pleaded guilty in federal court to improperly receiving $1.4 million in loans. The money was used to finance a chain of quick-oil-change franchises and for Walker's lavish lifestyle, which included an 80-ft (24-m) yacht named *Governor's Lady*. Walker said that he did not benefit personally from the transactions but offered no excuses.

Teacher Strike. The opening of the 1987–88 school year was delayed four weeks, as Chicago teachers went on strike over pay and class size. Agreement on a two-year contract was reached October 3, and the city's 430,000 public school students returned to class days later.

ROBERT ENSTAD, *"Chicago Tribune"*

© Eric Brissaud/Gamma-Liaison

On his way to Chile on March 31, Pope John Paul II denounced the regime there as "dictatorial." The following day, the pontiff was greeted in Santiago by President Augusto Pinochet, who declared that his military rule was necessary to save the country from "the hate, lies, and death culture" of Communism.

CHILE

Amid speculation that the government of Gen. Augusto Pinochet Ugarte would call a plebiscite to choose a presidential candidate in early 1988 instead of 1989, opposition parties began efforts to register millions of voters. Higher copper prices and agricultural exports marked an improved economic climate.

The Plebiscite. According to the 1980 constitution written by the four-member military junta, the junta will propose a single presidential nominee to stand for an eight-year term in a yes-or-no referendum in 1989. Opposition forces want a general election without a plebiscite, but have been unable to fashion a credible alternative.

Patricio Aylwin, newly elected leader of the Christian Democratic Party (PDC), and leaders of other political parties hoped that by registering 5 million of an estimated 8 million eligible voters, honest elections would be assured, and the nomination of General Pinochet rejected. By late October some 2.9 million Chileans had been issued new identity cards and registered. Aylwin called upon the armed forces to promote constitutional reforms that would guarantee free elections and equal time for competing candidates on the government-controlled television stations.

A law legalizing the formation of non-leftist political parties went into effect March 11. The law regulated the symbols and slogans parties can adopt as well as their internal organization, made it illegal for them to accept funding from foreign sources, and banned members of the military from becoming party members. In October, the junta stripped convicted Marxists of the right to free speech and empowered the government to suspend them from their jobs and to fine news organizations that published their views.

Human Rights. A British parliamentary human-rights group and Americas Watch, a New York-based human-rights organization, were among the groups charging the Chilean government with regularly using torture to obtain confessions, despite a 1986 agreement between the International Red Cross and Chile's secret police against such action.

In February it was announced that 390 exiles previously banned from Chile for political reasons would be allowed to return, in addition to the more than 600 who had been permitted to return earlier. Although the Interior Ministry claimed that only 461 exiles were now permanently banned from reentering Chile, the actual number was much higher; and few of those allowed to return have actually done so. Perhaps the most prominent returnee was Ariel Dorfman, who had been teaching at Duke University in North Carolina. His novel, *The Widows,* quickly sold 5,000 copies when it was published in a Spanish-language edition in July.

The Papal Visit. Most Chileans were pleased that the April 1–6 visit of Pope John Paul II had brought a "little summer" of free speech and "hopeful events," despite three incidents of violence. Eighteen opposition leaders—ranging from the extreme Right to the extreme Left—signed a statement before a meeting with the pope to express their commitment to a peaceful search for a revival of democracy. (Communist participants later said that they had not renounced violence as a means of ousting Pinochet, however.) The papal visit was accompanied by a broadening of newspaper and television coverage of political and economic news. *La Epoca,* a new newspaper owned by a prominent Christian Democrat, began publishing in March with an initial circulation of 55,000. (*El Mercurio,* the most popular pro-government newspaper, has a circulation of 65,000.)

Strikes. President Pinochet accepted the resignation of controversial businessman José Luís Federici as rector of the University of Chile on October 29. His replacement, Juán de Dios Vial Larrain, asked students and faculty to return to classes, which had been boycotted most of September and October. Rectors at three other universities also resigned because of government efforts to eliminate "unnecessary courses."

In October a strike called by the National Workers' Command (CNT) to demand an increase in the minimum wage from $45 to $90 monthly resulted in the deaths of three people in clashes with the police.

Economy. Chile's ability to repay its foreign debt of $21.4 billion was helped by rising copper prices and expanding agricultural, fishing, and forestry exports. A February agreement restructured part of the debt, reducing interest payments by $445 million in 1988. In addition, $1.7 billion in short-term credit was extended through 1989.

At midyear, Finance Minister Hernán Buchi said the economy was expected to grow by 5% in 1987, compared with 5.7% in 1986. Unemployment was expected to fall to 8.4%—compared with 13% in 1986—although these figures did not include workers involved in special emergency public-works projects.

Foreign Policy. Chile formally rejected a June request by the United States to extradite Juan Manuel Contreras and Lt. Col. Pedro Espinosa Bravo for plotting the 1976 murder in Washington, DC, of Orlando Letelier, a former cabinet minister and ambassador to the United States under President Salvador Allende. Both men were officers in DINA, Chile's national intelligence agency, at the time of the murder. Their accuser, also a former DINA member, had been secretly spirited out of Chile by U.S. officials. He was tried in Federal District Court in Washington, and sentenced to 5½ years in prison. An attempt to impose sanctions on Chile for its refusal to surrender the officers met with little response in the U.S. Congress.

CHILE • Information Highlights

Official Name: Republic of Chile.
Location: Southwestern coast of South America.
Area: 292,259 sq mi (756 950 km²).
Population (mid-1987 est.): 12,400,000.
Chief Cities (June 30, 1985): Santiago, the capital, 4,318,305 (including suburbs); Viña del Mar, 315,947.
Government: *Head of state and government,* Gen. Augusto Pinochet Ugarte, president (took power Sept. 1973). *Legislature*—Congress (dissolved Sept. 1973).
Monetary Unit: Peso (233.3 pesos equal U.S.$1, official rate Dec. 2, 1987).
Gross Domestic Product (1985): $16,100,000,000.
Economic Index (Santiago, 1986): *Consumer Prices* (1980 = 100), all items, 313.4; food, 286.5.
Foreign Trade (1986 U.S.$): *Imports,* $3,157,000,000; *exports,* $4,222,000,000.

The Chilean Minister of Government, Orlando Poblete Iturrate, charged Robert S. Gelbart, U.S. deputy assistant undersecretary of state, with interference in Chilean internal affairs. While on a mid-August visit to inaugurate an emergency-landing field for NASA space flights on Chilean-owned Easter Island, Gelbart had expressed the hope for free and open elections in Chile in 1988.

The Chilean consulate in Cochabamba, Bolivia, was dynamited on June 11, perhaps in retaliation for the Chilean rejection of a new corridor to the Pacific for Bolivia.

NEALE J. PEARSON
Texas Tech University

CHINA, PEOPLE'S REPUBLIC OF

The year 1987 ended with the course of political and economic reform in China confirmed and a new, young, technically competent set of leaders in place. It began, however, with student demonstrations in Beijing, the reaction to which appeared for a time to have overturned the carefully laid plans for reform and succession put in place by the most powerful political leader of the People's Republic, 83-year-old Deng Xiaoping.

Politics. During the first week of January, students in Beijing continued a series of protests that had begun the previous month. Protesting conditions at their universities and seeking more democracy in the political system, some 2,000 students marched in Beijing's Tiananmen Square. They believed, incorrectly as it later became clear, that Deng Xiaoping sympathized with their demands and was prevented from responding favorably to them by conservative middle-level bureaucrats.

Some of Deng's conservative colleagues took advantage of the student demonstrations to slow down the rapid pace of reform set by Deng and to attempt to replace reform-minded leaders with individuals holding more orthodox views. In the wake of the protests, the party's propaganda chief, Zhu Houze, was suspended and later purged. His replacement, Wang Renzhi, was considered a Marxist hard-liner. Also dismissed was Fang Lizhi, the vice-president of Science and Technology University in Hefei, scene of one of the first student demonstrations in December 1986.

At the highest level, on Janaury 16 the Politburo of the Central Committee of the Chinese Communist Party, augmented by members of the Party's Central Advisory Committee, met and accepted the resignation of Hu Yaobang, 71, as head of the party. Hu, who had held the post since 1980, was said to have been forced to resign. He was replaced by Prime Minister Zhao Ziyang, who became acting general secretary of the party while temporarily retaining

© Alvin Chung/Sygma

In Beijing's Tiananmen Square (left), *thousands of students demonstrated early in the year for democratic political reforms. The protests led to the dismissal of Hu Yaobang as head of the party and his replacement by Premier Zhao Ziyang* (below, right). *At the 13th party congress in October, paramount leader Deng Xiaoping* (below, left), *encouraged his aging colleagues to join him in retirement.*

© M. Philippot/Sygma

his position as premier. Hu's forced resignation was protested in a daring "open letter" to the Central Committee by 1,000 Chinese students and scholars in the United States.

Although Zhao Ziyang took the occasion of a Chinese New Year's speech on January 29 to reassure the Chinese people that the campaign against "bourgeois liberalism" would be confined to party members, the spring months were marked by a number of moves that seemed to suggest that reformers were on the defensive and conservatives were maneuvering to position themselves favorably prior to the 13th Party Congress in the fall. For example, a new State Media and Publications Office was established to monitor the press. Wielding the authority to close down any publication, the new office set out to evaluate China's 1,500 newspapers, 5,250 magazines, and 450 publishing houses. At the same time, new and more stringent regulations were enacted to control the flow of Chinese students and scholars abroad and to attempt to ensure their return.

The so-called conservatives in the Beijing leadership included several groups of political figures who shared a discomfort with the lack of clearcut policy guidelines and ideological parameters so eschewed by the practical-minded Deng. One such group in 1987 was headed by Peng Zhen, 85, who chaired the National People's Congress Standing Committee. In the absence of concrete guidelines, Peng's tendency was to move in the direction of greater party control. A second group looked toward the Soviet Union as a model for solving the nation's problems and thus favored more central planning and less local initiative. Included in this group were economist Chen Yun, 82, and Hu Qiaomu, 75. A third group, when confronted by the ambiguities of China's modernization, looked toward Marxist-Leninist orthodoxy for its guideposts. Deng Liqun, 72, who headed the Party's Propaganda Department during the anti-"spiritual pollution" campaign of 1983, and Central Advisory Committee Vice-Chairman Bo Yibo, 79, were exemplary of this group.

By late May the influence of these elderly conservatives apparently had begun to wane and, during the course of the summer, reform policies were agreed upon and appointments fixed for subsequent confirmation at the Party Congress. Shortly before the Congress convened, however, violent anti-Chinese demonstrations broke out on the streets of Lhasa, the capital of the Tibetan Autonomous Region (*see* special report, page 187). For a time it appeared that conservatives might use the uprising as a reason for attacking the reformers' relatively openhanded policies in the region, but that proved to be a mistaken prediction. The Congress opened on schedule at the end of October.

In his report to the Congress, Zhao endorsed the idea that China is in the "first stage of socialism"—a stage in which it is appropriate for market forces and central planning to exist side by side. He called for further economic reforms and, in the political sphere, for further circumscribing the role of the party to give greater scope for decision making to enterprise managers and local government officials. He also called for the introduction of a civil service to take the place of the arbitrary choice of officials based on personal connections.

As anticipated, the 68-year-old Zhao was confirmed as general secretary of the party despite his oft-repeated statements that he is better qualified to be premier than party head. Assisting him as members of the Standing Committee of the Politburo were Li Peng, 59; Qiao Shi, 63; Hu Qili, 58; and Yao Yilin, 70. While all four men were supporters of Zhao's program of reform, Li (because of his education in the Soviet Union) and Yao (because of his long experience in economic planning) were figures whose presence on the Standing Committee served to reassure the conservatives. With 175 members, the new Central Committee was smaller than its 209-member predecessor. The average age of its members was 55, four years younger than that of the 12th Central Committee. In November, Li Peng was appointed acting premier, succeeding Zhao in that post.

CHINA • Information Highlights

Official Name: People's Republic of China.
Location: Central-eastern Asia.
Area: 3,706,564 sq mi (9 600 000 km²).
Population (mid-1987 est.): 1,062,000,000.
Chief Cities (Dec. 31, 1985 est.): Beijing (Peking), the capital, 5,860,000; Shanghai, 6,980,000; Tianjin, 5,380,000.
Government: *General Secretary of the Chinese Communist Party,* Zhao Ziyang (chosen Oct. 1987); *Head of Government:* Li Peng, acting premier (took office Nov. 1987); *Head of State:* Li Xiannian (took office June 1983). *Legislature* (unicameral)—National People's Congress.
Monetary Unit: Yuan (3.722 yuan equal U.S.$1, August 1987).
Gross National Product (1986 est.): $262,000,000,000.
Foreign Trade (1986 U.S.$): *Imports,* $42,620,000,000; *exports,* $31,050,000,000.

As important as the new appointments were the resignations. Deng Xiaoping resigned as chairman of the Central Advisory Commission, giving evidence of his confidence in the newly appointed leadership and encouraging his aged colleagues to join him in retirement. With the resignation from the Central Committee of President Li Xiannian, 82, of Yang Dezhi, 77, chief of staff of the People's Liberation Army, and of the group of so-called "conservatives" discussed above, the way was cleared for a younger, reform-minded generation of leaders.

The Economy. While the slow pace of economic reform in 1987 could be attributed in part to the shifting political tides, it also was the result of purely economic factors. During the spring and summer, the State Commission for Economic Restructuring carried out a major review of economic reform since 1978. The review touched on several issues fundamental to the new economic course charted by Deng Xiaoping. First among these was the pace of reform. Should it be rapid and thus, inevitably, turbulent? Or should it be protracted and thus less dislocating? A second basic question concerned the implementation of reforms: Is the current piecemeal approach appropriate for the years ahead, or should a more systematic and comprehensive approach be adopted? And a third key issue involved the role of market forces in a socialist economy: Can free-market competition and central planning coexist? If so, how wide a scope should be given to market forces?

Industrial production grew a reported 9% during 1986, about half the rate of the previous year; the 18% recorded in 1985 was considered unhealthy by Chinese planners. Preliminary figures for 1987 suggested that the growth rate would be somewhere between 1985 and 1986 figures; average growth during the first three quarters was 15%.

The record year for grain output in China was 1984, when 405 million tons were produced. Because of an incentive system that encouraged the planting of other crops, grain production in the two subsequent years fell below that amount: 381 million tons in 1985 and 390 million tons in 1986. A goal of 405 million tons was set for 1987, and measures were taken to help ensure that the goal was met. The state quota was reduced, allowing more grain to move through the free-market system, where prices are higher. The supply of fertilizer was increased, and regulations were put in place to keep additional land from being taken out of grain production.

Plans for further reforms in the agricultural sector included consolidation of land through sales of land-use contracts to allow for more efficient cultivation. With the average Chinese household now farming less than 1 acre (.405 ha) of land, the goal was to increase the average plot size to at least 5 acres (2 ha) and then

SPECIAL REPORT/CHINA

Unrest in Tibet

AP/Wide World

The worst violence in three decades erupted in Lhasa, the capital city of China's autonomous region of Tibet, in late September and early October. Buddhist monks and other pro-independence demonstrators battled Chinese police.

On Sept. 27, 1987, for the first time in nearly 30 years, pro-independence demonstrators took to the streets of Lhasa, the capital of China's autonomous region of Tibet. Twenty-seven lamas (Tibetan Buddhist monks) defied Chinese law by carrying a Tibetan flag and, after refusing to desist, were arrested.

Four days later on October 1—China's National Day—Tibetan demonstrators again took to the streets, protesting the earlier arrests and calling for a "free Tibet," the expulsion of Chinese from the region, and the return of their spiritual ruler—the Dalai Lama—from his 28-year exile in India. The demonstrations quickly turned violent, with demonstrators stoning Chinese police and setting fire to a police station. The result was at least 6 deaths and 19 serious injuries.

A third demonstration, involving more than 100 monks, broke out on October 6—the 37th anniversary of China's military takeover. Sixty monks were arrested, bringing the total of those held in custody to more than 110 monks and an undetermined number of others. Some 600 Chinese militiamen were flown into Lhasa, and the demonstrations were quelled.

The Chinese government claims Tibet as a part of its territory. The region was brought under Chinese control in the early 18th century by the last Chinese imperial dynasty. Following the fall of the last emperor in 1911, the Dalai Lama proclaimed Tibetan independence. Because of civil war and the Japanese occupation, the Chinese were unable to reestablish their control over Tibet until 1950, when Mao Tse-tung's People's Liberation Army invaded the territory. Chinese troops suppressed a large-scale uprising nine years later, at which time the Dalai Lama fled to India. During the early years of the Cultural Revolution (1966–69) Red Guards repeatedly attacked Tibetan temples, leaving few of the 6,000 sacred sites unscathed.

The policy of the Chinese government toward Tibet, like its policy toward other areas inhabited by the 6% of China's population that are ethnic minorities, has varied between one of control and assimilation, and between one of autonomy and the preservation of cultural separatism. The Chinese government has viewed its policies toward Tibet since 1978 as generous and open. Substantial investment has been made by Beijing in the education of Tibetans and the economic and political development of the region. Moreover, the Communist regime contends, Tibetan society under the Dalai Lama was backward and oppressive. The Chinese leadership sees itself as playing a progressive role in Tibet, which like Taiwan, it considers an indivisible part of China and not economically or politically viable as an independent entity. By contrast, many Tibetans see the Chinese as exerting military control to exploit the region and suppress Tibetan nationalism. They see China's efforts at educating young Tibetans as an attempt to Sinify the younger generation.

In the United States, the Reagan administration and Congress had opposite reactions to the 1987 events in Lhasa. Putting the U.S. relationship with Beijing at the forefront, the administration expressed its regret at the bloodshed but associated itself with China's claim to sovereignty. Congress, having played host to the Dalai Lama in September and having heard his plan for negotiations with Beijing on Tibet's future status, sided with the demonstrators and deplored Chinese violation of Tibetan human rights.

JOHN BRYAN STARR

to begin mechanizing. By 1987, some 80 million of the rural work force of 350 million had shifted from agricultural pursuits to newly expanded rural industries. This trend will be encouraged further, with the goal of moving another 100 million workers out of agriculture and into industry. That would put about 60% of China's total work force in the industrial sector, up from 20% in 1980.

The political settlement that emerged from the October Party Congress appeared to have cleared the way for the issuing of a new law that would stipulate the responsibilities of the enterprise manager. Once this law is in place, a bankruptcy law passed for trial implementation by the Standing Committee of the National People's Congress in January 1987 could go into effect. Passage of the enterprise law also would clear the way for a resumption of price reforms, which were "postponed indefinitely" at the beginning of 1987.

By midsummer 1987, the Shanghai stock exchange, which opened in September 1986, had traded shares in nearly 1,500 enterprises, with a total turnover of more than $60 million. Shares are sold either to employees of the enterprise or to the public. A State Council circular issued in April 1987 placed limits on the number of enterprises that could sell shares and on the use to which the resulting funds could be put.

Foreign Affairs. China's generally warm relations with the United States suffered something of a setback in the fall of 1987 over China's alleged sale of up to $2 billion in Silkworm missiles and other arms to Iran. Protesting the sales, Washington suspended the granting of licenses allowing China to import high-tech equipment from the United States. Despite compelling evidence to the contrary, the Chinese government stoutly denied that it was supplying the missiles and called the U.S. charges "sheer fabrication." China has become the world's fifth largest exporter of arms (after the United States, the Soviet Union, Great Britain, and France), using these sales as a source of foreign exchange. Observers also suggested that China sought stronger ties with Iran as a counterweight to Soviet influence in neighboring Afghanistan.

China's relations with Japan cooled somewhat during the course of the year. In February a Japanese court of appeals awarded property in Kyoto to the government of Taiwan, an act that Beijing said violated the terms under which relations between Japan and the People's Republic were normalized in 1972. Also at issue were Chinese complaints over Japan's failure to help close the $4 billion deficit in bilateral trade and lingering questions about the treatment in Japanese school texts of the history of the Sino-Japanese war.

In May, Japanese journalist Shuitsu Henmi, a reporter for the newspaper *Kyodo,* was expelled from China for allegedly stealing state secrets. At issue were Central Committee documents, concerning the handling of student demonstrations and the dismissal of Hu Yaobang, that were published in *Kyodo* and other newspapers. The expulsion preceded by three weeks a visit to China by Yuko Kurihara, the head of Japan's Defense Agency.

Despite lingering disagreements on the political front, trade relations and scientific and cultural exchanges between China and the Soviet Union expanded significantly during the year. A longstanding disagreement over the location of the Sino-Soviet border in Siberia was resolved at the end of the summer. Two-way trade across that border, while still modest, was reported to be growing. The Chinese were interested in securing Soviet assistance in modernizing factories that were built with Russian aid during the 1950s, as well as in constructing major infrastructural projects in the western provinces. Among the latter is a new rail line that will link the Chinese city of Urumqi with Alma-Ata in the Soviet Union. At the same time, the Chinese continued to demand that progress be made in resolving the "three obstacles" to improved Sino-Soviet relations: the Soviet occupation of Afghanistan, Soviet assistance to Vietnam in its conflict in Cambodia, and the presence of Soviet troops and missiles on China's northern border. Because progress in each of these areas would be a boost to Mikhail Gorbachev's efforts at political and economic reform, there was reason to expect improvement in relations between Beijing and Moscow.

Efforts on both sides to mend Sino-Indian relations suffered a major setback during 1987, and a military clash between the two was only narrowly averted. China and India have had conflicting territorial claims in the area known as Arunachal Pradesh ever since the border war of 1962. Perhaps in response to the Indian government's decision to upgrade the status of the area from a centrally administered territory to a state, the Chinese began moving troops into neighboring Tibet. By early June it was reported that each side had amassed as many as 200,000 troops on the border, and Beijing and New Delhi traded accusations of border violations. The situation appeared to cool during the fall, at which time India appeared to take a neutral position toward the October riots in Lhasa—a potentially difficult situation given the fact that the Dalai Lama and many of his followers were residing in India.

In other foreign developments, China and Portugal early in the year reached agreement on the return of Macao to China in 1999, and the Communist parties of China and East Germany in June restored formal relations.

See also TAIWAN.

JOHN BRYAN STARR
Yale-China Association

CITIES AND URBAN AFFAIRS

In 1987 local governments in the United States entered their first full year without general revenue sharing funds, translating into a loss of about $4.6 billion to their treasuries. For the first time since the State and Local Fiscal Assistance Act was passed in 1972, a large majority of local governments did not receive direct federal assistance. Only two principal programs remained in federal urban aid: housing and community development funds of about $3.1 billion (down from $4 billion in fiscal 1981), and the Urban Development Action Grants (UDAG) program, with about $400 million for 1987 (about the same amount as for 1981). The budget for the U.S. Department of Housing and Urban Development (HUD) declined from $35.7 billion in fiscal 1980 to $14 billion by fiscal 1988 (from about 7% of the federal budget to 1%)—the largest reduction for any cabinet department during the Reagan years.

As a result, U.S. cities have attempted to increase taxes or find new sources of nontax revenue. Despite widespread public resistance to higher taxes, local governments have steadily increased revenues throughout the 1980s. As a result, expenditures have increased even though federal aid has dropped. From 1983 to 1986, local government spending went up 26%, to a total of $332 billion. In most cases, the revenues have come from higher user fees and charges for permits or licenses, or from increases in local government sales taxes.

The search for new revenue has not allowed all cities to avoid reductions in spending. A survey of 545 communities conducted by the National League of Cities showed that, through the first half of 1987, 52% had reduced capital spending and 26% had imposed hiring freezes or laid off employees, despite the fact that 58% of the communities had increased user fees and other charges.

Many cities have responded by lobbying state legislatures for new urban programs. States have responded in a variety of ways. Georgia and Texas passed legislation to allow their cities to collect sales taxes. A large number of states have provided funds to help shelter and feed the homeless. More than half the states have enacted enterprise zone legislation. Twelve states have passed legislation to help local governments pay the costs of carrying out state-imposed mandates. New Jersey, a leader, has capitalized a State Urban Development Corporation with $30 million, provided funds for for-profit neighborhood development corporations, and appointed an Urban Affairs Council to devise a state urban policy by late 1987.

But no state comes close to making up for all the lost federal dollars. Although 34 states realized a windfall of $6.3 billion in revenues as a result of the 1986 Tax Reform Act, their primary response has not been to invest in new urban or social programs, but to reform state tax codes by reducing individual and corporate rates and by broadening the tax base.

AP/Wide World

Annette Strauss, sister-in-law of former Democratic Party chairman Robert Strauss, was elected mayor of Dallas. She defeated Fred Meyer in an April runoff.

The 1986 Tax Reform Act posed considerable uncertainties. Due to the elimination of tax advantages for many forms of real-estate investment, redevelopment slowed significantly in several cities. In St. Louis, the Community Development Agency allocated funds to help redevelopment firms keep some renewal projects solvent. All across the United States, city officials and renewal experts were concerned that inner-city neighborhood renewal and commercial revitalization may slow precipitously once existing projects are completed.

Homelessness. Whether the number of homeless in the nation is 300,000 as estimated by HUD, or 3 million as claimed by advocacy groups, the problem of homelessness has reached crisis proportions in many U.S. cities. It is a problem with no easy remedy. Out of a national stock of 4 million public housing units, about 70,000 are lost each year because of age and poor maintenance. Waiting lists for public housing units are long: 200,000 in New York City; 44,000 in Chicago; 60,000 in Miami; 13,000 in Washington, DC. Although the federal government has shifted much of its housing subsidy to rent vouchers, many cities are finding that shortages of rental housing is a worse problem than poor housing.

A large number of public-private partnerships has been formed in an attempt to produce low-income housing. In such cities as New York, Chicago, Miami, Minneapolis, Chicago, Pittsburgh, Denver, and Oakland, nonprofit housing corporations have been formed to pool investors' capital and receive state and city housing funds. Fifteen states have created trust funds for housing assistance, programs that provide shelters for the homeless, assistance to nonprofit housing corporations, and loan funds to encourage home ownership. In July, President Reagan signed into law a bill authorizing more than $1 billion in emergency aid for the homeless over two years.

AIDS. Many cities have spent millions in tax dollars to reduce the spread of Acquired Immune Deficiency Syndrome (AIDS). In 1987 the cost of patient care, counseling, testing, and education rapidly escalated, threatening funding for existing municipal services. San Francisco spent $17.5 million for AIDS programs. Thirty states appropriated funds on AIDS programs for fiscal 1988 (compared with five in 1984). But concerned urban officials wanted this and other issues to receive national attention in the 1988 election campaign.

National groups representing city officials were laying the groundwork for influencing candidates in the 1988 elections. At its meeting in Des Moines in May, the National League of Cities' Election '88 committee announced a plan to spend up to $1 million to highlight urban issues during the campaign.

The U.S. Conference of Mayors adopted a "national urban investment" policy that called for increased federal money for AIDS, more money to assist local drug enforcement, more aid for the homeless, and a targeted revenue sharing program. The mayors' groups also asked mayors to delay endorsing candidates for the presidency in order to maximize their influence on campaign issues.

DENNIS R. JUDD
University of Missouri-St. Louis

COINS AND COIN COLLECTING

In honor of the bicentennial of the U.S. Constitution, the U.S. Mint in July began striking new $5 gold and $1 silver commemorative coins.

$1 silver, top, *and $5 gold commemorative coins were issued to mark the U.S. Constitution's bicentennial.*

Designs for the two coins were selected from the work of 11 invited artists as well as U.S. Mint engravers. A design submitted by sculptor Marcel Jovine, an Italian immigrant who went to the United States after World War II and now resides and works in New Jersey, was chosen for the $5 gold coin. The obverse displays a highly stylized eagle with a quill pen in its talons. For the $1 silver coin, a design created by Patricia Lewis Verani of Londonderry, NH, was selected. The reverse of the $1 coin portrays a cross section of Americans. Both commemoratives also feature the phrase "We The People" and data pertaining to the Constitution's bicentennial. Surcharges of $35 and $7, applied to the gold and silver coins, respectively, will be used solely to reduce the national debt.

The U.S. Bureau of Engraving and Printing (BEP) celebrated its 125th anniversary in 1987. Today the bureau produces not only paper money but also postage stamps and a variety of items of special interest to collectors at its 75-year-old facility in Washington, DC. Construction began on a second production facility in Fort Worth, TX, on April 25, 1987.

For the first time in its 50-year history, the Federation Internationale de la Medaille, a worldwide assembly of artists and medal enthusiasts, held its biennial congress and exposition in the United States. Medalists, directors of mints, museum curators, art critics, educators, and collectors from some 30 countries attended the conference in Colorado Springs, CO, September 11–15. The organization seeks to promote the medal as a prominent force in the world of art and numismatics.

In July 1987, Canadians began using a new smaller $1 coin, struck in aureate nickel (pure nickel coated in bronze), that depicts a loon, a bird synonymous with Canada. A revised version of Emanuel Hahn's traditional "voyageur" motif, depicting two early fur traders paddling a canoe before a northwoods scene, was to have been used on the reverse of the 11-sided coin. In late 1986, however, the master reverse dies were lost en route from the Royal Canadian Mint facility in Ottawa to its plant in Winnipeg, Man. Security concerns prompted the choice of Robert Carmichael's loon design as a replacement. If the $1 coin is accepted and circulated, the Canadian government plans to gradually phase out its $1 note.

MARILYN A. REBACK, *"The Numismatist"*

COLOMBIA

Violence from both right and left plagued Colombia during 1987. The most notable incident occurred on October 11, when Jaime Pardo Leal, leader of the leftist Patriotic Union (UP), was gunned down by unknown persons. The murder and subsequent rioting in Bogotá and other major cities proved once again that Colombia suffers from severe social ills. Despite an end to the extradition treaty between Colombia and the United States, the Colombian government increased its efforts against the "Drug Mafia." Although these efforts resulted in numerous arrests and destruction of several coca growing areas, the number of murders and abductions attributed to drug dealers continued to rise. The nation's social and political ills were partially offset by the economy, which performed at or above the level of most other Latin American countries during the year. In foreign affairs, a continuing boundary dispute between Colombia and Venezuela plagued relations between the two countries.

Politics. Colombia faced the total collapse of the cease-fire agreements negotiated with rebels in 1984. The country's largest guerrilla organization, the leftist Colombian Revolutionary Armed Forces (FARC), appeared to be heading toward a resumption of open conflict. The FARC, pointing to the assassination of more than 40 leftist politicians during the first half of the year, claimed that government forces had used the cease-fire to attempt to annihilate the opposition. The Pardo Leal killing only underscored what appeared to be a concerted campaign against the Left. The number of UP members killed since the party's founding in 1984 reached 451. In addition, a campaign of murder and intimidation at the University of Antioquia in Medellín resulted in the deaths of five students and two professors in two months.

The inaction of President Virgilio Barco Vargas only fueled dissatisfaction on the Left. An offer by the Catholic Church to mediate did not produce any new adherence to the tattered cease-fire. On the other side, the country's three largest guerrilla organizations—the FARC, the M-19, and the National Liberation Army (ELN)—stepped up their activities against the government. As of July 31, more than 1,600 deaths had occurred in clashes between government forces and the guerrillas.

Drugs. Reputed Colombian drug king Carlos Lehder Rivas was captured and extradited to the United States in February. But problems with the "Drug Mafia" worsened as the year progressed. In August a Colombian senator, Samuel Escruceria-Delgado, was arrested in Miami on drug charges. In January the Colombian ambassador to Hungary was shot and wounded by drug traffickers. And on June 25 the Colombian Supreme Court declared the 1979 extradition treaty with the United States unconstitutional. The decision hampered U.S. efforts to combat the international drug trade. By year's end an estimated 90,000 acres (36,500 ha) of coca were under cultivation.

Economy. Perhaps paradoxically, the Colombian economy performed exceptionally well during 1987. Through July, Colombia's trade balance showed a positive net of $113 million. Industrial production was up 6.88% during the year. In fact, the Colombian economy proved to be the most dynamic in all of Latin America during the 1980s, with an average annual per capita increase in gross national product of 4.1%. There were some negative signs: the cost of living rose 26.65% between July 1986 and July 1987, the fourth highest rise in the last 21 years. Imports rose by $480 million to $4.14 billion, although imports of primary goods rose more than three times as fast as all imports. In April, President Barco announced that Bogotá would have its own subway system in three years, and in September the president announced an ambitious development plan of 7.2 billion pesos (about $30 million) for the 1987–90 period.

Foreign Affairs. A dispute with Venezuela over territorial waters north of the Guajira Peninsula continued to simmer during the year. U.S.-Colombian relations did not appear to suffer from the ending of the extradition treaty between the two nations. In June the U.S. Department of State officially congratulated Colombia on its efforts against drug traffickers.

ERNEST A. DUFF
Randolph-Macon Woman's College

COLOMBIA • Information Highlights

Official Name: Republic of Colombia.
Location: Northwest South America.
Area: 439,734 sq mi (1 138 910 km²).
Population (mid-1987 est.): 29,900,000.
Chief City (Oct. 15, 1985): Bogotá, the capital, 3,982,941.
Government: *Head of state and government,* Virgilio Barco Vargas, president (took office Aug. 1986). *Legislature*—Parliament; Senate and House of Representatives.
Monetary Unit: Peso (258.00 pesos equal U.S.$1, Dec. 8, 1987).
Gross National Product (1986 U.S. $): $31,000,-000,000.
Economic Index (Bogotá, May 1987): *Consumer Prices* (1980 = 100), all items, 399.1; food, 425.6.
Foreign Trade (1986 U.S.$): *Imports,* $3,464,000,000; *exports,* $5,102,000,000.

COLORADO

The recession induced by low oil and mineral prices continued to squeeze Colorado in 1987. But as the year ended, statistics suggested the state's economy had bottomed out and was beginning a slow comeback.

Unemployment. The Colorado Department of Labor and Employment reported statewide unemployment reached a post-World-War-II high of 9.1% in March. Unemployment dropped to 7% in August, and the state reported the number of Coloradans with jobs increased by 15,600 during that month. Other economic indicators rose modestly through the summer and fall. But the economic slowdown resulted in the closing of some well-known companies, including the 92-year-old Denver Dry Goods chain and the Denver-based Petro Lewis Corporation. The Gates Corporation closed its Denver industrial belt factory, eliminating 800 jobs.

Economy. Colorado's new governor, Democrat Roy Romer, made repeated travels to other states, Europe, and Asia to lure new business. His trips earned him the nickname "Governor Roamer."

Romer and the Colorado Association of Commerce and Industry joined to promote "Blueprint for Colorado," aimed at reviving the state's economy by boosting its higher education and transportation facilities. Majority Republicans in the legislature responded to Romer's approach far more favorably than they had to the environmentalism preached by his predecessor, Richard Lamm (D). The legislature approved many of the proposals, especially in higher education.

The legislature also approved $36 million to help build a new state convention center in Denver, which will finance the rest of the more than $100 million project. The legislature also adopted a "flat" state income tax of 5%, down from the old maximum tax of 8%, to parallel the new federal income-tax law. A final economic development bill lessened regulations on communications companies within Colorado.

The legislature authorized two special governmental authorities to build a toll-collecting beltway to the east of the metropolitan area known as E-470 and a pilot mass-transit line in the southeast corridor popularly named "Wallyrail" after its prime backer, businessman George Wallace. Both projects relied heavily on private and local financing sources because of the tight state budget picture. By year's end, it was uncertain whether either could actually be built without more state or federal financial assistance.

AP/Wide World

Colorado Gov. Bob Romer took the bus to work during Denver's 90-day Better Air Campaign in the fall. The first-term Democrat also traveled extensively outside the state.

Economic news brightened in the autumn as U.S. West announced it would build a new $50 million research center in Colorado, a decision expected to bring 1,500 jobs to the state. In Golden, the Adolph Coors Co. settled a ten-year-old labor dispute with the AFL-CIO, which dropped its boycott against the company's beer. Summer tourism figures rose by 3.6% over 1986, boosting the total of the 1986–87 season to a healthy $5.4 billion.

Elections. The slow economy almost added Denver's Democratic Mayor Federico Peña to the unemployment rolls as Republican Don Bain topped a seven-way field in the city's nominally nonpartisan mayoral primary. But Peña rallied to win his second four-year term in the runoff, 79,694 to 76,648.

Politics. Two prominent Colorado Republicans ended the year as prominent Colorado Democrats. State Sen. Martha Ezzard of Cherry Hills Village resigned her seat in July and switched parties after a long-running fight with conservative colleagues. Republican Terry Considine was appointed to fill out Ezzard's term.

In October, Colorado Attorney General Duane Woodard also switched to the Democratic Party although, unlike Ezzard, he retained his office. Woodard had feuded bitterly with some of the legislature's conservative Republicans, and they had responded by cutting his budget sharply.

Former U.S. Sen. Gary Hart, who withdrew from the race for the Democratic presidential nomination in May, reentered the contest late in the year.

BOB EWEGEN, "The Denver Post"

COLORADO • Information Highlights

Area: 104,091 sq mi (269 596 km²).
Population (July 1, 1986): 3,267,000.
Chief Cities (July 1, 1986 est.): Denver, the capital, 505,000; Colorado Springs, 272,000; Aurora, 217,990; Lakewood, 122,140.
Government (1987): *Chief Officers*—governor, Roy Romer (D); lt. gov., Michael Callihan (D). *General Assembly*—Senate, 35 members; House of Representatives, 65 members.
State Finances (fiscal year 1986): *Revenue,* $5,995,000,000; *expenditure,* $4,952,000,000.
Personal Income (1986): $49,771,000,000; per capita, $15,234.
Labor Force (June 1987): *Civilian labor force,* 1,695,400; *unemployed,* 135,600 (8.0% of total force).
Education: *Enrollment* (fall 1985)—public elementary schools, 378,735; public secondary, 171,907; colleges and universities, 161,314. *Public school expenditures,* (1985–86), $1,901,000,000 ($3,740 per pupil).

COMMUNICATION TECHNOLOGY

Regarded as "the year of the Integrated Services Digital Network (ISDN)," 1987 in communications technology was marked by accelerated progress toward the goal of end-to-end, high-speed digital transmission and switching of combined voice, data, and video signals. With much of the new technology common to both computers and communications, the year's advances in microelectronics, microprocessing, software, and photonics (lightwave devices and systems) inaugurated what the experts have called "the second wave of the Information Age," in which public and private communications networks are being linked to increasingly intelligent terminal equipment for the movement and management of information.

Transmission and Switching. Optical fibers have become the dominant medium for wideband transmission lines, and their application is being expanded rapidly. Field trials in 1987 showed that lightwave systems can be extended to local loop interfaces. Connection to individual customers appeared to be only a few years in the future. Meanwhile, the world's highest-capacity commercial lightwave system was put into service by AT&T. It operates at a speed of 1.7 billion bits per second and is capable of carrying more than 24,000 phone calls at the same time over a single pair of glass fibers.

The year 1987 marked the 25th anniversary of the launching of AT&T's TELSTAR I, the world's first communications satellite, as well as the formation of COMSAT, the U.S. entry in the commercial satellite communications industry. From these beginnings just a quarter-century ago, instantaneous, worldwide television coverage of special events has become commonplace.

At laboratories in the United States, Japan, and Great Britain, research is being carried out on a new system of lightwave modulation and detection which may be the next great advance in optical communication. The new method, termed "coherent detection," can provide many closely spaced multi-gigabit (billions of bits) channels over light-guide fibers by the use of frequency-division multiplexing. Multiple channels are derived by using two lasers and electronic amplifiers and filters in a type of modulation similar to that used in radio or television receivers. Experimental coherent lightwave systems have achieved a rate of 2 billion bits per second over distances of almost 200 km (124 mi) with no intervening amplifiers. Ten such channels can be derived in the coherent system and transmitted over a single optical fiber. With further development, such a system would be capable of sending 10 million telephone conversations or 10,000 television channels on a light guide.

Wideband packet technology also is taking its place in the communications field. This is a way of combining voice, data, and image transmission by converting the signals into digital form (bits) and assembling the pulses into short groups, or "packets." The packets then can be sent as "spurts," each to its own designated address over one or several high-speed digital lines. Packets are a more efficient and less costly way to move and manage information. The technique, which is compatible with the ISDN, will find early application in local exchange and inter-exchange networks with heavy traffic loads.

Also introduced in 1987 was a new interoffice signaling system allowing local telephone companies to offer advanced calling services. In this system, all signaling functions are put on a separate, packet-switched network and sent on a channel independent of the message channel. Called "Common Channel Signaling (CCS)," it offers telephone users several new service features, such as tracing incoming calls by visually displaying the caller's phone number, forwarding calls, blocking incoming calls from selected numbers, and allowing only designated numbers to ring the phone. The CCS system ultimately will be linked to the nationwide long-distance network.

Communication Services. The area of personal communications—providing easy-to-use and economical service to people who are away from a fixed location—was an active one in 1987. The use of cellular mobile radio systems (with more than 800,000 subscribers in the United States), "beepers," and cordless telephones is rapidly increasing from year to year. In the near future, new digital mobile radio systems will be able to encrypt messages for privacy and will handle data traffic along with voice.

As of 1987 more than 5 million radio paging units were in service in the United States. An estimated 20 million units, with the ability to store, display, and print out messages, will be in use by 1990. Cordless telephones have undergone considerable improvement and are now being used in countries throughout the world. With the U.S. Federal Communications Commission (FCC) having opened up additional frequencies, the new cordless phones can automatically select an interference-free channel, store up to ten frequently called numbers for automatic dialing, and, with self-contained microphones and loud-speakers, make or receive calls without the use of a handset.

Advances in electronic speech-processing have created new ways in which humans can control and interact with computers and other machines. Encoding speech into digital impulses, synthesizing speech to allow a machine to speak, and automatic speech recognition are finding wide-spread applications in the com-

Today's Telephones

Since the breakup of the Bell System in 1984, U.S. consumers have returned some 70 million rented telephones and bought their own in equal or greater numbers. Competing for this vast market, a number of manufacturers have introduced a new generation of telephones with sophisticated electronic capabilities. An estimated 60% of all phones purchased in the United States today have some special feature. Cellular mobile telephones, below, *which use low-power microwave transmitters to cover small geographic "cells," now claim 800,000 U.S. subscribers; these phones are especially popular for automobile use. AT&T's* Speakerphone 420, below right, *features a line-powered speaker and one-touch dialing of 13 "memorized" numbers; some programmable or "smart" phones can memorize up to 100 numbers.* Battery-powered cordless telephones, right, *offer the sound quality of cord sets—plus the convenience.*

Courtesy of AT&T

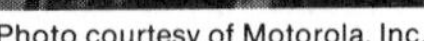

Photo courtesy of Motorola, Inc.

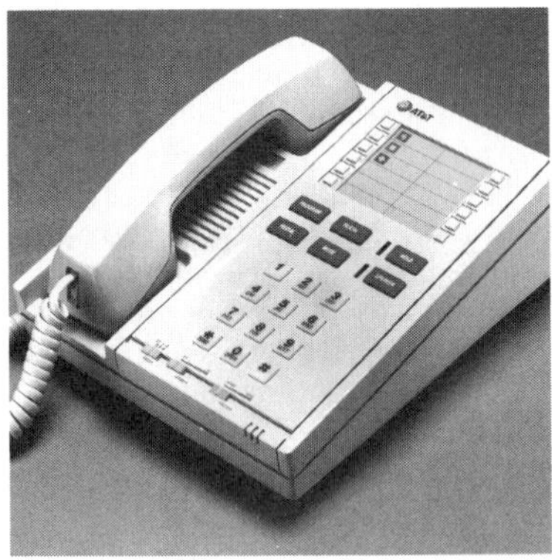

Courtesy of AT&T

munications field. Among the benefits are phone dialing by voice, voice store-and-forward systems (voice mail), data-base voice-access systems, voice control of computer terminals, and new electronic aids for the speech, hearing, and physically handicapped. Economical hardware has become available for incorporation into Private Branch Exchanges (PBXs), computer work stations, automatic machine controls, and voice-password security systems. Improved microelectronics also are being used to further the development of speech processors, which are currently limited to a vocabulary of about 1,000 isolated words or 50 continuous words independent of the speaker. In contrast, research in progress has the goal of a 20,000-word vocabulary, which would allow continuous speech, as in dictation to a word processor.

Microelectronics and Microprocessors. Introduced in 1987, the four-megabit dynamic random-access memory (DRAM) chip represents an impressive increase in capacity over the one-megabit chip available just one year earlier. The new integrated circuit consumes less power and creates less heat than its predecessor, while taking up no more space. Meanwhile, a 16-megabit chip was in the early stages of development in both Japan and the United States. When available for use as a memory in computers, this chip will be able to store as much information as contained in a 700-page book—but in an area of only about 1 sq. cm.

AT&T Bell Laboratories, IBM, and others are working to develop high-performance gallium arsenide integrated circuits for logic and memory functions in super high-speed computers and communications systems. Each chip will contain up to 5,000 logic gates and operate at a speed of more than 200 megahertz (200 million cycles per second).

With the shrinking dimensions of Very Large-Scale Integration (VLSI), a limit is being reached in the fabrication of metallic conductors to interlink chips and circuit boards. A technique of optical interconnection has been developed using a laser beam conducted along an optical waveguide and picked up by a photonic detector. Such a connection generates almost no heat and has the high reliability, long life, and same large band-width and freedom from electrical interference as lightwave technology.

M.D. Fagen
Formerly, AT&T Bell Laboratories

COMPUTERS

"Faster and cheaper" continued to be the guiding principle of the U.S. computer industry during 1987. Products based on powerful 32-bit microprocessors set new standards in personal computing, portable computers finally hit their stride, and businesses took increasing advantage of the enormous storage capabilities of CD-ROM (compact disc, read-only memory).

Products for the business market continued to represent the fastest-growing segment of the industry. A tremendous increase in applications programs made computing much more viable for all types of businesses. Word-processing, data-base, and spread-sheet programs remained the most popular applications, but a variety of others—such as expert systems, desktop publishing, and CAD/CAM (computer-aided design/manufacturing)—continued to grow rapidly. Also popular were memory-resident programs, which allow users to switch back and forth between a main program, such as a spread sheet, and a utility, such as a calendar or an outliner. New market segments included CASE (computer-aided software engineering) and MCAE (mechanical computer-aided engineering).

Personal Computers. In March, Apple introduced a pair of powerful Macintosh computers aimed chiefly at the office market. The Macintosh II is based on the 32-bit Motorola 68020 microprocessor: the Macintosh SE uses the relatively slower 16-bit Motorola 68000 microprocessor. Unlike earlier Macintoshes, the new machines allow users to insert specialized circuit boards to increase speed or memory or to perform special functions. They also offer optional disc-operating systems (DOS) compatibility, enabling users to run programs written for IBM PCs.

In April, IBM introduced its Personal System/2 series. The four new computers—Models 30, 50, 60, and 80—offer greater memory and speed as well as significantly improved graphics capabilities. In the following months, production of "classic" IBM PCs ceased.

IBM's new top-of-the-line machine, the Model 80, is based on the powerful Intel 80386 microprocessor. The machine's capabilities will not be fully exploited until after a new operating system, called OS/2, is released, reportedly in early 1988. OS/2, which also will be available for Models 50 and 60, will shatter the 640K memory barrier.

AT&T, Wyse Technology, and other manufacturers also announced new machines based on 32-bit microprocessors. Compaq, which in 1986 became the first major company to market 80386-based personal computers, expanded the line in 1987 with the introduction of five new models, including two portables.

Meanwhile, because a substantial market for PC-compatibles is expected to exist for some time, new clones of the old IBM PCs continued to be introduced during 1987.

The development of lighter and more capable battery-powered portables has caused sales of these machines to jump. Many models were introduced during 1987, some of them weighing less than 10 lbs (4.5 kg) yet packing all the power of an IBM PC.

Compact Discs. The same compact discs that have revolutionized the music industry are becoming cost-effective alternatives to microfilm and magnetic storage media. In the CD-ROM format, the discs can hold words, graphics, and any other type of digitized computer data. The data is read, or retrieved, by a laser in a special disc drive attached to a personal computer. CD-ROM greatly expands the memory storage capacity of computers—a single disc only 12 cm (4.7 inches) in diameter can store about 1,500 times as much data as can be stored on a typical floppy disc. Among the products introduced in 1987 was Microsoft's Bookshelf. This single CD-ROM disc holds a collection of ten reference works, including *American Heritage Dictionary, Roget's Thesaurus,* and *The World Almanac and Book of Facts.*

Although CD-ROM's greatest opportunities in the near future appear to lie in the business market, a new interactive technology introduced by General Electric also holds great promise for home and educational users. Called Digital Video Interactive (DVI), the technology allows 72 minutes of full-motion video, three-dimensional motion graphics, high-quality audio, and text to be encoded on a CD-ROM disc. One prototype DVI program uses these techniques to teach automotive school students how to remove a fuel pump. Another allows users to "walk" through a Mayan ruin. Still another lets people choose from a vast catalog of home furnishings.

Supercomputers. An advanced supercomputer system, the Numerical Aerodynamic Simulations Facility, was dedicated in March at Ames Research Center in Mountain View, CA. The system is based on a Cray-2, a four-processor supercomputer capable of a sustained rate of 250 million computations per second, with top speeds of 1.72 billion computations per second. It is being used to simulate extremely complex flight and weather phenomena for the first time. And by simulating aircraft configurations, it is reducing the time and cost involved in developing aircraft designs.

Cray Research has dominated the supercomputer market, though it is facing growing competition from other U.S. and Japanese companies. In May, for example, Honeywell-NEC unveiled its integrated line of SX 2 Series supercomputers, including the SX 2-400, billed as the fastest single-processor supercomputer in the world, with peak speeds of 1.3 billion calculations per second.

JENNY TESAR, *Free-lance Science Writer*

CONNECTICUT

Twenty-eight workers died in the April 23, 1987, collapse of an apartment building under construction in Bridgeport. It took rescue workers nine days to recover all the victims' bodies from the rubble. The L'Ambiance Plaza project, consisting of twin towers of 16 floors each, was 60% complete when it collapsed.

The Occupational Safety and Health Administration charged on October 22 that five companies working on the project knew or should have known that they were risking workers' lives because of inadequate engineering, design, and construction procedures. The federal agency proposed penalties totaling $5.1 million against the five companies. If enacted, it would be the largest penalty assessed since OSHA was established in 1971.

Investigators found that a hydraulic jack rod supporting the ninth floor in the west tower pulled away from a steel collar, triggering the collapse of the 320-ton cement floor and floors above it. The falling west tower pulled down the attached east tower.

CONNECTICUT • Information Highlights

Area: 5,018 sq mi (12 997 km²).
Population (July 1, 1986): 3,189,000.
Chief Cities (July 1, 1986 est.): Hartford, the capital, 137,980; Bridgeport, 141,860; New Haven, 123,450; Waterbury, 102,300.
Government (1987–88): *Chief Officers*—governor, William A. O'Neill (D); lt. gov., Joseph J. Fauliso (D). *General Assembly*—Senate, 36 members; House of Representatives, 151 members.
State Finances (fiscal year 1986): *Revenue,* $6,966,000,000; *expenditure,* $6,009,000,000.
Personal Income (1986): $62,502,000,000; per capita, $19,600.
Labor Force (June 1987): *Civilian labor force,* 1,778,500; *unemployed,* 57,700 (3.2% of total force).
Education: *Enrollment* (fall 1985)—public elementary schools, 321,203; public secondary, 140,823; colleges and universities, 159,348. *Public school expenditures* (1985–86), $2,157,000,000 ($4,888 per pupil).

Capital Punishment. Michael B. Ross, a 27-year-old insurance agent, became the first person condemned to die in Connecticut's electric chair since the U.S. Supreme Court upheld the death penalty in 1976. Ross was convicted June 6 of killing four young eastern Connecticut women. He was sentenced July 6 to die in the electric chair in August but was granted a stay of execution while his lawyers appealed his conviction and sentence.

Elections. Republican State Rep. Christopher Shays defeated Democrat Christine M. Niedermeier in a special 4th Congressional District election August 17. Shays would complete the unexpired portion of the two-year term of the late U.S. Rep. Stewart B. McKinney. McKinney, 56, died May 7 of AIDS-related pneumonia. McKinney, a Republican, was first elected to Congress in 1970. Shays' election maintained the 3–3 split between Democrats and Republicans in the state's House of Representatives delegation.

On November 3, Carrie Saxon Perry (D), a 56-year-old state representative, was elected mayor of Hartford.

Legislation. The 1987 session of the General Assembly adopted a record spending plan of $5.64 billion for the fiscal year that began July 1. The budget included money to add 2,858 jobs to the work force of about 52,000 state employees.

The state legislature also raised the minimum hourly wage to $3.75, beginning October 1. This gave Connecticut the highest hourly minimum wage in the nation. The same legislation increased the minimum to $4.25, effective Oct. 1, 1988.

Inadequate engineering, design, and construction procedures were cited as the reasons for the collapse of an apartment building under construction in Bridgeport, CT. Twenty-eight workers lost their lives in the disaster.

AP/Wide World

In another action, the legislature approved permanent state employees taking up to 24 weeks of unpaid leave within a two-year period after the birth or adoption of a child, or to care for a seriously ill child, spouse, or parent.

Smoking in public schools by students and teachers while schools are in session was banned. A law prohibiting the sale of tobacco products to persons under 18 also was enacted. The lawmakers killed an effort to outlaw smoking in restaurants.

The legislature once again rejected a bill prohibiting the use of leg-hold traps for catching animals. Advocates of humane treatment of animals have unsuccessfully sponsored the law in several legislative sessions.

ROBERT F. MURPHY, *"The Hartford Courant"*

CONSUMER AFFAIRS

"Consumer freedom of choice is the mainspring of our economic system, but the freedom of a blind man to match the colors of his costume is too limited in our time. Uninformed choice is not free." These were the words of one of the pioneers of the consumer movement, Colston E. Warne, who died on May 20, 1987. Warne was one of the founders of the Consumers Union and served as its president from its inception in 1936 to 1979. He was also instrumental in forming the International Organization of Consumers Unions in 1960 and served as its president for the next ten years.

Nothing of a startling nature took place in U.S. consumer affairs during 1987. The Consumer Price Index (CPI), the basic measure of inflation, increased at an annual rate of about 4%, compared with 1.9% in 1986. Just as the price of gasoline played an important part in keeping the inflation rate down in 1986, it played an important part in reversing the downward trend during 1987. The cost of medical care continued to lead the increase in prices.

Federal Consumer Activity. The proposed U.S. budget for fiscal 1988 as submitted by the Office of Management and Budget included the following appropriations for key consumer activities: Office of Consumer Affairs—$1.1 million, down 36%; Consumer Product Safety Commission—$34.4 million, down .6%; Federal Trade Commission—$69.9 million, up 7.5%; Food and Drug Administration—$449.7 million, up .4%; and the Consumer Information Center—$1.3 million, up 5.3%.

President Ronald Reagan proclaimed April 19–25, 1987, as National Consumers Week. The theme was "Consumers Celebrate the Constitution," tying in the event with the celebration of the 200th anniversary of the signing of the U.S. Constitution.

Two major U.S. consumer laws were enacted during the year. On March 17, President Reagan signed into law a bill establishing national energy conservation standards for large household appliances, a measure he once vetoed. The standards apply to 12 major home appliances, including refrigerators, stoves, and air conditioners. And on August 10, the president signed a law which, among other things, limited the length of time banks can hold consumers' deposited checks.

Credit Cards. The credit card war reached a new level of intensity during 1987, as issuers offered a variety of special inducements, new options, and, in some cases, lower interest rates. American Express introduced its Optima Card, an extended-payment service available only to American Express card members, at an interest rate of 13.5%. Exxon reduced its credit card interest rate from an average of 18% to 12.5%, except for those states which already mandated a lower rate. Major banks moved very slowly in lowering their credit card interest rates, but more and more credit card lenders vied for customers with sweepstakes prizes, membership in private clubs, and other special incentives.

Airline Service. Complaints against U.S. airlines increased rapidly during the year. Responding to the complaints, the U.S. Department of Transportation under its rulemaking authority required airlines to provide monthly flight performance data for public release. In the first report, for September, the rate of on-time arrival ranged from 67.4% for US Air to 84.5% for American. Northwest received the largest number of complaints concerning mishandled baggage.

Consumers and Cars. By late summer, the U.S. automobile industry was facing a major problem: an excessive inventory of 1987 cars just as the time was approaching to introduce the new 1988 models. General Motors, with a backlog of 1 million 1987 cars, offered interest rates as low as 1.9% for a two-year loan or a cash rebate of up to $2,000, depending on the car. Ford and Chrysler followed suit almost immediately to meet the competition.

Chrysler was caught in an embarrassing situation during the year, as the federal government filed charges against the company for selling as new up to 60,000 cars that had been driven (some more than 400 miles; 640 km) by Chrysler executives); some of the cars had even been damaged in accidents. Chrysler Chairman Lee Iacocca, in double-page advertisements in newspapers across the United States, stated: "Testing cars is a good idea. Disconnecting odometers is a lousy idea. That's a mistake we won't make again at Chrysler. Period." Warranties on the cars in question were extended for two years, and the company offered to replace the damaged vehicles with brand new 1987 cars of comparable value.

STEWART M. LEE
Geneva College

CRIME

Debate continued in 1987 over the precise nature of short-term changes in U.S. crime rates, but there was no disagreement that the three-year interlude of decreasing incidence had—or would shortly—come to an end. As has often been the case in recent years, the U.S. Federal Bureau of Investigation's (FBI's) Uniform Crime Reports (UCR), based on crimes known to the police, and the Bureau of Justice Statistics' National Crime Survey (NCS), based on interviews with a random sampling of U.S. households, came up with different conclusions about the precise nature of shifts in crime rates for 1986. But both surveys indicated a notable slowing of the previous decline in serious crime.

The UCR reported a 6% increase in the seven major categories of crime—murder, aggravated assault, rape, robbery, burglary, larceny-theft, and auto theft—during 1986. The total number of serious crimes was the highest since 1980, and experts predicted that crime would continue to go up for the remainder of the current decade. The increase was traced primarily to the growing number of persons coming into the 15-to-24-year-old age bracket, a group that commits a disproportionately large number of crimes. The previous slowdown in the escalation of crime resulted from the fact that children from the 1946–60 "baby boom" had aged out of their most crime-prone period.

The total number of major offenses tabulated by the UCR increased to 13.2 million, with violent crimes up 12% and property offenses rising 6%. Violent crimes had thus increased 45% since 1977, and property crimes had risen 18%. Upward movement in 1986 crime rates were reported in 44 of the 50 states. Downward trends were found only in Delaware, Indiana, Maine, Nevada, Montana, and North Dakota. The largest crime increase occurred in the South, where crime levels rose by 10.1%. The rise in the Northeast was 2.6%, in the Midwest 4%, and in the West 5.8%.

Conviction Rates. The striking escalation of crime in the South came despite the fact that this region has twice as high a conviction rate as any other area for persons arrested on felony charges. A U.S. Department of Justice study found 143 convictions for every 1,000 felony arrests in the South, compared with 58 in the West, 60 in the Northeast, and 78 in the Midwest.

Higher conviction rates also were found in less-populated areas of the country than in cities. Steven Schlesinger, director of the Bureau of Justice Statistics, explained the difference by the fact that crime in urban areas is so serious and so frequent that district attorneys become more selective about which cases they will prosecute; thus, many persons arrested in cities are never even brought to trial.

Victimization Statistics. Contrary to the UCR results, the National Crime Survey found "no measurable differences" between 1986 and 1985 in the number of U.S. households touched by any of the crimes tabulated: rape, robbery, assault, personal theft, household burglary, household theft, and motor-vehicle theft. This was the first year, the NCS reported, in which the percentage of households victimized by crime did not decrease significantly. Since its inception in 1975, the NCS has never shown a year-to-year crime increase. More than one fourth of U.S. households reported at least one resident to have been touched by violence or theft.

The NCS found that Americans were victimized by 34.2 million crimes during 1986. The survey found that 37% of all crimes were reported to the police, 5% more than in 1975. It remained unclear whether the rise in reporting was a consequence of greater confidence in the police, growing impatience with crime, or tighter requirements for recovery from insurance companies.

Escalating Criminal Justice Costs. Besides the influx of more people into the high crime-prone age brackets, the cessation of decreases in the crime rate has been traced to a slowdown in funding for criminal-justice work. Charles M. Friel, dean of the college of criminal justice at Sam Houston State University in Huntsville, TX, maintained that prison overcrowding, a function of the failure to fund new facilities, has led to the premature release of violent offenders and presented probation and parole officers with unmanageable caseloads of 300 or more persons. This produces, Friel argued, "a breakdown in proper supervision," which increasingly "puts the public at risk."

The costs of criminal justice continued to increase sharply. A study during 1987 indicated that such expenditures totaled $45.6 billion annually, or 2.9% of total government outlays. Of this amount, $22 billion was being used for police protection, $13 billion to build and run prisons and jails and to operate probation and parole departments, and $10 billion to carry out the business of the courts, prosecutors, legal services, and public defenders. Local governments were burdened with the largest part of this expense—$25.3 billion—while states were spending $15 billion and the federal government less than $6 billion. The cost to each citizen for operating the criminal justice system came to $191 annually.

Murder at the Workplace. Murder is a vocational peril that the Occupational Safety and Health Administration (OSHA) has ignored, charged the *American Journal of Public Health* (AJPH) in its October 1987 issue. Studies indicate odds of 2 in 100,000 annually that a male worker in the United States will be murdered while at work; that comes to a total of 1,600 homicides a year. In addition to police officers, taxi drivers, service-station attendants, and convenience-store workers are at particular risk.

Guns and Crime. The intense debate about the importance of gun control as a preventive measure against crime was further fueled during the year by a comprehensive study of the weapons behavior of a sample of 1,800 convicted adult male felons imprisoned in ten different states. The research, reported by James D. Wright of the University of Massachusetts, found that few felons—only one of six—purchased their guns from retail outlets. The majority said that they got the weapons from family members or friends on the street, or stole them. The felons, who are prohibited by the Gun Control Act of 1968 from acquiring guns when they are released from prison, nonetheless said that they thought it would be "no trouble at all" to get a weapon. Eighty percent said they could obtain a gun on the street within a few days or less. A majority insisted that if small, cheap handguns were banned, as has been proposed, they would merely locate bigger and more expensive handguns.

Interpreting these findings, James K. Stewart, head of the National Institute of Justice, argued that "vigorous enforcement and tougher penalties for those who commit crimes with firearms may be more effective than regulation." Critics of this interpretation insisted that gun-control laws could dry up the supply of weapons and thereby significantly diminish the ability of offenders to obtain guns either from retailers or on the street.

AIDS. The interplay between new social conditions and definitions of illegal activity was illustrated by a case in Minneapolis involving a prison inmate who bit two prison guards after testing positive for the AIDS (Acquired Immune Deficiency Syndrome) virus. The inmate was found guilty on two counts of assault with a deadly and dangerous weapon, his mouth and teeth. The offender, a 44-year-old heroin addict, was serving a seven-year sentence for credit-card fraud. Defense attorneys argued that though it is theoretically possible for AIDS to be transmitted through saliva, there was no scientific proof for that position. Earlier in the year, a man infected with the AIDS virus had been charged with attempted murder after he allegedly spat at police officers, but the judge dismissed the charge.

Organized Crime. A new twist to the sentencing of organized criminals occurred in June, when eight men convicted in New York as leaders of an international drug ring were ordered to contribute $2.5 million to a fund for the treatment of drug addicts. Sentences of 45 years in prison were imposed on the two main figures in the case: Gaetano Badalamenti, said by prosecutors to be a former leader of the Mafia in Sicily; and Salvatore Catalano, the boss of the drug ring, described as a top figure in the Bonanno crime family in New York. Testimony in the 17-month trial indicated that the defendants had acquired morphine base in Turkey and sold it in the United States, along with cocaine from South America. The men were alleged to have transferred about $60 million into overseas accounts. The street value of the heroin was said to be more than $1.6 billion. The case became known as the "pizza connection" because a network of pizza restaurants was used as fronts for many of the ring's drug deals.

More unusual than the sentence in the "pizza connection" case was the decree of a

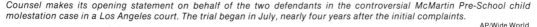

Counsel makes its opening statement on behalf of the two defendants in the controversial McMartin Pre-School child molestation case in a Los Angeles court. The trial began in July, nearly four years after the initial complaints.

AP/Wide World

AP/Wide World

John Gotti, the reputed boss of the Gambino crime family, and six co-defendants were acquitted on racketeering and conspiracy charges in a New York federal court in March.

Portland, OR, judge in August that a twice-convicted child molester had to move to a new home after finishing his prison term and to put a sign on his front door, proclaiming: "Dangerous Sex Offender. No Children Allowed." A similar sign had to be displayed on any car he drove. The defendant indicated that he would appeal the sentence terms.

Sentencing Commission. Controversy continued to mark the work of the seven-member U.S. Sentencing Commission. The commission, created by anticrime legislation in 1984 to overhaul the sentencing of federal offenders, submitted its guidelines in April 1987. The purpose of the commission was to reduce the wide disparity in criminal sentencing by spelling out prison terms for different offenses. Judges would be required to stay within the guidelines or to defend in writing their reasons for departing from them.

A report in *The Wall Street Journal* had charged that the committee's work was marked by "disarray, personal rivalries, and a lack of direction," and various groups and legal specialists had raised similar concerns. The commission's first draft report was withdrawn in September 1986 after critics maintained that it was too complex, relied too heavily on rigid mathematical formulas, and left too little discretion for judges. The commission's guidelines took effect on Nov. 1, 1987.

According to commission member Michael K. Block and research director William Rhodes, the final guidelines will have the following consequences:

• There will be a significant decline in the number of sentences that are reduced to probation. Currently, 41.4% of those convicted of crimes against a person receive probation. This proportion was projected to decline to 25.4% after the guidelines are implemented.

• The average time served for violent offenses will increase substantially.

• Except for burglary and income-tax fraud, where the average prison term will go up, the average time served for most property crimes will remain largely unchanged. Sentences for income-tax evasion, currently averaging about six months, were expected to increase to one year.

Overall, convicted federal offenders now serve an average of 15.8 months in prison. The guidelines were expected to increase the figure to 29.3 months.

Capital Punishment. The U.S. Sentencing Commission also had been tangled in debate regarding capital punishment. The view that a recommendation on the death penalty would so overshadow other proposals, and subject the report to bitter congressional debate, persuaded commissioners to put aside the issue.

The death penalty was inflicted with increasing regularity during the year, as legal obstacles to its use were swept aside by appellate courts. In California, three state Supreme Court justices who consistently had reversed death-penalty convictions failed to gain reaffirmation, a reflection of strong public support for capital punishment. In 1987, California had more than 200 of the nation's 2,000 prisoners awaiting execution on death row.

In Texas, Attorney General Jim Mattox called for the admission of cameras to the death chamber so that the public could see how a criminal is put to death. "For these things to be conducted in the still of the night with no crowds around, it is likely not to bring about the deterrent impact that the public would like it to have," Mattox noted. By September 1987, Texas had performed more than two dozen executions (all by lethal injection), the most in the nation since the U.S. Supreme Court restored the death penalty in 1976.

Amnesty International, the organization that won the Nobel Peace Prize in 1977 for its work against the use of torture in Third World countries, entered the death-penalty debate in the United States. It called capital punishment the "ultimate form of cruel, inhuman, and degrading punishment" and argued that "there is no place in civilized society for the gas chamber, the gallows, or the electric chair." Franca Sciuto, chairman of the organization's executive committee, pointed out that most European countries do not allow capital punishment despite popular sentiment in favor of it, and called upon U.S. legislators to follow suit. Short of complete abolition, Sciuto advocated a prohibition against the execution of juveniles and of mentally retarded persons. The first of these matters, involving a case from Oklahoma, was under review by the U.S. Supreme Court.

GILBERT GEIS
University of California, Irvine

CUBA

Although Cuba continued to be plagued by deep social and economic problems, in 1987 the Castro government maintained its orthodox Marxist style of economic management, rejecting the revisionist trend in the Soviet Union and other Communist bloc countries. Even though Castro conceded that the Cuban revolution was facing the most severe crisis in its 28-year-long history, he repeatedly asserted that the country's economic system would remain centralized, indicating that he himself would continue to make all major decisions.

Economy. The Cuban economy performed badly in 1987. In addition to the perpetual problem of government mismanagement, sugar and petroleum prices reduced hard currency reserves. (In 1986, Cuba earned $150 million in foreign currency by re-exporting Soviet oil. In 1987, however, Moscow shipped only enough petroleum to cover Cuba's internal needs.) Sugar production, which accounts for 70% of Cuba's exports and pays for most hard currency purchases, was estimated by Western sources at 6.9 million tons, about 500,000 less than in 1986. Adverse weather seriously affected the tobacco, livestock, and citrus sectors. Frozen out of the U.S. market, the country could not find buyers for its nickel production.

The shortage of foreign exchange caused Cuba again to stop interest payments on its $4 billion debt to Western banks, and to delay payments for Western imports. Tourism, a source of hard currency, increased slightly. But exports of citrus fruits, once envisioned by Castro as a promising dollar-earning commodity, fell sharply in 1987 because the crops did not meet world standards.

The Soviet Union continued to send Cuba goods to the value of $11 million a day, and Cuba's debt to the USSR rose to more than $30 billion, with an additional $19 billion owed to other Eastern bloc countries. The $49 billion debt did not include the cost of military aid.

Another indication of hard times ahead was a call by the Cuban Defense Minister Raul Castro for a cut in superfluous and wasteful expenditures for the armed forces.

Del Pino's Defection. Raul Castro's unusual admission of waste in the heretofore sacrosanct military followed a similar statement by Gen. Rafael del Pino, who had defected to the United States in May. Del Pino, one of Cuba's defense vice-ministers, also claimed that corruption was pervasive among government and party officials, and that there was discontent among the 37,000 Cuban troops in Angola.

Two months after General del Pino's defection, President Castro personally ordered the arrest of Luis Orlando Domínguez, head of the Civil Aeronautics Institute. Domínguez, who had been secretary general of the Union of Young Communists, was once touted as the prototype of the "new man" of the Cuban revolution. He was now charged with embezzling public funds and indulging in a luxurious and extravagant style of living. Although in publicly denouncing his former protegé Castro indicated that his case was not unique, Domínguez was the only official charged. He was tried, and given a 20-year prison sentence.

Relations with the United States. Cuba and the United States have not had diplomatic relations since 1961, but diplomatic contact was reestablished on a limited basis in 1977. Early in 1987, however, the senior U.S. diplomat in Havana, the chief of the U.S. Interests Section, was recalled to Washington in what was seen as another cutoff of relations. The September arrival in the Cuban capital of career diplomat John T. Taylor to fill the vacant post was the first solid indication of a thaw. Previously, the United States had given its approval for Cuban diplomats to travel to the Pan American Games in Indianapolis. Cuba reciprocated by permitting Washington to charter flights and transport supplies to the U.S. Interests Section in Havana.

In 1980 Castro allowed some 125,000 Cubans to emigrate to the United States through the Cuban port of Mariel. This huge and unexpected influx strained U.S. facilities in Florida, but the refugees were promised the opportunity to seek U.S. citizenship. It quickly became obvious, however, that Castro had included several thousand criminals and mental-hospital inmates among the émigrés. These were termed "excludable" by U.S. immigration authorities, and because they could not be deported—Castro refused to take them back—they were held in various prisons and detention camps. Other Mariel refugees, arrested and convicted of crimes committed in the United States, later joined them.

Through the years of their imprisonment, the jailed Cubans protested, staged hunger strikes, and rioted. Because the Supreme Court confirmed their "excludable" status, the Immigration and Naturalization Service (INS) could hold them indefinitely and without the

CUBA • Information Highlights

Official Name: Republic of Cuba.
Location: Caribbean.
Area: 42,803 sq mi (110 860 km^2).
Population (mid-1987 est.): 10,300,000.
Chief Cities (Dec. 31, 1984 est.): Havana, the capital, 1,992,620; Santiago de Cuba, 356,033; Camagüey, 287,392; Holguín, 194,113.
Government: *Head of state and government,* Fidel Castro Ruz, président (took office under a new constitution, Dec. 1976). *Legislature* (unicameral) —National Assembly of People's Power.
Monetary Unit: Peso (0.775 peso equals U.S.$1, August 1987).
Foreign Trade (1985 U.S.$): *Imports,* $8,593,000,000; *exports,* $8,567,000,000.

customary due process afforded ordinary prisoners. But some detainees were released under a revision process set up by the INS.

In December 1984, the United States and Cuba reached an agreement that allowed the deportation to Cuba of about 2,700 Mariel prisoners and the reception by the United States of a yearly quota of new Cuban immigrants. The deportations began in early 1985 but were ended by Cuba when Radio Martí, a Voice of America station, began broadcasts that May.

The United States and Cuba renegotiated the 1984 agreement in the autumn of 1987, and on November 20, Washington announced that 2,500 Mariel prisoners were to be repatriated. Cuban inmates at the Oakdale, LA, INS detention center and at the federal penitentiary in Atlanta, GA, rioted in protest, holding prison guards and other hostages. The takeovers ended peacefully after eight days in Oakdale and 11 days in Atlanta, with the U.S. Justice Department announcing a moratorium on deportations and pledging to reassess the status of prisoners eligible for parole and of the 3,600 who had completed their sentences.

GEORGE VOLSKY, *University of Miami*

CYPRUS

Cyprus celebrated the 27th anniversary of its independence from Great Britain on Oct. 1, 1987. It was still a divided country, however, as the result of a Turkish invasion in 1974, which left approximately 37% of the island under Turkish domination.

The southern part of Cyprus continued to be ruled by the internationally recognized Cypriot government under Greek Cypriot President Spyros Kyprianou, who represented the overwhelming majority of the population. In the territories occupied by Turkey, the "Turkish Republic of Northern Cyprus," proclaimed in 1983 and recognized only by Turkey, was headed by its President Rauf Denktas, a Turkish Cypriot. Greek and Turkish Cypriots were separated by a Green Line buffer zone, manned by the 300-member United Nations Peacekeeping Force in Cyprus (UNFICYP).

Obstacles to Reconciliation. All efforts to reach a permanent understanding between Greek and Turkish Cypriots—including mediation by the United Nations and strong initiatives by UN Secretary-General Javier Pérez de Cuéllar—proved unavailing. The de facto partition remained at the stalemate stage, with the two mainland governments each supporting their respective Cypriot populations.

In September 1987, Pérez de Cuéllar reported to the UN General Assembly that the Turkish military buildup, with an estimated 29,000 Turkish troops stationed on the island, might lead to a dangerous confrontation between the two sides. The Greek government maintained that the troops must be removed before the beginning of any meaningful negotiations. Although President Kyprianou wished the Cyprus question to be debated again by the UN General Assembly, Denktas opposed the type of discussion that has taken place there in the past. Indeed, it was the outcome of such a General-Assembly debate that disturbed Turkey and the Turkish Cypriots to the point of declaring their portion of the island independent in 1983. Kyprianou also favored the Soviet Union's proposal of an international conference on Cyprus. Denktas opposed the idea.

The Cyprus situation was further complicated in February 1987, in testimony by then U.S. Defense Secretary Caspar Weinberger before a congressional committee considering increased military aid to Turkey in fiscal 1988. The secretary admitted that some aid already given by the United States had been used by the Turkish forces in Cyprus. Greece strongly protested Weinberger's testimony.

During an address to the UN General Assembly on October 9, Kyprianou accused Turkey of importing some 65,000 mainland Turks to the island in an effort to increase the proportion of Turks to Greek Cypriots.

Women's Walk. "Women Walk Home," an organization of Greek Cypriot women, made two attempts to cross the Green Line in 1987 in order to bring to world attention the divisions and upheavals caused by the Turkish occupation, which had forced some 200,000 Greek Cypriots to flee their homes in 1974. An attempt to cross the Green Line in June was blocked by UN peacekeeping forces, but on November 22 some women managed to cross minefields and for the first time since 1974 to enter Turkish-occupied territory. They were turned back by UN and Turkish forces.

Economics. The Greek Cypriot territories continued to enjoy a strong economy. The occupied north, linked to the Turkish economy, did not. In October, the first Customs Union agreement with the European Community was signed by the Greek Cypriot government.

GEORGE J. MARCOPOULOS, *Tufts University*

CYPRUS • Information Highlights

Official Name: Republic of Cyprus.
Location: Eastern Mediterranean.
Area: 3,571 sq mi (9 250 km^2).
Population (mid-1987 est.): 700,000.
Chief Cities (1982 est.): Nicosia, the capital, 149,100; Limassol, 107,200.
Government: *Head of state and government,* Spyros Kyprianou, president (took office Aug. 1977). *Legislature*—House of Representatives.
Monetary Unit: Pound (0.492 pound equals U.S.$1, July 1987).
Gross Domestic Product (1984 est. U.S.$): $2,400,-000,000.
Economic Index (1986): *Consumer Prices* (1980 = 100), all items, 139.6; food, 146.7.
Foreign Trade (1986 U.S.$): *Imports,* $1,279,000,000; *exports,* $506,000,000.

AP/Wide World

Ordinary Czechs welcomed Mikhail Gorbachev to their homeland in April. The Soviet party boss discussed "plans and designs for the future" with Czech leaders.

CZECHOSLOVAKIA

The dilemma that Czechoslovakia's rulers have been facing in recent years became even more complicated in 1987: how to improve the mediocre performance of the country's economy by reducing stifling bureaucratic controls, without at the same time endangering the Communist Party's monopoly of power. "Restructuring" the economic system had become the official credo in Mikhail Gorbachev's Soviet Union, and the Communist leaders of Czechoslovakia felt duty bound to follow suit.

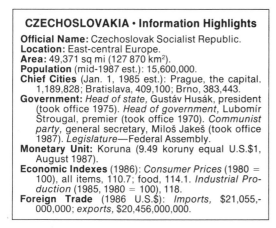

CZECHOSLOVAKIA • Information Highlights

Official Name: Czechoslovak Socialist Republic.
Location: East-central Europe.
Area: 49,371 sq mi (127 870 km²).
Population (mid-1987 est.): 15,600,000.
Chief Cities (Jan. 1, 1985 est.): Prague, the capital, 1,189,828; Bratislava, 409,100; Brno, 383,443.
Government: *Head of state,* Gustáv Husák, president (took office 1975). *Head of government,* Lubomír Štrougal, premier (took office 1970). *Communist party,* general secretary, Miloš Jakeš (took office 1987). *Legislature*—Federal Assembly.
Monetary Unit: Koruna (9.49 koruny equal U.S.$1, August 1987).
Economic Indexes (1986): *Consumer Prices* (1980 = 100), all items, 110.7; food, 114.1. *Industrial Production* (1985, 1980 = 100), 118.
Foreign Trade (1986 U.S.$): *Imports,* $21,055,000,000; *exports,* $20,456,000,000.

That leadership underwent a major change on December 17, when 74-year-old party chief Gustáv Husák resigned, apparently because of failing health. Miloš Jakeš, 65, a member of the Central Committee, was elevated to the post.

The Economy. The need for radical reform was once again underscored by uninspiring economic results in the first half of 1987. While modest quantitative increases were achieved in a number of industries, one third of the nation's industrial enterprises and one half of its construction firms failed to attain the planned levels of quality and technical advance. New apartment construction also failed to approach the goals set. Industrial production costs remained as high as in the first half of 1986 although the economic plan called for them to be lowered by at least 1.1%.

To cope with the economic malaise, the government introduced in July new types of controls on state enterprises closely patterned after those in the USSR. Organs of central government would now be in charge only of long-term production strategy and the setting of economic priorities, while the individual enterprises would be run by a director and an enterprise council elected by the workers' assembly in each plant. Enterprises would be fully self-accounting, and those unable to pay their own way would be closed. In an effort to improve inadequate services to the population, the party presidium announced that cooperatives and even individuals would be allowed to open catering establishments and small stores.

Foreign Relations. Attempts to revitalize the economy were accompanied by a concerted effort to improve Czechoslovakia's image abroad and thus to enhance the country's prospects for increased trade and the acquisition of much-needed Western technology. An impressive number of foreign statesmen, politicians, and delegations paid visits to Czechoslovakia. General Secretary Gorbachev was the first Soviet official since the Communist seizure of power in Czechoslovakia who was welcomed with genuine spontaneity by ordinary citizens. They hoped he would push the die-hard rulers of Czechoslovakia toward a more liberal course.

Human Rights. While many of the central controls over the economy were done away with or substantially reduced, no such action was considered in the area of human rights and religion. A slight improvement did occur in 1987 as police harassment of dissidents seemed to lessen, and the atmosphere at the conferences of various literary, cultural, and artistic organizations held in 1987 displayed more openness than had been the case in earlier years. But when a group of citizens decided to organize a Society of Friends of the United States, the ministry of the interior refused to grant the needed official approval.

EDWARD TABORSKY
The University of Texas at Austin

DANCE

Amid interest and excitement generated by new choreography and gifted young dancers, the dance world was affected or startled by several news events in 1987. These included an unexpected invitation to Mikhail Baryshnikov and Natalya Makarova, both of whom defected in the 1970s from the Kirov Ballet, to dance at a gala in Moscow. The invitation came from Yuri Grigorovich, the Bolshoi Ballet's artistic director, during a visit to New York early in the year to announce the Bolshoi's first U.S. tour since 1979. The offer fell through after the gala could not be organized on time and Baryshnikov said he would come only if the American Ballet Theatre, which he has directed since 1980, were invited later as well. The new Soviet policy of *glasnost* did, however, have an effect. At the end of the year, Rudolf Nureyev was allowed to see his ailing mother in the Soviet Union for the first time since his own defection from the Kirov in 1961.

On a sadder note, the year was marked by the death of some of the most important names in dance history. Antony Tudor, one of the 20th century's greatest ballet choreographers, died shortly after Nora Kaye, who had become a star at Ballet Theatre under his guidance. Tudor, who began his career in his native England, was often called the father of psychological ballet. In *Pillar of Fire, Dark Elegies, Jardin aux Lilas,* and other works, he demonstrated that the idiom of classical ballet could be extended into complex emotional expression and contemporary themes. Like Tudor, Miss Kaye was a charter member of Ballet Theatre in 1939; she was considered an unsurpassed dramatic ballerina. More recently, she served as a producer on dance-related films directed by her husband, Herbert Ross. In addition to *The Turning Point* (1977), these included *Dancers,* released in 1987 with Baryshnikov and other members of the Ballet Theatre in a modern story analogous to *Giselle*.

In the field of musical comedy, the death of Fred Astaire was followed by the deaths of Michael Bennett, the choreographer of *A Chorus Line* and *Dreamgirls,* and Bob Fosse, well-known for his choreography in Hollywood and on Broadway. Others who died included Choo San Goh, whose contemporary-style ballets were seen in many American and foreign troupes, including the Washington Ballet, where he was associate director.

Bennett's death was one of several in the performing arts attributed to AIDS (Acquired Immune Deficiency Syndrome). On October 5 at New York's Lincoln Center, 13 modern dance and ballet companies, under Jerome Robbins' supervision, staged a benefit called "Dancing for Life" and raised $1.4 million for AIDS research and care. The diversity on this program was echoed throughout the season.

Ballet. The most talked about company was the Bolshoi Ballet, which arrived in the United States with an array of new young stars. Grigorovich's choreography—in his restagings of such classics as *Raymona* and *Giselle* or in such new works as *The Golden Age*—was controversial. Although theaters were sold out at New York's Metropolitan Opera House and in three other cities, some critics felt Grigorovich had sacrificed the Bolshoi's dramatic expressiveness to a blander pure-dance approach. But others said he had given the Bolshoi a more streamlined contemporary look that maintained its traditional accent on bravura and virtuosity. The brilliance of the new generation of dancers was represented by Irek Mukhamedov, a powerful technician as the hero who rescues a cabaret dancer from Soviet gangsters during the 1920s in *The Golden Age,* a revised version of a 1930 ballet with music by Dmitri Shostakovich. Other new Bolshoi stars who left an impact were Andris Liepa, Nina Ananiashvili, Aleksei Fadeyechev, and the more established Ludmila Semenyaka.

For the second time in two years, the Kirov toured Canada and a few U.S. cities. Twenty-three U.S. cities, however, were visited by the Moscow Ballet, a group with guest artists and directed by the Bolshoi dancer Vyacheslav Gordeyev. Andrei Ustinov, a dancer on the tour, defected while in Dallas. The Kirov's Olga Likhovskaya danced in *Giselle* as a guest with the Warsaw Ballet from Poland.

The American ballet world saw a surge in creativity. Peter Martins found renewed inspiration in Baroque music with two premieres for the New York City Ballet: *Les Petits Riens* to Mozart and an all-male ballet, *Les Gentilhommes,* to Handel. Martins was equally inventive in a contrasting energetic work, *Ecstatic Orange,* set to music by a young American composer, Michael Torke. *Sinfonia Mistica,* choreographed by Paul Mejia to Penderecki's music, also was presented by the company. The Feld Ballet performed Eliot Feld's new *Embraced Waltzes*. The San Francisco Ballet attracted attention with two imaginative premieres, James Kudelka's *Dreams of Harmony* and William Forsythe's *New Sleep*.

The American Ballet Theatre offered one premiere, *Enough Said,* by company member Clark Tippett, but concentrated on revivals and a major new production of *The Sleeping Beauty,* staged by Kenneth MacMillan. The most splendid prince in this version was Julio Bocca, a 20-year-old Argentine dancer whose Ballet Theatre debut made him instantly popular. Bocca fused a strong technique with natural exuberance and gallant partnering. Ricardo Bustamante, a fiery soloist, and Wes Chapman, noticed for his purity, also came to the fore.

Other young dancers stood out in American ballet companies. In the Joffrey Ballet, Tina LeBlanc and Edward Stierle dazzled audiences

© 1987 Martha Swope

The American Ballet Theatre presented a new Kenneth MacMillan production of "The Sleeping Beauty," starring Julio Bocca and Cheryl Yeager. Bocca, a 20-year-old Argentinean, was cited as a "splendid prince" and a "classical dancer con brio."

with precise and fast footwork. The Joffrey made news with two productions. One was *The Nutcracker,* set in a 19th-century American household designed by Oliver Smith. This first *Nutcracker* for the company was conceived and directed by Robert Joffrey, co-choreographed by Gerald Arpino, and staged by Scott Barnard and George Verdak, who reconstructed dances from the 1940 Ballet Russe de Monte Carlo version.

A second Joffrey production attracted even more attention in its attempt to reconstruct Vaslav Nijinsky's lost choreography from the original 1913 version of the Igor Stravinsky ballet, *Le Sacre du Printemps.* Millicent Hodson and Kenneth Archer, two researchers who worked from notes and pictures, produced a colorful staging that conveyed the meaning of the ballet as conceived by the Russian painter, Nicholas Roerich. The stage action concerned the worship of the sun by a Slavic tribe. Meanwhile, the Tulsa (OK) Ballet Theatre revived *Mozart Violin Concerto,* a work created by George Balanchine in 1942 in Argentina.

Modern Dance. Another rare reconstruction came from the Alvin Ailey American Dance Theater with *The Magic of Katherine Dunham.* The 78-year-old modern dance pioneer supervised a program of her dances from the 1930s and 1940s, inspired by the black heritage in the Caribbean, the United States, and Latin America. The vibrant production values contributed to the staging's success. Ulysses Dove's *Vespers* also was performed by the Ailey troupe.

Martha Graham's *Celebration* from 1934 was revived to great acclaim for the first time in 50 years, surprising today's audiences with its abstract form and energy. *Persephone,* a premiere, was continually revised during the season by Miss Graham. Her company's New York engagement opened with an unusual gala: Baryshnikov and Nureyev appeared in *Appalachian Spring;* and Maya Plisetskaya, the Bolshoi star, appeared in *Incense.*

Modern dance premieres in 1987 included Merce Cunningham's *Shards, Fabrications,* and *Points in Space;* Paul Taylor's *Syzygy* and *Kith and Kin;* Twyla Tharp's *In the Upper Room* and *Ballare;* Erick Hawkins' *God the Reveller;* and Trisha Brown's *Newark.*

Maguy Marin, an experimental French choreographer, created a hit with *Cendrillon,* a dollhouse version of *Cinderella,* for the Lyons Opera Ballet. Her own company performed *Babel Babel* and *Eden* on similar themes of lost innocence. Visitors to the United States included the Paris Opera Ballet with Nureyev's version of *Cinderella,* the Ballet Rambert from England, the Netherlands Dance Theater, the Hungarian State Folk Ensemble, and the Belgian choreographers Anne Teresa de Keersmaeker and Wim Vandekeybus.

The Samuel Scripps-American Dance Festival award went to Alvin Ailey, the Kennedy Center Honors to Alwin Nikolais, and the Algur Meadows award to Merce Cunningham. The Capezio Award, honoring the centenary of the Capezio shoe firm, was given in a special presentation to Nureyev, Fosse, Astaire, and Jac Venza, the executive producer of the "Dance in America" series on public TV.

ANNA KISSELGOFF, *"The New York Times"*

DELAWARE

In 1987, the bicentennial year of the U.S. Constitution, Delaware celebrated its historic role as the first state to ratify the Constitution. Events throughout the year focused attention on the part played by Delaware's delegates to the constitutional convention in protecting the rights of the small states by ensuring equal representation for all in the U.S. Senate. (*See* feature article, page 37.)

While the bicentennial celebration went on, two prominent Delaware citizens emerged as contenders for the presidency in 1988. At the same time, many in the state became increasingly concerned with the consequences of rapid development caused by a long period of economic expansion.

Political Developments. Delaware's former Gov. Pierre duPont IV had announced his candidacy for the Republican presidential nomination in June 1986, and twelve months later U.S. Sen. Joseph Biden, Jr., declared that he would seek the Democratic nomination. Senator Biden, in particular, promised to make a substantial impact, attracting national attention as chairman of the Senate Judiciary Committee's televised hearings on the confirmation of Supreme-Court nominee Robert Bork. However, Biden's moment in the spotlight became a mixed blessing as allegations of plagiarism and distortion of his past academic and political record began to surface. As the highly contentious Bork hearings continued, Delaware's junior senator admitted to major errors in judgment and announced his withdrawal from the presidential race.

The Impact of Economic Growth. "Quality of life" became the buzzword for Delaware's civic and political leaders in 1987. The state's Financial Centers Development Act, designed to foster conditions favorable to banking, proved successful beyond expectations. Many banks brought their credit-card operations to Delaware, increasing the size of the work force, bringing unemployment to one of the lowest levels in the country (2.8%, seasonally adjusted, August 1987), and generally increasing the demand for housing, transportation, and public services.

Many Delawareans reacted against what they saw as a threat to their relatively quiet, unhurried way of life. "Quality of life" bills mandating stricter zoing and limiting development were introduced in the legislature; some were approved by the House of Representatives, but were not acted upon by the Senate during the regular legislative session. A special session was scheduled in December to complete work on the package. Meanwhile, pro- and anti-development debates went on at legislative hearings throughout the state.

Other Legislative Activity. In 1987 state revenues exceeded expenditures for the fourth year in a row. The legislature approved a revenue-sharing program to help local governments. Prison reform received a great deal of attention in the face of chronic prison overcrowding and repeated inmate escapes. Legislative hearings brought to light a long list of problems to be handled by a newly appointed corrections commissioner.

Environment. In a major 1987 victory for its strict laws protecting coastline areas for recreational use, Delaware won a court case against the Norfolk and Southern Company. The decision prevented the company from establishing a floating offshore coal transfer operation in Delaware Bay.

JEROME R. LEWIS
University of Delaware

DELAWARE • Information Highlights

Area: 2,045 sq mi (5 295 km²).
Population (July 1, 1986): 633,000.
Chief Cities (1980 census): Dover, the capital, 23,512; Wilmington, 70,195; Newark, 25,247; Elsmere, 6,493.
Government (1987–88): *Chief Officers*—governor, Michael N. Castle (R); lt. gov., S. B. Woo (D). *General Assembly*—Senate, 21 members; House of Representatives, 41 members.
State Finances (fiscal year 1986): *Revenue*, \$1,807,000,000: *expenditure*, \$1,415,000,000.
Personal Income (1986): \$9,498,000,000; per capita, \$15,010.
Labor Force (June 1987): *Civilian labor force*, 342,400; *unemployed*, 10,700 (3.1% of total force).
Education: *Enrollment* (fall 1985)—public elementary schools, 63,082; public secondary, 29,819; colleges and universities, 31,883. *Public school expenditures* (1985–86), \$385,000,000 (\$4,517 per pupil).

DENMARK

During 1987 attention in Denmark was focused on the country's volatile political situation.

Political Affairs. In a surprise move, Prime Minister Poul Schlüter called a parliamentary election in September, four months ahead of schedule. Although Schlüter may have hoped to take advantage of what he perceived as a favorable moment for his shaky coalition government, the result was a disappointment for him and his allies. With a turnout of 86% of the electorate, Schlüter's Conservative Party saw its representation in the 179-seat Folketing (parliament) reduced from 42 to 38. One of his coalition partners, the Center Democratic Party, gained 1 seat for a total of 9, but another, the Liberal Party, dropped from 22 seats to 19; the fourth member of the nonsocialist "Four-Leaf Clover" coalition, the Christian People's Party, fell from 5 seats to 4. The opposition Social Democrats—Denmark's largest party—also suffered a setback, losing 2 seats for a total of 54. The Socialist People's Party, a neutralist

AP/Wide World

Denmark's Prime Minister Poul Schlüter and his Conservative Party suffered a setback in September 8 parliamentary elections, but his governing coalition of four nonsocialist parties retained a slim majority.

group that opposes Danish membership in NATO and the European Community, registered the biggest gain, from 21 to 27. The anti-tax Progress Party, which seeks to limit Asian immigration, ended up with 9 seats (a gain of 3), and a new party known as Faelleskurs (Common Course), which combines Marxism with opposition to immigrants, surprised everyone by winning 4 seats.

As the nonsocialist parties still held a slim majority, Schlüter was reinstalled as premier, with Liberal Uffe Ellemann-Jensen as foreign minister. The other 20 ministries were shared among 8 Conservatives, 3 Center Democrats, 7 Liberals, and 2 members of the Christian People's Party. The weakened coalition, however, would need the support of the Progress Party and the Radical Liberals, who hold 11 seats, to remain in office.

Following the election, the leader of the Social Democrats, Anker Jørgensen, announced that he would retire from politics. He had served as chairman of the party for 15 years and had served twice as prime minister (1972-73 and 1975-82).

Greenland. Greenlanders, too, went to the polls in 1987, this being their fourth election since the introduction of home rule in 1979. Held on May 26, the election resulted in Siumut (Social Democrats) and Inuit Ataqatigiit (leftist nationalists) holding 11 and 4 seats, respectively, in the Assembly, with Atassut holding 11 seats. The first session of the new Assembly was held on June 9, at which time Jonathan Motzfeldt was reelected speaker and made the head of the coalition cabinet, consisting of five members from Siumut and two from Inuit Ataqatigiit.

Prior to the election there was some disagreement among the parties as to whether the modernization work on the U.S. radar base at Thule was in accord with the U.S.-Soviet ABM Treaty of 1978. Another matter of contention was the case of the 117 Greenlandic residents of the former village of Thule, who had been dispossessed from their living quarters when the Danish government had given the United States permission to build a radar warning station there. After the Greenlanders threatened to take the case to the International Court of Justice in The Hague, Netherlands, the Danish government decided to appoint an impartial three-member committee to try to solve the dispute.

Royal Travels. Early in the year, Queen Margrethe II and Prince Henrik visited Australia and New Zealand, the first such trip by a Danish monarch. The royal couple later traveled to France and Norway.

ERIK J. FRIIS
"The Scandinavian-American Bulletin"

DENMARK • Information Highlights

Official Name: Kingdom of Denmark.
Location: Northwest Europe.
Area: 16,629 sq mi (43 070 km²).
Population (mid-1987 est.): 5,100,000.
Chief Cities (Jan. 1, 1985 est.): Copenhagen, the capital, 1,358,540; Århus, 194,348; Odense, 136,803.
Government: *Head of state,* Margrethe II, queen (acceded Jan. 1972). *Head of government,* Poul Schlüter, prime minister (took office Sept. 1982). *Legislature* (unicameral)—Folketing.
Monetary Unit: Krone (6.4440 kroner equal U.S.$1, Nov. 10, 1987).
Gross National Product (1985 U.S.$): $38,400,-000,000.
Economic Indexes (1986): *Consumer Prices* (1980 = 100), all items, 151.8; food, 150.7. *Industrial Production* (1980 = 100), 126.
Foreign Trade (1986 U.S.$): *Imports,* $22,811,-000,000; *exports,* $21,201,000,000.

DRUGS AND ALCOHOL

Illegal drugs continued to be a significant problem in the United States during 1987, especially in urban areas, even though evidence indicated that use of most drugs had either leveled off or declined slightly. Alcohol abuse, while less publicized, also remained a problem with far-reaching consequences.

Usage. According to studies prepared for the National Institute on Drug Abuse (NIDA) of the U.S. Department of Health and Human Services, marijuana use, which peaked in 1978, continued to decline, as did usage of such hallucinogens as LSD and PCP. The use of cocaine, which had been increasing steadily since the late 1970s, appeared to be leveling off.

Most of the decline in drug usage was among the nation's better educated and higher income groups. For the inner-city poor, however, drug use—especially heroin and the inexpensive cocaine derivative crack—continued to be a growing problem. "We are dealing with two different worlds here," said Professor David F. Musto of the Yale University School of Medicine. "In the inner city, the factors that counterbalance drug use—family, employment, status within the community—often are not there. It is harder for people with nothing to say no to drugs."

Even though the number of drug users was declining, NIDA surveys indicated that tens of millions of Americans continued to use drugs. It was estimated, for example, that some 60 million Americans had tried marijuana and that about 25 million were using it regularly. More than 20 million had tried cocaine, while about 5 million were using it regularly. More than a half million Americans were addicted to heroin. Experts believed that Americans paid about $110 billion in 1986 for illegal drugs and that drug use in 1987 accounted for some $60 billion in crime, health problems, and lost productivity at the workplace.

Arrests. Well publicized "Say No to Drugs" campaigns kept the issue in the news. So, too, did reports of the year's largest drug arrests, which included:

• a 12-month investigation by undercover U.S. drug agents that resulted in 29 arrests in five cities and the seizure of some $300 million worth of cocaine and marijuana and the breakup of a Colombia-based drug cartel,

• one of the largest individual seizures ever recorded—one ton of cocaine worth an estimated $1 billion—by U.S. Drug Enforcement Administration (DEA) agents in Miami, FL,

• the arrest in Miami and subsequent conviction of Samuel Alberto Escruceria-Delgado, a member of the Colombian National Congress who federal officials said was the head of a large, drug-smuggling crime family, on charges that included conspiring to import and distribute cocaine,

• the breakup by DEA agents of New York City's biggest crack distribution organization, which sold as many as 10,000 vials of the substance a day.

Drug enforcement officials viewed these and other arrests and drug seizures with mixed feelings. On the one hand, the arrests proved that the nation's multibillion-dollar effort to enforce the drug laws had scored some notable successes. On the other hand, it was believed that law enforcement, even working at its optimum level, only intercepts 10–15% of the flow of illegal drugs. "We are very proficient at arresting drug dealers and users," said Washington, DC, Assistant Police Chief Isaac Fulwood, while discussing the fact that the nation's capital had a drug arrest rate of 21 per 1,000 residents, the highest in the nation. "But those arrest figures are a sad commentary on the situation in the District. I would take more pride in less arrests if that meant the problem had been abated."

Drug Use and AIDS. A serious new drug problem that surfaced for the first time in 1987 was the rapidly rising proportion of heroin addicts exposed to the AIDS (acquired immune deficiency syndrome) virus. Research has shown that AIDS can be spread from the sharing of needles, a practice that is common among intravenous users of heroin. It is believed that 20–100% of persons who are exposed to the virus eventually die from AIDS. In large cities, health officials are finding that significant numbers of intravenous drug users have been exposed to the AIDS virus, putting themselves, their sexual partners, and their children at grave risk. In New York City, for example, where there are an estimated 200,000 heroin addicts, more than 60% of the heroin users who entered into one drug treatment program tested positive for exposure to the virus.

Trafficking. Adding further to the problem was the lack of progress in anti-drug efforts in virtually all the countries that grow, process, and illegally export cocaine, heroin, and marijuana into the United States. In Bolivia, the major coca-growing country in the world, joint efforts by the United States and Bolivian law enforcement groups failed in 1987 to stem the nation's flourishing cocaine business. In Colombia, where drug-enforcement experts say 80% of the world's cocaine is processed and then smuggled overseas, organized criminal elements continued their illegal drug operations despite a "war" on narcotics declared by President Virgilio Barco Vargas.

Despite an extensive effort to combat drug trafficking, Mexico became the leading single-country source of heroin and marijuana entering the United States, as well as one of the main routes for cocaine processed in Colombia and smuggled northward. In 1986, Mexico passed Colombia to become the top foreign supplier of marijuana to the United States, according to the U.S. Drug Enforcement Administration. More than 40% of all marijuana shipped into the country comes from Mexico, the DEA reported. Nearly a third of the heroin reaching the United States consists of the so-called "black-tar" variety from Mexico. Meanwhile, the bulk of the world's heroin continues to pour virtually unabated out of the so-called Golden Triangle, where the borders of Thailand, Burma, and Laos meet.

Alcohol. While the drug problem garnered most of the headlines, alcohol abuse continued to be one of the United States' most serious health and social problems. Despite national campaigns against the dangers of alcohol, surveys indicated that alcohol use has remained essentially unchanged in recent years. A Gallup Poll released in August 1987, for example, found that 65% of respondents said they drank alcoholic beverages and that 38% of those who did drink had had one within 24 hours of being interviewed—figures that had not changed significantly since 1985.

Alcohol abuse is not uncommon among high-school and college students, and experts believe that as many as 15 million Americans are alcoholics or have other serious drinking problems. Alcoholism and alcohol abuse are implicated in half of all U.S. automobile accidents and homicides and in a fourth of all suicides; they are major factors leading to divorce and other problems brought to family courts, according to a report by the Office of Technology Assessment. It is estimated that the economic cost of alcoholism and alcohol abuse, measured primarily in lost work productivity, exceeds $100 billion a year.

MARC LEEPSON, *"American Politics"*

ECUADOR

The kidnapping of the president, extensive damage from a severe earthquake, continued deterioration of the financial situation, and mounting political tension as presidential elections on Jan. 31, 1988, approached, kept Ecuador in a state of agitation during much of 1987.

Kidnapping. President León Febres Cordero was seized on January 16 by a group of renegade Air Force officers at the Taura air base, located 285 miles (459 km) from the capital, Quito. The kidnappers called for the freedom of retired Air Force Gen. Frank Vargas Pazos, who had been imprisoned in 1986 after taking over another Air-Force base.

Febres was held hostage for 12 hours, during which time he signed an amnesty for Vargas and agreed not to take action against his captors. The president's action caused a furor in the national congress, which was controlled by the political opposition. An attempt to impeach Febres failed, however, when the Ecuadoran military threatened to shut the congress down.

ECUADOR • Information Highlights

Official Name: Republic of Ecuador.
Location: Northwest South America.
Area: 109,483 sq mi (283 560 km²).
Population (mid-1987 est.): 10,000,000.
Chief Cities (mid-1986 est.): Quito, the capital, 1,093,278; Guayaquil, 1,509,108; Cuenca, 193,012.
Government: *Head of state and government,* León Febres Cordero Ribadeneyra, president (took office August 1984). *Legislature* (unicameral)—Chamber of Representatives.
Monetary Unit: Sucre (196 sucres equal U.S.$1, financial rate, Oct. 14, 1987).
Gross National Product (1985 U.S.$): $10,700,000,000.
Economic Index (1986): *Consumer Prices* (1980 = 100), all items, 356.7; food, 459.6.
Foreign Trade (1986 U.S.$): *Imports,* $1,867,000,000; *exports,* $2,171,000,000.

Earthquake. Ecuador's vital petroleum industry was crippled when earthquakes on March 5 and 6 ruptured a key oil pipeline and killed at least 1,000 persons. The quakes caused an estimated $1 billion in damage and cut off petroleum exports, worth $1.2 billion a year in foreign-exchange income.

Prior to the quakes, Ecuador had been producing 240,000 barrels of oil a day, and oil exports accounted for 65% of the country's foreign-trade revenues. Within two months, the government opened an emergency pipeline from the country's oil-producing region in the Amazonian east to a connection with a Colombian pipeline on the Ecuador-Colombia border. The temporary pipeline enabled Ecuador to export 35,000 barrels a day through Colombian ports. In addition, Venezuela, a fellow member of the Organization of the Petroleum Exporting Countries (OPEC), provided Ecuador with 12.5 million barrels of oil over a four-month period for its internal consumption and shipped 7.5 million barrels to Ecuador's overseas customers. The damaged pipeline was repaired and reopened in mid-August.

Financial Problems. In the wake of the earthquake, Ecuador declared itself unable to meet debt-service payments of $550 million to foreign commercial banks in 1987. The country's overall external debt was $8.4 billion.

The government also imposed rigid austerity measures on the domestic economy, decreeing a 90% increase in gasoline prices, gasoline rationing, a 14% increase in bus and taxi fares, a price freeze on 17 basic foodstuffs, a 5% cut in government spending, and a freeze on public-sector hiring.

Political Tension. The year was marked by continual bickering between the executive and legislative branches of government. Attempts were made by the opposition-controlled congress to impeach cabinet officers, including senior minister Luis Robles Plaza. Nevertheless, the January 1988 presidential election was expected to be held without interruption.

RICHARD C. SCHROEDER, *"Visión" Magazine*

EDUCATION

Major concerns in U.S. education during 1987 included plans for a national board to certify teachers, court decisions which overturned two textbook censorship cases and declared Louisiana's "creation science" law unconstitutional, and rising college costs. In other countries, Britain's most ambitious state school reform since 1944 would introduce a national curriculum and, by parent vote, allow central government takeover of local schools.

School Reform. On April 5, U.S. Secretary of Education William J. Bennett blasted "education bureaucrats" in Indiana, Texas, Maine, and Michigan for cutting back on reform efforts because they felt costs were too high. Education leaders in these and other states disputed Secretary Bennett and insisted that reform indeed was threatened by insufficient funds. California Superintendent of Education Bill Honig said, "The concept . . . that you can have reform at no cost just doesn't work." An Oregon school official said, "To get school improvement, you need dollars. And we aren't getting the dollars." Other leaders said that school reform was "on track" and that the disagreement was "over what direction reform should take."

In a report commissioned by the MacArthur Foundation, titled *The Best of Educations: Reforming America's Public Schools in the 1980s*, author William Chance wrote that genuine reform will require better "professionalized teaching," early schooling, testing, and assessment. Chance maintained that to be professionals, teachers must accept differentiated merit pay, evaluation, and more rigorous, relevant training. The educational establishment has allowed students to be " 'schooled' without being 'educated'," he wrote. True reform needs a return to "public control."

Assessing the 1986–87 school year—which, he said, "was widely acclaimed as the year of reform"—*New York Times* education writer Fred Hechinger concluded that there had been "no revolutionary upsurge" in school reform, only small incremental change; he feared a decline without bold moves on the national level.

A report on high schools by the Southern Regional Education Board found that graduation requirements had become stricter and that more students were taking academic courses than in 1981. But student achievement must be more vigorously assessed to prove reform, the report held. And there was dismay at the 1985 dropout rate (22.3% in Maryland, 45.3% in Louisiana, and 29.4% nationwide).

To aid school reform, Secretary Bennett has advocated allowing parents to select alternative neighborhood schools. The National Education Association (NEA) disagreed, stating that when brighter children leave, poorer schools are worse off.

Former U.S. Education Secretary Terrel H. Bell contended that school reform benefits 70% of students, but not the 30% low-income minority. Tennessee's Education Commissioner Charles E. Smith said that school-reform ideas, such as merit pay for the best teachers, came from business and were "a top-down movement" with "no feeling of ownership" by local schools, teachers, and principals.

A report by the Congressional Budget Office issued in September expressed doubt that higher student achievement resulted from the

U.S. Secretary of Education William J. Bennett reports that, based on such criteria as graduation rates, standardized test scores, and teacher salaries, the nation's school systems "basically held steady" in 1986.

AP/Wide World

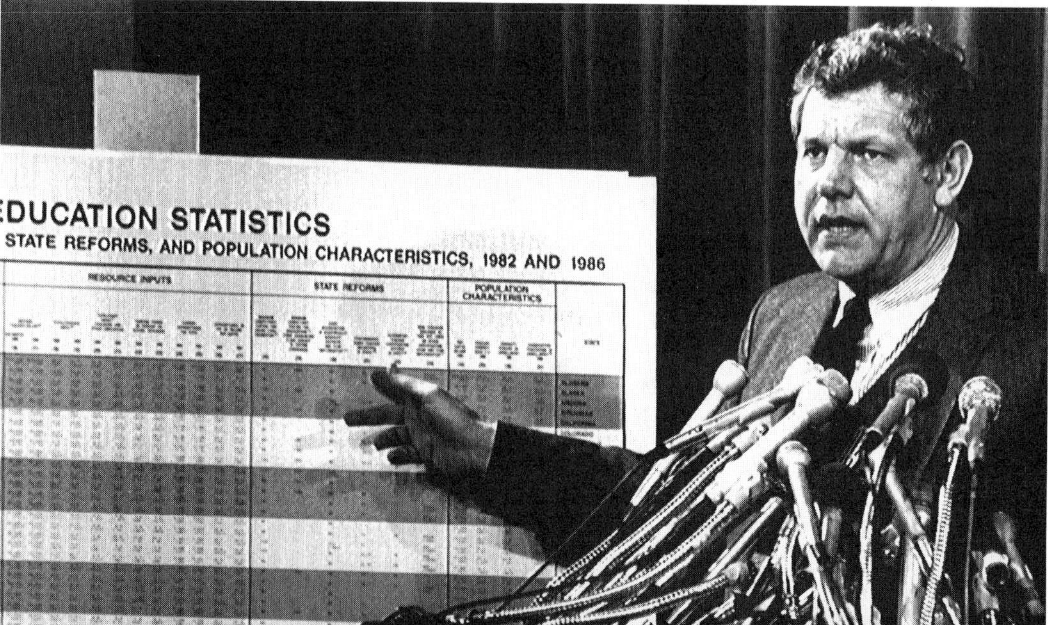

reform efforts. Higher scores antedated these programs. Scores might have risen without them.

Fundamentalism and the Courts. In August, U.S. federal courts overturned textbook censorship decisions in Hawkins County, TN, and the state of Alabama. A fundamentalist lawyer said, "We don't think this is the final decision. . . . It's just a whistle stop on the way to the U.S. Supreme Court." (See special report, page 214.)

The U.S. Supreme Court, by a 7-2 vote on June 19, declared unconstitutional Louisiana's 1981 law requiring public schools that teach evolution to teach creation science as well. Nobel laureates and scientific organizations had filed court briefs against the statute. A relieved Louisiana school administrator said, "We don't have the money now to be spending on bad science." A fundamentalist leader vowed, the Supreme Court "won't stay the same forever."

What Students Learn. In a plan issued in March, titled *The Nation's Report Card: Improving the Assessment of Student Achievement,* the U.S. Department of Education recommended enlarging the National Assessment of Educational Progress (NAEP), a federal program mandated in 1963 to test students in reading, writing, and math at least every five years. Under the new plan, the number of students tested would be increased from about 25,000 to more than 650,000, and the subject areas would be expanded to include science, technology, history, government, and geography. These and other changes would raise the cost of the testing program from $4 million to $26 million annually. Secretary Bennett approved the report and promised to seek funds for it. The prestigious National Academy of Education at Harvard University criticized the recommendation, warning that it might lead to a national curriculum. NEA President Mary Hatwood Futrell also expressed the fear that it would lead to a federally controlled national curriculum, as did the NAEP policy committee in a May 30 meeting.

Critical Reports. Two accounts of the same research gave U.S. 17-year-olds "failing marks" in literature and history. The findings were reported in *American Memory* by Lynne V. Cheney, chairwoman of the National Endowment for the Humanities, and in *What Do Our 17-Year-Olds Know?,* by the original researchers, Professor Diane Ravitch of Columbia University and U.S. Assistant Secretary of Education for Research Chester E. Finn, Jr. According to the latter $370,000 study, one third of those tested could not identify the Declaration of Independence as the document that formally separated the American colonies from Britain and many could not identify novels by Dostoevsky and Hemingway. The overall results revealed that only 55% of the 141 history questions and 52% of the 121 literature questions were answered correctly. The authors of both reports called for upgrading of teacher education; more communication between teachers and professors of education, history, and literature; and higher college admission requirements. Some educators expressed the belief that motivation to learn the national heritage was more important than memorizing facts.

U.S. public schools and higher education came under criticism in two best-selling books of 1987: Allan Bloom's *The Closing of the American Mind: How Higher Education Has Failed Democracy and Impoverished the Souls of Today's Students*; and E.D. Hirsch, Jr.'s *Cultural Literacy*. Bloom, a professor of philosophy, traces problems of today to the 1960s, when colleges gave in to activists, abandoned liberal arts, and taught "relevant" studies in which all ideas have equal value. He called today's students "sex-ridden moneygrubbers marching to rock music." Hirsch, a professor of English, maintains that by not teaching the unifying facts and values of Western culture, U.S. schools have produced a generation of cultural illiterates. Hirsch blasts the American educational philosopher John Dewey (1859–1952) for emphasizing learning skills rather than information. Both Hirsch and Bloom urge a return to liberal arts.

Harvard University President Derek Bok faulted the authors for using education as a scapegoat for social ills. A Chicago high-school principal with mainly Hispanic students said, "We've got to educate everyone—even the 35 IQs"; trouble begins before school in poor and noisy homes, he added. Blacks and women scored Bloom for calling black studies and women's studies low-level and irrelevant. One critic said, "The real bastions of democracy are probably *not* those elite universities to which Mr. Bloom constantly refers." Another critic argued that Hirsch's list of "what every American needs to know" reflects only what one cultural group thinks. Yet another suggests that the very popularity of both books argued against their theme: where but in a well-educated country would so many people read these two books critical of education?

Polls. A Phi Delta Kappa/Gallup Poll on August 27 found 76% of respondents in favor of tougher school standards, 80% for federal aid to school programs involving social problems, 71% for parents' choosing their children's schools, 44% for and 41% against vouchers to spend at either public or private schools, and 72% for required liberal arts degrees for teachers. The chief problems, according to the poll, were drug abuse, inadequate discipline, low financial support, few good teachers, poor curriculum and standards, overcrowding, and low moral standards. All in all, 12% (the highest since 1975) gave U.S. schools a grade of A,

31% a grade of B, 30% C, 9% D, 4% F, and 14% no opinion.

In a September Louis Harris poll for the Metropolitan Life Insurance Company, teachers blamed poor student performance on being left alone after school (51%); automatic promotion (44%); and schools not adapting to individual student needs (43%). Most teachers (85%) were satisfied with their profession.

Bilingual Education. Educators and politicians remained divided on how to educate the 1.5 million American 5–17-year-olds (500,000 in California alone) whose home language is not English. During the summer of 1987, members of the Los Angeles teachers union voted 78% for English-immersion teaching, helped by bilingual aides, and rejected the present approach of native-language transition to English. The union support of English immersion combined with Gov. George Deukmejian's summer veto of native-language transition may hasten English immersion nationally. California is among 14 states that have adopted English as the official language.

Education Secretary Bennett believes that bilingual education does not work and wants to expand from 4% to 25% congressional funding set aside for English-only instruction.

Teacher Certification. A 33-member planning group formed May 15 in San Diego launched the National Board for Professional Teaching Standards (NBPTS). Urged by a 1986 Carnegie Forum report, *A Nation Prepared: Teachers for the 21st Century,* NBPTS will set standards for teacher entrance, training, grading, ethical behavior, retention, advancement, censure, and dismissal. The purpose is to certify teachers nationally as competent professionals. Still unresolved was how NBPTS certification would fit in with the established certification standards of state departments of education. Many wondered how school administrators, local school-board members, and other education groups could be involved in the NBPTS program. The president of the American Association of School Administrators called NBPTS "an attempted takeover of American schools by the teacher unions. . . ." The president of the National School Boards Association said, "the final decision as to who's going to be hired" will still "rest with the local board of education." Some said that if NBPTS is to assure expert teachers, its members should be subject-matter specialists. Another suggested that: "The real issue is trust. Teachers don't trust superintendents and principals."

Doubt was cast on a recommendation by the Holmes Group to end the standard teacher requirement of an undergraduate major in education and require only fifth year teacher training. A leader of the National Council of Teachers of English emphasized the need for "the study of pedagogy, both at the undergraduate and graduate levels."

NBPTS's wider plan is to professionalize teaching; restructure schools to give teachers more autonomy; improve minority education; recruit more minority teachers; create a career ladder with salary steps based on experience, competency, and further education; and have "lead teachers" as highly paid school leaders.

A Louis Harris Poll in 1986 reported 87% public support for NBPTS. Ultimately, its 63 members will represent varied education interests. Board planning member Albert Shanker,

AP/Wide World

Teachers in Chicago began the 1987-88 school year on the picket line. After accepting a two-year agreement, calling for a 4% increase in the first year, striking teachers returned to work on October 5.

the president of the American Federation of Teachers, called it "a bold step forward" to capture the same respect, status, and remuneration that the public gives doctors and lawyears.

Teacher Pay. Teacher salary increases averaged 7.7% over 1984 to 1986. But the national average of $26,704 in 1987 was less than most professional salaries. The average starting salary for a new teacher was $17,800.

College Costs. The College Board in August found college tuition and fees up 5%-8% in 1987–88, outstripping inflation for the seventh consecutive year. Tuition and fees averaged $1,359 a year at public colleges and $7,110 at private colleges, up 6%-8% from 1986-87. Tuition and fees at two-year colleges averaged $687 per year for public institutions and $4,058 for private institutions, up 5%-6% from 1986–87. The higher education community disagreed vehemently with a claim by Education Secretary Bennett that colleges take advantage of federal aid to college students by raising their costs.

Governors' Reports. Believing that better education will lead to more jobs in their states, the National Governors' Association (NGA) in August issued three reports. One, titled *Educating Americans for Tomorrow's World: State Initiatives in International Education,* called on schools to produce workers who are internationally aware, computer literate, and proficient in English, math, geography, and foreign language. "We're involved in a global economy, and our future growth depends on how we do in international competition," said California Governor Deukmejian. Another NGA study, *Bringing Down the Barriers,* called for education or job training for welfare recipients. And the third study, *Results in Education: 1987,* noting that the states paid more than half of U.S. school costs in 1986, urged the reform movement to "use the current level of resources more effectively."

Great Britain. Prime Minister Margaret Thatcher's reelection in June assured vast changes in Britain's state schools. The Great Education Reform bill proposed by her Conservative government went to Parliament in November. It called for a national core curriculum for 90% of school time; more power for school heads over their largely Labour Party-oriented union teachers; parental vote to remove individual schools from largely Labour-dominated Local Education Authorities and to put them under central government funding and control; mandatory student testing at ages 7, 11, 14 and 16; and open-school enrollment with funds based on the number of students attracted.

Critics contended that the parental voting—or "opting out"—feature of the bill was a deliberate plan to weaken local (especially Labour-influenced) government and strengthen the Conservative national government, and possibly to cut back on comprehensive schools (which grew out of the democratizing Education Act of 1944) and strengthen privileged grammar schools. The critics argued that affluent parents would remove schools from local control and operate them as privileged schools, that national tests would funnel some children into nonacademic programs, and that free-choice schools benefit the affluent at the expense of the poor and minorities.

Despite school-enrollment declines, Labour critics blasted Thatcher's education record since coming to power in 1979: a decline in school funding from 14.3% to 12.7% of public expenditures; nursery schools for fewer than 25% of 3- and 4-year-olds; 1,575 primary schools and 312 secondary schools closed; 36,000 teaching jobs eliminated; university entrants reduced by 6,000 per year after 1980; and the value of student grants cut.

At the higher-education level, Prime Minister Thatcher planned to replace the semiautonomous University Grants Committee, which gives government funds to universities, with a University Funding Council, which would contract with individual universities for teaching and research funds that fit government priorities. Also planned were City Technology Colleges, which would be started with large industrial gifts and operated with funding from the national Department of Education and Science. The government also proposed to abolish university tenure, a move that has evoked little controversy because only about half of British universities grant tenure anyway and because more than 1,000 scientists and engineers leave Britain each year for better jobs abroad.

FRANKLIN PARKER
Northern Arizona University, Flagstaff

U.S. Public and Private Schools

	1987–88	1986–87
Enrollment		
Kindergarten through Grade 8	32,200,000	31,700,000
High school	13,500,000	13,700,000
Higher education	12,300,000	12,400,000
Total	58,000,000	57,800,000
Number of Teachers		
Elementary and secondary	2,600,000	2,600,000
Higher	700,000	700,000
Total	3,300,000	3,300,000
Graduates		
Public and private high school	2,737,000	2,677,000
Bachelor's degrees	1,001,000	995,000
First professional degrees	75,000	74,000
Master's degrees	294,000	293,000
Doctor's degrees	34,000	34,000
Expenditures		
Public elementary-secondary school	$168,600,000,000	$158,300,000,000
Private elementary-secondary	15,100,000,000	14,200,000,000
Public higher	81,300,000,000	75,600,000,000
Private higher	42,700,000,000	40,300,000,000
Total	$307,700,000,000	$288,400,000,000

Textbooks Under Criticism

Two U.S. federal court rulings and the vocal concern of certain educational and religious groups focused attention in 1987 on the textbooks being used in U.S. public schools. In late August, a federal appeals court in Alabama overturned a lower court ruling that had banned 44 textbooks because they promoted "secular humanism." The same week, a federal appeals court in Tennessee also reversed a lower court ruling, which had required schools in Hawkins County to excuse some children from class because their parents found the textbooks offensive to their religious beliefs.

In the Hawkins County case, the judge who had ruled in favor of the Christian fundamentalist families in 1986 said of textbook publishers: "They've almost whitewashed religion out of the schools. They've done it to try to satisfy everybody." Other observers agreed that textbook publishers, wanting to sell textbooks and fearful of offending critics, have been intimidated into removing religion from textbooks.

"The removal of religion as a subject of study," wrote a rabbi and a Lutheran minister in *The New York Times,* "has dismayed many responsible educators, parents, and mainstream religious leaders." The public schools, they insist, "have the right to teach *about* religion but not to teach which religious beliefs are correct."

Other reasons for watering down textbooks in religious, academic, and science content were cited by Fred M. Hechinger, education writer of *The New York Times.* He pointed out that as college enrollments skyrocketed and new textbook markets expanded, rapidly growing two-year colleges wanted textbooks more like those written for high schools. As conglomerates bought up textbook houses, editors, who were more often market experts than scholars, sought increased profits from a mass audience. As knowledge expanded, particularly in the sciences, the safest policy for editors was not to change texts submitted by authors, including questionable material. Thus, textbooks inevitably became larger, more expensive, often poorly written, and lightly edited.

Individuals and organizations that have faulted history and other textbooks for ignoring the role of religion include Secretary of Education William J. Bennett; Professors Diane Ravitch of Columbia University and Paul Vitz of New York University; People for the American Way, a liberal lobby opposed to censorship; Americans United for Separation of Church and State; the American Federation of Teachers (AFT); and the Association for Supervision and Curriculum Development (ASCD). An incisive report by ASCD, released on July 1, 1987, called for an end to "the curricular silence on religion." Such silence, it said, has permeated the classroom since the U.S. Supreme Court banned officially sanctioned prayer from public schools in 1962.

The ASCD deplored "bland" textbooks and the schools' "benign neglect" of the role religion has played in shaping U.S. and world history. It asserted that public schools must get over the mistaken notion "that matters of religion are simply too hot to handle." The ASCD report said, "The quest for religious freedom that fueled the establishment of this nation receives scant treatment at best in many textbooks." It added that the books "have even less to say about the profound part religious belief has played in more recent U.S. history," from the 19th-century abolitionist and temperance movements to the 20th-century civil-rights movement. "An elementary student can come away from a textbook account of the Crusades," for example, believing "that these wars to win the Holy Land for Christendom were little more than exotic shopping expeditions." Nor, it added, are the religious roots mentioned in such recent conflicts as between Iran and Iraq or in disturbances in Lebanon and Northern Ireland. Textbooks, the report continued, "contain few, if any, references to Christmas and Easter, or even to Thanksgiving . . . to say nothing of Jewish holidays or those of other religions."

Five world history textbooks were faulted in a July 29, 1987, report sponsored by the AFT, the Educational Excellence Network, and Freedom House. It called for courses and textbooks to focus on the historical struggle for democratic ideals. The five textbooks were said to be "bland, incomplete, lacking drama, and more interested in skills than in presenting ideas." The report said, "The basic ideas of Judaism and Christianity, which inform every debate over right and wrong and the place of the individual in society, are all ignored." Said AFT President Albert Shanker, "We are talking about understanding our ideals, about knowing our past—the unfortunate and the evil as well as the good. That is not indoctrination; that is education in the best sense of the word." Earlier in 1987 the AFT issued guidelines for teaching democratic values in U.S.

schools. The guidelines were endorsed by 150 politicians, educators, and other prominent citizens.

In a major 1986 study, psychology professor Paul Vitz also found that textbooks neglected religion and distorted family life by not stressing marriage and full-time parenting as the norm. He found little on patriotism and a neglect of business, labor, and altruism. He also noted that prominent contemporary political figures who were emphasized in many textbooks were almost exclusively "liberal." Observers claimed that this exclusion from textbooks of much of the American experience helps explain why federal district judges in Tennessee and Alabama have banned books, agreeing with fundamentalists that textbooks and school curricula are biased against religious convictions.

Education historian Diane Ravitch, who in 1986 examined readers used in most U.S. public schools, found them deeply disturbing. Concurring with the fundamentalists, she objected to their abundance of myth and fantasy. She was concerned about their neglect of classic literature. Late 19th-century educators and publishers saw their purposes as transmitting the best literature in the English language to young readers. Modern textbooks, written to satisfy complex readability and vocabulary control formulas, do not present classic literature by such authors as Nathaniel Hawthorne because his language does not fit such formulas. "Today's reader," she said, is "dumbed down" by readability formulas and is "blanded down" to remove anything that might offend interest groups in big states. Thus the readers strive to be cheerful, patriotic, multiethnic, nonsexist, and noncontroversial. She criticized this unrealistic image of society and praised the 19th-century McGuffey readers for including such classic writers as Hawthorne, William Shakespeare, Alfred Tennyson, and others.

Poetry, Ravitch noted, "accounted for 30% of . . . 19th-century readers. Today it is less than 3%." The golden age of the school readers faded in the 1920s with the introduction of standardized testing. Emphasis shifted from oral reading to silent reading, from teaching appreciation of literature to instructing children in the mechanics of reading for speed and efficiency, for timed tests, to answer true or false questions, or to fill in blanks or circle the correct answer. In the modern utilitarian era, she said, classic elements were dropped in favor of informational material and so-called realistic stories, as in the "Dick and Jane" readers. "Unless we expose children to the best literature," she said, we will lose them to television. She praised the California Reading

ROTHC
TEXTBOOK VIEW OF WORLD WITH ALL REFERENCE TO RELIGION REMOVED

© Boro/Rothco Cartoons

A cartoonist comments on a current controversial issue: the failure of U.S. textbooks to cover religious topics.

Initiative, a program instituted by State Superintendent of Public Instruction Louis (Bill) Honig to bring "real books" back to the classroom.

The California Board of Education on July 10, 1987, unanimously required that history textbooks include more facts on religion. The new requirement, part of a broad strategy to revamp the California history and social-science curriculum, calls for greater emphasis on the "major religions and ethical traditions throughout history" and the "role of religion in the founding of this country." Superintendent Honig called the strategy a "landmark" that confronts "head-on the erosion and dilution of the study of history." Because of California's large textbook market, its decisions sway the entire publishing industry and have national implications. Noting that textbook publishers are charged with deliberately avoiding controversial topics, a California educator held that "history without controversy isn't good history." He noted that the new California plan asks publishers to take on such controversial themes as the history of slavery, world human-rights issues, and dissent in Communist countries.

Pressure from scholars, educators, fundamentalists, and others have convinced publishers that textbooks are weak in religion, the classics, social studies, and science. Publishers, pushed by new content standards set by California and other states, seem ready to change.

See also articles on the states.

FRANKLIN PARKER

EGYPT

During 1987, President Hosni Mubarak was reelected and a new parliament (Peoples' Assembly) was chosen in Egypt despite continued terrorism by Muslim fundamentalist factions. The country's foreign debt escalated; in the diplomatic arena, relations were further mended with the Soviet Union and the Arab world.

Domestic Affairs. In February, President Mubarek decreed a referendum calling for early dissolution of parliament so as to legitimize his anticipated reelection later in the year. In a light turnout of the country's 14 million voters, elections for a new parliament were approved. In the voting for parliament on April 6, the National Democratic Party (NDP) won 308 seats, the Socialist Labor Party, 56, the Neo-Wafd, 36, and the Independents, 39; nine constituencies required new elections which the NDP later won.

Indicative of the rise in Islamic consciousness was formation during the election campaign of a combined electoral list including the Socialist Labor Party, the Liberal Party, and the Muslim Brotherhood. Although the list ran under the SLP label, more than half those elected on it were from the Muslim Brotherhood with little or no socialist orientation. Many used the slogan, "Islam is the solution." Although the NDP lost several seats, it still commanded a large majority, enough to provide Mubarak with the two thirds required to nominate him for a second six-year term. Two smaller parties, the Marxist National Unionist Progressives and the militant Muslim Umma Party, failed to gain the 8% of the vote required to place deputies in the legislature.

After his nomination by the People's Assembly in October, Mubarak, the only candidate, was chosen as president in a referendum on October 6 by a 97.1% majority, a decline from the 98.5% he received in 1981.

Upon taking office, the president placed special emphasis on the country's "terrible population explosion," which is now adding 1.2 million a year to the more than 50 million Egyptians. Other problems include the decline of arable land (now about 3% of the total) due to urban sprawl, the drain on government resources caused by subsidies on bread and other basic items, and cutbacks in national income resulting from loss of remittances sent by Egyptian workers in the economically depressed Persian Gulf region.

Deteriorating economic and social conditions fueled the trend toward fundamentalism, presenting the government with a choice between repression of or accommodation with militant Islam. On the one hand there was an attempt to bring responsible Islamic figures into the political system through the electoral process. The government made increasing use of Islamic symbols and permitted the Muslim Brotherhood, still officially banned, to become the largest opposition faction in parliament.

On the other hand, arrests and trials of Muslim militants continued. In February several people were arrested after a church was burned in a town south of Cairo and antigovernment demonstrations were organized at the university in Beni-Suef. Similar incidents continued throughout the year including attacks on or threats to American and Israeli diplomats, apprehension of several dozen members of an extremist Iranian-backed Islamic organization, and claims by defense lawyers that some 4,000 people were apprehended for suspected involvement in terrorist incidents.

Foreign Affairs. President Mubarak directed Egypt's foreign policy toward normalization of relations with the Soviet Union and the Arab world in an effort to improve the country's international economic situation. In April the finance minister reported that currency reserves for the year had plunged to $2 billion and that total foreign debt rose to $40 billion. During March and April a high level economic delegation from Egypt negotiated in Moscow for new terms of trade, assistance in upgrading Egyptian industrial plants, and postponement for 25 years of Egypt's $3 billion military debt to the Soviet Union. Later negotiations with Moscow were broadened to discuss restoration of normal bilateral relations and an international peace conference. These improved relations, Mubarak asserted, would not undermine relations with the United States.

Additional assistance was provided by the Paris Club, which in May agreed to reschedule some $12 billion of Egypt's debts, and by the Gulf Cooperation Council, which approved a $1 billion loan to help pay Egyptian military debts to the West. In November the Arab League, which had expelled Egypt in 1979 for making peace with Israel, voted to allow its members to restore ties with Cairo.

DON PERETZ
State University of New York, Binghamton

EGYPT • Information Highlights

Official Name: Arab Republic of Egypt.
Location: Northeastern Africa.
Area: 386,660 sq mi (1 001 450 km²).
Population (mid-1987 est.): 51,900,000.
Capital: Cairo.
Government: *Head of state,* Mohammed Hosni Mubarak, president (took office Oct. 1981). *Head of government,* Atef Sedki, prime minister (took office November 1986). *Legislature* (unicameral)—People's Assembly.
Monetary Unit: Pound (2.17 pounds equal U.S.$1, commercial rate, Nov. 17, 1987).
Gross Domestic Product (1985 U.S.$): $21,200,-000,000.
Economic Index (1986): *Consumer Prices* (1980 = 100), all items, 239.2; food, 255.0.
Foreign Trade (1986 U.S.$): *Imports,* $9,715,000,000; *exports,* $3,016,000,000.

ENERGY

The most important energy news in 1987 was the astounding progress in superconductivity, the ability of some materials to carry electricity without any loss of energy (*see* special report, page 427). Among existing technologies oil prices stabilized, and supplies were plentiful; electricity prices remained stable, but some areas of the United States experienced shortages for the first time in more than a decade; and, even though nuclear power generated record amounts of electricity, it continued to spark controversy around the world.

Although observers generally were upbeat about the short-term U.S. energy future, warning signs began to appear on the horizon. Government and private sources alike cautioned the nation about its growing dependence on imported oil, many fearing that another oil crisis is looming. In several parts of the country, voltage reductions (commonly called "brownouts") were imposed during the summer, when unusually hot weather created extremely heavy demand for electricity, threatening to overtax available supplies. And in New England, utility executives and critics were joined by financial experts in warning that if the region's economy continues to grow as predicted, there could be serious shortfalls in energy supply by the early 1990s.

© Steve Woit/Picture Group

Overall economic conditions and the Persian Gulf situation left the future of gasoline prices in doubt as 1987 ended. U.S. gas prices averaged just above $1 during the year.

Oil. In spite of increasing strife and uncertainty in the Persian Gulf, oil prices and supply remained stable throughout the year. With prices having ranged from $34 per barrel in 1982 to less than $9 in 1986, they leveled off early in 1987 and hovered in the $20 range until dropping dramatically in the aftermath of the unproductive December meeting of the Organization of the Petroleum Exporting Countries (OPEC).

Although Iran demanded an increase in production quotas and the benchmark price of petroleum (from $18 to $20 per barrel) to help finance its lingering war with Iraq, OPEC decided to extend its current quotas into 1988. This apparent disregard for the existing world oil glut resulted in an immediate drop in prices to below $15 per barrel. By year's end, the price had rebounded to about $16 per barrel, still below the official benchmark price of $18 per barrel.

In the first half of 1987, U.S. petroleum consumption increased by 2.1% to 16.4 million barrels per day. Coupled with a 6.1% decline in domestic production, the result was a substantial increase—28%—in oil imports. By year's end, the United States relied on foreign sources for 38% of its petroleum supplies, compared with 27% in 1986 and 35% in 1973, when the Arab oil embargoes sent the economy into a tailspin.

U.S. imports reached an average of nearly 6 million barrels per day in 1987, less than the record 8.5 million in 1977 but substantially higher than the 1985 low of 4.3 million. The U.S. Department of Energy predicted that imports may reach 8–10 million barrels per day by the mid-1990s. This increased dependence on imported oil prompted cautions from a number of fronts that the United States may be heading toward another oil crisis much like those of the mid-1970s and that self-sufficiency is necessary for national security.

A number of ideas have been proposed to help reverse this trend: imposing an import tax of $5–$10 per barrel, encouraging domestic production by easing environmental restrictions and repealing the "windfall profits" tax, or adding a federal gasoline tax of as much as $1 per gallon by the mid-1990s. With gasoline being the largest contributor to petroleum consumption, some experts saw the gasoline tax as a means not only of reducing consumption and helping cut the federal deficit, but also of forcing automakers to design cars that will get better than 26 miles per gallon (11 km/l), the average for U.S.-produced cars since 1984.

The U.S. oil industry continued to languish, hampered by competition from inexpensive foreign oil and the high capital costs of resuming domestic drilling and exploration. In once-booming, oil-intensive parts of the country, idle oil wells, empty office buildings, and nearly abandoned neighborhoods all stood as silent testimony to the effect of the energy crises of the past 15 years. Such scenes stood in stark contrast to much of the rest of the country, where the overall economy was booming. Americans were buying larger cars and increasing their gasoline consumption as prices remained affordable. Gasoline prices, which had dipped to an average 84.6 cents per gallon in 1986, returned to just over one dollar in 1987.

Natural Gas. U.S. demand for natural gas, at approximately 17 trillion cubic feet (480 billion m^3) per year in 1987, was expected to stay relatively constant in the future, increasing by less than 5%—to slightly under 18 trillion cubic feet (510 billion m^3) per year—by the end of the century, according to a study prepared by Wharton Econometric Forecasting Associates. Domestic production is expected to drop during this period, from its current level of approximately 16 trillion cubic feet (453 billion m^3) per year to just over 14.4 (408) by 2000. The shortfall will be made up by imports, mostly from Canada via new and existing pipelines. Meanwhile, if predictions of the American Gas Association come to pass, natural gas will be the fuel of choice for new electric generating plants built in the 1990s, thus creating a greater demand for the fuel.

Nuclear Power. Nuclear power supplied a record 16.6% of the electricity used in the United States during 1986, an increase of 7% over 1985. Nuclear power now supplies more electricity than any other fuel source except coal. In 1986, the 397 operating nuclear reactors in 26 countries provided approximately 16% of the world's demand for electricity. By the end of 1987, more than 110 nuclear plants were licensed in the United States, and more than 400 worldwide.

Scientists continued their investigations into the cause and potential long-term effects of the worst nuclear plant accident in history, that at the Chernobyl site in the Soviet Union on April 26, 1986. By year-end 1987, tens of thousands of the 135,000 people evacuated from the area still were not able to return, and it may be years before radiation levels in surrounding communities decrease to safe levels.

Experts remained divided over the extent and severity of the long-term effects of the radioactivity released in the days following the accident. The U.S. Environmental Protection Agency (EPA) predicted that among the 135,000 evacuees, there may be as many as 320 more fatal cancers than the 16,000 otherwise expected from this group during the next 70 years. Outside the evacuation zone, in a population of 75 million, the EPA predicted a statistical increase of less than 0.1% in the 9.5 million expected cancer deaths. The health effects are expected to be minimal in the rest of Europe and negligible in the United States.

The damaged Chernobyl 4 reactor is now buried under some 300,000 tons of concrete and 6,000 tons of metal, effectively preventing any further releases of radioactivity. Meanwhile, two of the remaining three Chernobyl reactors were restarted before the end of 1986, and the third was in operation by the end of 1987. Two additional units scheduled to be built at the site have been canceled.

In the United States public acceptance of nuclear power remained relatively strong, with two thirds of those surveyed saying they think nuclear energy is a good or realistic choice as an energy source for large-scale use, and three quarters citing nuclear power as an important energy source for meeting future needs.

There were renewed efforts in many parts of the country, however, to shut down operating nuclear plants and to keep others from starting or resuming operation. Most of these efforts were concentrated in New England, where activists argued that economics, emergency planning, waste disposal, and overall management were reasons to abandon nuclear power. In Maine voters defeated, for the third time, a referendum that called for the shutdown

© Sygma

Energy experts worldwide remained concerned about the lasting effects of the April 1986 disaster at the Soviet nuclear power plant in Chernobyl. In the USSR itself, technicians continued to check for radioactivity, right; *a new town was being built to house Chernobyl workers; and a third reactor at the plant was operational by year's end.*

of Maine Yankee nuclear plant. In New Hampshire construction of the Seabrook nuclear plant was completed, but the unit remained idle as the Nuclear Regulatory Commission (NRC) postponed issuing an operating license until emergency planning issues are resolved. In November the NRC accepted a utility-sponsored evacuation plan in lieu of one Massachusetts refused to submit, thus removing the major barrier to an operating license. The NRC predicted that plant operation could begin in early 1988, but Massachusetts officials pledged to bring the battle to court. Public Service Company of New Hampshire, Seabrook's largest owner, teetered on the brink of bankruptcy throughout much of 1987 and, in the last quarter, became the first major post-Depression utility to default on its bond obligations.

On Long Island, NY, the Shoreham Nuclear Plant also remained at the center of an emergency planning controversy, and was not allowed to increase power beyond the low-power (5%) license limit. Meanwhile, there was increased interest in a state takover of the Long Island Lighting Company, the owner of Shoreham.

The waste-disposal issue continued to create controversy, as federal authorities moved toward selection of the first national site for the disposal of used nuclear fuel, according to a schedule defined in the Nuclear Waste Policy Act of 1982. During 1987, the Department of Energy (DOE) proposed a five-year delay in the schedule for constructing a disposal facility, setting the completion date for Jan. 1, 2003. At year's end, the House of Representatives and the Senate directed DOE to proceed with development of a site in Nevada; authorized incentive payments of $10 million per year, to be increased to $20 million per year once the site begins operation; authorized the development of a centralized temporary storage facility; and declared a moratorium on the selection of any other sites.

The Low-Level Radioactive Waste Policy Act, passed by Congress in 1980 and amended in 1985, rquires each state to be responsible for all low-level radioactive waste produced within its borders. Some states joined together to form "compacts," while others decided to remain independent, all with the understanding that disposal sites must be in operation by 1993. By Jan. 1, 1988, all states were required to name the host state for the disposal facility, or face substantial surcharges from the three states which currently operate a low-level waste disposal facility.

The Price-Anderson Act, legislation enacted in 1957 establishing liability coverage for nuclear power plants in the event of an accident, technically expired on Aug. 31, 1987. The House of Representatives reauthorized modified legislation, but the Senate had not acted on it by year's end. The House version provided two tiers of coverage: $160 million from insurance pools and as much as $7 billion from other U.S. nuclear plants. Under the House bill, each licensed nuclear plant could be assessed a retrospective premium of up to $10 million per year for 6.3 years, or a total of approximately $7 billion for the more than 110 plants currently licensed in the United Staes. The bill also states that Congress will provide full compensation in the event that this coverage is exhausted. Pending final agreement in Congress, existing nuclear plants were covered under the terms of the previous legislation, which provides for a one-time assessment of $5 million per reactor.

Electric Utility Companies. Two words were heard frequently in utility company boardroom planning sessions during 1987: competition and deregulation. Electricity rates typically have been structured so that large commercial and industrial customers shoulder a disproportionate share of rates as a means of keeping residential rates manageable. With new technology making it possible for large companies to begin generating their own electricity, many are considering leaving the utility as a means of reducing overall operating costs. According to Henry Lee, an energy specialist with the John F. Kennedy School of Government at Harvard University, "This issue sends shivers up the spines of utility executives."

The spread of this self generation, along with the increase in cogeneration (generating electricity as a by-product of industrial steam production, for example) means that utilities face the potential loss of some of their largest customers, in some cases representing 5% or more of a utility's annual revenues. Certain fixed costs that these customers had been paying would have to be spread over all remaining customers, resulting in increased rates. This, in turn, would create a further financial inducement to other large customers to turn to non-utility sources of electricity.

There also has been pressure on some utilities to sell their excess electricity outside normal service areas. If this pressure is coupled with federal approval of long-distance wheeling —using existing transmission lines of other companies to sell power anywhere in the country—utilities will be facing stiff competition from one another as well as the loss of business from large, energy-self-sufficient companies.

With self generation becoming a very real possibility, with utility companies bidding against one another for large customers, and with the Reagan administration squarely behind deregulation, a fundamental change in the way utilities do business appeared to be on the way. No longer able to count on the protection of being a regulated monopoly, utilities throughout the country began instituting measures to increase efficiency and reduce costs.

ANTHONY J. CASTAGNO, *Energy Specialist*

ENGINEERING, CIVIL

The buildings, bridges, dams, and other accomplishments of civil engineers have as much impact on society as virtually every other professional achievement. So, too, do their failures. The year 1987 was marked by several major failures that left the discipline reeling with the question, "What went wrong?"

The most serious incident was the collapse of L'Ambiance Plaza in Bridgeport, CT. The apartment structure was being built using a method called lift-slab construction. Normally, each floor of a building is being built on top of the last floor. Lift-slab construction allows each floor to be cast in concrete on the ground, then hoisted into position *below* the floor before it. There it is permanently wedged into place. The technique has been used successfully around the world for decades.

Some part of the process failed at the L'Ambiance Plaza site on April 23. As one floor was being lifted into place, the building collapsed. Twenty-eight construction workers were killed. A federal investigation found "a serious disregard for basic, fundamental engineering practices," and the contractors responsible were fined a record $5.11 million.

The cause of the Schoharie Creek Bridge collapse in New York State, however, became clearer. Heavy spring rains had washed snow from the mountains of central New York. This water combined with the spillover from a nearby dam to convert the normally peaceful Schoharie Creek into a raging torrent. By April 5, the day of the disaster, near record amounts of water were flowing through the creek. The violently churning waters simply washed the river bed from beneath the footings of the bridge, a process called scour. The bridge collapsed taking ten lives, and severing the New York State Thruway.

A preliminary investigation into the disaster revealed that the bridge may have constricted the channel. A narrow channel means that water must move faster to pass through, and rapidly rushing water increases scour. According to the investigation, a state engineer who reviewed the plans for the bridge before it was built thought that the span should have been significantly wider than it was. By summer work had begun on a newly designed, $9.3-million structure that would be wider than the old bridge and constructed on more stable footing.

In Seattle, WA, officials blamed the collapse of a stadium under construction not on its design, but on the way it was being built. Investigators for the University of Washington said that the 15-story structure was not braced properly during construction.

Successes. The year could not entirely be called a "year of failures," however. It also marked the 50th anniversary of one of civil engineering's most unqualified successes, the Golden Gate Bridge in San Francisco. During its anniversary celebrations (*see* page 82), about 250,000 people jammed onto the bridge, applying to it what Gary Giacomini, president of the bridge district board, called "the greatest load factor of its life." In fact, the load flattened out the arch of its newly restored deck.

A six-year, $5-million facelift was completed at another landmark bridge. The structure, designed by John A. Roebling and spanning the Delaware River at Lackawaxen, PA, is the oldest surviving cable-suspension bridge in the United States. Originally it served as an aqueduct carrying the Delaware Canal across the river, and in 1908 it was converted into a road. But moving cars place different stresses on a structure than those of moving water. The difference took its toll. Although the bridge's cables had fared well, engineers had to replace its wooden deck with concrete.

Engineers also restored the deck of the Minneapolis City Hall and Courthouse, another National Historic Register landmark. Although the building had existed for more than 80 years, during a remodeling of the prison portion of the building, engineers discovered that the floors were weak. The original floor was made of steel beams braced against hollow clay tiles, then topped with a thin layer of concrete. At the time this structural system was quite innovative. But contemporary engineers decided to reinforce about 60 of these beams or reduce the loads on them by removing or replacing partitions.

Engineers in central Utah celebrated the completion of the Intermountain Power Project. Ten years and $1.6 billion in the making, the coal-burning plant will supply about 1600 mw of electricity, mostly to Los Angeles and several surrounding cities.

Also in Utah, the Great Salt Lake rose to its highest level in history. In 1985 the rising lake caused some $250 million in damage to shoreline property and businesses. If the lake rose just a few more feet, state officials feared the damage could easily top $1 billion. So in May 1986, the state approved an emergency $60-million plan to pump excess water from the lake into a natural basin in the nearby West Desert. Within a year, workers had begun construction on a pumping plant with a computer-based monitoring and control system. The watering pumps were brought in to remove the more than 10,000 gallons per minute (gpms) of groundwater that surfaced during plant excavation. It led Southern Pacific Railroad to build a 4-mi (6.4 km) discharge canal and use the 3 million yds^3 (2.29 million m^3) of earth workers excavated to raise the Southern Pacific embankment near West Pond. Work on the Bonneville and Newfoundland dikes which will flank at West Pond also was started.

HOWARD SMALLOWITZ
Formerly, "Civil Engineering" Magazine

Bridge Safety

In April 1987, ten persons lost their lives when a bridge over Schoharie Creek on the New York State Thruway collapsed. The accident focused attention on the issue of bridge safety.

AP/Wide World

According to a U.S. Department of Transportation report released in June, 42% of the nation's 575,000 bridges are either structurally deficient or functionally obsolete. Of the 131,562 bridges that are structurally deficient, 12,000 of them achieved that state in 1986. The report also said that only 11,383 bridges were upgraded in 1986 and moved out of the structurally deficient category. Commenting on the report, the president of the American Road and Transportation Builders Association (ARTBA), Daniel J. Hanson, Sr., said that $5 billion is needed over the next ten years to meet identified bridge capital needs. However, federal assistance for bridge rehabilitation and replacement was cut 20% in 1987 to $1.6 billion.

According to Hanson, the money for an expanded bridge program could be drawn from the $10 billion Highway Trust surplus. But because the Highway Trust Fund is considered a federal asset and makes the deficit appear smaller, using the money may be difficult. To free such funds, the ARTBA advocates two legislative actions: one exempting the federal-aid highway program from the spending restraints imposed by the Gramm-Rudman-Hollings balanced budget law and another for removing the trust fund from the unified federal budget.

Inspection. Funding is also central to bridge inspections, an issue which received renewed attention following the Schoharie bridge collapse. New York State plans to make underwater inspections of piers and abutments more frequent. State officials estimate that by the end of 1988, $2.7 million will have been spent to inspect 800 bridges below water.

As vital as underwater inspections are to bridge safety, there are no national standards for inspection procedures. State-highway officials are solely responsible for deciding what type of underwater inspection is done and how often. As a result, underwater inspections vary from state to state as does the training of the divers who perform them. The U.S. Navy, for example, uses engineer divers, as does the Massachusetts Department of Public Works which developed a program for underwater inspection in 1973. Its Office of Underwater Operation commissions part-time divers with engineering ratings. Using scuba equipment, divers make visual and tactile inspections and leave the underwater photography for problem areas.

According to Joseph Donahue, diving coordinator for the underwater operation, underwater visibility problems make filming impractical. Most of the documentation is done through sketches and, on the average, underwater inspections are conducted every two years. Four years is the maximum. For older bridges, or those with a problem, inspections are more frequent.

According to Lloyd Gifford, bridge management branch of the Federal Highway Administration (FHWA), Florida, Ohio, Arkansas, and other states also have implemented comprehensive underwater inspection programs. In April the FHWA proposed rules in the Federal Register that would make underwater inspections mandatory. In accordance with these new standards, bridges with fractures or those that warrant special consideration would have to be inspected at least once every five years. The rule also would allow states to vary inspection frequency. State officials could take into account a bridge's age, condition, and traffic volume and patterns and inspect accordingly.

MARION H. HART

ENVIRONMENT

The twin problems of ozone—its loss in the earth's upper atmosphere and its buildup at the earth's surface—again were the dominating environmental issues in 1987. Not far behind, quickly ascending the ladder of environmental concerns, was radon pollution. The year also saw a downgrading of sorts in concern over acid rain, new evidence of a potential health threat in magnetic fields associated with electric power lines, and new regulations to limit human exposure to serious pollutants.

Ozone Hole. The $2.2 billion international chlorofluoro-carbon (CFC) industry has for years challenged contentions that their chemicals play a role in destroying atmospheric ozone. But the recently identified seasonal development of an ever larger "hole" in the earth's stratospheric ozone layer, centered over Antarctica, focused escalating international concern during 1987 over the environmental ramifications of CFC emissions.

In March, scientists from the 1986 U.S. National Ozone Expedition to Antarctica reported data supporting a link between CFCs and stratospheric ozone loss. Their data showed an unexpected abundance within the hole of one chlorine-based molecule related to CFC use (chlorine dioxide). Two months later, researchers from the State University of New York at Stony Brook reported a similar finding: that concentrations within the hole of another CFC-related molecule (chlorine monoxide) were 100 times greater than normal.

But the most important data linking CFCs and the hole came from a six-week experiment ending in September 1987. Coordinated by the U.S. National Aeronautics and Space Administration (NASA), it flew aircraft into and under areas of the hole's greatest ozone loss. The resulting data not only confirmed the role of chlorine chemicals in destroying stratospheric ozone, but also found strong evidence that meteorological conditions help shape the hole's size and magnitude. A vortex of winds creates a self-contained "reaction vessel" within the stratosphere. Chlorine molecules trapped inside can rapidly break down ozone.

But these polar ozone losses represent just one manifestation of what appears to be global stratospheric-ozone losses. From 1978 to 1985, according to data reported in the July 10, 1987, issue of *Science*, global atmospheric ozone fell about 4%. In fact, the report said, "every indicator of [atmospheric] ozone abundance seems to be heading down."

Such findings helped galvanize the will of industrial nations to limit global CFC emissions. (The United States, a leader in calling for such limits, banned nonessential uses of CFCs in 1978.) At a September meeting in Montreal, Canada, 24 nations formally ratified an unprecedented agreement to freeze production of two key CFCs—known as CFC-11 and CFC-12—at 1986 levels. Signatories further pledged to reduce production 30% more by 1994 and to cut production to just 50% of 1986 levels by 1999. Signers also agreed to hold production of halons (a more ozone-damaging but less widely used class of chlorine- and bromine-based industrial chemicals) at 1986 levels.

In December, the United States became the first country to take internal legal steps to carry out the Montreal agreement, when the Environmental Protection Agency (EPA) proposed new, legally binding rules on the use of CFCs and halons. The freeze and subsequent rollback on production would follow the schedule agreed upon in Montreal.

Smog's Ozone. Ozone is not only the primary component but also the leading respiratory irritant in smog. While ozone is diminishing in the earth's upper atmosphere, it has become overly abundant in urban areas at the earth's surface. Generated by emissions of volatile organic compounds, especially hydrocarbons in vehicular exhaust, smog-ozone concentrations in 1987 exceeded the U.S. air-quality standard of 0.12 parts per million in more than 35 major U.S. metropolitan areas.

In April, the EPA announced that it would impose major sanctions against regions still failing the standard at year's end. Chief among the sanctions would be a construction ban on facilities (such as power plants, industrial boilers, oil refineries, and dry cleaners) that would emit 100 tons or more of ozone-generating pollutants. In June, EPA Administrator Lee M. Thomas identified the first 11 areas slated to receive such sanctions.

Radon. Radon, a naturally occurring gas, gained new recognition and notoriety during 1987, when EPA named it the leading U.S. air- and water-pollution problem. While radon itself is not a major health problem, its radioactive decay products—or "daughters"—are. They cling to respirable dust particles in the air and, once inhaled, attach to and irradiate the lung.

Outdoors, radon decay products are diluted to harmless levels. But if allowed to seep indoors, they can be trapped and accumulate to dangerous levels. In a ten-state indoor-radon survey released in August 1987, EPA found that 21% of the 11,600 homes surveyed had radon exceeding 4 picocuries per liter (pCi/l) in air—the level at which EPA recommends considering corrective action. Some home radon levels exceeded 150 pCi/l.

Though most radon enters buildings through cracks in their foundations, it also can seep into groundwater and be released by showering, bathing, cooking, washing, or flushing toilets. Although a new EPA survey found that 40% of U.S. drinking-water supplies probably contain high radon levels, the agency believes that these sources cause only a small

Waste Disposal

AP/Wide World

On March 22, 1987, a garbage scow, *above,* left Islip, Long Island (NY), with a cargo barely worth a glance compared with the mountains of solid waste produced in the United States and shipped across state lines daily. Yet within days, the *Mobro,* as the barge was called, raised a storm worthy of the North Atlantic itself and helped bring home to Americans the enormity of their waste-disposal problems.

The 3,186 tons (2 890 metric tons) of Islip garbage were destined to be landfilled near Morehead, NC, but city officials there backed out of the deal in the face of public opposition to "someone else's garbage" coming to their town. In the weeks that followed, the *Mobro* was turned away from five more states and three nations along the Atlantic coast and in the Gulf of Mexico before returning to New York, where the garbage was burned September 1 in a Brooklyn incinerator.

The barge's vain attempts to find a haven grabbed media attention, and the scow became the butt of jokes everywhere. But the case forced Americans to face the fact that alternatives to landfilling are urgently needed.

The United States discards more waste each day than any other nation in the world—a mountainous 400,000 tons (363 000 metric tons)—even as half the country's landfills are expected to reach capacity and close in three to five years. By the time a garbage dump at the Fresh Kills site on Staten Island is capped at the turn of the century, it will have become a virtual mountain.

Among major cities, Philadelphia was particularly hard-pressed to dispose of its waste in 1987. The city had to ship its incinerator ash all the way to Panama and truck much of its garbage to Ohio because it had run out of local disposal sites. Other cities routinely railed their garbage from 50 to 150 mi (80 to 240 km).

On average, garbage-disposal costs in 1987 doubled to $1 per ton for every mile the waste traveled over land. Tipping fees, the charges levied by landfill operators for accepting the garbage, were likely to rise severalfold in subsequent years as available space diminishes.

Largely because of transportation and tipping fees, Philadelphia's average disposal costs rose from $20 per ton in 1980 to $90 per ton in early 1987. New York's and Boston's disposal costs also were high, and the cities and towns of California were collectively approaching $1 billion annually in trash-disposal costs.

Beyond costs, the negative impact on the environment—principally in polluted groundwater and contaminated wells—from disposing of waste in poorly constructed landfills became more widely known. Favoring a large-scale recycling effort, environmental groups argued that urban solid waste contains metals more concentrated than the world's richest ores, paper representing thousands of hectares of forest, highly refined petrochemicals in the form of plastics, and countless tons of glass. The environmental groups called for an equitable share of the funding now going into solid-waste management to be used for major recycling programs. But engineering interests and most departments of public works favored incineration.

At year's end the lines were drawn. A cautious public, concerned over the perceived health hazards of incineration and the high capital expenditures involved, generally backed the environmentalists; city officials tended to favor incineration.

PETER TONGE

percentage of the 5,000 to 20,000 U.S. lung-cancer deaths per year now being attributed to indoor radon pollution.

Acid Rain. An EPA-convened panel of experts reported in April that acid rain is unlikely to damage few if any additional lakes in the U.S. Northeast during the next 50 years. The National Acid Precipitation Assessment Program (NAPAP), the umbrella organization coordinating U.S. acid-rain research, painted a similar picture. The NAPAP reported that few U.S. lakes have been damaged by acid rain and that the damage which has occurred is unlikely to increase dramatically in the future. Although NAPAP's annual report, published in July, acknowledged a link between acid rain and the buildup of acidification in northeast U.S. lakes, it said that similar regional acidification was not occurring in the West. Finally, it reported that ambient levels of acid precipitation have had almost no effect on U.S. crop yields, plant foliage, or seedlings.

These studies, which supported the Reagan administration's position that acid-rain levels did not yet justify introducing costly new controls on pollutants from coal-fired power plants, met strong criticism from several environmental organizations and the Canadian government. The Natural Resources Defense Council (NRDC), for example, charged that the NAPAP's reports were "political propaganda" and argued that the NAPAP had ignored new data contradicting its and the administration's conclusions. Moreover, NRDC faulted the NAPAP's approach—one that studies acid rain only, rather than as one of a potentially synergistic mix of toxic air pollutants.

ELF. There has been a quietly simmering controversy over the potential hazards posed by extremely-low-frequency (ELF) magnetic fields ever since a 1979 study first linked exposure to high-current power lines and an above-normal childhood death rate from certain cancers (especially leukemia). These fields occur wherever electricity flows through wires. The New York State Power Lines Project fanned the flames of the ELF controversy with its July 1987 review of 16 new scientific studies looking for possible ELF hazards.

Though most of the 16 studies found no adverse effects, there were a few exceptions. One University of North Carolina study, for instance, found roughly a twofold increased risk of cancer, especially leukemia, among children who lived closest to residential power lines or who had the most intense ELF exposures. Several other studies linked ELF fields to neurological changes. In one, pregnant rats exposed to the fields for 30 days developed temporary learning problems, and their offspring had permanent learning problems.

Chemical Exposures in the Home. Indoor air pollution bears little relation to what is in outdoor air, according to a massive EPA study published in September. A seven-year project, the first to measure directly individual human exposures to a host of toxic indoor-air pollutants, it found that concentrations of volatile organic chemicals were usually higher—often much higher—indoors than outdoors. Among the chemicals it found frequently polluting U.S. homes and their residents were several known or suspected carcinogens, including benzene, chloroform, and organic solvents. Smoking, painting, use of household cleansers, and visiting the dry cleaners were among the activities believed to contribute to the observed human contamination from indoor air. For example, the study found that room-air fresheners and toilet-bowl deodorants can place sustained, high levels of paradichlorobenzene, a carcinogen, in indoor air.

Another study, this one by researchers at the University of Southern California in Los Angeles, linked parental exposures to chemicals with an increased risk of leukemia in their children. A parent's workplace exposure to chlorinated hydrocarbon solvents (such as carbon tetrachloride) or household use of pesticides appeared to convey the highest leukemia risk to children. How the children become exposed to the chemicals—especially workplace chemicals—was still unknown, though there was some suspicion that they are contaminated by touching a parent's clothes or skin.

In August, the EPA prompted the maker of chlordane and heptachlor—leading termite-control agents—to halt the sale of the chemicals. In addition, the agency banned their application within or under inhabited buildings. A new study showed that even when properly applied, the chemicals can inadvertently pollute the air of treated homes for at least one year. The insecticides not only can cause liver disease and adverse nervous-system changes in animals, but they are also suspected human carcinogens.

There was also good news on the chemical pollution front. In May researchers at General Electric Company's research and development center announced that they had found microbes in river sediment that naturally degrade polychlorinated biphenyls (PCBs), suspected carcinogens contaminating many waterways and chemical dumps. Soil scientists at the University of California, Riverside, announced a related discovery in June: naturally occurring fungi which detoxify selenium-poisoned soils or water. Both microbes eventually could be harnessed to clean up the respective toxicants.

Regulations. In February, the U.S. Congress overrode a presidential veto to enact a bill reauthorizing the Clean Water Act. Ninety percent of the $20 billion committed to water cleanup would be used to fund new sewage treatment plants. Additional money would be used to begin a program to control "nonpoint" pollution—the type that runs off nonindustrial

National Park Service

Wheeler Peak, left, *is one of the natural splendors in Nevada's newly designated 120 sq mi (310* km^2*) Great Basin National Park. Conservationists applauded the dedication of Great Basin as the 49th U.S. national park in August. Meanwhile, along the 12,000 miles (19 000 km) of U.S. coast, conservationists became increasingly concerned about the lack of protection for overdeveloped and rapidly eroding beachfronts.*

© M. L. Miller/Picture Group

lands, including farms, city streets, and construction sites.

In July, the EPA announced its first standards for the eight most common volatile organic-chemical pollutants in drinking water. The list includes such known and suspected carcinogens as benzene, vinyl chloride, and carbon tetrachloride. In August, the U.S. Department of Labor issued new rules requiring all employers to tell workers about hazardous materials in the work environment and to train them in the safe use of those materials. Previously, only chemical and manufacturing industries had to furnish workers such "right-to-know" data.

Endangered Species. Trade in wildlife, a $5 billion international industry, endangers many animal species, according to TRAFFIC, a global network of trade monitors affiliated with the World Wildlife Fund. Although 95 countries have signed a treaty vowing to abstain from commercial trade in endangered species or unauthorized trade in threatened species, not all are living up to their pledge, TRAFFIC leaders reported at a July meeting in Washington, DC. In some cases, they alleged, ivory had been shipped with labels identifying it as "bees-wax," while rhino horns were transported as "spare parts." A detailed report of such infractions, issued at the TRAFFIC meeting, focused attention on Austria, France, and Japan as among the most serious violators of the Convention of International Trade in Endangered Species (CITES) since 1985.

See also ZOOS AND ZOOLOGY.

JANET RALOFF, *"Science News"*

In August, Marine Sgt. Clayton J. Lonetree, a former guard at the U.S. embassy in Moscow, was convicted of spying for the Soviet Union. He was sentenced to 30 years in prison.

AP/Wide World

ESPIONAGE

Two major intelligence-related incidents surfaced in 1987, causing national and international concern. The first case, the reported bugging of the still-unfinished U.S. embassy in Moscow, created new tension between the United States and the USSR. (*See* special report, page 228.)

The second incident disturbed segments of the U.S. government and populace as well as the foreign offices of many U.S. allies. The case focused on the activities of William Casey, late director of the Central Intelligence Agency (CIA), who was alleged to have had the major responsibility for certain covert actions about which Congress was never notified, and some of which were considered to have been against U.S. law. The Afghan freedom fighters fighting against the Soviet-backed regime in Kabul and the Angolan rebels fighting against the pro-Soviet government in the southern region of that country were both said to have received massive and secret U.S. support, under Casey's direction. Great controversy also surrounded Casey's role in the sale of arms to Iran and the transfer of funds to the contra guerrillas opposing the Sandinista government of Nicaragua.

Casey was incapacitated by a brain tumor in late December 1986, and died in May 1987. Reporter Robert Woodward claimed in his book *Veil* (1987) that Casey had told him that many of the allegations were true. President Ronald Reagan was among those who denied Woodward's claim.

CIA: Changing of the Guard. William Casey resigned as CIA chief on February 2 and President Reagan nominated Robert Gates, deputy CIA director, to take Casey's post. Congressional critics, however, charged that Gates had been too closely associated with Casey in the secret activities then being investigated and—convinced that he could not win Senate confirmation—Gates asked that his name be withdrawn.

On March 3, Reagan nominated William Webster, director of the Federal Bureau of Investigation (FBI), who had made his reputation by overhauling and modernizing the agency, to the CIA post. His nomination was readily accepted by the Senate. William Sessions replaced Webster at the FBI.

On August 7, Reagan acted to still the clamor over his failures to keep Congress aware of CIA activities. He notified the Senate Intelligence Committee that new rules governing covert action would be put into effect. All forthcoming presidential decisions on covert action would be written, not oral, except in extreme emergencies. No CIA covert action would be approved retroactively. The rules governing the CIA also would apply to covert actions outside the CIA, especially to other U.S. agencies and to private parties and foreign countries carrying out actions on behalf of the United States. And ongoing covert actions would be reviewed regularly by congressional intelligence committees and the National Security Council.

The Pollard Case. Jonathan Jay Pollard was sentenced to life imprisonment on March 4 after pleading guilty to a charge of spying for Israel. His wife received five years as his accomplice. Pollard had begun working for the U.S. Navy as an intelligence expert in 1979. He gained clearance to handle top-secret documents of the Navy, FBI, CIA, National Security Agency, and the State Department. He was therefore in a position to give his Israeli contacts highly sensitive material on U.S. diplomacy and defense.

The prosecution charged that Pollard had pilfered more secret documents than any other American spy. Many concerned American defense plans and weaponry. Others could be used by Israel to promote its international policies. Pollard would take the documents home, show them to his Israeli contacts, and then return them to their files.

The Navy was criticized in Congress and by the media for its lax security procedures, and for not acting on information that Pollard had psychiatric problems. The Israeli government denied complicity in the affair, but nevertheless refused to let U.S. investigators talk to Pollard's Israeli contacts. Although on May 28 the Israeli cabinet finally accepted responsibility, they asserted that no cabinet member could be blamed.

The Vanunu Case. Israel itself had a spy problem. Mordechai Vanunu, who was tried behind closed doors in Jerusalem on August 29, was charged with releasing secret information about Israel's nuclear capability to the *Sunday Times* of London.

Vanunu, who had worked at Israel's Dimona atomic installation, vanished from London shortly after the article appeared. Although he refused to say how he had been returned to Israel, letters he wrote from prison alleged that Shin Beth, Israel's intelligence agency, was spreading false reports about him. His motive in revealing the information was, he said, to promote disarmament and peace. He called himself "a prisoner of conscience."

Shin Beth came under fire for alleged lying about the use of violence in obtaining confessions. The Israeli cabinet said that no agent would be prosecuted, but that Shin Beth would be more closely monitored in the future.

Spying on Technology. During 1987 a number of nations accused the USSR of attempting to steal information about advances in Western technology and science.

The United States arrested four Americans in October on charges of conspiring to sell data on computer science from a firm in California's Silicon Valley. The information would have enabled the USSR to track U.S. submarines and missile flights more easily.

Six men and women were arrested in Paris when they attempted to obtain secrets regarding France's *Ariane* space program. Japan expelled a Soviet trade official in August for buying stolen information on aircraft instrumentation. Norway expelled four Russians in July for spying on Norwegian companies involved in underwater optics, acoustics, and oil exploration. Moscow denied all charges, and expelled French, Japanese, and Norwegian nationals in retaliation.

A Greek seized in Athens was accused of selling technological data to a Soviet contact. Some of the material involved the U.S. Stinger antiaircraft missile, as well as information about NATO defenses. The case caused political problems for Greek Prime Minister Andreas Papandreou, who is often accused of demonstrating a pro-Soviet bias in his foreign policy.

Other Major Spy Cases. The most damaging European case broke in August in Bonn, West Germany, where Margret Hoeke, who had been secretary to five West German presidents, was found guilty of treason for revealing state secrets to a KGB agent. The secrets included confidential messages between President Reagan and Chancellor Helmut Kohl.

Several Americans were accused of spying in foreign nations. Jon Pattis, an engineer in Iran, was sentenced there in April to ten years imprisonment as a CIA agent. Cuba seized Gladys Hernandez and her brother in May, accusing them of complicity with the CIA. In April, Poland accused U.S. embassy official Albert Mueller of spying. Nicaragua released American Sam Nesley Hall in January, terming the accused spy mentally unstable. In all these cases, Washington denied that the Americans worked for the CIA or any other intelligence agency.

Embassy Problems. On June 20 the Paris police threw a cordon around the Iranian embassy. They had been instructed to arrest Wahid Gordji, an Iranian without diplomatic immunity, who was wanted for questioning about five bombings in the Paris area that had killed several people and injured more than 150. Iran refused to surrender Gordji, and the embassy siege continued.

In Tehran, Iran surrounded the French embassy, demanding the surrender of Consul General Paul Torri whom they accused of espionage, and threatening to "bring all the spies in the embassy to Islamic justice." Although neither embassy incident seemed to involve actual espionage, there is no question that some embassies have been used as espionage centers as well as safehouses for terrorists. The special position that embassies occupy usually protects them from interference by their host nations.

The "Spycatcher" Imbroglio. The British controversy over *Spycatcher,* a book by former intelligence expert Peter Wright, ended only after the work had been published in the United States in 1987. Wright claimed that MI5, Britain's foreign intelligence agency, had conspired against Harold Wilson when he was prime minister; and that the late Sir Roger Hollis was a spy for the Russians when he headed MI5. The British government attempted to prevent the book's publication, to censor newspaper excerpts of it, and to suppress its publication in Australia. The publicity given the book by the government's efforts to suppress it made *Spycatcher* a bestseller when it finally became available. Wright's charges, however, remained in dispute.

VINCENT BURANELLI
Co-Author, "Spy/Counterspy"

Embassy Security

An international scandal caused by Soviet espionage at the U.S. embassy in Moscow in 1987 pointed out a problem about embassies in general—they are primary targets in spy wars between nations.

Embassies are repositories of highly secret information. Ambassadors receive orders from their governments, and transmit reports on the governments to which they are accredited. They keep records on everything of importance that comes to their attention, from military hardware to rumors about the stability of regimes. Their files cover plans to meet future contingencies, depending on the behavior of other nations. Therefore, embassy dispatch boxes, diplomatic pouches, code rooms, and "safe areas" are of great interest to unfriendly governments. Intelligence organizations try to retrieve the contents of enciphered phone calls, radio messages, telegrams, typed reports, and documents carried by couriers. Private discussions between ambassadors and other diplomats rank high on the list of sources to be penetrated, recorded, and used.

Embassies also are vulnerable to direct action. Situated in foreign lands, they are at the mercy of the local authorities. Many embassies have been seized by police or soldiers. Mobs throwing rocks have become common. Nothing could be done to save the U.S. embassy in Tehran in 1979 when a rabble stormed into it with the connivance of the Iranian government. Terrorist attacks no longer cause surprise.

For all of these reasons, embassy security is a major problem. From 1980 to 1985, the U.S. Congress appropriated more than $2 billion to be used in new embassy construction and improved protection. Congress had in mind mainly embassies in the Third World and Communist countries. In 1987, Communist espionage posed a special threat, more severe than anything of the kind in the past.

The Moscow Embassy. The security problem came to a focus in 1987 in the Soviet Union, where the United States was building a new embassy. The nearly finished structure was found to be riddled with electronic devices. U.S. observers believed that the Soviet intelligence agency (KGB) planted the bugs during construction work at a Russian factory. The Russian firm stated that the concrete could not be poured at the embassy site, and so that was done away from the site without American supervision.

The Russians denied all charges, and even produced bugs they said were planted by American agents at their Washington embassy. Americans, however, had the evidence. James Schlesinger, former director of the Central Intelligence Agency (CIA), directed a study of the Moscow complex. "As a nation," he said, "we failed to allow for the boldness, thoroughness, and extent of the penetration."

Some of the devices were so sophisticated that U.S. experts were puzzled by them, suggesting that the Soviet Union is ahead of the United States in electronic espionage. There were demands in Congress that the embassy building be torn down and rebuilt under strict U.S. supervision and, until that was done, the Russians not be allowed to occupy their new embassy in Washington.

The old U.S. embassy in Moscow also was found to be bugged. When Secretary Shultz visited Moscow and stopped at the embassy, he had to use a trailer to be sure that the KGB was not listening in. A second problem at the old embassy was staff irregularities. Some of the Marine guards were accused of violating rules by allowing Russian women into the building at night and of escorting them into areas off limits. Suspicion existed that the men gave information to the women, who could have been working for the KGB.

Defensive Measures. The security thread led to a series of proposals on what to do about it. The first area concerned electronics. The CIA and other intelligence organizations were ordered to overhaul the technology and bring the United States at least up to the level of the Soviet Union in this field. New methods of detecting bugs were given priority. Alarm systems that could not be turned off by embassy guards would be installed. Safety rooms might be raised on blocks to break contact with everyone outside. And the United States might use the diplomatic pouch carried by couriers for transmission of the most sensitive messages, bypassing electronic transmission.

The second problem area concerned staff. It was suggested that the sex angle be handled by selecting only married Marines for embassy jobs. They would be kept under surveillance in a tighter chain of command. Tours of duty would be shortened. Lie detector tests would be used more methodically. Local firms without clearance would not be hired for construction of sensitive embassy areas. Speaking more broadly, the State Department ordered all embassy personnel to be alert to the espionage threat.

VINCENT BURANELLI

ETHIOPIA

Ethiopia in 1987 adopted a new constitution that established a civilian Communist government. Renamed the People's Democratic Republic of Ethiopia, it held elections for a new people's assembly and underwent a change in military and economic leadership.

Political Changes. Communist party representatives from throughout the world attended celebrations in Ethiopia on September 12 to mark the 13th anniversary of the overthrow of Emperor Haile Selassie, the implementation of the new constitution, and Ethiopia's installation as a member of the Communist bloc. The chain of events began on February 1, when the constitution was approved by 81% of voters. According to Col. Mengistu Haile Mariam, the nation's leader, 96% of Ethiopia's 14 million voters participated in the referendum, the first ever held in Ethiopia.

According to the new constitution, the third in the country's history, the (Marxist) Workers' Party of Ethiopia (WPE) is the "vanguard" political organization. It is the only structure in the system that guides the direction of the state, laying "the foundation for the construction of the socialist system." The administration of state power lies in the hands of an 837-seat people's assembly known as the National Shengo, as well as a president, prime minister, state council, and council of ministers. All legislation must be approved by the Shengo, which selects the president, prime minister, and cabinet. The president is the head of state and commander-in-chief of the armed forces. The president sees to it that policy is carried out and, along with the Shengo, may initiate legislation. The prime minister supervises the ministries and the regional shengos.

In preparation for the new political order, a new defense minister, Air Force commander, and chief of staff of the armed forces were appointed in March; new ministers of finance and foreign trade and a new director of the Central Bank also were selected.

ETHIOPIA • Information Highlights

Official Name: People's Democratic Republic of Ethiopia.
Location: Eastern Africa.
Area: 471,776 sq mi (1 221 900 km^2).
Population (mid-1987 est.): 46,000,000.
Chief Cities (July 1980): Addis Ababa, the capital, 1,277,159; Asmara, 424,532; Dire Dawa, 82,024.
Government: *Head of state,* Mengistu Haile-Mariam, president (took office Sept. 10, 1987). Legislature—Parliament (National Shengo, established Sept. 9, 1987).
Monetary Unit: Birr (2.07 birr equal U.S.$1, June 1987).
Gross Domestic Product (1983–84 Est. U.S. $): $5,000,000,000.
Economic Index (Addis Ababa, 1985): *Consumer Prices* (1980 = 100), all items, 130.0; food, 122.6.
Foreign Trade (1986 U.S.$): *Imports,* $869,000,000; *exports,* $433,000,000.

In mid-June, an estimated 13.4 million Ethiopians participated in the voting for the first Shengo. All candidates were approved by the party. In addition to party chief Mengistu—who was named president—those elected to the Shengo included Foreign Minister Berhanu Bayih and three other key party figures: Fisseha Desta, named vice-president; Fikre-Selassie Wogderes, named prime minister; and Tesfaye Gebre Kidan, named to the state council.

Famine. To contend with the long-term problem of famine, Ethiopia moved forward with its resettlement and "villagization" (gathering peasants into centralized villages, where the government can provide services more easily) programs. Resettlement of families from drought-stricken areas of the north to more fertile regions in the south and southwest continued. By late 1987, in excess of 800,000 people had been resettled; the government program was targeting a total of 1.2 million. And by year's end, some 7 million peasants had been relocated from rural areas to centralized villages; plans called for the relocation of 30 million. Meanwhile, a prolonged dry spell created a new shortage of food. At least five million Ethiopians remained at risk of starvation.

Foreign Affairs. China extended a $5.3 million famine-relief loan; Great Britain pledged $3.9 million in emergency aid; and the United States indicated it would send 90,000 tons of food. In February an Ethiopian armored force crossed into Somalia in support of rebel troops there. The forces were repulsed, and some 300 Ethiopian soldiers were reported killed.

PETER SCHWAB
State University of New York at Purchase

ETHNIC GROUPS

As the United States marked the 200th anniversary of its Constitution, blacks, Hispanics, Asian Americans, and native Americans, witnessing the continued effects of retrenchment of affirmative-action programs as well as overt racist incidents, were reminded that the principles embodied in that document were far from being fully realized. The year also witnessed increasing awareness of the impact of shifting demographic trends on the future racial-ethnic composition of American society.

Blacks. U.S. blacks, numbering 26.4 million in 1987, continued to represent the largest of the nation's minority groups. In spite of media attention to the growing schism between black middle and lower classes, there was still a widening gap between whites and blacks of all classes in terms of family income and poverty level. The year saw a continuation of overt racism, including a January incident in all-white Forsyth County, GA, where about 1,000 whites jeered some 20,000 marchers who had come to protest the more than 75 years of exclusion

Carrie Saxon Perry, a 56-year-old Democrat and Connecticut state representative for seven years, was elected mayor of Hartford in November. She became the first black woman to head a major Northeastern city.

AP/Wide World

of blacks from the county. Also, the U.S. Equal Employment Opportunity Commission (EEOC) was investigating allegations of the existence of a social club called the "Road Niggers Association" within the Denver-based American Water Works Association. The U.S. Agricultural Stabilization and Conservation Service (ASCS) faced new charges of racial discrimination; oversight reviews found widespread abuses of civil-rights and equal-opportunity laws in the ASCS's Florida and Arkansas branches and suspected abuses in other branches.

The U.S. Supreme Court ruled that state death penalty statutes can be valid even if they are applied in a racially discriminatory manner. But there were also some decisions from the high court that benefited minority groups. It refused to hear a challenge by white fire fighters in Cincinnati, letting stand an affirmative-action plan for the promotion of blacks in the city's fire department. It upheld an affirmative-action plan in Alabama that provided promotions for equal numbers of white and black state troopers. And its expansion of an 1866 civil-rights law was expected to extend the range of litigation available for protection against discrimination.

Wilson Goode, a black, was reelected mayor of Philadelphia; Kurt Schmoke was the first black to be elected mayor of Baltimore; and Jesse Jackson announced his candidacy for president. Chicago Mayor Harold Washington, who was reelected in April, died suddenly November 25. He was succeeded by another black, Eugene Sawyer.

The major issues concerning blacks in 1987 were: continued high unemployment (12.4% in August), the continuing increase in number of female-headed households, high rates of out-of-wedlock births, and the high poverty rate for these households. Another prominent issue was the apparent reduction in black college enrollments, especially for black males. While women and other minorities have continued to increase their enrollments, blacks have lost ground in spite of an increase in absolute numbers of college-aged blacks. A report by the College Board indicated that entrance into the armed forces, employment, and attendance at non-collegiate postsecondary schools help explain the decline in college enrollment.

Hispanics. Hispanic Americans numbered 18.8 million in 1987, about 8% of the U.S. population. Consisting primarily of Chicanos (63%), Puerto Ricans, Cubans, and Central and South Americans, Hispanics are one of the most diverse minority groups in the United States. They are also the fastest-growing, having increased by 4.3 million since 1980. Their number is expected to double in the next 35 years.

This rapid growth was largely responsible for both the positive and negative trends seen in 1987. The good news was that the larger numbers meant that Hispanics were being "wooed" by consumer-product companies, the armed forces, and political hopefuls from both parties. The bad news was their increasing poverty rate, low educational achievement, and poor employment opportunities. The U.S. Census Bureau noted that there were 5.1 million Hispanics living in poverty—an increase of almost 500,000 during three years of national economic "recovery." Further, a University of Chicago study indicated that Hispanic school children were far more likely to attend segregated schools—which are largely overcrowded—than they were 20 years earlier. Moreover, Puerto Ricans and Chicanos have one of the highest dropout rates in the nation. Fewer than half of all Latinos are high-school graduates. Lower educational levels naturally affect employment, locking in many young Hispanics to menial, dead-end jobs.

Another important issue for Hispanics in 1987 was the English-only provisions being considered by 37 state legislatures—twice the number as in the previous year. This issue served as a major unifying force within the diverse Hispanic population. If passed, such legislation would have a devastating impact on the estimated 50% of the Hispanic community that is Spanish-speaking only.

The impact of the Immigration Reform and Control Act of 1986 also remained an issue. Fear that employers may be more cautious about hiring Hispanics without regard for their citizenship status may have been justified, since 121 employers had been cited by the Immigration and Naturalization Service by mid-1987. (The new law made the hiring of illegal aliens punishable by fine.) Also of interest was the impact of the law's amnesty provision, which allows illegal aliens who can document a continuous work and residence history since 1982 to apply for citizenship. With the provision scheduled to expire on May 4, 1988, only 784,000 of the estimated 2–4 million eligible aliens had applied by September 1987. The cost of applying was believed to deter many illegal aliens living below the poverty line.

Asian Americans. The 5.2 million Asian Americans represent a diverse group, ranging from third- and fourth-generation Chinese and Japanese Americans, to the more recently arrived Koreans and Indochinese. The issues facing this group in 1987 also were varied. Many of the newer arrivals, especially the Indochinese, struggled to adjust to a new language and culture, and bring themselves out of poverty; for the large number who settled in California, 58% were receiving welfare assistance. Federal officials tried to persuade some of the more than 800,000 Southeast Asian refugees to relocate to states where jobs and other opportunities were more plentiful. Angered refugee leaders in California called this "planned secondary resettlement" racist.

Meanwhile, the perception of Asian Americans as "overachievers" continued. Evidence that this perception was correct was strongest in the field of education. Asian-American students scored much higher than the average on college entrance math tests (lower than average in verbal skills) and made up a disproportionately high percentage of enrollment at the nation's top universities. But this high level of educational attainment also produced an increasingly visible backlash. In addition to a steady increase in number of violent anti-Asian incidents, some Asian Americans saw signs of discrimination at leading universities in the form of admissions quotas.

Native Americans. While still accounting for less than 1% of the U.S. population, native Americans represent a diverse group of tribes or nations, each having its own customs, beliefs, and practices. The unifying characteristic in 1987, according to a number of studies, was their continued disadvantaged social and economic status. One study found that native

© T. Capmion/Sygma

Wilma Mankiller, 41, became the first woman to be elected principal chief of the 75,000-member Cherokee Nation in Oklahoma. She had held the office since 1985.

Americans are still the poorest, the least educated (less than 17% attend college), and the least employed of any group in the United States. They also have the highest rates of diabetes, hepatitis, alcoholism, emotional disorders, and poor nutrition. Another study found that American-Indian newborns are 70% more likely than white babies to die during their first year.

Native Americans also have been the target of increased racial hostility. In April about 450 whites attacked eight Chippewa fishermen and their families at Lake Butternut, WI. Various anti-Indian groups also have organized to persuade Congress to end federal-tribal relationships and eliminate treaties and other agreements protecting Indian rights.

There were some positive signs, too, in 1987. Tribal leaders continued to improve their access to declining federal dollars. The Navajo Nation received legal authority to seek access to $30 million of federal Abandoned Mine Funds, which they had sought for more than ten years. In addition, the Burlington Northern Foundation offered a $130,000 grant to recruit native Americans to colleges and universities.

In July, U.S. Senators Pete Domenici (R-NM) and Dennis DeConcini (D-AZ) hosted the Navajo Economic Summit in Tohatchi, NM. The summit brought together some 40 corporate, state, and federal leaders to find ways to put the tribe's labor force to work.

LYNDA DICKSON
University of Colorado, Colorado Springs

© J. Langevin/Sygma

The leaders of the seven major industrial democracies met in Venice, Italy, June 8-10, for the 13th annual economic summit. On the diplomatic front, the leaders adopted a resolution calling for freedom of navigation in the Persian Gulf.

EUROPE

Until the devastating stock-market collapse in October, 1987 had been a year of optimism in Europe. Inflation was very low, and unemployment was declining; in most countries, growth was firm and sustainable. The 12-member European Community (EC) celebrated 30 years of solid achievement, including not least the smooth incorporation of Greece, Spain, and Portugal, its three most recent members. Rather than ousting governments from power, as they had done in most elections since the onset of recession in 1973, voters reelected their leaders, often with increased margins. After initial hesitation, West European governments welcomed the innovative policies of Soviet leader Mikhail Gorbachev and gave their support to Soviet-American negotiations on dismantling of intermediate-range nuclear missiles and to the subsequent treaty signed in Washington in December. At year's end, however, after the European stock exchanges had followed the vertiginous decline of the New York stock exchange, many Europeans feared the onset of recession or even depression.

Restored Economic Strength. For most of the year, Western Europe continued to enjoy the moderate boom that had begun in 1981, although the leadership in this revival was taken by Britain and Italy, countries that had shown the weakest performances in the 1970s, rather than by West Germany, which even saw its production fall in the first quarter. Britain increased its growth rate from 2.7 to 4%, reduced inflation to less than 5%, and cut unemployment by 2%. Believing that public confidence in her monetarist policies and opposition to union wage demands was high, Prime Minister Margaret Thatcher called elections in June in which the Conservative Party was swept back to a third term in office with an absolute majority of 101 seats.

In Italy, the economy grew at a steady 3% rate, and its industrial companies, restructured after reductions of up to one quarter of their work force, showed profits five times higher than in 1980. When quarrels with his Christian Democratic coalition partners forced Socialist Prime Minister Bettino Craxi to resign after an unprecedented 44 months in office, the electorate showed approval of the coalition's record by sending both Socialists and Christian Democrats back with increased parliamentary representation. Even in West Germany, voters in January showed less concern over economic slowdown than satisfaction in a fall of 1.5% in unemployment and the absence of inflation, and returned to power Chancellor Helmut Kohl's coalition of Christian Democrats and Free Democrats.

Renewed Euro-Confidence. The "Euro-Pessimism," or lack of faith in the institutions of the European Community, which had been prevalent in the 1970s, lessened markedly during the early part of the year. In part, the renewed confidence was due to the successful beginning of the integration of the weak economies of the new southern European members with those of the nine existing members. Greece, which had joined the Community in 1981, had profited from markets in the EC for its agricultural exports and from modernization and job-training grants for its more backward regions. The Greek stabilization plan, implemented in 1986–87 for the purpose of cutting public deficits and reducing inflation, was backed with a loan of $1.75 billion by the Community.

Spain, which with Portugal joined the EC in 1986, began the seven-year process of abolishing its tariffs with the other EC members, and saw immediate increases in both exports to and imports from the Community, while its foreign exchange reserves rose by more than $3 billion. Portugal continued to recover from its deep recession of 1983–85, achieving a favorable payments balance of more than $1 billion and a reduction of inflation to 8%. Attributing these achievements to the free-market policies of Social Democratic Prime Minister Anibal Cavaço Silva, who had promised to follow the example of Britain's Thatcher and France's Prime Minister Jacques Chirac of privatization, the sale to private individuals of nationalized industries, the voters gave him a sweeping endorsement in July, returning him to power with 50.15% of the vote.

Perhaps the most significant proof of renewed faith in the EC was the progress made toward achieving a totally integrated market by 1992. In 1985, the European Commission, feeling that too many barriers remained to conversion of the Community into "an area without internal frontiers," as envisaged in the original Treaty of Rome (whose 30th anniversary was celebrated with due pomp in March 1987), proposed 300 changes needed to complete the internal market. In 1986, the Community heads of government agreed to amend the Treaty of Rome for the first time, by passage of a Single European Act, which would improve Community decision making and remove all existing barriers to totally free economic relations in the Community. Agriculture remained, however, a major Community problem. Subsidies to European farmers, whose surpluses were purchased and stocked by the EC and other agricultural programs, cost the Community more than $26 billion in 1987, threatening it with bankruptcy. Moreover, attempts to rid the Community of its stocks by selling butter, beef, and cereals to Third World countries at low prices, caused conflict with other agricultural exporters like the United States. The summit conference of heads of government in Copenhagen in December failed to reach agreement on reducing agricultural subsidies and changing the EC's method of financing its budget.

Improving East-West Relations. West European confidence in the future was strengthened, as relations improved with Communist Eastern Europe and the Soviet Union. Soviet Party Secretary Gorbachev persuaded Western leaders who visited Moscow that, in order to gain freedom to restructure the Russian economy, he sought not only improved economic relations with the West but also a genuine scaling down of the arms race. He seemed, too, to be encouraging the East European powers to follow similar policies both at home and in their foreign relations. The Soviet Union dropped its opposition to recognition of the European Community, and pressed for a formal agreement on cooperation between the Communist bloc's Council for Mutual Economic Assistance (COMECON) and the EC. After the Soviet Union withdrew its disapproval, East German party leader Erich Honecker was able to pay an official visit to West Germany in September, where he and Chancellor Kohl signed three agreements on technical cooperation. A month later Hungarian Prime Minister Károly Grósz also visited Bonn to sign educational and technical agreements. The West German government also decided to support Soviet-American attempts to reach agreement on an Intermediate-Range Nuclear Forces Treaty eliminating medium-range missiles, by reluctantly agreeing to dismantle its 72 Pershing nuclear missiles as part of an overall agreement. Soviet and U.S. negotiators were finally able to prepare the treaty for signature by Gorbachev and President Ronald Reagan during their summit meeting in Washington in December.

Crash on the Stock Exchanges. The interdependence of Europe and the United States was dramatically brought home by the almost simultaneous transmission of the shock of the Wall Street crash of "Black Monday," October 19, when American shares lost 22.6% in one day, to all the West European markets. Within hours, losses reached 10% in London, 13% in Frankfurt, and 9% in Paris. During the following weeks, as the New York exchange continued its violent oscillations and the dollar dropped lower, the European economy was severely shaken. Losses in stock values were enormous. In Paris, for example, the stock market lost more than $65 billion between its peak in April and November. Planned sales of nationalized companies had to be postponed. When new share offerings could not be sold, companies found themselves short of capital they had expected to be able to raise for expansion. Continual, large interventions by the central banks were necessary to slow the fall of the dollar which was threatening European competitiveness on both the American and Third World markets. Companies which had invested in the financial markets to profit from booming prices were facing major losses. Although at the end of the year, there was as yet no sign of a falloff in consumer demand with its consequent industrial layoffs, European business and political leaders were unanimous in warning that, without major reductions in the American budgetary and commercial deficits, Europe ran the very real risk of following the United States into recession in 1988.

F. ROY WILLIS
University of California, Davis

FAMILY

The effects of shrinking household size and other changes in U.S. family life were widely apparent in 1987. Census figures for 1986 put the number of persons in the average U.S. household at 2.67, the lowest ever reported. The decrease was part of a long-term trend—in the 1800s, the average household consisted of about 5 people—that was attributed in part to the aging of the population, increases in the numbers of single parent families and people living alone, and a decrease in the number of children per family. Census officials predicted that the decline would continue despite a slight drop in the U.S. divorce rate (still the highest in the world) and an increase in the number of young adults who continue to live with their parents past the age of 18.

At the same time, with more women in the work force, families were spending less free time on household chores and more time enjoying themselves. A study by Johnson Wax showed that the average family spent 15.8 hours per week on family activities, 14.4 hours watching TV, 9.1 hours on housework, 9.1 hours preparing meals, 5.7 hours reading, and 5.3 hours on crafts and hobbies.

Teenagers in the family were apt to be out working. As members of the "baby bust" generation—those born between 1965 and 1980, when the U.S. birthrate dropped sharply—they could take their pick of part-time jobs. The baby bust also affected schools, where enrollment dropped, and parents of young children, who found it hard to find babysitters.

Child Care. Child care remained a problem for working parents in 1987. With nearly 70% of mothers of school-age children in the work force, calls for government help increased. A bill was introduced in the U.S. House of Representatives in 1987 to establish a national clearinghouse for child-care information, and the Senate held hearings on the shortage of affordable care. Typical day-care costs were running about $3,000 a year, putting the service out of reach for many poor families. But with the federal budget deficit at record levels, many people expected more help to come from the private sector than from government. One possible model was the California Child Care Initiative, begun in 1985, in which corporations and government agencies split the cost of training day-care providers.

The United States remained the only Western industrialized country without government-mandated leave for parents of newborn children. In both houses of Congress, bills to require companies with 15 or more employees to provide up to 18 weeks of unpaid parental leave ran into stiff opposition from business lobbies during the year. Laws requiring maternity leave were in effect in several states; California's law was upheld in a 1987 U.S. Supreme Court ruling, *California Savings and Loan Association v. Guerra*. Minnesota and Oregon passed laws requiring parental leaves for mothers and fathers, and similar laws were under consideration in other states.

Family Violence. Reports of child abuse rose 55% in the first half of the 1980s, according to a congressional survey. Much of the increase was attributed to greater public awareness of the problem. Meanwhile, a study by the National Committee for Prevention of Child Abuse showed that in 24 states, deaths of abused and neglected children rose 29% from 1985 to 1986. The study's authors blamed deteriorating conditions among poor people and the fact that many state agencies were stretched too thin to cope with the rising number of cases of abuse and neglect.

The increased focus on child abuse, and sexual abuse in particular, produced a backlash of sorts. A number of abuse cases ended in acquittals or dropped charges, and the angry defendants filed defamation and negligence suits. Several parents' groups spoke out against local and state agencies that investigated abuse reports, protesting what they saw as a "witch-hunt" approach that led to government interference in family life. However, agency officials said that the vast majority of reports of abuse were genuine.

Foster Care and Adoption. In the past, many cases of child abuse and neglect led to the breakup of the family, with children being bounced from foster home to foster home. While some 250,000 U.S. children were in foster homes in 1987, many agencies were changing their emphasis and striving to keep families together through counseling and other forms of help. The foster care system itself was changing, too, with several states offering increased training and incentives to foster parents in the hope of providing more stable environments for children placed with them.

While social service agencies sought to help unwanted and abused children, many childless couples were turning to adoption and other alternatives to natural conception and pregnancy, such as surrogacy. (*See* page 55.)

Incomes. The U.S. median family income increased more than 4% (after adjustment for inflation) in 1986, but single-parent and minority families failed to keep pace. A survey of 47 cities found that, for the first time, families with children made up the largest segment of the homeless. For single parents, the average child-support payment was found to have dropped 12.4% from 1983 to 1985. However, under a new federal enforcement program, these parents in 1986 collected more than $3 billion in unpaid child support. And many older Americans found their financial position improving, although poverty remained a problem among elderly women who lived alone.

ELAINE PASCOE, *Free-lance Writer*

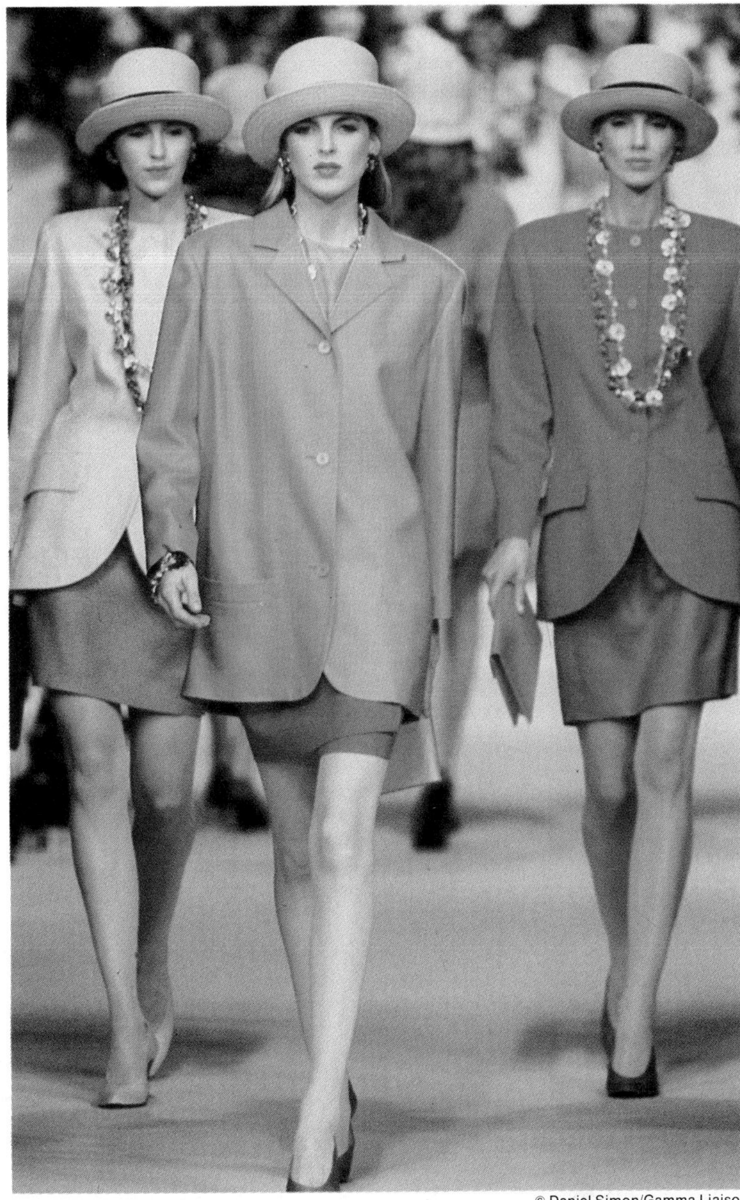

Legs! Legs! Legs!—the big fashion statement in 1987 was the shorter skirt. Rising hemlines coupled with the long jacket created the "long-over-short" look that was increasingly popular in the fall.

© Daniel Simon/Gamma Liaison

FASHION

The biggest fashion news in 1987, as well as the most controversial, was the rising hemline and a return—on runways, at least—of the miniskirt. The controversy saw retailers and manufacturers accused of promoting shorter skirts to bolster dwindling apparel sales and plummeting retail stock prices and feminists decrying what they considered an attempt by a threatened macho male establishment to return women to their former status of malleable sex objects. The resulting media blitzkrieg, however, overlooked the fact that there was still a wardrobe of lengths, from mid-calf to mid-thigh, available, though the most prevalent hemlines hovered near the knee.

Silhouette. While hemlines grabbed the headlines, there were also significant and new changes in proportion and silhouette. Gone was the mannish mien of past seasons with its square padded shoulders and oversized looks; a softer, more rounded and distinctly feminine figure was emerging, deeply cinched at the waist and curved above and below to achieve an hourglass effect. For day it appeared as a cropped, fitted, or tightly-belted jacket over a narrow skirt that was draped or wrapped to mold the hips; for evening, a bustier or other figure-molding bodice over a bouffant skirt, buoyed by crinolines or petticoats. Another favorite silhouette featured the proportions of long over short—a soft, flared but fluid, three-quarter or seven-eighths tunic, coat, or jacket worn over the narrow short skirt. Often high waisted or empire, the tops were of trapeze or A-line shape that created a fresh and feminine look.

Fabric. Quality fabrics, leathers, and suedes were still important in all major lines while denim, the darling of the couture in 1986, retained its popularity and was stronger than ever in the sportswear area in new overdyed, cracked, or distressed versions. Jerseys and double knits became the backbone of the new softer, body-hugging or fluid flyaway dresses and tunic tops as well as for many of the pants that were shown as an alternative to the shorter skirts. But the most important new fashion innovation was in the stretch fabrics that were used in important American designers' lines. Donna Karan's bodysuits, draped skirts, and fitted jackets owed much of their success to the spandex additive in the jerseys, cavalry twill, wool crepes, and cashmere and wool velours that she used to provide fit and the freedom of movement that she felt active women wanted. Calvin Klein used stretch gabardine for his trim trousers and slim suits for day. These signature looks were translated into stretch velvet for evening. From poplin and pique to lace and tulle—it was new if it was stretch.

Patterned fabrics in black-and-white checks were hits of the fashion season, as was the return of the form-fitting, distinctly more feminine silhouette that created an hourglass-figure effect.

© P. Vauthey/SYGMA

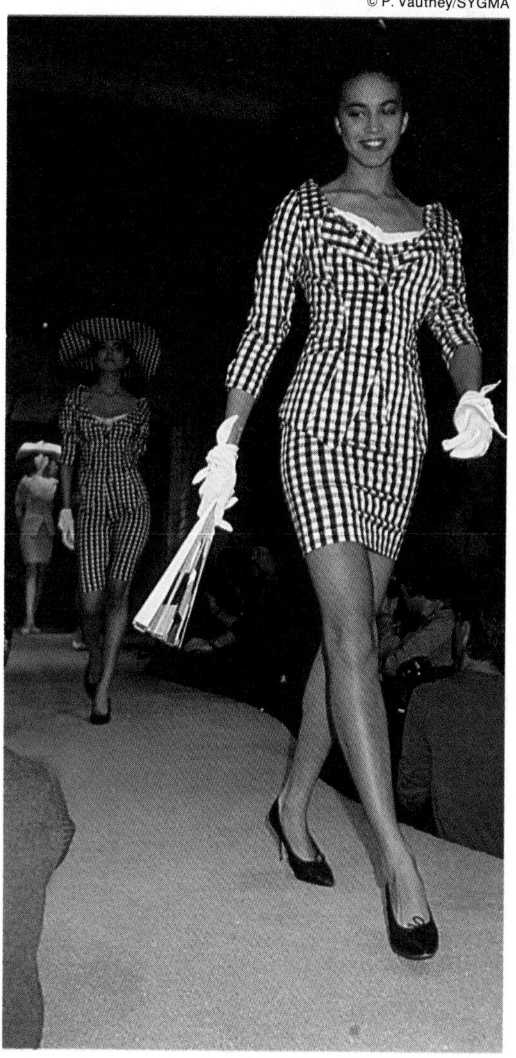

Another new fabric development was the introduction and use of washable silks. Available in broadcloth, shantung, and crepe weaves, these fabrics extended the use of silk into areas such as sportswear and swimwear, where practicality and easy care were paramount.

Colors. Black was fall's strongest color in apparel, perfect to pair with brights or the newer pure pales or to mix with white in checks, Prince-of-Wales plaids, or in dotted or striped patterns. Browns, ranging from deep bitter chocolate to warm, reddened chestnut hues were a close second in importance. Brights, such as cerise, kelly green, royal, turquoise, and scarlet, were accents to black and the browns both for day and evening, and clear, strong pastels emerged as key colors leading into spring 1988.

Jungle fever in the form of animal and reptile prints still fascinated designers. From zebras to jaguars and pythons to crocodiles, animal markings were printed on fabrics or leathers—such as Bill Blass' leopard- and zebra-stenciled calfskin skirts—and in knits—such as Valentino's popular ocelot-patterned, cashmere sweater sets.

Accessories. In accessories, jewelry came to the forefront largely due to the auctions of two remarkable collections: the legendary and unique pieces of the late Duchess of Windsor, glittery and costly, and Diana Vreeland's personal wardrobe of fabulous costume jewelry, classics from Chanel, St. Laurent, and Kenneth Jay Lane. These collections epitomized the best in jewelry design of the 1930s, '40s, and '50s and inspired look-alike brooches, necklaces, and bracelets, reviving an interest in estate jewelry of those periods.

Other important accessory items were integral parts of the new look, including the opaque or textured stocking, the high-heeled suede pump, or the over-the-knee, often thigh-high boots that were highlighted by the shorter skirts. Nipped-in waists depended on belts, the wider the better, and none were as inventive as Louis del Olio's leather waist-cinchers with attached peplums. Hoods replaced hats and were attached to coats, dresses, and sweaters in snug, head-hugging versions or face-framing soft cowls.

This was a time for trims—buttons, bows, and braids. Showstopping extremes included Jean-Paul Gaultier's suits, studded with multicolored, multisized buttons; Yves St. Lau-

The Latest for Children

© Theo Westenberger

Children have become increasingly fashion conscious. Such materials and items as denim and treated denim, Western jackets, miniskirts, high-topped sneakers, and oversized sweaters were popular with the younger set in 1987.

Downsized and upscale are the words that best describe today's children's fashion. As young consumers, trendy and label conscious, copy their parents' status attitudes and symbols, manufacturers and retailers happily cater to this growing "Me II" generation.

Boutiques stocked with mini-couture from such international designers as Burberry, Giorgio Armani, Ralph Lauren, Saint Laurent, Benetton, and Dior—with prices as *haute* as their styling—were springing up throughout the world. Moderate-priced manufacturers were mining this golden market as well, with such firms as Liz Claiborne, The Gap, Esprit, and Lands' End scaling down their adult lines for their customers' offspring. And to keep abreast of trends, there were "collections"—Pitti Bimbo in Florence and Mode Enfantile in Paris, for example—to which buyers and press flocked.

While designer labels were important, videos and television shows, spawning young Madonnas and Don Johnsons, and sitcoms featuring kids set fashion trends for preschoolers through teens. The licensing of cartoon characters for a wide range of fashion items for children grew, and food companies, capitalizing on their familar brand names, were promoting clothing with Jello labels, Oreo logos, or lines of Popsicle Playwear.

Denim, a perennial for children's wear, gained status because of its importance in adult ready-to-wear. Classic indigo and treated denims—such as the acid-washed, frosted, or overdyed versions—were used in jeans, prairie skirts, and Western jackets as well as the newer miniskirts and overalls. It was also often "dressed up" with ruffles, lace, ribbon, studs, or sequins.

Primary colors and bold graphics made oversized sweaters and fleece tops particularly "hot" items and went well with pants, skirts, or tights in black, which was the most popular color in children's wear. Designer lines mixed brightly colored plaids and stripes in sophisticated ways and featured animal prints—most notably, leopard and zebra—in a variety of ways.

In the accessory area, backpacks, brightly colored or patterned suspenders, ankle boots, and multicolored high-topped sneakers were seen on both boys and girls, while patterned tights and big hair bows were sassy accents on miniskirted misses. But the biggest fad was for patches and badges, worn in batches on jackets, sweaters, book bags, hats, and other apparel and accessory items.

Social calendars filled with upwardly mobile activities—tea dances, etiquette classes, and recitals—were occasions for young debs to come out in off-the-shoulder froufrou dresses that were miniatures of Mom's Calvin or Oscar. Their escorts sported the latest Italian-styled suits or, on occasion, a tuxedo. On the horizon were upscale grooming products, cosmetics, and fragrances for the ten and under crowd.

ANN M. ELKINS

© Daniel Simon/Gamma Liaison

© P. Vauthey/SYGMA

Among the most talked-about couturiers of the year was Paris designer Christian Lacroix, above, *who has created a new image for the House of Patou since taking it over in 1981.*

© Wilfrid Rouff

Other trends of the fashion year were found in the elaborately beaded jacket for evening wear, left, *and in such dramatic accessories as the choker of black beads and tassels which set off decolleté formal gowns.*

rent's and Oscar de la Renta's evening jackets sprinkled with beaded or sequined bows; Givenchy's black velvet sheath with oversized shocking pink taffeta bows marching down its side. Black and gold passementerie were curved in Camargue motifs on Christian Lacroix's designs, and at Chanel, Karl Lagerfeld was lavish with braid and fringe; at Dior, chokers of jet beads with tassels accessorized décolleté ballgowns.

Fur trims and accessories were strong, too. Mink, Persian lamb, and similar furs edged hems and necklines, and were used for collars and cuffs on suits and coats. At Chantal Thomas fur was even shaped into bustiers with matching "bracelets," and Claude Montana designed a mink sleeve to slip on his sweaters. Perky fur toques and oversized berets appeared in many collections as did fur muffs, shawls, and scarves. There was even a return of the mink stole.

Menswear. Menswear rejected the fanciful fun to be found in women's wear and became more studied. The emphasis was on gentlemanly dressing with an international blend of English style, Italian flair, and American ease in a combination of lighter-weight fabrics, less construction, and easier, more ample cuts. The jackets of 1987 had broader, sloping shoul; ders; an expanded chest that narrowed for a defined waistline; and a slim hip. The lapels were wider, and vents were gone. Shirts were straight cut, mostly striped, and trousers were pleated for ease at the waist but tapered to the cuff. Topcoats, roomy enough to accommodate the easier suits, were fur-trimmed tweeds, meltons, or camel's hair or casual shearling or loden duffles.

Sweaters in subtle, abstract patterns or sophisticated colors were often stylish enough to replace a blazer or substitute for a smoking jacket; vests, with lapels, done in bold colors or patterns were one way for a cosmopolitan male to show flair. Other worldly accents were braces, pocket squares, belts in exotic leathers, and elegantly patterned silk ties.

ANN M. ELKINS
Fashion Director, "Good Housekeeping"

FIJI

A wave of Fijian nationalism brought cardinal change to that multiracial South Pacific island nation in 1987. Events were shaped by two military coups—the second confirmatory of the first—and prolonged political turmoil, with abrogation (in September) of the constitution by coup leader Col. Sitiveni Rabuka, a dedicated indigenous Fijian nationalist.

The turmoil began in the wake of a general election in early April, in which for the first time since independence in 1970 the predominantly Fijian-backed Alliance Party lost to a coalition of the Indian-supported National Federation Party (NFP) and the multiethnic Labor Party. The Labor-NFP administration, led by Timoci Bavadra, took office on April 13 with a 28–24 parliamentary majority. Its foreign policy included plans to move toward nonalignment, while in domestic affairs a pro-union stance was foreshadowed. For indigenous Fijian leaders—and especially the militant anti-Indian Taukei Movement—the change in government raised concerns over a perceived threat to Fijian primacy in land ownership and fears about a weakening of Fiji's strategic alignment with the West.

On May 14, Colonel Rabuka led a small group of Army soldiers into Parliament House, seized Bavadra and other government members, and proclaimed a military takeover. Rabuka proceeded to form an administration that included Ratu Sir Kamisese Mara, the preelection Alliance Party prime minister. The governor-general, Ratu Sir Penaia Ganilau, swore in Rabuka as chairman of a Council of Ministers on May 17. Bavadra was released from detention on May 19, but calls by Commonwealth leaders for restoration of constitutional processes and parliamentary democracy went unheeded. As Fiji's sovereign, Queen Elizabeth II made known her concern.

Rabuka planned a parliamentary system with enough seats reserved for indigenous Fijians to assure their control over national policy: a single 67-seat legislature with a balance of Melanesian and non-Melanesian elective members (28 each), plus eight members nominated by the indigenous Great Council of Chiefs. In all, the Indian component would be limited to 20 members; other "general electors" would elect eight members; Fiji's Rotuman population would elect one. The key political posts could be filled only by indigenous Fijians.

Rabuka was able to gain Mara's formal support, but he was strongly opposed by Bavadra and was unable to win over Governor-General Ratu Ganilau. In late September, Rabuka led a second bloodless coup, taking over two newspapers and the commercial radio station and imposing a curfew. Ganilau's efforts to maintain what authority he could, and Rabuka's efforts to bend rather than break him, ended with the abolition of the office of governor-general and the proclamation of the Republic of Fiji on October 6. On October 15, Queen Elizabeth released a statement accepting the end of the tie with the British crown.

Then in early December, Rabuka stepped down as head of state and government, appointing Ganilau as the first president of the new republic and naming Mara prime minister.

The political crises had serious economic consequences. Tourism dropped off sharply, as security-conscious international travelers shunned the islands. The sugar crop, a major export earner, suffered from the interruption of harvesting at the height of the season. And in Suva, shops and banks were closed during the crisis periods because of looting.

R.M. YOUNGER

FIJI • Information Highlights

Official Name: Fiji
Location: South Pacific Ocean
Area: 7,054 sq mi (18 270 km²)
Population (mid-1987 est.): 700,000.
Chief City: Suva, the capital.
Government: *Head of state,* Ratu Sir Penaia Ganilau (took office December 1987). *Head of government,* Ratu Sir Kamisese Mara (took office December 1987).
Gross Domestic Product (1986 est.): $1,099,000,000.

FINLAND

Politics dominated the year in Finland, as parliamentary elections gave conservatives a role in government for the first time in 20 years.

Political Affairs. On March 15 and 16 the Finnish people elected a new Parliament for a four-year term. The results indicated a swing to the right, with the Conservative Party gaining nine seats and emerging as the country's second biggest party with 53 representatives. The Social Democrats, with 56 seats, remained the party with the largest representation in Parliament. The Center Party gained two seats for a total of 40. The Swedish People's Party took 13 seats; the Christian Party, 5; the Rural Party, 9; and the Greens, 4. The larger of Finland's two communist parties, the Democratic Union, ended up with 16 seats, and its splinter party, the Democratic Alternative, won 4.

The changes in Parliament led to the formation of a new cabinet, based on unprecedented cooperation between the Conservatives and the Social Democrats. The Conservatives, who entered the government for the first time since 1966, were given six of the ministries, with Harri Holkeri becoming prime minister. Former Prime Minister Kalevi Sorsa, of the Social Democrats, became deputy prime minister and foreign minister. The other 16 ministries were shared among seven Social Democrats, six Conservatives, two ministers from the

FINLAND • Information Highlights

Official Name: Republic of Finland.
Location: Northern Europe.
Area: 130,127 sq mi (337 030 km²).
Population (mid-1987 est.): 4,900,000.
Chief Cities (Dec. 31, 1984): Helsinki, the capital, 484,263; Tampere, 168,150.
Government: *Head of state,* Mauno Koivisto, president (took office Jan. 27, 1982). *Head of government,* Harri Holkeri, prime minister (took office April 30, 1987). *Legislature* (unicameral)—Eduskunta.
Monetary Unit: Markka (4.0935 markkaa equal U.S.$1, Nov. 23, 1987).
Gross National Product: (1985 U.S.$): $54,400,000,000.
Economic Indexes (1986): *Consumer Prices* (1980 = 100), all items, 155.9; food, 163.0. *Industrial Production* (1980 = 100), 117.
Foreign Trade (1986 U.S.$): *Imports,* $15,325,000,000; *exports,* $16,340,000,000.

Swedish People's Party, and one minister from the Rural Party.

Presidential elections were scheduled for January 1988. The incumbent, Mauno Koivisto, a Social Democrat, was expected to receive the support of the Rural Party and the so-called Koivisto Movement in addition to that of his own party. The Conservatives nominated Harri Holkeri. Kalevi Kivistö, a provincial governor, received the support of the Democratic Union; the Democratic Alternative declared for its secretary-general, Jouko Kajanoja; and the Center Party nominated its leader, Paavo Väyrynen.

The Holkeri government set as its goal a 3% annual growth rate in gross national product (GNP) during the four-year term of Parliament. The rate was .5% above the planned growth in the industrial countries of Western Europe. Also foreseen were a rise in exports and a 5% reduction in unemployment in 1988.

Parliament on June 2 adopted constitutional reforms that had been approved by the previous legislature. The proposal to introduce a system of advisory voting (a kind of referendum) was approved unanimously. Also introduced were changes transferring some minor decision-making powers from the president to Parliament. For example, Parliament and the speaker must be consulted on the appointment of a new cabinet and on setting the closing date of a parliamentary session. Direct presidential elections were also introduced.

Independence Anniversary. December 6 marked the 70th anniversary of Finnish independence. Made a part of the Swedish realm during the Middle Ages and ceded to Russia in 1809, Finland became an independent republic on Dec. 6, 1917. Patriotic celebrations and activities were held throughout the year, including traveling exhibitions on Finnish heraldry and the history of the Finnish flag, with the main festivities on the National Day.

ERIK J. FRIIS
The Scandinavian-American Bulletin

FLORIDA

Pope John Paul II opened his 1987 tour of the United States in Miami on September 10. (*See* RELIGION.) While in Florida, the pope had meetings with President Ronald Reagan and with a delegation of American Jewish leaders. The pope then traveled to Miami's Tamiami Park, where 200,000 people gathered for what was to be the first outdoor mass of his U.S. tour. However, the papal mass was cut short by a violent thunderstorm.

In November, Mayor Xavier Suarez of Miami, the first Cuban-American to lead the city, was returned for a second term in a runoff vote against former Mayor Maurice Ferre.

Legislation. Two major bills pushed by Gov. Bob Martinez and passed during the regular legislative session were the targets of outspoken criticism.

First, establishment of a statewide gun permit that wiped out stricter ordinances also created a loophole that allowed open display of handguns, triggering complaints from law enforcement officers. Second, a 5% sales tax on a variety of professional services—the largest tax increase in state history—prompted angry attacks from business factions. Especially outraged were national advertisers, who would be taxed on the proportion of their total advertising that appeared in Florida.

Martinez called a special legislative session to correct the gun-law flaw and repeal the services tax. The legislators banned open sidearms and late in the year agreed with his reversal on the service tax issue. The levy was repealed, but the state sales tax was raised one penny to offset the expected $1 billion in lost revenues.

Other major new laws provided for the cleanup of Lake Okeechobee and other polluted waters, $67 million for new prisons (overcrowding had become so acute that thousands of inmates were released early to make room for more prisoners), and an expanded indigent health-care plan. Martinez also won approval for his budget plan, control over the new lottery, and confirmation of key appointees.

Economy and Tourism. The state's unemployment rate remained among the lowest in the nation. The citrus industry was buoyed by two factors: the epic every-other-year freezes that started in 1983 skipped 1987 and spared growers monumental losses, and the grapefruit crop was the largest in six years with strong sales in Europe and Japan.

Florida's population continued to grow. According to state projections based on U.S. Census Bureau figures, Florida passed Massachusetts as the fifth most populous state on June 30 with 11,934,360 people.

Bayside Marketplace, Miami's $93 million showplace on the water, opened on April 8 amid fireworks and upbeat music. The 16-acre

© Walter Marks/Metro-Dade County

Bayside Marketplace, a 16-acre, $93 million retail and entertainment center on the Miami waterfront, opened in April. The complex is the centerpiece of the city's revitalization.

(6.5 ha) retail and entertainment center, which features shops and restaurants, is considered the backbone of Miami's revitalization.

On Miami Beach, the main street in the Art Deco district was fast becoming a true vacation destination, with its share of history, sun, surf, and nightlife. Ocean Drive, where many neglected old hotels were being restored to their 1930s splendor, was the scene of activity Miami Beach had not experienced in two decades.

The Tampa Bay Performing Arts Center opened in Tampa in September. The new cultural center, which houses three theaters, is located on the Hillsborough River. Scheduled performers for the opening season included the Leningrad State Symphony and the American Ballet Theatre.

Sports and Games. The state spent many months working out lottery plans. It hired the Illinois lottery director and prepared for the first scratch-off games to start Jan. 15, 1988. Much of the revenue was earmarked for education.

After 20 years of playing in the Orange Bowl, the Miami Dolphins moved to their new stadium in north Dade County. Named for its National Football League team owner, Joe Robbie Stadium, seating 74,993, was called one of the finest facilities in the league. However, the first regular-season, home game against the defending champion New York Giants was canceled because of the NFL Players Association strike.

An arena took shape in downtown Miami, where the newest National Basketball Association franchise will play. The Miami Heat will take the court in the 1988–89 season.

Finally, after years of haggling, Sunday horse racing became a reality.

GREG MELIKOV
State Desk, "The Miami Herald"

FLORIDA • Information Highlights

Area: 58,664 sq mi (151 939 km²).
Population (July 1, 1986 est.): 11,675,000.
Chief Cities (July 1, 1986 est.): Tallahassee, the capital, 119,480; Jacksonville, 610,030; Miami, 373,940; Tampa, 277,580; St. Petersburg, 239,480.
Government (1987): *Chief Officers*—governor, Bob Martinez (R); lt. gov., Bobby Brantley (R). *Legislature*—Senate, 40 members; House of Representatives, 120 members.
State Finances (fiscal year 1986): *Revenue,* $15,815,000,000; *expenditure,* $13,740,000,000.
Personal Income (1986): $170,980,000,000; per capita, $14,646.
Labor Force (June 1987): *Civilian labor force,* 5,882,900; *unemployed,* 312,600 (5.3% of total force).
Education: *Enrollment* (fall 1985)—public elementary schools, 1,086,250; public secondary, 476,622; colleges and universities, 451,392. *Public school expenditures* (1985–86), $5,391,000,000 ($3,731 per pupil).

FOOD

Two conflicting developments in 1987 left U.S. consumers disoriented in their search for a healthy diet and damaged the credibility of the food industry and one of its governmental regulators. One major trend, confirmed by many sources, was that U.S. consumers continued to switch foods in search of good health —for example, from red meat to fish and chicken. However, it was also revealed that chicken meat in the United States was frequently unsafe to eat, having been contaminated during processing.

Food Safety. Information about the health hazards from poultry processing emerged from a National Academy of Sciences (NAS) report issued in May, from a series of feature stories by investigative reporter George Anthon, and from hearings by a Senate Governmental Affairs subcommittee. The NAS report stated that U.S. citizens have suffered several million cases of food poisoning each year from chicken contaminated by salmonella and other microorganisms. Contamination was caused by high-speed processing machines which killed, defeathered, and eviscerated chicken carcasses. Surveys by the U.S. Department of Agriculture (USDA) and state agencies indicated that 35% to 65% of chickens leaving U.S. processing plants were contaminated with salmonella and other harmful bacteria.

Consumer groups and some members of Congress demanded that the industry clean up its act—even eliminate automatic processing or brand chicken carcasses "hazardous to health." Food-industry representatives suggested instead that consumers be trained to cook chicken thoroughly in order to destroy salmonella. The poultry investigation came at a time when both the industry and its regulatory agency—the Food Safety and Inspection Service (FSIS)—had been arguing that the private sector should be given more responsibility for policing itself. With the chicken market booming, it had been argued that the industry would take pains to maintain a reputation for a wholesome product. The disclosures of 1987 thus jeopardized the reputation of both the poultry industry and the FSIS.

Salmonella occurring in processed poultry was indicative of a worldwide problem of food-borne diseases. A 1987 exposé of the U.S. meat-packing industry reported unsafe conditions reminiscent of Upton Sinclair's turn-of-the-century novel, *The Jungle*. A World Health Organization (WHO) publication stated that illness caused by contaminated food was a leading cause of suffering and death in the developing world, while diarrheal diseases also killed millions of children in those countries each year. WHO urged that national governments give more attention to the impact of food-borne disease.

Food Supplies. At a time when the world's grain bins were bulging (*see* AGRICULTURE), there were still large pockets of hunger. Indeed there were some malnourished people in virtually every country in the world. At an Amsterdam, the Netherlands, meeting of food experts in February, it was agreed that sub-Saharan Africa remained in a condition of persistent poverty and food shortage, with lagging agricultural production. And Ethiopia and Mozambique experienced drought again in 1987, a possible prelude to another famine. Economists identified the cause of hunger in the world today as the lack of sufficient income of people in market economies to buy food—or that prices are higher than they can afford to pay. Governments of many developing countries, using subsidies and regulation, tried to keep food prices down, if only to prevent urban riots; but when food prices were low, farmers lacked incentive to produce adequate supplies.

Dietary Products and Trends. The Hormel Company, which in 1987 marked the 50th anniversary of SPAM (for spiced ham), also released a new miracle food during the year: a ready-to-eat main dish called Top Shelf, which reputedly could be stored at room temperature for 18 months before being popped into the microwave. Hormel and certain other corporate processors were abandoning their traditional meat-packing plants, engaging instead in finishing food for home consumption.

In response to the demand for speed and convenience in cooking, the microwave was rapidly replacing the oven, and even the range. Products for the microwave, including frozen dinners, popcorn, pancakes, and even cake mixes, were booming. Meanwhile, one of the oldest convenience foods—breakfast cereal—remained as ubiquitous and profitable as ever. Indeed, 90% of all breakfasts in the United States were still consumed at home, which made cold cereal one of the hottest markets.

For meals eaten outside the home, convenience and speed were high priorities. Fast-food places such as McDonald's were pulling customers away from the chain restaurants and from locally owned restaurants, too. The fast-food places provided some comparable foods, such as prepared salads, but with faster service. Pizza chains also were finding that profit and expansion came from providing quick service and, even more important, from fast home delivery. See also THE CONVENIENCE BOOM, page 63.

Dietary Changes. Food preferences and behavior, once thought to be among a culture's stablest values, were changing radically. In Asia, taste and income shifts were leading to more imports of wheat, vegetables, and livestock feed, while rice, a traditional food, was usually available for export.

In the United States, food processors, restaurateurs, and grocers generally seemed to be in agreement about the direction of change. The National Restaurant Association reported that "owners see low-calorie meals as the wave of the future." A survey of newspaper food reporters published in the magazine *Progressive Grocer* revealed a consensus that consumers would be shopping for more low-calorie items, fresh produce, fish and seafood, and less red meat.

Similar dietary trends were found in a survey of consumers administered by the U.S. Human Nutrition Information Service. Women in the survey reported eating only half as much beef and only a third as much pork as those surveyed a decade earlier, while consuming more fruit and milk. Women and children alike were switching to low-fat milk and to low-calorie carbonated soft-drinks. Men in the survey had sharply reduced intake of beef and pork and were eating less poultry and eggs; fish consumption was up 50% from 1977. Men also were consuming more nuts, fruits, grain mixtures, and low-calorie soft drinks. And men reportedly were receiving more than one third of their nutrients from foods obtained away from home, up from one fourth in 1977. Younger men were snacking more: 40% said they ate five or more times each day.

DONALD F. HADWIGER
Iowa State University

© François Lochon/Gamma Liaison

France's "cohabitation" government continued in 1987. Under the system, Prime Minister Jacques Chirac, left, *has tried to dominate domestic affairs, while his counterpart, Socialist President François Mitterrand, has overseen foreign affairs and diplomatic matters.*

FRANCE

France's political life in 1987 was dominated by the approaching presidential elections in the spring of 1988. Skirmishing and frequent revelations of political scandals, or *affaires,* attracted wide attention. Socialist President François Mitterrand remained firmly in control of foreign policy under a power-sharing arrangement with conservative Prime Minister Jacques Chirac known as "cohabitation." Chirac, seeking to display predominance in domestic affairs, emphasized his government's reform program, notably privatization of leading companies and banks, which was expected to be a major campaign issue.

Politics. The year began in a crisis atmosphere as a wildcat strike by workers and train engineers on the state-owned railroad spread to the Paris transport network, docks, and electricity works throughout France. In what was regarded as the largest strike in the public sector in 20 years, workers and unions were challenging Chirac's plan to introduce merit-based promotion rules on the railroad and to hold down wage increases to 2–3%. Although the government weathered the walkouts, and the public saw restored service by January 13, the Chirac government was forced to grant wage increases of just over 3%, and it shelved the promotion scheme. Commentators noted that the compromise agreements reflected Chirac's growing hesitation to implement reforms aimed at shrinking the government's role in the economy.

French police, in a spectacular, nonviolent raid on February 21, arrested four people identified as leaders of the Direct Action terrorist group. The arrests were regarded as a major triumph for the "law-and-order" Chirac government. Direct Action was believed to have been responsible for nearly 80 bombings and other terrorist attacks since 1979. In a related victory for the government a week later, a special seven-magistrate panel in Paris sentenced a suspected Arab terrorist, Georges Ibrahim Abdallah, to life in prison for involvement in three attacks on foreign diplomats including two U.S. officials. Although a victory for the government, the harsh sentence was expected to complicate negotiations for the release of French hostages in the Middle East.

On April 7, Chirac opened the new session of the National Assembly with a warning to his conservative coalition to avoid infighting that could damage chances of winning the two-round presidential elections scheduled for April 24 and May 8, 1988. His warning was directed mainly at former Prime Minister Raymond Barre, actively campaigning as a probable presidential candidate with the support of the Union for French Democracy (UDF), a center-right party and junior coalition partner with Chirac's ruling Gaullist Rally for the Republic (RPR). The UDF had recently broken ranks with Chirac over defense issues and stricter nationality requirements proposed by the government.

The Socialist Party, at a special congress in Lille April 3–5, began debating what became a predominant, intriguing question throughout the year: who would be the party's candidate for president? Mitterrand was widely viewed as the party's best hope, but the 71-year-old president declined to reveal his intentions. A poll of the Socialists' executive committee showed that Michel Rocard, a moderate and former agriculture minister, was the party's favorite choice after Mitterrand. He was trailed by former Prime Minister Laurent Fabius.

Jean-Marie Le Pen, leader of the extreme right wing National Front, announced his presidential candidacy on April 26, placing new pressures on Chirac's coalition. Le Pen had used emotional issues, such as calls for restricting Arab immigration, to build support for his party, backed by about 10% of the electorate. Although Le Pen was not expected to survive the first round, his campaign appeared to be motivated by determination to win a ministerial post in a new conservative government.

In what some commentators described as a major blow to his political ambitions, Le Pen in a statement on September 13 referred to the Nazi gas chambers as "a detail of the history of the Second World War." French political and religious leaders widely condemned the statement as a reflection of Le Pen's anti-Semitism. Le Pen denied the allegations five days later, insisting that criticism of his statement had been stirred up by the "pro-immigrant lobby" and the "apparatus of the Left."

Embarrassment for the Socialists intensified during early October as the National Assembly and the Senate voted to establish a parliamentary high court to impeach Christian Nucci, minister for development in the Socialist government. He was accused of diverting more than 5 million francs (close to $1 million) from a publicly financed organization into his own party treasury, or his political expense account. Nucci said the cash was taken without his knowledge, amid speculation that the parliament will not reach a verdict until after the presidential election.

By late December, Mitterrand was running ahead of all likely candidates in the polls, and although he still was insisting he had not yet decided on whether to seek reelection, the leader was acting increasingly like a candidate. Amid whirlwind trips around the country and appearances on television talk shows, Mitterrand leveled biting attacks against Chirac's government.

Economy. Although France entered 1987 with growing pressures on its low rate of inflation, prospects for moderate growth improved throughout the year. But unemployment worsened, while the country's external deficits remained a major constraint on government-expansion plans. The government's five-year privatization plan affecting major banks and companies was widely regarded as a major achievement, although its future was clouded by the world monetary crisis after mid-October, which depressed prices on the Paris Bourse.

Finance Minister Edouard Balladur announced February 5 that during 1986 France had a balance-of-payment surplus of 25.4 billion francs (approximately $5 billion), the first since 1979 (and compared with a 1.5 billion franc, $300 million, deficit in 1985). Early in 1987, however, France's 1986 trade surplus of 500 million francs ($100 million) turned into a deficit. The national statistics institute predicted the 1987 trade deficit would reach 30-35 billion francs ($6–7 billion), which was expected to push the balance of payments into the red as well.

Balladur and public officials, however, criticized the institute and private forecasters for "excessive pessimism," amid rumors early in the year that Balladur and Chirac would stimulate the economy, possibly through accelerated tax cuts or increased government spending. In early March the Organization for Economic Cooperation and Development (OECD) warned that the government had "little scope" for stimulative action without provoking increased inflation.

Despite more optimistic claims by the finance ministry, the OECD in late December predicted that France's economic growth would fall to 1½% in 1987 and 1988 from the previous year's rate of 2%. The OECD, confirming ministry assessments, also said that unless French growth reached a minimum rate of 3% annually, unemployment would continue rising. The jobless rate was projected at 11.5% for 1988, up from 10.6% in 1987, representing just over 3 million persons, and one of the highest rates in Western Europe.

The privatization program stirred widespread political controversy throughout the year but was generally considered a financial success for the government. By October a total of 23 operations had been carried out successfully, representing a market value of about 100 billion francs ($20 billion). The goal, under a 1986 law, is to privatize a total of 65 groups, including 26 major industrial, banking, and insurance groups.

Socialist leaders and some conservatives, including former Prime Minister Barre, alleged that Balladur had been deliberately underpricing privatized stocks and had shown excessive favoritism to political friends when awarding shares to the "hard core" of investors. These groups, designated by the finance ministry,

FRANCE • Information Highlights

Official Name: French Republic.
Location: Western Europe.
Area: 211,208 sq mi (547 030 km²).
Population (mid-1987 est.): 55,600,000.
Chief City (1982 est.): Paris, the capital, 8,706,963.
Government: *Head of state,* François Mitterrand, president (took office May 1981). *Chief minister,* Jacques Chirac, prime minister (took office March 1986). *Legislature*—Parliament: Senate and National Assembly.
Monetary Unit: Franc (5.6564 francs equal U.S. $1, Dec. 8, 1987).
Gross Domestic Product (1985 U.S.$): $510,-000,000,000.
Economic Indexes (1986): *Consumer Prices* (1980 = 100), all items, 162.0; food, 164.4. *Industrial Production* (Oct. 1987, 1980 = 100), 105.
Foreign Trade (1986 U.S.$): *Imports,* $128,836,-000,000; *exports,* $119,435,000,000.

© Brian Willer Photography

Canada's Prime Minister Brian Mulroney and Quebec Premier Robert Bourassa (front) *welcomed representatives of 37 French-speaking nations, including France's President Mitterrand* (right), *to Quebec City for a second francophone summit.*

control the largest blocks of shares in the companies. Balladur brushed off the charges.

The 1988 budget, presented to the Council of Ministers on September 16, sought a 2.78% increase in spending, to 1.083 trillion francs (about $215 billion). Revenues were projected to rise 4.73% despite planned tax cuts, including income-tax reductions, which the government was expected to emphasize in the approaching presidential election. According to Balladur, the budget deficit was expected to drop to 115 billion francs ($23 billion) from 129 billion francs ($26 billion) in 1987. Inflation was projected to slow to 2.5% in 1988, compared with 3.4% in 1987 and 2.1% in 1986.

In the largest single foreign investment project of the year, Chirac on March 24 signed a contract with Walt Disney Productions for the building of Europe's first Disneyland amusement park. The first phase of the project will require an investment of 15 billion francs, ($3 billion), with Disney Productions owning one sixth of a new company that would oversee construction at a site on the eastern outskirts of Paris. Completion of Eurodisneyland, which will also include a hotel and business center, was planned for 1992.

Foreign Affairs. As part of France's continued military involvement in Chad, and in response to raids on Chadian targets by Libyan jets, French Jaguar fighter-bombers on January 7 "neutralized" Libyan radar stations at a military site at Wadi Doum, in northern Chad. Amid continued skirmishing, French forces on September 7 shot down a Libyan Tupolev-22 bomber over N'Djamena, Chad's capital, killing the plane's three crewmen.

France tried to play down the incident, but the Reagan administration viewed the conflict as a way of increasing pressure on Libya, which created new tensions with Paris. The United States had already provided Chad an extra $32 million in military aid during 1987 and, reportedly, satellite maps of Libyan positions. French Foreign Minister Jean-Bernard Raimond on September 8 said that the U.S. administration was "perhaps giving Chad advice that is different from ours . . . but what is best for the Chadians and Africans is the French policy."

Foreign arms sales by French industry became the center of several controversies. On April 2, the U.S. State Department submitted reports to Congress on arms sales to South Africa by French and Italian companies, violating a United Nations embargo. Classified versions of the reports supposedly contained assertions that Paris and Rome were aware of the arms trade. Chirac, who was visiting Washington, said he was "surprised" by the U.S. report and told newsmen France had stopped arms shipments to South Africa ten years earlier.

A secret military report published November 4 by a Paris newspaper said that President Mitterrand was informed in 1984 that a French arms firm, Luchaire, was illegally exporting artillery shells to Iran. (France had embargoed arms sales to Iran in 1980.) The report, prepared by Jean-François Barba, the inspector general of the armed forces in the Chirac government, immediately became the center of a Left-Right political battle and was compared to the Iran-contra affair in the United States. It said the shipments had occurred from 1983 to 1986 and that revenues from some of the sales had been diverted to the Socialist Party.

The "Luchaire affair" immediately focused national debate on the financing of political

© J. Pavlovsky/Sygma

In July, French police began guarding the Iranian Embassy, where they believed an Iranian wanted for questioning was hiding. France broke off relations with Iran in midmonth.

parties in France and on Mitterrand's role in policy-making, while adding to public confusion about France's policy regarding the Iran-Iraq war. The Barba report also revealed details of how the Socialists were involved in using arms trading with Iran as a means of obtaining the release of French hostages in Lebanon. The Socialists tried to play down the affair's political importance, with a spokesman for Mitterrand saying in early November that the president would make no comment, emphasizing that the affair was under judicial investigation.

These revelations about Iran came several months after a dramatic standoff involving the besieged French and Iranian embassies in Tehran and Paris, following France's decision to break off diplomatic relations with Iran on July 17. The incident appeared to mark the end of French efforts to "normalize" relations with Iran. Evidencing the growing strains in relations between Chirac and Mitterrand over foreign policy, the French president emphasized that the friendlier policy toward Iran had been instituted by the prime minister.

Late in November, however, two French hostages were released in Lebanon by pro-Iranian forces. The Franco-Iranian accord that led to the release—including promise of partial repayment by France of a large debt owed to Iran and the eventual restoration of diplomatic relations between the two countries—was severely criticized by Britain, the United States, and much of the Arab world. Early in December, Chirac assured his European allies that France had paid no ransom.

Tensions with the Soviet Union surfaced during a visit by Chirac to Moscow, May 14–16. This followed France's arrest of several alleged Soviet spies working on development of the European space launcher Ariane and Soviet opposition to France's plans to modernize its nuclear strike force. On the first day of Chirac's visit, Soviet leader Mikhail Gorbachev made a surprise appearance at a Kremlin banquet for Chirac. But Nikolai Ryzhkov, the premier, noted "dents" and "complexities" that had recently marred French-Soviet relations. Chirac said improved relations would depend on improved Soviet action on human rights and on withdrawal of Soviet forces from Afghanistan.

As part of a determined effort to improve relations with West Germany—and to distance himself from Chirac—Mitterrand told German Chancellor Helmut Kohl on May 21 that he favored the "double-zero" disarmament option on Euromissiles. The statement came on the first of a two-day summit meeting in Paris between the two leaders, and appeared to conflict with the position taken by Chirac earlier, questioning the Soviet offer. Asked to comment on the apparent conflict, Mitterrand told newsmen: "France speaks with one voice. You have heard it."

A month later, Mitterrand said he welcomed a proposal by Kohl to form a joint French-German army brigade. At a news conference in Bonn on June 19, Kohl said the brigade would be an "experiment" and would not conflict with "close ties" with the United States in the North Atlantic Treaty Organization (NATO). Mitterrand, several days later, said that the project could be the "embryo of a European defense structure," but he ruled out any return by France to the unified NATO command structure. Traditional Gaullists, such as former Prime Minister Michel Debré, said they were reluctant to give up any French autonomy in defense, particularly to the Germans.

Nevertheless, at the conclusion of French-German military war games in Germany, September 21–24, Mitterrand announced that the two governments would be establishing a joint defense council by January 1989. The French leader said that its goal would be to "coordinate decisions and harmonize analyses in the areas of security, defense, research, armament, and the organization and deployment of joint units." Mitterrand also invited other European allies to join the council. Political observers said Mitterrand's gesture was aimed at reinforcing his position as the nation's predominant force in diplomatic and foreign affairs.

AXEL KRAUSE
"International Herald Tribune," Paris

© Robert C. Lautman

The 4.2 acre (1.7 ha) Enid A. Haupt Garden at the Smithsonian Institution in Washington, DC, was opened on May 22, 1987. A large Victorian parterre dominates the center garden and leads to the entrance (top center).

GARDENING AND HORTICULTURE

The number one outdoor leisure activity in the United States continued to be gardening, according to a 1986–87 survey conducted by the Gallup Organization for the National Gardening Association. The survey found that 78% of U.S. households (69 million) were involved in at least one form of gardening activity.

New Garden. The Enid A. Haupt Garden at the Smithsonian Institution in Washington, DC, was opened to the public in May 1987. This fully mature, colorful, 4.2 acre (1.7 ha) garden provides the illusion of visiting the grounds of a fine old estate. To accomplish the fully mature impression, specimen plants with root balls as large as 8 ft (2.4 m) in diameter and weighing more than 4 tons were transplanted into the garden which is situated above the underground quadrangle complex housing the new National Museum of African Art, the Arthur M. Sackler Gallery, and the International Center. The Enid A. Haupt Garden, with its 13 matched pairs of 20-ft (6-m) high saucer magnolias planted to form *allées* of springtime splendor, 15 little-leaf lindens, each standing 18-ft (5.5-m) high, planted along the main entrance, and a 40-ft (12.2-m) high weeping beech against the Castle facade, was completed at a cost of $3 million, which was donated by Mrs. Enid Annenberg Haupt.

Award Winners and Honors. The All-America Rose Selection Award (AARS) for 1988 was announced for three outstanding new varieties of roses, including one variety of each category —grandiflora, floribunda, and hybrid tea. "Prima Donna," a deep pink grandiflora with 4-inch (10-cm) blooms of 35 petals each, was introduced by DeVor Nurseries, Pleasanton, CA, and hybridized by Takeshi Shirakawa, Gamagori-shi, Aichi Ken, Japan. "Prima Donna" has shown itself to be a proven performer with the florist and commercial greenhouse trade. "Amber Queen" received the award as a floribunda rose. With a height of 3–3.5 ft (.9–1.1 m), "Amber Queen" produces strongly fragrant flowers, with golden yellow tinged with apricot petals, 2.5–3 inches (6.4–7.6 cm) across, on lustrous, dark green, disease-resistant plants. "Amber Queen" was hybridized by Jack Harkness, Suffolk, England, and introduced by Roses by Fred Edmunds, Wilsonville, OR. "Mikado" (var Koh-Sai) hybrid tea produces flowers of 4–5 inches (10–12.7 cm) with brilliant red shaded to yellow at the base and deep coral-pink washed with yellow on reverse. With very good mildew resistance, "Mikado" was hybridized by Seizo Suzuki, Keisei Rose Nursery, Tokyo, Japan, and introduced by Conard-Pyle Company, West Grove, PA.

William J. Park, president of George W. Park Seed Co., Greenwood, SC, was presented the All-America Selections (AAS) Silver Medallion in January 1987 for a lifetime of professional excellence, integrity, and distinguished service to the AAS and the home-garden industry. Joseph Harris of Rochester, NY, was awarded the Gold Medal of Horticulture by the New York State Nurserymen's Association. Under Harris' direction, the Joseph Harris Company, founded by his grandfather in 1879, introduced hundreds of varieties of flowers and vegetables with improved productivity and growth characteristics.

New Publication. *Diseases of Trees and Shrubs* by W.A. Sinclair, H.H. Lyon, and W.T. Johnson was published by Cornell University Press in 1987. With more than 1,700 full-color plates and 576 pages, this nontechnical reference book focuses on plant problems that can be seen with the naked eye.

RALPH L. SNODSMITH
Ornamental Horticulturist

GENETICS

The year 1987 in genetics was highlighted by a controversial public-policy decision and continuing advances in scientific research.

Patenting New Genetic Forms. In a series of decisions beginning in 1980, the U.S. Supreme Court and the Patent and Trademark Office of the U.S. Department of Commerce have allowed the patenting of certain organisms with unique characteristics produced through gene splicing (recombinant-DNA technique). Over the years, some 200 patents have been granted for bacteria, viruses, and plants that had been genetically modified. In April 1987, the Patent Office extended the policy by allowing patents for new forms of animal life created through gene splicing. The decision expands considerably the commercial possibilities for genetic engineering and will help stimulate new work in this field. However, it also has fueled a vigorous ethical debate. Opponents contend that the creation of new forms of animal life is a dangerous and improper intrusion into nature.

Gene Splicing. In recombinant-DNA technique, genes are removed from one organism and inserted into another. Since the first such procedure in 1973, thousands of transfers have been performed in animals and plants as well as microbes.

Extending gene splicing even further, another team of California researchers succeeded in transferring a gene from an animal to a plant. The animal gene, from the firefly *Photinus pyralis,* is the one that codes for the enzyme luciferase. The enzyme catalyzes a chemical reaction between luciferin, a small organic molecule, and adenosine triphosphate (ATP), the cell's energy storage molecule. When all three are present, luciferin reacts with ATP and emits light. In this experiment, the luciferase gene was transferred to a tobacco plant, and when the roots of the plant were placed in a luciferin solution, the plant began to emit light. This demonstrated that animal genes, under the proper conditions, will function normally in plant cells. If the reverse were also found to occur, as believed, there would be no insurmountable barriers to the transfer of genes between the animal and plant kingdoms.

Human XX Males. In humans and other mammals, sex is determined by the presence or absence of the Y chromosome. Males are normally XY, females XX. However, about one child in 20,000 human male births has normal male genitalia but an XX chromosomal composition. Recent work by scientists in Finland has explained the underlying genetics of XX male births.

It was already known that the maleness of an XY individual is determined by one or more genes located in the shorter segment of the Y chromosome. To ascertain the exact location, the researchers took a number of shorter segments from the Y chromosomes of normal XY males and made them radioactive. These segments, which contained the male-determining genes, would bind to any chromosome that contained the same type of genes. When the Y-chromosome segments were mixed with the chromosomes of various XX males, they were found to bind to only one X chromosome of each XX male. Apparently, during sperm formation in the father of each XX male, an exchange of genetic material between the X and Y chromosomes had transferred male-determining genes from the Y chromosome to the X chromosome. The subsequent union of sperm and egg must have involved the sperm cell with the X chromosome containing the male-determining genes.

Transcription. Geneticists have long believed that only one strand (sense strand) of a double-stranded DNA (deoxyribonucleic acid) molecule contains the actual genes transcribed into RNA (ribonucleic acid). The opposite strand (antisense strand) was believed to function only in the replication of the DNA molecule by providing the template upon which the new sense strand would be built. Correspondingly, the old sense strand would act as a template for the formation of a new antisense strand during replication.

Recently, however, scientists studying transcription have reported obtaining RNA transcripts from both strands for the same DNA sequence. In each case, the RNA transcript from the sense strand is translated into a known protein. It is not yet known whether the RNA transcript from the antisense strand is translated or remains as RNA, but the fact that both strands of a DNA molecule can be transcribed enlarges considerably the potential size of the genome in double-stranded organisms.

Manic Depression. An estimated 2.4 million Americans suffer from manic depression, or bipolar disorder, characterized by alternating periods of extreme elation and extreme depression. (Symptoms normally appear between ages 15 and 35.) Having identified families in which the disorder has appeared in several generations, a group of researchers used DNA-cutting enzymes to examine chromosomes for particular sized segments that might be present in affected individuals but absent from normal ones. They discovered such a DNA section near the shorter end of chromosome #11 which contained genes both for the protein insulin and for a protein found in benign forms of cancer. The genes for the two proteins are not believed to cause manic depression, but, quite by chance, they are located near the gene for bipolar disorder. Thus, the discovery presents the first genetic marker for a mental illness and allows identification of children who are at risk for bipolar disorder later in life.

See also BIOTECHNOLOGY.

LOUIS LEVINE, *City College of New York*

GEOLOGY

The worst U.S. earthquake of 1987 occurred on October 1, when the area of Los Angeles experienced its strongest quake since the 1971 event that killed 65 people. Measuring 5.9 on the Richter scale, the quake had its epicenter between Whittier and Pasadena. Three minutes later came a severe aftershock of 5.3, and within a day 16 more aftershocks measuring 3.0 or higher had been recorded. Six persons were killed, and damages exceeded $200 million.

Seismologists at first blamed the shocks on the Whittier-Elsinore fault, the vertical type of fault—highly visible in California—that lies between crustal plates moving in different directions. Later studies showed that this fault was not involved, however, and suggested a far deeper epicenter in a thrust-type fault where one plate rides over another. The worrisome fact for quake prediction efforts in the area is that geological knowledge of the deep-lying sites there is less developed than for vertical faults, and the only more observable features with which they are linked are near-surface folds in sedimentary rock.

Two strong earthquakes also struck Ecuador. The shocks, one of magnitude 7.0, rocked the nation's northeastern mountains on March 5 and 6. They were followed by hundreds of aftershocks that triggered severe flooding and mudslides, leaving as many as 100,000 people homeless and an estimated 1,000 dead or missing. One month earlier, on February 8, a major quake and resulting landslides destroyed villages on a Papua New Guinea island, leaving several hundred people homeless. The initial tremor measured 7.6 and was followed on February 10 by a 5.4 aftershock. Strong earthquakes also were recorded in Chile, Nicaragua, Alaska, China, and Japan.

Plate Tectonics and Earth Structure. Earth scientists know that the Earth's crust and upper mantle, or lithosphere, is divided into several large, slow-moving plates, but the causes and rates of plate movement are not yet fully understood. Employing large radio antennas to record signals from distant quasars as reference points, scientists have studied these rates of movement. The best data thus far obtained have been for the relatively fast-moving Pacific plate. Over the past three years, for example, the distance between Hawaii and a site near Fairbanks, Alaska, has decreased by 52.3 millimeters (2 inches) per year, and Hawaii is also approaching Japan at a rate of 83 millimeters (3.2 inches) per year.

Various causes of plate movement have been proposed. In 1987, results from a computer model of possible mechanisms have suggested that plates provide their own motive force through the pull of cooling ocean plates as they sink into deep-sea trenches. Other studies suggest that great heat may be another driving mechanism, since California scientists have determined that the Earth's core is much hotter than had once been thought and even hotter than the surface of the Sun—more than about 6,650° C (about 12,000° F). This heat may seep from the core to the mantle, generating currents that move crustal plates. The semi-molten upper mantle itself has been found to have a "lumpy" structure rather than a uniform consistency, as had originally been supposed. At depths of 97 km (60 mi) to 290 km (180 mi), seismic waves reveal rock pockets ranging from about 5 km (3 mi) to 100 km (62 mi) in diameter. These mantle variations could be the result of temperature differences and changes in rock composition, and these in turn might be related to plate movements.

Earliest Life Forms. Newly discovered microfossils from western Australia appear to be the oldest oxygen-bearing bacteria yet described. The fossils indicate that physiologically advanced photosynthesis may have occurred as early as 3.5 billion years ago. They also suggest that life may have originated some 4 billion years ago, or only 500 million years after the birth of the planet. Fossils from rocks dating about 488 million years old, in the Late Ordovician period, represent the oldest known trace fossils of nonmarine origin. They take the form of networks of tubular burrows, ranging from 2 to 21 millimeters (.08-.8 inches) in diameter, that occur in strata that are typical of ancient buried soils. Their origin is not certain, but they may have been made by millipedes. The fossils suggest that colonization of land began much earlier than was once thought.

Dinosaur Remains. Rocks in Montana 75 million years old yielded the remains of a new type of horned, or ceratopsid, dinosaur. Named *Avaceratops lammersi,* the plant-eating animal weighed about 180 kg (400 lb) and was about 2 m (6.5 ft) long and almost 1 m (3 ft) high.

The oldest known dinosaur eggs were found in Upper Jurassic strata in western Colorado. Estimated to be 145 million years old, the eggs shed new light on the nesting habits of dinosaurs. Shells arranged in at least 6 layers of nests suggest that some dinosaurs sought isolated nesting sights and used them repeatedly. Dinosaur nests, some containing baby dinosaur skeletons, also were found in central Texas. In Mongolia's Gobi Desert, where the first such eggs were discovered in 1922, fragments of dinosaur eggs were found arranged upright and surrounded by strawlike plant fibers, further supporting the close evolutionary link thought to exist between dinosaurs and birds. This link is also indicated by a dinosaur brain case found in Alberta, Canada, whose delicate structure resembles that of modern birds.

Findings in Amber. A possibly startling discovery concerning the environment in which the dinosaurs lived was announced at the annual meeting of the Geological Society of America in Phoenix, AZ. Researchers described the process by which they had crushed Canadian amber dating from Cretaceous times to obtain tiny samples of ancient atmosphere trapped in bubbles in the hardened resin. Using advanced spectroscopic techniques, the samples were found to be more than 10% richer in oxygen than is the modern atmosphere. If confirmed, the result has implications for evolutionary theory and concepts of how the Earth's climate has formed and changed.

WILLIAM H. MATTHEWS III
Lamar University

GEORGIA

In 1987, Georgia drew attention for its economic growth, the nation's largest civil-rights demonstration in 20 years, and the choice of Atlanta to host the 1988 Democratic convention. The takeover of a federal penitentiary in Atlanta by Cuban immigrant detainees dominated the news for 11 days in late November and early December (*see* CUBA).

Rural Forsyth County north of Atlanta became a symbol for racial intolerance when 20,000 civil-rights advocates marched to protest the county's all-white status. The rally brought people from throughout the nation, international media coverage, 3,000 national guardsmen, and such well-known civil-rights leaders as Coretta Scott King, Joseph Lowery, and Benjamin Hooks.

Economic Growth. As Gov. Joe Frank Harris embarked on a second term, Georgia, in general, continued to experience economic growth, despite the fact that the state led the nation in the number of farms nearing foreclosure. Seventeen foreign companies established their U.S. headquarters in Georgia bringing the total to 252. RJR Nabisco, Inc. and the American Cancer Society announced plans to relocate their headquarters in Atlanta.

For the second consecutive year Gwinnett County in metro Atlanta was the fastest growing county in the nation. Home sales in Atlanta continued to increase despite higher mortgage interest rates; and metro Atlanta's service-based economy showed a 33% job growth over the first half of the 1980s.

Just as the elegant Post Modern IBM Tower rose to its full height over the city, developers announced that the same architects—Phillip Johnson and John Burgee—would design a landmark, 50-story office complex on Peachtree in downtown Atlanta. Nearby in Midtown, development began on a 16-acre (6.5-ha) complex around the rapid-rail station.

Assuming approval by the Turner Broadcasting Service (TBS) board of directors, Ted Turner planned to market a new cable television channel, Turner Network Television (TNT). The channel would feature popular sporting and awards events.

The Bond Affair. Former state Sen. Julian Bond and other Atlantans were accused by his estranged wife of cocaine use. There were suggestions that Mayor Andrew Young had attempted to influence Alice Bond's decision to testify and allegations that two Atlanta police narcotics officers were transferred abruptly before completion of the investigation. A special mayoral panel was appointed, and a federal grand jury probed the possible obstruction of justice. Due to lack of evidence, however, no formal charges were brought and no indictments were returned regarding the issue of obstruction of justice. The matter of drug use remained under investigation.

Legislation. Insurance and tort reform were primary issues as state legislators attempted to limit the rights of injured parties to sue and to hold down escalating insurance rates. Legislative packages put a $250,000 limit on most punitive damage awards and allowed physicians limited immunity from malpractice suits involving charity care. The insurance commissioner was given more power to review proposed rate increases.

Other new legislation requires parental approval for girls under 18 seeking an abortion; bans the sale of tobacco products to anyone under 17; and restricts computerized telephone calls to certain hours of the day and requires the consent of the receiver of such calls. Major legislation that was defeated included bills to decriminalize heterosexual sodomy, ban nude dancing at night clubs, dismantle a pari-mutuel betting referendum, require seat belts, and demand testing for AIDS for Georgians undergoing routine blood testing. In order to finance projects for education, highway development, and tourism, the General Assembly voted to issue $590 million in bonds.

KAY BECK, *Georgia State University*

GEORGIA • Information Highlights

Area: 58,910 sq mi (152 576 km^2).
Population (July 1, 1986): 6,104,000.
Chief Cities (July 1, 1986 est.): Atlanta, the capital, 421,910; Columbus, 180,180; Savannah, 146,800.
Government (1987): *Chief Officers*—governor, Joe Frank Harris (D); lt. gov., Zell Miller (D). *General Assembly*—Senate, 56 members; House of Representatives, 180 members.
State Finances (fiscal year 1986): *Revenue,* $9,391,000,000; *expenditure,* $8,530,000,000.
Personal Income (1986): $82,078,000,000; per capita, $13,446.
Labor Force (June 1987): *Civilian labor force,* 3,101,700; *unemployed,* 158,400 (5.1% of total force).
Education: *Enrollment* (fall 1985)—public elementary schools, 756,752; public secondary, 322,842; colleges and universities, 196,826. *Public school expenditures* (1985–86), $2,960,000,000 ($2,980 per pupil).

© Patrick Piel/Gamma-Liaison

In a diplomatic breakthrough, West German Chancellor Helmut Kohl (left) *welcomed East Germany's Erich Honecker* (right) *in Bonn, September 7. Honecker's five-day visit to the Federal Republic was the first by an East German head of state.*

GERMANY

Relations between the two German states—the Federal Republic of Germany (FRG or West Germany) and the German Democratic Republic (GDR or East Germany)—reached a new high level in September 1987, when Erich Honecker became the first leader of East Germany to step onto West German soil. His long-awaited five-day visit, which had been nixed twice before (in 1984 and 1985) by the Soviet Union, represented a culmination of 15 years of steadily improving relations. This period has been characterized by greatly increased economic activity financed in part through multibillion-dollar credits from West Germany, extensive scientific and technological cooperation, and a sharply increased flow of visitors from East Germany to the West. During 1987, one million East Germans under the pension age were allowed to visit the Federal Republic, up from only 50,000 in 1985. The total number of East Germans who traveled to the West in 1987 rose to more than 2.6 million, or about 15% of the GDR's population.

For Honecker the visit meant that the Federal Republic, after almost 40 years, had finally recognized the GDR as a sovereign and legitimate state. For Chancellor Helmut Kohl it was an opportunity to demonstrate to West Germans that his government remained committed to reuniting the nation and to pressing the East Germans for improvements in human rights.

Although welcomed by FRG President Richard von Weizsäcker as a "German among Germans," Honecker emphasized that the division of the country is irreversible and that capitalism and socialism are as incompatible as "fire and water." While continuing to disagree on such major questions as reunification and the Berlin Wall, both leaders signed new agreements on scientific and technological cooperation, environmental protection, and nuclear reactor safety. West Germany also extended new loans to the GDR for highway and rail improvements. The visit ended on an optimistic note when Honecker expressed his hope that some day the "borders will not separate us, but will unite us."

Federal Republic of Germany (West Germany)

The most significant domestic political event in West Germany during 1987 was the January national election, the 11th in the republic's history, at which voters returned the government of Chancellor Helmut Kohl, albeit with a reduced majority. Kohl's Christian Democratic Union (CDU), along with its Bavarian sister-party, the Christian Social Union (CSU), saw its portion of the vote drop from 48.8% to 44.3%, its lowest level since 1949. But the chancellor's coalition partner, the Free Democratic Party (FDP) led by Foreign Minister Hans-Dietrich Genscher, increased its share of the vote from 7.0% to 9.1%. The ma-

Entscheidung
für Deutschla
CDU
Damit der
Friede sicher
bleibt
und deutsche
Interessen
zählen.
Den Besten für Deutschland: Johannes Rau.

© R. Bossu/Sygma

In West German national elections January 25, Chancellor Helmut Kohl (left) *was returned to office, but with a reduced majority. The major opposition party, the Social Democrats of Johannes Rau* (right), *also suffered a loss of support.*

jority opposition party, the Social Democrats (SPD) also lost support, dropping from 38.2% to 37.0%, their poorest performance since 1961. And the other parliamentary opposition party, the Greens, increased their vote from 5.6% to 8.3%. Thus, the nation's two major parties—the CDU and SPD—both lost support at the same election for the first time in the history of the republic, and the two smaller parties, the FDP and the Greens, were the beneficiaries of the voter discontent.

As a result of the elections, the new 497-seat Bundestag (lower house) included 223 CDU/CSU members (down 21), 186 Social Democrats (down 7), 46 Free Democrats (up 12), and 42 Greens (up 15).

As 1987 progressed, the political fortunes of Chancellor Kohl's party did not improve. At four state elections in May and October, the party lost support because of the slow economy, internal party conflicts, and scandals. The CDU was shaken in September when the young premier of the northern state of Schleswig-Holstein, Uwe Barschel, was accused of using government agencies and funds for a Watergate-style "dirty tricks" campaign against his Socialist challenger. Shortly before he was to testify before a parliamentary investigating committee, Barschel, who had been in ill health from an airplane accident, was found dead in a Zurich hotel room, apparently a case of suicide.

The Social Democrats' defeat in January was followed later in the year by the resignation and virtual retirement from political life of the former chancellor and long-time party chairman, Willy Brandt. The winner of the 1971 Nobel Peace Prize, Brandt was widely acclaimed outside of Germany as a "good German" and a symbol of a postwar society that had overcome its Nazi past. Within Germany, Brandt in recent years was identified with the left wing of the SPD and was considered a divisive force within the party. He was succeeded as party chairman by Hans-Jochen Vogel. Under Vogel's leadership the SPD had mixed success in 1987, gaining votes in two state elections but losing in three others.

The Free Democrats followed their strong showing at the national election with gains in five consecutive state polls. A key factor in the FDP's success was the party's support for the "double-zero" missile option, i.e. the removal of both short- and medium-range missiles from Europe, which eventually became the basis for the U.S.-Soviet agreement signed in December. By supporting the option, which was opposed by the Christian Democrats throughout much of the year, the FDP could present itself as the peace and disarmament advocate within the government.

It was a difficult year for the Greens, Germany's environmentalist and peace party. Although they gained at the national election and at several state elections, their governing coalition with the SPD in the state of Hesse collapsed in February, and the party went into opposition. The Greens remained deeply divided between two factions: the Fundamentalists, who opposed any coalition with the Social Democrats; and the Realists, who wanted the party to participate in governing coalitions wherever possible. The party's image in 1987 also was damaged by its advocacy of a citizen boycott of the national census, which, after numerous delays, finally was conducted in May.

Economy. The West German economy in 1987 was sluggish. The weak U.S. dollar and increased energy prices reduced exports from their record 1986 levels and held the real growth rate to about 1.5%. This was insufficient to cause a significant drop in unemployment, which remained at roughly two million, or about 8.5% of the work force. The high unemployment was an important issue at the 1987 national election and contributed to the poor performance of the Christian Democrats. Inflation, however, was very low, at about 1.0%. To stimulate economic growth, the Kohl government approved tax cuts of $8.2 billion in 1988 and about $12 billion in 1990 (following a $5 billion reduction in 1986). Corporate-tax rates on undistributed profits also were to be cut in 1988, from 56% to 50%. Government spending increased by only 2.4% in 1987, and the federal budget deficit was about $16 billion. The decline in revenue caused by the tax cuts would be made up in part by the proceeds from the government's privatization program: Bonn was to sell its 47% stake in energy, chemical, and aluminum enterprises and its 16% share of the Volkswagen company to private investors.

In another move to boost the sluggish economy, Bonn late in the year announced a program to encourage capital spending. The plan involved cutting the rates and increasing the amount of credit available from the state reconstruction loan corporation established after World War II.

Environment. In the aftermath of the 1986 Chernobyl disaster and massive chemical spills in the Rhine, concern about the environment remained high throughout 1987. In April the governing coalition joined the opposition Social Democrats in supporting a constitutional amendment establishing environmental protection as a national goal. The amendment would increase the power of the federal government to enact programs binding on state and local governments as well as individuals and corporations. Previously, this authority had been reserved largely to the states. The Greens opposed the measure and proposed a still stronger amendment which would have made environmental protection a fundamental right.

Foreign Policy. West Germany's relationship with the United States during 1987 was highlighted by differences over economic policies and arms control. Throughout the year, the Reagan administration and especially U.S. Secretary of the Treasury James Baker urged the Germans, as one of the world's leading trading nations, to speed up their economy in order to increase the demand for American goods and help reduce the U.S. trade deficit. Given West Germany's high unemployment, low inflation, and meager growth rate, Washington argued, there was ample room for Bonn to expand its economy through lower interest rates and increased government spending. West Germany's European neighbors generally agreed with the U.S. position, but both the Kohl government and the German Central Bank (*Bundesbank*), downplayed Germany's economic influence and pointed instead to the huge U.S. budget deficit as the primary cause of the U.S. trade imbalance.

This West German-U.S. impasse became a major factor in the international financial crisis which began with the plunge on the New York Stock Exchange in October. When Bonn in the week preceding the October 19 crash increased one of its key interest rates, Secretary Baker warned the Germans that unless they stopped raising rates and restraining their economy, the United States would take no steps to prevent a drastic decline in the value of the dollar. Most West German economic policymakers and especially the governors of the Central Bank had given greater priority to keeping inflation low than to reducing unemployment or stimulating economic growth. But in early November, responding to growing pressure from the United States and its European neighbors, the Central Bank with the support of the Kohl government did lower interest rates in an effort to calm the volatile world financial markets. Bonn then challenged Washington to make the next move by reducing its budget deficits. An unchecked dollar, many German experts argued, would upset world trade and investment patterns and ultimately bring on a worldwide recession.

Until June the Bonn government was divided over the double-zero missile option. Some officials in the Kohl government and his CDU party criticized the U.S. proposal as a sellout of West German interests, which would leave the country vulnerable to superior Warsaw Pact conventional forces. Foreign Minister Genscher, however, took Washington's position that even after the double-zero option had been implemented the West would still have enough nuclear punch in battlefield weapons, bombers, and intercontinental missiles to deter a Soviet attack. Genscher's position ultimately prevailed, and Bonn accepted the U.S. plan.

Bonn's relations with the Soviet Union showed improvement in 1987 despite the uproar created in May by a 19-year-old West German, Mathias Rust, who piloted a small private plane through more than 400 mi (650 km) of heavily guarded Soviet air space and landed in Moscow's Red Square on a self-described "mission of peace." His flight prompted the dismissal of the Soviet defense minister and the air marshal responsible for Moscow's defense. Rust was tried by a Soviet court in September and received a four-year prison term.

In July, President von Weizsäcker's six-day visit to Moscow opened the way for a series of high-level contacts between Moscow and Bonn. The Kohl government's decision in August to dismantle the 72 Pershing 1A missiles,

(Continued on page 256.)

Berlin's 750th Anniversary

© Dallas and John Heaton /Click, Chicago

West Berlin underwent extensive redevelopment in honor of its 750th anniversary in 1987.

The 750th anniversary of Berlin was celebrated throughout 1987 in both halves of the divided city. Britain's Queen Elizabeth, U.S. President Ronald Reagan, French President François Mitterrand, and Soviet leader Mikhail Gorbachev led the parade of prominent leaders to Germany's former capital.

Various attempts by authorities on both sides to organize at least some token anniversary celebrations for the whole city were unsuccessful as the city's 42-year-old East–West division could not be bridged even temporarily in the anniversary year. East German leader Erich Honecker invited West Berlin's Mayor Eberhard Diepgen to festivities in East Berlin, and Diepgen returned the favor by asking Honecker to participate in corresponding celebrations in the West. Both leaders eventually declined the invitations.

The continuing competition between the two ideologies and political systems that each part of the city represents influenced many of the anniversary events. In early June, a three-day open-air rock-music festival in West Berlin just beyond the Wall dividing the city caused the most serious public disturbance in East Berlin since the late 1970s. Thousands of East German rock-music fans and police clashed on three consecutive nights. The young people were protesting the East German police lines erected to keep them from gathering near the Wall to listen to the rock stars.

The anniversary also prompted a building boom in both parts of the city. In the East a new Grand Hotel was being built on the famous Unter den Linden avenue. Along the Friedrichstrasse, another major street in the city's center, 4,000 new apartments were built, and an equal number were restored. In West Berlin, $1.5-billion worth of new buildings, designed by world famous architects under the sponsorship of the International Building Exhibition, were completed for the anniversary. Many of the buildings, mostly apartments for about 35,000 middle- and working-class tenants, have received international acclaim.

In spite of the failed policy of "mutual invitations," both sides want to improve relations. West Berlin's leadership is seeking more generous arrangements for its citizens to visit East Berlin. Both governments want closer cooperation on transport and environmental problems. Mayor Diepgen has proposed that West Berlin, which produces all its own electricity, draw power from East Germany. The East could in turn receive power from the West German grid at peak hours.

History. The village of Berlin grew up on the east bank of the Spree River in the 13th century. By the 15th century, it was an important trading center in the province of Brandenburg. In 1470 it became the official residence of the Hohenzollerns, the rulers of Brandenburg and the future royal house of the German Reich. During the Thirty Years' War (1618–1648), the city was occupied by opposing armies, burned, and stricken by epidemics. Under the Great Elector, Frederick William of Hohenzollern (1640–1688), Berlin became one of Germany's major cities. His son, Frederick I, became the first king of Prussia in 1701, and made Berlin his capital.

As the capital of the German Empire (1871–1918), Berlin experienced meteoric growth. Its population rose from 826,000 in 1871 to 3.7 million by 1910. By the late 1920s, it was the world's third largest city and the biggest industrial center in Europe.

Berlin remained Germany's capital through the Weimar Republic (1919–1933) and Hitler's Third Reich. The city was conquered by Soviet troops in the last few days of World War II. As agreed, the city was put under the joint administration of the four victorious powers. Each of them—France, Great Britain, the USSR, and the United States—occupied a sector of the city, which together formed an enclave in the middle of the overall Soviet occupation zone.

As the East–West conflict worsened, the joint four-power administration of Berlin proved impossible. Under Soviet pressure, the city was politically and administratively split in 1948. But the Soviet Union did not want to tolerate the existence of a Western enclave within its zone and tried to force the Western powers out of the city with the Berlin Blockade in 1948 and the Nikita Khrushchev ultimatum in 1958. Both attempts failed, and in 1961 as the number of East Germans fleeing into West Berlin increased to nearly 1,000 per day, East Germany, with Soviet backing, sealed off the East–West sector by constructing a wall across the city.

The Wall stopped the flow of refugees and enabled the Communist regime to consolidate its rule over the remaining 17 million inhabitants of the former Soviet zone. Since a 1971 four-powers agreement, which was intended to ease tensions, the city's political situation has stabilized. The East German state has been recognized by the West, and Western access rights to West Berlin across East German territory have been respected by the Soviet Union.

DAVID P. CONRADT

© Patrick Piel/Gamma-Liaison

A major building and beautification program also was underway in East Berlin during the anniversary year. New or redeveloped housing was emphasized.

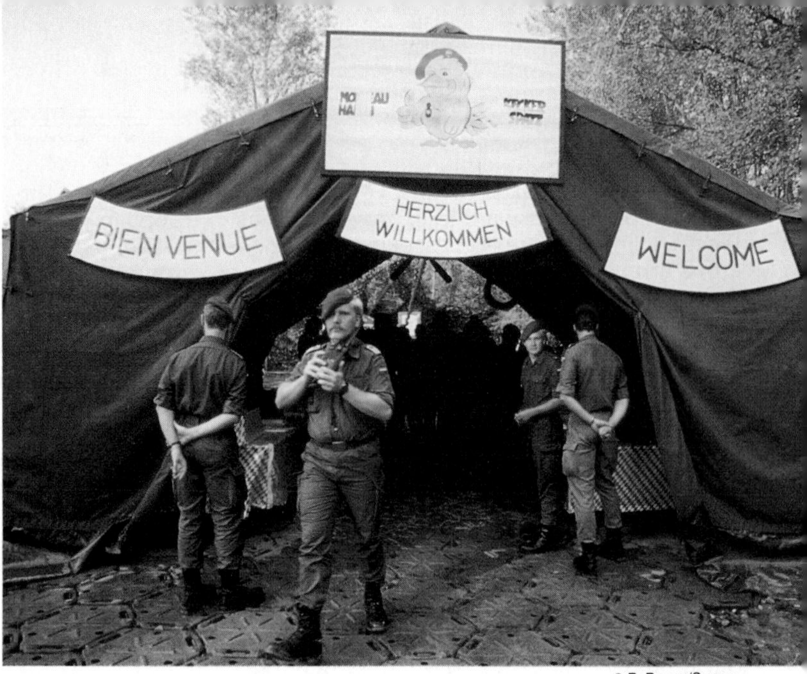

Growing military cooperation between West Germany and France was highlighted by four days of joint war games, dubbed "Bold Sparrow," in September.

© R. Bossu/Sygma

which the Soviets requested as part of the U.S. arms control treaty, markedly improved the climate between the two governments. A new agreement providing for cooperation in the peaceful use of atomic energy, including the problem of radioactive waste disposal, also was completed. Soviet General Secretary Mikhail Gorbachev, whom Chancellor Kohl in 1986 compared to the Nazi propaganda boss Josef Goebbels, was expected to make an official visit to Bonn in 1988.

West Germany's relations with France in 1987 featured intensified military cooperation, including the creation of a fully-integrated Franco-German brigade. In September the two countries conducted joint military maneuvers in West Germany. Nicknamed "Bold Sparrow," the exercises were the largest ever engaged in by France outside its territory. Officer exchange programs also increased, and the two countries agreed to proceed with the production of a new antitank helicopter. Some French and German political leaders, including former Chancellor Helmut Schmidt, envision France and Germany as the twin pillars of a new European defense force which would lift the burden of defending the continent from the United States.

Within the European Community (EC), Bonn in 1987 continued its efforts to mediate the controversy between Great Britain and the other members over agricultural subsidies. About 70% of the EC's $41 million budget was going to farm support, a figure which the British wanted reduced. At a two-day conference of EC leaders in late June, widely viewed as a test of Europe's political cohesion, no agreement was reached on spending cuts or reduction of the huge surpluses of agricultural products. Since West German payments account for about 60% of the EC annual income, Bonn attempted to forge a compromise which would keep future spending in line with the growth of national economies and reduce the proportion given to farmers. British Prime Minister Margaret Thatcher, however, contended that earlier pledges to hold spending in line were not being fulfilled. Chancellor Kohl predicted that the dispute would drag on in 1988.

West Germany, and in particular its many beer drinkers, were disappointed by a 1987 decision of the European Court, which ruled that the country's 450-year-old beer purity law was an impediment to free trade. Under the law only water, hops, malt, and yeast could be used in making beer sold in the country. Foreign beer, containing preservatives or ingredients such as millet or soya, could not be exported to the Federal Republic. The court's decision paved the way for foreign beer producers to enter the huge West German market and compete with the country's 1,200 breweries.

WEST GERMANY • Information Highlights

Official Name: Federal Republic of Germany.
Location: North-central Europe.
Area: 95,977 sq mi (248 580 km²).
Population (mid-1987 est.): 61,000,000.
Chief Cities (June 30, 1985): Bonn, the capital, 292,600; West Berlin, 1,852,700; Hamburg, 1,585,900; Munich, 1,266,100.
Government: *Head of state,* Richard von Weizsäcker, president (took office July 1, 1984). *Head of government,* Helmut Kohl, chancellor (took office Oct. 1982). *Legislature*—Parliament: Bundesrat and Bundestag.
Monetary Unit: Deutsche mark (1.689 D. marks equal U.S.$1, Nov. 17, 1987).
Gross National Product (1985 U.S$): $628,200,-000,000.
Economic Indexes (1986): *Consumer Prices* (1980 = 100), all items, 120.7; food, 117.6. *Industrial Production* (1980 = 100), 107.
Foreign Trade (1986 U.S.$): *Imports,* $189,484,-000,000; *exports,* $242,411,000,000.

German Democratic Republic (East Germany)

The reform program of Soviet leader Gorbachev presented major problems for the East German regime during 1987. Politically the GDR has been the most orthodox Communist state in Eastern Europe, and it also has maintained the highest standard of living of any country in the bloc—including the USSR itself. East German Communists thus contended that Gorbachev's reforms were not needed there and downplayed his calls for openness, democratization, and "new thinking." The Soviet leader's November speech assailing the "enormous and unforgivable" crimes of Josef Stalin and praising the attempted reforms of the Nikita Khrushchev era was given only limited and unenthusiastic coverage in the East German media. Shortly before the Gorbachev speech, the East German party newspaper *Neues Deutschland* condemned the Soviet film *Repentance* (one of the first to emerge under the Kremlin's policy of greater cultural freedom), which is critical of the Stalin era as "nihilistic" and "inhuman."

Earlier in the year, East German party functionaries were advised to avoid the Soviet Institute for Science and Culture in East Berlin, which was sponsoring lectures by Soviet party officials on Gorbachev's new policies. Some East German intellectuals were prohibited from attending the lectures.

The fears of hard-line party elites about the new Soviet course were heightened as reports circulated that Gorbachev's choice for successor to the 75-year-old Honecker was Hans Modrow, the chief of the Dresden party organization. Modrow is regarded as one of the key figures in the East German Communist party's small reform faction.

There were, however, some signs of "new thinking" in East Germany during 1987. In June the Honecker regime announced a general amnesty for thousands of political and other prisoners, and East Germany became the first Communist state to abolish the death penalty. Prisoners serving life sentences had their terms commuted to 15 years. The amnesty ostensibly was proclaimed to celebrate the 38th anniversary of the GDR's founding, but many observers interpreted the decision as an attempt to improve the country's human-rights image in the West prior to Honecker's visit to the Federal Republic.

Economy. The East German economy in 1987 was plagued by continuing problems in trade with Western nations. After seven years of steady growth, East German exports to the West declined. While the GDR remains a major economic power within the Communist bloc, many of its products do not meet Western quality standards. Its planned economy has many deficiencies in marketing, design, and new-product planning, and it is slow to adapt to changes in Western consumer preferences. Textile producers, for example, continue to offer styles and colors long out of fashion in the West. Faced with a growing Western trade deficit, the GDR in early 1987 began to exchange large amounts of its currency for West German marks. This caused a sharp decline in the real value of the East German mark. Other economic difficulties in 1987 included lower rates of capital investment and growth, as well as an increase in Western debt from \$6.5 billion to \$8 billion. The current five-year plan—targeting annual increases of 4.4% in national income and 8.3% in industrial production for the period 1986–90—was behind schedule.

Environment. The GDR made little progress in 1987 toward cleaning up its environment, considered by experts to be one of the most polluted in Europe. The number of smog alarms rose sharply during the year, and the Elbe river, which separates the two German states, was by far the most polluted waterway in Central Europe. The country's heavy reliance on brown coal or lignite, a major pollutant, actually increased in 1987 and was not projected to decline until 1991, when several nuclear power plants were scheduled to become operational. Another major source of pollution is the Trabant and Wartburg automobiles, which have no exhaust emission control devices.

The Society for Nature and the Environment, which was formed in the early 1980s and is not controlled by the party, numbered about 60,000 members in 1987 and sponsored several low-key demonstrations and petition drives to alert the public to the deteriorating environmental situation. The government, meanwhile, was hoping to receive additional technical and financial assistance from West Germany for its cleanup programs.

DAVID P. CONRADT
University of Florida

EAST GERMANY • Information Highlights

Official Name: German Democratic Republic.
Location: North-central Europe.
Area: 41,826 sq mi (108 330 km^2).
Population (mid-1987 est.): 16,700,000.
Chief Cities (Dec. 31, 1984): East Berlin, the capital, 1,196,900; Leipzig, 555,800; Dresden, 520,100.
Government: *Head of state,* Erich Honecker, chairman of the Council of State. *Head of government,* Willi Stoph, chairman of the Council of Ministers. General Secretary of the Socialist Unity (Communist) Party, Erich Honecker (took office 1971). *Legislature* (unicameral)—Volkskammer (People's Chamber).
Monetary Unit: DDR mark (2.38 DDR marks equal U.S.\$1, June 1986).
Gross National Product (1985 U.S.\$): \$174,700,-000,000.
Economic Index (1986): *Industrial Production* (1980 = 100), 127.
Foreign Trade (1985 U.S.\$): *Imports,* \$25,268,-000,000; *exports,* \$25,684,000,000.

GREAT BRITAIN

The most important event in Great Britain during 1987 was the general election on June 11, which resulted in a third successive victory for Prime Minister Margaret Thatcher and her Conservative Party. (*See* special report, page 260.) The election provided a context in which the major developments of the year could be viewed. The campaign focused on the central issues facing the nation, and the results helped to strengthen existing trends. The Conservatives fought the campaign on a platform of further radical reforms at home and a strong Britain abroad. The underlying issue, however, was the economy. Had the country's undoubted economic growth simply made the rich richer and the poor poorer? Was there an increasing "underclass"—a word that entered the British political vocabulary for the first time —that was falling further behind the rest? In particular, was the gap between the affluent south and the poorer north becoming dangerously wide? Not least, was the economic growth sustainable, or was it a deliberately engineered preelection boom?

Economy. Since 1982, Great Britain had experienced a relatively high economic-growth rate of approximately 3% annually. The strong performance of the nation's economy during 1987 was evidenced by a growth rate of about 4%. The biggest blot on the economic landscape, however, was the continuing high level of unemployment. In September 1986 it had reached 12.0% of the work force, or about 3.3 million people. The figure began to drop during the autumn of that year, and the decline continued during 1987. In October it fell to 9.8%, the first time in five years that the rate was below 10%. The decline in unemployment was a significant boon to the Conservatives in their election campaign. If the figure had continued rising, as it had for the previous seven years, it would have been much harder to persuade the electorate that the government's policy of promoting a free-market economy was beginning to work.

And there was another economic development beneficial to Prime Minister Thatcher. While public expenditures were being controlled tightly, government revenues rose—partly as a result of taxes and royalties from North Sea oil. Thus, in the government's 1987–88 budget, unveiled March 17, Chancellor of the Exchequer Nigel Lawson could propose an unusual hat trick: a slight reduction in the personal-tax rate, an increase in spending on public services, and a decline in public-sector borrowing to about 1% of the gross domestic product.

The Labour Party charged that the chancellor was playing politics in advance of the election. Once the election was over, however, it seemed likely that Lawson, who remained chancellor, would be able to perform a similar feat in 1988–89. His autumn financial statement, which sets the framework for the next year's budget, pointed to further tax cuts, selective public-spending increases in such areas as health and education, and a net borrowing requirement that would be almost negligible.

On the international economic front, the situation was more volatile. The British government worried increasingly about possible protectionist moves in the United States. It also became alarmed by the decline of the U.S. dollar, when an agreement by the major industrial democracies in Paris during February to stabilize exchange rates seemed not to be functioning. Following a few initial hiccups, however, this so-called Louvre Accord appeared to bring on a period of calm in the international markets. That was shattered by the crash on the New York Stock Exchange on October 19. The resulting uncertainty was of particular concern to Great Britain because, although the pound-dollar rate is no longer the one that matters most, the British currency is still not a full member of the European Monetary System. The pound can therefore oscillate wildly during periods of international instability.

Despite the healthy economic-growth rate, which has been impressive by international standards, inflation was not brought fully under control, and the government's aim at achieving stable prices was not met. Several times since 1983, the inflation rate has fallen to about 3%, but it has repeatedly gone up again and ended 1987 at about 5%. A principal cause has been the level of wage settlements, which have been running at an annual rate of about 8% during the 1980s.

Domestic Policies. After the election the Conservative government immediately set about implementing the domestic reforms it had promised during the campaign. These included radical changes in education, whereby a national core curriculum will be introduced and schools will be allowed to opt out of the control of local authorities and obtain support from the central government instead. The private housing market will be further deregulated, and an element of competition will be injected into the national health service. Perhaps most controversially of all, the system of domestic tax rates, whereby householders pay a local tax on their property, is to be abolished and replaced by a community charge levied on all citizens age 18 and over. Immediately after the election, Prime Minister Thatcher also announced a campaign to revive the nation's inner cities where, especially in the north, the Conservatives had fared badly.

All of these measures would take time to go through Parliament and were not expected to take effect before mid-1988 at the earliest. They faced some prospect of opposition in the

House of Lords on the grounds that the government was becoming excessively centralist and taking power away from the local authorities. In the House of Commons, however, the Conservatives seemed safe. The Labour Party showed little sign of recovering from its third electoral defeat in a row, and the Social Democratic Party (SDP) was split between those who, like party leader David Owen, wanted to remain independent and those who wanted to merge with the Liberals. In early August the party rank and file voted to merge with the Liberals, and Owen resigned. Robert Maclennan was elected to succeed Owen as SDP leader. By the end of the year, however, the merger talks were going badly.

Foreign Affairs. Prime Minister Thatcher appeared to be increasingly self-confident in promoting her foreign policy during 1987. At the Commonwealth Conference in Vancouver, British Columbia, in October, she resisted pressure from all 46 other members to impose further economic sanctions against South Africa. In the European Community (EC), she determined that the common agricultural policy—subsidizing surplus production—has led to huge food stocks and should be reformed. She incurred the anger of the other Western European governments for being more concerned with British interests than with the development of the EC, and the meeting of European heads of government in Copenhagen, Denmark, in December produced little more than another fight over farm prices.

Perhaps Thatcher's greatest coup in foreign policy was to establish a close working relationship with Soviet General Secretary Mikhail Gorbachev, whom she visited in Moscow in March and who held talks with her in London on his way to Washington in December to sign the agreement on the elimination of Intermediate Nuclear Forces (INF). During the latter discussions, the British prime minister stated her own view that after the INF treaty there should be no further nuclear weapons reductions in Europe until there was progress on conventional arms control. She insisted that Great Britain still had a special relationship with the United States and had no fears that U.S. troops would be withdrawn from Europe. Some sharp criticism of U.S. economic policy, however, came from Chancellor Lawson.

In the Persian Gulf conflict, the British leadership at first refused requests from Washington to back up U.S. minesweeping efforts, but the discovery of mines in the Gulf of Oman forced Thatcher to change her mind and send a small fleet of minesweepers in mid-August. On September 21, the British-registered tanker *Gentle Breeze* was ambushed by an Iranian gunboat, killing one Filipino crewman and injuring 33 others. In response to the attack, Britain closed Iran's arms procurement office in London and joined the United States in calling for a UN arms embargo against Iran.

In an earlier diplomatic confrontation, the second-ranking British diplomat in Tehran was arrested and beaten in late May, and London responded by closing an Iranian consulate. Tehran, in turn, expelled five British diplomats. The series of expulsions continued until each side had only one caretaker diplomat left in the other's capital.

In Northern Ireland, the second anniversary of the Anglo-Irish agreement, allowing

(Continued on page 262.)

*Prime Minister Margaret Thatcher (*right*) held several hours of talks with Soviet leader Mikhail Gorbachev (*left*) at Brize Norton, England, December 7. Gorbachev was on his way to Washington to sign the U.S.-Soviet arms control agreement.*

AP/Wide World

Margaret Thatcher Wins a Third Term

Prime Minister Margaret Thatcher's resounding victory in Great Britain's June 11 general election earned the Conservative Party leader an honored place in the history books. Not since the Napoleonic era, when Lord Liverpool served as prime minister from 1812 to 1827, had a British prime minister been elected to three consecutive terms. (Thatcher had been elected in 1979 and reelected in 1983.) Although the Tory majority slipped to 101 seats in the 1987 voting—from 144 seats in 1983—it was still the second-largest majority achieved by any British party since World War II.

The margin of Thatcher's victory, which took even her supporters by surprise, means that she is virtually certain, short of a revolt within her Conservative Party, of pushing her legislative program through Parliament.

With 42.3% of the popular vote (down from 42.4% in 1983), the Conservatives won 375 seats in the 650-seat House of Commons. The principal opposition would come from Neil Kinnock's Labour Party, which earned 32.8% of the vote (up from 27.5%) and increased its representation by 21 seats, to 22%. The Alliance, a centrist coalition of the Liberal and Social Democratic parties, had hoped to overtake the Labour Party as the principal opposition but polled only 22.5% (down from 25.4%) and returned only 22 members of Parliament (MPs), down five from 1983.

Although there was no material shift in the balance of power, the composition of the House changed in two important respects: there would be more women, up from 28 to 41, and, for the first time in more than half a century, five nonwhites, all Labour.

Significance. The election result was decisive confirmation of Thatcher's dominance in British politics. Her eight-year term of office had already allowed her to set up a comprehensive political agenda and to shift the country's political center of gravity farther to the right than any previous Conservative prime minister since World War II. Her pursuit of a free-enterprise culture and her dedication to free-market economic policies had made "Thatcherism" a familiar term in the world's political lexicon. In many parts of the world, where enthusiasm for state control has waned, "Thatcherism" is often viewed as an antidote for socialism. An intensely pragmatic woman, she once defined Thatcherism as mere "common sense."

Thatcher's strong victory after holding power for so long also carried considerable international significance. Her highly acclaimed visit in March–April 1987 to the Soviet Union, where she held marathon talks with Soviet leader Mikhail Gorbachev, boosted her image as an international stateswoman. She was already the Western world's longest-serving major leader, having assumed office some 20 months before U.S. President Ronald Reagan. As a pillar of the North Atlantic Treaty Organization (NATO), she regarded reelection as crucial to the continuity of the Western military alliance. This was particularly important to her because President Reagan, a close ally and friend, cannot constitutionally serve beyond his second term, which ends in January 1989. Prime Minister Thatcher, however, faces no legal bars to standing for a fourth term in 1992, if she so desires.

The 1987 election also held potentially profound strategic consequences. For the first

In June, Margaret Thatcher, 61, led Britain's Conservative Party to a third consecutive victory at the polls and gained a chance to complete her "unfinished revolution."

time since World War II, the opposition Labour Party broke with the national political consensus on the need for a bipartisan nuclear defense policy. Labour's new leader, Neil Kinnock, succeeded in taking the party beyond its 1983 manifesto in calling unequivocally for a unilateral nonnuclear policy. This included abandonment of Britain's nuclear deterrent and the removal of all U.S. nuclear weapons and bases from British soil. The proposals caused alarm among many of Britain's NATO partners, who thought it would undermine the Western alliance. President Reagan, in particular, did not hide his concern.

Timing. Controversy over Labour's nonnuclear defense policy was one of the first indications that the party's election campaign would face difficulties. Another troubling sign for Labour was the emergence of the so-called "loony left." The term referred to party militants in the London area whose preoccupation with gay rights, black activism, opposition to inner-city policing, and costly social programs embarrassed more conventional Labour supporters elsewhere in the country.

But there were other factors beckoning the prime minister—who has probably the most highly developed political antennae of any figure on the British scene—to opt for an early election. She was not obliged to call an election until the expiration of her five-year term in July 1988, but as spring moved toward summer, her prospects of being reelected improved markedly. The economy was booming, despite rising unemployment, and the Conservatives—the party most inclined to beat the patriotic drum—were quick to point out that Britain's economy was now growing faster than that of both the United States and its major European partners. A 2% tax cut, unveiled during the March budget, began working its way through to individual pay packets in May. And during that same month, local government elections, which traditionally go against the government in power, brought gains for the Conservatives and losses for the Labourites.

The temptation to exploit these favorable circumstances, particularly after Thatcher's highly successful trip to the Soviet Union the previous month, now became irresistible. On May 18, just a week after the council election results, the prime minister announced the suspension of Parliament and called for national elections. Under the parliamentary system, only 17 working days are required between the calling of an election and the polling date.

Political Climate. As the campaign started, the Conservatives were comfortably ahead with a rating consistently above 40%. Labour stood at about 33%, with the Alliance farther back at 25%. Yet in some respects the circumstances were not as propitious for the Conservatives as they had been in the last two elections.

Unlike the situations in 1979 and 1983, there was no single issue that dominated the 1987 campaign. In 1979, Mrs. Thatcher, in the aftermath of mounting labor problems, had called for a strong government to show who was running the country. Her appeal prevailed, and she immediately set about curbing the power of the trade unions. In 1983, the patriotic fervor aroused by Britain's spectacular victory in the 1982 Falklands War ensured that a tidal wave of popular support would keep Prime Minister Thatcher in power.

In 1987, however, government advisers were apprehensive that, after eight years of her rule, voters might tire of Margaret Thatcher and opt for a fresh face in the young, energetic, but inexperienced Neil Kinnock. Moreover, Mrs. Thatcher, a combative figure who made no secret of preferring confrontation to conciliation or consensus in facing up to national problems, was intensely disliked in working-class manufacturing areas. These were the areas hardest hit by unemployment and where Labour traditionally scores well—such as Wales, Scotland, and northern England. In the eight years since Thatcher came to power, unemployment had risen from one million to three million, and the number of people living in poverty had doubled. Among the prime minister's more moderate supporters, there was concern that her strengths might now be viewed as liabilities. Much was made of her possibly being a divisive figure. As for the opposition, Labour leader Kinnock was quick to exploit the image of Thatcher as an uncaring woman who had divided the country by privilege.

Indeed, the Labour Party was widely credited with winning the campaign and projecting a more likeable and photogenic leader. The results of the election, however, revealed that those who had voted for Thatcher in 1983 remained unusually loyal.

The Great Britain envisioned by Prime Minister Thatcher is a nation in which the government rolls back the restrictions and controls of the state, eliminates socialism, and encourages all citizens to participate in a home-owning, property-owning democracy. The extent of such change since Margaret Thatcher came to power in 1979 indicates just how successful she has been in winning her argument and changing the social, economic, and political face of her nation.

DAVID WINDER

AP/Wide World

The Townsend-Thoresen ferry "Herald of Free Enterprise" capsized March 6 shortly after setting out for Dover, England, from the Belgian port of Zeebrugge. Some 180 passengers and crew members were killed.

Dublin a voice in British policy in Ulster, was marked on November 15. Despite the continued resistance of Ulster Unionists, it began to appear that the accord was a lasting one. Unionist Members of Parliament (MPs) had reacted to it by boycotting the British Parliament, but took their places again after the general election. One of the most prominent opponents of the agreement, Enoch Powell, lost his seat in the election. In the Irish Republic, the agreement survived the election of Charles Haughey as prime minister in March. Haughey originally had called for substantial revision of the agreement but changed his position and went along with the existing terms. (*See also* IRELAND.)

On November 8, Remembrance Sunday, an Irish Republican Army (IRA) bomb went off in the northern town of Enniskillen, killing 11 people. Television pictures were broadcast around the world, and the IRA leadership performed the unusual act of apologizing for attacking civilian targets. Only a few days earlier, a ship carrying large quantities of arms apparently destined for the IRA was intercepted by the British with the help of French and U.S. intelligence; the cargo was seized in Libya. As a result, Britain and Ireland agreed further to strengthen their security cooperation. During the course of the year, the British government also promised to introduce antidiscrimination legislation in the workplace in Northern Ireland, to some extent in response to U.S. pressure.

Other. There were no royal weddings or great court events of the kind that had been witnessed in previous years. Indeed 1987 was marked by increasing criticism of the royal family, especially its younger members, by the popular press. There were repeated rumors, never wholly denied, of an estrangement between Prince Charles, the heir to the throne, and Lady Diana, the princess of Wales.

In the worst peacetime disaster in the history of English Channel shipping, the British ferry *Herald of Free Enterprise* capsized March 6 shortly after leaving the Belgian port of Zeebrugge. More than 400 passengers and crew members were rescued, but the death toll exceeded 180. The south of England was struck by the worst hurricane in 300 years on October 15. At least 18 people were killed, and an estimated 15 million trees were destroyed.

Thirty people were killed and dozens injured when a fire broke out during rush hour on November 17 in London's King's Cross underground (subway) station. The cause was identified as a burning cigarette, and there was a widespread outcry that safety standards were not being maintained. For all the country's increasing affluence, there was still a feeling that public services were being unduly starved of resources. The fire in the London underground—one of the most antiquated systems of its kind in the world—was a spectacular reminder.

Great Britain and France finally began construction of the channel tunnel, a project that had been discussed since the beginning of the 19th century. It is expected to take its first rail traffic in 1993.

MALCOLM RUTHERFORD
"Financial Times," London

GREAT BRITAIN • Information Highlights

Official Name: United Kingdom of Great Britain and Northern Ireland.
Location: Island, western Europe.
Area: 94,525 sq mi (244 820 km²).
Population (mid-1987 est.): 56,800,000.
Chief Cities (mid-1985 est.): London, the capital, 6,767,500; Birmingham, 1,007,500; Glasgow, 733,800; Leeds, 710,500; Sheffield, 538,700.
Government: *Head of state,* Elizabeth II, queen (acceded Feb. 1952). *Head of government,* Margaret Thatcher, prime minister and First Lord of the Treasury (took office May 1979). *Legislature*—Parliament: House of Lords and House of Commons.
Monetary Unit: Pound (0.5302 pound equals U.S.$1, Dec. 31, 1987).
Gross National Product (1985): $443,200,000,000.
Economic Indexes (1986): *Consumer Prices* (1980 = 100), all items, 146.3; food, 135.7. *Industrial Production* (1980 = 100), 110.
Foreign Trade (1986 U.S.$): *Imports,* $126,200,000,000; *exports,* $107,013,000,000.

© Richard H. Smith/Dominic Photography

© Catherine Ashmore/Dominic Photography

Among major contributors to the artistic well-being of British opera and theater in 1987 were Margaret Price (left) in the Royal Opera's "Norma," and Anthony Hopkins and Judi Dench in "Antony and Cleopatra," at the National Theatre.

The Arts

In a year in which the Arts Council estimated that its present budget of £128 million (about $200 million) was currently worth less in real terms than funding in 1982, its secretary general Luke Rittner worked hard to make a case for increased government money. Arts Minister Richard Luce, however, made some tough predictions that arts institutions might have to look for private sponsors while relying on state money for "core funding."

Theater. The Royal Shakespeare Company (RSC), after one lackluster season in 1986 at its Barbican Theatre in London, was in debt and was happy to accept £1 million (about $1.6 million) sponsorship over three years from the Royal Insurance Company to wipe out the debt. The RSC continued as artistically strong as it was financially unsound with productions in Stratford of *The Merchant of Venice* with Antony Sher a brilliant Shylock; and *The Revenger's Tragedy* at the Swan Theatre next door, with Sher playing Vindice. *Twelfth Night,* with Harriet Walter as Viola, and an arresting Jonathan Miller production of *The Taming of the Shrew* (more a treatment for the maladjusted) were other Stratford programs.

In London, the RSC mounted a Jean Genet retrospective and a premiere of the Russian play abut the nuclear disaster at Chernobyl, *Sarcophagus* by Vladimir Gubaryev. The National Theatre achieved a varied and well-performed year from Michael Gambon as a moving Eddie Carbone in *A View from the Bridge;* through Judi Dench's "glorious Cleopatra" (the *Observer*), opposite Anthony Hopkins as Antony; and ending with Dench and Tim Piggott-Smith in *Entertaining Strangers,* a country play about Thomas Hardy's Wessex, by David Edgar and directed by Peter Hall.

New companies emerged, including the English Shakespeare Company led by director Michael Bogdanov and actor Michael Pennington in the *Henry IV, Parts 1 and 2,* and *Henry V* plays at the Old Vic; and the Renaissance Company led by Kenneth Branagh. Philip Prowse at the Glasgow Citizens Theatre designed and directed a mesmerizing production of *Anna Karenina.* Among the best new plays were Caryl Churchill's *Serious Money,* which had a cult following in the financial circles it set out to satirize; Stephen Bill's *Curtains;* Alan Ayckbourn's *A Small Family Business,* at the National; Peter Gill's *Mean Tears;* and Peter Nichols' *A Piece of My Mind.*

Music. The Royal Opera House, Covent Garden, had a varied year under its new musical director, Bernard Haitink, with Jeffrey Tate as new principal conductor. The year opened with Margaret Price in magnificent voice in *Norma* and Placido Domingo a majestic Otello. Gwyneth Jones in *Die Frau ohne Schatten* also drew excellent notices. Less well received was the British premiere of Finnish composer Aulis Sallinen's new work, *The King Goes Forth to France.* Covent Garden brought Domingo in *La Bohème* by screen to the Piazza in Covent

Garden, an innovation that will be repeated. The English National Opera scored triumphs with two Josephine Barstow performances in *Lady Macbeth of Mtsensk* and *Salome*. The Scottish Opera presented a brilliant *Madame Butterfly,* directed by Nuria Espert, while Opera North in Leeds presented for the first time in Britain, Strauss' *Daphne,* written in 1937. Among distinguished visitors, the Kirov Opera from Leningrad brought their productions of *The Queen of Spades* and *Boris Godunov*. The Almeida Festival in London presented five weeks of contemporary music, and on the South Bank, Harrison Birtwistle chose his own festival repertory, including very little of his own music. A broad ranging Promenade season at Albert Hall provided a summer of high quality, and Simon Rattle's performances with the City of Birmingham Orchestra continued to be highlighted throughout the year. The death of Peter Schidlof on August 16 brought to an end Britain's famous Amadeus String Quartet.

Dance. The London Festival Ballet sharpened its reputation in 1987 under the leadership of Peter Schaufuss, reviving Frederick Ashton's *Apparitions,* once Margot Fonteyn's star vehicle, for Natalia Makarova. Ballet Rambert changed its name to the Rambert Dance Company to show its shift of emphasis to modern works, and mounted *Pulcinella,* new from Richard Alston. Ashley Page's *Pursuit* was one of the new works given by the Royal Ballet, and Sadlers Wells presented *Allegri Diversi,* one of David Bintley's most satisfying new works so far. London Contemporary Dance Theatre celebrated its 21st anniversary with a new Robert Cohan work, *The Phantasmagoria*.

"Pursuit," choreographed by Ashley Page, was one of the new works presented by Britain's Royal Ballet, Covent Garden, during its 1987 season.

© Catherine Ashmore/Dominic Photography

Among the many visiting companies were the National Ballet of Canada, the Bolshoi Ballet Academy, and the Merce Cunningham Dance Company, the most distinguished of modern groups. Britain's Royal Ballet visited Moscow for the first time in many years.

Fine Arts. The Royal Academy started the year with a major retrospective of "British Art in the 20th Century," tracing the years from Walter Sickert's Postimpressionism to the current fantasies of Gilbert and George. A show of Greek frescoes and icons followed, as well as master drawings from the Woodner Collection, before the large-scale winter show "The Age of Chivalry: Art in Plantagenet England 1200–1400." The Tate Gallery opened its new Clore Gallery to house the J. M. W. Turner bequest, making it a permanent center for Turner studies. The artist's gift to the nation included more than 300 oils, 20,000 drawings, and almost 300 sketchbooks. The gallery itself was designed by James Stirling. In its other galleries, the Tate mounted a retrospective of Naum Gabo and a magical Mark Rothko exhibition, finishing the year with "Hogarth and British Painting 1700 to 1760." At the Barbican Gallery, a popular exhibition of London through the eyes of the great painters from Canaletto to Monet was followed by "The Edwardian Era." At the Hayward Gallery, a controversial Le Corbusier show was followed at the year's end by a major retrospective of Diego Rivera. The end of Sir Michael Levey's period as director of the National Gallery was marked by a show of "Selected Acquisitions: 1973 to 1986."

Film and Television. The London Film Festival in November opened with Mike Hodges' *A Prayer for the Dying* and ended with *Cry Freedom,* Richard Attenborough's version of the life of Steve Biko, murdered in South Africa. Among other notable British films of the year were Peter Greenaway's *The Belly of an Architect,* Merchant-Ivory's film version of an E. M. Forster novel, *Maurice,* David Leland's *Wish You Were Here,* John Boorman's *Hope and Glory,* Stephen Frears' *Prick Up Your Ears,* and Nicholas Roeg's *Castaway*.

Among new plays written for television, Bill Nicholson's story of the discovery of DNA, *Life Story,* with Tim Piggott-Smith, Jeff Goldblum, and Juliet Stevenson, won prizes for BBC drama, as did Simon Gray's *After Pilkington,* starring Bob Peck. One of the most entertaining series was called simply *Acting,* in which Michael Caine, Jonathan Miller, and Simon Callow demonstrated the finer points of their art.

MAUREEN GREEN
Free-lance Writer, London

GREECE

During 1987 the government of Prime Minister Andreas Papandreou, leader of the Panhellenic Socialist Movement (PASOK), faced religious, political, and international problems.

Church-State Relations. The gravest clash in church-state relations in decades erupted in March when the Papandreou government announced pending legislation to take over vast holdings of the Greek Orthodox Church, whose tenets form the state religion. Archbishop Seraphim, head of the church in Greece, denounced the government's plan, as did the Holy Synod and church leaders throughout the country. So bitter was the dispute that on Greek Independence Day, March 25, the archbishop and other bishops held a separate ceremony, boycotting the traditional service attended by the Greek president at the Athens Cathedral.

A modified version of the legislation was passed early in April and was challenged by the church hierarchy. Constantine Mitsotakis, leader of the parliamentary opposition, said that if his New Democracy Party came to power the law would be rescinded. For support, the hierarchy turned to Ecumenical Patriarch Dimitrios I, the spiritual leader of the world's Orthodox, whose episcopate is in Istanbul, Turkey. In August the Greek Council of State took action to suspend implementation of the new legislation. Following negotiations between Archbishop Seraphim and Prime Minister Papandreou, the government and the church announced in early November that they had reached a mutually agreeable solution regarding church property. In mid-November, Ecumenical Patriarch Dimitrios I visited Greece, where he was enthusiastically received by church and government leaders.

Internal Events. Papandreou was beset by many significant problems other than the church dispute during the year. He made major changes in his cabinet in February and September. These were the 12th and 13th times he had made changes in the cabinet since taking power in 1981. Beset by charges of corruption in his government, he won a parliamentary vote of confidence in May 1987, which strengthened his position. The prime minister's position was further aided by intense internal bickering within the New Democracy Party. The dissent fragmented Papandreou's major opponents and weakened New Democracy's call for early elections before June 1989, the latest they would be required constitutionally.

Papandreou became the object of exceptionally wide newspaper coverage and criticisms for an alleged affair with a married, 33-year-old former flight attendant, a situation that many observers felt had a political impact. The 68-year-old prime minister has been married for 36 years to his second wife, the American-born Margaret Papandreou, with whom he has four children.

AP/Wide World

A Greek Orthodox priest demonstrates against Greece's new law granting the government control over the church's vast holdings. After negotiations, the government and the church reached an agreement in November.

Foreign Affairs. Greek-Turkish relations remained strained during 1987, particularly due to a dispute over territorial waters in the Aegean Sea, the role of each country in the North Atlantic Treaty Organization (NATO), and Turkey's occupation of Cyprus since 1974. In March the dispute over oil rights in the Aegean almost led to a military confrontation between Greece and Turkey.

In U.S. relations, the Papandreou government showed alternating periods of friendship and irritability. In November, following months of negotiations, formal discussions started on the possibility of allowing American military bases to remain in Greece after a 1983 agreement expires in 1988. But Papandreou stressed that any accord would be subject to a

GREECE • Information Highlights

Official Name: Hellenic Republic.
Location: Southwestern Europe.
Area: 50,942 sq mi (131 940 km^2).
Population (mid-1987 est.): 10,000,000.
Chief Cities (1981 census): Athens, the capital, 885,737; Salonika, 406,413; Piraeus, 196,389.
Government: *Head of state,* Christos Sartzetakis, president (took office March 1985). *Head of government,* Andreas Papandreou, prime minister (took office Oct. 1981). *Legislature*—Parliament.
Monetary Unit: Drachma (131.48 drachmas equal U.S.$1, Dec. 8, 1987).
Gross National Product (1985 U.S.$): $32,800,000,000.
Economic Indexes (1986): *Consumer Prices* (1980 = 100), all items, 314.8; food, 315.9. *Industrial Production* (1980 = 100), 108.
Foreign Trade (1986 U.S.$): *Imports,* $11,314,000,000; *exports,* $5,650,000,000.

referendum by the Greek people. The issue of the bases was further complicated by several terrorist attacks on American personnel and property, which the Papandreou government condemned. The statue of President Harry S. Truman, damaged in a terrorist attack in 1986, was restored to its place in Athens in August.

With its Balkan neighbors to the north—all Communist states—the Papandreou government tried to maintain friendly relations. A 47-year state of war with Albania, dating from the World War II era, was finally ended in August 1987. But the move was criticized by the Greek opposition and by groups within Greece supporting the Greek-Orthodox minority in southern Albania.

Economy. Work was started on a $600 million alumina plant, an enormous Soviet investment in Greece; and an agreement was signed for Greece to purchase natural gas from the Soviet Union. The Greek government also actively continued to seek more foreign investment in Greece and to persuade Greek businessmen to reinvest their profits in the country. Austerity measures introduced in October 1985 to bolster the nation's economy continued to provoke widespread dissatisfaction, strikes, and demonstrations. Papandreou announced that some salary increases would be allowed in January 1988, but National Economy Minister Costas Simitis resigned suddenly in November 1987 over the timing of the measure.

Education. Students throughout Greece became restive during 1987 over government policies on higher education. Their discontent became particularly apparent beginning in September. In November a huge crowd of students marched on the ministry of education in Athens, calling for more funding for public universities, the elimination of private schools of higher education, and other reforms.

The University of Athens celebrated its 150th anniversary during 1987. It was founded in 1837 during the reign of King Otho I, the first king of modern Greece.

Royal News. In June the life of Prince Paul, eldest son of the deposed King Constantine II, was saved after a serious automobile accident in England. Earlier in the year the prince had finished a course at the Royal Military College, Sandhurst.

GEORGE J. MARCOPOULOS, *Tufts University*

HAWAII

Former Philippine President Ferdinand Marcos, who has been living in Hawaii since his ouster in 1986, received a one-year extension of his "parole status" from the U.S. government. He almost lost the protection in January because of an apparent attempt to return to his homeland without U.S. approval. Marcos left his seaside sanctuary for quieter, better-secured quarters in a hillside mansion overlooking Honolulu.

Politics. Honolulu Mayor Frank F. Fasi, a former Democrat turned Republican, was the target of impeachment proceedings after a State Circuit Court jury found him and two other city officials guilty of misusing taxpayers' money to promote a large housing project in Central Oahu. The citizens' civil suit was brought against Fasi by a public interest group, "Hawaii's Thousand Friends." The jury ruled that Fasi and the other officials had to pay back nearly $500,000 spent on advertising, planning, and consulting for the 1,500-unit project. After the verdict attorneys for the Thousand Friends demanded that Fasi resign. When he refused, impeachment papers were filed, but they were thrown out of court.

Nature. An eruption on the south flank of the 13,677-ft (4,169-m) Mauna Loa volcano that began in 1983 continued to destroy homes in the Puna district of the Island of Hawaii. The total damage passed the $15 million mark, with more than 55 homes consumed by fiery molten lava, most of them in the Royal Gardens subdivision. Fortunately for the residents the lava

HAWAII • Information Highlights

Area: 6,471 sq mi (16 759 km^2).
Population (July 1, 1986): 1,062,000.
Chief Cities (1980 census): Honolulu, the capital (1986 est.), 372,330; Pearl City, 42,575; Kailua, 35,812; Hilo, 35,269.
Government (1987): *Chief Officers*—governor, John D. Waihee III (D); lt. gov., Benjamin J. Cayetano (D). *Legislature*—Senate, 25 members; House of Representatives, 51 members.
State Finances (fiscal year 1986): *Revenue,* $2,945,000,000; *expenditure,* $2,472,000,000.
Personal Income (1986): $15,814,000,000; per capita, $14,886.
Labor Force (June 1987): *Civilian labor force,* 508,900; *unemployed,* 22,100 (4.3% of total force).
Education: *Enrollment* (fall 1985)—public elementary schools, 111,564; public secondary, 52,605; colleges and universities, 49,937. *Public school expenditures* (1985–86), $568,000,000 ($3,766 per pupil).

flow was slow, enabling them to leave their homes with most of their belongings. Some persons even vowed to rebuild after the lava cools and hardens. One of the few pluses about the eruption: it increased the size of the island by dozens of acres.

Yachting. Honolulu competed with San Diego for the right to hold the next America's Cup Yacht Race in Hawaiian waters—and lost. But the months-long controversy over which city should be selected had a positive side for Honolulu. It made Hawaiians realize the need for better docking and anchorage facilities for sailboats. At year's end, despite the initial setback, Hawaii was being considered as a possible site for a 1988 race when the San Diego Yacht Club, holders of the Cup, accepted a challenge from a New Zealand yachtsman.

Construction. Legal obstacles to the construction of a third tunnel through the Koolau Mountains separating Honolulu from Windward Oahu appeared to be overcome when the State Transportation Department began driving piles for a massive overpass. Environmental groups managed to stall the "H-3" superhighway for nearly 20 years by going to the courts, claiming the project endangered rare plants, animals, and Hawaiian petroglyphs (rock carvings). The delays meant that the construction costs for the tunnel and approach roads might rise from about $150 million to nearly $1 billion by the time the ten-year job is completed. About 2,500 construction workers were expected to be employed each year.

Tourism. Hawaii's tourist industry enjoyed another banner year with visitors outnumbering local residents by a 5-to-1 margin. Hotel and condominium owners were encouraged to build more accommodations, and the present inventory of about 65,000 rental units was expected to nearly double by the mid-1990s. Many of the Waikiki hotels have been acquired by Japanese nationals.

CHARLES TURNER, *Honolulu*

HONG KONG

Sir David Wilson was sworn in as Hong Kong's 27th governor on April 9. He replaced Sir David Akers-Jones, who had served as acting governor after the sudden death of Sir Edward Youde in December 1986.

Government. The new governor faced growing public pressure to allow direct elections to Hong Kong's Legislative Council beginning in 1988. Proponents believed that instituting direct elections under the British would ensure some self-rule for Hong Kong after it becomes part of China in 1997. But Beijing strongly opposed any change in Hong Kong's political system before that date. And Britain's seeming reluctance to grant Hong Kong a measure of democracy was seen by some as an effort to please Beijing and thus preserve British-Chinese relations.

A "Green Paper" on the development of representative government was published in May, and an office was set up to collect public opinion. The results of the polls, published November 4, revealed that 67% of respondents opposed direct elections in 1988.

In March the Legislative Council passed into law the Public Order (Amendment) Bill, which made it an offense for any person to publish false news likely to cause public disorder. The passing of the bill was viewed by some as another attempt by the Hong Kong government to please Beijing. In February the government announced that Chinese immigrants who obtained a Macao identity card before January 1980 would be permitted to visit Hong Kong.

Economy. The Hong Kong stock exchange was severely affected by the international stock-market plunge October 19. (*See* STOCK MARKET.) After major losses, the Hong Kong exchange suspended trading October 20. Its reopening a week later was made possible by a $256 million rescue plan for bankrupted stockbrokers, funded by the government and large banks and brokerage firms.

Among the other external factors determining Hong Kong's economic performance were a continued reduction in demand for exports to China and the threat of increased protectionism from the United States, which typically buys more than 45% of Hong Kong's exports.

The port of Hong Kong overtook New York as the world's second busiest container port, handling nearly 2.8 million 20-foot equivalent units (TEUs) in 1986. By 1992, Hong Kong's container-handling capacity was expected to increase to 3.5 million TEUs, challenging Rotterdam's leading capacity.

With its low, simple tax structure and excellent international communications and transport systems, Hong Kong continued to provide a favorable environment for industrial investment. The three major industries for overseas investments were electronics, nonmetallic mineral products, and textiles and clothing.

New Passports. The new British National (Overseas) passport, or BN(O), was issued on July 1 to replace the British Dependent Territory Citizen (BDTC) passport. Also issued was a new Permanent Identity Card (PID) giving the holder a right of abode in Hong Kong. With the BN(O) passport and PID, the 11,000 non-Chinese BDTC passport holders in Hong Kong would have the right to reside in the territory, although BN(O) status is not transmissable to the next generation. By June, 19 countries—including the United States, Japan, France, and West Germany—had recognized the BN(O) passport as a valid travel document.

DAVID CHUENYAN LAI
University of Victoria, British Columbia

A housing developer inspects the panelized townhouses he is constructing in a New York suburb. Such construction permits sections of walls, floors, and roofs to be assembled in a factory and then transported to the site. Such prefabrication saves time and lowers costs.

AP/Wide World

HOUSING

The performance of the U.S. housing market was mixed in 1987, and an October stock market decline had major implications for the housing sector as well as for the overall economy. Total housing production for the nation as a whole fluctuated considerably as the year progressed. Markedly different performances also were turned in by components of the housing market. The market for single-family homes fared much better than the market for rental properties. Furthermore, certain regions of the country had a good housing year, while others suffered depressed housing markets.

Total Production. The production of housing in the United States was strong during the early months of 1987, as housing starts ran at an annual rate of about 1.8 million units—equivalent to the strong 1986 pace. However, housing starts were considerably lower during the balance of the year, and the total for 1987 was approximately 1.65 million. This was the nation's lowest production level since the recession year of 1982 when housing starts fell to 1.06 million units.

Single-Family Housing. The production and sale of single-family homes fluctuated during 1987 largely in response to shifts in market interest rates. Home-mortgage rates fell to about 9% by March, the lowest level since 1978, and starts of single-family units surged into the 1.2–1.3 million unit range. Between March and mid-October, however, long-term, home-mortgage rates climbed by about 3 percentage points, and single family housing starts fell to an annual rate of about 1.1 million.

A dramatic fall in the stock market on October 19, "Black Monday," broke the upward momentum in interest rates. Mortgage rates were lower for the balance of 1987, but they remained well above the lows that had been reached in March. Consumer confidence may have been shaken to some degree by the stock market collapse. But the fall did not appear to have a negative impact on single-family housing during the fourth quarter. In fact, in some areas it appeared that the drop in the stock market stimulated interest in housing and real estate as an investment alternative.

The adjustable-rate mortgage (ARM) was a major factor in the single-family housing market during 1987. When long-term mortgage rates were falling to their cyclical lows during the first quarter, there was relatively little use of ARMs by lenders and buyers; in fact, less than one fifth of home sales were financed by ARMs early in the year. But as interest rates climbed, the importance of ARMs increased. By fall, 60% of all conventional home loans had adjustable-rate features, and this pattern persisted through the balance of the year.

The ARM has truly become a major "safety valve" in the home-mortgage market, helping buyers stay in the market when interest rates are rising. During the second half of 1987, home buyers could get ARMs with initial interest rates roughly 3 percentage points below prevailing rates on fixed-rate mortgages.

Multifamily Housing. The rental-housing market in the United States had a difficult year in 1987. The production of multifamily structures, which are built primarily for rent, deteriorated for the second consecutive year. Starts of multifamily units fell to an annual rate of about 450,000 units in the fourth quarter, down about 40% from the recent high in early 1986.

The weakening of the multifamily housing market reflected two major and interrelated factors: high vacancy rates in rental housing and the Tax Reform Act of 1986. In 1987, rental vacancies hit the highest level in more than 20 years, climbing to more than 8% of the stock of rental housing in the United States. In apartment buildings with five or more units, the vacancy rate rose to more than 11%. The Tax Reform Act of 1986 substantially reduced tax incentives for investment in multifamily rental housing. Since passage of such legislation that would adversely affect investors in multifamily housing actually was anticipated widely by late 1985, the impact of tax reform pervaded the rental-housing market during both 1986 and 1987.

Regional Housing Markets. There have been extraordinary differences in the performance of housing markets in different parts of the United States in recent years, and 1987 was no exception. The strongest markets were in areas with diversified economic bases having strong reliance on high-tech, defense, and service industries—such as the Northeast, Florida, and the West Coast. The weakest housing markets were in areas with economic bases highly concentrated in oil and agriculture. Declines in world prices of petroleum and agricultural commodities have taken a heavy toll in such states as Texas, Louisiana, Oklahoma, Arkansas, and Alaska.

Housing markets in the industrial Northwest, commonly dubbed the "rust belt," weakened badly in the early and mid-1980s as a combination of factors made the U.S. industrial sector less competitive in world markets. However, this area of the country has been recovering economically, and housing markets have been bouncing back in the process. A lower dollar on foreign-exchange markets and greater industrial efficiency at home contributed to the recovery.

National Housing Policy. Federal expenditure programs in support of housing were trimmed in 1987, continuing a trend begun about 1980. Because of these cuts and other factors, several housing-policy issues gained increasing prominence in 1987. These issues included: 1) erosion of home-ownership affordability, particularly among younger households who normally are first-time buyers; 2) a growing affordability problem for low-income renter households; 3) an impending exit of low-income rental units from the stock of housing reserved for such households; and 4) an increasingly visible homeless problem.

The U.S. government responded to these issues in two ways. First, the Housing and Community Development Act of 1987 was enacted just before year's end, reauthorizing a variety of housing-finance institutions and continuing most federal housing programs into 1988 and 1989 at their 1987 levels. Second, congressional leaders set in motion a broad effort to review the state of housing in the United States and to shape a major bill to be considered in 1988. This effort involved three phases. First, housing-interest groups were asked to provide input as a prelude for major housing legislation. Second, a series of academic studies were commissioned on various housing-policy issues, and conferences were held to present and discuss these studies. Third, a blue-ribbon panel of senior housing-industry practitioners was convened, and their recommendations were presented to the Congress. The congressional committees overseeing housing would utilize the output from these three phases as they attempt to fashion a bipartisan bill to address housing problems—within the context of tight federal budget restrictions.

Home-ownership Rates. Home-ownership rates in various countries reflect a combination of economic and social forces as well as government policies that encourage or discourage home ownership. In the United States, the home-ownership rate trended upward from 44% in 1940 to nearly 66% by 1980, before edging down to about 64% in 1987. The long-term upward trend in the U.S. home-ownership rate reflected a combination of economic and demographic factors along with a variety of government policies that encouraged home-ownership. The reversal since 1980 reflects both underlying demographic forces and a problem of affordability for younger, first-time buyers striving to achieve home ownership.

Data on home-ownership rates outside the United States are extremely sketchy. The highest rate among major industrialized countries appears to be in Australia, where 68% of all households owned their own homes in the early 1980s. The home-ownership rate in Japan has been on an upward trend since the early 1970s, and by 1987 was apparently very close to the U.S. rate (64%).

The most striking change in home-ownership rates has been occurring in Great Britain. The rate was only 56% in 1980, but it surpassed 63% by 1985 and equaled or exceeded the U.S. home-ownership rate by 1987. The surge in Great Britain's home-ownership rate is traceable at least in part to a law passed by Prime Minister Margaret Thatcher's Conservative government in 1980. This law enables renters of publicly subsidized or "council" housing to purchase the units they occupy, at substantial discounts that range up to 50% of market value. In the first three years after passage, some 250,000 households bought their council units, adding more than 10% to the overall ownership rate, and such sales continued through 1987.

KENT W. COLTON and DAVID F. SEIDERS
National Association of Home Builders

HUNGARY

In 1987, Hungary saw the start of a three-year economic austerity program as well as insistent demands for political democratization and bolder challenges to the regime of aging Hungarian Communist Party leader János Kádár.

Economy. Hungary's 20-year-old experiment with economic liberalization seemed to have ended in a general catastrophe—double-digit inflation, a steadily rising cost of living, a chronic budget deficit, dwindling exports, and one of the world's largest per capita foreign debts.

With gloomy predictions for the indefinite future, the regime launched a series of draconian "stabilizing" measures. In March the forint was devalued by an average of 8% against most world currencies. In August the government permitted a sharp rise in prices for a broad range of consumer products and necessities, including flour, bread, gasoline, fuel oil, electricity, and cigarettes. In 1988, Hungarians would begin paying personal income taxes (about 8% for average wage earners, but as high as 60% for those with second and third jobs), as well as a value-added tax on most goods and services (amounting to another 8%).

The forcing of inefficient state enterprises into bankruptcy and revamping the oversized administrative system were expected to add more than 200,000 persons to the ranks of the unemployed. Some nongovernmental critics blamed the Council for Mutual Economic Assistance (COMECON), the Soviet bloc economic organization, for hampering Hungary's economy by discouraging competition and innovation and the free production and exchange of goods. Others attacked the major misallocation of Hungary's investment funds to such party-favored projects as the natural gas pipeline from Siberia to Eastern Europe and the large joint hydroelectric project on the Danube River.

HUNGARY • Information Highlights

Official Name: Hungarian People's Republic.
Location: East-central Europe.
Area: 35,919 sq mi (93,030 km^2).
Population (mid-1987 est.): 10,600,000.
Chief Cities (Jan. 1, 1986): Budapest, the capital, 2,075,990; Debrecen, 211,823; Miskolc, 211,660.
Government: *Head of state,* Károly Németh, president of the presidential council (took office June 1987). *Head of government,* Károly Grósz, premier of the council of ministers (took office June 1987). Secretary general of the Hungarian Socialist Workers' Party, János Kádár (took office 1956). *Legislature* (unicameral)—National Assembly.
Monetary Unit: Forint (47.627 forints equal U.S.$1, August 1987).
Economic Indexes (1986): *Consumer Prices* (1980 = 100), all items, 146.5; food, 138.7. *Industrial Production* (1980 = 100), 111.
Foreign Trade (1986 U.S.$): *Imports,* $9,613,000,000; *exports,* $9,183,000,000.

Dissent. Public economic criticisms were increasingly coupled with calls for political liberalization within the party and government, including real power for the parliament and a multiparty political system. There was growing disenchantment with the ineffective leadership of the 75-year-old Kádár himself.

In November 1986, the Hungarian Writers' Union decried the general decline of the nation, citing a declining adult life expectancy, a steadily decreasing population, rising alcoholism, and the highest recorded suicide rate in the world. The union also demanded Western-type democracy and neutrality for Hungary. On March 15, 1987, as part of the official commemoration of the Hungarian Revolution of 1848, some 1,500 persons, mostly students, marched for three hours about Budapest. Led by a group calling itself "the democratic opposition," they chanted for freedom of speech, press, and assembly, a Hungary free of dominating foreign (i.e., Soviet) influences and troops, and the erection of a memorial to Imre Nagy, prime minister during the Soviet invasion of 1956.

In response the government adopted a less tolerant stance toward "insolent and aggressive" dissenters. It began to deny exit visas to political opponents, confiscate underground publications, and ban the works of dissident Hungarian authors published abroad. In June, Károly Grosz, a conservative and a chief contender for Kádár's post, became premier.

Other. In September, Hungary and Israel announced agreement on establishing diplomatic interest sections in each other's capitals.

JOSEPH FREDERICK ZACEK
State University of New York at Albany

ICELAND

Iceland's Independence-Progressive coalition government, formed in 1983, completed its term of office in the spring. In the April 25 election, the Independents won 18 seats of the newly enlarged (from 60 to 63 seats) Althing, or Parliament; the Progressives, 13; the Social Democrats, 10; the People's Alliance, 8; and the Women's Alliance, 6—up from 3 seats in the previous election. One seat was won by an independent. Former Industry Minister Albert Gudmundsson was forced to resign from the Independence Party, and founded the new Citizens' Party, which won 7 seats. The 1987 election was the first in which 18- and 19-year-olds were allowed to vote. Some 90% of the total electorate voted. A coalition of Independents, Progressives, and Social Democrats formed a government after ten weeks of negotiations, and took office on July 8.

Economy. Growth in Iceland's gross national income was 8.6% in 1986, the highest figure in all the industrial countries, and was forecast at 9.3% for 1987. Although inflation

ICELAND • Information Highlights

Official Name: Republic of Iceland.
Location: North Atlantic Ocean.
Area: 39,768 sq mi (103 000 km²).
Population (mid-1987 est.): 200,000.
Chief Cities (Dec. 1, 1986): Reykjavík, the capital, 91,497; Akureyri, 13,761.
Government: *Head of state,* Vigdís Finnbogadóttir, president (took office Aug. 1980). *Head of government,* Thorsteinn Pálsson, prime minister (took office July 1987). *Legislature*—Althing: Upper House and Lower House.
Monetary Unit: Króna (38.9 krónur equal U.S.$1, August 1987).
Gross National Product (1986 U.S.$): $3,731,-000,000.
Foreign Trade (1986 U.S.$): *Imports,* $1,115,000,000; *exports,* $1,096,000,000.

dropped to 13% in 1986, it was expected to rise to about 20% for 1987. A strong import demand, the result of an increase in real incomes and purchasing power, meant that the current account of the balance of payments was expected to show a large deficit, in contrast with the 550 million krona (about $15 million) surplus in 1986. To counteract these trends, the government brought in a 10% sales tax on all except some staple foods and on a range of services, while abolishing various exemptions from the 25% sales tax. Fees of 1% to 3% on foreign borrowing also were introduced. Changes in currency regulations and a liberalization of capital transfer to and from Iceland were planned to encourage foreign investment. Terms of trade improved, and growth in GDP was predicted at 6.6% (1986: 6.3%). The foreign debt was forecast at 40% of GDP (1986: 47%). The exchange rate of the krona was kept stable for the second year in succession.

Unemployment, one of the lowest rates in the world, remained at under 1%. Labor shortages were felt in all fields of industry, and to ease the labor situation, more workers were hired from abroad. The fishing industry enjoyed a successful year, with increased catches and high fish prices abroad. General wage agreements in December 1986 allowed for slight increases in 1987, and further increases took place during the year in view of price rises.

General. Disagreement with the United States over Iceland's research whaling—which the United States claimed was merely disguised commercial whaling—led to whaling being halted for the duration of talks, shortly after the season began in June. The United States later agreed not to impose economic sanctions on Iceland, and research whaling was permitted to continue.

A new international air terminal opened in April, bringing about the complete separation of civil aviation and NATO defense facilities at Keflavík. A privately built shopping mall was opened in Reykjavík in August, housing more than 70 establishments.

ANNE COSSER, *Reykjavík*

IDAHO

New found harmony between a Republican legislature and a Democratic governor—with Cecil Andrus returning to the governor's office after a ten-year absence—began the year as legislators followed Andrus' call to prime the pumps of education and economic development. Recent years of economic stagnation appeared to be giving way to new growth in later months. In September unemployment sank below 5% for the first time since 1979, but analysts said it was too early to predict a sure rebound.

Legislature. A spirit of bipartisan cooperation helped legislators meet and then exceed challenges presented by Andrus. Putting aside the rancor that had characterized their dealings with former Gov. John Evans, lawmakers increased funding for public schools by 7.8% and for higher education by 12.1%. They also pumped $2 million into the state's Department of Commerce, an increase of 168%. The bolstered spending was backed by a permanent sales tax increase to 5 cents and raises in income tax rates. After several unsuccessful attempts in previous years, the legislature also raised the state's drinking age from 19 to 21 and agreed to spend $20.8 million for a new maximum-security prison to relieve overcrowding at the existing penitentiary.

Economy. Signs of recovery included reopening of the Lucky Friday and Sunshine silver mines in the Panhandle and the Conda mine in the southeast, a commitment by Trus Joist to a new plant in the Twin Falls area, and increases in Micron Technology's work force in the Boise valley. But they were tempered by Tupperware's decision to close its Jerome plant, layoffs at the Thompson Creek molybdenum mine near Challis, and streamlining by Union Pacific.

Crime. Convicted "Mountain Man" killer Claude Dallas, who made the FBI's ten most-wanted list after escaping from the state prison

IDAHO • Information Highlights

Area: 83,564 sq mi (216 432 km²).
Population (July 1, 1986): 1,003,000.
Chief Cities (1980 census): Boise, the capital (July 1, 1986 est.), 108,390; Pocatello, 46,340; Idaho Falls, 39,590.
Government (1987): *Chief Officers*—governor, Cecil Andrus (D); lt. gov., C. L. Otter (R). *Legislature*—Senate, 42 members; House of Representatives, 84 members.
State Finances (fiscal year 1986): *Revenue,* $1,744,000,000; *expenditure,* $1,517,000,000.
Personal Income (1986): $11,250,000,000; per capita, $11,223.
Labor Force (June 1987): *Civilian labor force,* 488,200; *unemployed,* 34,200 (7.0% of total force).
Education: *Enrollment* (fall 1985)—public elementary schools, 149,380; public secondary, 59,289; colleges and universities, 42,668. *Public school expenditures* (1985–86), $480,000,000 ($2,390 per pupil).

in March 1986, was arrested March 8 at Riverside, CA. But Dallas was acquitted of an escape charge after he convinced a Boise jury that prison guards who were out to get him forced his escape. He was sent to Nebraska to complete his 30-year term for the 1981 slayings of game wardens Bill Pogue and Conley Elms.

Former Republican Congressman George Hansen, paroled December 1986 after serving six months for filing false financial disclosure forms, was arrested April 15 at Omaha, NE, for violating parole conditions. Hansen was released from prison September 29 after serving 11½ months of a 5- to 15-month sentence.

The Rev. Richard Butler, founder of the Aryan Nations group near Coeur d'Alene, was indicted with 14 other white supremacists April 14 for allegedly conspiring to overthrow the government through assassination of public officials. Butler remained out on bail the rest of the year.

Death. Supreme Court Justice Charles Donaldson, 68, died October 9 of a heart attack. After joining the five-member court in 1969, he frequently served as a swing vote in controversial cases. His seat was not filled in 1987.

JIM FISHER, Editorial Writer
"Lewiston Morning Tribune"

ILLINOIS

For Illinois taxpayers it was like déjà vu. As he had after his first election victory, Gov. James R. Thompson disclosed early in 1987 that the state needed more tax money. The fiscal problem came to light only weeks after Thompson had assured voters in his reelection campaign that state coffers were in good shape. While the governor mapped out a plan for new taxes, the state was forced to borrow $100 million.

To meet the problem, Thompson's administration proposed hikes in the state income tax and a 9.5 cents-a-gallon increase in the gasoline tax. The Democratic-controlled state legislature balked at Thompson's tax proposals and passed only a bare-bones budget before adjourning. Thompson blamed Democratic leaders for the defeat of his tax proposals; the Democrats blamed the Republican governor for failing to win support from members of his own party. Thompson had threatened to lay off 3,000 state employees if his tax plan was not passed. The cutbacks in mental health, corrections, and other state programs were not quite so dramatic, however.

Economy. The state's employment level reached a record 5.4 million in September, as unemployment dropped to 6.4%, its lowest level in nine years. (In 1986, unemployment stood at 8.1%.) Total nonfarm employment grew by 44,000 in 1987 because of gains in retail trades, services, finance, and transportation.

ILLINOIS • Information Highlights

Area: 56,345 sq mi (145 934 km²).
Population (July 1, 1986): 11,553,000.
Chief Cities (July 1, 1986 est.): Springfield, the capital, 100,290; Chicago, 3,009,530; Rockford, 135,760.
Government (1987): *Chief Officers*—governor, James R. Thompson (R); lt. gov., George H. Ryan (R). *General Assembly*—Senate, 59 members; House of Representatives, 118 members.
State Finances (fiscal year 1986): *Revenue,* $19,437,000,000; *expenditure,* $17,823,000,000.
Personal Income (1986): $180,052,000,000; per capita, $15,586.
Labor Force (June 1987): *Civilian labor force,* 5,817,600; *unemployed,* 451,600 (7.8% of total force).
Education: *Enrollment* (fall 1985)—public elementary schools, 1,246,496; public secondary, 579,982; colleges and universities, 678,689. *Public school expenditures* (1985–86), $5,629,000,000 ($3,621 per pupil).

Crime. Stephen B. Small, a Kankakee media heir and the great-grandson of an Illinois governor, was buried alive and apparently suffocated in September, as kidnappers unsuccessfully sought a $1 million ransom. The state said it would seek the death penalty against a young man and woman charged with the kidnapping and murder.

In August former Democratic Gov. Daniel Walker pleaded guilty to federal fraud and perjury charges. He was accused of having taken improper loans from the bank he had headed until its failure in 1986.

The case of convicted rapist Gary Dotson was revived in the headlines when the Illinois Prisoner Review Board revoked his parole. Dotson made international news in 1985, when Governor Thompson commuted his 25 to 50 year sentence after his accuser recanted her trial testimony about the rape. The parole revocation came after Dotson's wife had him arrested on a battery charge. Recent convictions against Dotson for drunken driving also played a role in the revocation decision.

AIDS Laws. In September, Illinois became the first state to enact a series of laws designed to detect AIDS (Acquired Immune Deficiency Syndrome) through broad-based testing programs. Along with Louisiana, Illinois made AIDS virus-antibody testing mandatory as a prerequisite to marriage, a requirement that would take effect on Jan. 1, 1988. Other laws, however, were unique to Illinois and included AIDS testing for convicted sex and drug offenders; required education about AIDS as well as about sexual abstinence in public schools grades six through twelve; required doctors to notify school principals if students test positive for AIDS antibodies; and ordered the quarantine of some AIDS victims under certain circumstances. Wrongful release of confidential test results would be treated as a criminal offense.

ROBERT ENSTAD, *"Chicago Tribune"*

INDIA

As it marked the 40th anniversary of its independence, India during 1987 was a troubled country, with continuing communal violence and political terrorism, a prime minister—Rajiv Gandhi—who was suffering a serious loss of credibility, a divided ruling party—the Congress (I)—and an even more fragmented opposition, the worst drought of the century, a mixed economic picture, and growing involvement in the Sinhalese-Tamil struggle in neighboring Sri Lanka.

Political Affairs. For Prime Minister Gandhi the year was a particularly trying one, as he faced a marked decline in credibility, growing disenchantment with his autocratic style of governing, charges of corruption in his administration, alienation from many of his once-close associates, and continued frustration in his attempts to stem the tide of communal violence, especially in Punjab. Since national elections were not due until December 1989, and since the opposition to his Congress (I) party held only 122 of the 543 seats in the Lok Sabha (lower house)—and these divided among 16 often bickering parties—he was in no danger of being overthrown by normal constitutional processes. But his increasing political problems were reflected by frequent changes in the cabinet and by a number of resignations or dismissals in both the party and the government.

The most highly publicized resignation was that of Defense Minister Vishwanath Pratap Singh, one of the most effective members of the cabinet, on April 12. The resignation came amid charges that Singh had intended to embarrass the prime minister in a new corruption probe pertaining to a $300 million submarine purchase from West Germany. K. C. Pant was named as the new defense minister. Singh later was expelled from the Congress (I) and became one of the most popular leaders of the opposition.

The year also saw two noteworthy changes in the ministry of external affairs. In January, Foreign Secretary A. P. Venkateswaran, one of India's most senior career diplomats, resigned following a public rebuke by the prime minister—an action for which Gandhi was widely criticized. K. P. S. Menon, who had been serving as ambassador to China, was named to the post. Then in July, Minister of External Affairs Narayan Dutt Tiwari was shifted to the finance ministry. Gandhi, who had temporarily held the finance post, among others, relinquished that portfolio and took over external affairs.

An acrimonious dispute between Prime Minister Gandhi and President Giani Zail Singh became public knowledge in March, when an Indian newspaper published a letter from the president accusing Gandhi of not showing proper respect for the office of president and of not following "certain well-established conventions," especially in not keeping him informed on important matters.

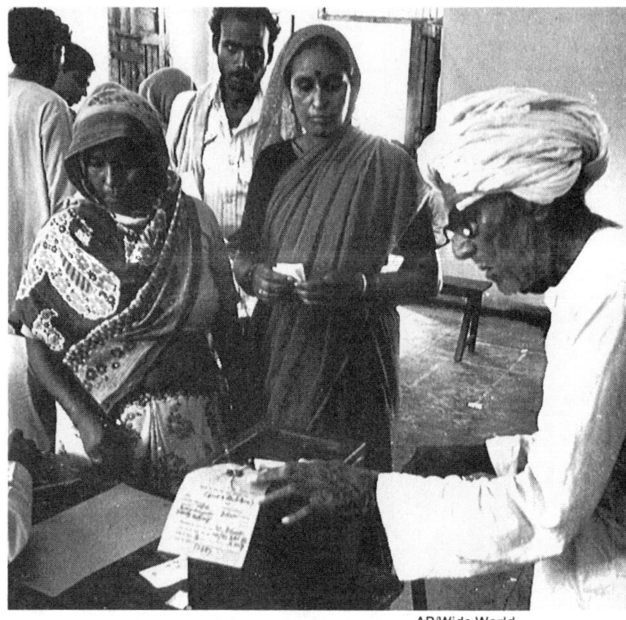

AP/Wide World

Voters in India's northwestern state of Haryana cast their ballots in state-assembly elections June 17. The results were a political setback for Prime Minister Rajiv Gandhi.

President Singh in June affirmed that he would not stand for reelection in presidential balloting the following month. Vice-President Ramaswami Venkataraman, the 76-year-old Congress (I) candidate, won 71% of the vote in the July 13 election and took office as India's eighth president on July 25. Shankar Dayal Sharma, a consensus candidate of the Congress (I) and opposition parties, was sworn in as vice-president.

Leaders of the non-Communist opposition parties met repeatedly during the year to organize a more unified front against the Congress (I). Most of these efforts proved ineffectual, but two developments in September seemed to promise more fruitful results. One was a large meeting in Mathura in Uttar Pradesh to promote the new People's Front, a movement in which Vishwanath Pratap Singh was a leading figure. The second was a meeting in Surajkund in Haryana, convened by Devi Lal, the new chief minister of Haryana, and attended by leaders of nine opposition parties.

During the course of the year, the ruling Congress (I) suffered a series of reverses in elections to state legislative assemblies. In Mizoram, holding its first election in February, Congress (I) candidates won only three seats, while a local tribal party, the Mizo National Front, won a majority and formed the state's first government. In March, important elections were held in Kerala, West Bengal, and Jammu and Kashmir. In the latter state, an al-

AP/Wide World

Residents of Mehsana in the southwestern state of Gujarat wait patiently to fill their waterpots, as much of India is hit by the worst drought of the 20th century.

liance of the National Conference (JKNC) and the Congress (I) won 70 of 76 seats (36 going to JKNC candidates), and a coalition government, headed by JKNC leader Farook Abdullah, was formed. In Kerala and West Bengal, the Congress (I) was routed by Left Front alliances headed by the Communist Party of India —Marxist (CPM).

In the northwestern state of Haryana—which, unlike the other states, had been a Congress (I) stronghold—an alliance of two main opposition parties, the Lok Dal (B) and the Bharatiya Janata Party (BJP), won four fifths of the seats in state-assembly elections on June 17; the Congress (I) won only five seats. This was the party's sixth defeat in the previous seven state elections it had contested under Prime Minister Gandhi.

Religious and communal violence continued to take a heavy toll, especially in the north. In May more than 150 people were killed in Hindu-Muslim clashes in Meerut and New Delhi. Violence was most frequent in the Sikh-majority state of Punjab, as it had been for the past three years. In July, 75 persons were killed in attacks by Sikh terrorists in Punjab and Haryana, and several Sikhs were killed in rioting by Hindus across northern India. Sikh militants continued to resort to terrorism to press their demands for greater autonomy, or even independence, for Punjab.

In February the chief minister of Punjab, Surjit Singh Barnala, the relatively moderate leader of the Akali Dal, the main Sikh political party, was excommunicated by the five high priests of the Sikh faith. Barnala remained in power but was increasingly unable to deal with the mounting violence. On May 11—with the death toll from Sikh terrorist attacks already exceeding 300 for the year, and with up to 70,000 police and paramilitary forces in the state unable to preserve law and order—Prime Minister Gandhi dismissed the Barnala government and brought Punjab under central-government rule. Gandhi warned repeatedly that he would not tolerate "communal and secessionist" activities, but his efforts to curb the violence were largely unavailing. He was widely criticized for being either too soft or too forceful in dealing with the Sikh terrorists.

Mizoram and Arunachal Pradesh on February 20 officially became the 23rd and 24th states, respectively, in the Indian Union, and Goa became the 25th on May 30.

The Economy. India's economic picture during 1987 was mixed. Promising trends in food grain production were reversed substantially by the worst drought of the century in most of the country (and by unusually severe floods in the northeast and east). By the end of the year, the adverse effects of the drought were manifest in many sectors of the economy. After years of virtual self-sufficiency in food, it seemed apparent that India would have to resume substantial food imports.

In spite of the drought, the overall economic growth rate reached about 5%, with industrial growth at 7–9%. There was concern about marked increases in expenditures not contemplated in the Seventh Five-Year Plan (1985–90), especially since these might adversely affect the plan's progress. Exports increased at a higher rate than imports, leading to a decline in the trade deficit, but the trade balance remained distinctly unfavorable.

To achieve the goals of the Five-Year Plan, additional external financing would be required. This would add to the already serious problem of India's rapidly increasing external indebtedness and debt servicing; the latter amounted to about 19% of current government receipts.

The government's budget for fiscal 1987–88, presented to Parliament on February 28 by Prime Minister Gandhi, called for a 23% increase in defense spending, a strengthening of the public sector, greater momentum for antipoverty programs, a higher priority to education and housing, and measures to increase exports and curb imports. Total expenditures were budgeted at Rs. 629.42 billion (U.S. $48.1 billion), with receipts envisioned at Rs. 569.32

INDIA • Information Highlights

Official Name: Republic of India.
Location: South Asia.
Area: 1,269,340 sq mi (3 287 590 km^2).
Population (mid-1987 est.): 800,300,000.
Chief Cities (1981 census): New Delhi, the capital, 5,157,270; Bombay, 8,243,405; Calcutta, 3,288,148.
Government: *Head of state,* Ramaswami Venkataraman, president (took office July 25, 1987). *Head of government,* Rajiv Gandhi, prime minister (took office Oct. 31, 1984). *Legislature*—Parliament: Rajya Sabha (Council of States) and Lok Sabha (House of the People).
Monetary Unit: Rupee (12.9366 rupees equal U.S.$1, Dec. 1, 1987).
Gross National Product (fiscal 1985–86 U.S.$): $190,000,000,000.
Economic Indexes (1986): *Consumer Prices* (1980 = 100), all items, 169.4; food, 168.7. *Industrial Production* (1980 = 100), 149.
Foreign Trade (1986 U.S.$): *Imports,* $14,657,000,000; *exports,* $9,107,000,000.

billion ($43.5 billion), leaving a deficit of Rs. 60.10 billion ($4.6 billion).

At the close of a meeting in Paris in mid-June, the Aid India Consortium announced a commitment of $5.4 billion in concessional aid, an increase of 23% over the recommendation for 1986–87. The Consortium commended India's economic achievements, especially its efforts to eliminate poverty, undertake reforms in trade and industry, improve the trade balance and reduce the current-accounts deficit, and increase exports.

Involvement in Sri Lanka. India during 1987 became more deeply involved in the troubled internal affairs of Sri Lanka than ever before in modern times. Relations between the two countries reached a new low during the first six months of the year, as India demonstrated its sympathies with the Tamils in Sri Lanka in their fight against the majority Sinhalese. The support was most vocal and tangible in Tamil Nadu, the Indian state closest to Sri Lanka and the home of some 50 million Tamils. In the early part of the year, tough messages and public criticisms were exchanged between the two governments and their leaders. Indian spokesmen criticized the decision of the Sri Lankan government to mount a major military offensive against the Tamil rebels in the northern and eastern provinces. In late May, Prime Minister Gandhi urged Sri Lanka's President Junius R. Jayewardene "to observe restraint" in dealing with the Tamils. He openly criticized the military operations and accused Jayewardene of deceiving him. Sri Lankan officials, in turn, charged that India was exacerbating the internal conflict by supporting the Tamil cause.

A major crisis in Indo-Sri Lankan relations developed in early June, when India dispatched 19 boats with food and medical supplies for Tamils in the rebel-held Jaffna Peninsula. But the boats were halted by Sri Lankan naval vessels in the Palk Strait and, after a few tense hours, turned back. Prime Minister Gandhi proceeded to dispatch five Indian Air Force planes, escorted by four fighters, to drop "humanitarian relief" supplies in the Jaffna Peninsula. Colombo bitterly protested this alleged violation of its sovereignty and integrity.

In the weeks that followed, however, Indian involvement in Sri Lanka increased markedly, this time at the request of the Colombo government. India in effect became a party to the civil strife in Sri Lanka rather than a mediator, as it had originally intended. In early July, at Gandhi's request, the two leaders began a series of secret talks aimed at resolving the Sri Lankan civil war. After three weeks of negotiations, the leaders reached a major accord—signed in Colombo on July 29—"to establish peace and normalcy in Sri Lanka." The agreement was immediately denounced by both Tamil and Sinhalese factions in Sri Lanka. On the day after the signing, as Prime Minister Gandhi was reviewing a Sri Lankan honor guard before leaving for Delhi, a Sinhalese soldier suddenly struck him with a rifle butt; Gandhi suffered only minor injuries.

Among the key provisions of the July 29 accord was that the government of India would "underwrite and guarantee" its implementa-

AP/Wide World

Prime Minister Gandhi (left) *and Sri Lanka's President Junius Jayewardene met in Colombo in July and signed an agreement to end the four-year-old rebellion of Sri Lanka's Tamil minority.*

tion. At Jayewardene's request, Gandhi dispatched several thousand Indian troops—a force that grew to nearly 20,000—to the Jaffna Peninsula. The troops immediately became engaged in military operations against Tamil rebels, who—along with Tamil civilians—suffered a heavy loss of life. Even moderate Tamils had a change of attitude toward India—a country to which they had looked for support but which they now saw as a collaborator of the Sinhalese-dominated government in Colombo. In India, too, the military intervention in Sri Lanka was criticized. (*See also* SRI LANKA.)

Other Foreign Affairs. After an apparent improvement in Indo-Pakistani relations during 1986, tensions were high in early 1987. India massed some 150,000 troops, presumably engaged in military exercises, along the border, and Pakistan responded with its own troop deployment. Delhi had been increasingly concerned about Pakistan's reported arms buildup, the impending supply of more sophisticated U.S. military equipment, and Islamabad's support for disaffected Sikhs in the border state of Punjab. Relations improved somewhat in February, after Pakistan's President Zia ul-Haq met with Prime Minister Gandhi in New Delhi. Two rounds of negotiations at the foreign secretary level then led to an agreement for a bilateral troop withdrawal from the border regions. But relations between the two South Asian rivals remained uneasy throughout the year. India resented Pakistani criticisms of its deployment of troops to Sri Lanka. And it raised strong objections to a reference to Kashmir by Pakistan's Prime Minister Mohammed Khan Junejo in a September address to the UN General Assembly. During a November meeting of the South Asia Association for Regional Cooperation (SAARC) in Nepal, Prime Minister Gandhi and President Zia agreed to resume the Indo-Pakistan dialogue.

Sino-Indo relations remained chilly despite an exchange of visits by high-level officials and another round of talks on border issues. Beijing resented Indian criticisms of Chinese moves in Tibet (*see* special report, page 187), and it expressed its displeasure at the elevation of the border area of Arunachal Pradesh to full statehood. Each country alleged that the other was amassing troops along the border and was interfering with the internal affairs of the other.

India's economic and military ties with the Soviet Union continued to be extensive. After several Indian defense purchases were stalled by scandals involving Indian officials and Western arms firms, the Soviet Union increased its supply of military equipment. During an official visit to the Soviet Union in early July, Prime Minister Gandhi held two rounds of wide-ranging talks with General Secretary Mikhail Gorbachev, unveiled a statue of his mother—the late Prime Minister Indira Gandhi—in a square in Moscow renamed after her, praised the year-long Festival of India that was being held in more than 100 Soviet cities and towns, and joined Gorbachev in signing a long-term agreement on science and technology. In November, Prime Minister Gandhi and Soviet Premier Nikolai Ryzhkov inaugurated a Festival of the USSR in India and unveiled a statue of Lenin in Nehru Park in New Delhi.

Indian assessments of relations with the United States varied considerably during the course of the year. During the early part of the year, with the Reagan administration proposing a major military and economic aid package for Pakistan, several members of the Indian Parliament expressed the view that Indo-U.S. relations had touched a new low. A few months later, Prime Minister Gandhi stated that there had been "a tremendous improvement" in relations. Nevertheless, India continued to object vigorously to the U.S. supply of sophisticated military equipment to Pakistan.

In October prolonged and often tense Indo-U.S. negotiations over the sale of an advanced American super-computer to India culminated in a compromise agreement for the purchase of a Cray XM P-14 and a more general agreement on future super-computer deals. Pentagon officials and others in the Reagan administration and the U.S. Congress had expressed reservations about the proposed arrangement, on the grounds that it would jeopardize the national security of the United States and that India might allow the super-computer to fall into the hands of the Soviet Union. The implementation of the agreement would mark the first time that the United States had made a super-computer available to a nation with close ties to Moscow.

In late October, after attending the Commonwealth Heads of Government Conference in Vancouver, Canada, Prime Minister Gandhi made an official three-day visit to the United States. The trip was marked by cordial meetings with U.S. officials and by protest demonstrations, mainly by dissident Sikhs, in each of the cities he visited. In New York he conferred with several heads of state and addressed the UN General Assembly. In Washington on October 20, he met with President Reagan.

India also played host to several diplomatic gatherings during 1987. In January the presidents of Algeria, Congo, Peru, Yugoslavia, and Zambia; the prime minister of Zimbabwe; the foreign minister of Argentina; and the chief of general staff of Nigeria all traveled to New Delhi to participate in a two-day summit meeting of the Africa Fund, of which Prime Minister Gandhi was chairman. In October, 300 delegates from 30 Asian countries attended the four-day Asian Relations Commemorative Conference in New Delhi, marking the 40th anniversary of the Asian Relations Conference.

NORMAN D. PALMER, *Professor Emeritus*
University of Pennsylvania

INDIANA

An education program and a package of new tax laws dominated debate in the regular 61-day session and necessitated a one-day special session for the 1987 Indiana General Assembly. Mayoralty races, sports events, and a midsummer heat wave also headlined news stories during the year.

Legislature. Despite months of bitter debate and 144 versions of the bill, legislators required a brief special session to approve the A+ Program for Educational Excellence sponsored by Gov. Robert D. Orr and Superintendent of Public Instruction H. Dean Evans. Considered by some as nationally significant educational reform, the A+ Program includes a comprehensive statewide testing program to determine student achievement; a performance-based accreditation system to increase schools' accountability for good education; a five-day extension of the school year to 180 days; a program to help students at risk of failing because of their environment; free textbooks for poor children; and a college-loan forgiveness plan for minority students who become teachers. Opponents of the measure feared the increased state control over local school corporations, disapproved of the enormous tax increases necessary to fund the program, and questioned the provisions' effectiveness in improving student performance.

Also passed by the General Assembly were significant, hotly contested measures that regulated smoking in government buildings, schools, and licensed health-care facilities and raised to 65 mph (105 km/h) the speed limit on rural interstate highways. Legislators also approved a proposed constitutional amendment that would repeal the state's ban on lotteries and pari-mutuel betting. The measure must pass a statewide referendum.

Budget. Faced with funding the A+ Program, the General Assembly approved a two-year, $15.84 billion budget that was approximately $700 million higher than the State Budget Committee recommended. Most of the increase, about $550 million, was for education. In addition to funds for elementary and secondary schools, the legislature increased bonding authority for university-building programs. It also authorized additional aid to state-supported universities in order to lower projected student fee increases but failed to provide enough money to improve faculty salaries. Also included in the budget were $20.5 million for Aid to Families with Dependent Children, $1.5 million for a home health-care system for the elderly and disabled, and $10.4 million for major salary increases over a two-year period for judges, the governor, lieutenant governor, attorney general, and superintendent of public instruction. The legislature also provided funds to continue the state's efforts to upgrade its mental hospitals and correctional institutions.

> **INDIANA • Information Highlights**
>
> **Area:** 36,185 sq mi (93 720 km²).
> **Population** (July 1, 1986): 5,504,000.
> **Chief Cities** (July 1, 1986 est.): Indianapolis, the capital, 719,820; Fort Wayne, 172,900; Gary, 136,790.
> **Government** (1987): *Chief Officers*—governor, Robert D. Orr (R); lt. gov., John M. Mutz (R). *General Assembly*—Senate, 50 members; House of Representatives, 100 members.
> **State Finances** (fiscal year 1986): *Revenue,* $8,485,000,000; *expenditure,* $7,548,000,000.
> **Personal Income** (1986): $72,294,000,000; per capita, $13,136.
> **Labor Force** (June 1987): *Civilian labor force,* 2,767,100; *unemployed,* 172,300 (6.2% of total force).
> **Education:** *Enrollment* (fall 1985)—public elementary schools, 654,061; public secondary, 312,045; colleges and universities, 250,567. *Public school expenditures* (1985–86), $2,670,000,000 ($2,973 per pupil).

To pay for the mammoth budget, lawmakers raised the individual state income tax rate from 3% to 3.4%, increased the corporate adjusted gross income tax rate from 3% to 3.4% and the corporate supplemental net income tax rate from 4% to 4.5%, and approved a school-funding formula estimated to increase property taxes by $44.2 million in 1988 and another $44 million in 1989.

Urban Elections. In November, Thomas V. Barnes captured 95% of the vote to be elected mayor of Gary. Barnes, a 50-year-old black lawyer, had defeated Richard G. Hatcher, the nation's longest-serving black mayor of a major city, in a May Democratic primary. Meanwhile in Indianapolis, William P. Hudnut III (R) was reelected to a fourth term. Earlier it was discovered that Hudnut had applied for other jobs, including the presidency of a university, and he had to promise to withdraw his applications if reelected.

Other. Beginning with Indiana University's victory in the NCAA men's basketball tournament in March, athletics highlighted 1987 in Indiana. Early in August, 4,700 athletes from all 50 states and 70 foreign countries participated in the International Summer Special Olympic Games in South Bend. Also in August, Indianapolis and surrounding counties hosted the 10th Pan American Games, the first to be held in the continental United States since 1959. (*See also* SPORTS.)

Despite a record-setting midsummer heat wave, earlier spring and summer rains prevented major agricultural losses in the state. An increasing number of foreign-owned factories and businesses established throughout the state brought social, educational, and economic benefits, as well as problems, to Indiana during 1987.

LORNA LUTES SYLVESTER
Indiana University, Bloomington

Hoosier Hysteria

Indiana High School Athletic Association, Inc.

Everyone in Indiana is a basketball fan. A standing-room-only crowd of 17,400 witnessed the finals of the 1987 high-school boys' tournament at Market Square Arena in Indianapolis.

The sport of basketball holds a special place in the life of Indiana, and 1987 was a special year for Indiana basketball. The movie *Hoosiers,* about a small-town high-school team in the early 1950s, earned two Academy Award nominations and was acclaimed by audiences and critics throughout the United States. John Feinstein's book *A Season on the Brink* stirred new controversy about Indiana University basketball coach Bob Knight and became a national best-seller. And in March, I.U.'s Hoosiers won the National Collegiate Athletic Association (NCAA) men's basketball championship for the fifth time. It was Hoosier hysteria at its highest.

Despite nationally prominent university teams and coaches, Indiana's obsession with basketball has always centered on high-school competition. Every March all but a handful of the state's nearly 400 high schools enter a team in the four-week statewide tournament. In 1987 some 940,000 fans attended the boys' tournament series; more than 190,000 followed the girls through their final game. And the tournament was only the finale. During the 1986–87 regular season, literally millions of Hoosiers attended high-school games in their hometowns. Eighteen of the 20 largest high-school gymnasiums in the country are located in Indiana. The field houses in Anderson and New Castle seat approximately 9,000 spectators. The Seymour High School gym holds more than six times the student enrollment of 1,346. Rural North Knox High School, with a student population of about 550, has a gym that seats about 4,000. These are examples, not exceptions. Boys' teams at some of the state's largest schools played before as many as 150,000 spectators during the 1986–87 season. Girls' games draw fewer fans, but attendance in 1986–87 was higher than in the preceding years.

Explaining Hoosier hysteria is as difficult as defining the word Hoosier itself. Basketball has always belonged peculiarly to Indiana (though admittedly the passion is nearly as intense in a few neighboring states). Even Dr. James Naismith, who invented the game in Massachusetts, reputedly said in 1939, "Basketball really had its origin in Indiana, which remains today the center of the sport." According to tradition, Indiana basketball began in Crawfordsville in 1893, two years after Naismith first laid out the rules. It was a winter sport, played indoors, and Indiana was a rural state. Basketball gave farm families something to do between fall harvesting and spring planting. For the state's isolated farmsteads and myriad small towns, the Friday night basketball game became the focus of community life.

Today Indiana is more than 64% urban, but no single metropolitan area—not even Indianapolis—dominates the state. Instead, a scattered urban population in dozens of middle-sized cities retains many traditional rural characteristics that influence the economic, political, and social development of the state. Included is a love of basketball, which remains a major cohesive force in Hoosier life.

LORNA LUTES SYLVESTER

INDONESIA

The year in Indonesia was marked by a worsening economic situation and general elections that returned President Suharto's ruling Golkar coalition to power.

Economy. Indonesia's economy, heavily dependent on oil-export earnings, suffered because of low oil prices. The 1987–88 budget dropped nearly 27%; many infrastructure development projects had to be postponed; and budget cuts in some areas, including higher education, exceeded 65%. While some economic reforms, including radically altering the system of import-export licensing, were contemplated, the magnitude of the fiscal problem was such that planners felt forced to rely even more heavily than before on foreign loans and aid. The World Bank predicted that by 1995 the country's indebtedness would reach $43.5 billion, or half the current gross national product. President Suharto and his economic advisers resisted suggestions that Indonesia negotiate with lenders for rescheduled payments.

The economic crisis was anticipated to have broad repercussions. In agriculture, for example, international advisers—who earlier had praised Indonesia's difficult achievement of self-sufficiency in rice production—now counseled that government fertilizer subsidies were too expensive, that overuse of pesticides was creating resistant pest strains, and that diversification of staple crops was necessary. The development of high-tech industries, for some time a priority of the Suharto government, for the first time came under criticism from within the close circle of presidential advisers. In February, President Suharto announced the privatization of various state enterprises.

Politics. Elections for the national legislature were held in April. Although the government had feared disorder due to Muslim critics and the failing economy, the elections were the quietest in memory. Official results indicated an overall voter turnout of 91.3%. No one doubted that Golkar would win handily. However, the appearance in the campaign of the memory of former President Sukarno, who died in 1970 after being deposed by Suharto in 1966, came as something of a surprise.

INDONESIA • Information Highlights

Official Name: Republic of Indonesia.
Location: Southeast Asia.
Area: 735,355 sq mi (1 904 570 km²).
Population (mid-1987 est.): 174,900,000.
Chief Cities (Dec. 31, 1983 est.): Jakarta, the capital, 7,347,800; Surabaya, 2,223,600; Medan, 1,805,500; Bandung, 1,566,700.
Government: *Head of state and government,* Suharto, president (took office for fourth five-year term March 1983). *Legislature* (unicameral)—People's Consultative Assembly.
Monetary Unit: Rupiah (1,647.0 rupiahs equal U.S.$1, Dec. 31, 1987).
Gross National Product (1986 U.S.$): $85,000,000,000.
Economic Index (1986): *Consumer Prices* (1980 = 100), all items, 168.2; food, 162.1.
Foreign Trade (1986 U.S.$): *Imports,* $10,718,000,000; *exports,* $14,805,000,000.

AP/Wide World

A Delta rocket carrying Indonesia's new communications satellite, Palapa B2P, lifts off from Cape Canaveral in March.

Sukarno and his vice-president, Mohamad Hatta, had been accorded hero status by the government, but the intent was not to rehabilitate the former president politically. Crowds gathered to see the late leader's picture displayed at rallies for the Indonesian Democratic Party (PDI) or to listen to the campaign speeches of his daughter, Megawati, who was elected to parliament. Most of the enthusiasm came from voters too young to have experienced the Sukarno era, and analysts generally put the support down to nostalgia or faddism rather than to the rise of a new political movement.

Foreign Affairs. Soviet Foreign Minister Eduard Shevardnadze visited Indonesia during a March tour of Asia and met with President Suharto and Foreign Minister Mochtar Kusumaatmadja. The continuing occupation of Cambodia by Soviet-backed Vietnam was reported to be a major issue of discussion. On March 12, Vietnam's Foreign Minister Nguyen Co Thach announced that his country would seek a political solution to the situation through discussions with China and the Association of Southeast Asian Nations (ASEAN). (Indonesia is the official mediator of the ASEAN nations regarding Cambodia.)

Four months later, Foreign Minister Kusumaatmadja traveled to Vietnam for further talks on the Cambodian issue. A communiqué issued at the end of the visit stated that an understanding had been reached for an "informal meeting" of the various Khmer factions.

INDUSTRIAL PRODUCTION

U.S. industrial production, reflecting sharply increased demand at home and abroad, tripled its rate of growth in 1987. Manufacturing industries were the main beneficiaries of a declining exchange rate of the U.S. dollar against other currencies, which made U.S. goods less expensive for customers abroad and foreign merchandise more expensive for buyers in the United States. Major U.S. trading partners, including Japan and West Germany, reflected the dollar's depreciation in slow production rates in the first half of 1987. Newly industrializing countries, especially those whose currencies are tied to the U.S. dollar, continued rapid growth.

Following gains of 1.1% in 1986 and 1.9% in 1985, U.S. industries posted an estimated 3.5% gain in 1987, as measured by the Federal Reserve Board's index of industrial production. It was the best performance since the 11.2% jump in 1984, following the recession. Much of the credit for the revival of production belongs to the decline of the dollar against such major currencies as the West German mark and the Japanese yen. The dollar has depreciated more than 50% against both since the dollar reached its high in late February 1985.

Manufacturers racked up a 4% increase for the year, as production began to speed up at midyear at rates topping previous-year levels by more than 5%. Computer manufacturers came back strongly, posting a 4.3% gain after suffering a 2.2% production loss in 1986. Steelmakers pushed production up 8%, close to 88 million tons in 1987, after a 7.5% drop in raw metal poured in 1986. The industry, after severely trimming capacity to about 110 million tons as compared with nearly 160 million tons in 1975, operated at about 80% of capacity at year-end. Aerospace industries increased output for the sixth year in a row. With shipments topping $100 billion, the industry delivered 355 large aircraft, compared with 310 in 1986. General aviation, producers of small craft, delivered only 1,160 machines, down from 1,495 in 1986 and a far cry from the 17,000 units delivered in both 1978 and 1979. Domestic automakers turned out a record number of trucks in 1987—3.8 million, but car production dropped to 7.1 million from 7.8 million in 1986.

U.S. consumer electronics producers increased shipments more than 4% in 1987, but they supplied only 40% of the domestic market. Household appliance manufacturers increased production by 6%, boosting shipments to a record $16.6 billion. The pharmaceutical industry, too, improved sharply—output rose 8% during 1987, in contrast to 1.6% in 1986. Electronic components production jumped 12% compared with 8% in 1986, despite a shakeout of manufacturers.

International Production. With more foreign firms establishing operations in the United States and with domestic demand increasing, U.S. production at year-end topped 1986 levels by 5.4%. Changes for other countries were increases of 23.8% for Australia, 0.6% for Belgium, 7.4% for Canada, and 1.9% for France, a decline of 1.1% for West Germany, a 0.9% increase for Italy, a 4.9% increase for Japan, a

U.S. sales of consumer electronics goods were expected to approach a record $30 billion for 1987. Domestic manufacturers increased shipments by more than 4%, but foreign producers still accounted for about 60% of the U.S. market.

AP/Wide World

2.2% drop for the Netherlands, a 4.4% gain for Spain, a 6.3% increase for Sweden, a 2.8% drop for Switzerland, and a 2.2% gain for the United Kingdom.

All signs pointed to continued growth in Asia's newly industrializing countries. In 1986, South Korea sprinted ahead with a 19% increase, as production was spurred by the success of its Hyundai motor car. South Korea has doubled manufacturing production since 1980. Taiwan pushed production up 16%, and Hong Kong posted a 15% gain. Singapore raised industrial production 5% in 1986.

Employment and Productivity. In contrast to the brisk 3.2% growth in 1987 total U.S. employment, jobs in goods-producing industries rose only 0.7%. Construction jobs increased 2.4%, but mining recorded a 5.5% loss. Manufacturing employment began to grow noticeably after mid-year, adding 300,000 jobs between June and year-end. That put growth for the year at 0.8%.

Jobs in durable goods manufacturing edged down by 0.2% to 11.2 million, as motor-vehicle producers, machinery manufacturers, instrument makers, electrical and electronic equipment manufacturers, and the primary metals group trimmed their payrolls. Among primary-metal industries, the big exception was steel, as jobs in blast furnaces and basic steel products posted a better than 30% gain over the 1986 average. Job gains in the 3% range were also recorded for furniture and fixtures, lumber and wood products. Miscellaneous manufacturing—toys, sporting and athletic goods, jewelry, pens, pencils, art supplies, and musical instruments—also posted a modest job gain.

Nondurable goods industries added 2.3% more workers to their payrolls, raising the annual average to 7.9 million. Continuing their long decline were tobacco manufacturers, whose employment dropped 3%, and the leather and leather products group with a 0.3% decline. Jobs dropped nearly 6% in the petroleum and coal products industry group.

The U.S. manufacturing sector has improved its productivity at a remarkable rate in the 1980s. Output per hour rose 3% in 1987, after posting a 3.7% gain in 1986. That followed a 5.1% increase in 1985 and a 5.8% jump in 1984. So far in the 1980s, productivity has grown at a 3.9% annual rate, compared with the 2.3% growth rate in the 1970s.

After reaching a record 21 million in 1979, factory jobs have dropped 9%, reflecting productivity gains as well as import competition. Manufacturing jobs as a proportion of total nonfarm employment has declined from 31% in 1960 to about 19% in 1987. However, manufacturing output as a proportion of total output, or gross national product, has held fairly steady, ranging from 20.3% in 1960 to 22% in 1987. Thus, manufacturing's role in the U.S. economy has not declined, if production is the criterion. It is a different story when it comes to employment. Given the emphasis on improving manufacturing processes, employment gains will not keep pace with output gains.

U.S. Industrial Production

	Percent Change 1985 to 1986	Index (1977=100) 1986 level	Percent Change 1986 to 1987
Total Production	1.1	125.1	3.5
Mining	−7.8	100.4	−0.7
Utilities	−2.5	108.5	0.9
Manufacturing	2.2	129.1	4.0
Consumer Goods	3.6	124.0	3.0
Business Equipment	−0.5	139.5	3.3
Defense and Space Equipment	6.2	182.0	3.8
Durable Manufactures	0.6	128.4	3.2
Lumber and products	8.4	124.1	4.4
Furniture and fixtures	4.3	143.8	5.9
Clay, glass and stone products	3.4	118.2	0.3
Primary metals	−6.7	75.1	7.3
Fabricated metal products	0.8	108.0	2.0
Nonelectrical machinery	0.8	145.0	4.7
Electrical machinery	−1.6	165.7	4.0
Transportation equipment	3.8	127.5	0.8
Nondurable Manufactures	4.4	130.1	5.1
Foods	3.1	134.4	2.8
Tobacco products	−3.0	97.1	4.8
Textile mill products	6.9	109.2	6.0
Apparel products	2.6	103.1	4.4
Paper and paper products	6.9	136.5	5.3
Printing and publishing	6.3	160.9	0
Chemicals and products	4.4	132.0	6.0
Petroleum and products	6.6	92.7	0.2
Rubber and plastic products	3.6	151.4	8.9
Leather and products	−10.2	61.4	−2.7

Source: Board of Governors of the Federal Reserve System

Industrial Production: International Overview

1980=100

	1981	1982	1983	1984	1985	1986	1987*
Industrial Countries	100	97	100	107	110	111	114
Australia	103	98	92	99	103	108	130
Japan	101	101	105	117	122	122	123
Austria	98	98	99	104	108	110	N.A.
Belgium	97	98	99	102	104	105	N.A.
Canada	101	90	95	104	108	108	111
Denmark	100	102	106	117	122	128	N.A.
Finland	103	104	107	111	116	116	123
France	98	98	99	100	101	102	104
Germany, West	98	95	95	98	103	105	107
Great Britain	97	98	102	103	108	110	113
Ireland	105	104	111	125	127	130	N.A.
Italy	98	95	92	95	97	99	102
Luxembourg	94	95	100	114	121	125	N.A.
Netherlands	98	94	97	101	105	106	110
Norway	99	99	108	117	111	126	132
Spain	99	98	101	102	104	107	110
Sweden	98	97	101	109	111	111	116
Switzerland	99	94	94	98	102	107	N.A.
United States	102	95	101	112	115	114	118

Source: International Monetary Fund
*Preliminary estimates N.A. not available

Mining. Mining output registered a 0.7% loss on the Federal Reserve Board's index of industrial production. The loss reflected a 4.6% drop in crude-petroleum production from a rate of 8.68 million barrels per day in 1986. Natural-gas production also declined in 1987, dropping 2% from the 16.04 trillion cubic feet extracted in 1986. But coal production reached a record 910 million tons, up 2.2% from 1986.

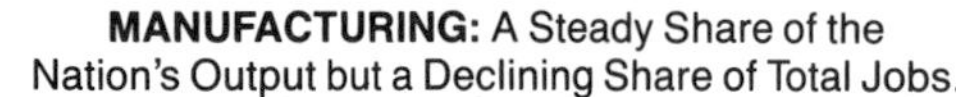

MANUFACTURING: A Steady Share of the Nation's Output but a Declining Share of Total Jobs.

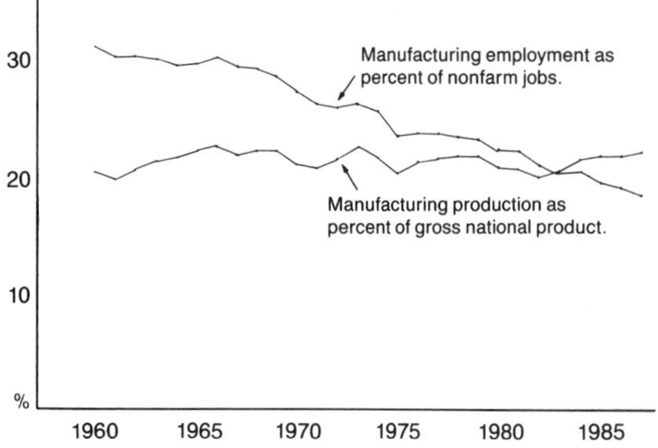

Nonfuel-mineral mining produces some 90 minerals, including copper, iron, gold, silver, and lead, and such nonmetallic minerals as stone, sand and gravel, clays, phosphatic rock, salt, soda ash, and boron. On a constant-dollar basis, the value of mineral production in 1987 was 3.7% higher than in 1986, but only 1.2% higher than in 1972. While jobs in nonmetallic-mineral mining dropped 1.6% in 1986 to 106,800, metal-mining jobs increased 2.9% to 42,300. That gain reflected a large increase in gold-mining production.

Copper mining also posted a strong increase in 1987, about 10%, as strong demand pushed prices to a seven-year high. About half of American producers left the business since 1982, as low cost producers to Zaire, Chile, and Zambia rendered U.S. firms uncompetitive. Surviving U.S. producers slashed production costs, not only by work-force reductions but also by introducing new technology. Known as "solvent extraction electrowinning," the new method cuts production costs by as much as one half compared with previous techniques. Thus, U.S. copper mines employed just about one third of the workers they employed in 1980 to produce 1.3 million tons of copper in 1987, 200,000 tons more than was produced in 1980.

Value of New Construction Put in Place in the United States (Billions of 1982 dollars)

	1986	1987*	Percent Change
Total new construction	347.8	348.5	0.2
Private construction	283.6	282.0	−0.2
Residential buildings	168.6	173.7	3.0
Nonresidential buildings	79.8	74.3	−6.9
Industrial	12.0	10.8	−10.0
Office	25.0	22.1	−11.6
Hotels and motels	6.5	6.2	−4.6
Other commercial	24.7	22.1	−7.7
Religious	2.4	2.3	−2.7
Educational	2.1	2.9	38.1
Hospital and institutional	4.7	4.9	4.3
Miscellaneous buildings[1]	2.4	2.4	12.5
Telephone and telegraph	7.7	7.7	0
All other private[2]	2.1	2.0	4.7
Public construction	64.3	66.5	3.4
Housing and redevelopment	1.3	1.3	0
Industrial	1.5	1.3	−10.4
Educational	7.4	7.3	−1.1
Hospital	1.8	1.9	8.6
Other public buildings[3]	8.7	9.6	10.3
Highways and streets	20.2	20.2	0
Military facilities	3.4	3.4	0
Conservation and development	4.4	5.0	13.6
Sewer systems	7.7	8.7	13.3
Water supply facilities	3.2	3.4	5.8
Miscellaneous public[4]	4.8	4.6	−4.8

Source: Bureau of the Census * preliminary
[1] Includes amusement and recreational buildings, bus and airline terminals, animal hospitals, and shelters, etc. [2] Includes privately owned streets and bridges, parking areas, sewer and water facilities, parks and playgrounds, golf courses, airfields, etc. [3] Includes general administrative buildings, prisons, police and fire stations, courthouses, civic centers, passenger terminals, postal facilities. [4] Includes open amusement and recreational facilities, power generating facilities, transit systems, airfields, open parking facilities, etc.

Business Investment. Spending on new plant and equipment gathered strength in the second half of 1987. After dropping 3.1% in the first quarter and gaining a meager 0.7% in the second, business investment increased 4.7% in the third and 6.3% in the fourth quarter of 1987. That brought the increase for the year to 2.3% in real terms, in contrast to a 2.6% drop in 1986. In current dollars, the 1987 business investment totaled $390.6 billion.

After declining in the first half, plant and equipment spending by manufacturing industries took on boom proportions in the third and fourth quarters. The steel industry increased investment by 38%, and textiles showed a 16% gain for the year. Manufacturing as a whole increased investment 3%, mining 0.6%; transportation reduced investment by 0.4%, public utilities 5.5%—mostly by electric utilities, but commercial enterprises increased investment by 4.2% in 1987.

Construction. Construction activity slowed considerably in 1987, edging up a mere 0.2% in constant-dollar terms. During the 1982–86 span, construction was put in place at annual growth rates that averaged 9%. That booming period followed four years of decline in 1979–82, when construction activity declined at an annual rate of 6%.

Residential construction, boosted by additions and improvements, increased 3% in 1987, measured in terms of 1982 dollars. The gain came despite a 10% drop in housing starts from 1986, when 1,805,400 new privately owned homes were started. While single-family starts held up fairly well, apartment building starts lagged 27% behind the 1986 total.

Business construction declined nearly 7%, measured in 1982 dollars. Changes in tax laws adversely affected office construction, which had enjoyed a tax-favored boom for several years. It dropped nearly 12% for the second year in a row. The public sector posted a better than 3% gain in 1987, as construction was stepped up to provide more sewer systems, water-supply facilities, and a wide range of public buildings such as prisons and civic centers.

AGO AMBRE
U.S. Department of Commerce

INSURANCE, LIABILITY

The U.S. liability insurance crisis abated in 1987. Coverage became more widely available than it had been in previous years, when entire categories of professionals, businesses, and local governments were faced with premium increases of as much as 1,000% or outright policy cancellations. Individuals, corporations, and public entities that provide high-risk services or products were forced to accept the rate hikes or "go bare," continuing to operate without liability insurance.

For some, the crisis of 1985–86 was not over yet. Affordable malpractice insurance was still lacking in many states, especially Florida, Illinois, Michigan, and New York, as well as the District of Columbia. The largest medical malpractice insurer in the Miami area, for example, raised premiums by nearly half during the summer, forcing many surgeons to stop operating and dozens of area hospitals to shut down their emergency rooms. In addition, some professionals, such as psychiatrists and accountants, have only recently become frequent targets of malpractice actions, making it harder for these groups to obtain liability coverage at any price.

But with few exceptions, liability insurance in 1987 was easier to come by and less expensive than it was in 1986. For one thing, the industry itself was emerging from its most recent cyclical downturn. The nation's property and casualty insurers turned their 1985 loss of $5.6 billion into a profit of an equal amount in 1986. The higher profits enabled the industry to lower premiums. Another factor was a new federal law, the Risk Retention Amendments, passed by the U.S. Congress in October 1986, to provide alternatives to commercial liability insurance.

The new legislation allows professionals and others to organize in order to buy coverage on a group basis or to pool funds for the purpose of self-insurance. As of late 1987, such "risk retention groups" had been set up in at least 26 states. One example was Corporate Officers & Directors Assurance, an association of about 50 companies set up to provide liability coverage for the members of their boards of directors, a category of professionals that had found commercial insurance increasingly hard to obtain because of a large product-liability suits brought against their companies in recent years.

Consumers have welcomed the change, which not only has made insurance more widely available but also has provided coverage at cut rates, in some instances half those commercial insurers charge for comparable policies. However, the law has run into trouble. The 50 states, not the federal government, are responsible for regulating the insurance industry, and many state-insurance commissioners have objected to risk retention groups, saying they may not be financially sound enough to cover catastrophic losses that might arise from steep damage claims.

In any case, the Risk Retention Amendments address only one aspect of the recent insurance crisis. Other reform efforts at the federal level have floundered amid the continuing controversy over who is to blame for the scarcity of affordable liability coverage. Consumer groups and members of the legal profession maintain that the insurers create their own "crises" by engaging in rate wars to drive out competitors. As rates plummet, claims begin to exceed premiums, and insurers are forced to raise their rates again, creating a cyclical pattern of boom and bust that ultimately hurts consumers.

The insurance industry defends its actions and blames the drastic premium hikes and policy cancellations of 1985–86 on what it calls an overly litigious society and a legal system that allows citizens, and their lawyers, to extract exorbitant awards in liability suits. Insurers are especially critical of the tendency of juries across the United States to grant increasingly high awards not only to compensate plaintiffs for their actual economic losses, but also for the "pain and suffering" they have sustained.

Further congressional reform initiatives remain hostage to these two competing claims. As a result, the greatest strides toward resolving the insurance problem continue to be made at the state level, where legislators have tended to support the insurer's position. Their most common solution has been to modify the system of tort law, which allows citizens to sue professionals for malpractice or manufacturers for selling dangerous or lethal products. As of Oct. 31, 1987, according to the American Tort Reform Association, all but 12 states and the District of Columbia had passed some form of tort-reform legislation. Although the provisions vary from state to state, most of these laws limit the amount of money plaintiffs can receive for noneconomic damages such as "pain and suffering" in product-liability and malpractice suits.

It remains uncertain whether the recent spate of reform efforts will suffice to break the insurance-crisis cycle. Although the industry reported substantial profits in 1986, the crisis has emboldened frustrated policyholders to seek alternative sources of liability coverage. Barely a year after they were introduced, self-insurance associations already represented about one third of the liability market. As commercial insurers are forced to compete for the rest of the market, they may set off another price war that could once again leave consumers holding the bag.

MARY H. COOPER
"Editorial Research Reports"

INTERIOR DESIGN

Interior design gained ground in 1987 in its progress from being an optional luxury to becoming a necessity in American homes and offices. This was especially true on the commercial front—offices, stores, and institutions. *Interior Design* magazine, for example, estimated that firms specializing in commercial design have enjoyed an annual growth rate of about 24% since the late 1970s. In the United States, total annual expenditures for design services and furnishings ordered through designers now are estimated at $37.5 billion, about $30 billion in the commercial field and $7.5 billion for residential furnishings and design services.

Decorating Services. During 1987, the general public gained greater access to decorating services through several avenues, including expansion of referral services which match clients with designers and the release of a number of videos on decorating subjects. The decorator referral services, which now are found in many large cities, are free or available at low cost to consumers. Designers pay a fee to be listed and have examples of their work kept on file. What is believed to be the first video by an interior designer showing how to redecorate an existing home was released in 1987. It joined a growing number of videocassette tapes on such subjects as installing wall coverings, doing other home projects, and landscaping.

The country-style kitchen, below, *is featured on a 1987 how-to-decorate video. The country look continued to be very popular with the American public.*

Renovation and Traditional Style. Whether it is residences or commercial buildings, the value of renovations now is outpacing new construction which in the 1970s accounted for the lion's share of design projects. This emphasis on restoring older buildings may help account for the continued appeal of traditional decorating styles. The increasing popularity of traditional decorating styles is shown in a growing number of furniture, wall-coverings, fabric, and lamp reproductions; in continued sales records for auction houses specializing in decorative arts; and in the rooms featured in the pages of decorating and shelter magazines.

Nineteenth-century formal styles dominated at a number of decorator show houses during 1987. In addition, almost all the entries in the well-known S.M. Hexter Co. competition for designers featured traditional rooms. The winning residential entry was a living room in a 19th century restored town house that featured such details as original wood floors covered with an antique Aubusson rug, extensive neoclassical architectural detailing, and walls painted with a finish simulating plaster. On the other hand, as is also typical in current traditional rooms, ample electronic equipment and the latest in lighting also were installed unobtrusively.

Today's return to tradition is not a search for complete authenticity, as had been true in earlier revivals. Instead, current design themes from the past merely soften and make more comfortable interiors which also possess the latest innovations in appliances, home electronics, efficient heating and cooling, and lighting.

Reasons advanced for the continued appeal of tradition center around the home as a place of respite. June Felber, vice-president of the Hexter Co., pointed out that most public spaces and offices are furnished in contemporary functional styles. "We spend so many hours in these places that we feel comfortable escaping to another era at home," the decorator declared.

Competency. During 1987, U.S. interior designers continued their national drive to limit use of the term interior designer to those who established minimum competency through a degree from an interior-design program, experience, and/or examination. In 1987, Washington, DC, became the fourth jurisdiction to adopt licensing or title registration for interior designers. (Alabama, Connecticut, and Louisiana are the others.) Similar legislation was under consideration in approximately seven other states. Opposition to such licensing has arisen, and in some states designers now are fighting encroaching legislation introduced by architects.

BARBARA MAYER, *The Associated Press*

INTERNATIONAL TRADE AND FINANCE

Just as 1929 cannot escape being thought of as the year of a major stock-market crash on "Black Tuesday," October 29, so 1987 probably will be long remembered for "Black Monday," October 19. Not only did stock prices tumble dramatically on Wall Street, but that day or the next they fell like stones in most of the major security markets of the world. The debacle had sweeping consequences both in U.S. economic affairs and in international finance and trade.

Stock Market Crash. The Black Monday collapse was huge by any standard. The Dow Jones industrial average plunged a record 508.32 points, or 22.6%, to 1,738.74; that compared with a drop of "only" 12.8% on Oct. 29, 1929. If the August peak for the U.S. market is taken as a base, stocks dropped nearly 28% altogether. In other countries the West German stock market was down 41.2% from its peak in April 1986 to mid-November 1987. The French stock market peaked in late March 1987 and dropped 37.8% by November 20. The British stock market reached its highest level in mid-July 1987 and was down 35.6% by mid-November. Japan's Nikkei index peaked during the week of October 16 and stood only 15% lower in mid-November.

In the immediate aftermath of the Wall Street crash, U.S. economists quickly marked down their forecasts of the nation's economic growth by one or two percent. But as 1987 rolled on, they were beginning to wonder if the growth slump anticipated as a result of a loss in wealth in the stock market of some $1 trillion would materialize. The nation's economic recovery, which enjoyed a fifth birthday in November, advanced at a handsome pace. Christmas shoppers seemed unfazed by any loss of wealth. Business orders for plant and equipment were picking up, as were sales abroad. With a weakened dollar, U.S. exports were starting to boom.

By early autumn the economic upturn already had become the longest peacetime expansion in modern times. Inflation remained moderate, about 4%. Most economists did not expect the market bust to kick off a repeat of the Great Depression that followed the 1929 market collapse. They presumed the policy mistakes of the 1930s would not be repeated. The 1929 crash was followed by widespread bank failures, a shrinkage in the nation's money supply, and the passage of the highly protectionist Smoot-Hawley bill. Taking to heart the lessons of the Great Depression, the Federal Reserve System (the Fed) in 1987 was ready to defend the commercial banks from any loss in depositor confidence. The day after the crash, the new Fed chairman, Alan Greenspan (*see* BIOGRAPHY), issued a one-sentence statement affirming the central bank's "readiness to serve as a source of liquidity to support the economic and financial system." Indeed, in the post-crash days the Fed injected a huge slug of reserves into the banking system to ward off any danger of recession or worse. Nonetheless, as the year wore on, economists were still worrying about Fed monetary policy, wondering if it remained too tight. Some argued that the Fed's relatively firm credit policy in the months prior to October was one cause of the market bust.

Market observers had numerous explanations for the speed of the 1987 crash. In a post-crash survey, Yale University Professor J. Shiller asked individual and institutional investors about what factors influenced the panic on Wall Street—the falling dollar, U.S. military actions in the Persian Gulf, an overvalued market, a recent rise in the prime rate commercial banks charge their best customers, the federal deficit, the balance of trade, the producer price index, a rush of profit takers, portfolio insurance, Wall Street rumors, investor hunches, investor anxiety, a contagion of fear. From the results, economist Shiller concluded that though portfolio insurance was probably a factor in the crash, "The primary cause appears to have been that already nervous investors were trying desperately to guess when other investors were going to sell." In other words it was old-fashioned investor panic—fear feeding fear in an overvalued market.

The market "meltdown" had a number of consequences that some economists regarded as positive. For one thing short-term interest rates, which had been rising, dropped sharply as investors sought safety from stocks by shifting their money into U.S. Treasury bills or other "near money" investments. With longer-term interest rates also falling, economists hoped consumers would be less reluctant to take on mortgages to buy new homes or add to their other debts.

Another result was a sharp decline in the value of the dollar on foreign exchange markets. This started before the crash and accelerated after the fall in U.S. interest rates. By the end of November, the dollar's average value on a trade-weighted basis was down 12.4% from 12 months earlier, according to a measure compiled by the Federal Reserve Bank of Atlanta that takes account of 18 major currencies. It was down 31.2% from its peak on Feb. 25, 1985. This drop put the dollar back to its average value in late 1980.

The greenback was further damaged in December when the U.S. Department of Commerce announced a record trade deficit for October of $17.6 billion. The Japanese yen moved up on foreign exchange markets to 130.30 per dollar, a record low for the dollar since the late 1940s. The West German mark and British pound also strengthened. Despite the earlier weakness of the dollar, economists were anticipating a record U.S. trade deficit of nearly $175 billion for 1987, up from $170 billion in 1986. The dollar's earlier weakness had already boosted the volume of U.S. exports substantially, but not enough to offset more costly imports of oil, cars, and other products.

The stock-market crash, many analysts figured, also would weaken the possibility that a tough, protectionist omnibus trade bill which Congress had been considering in 1987 would actually be passed in 1988. Many Congressmen were afraid of being tagged with the Smoot-Hawley label. On the other side the delay in reducing the trade deficit beyond what many economists anticipated was promoting feelings that Congress must take concrete action.

As for the other major deficit, the U.S. budget deficit, the stock-market crash spurred President Reagan to announce that he would negotiate with congressional leaders on a deficit-reduction program, and even consider going along with a boost in taxes, something he had up to then ruled out. After four weeks of arduous negotiations, a deal was worked out with congressional leaders on November 20. It called for a total of $30.2 billion in deficit reduction, which included $9 billion in new taxes, $12.8 billion in budget cuts, and $5 billion in asset sales. Another $45.85 billion in deficit reductions was promised for fiscal 1989. Congress then started considering the 1988 proposals. Without their implementation, automatic spending cuts of $23 billion would have taken place under provisions of the Gramm-Rudman-Hollings balanced-budget legislation passed in 1985. Certainly congressional action was seen as necessary to keep the budget deficit on a downward path. In any case, as a proportion of national output, the U.S. deficit was already at lower levels than that of such countries as France, Italy, and Japan, and not much above even that of West Germany.

International Economic Coordination. Another product of the market crash was a greater interest in international economic coordination to prevent the dollar from dropping further. As the year drew to a close, there was much talk of another meeting of the Group of Seven nations—the United States, Japan, West Germany, Great Britain, France, Italy, and Canada. One of the earlier significant economic events in 1987 had been an accord on exchange-rate stability among the Group of Seven. The so-called Louvre accord, signed on February 22 in Paris, set exchange-rate bands for the dollar against major currencies. Although the exact ranges were never disclosed, the agreement was generally credited for keeping the dollar between 1.75 and 1.90 West German marks and between 140 and 155 Japanese yen for most of the year until after the stock-market crash. In September 1985, the Group of Five (the same nations minus Canada and Italy) had agreed at a meeting in New York to encourage a further decline in the dollar. At the Paris meeting, the Group of Seven wanted to stabilize the dollar.

However, international economic coordination did not always prove effective in controlling exchange rates. It was only a few weeks before the crash, during the gathering of finance ministers and central bankers in Washington for the joint annual meeting of the World Bank and the International Monetary Fund (IMF), that the Group of Seven recommitted themselves to cooperating closely "to foster the stability of exchange rates around current levels." But when the U.S. government had to choose between supporting the dollar with high interest rates and pumping up the money supply to make sure the stock-market crash did not turn into a serious economic slump, the latter domestic concern took precedence over international policy coordination.

Most governments similarly followed domestic political priorities. West Germany most of the year resisted U.S. pressures to step up domestic economic growth and thus encourage more imports and discourage exports. The government feared that expansionary measures might prompt more inflation—a political taboo in Germany, where many older people have experienced hyperinflation and drastic currency reform. However, a few weeks after the crash and worried about the possibility of a world slump, Bonn moved to lower domestic interest rates. Then in December the cabinet decided to pass a "stimulation program" under which the government-controlled bank for reconstruction was to offer 21 billion marks (about $13.75 billion) in additional credit over the next three years to state and local governments and to smaller business firms. Many West German experts regarded the move as more symbolic than economically important.

Japan was under less pressure from Washington to boost its economy because it had announced a $43 billion stimulus package just before the annual summit of major industrialized democracies, held in Venice, Italy, June 8–10. Despite the usual media splash, the Group of Seven leaders, including President Reagan, were unable to agree on any new actions to stabilize the dollar, fend off world recession, or curb the huge U.S. budget and trade deficits. The best they could do was adopt vague language in a nine-page communiqué calling on their finance ministers to propose "additional appropriate policy measures" in the future if "world economic growth is insufficient."

Debt. Because of its huge balance-of-payments deficit, the United States was piling up a greater and greater international debt. One often-cited estimate was that foreign assets in the United States exceeded U.S. assets abroad by $414 billion at the end of 1987. According to

AP/Wide World

In Acapulco, Mexico, in November, eight Latin American leaders agreed that the repayment of the region's large foreign debt "should be adjusted to the capacity of each country to pay" and that there should be "limits on interest rates."

some economists, however, that number is an exaggeration. For one thing, it measures the value of direct investment in plant and equipment by looking at book value—that is, the cost of the original investment. Because much U.S. investment was made decades ago, they argued, it should be worth far more today; foreign investment in the United States, on the other hand, flourished in more recent years, and its current value would have risen less. Nevertheless, economists noted that the United States has become the world's largest debtor nation and will have to service that debt in the years ahead. This could slow any growth in U.S. living standards.

A considerably smaller debtor, Brazil, caused some nervousness when in February it suspended interest payments on its $68 billion in foreign bank debt. Not until early November was a deal reached with commercial creditor banks whereby Brazil would get some new money and resume interest payments at the start of 1988.

During the World Bank-IMF meeting, U.S. Treasury Secretary James A. Baker III tried to lessen tensions over developing-country debts by proposing various measures to make it easier for them to meet debt-service payments. He called on the IMF to be more lenient in its demands for economic reforms by developing countries, urging it to take into consideration progress in such areas as market-oriented pricing, privatization and reform of government-owned enterprises, and trade and investment liberalization when considering a nation's program performance. He suggested the creation of a new External Financing Facility within the IMF that would take account of "unforeseen developments" affecting the ability of nations to carry out "standby programs" aimed at improving their international-payments positions. But his suggestions left intact the present strategy of handling the debtor crisis by dealing with each nation on a case-by-case basis.

Unsatisfied with their treatment, eight Latin American debtor nations—Argentina, Brazil, Colombia, Mexico, Panama, Peru, Uruguay, and Venezuela—met in Acapulco, Mexico, for four days in late November. The leaders agreed to seek a joint approach in negotiations with foreign banks and to push for lower interest payments on their collective $350 billion in debts. They stopped short of forming a debtors' cartel and sidestepped other radical proposals. But they did try to link their debt payments to access for their exports in the industrialized world. They also spoke of creating "mechanisms" that would enable them to benefit from the discounts of 40% and more offered on their loans when commercial bankers sell these to investors such as multinational companies.

Free Trade Pact. Another highlight of 1987 was the initialing by Canada and the United States of a free-trade agreement on October 3. After further tough negotiations, the two sides approved a legal text on December 7. If ratified by the Canadian Parliament and U.S. Congress in 1988, the deal—calling for the elimination of most tariffs between the two nations within a maximum of ten years—will begin on Jan. 1, 1989. The agreement also will remove many other barriers to trade and commerce. Canada and the United States were already the world's largest trading partners. (*See* page 165.)

See also STOCKS AND BONDS; UNITED STATES—The Economy; and articles on other individual countries.

DAVID R. FRANCIS
"The Christian Science Monitor"

IOWA

The Iowa General Assembly increased appropriations for public education by more than $92 million. The bill increased the beginning teacher's minimum salary to $18,000 and granted an increase to the average annual salary of public schoolteachers of about $3,000. In addition, tuition tax deductions of up to $1,000 were given to Iowans who itemize their taxes.

A total appropriation package of nearly $2.42 billion was passed. Gov. Terry Branstad (R) claimed it was about $25.6 million higher than his recommended budget. Other newly enacted legislation established a 65 mile per hour (105 km/hr) speed limit on the rural interstate highways; approved a groundwater protection plan that would involve $64.5 million over five years for education, research, and regulation; and provided for a laser research center at the University of Iowa and a molecular biology building at Iowa State, both a part of a $65.5 million building program at the Board of Regents institutions. The legislature also required women covered by the state indigent care program in a nine county area around Iowa City to have their babies delivered at the University of Iowa Hospitals; indigent women in the other 90 counties could have their babies with state support in local hospitals.

Also during the regular session the legislature "coupled" the state income taxes for corporations to the new federal tax but did not "couple" the individual personal income tax with the federal formula. No change was made in the rates at which personal income taxes would be collected. The legislation, however, did retain federal-income-tax deductibility on personal income taxes. In a three-day special session called by the governor after the regular session adjourned in May, the Iowa House and Senate could not agree to a revision of the state personal income tax formula. A second special session reduced personal income tax rates but retained federal tax deductibility.

The salary of the governor was increased from $64,000 to $70,000, effective in July 1987. The measure also increased salaries of the members of the Iowa General Assembly by $2,000 to $16,000, effective in January 1989. The increase, the first since 1985, was a raise of 29%. All state employees received salary increases with the largest going to the faculties of the Board of Regents institutions at Northern Iowa, the University of Iowa, and Iowa State University.

Agriculture and the Economy. In 1987 the number of Iowa farms was reduced by nearly 2,000 to a total of 107,000. The average farm size increased to 313 acres (127 ha). For the first time in six years the value of farmland increased. Iowa's corn crop averaged 133 bushels per acre, ranking the state first in total yield. Soybeans averaged 41 bushels per acre ranking the state second in total production to Illinois. Both the corn and soybean harvests were some 13% lower than in 1986 because of a major reduction in acres planted.

Iowa's unemployment rate in June 1987 was 4.5%, 1.5 percentage points lower than the national average. The Iowa City metropolitan area had the lowest unemployment rate of any U.S. metro area.

Health News. Iowa optometrists will be allowed to treat patients with drugs for glaucoma. Formerly only ophthalmologists were permitted to prescribe drugs for glaucoma.

Cigarette smoking is restricted in Iowa's public establishments, including offices, hospitals, schools, museums, and stores. All such places must designate smoking and nonsmoking areas. Persons not complying may be fined $10.

RUSSELL M. ROSS, *University of Iowa*

IOWA • Information Highlights

Area: 56,275 sq mi (145 753 km²).
Population (July 1, 1986): 2,851,000.
Chief Cities (July 1, 1986 est.): Des Moines, the capital, 192,060; Cedar Rapids, 108,390; Davenport (July 1, 1984 est.), 102,129.
Government (1987): *Chief Officers*—governor, Terry E. Branstad (R); lt. gov., Jo Ann Zimmerman (D). *General Assembly*—Senate, 50 members; House of Representatives, 100 members.
State Finances (fiscal year 1986): *Revenue,* $5,314,000,000; *expenditure,* $4,852,000,000.
Personal Income (1986): $38,053,000,000; per capita, $13,348.
Labor Force (June 1987): *Civilian labor force,* 1,475,400; *unemployed,* 66,100 (4.5% of total force).
Education: *Enrollment* (fall 1985))—public elementary schools, 324,332; public secondary, 161,000; colleges and universities, 152,897. *Public school expenditures* (1985–86), $1,627,000,000 ($3,568 per pupil).

IRAN

For the Islamic Republic of Iran, 1987 was a turbulent year on several fronts. Domestically, a long-simmering power struggle came out in the open following the November 1986 revelation of arms shipments from the United States. (*See* feature article, page 26.) On the foreign front, the war with Iraq entered its eighth year in September, the "tanker war" in the Persian Gulf reached new levels of tension, and relations with foreign governments in general reached an unprecedented low.

Domestic Affairs. A move within Iran's 270-seat Majlis, or parliament, to conduct an investigation into the arms-for-hostages swap was squelched only after personal intervention by Ayatollah Ruhollah Khomeini. Divisions among the ruling mullahs, however, did lead to two major developments. The dominant Islamic Republic Party was abolished in June, in part to prevent a formal split. In a rare comment on domestic politics, Ayatollah Khomeini warned at the time that "sowing discord is one of the greatest sins." The move was important because of scheduled parliamentary elections in 1988; the party's dissolution left the candidate nomination process more susceptible to manipulation by rival factions at a crucial juncture. Many Iranians believe the aged and ailing Khomeini will die during the next four-year Majlis session; whichever faction dominates the next parliament is thus expected to set the tone of the post-Khomeini era.

Then in August, Mehdi Hashemi, a leading militant who first leaked the story of the May 1986 visit to Tehran by former U.S. National Security Adviser Robert MacFarlane and others, was tried, convicted, and sentenced to death for murder, sabotage, and treason. Hashemi headed the World Organization of Islamic Liberation Movements, an umbrella for militant Islamic groups throughout the Middle East and a vehicle for exporting Iran's brand of religious zealotry. Most importantly, however, Hashemi was a protégé of Ayatollah Ali Montazeri, Khomeini's designated heir, and his execution in September was widely interpreted as a signal that Montazeri's personal influence had waned.

The power struggle centers not only on rival personalities vying for supremacy after Khomeini's death. Also at stake is the future course of the revolution. At one end of the political spectrum are those who want to settle down to the business of creating the world's only modern theocracy and implementing reforms. Iraq's invasion of Iran in 1980 came just 20 months after the 1979 revolution, and most major reforms—particularly economic—were put on hold while resources were diverted to the war. This faction, referred to as the "moderates" or "normalizers," favors ending the war as soon as possible and normalizing Iran's place in the world, in part for economic reasons. In terms of tactics, the moderates advocate making Iran the model Islamic society which other communities will voluntarily want to imitate. Speaker of Parliament Ali Akbar Hashemi Rafsanjani, who was implicated in the arms-for-hostage swap, has been widely viewed as the leading "normalizer."

At the other end of the spectrum are those who advocate perpetual revolution, not only in the name of Iran or the Muslim world but also in the name of the Third World's "oppressed." They hope to create a new power bloc capable of defying both superpowers and challenging conventional capitalist and socialist ideologies, in effect creating a "new way" for Third World countries to conduct domestic and foreign affairs. Many on this side are prepared to condone violence to promote their aggressive ends. Montazeri is considered a militant, although Interior Minister Ali Akbar Mohtashimi

AP/Wide World

Speaker of Parliament Ali Akbar Hashemi Rafsanjani (right), *a moderate, is reportedly the second most powerful figure in Iran, after Ayatollah Ruhollah Khomeini* (left).

emerged in 1987 as another powerful leader of this camp.

Tehran's theocrats do not, however, fall neatly into categories. Some who are militant on foreign policy and the war are, for example, conservative on economic issues. The power struggle also is riddled with a labyrinth of subplots. Because of the fallout from dealings with the "Great Satan" (the United States), the militant factions appeared to be in ascendancy throughout most of 1987.

War Fronts. Militarily, the seventh year of the Gulf war witnessed a series of Iranian offensives code-named "Karbala" (after a Shiite holy city in Iraq) against Iraq's strategic southern port city of Basra. Iran boasted that this would be "the final offensive," but only marginal gains were made during the spring in breaking through Iraq's tough defense barrier. The offensives did, however, bring Iran within artillery range of Basra, an important psychological achievement, albeit at a staggering cost in human life.

The casualty toll, estimated to have surpassed 750,000 since the beginning of the war in 1980, and the recognition that mass offensives would not easily or quickly defeat Iraq appeared at least partially responsible for a shift in Iran's demands for an end to the conflict. Iran's two long-standing preconditions had been reparation for material losses suffered over the previous seven years and the ouster of Iraqi President Saddam Hussein's Baathist regime. But in response to a United Nations peace effort launched during the summer, Tehran said it would be satisfied if a commission just named President Hussein the "aggressor" in the conflict. Repeated efforts by UN Secretary-General Javier Pérez de Cuéllar to bridge the gap were, however, unsuccessful in 1987.

The shift did not represent a change in Iran's commitment to carry through with the war until it wins some tangible achievement, in particular security along a border that has been the scene of sporadic conflicts for centuries. Indeed, Iran's arms-production capability was considerably improved in 1987, and the paramilitary Revolutionary Guards established their own small naval and air force to supplement the conventional military's capabilities. Iran's Supreme Defense Council also managed to replenish and upgrade its arsenal, most notably with Chinese-made Silkworm missiles, despite the renewed U.S. campaign to block arms sales to Tehran from China, North Korea, the Eastern European bloc, and Western Europe. In response to an escalation of Iraq's air and sea attacks, Iran in November began to mobilize for what its leadership pledged would be a new offensive.

Tension in the Persian Gulf reached a new high with the U.S. decision to reflag 11 Kuwaiti oil tankers, which began in July, and to deploy more than two dozen warships to protect freedom of navigation. The move followed a Soviet decision to lease three small tankers to Kuwait, whose ships had been frequent targets in the Gulf's strategic sea-lanes. Iran frequently hit ships belonging to Kuwait, a financial and political supporter of Iraq, in retaliation for Iraqi attacks on tankers carrying Iranian oil. The U.S. decision was also an attempt to restore credibility in moderate Arab eyes after the Iran-contra revelations.

Iran, which interpreted the move as a de facto U.S. alliance with Iraq, charged that it was being unfairly blamed for the tanker war and unfairly threatened by the United States. Iran's constant verbal intimidation and military harassment almost led to a full-scale showdown, with three direct confrontations during September and October. An Iranian ship seen laying mines was attacked and seized by U.S. forces; Revolutionary Guard patrol boats exchanged fire with U.S. helicopter gunships; and, after an Iranian missile hit a reflagged tanker in Kuwaiti waters, U.S. warships destroyed an Iranian offshore oil platform that had become a military staging post. As a result of what the Reagan administration called "unprovoked attacks" and Iran's refusal to accept UN Resolution 598 on a cessation of hostilities, the White House in late October imposed an embargo on all imports from Iran and on all U.S. sales of equipment that could be "militarily useful" to Iran.

Iran's relations with the outside world generally hit their lowest point since the 1979–81 U.S. hostage trauma, ending a two-year period during which Tehran had experimented with a cautious open-door policy. Relations with Saudi Arabia, which had warmed after a 1985 summit, deteriorated as the result of a clash between Iranian pilgrims and Saudi security forces during the annual *Hajj,* the Muslim pilgrimage to Mecca. Saudi attempts to block an Iranian demonstration on July 31 led to riots in which more than 400 people were killed. Both sides accused the other of firing weapons, which is forbidden near Islam's holiest site. The Mecca riots led to scathing threats from Tehran against the Saudi monarchy, while Saudi Arabia attempted to mobilize the 22-member Arab League to break relations with the Islamic Republic.

In separate confrontations, Iranian diplomats in Tunisia and Egypt were expelled for allegedly inciting local Islamic fundamentalist groups. Kuwait followed suit after three Iranian missile attacks on Kuwaiti property. Relations with France and Great Britain also deteriorated over incidents involving Iranian diplomats. Paris, which had launched a rapprochement effort with Tehran in 1986 to help free French hostages held by pro-Iranian groups in Lebanon, ended up breaking relations in July, although the crisis was partially defused after two French hostages were freed in Lebanon in November. Great Britain deported several Iranian envoys, leading Iran to follow suit.

The only major improvement in foreign relations occurred with the Soviet Union. A series of high-level meetings led to economic agreements on railway and pipeline links. But a warmer long-term alliance was doubtful because of Soviet military aid to Iraq and its eight-year occupation of Afghanistan.

By the end of 1987, revolutionary Iran, which just one year earlier had appeared to be settling down, once again was isolated and defiantly threatening to take on any nation that challenged the Islamic Republic.

See also MIDDLE EAST.

ROBIN WRIGHT
Carnegie Endowment for International Peace

IRAN • Information Highlights

Official Name: Islamic Republic of Iran.
Location: Southwest Asia.
Area: 636,293 sq mi (1 648 000 km^2).
Population (mid-1987 est.): 50,400,000.
Chief City (1986 census): Tehran, the capital, 5,770,000.
Government: *Supreme faqih,* Ayatollah Ruhollah Khomeini, *Head of state,* Ali Khamenei, president (took office Oct. 1981). *Head of government,* Mir Hosein Musavi-Khamenei, prime minister (took office Oct. 1981). *Legislature* (unicameral)—Islamic Consultative Assembly.
Monetary Unit: Rial (71.654 rials equal U.S.$1, August 1987).
Gross National Product (1986 U.S.$): $82,400,-000,000.
Economic Index (April 1986): *Consumer Prices* (1980 = 100), all items, 227.2; food, 242.9.
Foreign Trade (1986 est. U.S.$): *Imports,* (est.) $10,000,000,000; *exports,* $7,800,000,000.

IRAQ

Iraq in 1987 displayed a growing capacity to survive its continuing war with Iran, proving itself decidedly resilient in political and economic, no less than military, terms.

The year began with Iraq under major stress. The revelation of secret U.S. arms sales to Iran (*see* feature article, page 26) shattered an embryonic U.S.-Iraqi trust and subverted U.S. policy toward the Persian Gulf war. In January, Iranian forces came within a few miles of the southern Iraqi city of Basra, using artillery barrages to expel large segments of the population before being pushed back in March. Then in May, Iraq's inadvertent attack on the U.S. Navy frigate *Stark,* which killed 37 American sailors, placed added strain on relations between Baghdad and Washington—even though the Iraqi regime apologized for the "unintentional" incident.

Domestic Impact. Iran's offensive initially posted an acute political challenge to Iraq, though it ended in disaster for Iran. As with earlier offensives, there were no signs of a political collapse or significant opposition to the Iraqi government. Instead, observers reported a strong national consensus in support of President Saddam Hussein and the view that the conflict is a legitimate war of defense, waged not only on behalf of Iraq, but the rest of the Arab world as well.

Domestic support for President Hussein during this period confirmed the wartime growth of national identity in Iraq. Most significant has been the stability of its Shia community, which comprises 55–60% of the population. Because they belong to the same Islamic sect as nearly all Iranians, Iraq's Shiites had been viewed as vulnerable to the revolutionary ideology of Iran's religious leader, the Ayatollah Ruhollah Khomeini. But Iraq's Shia community appeared to put national feelings before religious ones, and the resulting consolidation of Iraq's polity constitutes perhaps the most far-reaching political consequence of the war.

Nevertheless, the regime's record of stability was not perfect. In September, unknown dissidents (believed to be Iran-backed Shiite extremists) staged an attack on a government rally in the town of Baquba, 30 mi (48 km) northeast of Baghdad. Foreign diplomats reviewing the parade reported upward of 100 casualties in the opposition's most daring raid in five years, a clear attempt to tarnish President Hussein's image of control. Iran also increased its cooperation with Kurdish insurrectionists, mounting attacks against government installations in oil-rich northern Iraq. This provoked the Baghdad regime to raze scores of Kurdish villages and relocate thousands of inhabitants to other areas of Iraq. The campaign strained the government's relations with the Kurdish minority—as did a bombing raid by Turkish warplanes in March—but the overall situation did not pose a direct or serious threat to Iraq's national security.

Economy. Economic improvisation has been a centerpiece of Iraq's survival strategy, and 1987 was no exception. In September the government let a contract with several foreign companies complete a large oil-export system across Saudi Arabia. Scheduled for completion sometime in 1989, the pipeline will carry some 1.6 million barrels a day to the Red Sea. The expansion of Iraq's pipeline network will enable it to export as much oil—more than 3 million barrels a day—as it did before the war. It thus symbolizes Iraq's return to economic power and confirms its capability, if need be, to finance the war effort against Iran for many years to come.

Iraq in 1987 also underwent a bold program of economic reform, centered on privatization and a radical reduction of the government's role in the socialist economy. Dozens of state-owned enterprises in the agricultural and service sectors were sold off; trade unions were abolished; and half the shares of nationally owned Iraqi Airways were to be offered for sale to the public. In addition, an entire stratum of bureaucracy—the "state organizations"—was effectively eliminated. Responsibility now lies with the government ministries and economic and industrial enterprises that generate most of Iraq's domestic output. Several ministries were merged and/or streamlined, and most received new ministers.

Foreign Affairs. Iraq also moved to shore up ties with the two Arab states opposing it in the war with Iran. In September, a joint communiqué with Libya was issued, a sign of much improved relations that fell short of normal diplomatic ties. More importantly, November's Arab summit in Amman allegedly produced a full reconciliation between Saddam Hussein and Syria's President Hafiz al-Assad. The two had met secretly in April in a bid to ease Syrian support for Iran.

FREDERICK W. AXELGARD
Fellow in Middle East Studies
Center for Strategic and International Studies

IRAQ • Information Highlights

Official Name: Republic of Iraq.
Location: Southwest Asia.
Area: 167,923 sq mi (434 920 km²).
Population (mid-1987 est.): 17,000,000.
Chief City (1981 est.): Baghdad, the capital, 3,400,000.
Government: *Head of state and government,* Saddam Hussein, president (took office July 1979).
Monetary Unit: Dinar (0.311 dinar equals U.S.$1, August 1987).
Gross National Product (1986 est. U.S.$): $35,000,000,000.
Foreign Trade (1986 est. U.S.$): *Imports,* $9,500,000,000; *exports,* $7,450,000,000.

IRELAND

After more than four years in power, Prime Minister Garret FitzGerald's Fine Gael and Labour Party coalition foundered on the reefs of an austerity budget. His successor faced the same problems of an ailing economy.

Election. Since 1982, FitzGerald had tried to promote a policy of "fiscal rectitude," in the hope of stimulating economic growth. But the heavy burden of welfare benefits and sluggish productivity had hampered the government's ability to lower the budget deficit of almost 1.4 billion Irish pounds (about $2 billion) or 8.5% of the country's gross national product (GNP).

In his budget of Jan. 20, 1987, FitzGerald recommended more stringent spending cuts, which proved unacceptable to the four Labour ministers in his cabinet who resigned in protest. FitzGerald then asked President Patrick Hillery to dissolve the Dail (House of Representatives) and call for a general election on February 17.

After a campaign full of recriminations about rising unemployment, taxes, and interest rates as well as reductions in social services, the Fianna Fail party, led by former Prime Minister Charles J. Haughey, won 81 of the 166 seats in the Dail, and 44.1% of first preference votes. Fine Gael finished a distant second with 51 seats and 27.1% of the votes cast. To the dismay of Labour supporters, who accounted for only 12 seats and 6.5% of the vote, the newly formed (1985) Progressive Democrats, headed by a former Fianna Fail minister, Desmond O'Malley, secured 14 seats in the Dail and almost 12% of the vote. For the first time since 1922 the radical nationalist Sinn Fein party entered the electoral contest, even though the law prevented its candidates from appearing on radio or television. Only 2% of the electorate voted Sinn Fein, which won not a single seat.

With the votes counted, the combined forces of those opposing Fianna Fail in the Dail came to 82, which equaled the number of Haughey's supporters. This deadlock forced the speaker to cast the deciding vote, and Haughey was elected prime minister on March 10 by 83 to 82 votes (with one abstention). The principal ministers of Haughey's third administration included Brian Lenihan (deputy prime minister and foreign affairs.)

In response to the election results, FitzGerald decided to resign as leader of Fine Gael, a position he had held for almost ten years. On March 21 the party elected a new leader, Alan Dukes, aged 41, who had held three cabinet posts in the previous government. Widely regarded as more liberal in his politics than several rivals for the post, Dukes won the support of Fine Gael members who worried about the ability of the Progressive Democrats in the election to lure away supporters of Fine Gael.

IRELAND • Information Highlights

Official Name: Ireland (Eire).
Location: Island in the eastern North Atlantic Ocean.
Area: 27,135 sq mi (70 282 km²).
Population (mid-1987 est.): 3,500,000.
Chief Cities (1981 census): Dublin, the capital, 525,882; Cork, 149,792; Limerick, 75,520.
Government: *Head of state,* Patrick J. Hillery, president (took office Dec. 1976). *Head of government,* Charles Haughey, prime minister (took office March 1987). *Legislature*—Parliament: House of Representatives (Dail Eireann) and Senate (Seanad Eireann).
Monetary Unit: Pound (0.6651 pound equals U.S.$1, Oct. 26, 1987).
Gross National Product (1985 U.S.$): $14,300,000,000.
Economic Indexes (1986): *Consumer Prices* (1980 = 100), all items, 185.2; food, 167.2. *Industrial Production* (1980 = 100), 130.
Foreign Trade (1986 U.S.$): *Imports,* $12,610,000,000; *exports,* $13,161,000,000.

Economy. Although Fianna Fail leaders had attacked FitzGerald's economic policies, they introduced a budget on March 31 that cut even deeper into health and social services. Hoping to lower the deficit, Finance Minister Ray MacSharry announced a freeze on all wages and hiring in the public sector. Government grants to hospitals were slashed, prompting a number of doctors to call for strike action. The Haughey government thus found itself wrestling with the same problems as its predecessor—in particular an unemployment rate of more than 20% and a budget deficit equivalent to more than 7% of GNP. While the politicians debated ways of economizing, young people had little to look forward to in the way of jobs.

European Referendum. On May 26 a referendum was held to resolve the impasse over the Single European Act of the European Community. By a majority of 755,423 to 324,977 votes, the Irish electorate approved this measure, already endorsed by the other 11-member nations, which called for "closer cooperation" on matters relating to European security. Although both houses of Parliament had approved the terms of the act in December 1986 and the president had given it his official blessing, an Irish citizen obtained a court injunction against ratification on the grounds that it violated the constitution and jeopardized the country's right to remain neutral in the event of a European war. The results of this vote made possible the act's coming into effect on July 1.

Strife. The political and sectarian struggle within Northern Ireland continued to spill over into the Republic. For his 1986 role in leading a loyalist procession across the border and into the town of Clontibert, which ended in riotous disorder, Peter Robinson, the deputy leader of the Democratic Unionist Party, was found guilty of "unlawful assembly" by a Dublin court. A member of Parliament for Belfast East, he was fined about $21,000.

L. PERRY CURTIS, JR., *Brown University*

AP/Wide World

Prime Minister Yitzhak Shamir (left) *of the Likud bloc and Deputy Prime Minister and Foreign Minister Shimon Peres* (right) *of the Labor Party headed Israel's national unity government but did not see eye to eye on several key issues.*

ISRAEL

Israel's national unity government continued to be plagued during 1987 by disputes between the center-left Labor Party and the right-wing Likud bloc over domestic and foreign-policy issues. The outbreak in December of rioting in the occupied territories presented the government with a serious challenge. In foreign affairs the principal disagreement was whether or not to support the convening of an international Middle East peace conference.

Domestic Affairs. The cabinet voted in August to scrap Israel's most costly defense project, the Lavi jet-fighter plane. The seven-year-old project had been seen as a key to the development of the nation's defense plans and the basis for expansion of its high-tech industry, especially in the aeronautics field. The venture was backed by several billion dollars in U.S. military aid, but Washington had called on Israel to abandon it because equivalent aircraft could be supplied by the United States at much lower cost. The leaders of Israel's Labor Party, supported by top military and air-force commanders, voted to suspend construction, while Prime Minister Yitzhak Shamir and most of his Likud bloc supported continuation. In protest against the decision, Likud Minister Without Portfolio Moshe Arens resigned in September. The short-term costs of canceling the Lavi were expected to be hundreds of millions of dollars in lost contracts, the laying off of thousands of engineers and aircraft industry employees, and other dislocations.

Economic planners perceived cancellation of the Lavi project as a contribution to fiscal stability and the improvement of the overall economy. By year's end, the annual inflation rate had dropped to 20% (from its 1985 high of 500%) without any rise in unemployment. The shekel seemed stable against the U.S. dollar, and the $23.3 billion state budget was brought almost into balance after running annual 12–15% deficits for some 15 years. While continued austerity and limitations on hiring in the public sector were major factors in the economic stabilization, massive U.S. assistance also played a vital role. In addition to the "normal" $3 billion in military and economic aid, the United States for the second year in a row gave Israel an extra $750 million as an incentive to take steps unpopular with the public. These included a 9.75% devaluation of the shekel in January, reductions in food subsidies, and cutbacks in a number of projects beside the Lavi.

Despite the overall economic improvement, the country's large labor federation, the Histradut, called several strikes to demand higher wages and a shorter workweek, paralyzing air traffic and cutting off radio and television broadcasts at various times during the year.

Disputes over the propriety of activities by Israel's security services continued, with attention focusing on Shin Bet, the primary agency used to combat internal guerrilla activity. In May the Israel Supreme Court ruled that the Shin Bet had framed a Muslim officer in the Israeli army and sentenced him unjustly to 18 years in prison. This led to a cabinet-ordered inquiry, which reported in October that Shin Bet had consistently committed perjury in covering up its use of physical force and other pressures to extract confessions.

Several noteworthy legal trials were under way during 1987. Proceedings against John Demjanjuk, a naturalized U.S. citizen who was extradited to Israel on charges of collaborating with the Nazis in the murder of Jews at the Treblinka death camp, continued throughout the year. Mordechai Vanunu, a former technician employed by Israel's nuclear energy industry, was charged with selling nuclear secrets to a London newspaper in 1986. And in March, four prominent Israelis who had been part of a 22-member delegation of antiwar campaigners at a conference in Romania were charged with violating a provision of the Prevention of Terrorism Ordinance banning Israelis from any contact with members of the Palestine Liberation Organization (PLO).

After a chaotic session in 1986, the Herut Party reconvened in March and calmly reelected Prime Minister Yitzhak Shamir, 73, as chairman. His close associates, Ariel Sharon and Moshe Arens, also received key posts.

Shortly after the convention, Shamir clashed openly with Shimon Peres, the Labor Party leader and minister of foreign affairs, over the latter's plan for an international Middle-East peace conference. Shamir described the Peres proposal as a "perverse and criminal" idea that must be "wiped off" the cabinet agenda. Peres responded with charges that Shamir was engaging in "hatred" and "character assassination." After several meetings in May of the ten-member inner cabinet (five members each from Labor and Likud), no decision was reached on a unified peace policy. Amnon Rubinstein, the leader of the small left-of-center Shinui (Change) Party resigned as minister of communications, and the three Shinui representatives in the Knesset (parliament) withdrew their support for the government.

On December 9 violent unrest—mostly by rock-throwing youths—erupted in the occupied Gaza Strip and quickly spread to the West Bank. In the ensuing weeks Israeli army efforts to quell the continuing rioting resulted in numerous Palestinian deaths and injuries. International protest mounted in January 1988, when Israel deported several Arabs. The government then imposed round-the-clock curfews in Palestinian centers.

Foreign Affairs. Despite the threat to the unity of the national unity government, Foreign Minister Peres insisted that Israel's best chance to make peace with Jordan and the Palestinians was through an international conference. He agreed with Jordan's proposal for an open meeting that would include the five permanent members of the UN Security Council, to be followed by face-to-face parleys between Israel and a joint Jordanian-Palestinian delegation. After the opening of direct negotiations, the five powers would play no direct role except as mutually agreed to by Israel and Jordan. While Jordan refused to attend a conference without the Soviet Union, Israel's cabinet's conditions for Moscow's participation included the restoration of diplomatic ties broken by Moscow in 1967 and the removal of restrictions on the exodus of Soviet Jews.

Peres elaborated on his proposals—worked out in dozens of secret meetings with Jordan's King Hussein—at the September session of the UN General Assembly in New York. Additional points included the establishment of separate negotiating committees representing Israel and Syria, and a third with Lebanon; each committee would engage in direct face-to-face negotiations. There would be no imposed settlements by the conference as a whole and no veto on agreements reached between Israeli and Arab negotiators. The conference would strive to "solve the Palestinian problem in all its aspects."

U.S. Secretary of State George Shultz flew to Jerusalem in October for separate talks with Shamir and Peres in an effort to end their disagreement on the proposed conference, but he was unable to break the deadlock. Peres also pursued his initiative through direct parleys with Egyptian officials during February.

In Africa, Israel scored a small success during June when Togo became the fifth black African nation to restore diplomatic relations, ended when 29 African states broke ties in 1973. During the year, Israel reassessed its ties with South Africa and in September adopted a series of sanctions affecting trade, cultural exchange, and tourism. Further government investment in or loans to South Africa were banned, and steel imports from the country were frozen. No new military-sales contracts were to be signed.

In July, for the first time in 20 years, a delegation of Soviet diplomats visited Israel, to survey property belonging to the Russian Orthodox Church and to renew the passports of Soviet citizens. In other contacts, the Soviet and Israeli foreign ministers discussed proposals for the Middle-East conference and for renewed diplomatic exchanges.

Relations with the United States were set back when it was revealed that convicted spy Jonathan Pollard, a former U.S. Navy intelligence analyst, had been employed by Israeli agents to collect secret military information.

Israeli officials were implicated in the investigation by the U.S. Congress of secret diplomacy and arms sales by White House officials with the government of Iran and the diversion of funds to Nicaraguan "contra" rebels. (*See* feature article, page 26.)

DON PERETZ
State University of New York, Binghamton

ISRAEL • Information Highlights

Official Name: State of Israel.
Location: Southwest Asia.
Area: 8,019 sq mi (20 770 km²).
Population (mid-1987 est.): 4,400,000.
Chief Cities (June 4, 1983 est.): Jerusalem, the capital, 428,668 (including East Jerusalem); Tel Aviv-Jaffa, 327,625; Haifa, 235,775.
Government: *Head of state,* Chaim Herzog, president (took office May 1983). *Head of government,* Shimon Peres, prime minister (took office Sept. 14, 1984). *Legislature* (unicameral)—Knesset.
Monetary Unit: Shekel (1.5625 shekels equal U.S.$1, Dec. 8, 1987).
Gross National Product (1986 est U.S.$): $21,000,-000,000.
Economic Indexes (1986): *Consumer Prices* (1980 = 100), all items, 33,322.5; food, 33,412.2. *Industrial Production* (February 1987, 1980 = 100), 125.
Foreign Trade (1986 U.S.$): *Imports* $9,347,000,000; *exports,* $6,846,000,000.

ITALY

After a record-breaking 3½ years, the government of Socialist Prime Minister Bettino Craxi gave way in July 1987 to a Christian Democratic government under Giovanni Goria. Craxi nonetheless remained Italy's most powerful figure.

Domestic Affairs

The year 1987 began with Prime Minister Craxi's five-party coalition of Socialists, Christian Democrats, Social Democrats, Republicans, and Liberals still in office. Since becoming prime minister on Aug. 4, 1983, Craxi had overseen Italy's economic growth rate increase to about 3% a year. Inflation had fallen from 15% to about 5%, thanks to his cutting back the *scala mobile* system of indexing wages to inflation, and to lower oil prices. Unemployment (13%) and the huge budget deficit (16% of gross domestic product, or GDP) had at least remained stable. The government also had jailed numerous terrorists and drug traffickers.

What had not changed in Italy under Craxi was the essential balance among the three main political blocs. The Communists, the Christian Democrats, and, in between, the four small "laic" or secular parties each attract about one third of the vote in Italy. Ever since the Cold War, the Communists have been excluded from ministerial positions. The Socialists, one of the four "laic" parties, had polled 11.4% of the vote in the 1983 parliamentary elections and were eager to increase their strength. The Christian Democrats, accustomed to having headed every post-World War II government until 1981, were determined to regain their hegemony.

In July 1986, Craxi was compelled to engage in protracted negotiations with Christian Democratic Party Secretary Ciriaco De Mita, the political rival he most dislikes. These talks resulted in Craxi's reluctantly agreeing to a bargain to keep the premiership until March 1987 and then relinquish it to the Christian Democrats, who could hold it until 1988.

Fall of the Craxi Government. But, like so many political deals in Italy, this one came unhinged. In February 1987, Christian Democrats, in a new row over the premiership, threatened to withdraw from the coalition. The government also faced a no-confidence vote raised by the Communists. On February 17, Craxi announced that the coalition accord no longer was in effect, and hinted that he would seek new elections. Apparently he thought his own party could do better in early elections while he was still premier. But on March 3, Craxi resigned the premiership.

On March 9, Italy's President Francesco Cossiga asked Giulio Andreotti, a veteran

AP/Wide World

Treasury Minister Giovanni Goria, a 44-year-old Christian Democrat, was sworn in as Italy's premier in July. His five-party coalition later was reinstated after a cabinet crisis.

Christian Democrat, to form a new government. The Socialists rejected Andreotti and predicted a lengthy crisis. On March 27, President Cossiga asked Nilde Iotti, the Communist president of the Chamber of Deputies, to try her hand at proposing a new government. She was the first Communist and first woman to be given such an assignment in Italy. She quickly failed.

Then, on April 1, President Cossiga decided to withdraw his acceptance of Craxi's March 3 resignation, thus forcing him to face a formal debate and confidence vote—which, if Craxi lost, would necessitate new parliamentary elections. The main debate centered on whether to hold in June the referendums proposed by Craxi on the future of nuclear energy in Italy and on legal accountability of the judiciary. The Christian Democrats preferred to avoid referendums and let Parliament decide the nuclear energy question.

Declaring that the political crisis could be resolved if all sides showed reason, Craxi expressed readiness to support a Christian Democratic premier until regular parliamentary elections in 1988. (That was essentially what he had agreed to in 1986.) This time, however, the Christian Democrats turned down his offer. And fearing that they would be blamed for bringing down Craxi's government, they pulled their ministers out before the confidence vote. On April 9, Craxi submitted his resignation for the second time in the protracted imbroglio.

At last, on April 18, Amintore Fanfani, the 79-year-old president of the Senate (Italy's second-highest official by protocol), was sworn in to head a minority Christian Democratic government. As was expected, Fanfani quickly lost a confidence vote, thus permitting Cossiga to dissolve Parliament on April 28 and call for general elections on June 14, one year ahead of schedule. The caretaker Fanfani government, with Giulio Andreotti continuing as foreign minister, took responsibility for hosting in Venice the June meeting of the seven major industrial nations.

The Campaign and Election. Parliamentary elections in Italy usually do not revolve around personalities. But this time, Craxi was the focus. His campaign got off to a shaky start with the defection to the Communist Party of five prominent Socialists. The Italian Communist Party, which now accepts a market economy, submerged traditional Marxist issues, stressing instead protection of the environment, women's rights, and concern for the young. About 40% of the Communist candidates were women.

The Christian Democrats gratefully accepted the unexpected help of Italy's bishops, who, with approval from Pope John Paul II, urged Catholics to vote for a party whose family policies were "compatible with the Christian faith." This pronouncement greatly irritated non-Catholics.

Despite their growing boredom, 88% of the electorate went to the polls on June 14. Voting under a system of proportional representation, they endorsed the concept of Socialist-Christian Democratic partnership. Although Italy's balance of political forces did not change very much, four parties improved their standings. The Christian Democrats won 34.3%, a rise of 1.4% over the 1983 elections. Craxi's triumph was the greater, however, for his Socialists performed their best yet—14.3%, a rise of 2.9%. The Greens, a brand-new environmentalist and antinuclear party, attracted 2.5% of the vote. The Proletarian Democrats, a hard-line Marxist party, got 1.7%, a gain of 0.2%.

All of the other parties lost strength. Thus, the Communists fell 3.3% to 26.6%—their lowest level since 1963 and their third consecutive drop. Most of the defections went to the Socialists and extreme Left. The three "laic" center parties that had been in Craxi's coalition government also declined—the Republicans losing 1.4% to 3.7%; the Social Democrats falling 1.1% to 3.0%; and the Liberals dropping 0.8% to 2.1%. The maverick Radicals fell 0.4% to 2.6%. The neo-Fascist Italian Social Movement (MSI) polled 5.9%, down 0.9%.

In the wake of the Communist Party's poor showing, its Central Committee, meeting in a stormy session, elected Achille Occhetto to be heir-apparent to the 69-year-old party secretary Alessandro Natta.

The Goria Government. A battle royal between the Christian Democrats and the Socialists persisted for several weeks after the election. Craxi refused to enter personally into a new coalition under Christian Democratic leadership, but he did agree to let his Socialist Party take part. The new government was to be headed by Giovanni Goria, the outgoing Christian Democratic treasury minister and a youthful disciple of the Christian Democratic party leader, Ciriaco De Mita. (*See* BIOGRAPHY—Goria, Giovanni.) On July 26, Goria reported to President Cossiga that he had formed a new government composed of the same five parties (the *pentapartito*) as that of Craxi.

The Socialist Party's reluctant acquiescence to the advent of the Goria government temporarily obscured the fact that Craxi really seeks a major change in Italy's postwar political structure—the formation of an alternative, leftist government that would exclude, for the first time, the "hegemonic-minded" Christian Democrats. Such a government of the Left would include the Social Democrats, the Republicans, and also the Communists, now that they have accepted a pluralistic political system. The Radicals and Greens also might be included. Such a seismic shift toward a two-bloc political structure would probably have to await another parliamentary election, however.

In the fragile Goria government, most of the 15 Christian Democratic ministers were old hands. Giulio Andreotti returned to the foreign ministry. Amintore Fanfani took on the ministry of the interior. These familiar Christian Democratic faces risked being outshone by the Socialist Party's eight appointees, among whom were some vigorous personalities who had made their reputations outside politics.

Referendums. In a complex referendum that had to be postponed from June until November

ITALY • Information Highlights

Official Name: Italian Republic.
Location: Southern Europe.
Area: 116,305 sq mi (301 230 km²).
Population (mid-1987 est.): 57,400,000.
Chief Cities (Dec. 31, 1985): Rome, the capital, 2,826,488; Milan, 1,515,233; Naples, 1,206,010.
Government: *Head of state,* Francesco Cossiga, president (took office July 1985). *Head of government,* Giovanni Goria, prime minister (sworn in July 29, 1987). *Legislature*—Parliament: Senate and Chamber of Deputies.
Monetary Unit: Lira (1,164.5 lire equal U.S.$1, Dec. 31, 1987).
Economic Indexes (1986): *Consumer Prices* (1980 = 100) all items, 201.5; food, 190.2. *Industrial Production* (1980 = 100), 99.
Foreign Trade (1986 U.S.$): *Imports,* $99,937,000,000; *exports,* $97,835,000,000.

8, Italians went to the polls in an unusually low turnout. By majorities of about 80% they voted in favor of five measures that Craxi had first proposed in 1986.

The three that pertained to nuclear energy will almost surely make it difficult for Italy to build new nuclear-energy plants. One of the measures dissolved a commission of inquiry into wrongdoing by politicians. In the future, such investigations will be left up to Parliament itself. The most controversial measure removed magistrates' immunity from damage suits by citizens who feel they were wrongfully arrested or imprisoned.

New Cabinet Crisis. On November 14, the 15-week-old Goria government resigned after the small Liberal Party withdrew from the coalition in a dispute over the budget deficit. The Liberals insisted that the coalition policy was to reduce the deficit through spending cuts.

One week later, the five-party government was reinstated after Goria promised the Liberals he would restore projected tax cuts if inflation did not rise unexpectedly in 1988.

Economy. On November 25, the unions called nationwide work stoppages to protest the government's failure to provide immediate tax cuts. The strike also was seen as a test of how well the once-powerful unions commanded the support of the work force. The strikes were most effective (80%) in transportation and industry, but only about 60% effective in the health-care, credit, and public-administration sectors.

Italy has the most expansionary fiscal policy of any big industrial economy and risks being caught in a debt trap. Government borrowing amounted to 13% of GDP in 1986. In Italy social security and pension contributions represent a bigger share of an employer's total labor costs than anywhere else in Western Europe. Italy's relative prosperity of recent years has not been equally shared. Average income per capita in the South is half that of the North, while unemployment is twice as high. The national rate of unemployment rose in September 1987 to 14.3%. In the working-age bracket under 25, one out of three Italians is jobless.

The entire year of 1987 was a poor one for the Milan bourse. After the Wall Street crash of October 19, the Milan stock price indexes were 24.3% lower than they were a year earlier.

Despite these problems, Italians boasted that their economy had overtaken Britain's. But to sustain such a claim, they had to add to the official statistics Italy's huge (15%) unrecorded "black," or underground, economy.

Law and Order. In February, Italian authorities issued an arrest warrant for American Archbishop Paul Marcinkus, head of the Vatican bank, in connection with the Milanese Banco Ambrosiano bank collapse and scandal of 1982. The Vatican insisted that Marcinkus was immune from Italian prosecution. On July 17, an Italian appellate court conceded this point.

Red Brigade terrorists assumed responsibility for the March 20 killing in Rome of Italian Air Force General Licio Giorgieri, a senior officer in the space weapons program. On June 9, rocket and car-bomb attacks struck the U.S. and British embassies in Rome.

In September, Licio Gelli, head of the once powerful, secret P2 lodge of Italian Masons, surrendered to authorities in Switzerland, where he had escaped from jail four years earlier. Gelli is wanted in Italy on many charges, including fraudulent bankruptcy in connection with the 1982 collapse of Milan's Banco Ambrosiano, and of conspiring to protect the right-wing terrorists who killed 85 people in the bombing of the Bologna railway station in 1980. The trial of these terrorists got under way in Bologna in 1987 after long delays.

The longest Mafia trial in history ended in Palermo, Sicily, in mid-December. A total of 338 of 452 defendants accused of involvement in a major crime ring financed by heroin traffic to the United States were found guilty.

Foreign Affairs

Because of Italy's impending election, President Ronald Reagan canceled a proposed state visit to Italy in May. He did spend a week in Venice in June, however, for the meeting of the major industrial powers. He also visited Pope John Paul II.

At the Venice conference, Italian officials claimed credit for inserting the word "just" into the call for "the adoption of just and effective measures" by the United Nations Security Council, in an effort to end the war between Iraq and Iran. This phraseology implied equal treatment for the two belligerents.

In early August, Italy rejected a U.S. request to send minesweepers and escort vessels into the Persian Gulf to help protect neutral shipping. But in September, after an Italian merchant ship had been attacked, the Goria government, under pressure from Craxi, reversed itself and sent naval contingents to protect Italian shipping. Later, Italians were chagrined to learn that some of Iran's mines allegedly had been supplied by an Italian company.

Italy expressed enthusiastic approval for the U.S.-Soviet arms-control treaty of December 8 eliminating intermediate-range nuclear forces, including cruise missiles based in Sicily. Goria himself strongly endorsed the treaty during a visit to Washington in mid-December. The prime minister, however, urged President Reagan to be flexible in future negotiations with the Soviets concerning the Strategic Defense Initiative (SDI).

CHARLES F. DELZELL, *Vanderbilt University*

Noboru Takeshita leads the cheering after being named president of Japan's ruling Liberal Democratic Party on October 31. The 63-year-old former finance minister succeeded Yasuhiro Nakasone in the premiership November 6.

AP/Wide World

JAPAN

Despite a steep rise in the yen's exchange value, Japan's global trade surplus in 1986 increased almost 80% over that of the previous year, to total $82.7 billion. Trade surpluses with the United States and the European Community (EC) reached record highs of $51.5 billion and $16.7 billion, respectively, according to the Finance Ministry. Although exports to the United States declined in yen terms, they increased 17.8% in dollar value. Trade issues therefore completely dominated U.S.-Japan relations during 1987.

Japan had come to account for 10% of the world's gross national product (GNP). And yet Japanese remained fearful of a "hollowing out" of their industrial base, as corporations continued expansion of plants into the United States. In January the unemployment rate rose to 3%, the highest level since reporting began in 1953. Although only half the U.S. jobless rate, the Japanese figure meant that some 2 million workers were unemployed.

During most of 1987, Yasuhiro Nakasone continued to serve as president of the ruling Liberal-Democratic Party (LDP) and thus as prime minister. In September 1986, however, the party had denied him a third presidential term, simply extending his tenure to Oct. 30, 1987. The intraparty succession struggle was won by Noboru Takeshita (*see* BIOGRAPHY), who became prime minister in November.

Domestic Affairs

From the beginning of 1987, the Nakasone cabinet suffered from a recession in industry, foreign pressure on trade issues, an unpopular tax proposal, and declining public support. In an opinion survey released March 28, nonsupport for the prime minister reached a record 66% (climbing from 38% in December).

Party Politics. When the Diet (parliament) reconvened on January 25, the LDP—with its conservative allies—controlled 309 of the 512 seats in the (lower) House of Representatives and 143 of the 252 seats in the (upper) House of Councillors. The Japan Socialist Party (JSP), with 87 seats in the lower and 41 seats in the upper house, made up the chief opposition. Other minority parties included the Clean Government Party (Komeito), the Democratic Socialist Party (DSP), and the Japan Communist Party (JCP).

In September 1986, Takako Doi had been selected as leader of the JSP, the first woman to head a major party in Japan. The party adopted an action program for 1987 stressing the need to become a West European-style socialist party and to appeal to the younger generation. Together with the Komeito's new chairman, Junya Yano, and the DSP head, Saburo Tsukamato, Doi agreed to oppose the LDP's plans for tax reform, for increased defense spending, and for participation in the U.S. Strategic Defense Initiative (SDI) or "Star Wars" program.

Opposition parties immediately confronted the LDP in the Diet and refused to enter debate. On March 4, just one day after proceedings resumed, the JSP again boycotted public hearings on the fiscal 1987 budget scheduled for March 13–14. Normality was restored when the LDP agreed to await the outcome of local elections set for April 12 and settled for a provisional budget to cover the first 50 days of the fiscal year beginning April 1.

The major issue in this struggle was a 5% value-added sales tax proposed by the Nakasone cabinet. Although the prime minister had promised in his campaign for the general election in 1986 not to initiate a broad-based tax, the sales tax appeared as part of his long-range tax reform. Even business associations, normally allies of the LDP, opposed the new tax.

On March 8 a JSP candidate overwhelmingly had won an upper house by-election in Iwate Prefecture, a conservative stronghold. Then on April 12 the LDP lost more than 100 seats in 44 prefectural assemblies, as well as gubernatorial posts in Fukuoka and in Hokkaido. Finally, on April 23—on the eve of the prime minister's scheduled visit to Washington—the LDP dropped its controversial sales-tax plan in order to obtain passage of the 1987 budget. Some media members predicted that Nakasone would have to yield leadership before expiration of his LDP presidential term in October.

There was no lack of potential successors. On May 1, Deputy Prime Minister Shin Kanemaru urged the LDP secretary-general, Noboru Takeshita, to form his own faction in order to prepare for the fall presidential race. On May 14 the former LDP vice president, Susumu Nikaido, announced that he would be a candidate. He and Takeshita thus began maneuvers to succeed to the leadership of the largest faction within the LDP, with 141 members.

Nominally led by the ailing former Prime Minister Kakuei Tanaka, this faction had been entrusted to Nikaido, who nevertheless commanded only about 20 members. On July 29 the Tokyo High Court upheld the 1983 conviction of Tanaka in the Lockheed Corporation bribery case and, although he planned further appeal, the former leader faded from active politics. Meanwhile, Takeshita made his move.

On July 4 the secretary-general announced formation of the first new major faction in the party in 15 years. Called the Keiseikai, the group won the support of about 120 members of the old Tanaka faction. Takeshita also formed an alliance with a former foreign minister, Shintaro Abe, who headed an 85-member faction. On July 2, finance Minister Kiichi Miyazawa entered the presidential race. He chaired an 88-member faction. The press referred to Miyazawa, Abe, and Takeshita as the "three new leaders" and predicted that Nakasone's successor would emerge from among this group.

After negotiations among the aspirants failed to reach a compromise, Prime Minister Nakasone named Takeshita to the party presidency. On October 31 at an extraordinary convention of the LDP, Noboru Takeshita was selected to be president and, as head of the majority party, was elected prime minister by the Diet on November 6.

Economy. Once the Nakasone cabinet surmounted the opposition boycott of Diet proceedings, it won approval of an austerity budget for fiscal 1987 with the smallest increase (0.02%) in expenditures in 32 years. Balanced at a total of 54.1 trillion yen (about $360 billion), the budget decreased dependency on bonds below 20% for the first time. Late in 1986 the government did, however, decide to allocate 3.5 trillion yen (about $23 billion) for defense. It was the first time since 1976 that military costs exceeded a politically established ceiling of 1% of total GNP.

On March 17 the Economic Planning Agency (EPA) announced that the Japanese economy had ended 1986 with a 2.5% real growth rate, the lowest increase in 12 years. The EPA attributed the decline to a steep plunge in consumer spending. The Ministry of International Trade and Industry (MITI) reported that mining and manufacturing output in 1986 declined 0.3% from a year earlier, the first annual decline in 11 years. Output stood at an index of 121.5 (1980 = 100). MITI blamed the drop on the deflationary impact of the strong yen.

In May, according to the Statistics Bureau, Japan's labor force totaled 61.7 million; unemployed numbered 1.9 million for a record 3% jobless rate. Inflation was, however, moderate, the national consumer price index standing at 101.2 in May (April = 101.0; 1985 = 100).

On April 17, the LDP unveiled a package of emergency economic measures designed to revive the slumping domestic economy. When Prime Minister Nakasone visited President Reagan at the end of April, he promised further stimulation of domestic demand in order to offset the towering trade surplus. On June 23 the cabinet approved a 2.08 trillion yen (about $13.9 billion) supplementary budget for fiscal 1987. This brought total government spending to a total of 56.18 trillion yen (about $375 billion), up 4.4% over the previous year.

Japan's central bank also joined in the campaign to stimulate the domestic economy. The Bank of Japan carried out the long-awaited reduction of the official discount rate to a record low of 2.5% effective February 23.

Railroad Reorganization. Just after midnight April 1, a C-56 steam engine pulled out of the Shiodome Station in Tokyo to commemorate the end of the 115-year history of the Japanese National Railways (JNR, "Kokutetsu"). Freighted with a $250 billion deficit, the JNR was deregulated into six regional passenger systems and a freight firm. Some 200,000 rail workers took over operation of the private federation under the new logo, "JR." The new General Federation of Rail Workers' Unions (*Tetsudororen*) claimed a total membership of 125,000.

Obituaries. On February 3 Prince Takamatsu, 82, younger brother of emperor Hirohito, died in Tokyo. A graduate of the naval academy in 1924, he was appointed to the rank of captain in 1942. After World War II he served as president of the Japanese Red Cross Society.

On August 7 former Prime Minister Nobusuke Kishi, 90, died of heart failure in a Tokyo hospital. Kishi, a bureaucrat turned politician, served as prime minister 1956–58 and 1958–60 and was instrumental in achieving revision of the U.S.-Japan security treaty in 1960.

Foreign Affairs

Facing a trade crisis, Japan is at a "historic turning point" and must voluntarily cut its trade imbalances in order to win respect as a responsible nation, according to an annual Foreign Ministry report released in July. That 1987 Diplomatic Blue Book also proposed that Japan improve defense capabilities without becoming a military giant, increase its foreign economic aid, and expand international exchanges in culture and science.

Finance and Trade. Early 1987 saw strenuous attempts to stabilize currency values among the so-called G-7 powers (Japan, United States, Canada, Britain, France, West Germany, and Italy). At the end of 1986, Japan's currency had closed at 160.10 yen to the U.S. dollar. On January 9, the Bank of Japan brought an estimated $2 billion on the Tokyo foreign exchange market, a record for one day. Nevertheless, after Finance Minister Miyazawa met Treasury Secretary James Baker in Washington January 21, the dollar fell further to 151.50 yen. On February 22 in Paris, six of the G-7 powers (less Italy) agreed to "cooperate closely" to stabilize the dollar at about 153 yen. Despite massive intervention by the central banks, by March 30 the dollar had fallen even further to 144.70 yen.

On April 8 the G-7 met again in Washington and agreed that the dollar had fallen enough. The governments put in place mechanisms designed to stabilize the dollar at around 144 yen, a level that the markets immediately tested. On April 27 the dollar dropped to 137.70, a record low since the yen was revalued after World War II. In their meetings April 30-May 1 in Washington, Prime Minister Nakasone and President Reagan agreed that further decline of the dollar would be "counterproductive." In July the dollar was hovering around the 150 level, but following the October stock crash it was again fluctuating in the 130s.

It had been assumed that appreciation in the value of the yen (making exports more expensive) would soon bring corrections in Japan's trade balance. On May 1, however, the Finance Ministry announced that in fiscal 1986 (ended March 31, 1987) Japan's trade and current account surpluses leapt to record highs of $101.4 billion and $93.8 billion, respectively.

Aided by the strong yen, Japan actually increased investment in the United States. By April, Japanese capital flow into the United States totaled $135 billion, greater than that of any other nation except Britain.

AP/Wide World

Activity was frenzied on the Tokyo exchange during 1987, as efforts to stabilize the values of Western currencies failed. The U.S. dollar hit record lows.

U.S. Relations. In 1987 trade friction dominated other issues in U.S.-Japan relations. A steady stream of American visitors to Japan warned of increasing protectionist sentiment in Congress: for example, Under Secretary of Commerce Bruce Smart (January); George Deukmejian, governor of California, and Roger B. Smith, chairman of General Motors (February); Secretary of State George Shultz (March); and Clayton Yeutter, trade representative, Secretary of Agriculture Richard Lyng, and David Halberstam, Pulitzer Prize-winning author (May).

Bowing to intense pressure from Reagan administration officials, on March 16 plans for the sale of the Fairchild Semiconductor Corporation to Fujitsu, Ltd., were dropped. Primary objections revolved around U.S. national security, but officials in Washington conceded that mounting trade friction was also a factor.

On March 27, President Reagan announced the first trade retaliation against Japan in postwar history. A 100% duty on 19 electronic products, accounting for $300 million in imports annually, was set to go into effect April 17. The United States charged that Japan had failed to comply with a semiconductor accord signed in July 1986 and was engaged in underpricing ("dumping"), particularly in third countries. Tokyo threatened to revoke the chip accord and to appeal under the General Agreement on Tariffs and Trade (GATT).

At the Venice summit of advanced industrial democracies (June 8–10), President Reagan informed Prime Minister Nakasone that sanctions were being eased. Indeed, the virtual absence of "Japan-bashing" at the conference was attributed to a softening American attitude. "The summit produced satisfactory results," Chief Cabinet Secretary Masaharu Gotada concluded. American criticism flared up again, however, one month later.

On July 1 the Toshiba Corporation announced that its chairman and its president would resign to take responsibility for illegal sales of militarily sensitive technology by a subsidiary company. Between 1982 and 1984, Toshiba Machine had sold eight high-tech milling machines to the Soviet Union in violation of rules made by the Coordinating Committee for Export Control (COCOM). The resignations followed U.S. Senate approval by a 92–5 vote of an amendment to an omnibus trade bill that would ban all Toshiba exports to the United States for at least two years.

Despite trade problems, on July 21, Japan became the fifth U.S. ally to join in research for the Strategic Defense Initiative. Ambassador Nobuo Matsunaga joined Defense Secretary Caspar Weinberger in Washington to sign the framework agreement. Tokyo's move to cooperate in the "Star Wars" program, according to *Pravda* in Moscow, signaled Japan's increasing participation in a space arms race.

Soviet Relations. For several other reasons, relations with the USSR steadily deteriorated during 1987. Early in the year the Japanese press speculated over the possibility of a visit by Soviet General Secretary Mikhail Gorbachev. Negotiations toward such a trip were stalled, however, by the continued rigidity of Moscow over a boundary issue. Tokyo insisted that talks toward a long-delayed peace treaty should take into account its claims to what Japanese called "the northern territories," islands north of Hokkaido under Soviet occupation since World War II. Soviet officials dismissed the claims as an obstacle to a Gorbachev visit.

JAPAN • Information Highlights

Official Name: Japan.
Location: East Asia.
Area: 143,749 sq mi (373 310 km²).
Population (mid-1987 est.): 122,200,000.
Chief Cities (Oct. 1, 1985 est): Tokyo, the capital, 8,353,674; Yokohama, 2,992,644; Osaka, 2,636,260; Nagoya, 2,116,350.
Government: *Head of state,* Hirohito, emperor (acceded Dec. 1926). *Head of government,* Noburu Takeshita, prime minister (took office Nov. 1987). *Legislature*—Diet: House of Councillors and House of Representatives.
Monetary Unit: Yen (121 yen equal U.S.$1, Dec. 31, 1987).
Gross National Product (1986 U.S.$): $1,979,000,000.
Economic Indexes (1986): *Consumer Prices* (1980 = 100), all items, 115.2; food, 114.6. *Industrial Production* (1980 = 100), 121.
Foreign Trade (1986 U.S.$): *Imports,* $126,408,000,000; *exports,* $209,153,000,000.

On August 20 the Soviet Union ordered two Japanese, a naval attaché and a businessman, to leave the country. Tokyo countered by expelling a Soviet deputy trade representative. These were the first expulsions since the war and the latest moves in exchanges of spy charges and countercharges. Meanwhile, on August 4 in an interview with the Kyodo News Service, Ivan Kovalenko, who is in charge of Soviet-Japan trade relations, continued to denounce decisions in the Toshiba case. "Having yielded to U.S. pressure," he said, "Japan is losing the right to decide what to sell to the world."

Northeast Asia. After the resignation in January of Hu Yaobang, a Chinese Communist Party leader known to be friendly with Prime Minister Nakasone, relations with Beijing cooled. In a meeting with a JSP delegation in Beijing on July 29, President Li Xiannian warned that Tokyo's decision to eliminate the ceiling on defense spending had given rise to concern over a reemergence of militarism in Japan. Li also referred to what supreme leader Deng Xiaoping had declared was a violation of the 1978 Japan-China friendship treaty. In February a Japanese court had recognized the right of Taiwan to maintain possession of a Chinese student dormitory in Kyoto. To China's protest, Nakasone pointed to the independence of the judiciary in Japan, but he added that his government had no plans to abandon the one-China policy that recognized Beijing as the sole legitimate government of China.

Taiwan was also involved indirectly in an incident that affected Japan and the two Koreas. On February 7, Japan had transferred 11 defectors from North Korea via Taiwan to Seoul in South Korea. North Korea, with which Japan has no formal relations, was angered and stated that it would not return Japanese fishermen who had drifted into North Korean waters.

Southeast Asia. At a meeting held June 18–20 in Singapore, Foreign Minister Tadashi Kuranari pledged Japan to provide $20 billion in public- and private-sector aid to spur economic development in Southeast Asia over the next three years. The promise was made to Association of Southeast Asian Nations (ASEAN) foreign ministers and to delegates of six so-called dialogue partners. ASEAN, established in 1967, is a loose regional association linking Brunei, Indonesia, Malaysia, the Philippines, Singapore, and Thailand. The dialogue partners include Japan, the United States, Canada, Australia, New Zealand, and the European Community. "We will take fully into account the needs of the ASEAN countries, Japan's most important economic cooperation partners," Kuranari announced.

See also feature article, INDUSTRIAL COMPETITIVENESS, page 47.

ARDATH W. BURKS, *Rutgers University*

Jordan's King Hussein (left) gained a measure of prestige when he welcomed Iraq's President Saddam Hussein and 14 other Arab League heads of state for an emergency meeting in Amman, November 8–11. The group unanimously passed a resolution supporting Iraq and condemning Iran in the Persian Gulf war.

AP/Wide World

JORDAN

The year 1987 for Jordan was one of tranquility and peaceful development internally, and of energetic diplomatic activity, which was at least partially successful, on the foreign front.

Domestic Affairs. There were no clashes with student or other demonstrators such as those that had occurred at Yarmuk University in May 1986. While one reason may have been the severity with which the government had clamped down on all dissident groups, it was also true that the regime had embarked on a large-scale review of the whole educational system in order, in the words of King Hussein, "to modernize existing programs and curricula on all levels in accordance with the requirement of economic and social changes." Supervision was entrusted to Crown Prince Hassan, the king's brother.

The dinar remained stable throughout the year, reflecting a satisfactory pace of economic growth and adequate foreign exchange reserves. Some natural gas was discovered in Jordan during 1987, which, if successfully developed, would be a great boon to the energy-poor country. Jordan and Syria reached an agreement in the fall on construction of the Al Wahdah Dam on the Yarmuk River to increase the water supply and generate electricity.

The creation of a People's Army, announced in 1986 as a supplement to regular Jordanian forces, did not seem to advance greatly. Nor was much heard in 1987 of the vast $750 million plan, announced in fall 1986, for the economic development of the West Bank. The wealthier Arab states, whose aid is essential, had shown little interest. A more modest scheme surfaced in February 1987, when Saudi Arabia and Kuwait pledged $14.5 million to a joint Palestine Liberation Organization (PLO)-Jordan fund to aid the Palestinians of the West Bank. Yasir Arafat's senior deputy in the PLO, Khalil Wazir—who had been expelled from Jordan in 1986—visited Amman in mid-February to discuss the use of the funds. This, however, militated against rather than aided King Hussein's hopes of gaining the support of the Palestinians and weaning them from the PLO.

Perhaps the most interesting point of policy announced by King Hussein during 1987 was his decision to postpone elections to the House of Representatives, thus prolonging the life of a parliament first elected in 1967. The constitutional amendments of 1984 and the implementing electoral law of 1986 provided for the expansion of the lower house from 60 to 142 seats and for equal representation of the West Bank in the form of 71 new members. The official reason for the postponement was that the time had been too short to work out the administrative consequences of the new law.

Foreign Affairs. The two main themes of Jordanian foreign policy continued to be the efforts to achieve Arab unity and to create a compromise peace ending the Arab-Israeli conflict. There was a sustained effort to mobilize support for the idea of an international peace conference on the Middle East, with King Hussein touring European capitals in March and April, while Prime Minister Zaid Rifai visited Washington in early April. (The king had re-

JORDAN • Information Highlights

Official Name: Hashemite Kingdom of Jordan.
Location: Southwest Asia.
Area: 37,737 sq mi (97 740 km²), includes West Bank.
Population (mid-1987 est.): 3,700,000.
Chief Cities (Dec. 1983): Amman, the capital, 744,000; Zarqa, 255,000; Irbid, 131,200.
Government: *Head of state,* Hussein I, king (acceded Aug. 1952). *Head of government,* Zayd al-Rifa'i, prime minister (appointed April 4, 1985). *Legislature*—Parliament: House of Representatives and Senate.
Monetary Unit: Dinar (.33100 dinar equals U.S.$1, Dec. 2, 1987).
Economic Index (1986): *Consumer Prices* (1980 = 100), all items, 129.9; food, 122.9.
Foreign Trade (1986 U.S.$): *Imports,* $2,432,000,000; *exports,* $647,000,000.

fused an invitation to visit the United States, to express his disapproval of the U.S. arms sales to Iran.) Hussein regarded right-wing Israeli opposition as the main stumbling block to a conference, though he did hold meetings, at first secret, with Israel's Foreign Minister Shimon Peres in the spring.

The rapprochement with Syria continued, as did the chill between Jordan and the PLO. Hussein and Arafat did meet, however, at the Islamic Conference in Kuwait in late January, as well as at the Arab League conference in Amman in early November. This latter event was a great feather in the cap for Jordanian diplomacy. In addition to the prestige of hosting the parley, Hussein witnessed several substantive agreements that were in line with Jordanian policy. Jordan, a consistent supporter of Iraq and opponent of Iran, saw the adoption by the Arab states of an anti-Iranian resolution which Syria (Iran's consistent supporter) did not dissent from; and the conference sanctioned the reestablishment of normal relations with Egypt, which Jordan had done in 1984.

ARTHUR CAMPBELL TURNER
University of California, Riverside

KANSAS

The Kansas economy continued to be affected by depressed agricultural prices and the sagging oil industry. Lower than estimated state revenues resulted in a 3.8% cut by state agencies for the fiscal year ending in June. Early spring blizzards caused losses in the cattle industry.

Agriculture. The 1987 wheat crop totaled 366.3 million bushels with an average yield of 37 bushels per acre. This was 9% larger than the 1986 crop but smaller than estimated in the spring due to rains that delayed the harvest. For the fourth consecutive year, Kansas farmers ranked first in the nation in milo (sorghum grain) production with a total of 277.5 million bushels. The average per acre yield was 75 bushels. Corn production of 156 million bushels was down 14% from 1986 on 10% fewer acres. The soybean crop was estimated to reach 65.1 million bushels, the largest on record. Crop prices were slightly higher than a year earlier but still were considered low.

Weather. Two spring blizzards hit most of western Kansas on successive weekends in late March, closing highways, stranding travelers, and causing power outages. The first storm had winds in excess of 70 miles per hour (113 km/hr) and reduced visibility to zero. The second blizzard, affecting the same area as the first, had heavy snow with winds of 30 to 50 miles per hour (48–80 km/hr), causing 6-foot (1.8-m) drifts in many areas. The blizzards came at the time spring calves were being born and ranchers in some areas lost 50% of their new calves. There also was damage to older stock. The Kansas National Guard provided haylifts for stranded herds. Losses were estimated to be several million dollars. Fifty-two counties were placed on the list to receive disaster relief.

Legislation. One of the first actions taken by the 1987 Kansas legislature was to cut $60 million from previously appropriated funds for state agencies to meet a projected shortfall of revenues. This amounted to a 3.8% cut of budgets that had been approved in the 1986 session.

The biggest disappointment for newly inaugurated Gov. Mike Hayden was the Senate's failure to pass a bill reinstating capital punishment. Support for capital punishment had been a major issue in Hayden's campaign for office. Bills establishing liquor by the drink, a state lottery, and pari-mutuel wagering were passed to implement three constitutional amendments approved by voters in the 1986 elections.

A special task force, established to study highway construction needs and financing plans, developed a plan that was endorsed by Governor Hayden. The governor called a special session of the legislature to consider the $1.71 billion proposal in late August. Hayden had spent part of the summer traveling the state to build support for the plan. Meeting in the first special session in 21 years, the legislature failed to take action on the program supported by Hayden or other alternative proposals and adjourned after six days. The Republican governor blamed the Democrats for blocking action on the plan.

Newsmakers. U.S. Sen. Robert Dole (R) officially announced his candidacy for the presidency in his hometown, Russell, KS, on November 9. Former Gov. Alfred M. Landon, the 1936 Republican presidential candidate, died on October 12.

PATRICIA A. MICHAELIS
Kansas State Historical Society

KANSAS • Information Highlights

Area: 82,277 sq mi (213 098 km²).
Population (July 1, 1986): 2,461,000.
Chief Cities (July 1, 1986 est.): Topeka, the capital, 118,580; Wichita, 288,060; Kansas City, 162,070.
Government (1987): *Chief Officers*—governor, Mike Hayden (R); lt. gov., Jack D. Walker (R). *Legislature*—Senate, 40 members; House of Representatives, 125 members.
State Finances (fiscal year 1986): *Revenue,* $3,948,000,000; *expenditure,* $3,522,000,000.
Personal Income (1986): $36,042,000,000; per capita, $14,650.
Labor Force (June 1987): *Civilian labor force,* 1,277,700; *unemployed,* 59,300 (4.6% of total force).
Education: *Enrollment* (fall 1985)—public elementary schools, 285,671; public secondary, 124,558; colleges and universities, 141,359. *Public school expenditures* (1985–86), $1,439,000,000 ($3,914 per pupil).

KENTUCKY

Because 1987 was a gubernatorial election year in Kentucky, the dominant theme throughout the year was electoral politics. A second persistent theme was the financial problems facing the state.

Gubernatorial Election. The winner of the May 26 Democratic primary was Wallace Wilkinson, a 45-year-old millionaire businessman and developer, who had never held elective office before. Wilkinson won 35% of the vote in a five-man race. Throughout most of the campaign the front-runner was John Y. Brown, Jr., who had been governor (1980–84). His closest challenger was Lt. Gov. Steve Beshear. Running well behind were Wilkinson, former Gov. Julian Carroll, and Grady Stumbo, a doctor who finished third in the 1983 gubernatorial primary.

The 1987 Democratic gubernatorial primary broke all spending records. More than $12 million was spent, including $4 million by the winner, Wallace Wilkinson. Although Wilkinson loaned his campaign half of that amount, he was reimbursed fully by contributions after the primary. Another surprising feature of the 1987 campaign was the rapid changes in voter preferences. One month before the primary Brown led with 36%, and Wilkinson had only 9%, while almost one fifth were undecided. Wilkinson apparently gained about 10 percentage points in the last few days of the campaign to win by a 9 percentage point margin over Brown.

The Republican campaign for governor collapsed at the beginning of the year when Larry Forgy, the consensus choice of Republican leaders, pulled out of the race. The winner of the primary was John Harper, a relatively unknown legislator. Wilkinson outspent Harper at least 10 to 1 in the general-election campaign, and was elected in November with 65% of the vote. Only 29% of the voting-age population voted—the lowest proportion of turnout in a gubernatorial election in the 20th century.

AP/Wide World

Wallace Wilkinson, a 45-year-old businessman, was the surprise winner of the Democratic primary for governor of Kentucky and won 65% of the vote in the November election.

KENTUCKY • Information Highlights

Area: 40,410 sq mi (104 660 km²).
Population (July 1, 1986): 3,728,000.
Chief Cities (July 1, 1986 est.): Frankfort, the capital (1980 census), 25,973; Louisville, 287,460; Lexington-Fayette, 213,600.
Government (1987): *Chief Officers*—governor, Wallace Wilkinson (D); lt. gov., Brereton Jones (D). *General Assembly*—Senate, 38 members; House of Representatives, 100 members.
State Finances (fiscal year 1986): *Revenue*, $6,710,000,000; *expenditure*, $5,706,000,000.
Personal Income (1986): $41,902,000,000; per capita, $11,238.
Labor Force (June 1987): *Civilian labor force*, 1,703,100; *unemployed*, 155,300 (9.1% of total force).
Education: *Enrollment* (fall 1985)—public elementary schools, 448,768; public secondary, 195,065; colleges and universities, 141,724. *Public school expenditures* (1985–86), $1,651,000,000 ($2,853 per pupil).

State Finances. The sluggish economy in Kentucky led to revenue shortfalls and several budgetary cutbacks during 1987. Experts predicted a gap between probable revenue and the costs of existing state programs of more than $400 million during the 1988–90 biennium. The stock-market crash late in 1987 created further pessimism about Kentucky's economy in the years ahead.

These gloomy economic forecasts prompted considerable debate during the gubernatorial campaign about the possibility of a tax increase. Wallace Wilkinson, however, firmly opposed higher taxes, and proposed instead the adoption of a state lottery. The popularity of the lottery was apparently a major factor in Wilkinson's upset primary victory. If the legislature approves, the voters in 1988 will be asked to approve a constitutional amendment authorizing a state lottery.

Workmen's Compensation. During a special session called by Gov. Martha Layne Collins in October, the legislature fundamentally revised the workmen's compensation program. In order to put a halt to skyrocketing costs, it cut back the level of benefits for future recipients. Because the heaviest financial burden comes from black-lung cases, the legislature changed the formula so that the coal industry would bear a larger proportion of costs and thus reduce the burden on other state industries.

MALCOLM E. JEWELL
University of Kentucky

KENYA

Long-standing good relations between Kenya and the United States were strained in 1987 when the United States joined Amnesty International, some Kenyans, and others in criticizing alleged Kenyan human-rights abuses. Kenyan tourism was not affected, however, nor was U.S. economic assistance, which amounted to approximately $53 million in 1987. Significantly, however, the U.S. Congress made future assistance contingent upon an improvement in Kenya's human-rights record.

Human Rights Issues. According to Amnesty International, since 1986 more than 100 persons had been detained and at least two of them died while in prison. There also were charges of confessions obtained under duress and of unfair trials. This was seen as a calculated effort on the part of the Kenyan government to silence political opponents, particularly supporters of a secretive antigovernment known as *Mwakenya*.

During an official visit to Washington in March 1987, President Daniel arap Moi was embarrassed by a *Washington Post* story on the brutal death of Peter Karanja, a Kenyan businessman. The official version was that Karanja died of natural causes, but, according to Amnesty International, three weeks after he had been taken into custody in good health he died with clear evidence that he had been tortured.

President's Reactions. President Moi's response was to accuse Kenya's critics of malicious propaganda, and he attempted to divert such criticism by linking local dissidents with external threats, especially from Libya. In a June reshuffle of the Kenyan cabinet, Moi demoted Foreign Minister Elijah W. Mwangale to the agriculture ministry, and appointed Zachary Onyonka as foreign minister. Moi apparently felt that Mwangale had failed in his official efforts to counteract these criticisms.

Kenya's President Daniel arap Moi (left) *met with top U.S. officials—including Defense Secretary Weinberger—during March. Human rights and South Africa were key issues.*

AP/Wide World

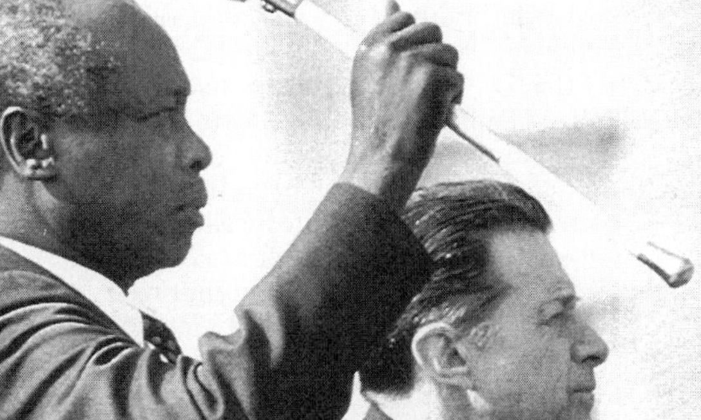

KENYA • Information Highlights

Official Name: Republic of Kenya.
Location: East Coast of Africa.
Area: 224,961 sq mi (582 650 km²).
Population (mid-1987 est.): 22,400,000.
Chief Cities (1983 est.): Nairobi, the capital, 1,047,951; Mombasa, 409,616.
Government: *Head of state and government,* Daniel T. arap Moi, president (took office Oct. 1978). *Legislature* (unicameral)—National Assembly, 170 members.
Monetary Unit: Kenya shilling (16.516 shillings equal U.S.$1, Aug. 1987).
Gross Domestic Product (1985): $4,800,000,000.
Economic Index (1986): *Consumer Prices,* (Nairobi, 1980 = 100), all items, 215.2; food, 187.1.
Foreign Trade (1986 U.S.$): *Imports,* $1,613,000,000; *exports,* $1,200,000,000.

In July, 72-year-old Oginga Odinga, who had been vice-president from independence in 1963 until 1966, read a highly critical open letter to Moi before a group of reporters. While no Kenyan newspaper printed the letter, it received wide international coverage. Odinga, who is from Kenya's second-largest ethnic group, the Luo (the Kikuyu are the largest), criticized government restrictions on freedom of speech and expression and called for the return to a multiparty system. At a nationally broadcast public rally, Moi rejected Odinga's suggestion and claimed that in the past the multiparty system had led to ethnic tensions and rivalries.

The Economy. Kenya's economic problems continued to mount as well. The Kenya shilling sank to a new low against the U.S. dollar in June. Coffee, which represents 40% of Kenya's exports, earned less in 1987 as a result of a world price slump, and foreign indebtedness increased. The debt-service ratio rose from the 7% prevalent in recent years to 20% of foreign currency earnings needed just to meet annual interest and repayments. Because of its very high population growth rate (4.2%), it has been estimated that Kenya requires a 4.5% annual economic growth rate just to keep per capita gross national product (GNP) from falling, an unrealistically high figure even under favorable economic conditions.

AIDS. Minister of Health Kenneth Matiba, in announcing that the official number of Acquired Immune Deficiency Syndrome (AIDS) cases had doubled to 625 since the last official account, acknowledged that the actual number might be much greater. He launched a new program against AIDS, funded with close to $4 million from Western donors.

PATRICK O'MEARA AND
N. BRIAN WINCHESTER
Indiana University

AP/Wide World

Despite political unrest, the South Korean capital of Seoul bustled. The nation's economy continued its rapid recovery, and the city prepared for the 1988 Olympic Games, expected to be a major boost to the economy and to South Korea's image.

KOREA

The salient event of 1987 in Korea was the first open presidential election in South Korea in 16 years. The candidate of the ruling party won, against a divided opposition, sparking protests by young dissenters against electoral fraud. Most South Koreans, however, appeared to accept the results of the election.

Republic of Korea (South Korea)

In 1987, South Korea narrowly but successfully avoided the alternative extremes of prolonged political disorder and martial law.

Politics and Government. As the year opened, an escalating political confrontation was in progress between the ruling Democratic Justice Party (DJP) and the principal opposition party, the New Korea Democratic Party (NKDP), over constitutional revision. The former wanted a parliamentary system, under which the real power would be the prime minister, who would be chosen by the DJP-dominated National Assembly. The NKDP demanded a presidential system, with the president to be elected by direct popular vote rather than by an electoral college susceptible to manipulation by the DJP as under the existing constitution.

The opposition was divided over whether to compromise with the DJP on the constitutional question. The two most influential members of the NKDP, Kim Young Sam and Kim Dae Jung, were unwilling to do so and broke away to form their own party, the Reunification Democratic Party, the name being intended to indicate a high level of interest in unification with Communist-controlled North Korea. President Chun Doo Hwan, the leader of the DJP, promptly announced (on April 13) that the constitutional dialogue was suspended and the next presidential election would be held under the existing constitution, with victory almost certain to go to the DJP candidate (not Chun, since he was ineligible to succeed himself). This announcement provoked a huge uproar from both the moderate wing (the opposition parties) and the militant wing (radical students and intellectuals and some members of the large Christian community) of the opposition. Both wings also felt outraged by the violent deaths of students from time to time, either while in the custody of the frequently brutal police or while involved in demonstrations.

The uproar grew even greater when, on June 10, the DJP formally announced that its presidential candidate would be Roh Tae Woo, a former general like President Chun, as well as Chun's close colleague. There were serious and violent demonstrations in Seoul and other cities, which the numerous and well equipped riot police tried vigorously to suppress by means that included a particularly virulent and long-lasting form of tear gas.

So forceful was the behavior of the police that the demonstrating students began to attract significant sympathy and support, for the first time, from elements of the urban middle and industrial working classes. This was naturally most disturbing to the DJP and the government. Encouraged, the students grew bolder and more effective in fighting the riot police. On June 19, the demonstrators succeeded in disarming and taking prisoner a substantial number of riot police.

Emergency consultations then were held within the ruling elite, including the army leadership. There were two basic options. One was to declare some form of martial law, bring in the army, and crack down hard on the demonstrators, as had been done in May 1980 but with very adverse effects on the regime's image at home and abroad. The other was to ride more or less with the political tide, as the army had done in 1960, when demonstrations precipitated the fall of President Syngman Rhee.

Several factors determined a prompt choice of the second option. One was the unwillingness of a significant number of the generals to intervene, and the preference of most of the DJP members of the National Assembly for a political rather than a military solution. Another was a calculation that essential nonintervention was the course most likely to promote stability in 1988, a year of crucial importance to the establishment because a new president would be inaugurated in what had been predicted to be a peaceful transition and the Olympic Games would be held in Seoul. The Olympics were taken very seriously as a potential mark of maturity for the Republic of Korea. The United States strongly opposed military intervention, favoring some sort of compromise between the DJP and the opposition.

Perhaps most important of all, Roh Tae Woo, who had been serving as the leader of the DJP contingent in the National Assembly, decided that he did not want to be imposed as president on a deeply divided country and preferred to take his chances on a popular vote. On June 29, accordingly, he made a statesmanlike declaration supporting the opposition's demands for a popularly elected president, restoration of the political rights of Kim Dae Jung (regarded by the military as a dangerous leftist and still nominally serving a 20-year sentence for sedition), the release of political prisoners, measures to promote human rights and freedom of the press, and elective rather than appointed institutions of local government. He did not, however, specifically propose curbing the behavior of the police toward demonstrators and prisoners. He added that he would withdraw from the presidential race if his proposals were not endorsed by President Chun. Chun did endorse them on July 1.

These dramatic developments constituted at least a potential alteration of fundamental importance in the political situation and led promptly to the resumption of talks on constitutional revision between the DJP and the opposition. The resulting draft, which provided for direct presidential elections, enhanced civil rights, and a stronger role for the National As-

South Korea's December election pitted the government-backed Roh Tae Woo, top, *against the opposition's Kim Dae Jung,* center, *and Kim Young Sam,* bottom. *Roh won.*

Photos AP/Wide World

sembly, was approved by the Assembly on October 12 and by a majority of over 90% in a popular referendum on October 27.

The prospect of a relatively open presidential election naturally generated a lively campaign. Kim Young Sam and Kim Dae Jung were unable to agree on which of them should be the opposition candidate for the obvious reason that each wanted to play that role. Kim Dae Jung held off announcing his candidacy for a time in the hope that his nomination for a Nobel Peace Prize would be successful and would immunize him against military pressure of any kind, but after he failed to win the prize he broke away from the Reunification Democratic Party and formed his own party, the Party for Peace and Democracy. At about the same time, in early November, Kim Young Sam formalized his status as the candidate of the Reunification Democratic Party. Roh Tae Woo was campaigning vigorously meanwhile as the candidate of the DJP. There was also a fourth major candidate, Kim Jong Phil (New Democratic Republican Party), who had been an important political figure during the presidency of Park Chung Hee (1961–79).

Meanwhile, student demonstrations continued, and labor unrest became a serious problem for the first time in the history of the Republic of Korea. Strikers against a large number of firms won various concessions that fell short of their maximum demands but were the object of considerable police repression. President Chun, who was inevitably viewed as something of a lame duck, did his best to retain control of events and to counter the tendency of Roh Tae Woo to crowd him out of the spotlight, an example being a visit by Roh to the United States in September.

With some 90% of registered voters turning out, Roh Tae Woo won the December 16 balloting, with 36.6% of the vote; Kim Young Sam followed with 28%, and Kim Dae Jung garnered 26.9%. Young dissenters demonstrated against Roh's victory, charging that it was rigged. Other South Koreans, however, noting that the combined vote for the "two Kims" was 55%, expressed anger that the opposition had been unable to settle on a single candidate, who well might have defeated Roh. The U.S. administration quickly congratulated Roh but withheld judgment on the cheating issue.

Economic Developments. The economy, continuing its recovery from its bad year in 1985, grew rapidly in 1986 (12.5%) and 1987 (12.2%). Growth rates were high in both the manufacturing and the service industries. Presumably, this good performance was due in part to the fact that the government, active as usual in economic matters, had implemented in 1986 a program of "structural reform" consisting of limited liberalization of restrictions on imports, tax reform, and a new tax code, the more or less compulsory liquidation of financially troubled firms, and the redirection of investment funds toward industries considered economically "strategic."

Bad summer floods seriously affected agricultural production in several areas in 1987.

Expanded domestic demand began to make a significant contribution to South Korea's prosperity, which previously had been fueled largely by export-led growth based in part on a systematically undervalued currency.

Foreign trade nonetheless continued to play a crucial role in the South Korean economy. The 1986 total of $63.5 billion (both exports and imports) had included South Korea's first trading surplus ($4.25 billion). This fact reflected not only South Korea's industrial strength but also the declining prices of some of its major imports, such as oil and commodities. There was a deficit of $5.44 billion with Japan, in spite of which the Japanese government took measures to reduce imports of Korean textiles and apparel. There was a sizable, largely unpublicized, trade with China. South Korea had a surplus of $7.34 billion with the United States, which caused some concern on both sides even though it was only a small part of a much larger overall American trading deficit. Although the won appreciated slightly in relation to the dollar, Seoul continued to resist U.S. pressure for a major upward revaluation. Similarly, liberalization of tariffs on and nontrade barriers to American goods, in response to pressure from Washington, occurred on a limited scale, and mainly in commodities such as tobacco rather than in fields incorporating high-industrial technology. Like many others, South Koreans worried about a possible upsurge of U.S. protectionism.

Systematic official measures reduced the external debt somewhat in 1986, to approximately $44.5 billion. Despite the large size of this figure, South Korea was considered creditworthy abroad because of the dynamism of its economy and its good repayment record.

SOUTH KOREA • Information Highlights

Official Name: Republic of Korea.
Location: Northeastern Asia.
Area: 38,023 sq mi (98,480 km²).
Population (mid-1989): 42,100,000.
Chief City (Oct. 1985 est.): Seoul, the capital, 9,798,057.
Government: *Head of state,* Chun Doo Hwan, president (formally inaugurated March 1981). *Head of government,* Kim Chung Yul, prime minister (appointed July 1987). *Legislature*—National Assembly.
Monetary Unit: Won (807.7 won equal U.S.$1, Aug. 1987).
Gross National Product (1986, 1986 prices): $94,100,000,000.
Economic Indexes (1986): *Consumer Prices* (1980 = 100), all items, 144.2; food, 141.0. *Industrial Production* (1980 = 100), 195.
Foreign Trade (1986 U.S.$): *Imports,* $31,584,000,000; *exports,* $34,714,000,000.

In an effort to restrict the outflow of funds for nonessential purposes, Seoul continued to limit severely the number of passports issued to South Koreans wishing to travel abroad as tourists, while doing its best to encourage tourism on the part of foreigners in Korea. The 1988 Olympics were expected to boost foreign spending in Korea substantially.

International Relations. Not only the domestic politics but also the foreign policy of South Korea centered in large part on an official determination to ensure the security and success of the Olympic Games. In addition to enhancing South Korea's general international image, the games were seen as potentially improving its position with respect to the North Korean adversary. If by any chance North Korea participated, it would be doing so on Seoul's ground and more or less on its terms. There appeared to be no chance that North Korea would succeed in persuading more than a handful of leftist governments to join it in boycotting the games. It was virtually certain that the major Communist countries, including the Soviet Union and China, would participate, probably with beneficial effects on their (nondiplomatic) relations with South Korea and an adverse impact on their ties with North Korea.

The games were only one, although a very important, aspect of an active South Korean diplomacy reflecting an upsurge of nationalism on the part of both the ruling elite and the opposition. One facet of this trend was a desire to minimize dependence on the United States by improving ties with other non-Communist countries. In this spirit, then Prime Minister Lho Shin Yong visited five West European countries in January-February. His first stop was the Netherlands, with which many South Koreans feel a special affinity because it shares with the Republic of Korea an economic dynamism as well as a determination to avoid domination by its larger neighbors.

Such developments notwithstanding, South Korea's most important single external relationship continued unquestionably to be the one with the United States. This was true despite a considerable increase in anti-Americanism in various forms within both the establishment and the opposition. The U.S. alliance appeared essential to South Korea's security from attack by North Korea, and the American market was vital to the prosperity of South Korea's export industries and indeed its entire economy.

Various statements, especially some by Secretary of State George Shultz and Assistant Secretary of State Gaston Sigur, showed clearly that the U.S. government strongly supported political liberalization in South Korea and compromise between the ruling party and the opposition, and it objected to the idea of military intervention. These statements amounted to pressure on Seoul, and probably played some, although not a decisive, part in the tendency toward liberalization. The United States also encouraged a resumption of dialogue between the two Koreas and with Seoul's acquiescence began to allow its diplomats to respond to overtures from North Korean counterparts in third countries. Economic issues between South Korea and the United States remained fairly serious; South Korea feared an erosion of its access to the American market, and the United States wanted freer access to the South Korean market.

Democratic People's Republic of Korea (North Korea)

Two main issues confronted the North Korean leadership in 1987: uncertainties surrounding the implementation of the plan of the 75-year-old leader Kim Il Sung to be succeeded by his son Kim Jong Il and North Korea's role (if any) in the 1988 Olympic Games.

Domestic Affairs. Kim Il Sung's health was the subject of recurrent rumors; he was reported to have suffered a stroke in June, but by early July he was well enough to receive the Indonesian foreign minister. In any event a succession was clearly more or less imminent, and Kim had been preparing for it for more than a decade by grooming his son Kim Jong Il, who appears to be a spoiled playboy, as his successor. This has been done in part through repeated—rather than continual—bursts of adulatory publicity, one episode of which marked the first few months of 1987. It also appears that the younger Kim has been entrusted by his father from time to time with temporary control over policy, but that the elder Kim has resumed authority in the intervals. It is unlikely that Kim Jong Il's effort to succeed his father is universally popular in North Korea; there have been plausible reports, for example, of opposition from elements of the military leadership.

The army may also resent the reported demobilization of some 150,000 men to work on labor projects, possibly including new dams being built north of the Demilitarized Zone (be-

NORTH KOREA • Information Highlights

Official Name: Democratic People's Republic of Korea.
Location: Northeastern Asia.
Area: 46,540 sq mi (120 450 km²).
Population (mid-1987): 21,400,000.
Chief Cities (July 1980 est.): Pyongyang, the capital, 1,445,000; Hamhung, 780,000.
Government: *Head of state,* Kim Il-sŏng, president (nominally since Dec. 1972; actually in power since May 1948). *Head of government,* Li Gun Mo, premier (appointed December 1986). *Legislature* (unicameral)—Supreme People's Assembly. The Korea Workers' (Communist) Party: General Secretary, Kim Il-sŏng.
Gross National Product (1985 U.S.$): $24,000,-000,000.

tween North Korea and South Korea) and reconstruction programs following a devastating typhoon that struck in 1986.

Conscious that its economic development has lagged badly behind that of its neighbors, Communist and non-Communist alike, Pyongyang launched a loudly publicized Seven Year Plan covering 1987–93. Apart from evidencing an interest in increased exports and even in foreign investment in North Korea, the plan was marked by the usual priority for heavy industry. The military budget—announced as about 14% of the total budget but in reality probably considerably higher—was clearly a drag on the rest of the economy.

International Relations. Pyongyang had felt badly aggrieved by the award of the prestigious privilege of hosting the 1988 Olympics to Seoul, the capital of its rival and adversary. The initial North Korean response, a demand to cohost the games, was both unacceptable to South Korea and impractical and was rejected by the International Olympic Committee. The latter, eager nevertheless to avoid a nasty confrontation and to contribute if possible to better relations between the two Koreas, then offered to allow Pyongyang to host five of the events. Pyongyang regarded this as insufficient and apparently decided to boycott the games.

The North Korean economy has clearly needed to open itself to the outside world, and some moves in that direction—such as efforts to encourage investment and tourism from abroad—have in fact been made, but on a much more limited scale than in China. Pyongyang's hopes for more beneficial economic relations with the outside world sustained a severe blow in August, when a group of West European banks declared it to be in default on about $770 million of its external debt and initiated legal proceedings to seize a corresponding amount of North Korea's overseas assets.

As in the past, North Korea continued to maneuver between its two allies, the Soviet Union and China, without "tilting" completely toward either. In recent years, Moscow's influence has tended to outweigh Beijing's by virtue of Soviet ability and willingness to transfer modern weapons systems, in exchange for overflight and port-call privileges. On the other hand, North Korea maintains its wary political cooperation with China. Kim Il Sung visited China in May, and Kim Jong Il reportedly did the same, in secret, during August. Beijing's evident intent to attend the 1988 Olympics in Seoul was probably among the matters discussed. As for many years past, it was reasonably clear that neither Moscow nor Beijing wanted North Korea to attack South Korea again but that both felt a compulsion to avoid antagonizing Pyongyang. Hence, both were coming to accept, although informally and apparently with distaste, Kim Jong Il as his father's successor.

North Korea achieved a diplomatic success of sorts by hosting in June a meeting of foreign ministers of countries belonging to the Nonaligned Movement, of which North Korea is rather incongruously a member.

The Two Koreas

As for many years past, a controlled but dangerous hostility continued to dominate the relationship between North Korea and South Korea.

The Military Balance. Even though Pyongyang made no overt move during the political instability of 1987 in South Korea, Seoul has been very concerned over a potential "water bomb" in the form of a large dam being built north of the Demilitarized Zone and capable eventually, in theory, of releasing enough water to flood Seoul. To counter this threat, real or imaginary, Seoul began work on a containing dam and offered Pyongyang electric power if it would stop construction of its dam.

Pyongyang's claim to have demobilized a large part of its armed forces and an accompanying demand that South Korea reciprocate were rejected with skepticism by the other side. North Korea protested vigorously, as always, against the annual Team Spirit exercises involving South Korean and U.S. troops, held east of Seoul.

Political Contacts. Mutual hostility and suspicion continued to guarantee that each side would reject any overture from the other.

Talks between the two sides had been broken off by the North in January 1986. Proposals by Seoul for resumption in some form, such as a summit meeting or a foreign minister's meeting, were rebuffed. Pyongyang's preference is for talks involving not only the two Koreas but also the United States, with which North Korea hopes to negotiate the withdrawal of U.S. forces from the South. To date this idea has been unacceptable to Seoul and therefore also to Washington. The old North Korean proposal for a confederation was revived in 1987 but rejected by Seoul, which feared a trick.

The South Korean opposition tends to be less afraid of North Korea than the establishment is and claims to be more interested in contacts conceivably leading to unification. Militant elements probably want to embarrass the government or even see it brought down in the course of engagement with the North, regardless of the consequences.

The ruling DJP has come around to favoring "cross-recognition" of both Koreas by the major powers, preferably after the Olympics. The United States and Japan would recognize Pyongyang; the Soviet Union and China would recognize Seoul. Pyongyang has not accepted this idea.

HAROLD C. HINTON
The George Washington University

LABOR

Although joblessness remained a widespread concern, the unemployment rate fell in the United States and some other large countries in 1987. Despite declines in the percentage of organized workers in a number of industrialized countries, unions often still had an important impact on labor relations and public policy.

United States

The improvement in the U.S. unemployment situation came as a surprise to most forecasters. As jobs expanded by 2.8 million in 12 months, the civilian jobless rate dipped under 6% in September for the first time since late 1979. The number of unemployed, slightly more than 7 million, had increased by 850,000 in the eight years, but civilian employment in that period rose by far more, 13.2 million.

Out of the total labor force of 121.6 million (persons age 16 and over working or looking for work), 114.5 million held jobs—112.8 million civilians and 1.7 million members of the armed forces stationed in the United States. Nearly 54 million women, or 56% of females of working age (compared with 76% of males), were in the labor force and accounted for 44% of that labor force. Seven out of every ten mothers with school-age children worked outside the home.

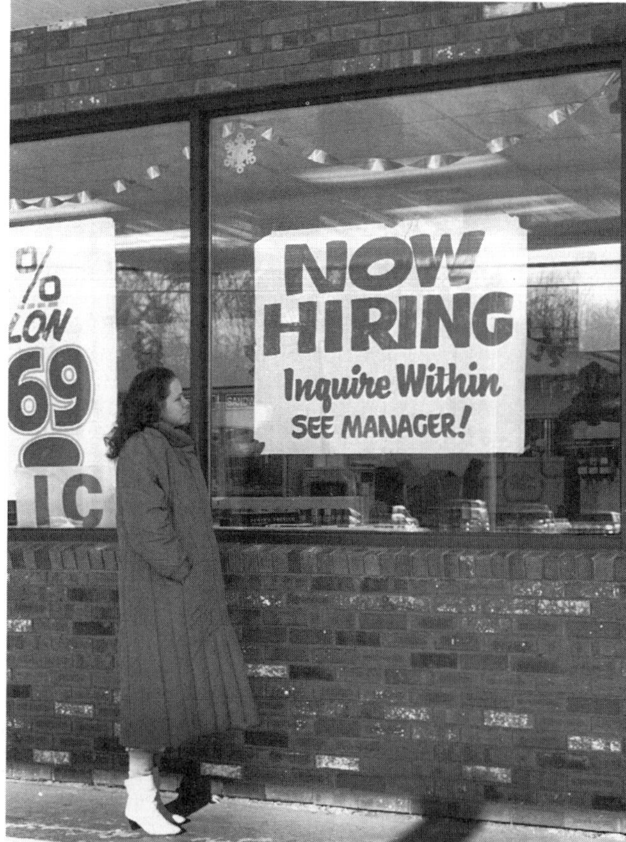

© Paula Kobylarz

With fewer young people in the U.S. work force, help-wanted posters were common in the service industries. By December, the nation's unemployment rate had dropped to 5.7%.

In some cities and suburbs, jobs went begging, especially in service occupations, partly because the population of 18-to-25-year-olds was shrinking and because fewer of those young people were in the labor force. But some areas and groups did not share in the bright labor-market picture. Double-digit unemployment rates still lingered in some cities of Michigan, Texas, Louisiana, and Florida. About 5 million persons were working part-time only because no full-time jobs were available. Another one million, discouraged by employment prospects, had stopped looking for work. The black unemployment rate, 12.3%, was roughly seven percentage points higher than that of whites.

Earnings and Costs. The nation's 83 million wage and salary workers with full-time jobs averaged $371 in weekly earnings in the third quarter, a real (inflation-adjusted) increase of a little less than 1% over a year earlier. Women in full-time jobs had weekly earnings of $301, compared with $428 for men. The figures reflected a gradual decrease in the male-female pay gap; the female-to-male earnings ratio of 70.3% was up a full percentage point from a year earlier and 4.5 points from 1983. Average weekly earnings of nonsupervisory workers in manufacturing industries in September were $406, a 2% drop in real terms over the previous year.

Employees in private industry (including executives) averaged benefits worth 21% of total earnings, or 32% including vacations and other paid leave, according to a special annual study of March labor costs by the Bureau of Labor Statistics. Taking into account earnings and all benefits, including paid leave, employee compensation costs rose by 3.4% over the 12-month period ending in September, roughly the same as the increase in the corresponding period a year earlier.

Productivity. Labor productivity, measured by volume of output per hour of work, continued a welcome upswing that began in 1986. The increase in the third quarter was the strongest in 18 months, as the output of private businesses other than farms expanded at an annual rate of 5.5% over the previous quarter, while the number of hours worked increased at only a 1.8% pace. The biggest gain in output, 7.4%, came in manufacturing. While productivity climbed 3.6% during the third quarter for all nonfarm businesses, it was up 3.8% for manufacturing alone. As a result, unit labor costs in manufacturing actually declined by 2.3% from the second quarter in 1987 and 2.4% from the third quarter in 1986.

Collective Bargaining. Under major labor contracts covering 1,256,000 U.S. workers, settlements reached in the first nine months of 1987 provided wage increases of 2.3% annually over the life of the contracts. That was 0.2% points lower than increases granted the last time parties to these settlements negotiated, usually two or three years earlier. Of late both salaries and total compensation costs have been rising at a rate twice as fast for workers without union contracts as for those with them, although the average pay of nonunionized workers remains lower (27% lower in 1986).

Under new three-year contracts with Ford and General Motors, the United Auto Workers accepted modest wage increases in a trade-off whereby the workers received stronger job security and management got greater flexibility in work rules. The agreements were reached, in mid-September with Ford and early October with General Motors, without coming close to a strike.

The ill-fated three-week strike of National Football League players in the fall was a highly publicized exception to the general rule: striking had grown further out of favor as a union tactic in 1987. The percentage of working time lost because of work stoppages was at the lowest level since 1939, when the Labor Department started collecting those figures.

AFL-CIO. The highlight of the 17th biennial convention of the American Federation of Labor-Congress of Industrial Organizations (ALF-CIO) in October was the re-affiliation of the International Brotherhood of Teamsters, which with 1.7 million members is the country's largest union. This brought the AFL-CIO's total membership to about 14.5 million.

The Teamsters came under well-publicized threats from the Justice Department to remove its 21-man executive board and place the whole union in the hands of a court-appointed trustee because of the department's belief that the union was controlled by criminals. In welcoming the Teamsters back to the "house of labor" after a 30-year absence, AFL-CIO President Lane Kirkland repeated an earlier executive-council statement: "A government-supervised trade union, like an employer-supervised union, is a contradiction in terms." He promised to oppose a government takeover by all legal means, including the filing of charges with the International Labor Organization. At the same time, Kirkland stressed "our support for full and vigorous law enforcement aimed at those who seek to prey on our movement."

The convention's position on the 1988 presidential election was in sharp contrast to that of the convention four years earlier, when the AFL-CIO warmly welcomed Walter Mondale and endorsed him for the presidency eight months before he obtained the support of sufficient delegates for the Democratic Party nomination. This time, after polling its membership and finding no consensus, the AFL-CIO postponed a decision on endorsement. Instead it adopted a strategy of getting unionists elected as delegates to party caucuses and conventions, in hopes that it will be able to rally behind a candidate early in 1988.

Ann Dore McLaughlin, 46-year-old former assistant secretary of the treasury and undersecretary of the interior, took the oath as secretary of labor on December 17. Her husband, television-commentator John McLaughlin, held the Bible.

AP/Wide World

Aware of a continuing need to improve its public image, the AFL-CIO adopted a two-year, $13 million media campaign called "Union, Yes."

Social Legislation. With both houses of the U.S. Congress controlled by the Democrats, there was an upsurge in the introduction of AFL-CIO-supported bills affecting federal labor and social policy. Almost all of the bills, however, were held over to 1988, as senators and congressmen became engrossed in the Iran-contra hearings, negotiations on the federal budget, and other priorities.

Faced with criticism from labor and other groups, the Occupational Safety and Health Administration (OSHA) took new interest in enforcing existing laws. *Business Week* headlined: "OSHA Awakens from Its Six-Year Slumber." In July, OSHA proposed a $2.6 million fine against IBP Inc., the nation's largest meatpacking firm, for allegedly doctoring accident and illness records, and then in October followed with a record $4.2 million in penalties against Bath Iron Works, a shipbuilding and repair facility in Maine. With 3.5 million workplaces under its jurisdiction, OSHA had 1,036 inspectors in 1987, down by 300 from 1980.

Another federal agency, the Federal Pension Benefit Guaranty Corporation, which insures the pensions of one out of three U.S. workers, was swamped by demands on its resources by corporations (chiefly steel companies) in bankruptcy proceedings. Because it assumed the pension payments of those firms' retired workers, the agency found itself at the point of insolvency with a deficit of $4 billion, and asked Congress to revise the bankruptcy and other laws to put less of the burden of business failures on the taxpayer. Further, unions and senior-citizen groups pressed for changes in a pension law that allows companies to withdraw "surplus" monies from retirement funds instead of saving them for future cost-of-living adjustments.

Department of Labor. After two-and-a-half years on the job, Secretary of Labor William E. Brock resigned in October to run the presidential campaign of Senate Minority Leader Bob Dole. To succeed him, President Reagan selected Ann Dore McLaughlin, who until March was undersecretary of interior. Brock's record at the Labor Department included deflecting a Justice Department move to end numerical goals for the hiring of women and minorities by contractors.

Canada

The unemployment rate in Canada—which in recent years has moved in tandem with that of the United States but at a level 2–3% higher —dropped to 8.6% in September. Employment, which reached the 12 million mark in September, grew at roughly the same pace as in 1986: 3% in the 12-month period ending in August. With 5.7 million women employed or looking for jobs, the rate of female participation in the labor force reached a new high in July: 57.6%, fractionally higher than the U.S. rate. Most workers had a decline in real income, as average wages remained almost level while prices rose 4%.

Union membership grew by 1.4% to nearly 3.8 million, but dipped very slightly as a percentage (from 37.7% to 37.6%) of the faster-growing total of nonagricultural wage and salary workers.

The Canadian Labour Congress (CLC), which with more than two million members is by far the nation's largest labor center, clashed sharply with the Progressive Conservative-led national government over the proposed U.S.-Canadian free-trade agreement. In October, when the U.S. and Canadian governments agreed on a comprehensive bilateral free-trade pact, Bob White, president of the 150,000-member Canadian Auto Workers, denounced it for setting Canada on a course to "a Rambo, dog-eat-dog society with no ability to maintain our social programs or to structure our own economy." (*See* special report, page 165.)

International

A downward trend in unemployment also favored a few Western European nations, most notably Great Britain, whose jobless rate declined from 12% in September 1986 to 9.8% in October 1987. Belgium, France, the Netherlands, and Spain, however, still maintained double-digit rates ranging from 11% to 20%, levels more or less the same as in 1986. Unemployment in Japan in early 1987 topped 3%, the highest in decades, but then dropped to 2.8% during the summer months.

British-government claims of a "job creation miracle" were backed by a 372,000 increase in employment during the 12-month period ending in June, whereas Western Europe generally had a sluggish job-creation record. Most of Britain's new jobs were in service industries. A 3.7% job gain in services also enabled Japan to increase its employment levels slightly to 60 million in 1987; jobs in manufacturing actually declined by 1.8%.

Wage increases almost everywhere were modest, especially when adjusted for inflation. In Japan the unions' annual spring-wage offensive managed to win an average pay increase of 3.5%, down from 1986's 4.5%, which already was a record low. In Australia most workers took a cut in real wages amid the economic problems of 1986–87, including a sinking world demand for Australian commodities.

Shorter Hours. In West Germany, where negotiated wage increases averaged 3.6%, the same as in 1986, some unions broke with tradition and agreed to contracts having a duration of more than a year. The powerful German Metalworkers union, which with 2.6 million members is the world's largest union, for the first time signed a three-year contract. In return the employer federation accepted movement toward the union's goal of a 35-hour workweek: the average weekly working time will be cut in two steps from 38½ to 37 hours by 1989.

In Japan a gradual reduction of working hours would be achieved through legislation rather than collective bargaining. Making the first revision in the country's labor-standards law since it was adopted in 1947, the Japanese Diet (parliament) cut the standard workweek from 48 to 46 hours for larger companies, effective April 1988. Firms with fewer than 300 workers, which employ almost 90% of all those on a payroll, will be given until 1991 to put the same reduction into effect. Existing overtime premiums of 125% remained in effect.

The changes in Japan and West Germany did not signal a wide trend. The length of weekly working hours, whether set by legislation or labor-management agreement, has generally remained on a plateau for years. In most export-driven economies, such as Hong Kong, South Korea, and Malaysia, that plateau has stayed high—at 60 hours or more per week for millions of working men and women, and sometimes children.

Labor Costs. In a study of the effect of exchange-rate fluctuations on hourly labor costs (including benefits) in manufacturing, the British magazine *The Economist* reported: "In 1985 America's labor costs were 63% higher than Japan's and 39% above West Germany's." However, the study found, "With today's weaker dollar, American workers cost 20% less than those in West Germany and roughly the same as in Japan." Moreover, it was shown, when productivity and labor costs are combined, the United States in mid-1987 produced 5–20% more per hour of labor costs than did any other major economic power. The study did not include Asia's newly industrialized countries, whose currencies are tied closely to the U.S. dollar.

Consolidation in Japan. In November union organizations representing 5.6 million workers in private Japanese businesses merged into a new national center called the Japanese Private Sector Trade Union Confederation, or Rengo. Rengo was expected to play a much more influential role on the political scene than did the two big national confederations—Domei, with 2.4 million members, and Churitsuroren, with 1.3 million—which it absorbed. The new center signaled its orientation by affiliating itself with the International Confederation of Free Trade Unions, the non-Communist world union body headquartered in Brussels, Belgium.

Until the birth of Rengo, another group, the traditionally left-of-center General Council of Trade Unions of Japan, or *Sohyo*, was the largest national labor center. However, of its 4.2 million members, 1.8 million in the private sector were gradually shifting to Rengo. At its convention in July, Sohyo decided to dissolve itself in 1990, when most of its public-sector affiliates were expected to blend into Rengo. A far-left minority faction within Sohyo planned to form its own organization at that time to continue the pursuit of political goals, such as opposing Japan's security treaty with the United States.

Labor Influence. One pressure behind Japanese labor unity was that union membership, which peaked at 56% of the work force in 1948, decreased to a post-World War II low of 28.2% in 1987. On the other hand, union membership remained both stable and high in a number of other countries—especially Australia (58%), where the Australian Council of Trade Unions forms the bulwark of the governing Labor Party; and in the Nordic countries—Sweden (82%), Norway (60%), Finland (80%), and Denmark (more than 90%)—where unions have a strong voice not only in politics but in management as well. But the relative status of organized labor in other industrial countries, especially the United States (down to less than 18%), continued to stimulate speculation that unions have had their day and are bound to die out as institutions in the modern world.

Certain events in 1987 indicated that membership size, while vastly important, could not be relied on as the sole measure of union strength and influence. In three widely separated countries where only a small minority of workers are united in organizations not under government control, unions stood out as a force on which millions pinned their hopes for the future:

• In Poland, although the government has seized its assets and suppressed its formal structure, the banned Solidarity trade-union confederation retained the loyalty of a large mass of workers. With an informal national council, Solidarity continued to operate in the underground and to serve as a restraining influence on Communist authorities.

• In South Korea workers formed 1,500 local unions within a five-month period, and, thus reinforced, the Federation of Korean Trade Unions successfully pressured the government to adopt long-demanded reforms in labor law and practice.

• In South Africa the newly emerging black labor unions demonstrated their strength with a two-day general strike by an estimated 1.5 million workers during the whites-only parliamentary elections in May. According to a researcher at the independent South African Institute of Race Relations, the nation's black unions have become the "major vehicle" in the struggle against apartheid.

ROBERT A. SENSER, *Free-lance Labor Writer*

Preserving the English Language

Few students of the English language would disagree that the information and media explosion in America has brought with it a flood of bad language—improper grammar, incorrect word usage, and ambiguous or nonsensical phrases. In recent years, however, in part because of the efforts of a handful of language "watchdogs," there are increasing signs of a new concern for clear, concise self-expression. Individuals such as Edwin Newman, Richard Mitchell, and William Safire have written extensively on English grammar and word usage, to growing audiences. Groups such as the Unicorn Hunters, the Committee on Public Doublespeak, and the Society for the Preservation of English Language and Literature (SPELL) publish newsletters that have thousands of subscribers. In corporations and classrooms, greater attention is being paid to proper, precise use of the language. Most major metropolitan newspapers in the United States now carry columns that focus on grammar and style. Dozens of "grammar hot lines," many sponsored by college English departments, have cropped up across the nation.

Words—Written and Spoken. The heightened interest in good language may mark the end of a long-standing debate, nurtured by linguists and educators, over the importance of written versus spoken language. While the debate lasted, less and less formal grammar was taught in U.S. schools. Students were encouraged to express themselves even if they had nothing to express. Taught to write the way they speak, Americans stopped using language as a tool for genuine thinking and understanding. Opinions based on reason and knowledge were replaced by notions based on gut feeling. We found ourselves living in an age of slogans.

As many people are now realizing, what we need most is rigorous language instruction for students at the elementary-school level. This means, of course, that teachers themselves must know the difference between proper and improper usage. Unless correct word usage is taught in schools, we will continue to lose the distinctions, for example, between "disinterested" and "uninterested," "fewer" and "less," "comprise" and "compose," and "tragic" and "sorrowful." Proper (written) usage will be indistinguishable from informal (spoken) usage. We will lose the subtle but important distinctions between words. Distinctions and subtleties of meaning are both useful and necessary for expressing ideas, and, as the philosopher Suzanne Langer has pointed out, it is the expression of ideas that accounts for the traits—such as ritual, art, science and speech—which set us apart from animals.

Some Examples of Correct Usage

Comprise-Compose. Comprise means to contain or include. Compose means to form by putting together. For example, the transit system comprises four subway and nine bus lines. The author outlined the 24 chapters that composed his book.

Disinterested-Uninterested. Disinterested means unbiased or impartial. Uninterested means bored or indifferent. For example, Jane was a disinterested witness at the trial. John was an uninterested spectator at the game.

Fewer-Less. Fewer should be used in reference to a number of persons or things; less refers to quantity. For example, the farmers are growing less corn this year. Fewer than 300 farmers participated in the demonstration. N.B. exceptions: Use less when the number is one or when a specified number suggest a quantity or sum (less than $10 million).

Tragic-Sorrowful. Tragic refers to a situation of, marked by, or expressive of a lamentable, dreadful, or fatal event or affair, calamity, disaster. Sorrowful means full of or marked by deep distress and regret. For example, the young brother and sister were killed in a tragic auto accident. The death of the wonderful 99-year-old woman was a sorrowful event for her many friends.

The Need for Rules. Proper grammar is as important as proper word usage. Words express meaning in two ways. They carry meaning in their own right, denoting specific objects or concepts, and, in relation to other words, they express more complex ideas. Grammar is a system of rules, a formal structure that allows individual words to function in relation to others and produce meaning. "He ain't never going to lose" may be understood as "he is never going to lose," but the erosion of grammar is the erosion of meaning. To take the extreme view, if we dispense with grammar, eventually we will be unable to understand each other. To be less extreme, we may already understand each other less well than ever before.

Even the most ardent defenders of proper grammar and usage know full well that language changes. To think or wish otherwise would be foolish. Although the watchdogs may differ in how much they are willing to accept as change, they do agree that changes may be controlled, that they may be judged good or bad, that some produce vitality in the language, and that some result in cliché or loss of meaning. In other words, they accept that language changes, but they insist on vigilance.

W.S. PENN, *Michigan State University*

LAOS

Policies adopted at the fourth congress of the Communist Lao People's Revolutionary Party (LPRP) late in 1986 governed political and economic life in Laos in 1987. Efforts to rejuvenate the LPRP and to introduce greater market incentives into the economy reflected measures taken in neighboring Vietnam, which largely controls the Laotian party and government.

Politics. The fourth party congress added some younger members to the Politburo and Central Committee. Phoumi Vongvichit continued as acting president. The foreign minister and second-ranking Politburo member were dropped from the executive secretariat of the Central Committee for reasons of health or age.

Economics. The second five-year plan (1986–90), also approved at the party congress, calls for improvements in food production, forestry, industry, and transportation. Grain (mainly rice) production is to rise from 1.4 million tons in 1985 to 2.2 million tons in 1990. Presumably much of the increased production will be traded to Vietnam and other Soviet-bloc countries for needed imports of fuel, fertilizer, and machinery. Soviet-bloc countries provide Laos with about $80 million a year for road-building and other development projects, but much of the money is wasted through mismanagement.

Foreign Relations. Laos sought to improve relations with nearby China and Thailand as well as with the United States. A Chinese delegation's visit to Vientiane in December 1986 produced no immediate results, however, and Thai-Lao relations remained cool because of a border conflict. The Lao accused both China and Thailand of harboring large resistance armies of Laotian refugees. Yet Thailand was the main hard-currency trading partner of Laos, and the Lao hoped to increase exports of surplus electric power to Thailand.

The main U.S.-Lao issue was Washington's desire for a full accounting of Americans missing in action. An official U.S. mission visited Vientiane in August, and the Lao vice foreign minister went to Washington during the UN General Assembly session in the fall.

PETER A. POOLE
Author, *"Eight Presidents and Indochina"*

LAOS • Information Highlights

Official Name: Lao People's Democratic Republic.
Location: Southeast Asia.
Area: 91,430 sq mi (236 800 km²).
Population (mid-1987 est.): 3,800,000.
Government: *Head of state:* Phoumi Vongvichit, temporary president; *Head of government,* Kaysone Phomvihan, chairman. *Legislature* (unicameral)—National Congress of People's Representatives.

LATIN AMERICA

As in the previous five years, Latin America in 1987 struggled with mounting external debt and sluggish economic growth. According to preliminary estimates by the UN Economic Commission for Latin America and the Caribbean (ECLAC), the Latin American economies, among the most dynamic in the world in the 1960s and 1970s, grew by less than 3% in 1987. For six consecutive years, the region has failed to reach 4% in annual growth of the gross domestic product (GDP).

In many countries of the region, according to the Inter-American Development Bank (IDB), "falling living standards have begun to threaten both political and economic development." Nonetheless, states the IDB, there has been a "profound transformation" in the Latin labor market that sets the stage for "very favorable" economic, social, and political developments in the future.

Debt Problem. The region's aggregate external debt, which stood at $325 billion at the onset of the debt crisis in 1982, reached $400 billion in 1987. Two important debtor countries, Brazil and Ecuador, began to withhold debt-service payments during the year, citing the need to conserve funds for internal investment to stimulate renewed economic growth.

After an early run-up, oil prices began to soften at midyear, leading to speculation that big petroleum exporters like Mexico and Venezuela also could find themselves short of the foreign exchange needed for debt service. Concern mounted when interest rates began rising later in the year, since most of Latin America's debt was contracted at floating rates that vary with market conditions.

As a result, several big money-center banks, led by Citicorp, began to move nonperforming assets—loans that are not being repaid—off the books and into secondary markets at large discounts. In some cases, the debtor countries themselves purchased the loans at considerably less than face value. In July, for example, the Bank of America announced that a consortium of banks would permit Bolivia to repurchase part of its debt at a substantial discount. Some commercial banks also offered to swap part of the debt for equity in productive Latin American enterprises.

Trade. For the fifth year in a row, Latin American countries registered a surplus in their trade with the United States in 1986. The surplus of $13.2 billion was due not to an expansion of exports, but to a decline in imports, reflecting the austerity conditions in much of the region. The value of Latin America's foreign trade, which reached $200 billion in 1981, dropped to less than $150 billion in 1986.

Rising protectionism in the industrialized countries elicited strong Latin American protest in 1987. The Latin governments were es-

AP/Wide World

President León Febres Cordero of Ecuador (at left, in glasses) *is welcomed in Quito after his release by rebellious air force troops who took him hostage January 16. He was held for 12 hours and set free after acceding to demands.*

pecially concerned about an omnibus trade bill pending in the U.S. Congress during much of the year. The bill would require retaliation against countries that consistently run trade surpluses with the United States.

A special trade committee of the Organization of American States (OAS) said that passage of the bill would "make it more difficult for the countries of Latin America and the Caribbean to obtain the income they need for their economic and social development and for meeting their burdensome international financial commitments."

The countries of the region also showed a willingness to negotiate bilateral trade agreements, bypassing the multilateral mechanisms of the General Agreement on Tariffs and Trade (GATT). The United States signed a landmark trade liberalization pact with Canada and negotiated a more limited bilateral arrangement with Mexico. Argentina, Brazil, and Uruguay signed bilateral accords to open the way for increased Southern Cone regional trade, effective Jan. 1, 1987.

Labor Force. In an analysis of the Latin American economies, the IDB found major changes in the structure and composition of the labor force from 1950 to 1980. There has been a massive shift from agriculture to industry. The IDB reported the number of people employed in industry and services increased 2.9 times and 3.4 times, respectively, while output in those sectors multiplied six times. In contrast, agricultural output tripled during the period, and the farm-work force grew by only 30%.

The IDB also found that the number of working women had increased significantly. Between 1950 and 1980, the number of men in the Latin American work force rose by 94%, but working women's ranks more than tripled, growing from 9.8 million to 30.9 million. In 1950, women constituted 18% of the economically active Latin American population; by 1980 the proportion was 26%.

Politics. The region's difficult economic situation put increasing strains on Latin American governments during 1987. Military establishments in Argentina, Brazil, Ecuador, and Peru grew restive with the inability of civilian governments to cope with the debt and stagnant growth. In Argentina, the centrist government of President Raúl Alfonsín suffered a serious loss in gubernatorial and congressional elections in September. In Peru, a stubborn Maoist insurrection continued.

The democratic current in most of the hemisphere, however, remained strong. Presidential elections were scheduled in Ecuador in January 1988, in Mexico in July, and in Venezuela in December 1988. Bolivia had municipal elections in December 1987, and congressional elections were scheduled in El Salvador in March 1988.

International. The USSR made important diplomatic and political advances in Latin America in 1987. In October, Soviet Foreign Minister Eduard Shevardnadze visited Brazil, Argentina, and Uruguay. The Soviet Union is Argentina's largest export customer and also supplies the bulk of the Peruvian army's military equipment. The USSR has diplomatic relations with 16 Latin American countries, compared with only five 30 years ago.

In view of the serious economic situation, the IDB sought a capital increase in 1987. The United States blocked the request and demanded veto power over IDB loans. The United States fell $50 million behind in its scheduled contribution to the OAS, impairing the organization's ability to function.

Health. Although the incidence of AIDS (Acquired Immune Deficiency Syndrome) is lower in Latin America than in the United States, the disease is on the rise, especially in the Caribbean. The Pan American Health Organization (PAHO) reported 2,631 cases in Latin America in December 1986; PAHO reported only 352 cases in the region in 1983.

RICHARD C. SCHROEDER, *"Visión" Magazine*

LAW

It was another year of transition for the U.S. Supreme Court, as Justice Lewis F. Powell announced in the closing minutes of the 1986–87 term that he was retiring at age 79. As the nation celebrated the 200th anniversary of the signing of the Constitution (*see* feature article, page 37), the dramatic retirement overshadowed some important rulings by the court and set the stage for a bruising confirmation battle over his successor.

President Ronald Reagan, hoping to place his conservative imprint on the court for years to come, selected Federal Appeals Court Judge Robert H. Bork (*see* BIOGRAPHY) to fill the vacancy. But the nomination was defeated in the Democratic-controlled Senate following an intense, marathon fight. Bork's opponents portrayed him as a right-wing ideologue whose appointment could topple three decades of civil-rights achievements. President Reagan's second nominee was Judge Douglas H. Ginsburg, another conservative from the U.S. Court of Appeals for the District of Columbia. But Ginsburg withdrew from consideration ten days later, after disclosure that he had smoked marijuana in the past. The president's next choice was 51-year-old federal Judge Anthony Kennedy of California, who had served for 12 years on the Ninth Circuit Court of Appeals.

The term itself was marked by some notable successes for court liberals, led by 81-year-old Justice William J. Brennan. He wrote important opinions for the court as it strengthened the wall of separation between church and state, bolstered affirmative-action programs for women and racial minorities, and extended legal protection to people afflicted by contagious diseases such as Acquired Immune Deficiency Syndrome (AIDS).

In the lower courts, there were important developments over issues of surrogate motherhood, church-state relations, and the right-to-die. It was also a busy year for discussion of American ethics, including cases dealing with insider stock trading and corruption charges against government officials.

In international law, such major world trouble spots as the Persian Gulf and Central America continued to raise charges and countercharges of violations of international norms. The U.S. administration, in a move to deny international legal protection to terrorists and anti-Western guerrillas, decided against ratification of a revised protocol—signed by the United States in 1977—of the 1949 Geneva Convention.

UNITED STATES

Supreme Court. The shifting center on the high court again determined the outcome of key closely watched cases. In addition to Powell, Justices Byron R. White, Harry A. Blackmun, and Sandra Day O'Connor were the moderate conservatives whose votes were crucial. Scalia, the court's newest member and Reagan's second appointee after O'Connor, generally came down on the conservative side. But Scalia demonstrated independence on occasion in disagreeing with Rehnquist, the court's leading conservative. Scalia also enlivened the court's oral argument sessions with a refreshing zest for the give-and-take of constitutional debate and legal interpretation.

AP/Wide World

U.S. Supreme Court Justice Lewis F. Powell, 79, retired at the end of the 1986–87 session, citing age and health.

Scalia and Rehnquist were the only dissenters in the term's most important ruling on religious freedom and separation of church and state. The justices held that states may not require the teaching of "creationism" in public schools where evolution is taught (*Edwards v. Aguillard*).The court called such a law a thinly veiled and unconstitutional attempt to promote religion. The ruling was hailed by civil libertarians, who said it will help safeguard the independence of educators from fundamentalist efforts to alter school curricula. In another religion case, the court held that churches and other religious institutions may refuse to hire anyone not of their faith even for nonreligious jobs. The court said that such employers are exempt from a federal law banning employment discrimination based on religion (*Corporation of Presiding Bishops v. Amos*). And the justices also ruled that states may not deny unemployment benefits to workers fired for refusing to work on their sabbath (*Hobbie v. Unemployment Appeals Commission*).

The court buttressed the rights of the handicapped in ruling that people physically impaired by contagious diseases—including tuberculosis and AIDS—are protected by a federal law banning discrimination against the handicapped (*Nassau County School Board v. Arline*). The decision was a defeat for the Reagan administration, which argued initially that the fear of contagion could be grounds for excluding someone from protection of the law.

In the area of military affairs, the court said that members of the armed forces may be court-martialed for crimes unrelated to their military duty (*Solorio v. U.S.*). The justices also barred members of the military from suing the government or its agents for even deliberate violations of their constitutional rights. The court blocked a lawsuit by a former soldier given LSD without his knowledge in secret chemical warfare tests (*U.S. v. Stanley*).

In a ruling that will help aliens seeking political asylum in the United States, the court held that refugees should be allowed to remain in the country if they have a "well-founded fear" of persecution if they are forced to return to their homeland (*INS v. Cardoza-Fonseca*).

The term was marked by a number of important criminal-law decisions, perhaps the most important of which upheld the use of preventive detention. The court ruled that persons accused of crimes may be denied bail before trial if deemed dangerous to the community. Public safety may in some circumstances outweigh the traditional presumption of innocence until proven guilty (*U.S. v. Salerno*). The court also said that federal judges should consider community safety before ordering the release of a criminal defendant whose state-court conviction they overturn (*Hilton v. Braunskill*).

In a ruling favoring the accused, the justices said that police who have entered a home lawfully because they suspect an emergency may not, without a court warrant, move items to check their serial numbers if they think the items are stolen (*Arizona v. Hicks*). But the court also held that honest mistakes by police officers may excuse what otherwise would be an unconstitutional search of someone's home. The case involved the search of the wrong apartment by police who had a warrant for another premises (*Maryland v. Garrison*).

The court also held that criminal suspects whose constitutional rights have been violated sometimes may be asked to give up their right to sue in exchange for the dropping of charges against them (*Newton v. Rumery*). Also, the justices said that courts cannot ban all testimony by defendants whose memories have been helped by hypnosis (*Rock v. Arkansas*); ruled that federal courts may force state officials to extradite fugitives to other states (*Puerto Rico v. Branstad*); and held that defendants accused of sexually abusing children do not have the right to be present at pretrial hearings conducted to determine the children's competency to testify (*Kentucky v. Stincer*).

In perhaps the last sweeping legal challenge to capital punishment, the court said that state death penalty laws can be valid even if statistics indicate they are carried out in racially biased ways. The court upheld Georgia's law even though convicted killers of white people in the state are far more likely to be sentenced to death than those convicted of killing blacks (*McCleskey v. Kemp*). The court also held that accomplices may be sentenced to death in murder cases if they displayed a "reckless indifference" for human life although they did not kill anyone or intend to kill anyone (*Tison v. Arizona*). But the court ruled that states may not make death sentences mandatory for prison inmates who kill other inmates or guards while serving life terms (*Sumner v. Shuman*).

Marking another important year for women's rights, the court said that states may force Rotary International and perhaps numerous other male-only clubs to admit women as members (*Rotary International v. Rotary Club of Duarte*). The court also said that states may require employers to give pregnant workers job protection not available to other employees. It upheld a California law requiring employers to grant unpaid leaves of absence to women unable to work because of pregnancy (*Cal Fed v. Guerra*). But the court also said that states are under no special legal obligation to pay unemployment benefits to women who lose their jobs after taking maternity leave (*Wimberly v. Labor and Industrial Relations Commission*).

The court buttressed affirmative action in two key decisions. It ruled that employers may give special preferences in hiring and promoting women and members of racial minorities to create a more balanced work force even without admitting past discrimination (*Johnson v. Transportation Agency*). And, in upholding a plan for promotion of equal numbers of black and white Alabama state troopers, it said that racial quotas may be used to hasten promotions of racial minorities (*U.S. v. Paradise*).

In a pair of cases, the court said that civil-rights laws dating back to the Civil War and primarily aimed at helping blacks may be used to ban and punish discrimination against Arabs and Jews (*St. Francis College v. Al-Khazraji* and *Shaare Tefila Congregation v. Cobb*).

In defeats for government regulators, the court also handed down two major rulings strengthening individual property rights. The court said that landowners must be compensated when government regulations bar them even temporarily from using their property (*First English v. Los Angeles County*). And the justices ruled that state and local governments are limited in granting access to private land and may have to pay the owners for allowing such access (*Nollan v. California*).

Finally, in the area of free speech, the court said that the government is not engaging in unlawful censorship by labeling as "political propaganda" three Canadian films on acid rain and nuclear war (*Meese v. Keene*). The court also forbade government-run airports from imposing sweeping bans on free speech in trying to prevent distribution of leaflets and soliciting of donations in terminals (*Board of Airport Commissioners v. Jews for Jesus*). The justices ruled that the U.S. Olympic Committee has absolute control over all commercial and promotional uses of the word "Olympic" and acted within its authority in barring a homosexual group from sponsoring an athletic event called the Gay Olympics (*San Francisco Arts v. U.S. Olympic Committee*). And, in a ruling that could make it more difficult to obtain convictions under state obscenity laws, the court said that juries should not use local standards of taste in deciding whether sexually oriented material has redeeming value (*Pope v. Illinois*).

Local Justice. In the lower courts, probably no case attracted more national attention than one involving the issue of surrogate motherhood. A judge in New Jersey said that Mary Beth Whitehead must honor a contract and surrender the baby she bore for a childless couple, William and Elizabeth Stern. The so-called "Baby M" case marked an important turning point in the controversy over surrogate motherhood. But Mrs. Whitehead vowed to continue her fight, and the debate over the issue in her case and around the nation is certain to rage on. (*See* feature article, page 55.)

The battle between Christian fundamentalists and educators heated up as school officials in Alabama successfully overturned a book-banning ruling by federal Judge W. Brevard Hand. The judge said that secular humanism is a religion and that 44 textbooks which espouse such views may be banned from public schools. But a three-judge panel of the 11th U.S. Circuit Court of Appeals overruled Hand and restored the books to the classroom.

The panel's decision in August came just three days after the 6th U.S. Circuit Court of Appeals dealt fundamentalists another setback. That appeals court dismissed a lawsuit filed by Tennessee fundamentalists seeking to shield their children from "godless" textbooks. The court held that the 1st Amendment rights of seven families were not violated by public-school textbooks that the plaintiffs said offended their Christian beliefs. The ruling also threw out a lower court order awarding those families more than $50,000 to pay for private school tuition and other expenses.

In another case from New Jersey, that state's Supreme Court made it easier for hopelessly ill patients and their families to decline life-sustaining treatment. In three right-to-die cases, the state court sanctioned an end to force-feeding and hydration of the patients. The cases involved an elderly woman in "a persistent vegetative state" who made it clear while she was healthy that she did not wish to be kept alive by extraordinary measures; a mentally competent young woman with a terminal degenerative illness who asked to be allowed to die; and a 31-year-old woman in an irreversible coma who had not made it entirely clear whether she would want to be kept alive by a feeding tube. In the latter case the court bowed to the wishes of the woman's husband.

The issue of drug testing in the workplace, which was expected soon to reach the U.S. Supreme Court, prompted a ruling in New York against mandatory testing. The New York Court of Appeals, that state's highest court, said that school teachers may not be tested without a reasonable suspicion that they are engaging in drug abuse. The Patchogue-Medford school district had ordered its untenured teachers to submit urine samples for drug analysis as part of their routine physicals. The court of appeals, in a suit by the teachers' union, said the urine tests administered without a court warrant infringed on the reasonable privacy rights of the teachers.

JIM RUBIN, *The Associated Press*

AP/Wide World

The Pit Bull Dispute

One of the most widespread legal issues in U.S. state and local jurisdictions during 1987 had to do with an often-vicious breed of dog known as the "pit bull." Descended from the fighting bulldogs of the 19th century, the American pit bull is a squat, muscular, oval-headed terrier with steel-trap jaws and a fight-to-the-death instinct. From 1983 through 1987, the pit bull has been responsible for nearly two dozen bite-related deaths and numerous other brutal attacks in the United States. With the breed becoming increasingly popular, mounting fear has led at least three dozen states and communities since 1985 to pass laws aimed at dogs that bite people or at pit bulls in particular. The courts, however, have struck down a number of these statutes as too vague. Proponents of the breed claim that the pit bull is not naturally vicious and blame the attacks on improper treatment and training.

International Law

The revelation that U.S. officials had secretly sold arms to Iran and diverted part of the profits to the "contra" rebels in Nicaragua produced international as well as domestic repercussions in 1987, but few of these were matters of law—an indication that global norms are far more permissive than national rules of behavior, at least for superpowers.

Subsequent U.S. actions, however, raised several legal issues. The Reagan administration operated within maritime law in beefing up its fleet in the Persian Gulf to protect Kuwaiti tankers that were reregistered in July and flew the American flag. A UN Security Council resolution in July demanded a cease-fire in the Iran-Iraq war. It raised a new legal issue by proposing an international commission that would rule on responsibility for the conflict—a finding that could lead to legal obligations for billions of dollars in reparations.

In October, when Washington imposed an embargo on trade with Iran, the Tehran regime protested. It cited a 1981 pact, for the freeing of 52 Americans held hostage in Tehran, in which Washington pledged not to "intervene directly or indirectly, politically, or militarily, in Iran's internal affairs."

The case involving U.S. support of Nicaraguan contras (prior to the Iran arms sales diversion) remained on the docket of the International Court of Justice at The Hague. The 15-judge panel, known as the World Court, in 1986 had found the United States guilty of violating international norms. Now the court would have to define the amount of reparations if the two parties could not agree on it. The United States continued to reject the World Court's jurisdiction. Nicaragua, meanwhile, had brought two related cases in July 1986, involving the alleged granting of havens to the contras by neighboring Costa Rica and Honduras. The Sandinista government dropped its case against Costa Rica in August 1987, but the case against Honduras continued.

A five-judge panel of the court issued a unanimous ruling in December 1986 to resolve a frontier dispute between the African nations of Mali and Burkina Faso, a decision both nations accepted. A second five-judge panel was formed in March 1987 to hear a case between Italy and the United States involving the confiscation by Rome of an electronics factory that was wholly owned by two American corporations. And a third World-Court panel, also consisting of five judges, was named in May 1987 to deal with a frontier dispute between El Salvador and Honduras.

The only other case before the court in 1987 was the appeal of a UN personnel edict. The case involved a Soviet citizen, Vladimir Yakimetz, who defected while working in New York. His contract was not renewed, at Soviet insistence, despite positive ratings of his work. The court voted to back the UN's dismissal.

UN Secretary-General Javier Pérez de Cuéllar announced new rules in November on access to archives of the UN War Crimes Commission, a 17-nation body that disbanded in 1948 and left its records with the UN. For almost 40 years the files, including dossiers on some 25,000 people the commission deemed eligible for prosecution as war criminals, had been available only to governments. But when it was revealed that the files contained data on the former UN secretary-general, accused Nazi war criminal, and current president of Austria Kurt Waldheim, pressure for increased access grew. After consulting officials of the 17 former commission members, Pérez de Cuéllar announced the opening of the files to journalists and historians accredited by their governments.

The UN General Assembly in 1987 endorsed an international declaration on the "nonuse of force" in disputes. It also began discussion aimed at drawing the line between illegal acts of terrorism and legitimate acts of national liberation.

The UN Commission on International Trade Law reached agreement in 1987 on two issues of use in the world of commerce. One was a treaty on internationally negotiable instruments, an attempt to define rules permitting common-law and civil-law systems to pass into each others' zones with fewer problems and thus facilitate broader trade in commodities between the two zones. The second agreement was a manual for drafting contracts for the opening of factories in the Third World that require little technical input from the recipient country, plants known as "turnkey" operations. The manual enables lawyers in developing countries to protect their clients' interests when negotiating such arrangements.

The global epidemic of Acquired Immune Deficiency Syndrome (AIDS) prompted governments to consider new legal measures in 1987. Some 120 nations, meeting in Paris in October, agreed informally that no government would require compulsory testing for the deadly disease at international borders. Several nations, including India and Kuwait, and the West German state of Bavaria, had already passed domestic legislation mandating AIDS tests for some foreigners. The Paris delegates also agreed that AIDS tests would not be performed on individuals without their knowledge.

Legal issues also plagued a French-sponsored expedition to salvage valuables from the wreck of the *Titanic* off the coast of Newfoundland. The U.S. Senate passed a bill in August barring salvage items from sale or display in the country. But experts in maritime law noted that both ancient and modern codes recognize the legitimacy of such activities.

MICHAEL J. BERLIN, *"The Washington Post"*

Photos, AP/Wide World

Civil war continues in Lebanon. A car, top, *is destroyed during fighting between Shiite Muslims and Communist forces. A Fijian UN trooper,* above, *checks a woman's ID.*

LEBANON

Lebanon's landmark development in 1987 was the alarming breakdown in nearly all sectors of the economy. No event since the outbreak of civil war in 1975 has threatened the livelihood of the average Lebanese more than the drastic drop in the exchange value of the Lebanese pound against foreign currencies. At the political and military levels, Lebanon continued to serve as the open battleground for no fewer than four regional powers vying for influence and control. Internally, the situation gained increasing complexity as a result of the Syrian-orchestrated boycott of the Christian president by the Sunni Muslim prime minister, the Shiite Muslim speaker of the parliament, and other cabinet ministers. The one optimistic note was the noticeable decline in the level of random violence, particularly the indiscriminate shelling of civilian areas. Another kind of violence—state-sponsored terrorism and kidnapping of Westerners—became a sophisticated, professional operation.

The Economic Crisis. After 1984 the civil war shifted from the political and military fronts to the socioeconomic front. The downturn in Lebanon's economic fortunes began in 1984, accelerated in 1985–86, and reached the breaking point in 1987. Frightening are both the devastating consequences of the crisis and the absence of any remedy in the foreseeable future. The ongoing civil conflict has deepened sectarian fragmentation and paralyzed state institutions, making it difficult for any government authority to undertake policies that could halt or reverse the economic deterioration. Additionally, the government's expansionary fiscal policy has resulted in wasteful spending, and its reckless monetary policy has helped strain relations between the central bank and commercial banks.

A grave manifestation of the economic crisis was the loss of confidence in the national currency. The spiral drop in the exchange value of the Lebanese pound, from 87 pounds per U.S. dollar early in the year to 437.02 by late December, was unprecedented in Lebanon's modern history. Gradually, the Lebanese economy is being "dollarized" as most commercial transactions are conducted in U.S. dollars. By year's end, 81.5% of bank deposits were in foreign currencies, compared with 43.5% in December 1985.

Other economic indicators achieved records. With an estimated budget deficit in 1987 of 95 billion Lebanese pounds and a large public debt, Lebanon's ratios of budget deficit and public debt to national income are among the highest in the world. The deficit, financed primarily by the domestic economy, along with rapidly increasing import prices (Lebanon is an importer of most basic food items), drove inflation to an annual rate in excess of 500%. (Prior to 1975, inflation was less than 4%.) The one positive by-product of the crisis was the revitalization of the industrial sector, which gained a competitive edge in a broadening export market throughout the nations of Europe and the Arab world.

The lifting of subsidies on petroleum products and wheat in September helped curb the multibillion-dollar smuggling operations into neighboring countries, especially Syria, where prices of these commodities are higher. This measure, however, had only a marginally positive effect on the crisis. Recurrent shortages of certain food products, electric power cuts, and insufficient water supply were more frequent in 1987 than in previous years.

For the first time since the mid-1970s, the confederation of Lebanon's labor unions, composed of a multisectarian membership, organized a nationwide strike in October and held demonstrations throughout the country to force the government to take measures to alleviate economic hardships. Strikes also were organized by the teachers' unions demanding salary raises and social benefits to compensate for the drop in their real income. Although these moves reflected the widespread popular discontent with the overall economic situation, demands could not be met under the current circumstances.

Domestic Political Developments. For more than five months, from January to June, newspapers speculated on the possibility of reopening channels of communication between President Amin Gemayel and Syrian President Hafez al-Assad, as a first step toward ending the political boycott exercised by Lebanon's most influential Muslim leaders. The boycott began following the failure early in 1986 of the Syrian-sponsored Tripartite Agreement, signed in Damascus in December 1985 by rival Lebanese militia leaders.

President Gemayel's attempts to break the deadlock by proposing reform plans and by enlisting the support and mediation of a number of Arab countries, notably Algeria, did not soften the Syrian position. At the Arab summit held in the Jordanian capital in October, Arab leaders paid little attention to the Lebanese crisis, and even Lebanon's request for economic aid was not granted.

Government paralysis reached a peak following the assassination of Prime Minister Rashid Karami on June 1 by an explosive device placed under his seat in a Lebanese Army helicopter. Not surprisingly, the identity of Karami's assassins will never be known with any certainty. There were other politically motivated assassinations (or assassination attempts) in 1987 aimed at highly visible political and religious figures. With the exception of the abortive attempt to assassinate former President Camille Chamoun in January in East Beirut, most other attacks took place in the western sector of the city. (Chamoun died at age 87 of heart failure on August 7.) Two prominent victims were a leading Sunni religious authority, Shaykh Subhi Al-Salih, and President Gemayel's Sunni Muslim adviser, Muhammed Shuqair. The latter was one of the few Muslim politicians who continued to cooperate with the president.

Another important development was the abrogation of the 1969 Cairo Agreement, signed between the Lebanese government and the Palestine Liberation Organization (PLO), and of the May 17 Accord of 1983 (signed between Lebanon and Israel) on May 21 by the Lebanese parliament. The National Assembly, elected in 1972, was composed of 79 members (of a total of 99), with 20 deputies having died.

Divisiveness was not confined to state institutions and major communal groups; it spread to each community and, more precisely, to the sectarian militias claiming to represent their respective groups. In the Christian areas, the Lebanese Forces (the major Christian militia), led by Samir Geagea, was engaged in a bitter conflict with supporters of President Gemayel over the control of the Phalangist Party, now under revisionist leadership not in agreement with the traditional party line of the Gemayel family. In areas controlled by the Shiite militia Amal (led by cabinet minister Nabih Berri) and the Druze militia of the Progressive Socialist Party (led by cabinet minister Walid Jumblat), the situation was highly unpredictable. These two militias, along with a few others, notably the militia of the militant Shiite Party of God *(Hizballah),* were at odds on basic issues.

The making and breaking of alliances among these groups, reflecting Syria's changing policies toward Lebanon, culminated in the bloody street fighting in West Beirut in February. This round of violence, which resulted in more than 200 deaths, ended only after Syrian troops entered the city to redress the balance in favor of Amal, Syria's major ally. This time, unlike Syria's military deployment in 1976 as part of the Arab Deterrent Forces, the Syrian army was not invited by the Lebanese government. Nor did it need an official invitation, for Syrian forces, now under no official mandate by the Arab League, have unimpeded access to more than 60% of Lebanese territory.

Syria's Agendas in Lebanon. Since 1975–76 Syria has changed its policies and priorities in Lebanon with every variation in the regional balance of power, particularly in relation to the Arab-Israeli-Palestinian conflict. In 1987, Syria did not pursue any major political or military offensive in Lebanon. But Damascus had two broad objectives: first, to deepen its presence in Lebanon by weakening government institutions and depriving any leader or state authority of sufficient power to tip the balance in ways unfavorable to Damascus; second, to maintain the upper hand in areas under its military control by exercising a divide-and-rule tactic designed to preserve a precarious status quo among the various groups that gravitate in Syria's orbit.

In the period that preceded the signing of the U.S.-sponsored Lebanese-Israeli Accord of May 17, 1983, Syria had to deal with the potential threat of a united Lebanon under a strong central government and with increasing Israeli influence on certain Christian groups. By 1987, however, neither the limited Israeli presence in southern Lebanon nor Christian opposition to Damascus constituted any real threat to the Syrian regime in Lebanon.

Since the Israeli withdrawal from the south in 1985 (except for a security buffer zone controlled by the Israeli-backed South Lebanon Army), there had been a working arrangement between Israeli and Syrian forces in Lebanon. In 1987, Israel maintained a defensive posture. Occasional attacks undertaken by Iranian-backed Islamic movements resulted in no change in the balance of power on the ground. In addition to the tacit understanding between Syria and Israel, the latter kept communication lines open with the Druze militia in the Chouf mountains and the Shiite Amal militia in the south.

If Syria faced no imminent threat from either Lebanese factions or Israel, this did not apply to Syrian-Palestinian relations in Lebanon. Damascus was the greatest obstacle facing PLO Chairman Yasir Arafat in his quest to regain control over Palestinian camps in Lebanon. Since 1983, President Assad has been engaged in an all-out war against Arafat, first by supporting a mutiny within Arafat's core guerrilla group, al-Fatah, aimed at creating a substitute leadership to Arafat's, and later by investing political capital, military power, and prestige in fighting Arafat's forces in Lebanon. By 1987, neither party had been able to score a decisive victory.

Assad was unable to destroy Arafat's legitimacy, and Arafat could not beat Assad's army and pro-Syrian militias. This conflict is what is commonly known as "the war of the camps" in Beirut, Sidon, and Tyre between Palestinian forces and the Syrian-backed Amal militia. Fighting continued intermittently throughout the year, especially in January, February, and September. Military confrontations could not be ended despite high-level mediation by Algeria, Libya, and Iran. An agreement was signed between Amal and Palestinian representatives on September 11, but like its predecessors, it was no more than a convenient cease-fire before the eruption of another round of fighting.

The more interesting Syrian agenda in Lebanon concerns Syria's relations with Iran. Although Syria brought Iranian revolutionary guards to Lebanon in 1982 and worked closely there with various Iranian-backed terrorist groups, in 1987 Syria began to revise some of its tactics regarding Ayatollah Khomeini's Iranian regime. The first major military confrontation between Syrian troops and *Hizballah,* Iran's main ally in Lebanon, took place in February. But Damascus was careful to distinguish between the essentially strategic relationship it sought to maintain with Iran (at war with Iraq, Syria's foremost Arab enemy) and its hostility to Iran's unruly client *Hizballah,* whose leadership was accused of cooperating with Arafat's forces, Syria's principal enemy in Lebanon.

The Business of Terrorism. Terrorism, involving the kidnapping of foreign nationals and random acts of violence against Lebanese and non-Lebanese targets, underwent a qualitative change in 1987. It was no longer the activity only of "crazy fanatics." Rather, it was an organized business enterprise run by professional terrorists and sophisticated politicians who have come to understand (and exploit) the loopholes of Western democratic systems and the power of public opinion. Of course, it is only in a country like Lebanon—the "no-man's land" of the Middle East—where terrorists can so readily put their skills into practice, and where states can kidnap citizens of other states without being held responsible for the deed.

In 1987 hostage-taking served objectives other than strictly political. Examples include two Germans, both kidnapped in January. One was released for money in September but the other detained in retaliation for the arrest in Frankfurt of a Lebanese hijacker. Several Lebanese and nationals of Arab countries were also the targets of kidnapping for ransom.

See also TERRORISM.

FARID EL-KHAZEN
American University of Beirut

LEBANON • Information Highlights

Official Name: Republic of Lebanon.
Location: Southwest Asia.
Area: 4,015 sq mi (10 400 km^2).
Population (mid-1987 est.): 3,300,000.
Chief Cities (1980 est.): Beirut, the capital, 702,000; Tripoli, 175,000.
Government: *Head of state,* Amin Gemayel, president (took office Sept. 1982). *Head of government,* Salim al-Huss, acting prime minister (named June 1987). *Legislature* (unicameral)—National Assembly.
Monetary Unit: Lebanese pound (437.02 pounds equal U.S.$1, Dec. 29, 1987).
Foreign Trade (1985 U.S.$): *Imports,* $2,200,000,000; *exports,* $482,000,000.

LIBRARIES

Libraries in the United States in 1987 were affected by legislation enacted in 1981 and 1985 for the purpose of reducing the federal deficit. The Gramm-Rudman-Hollings Act had categorized libraries as nondefense spending; consequently, libraries suffered the total impact of reductions. Aggravated further by the falling value of the U.S. dollar, library funding was limited in 1987. Some improvements were noted however, including the U.S. House of Representatives' approval of the Second White House Conference on Libraries and Information Services (WHCLIS), scheduled for some time between Sept. 1, 1989, and Sept. 1, 1991, and the School Improvement Act of 1987, which relates to school library and media centers.

Legislation. The fiscal year 1988 Labor, Health, and Human Services Education Appropriations Bill (HR3058) represents the first funding of the new Higher Education Act (HEA) Title II-D, College Library Technology and Cooperative Grants. Funded at $5 million, HEA-II-D provides grants for equipment needed to share college-library resources, joint-use library facilities, and special needs utilizing technology to enhance library or information science. With its funding at $85 million, the Library Services and Construction Act (LSCA) I has been increased $5 million from the 1987 appropriation. LSCA III was funded at $20 million, an increase of $2 million.

Economic News. Generally the salaries of librarians were increasing. The average (mean) beginning salary for women in 1986 was $20,718, a 5% increase over 1985; for men the beginning salary was $21,498, a 6% increase.

The dollar's fall abroad caused research libraries in the United States to reduce severely the purchase of foreign publications. The drop in purchasing power of the U.S. dollar has averaged 40% since the summer of 1986.

Library Education. Three American Library Association (ALA) accredited library schools —Emory University in Atlanta, the University of Southern California, and Vanderbilt University in Nashville—announced in academic year 1986–87 that they would cease operation. Various functioning schools changed their names to include "information" in the titles. The University of Hawaii's library school was renamed the School of Library and Information Studies. Similar changes were made by Dalhousie University (Nova Scotia), Northern Illinois University, and the State University of New York at Albany.

School Match, a Westerville, OH, firm that helps individuals and corporations evaluate schools, reported that of all expenditures that influence a school's effectiveness—including those for facilities, teachers, and guidance services—the level of expenditures for library and media has the highest correlation with student achievement.

Copyright Hearing. Librarians and publishers testified April 8 and 9 at a public hearing on section 108 of the Copyright Act of 1976 relating to library photocopying. They held that because the balancing between the rights of copyright holders and the needs of library users was being achieved, no change in the present copyright legislation should be made.

Library of Congress. Dr. James H. Billington, an author, historian, educator, and administrator, was sworn in as the nation's 13th Librarian of Congress on September 14. He succeeded Dr. Daniel J. Boorstin. Many librarians were against the appointment because of Billington's lack of experience as a librarian.

Associations. By September 1987, ALA membership totaled 45,145. Thomas Galvin, the association's executive director, announced that revenues for 1987 totaled $9,034,538, an increase of 18% over the proceeding year.

The ALA's 106th annual conference was held in San Francisco, CA, June 27–July 2. ALA President Regina Minudri's theme was "Diversity: The Challenge to American Libraries." The 17,206 registrants surpassed New York's record 16,530 in 1986. At the end of the conference, Dr. Margaret Chisholm was inaugurated president, and Dr. F. William Summers of Florida State University was president-elect.

The Canadian Library Association (CLA) held its 42d annual conference in Vancouver, B.C., June 11–16. Attracting 1,778 delegates, the conference was a great success according to incoming President William Converse.

The International Federation of Library Associations and Institutions (IFLA) met in Brighton, England, August 16–22. Paul Nauta, director of the Frederick Muller Academy Library School in Amsterdam, the Netherlands, was appointed its secretary general.

RICHARD KRZYS, *University of Pittsburgh*

LIBRARY AWARDS OF 1987

Beta Phi Mu Award for distinguished service to education for librarianship: Sarah K. Vann, professor emeritus, University of Hawaii

Randolph J. Caldecott Medal for the most distinguished picture book for children: Richard Egielski, *Hey Al* (story by Arthur Yorinks)

Melvil Dewey Award for recent creative professional achievement of a high order: Herbert S. White, dean, School of Library and Information Science, Indiana University

Grolier Award for unique contributions to the stimulation and guidance of reading by children and young people: Lillian Morrison, former coordinator, Young Adult Services, New York Public Library

Joseph W. Lippincott Award for distinguished service to the profession of librarianship: Edward G. Holley, former dean, School of Library Science, University of North Carolina

John Newbery Medal for the most distinguished contribution to literature for children: Sid Fleischman, *The Whipping Boy*

LIBYA

Components of the Libyan army and air force supporting rebels in northern Chad were driven out of that country in 1987 by Chad's Western-trained and -equipped military. The costly fighting in Chad damaged Libya's already reeling economy. Efforts to revitalize it led to a warming in relations between Libya and several neighbors. Events in Chad also contributed to a decline in active Libyan support for radical movements throughout the world, although U.S. officials insisted that this quiescence stemmed from Libyan fear of a repeat of the U.S. raid of April 1986. Revelations in the U.S. press about that attack, and about general U.S. policy toward Libya in recent years, disclosed that the United States had, on several occasions, sought to oust Libyan leader Muammar el-Qaddafi.

Conflict with Chad. Libyan forces inside Chad were in disarray from the very beginning of the year. Chad's army overran the garrison at Fada on January 2 and maintained the upper hand in the heavy fighting that followed, culminating in the capture of the crucial Libyan air base at Wadi Doum on March 22. Deprived of effective air cover, the Libyans withdrew from Faya-Largeau, an oasis they had occupied since 1983 and their last stronghold in Chad, a few days later.

Chad's victory stemmed not only from its own newly found unity, but also from the declining morale of the Libyan military. Disgruntled by their inadequate training and the harsh conditions of service in northern Chad, most Libyan soldiers had little enthusiasm for the war. Their malaise was heightened as they sustained thousands of casualties in the early months of 1987, resulting in defections and a general breakdown in the army's discipline. Consequently, as Chadian forces pressed their advantage at the end of March, a disorderly Libyan retreat ensued. Military matériel, including an arsenal of Soviet-supplied weaponry with an estimated value of as much as $1 billion, was abandoned.

LIBYA • Information Highlights

Official Name: Socialist People's Libyan Arab Jamahiriya ("state of the masses").
Location: North Africa.
Area: 679,359 sq mi (1 759 540 km²).
Population (mid-1987 est.): 3,800,000.
Chief Cities (1980 est.): Tripoli, the capital, 1,223,000; Benghazi, 530,000.
Government: *Head of state,* Muammar el-Qaddafi (took office 1969). *Legislature*—General People's Congress (met initially Nov. 1976).
Monetary Unit: Dinar (0.297 dinar equals U.S. $1, August 1987).
Gross Domestic Product (1986 est. U.S.$): $20,000,000,000.
Foreign Trade (1986 U.S.$): *Imports,* $5,000,000,000; *exports,* $5,000,000,000.

Renewed fighting erupted in August as Chad accused Libya of new incursions. In a counterattack, Chad occupied positions in the Aozou Strip, a disputed territory on the frontier between the two countries, for several weeks. Early in September the hostilities entered a new phase. Chad invaded Libya proper, for the first time since the conflict had begun in 1980, to destroy an airfield from which it claimed bombing raids on northern Chad were being launched. In retaliation, Libyan planes attempted, but failed, to bomb Ndjamena, Chad's capital.

Both sides again suffered high casualties in the fighting, and both agreed to abide by the terms of a cease-fire proposed on September 11 by the Organization of African Unity (OAU). Although Libya strengthened its hand by recruiting Lebanese Druze militiamen for service in the event of renewed combat, the cease-fire held. In conjunction with it, the OAU also took on the task of mediating the long-standing dispute over the Aozou Strip. The process of documenting the conflicting claims was expected to be a lengthy one, and a final decision was not anticipated for some time.

Economy. The expense of Libya's military involvement in Chad aggravated existing problems in its economy. Although U.S. economic sanctions, imposed in 1986, had little impact on Libya, the generally depressed price of oil on world markets did. Oil revenues in 1987 exceeded those of the previous year, reaching nearly $8 billion, but were grossly inadequate to support both domestic development and military spending. Inefficiency in many state-operated industries, as well as in the agricultural sector, combined with Libya's declining ability to pay for vital imports to create shortages of consumer goods. To secure badly needed revenues, the government sold its shares in Fiat, the Italian automotive company. Some of the $3 billion earned in this transaction was used to purchase badly needed foodstuffs.

Support for Radicals. Colonel Qaddafi's focus on the war with Chad resulted in a decrease in, but not an end to, Libyan support for radical movements worldwide. Governments as far afield as Spain and Australia alleged that Libya was fomenting unrest in areas they deemed crucial to their interests. In February, Spain arrested several Libyans in the Canary Islands, accusing them of plotting with islanders seeking to create an independent government there. In May, Australia closed the Libyan People's Bureau (as the country's embassies are styled) in Canberra on the grounds that Libya had attempted to incite Australia's Aboriginal population and had aided guerrilla movements in French New Caledonia and the Indonesian provinces of Irian Jaya and East Timor.

In October, French authorities seized a vessel loaded with Libyan weapons and manned

AP/Wide World

Libyan leader Col. Muammar el-Qaddafi (right) *met in August with Baptist minister Graham Ferguson Lacey* (left), *who was seeking information about Anglican Church envoy Terry Waite, who disappeared in Lebanon in January. While Qaddafi's attention focused on the war with Chad throughout 1987, he continued to maintain ties with radical movements worldwide.*

by individuals linked by security forces in Dublin with the Irish Republican Army (IRA). The incident produced a resounding denunciation by the British government of Libya's willingness to arm and support the IRA, which Britain regards as a dangerous terrorist organization.

U.S. Relations. U.S. officials suggested that Libya's lowered profile stemmed from fear of a repeat of the air raids on Tripoli and Benghazi in April 1986. Qaddafi used the first anniversary of those attacks as an opportunity to censure the United States, charging that its main purpose in carrying out the raids had been to assassinate him. The Reagan administration vehemently denied this accusation, but articles published in *The New York Times* in February, based on interviews with officials in the Central Intelligence Agency (CIA), the National Security Council (NSC), and other agencies of the U.S. government, asserted that Qaddafi's death was the primary objective of the mission.

Other information concerning American policy toward Libya during the Reagan presidency was unearthed by journalists in 1987. In 1983, Egypt and the United States conspired to create a situation intended to deceive Libya into believing that a coup under way in Khartoum, capital of Sudan, required Libyan support to succeed. The American hope was that Libya would attack Sudan, thus providing Egypt, which had a defense treaty with Sudan, with an excuse to destroy Libya's air force, aided by U.S. logistical support. The plan collapsed when unusual military movements by both the United States and Egypt were reported in the press, alerting Libya to an impending danger.

In the wake of the hijacking of Trans World Airlines (TWA) flight 847 in June 1985, the NSC and CIA again devised a plan for a joint Egyptian-U.S. operation against Libya. Although there was no evidence of Libyan involvement in the hijacking, key intelligence officials believed that Colonel Qaddafi represented the safest and most visible target for an antiterrorist endeavor. A proposal for an Egyptian invasion of Libya backed by U.S. air support was ultimately shelved because of the opposition of the Departments of State and Defense and Egyptian President Hosni Mubarak's unwillingness to go along with the scheme.

Relations with Neighbors. Revelations such as these no doubt increased Libya's desire to lessen its isolation and initiate better relations with some of its stronger neighbors. Contacts with Algeria intensified during 1987, resulting in several joint economic ventures. These included the construction of a spur into Libya from the natural-gas pipeline linking Algeria to Europe through Tunisia and a series of projects in the Sahara along the Algerian-Libyan frontier. The warming of relations between the two countries provided Algeria with a convenient market for its expensive natural gas, while Libya benefited by gaining access to the more highly industrialized Algeria's advanced technology.

Libyan efforts to draw Algeria into a political union, however, were not successful. Qaddafi's hopes for such an undertaking were dashed when the Algerian government recommended that, rather than forging a new entity, Libya adhere to the Treaty of Friendship signed in 1983 by Algeria, Mauritania, and Tunisia, asserting that such a linkage would greatly enhance the prospects for unity among all the countries of Arab North Africa. Libya, however, declined to accept the Algerian invitation to join the pact.

In a gesture of goodwill toward another of its neighbors, Libya agreed to compensate some 40,000 Tunisian workers who had been expelled from the country in 1985 as the result of a conflict between Tunis and Tripoli. Libya's decision not to interfere in Tunisia in November when the aging President Habib Bourguiba was ousted by his prime minister, Zine El Abidine Ben Ali, despite Ben Ali's promises to carry on the pro-Western policies of the former president, was another indication of Libya's desire to remain on good terms with its North African neighbors.

KENNETH J. PERKINS
University of South Carolina

LITERATURE

Overview

Just as great works of literature are said to reflect the essence of their times, so other events in the world of letters may underscore contemporary political and social trends. Such was the case in 1987, as issues of censorship arose in several countries, Great Britain moved to suppress publication of a book by a former counterintelligence agent, the reform-minded Soviet leadership seemed to loosen literary strictures, and a preeminent Soviet émigré poet was named the winner of the Nobel Prize. In the United States during 1987—designated as the "Year of the Reader"—there was controversy over school textbooks (*see* special report, page 214), and a new poet laureate was appointed.

Censorship. Perhaps no English-language work was the cause of greater controversy than *Spycatcher,* the memoirs of former British M-15 counterspy Peter Wright. In Great Britain, the government began legal proceedings against three newspapers for publishing excerpts in defiance of a 1986 ban under the nation's secrecy laws, and The Law Lords—Britain's highest court—upheld the initial injunction. The Thatcher administration also attempted to stop the book's publication in Australia, but a judge there ruled against the request. *Spycatcher* was published in the United States during the summer and quickly rose to the top of best-seller lists.

Elsewhere, in a reported crackdown on intellectuals following a wave of political protests, the Chinese Communist Party early in the year expelled Wang Ruowang, a prominent Shanghai author. In Chile, military authorities were reported to have burned some 15,000 copies of *The Adventures of Miguel Littin While Underground in Chile* by 1982 Nobelist Gabriel García Márquez of Colombia. As part of a crackdown on dissidents, Hungary refused to send 13 books by several native authors to an international book fair in West Germany. A French publishing company issued the autobiography of Poland's Lech Walesa, after pages had been smuggled back and forth for a year. In February the Soviet news agency Tass reported that the ban on *Dr. Zhivago,* a novel by 1958 Nobelist Boris Pasternak set during the Bolshevik Revolution, would be lifted and that the book would be published in the USSR in 1988. In April a Soviet literary journal began publishing installments of Anatoly Rybakov's *Children of the Arbat,* a long-suppressed novel set during Joseph Stalin's reign of terror.

Nobelist. As restraints on Soviet artists and writers appeared to be easing, the Swedish Academy awarded the 1987 Nobel Prize for Literature to the exiled Soviet-Jewish dissident Joseph Brodsky. A 47-year-old poet and essayist, Brodsky was cited by the Academy for "an all-embracing authorship, imbued with clarity of thought and poetic intensity." As a young underground poet in his native Leningrad, Brodsky was convicted in the mid-1960s of being a "social parasite" and spent 18 months in a state labor camp in the Arctic. After being expelled from the Soviet Union in 1972, he settled in the United States, where he became a citizen five years later. His poetry collections, which he helped translate into English, include *Selected Poems* (1973), *A Part of Speech* (1977), and *History of the Twentieth Century* (1986). *Less Than One,* a book of essays written in English, appeared in 1987.

U.S. Poet Laureate. Richard Wilbur, a 66-year-old poet, translator, and lyricist, was named to succeed Robert Penn Warren as the official U.S. poet laureate beginning in September. The appointment, made by then Librarian of Congress Daniel Boorstin, was for a renewable one-year term. Wilbur, a New York City native who was raised on a farm in New Jersey and now lives in Cummington, MA, won the Pulitzer Prize in 1957 for his third book of poetry, *Things of This World.* He also is known among scholars for his translations of the French dramatists Molière and Racine.

The 47-year-old exiled Soviet poet and essayist Joseph Brodsky was awarded the 1987 Nobel Prize for Literature.

AP/Wide World

AP/Wide World

In her acclaimed fifth novel, "Beloved," Toni Morrison brought sophisticated new insights to the cruelty and loathsomeness of slavery in pre-Civil War America.

American Literature

Although many of the best-selling and best-loved works in American literature have been by women, the orientation of American literary studies traditionally has been toward male writers. Since the 1960s, however, not only have many women found a stronger voice in fiction and poetry, but they have also, in growing numbers, risen to positions of influence as editors, publishers, agents, academics, and critics. In 1987 the fruits of that liberation of energy were seen everywhere. Books by women regularly got major reviews, were widely promoted, and represented some of the best writing being done.

Novels. Toni Morrison's *Beloved* was perhaps the most important new novel of the year. Set in pre-Civil War America, it confronts the horror of slavery by means of an artistically sophisticated narrative that is both a ghost story and a shatteringly accurate depiction of life under human bondage. A mother, having been driven to kill her own baby so that it will not grow up as a slave, creates a haunting that can never leave the American conscience.

Marge Piercy's *Gone to Soldiers,* a psychologically astute and culturally rich epic novel of World War II, was one of a number of serious explorations of political, social, and philosophical themes by American women writers during 1987. Similarly ambitious, Joan Silber's *In The City* looks at Greenwich Village life over several decades. Diane Johnson's *Persian Nights* is set in Iran before the fall of the shah in 1979. Ruth Prawer Jhabvala's *Three Continents* ranges around the world in her depiction of the seductive appeal of a corrupt religious cult. And Cynthia Ozick's *The Messiah of Stockholm* deals with the complexity of differentiating reality and illusion through a Polish refugee who assumes a false identity.

Some fine novels did stay closer to home. Alice McDermott's *That Night* imaginatively recreates the underlying tensions of 1960s American suburbia. Josephine Humphreys' *Rich in Love* focuses on a deteriorating marriage as seen by a 17-year-old girl. And Southern women writers continued to explore the complex problems of their relationship to their heritage, as in Gail Godwin's *A Southern Family* and Jill McCorkle's *Tending to Virginia.*

More evidence of the continued vitality of the novel in American culture was the number of practitioners who had made their reputations in other fields. In *And We Are Not Saved,* the eminent law professor Derrick Bell deals with the difficulties of achieving racial justice. James Dickey, one of the most successful U.S. poets, produced *Alnilam,* a difficult and poetic novel involving a man's search for an answer to his son's death. Two well-known feminist activists wrote novels—Andrea Dworkin's controversial *Ice and Fire* and Robin Morgan's painfully honest *Dry Your Smile.* The president of E.P. Dutton, Richard Marek, gives an inside view of publishing in *Work of Genius.* Columnist and onetime presidential speech-writer William Safire's *Freedom* details (hypothetically) two crucial years in the life of Abraham Lincoln.

In a year that saw a number of important works by women authors, Marge Piercy's ambitious and wide-ranging novel of World War II, "Gone to Soldiers," stood out.

© Tom Victor/courtesy of Summit Books

© Tom Victor/courtesy of Farrar Straus and Giroux

A longtime practitioner of the "New Journalism"—a form which was to have replaced fiction—Tom Wolfe produced a successful first novel, "The Bonfire of the Vanities."

Tom Wolfe, the notorious bad boy of cultural and political criticism, capitulated to the lure of the traditional novel; his *The Bonfire of the Vanities* is a mercilessly accurate dramatization of class conflicts and social customs in New York City. And Thomas McMahon, a research scientist at Harvard University, produced his third impressive novel, *Loving Little Egypt,* an intellectual comedy involving sightless people setting up information networks.

Southern fiction remained in a state of evolution, as tne tragic Gothic world of William Faulkner continued to be replaced by the ironic dislocations of the "New South." The trend was exemplified in 1987 by Walker Percy's *The Thanatos Syndrome,* a mystery novel and an inquiry into private and public morality involving a town that is unknowingly the subject of a mass experiment. And there was a renewed emphasis on the grotesque in Southern writing: Padgett Powell's *A Woman Named Drown,* T.R. Pearson's *The Last of How It Was,* James Wilcox's *Miss Undine's Livingroom,* and Barry Hannah's *Hey Jack!* all exploit their comic possibilities more than their tragic potential through an emphasis on eccentric characters and bizarre situations.

Other regional writers also showed a strong sense of place and history. T. Coraghessan Boyle's *World's End* focuses on an idealistic community in New York's Hudson River Valley, ranging from the 17th-century settlers to post-World War II political and social tensions. Ivan Doig's *Dancing at the Rascal Fair* conjures up the people and places that create Montana.

Among new works by older writers, Saul Bellow's *More Die of Heartbreak* shows his growing insight into the pains of love and the costs of wealth. John Barth's *The Tidewater Tales* continues his simultaneous creation and dissection of imaginative writing through a professor whose specialty is the Art of Everdiminishing Fiction. And most impressive, Wallace Stegner's *Crossing to Safety* sees deep into American society through the interaction of two couples over many years.

Scott Turow's first novel, *Presumed Innocent,* was one of the biggest successes of 1987. Its grittily authentic portrait of police procedure, lawyers' machinations, and municipal corruption is energized by a fast-moving plot full of clever twists and turns.

Short Fiction. Short-story collections continued to attract significant attention and seemed to have regained their rightful importance in American literature. John Updike's *Trust Me* lent credence to the argument that his best work is his short fiction. The 22 stories in this collection are resonant with emotional tension, sensual evocation, psychological complexity, and philosophical possibility. Jayne Anne Phillips' *Fast Lanes* suggests that she, too, is more at home in short stories than in the novel. And James Purdy's *The Candles of Your Eyes* again proves that he can be as suggestively compelling and as convincingly sad as any contemporary short-story writer.

The short novel, considered too long for magazine publication but too short to appear as a book, has become the least marketable of all literary forms. Nevertheless, the publication of shorter novels by such writers as Cynthia Ozick and Philip Roth, and the 1987 success of Jane Smiley's *The Age of Grief* may signal the revival of this classic form. Smiley's observant domestic tale reverses conventional wisdom in speaking of the avoidance of communication to preserve a relationship.

The most spectacular family achievement of the year was the triple publication by the Barthelme brothers. Donald Barthelme's *Forty Stories* demonstrate his witty transformations, parodies, and revitalizations of literary conventions. Younger brother Frederick Barthelme's *Chroma* continues his depictions of the emotionally atrophied lives of the modern world. And the youngest brother Steve Barthelme's *And He Tells the Little Horse the Whole Story* signals a new talent who is unafraid to deal with strangeness and violence.

Despite the widely publicized homogenization of American society, writers were still finding vitality in the nation's ethnic enclaves and subcultures. Daniel Menaker's *The Old*

Left focuses on an aging New York radical with rich memories of old battles. Lynne Sharon Schwartz's aptly titled *The Melting Pot* concerns the ironies of cultural conflict. And Steve Stern's *Lazar Malkin Enters Heaven* invests a contemporary Jewish community in the American South with all the magic and mystery of Old World ghetto life.

Culture and Criticism. A number of new books in 1987 spurred lively debate about American education. Ernest L. Boyer's *College: The Undergraduate Experience in America* argues that universities have lost their vision and intellectual integrity and have become little more than vocational training schools. E.D. Hirsch, Jr.'s *Cultural Literacy: What Every American Needs to Know* focuses more on primary and secondary education. In it, Hirsch argues that historical facts, proverbial expressions, literary references, and religious allusions long considered part of common knowledge have been largely forgotten. He calls for a national core curriculum to deal with the problem and supplies a list of names and terms he believes every American should be able to recognize. The most sustained attack on the lack of a rigorous humanistic curriculum came from University of Chicago philosophy professor Allan Bloom; *The Closing of the American Mind* is aggressively subtitled *How Higher Education Has Failed Democracy and Impoverished the Souls of Today's Students*. Taking another track, Russell Jacoby's *The Last Intellectuals: American Culture in the Age of Academe* celebrates thinkers who stayed away from the university—which he sees as a baneful force on intellectual independence.

One of the most talked-about books of the year was "The Closing of the American Mind," an indictment of U.S. education by University of Chicago Professor Allan Bloom.

AP/Wide World

History and Biography. Good biographies and autobiographies not only reveal the details of lives, but they also provide new insights into history. In *Nixon: The Education of a Politician 1913–1962,* Stephen E. Ambrose argues that the former president had many virtues for which he has not been recognized. And if politicians get reconstructed in biographies, writers and artists tend to be deconstructed. Kenneth Lynn's *Hemingway* proposes that his mother's attempt to treat him as a girl was at the center of his attitudes toward life and death. Stephen B. Oates' *William Faulkner* emphasizes insecurity and the need for affection as the source of his tension. The biographies of two modernist black writers are more useful in correcting the neglect of literary history: Cynthia Earl Kerman and Richard Eldridge's *The Lives of Jean Toomer,* and Wayne F. Cooper's *Claude McKay*.

Autobiographies, while not authoritative, are intrinsically interesting and inevitably revealing in that they reflect the author's own interpretation of his or her life. That was the premise for Alex Harris' *A World Unsuspected,* a collection of "Portraits of Southern Childhood" by 11 American writers, including Barry Hannah, T.R. Pearson, Bobbie Ann Mason, and James Alan McPherson.

Childhood memories can be provocative, but the accounts of long careers create the human texture of social history. Arthur Miller's *Timebends* details the political pressures put on him during the decades in which he was producing his greatest plays, as well as his marriage to Marilyn Monroe. In *With All My Might,* Erskine Caldwell reminisces about his battles with publishers and critics as his work fell out of favor.

Poetry. Good poetry moves at a pace of its own. Timeless, meditative, it seems untouched by the fads and fancies of the more commercial prose forms. The 30 years of work collected in W.D. Snodgrass' *Selected Poems* demonstrates changes in interest and forms, but it also reflects the growth of the poet as he wrestles with language and the world around him. A number of other works also demonstrated that American poetry is more open than ever to new explorations and new voices. William Matthews' *Forseeable Futures* and David Wagoner's *Through the Forest: New and Selected Poems 1977–1987* are, at times, unabashedly funny. Sharon Olds' *The Gold Cell* and Daniel Halpern's *Tango* contain miniature narratives. And Jorie Graham's *The End of Beauty* contains suggestive and mysterious fragments of language which require the deepest attention.

JEROME STERN, *Florida State University*

AMERICAN LITERATURE: MAJOR WORKS | 1987

NOVELS

Barth, John, *The Tidewater Tales*
Bell, Derrick, *And We Are Not Saved*
Bell, Madison Smartt, *The Year of Silence*
Bellow, Saul, *More Die of Heartbreak*
Bottoms, David, *Any Cold Jordan*
Boyle, T. Coraghessan, *World's End*
Buechner, Frederick, *Brendan*
Calisher, Hortense, *Age*
Capote, Truman, *Answered Prayers*
Caputo, Philip, *Indian Country*
Cheever, Susan, *Doctors and Women*
Crews, Harry, *All We Need of Hell*
Dickey, James, *Alnilam*
Dworkin, Andrea, *Ice and Fire*
Elkin, Stanley, *The Rabbi of Lud*
Ellis, Bret Easton, *The Rules of Attraction*
French, Marilyn, *Her Mother's Daughter*
Godwin, Gail, *A Southern Family*
Grumbach, Doris, *The Magician's Girl*
Hannah, Barry, *Hey, Jack!*
Higgins, George V., *Outlaws*
Humphreys, Josephine, *Rich in Love*
Janowitz, Tama, *A Cannibal in Manhattan*
Jhabvala, Ruth Prawer, *Three Continents*
Johnson, Diane, *Persian Nights*
Jong, Erica, *Serenissima: A Novel of Venice*
Just, Ward, *The American Ambassador*
Kotzwinkle, William, *The Exile*
Major, Clarence, *Such Was the Season*
Marek, Richard, *Works of Genius*
McCorkle, Jill, *Tending to Virginia*
McDermott, Alice, *That Night*
McElroy, Joseph, *Women and Men*
McMahon, Thomas, *Loving Little Egypt*
McMurtry, Larry, *Texasville*
McPherson, William, *To the Sargasso Sea*
Morgan, Robin, *Dry Your Smile*
Morrison, Toni, *Beloved*
Novak, Barbara, *Alice's Neck*
Nunn, Kem, *Unassigned Territory*
Oates, Joyce Carol, *You Must Remember This*
Olson, Toby, *Utah*
Ozick, Cynthia, *The Messiah of Stockholm*
Pearson, T.R., *The Last of How It Was*
Percy, Walker, *The Thanatos Syndrome*
Piercy, Marge, *Gone to Soldiers*
Plimpton, George, *The Curious Case of Sidd Finch*
Powell, Padgett, *A Woman Named Drown*
Safire, William, *Freedom*
Silber, Joan, *In the City*
Simmons, Charles, *The Belles Lettres Papers*
Thurm, Marian, *Walking Distance*
Turow, Scott, *Presumed Innocent*
Vidal, Gore, *Empire*
Vonnegut, Kurt, *Bluebeard*
Wideman, John Edgar, *Reuben*
Wilcox, James, *Miss Undine's Livingroom*
Wolfe, Tom, *The Bonfire of the Vanities*

SHORT STORIES

Abbott, Lee K., *Strangers in Paradise*
Auchincloss, Louis, *Skinny Island*
Barthelme, Donald, *Forty Stories*
Barthelme, Frederick, *Chroma*
Barthelme, Steve, *And He Tells the Little Horse the Whole Story*
Baumbach, Jonathan, *The Life and Times of Major Fiction*
Bell, Madison Smartt, *Zero db*
Benedict, Pinckney, *Town Smokes*
Coover, Robert, *A Night at the Movies*
Ford, Richard, *Rock Springs*
Gordon, Mary, *Temporary Shelter*
Hall, Donald, *The Ideal Bakery*
Keillor, Garrison, *Leaving Home*
Kercheval, Jesse Lee, *The Dogeater*
Menaker, Daniel, *The Old Left*
Phillips, Jayne Anne, *Fast Lanes*
Purdy, James, *The Candles of Your Eyes*
Ruta, Suzanne, *Stalin in the Bronx*
Schwartz, Lynne Sharon, *The Melting Pot*
Smiley, Jane, *The Age of Grief: A Novella and Stories*
Stern, Steve, *Lazar Malkin Enters Heaven*
Tallent, Elizabeth, *Time With Children*
Updike, John, *Trust Me*
Woodman, Allen, *The Shoebox of Desire*

POETRY

Berry, Wendell, *Sabbaths*
Bronk, William, *Manifest: And Furthermore*
Clampitt, Amy, *Archaic Figure*
Duncan, Robert, *Ground Work II: In the Dark*
Graham, Jorie, *The End of Beauty*
Halpern, Daniel, *Tango*
Johnson, Denis, *The Veil*
Justice, Donald, *The Sunset Maker: Poems/Stories/ A Memoir*
Kizer, Carolyn, *The Nearness of You*
Levertov, Denise, *Breathing the Water*
Llewellyn, Chris, *Fragments From the Fire: The Triangle Shirt-waist Company Fire of March 25, 1911*
Matthews, William, *Foreseeable Futures*
Menashe, Samuel, *Collected Poems*
Meredith, William, *Partial Accounts: New and Selected Poems*
Olds, Sharon, *The Gold Cell*
Rakosi, Carl, *The Collected Poems of Carl Rakosi*
Sanders, Edward, *Thirsting for Peace in a Raging Century: Poems 1960–1985*
Simic, Charles, *Unending Blues*
Snodgrass, W.D., *Selected Poems 1957–1987*
Stafford, William, *An Oregon Message*
Swenson, May, *In Other Words: New Poems*
Wagoner, David, *Through the Forest: New and Selected Poems, 1977–1987*

CULTURE AND CRITICISM

Banta, Martha, *Imaging American Woman: Idea and Ideals in Cultural History*
Bloom, Allan, *The Closing of the American Mind*
Boyer, Ernest L., *College: The Undergraduate Experience in America*
Didion, Joan, *Miami*
Dillard, Annie, *An American Childhood*
Donoghue, Denis, *Reading America*
Fraser, Kennedy, *Scenes From the Fashionable World*
Gray, Francine duPlessix, *Adam & Eve And the City*
Hersey, John, *Blues*
Hirsch, E.D., *Cultural Literacy*
Hite, Shere, *Women and Love: A Cultural Revolution in Progress*
Jacoby, Russell, *The Last Intellectuals: American Culture in the Age of Academe*
Kendrick, Walter, *The Secret Museum: Pornography in Modern Culture*
Lees, Gene, *Singers and the Song*
Rosenberg, Charles E., *The Care of Strangers: The Rise of America's Hospital System*
Simpson, Eileen, *Orphans: Real and Imaginary*
Trillin, Calvin, *If You Can't Say Something Nice*

HISTORY AND BIOGRAPHY

Ambrose, Stephen E., *Nixon: The Education of a Politician 1913–1962*
Bender, Thomas, *New York Intellect: A History of Intellectual Life in New York City, From 1750 to the Beginnings of Our Own Time*
Caldwell, Erskine, *With All My Might*
Cooper, Wayne F., *Claude McKay: Rebel Sojourner in the Harlem Renaissance*
Cox, Archibald, *The Court and the Constitution*
Davis, Linda H., *Onward and Upward: A Biography of Katherine S. White*
Donald, David Herbert, *Look Homeward: A Life of Thomas Wolfe*
Ettinger, Elzbieta, *Rosa Luxemburg: A Life*
Gill, Brendan, *Many Masks: A Life of Frank Lloyd Wright*
Grunfeld, Frederic V., *Rodin*
Harris, Alex, ed., *A World Unsuspected: Portraits of Southern Childhood*
Kerman, Cynthia Earl, and Eldridge, Richard, *The Lives of Jean Toomer*
King, Mary, *Freedom Song: A Personal History of the 1960s Civil Rights Movement*
Lynn, Kenneth S., *Hemingway*
McCarthy, Mary, *How I Grew*
McCormick, John, *George Santayana: A Biography*
Miller, Arthur, *Timebends: A Life*
Miller, James, *"Democracy is in the Streets"* From Port Huron to the Siege of Chicago
Novak, William, *Man of the House: The Life and Political Memoirs of Speaker Tip O'Neill*
Oates, Stephen B., *William Faulkner: The Man and the Artist*
Washington, Mary Helen, *Invented Lives: Narratives of Black Women 1860–1960*
Woodress, James, *Willa Cather: A Literary Life*

Children's Literature

Children's book publishing continued to enjoy a healthy growth trend thanks to the strength of the bookstore market. Paperback romances, baby books, attractive versions of the classics, and lush picture books have become key components of booksellers' stock. There is some question, though, whether the race to capture the buying public with books that assure sound financial return will affect negatively the ability of some houses to continue to offer quality fiction. However, first-rate reading for a range of ages and tastes still is quite available on library shelves.

The American Library Association's prestigious Newbery Award went to Sid Fleischman for *The Whipping Boy,* a tale of a spoiled prince and his streetwise whipping boy whose wits save them both outside the safety of the castle walls. And the Caldecott Medal was awarded to Richard Egielski for *Hey, Al,* a fable about a man who learns that paradise may be no farther away than his humble home.

Recommended Books. Among 1987's noteworthy picture books were Reeve Lindbergh's *The Midnight Farm,* illustrated by Susan Jeffers, and Bert Kitchen's *Animal Numbers. The Midnight Farm,* about a mother who leads her not-very-sleepy child on a nighttime tour of the house and barnyard, is graced with rich, intricate full-color drawings that romanticize the story's country setting. Kitchen's *Animal Numbers* is a visually spare but very compelling book. Tana Hoban's *26 Letters and 99 Cents* is a nonfiction picture book that is actually two books in one. Turn the pages one way for a colorful photographic look at the alphabet; turn the book about for a graphic, concise introduction to coins and the amounts they stand for. Another novelty book that reflects a skilled artist's inventiveness is Ann Jonas' *Reflections.* Here the pictures can be read two entirely different ways: right side up and upside down.

Children in the middle grades (ages 9–12) would find Bill Brittain's *Dr. Dredd's Wagon of Wonders* a good tale of creepy suspense, as a diabolical villain tries to destroy a small town whose residents resist his evil power. In a quite different vein is Mildred Taylor's bittersweet *The Gold Cadillac.* Taylor, a Newbery Award-winning author, recalls an episode from her 1950s' childhood that demonstrates the love her family shared as they wrestled with the impositions of the time's racially segregated society. Lovers of fantasy will find forceful storytelling in Susan Price's *The Ghost Drum: A Cat's Tale.* The story has a Russian setting and a memorable young witch for a heroine.

Books for junior-high-school readers (ages 11–13) offered some of the meatiest reading for children. In *Sons from Afar,* Cynthia Voight continues her saga of the Tillerman family. Otto R. Salassi's *Jimmy D., Sidewinder, and Me* is a down-home story of a youth who hustles at pool and learns to gamble yet keeps his honor intact. And Lois Lowry's *Rabble Starkey* presents a memorable story of a mother and daughter.

Nonfiction also offered a rich lode of reading. Brent and Melissa Ashabranner's *Into a Strange Land: Unaccompanied Refugee Youth in America* documents the wrenching story of immigrant minors. In the year of the 200th anniversary of the Constitution, young people could find some of the liveliest reading on the document in Jean Fritz's entertaining *Shh! We're Writing the Constitution.* Folklore scholars will want to note Julius Lester's retelling of the Brer Rabbit stories in *The Tales of Uncle Remus: The Adventures of Brer Rabbit.* The book's enlightening introduction offers an instructive look at the history and evolution of the stories, which still stand as one of the richest sources of black-American folklore.

DENISE MURCKO WILMS
Assistant Editor, "Booklist"

SELECTED BOOKS FOR CHILDREN

Preschool–Age 6 and Picture Books
Blos, Joan, *Old Henry*
Chaiken, Miriam, *Exodus*
dePaola, Tomie, *An Early American Christmas*
Gould, Deborah, *Grandpa's Slide Show*
Hendershot, Judith, *In Coal Country*
Hoban, Tana, *26 Letters and 99 Cents*
Kellogg, Steven, *Aster Aardvark's Alphabet Adventures*
Purdy, Carol, *Least of All*
Steptoe, John, *Mufaro's Beautiful Daughters*
Willard, Nancy, *The Voyage of the Ludgate Hill: Travels with Robert Louis Stevenson*

Ages 9–12
Byars, Betsy, *A Blossom Promise*
Cole, Brock, *The Goats*
Cooper, Ilene, *The Winning of Miss Lynn Ryan*
Cresswell, Helen, *Moondial*
Freedman, Russell, *Indian Chiefs* (nonfiction)
Giblin, James Cross, *From Hand to Mouth* (nonfiction)
Hearne, Betsy, *Eli's Ghost*
Jacques, Brian, *Redwall*
Lisle, Janet Taylor, *The Great Dimpole Oak*
MacGowen, Tom, *The Magician's Apprentice*
Shreve, Susan, *Lucy Forever and Miss Rosetree, Shrinks*
Simon, Seymour, *Mars* (nonfiction) and *Uranus* (nonfiction)

Young Teens
Alcock, Vivien, *Mysterious Mr. Ross*
Cannon, Bettie, *Bellsong for Sarah Raines*
Cassedy, Sylvia, *M.E. and Morton*
Chetwin, Grace, *Riddle and the Rune*
Dunlop, Eileen, *The House on the Hill*
Fox, Paula, *Lily and the Lost Boy*
Howker, Janni, *Isaac Campion*
Paulson, Gary, *Hatchet*
Snyder, Zilpha Keatley, *And Condors Danced*
Wells, Rosemary, *Through the Hidden Door*

Young Adults
Bridgers, Sue Ellen, *Permanent Connections*
Gordon, Ruth, ed., *Under All Silences* (poetry anthology)
Gordon, Sheila, *Waiting for the Rain*
Janeczko, Paul, ed., *Going Over to Your Place* (poems)
MacLean, John, *Mac*
Pullman, Philip, *The Ruby in the Smoke*
Townsend, John Rowe, *Downstream*

Canadian Literature: English

Canadian writers were busy in 1987, especially in the areas of biography and autobiography.

Nonfiction. Journalists and television personalities were the subjects of some noteworthy books during the year. The popular Pierre Berton produced *Starting Out,* in which he covers his early years, up to 1947, and then his adventures as a reporter. Newscaster Knowlton Nash's second volume of memoirs, *Prime Time at Ten,* deals with his career with the Canadian Broadcasting Corporation. Gordon Sinclair's life as a journalist and television personality was the subject of Scott Young's biography, *Gordon Sinclair: A Life . . . and then Some.* Other biographies of interest included Farley Mowat's *Virunga,* describing the life and murder of anthropologist Dian Fossey and Jim Taylor's *Rick Hansen, Man in Motion,* about the man who circled the globe in a wheelchair to raise C$20 million for spinal cord research. Lawyer Eddie Greenspan reminisced in *Greenspan, in Defence Of,* while Susan Riley discussed a little-reported aspect of politics in *Political Wives: The Lives of the Saints.* Another political biography was that of New Democratic Party stalwart Tommy Douglas, *The Road to Jerusalem,* by Thomas H. McLeod and Ian McLeod. Sandra Djwa produced in *The Politics of the Imagination,* a biography of F. R. Scott. *Stephen Leacock: A Reappraisal,* edited by David Staines, is a collection of essays on Canada's famed humorist.

Other nonfiction was also much in evidence. Peter C. Newman's *Caesars of the Wilderness* is the second volume of his history of the Hudson's Bay Company. C.P. Stacey and Barbara Williams contributed *The Half Million,* and Daniel Dancock wrote *Spearhead to Victory. Our American Cousins,* edited by Thomas S. Axworthy, shows many views of the United States. Linda McQuaig's *Behind Closed Doors* has a caustic subtitle: *How the Rich Won Control of Canada's Tax System . . . And Ended Up Richer.* Margaret Atwood edited *CanLit Foodbook,* and Northrop Frye wrote *On Education.* Books on the law included *Everyday Law,* by Jack Batten and Marjorie Harris, and *Talk to My Lawyer,* by James Gray.

The vexed issue of Canadian immigration inspired *Justice Delayed: Nazi Criminals in Canada,* by David Matas and Susan Charendoff; *Haven's Gate,* by Victor Malarek; and *Double Standard,* by Reginald Whitaker. Another annoying issue, the problems of the nation's postal service, is examined by David Stewart-Patterson in *Post Mortem.*

Politics captured readers' interest in such works as *The Insiders,* John Sawatsky's look at Ottawa lobbyists; Claire Hoy's *Friends In High Places,* on patronage in the federal government; and Rod McQueen's *Inside the Sinclair Stevens Affair,* detailing the lengthy investigation into federal cabinet minister Stevens' blind trust. The investigation also inspired *Sinc: The Inside Story of Sinclair Stevens,* by Margaret Polanyi and others.

Poetry. Among the year's volumes of poetry were Irving Layton's *In My Father's House,* a collection of his poems about the Jews and their history; Ralph Gustafson's *Winter Prophecies;* Douglas LePan's *Weathering It;* J. Michael Yates' *Schedules of Silence;* Al Purdy's *The Collected Poems of Al Purdy;* and George Bowering's *Delayed Memories and Other Poems.* Senior poet Dorothy Livesay's *The Self-Completing Tree* draws on some 60 years of her writings, and Gwendolyn MacEwan contributed *Afterworlds.* Nancy-Gay Rotstein's *China: Shockwaves* gives poetic utterance to her impressions of China.

Fiction. Short-story collections included W.P. Kinsella's *Red Wolf, Red Wolf;* Margaret Atwood's *Bluebeard's Egg,* about women who have parted company from one man and are uncertainly joined to another; and Fraser Sutherland's *In the Village of Alias.*

Interesting novels of the year were Jane Rule's *Memory Board,* examining the life of a family; Brian Moore's *The Colour of Blood; The Honorary Patron,* by Jack Hodgins, set on Vancouver Island; and Charlotte Vale's *Illusions.* Second novels were produced by poet Susan Musgrave, with *The Dancing Chicken,* and Susan Haley, with *Getting Married in Buffalo Jump.* Gordon Bowering's unusual Western, *Caprice,* found the heroine searching for her brother's killer in anything but the traditional manner. Michael Ondaatje's *In the Skin of the Lion* is a fanciful history of Toronto in the two decades following World War I.

DAVID SAVAGE
Free-lance Writer, Vancouver, B.C.

English Literature

Most of Britain's leading novelists produced new works in 1987. *Close Quarters* by William Golding was a sequel to *Rites of Passage,* continuing the tale of an 18th-century sailing ship bound for Australia. Bruce Chatwin's *The Songlines* was also preoccupied with Australia and presented an original, philosophical quest among present-day aborigines. Ruth Prawer Jhabvala contributed *Three Continents,* a story of 19-year-old twins. William Boyd's fictional autobiography of a filmmaker, *The New Confessions,* won praise, as did Anita Brookner's meticulous, stylish *A Friend From England.* J.G. Ballard's *The Day of Creation* was an adventure story packed with events, and Ian McEwan's *A Child in Time* was McEwan in a less chilling mood. Margaret Drabble's *The Radiant Way* was greeted by some as

Camera Press from Photo Trends

Penelope Lively won the 1987 Booker McConnell Prize, Britain's top literary award, for her novel "Moon Tiger," set in Cairo during the 1940s. Lively was born in Cairo in 1933.

serious, by others as portentous, as it surveyed late 20th-century Britain. Lisa St. Aubin de Teran produced *Black Idol* and Fay Weldon *The Hearts and Lives of Men.* Australian Thomas Keneally recreated the convict society of early Australia in *The Playmaker,* and A.L. Barker's *The Gooseboy* won critical acclaim. Alice Thomas Ellis contributed another study of oddity with *The Clothes in the Wardrobe.* Jane Ellison mocked the English publishing scene in her satire *Another Little Drink.*

When the judges for the Booker McConnell Prize for fiction announced their shortlist in October, however, none of these novels had been selected. Instead they let their final judgment fall on Iris Murdoch's densely plotted *The Book and the Brotherhood;* Peter Ackroyd's novel *Chatterton,* imaginatively recreating through the character of Charles Wychwood the life of the poet Thomas Chatterton, who in fact had died at age 18 in 18th-century London; Nigerian Chinua Achebe's *Anthills of the Savannah,* surveying the rise of military dictatorship; Brian Moore's *The Colour of Blood,* centering on a cardinal on the run in an authoritarian state; Penelope Lively's *Moon Tiger,* set in Cairo during the 1940s; and Nina Bawden's *Circles of Deceit.* The judges finally settled on Penelope Lively to receive Britain's top literary award.

Nonfiction. It was a good year for biographies and other nonfiction. Richard Ellman's biography of Oscar Wilde, *Wilde: Life and Works,* was long awaited; the only misfortune was that Professor Ellman did not live to receive the praise for his 15 years of endeavor. Among other biographies, Claire Tomalin's *Katharine Mansfield* and Leon Edel's *Henry James* were appreciated. Kerry Downes' life of *Sir John Vanbrugh* reminded readers of the subject's achievements in two unrelated fields, architecture and play writing. Simon Callow wrote a moving tribute to his most admired actor *Charles Laughton.* Anthony Howard published *Rab,* a highly readable biography of R.A. Butler, fondly known to British political circles as the best prime minister Britain never had. Rupert Brooke's centenary was celebrated with a history of his circle, *The Neo Pagans,* and republication of letters and collected poems and memoirs for an audience which now refuses to regard him with the former idolatry. Two autobiographies stood out: the traveler Wilfrid Thesigner's account of his life as a desert explorer, *The Life of My Choice,* and the first volume of racy recollections entitled *Little Wilson and Big God* from Anthony Burgess. Robert Hewison, in *The Heritage Industry,* penned a caustic polemic on the dangers of turning all of Britain into an island museum. Among travel writing, Quentin Crewe's *Touch the Happy Isles* was applauded as a favorite Caribbean book.

Poetry. Ireland's Brendan Kennelly produced *Cromwell,* a volume of knockabout poems on that hated figure from British history filled with both historical and present-day horrors that pointed to a tradition of evil living on. Irish poet Seamus Heaney produced a new and masterly volume, *The Haw Lantern,* that included a sonnet sequence concerning the death of his mother. From Protestant Northern Ireland came *Poems 1956–1986,* by James Simmons, that included hard-hitting verses on the local violence. From Northern Ireland also came *Meeting the British,* miniaturist probings from Paul Muldoon. Roy Fuller, 75, produced *Consolations,* meditations on old age. The major event of the poetry year for many, however, was the appearance of *Collected Poems,* by George Barker, a massive volume from a poet admired by Yeats and still writing.

MAUREEN GREEN
Free-lance Writer, London

World Literature *

Books by Hispanic, Germanic, and Third World authors stood out most prominently among the non-English literary works published at the close of 1986 and during 1987, both in quantity and in quality. Russian and East European literature made respectable showings, among émigrés as well as at home, but it was definitely an off year for most other European writers, particularly the perennially strong French and Italians.

Hispanic. From Spain came three noteworthy new titles. The octogenarian poet-artist Rafael Alberti continued his productive career with a new selection of verse, titled *Children of the Dragon;* the mood is more somber than in much of his earlier works, imparting a sense of dark finality. Juan Goytisolo's novel *In the Kingdom of Taifa,* a sequel to the previous year's *Game Preserve,* continues his examination of the contradictions and conflicts in Spain's history. And the novelist Gonzalo Torrente Ballester collected many of his best recent essays on literary-cultural topics in *Delicacies in the Gulf.*

From Spanish America came even richer offerings. The long-awaited *Christopher Unborn* by Mexican novelist Carlos Fuentes presents a satiric, metafictional look at the Mexico City of the near future (1992, the 500th anniversary of Columbus's discovery of the New World), a horrifyingly filthy, overpopulated, rat-infested ruin of a metropolis. Fuentes' countryman, Octavio Paz, Latin America's leading poet, brought out a bilingual edition of his collected verse of the last 30 years—nearly 200 pieces in all—with English renderings by such noted poets as Elizabeth Bishop, Denise Levertov, and Charles Tomlinson. The 1982 Nobel laureate Gabriel García Márquez of Colombia returned to the chronicle form of *A Death Foretold* for his account of *The Clandestine Adventure of Miguel Littín in Chile,* a brisk, sometimes thrilling account of the Chilean filmmaker's secret 1985 visit to his homeland to film "the reality of his country after twelve years of military dictatorship." A far more sober and complex view of the Chilean situation is found in *Hopelessness,* the exile author José Donoso's first major work in a decade; alternately hallucinatory and graphically naturalistic, mirroring the national dilemma in the personal traumas of its protagonist, the book in every way lives up to its title as a "document on despair."

Germanic. Leading the parade of significant new German-language works in 1987 was *Secret Heart of the Clock,* the notebook and diary writings of 1981 Nobel laureate Elias Canetti from the years 1973–85; a loose mix of aphorisms, confessions, observations, and ideas, the texts offer a challenging, engaging look into Canetti's artistic world and work. The young Austrian Peter Handke brought out two new books during the year: the novella *Afternoon of a Writer* follows its protagonist on an "uneventful" afternoon walk through his modest-size city, viewing its people, places, and phenomena through his hyper-perceptive eyes and thus conveying how an artist "sees" what lies perfectly visible for all but goes unnoticed by most; and *The Absence,* billed as a fairy tale, tracks its four archetypal characters (an old man, a soldier, a woman, and an actor) across continents and eras on a quest born of vague allusive longings and mystically sensed needs.

The West German novelist Martin Walser's novelette *Dorle and Wolf* astutely explores the psychological and psychosocial consequences of divided loyalties through the story of the East German double agent Wolf Ziegler and his attempts to quit his dual life and remain with family, friends, and a government job in the West. Gabriele Wohmann offers lighter and rather more romantic fare in *The Sound of the Flute,* a generational drama featuring chance meetings, brief affairs with lingering afterglows, and the binding threads of memory, small duplicities, and family loyalties. Peter Härtling constructs his sensitive novel *Waiblinger's Eyes* around the historical figure of Wilhelm Waiblinger, an early 19th-century poet and friend of Friedrich Hölderlin whose brief life ended by his own hand. The 75-year-old Luise Rinser spins a Kafkaesque dream novel in *Silverguilt,* whose first-person narrator is led on a fantastic journey toward knowledge, purgation, and redemption.

* Titles translated.

Octavio Paz, the Mexican poet, essayist, and critic, saw "Convergences," his series of essays, published in 1986.

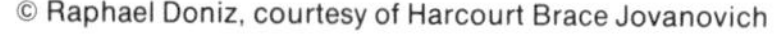

© "Time" Magazine

Anatoli Rybakov was at the center of an eagerly awaited Soviet literary event, the publication of his long-suppressed novel, "Children of the Arbat," set in the Stalin period.

Russian and Eastern European. Four émigrés led the year's production in Russian literature: two poets and two prose writers. *Homage to Urania* by Joseph Brodsky, the 1987 Nobelist, collects several recent publications with accompanying English translations, including the masterful "Gorbunov and Gorchakov" and the celebrated "Roman Elegies" cycle. *Beyond the Limit* fully introduced Irina Ratushinskaya to American readers with a 47-poem cycle written during her incarceration at a "strict regime" camp for women political prisoners. The Borgesian side of prose writer and critic Abram Tertz (pen name of Andrei Sinyavsky) was revealed to Western readers in the collection *Fantastic Stories*. The novel *Moscow 2042* by Vladimir Voinovich is a futuristic satire of both the Soviet state and the messianic aims of such prominent exiles as Aleksandr Solzhenitsyn.

From Eastern Europe came three very interesting new books. The Polish novelist Tadeusz Konwicki mixed novel and diary in intriguing fashion in *Moonrise, Moonset,* a fictionalized memoir of his participation in both the anti-Nazi underground of 1944–45 and the Solidarity movement of 1980–81. *A Cup of Coffee with My Interrogator* by Ludvík Vaculík is the first collection of the banned Czech writer's chronicles and essays to appear anywhere outside Prague's clandestine literary network and contains short, witty commentaries on "everything from Gandhi to *glasnost*." Meto Jovanovski's *Cousins,* reportedly the first Macedonian novel to be translated into English, follows the comically inept country cousins Srbin and Shishman through their bumbling encounters at the front lines of a war involving Serbs, Bulgarians, Greeks, and the French; the result is an open indictment of fanaticism and warmongering that proves entertaining and of more than passing literary interest.

Other European and American. Important new works from other European and American writers were rather sparse in 1987. From France, only the octogenarian Julien Green's newest novel deserves special mention: *The Distant Country* evokes the pre-Civil War U.S. South in an elegantly told panorama of passion and intrigue. The Romanian playwright Marin Sorescu came to the attention of the West with the bilingual publication of *Vlad Dracula the Impaler,* a stark drama in which the figure of Vlad Tepes, or Dracula, is presented as "an enlightened madman and martyr who inflicts pain and suffering in the belief that he can overcome evil." Ismail Kadare, Albania's sole true claim to membership in the European literary community, was represented by no fewer than three new publications: *Chronicle in Stone,* only the second of his dozen-plus novels to have appeared in English as yet, chronicles the fate of the author's beautiful, fabled, walled native city of Gjirokastër (Greek: Argyrocastron) under its successive occupations during World War II; *The Black Year,* published in French translation in 1987, recounts the political and military machinations in and around the court of the German prince Wilhelm von Wied following his ascent to the throne of the new Albanian state in March 1914; and *Epoch of Writings,* published in Tiranë, collects two recent short novels and eight short stories dealing with different eras of Albania's "haunted history." Greece's famed poet Yannis Ritsos issued the eighth installment of a planned nine-volume prose cycle, *The Questions Diminish,* featuring dramatic monologues and expository tales involving figures both mythical and earthly. The Swedish Academy member Lars Gyllensten produced *Seven Wise Masters about Love,* an exquisitely crafted set of love stories that together constitute "a discrete education in the stages of moral education," to cite one critic. And from Brazil, the dazzling talents of novelist Marcio Souza were on display in *The Flying Brazilian,* an irreverent fictionalized biography of aviator Alberto Santos Dumont.

Third World. Third World authors offered both great diversity and high quality in their 1987 productions. From the Near East, for example, came new works by leading writers of Israel, Egypt, and Turkey. The Hebrew novelists Aharon Appelfeld and Yehoshua Kenaz used enchantingly dream-like prose and a deceptively simple style in *To the Land of the Reeds* and *After the Holidays,* respectively, to evoke on the one hand the Jewish world of 1939 in Central and Eastern Europe, and on the other the early years of Jewish Palestine prior to World War I. Egypt's finest active fiction writer, Naguib Mahfouz, saw his sensitive recent novel of the poverty and suffering of an

Egyptian family during World War II, *The Beginning and the End,* brought out in English translation to considerable international acclaim. The Persea Books (New York) edition of the late Nazim Hikmet's *Selected Poetry* is the closest thing yet to a "Best of Hikmet" volume in English (or any other major language), incorporating numerous new translations with previously published pieces.

New works by three long-established writers from three widely dispersed regions highlighted the year in African letters. In *These Sweet Fruits of the Breadfruit Tree* the Congolese novelist Tchicaya U Tam'si produced one of the most provocative and challenging works in several years from Francophone Africa, a complex study in political intrigue and psychological-ethical questions built around the trial of a putative mass murderer. In *The Rain,* the Algerian Francophone author Rachid Boudjedra probes the dark inner world of a suicidal young Arab woman. At the other end of the continent, the revered South African author and critic Es'kia Mphahlele brought out *Afrika My Music,* an autobiography covering the years 1957–83.

Courtesy of The Seal Press

Herbjørg Wassmo won the Nordic Literature Prize for 1987 for her novel "Hudløs himmel" ("Sensitive Sky"). She is the first Norwegian woman writer so honored.

From the Caribbean in 1987 came one major new book, one important reissue, and one notable translation. Derek Walcott of Trinidad, one of the finest English-language poets anywhere in the world, published *The Arkansas Testament,* his first large new volume of verse since his *Collected Poems,* of 1985. The reissue of *Natives of My Person,* a 1971 novel by George Lamming, brings to the attention of a new generation of readers what is perhaps the Barbadian author's most significant and most ambitious work, an account of a 17th-century British colonizing expedition that moves on allegorical as well as historical and realistic levels. *Cathedral of the August Heat* introduces the English-reading public to the Haitian poet-journalist Pierre Clitandre's epic novel of prerevolutionary life among the lowest of the low in Port-au-Prince, replete with the flavor of Caribbean folklore and the force of bloody naturalism.

Asian and Pacific. Old and new masters alike were prominent in Asian and Pacific writing in 1987. India's grand old man of letters, R. K. Narayan, created another in his long line of engaging Malgudi poseurs in the mysterious but compulsively engaging raconteur Dr. Rann, the protagonist of *Talkative Man.* Japan's venerated fiction writer Masuji Ibuse, now almost 90, saw his two finest short novels disseminated to a worldwide audience in faithful English translations bound in a single volume: *Waves,* a fictitious war diary from the 12th-century conflict between the Heike and Genji clans; and *Isle-on-the-Billows,* a lighter piece set during the later years of the Tokugawa shogunate in the 19th century. The novel many consider the finest of Japan's modern period, Shimazaki Toson's *Before the Dawn* (1935), a massive yet thoroughly absorbing drama of the changes wrought in ordinary lives by Perry's opening of Japan in 1853, was finally published in English translation. Also making its first appearance in English was *The Old Capital* by Nobel laureate Yasunari Kawabata, the ethereal, atmospheric tale of a young Kyoto woman's filial devotion and self-realization. *Leaden Wings,* an absorbing 1980 novel of daily life in modern China by Zhang Jie, became one of the first larger recent works of Chinese fiction to appear in translation in the West.

Along the Pacific Rim, Indonesia's Ismail Marahimin's haunting World War II novel *And the War is Over* received the prestigious Pegasus Prize for 1987, an award whose purpose is "to introduce American readers to distinguished works from countries whose literature is rarely translated into English." *Wings of Stone* continues Linda Ty-Casper's recent series of novels about sociopolitical events in her native Philippines. The half-aboriginal (and pseudonymous) B. Wongar published his third novel set in Australia's primitive bush country, *Gabo Djara,* a moving allegory about a culture facing potential devastation from uranium mining and nuclear testing. And lastly, New Zealand's Keri Hulme followed the enormous worldwide success of her novel *The Bone People* with a collection of short fiction titled *Te Kaihau / The Windeater,* most of whose stories blend the uniqueness of her native Maori culture with the European culture of modern New Zealand.

WILLIAM RIGGAN, "*World Literature Today*"

LONDON

During a period of soaring prices for land and property in London, a variety of plans have been put forward to reclaim parts of the city for new uses and for a widely mixed citizenry.

Reclamation and Development. Concern for the condition of Great Britain's inner cities was highlighted by a visit from Prince Charles to London's Brick Lane, a conglomeration of mainly Asian-inhabited garment factories. Brick Lane is located near Spitalfields, many of whose 18th-century houses already have been bought up and renovated.

The efforts of the Soho Society, backed by a stiff new policy from the Westminster City Council—requiring the licensing of pornography stores and limiting their number to only five—have helped nearly eliminate the pornography industry from Soho, which has returned to some of its pre-World War II smartness. New clubs, like the media-favorite Groucho's, and fashionable brasseries have opened up among the district's old theaters and restaurants. Many new residents are moving in and renovating 18th-century cottages. Although the Soho Society is promoting housing for the moderate-income citizenry, high prices already are keeping out most non-yuppies.

As a result of London's most ambitious new reclamation project, city development—which for centuries had moved generally westward—now is moving eastward. The largest area of reclamation is Docklands, the rotting wharves and loading docks along the Thames; it is an area that declined with London's eclipse as a leading port. In 1987, after six years of planning and seeking investment, the London Docklands Development Corporation announced that the reclaimed area will provide 25,000 new homes (in all price ranges) and 80,000 new jobs by 1990. The Royal Docks section is regarded as the largest urban development site in the world, while Canary Wharf is expected to be the biggest commercial development in Europe. The latter, located near the city's major financial institutions, will be the principal site of new office construction after 1988.

Transit. The new London City airport of Stolport was officially opened in October 1987. Meanwhile, proposals for 13 mi (21 km) of new road linking Limehouse with the Royal Docks were put forward. And on July 31, Queen Elizabeth II presided over the opening of the Dockland Light Railway, an automatic driverless elevated train system linking central London with the rapidly developing Docklands area. The 7.5 mi (12 km) of track link 15 new stations from Island Gardens to Tower Gateway near the Tower of London. Fire broke out in the King's Cross subway station on November 18. The blaze in London's busiest underground station killed 30 persons.

MAUREEN GREEN, *Free-lance Writer, London*

LOS ANGELES

Urban growth control was the theme of Los Angeles city and suburban politics in 1987. Also during the year, the Colosseum commission and the Rapid Transit District board came under criticism, a major earthquake rocked the area, and the Getty Museum was the subject of scandal.

Politics. The growth control issue sharpened during 1987. By initiative, city voters cut in half the building density to be allowed on 75% of the city's commercial and industrial land. Many suburbs made efforts to preserve local life-styles with land-use restrictions, some adopted by voter initiative. Typically, these would allow only single-family houses, set a limit on the rate of issue of building permits, require voter approval for certain zoning changes, or require developers to pay the full cost of new infrastructure. Such measures were expected to push development outward and to decrease urban density, thereby promoting urban "sprawl."

Mayor Tom Bradley appointed the city's first housing coordinator to bring together agencies to preserve and construct lower-cost housing. The city's supply of "affordable" housing has been decreasing. The mayor also announced plans for 2,000 housing units for the homeless.

The June election produced one upset. City Council President Pat Russell was defeated by Ruth Galanter, who accused the former of failing to support growth control. Perhaps another factor was a nearly fatal knife attack upon Galanter in her home shortly before the election.

Asserting that no one was in charge of transportation planning and construction in the Los Angeles area, the state legislature attempted to abolish the regional and county transit boards and replace them with a single ex officio board of elected officials, but the governor vetoed the bill. Subway construction proceeded slowly.

Earthquake. The area experienced a major earthquake (Richter 6.1) in the early morning of October 1. It killed six persons, injured perhaps 100 others, damaged more than 100 structures, and briefly disabled city services.

Other. The Colosseum commission also came under fire when the pro football Raiders announced that they would move out of that stadium and build a new one in Irwindale. The Lakers won their fourth NBA title since 1980, defeating the Boston Celtics in six games.

In February the *Times* of London revealed that Jiri Frel, curator of antiquities for the Getty Museum in Malibu, had accelerated the rate of donated acquisitions by overestimating their value for tax purposes. Frel resigned.

CHARLES R. ADRIAN
University of California, Riverside

LOUISIANA

A Louisiana political era ended in the fall, 1987, when incumbent Gov. Edwin W. Edwards dropped out of the governor's race after trailing a challenger, U.S. Rep. Charles E. (Buddy) Roemer 3d, in the primary election. Roemer, a 44-year-old Democratic congressman from Bossier City, led Edwards with 522,344 votes to 452,513, out of 1,597,591 cast. Although a runoff was scheduled because Roemer failed to obtain a majority, Edwards announced his withdrawal soon afer the primary election. The incumbent, who was seeking his fourth term as governor, had obtained only 28.3% of the primary votes and apparently realized he had little chance in the runoff.

Trailing the two front runners were six other candidates. The principal challengers were U.S. Rep. Robert Livingston of Metairie, U.S. Rep. W.J. (Billy) Tauzin of Houma, and Secretary of State Jim Brown of Baton Rouge. In the state's open-primary system, candidates of all parties run together. Livingston, the only Republican, had been considered Edwards' toughest challenger early in the campaign.

Charles E. (Buddy) Roemer staged a successful campaign for Louisiana's governorship in 1987. A graduate of Harvard, he has served in the U.S. House since 1981.

AP/Wide World

LOUISIANA • Information Highlights

Area: 47,752 sq mi (123 677 km²).
Population (July 1, 1986): 4,501,000.
Chief Cities (July 1, 1986 est.): Baton Rouge, the capital, 241,130; New Orleans, 554,500; Shreveport, 220,380; Houma (1984 est.) 101,998.
Government (1987): *Chief Officers*—governor, Edwin W. Edwards (D); lt. gov., Robert L. Freeman (D). *Legislature*—Senate, 39 members; House of Representatives, 105 members.
State Finances (fiscal year 1986): *Revenue,* $8,359,000,000; *expenditure,* $8,218,000,000.
Personal Income (1986): $50,382,000,000; per capita, $11,193.
Labor Force (June 1987): *Civilian labor force,* 1,950,000; *unemployed,* 219,200 (11.2% of total force).
Education: *Enrollment* (fall 1985)—public elementary schools, 571,321; public secondary, 221,383; colleges and universities, 177,176. *Public school expenditures* (1985-86), $2,207,000,000 ($3,046 per pupil).

Roemer, who would be inaugurated in March 1988, carried 37 of the state's 64 parishes. Edwards won only 20 parishes, including the city of New Orleans. Tauzin, like Edwards a Cajun, captured four parishes in predominantly French areas, and Livingston won three New Orleans suburban parishes. Early polls had shown Roemer far back in the pack, but in mid-campaign he began a rapid climb in popularity, particularly after he received the endorsements of most of the state's major newspapers.

All of the challengers ran on a platform stressing the need for a change in state leadership. They pointed to the state's dire economic situation, questioned Edwards' honesty and integrity, and decried Louisiana's poor image. Roemer appealed to voters by refusing to accept contributions of more than $5,000 from any individual or cash, loans, or money from political-action committees.

Only a few years ago, Edwards had been considered the most popular and influential Louisiana politician since Huey P. Long. He won two consecutive terms as governor, in 1971 and 1975, and then was forced by constitutional provisions to sit out one term before he was again elected governor in 1983. But his most recent term became a disaster. He was twice tried on federal racketeering charges—the first resulting in a hung jury and the second in acquittal. And as the end of the oil boom sank Louisiana into an economic quagmire, Edwards proposed casino gambling and a lottery as solutions, but the state legislature refused those proposals. By the time of the October election, Louisiana faced a cumulative deficit of $350 million to $500 million. Some said that unless new revenue sources were found the state would not be able to meet its payrolls by mid-1988.

In other major statewide races, former Secretary of State Paul Hardy defeated incumbent Lt. Gov. Bobby Freeman; State Rep. Fox McKeithen was elected secretary of state; Attorney General Billy Guste was reelected; and State Rep. Mary Landrieu was elected treasurer. Voters elected a more conservative legislature, ousting a number of lawmakers close to Edwards.

Legislation. The 1987 legislature gave the governor the right to borrow up to 20% of anticipated annual revenues to deal with cash-flow problems, which opponents said was a scheme to mask the state deficit until after the elections. The legislature also approved off-track racehorse betting and partial reform of insurance-liability laws.

Other News. In November the seizure of a federal detention center in Oakdale by Cuban inmates captured the attention of the state and nation. The refugees were protesting federal government plans to return them to Cuba by seizing 26 hostages and holding them for eight days. The crisis was resolved on November 29 after the government agreed to give individual hearing to the refugees to determine whether or not they should return to Cuba. (*See also* CUBA.)

In midyear plans were announced to divert part of the Mississippi river's flow to marshes in an effort to halt saltwater intrusion and erosion of the state's coastline, which is losing 40–60 sq. mi. (104–155 km²) a year.

JOSEPH W. DARBY III
"The Times Picayune"

MAINE

The worst flood in the history of Maine's weather records began on April 1, 1987, and continued for two more days. National Weather Service hydrologist Jerry French termed the high waters a "once in 500 years event." Hardest hit were communities along the Kennebec River, which crested at a record 21 ft (6.4 m) above flood stage. Other raging rivers included the Androscoggin, the Penobscot, and the Piscataquis, but in spite of the flooding—which wiped out bridges, highways, factories, and homes—no lives were lost. Damage estimates topped $100 million, and President Ronald Reagan declared six counties disaster areas. Many landmarks, including the 130-year-old covered bridge at Lows, one of the nation's oldest, were destroyed.

Forecasters had failed to predict the deluge, but as the waters receded, the heavy snows of January combined with almost 6 inches (15 cm) of rain during the last three days in March were said to be responsible. As the year ended, repairs were in progress.

The Economy. With an economic growth rate of 12% for the year and an unemployment rate well below 5%, the state's economy accelerated steadily, leaving many employers wondering if they could fill the available jobs. At one point during one of the busiest and most crowded tourist seasons in the state's history, staff shortages forced several restaurants to close one day a week and hotels to trim their services.

"Over the past few years, Maine has been enjoying in economic renaissance," said State Planning Director Richard Silkman, "with growth rates that haven't been seen here in more than a century." But while per-capita income rose 7%, the second highest rate in the nation, growth was not without its problems.

Housing starts for the past three years had increased from the previous year at a rate eight times the national average, and populations in the three southern counties had doubled since 1960. Acadia National Park is now the second most visited park in the nation, and many other state parks were filled to capacity during the summer season.

In response to these pressures, some 40 Maine communities have voted in favor of halting all building for one or more years while they try to cope with the already existing growth. And a $35 million public-land acquisition fund was approved by Maine voters in November. Voters also rejected a plan to shut down the Maine Yankee nuclear plant in 1988.

The robust economy helped Gov. John Y. McKernan, Jr., enjoy a trouble free first year in office. As a Republican who has to deal with a Democratic House and Senate, McKernan was expected to have some problems. But none materialized, and Maine's 113th legislature was notable for its moderation.

Other News. The year 1987 was also the year a lobster first appeared on the state's auto license plates; the year Rockport's famous Andre the Seal died of old age; and the year when the U.S. First Circuit Court of Appeals ended all speculation about the future of the Maine Guides, the state's only professional baseball team. The recent sale of the Guides, the court said, meant that the team would have to move to Scranton, PA.

JOHN N. COLE, *"Maine Times"*

MAINE • Information Highlights

Area: 33,265 sq mi (86 156 km²).
Population (July 1, 1986): 1,174,000.
Chief Cities (1980 census): Augusta, the capital, 21,819; Portland, 61,572; Lewiston, 40,481; Bangor, 31,643.
Government (1987): *Chief Officer*—governor, John R. McKernan, Jr. (R). *Legislature*—Senate, 33 members; House of Representatives, 151 members.
State Finances (fiscal year 1986): *Revenue*, $2,389,000,000; *expenditure*, $2,156,000,000.
Personal Income (1986): $15,007,000,000; per capita, $12,790.
Labor Force (June 1987): *Civilian labor force*, 589,600; *unemployed*, 23,700 (4.0% of total force).
Education: *Enrollment* (fall 1985)—public elementary schools, 140,413; public secondary, 65,688; colleges and universities, 52,201. *Public school expenditures* (1985-86), $647,000,000 ($3,346 per pupil).

MALAYSIA

Prime Minister Mahathir bin Mohamad narrowly withstood an election challenge to his party leadership. Racial tensions later in the year prompted the arrests of more than 100 oppositionists. The economy showed modest growth.

Politics. In party elections April 24, Prime Minister Mahathir defeated Minister of Trade and Industry Tengu Razaleigh Hamzah, 761–718, to win a third term as president of the ruling United Malays National Organization (UMNO). It was the first direct challenge to a sitting president in the party's 41-year history. Ghafar Baba, whom Mahathir had chosen as deputy prime minister following the 1986 resignation of Musa Hitam, won by 41 votes over Musa for the party deputy presidency. In the aftermath of the vote, cabinet members who supported the Razaleigh-Musa challenge either resigned or were replaced.

In Sarawak, the National Front coalition retained control of the state government in April elections despite the defection of one of its largest member parties, the Sarawak Dayak party (PBDS). The PBDS won more seats than any single party but found itself in the opposition. In Sabah, the sudden death of the United Sabah National Organization (USNO) president, Hamid Mustapha, upset plans to merge the party with UMNO.

Still suffering from the failure of largely Chinese savings cooperatives closely linked with the party, the Malaysian Chinese Association (MCA) threatened to pull out of the National Front coalition and thereby prompted the government to intervene to protect depositors. Incumbent leaders of the other major Chinese party in the National Front, Gerakan, were easy winners in June party elections.

Domestic Affairs. The Communist Party of Malaya has been in armed revolt against the government, mostly from jungle bases in southern Thailand, since 1948. In early 1987, however, an offer of amnesty from the Thai government, combined with military pressure, led to mass defections during March and April. The number of Communist Party members still in the jungle reportedly was reduced to fewer than 1,000.

In late October, amid rising tension between Malays and the nation's ethnic Chinese minority, the government arrested 106 opposition figures, many of them ethnic Chinese—including Lim Kit Siang, the leader of the Democratic Action Party. The government action, which also included the shutdown of four newspapers, was taken under a law against subversives and terrorists. Prime Minister Mahathir said that the law was invoked to avoid the kind of racial rioting that broke out in 1969. Many of those arrested later were released.

Economy. In 1987, modest recovery in petroleum prices and strengthening export markets for other commodities, especially electronics and textiles, led to growth projections of more than 2% for the year. The country also recorded its first surplus in current account balance of payments in eight years.

Prior to his arrest in October, Lim Kit Siang forced a delay in the signing of a contract that would turn over the 560-mi (900-km) north-south highway to a private company of which UMNO is a major owner. Lim's court case was based on the claim that cabinet members who approved the contract will benefit directly. The government, however, described the contract as part of its continuing privatization program and as a means to build the remaining 311 mi (500 km) of the highway.

K. MULLINER, *Ohio University*

MALAYSIA • Information Highlights

Official Name: Malaysia.
Location: Southeast Asia.
Area: 131,900 sq mi (329 750 km²).
Population (mid-1987 est.): 16,100,000.
Chief City (1980 census): Kuala Lumpur, the capital, 937,875.
Government: *Head of state,* Mahmood Iskandar Ibni Sultan Ismail (elected Feb. 9, 1984). *Head of government,* Mahathir bin Mohamad, prime minister (took office July 1981). *Legislature*—Parliament: Dewan Negara (Senate) and Dewan Ra'ayat (House of Representatives).
Monetary Unit: Ringgit (Malaysian dollar) (2.517 ringgits equal U.S.$1, August 1987).
Economic Index (1986): *Consumer Prices* (1980 = 100), all items, 126.4; food, 123.4.

MANITOBA

Relations between government and business dominated Manitoba news in 1986–87. Several Crown (government) corporations showed large losses. In the private sector, political considerations cost Manitoba a major federal contract for aircraft repairs. The federal government, on the other hand, bolstered Winnipeg's construction industry by initiating urban-renewal projects, and provincial support of a takeover bid by Ford Motors may have saved 1,200 jobs.

Business and Government. Two long-established Crown Corporations announced major losses in 1986–87. Deals with Saudi Arabia cost MTX, the export subsidiary of the Manitoba Telephone System, more than C$25 million. The Manitoba Public Insurance Corporation (MPIC) had similar losses, and saw its reserves virtually wiped out. Critics suggested that the MPIC had set car-insurance rates too low during the 1986 election year. The government claimed that the losses came from out-of-province reinsurance, a field from which MPIC would withdraw.

The provincial government tried to move into the field of natural-gas distribution when it

MANITOBA • Information Highlights

Area: 250,946 sq mi (649 950 km^2).
Population (1986 census): 1,071,232.
Chief Cities (1986 census): Winnipeg, the capital, 594,551; Brandon, 38,708; Thompson, 14,701.
Government (1987): *Chief Officers*—lt. gov., George Johnson; premier, Howard Pawley (New Democratic Party). *Legislature*—Legislative Assembly, 57 members.
Provincial Finances (1987–88 fiscal year budget): *Revenues,* \$3,772,608,800; *expenditures,* \$4,187,-860,300.
Personal Income (average weekly earnings, July 1987): \$411.29.
Labor Force (September 1987, seasonally adjusted): *Employed* workers, 15 years of age and over, 539,000; *Unemployed,* 41,000 (7.6%).
Education (1987–88): *Enrollment*—elementary and secondary schools, 219,500 pupils; postsecondary—universities, 19,530; community colleges, 3,900.
(All monetary figures are in Canadian dollars.)

announced a takeover of Inter-City Gas, the major supplier of domestic natural gas. In June, Premier Howard Pawley said that the new Public Gas Corporation would save customers \$50 million yearly. However he reduced this estimate and cancelled the action.

Versatile Implements of Winnipeg—which had been on the verge of collapse in mid-1986 due to the failure of a buyout bid by their competitors, Deere and Co.—was taken over by Ford in late 1987, after the provincial government had intervened. Provincial government lobbyists were less successful with Bristol Aerospace, another major Winnipeg employer. Bristol had bid on a long-term maintenance contract for Canada's CF-18 fighters. After a struggle involving the federal government and the Saskatchewan provincial government on the one hand, and all three Manitoba political parties on the other, the contract—worth more than \$1 billion and 347 jobs—went to the highest bidder, Canadair of Montreal.

The federal government supplied major funding for an innovative urban-renewal scheme in Winnipeg. Portage Place, which combines shopping mall, office complex, housing projects, and a system of overhead walkways, opened in September 1987. It cost more than \$200 million, much of it in federal grants.

Unemployment in Manitoba ranged from a high of 7.9% to a low of 6.7% during the first nine months of 1987.

French Language Services. The year 1987 saw the climax of a longstanding conflict in Manitoba over French-language services. The Canadian Supreme Court had ruled that all provincial laws were unconstitutional unless they were written in both English and French. In March 1987, the Manitoba government introduced a single, 9,000-page bill containing the most important statutes of the province in both languages.

MICHAEL KINNEAR
The University of Manitoba

MARYLAND

The Sept. 15, 1987, Democratic primary for Baltimore mayor was decided by barely 5,000 votes of about 155,000 cast, as city State's Attorney Kurt L. Schmoke, 37, edged out incumbent Clarence H. "Du" Burns, 69.

Burns, a veteran of 40 years in politics, was president of the City Council and ascended to the mayor's office after William Donald Schaefer was elected governor of Maryland in 1986. Schmoke had served only five years in elected office.

Burns was the city's first black mayor, and the primary set up Schmoke to become the first elected black mayor. His November 3 general election victory over Republican Samuel A. Culotta was considered a formality in a city where registered Democrats outnumber registered Republicans by more than 10 to 1.

Economy. The year's Chesapeake Bay oyster harvest was devastated by the parasite known as "multinucleate sphere unknown (MSX)," which thrives in waters where area droughts result in high salinity. Scientists estimated MSX would destroy up to 80% of the bay's oysters. They based their hopes for eventual recovery of the industry on developing a disease-resistant oyster within a decade. To compound the woes of watermen, a multistate shellfish industry organization insisted that the state prohibit harvesting oysters immediately after heavy rains, when water contamination from land runoff is most severe.

In Baltimore's mayoralty race, Kurt L. Schmoke, a graduate of Yale and Harvard, defeated incumbent Clarence Burns in the Democratic primary and was elected in November.
AP/Wide World

The General Assembly repealed the state's "blue laws," which limited commercial activity on Sunday. A state appellate court rejected an attempt to bring to referendum the legislature's decision to build a $200 million sports stadium complex in downtown Baltimore.

Mandel Case. In November a federal judge threw out the 1977 mail fraud and racketeering convictions of former Gov. Marvin Mandel and five close associates, in light of a U.S. Supreme Court ruling in June that sharply narrowed the applications of the law. Mandel had been accused of accepting thousands of dollars in bribes and gifts in return for influencing legislation to benefit his friends. He had served 19 months when President Reagan commuted his three-year sentence in 1981. He said he would seek to be reinstated to the bar, and federal prosecutors said they would appeal the District Court decision.

Indictments. In the wake of the June 1986 cocaine-induced death of University of Maryland basketball star Len Bias, four young men were indicted. Charges against three of them were dropped and two agreed to testify against Bias' friend Brian Lee Tribble. Tribble was accused of supplying the cocaine that killed Bias and was charged with cocaine possession and distribution. He was tried and acquitted.

An Amtrak passenger train crashed into three Conrail locomotives on January 4 in Chase, about 20 mi (32 km) east of Baltimore, resulting in a derailment in which 16 persons died and more than 170 were injured. Conrail engineer Ricky L. Gates was indicted on manslaughter charges in Amtrak's worst disaster. The residents of the surrounding community later were honored by the White House for taking in the crash survivors and aiding the massive rescue effort that followed the accident.

Two brothers from a prominent political family, former Democratic state Sen. Clarence Mitchell III and Democratic state Sen. Michael B. Mitchell, were indicted. They were tried and convicted of conspiring to interfere with the congressional inquiry into activities of Wedtech Corporation, a New York defense contractor. They were accused of accepting $110,000 from Wedtech and promising to influence their uncle, U.S. Rep. Parren J. Mitchell, then chairman of the House Small Business Committee, in the committee's investigation of Wedtech's activities.

State Law Voided. In a 5–4 vote, the U.S. Supreme Court on June 15 voided a Maryland law that allowed "victim impact" statements to be presented to juries deliberating death sentences. The ruling did not affect such testimony, concerning the effect of a crime on the victim and family, in noncapital sentencings.

PEGGY CUNNINGHAM
"The Evening Sun," Baltimore

MARYLAND • Information Highlights

Area: 10,460 sq mi (27 092 km²).
Population (July 1, 1986): 4,463,000.
Chief Cities (1980 census): Annapolis, the capital, 31,740; Baltimore (July 1, 1986 est.), 752,800; Rockville, 43,811.
Government (1987): *Chief Officers*—governor, Donald Schaefer (D); lt. gov., Melvin A. Steinberg (D). *General Assembly*—Senate, 47 members; House of Delegates, 141 members.
State Finances (fiscal year 1986): *Revenue,* $9,140,000,000; *expenditure,* $8,132,000,000.
Personal Income (1986): $75,272,000,000; per capita $16,864.
Labor Force (June 1987): *Civilian labor force,* 2,437,600; *unemployed,* 101,500 (4.2% of total force).
Education: *Enrollment* (fall 1985)—public elementary schools, 446,3[illegible]1; public secondary, 225,239; colleges and universities, 231,649. *Public school expenditures* (1985–86), $2,663,000,000 ($4,349 per pupil).

MASSACHUSETTS

Continued strong economic growth and the presidential campaign of Gov. Michael Dukakis highlighted Bay State news in 1987.

Forecasters were betting that the Massachusetts economy would remain in good shape through 1988 in spite of October's sharp drop in stock market prices. Unemployment in September was 2.5%, down from 4.0% in September 1986. There were 68,000 new jobs, causing serious worker shortages in some areas, particularly nursing, retail help, and food services. Employers were paying premium wages to hire or retain employees. Average wages in manufacturing were up more than 6.4% from the previous year.

The state's economic growth continued to be fueled by the high-tech industries in which many firms combine research and development with direct manufacturing under one roof. Computer-software firms, such as Lotus Development Corporation, posted record sales and profits. Computer-hardware firms, such as Wang Laboratories and Digital Equipment Corporation, had a more difficult time keeping momentum, but continued growth was seen as indicated by Digital's huge private exposition held in September on a number of cruise ships in Boston harbor.

Politics. Governor Dukakis was frequently out of the state campaigning for the Democratic presidential nomination in 1988. The Dukakis campaign drew much support from Massachusetts Democrats, who helped give the governor an early lead in money raised among Democratic contenders.

In April, Dukakis announced that his chief of staff and closest adviser, John Sasso, was resigning from state service to head the campaign. Sasso was replaced by Hale Champion of Harvard's Kennedy School of Government, an experienced administrator who had spent many years at the Boston Redevelopment Au-

AP/Wide World

Boston Mayor Raymond L. Flynn and his wife Kathy greet supporters on election night. The Democrat, who claimed credit for easing Boston's racial tensions, won reelection with 67% of the vote.

thority. Sasso was later forced to resign from the campaign when he leaked to the press damaging information about Delaware Sen. Joseph Biden—a competitor of Dukakis.

Dukakis' presidential campaign ambitions were believed to strengthen his continuing opposition to the opening of the Seabrook nuclear power plant on the Massachusetts-New Hampshire border. Dukakis refused to submit an evacuation plan for the Massachusetts town which lay within 10 mi (16-km) of the plant, thus preventing the Nuclear Regulatory Commission from granting a start-up license. The Seabrook plant has become increasingly unpopular in New Hampshire, and Dukakis' move was seen as helping to maintain his lead in that state's presidential preference primary in early 1988.

Relations between the legislature and the governor were more cooperative than in previous years, but some disputes did occur. One, early in the year, involved plans to distribute the large tax surplus garnered from the rapidly growing economy. A compromise was eventually reached in which a limited income-tax cut, funding of state pension programs, and a "rainy day" escrow were approved. Another conflict took place in the autumn, when the legislature balked at approving a "universal health care" measure which was heavily promoted by the governor. The bill would establish health insurance for the estimated 600,000 persons not covered by conventional plans. Eventual passage was predicted. Hospitals were alarmed by the proposed reductions in reimbursements.

In Boston, incumbent Mayor Raymond Flynn was elected to a second term, defeating Councilman Joseph M. Tierney.

Transportation. Two important developments in transportation occurred during the year. The first was federal funding of continued planning to reconstruct the elevated highway which runs through the downtown Boston area known as the Central Artery, along with construction of a third vehicle tunnel under Boston harbor connecting with the airport. The controversial project was initially rejected by federal officials but strong support from the Massachusetts congressional delegation kept the plan alive. The second issue involved Logan International Airport, the world's eighth busiest, with about 2.5 million passengers each month. Airport officials announced plans to require airlines to schedule flights at off-peak hours to reduce congestion that has resulted in delays and dangerous conditions. Airport officials also launched a series of radio, television, and print commercials aimed at discouraging people from driving to the airport.

HARVEY BOULAY, *Rogerson House*

MASSACHUSETTS • Information Highlights

Area: 8,284 sq mi (21 456 km²).
Population (July 1, 1986): 5,832,000.
Chief Cities (July 1, 1986 est.): Boston, the capital, 573,600; Worcester, 157,700; Springfield, 149,410.
Government (1987): *Chief Officer*—governor, Michael S. Dukakis (D); lt. gov., Evelyn F. Murphy (D). *Legislature*—Senate 40 members; House of Representatives, 160 members.
State Finances (fiscal year 1986): *Revenue,* $13,121,000,000; *expenditure,* $12,449,000,000.
Personal Income (1986): $103,353,000,000; per capita, $17,722.
Labor Force (June 1987): *Civilian labor force,* 3,136,800; *unemployed,* 97,000 (3.1% of total force).
Education: *Enrollment* (fall 1985)—public elementary schools, 559,057; public secondary, 285,273; colleges and universities, 421,175. *Public school expenditures* (1985–86), $3,245,000,000 ($4,255 per pupil).

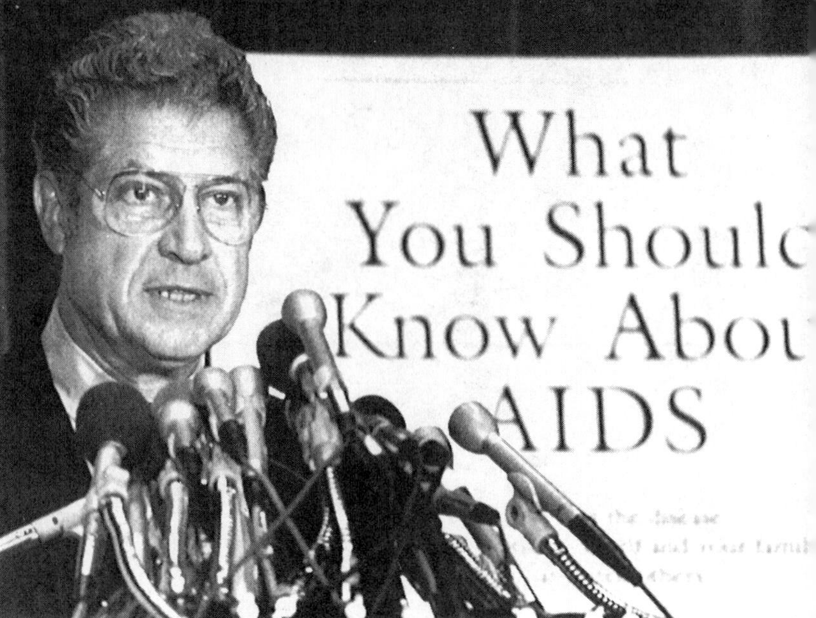

U.S. Department of Health and Human Services Undersecretary Don Newman announced in September the federal government's first AIDS awareness and prevention campaign, complete with television, radio, and print advertisements. The campaign follows by only a few months President Ronald Reagan's appointment of a 13-member AIDS commission, which is to complete a report by June 1988 advising the government on broad aspects of the AIDS problem, including medical, legal, social, economic, and ethical issues.

AP/Wide World

MEDICINE AND HEALTH

Promising gains were made during 1987 in treating Parkinson's disease, high cholesterol levels, and other medical problems. During the year scientists announced that certain cancers could be related to genetic defects. But all this progress was overshadowed by the specter of AIDS (Acquired Immune Deficiency Syndrome) and the complex legal and ethical issues associated with the disease. Ever-increasing medical costs and the attempt to legislate catastrophic medical insurance also garnered headlines, as did the practice of surrogate motherhood. (*See* feature article, page 55.)

AIDS. The epidemic of AIDS continued to grow, with experts predicting grimmer times in the years ahead. The World Health Organization estimated that 5 to 10 million people carried the virus by 1987, and as many as 3 million of them were likely to develop the disease by 1992. The U.S. Centers for Disease Control in Atlanta estimated that 1.5 million Americans were infected, and it projected 270,000 cases of disease and 179,000 deaths by the end of 1991. (By late 1987 approximately 48,000 cases and 27,000 deaths had been recorded in the United States.)

The AIDS virus may remain inactive within the human body for years, causing no symptoms of disease though remaining capable of being spread to others. Because there is no way to determine how many people are actually infected, it is difficult to forecast future problems, needs, and costs. Though forecasts are disparate, none are encouraging. For instance, many experts believe it will cost as much as $16 billion to provide medical care for AIDS victims in the United States in 1991, as compared with the $1.1 billion spent in 1986.

Painful issues confront society as it tries to help AIDS victims and at the same time protect others against the disease. Numerous programs to test for the AIDS virus were proposed or instituted during 1987. In June, U.S. President Ronald Reagan called for testing of federal prisoners and would-be immigrants, and the West German state of Bavaria began testing all prostitutes, drug addicts, prison inmates, and applicants for government jobs. In September the Soviet Union began testing foreigners entering the country who planned to stay for more than three months. In October, Houston's Methodist Hospital announced it would ask all entering patients to take the test.

Many medical and legal experts opposed mandatory testing, contending that it would not slow the spread of infection and that it infringed on individuals' rights. In addition, people who become infected with the virus may not develop antibodies for more than a year. Commonly used tests for AIDS actually detect antibodies rather than the virus itself. Thus people who test negative may in fact be infected, and the negative test may result in a false sense of security among them, their sexual partners, health-care workers, and others.

Fear of contracting AIDS forced some physicians and other health-care workers to refuse to treat AIDS patients. In November the American Medical Association ruled that physicians have an ethical obligation to treat such patients.

AIDS patients have complained that the U.S. government was slow to approve potentially helpful drugs, including drugs such as ribavirin that were being marketed in other countries. Early in 1987, ICN Pharmaceuticals of Costa Mesa, CA, claimed that ribavirin inhibited replication of the AIDS virus during early stages of infection. Thousands of Americans traveled to Mexico to purchase the drug, which is available there without a prescription. Data contradicting ICN's claims was released in June, following a study of ribavirin carried out at six medical centers around the United States. The study indicated that ribavirin had no significant effect in preventing death or slowing the progression of AIDS.

In March, azidothymidine (AZT) became the first drug approved by the Food and Drug Administration (FDA) for the treatment of AIDS. AZT inhibits the reproduction of the AIDS virus, helping to prolong the lives of some patients. However, it is extremely toxic, and many AIDS victims are unable to tolerate it.

In May the federal government announced that it would make experimental drugs more quickly available to patients with AIDS and other "immediately life-threatening diseases." The rule applies only to drugs that are undergoing clinical trials designed to prove the drugs' safety and efficacy.

Syphilis and Gonorrhea. A 35% increase in the incidence of the sexually transmitted disease (STD) syphilis was reported by U.S. officials. Most of the increase occurred in New York City, Los Angeles County, and Florida, primarily among black and Hispanic heterosexuals.

There also was an alarming increase in cases of penicillin-resistant gonorrhea. Other antibiotics can be used to treat the disease, but gonorrhea bacteria were developing resistance to these as well. U.S. Army researchers reported that servicemen infected with gonorrhea in Korea had strains that could withstand spectinomycin, and they expected this resistance to spread to the United States.

Cancer. Can nutrients prevent cancer? Although health-food enthusiasts have long claimed that supplements of vitamin A and other nutrients help prevent or retard the development of cancer, little scientific data supports this view. Now close to two dozen major studies are underway to determine whether nutrient supplements can be used to reduce the incidence of cancer, particularly in cigarette smokers and other high-risk individuals. Definitive results are not expected for at least five to ten years.

Early detection of cancer is often the key to saving lives. For example, routine mammography (breast X rays) can reduce the death rate from breast cancer by 30%, largely because the procedure can detect tumors while they are still very small, when treatment is most likely to be effective. But the American Cancer Society reported that only 10% to 15% of American women who should have mammograms have ever had them. Only when a well-known public figure has surgery for breast cancer does the number of women seeking mammograms increase. Following Nancy Reagan's surgery for breast cancer in October, the number of women making appointments for mammograms nearly doubled.

Studies by biochemist Edsel T. Bucovaz at the University of Tennessee indicate that heightened levels of B-protein in the blood often signal the presence of cancer, giving the substance the potential of acting as a biological marker to detect cancer in its early stages. Bucovaz and his colleagues also reported that the level of B-protein in cancer patients increases as the cancer progresses. By measuring these patients' B-protein levels, physicians can keep tabs on the advance or remission of the disease.

During 1987 scientists revealed that genetic defects contribute to the development of a number of diseases, including certain types of lung, breast, and colorectal cancers. At least some of the studies suggested that genes that normally control cell growth are inactivated or missing in the patients, leading to excessive cell growth and the formation of cancerous tissue.

New evidence linking papilloma viruses to cancers was reported by several researchers. More than 50 types of papilloma viruses have been identified. They are widespread and best known for causing warts. Those that infect the genital tract, however, have been implicated in cervical cancer and other malignancies. A team at the German Cancer Center estimated that papilloma viruses can be detected in at least 80% of all cervical cancers, leading other experts to suggest that the viruses are probably present in all such cancers. The relationship between the viruses and cancer is not yet known, though most researchers believe the viruses actually contribute to the development of the disease.

A substance called interleukin-2 showed some promise as a treatment for advanced cancers that do not respond to other therapies. Interleukin-2 is produced by the body and stimulates the formation of white blood cells. The results of one study released in 1987 stated that nine out of 152 patients had complete remission following treatment, 20 showed significant improvement, and others had minor improvements.

Alzheimer's Disease. Research teams found evidence that a defective gene causes the hereditary form of Alzheimer's disease (*see* BIOCHEMISTRY), a degenerative brain disorder that develops in middle or later life and for which there is no known cure.

The first drug to show promise of reducing memory loss in victims of Alzheimer's disease was tetrahydroaminoacridine (THA). Clinical trials of THA were halted by the FDA in October, however, after 20% of the test subjects experienced undesirable changes in liver chemistry.

In the first study on the economic toll of Alzheimer's disease, the *Journal of Public Health* reported that the cost to the United States was between $27 billion and $31 billion a year—a figure that is expected to increase dramatically because of the increasing number of older people.

Cholesterol Levels. Cholesterol is a fatty substance needed for such functions as making cell membranes. Excessive blood cholesterol levels, however, can cause atherosclerosis. This disease, characterized by the formation of fatty deposits that clog arteries, is the cause of heart attacks that kill hundreds of thousands of Americans each year. Scientists at the University of Southern California School of Medicine reported in June the first "clear evidence" that an intensive regimen of drugs and low-cholesterol dieting can slow and even reverse the formation of fatty deposits, thereby lowering the risk of heart disease.

In October the federal government issued detailed guidelines for identifying and treating people whose blood cholesterol levels are undesirably high. The guidelines recommended that such people follow a stringent low-cholesterol diet, followed, if necessary, by treatment with drugs.

In September the FDA approved lovastatin, a drug shown to reduce total cholesterol levels by 32% and levels of low-density lipoproteins (LDLs), the so-called "bad" cholesterol, by up to 39%. Long-term safety of lovastatin has not yet been established, however, so it is not expected to be considered a drug of first choice for treatment of high cholesterol.

Another anti-cholesterol drug, gemfibrozil, reduces total cholesterol levels only slightly. But a study conducted in Finland found that gemfibrozil significantly lowered the risk of heart disease in men with dangerously high cholesterol levels. The drug appears to work by increasing the blood level of high-density lipoproteins (HDLs), a "good" form of cholesterol, while decreasing LDL levels.

If two or more of the coronary arteries that carry blood to the heart muscles are blocked by the buildup of fats and other deposits, surgeons generally perform coronary bypass surgery, removing sections of one or more veins from the patient's leg and using them to form a detour around the blocked arteries. A low-cholesterol diet and possibly drugs may be recommended when only one coronary artery is blocked.

An alternative to bypass surgery, but still experimental, is laser angioplasty. A laser is connected to a catheter encasing bundles of optical fibers. The catheter is threaded through arteries until it reaches the deposits. The laser is then fired, sending pulses of energy through the optical fibers. The energy breaks down the deposits into carbon dioxide, hydrogen, and other harmless molecules.

Surgical Advances. In a complex 22-hour operation that captured wide attention, seven-month-old twin boys born joined at the back of their heads were separated at Johns Hopkins Hospital in Baltimore. In addition to sharing a large area of the skull, the infants had shared a vital vein, necessitating reconstruction of the severed vessel in each child. During the hour it took to reconstruct the vein, the infants were in a state of "suspended animation," their blood supplies drained from their bodies and their hearts stopped. The twins suffered at least minor brain damage during the operation and their recovery was slow and difficult.

An unusual transplant operation took place at Johns Hopkins in May. A healthy heart was removed from a 28-year-old man suffering from cystic fibrosis, a disease that blocks lung passages, interfering with breathing. The heart was implanted into another man who suffered from heart disease. And the cystic fibrosis patient received the heart and lungs of an accident victim. The doctors who performed the operation believe that heart-lung transplants are more likely to succeed than lung transplants alone, an opinion not shared by all transplant specialists.

In October an infant just hours old became the youngest person to undergo a heart transplant operation. Doctors at Loma Linda Medical Center in California transplanted a new heart into the baby boy, who had a heart defect that causes death soon after birth.

Another type of transplant surgery offered hope to victims of Parkinson's disease, a neurological disorder characterized by tremors and loss of muscle control. In April scientists in Mexico reported dramatic improvement in Parkinson patients following the transplantation of adrenal tissue into the brain. The adrenal glands produce norepinephrine, a hormone that is chemically similar to dopamine, a substance produced by the brain that carries messages between nerve cells. The amount of dopamine is believed to be deficient in Parkinson victims.

Diet and Dieting. In April the American Medical Association and three nutrition organizations released guidelines for dietary vitamin and mineral allowances. The groups stated that most Americans obtain adequate nutrients from their diets and do not need vitamin or mineral supplements. Furthermore, they warned that regular intake of large doses of supplements may cause serious medical problems, such as birth defects.

A study codirected by Drs. Steven L. Gortmaker of the Harvard School of Public Health and William H. Dietz of the New England Medical Center in Boston found that the proportion of overweight American children between the ages of 6 and 17 has increased more than 40% in the last 15 years. Although the study did not examine the causes of this increase, the researchers speculated that eating salty, fatty fast foods on a regular basis and the general decline in physical activities can be blamed for much of today's high level of childhood obesity.

Osteoporosis. Following menopause, many women become susceptible to osteoporosis, a condition characterized by thinning and weakening of the bones. Claims made earlier in the decade that increased calcium intake would help prevent osteoporosis led millions of women to take daily supplements of the nutrient. Recent studies conducted in the United States and Denmark found little if any evidence to support the claims for calcium. On the other hand, decreasing production of the hormone estrogen by postmenopausal women does appear to cause bone loss. This can be counteracted by estrogen replacement therapy (ERT).

Other factors that have been shown to play roles in osteoporosis include cigarette smoking, heavy alcohol consumption, lack of exercise, and therapeutic drugs such as cortisone. Women who are small and thin or who have undergone premature menopause also have a higher than average chance of developing osteoporosis.

Nursing Shortage. A serious shortage of nurses threatened the quality of health care in U.S. hospitals. The profession's lack of status, relatively low salaries, and long and difficult hours are among the reasons cited for the decline. In the short term, part of the problem might be alleviated by speeding up the computerization of medical record-keeping and by hiring secretaries and administrators to perform many of the nonmedical tasks now handled by nurses. However, because of a substantial decline in enrollment in nursing schools, experts foresee a much more difficult problem during the 1990s.

To attract more people to the profession, schools revised their nursing programs, offering more flexible class schedules, accelerated programs, and new scholarships, loans, and free-tuition plans.

Meanwhile, some hospitals faced the loss of federal certification because of insufficient staffing, and at least one state offered bonuses of $3,000 or more to attract nurses to work in its psychiatric hospitals.

Dentistry

More people than ever have access to and are receiving dental care. Nonetheless, there is an oversupply of dentists and, as a result, declining applications to dental schools, which may create problems in the coming years. In March, Georgetown University announced that it would close its prestigious dental school by 1990. Georgetown President Timothy S. Healy pointed out that the school's applications had decreased 70% and that "those students who are choosing dentistry are less qualified than in previous eras, and the mean grade-point average of entering classes is dwindling to unacceptable levels."

Gum Disease. Periodontitis, or gum disease, is one of the most common and costly health problems in the United States today. Indeed, more tooth loss results from periodontitis than from tooth decay.

A precursor to periodontitis is a buildup of bacterial plaque on the teeth, resulting from inefficient or insufficient cleaning. The bacteria produce toxins that irritate neighboring gum tissue, causing it to become red and quick to bleed. Chronic infection gradually leads to the formation of pockets between the teeth and the gums, plus the destruction of the tissues and bone that support the teeth. As a result, the teeth become loose and may even fall out.

Considerable disagreement exists concerning the treatment of periodontitis. Particularly controversial is the use of surgery to reduce the size of pockets and expose teeth surfaces for easier cleaning. The procedure is quite common. Some dentists, however, say that more conservative cleaning treatments are frequently just as effective, and that surgery is often performed needlessly.

Cosmetic Dentistry. For many dentists, cosmetic dentistry is the fastest-growing part of their practice. Jeffrey Morley, president of the American Academy of Cosmetic Dentistry, noted that the amount of cosmetic work done by dentists has tripled since the early 1980s. The increase has resulted largely from the development of better materials, such as porcelain and acrylic laminates—thin veneers that are applied to the surface of a patient's teeth and bonded into place.

Dental Implants. Another technique that is becoming widely used is osseointegration—attaching artificial teeth permanently to the jawbone. A decade-long study has shown that osseointegration not only works but can be healthier and more efficient than traditional "false teeth."

The procedure, developed in Sweden in the 1960s, involves the implantation of hollow, threaded titanium cylinders in the jaw. Over a period of several months, the jaw tissue grows around the cylinders, forming a permanent bond with the implants. Then a titanium post is screwed into each cylinder. Finally, the patient's new artificial teeth are attached to these posts.

Like natural teeth, implants do not move when the person chews. They do not need to be removed for cleaning and they distribute the stress of chewing more naturally within the jaw than do traditional dentures.

JENNY TESAR
Medicine and Science Writer

Smoking in Public Places

Smoking is the leading preventable cause of death in the United States, contributing to at least 360,000 deaths annually, including one third of all cancer and heart-disease fatalities. These were some of the findings of the 1986 report of U.S. Surgeon General C. Everett Koop (*see also* BIOGRAPHY).

The health hazards to smokers have been known for more than two decades, during which time the number of smokers in the United States has plummeted from 42% to less than 30% of the national population. But the major focus of the latest surgeon general's report is not the dangers to smokers themselves but the dangers to those who innocently inhale others' smoke—the "passive" or "involuntary" smokers. According to the report, titled "The Health Consequences of Involuntary Smoking," evidence "clearly documents that nonsmokers are placed at increased risk for developing disease as the result of exposure to environmental smoke." The conclusion is corroborated by a number of independent researchers.

© Mark Reinstein/Gamma-Liaison

Armed with evidence they have long suspected, antismoking groups have become increasingly vocal and have influenced a number of sweeping legislative and policy changes in recent years. As of 1987, some 40 states had restrictions on smoking in public places, including restaurants, trains, buses, and even workplaces. There were also about 800 local ordinances against public smoking. The U.S. Congress passed a measure to ban smoking on domestic flights of two hours or less, and it considered bills to ban tobacco advertising, raise excise taxes on cigarettes, and strengthen smoking regulations in federal buildings. Although there is strong sentiment in Congress in favor of such legislation, members from the tobacco-growing states remain a powerful opposition.

Amid fears of health-related lawsuits from nonsmokers, private industry is acting as well. Some 30% of U.S. corporations now limit employees' smoking on the job, and the National Center for Health Promotion predicts that the number will grow to 80% before 1990. Most industrial restrictions are flexible, but some, like those at the Chicago-based USG Corporation, entirely ban smoking by employees. (In the case of USG, evidence indicates that mineral fibers used in their plants could have especially harmful effects on smokers.)

The $32-billion tobacco industry insists that evidence of the dangers of "passive smoking" is inconclusive and that public bans are inappropriate, premature, and discriminatory. Nevertheless, according to a December 1986 Gallup Poll, 87% of all Americans and 80% of current smokers support measures restricting smoking.

In the face of such stiff opposition, The Tobacco Institute, the major lobbying group for the tobacco industry, has been conducting a massive public-relations campaign that has seen its staff double to 90 over the past decade. And industry leaders are beginning to present alternatives to the public.

One such alternative is a cigarette substitute—rolled paper impregnated with nicotine—which is puffed on by smokers but not lighted. The product provides smokers with nicotine they require but does not affect anyone around them.

Another alternative will be test-marketed in 1988 by the R. J. Reynolds Company. This "smokeless" cigarette heats the tobacco rather than burns it and, as such, produces no ash, odor, and virtually no smoke from the lighted end. The American Lung Association, however, believes this product is not a safe alternative for either the active or passive smoker.

While the scientific and political debates continue, public sentiment against smoking is gaining rapidly. Surveys reveal that 94% of the U.S. population believes that smoking is hazardous to health and that nearly 90% of all smokers would like to kick the habit. To meet that demand, a number of self-help groups are springing to life, and smokers who want to quit were expected to pay an estimated $100 million for their services in 1987—a figure likely to double by 1989.

DENNIS L. MAMMANA

Catastrophic Health Insurance

The U.S. Congress in 1987 acted to help the nation's elderly and disabled citizens pay for the treatment of "catastrophic" illnesses with legislation that would extend Medicare coverage to include a large portion of the costs associated with prolonged medical treatment. Measures passed separately by the Senate and the House of Representatives were aimed at sheltering the Medicare program's 31 million beneficiaries, whose incomes are often limited and fixed, from health-care bills that threaten many with financial ruin. Final action on the measure was expected in early 1988.

The problem of "catastrophic" health costs has grown worse in recent years. Health-care costs in general have shot up, rising by 7.7% in 1986, even as the rate of inflation registered a modest 1.1% increase. And because demand for health care can only increase with the expanding elderly population, there is no end in sight to runaway health-care inflation: By the end of 1987, a projected $497 billion will have been spent on health care for the year, up 8.4% from 1986.

The issue of federally funded health insurance long has been a matter of dispute among lawmakers. Sen. Edward M. Kennedy (D-MA) and other supporters of national health insurance point to the effectiveness of programs currently provided in Canada and Western Europe. For their part, conservatives have resisted even limited measures to expand Medicare, which since 1965 has provided health coverage to the elderly and the disabled, as steps toward "socialized medicine." But such objections faded in the face of the growing need for protection from catastrophic expenses. Before Congress acted, President Reagan proposed a catastrophic insurance measure of his own, which he later abandoned out of concern for the growing federal budget deficit.

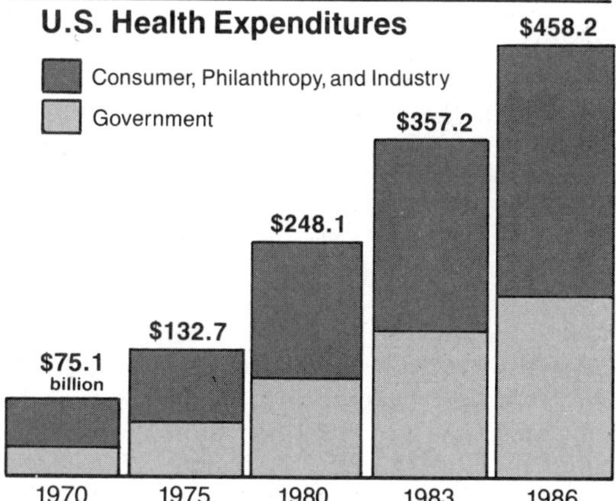

Source: U.S. Health Care Financing Administration

Although measures passed by the House in April and by the Senate in October differ in terms of coverage and needed to be resolved by a conference committee, President Reagan pledged to sign into law a compromise measure that resembles the Senate version. This measure contains several innovative elements that may affect future legislation on social programs.

In a departure from existing Medicare, Medicaid, and Social Security programs, catastrophic insurance would be financed by the beneficiaries themselves, and so would not add to the budget deficit. The Senate bill also would introduce means-testing to Medicare. For the first time, premiums for the new coverage would vary according to beneficiaries' income, ranging from $13 per year for those with annual incomes of no more than $11,000, to as much as $1,600 per year for beneficiaries with $120,000 or more in yearly income. Finally, the new coverage for the first time would include benefits for prescription drugs, which would be financed in large part out of the premium increases.

In return, the elderly would pay no more than $1,850 per year for health-care services provided under Medicare. The drug benefit, to be phased in over three years beginning in 1990, would cover 80% of the cost of prescription drugs above an annual $600 deductible. Another deductible, of $540 per year, would be the most any beneficiary would pay for hospital stays, no matter how long.

While spokesmen for the elderly welcomed the congressional action on catastrophic health insurance, other critics of the U.S. health-care system say it does not go far enough. As more and more workers are employed in the service sector, where such traditional employee benefits as health insurance often are not provided, growing numbers of Americans of all ages—as many as 37 million in 1986, according to the U.S. Census Bureau—are without health coverage of any kind. But the federal government, still searching for ways to cut the budget deficit, is unlikely to come to their aid in the foreseeable future. The uninsured, therefore, will have to look increasingly to the states for help.

MARY H. COOPER

Mental Health

There were significant advances in several areas of mental-health research and treatment in 1987.

Manic-Depressive Illness. Important new findings on the genetics of manic-depressive disease were reported by grantees of the National Institute of Mental Health (NIMH). Manic-depressive illness, also known as bipolar affective disorder, afflicts between 1 and 2 million Americans. Individuals with the disease experience extreme mood swings in which feelings of deep—often incapacitating—depression alternate with periods of intense activity.

Using sophisticated molecular-genetic techniques, a multidisciplinary team of scientists located a gene associated with manic-depressive disease on chromosome 11 in blood samples collected from an Amish family in Pennsylvania. This was the first demonstration of a possible genetic basis for one of the major mental disorders, and it opened a new direction for research in psychiatry.

The researchers—from the University of Miami, Yale University, and the Massachusetts Institute of Technology—reported on a ten-year study of manic-depressive illness among the Amish. Although the disease is not more common among the Amish than in the general population, genetic studies are easier to pursue in a well-defined and geographically stable community where there is little criminal behavior, violence, divorce, or alcoholism. In general, the Amish tend to have large families and keep detailed genealogical records.

As the focus of study, the researchers chose an extended family with 81 members. Fourteen had been diagnosed as manic-depressive and five as severely depressed. When the genetic profiles of these 19 people were compared to those of the unaffected family members, differences in the region of chromosome 11 became apparent. The researchers concluded that there is a gene in that location which predisposes the individual to manic depression. A parent who is subject to manic depression has a 50% chance of passing the gene on to his or her child. The fact that up to 85%, rather than 100%, of the individuals with the gene develop the disease suggests that there are other factors, perhaps environmental, that influence onset of the illness.

Depression. The NIMH in collaboration with private organizations continued to plan for a major national program, called D/ART (Depression/Awareness, Recognition, and Treatment), to educate the public, physicians, and mental-health specialists about depressive disorders, their symptoms and treatment. The primary goal of D/ART, which will begin in May 1988, is to alleviate suffering due to depressive disorders. Fully 25% of all women and 11.5% of all men in the United States will have a depressive episode during their lifetimes. The annual cost to the nation is more than $16 billion, of which more than $10 billion is due to time lost from work. Evidence suggests that many people suffer needlessly. Available treatments could help 80–90% of those who are experiencing a serious depression, but only 1 in 3 people with a depressive disorder seeks mental-health treatment.

Youth Suicide. In 1987 there was increased concern about the difficult problem of youth suicide. The suicide rate for people aged 15 to 24 has almost tripled in the past 30 years. Suicide is now the second leading cause of death for people in this age group. The causes of youth suicide are not yet known. There is some evidence that suicide is not as frequently associated with depression in young people as in adults. Many young suicide victims did not have a major mental illness but had a history of impulsive, aggressive, or antisocial behavior, often complicated by substance abuse.

To better understand the factors underlying youth suicide and find a means to prevent it, investigators are conducting a study to develop psychological profiles of young people who committed suicide. People close to the victim will be interviewed to determine what his or her mental state was prior to the suicide. The investigators will also attempt to determine how young people who completed suicide differ from suicide attempters, and will gather data on the victims' families to learn whether there are family characteristics that correlate with youth suicide.

Schizophrenia. In a large-scale study involving several research centers, scientists determined that the drug clozapine is effective in many people with schizophrenia who do not benefit from the drugs traditionally used in the treatment of this disorder. In fact, the study found that 30% of schizophrenic patients who do not respond to other antipsychotic drugs have a favorable response to clozapine. This means that many "chronic" schizophrenia patients can be helped by clozapine treatment. However, the drug can have serious side effects, and patients need to be carefully monitored while they are taking it.

To hasten progress toward conquering schizophrenia, the NIMH is fostering a national plan for schizophrenia research.

Dual Diagnosis. Also in 1987, the NIMH awarded 13 Community Support Program (CSP) demonstration grants to state mental-health authorities to develop effective local programs and approaches for treating individuals with a dual diagnosis of mental illness and substance abuse. According to a report prepared for NIMH, there is an immediate need for programs to treat such people.

FRANK J. SULLIVAN
Acting Director
National Institute of Mental Health

© Neefus/Earth Scenes

An unexpected snowstorm struck six northeastern states on October 4. The storm, the earliest one on record to hit the region, caused heavy damage to trees and power lines. Some areas were left without electricity for days.

METEOROLOGY

Meteorologists in 1987 observed a large ozone "hole" in the Antarctic stratosphere that may be related to the special south polar weather conditions and high concentrations of chlorofluorocarbons. New weather satellites were launched, and two important field experiments were conducted. A modest El Niño and droughts in Southeast Asia and North Africa modified normal weather conditions.

Air Chemistry. A "hole" again appeared in the stratospheric ozone layer over Antarctica during September and October. Measurements showed the largest reduction in ozone content over the widest area since the phenomenon was first recorded in 1983. Although the causes of the Antarctic ozone hole are still not fully understood, possible causative factors for this depletion emphasize the special south polar meteorological conditions and the chemical reactions involving high concentrations of human-generated chlorofluorocarbons. Some scientists have theorized that as the sun appears after the dark Antarctic winter, the chlorine adhering to ice crystals in the atmospheric clouds is converted by the sunlight from passive to active molecules that react with and destroy the ozone. In November scientists reported that these reactions were duplicated in the laboratory.

The role of air pollution in changing the environment continues to be more clearly evaluated. The number of acidic lakes (one result of acid rain) in the northeastern United States is unlikely to show a significant increase in the next few decades at present air-pollution levels, while an increase can be expected in the southern Blue Ridge Mountains in the southeastern United States. Pollution-related damage to forests is visible in parts of Europe, and even China, but researchers note that air pollution has many sources, making it hard to lead a focused cleanup campaign.

Observing Systems. Early in the year the complement of U.S. meteorological satellites was brought up to full strength with two successful launches. NOAA-10 was placed in a polar orbit in January, and a new GOES-EAST was placed in geosynchronous orbit in February. New groups of satellites being planned for the 1990s will provide expanded capabilities for monitoring the earth's atmosphere, oceans, and land surface. A problem to be resolved is the means for handling the enormous flood of data that these new satellites will generate. It is likely that meteorologists will have access to 100 times as much satellite data in 1995 as in 1987.

On the ground the National Oceanic and Atmospheric Administration (NOAA) continued to plan the deployment of 30 instruments called Profilers, to begin in late 1988. The Profiler uses a relatively new technology that measures winds at many levels in the atmosphere above the site by sending pulses of microwave energy nearly vertically, then measuring the Doppler shift of the energy reflected back at various heights. Doppler shifting occurs because particles moving toward/away from the Profiler reflect microwaves with a slightly higher/lower frequency than the original signal.

The NEXRAD (next-generation radar) system encountered a slowdown because of difficulties in producing this ground-based system. It incorporates modern electronic technology and computer-based information processing as well as measurements of the Doppler shift to provide data about such conditions as wind shear.

Field Experiments. Two intensive field observation programs were conducted in 1987 at opposite ends of the United States. From January to March the Genesis of Atlantic Lows Experiment (GALE) was conducted along the Carolina coast. This region is sometimes the birthplace of a "bomb," a storm system that quickly intensifies. Although no bombs developed in the GALE study, much important data was obtained, including precursors to storms that later intensified outside the study area.

In July, San Nicolas Island, CA, was the base for the First International Regional Experiment (FIRE) sponsored by the International Satellite Cloud Climatology Program (ISCCP). The goal was to develop detailed data on the blankets of stratocumulus clouds that cover sections of the world's oceans, including the Pacific near California. These cloud blankets contribute to the regional and global climate by reflecting sunlight back into space and bringing moisture to the tropics.

El Niño. During 1987 the tropical Pacific Ocean experienced the first El Niño, a warm-water current off the coast of Peru, to occur since the all-time record event of 1982–83. Experimental forecasting techniques had foreshadowed the current El Niño in late 1986, although a slow start cast doubt on its occurrence until the spring of 1987. The El Niño of 1987 was modest in comparison to the 1982–83 event. Partly as a result of the 1982–83 event, researchers were spurred to find and understand links between the El Niño and other meteorological and oceanographic changes. The causal links are not always obvious because too few El Niños have been observed to separate its effects from other natural fluctuations.

Droughts. In 1987 the summer monsoon produced less than normal rains over much of Southeast Asia. Indonesia and the Pakistan-India border were hardest hit. In other regions, such as southeastern India, the rainfall was low at the beginning of the season, which disrupted the planting schedule and reduced crop yields. The Philippines also suffered early drought, while eastern India and Bangladesh did experience normal amounts of rainfall. Many of these anomalies are consistent with the anomalies experienced in other El Niño years.

On the average, the summer rains in North Africa were more sporadic and occurred over a shorter timespan than usual. The reduced rainfall and the influence of the sahel wind helped to reduce 1987's crop yields.

The southeastern United States returned to near-normal conditions after extremely dry conditions in 1986. Nonetheless, small portions of the mid-Atlantic states experienced very dry conditions for the second spring in a row.

Voyager. In December 1986, the Voyager aircraft made a record-setting flight around the world without stopping or being refueled, and the forecasting effort that accompanied this project provided a crucial margin of success. On the one hand, tailwinds were required for the Voyager to make the trip without refueling. At the same time, the Voyager had to avoid stormy conditions to prevent damage to the airframe and crew. A wide variety of information was used, including the forecasts routinely prepared by the National Weather Service (NWS), satellite images from three different satellites, and reports by the Voyager's crew. Noteworthy weather encounters included skirting Typhoon Marge, penetrating afternoon thunderstorms over Africa, and escaping unforeseen nighttime thunderstorms over the Atlantic Ocean. Calculations showed that the Voyager would have been forced to land short of its goal if the flight-average tailwind had been only 1.5 knots (0.8 m/s) slower!

Other Weather Highlights. For much of the year northern Canada had below-normal temperatures, continuing the pattern from the last half of 1986. As a result, ice breakup was two to three weeks later than normal. Southern Canada, Alaska, and parts of the northern United States were warmer than normal for the first half of the year. On March 8, Milwaukee, WI, experienced a temperature change from 71°F (22°C) to 41°F (5°C) in just 30 minutes. On August 9, Miami, FL, tied its all-time record for maximum temperature of 98°F (37°C).

The northeastern United States had a stormy winter, experiencing the "double-header" snowstorms in the period January 21–26, another on February 23, and another in central New England April 28–29. The first three storms each dumped 10 inches (25 cm) or more of snow on the Washington, DC, area, making the winter one of the snowiest on record there. The Washington area was also the focus of the unusual Veteran's Day storm, accumulating up to 15 inches (38 cm) on November 11, a new record for the month. In the same storm, Norfolk, VA, set a record for the earliest measurable snowfall, and lesser amounts of snow fell as far north as Boston, MA.

The tornado season was about average. The most devastating tornado of the year occurred in Edmonton, Alba., on July 31. The death toll of 27 ranked as Canada's third worst, and the damage (in excess of $250 million) established a new record for Canadian tornadoes.

Meanwhile, the Atlantic hurricane season only saw six named storms, two less than normal. Three reached hurricane status.

GEORGE J. HUFFMAN, *University of Maryland*

Minister of Budget and Planning Carlos Salinas de Gotari (left) was named in October as the presidential candidate of the ruling Institutional Revolutionary Party (PRI). The nomination virtually assured that he would be elected Mexico's next president in the July 1988 balloting.

AP/Wide World

MEXICO

In October, the identification of the government party's presidential candidate ended months of political jockeying. Splits within the ruling party, however, encouraged the Left to unite for the first time. The nation stumbled through another year of government austerity, economic stagnation, high inflation, and foreign-debt renegotiation.

Politics. Much of 1987 was spent in political maneuvering as presidential aspirants sought to gain the designation by incumbent President Miguel de la Madrid as the nominee of the government party, the Institutional Revolutionary Party (PRI), the almost certain winner in the 1988 elections. Early in the year, PRI dissidents, calling themselves the Democratic Current, launched a public campaign to democratize the presidential nomination process by demanding that the PRI use a party primary. But the old-style party officials refused to budge and booted the leaders of the Democratic Current out of party posts. The episode marked a serious rift in PRI ranks because the dissident leaders—Porfirio Muñoz Ledo, a former PRI president, and Cuauhtémoc Cárdenas, a former state governor and son of Mexico's most popular 20th-century president, Lázaro Cárdenas—were highly respected.

One result of the incident was the unprecedented announcement in August of six pre-candidates for the PRI nomination and their public campaigns to gain support for the nomination. Few serious observers saw this as anything but a diversionary tactic, for it was clear that de la Madrid would make the selection.

In October, the PRI named as its candidate Dr. Carlos Salinas de Gotari, minister of budget and planning and one of the pre-candidates. Like the incumbent, the candidate's first elective political office would be the presidency. Salinas was an unusual selection for several reasons. At 39 years of age, he was younger than usual for a Mexican president. In addition to a degree from the national university, he also earned three graduate degrees from Harvard University. A criticism of recent Mexican political leaders has been that too many hold foreign university degrees and are thus out of touch with Mexico. Finally, Salinas was the chief architect of Mexico's unpopular economic austerity program. His selection was seen as an effort to reassure foreign banks, international lending agencies, and domestic and foreign investors that Mexico would continue to follow a plan of economic austerity and honor its foreign debt.

Dissension within the PRI and growing dissatisfaction with government policy encouraged the Left to unify into a single political party for the first time and support a single presidential candidate. In March, the Mexican Unified Socialist Party (which includes the Mexican Communist Party), the Mexican Workers Party, and three smaller parties joined forces as the Mexican Socialist Party. In September, the new party nominated Heberto Castillo, a 59-year-old engineer and longtime leftist leader, for the presidency. That Castillo was selected through a party primary was intended to embarrass the government and the PRI and to emphasize that the Left is democratic. Although Castillo had no chance of being elected president, the unification of the Left promised to give it greater political influence.

The leading opposition party, the rightist National Action Party (PAN), was expected to nominate Jesús González Schmall. In recent years, PAN had been the major threat to total PRI control, especially in the northern states.

In response to the rise of opposition, President de la Madrid had Congress change the electoral system to increase opposition participation in Congress and ensure fairer elections. The Chamber of Deputies was increased from 400 to 500 seats, and minority parties were guaranteed a minimum of 30% and as much as 40% of the seats. The new federal electoral code also created an Independent Electoral Tribunal, composed of representatives nominated by each political party and confirmed by Congress. Opposition demands that the Federal District, where PRI fares poorly in elections, become the new state of Anahuac prompted the government to create the Representative Assembly of the Federal District.

Education. In the largest protest movement since 1968, students at the national university struck for 18 days early in the year to protest a reform program initiated by the university administration. The proposed reform would have raised annual tuition from 200 pesos (about 20 cents in U.S. currency) to 5,000 pesos and tightened admission standards in the overcrowded 300,000-student institution. Faced with the possibility of a serious student uprising, the government and university administration caved in to student demands that the changes be suspended and agreed to appoint a student-faculty-administrator committee to propose a different mechanism through which changes might be implemented. The committee agreed to university-wide elections to elect a university congress to consider reforms.

Economy. The economy continued to be sluggish during the year, with only a few bright spots. Prices rose about 135%, the peso continued to tumble downward, and real wages fell even further. Increased world oil prices boosted oil revenues 40% and brought a current-account surplus. Total foreign reserves reached $14.6 billion by September and were expected to reach $15 billion by year's end. Petroleum exports, which largely accounted for these gains, represented only 4% of the gross domestic product. Nonpetroleum exports increased 26% in the first half of the year, led by manufacturing exports, which increased 46%.

MEXICO • Information Highlights

Official Name: United Mexican States.
Location: Southern North America.
Area: 761,602 sq mi (1 972 550 km²).
Population (mid-1987 est.): 81,900,000.
Chief Cities (1980 census): Mexico City (Federal District), the capital (1983 est.), 9,663,360; Guadalajara, 1,626,152; Monterrey, 1,090,009.
Government: *Head of state and government,* Miguel de la Madrid Hurtado, president (took office Dec. 1982). *Legislature*—National Congress: Senate and Federal Chamber of Deputies.
Monetary Unit: Peso (2,283 pesos equal U.S.$1, floating rate, Dec. 4, 1987).
Gross Domestic Product (1985 U.S.$): $147,200,-000,000.
Economic Indexes (1986): *Consumer Prices* (1980 = 100), all items, 1,978.7; food, 1,921.1. *Industrial Production* (1980 = 100), 101.
Foreign Trade (1986 U.S.$): *Imports,* $11,995,-000,000; *exports,* $15,774,000,000.

The Japanese Export-Import Bank agreed to finance most of a $700 million oil pipeline from the oilfields on the Gulf of Mexico to the Pacific Coast. The Honda Motor Company of Japan began building a $40.8 million motorcycle plant near Guadalajara in order to take advantage of Mexico's inexpensive labor market.

Economic activity increased in the second half of 1987 and was expected to increase even more in 1988 as the government reversed previous policy to stimulate the economy for the 1988 elections. Government expenditures accounted for 53.6% of the gross domestic product. In spite of the government's agreement with the International Monetary Fund (IMF) to decrease public expenditures, deficit spending was increased to 18% of the gross domestic product instead of the 10% targeted by the IMF. Public investment was budgeted to grow 15% in real terms instead of declining as originally planned.

Looking to boost exports with a currency devaluation, the government in the fall floated the peso, allowing it to fend for itself on the free market. In mid-November, however, the exchange rate plunged more than expected, reaching 2,830 to the dollar. It recovered somewhat in the following weeks, but in mid-December the government devalued the peso by 22% to bring it more in line with the free-market rate of about 2,350 to the dollar.

Foreign Debt. In his state of the union address on September 1, President de la Madrid called on international banks and industrialized nations to be more flexible in negotiating debt payments with Third World countries. He argued that creditors must share responsibility with a debtor nation for the size of the latter's international debt. While assuring the international financial community that Mexico would meet its obligations, he warned that the nation had gone as far as it possibly could in adopting an austerity program. The Mexican foreign debt of more than $100 billion was one of the world's largest, and debt service cost the nation more than 35% of its export earnings. As interest rates rose and uncertainty increased in creditor nations late in the year, pressure mounted to break loose from the IMF agreement and repayment of the total debt in order to meet domestic needs.

Foreign Policy. Relations with the United States continued to be cordial, but Mexico expressed concern about the possible adverse effects of U.S. trade protectionism and its new immigration and naturalization law. Mexico supported the Central American plan for a negotiated peace in El Salvador and Nicaragua. Soviet-Mexican relations improved as the foreign ministers of each nation exchanged visits. Trade relations with Japan, China, and Latin America were expanded.

DONALD J. MABRY
Mississippi State University

MICHIGAN

The second-worst U.S. airplane crash in history, a visit by Pope John Paul II, the death of auto giant Henry Ford II, and continuing controversy over tax-paid abortions for the poor were news highlights in Michigan during 1987. Michigan also celebrated the 150th anniversary of its statehood during the year.

Airliner Crash. On August 16, Northwest Airlines Flight 255 crashed onto a highway while taking off from Detroit Metropolitan Airport, killing 154 of 155 passengers and two people on the ground. Investigators said the pilots had not set the wing flaps for a normal takeoff, and an electrical-power interruption prevented a warning system from alerting the pilots to the failure. Further investigation was to be conducted to complete an analysis of the crash. The sole survivor was four-year-old Cecelia Cichan of Tempe, AZ. Her father, mother, and six-year-old brother all died in the crash. While Cecelia, originally listed in critical condition with burns and broken bones, fought for life, the nation showered her with gifts. She left the hospital October 9.

Papal Visit. Pope John Paul II, in a whirlwind two-day visit to Detroit, Hamtramck, and Pontiac, September 18–19, said the advancement of technology should take a back seat to concern for the well-being of workers and society. Preaching to relatively small but respectful crowds, the pontiff's messages stressed the dignity of the worker, solidarity among nations, and the responsibilities of individuals. The visit to Michigan, the first ever by a pope, was part of a ten-day, nine-city U.S. tour. The pope drew his largest Michigan audience on September 19, when 90,000 attended a Mass in the Pontiac Silverdome.

Ford Dies. Auto giant Henry Ford II died September 29 after being hospitalized for 17 days with pneumonia. The body was cremated after a private funeral service. Ford's will, filed in Palm Beach, FL, where Ford maintained a residence, provided that most of his estimated $250 million fortune be placed in trust, with the income going to his widow, Kathy DuRoss Ford, during her lifetime. Trust holdings included 1.96 million shares of Ford Motor Company stock. (*See* OBITUARIES.).

Abortion Controversy. In October the Michigan Supreme Court ruled that a legislative ban on taxpayer-funded abortion for poor women could not take effect until 90 days after the end of the current legislative session, or about March 30, 1988. The court acted on an appeal filed by Right to Life of Michigan and the state attorney general's office. The suit was prompted by the legislature's enactment of a veto-proof ban following a petition drive by antiabortion groups that claimed the measure should take effect immediately. Gov. James J. Blanchard had vetoed past legislation restricting Medicaid funding of abortions, but he had no power to veto the citizen-initiated ban. Pro-choice supporters filed suit, contending that the prohibition should not have immediate effect. The Supreme Court action had the effect of allowing pro-choice forces time to continue a petition drive in an attempt to force a vote on the ban before it took effect. Michigan spent about $5.8 million for 18,600 abortions in 1986.

Economy and Business. In August, Mazda Motor Corporation began manufacturing the company's first U.S.-built cars at a new plant in Flat Rock, south of Detroit. The $550 million plant began operations with a work force of 1,200 and was expected to employ 3,500 people by the end of 1988.

Hearings on a proposed joint-operating agreement between the Detroit *News* and Detroit *Free Press,* the city's two major newspapers, were held during the summer. Testimony and written arguments were submitted to Administrative Law Judge Morton Needleman who was to make a formal recommendation to U.S. Attorney General Edwin Meese. Approval of the joint-operating agreement would allow the two newspapers to merge business operations and share profits while maintaining separate editorial staffs.

Detroit's People Mover, an elevated 2.9-mile (4.7-km) rail service circling the downtown area, began operation August 1, attracting 40,000 riders a day during its first eight days, when rides were free. The $200 million system opened seven months behind schedule and $65 million over budget.

The United Auto Workers Union, negotiating for new contracts with major auto manufacturers, reached agreement with Ford Motor Company and General Motors Corporation without resorting to threatened strikes. Negotiations continued with Chrysler Corporation.

CHARLES W. THEISEN, *"The Detroit News"*

MICHIGAN • Information Highlights

Area: 58,527 sq mi (151 586 km²).
Population (July 1, 1986): 9,145,000.
Chief Cities (July 1, 1986 est.): Lansing, the capital, 128,980; Detroit, 1,086,220; Grand Rapids, 186,530; Warren, 149,800; Flint, 145,590; Sterling Heights, 111,960.
Government (1987); *Chief Officers*—governor, James J. Blanchard (D); lt. gov., Martha W. Griffiths (D). *Legislature*—Senate, 38 members; House of Representatives, 110 members.
State Finances (fiscal year 1986): *Revenue,* $20,507,000,000; *expenditure,* $17,563,000,000.
Personal Income (1986): $135,113,000,000; per capita, $14,775.
Labor Force (June 1987): *Civilian labor force,* 4,574,700; unemployed, 408,300 (8.9% of total force).
Education: *Enrollment* (fall 1985)—public elementary schools, 1,103,969; public secondary, 585,859; colleges and universities, 507,293. *Public school expenditures* (1985–86), $5,844,000,000 ($3,789 per pupil).

MICROBIOLOGY

Cerebrospinal meningitis, a disease caused by the bacterium *Neisseria meningitidis,* is characterized by an inflammation of the membranes surrounding the brain and spinal cord. The bacteria also may enter the bloodstream, where they produce a septicemia (blood poisoning) that can result in death. The disease first appeared in Norway in 1974, and outbreaks have occurred subsequently in other parts of Europe, South Africa, Chile, Cuba, and, in the United States, in Florida.

Recently, Dr. Dominique Caugant at the University of Rochester (NY), together with colleagues at other institutions, examined cultures of *N. meningitidis* that had been collected at various times and places. They analyzed the cultures for electrophoretic variation in 15 enzymes and found that the bacteria responsible for the current Norwegian epidemic and the recent increases in incidence of the disease in other countries formed a distinct group, which they called Electrophoretic Type #5 (ET-5). The researchers also established that the first cases of the disease caused by ET-5 occurred in Denmark in 1976, Britain in 1978, Germany and The Netherlands in 1980, and France in 1981. Elsewhere, ET-5-caused cases of the disease first occurred in South Africa and Cuba in 1980, Florida in 1981, and Chile in 1985. It seemed clear that ET-5 spread across Europe along a north-south axis. Although it is not yet possible to trace the spread to Chile, South Africa, and Cuba from places in Europe, it is believed that the cases in Florida are associated with the influx of Cuban immigrants in 1980.

Reproduction in Volvox. When they occur in small ponds, both male and female colonies of *Volvox carteri,* a species of green flagellates, reproduce asexually during the spring. Before the pond dries up in summer, the colonies become sexually mature, producing sperm and eggs, respectively. Gametic fusion results in the formation of dormant, overwintering zygotes. The immediate stimulus for the transition from asexual to sexual stages is the production, by one of the male colonies, of a protein which acts as an inducer of sexuality in surrounding colonies.

At Washington University in St. Louis, Drs. D. L. and M. M. Kirk recently conducted a series of experiments in which *V. carteri* in asexual stages were exposed to heat shock. They found that all of the colonies exposed to heat produced the inducer protein. Thus, the environmental factor that induces sexuality in this organism apparently is the rise in water temperature in early summer. It is not yet known, however, why the male normally produces the inducer, since both sexes were capable of doing so under experimental conditions.

A New Risk From Undercooked Pork. Toxoplasmosis is a disease caused by the protozoan *Toxoplasma gondii,* which, upon ingestion, invades the lungs, liver, heart, skin, muscles, and brain. The parasite also can pass from a pregnant woman to her developing child. This has resulted in some 3,300 children being born with the disease each year in the United States. Those with severe infections can suffer from blindness, mental retardation, and even death.

It was long believed that humans become infected with *T. gondii* mainly from the handling of pet cats, whose feces often contain the parasite. Recently, however, Dr. Jitender Dubey and his team at the U.S. Department of Agriculture discovered that pigs also are a source of the parasite. The researchers estimated that as many as one in three pigs is infected with *T. gondii.* As in the case of the well-known trichina (round worm) parasite, eating undercooked pork creates a danger of infection. While the threat of trichinosis has been lessened in recent years by improvements in animal care and by special breeding programs, the discovery that *T. gondii* is a pig parasite continues to make eating undercooked pork hazardous to human health.

Archaebacteria. Bacteria are organisms whose cells have no subcellular structures. That is, they possess no nuclei, mitochondria, endoplasmic reticulum, etc. Recent research has revealed two distinct types of bacteria, based on differences in the RNA sequences of their ribosomes, chemical compounds in their cell walls, and mechanisms of transcription and translation. Bacteria, therefore, are now classified as belonging to one of two major groups: *eubacteria,* whose members include typical bacteria, blue-green bacteria, purple photosynthetic bacteria, and others; and *archaebacteria,* whose members include the various primitive bacteria.

As pointed out recently by Dr. Karl Stetter and his colleagues at the University of Regensburg in West Germany, the archaebacteria classification consists of a number of distinct subgroups. One subgroup is found in bogs, streams, and lakes whose sediments are rich in decaying vegetation. These microbes obtain energy by combining carbon dioxide and hydrogen to form methane. A second subgroup is usually found in hot sulfur springs, where they obtain energy either by combining sulfur and hydrogen to form hydrogen sulfide or by combining sulfur with oxygen to form sulfuric acid, depending on the availability of oxygen.

Some archaebacteria are able to live in environments characterized by high temperature, high acidity, and the absence of oxygen. These are thought to be the conditions that prevailed on Earth during the initial stages of organism development. Archaebacteria represent the simplest form of life on Earth today, and their continued study undoubtedly will provide important information on early cellular evolution.

LOUIS LEVINE, *City College of New York*

MIDDLE EAST

The volatile and dangerous situation in the Middle East underwent some marked changes in focus, if not in substance, during 1987. The weary and bloodstained anarchy of Lebanon, while as bad as ever, ceased to attract much general notice. The problem of Arab-Israeli relations erupted in new violence during December but seemed to be of diminished concern, even to Arab states, throughout much of the year. Instead, the primary concern of the Middle Eastern states and of powers outside the region moved to the Iraqi-Iranian war and the numerous incidents arising out of it.

The Iraqi-Iranian War: Dimensions. The conflict moved into its eighth year in September, the anniversary of Iraq's initial attack, but it seemed no nearer an end than in earlier years. The objectives of the two sides remained totally irreconcilable. Iraq's presumable intention in commencing the war, to strike some crippling blow at the regime of religious fanaticism that replaced Shah Mohammed Reza Pahlavi in 1979, had failed before the war was a year old; since then its aim has been merely to survive. Iran's proclaimed purpose, now as in 1980, has been to replace what it calls the godless regime in Baghdad and to exact enormous sums in compensation from Iraq and the states that have supported it. The cost of the war in human lives cannot be known for certain, but a U.S. State Department estimate early in 1987 put the total at approximately a quarter-million for Iraq and three quarters of a million for Iran (a ratio that closely parallels the ratio in population of the two countries).

Following a prolonged period of relative quiet on the southern front, the Iranians in January 1987 launched a major offensive, dubbed "Karbala-5," with the objective of capturing Basra, Iraq's second-largest city. By incurring tremendous casualties, Iran did advance through Iraqi territory and came within 10 mi (16 km) of Basra. But the fighting eventually stalemated, and the offensive was called off in late February after six weeks of the heaviest fighting of the war. There was little more in the way of serious military activity on the southern front for the rest of the year, though Iran claimed in the fall to be amassing enormous forces for a decisive major offensive. At midyear Iranian forces made some progress in the Kurdish north, employing the standard tactic of exploiting the discontent of Kurdish tribesmen with the Baghdad government.

However, the main focus of attention in 1987 was not the land war but the innumerable incidents of violence occurring on the waters and around the shores of the Persian Gulf. Indeed the dramatic change in Middle Eastern affairs during the year was the escalation of the Gulf shipping war and the involvement of major outside powers.

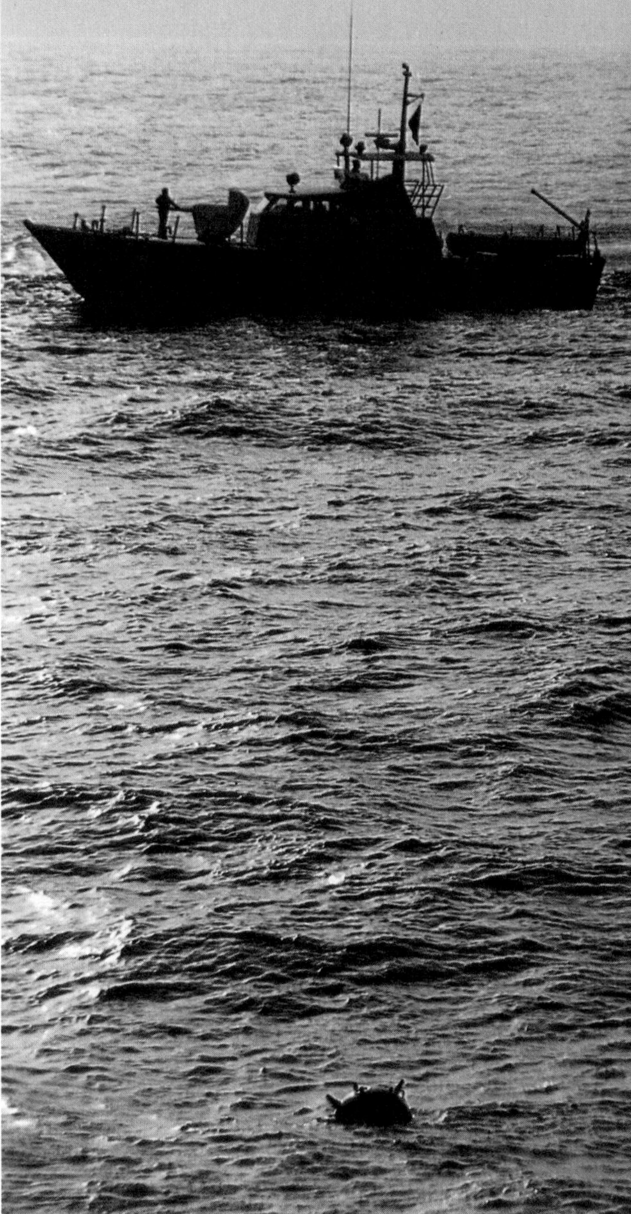

AP/Wide World

A United Arab Emirates coastguard boat spots a mine in the Gulf of Oman. More than 100 commercial vessels were attacked or damaged by mines in the Persian Gulf region.

Attacks on shipping in the Gulf were not novel in 1987. The war had entered this new and more ominous stage in May 1984, when Iraq proclaimed a 50-mi (80-km) war zone around Kharg Island, Iran's oil-export terminal in the upper Gulf, and began raids on tankers and the terminal itself. The primary Iraqi objective was to stymie Iran's oil-exporting industry (on which its economy entirely depends) and so force it to the negotiating table. The ploy did not succeed. Iran's exports, though reduced, have continued, partly through the use of smaller shuttle tankers to take oil to less vulnerable ports on the lower Gulf. Since all of Iraq's oil exports are transported by pipelines, it was not vulnerable to retaliation in kind. Iran nevertheless began reprisals, which have continued intermittently ever since, by attacking ships calling on the ports of other Arab states on the Persian Gulf. By the end of 1986, approximately 100 commercial vessels had been subject to attack in the Gulf. These developments brought home to the conservative, monarchical Arab gulf states the dangers posed by the revolutionary regime. They protested vehemently against Iran, began to line up more clearly on the side of Iraq, and took some steps to organize their defenses through the machinery of the Gulf Cooperation Council.

Situation of Kuwait. Of all the Gulf states, the most vulnerable is Kuwait. A tiny emirate wedged between Iraq and Saudi Arabia, with a population of only 1.9 million, Kuwait is also fantastically rich, with enormous oil reserves. Many of the developments of 1987 turned on the question of its vulnerability. Kuwait has earned the hostility of Iran, since its port forms one of Iraq's supply routes and since it has been one of Iraq's principal financial backers. With the capture of Al Faw in early 1986 and the attack on Basra in early 1987, Iranian forces moved so close to Kuwait that the gunfire and explosions were clearly audible in the emirate. Over the years of the war, Kuwaiti territory has been bombed by Iran on a number of occasions—accidentally or as a gesture of intimidation.

In January 1987, Kuwait hosted the fifth summit meeting of the Organization of the Islamic Conference, attended by delegations from 44 nations. Iran boycotted and threatened the meeting but, under tight security, the three-day summit proceeded without incident. Kuwaiti oil sites were subjected to a number of terrorist bombings on January 19, with similar incidents recurring in May. When the United States took action in the spring to protect Gulf shipping, the immediate purpose was to ensure safe passage for Kuwaiti tankers, since these seemed to be most at risk.

The Tanker War: U.S. Involvement. The question might well be raised, why the United States chose to intervene in the Gulf shipping war in 1987, since the threats to essential oil traffic through the Strait of Hormuz were not, in fact, any more serious than they had been for two years. There appeared to be two key factors. One was a need for significant U.S. action to regain prestige and credibility in the Arab world. The revelations of the Iran-contra affair (*see* feature article, page 26) appalled and outraged the Arab states, especially those that had been most friendly to, and most trusted, the United States. One symbol of the Arab reaction was the refusal in March by both King Hussein of Jordan and President Hosni Mubarak of Egypt to accept invitations to visit Washington for talks. The second factor was the emerging likelihood of considerable Soviet naval activity in the Gulf.

U.S. naval strength in the region already had been stepped up. Since the fall of 1986, a U.S. aircraft carrier had been stationed in the Gulf of Oman, just outside the Strait of Hormuz. In March 1987, Kuwait refused an offer of direct U.S. naval escorts for its tankers, but then in May entered into arrangements with both superpowers. Kuwait would lease three Soviet oil tankers which would receive Soviet protection; and it would allow 11 of its tankers to sail under the U.S. flag and receive U.S. naval protection. Even as these arrangements were pending, however, there were reminders that even superpower involvement carried risks. On May 6, Iranian gunboats attacked a Soviet freighter, causing minor damage, and on May 16 a Soviet tanker struck a mine off Kuwait. Much more serious was the damage on May 17 to the U.S.S. *Stark,* a frigate patrolling international waters off Bahrain. The vessel was hit by Exocet missiles from an Iraqi plane, killing 37 U.S. sailors. Baghdad quickly apologized for what it insisted was an accident, and Washington accepted the apology.

The first of the 11 reflagged Kuwaiti tankers, the *Bridgeton,* entered the Persian Gulf on July 22 escorted by three U.S. warships. Two days later it struck a mine. From then on, the U.S. Navy escorted the reflagged ships in a series of convoys. Another major incident was an Iranian missile attack on October 16 against an empty U.S.-flagged tanker, the *Sea Isle City,* in Kuwaiti territorial waters. The missile in this case was a Chinese-made "Silkworm," a weapon with which China recently had been supplying Iran. Great concern had been expressed earlier in the year, when a number of these missiles reportedly were installed along the Strait of Hormuz. Iran held out the threat that, if Iraqi air attacks made the Gulf unusable by them, they could make it unusable by all. By year's end, however, the Silkworms at Hormuz had not been employed.

Mines were another largely new threat in the Persian Gulf during 1987. The United States, unlike Western European nations, has little in the way of minesweeping ships, but on July 31 it did order minesweeping helicopters to the Gulf. Its Western European allies at first expressed reluctance to join in the operation, but Great Britain and France announced on August 11 that they were sending minesweepers, an example followed in September by Italy, the Netherlands, and Belgium.

Rioting in Mecca. Another event of importance to the entire region occurred on July 31 in Saudi Arabia. Gulf tension was raised when hundreds of Muslims on their annual pilgrimage to Mecca were killed in an outbreak of rioting and subsequent clashes with Saudi police. The United States and most Arab countries accepted the Saudi account of the incident: that Iranian pilgrims had been involved in violent anti-U.S., anti-Israeli demonstrations; that the

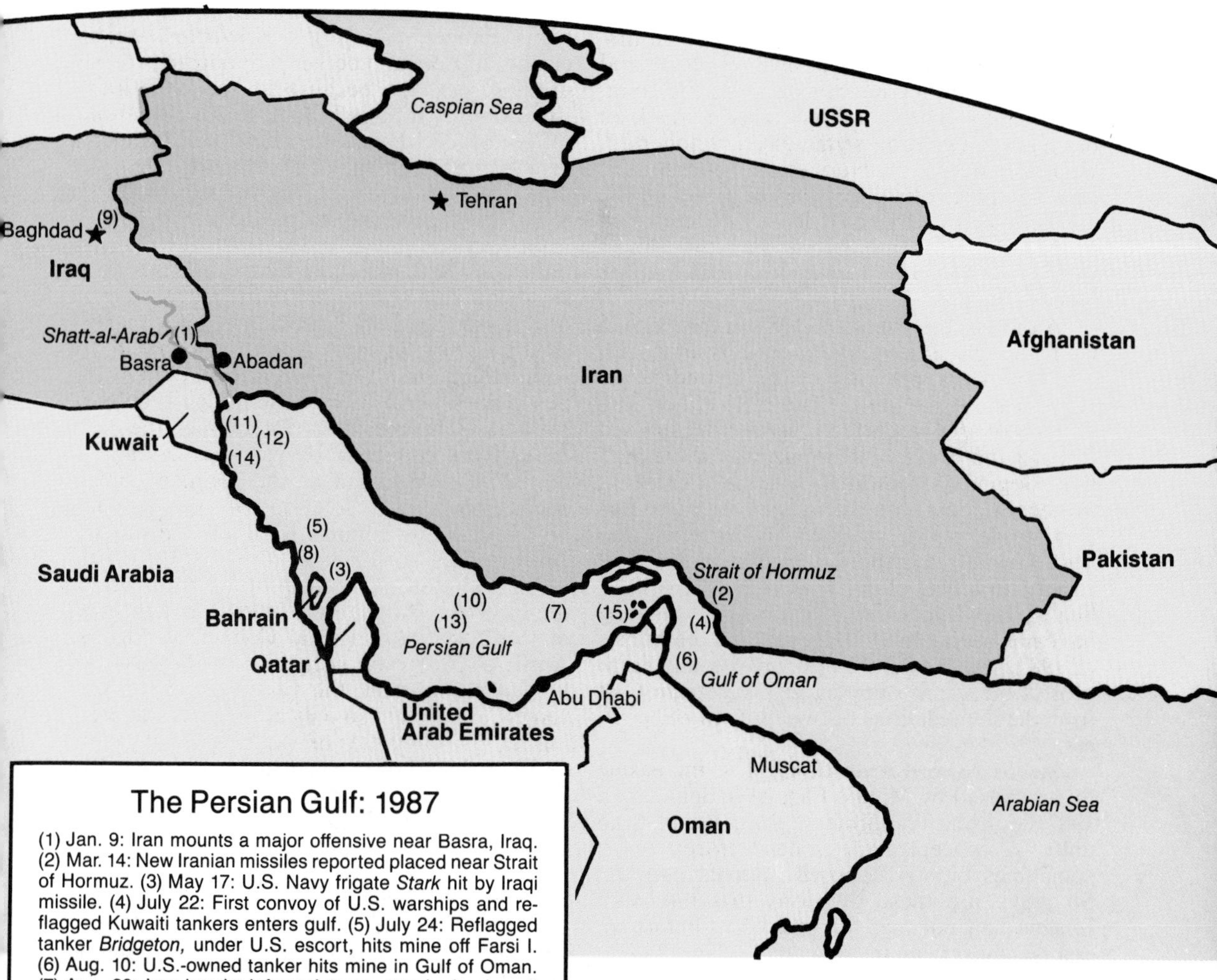

The Persian Gulf: 1987

(1) Jan. 9: Iran mounts a major offensive near Basra, Iraq. (2) Mar. 14: New Iranian missiles reported placed near Strait of Hormuz. (3) May 17: U.S. Navy frigate *Stark* hit by Iraqi missile. (4) July 22: First convoy of U.S. warships and reflagged Kuwaiti tankers enters gulf. (5) July 24: Reflagged tanker *Bridgeton,* under U.S. escort, hits mine off Farsi I. (6) Aug. 10: U.S.-owned tanker hits mine in Gulf of Oman. (7) Aug. 29: Iraq breaks informal truce, attacks Iranian oil installations. (8) Sept. 21: U.S. helicopter disables Iranian vessel allegedly laying mines. (9) Oct. 5, 6: Iranian missiles hit residential areas in Baghdad. (10) Oct. 5: Iraqi planes strike Iranian oil installations at Lavan I. and other sites. (11) Oct. 15: U.S.-owned tanker *Sungari* hit by Iranian missile in Kuwaiti waters. (12) Oct. 16: Reflagged tanker *Sea Isle City* hit by Iranian missile. (13) Oct. 19: U.S. forces shell two Iranian oil platforms used as bases for raids and board a third to knock out communications. (14) Oct. 22: Iranian missile strikes Kuwait's main offshore oil terminal. (15) Dec. 12: Culminating a week of attacks by Iran and Iraq on gulf shipping, an oil tanker carrying the Cypriot flag is set ablaze and sunk; a U.S. warship rescues the crew.

Saudi police had fired no shots and that the casualties had occurred in a stampede; and that some 400 people had been killed, nearly all of them Iranians, with another 650 injured. The Iranian version was that peacefully-marching pilgrims had been attacked by police gunfire in a U.S.-Saudi plot, and that more than 600 had been killed and 4,500 injured. The next day, angry mobs in Tehran sacked the Saudi and Kuwaiti embassies, and the French embassy was stoned. Leaders of the Iranian regime called on Muslims to wrest control of Islamic holy sites from Saudi Arabia.

UN Resolution. After the United Nations had fumbled for nearly seven years with the problem of the Iraqi-Iranian war, the Security Council on July 20 agreed unanimously to Resolution 598, calling for an immediate cease-fire "on land, at sea, and in the air" to allow peace negotiations to begin. Iraq, of course, was willing to agree, but Iran neither agreed nor disagreed. In talks with UN Secretary General Javier Pérez de Cuéllar, it avoided commitment, playing for time to year's end.

Tanker War Renewed. The UN resolution was followed by a perceptible lull in Gulf fighting for six weeks. Iraq did carry out some air raids on Iranian installations on August 10, but there were no major incidents until August 29. Iraq then launched widespread attacks for five days in succession on oil terminals, ships, and some land targets. Iran responded with its typical hit-and-run attacks from small ships. In short, as *The Economist* of London observed, "The Gulf returned to normal on August 29." For the remainder of the year, events took much the same "normal" course.

The United States retaliated for the *Sea Isle City* attack of October 16 three days later, when it destroyed an Iranian oil platform that had been converted to a military command post. This warning did not dissuade the Iranians from committing a direct missile attack on the main Kuwaiti oil terminal on October 22. On December 14, the Norwegian tanker *Susangird* was twice attacked by Iraqi planes in the northern Gulf, leaving at least two crewmen dead and 20 missing. More than two dozen ships were raided by Iran or Iraq in December alone.

All in all, the events of 1987 in the Persian Gulf, though striking, were entirely inconclusive. The naval presence of the United States and other outside parties had little effect. The number of U.S.-escorted convoys that passed through the Strait of Hormuz was about half that originally projected by the Pentagon. Moreover, most of them did not even carry Kuwaiti crude, but oil products and liquefied gas. The Kuwaitis transported nearly all their oil exports in a fleet of about 40 other ships. And finally, the Iranian attacks on Gulf shipping have not been inhibited. Despite all the efforts of 1987, the Western world proved unable to protect merchant shipping in the Persian Gulf from the depredations of two quite minor powers.

Moves Toward Arab Unity. The increasing threats posed by Middle East developments in 1987 did, ironically, promote the cause of Arab unity—a concept made difficult to realize by sometimes bitterly opposed national policies. So grave are these divisions that the Arab League had not met for five years before an emergency session in Amman, Jordan, in early November. Minor steps toward reconciliation had occurred earlier in the year. At the Islamic summit in Kuwait during January, King Hussein of Jordan met with PLO (Palestine Liberation Organization) leader Yasir Arafat for the first time since their breach of relations in February 1986. Presidents Mubarak of Egypt and Assad of Syria, the latter an implacable enemy of Israel, also met at the Kuwait summit, for the first time since 1981. Assad and President Saddam Hussein of Iraq met inconclusively in April. And later in the spring, former U.S. President Jimmy Carter, returning from Syria, reported, surprisingly, that Assad was ready to sit down with Israel as participants in a general Mideast peace conference.

The upheavals in Mecca at the end of July seemed to increase Arab apprehensions greatly, facilitating the Arab League summit in Amman, November 8–11. This was an extraordinary event. Time alone will tell how real were the gestures of reconciliation and unity, but it seemed possible that the meeting would prove to be a real turning point. The main achievement was a demonstration of united Arab support for Iraq in its war against Iran. Syria's President Assad, long Iran's only Arab supporter, acquiesced—perhaps because the Iranian connection has not prevented serious clashes in Lebanon between Syrian and Iranian proxies, perhaps because of the undesirable isolation that it brought him. Risking a cutting-off of needed Iranian subsidies, Assad gained a promise of Arab financial support. Thus, by diplomatic adroitness, he moved from isolation to center stage in the Arab world.

Assad's adroitness also was shown in not opposing the sanctioning by the conference of renewing diplomatic ties with Egypt (which only Jordan had done previously). Reconciliation with Egypt was directly motivated by panic about Iran. Only Egypt could offer serious military opposition to the Iranians; military planning talks between Egypt and the Gulf states were convened by year's end. Another united Arab decision at the Amman conference, endorsing Resolution 598, put pressure on Moscow to commit itself or alienate the Arab world.

In a kind of microcosm of the Arab world, the PLO also sought unity in 1987. In a meeting of the Palestine National Council at Algiers, April 20–26, Arafat secured a reaffirmation of his leadership from the varied factions represented. But he did so only at the price of agreeing to a statement of policies much more extreme than those he had lately espoused. The Egyptian government reacted by closing 14 major PLO offices. In October the U.S. State Department closed the PLO office in Washington.

Israel: Conference Proposals. In addition to preparing for and hosting the Arab summit, Jordan was active diplomatically in promoting the idea of a general conference on the Palestinian problem and the Arab-Israeli conflict. This idea gained endorsement from most interested parties, including the Israeli foreign minister, Shimon Peres, but notably not from the Israeli prime minister, Yitzhak Shamir. Indeed, the power-sharing arrangement currently in effect in Israel makes any serious move away from the status quo very unlikely.

The Soviet Union, which hopes to be represented at any such general conference, edged a little nearer to the restoration of diplomatic relations with Israel. A general thaw in Israeli relations with Eastern Europe also was in progress; Israel and Hungary agreed to set up interests sections in each other's capitals.

The seriousness of the unsolved problems in Israeli-Palestinian relations—generally disregarded during most of the year—was demonstrated by outbreaks of street violence in Gaza and the West Bank during December. Israeli troops moved in en masse, arresting hundreds of Arabs and leaving more than two dozen dead. The Israeli government blamed the uprising on organized terrorist groups.

See also articles on individual countries.

ARTHUR CAMPBELL TURNER
University of California, Riverside

MILITARY AFFAIRS

Although there was no dearth of activity on the part of smaller nations, the superpowers continued to dominate world military affairs during 1987. They sparred over the Strategic Defense Initiative (SDI, or "Star Wars"), continued to develop new strategic nuclear weapons, and considered the potential military consequences of the agreed-upon removal from Eastern and Western Europe of intermediate-range ballistic missiles (*See* ARMS CONTROL).

SDI. As has been the case since its introduction by President Ronald Reagan in 1983, the U.S. plan to build a defense against Soviet ballistic-missile attack continued to encounter widespread opposition. In April a panel of physicists from the American Physical Society issued a report claiming that so many breakthroughs in advanced technology still needed to be made that it would take 10 to 15 years just to determine whether the project is feasible. The advanced technologies examined by the panel were such "directed-energy weapons" as lasers, which travel at the speed of light, and particle beams, which travel at slightly less than the speed of light. In addition to pointing out the formidable scientific difficulties in building an advanced-technology space-based defense system, the panel questioned whether such a system could survive a direct attack. The panel did not even address what many consider the most difficult of all technical requirements—the computer hardware and software necessary to orchestrate the SDI systems during the 30 minutes it would take for a Soviet warhead to travel from its launch site to a target in the United States.

For its part, the Strategic Defense Initiative Organization (SDIO), which is responsible for coordinating research on the project, said it found the conclusions of the report "subjective and unduly pessimistic about our capability to bring to fruition the specific technologies needed for a full-scale development decision in the 1990s." The SDIO also stated that, since the completion of the physicists' study in the autumn of 1986, "significant progress" had been made.

Later in the year, a report from the Lawrence Livermore (CA) government weapons laboratory argued that rapid-fire satellite guns which would shoot small projectiles (kinetic kill vehicles) at Soviet missiles would not be effective. However, knowledgeable observers about the subject noted that the federally supported laboratory had an institutional bias against such space guns because its primary research was in the area of directed-energy weapons.

Another source of hostility to the president's space defense plan was the U.S. Congress, where a number of Democrats in particular doubted the technical feasibility of SDI technology. In December,Congress cut the president's 1988 SDI budget from $5.8 billion to $3.9 billion.

Despite such criticism, President Reagan's chief advisers, then Secretary of Defense Caspar Weinberger and Lt. Gen. James Abrahamson, the SDIO director, suggested that sufficient technical evidence had been obtained to permit a decision to start deploying kinetic kill vehicles in space by the early or mid-1990s. This view was supported by a private group called High Frontier, headed by retired Army Gen. Daniel O. Graham. The group's leaders crisscrossed the country urging the public to lobby their congressmen to fund the president's SDI request.

While Americans argued about their SDI, speculation and controversy abounded concerning the evolution of Soviet strategic defense efforts. Most Western observers agreed that the Soviets were engaged in SDI-type research and development, a fact confirmed by General Secretary Mikhail Gorbachev in December. There was debate, however, on exactly what the Soviets had achieved and the degree to which their accomplishments threatened the United States. The debate over Soviet SDI activity heated up as a result of several events. One was the publication by a Swedish news company of satellite pictures showing a new Soviet laser laboratory near Dushanbe, the capital of the Tadzhik Republic. Experts disagreed as to whether the facility housed only experimental lasers or some that corresponded to the first phase of the American SDI. According to U.S. Air Force Gen. John Piotrowski, chief of the Space Command, some of the Soviet lasers could knock out U.S. reconnaissance satellites operating at an altitude of 400 mi (650 km) and could damage those orbiting as high as 750 mi (1 200 km). The general also stated, however, that U.S. military communication satellites in geosynchronous orbit (stationary relative to a fixed point on earth), which operate at an altitude of 22,300 mi (36 000 km), are not threatened. Another event that caused concern over the Soviet SDI effort was the arrest of three men who were charged with conspiring to sell to the Soviets U.S. computer technology suitable for SDI application.

Strategic Offensive Systems. Both the United States and Soviet Union continued to modernize their delivery systems by which nuclear weapons could be carried to the other nation. Late in the summer, the White House announced that the Soviet Union had become the first nation to deploy an ICBM (intercontinental ballistic missile) capable of being launched from railroad cars. Known as the SS-24, the missile carries ten nuclear warheads with a range of approximately 6,200 mi (10 000 km). The Reagan administration criticized the Soviets for deploying a weapon whose numbers would be difficult to verify (because it could be moved along the vast length of the Soviet rail system) and contended that the SS-24 would inject a destabilizing factor into strategic relationships. Others, however, took a more positive view of the Soviet activity, contending that a changeover from fixed-based ICBMs, which invite a first strike, to mobile missiles, which can survive such an attack, adds stability to the nuclear relationship. The Soviets previously had demonstrated a capability to launch another missile, the SS-25, from a tank-like vehicle. For its part, the United States also continued development of a mobile ICBM—the Midgetman—which could be moved across vacant government-owned land by means of a tracked vehicle.

Two of the most advanced additions to the U.S. strategic nuclear force encountered problems during 1987. The B-1 jet bomber, a replacement for the aging B-52s, was criticized by members of Congress for having major technical problems. The Air Force, however, reaffirmed its confidence in the new plane. One of the planes crashed in the autumn, but an investigation indicated that there had been no technical malfunction; the accident was blamed on a flock of birds being sucked into an engine. Meanwhile, members of the House Armed Services Committee were critical of the accuracy of the nation's newest missile, the ten-warhead MX (dubbed the "Peacekeeper" by the Pentagon).

The year 1987 marked the 30th anniversary of the launching of the first earth satellite (and, by inference, the capability to build an ICBM) by the Soviet Union. The anniversary occasioned a number of U.S. government and private analysts to review the Soviet record of military space achievements. Many of these analysts suggested that, given the postponement of the U.S. space shuttle program, the Soviets could be expected to move far ahead in the military utilization of space, including the use of their orbiting space station MIR for military experimentation.

Consequences of the INF Treaty. A number of military strategists worried that if the United States and Soviet Union signed a treaty to remove intermediate-range nuclear forces (INF) from Europe, NATO would be endangered. Part of their concern was that even if short-range battlefield nuclear weapons were preserved, the manpower superiority of Soviet and Warsaw Pact forces would work to the disadvantage of the West Europeans. Those holding this view maintained that, in the eventuality of war, the United States would have to use strategic nuclear weapons based at sea or on U.S. soil, or else lose Western Europe. Suggested ways to compensate for the Soviet advantage included pressuring the NATO allies to contribute more conventional capability to the alliance and introducing more high-technology weapons to the NATO units. Such equipment would include very accurate non-nuclear weapons for use against Soviet tank armies.

Former U.S. Secretary of State and National Security Adviser Henry Kissinger presented a gloomy assessment of the potential damage to NATO should the INF Treaty be signed. Adoption of the treaty, he argued, would enable the Soviets to move closer to a long-standing objective—decoupling the United States from its NATO allies. And, he contended, the removal of American intermediate nuclear forces likely will trigger three consequences: cast doubt about Washington's commitment to defend Europe, reduce U.S. influence among the NATO nations, and cause the Europeans to seek new defense policies. With respect to the latter, some nations might proceed from the removal of intermediate-range nuclear forces to the removal of battlefield nuclear weapons; other nations, however, might enhance their independent nuclear forces. As an alternative to the INF treaty, Kissinger called on Washington to endorse the strengthening of existing nuclear forces by Great Britain and France, while encouraging the NATO allies to develop a more cooperative defense posture among themselves to offset the erosion of the U.S. presence.

Resignations and Dismissals. Early in November, President Reagan announced the resignation of his secretary of defense for nearly seven years, Caspar Weinberger. No official reason was given, but it was widely reported that Weinberger wanted to spend more time with his ailing wife. Friends of Weinberger, led by President Reagan, praised him for building up the nation's defense in the face of a growing Soviet military threat. According to the president, Weinberger had brought to his government service "courage, consistency, loyalty, together with uncommon brilliance, decisiveness, and determination." Critics charged that the Weinberger years had been marked by a lack of effective leadership and obscure policy objectives.

At the same time that he announced Weinberger's resignation, President Reagan nominated his national security adviser, Frank Carlucci (*see* BIOGRAPHY), to be the new secretary of defense. Replacing Carlucci at the National Security Council (NSC) would be Lt. General Colin Powell, an NSC deputy.

In the Soviet Union, a change in top military leadership was occasioned by an odd event in May. A young West German pilot flew a small private plane hundreds of miles through Soviet air space and landed it in Moscow's Red Square. In the aftermath, Defense Minister Sergei Sokolov and the Air Defense Forces chief Alexandre Koldunov were removed. Army Gen. Dmitri Yazov, 63, was named as the new defense minister.

ROBERT M. LAWRENCE
Colorado State University

Today's Marine Corps

© David H. Wells/The Image Works

Shortly after taking over as the new commandant of the U.S. Marine Corps on July 1, 1987, Lt. Gen. Alfred M. Gray, Jr., declared that "there are going to be major changes in the way we [the Marines] do business." According to the 59-year-old Korean War veteran, the Marines' "standards of excellence are going to go up" and "that's nonnegotiable."

Indeed the previous four years were tough ones for the Marine Corps. It began in 1983 when 241 servicemen died in a terrorist bombing of a Marine barracks in Beirut, Lebanon. The official investigation of the tragedy was critical of Marine leadership for failing to prepare adequate defensive measures for troops placed in an obviously dangerous situation. Problems of a much different kind surfaced in 1987. Marines, on active duty and retired, winced when allegations were made that Marine guards at the U.S. embassy in Moscow, and elsewhere, had traded intelligence secrets for sex. As the reports accumulated of guards allegedly permitting Soviet intelligence (KGB) agents access to the Moscow embassy, the Corps suffered through an unprecedented period of rebuke and ridicule. The April 20 issue of *Time* carried on its cover the likeness of a Marine guard with a black eye and the caption, "SPY Scandals—Marine Corps Woes."

By early summer the spy-sex affair took a new turn, which in its way also was damaging to the Corps. Friends and relatives of the accused guards claimed that the Marines had blown the matter out of proportion, and that false confessions had been obtained improperly by Naval Intelligence Service investigators. In spite of the charges, Sgt. Clayton J. Lonetree became the first Marine to be tried for spying. In late August he was found guilty and sentenced to 30 years in prison (*See also* ESPIONAGE.)

The Marine Corps received additional publicity as the congressional investigations of the Iran-contra affair focused on a Marine officer, Lt. Col. Oliver North. After receiving a grant of limited immunity, the fired National Security Council staff member told of helping to sell arms to Iran, then clandestinely diverting the funds to support the contras fighting the Sandinista government in Nicaragua. There were those who saw North as an example of the gung ho Marine, blindly following orders. In this case it appeared to some that there was failure to distinguish between loyalty to a president and the duty to support the Constitution and the nation's laws. On the other hand, opinion polls indicated that a majority of Americans considered North a patriotic officer who did his duty as he saw it.

By late 1987, the Marine Corps, a force of some 200,000, was addressing the question of how it could best serve U.S. foreign-policy interests in the complex world of the late 20th and early 21st century. Competition for status as an elite strike force is keen from special Army and Air Force units. The Corps, which was established in 1775 and is a separate service within the Department of the Navy, has removed some of the most rigorous aspects of basic training. The Corps claims, however, that it still produces a tough and disciplined fighting "leatherneck," willing to observe its code of *Semper Fidelis* ("Always Faithful").

ROBERT M. LAWRENCE

MINNESOTA

The Minnesota Twins created statewide bedlam by winning the World Series for the first time. An upturn in the farm economy, antitakeover legislation, and a standoff over an early presidential primary were among other top events in Minnesota in 1987.

Politics. In an effort to be one of the earliest states expressing a presidential preference, the state legislature set Feb. 23, 1988, as precinct caucus day, rousing the ire of the Democratic National Committee. Seeking to enforce its rule that no caucuses be held before March 8, the committee threatened not to seat the state's delegation at the 1988 convention. A compromise was reached, but Minnesota will have downgraded hotel rooms and poor seating on the convention floor.

Governor Perpich commanded sustained public attention through a number of well-covered public actions. Among them: he announced that for occasions demanding some formality, he would use "Rudolph G." instead of the "Rudy" Minnesotans are accustomed to. The governor refused to attend the dedication of the World Trade Center in St. Paul, a project he had sponsored, because of what he regarded as bad treatment by the press.

The governor's effort to invalidate an act that would have allowed the use of state national guard troops overseas despite his veto was denied by the courts. (Minnesota's national guard was used in exercises in Honduras.)

Former Vice-President Walter Mondale resumed living and practicing law in Minneapolis, giving rise to speculation that he may try to return to the U.S. Senate in 1990.

The Economy. After several years of acute distress, farmers experienced an economic upturn, the result of higher prices for livestock, increased subsidy payments, and lower production costs. The sharp decline in land values appeared to have halted.

MINNESOTA • Information Highlights

Area: 84,402 sq mi (218 601 km²).
Population (July 1, 1986): 4,214,000.
Chief Cities (July 1, 1986 est.): St. Paul, the capital, 263,680; Minneapolis, 356,840; Duluth (1980 census), 92,811.
Government (1987): *Chief Officers*—governor, Rudy Perpich (DFL); lt. gov., Marlene Johnson (DFL). *Legislature*—Senate, 67 members; House of Representatives, 134 members.
State Finances (fiscal year 1986): *Revenue,* $9,540,000,000; *expenditure,* $8,581,000,000.
Personal Income (1986): $63,184,000,000; per capita, $14,994.
Labor Force (June 1987): *Civilian labor force,* 2,284,100; *unemployed,* 110,400 (4.8% of total force).
Education: *Enrollment* (fall 1985)—public elementary schools, 467,957; public secondary, 237,183; colleges and universities, 221,162. *Public school expenditures* (1985–86), $2,542,000,000 ($3,864 per pupil).

The opening of the $120 million World Trade Center in St. Paul and the Conservatory Retail Center in Minneapolis highlighted redevelopment in the Twin Cities. Minneapolis also saw completion of the 31-story Lincoln Centre office building and continuing work on the 55-floor Norwest Bank Building.

The Minnesota legislature made it more difficult for state business firms to be acquired in hostile takeovers when it passed protective legislation intended to halt takeover of the Minneapolis-based Dayton-Hudson Corporation. The legislature also established the Greater Minneapolis Corporation, with potential financing of $100 million or more, to promote economic development and jobs.

Education. At the University of Minnesota, a faculty task force recommended that the School of Dentistry and the College of Veterinary Medicine be closed, in line with a program aimed at focusing resources on fewer but higher quality programs. The recommendations were rejected by the Regents.

The site of a new state-financed arts high school was shifted from Minneapolis to St. Paul when the Minneapolis city council attached conditions that the school's board found unacceptable. The project was heading for a stormy time in the 1988 legislature.

Items of Interest. Garrison Keillor ended his National Public Radio program, *"Prairie Home Companion,"* on June 13. The Minnesota Zoo lost its star attraction, the beluga whale, Bigmouth, and attendance dropped sharply, creating a cloudy future for the zoo.

ARTHUR NAFTALIN, *University of Minnesota*

MISSISSIPPI

Quadrennial state and local elections, a wide-ranging federal investigation of corrupt county purchasing practices, and two legislative sessions claimed major attention in Mississippi during 1987. Other items of considerable interest were the state of the economy and an October political announcement by the state's senior U.S. senator.

Elections. In the November gubernatorial election, state auditor Raymond Mabus, Jr., a reform-minded, 39-year-old Harvard law graduate who had won the Democratic gubernatorial nomination with record-setting August primary victories, defeated Republican nominee Jack Reed, a 64-year-old Tupelo businessman and former state board of education member. Mabus captured 53% of the more than 700,000 votes cast and carried 59 of 82 counties. Reed's surprisingly strong showing (47%) was the best of any Republican candidate for statewide office in the 20th century, but other Republicans seeking state office were swamped by Democratic opponents representing, for the most part, a new generation of political leaders.

© Greg Campbell/"Time" Magazine

With the overwhelming support of state blacks, Democrat Ray Mabus, 39, a Harvard-educated lawyer, was elected governor of Mississippi. His victory was cited as a refutation of any Republican-oriented "realignment" of Southern politics.

Legislative seats and local posts continued to be dominated by Democrats.

An amendment to repeal the constitutional ban on interracial marriages, struck down by federal courts years ago, was approved by a narrow margin (52 to 48%). Nine other amendments won overwhelming acceptance.

County Corruption. Nine county supervisors and an equipment salesman were indicted February 12 on charges of bribery, extortion, and mail fraud as the result of "Operation Pretense," a two-year federal undercover investigation of kickbacks and other illegal buying practices. By year's end, indictments had spread to nearly one third of the counties, and more than one tenth of all supervisors had been arrested along with a county-road foreman and several salesmen. A small number of these were convicted, and most of the remainder entered guilty pleas. The ongoing probe was cited as one reason why some 40% of incumbent supervisors resigned, retired, or were defeated in either the primaries or the general election.

The Legislature. The 1987 legislature will probably be remembered more for the rules changes adopted by the House of Representatives than for the legislation that was enacted during the 90-day session. On January 9, House dissidents substantially diluted the power of the speaker, prompting C. B. "Buddie" Newman, who had held that position since 1976, to decide against seeking reelection to the House for the term beginning in January 1988. The major accomplishments of the session were the passage of a $1.6 billion highway program and the balancing of the state budget with "windfall" monies. A proposal to allow voters to decide on calling a constitutional convention was killed by the House Constitution Committee.

A special session called by Gov. Bill Allain in August enacted legislation aimed at strengthening Mississippi's bid for the Superconducting Super Collider to be built by the federal government. In addition, lawmakers appropriated $27.5 million for universities and junior colleges, literacy programs, and repair of state buildings.

Other Items. The unemployment rate declined during the year, and rising agriculture and energy prices helped fuel a moderate expansion in the economy. . . . On October 19, U.S. Sen. John C. Stennis (D), 86, announced that he would not seek election to an eighth term in 1988, leading two Congressmen—Wayne Dowdy (D, 4th district) and Trent Lott (R, 5th district)—to declare their intention to run for the seat. . . . A prolonged drought led to wildfires that destroyed thousands of acres of public and private lands during October and November.

DANA B. BRAMMER
The University of Mississippi

MISSISSIPPI • Information Highlights

Area: 47,689 sq mi (123 515 km²).
Population (July 1, 1986): 2,625,000.
Chief Cities (1980 census): Jackson, the capital (July 1, 1986 est.), 208,440; Biloxi, 49,311; Meridian, 46,577.
Government (1987): *Chief Officers*—governor, William A. Allain (D); lt. gov., Brad Dye (D). *Legislature*—Senate, 52 members; House of Representatives, 122 members.
State Finances (fiscal year 1986): *Revenue,* $4,434,000,000; *expenditure,* $3,836,000,000.
Personal Income (1986): $25,504,000,000; per capita, $9,716.
Labor Force (June 1987): *Civilian labor force,* 1,157,600; *unemployed,* 112,900 (9.8% of total force).
Education: *Enrollment* (fall 1985)—public elementary schools, 329,981; public secondary, 141,214; colleges and universities, 101,180. *Public school expenditures* (1985–86), $997,000,000 ($2,305 per pupil).

MISSOURI

As a result of the decade-old court battle to desegregate the Kansas City School District, children began attending magnet schools designed to attract white students from the suburbs to study foreign languages, computers, the arts, and a variety of other specialized subjects in the predominantly black Kansas City district. During the first month of classes, U.S. District Judge Russel G. Clark nearly doubled property taxes in the district and raised the state income tax on people working in the district by 25% to help pay the costs of desegregation.

Politics. U.S. Rep. Richard Gephardt, a St. Louis Democrat, announced his candidacy for the presidency and campaigned heavily in Iowa, emerging as one of the early leaders in the race for the 1988 Democratic nomination.

Kansas City Mayor Richard Berkeley was reelected to a third straight term, winning 62% of the vote to defeat City Councilman Jim Heeter.

Business. Following a federal investigation, a grand jury indicted Chrysler Corporation for selling luxury cars after executives at the company's plant in suburban St. Louis had driven them—sometimes for more than 400 mi (640 km)—with their odometers disconnected. Evidence indicated that the practice had been going on for more than 30 years. Chrysler admitted unhooking odometers as part of a program to test cars on the road, but said the practice was not illegal. Company President Lee Iacocca apologized and offered new Chryslers to any consumers who had bought cars driven in the program.

Kroh Brothers Development Co., a Kansas City real-estate developer with operations nationwide, collapsed under the weight of nearly $800 million in debts. Accused by creditors of fraudulently obtaining personal loans, brothers George P. Kroh and John A. Kroh, Jr., were forced into personal bankruptcy, along with their company and many of its partnerships.

State Government. The Missouri General Assembly approved development of a 200-mile (320-km) hiking and biking trail along an abandoned railroad line, but property owners along the scenic route through central Missouri filed suit to block development of the trail.

Legalized gambling efforts faced difficulties. Three years after Missouri voters approved pari-mutuel betting on horse races, not a single developer had been able to attract the financial backing needed to get a license to build a race track. The Missouri Lottery, which started in 1986, was criticized for exceeding the constitutional limit on spending for administration. The General Assembly refused to pass legislation allowing lottery officials to spend more than 10% of proceeds on administration. In hopes of boosting sales, Missouri decided to join a multistate lottery designed to produce bigger jackpots than individual states can offer.

Mass Murders. The tiny southern Missouri town of Elkland was stunned September 25 by the news that 14-year-old Kirk Buckner had killed his parents, his three younger brothers, and his aunt before dying himself in a struggle with his uncle. But ten days later, the dead youth was exonerated and his uncle, John Schnick, was charged with seven counts of first-degree murder. Earlier in September, five supermarket employees in St. Louis were shot and killed during a robbery.

STEPHEN BUTTRY
"The Kansas City Times"

MISSOURI • Information Highlights

Area: 69,697 sq mi (180 516 km²).
Population (July 1, 1986): 5,066,000.
Chief Cities (July 1, 1986 est.): Jefferson City, the capital (1980 census), 33,619; Kansas City, 441,170; St. Louis, 426,300; Springfield, 139,360; Independence, 112,950.
Government (1987): *Chief Officers*—governor, John Ashcroft (R); lt. gov., Harriett Woods (D). *General Assembly*—Senate, 34 members; House of Representatives, 163 members.
State Finances (fiscal year 1986): *Revenue,* $7,491,000,000; *expenditure,* $6,477,000,000.
Personal Income (1986): $69,856,000,000; per capita, $13,789.
Labor Force (June 1987): *Civilian labor force,* 2,601,700; *unemployed,* 156,800 (6.0% of total force).
Education: *Enrollment* (fall 1985)—public elementary schools, 544,197; public secondary, 250,910; colleges and universities, 241,146. *Public school expenditures* (1985–86), $2,256,000,000 ($3,155 per pupil).

MONTANA

In 1987, Montana moved into the national spotlight when a Montana State University professor was reprimanded by federal environmental authorities. The state's voters and lawmakers continued to be preoccupied with proposals for tax reform.

EPA Controversy. Plant pathologist Gary Strobel was cited in August by the Federal Environmental Protection Agency (EPA) for having injected elm trees with genetically altered material in violation of federal regulations. Strobel had deliberately defied the EPA to protest its controls over his research into Dutch elm disease. The controversy ended in September when Strobel destroyed the trees.

Legislation. State lawmakers rejected four bills that would have created the state's first sales tax, and turned down all other bills designed to reform personal and property taxes. Instead they approved a 10% income-tax surcharge to cut an expected revenue shortage. Nevertheless, state government had to take $34 million from the education trust account to balance its general-fund budget.

MONTANA • Information Highlights

Area: 147,046 sq mi (380 848 km²).
Population (July 1, 1986): 819,000.
Chief Cities (1980 census): Helena, the capital, 23,938; Billings, 66,798; Great Falls, 56,725.
Government (1987): *Chief Officers*—governor, Ted Schwinden (D); lt. gov., George Turman (D). *Legislature*—Senate, 50 members; House of Representatives, 100 members.
State Finances (fiscal year 1986): *Revenue,* $1,754,000,000; *expenditure,* $1,643,000,000.
Personal Income (1986): $9,666,000,000; per capita, $11,803.
Labor Force (June 1987): *Civilian labor force,* 407,500; *unemployed,* 24,600 (6.0% of total force).
Education: *Enrollment* (fall 1985)—public elementary schools, 107,918; public secondary, 45,951; colleges and universities, 35,958. *Public school expenditures* (1985–86), $600,000,000 ($4,337 per pupil).

Montana's petroleum-producing counties were hurt by a referendum approved by voters that capped property taxes at their 1986 levels. Petroleum-rich counties set their tax rates at low levels during the early 1980s because the tax on high-priced oil easily filled their needs. As the price of oil plummeted in 1986 and 1987, the referendum precluded them from raising rates to maintain their cash flow.

Many of the legislature's efforts were aimed at attracting industry. Lawmakers approved money for formal presentation to try to attract the federal government's Superconducting Super Collider and a telephone research laboratory. Rangeland, north of Billings, was selected as Montana's proposed site for the Super Collider.

In addition, the legislature approved a 4% tax on motel rooms and halved the state's 30% coal severance tax. But lawmakers increased the workers compensation tax on employers, which already was among the highest in the nation. The legislature also passed a health-care information act, which protects the confidentiality of medical records.

Railroads. In July, the Burlington Northern Railroad (BN) agreed to sell or lease 600 mi (966 km) of its southern line through the state to Montana Rail Link, a corporation headed by Dennis Washington of Missoula, who reopened the closed Anaconda Corporation copper mine at Butte in 1986.

Numerous protests from groups, including the state Public Service Commission, grain shippers, and labor unions, were filed after the Interstate Commerce Commission (ICC) declined to fully review the proposal. Completion of the sale was awaiting a decision on the protests. The proposed sale was announced only two months after the ICC accused BN of predatory pricing in setting grain shipping rates in Montana.

Weather. Montana's mountains entered spring with record-low snowpack, which worried irrigators and wildlife officials. Rain fell during nearly every week throughout the summer, however, reducing the need for irrigation and boosting crops to near-record production levels.

Other Items. Montana's first state lottery opened in June. In August, Gov. Ted Schwinden declared that he would not run for reelection in 1988.

ROBERT C. GIBSON
Regional Editor, "The Billings Gazette"

MOROCCO

The 11-year-old war in the Western Sahara remained stalemated throughout 1987. Morocco maintained military superiority on the ground, while the Algerian-backed Polisario Front guerrilla movement and its political arm, the Sahrawi Arab Democratic Republic (SADR) retained the diplomatic advantage (Belize, for example, in November 1986 became the 67th state to open diplomatic relations with SADR).

Foreign Affairs. Despite the meeting on May 4 between King Hassan II and Algeria's President Chadli Benjedid, brokered by King Fahd of Saudi Arabia, Moroccan-Algerian relations showed no marked improvement. This was due almost entirely to the inability of either side to compromise its position over the Sahara. There were no immediate prospects for this situation to change despite several dramatic Polisario military offensives. A new series of intensive attacks began in late May and continued through early July, ending with a wide-ranging battle on August 21 in which, according to Polisario sources, 195 Moroccan soldiers were killed.

Algerian-Moroccan contacts nonetheless continued, with meetings between both countries' foreign ministers taking place in Yugoslavia on June 3-4. Also, Algeria's foreign minister paid a surprise courtesy visit to King Hassan in Casablanca on July 11, prior to the king's visit to the United Kingdom. Despite these diplomatic initiatives, Morocco was put in a serious defensive position with the surprise announcement on October 7 that Algeria and Libya had reached agreement in principle on a treaty of political unity.

The other major foreign-policy concern involved Spain. At the start of July the Spanish foreign minister discussed three central issues with his Moroccan counterpart in Rabat: the Spanish North African enclaves of Ceuta and Melilla, where the minority Muslim population has demanded greater political and economic rights; the renewal of the Spanish-Moroccan fishing treaty; and the question of transit rights for Moroccan exports across Spain. Although none of these issues was resolved to Morocco's satisfaction in 1987, cordial Spanish-Moroccan

© Benyatouille/Gamma-Liaison

The wedding of Princess Lalla Asmaa, the daughter of King Hassan II, and Khalid Benchentouf, son of a member of parliament, was a happy occasion in Morocco during 1987. The principal ceremonies took place on June 6 in Marrakech.

contacts were maintained. Temporary agreements were reached when Morocco extended Spanish fishing rights through Dec. 31, 1987, and Spain agreed to permit free transit of Moroccan industrial and agricultural exports through its country.

Domestic Affairs. Reacting to widespread discontent with the nation's system of educational recruitment, King Hassan announced on June 27 that the baccalaureate examination, the essential qualification for access to higher education, would be abandoned in May 1988 and replaced by a diploma that would reflect an average of academic performance in annual examinations over the previous three years.

The formal presentation of the new 1988–92 five-year development plan was initiated at the start of May in a letter from Hassan to the prime minister, Azzedine Laraki, outlining the plan's principles. The plan will emphasize regional planning, the rural sector and the private sector—particularly small and medium-sized businesses—education, and the provision of adequate drinking water and services.

World Bank estimates suggested a general if slow improvement in the Moroccan economy over ten years. The per capita gross national product would rise by 4.7% in the 1985–90 period and 4.8% in 1990–95. Late economic indicators confirmed the encouraging developments in the Moroccan economy in 1986. Budgetary performance was far better than projected in 1986, with the actual deficit to be covered by the treasury falling from 8.9% of the gross domestic product (GDP) in 1985 to 6.6% of GDP in 1986. The improvement was due both to successful rescheduling of public foreign debt and to a significant underspending on budgetary commitments. On May 18, Morocco became the 94th member of the General Agreement on Tariffs and Trade (GATT).

Hassan permitted the return from exile of Mohammed Basri, the former socialist leader who was condemned to death four times in absentia.

JOHN P. ENTELIS, *Fordham University*

MOROCCO • Information Highlights

Official Name: Kingdom of Morocco.
Location: Northwest Africa.
Area: 172,413 sq mi (446 550 km^2).
Population (mid-1987 est.): 24,400,000.
Chief Cities (1982 census): Rabat, the capital, 518,616; Casablanca, 2,139,204; Fès, 448,823; Marrakech, 439,728.
Government: *Head of state,* Hassan II, king (acceded 1961). *Head of government,* Azzedine Laraki, prime minister (appointed Sept. 30, 1986). *Legislature* (unicameral)—Chamber of Representatives.
Monetary Unit: Dirham (8.375 dirhams equal U.S.$1, August 1987).
Gross Domestic Product (1986 U.S.$): $11,900,-000,000.
Economic Indexes (May 1987): *Consumer Prices* (1980 = 100), all items, 178; food, 181.6. *Industrial Production* (1984, 1980 = 100), 108.
Foreign Trade (1986 U.S.$): *Imports,* $4,069,000,000; *exports,* $2,260,000,000.

MOTION PICTURES

Movies generally lag behind trends in society but tend to catch up eventually when producers become convinced of what the public wants or is ready to accept. Numerous films released in 1987 reflected efforts to fall in step with changes in attitude.

It is significant that one of the year's major hits, *Fatal Attraction,* was a cautionary tale capable of throwing a scare into men and women about the dangers of casual relationships. The film, directed by Adrian Lyne, pitted superb actress Glenn Close against Michael Douglas in a frightening thriller about how a married man's life is shaken up as a result of what he thought would be a simple, brief fling.

Concern for the problems of career women in the wake of the feminist revolution was slickly tapped into by the comedy *Baby Boom.* Diane Keaton excelled as an executive who suddenly has the responsibility of caring for a baby, and the clash between career and domesticity provided the basis for laughter and sentiment.

Babies turned up in movies with more frequency than usual. *Three Men and a Baby* was an American remake of the French comedy *3 Men and a Cradle* (1986). Both capitalized on the idea of men having more to do with caring for children in contemporary society and gave audiences occasion to laugh at their incompetence. *Raising Arizona* was an offbeat comedy about a former convict and his wife who satisfy their yearning for a baby by kidnapping one.

The world of business and finance received contemporary treatments. Michael J. Fox played a yuppie trying to succeed in the comedy *The Secret of My Success.* Oliver Stone followed his *Platoon* (1986) with *Wall Street,* dramatizing pressures and manipulations in financial circles akin to recent headlines. James L. Brooks' *Broadcast News* took a fresh look at network television.

Most dramatic of all was the upsurge of films dealing with the Vietnam War, a subject that had been shunned for years. Stanley Kubrick's jolting *Full Metal Jacket,* examining the dehumanizing effect of both training for war and combat itself, followed the release and immense success of Stone's *Platoon,* which won four Oscars, including the best-picture award. John Irvin's *Hamburger Hill* also looked at what it was like to have fought in Vietnam. There was a different perspective on the war in Francis Coppola's *Gardens of Stone,* scanning the Vietnam conflict from the viewpoint of soldiers assigned to burial duty at Arlington National Cemetery. There were plans to rerelease *Go Tell the Spartans,* a 1978 film dramatizing the early days of America's fateful involvement that quickly disappeared from the movie theaters at the time of its original release.

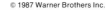

Arguments about public policy toward South Africa's perpetuation of apartheid made Richard Attenborough's *Cry Freedom* a timely drama. Denzel Washington played murdered black leader Stephen Biko and Kevin Kline portrayed Biko's friend and supporter, newspaper editor Donald Woods, whose escape from South Africa was recounted in the stirring epic. *No Way Out,* depicting a corrupt cover-up in the Pentagon, traded on the public's conditioning, created by a steady diet of in-

Stanley Kubrick's powerful "Full Metal Jacket" was one of a number of new films dealing with the Vietnam War.

formation of duplicity in Washington. So did *Suspect,* starring Cher as a court-appointed lawyer whose defense of a derelict accused of murder uncovers a scandal.

Maurice, a period film of producer Ismail Merchant and director James Ivory based on E.M. Forster's novel, reflected current candor in dealing with homosexuality, as did *Prick Up Your Ears,* Stephen Frears' film about the life of murdered British playwright Joe Orton. *Too Outrageous,* a Canadian-made sequel to *Outrageous* (1977), mentioned AIDS as a cause of a death, thereby recognizing present anxieties.

Rediscovering the Past. While many films were rooted in the present, others harked back to the past. One example was *Matewan,* directed by John Sayles, which recalled the violent 1920 coal-mine battles in West Virginia as labor attempted to organize in the face of brutal resistance by the mine owners. In *Radio Days,* Woody Allen looked with nostalgia at the pre-television era when radio was the unifying communication in the home. British director John Boorman's autobiographical *Hope and Glory* viewed World War II in England from the perspective of a youngster growing up in the midst of the excitement and tragedies of the period. The short but meteoric career of rock 'n' roll singer Ritchie Valens, who died in the same plane crash as Buddy Holly, was dramatized in *La Bamba.* The career of composer-singer Chuck Berry was recalled in *Chuck Berry Hail! Hail! Rock 'n' Roll,* a documentary by Taylor Hackford. The Disney Company re-released its classic *Snow White and the Seven Dwarfs* to mark the 50th anniversary of the animated favorite (*see* page 82). The new James Bond adventure, *The Living Daylights,* this one starring Timothy Dalton, served to highlight the 25th anniversary of the 007 films, an occasion for a nostalgic retrospective at the Museum of Modern Art in New York. Also in the realm of anniversaries, Hollywood celebrated its 100th birthday (*see* feature article, page 70).

The durable writing of Tennessee Williams received fresh attention with Paul Newman's production of *The Glass Menagerie,* starring Joanne Woodward (Mrs. Paul Newman). The particularly sensitive and brilliantly acted film did justice to the play. In a more popular vein, the former hit television series *The Untouchables* spawned a new film by Brian De Palma under the same title. Starring Kevin Costner as Treasury man Eliot Ness, *The Untouchables* was a salute to the Hollywood gangster films of old.

The pangs of nostalgia were especially evident in *The Whales of August,* which featured captivating performances by the now elderly actresses Lillian Gish, Bette Davis, and Ann Sothern, and veteran actor Vincent Price. Davis, all but unrecognizable as a result of illness and aging, nevertheless still was riveting with her familiar, distinctive voice and her bravura performance as a blind woman cared for by her sister. The film, directed by Lindsay Anderson, afforded fans of the stars an unusual opportunity to reflect on their impressive careers.

Outstanding Acting. The year was rich in other noteworthy performances, some of them superior to the films that they enhanced. Faye Dunaway showed a new dimension to her acting by portraying an alcoholic in *Barfly,* a film in which Mickey Rourke also extended himself as a slovenly, habitually drunken writer living on skid row. A virtually unknown actress, Rachel Levin, gave a gripping performance in *Gaby—A True Story* as Mexican-born author Gabriela Brimmer, who grappled with cerebral palsy that left her almost entirely paralyzed. Norma Aleandro, noted for *The Official Story* (1985), was deeply moving as her caring companion.

Marcello Mastroianni, who has remained popular throughout his prolific career, once again charmed audiences with *Dark Eyes,* directed by Soviet filmmaker Nikita Mikhalkov. Barbara Hershey won the Cannes Film Festival's best actress award for her portrayal of a backwoods woman in Louisiana in *Shy People,* although the film itself left much to be desired. Anne Bancroft and Anthony Hopkins were exceedingly good in *84 Charing Cross Road,* filmed from Helene Hanff's memoir about her infatuation with a British bookstore.

French actor Gérard Depardieu was memorable as the frustrated farmer in *Jean De Florette,* Claude Berri's movie based on the two-part novel by Marcel Pagnol. Yves Montand was also a standout in the film, and even better in the second part, *Manon of the Spring.* Steve Martin garnered laughs as a modern Cyrano in *Roxanne.* Bette Midler and Shelley Long made a delightful team in *Outrageous Fortune,* and Richard Dreyfuss was excellent in both *Tin Men* and *Stakeout.* James Woods made the most of an odd role as a hitman in *Best Seller,* while Brian Dennehy was striking as the cop/author whom he pressures into writing his story.

Kim Basinger was emerging rapidly as a fine comedienne; two films, *Blind Date* and *Nadine,* emphasized her comic talent. Ellen Barkin made a bid to become a major star with her work in *The Big Easy* as a district attorney fighting corruption in New Orleans. Among rising actors, Dennis Quaid, in the same film, flashed charisma as the target of the inquiry and also as the impetuous juror in *Suspect.*

Directing Turns. Some of the noteworthy exhibitions of talent were by directors, old and young. John Huston, who died during 1987, made his last film, *The Dead,* based on *Dubliners* by James Joyce. Norman Mailer made an idiosyncratic *film noir, Tough Guys Don't Dance,* based on his book. Woody Allen had

© Alive Films, photo by Jonathan Levine

Lillian Gish (left) and Bette Davis, two legends of motion pictures, were united in "The Whales of August." Gish and Davis, who together make up an association with the silver screen stretching from 1914 through Hollywood's golden age to the present, play two sisters sharing what could be their final summer on the Maine coast.

MOTION PICTURES | 1987

ANGEL HEART. Written and directed by Alan Parker, based on the novel *Falling Angel* by William Hjortsberg. With Mickey Rourke, Robert De Niro, Lisa Bonet.

BABY BOOM. Director, Charles Shyer; screenplay by Mr. Shyer and Nancy Meyers. With Diane Keaton, Sam Shepard, James Spader.

BARFLY. Director, Barbet Schroeder; screenplay by Charles Bukowski. With Mickey Rourke, Faye Dunaway.

BEVERLY HILLS COP II. Director, Tony Scott; screenplay by Larry Ferguson and Warren Skaaren. With Eddie Murphy.

BEYOND THERAPY. Director, Robert Altman; screenplay by Christopher Durang and Mr. Altman. With Julie Hagerty, Jeff Goldblum, Glenda Jackson, Tom Conti.

THE BIG EASY. Director, Jim McBride; screenplay by Daniel Petrie, Jr., and Jack Baran. With Dennis Quaid, Ellen Barkin, Ned Beatty.

BLACK WIDOW. Director, Bob Rafelson; screenplay by Ronald Bass. With Debra Winger.

BLIND DATE. Director, Blake Edwards; screenplay by Dale Launer. With Kim Basinger, Bruce Willis.

BROADCAST NEWS. Written and directed by James Brooks. With William Hurt, Albert Brooks, Holly Hunter.

CRY FREEDOM. Director, Sir Richard Attenborough; screenplay by John Briley, based on the books *Biko* and *Asking for Trouble* by Donald Woods. With Denzel Washington, Kevin Kline.

DARK EYES. Director, Nikita Mikhalkov; screenplay by Alexander Adabachian and Mr. Mikhalkov, with the collaboration of Suso Cecchi D'Amico, based on the short stories of Anton Chekhov. With Marcello Mastroianni, Silvana Mangano, Marthe Keller.

THE DEAD. Director, John Huston; screenplay by Tony Huston, based on James Joyce's short story. With Anjelica Huston, Donal McCann.

DEAD OF WINTER. Director, Arthur Penn; screenplay by Marc Shmuger and Mark Malone. With Mary Steenburgen, Roddy McDowall.

DIRTY DANCING. Director, Emile Ardolino; screenplay by Eleanor Bergstein. With Jennifer Grey, Patrick Swayze, Jerry Orbach, Jack Weston.

DUET FOR ONE. Director, Andrei Konchalovsky; screenplay by Tom Kempinski, Jeremy Lipp, and Konchalovsky. With Julie Andrews, Alan Bates.

84 CHARING CROSS ROAD. Director, David Jones; screen play by Hugh Whitemore. With Anne Bancroft, Anthon Hopkins.

EMPIRE OF THE SUN. Director, Steven Spielberg; screen play by Tom Stoppard. With Christian Bale, John Mal kovich.

FATAL ATTRACTION. Director, Adrian Lyne; screenplay by James Dearden. With Michael Douglas, Glenn Close, Anne Archer.

FULL METAL JACKET. Director, Stanley Kubrick; screenplay by Mr. Kubrick, Michael Herr, and Gustav Hasford, based on the novel *The Short Timers,* by Mr. Hasford. With Matthew Modine, Adam Baldwin, Vincent D'Onofrio, Lee Ermey.

GABY—A TRUE STORY. Director, Luis Mandoki; screenplay by Martin Salinas and Michael James Love. With Liv Ullmann, Norma Aleandro, Rachel Levin.

GARDENS OF STONE. Director, Francis Coppola; screenplay by Ronald Bass, based on the novel by Nicholas Proffitt. With James Caan, Anjelica Huston, James Earl Jones.

THE GLASS MENAGERIE. Director, Paul Newman; playwright, Tennessee Williams. With Joanne Woodward, John Malkovich, Karen Allen, James Naughton.

GOOD MORNING, VIETNAM. Director, Barry Levinson; screenplay by Mitch Markowitz. With Robin Williams.

HAMBURGER HILL. Director, John Irvin; screenplay by Jim Carabatsos. With Courtney Vance, Dylan McDermott, Tegan West.

HOOSIERS. Director, David Anspaugh; screenplay by Angelo Pizzo. With Gene Hackman, Barbara Hershey, Dennis Hopper.

HOPE AND GLORY. Written and directed by John Boorman. With Sarah Miles, David Hayman, Derrick O'Connor, Susan Wooldridge, Sammi Davis, Ian Bannen, Sebastian Rice Edwards.

HOUSEKEEPING. Written and directed by Bill Forsyth, based on the novel by Marilynne Robinson. With Christine Lahti, Sara Walker, Andrea Burchill.

HOUSE OF GAMES. Written and directed by David Mamet, based on a story cowritten by Jonathan Katz. With Lindsay Crouse, Joe Mantegna.

IRONWEED. Director, Hector Babenco; screenplay by William Kennedy, from his novel. With Jack Nicholson, Meryl Streep.

ISHTAR. Written and directed by Elaine May. With Warren Beatty, Dustin Hoffman.

JEAN DE FLORETTE. Director, Claude Berri; screenplay by Mr. Berri and Gérard Brach. With Yves Montand, Gérard Depardieu.

LA BAMBA. Written and directed by Luis Valdez. With Lou Diamond Phillips, Esai Morales.

THE LAST EMPEROR. Director, Bernardo Bertolucci; screenplay by Mark Peploe with Mr. Bertolucci. With John Lone, Joan Chen, Peter O'Toole.

THE LIVING DAYLIGHTS. Director, John Glen; screenplay by Richard Maibaum and Michael G. Wilson. With Timothy Dalton.

MANON OF THE SPRING. Director, Claude Berri; screenplay by Mr. Berri and Gérard Brach from the novel *L'Eau des Collines*, by Marcel Pagnol. With Yves Montand, Daniel Auteuil, Emmanuelle Béart.

MATEWAN. Written and directed by John Sayles. With Chris Cooper, James Earl Jones.

MAURICE. Director, James Ivory; screenplay by Kit Hesketh-Harvey and Mr. Ivory, based on E. M. Forster's novel. With James Wilby, Hugh Grant.

MOONSTRUCK. Director, Norman Jewison; screenplay by John Patrick Shanley. With Cher, Nicolas Cage.

MY LIFE AS A DOG. Director, Lasse Hallstrom; screenplay by Mr. Hallstrom, Reidar Jonsson, Brasse Brannstrom, Per Berglund. With Anton Glanzelius.

NADINE. Written and directed by Robert Benton. With Jeff Bridges, Kim Basinger, Rip Torn, Gwen Verdon.

NO WAY OUT. Director, Roger Donaldson; screenplay by Robert Garland. With Kevin Costner, Gene Hackman, Sean Young, Will Patton.

NUTS. Director, Martin Ritt; screenplay by Tom Topor, Darryl Ponicsan, Alvin Sargent. With Barbra Streisand, Richard Dreyfuss.

ORPHANS. Director, Alan J. Pakula; screenplay by Lyle Kessler, based on his play. With Albert Finney, Matthew Modine, Kevin Anderson.

OUTRAGEOUS FORTUNE. Director, Arthur Hiller; screenplay by Leslie Dixon. With Bette Midler, Shelley Long.

PLANES, TRAINS AND AUTOMOBILES. Written and directed by John Hughes. With Steve Martin, John Candy.

PRICK UP YOUR EARS. Director, Stephen Frears; screenplay by Alan Bennett, based on the book by John Lahr. With Gary Oldman, Alfred Molina.

THE PRINCESS BRIDE. Director, Rob Reiner; screenplay by William Goldman, based on his novel. With Cary Elwes, Robin Wright, Mandy Patinkin.

PROJECT X. Director, Jonathan Kaplan; screenplay by Stanley Weiser. With Matthew Broderick.

RADIO DAYS. Written and directed by Woody Allen. With Mia Farrow, Seth Green, Julie Kavner, Michael Tucker, Dianne Wiest.

RAISING ARIZONA. Director, Joel Coen; screenplay by Ethan and Joel Coen. With Nicolas Cage, Holly Hunter.

REPENTANCE. Director, Tengiz Abuladze; screenplay by Mr. Abuladze, Nana Djanelidze, Rezo Kveselava. With Avtandil Makharadze.

ROXANNE. Director, Fred Schepisi; screenplay by Steve Martin, from the play *Cyrano de Bergerac* by Edmond Rostand. With Steve Martin, Daryl Hannah, Shelley Duvall.

THE RUNNING MAN. Director, Paul Michael Glaser, screenplay by Steven E. de Souza, based on a novel by Stephen King. With Arnold Schwarzenegger.

SEPTEMBER. Written and directed by Woody Allen. With Elaine Stritch, Mia Farrow, Dianne Wiest, Sam Waterston, Denholm Elliott, Jack Warden.

THE SICILIAN. Director, Michael Cimino; screenplay by Steve Shagan, based on the novel by Mario Puzo. With Christopher Lambert.

SOMEONE TO WATCH OVER ME. Director, Ridley Scott; screenplay by Howard Franklin. With Tom Berenger, Mimi Rogers, Jerry Orbach, Lorraine Bracco.

SPACEBALLS. Director, Mel Brooks; screenplay by Mr. Brooks, Thomas Meehan, and Ronny Graham. With Mel Brooks, John Candy, Rick Moranis.

STAKEOUT. Director, John Badham; screenplay by Jim Kouf. With Richard Dreyfuss.

STREET SMART. Director, Jerry Schatzberg; screenplay by David Freeman. With Christopher Reeve.

SUPERMAN IV: THE QUEST FOR PEACE. Director, Sidney J. Furie; screenplay by Lawrence Konner and Mark Rosenthal. With Christopher Reeve.

SUSPECT. Director, Peter Yates; screenplay by Eric Roth. With Cher, Dennis Quaid, Joe Mantegna.

SWIMMING TO CAMBODIA. Director, Jonathan Demme; screenplay by Spalding Gray. With Spalding Gray.

THREE MEN AND A BABY. Director, Leonard Nimoy; screenplay by James Orr, Jim Cruickshank, based on *Trois Hommes et un Couffin* by Coline Serreau. With Tom Selleck, Steve Guttenberg, Ted Danson.

THROW MOMMA FROM THE TRAIN. Director, Danny DeVito; screenplay by Stu Silver. With Mr. DeVito, Billy Crystal.

TIN MEN. Written and directed by Barry Levinson. With Richard Dreyfuss, Danny DeVito, Barbara Hershey.

TOUGH GUYS DON'T DANCE. Written and directed by Norman Mailer. With Ryan O'Neal, Isabella Rossellini.

THE UNTOUCHABLES. Director, Brian De Palma; screenplay by David Mamet. With Robert De Niro, Sean Connery, Kevin Costner.

WALKER. Director, Alex Cox; screenplay by Rudy Wurlitzer. With Ed Harris, Marlee Matlin.

WALL STREET. Director, Oliver Stone; screenplay by Mr. Stone and Stanley Weiser. With Michael Douglas, Charlie Sheen, Daryl Hannah, Martin Sheen.

THE WANNSEE CONFERENCE. Director, Heinz Schirk; screenplay by Paul Mommertz. With Dietrich Mattausch, Gerd Bockmann.

WEEDS. Director, John Hancock; screenplay by Dorothy Tristan and Mr. Hancock. With Nick Nolte.

THE WHALES OF AUGUST. Director, Lindsay Anderson; screenplay by David Berry. With Bette Davis, Lillian Gish, Vincent Price, Ann Sothern.

THE WHISTLE BLOWER. Director, Simon Langton; screenplay by Julian Bond, based on the novel by John Hale. With Michael Caine, James Fox, Sir John Gielgud.

WHO'S THAT GIRL. Director, James Foley; screenplay by Andrew Smith and Ken Finkleman. With Madonna.

THE WITCHES OF EASTWICK. Director, George Miller; screenplay by Michael Cristofer, based on the book by John Updike. With Jack Nicholson, Cher, Susan Sarandon, Michelle Pfeiffer.

THE WOLF AT THE DOOR. Director, Henning Carlsen. With Donald Sutherland, Max Von Sydow.

© Gamma-Liaison

Kevin Costner (foreground), *a new Hollywood leading man, teamed with veteran actor Sean Connery in "The Untouchables," a film based on lawman Eliot Ness' book and the popular television series, and depicting Chicago during the Prohibition era.*

the distinction of providing two new films during the same year; he followed *Radio Days* with *September,* which had a Vermont country setting instead of his familiar New York City locations.

Playwright David Mamet tried directing with his unusual *House of Games,* a study in con artistry. Alan Pakula adapted the stage play *Orphans*. Critics detected a bright new filmmaking talent in Robert Townsend, who produced, directed, and starred in *Hollywood Shuffle,* a personal comedy spoofing the problems a black actor encounters in Hollywood. Director Rob Reiner provided mirth for family audiences with *The Princess Bride,* a frothy satire on fairy tales. Hector Babenco, who scored with *Kiss of the Spider Woman* (1985), was back with *Ironweed,* starring Jack Nicholson and Meryl Streep.

Business. A sharp increase in movie production resulted in a particularly crowded schedule of releases. Many films primarily aimed at the videocassette market must open in a theater in order to satisfy contract stipulations geared to guaranteeing exposure that will help the videocassette sales and rentals. In New York, distributors complained of a shortage of theaters in which to open their films. Sometimes the way was cleared as a result of the quick failures of films on which hopes for long runs had been pinned. *Ishtar* was the supreme example of a costly flop.

Cineplex Odeon, the rapidly expanding Canadian-based company in which Universal holds a half interest, ran into protests from notables in the entertainment world when it added the Regency Theater in New York to its roster of some 1,500 movie houses. The acquisition signaled the end of repertory cinema at the Regency, where buffs had flocked to see movie classics. In response to the objections, Cineplex Odeon opted to devote its New Carnegie to repertory.

The battle over coloring old black and white films continued to rage. The anti-coloring forces lost a round when the Library of Congress ruled that a colored version was an original work entitled to a copyright of its own. Notables in the film world testified against the practice at congressional hearings. Woody Allen, for example, called coloring black and white movies "sinful."

Hollywood adhered to its familiar ways of operating. David Puttnam, the independent producer who made *Chariots of Fire* (1981), came to Columbia Pictures as its new president with plans to do things his way. He spoke frequently about the need to cut budgets and pay stars less money, thereby alienating many who preferred the status quo. Puttnam found increasing opposition to his plans and resigned midway through his three-year contract.

WILLIAM WOLF
New York University

MOZAMBIQUE

By 1987, Mozambique's decade-old civil war had almost destroyed an economy already among the world's poorest.

Domestic Affairs. President Samora Machel's death in October 1986 ushered in a new head of state, Joaquim A. Chissano, at a time when the government was attempting to retreat from its doctrinaire socialism. President Chissano's major problem was the escalation of the civil war with the Mozambique National Resistance Movement, or Renamo. The poorly trained Mozambique army proved no match for the South African-supported Renamo forces, which controlled up to 70% of the countryside. A Renamo attack on July 18 in Homoine northeast of Maputo killed 386 and wounded 76 civilians. Another attack on October 29 near the town of Taninga north of the capital left a reported 211 civilians dead. Maputo was spending 45% of its budget on the war effort. Government sources estimated that the war had inflicted $5 billion in damage to the economy, killed 100,000 people, and created 1.5 million refugees.

Economy. The war severely limited even traditional agriculture, already damaged by years of drought. Western creditor governments in June granted the best terms ever to reschedule Mozambique's $3.2 billion debt over 20 years. The nation's exports fell to only $82 million in 1987. And, with drought conditions compounding civil strife, an estimated one third of Mozambique's 14 million people needed emergency food.

Foreign Affairs. Despite the 1984 Nkomati agreement, South Africa continued its support of Renamo as well as its policy of economic destabilization. Mozambique received credits, food, and military supplies from Cuba, the Soviet Union, and Eastern bloc nations. Its greatest supporter was Zimbabwe, which deployed 15,000 men to guard rail and oil lines to the port of Beira. Malawi, although allowing bases for Renamo, also deployed troops to protect its links with the Mozambique port of Ncala. Great Britain and Zimbabwe were training Mozambique army units.

HARRY A. GAILEY, *San Jose State University*

MOZAMBIQUE • Information Highlights

Official Name: People's Republic of Mozambique.
Location: Southeastern coast of Africa.
Area: 309,494 sq mi (801 590 km^2).
Population (mid-1987 est.): 14,700,000.
Chief City (1984 est.): Maputo, the capital, 903,621.
Government: *Head of state,* Joaquim A. Chissano, president (took office November 1986). *Head of government,* Mário da Graca Machungo, prime minister (took office July 1986). *Legislature* (unicameral)—People's Assembly.
Gross National Product (1986 est. U.S.$): $1,300,000,000.

©James Heffernan/Metropolitan Opera

Franco Zeffirelli's lavish production of Puccini's "Turandot" at New York's Metropolitan Opera drew gasps from audiences and mixed reviews from critics. The production starred soprano Eva Morton in the title role and tenor Placido Domingo.

MUSIC

With all that was new in the world of music during 1987, a special place was held for acknowledged masters—living and dead—and for great works of the past in the classical realm as well as in the musical theater, pop industry, and jazz.

George Gershwin, who fit neatly into all and none of these categories, was celebrated on the 50th anniversary of his death with a monthlong tribute at the Brooklyn (NY) Academy of Music. The conductor Michael Tilson Thomas led a gala concert with a galaxy of contemporary stars.

In classical music, the Soviet-born cellist and conductor Mstislav Rostropovich was honored on his 60th birthday, March 27, with a musical tribute at the Kennedy Center in Washington, DC; celebratory concerts already had been held in New York and Boston. In Chicago, music director Sir Georg Solti was honored for his 75th birthday, October 21. In August, music lovers mourned the death of the Austrian-born violist Peter Schidlof and the consequent demise of the great Amadeus String Quartet, which he founded with three other refugees from Hitler's Europe.

Pop music fans marked the 20th anniversary of the release of a ground-breaking Beatles album and the tenth anniversary of the death of Elvis Presley. A number of rock 'n' roll hitmakers of the 1960s returned to the limelight.

Jazz was winning new audiences with innovative musical statements, but homage was paid to such pioneers as Ella Fitzgerald, Lionel Hampton, and the late Louis Armstrong.

Classical

Orchestras. The symphonic orchestra as an American institution began to show signs of real evolution in 1987. The inclusion of new American works in the regular repertory of orchestral subscriptions became normal practice. More orchestras were divided into performing groups of varying sizes and types, employing musicians in different ways, and offering audiences a repertory extending beyond the strictly symphonic. More orchestras were dividing up the directors' artistic responsibilities, using staff and guest conductors for music in which the regular music directors were not best suited.

Composers-in-residence with major symphonies were given greater advisory and performing responsibilities for the new music performance and educational activities of their orchestras. The roles played by composer Jacob Druckman at the New York Philharmonic, Charles Wuorinen at the San Francisco Symphony, and John Harbison at the Los Angeles Philharmonic were representative of that trend.

Professional chamber orchestras grew in number and institutional strength, the leading examples being the St. Paul (MN), Orpheus (New York City), Los Angeles, San Diego, Fort Worth (TX), San Francisco, Montgomery (Washington, DC), and Mostly Mozart (New York City). The St. Paul Chamber Orchestra seemed to sum up the changes in the symphonic concept when it announced, effective September 1988, that it would replace the conventional single artistic directorship with a three-member directorial team: Christopher Hogwood as music director, Hugh Wolff as principal conductor, and composer John Adams as "creative chair."

Gradually, a number of orchestras that had been in deep economic trouble began working out their difficulties by restructuring fund-raising efforts and management and by negotiating contracts that called for some concessions by the musicians. A strike by the Detroit Symphony, begun on September 21 when the association announced a mandatory 11% wage cut, ended on December 14 with the signing of a contract in which the musicians' salary goals would be achieved in the third year, contingent on the success of a two-year campaign to eliminate a $4.1 million deficit. Other orchestras out of the woods, but barely, included: the New Orleans Symphony; the Denver Symphony; the San Diego Symphony, playing a reduced season after a one-year cessation; the Rochester Philharmonic, playing on an interim agreement until January 1988; and the Omaha Symphony. Musicians of the San Antonio Symphony, asked to take a 47% pay cut, formed their own Orchestra San Antonio with Akira Endo as principal conductor.

Sir Georg Solti, music director of the Chicago Symphony since 1969, was the subject of a major celebration with an elaborate gala concert and party on October 9 for his 75th birthday (October 21). Raymond Leppard became music director of the Indianapolis Symphony at the beginning of the season. Yoel Levi, a Romanian-born Israeli, was announced as the Atlanta Symphony's music director beginning in 1988, after Robert Shaw, 71, retires.

New Music. Ralph Shapey's *Symphonie Concertante,* a soloistic composition for 100 players, was introduced by the Philadelphia Orchestra, Riccardo Muti conducting, on April 2; it was the third of six works commissioned in celebration of the bicentennial of the U.S. Constitution. George Perle, the 1986 Pulitzer Prize winner, was featured in three of six concerts on the Tanglewood Festival's Contemporary Music weekend, July 30–August 2, with his *New Fanfares, Concertino for Piano,* and *Songs for Praise and Lamentation,* a work for chorus and orchestra. Seiji Ozawa conducted Donald Martino's *The White Island,* a Boston Symphony commission, on April 8.

Festivals. Louisville, KY, whose Louisville Orchestra boasts a 50-year history of new music commissioning, performing, and recording, produced a ten-day festival, called Sound Celebration, September 20–29, that was regarded as an artistic success; the Soviet composer Sofia Gubaidulina's *Third String Quartet* won especially high praise. The Los Angeles Festival, successor to the 1984 Olympic Arts Festival, featuring some 30 performing companies from 11 countries, was held September 3–27. Most of the music events were in the avant-garde wing, including the John Cage Celebration, performances by specialized performers and groups; and a 70-minute electronic work, *Hungers,* with music by Morton Subotnick and featuring Joan La Barbara.

The 52nd Ravinia Festival of the Chicago Symphony celebrated anniversaries—the 30th of Margaret Hillis' Symphony Chorus, which sang Schoenberg's *Gurrelieder* and Mahler's *Eighth Symphony;* the 20th of Edward Gordon

The Brown Theater at Houston's $70 million Wortham Center was inaugurated October 15 with a production of "Aida," with Mirella Freni (right) *and Stefania Toczyska* (left).

© Jim Caldwell

as the festival's executive director; and the 15th of James Levine as music director.

Opera. The trend toward the dominance of the opera producer reached a kind of climax with the only new work introduced in 1987 by a major U.S. opera company, *Nixon in China*. The producer-director Peter Sellars not only conceived the bold idea but chose the composer (John Adams) and librettist (Alice Goodman) and supervised the production right through its premiere by the Houston Grand Opera on October 22. The strongest element was Goodman's libretto, which took a searching look at the former president's 1972 visit, and Sellars' staging was tight and focused. Though Adams' minimalist style, in its simple and repetitious nature, focused attention on Goodman's text, a faulty performance and amplification strategy made the words largely unintelligible. *Nixon in China* was the second event to be staged at the Alice and George Brown Theater in Houston's $70 million Gus S. Wortham Theater Center. The facility was inaugurated on October 15 with a production of Verdi's *Aida*. A prior intercompany commitment ensured additional performances of *Nixon* in December at the Brooklyn Academy of Music, in February at the Kennedy Center, and in June at the Holland Festival.

The interpretive liberties taken by opera producers were a major issue in the press. Among those heavily criticized were Franco Zeffirelli for his extravagant *Turandot* at New York's Metropolitan Opera, and Peter Sellars for his controversial staging of *Don Giovanni* at the Summerfare Festival in Purchase, NY.

In May, the Metropolitan's general manager, Bruce Crawford, announced that the opera house was artistically and financially unsuited for contemporary opera. The Met canceled its 1981 contract for Jacob Druckman's *Medea* and deferred, perhaps indefinitely, plans to present the opera commissioned of John Corigliano in 1980, *A Figaro for Antonia*.

There were a few adventurous premieres by regional companies during 1987. One example, *Beauty and the Beast* (1984) for a cast of six, music and libretto by the British composer Stephen Oliver, was well received in its American premiere at the Opera Theater of St. Louis, June 11. The Santa Fe Opera, which had given the American premiere of Shostakovich's *The Nose* in 1965, revived it on August 7. The Los Angeles Music Center Opera, potentially a new addition to the ranks of major American companies, was perhaps less impressive in its second year than in its first. However, its new production of Wagner's *Tristan und Isolde*, designed by David Hockney and directed by Jonathan Miller, was striking and individual; the musical performance was distinguished, with Zubin Mehta conducting the Los Angeles Philharmonic and with Jeanine Altmeyer and William Johns in the title roles.

Opera America's survey of the 1985–86 season, covering 84 member companies in the United States and Canada, reported a total of 2,054 main-stage performances of 415 full productions. The total audience was 3,379,000, an increase of 3.8% over the previous year.

International Music Relations. The pianist Vladimir Feltsman, one of the Soviet Union's star artists, became its leading musical émigré to the United States in early August. Feltsman's eight-year struggle to leave the USSR was resolved during a visit to Moscow by U.S. Secretary of State George Shultz. Feltsman became an instant U.S. celebrity, performing at

Courtesy of Chicago Symphony Orchestra

Sir Georg Solti, the Hungarian-born music director of the Chicago Symphony, was honored for his 75th birthday with a gala concert in October. The evening featured his first U.S. appearance as a solo performer, in a Mozart piano concerto.

Courtesy of American Music Theater Festival

The highlight of Philadelphia's 1987 American Music Theater Festival, one of the nation's foremost showcases for new and unusual music theater works, was "The Man Who Mistook His Wife for a Hat," by the British composer Michael Nyman.

the White House on September 27, taking up a professorship at the State University of New York in New Paltz, and making his U.S. public debut in Carnegie Hall on November 11.

A musical exchange between Boston and Moscow, to take place in March–April 1988 and involving 100 Soviet performers and 12 composers in joint concerts with Americans, was announced on September 17. Sarah Caldwell, the director of the Opera Company of Boston, and the composer Rodion Shchedrin are co-directors of the three-week Festival of Soviet Music. Gilbert Levine was appointed music director of the Cracow (Poland) Philharmonic from December 1987 through the end of the 1991 season, becoming the first American to hold such a position in Eastern Europe.

Among the many orchestras that visited the United States during 1987 was the Central Philharmonic of China, from Beijing, making its U.S. debut. Regarded as the best of China's 20 orchestras, the Central Philharmonic toured 24 U.S. cities in October and November.

New Performing Arts Centers. A $52 million Performing Arts Center was opened in downtown Tampa, FL, featuring three theaters of 2,400, 900, and 300 seats, respectively. On September 25, the city of Pittsburgh unveiled its Benedum Center for the Performing Arts, a former movie palace restored at a cost of $42 million. The reopening of New York's renovated Carnegie Hall on Dec. 15, 1986, was followed by months of controversy; criticism centered on the effects on the legendary acoustics as well as the failure to improve audience traffic. The Los Angeles Philharmonic received a gift of $50 million for a new symphony hall.

In other countries, the most impressive facility inaugurated in 1987 (on October 6) was the National Chiang Kai-Shek Cultural Center in Taipei, Taiwan, built at a cost of $263 million. The facility includes the National Theater, with an opera house seating 1,522 and a theater seating 500, and the Concert Hall of 2,070.

Awards. The $75,000 Carnegie Hall International American Music Competition was won by William Sharp, a baritone from Kansas City, MO. The British composer Harrison Birtwistle won the University of Louisville's $150,000 Grawemeyer Award for his opera, *The Mask of Orpheus,* premiered at the London Coliseum in May. John Harbison received the 1987 Pulitzer Prize for his composition *Flight Into Egypt*.

Leonard Bernstein received both the Albert Schweitzer Music Award and the MacDowell Medal. The Schweitzer Award, given by the Creo Society for a life's work dedicated to music and humanity, was presented on April 21 at New York's Avery Fisher Hall. On August 9, at the MacDowell Colony in New Hampshire, Bernstein also became the ninth American composer to be awarded the MacDowell Medal. The violinist Nathan Milstein, 83, was one of five recipients of 1987 Kennedy Center Honors for career achievement. The composer William Schuman, 77, was among 11 recipients of the National Medal of the Arts.

ROBERT COMMANDAY
Music Critic, "San Francisco Chronicle"

Wynton Marsalis (right), *Art Farmer* (center), *and Roy Eldridge* (left) *were among the top trumpeters who gathered at the Queens, NY, home of the late Louis Armstrong for a special musical tribute.*

© Mario Ruiz/ Picture Group

Jazz

Showing signs of a strong popular resurgence, jazz in 1987 was claiming new audiences with innovative statements by established and young talents alike. Saxophonist Ornette Coleman, guitarist Pat Metheny, the Modern Jazz Quartet, trumpeter Wynton Marsalis, and a host of others were pioneering new directions and sparking a new vitality in the music and the industry. Record labels were issuing more jazz on albums, cassettes, and compact discs. Radio stations were expanding jazz programming. And jazz festivals were bigger, more wide-ranging, and better sponsored.

Also evident in 1987 was the movement of jazz musicians from studio work to playing on the road in jazz combos, and from the pure jazz scene into jazz education. The former trend was typified by the new Gadd Gang (Steve Gadd, drums; Richard Tee, keyboards; Cornell Dupree, guitar; Eddie Gomez, acoustic bass; and Ronnie Cuber, baritone and soprano sax). Their first record, *The Groove,* exceeded 100,000 sales in Japan, and these well-established New York studio players went on their second Japanese tour in July.

Among the top jazz musicians with college or high-school teaching posts in 1987 were: Stan Getz, Rufus Reed, and Jim McNeely at Stanford University; Bill Potts at Montgomery College; Carla Bley, Steve Swallow, Lee Konitz, and Harold Danko at Concordia College (Quebec); Artie Shaw at Drake University; Branford Marsalis at Arts High School in Dallas; and Wynton Marsalis at Whitney Young High School in Chicago.

Collections and Tributes. Executors of the estate of the late Louis Armstrong donated to Queens College in New York City the great trumpeter's 30-year collection of jazz recordings (many unreleased), correspondence, and photographs. The school established a special archive to house the collection, and a number of top trumpeters—including Dizzy Gillespie, Wynton Marsalis, Roy Eldridge, Dexter Gordon, Art Farmer, and Clark Terry—gathered at "Satchmo's" former home in Queens for a special musical tribute.

Another major event was the release of the revised 1973 *Smithsonian Collection of Classic Jazz.* Expanded from six to seven LPs (five cassettes), the compilation—by Martin Williams of the Smithsonian Institution—provides an overview of the entire jazz tradition.

Awards. A number of jazz greats won special awards in 1987. Ella Fitzgerald received the National Medal of Arts in a White House ceremony. Ray Charles received The Kennedy Center Award for Excellence (late 1986). Lionel Hampton was honored as BMI's first One of a Kind Award winner. And Dexter Gordon was nominated for an Oscar for his role in the film *'Round Midnight*.

Winners of the 35th annual *Down Beat* International Critics Poll were: Johnny Dodds—Hall of Fame; David Baker—lifetime achievement award; Pat Metheny's and Ornette Coleman's *Song X*—record of the year; Duke Ellington's *The Blanton/Webster Years* and Thelonious Monk's *The Complete Riverside Recordings*—reissues of the year; Gil Evans—big band; Art Blakey's Jazz Messengers—acoustic group; Carla Bley—composer; Lester Bowie—trumpet; Ray Anderson—trombone; Ornette Coleman—soprano saxophone; Sonny Rollins—alto and tenor sax; Gerry Mulligan—baritone sax; Cecil Taylor, piano; Jim Hall—guitar; Charlie Haden, acoustic bass; and Max Roach, drums.

Deaths. The jazz world in 1987 mourned the deaths of three giants: bandleader Woody Herman; bandleader and drummer Buddy Rich; and producer/critic/talent scout John Hammond. (*See* OBITUARIES.)

DOMINIC SPERA, *Indiana University*

© Neal Preston/Camera 5

The group U2 reached superstardom in 1987 with the hit album "The Joshua Tree" and an extensive U.S. tour.

Popular

Pop music in 1987 saw no new trends but thrived with a celebration of music of the past, the continued success of established stars, and the consolidation of such popular teenage genres as rap and heavy metal. The increased popularity of the compact disc gave the record industry its most profitable year ever, despite the fact that unit sales were down. Twenty years after the release of *Sgt. Pepper's Lonely Hearts Club Band,* baby-boom consumers snapped up the Beatles' complete works as they were systematically released on CD.

In August, fans of Elvis Presley converged on his Memphis home, Graceland, to commemorate the tenth anniversary of his death. The anniversary also was marked with television specials, books, and the release of new collections of Presley's music. (*See* page 83.)

The rock 'n' roll movie smash of the summer was *La Bamba,* the story of Ritchie Valens, the Latin rocker who died in the same 1959 plane crash that killed Buddy Holly. Valens' music was performed on the soundtrack by Los Lobos, a highly regarded Los Angeles band who scored a commercial breakthrough when the movie's title song became a No. 1 hit.

The year's other big rock 'n' roll movie was *Hail! Hail! Rock 'n' Roll,* a revealing portrait of Chuck Berry that chronicled his influence and included a concert segment in which the 60-year-old rock master was joined by such musicians as Eric Clapton, Linda Ronstadt, and Keith Richards. The latter also served as the film's musical director.

But not everything was old. U2, who tasted the spotlight as the linchpin group of 1986's multi-star tour to benefit Amnesty International, became major stars in 1987. *The Joshua Tree,* a dark and brooding album emotionally defined by one of its hit singles, "I Still Haven't Found What I'm Looking For," sold more than 3 million copies. The group toured extensively, sold out at every stop, and maintained an intense rapport with its audience.

Paul Simon won a Grammy for his successful 1986 LP, *Graceland,* and toured with an entourage of African musicians to good reviews. The extraordinary South African a capella group Ladysmith Black Mambazo gained the most exposure from the tour, which ended with a series of benefit concerts. *Graceland* continued to spark controversy due to charges that Simon had ignored the cultural boycott of South Africa by recording half of the album in that country with native musicians.

Bruce Springsteen, who culminated his recent ascendance to mass popularity with 1986's five-record live set, surprised everybody by releasing a new studio record in the fall of 1987. *Tunnel of Love,* an intimate collection of love songs recorded with little backup from his E Street Band, was perceived by many to be an attempt by the singer to avoid hoopla and speak from the heart.

Not so Michael Jackson. *Bad,* his first release since 1982's *Thriller,* the best-selling LP of all time, was accompanied by a firestorm of media coverage and a long-form video of the title tune directed by Martin Scorsese. Much was made of Jackson's cosmetic surgery and his constant companion, a chimpanzee named Bubbles, who accompanied him to the September kickoff of his world tour in Japan.

Whitney Houston followed up her self-titled debut album with an LP called *Whitney.* Sounding like a virtual mirror image of its predecessor, the album was a carefully coiffed collection of ballads and dance tunes aimed at a wide, biracial audience. Smokey Robinson, whose soulful style has not changed all that much in the past 25 years, returned to the charts with *One Heartbeat*.

More adventurous music was produced by Prince, whose *Sign O' the Times* provided the musical score for a concert film of the same name. The year also saw something of a blues revival: singer and guitarist Robert Cray, who serves his blues with a side order of Southern soul, enjoyed an unprecedented million-selling hit with *Strong Persuader*.

Other notable releases during the year included John Cougar Mellencamp's *The Lonesome Jubilee,* a hard-rocking, socially conscious follow-up to his breakthrough album *Scarecrow,* and Sting's . . . *Nothing Like the Sun,* which expanded on the pop-jazz format the former Police singer has pursued in his solo career. Robbie Robertson, the songwriter famous for his work with The Band, brought to an end a decade of silence by releasing his first solo album. Other debuts included those by the multi-styled singer Terence Trent D'Arby and the pop group Crowded House.

The comeback band of the year was undoubtedly the Grateful Dead, whose *In the Dark* LP, the group's first in six years, featured the Dead's first ever Top 10 single, "Touch of Grey." For the past decade, the Dead have been among the most successful touring acts in pop music.

Pop-chart observers were further struck by a sense of déjà vu, as such old hit makers as Pink Floyd, Yes, the Bee Gees, and Lynyrd Skynyrd returned to the limelight.

Rap music, a hard-edged black music that originated in inner-city New York, made unexpected strides into the mainstream, particularly when it was linked to another pop style that has traditionally earned little respect, heavy metal. The combination, first exploited when Run-D.M.C. had a huge hit interpreting Aerosmith's "Walk This Way," came to full fruition with the success of the Beastie Boys, a white trio whose album, *Licensed to Ill,* hit No. 1 and who gained considerable notoriety for their provocatively tasteless stage show. Run-D.M.C. and the Beastie Boys toured together during the summer in an unusual and highly publicized attempt to draw an integrated audience. The year's other break-out rapper was L.L. Cool J, who showed that black rappers could also benefit from the expanding audience for hard rhythms and catchy rhyme.

Heavy metal did not need rap to thrive in 1987 as the album charts were dominated by hit albums by such rookie acts as Cinderella, Whitesnake, Poison, and the work of such already established bands as Aerosmith and Mötley Crüe. Bon Jovi, a band that tempers its heavy metal into a more traditional hard-rock format, was the year's break-out group, with its *Slippery When Wet* LP selling some 8 million copies. Def Leppard, whom many credit with anticipating the current metal rage with its 1982 album *Pyromania,* returned with another hit album, *Hysteria*.

Country music continued to be enlivened by the "new traditionalists," who adhere to traditional country styles in lieu of the recorded sweetening that Nashville has long employed in an attempt to cross over to the pop charts. Randy Travis, best known for his ballads, became a commercial powerhouse with his second big-selling album.

Steve Earle continued to attract both country and rock fans, as did the slightly more traditional Dwight Yoakum. Others who found their country success translating into pop notoriety included the Judds, Reba McIntire, the Forrester Sisters, and George Strait. *Trio,* a long-awaited collaboration by Dolly Parton, Linda Ronstadt, and Emmylou Harris, was a major hit on both the country and pop charts.

On Broadway, the British continued to dominate the world of musicals, with *Les Misérables* winning the Tony Award as best musical. Liza Minnelli returned for a well-received extended engagement at New York's Carnegie Hall that reaffirmed her reputation as the queen of the cabaret.

JOHN MILWARD
Free-lance Writer and Critic

The Grateful Dead and Bob Dylan (center)—*enduring symbols of the 60s counterculture—made a joint six-city tour.*

© Peter Lovino/Gamma-Liaison

AP/Wide World

Nebraska Gov. Kay Orr (right), *named David Karnes* (left), *a 38-year-old Republican businessman from Omaha, to the U.S. Senate seat vacated by the death of Edward Zorinsky.*

NEBRASKA

For a nonelection year, 1987 was a politically turbulent one in Nebraska. The year began with the city of Omaha, for the first time in its history, recalling its mayor. A citizens' group had organized the recall petition drive after Mayor Mike Boyle fired the police chief in October 1986, following a long-running feud with the Omaha police department. The recall drive was successful, and in mid-January a special election forced the mayor out of office. He was replaced by Bernie Simon, a member of the City Council.

Early in March, U.S. Sen. Edward Zorinsky, a Democrat, died suddenly of a heart attack. Gov. Kay Orr appointed a relatively unknown businessman, 38-year-old Republican David Karnes, to fill the remainder of Zorinsky's term. Although Karnes promptly began campaigning to retain the Senate seat, a July poll showed Republican Congressmen Douglas Bereuter and Hal Daub well ahead of him in public support. In the Democratic camp, the popular former governor Robert Kerrey was in front.

NEBRASKA • Information Highlights

Area: 77,355 sq mi (200 350 km²).
Population (July 1, 1986): 1,598,000.
Chief Cities (July 1, 1986 est.): Lincoln, the capital, 183,050; Omaha, 349,270; Grand Island (1980 census), 33,180.
Government (1987): *Chief Officers*—governor, Kay Orr (R); lt. gov., William E. Nichol (R). *Legislature* (unicameral)—49 members (nonpartisan).
State Finances (fiscal year 1986): *Revenue,* $2,334,000,000; *expenditure,* $2,205,000,000.
Personal Income (1986): $21,957,000,000; per capita, $13,742.
Labor Force (June 1987): *Civilian labor force,* 824,300; *unemployed,* 38,700 (4.7% of total force).
Education: *Enrollment* (fall 1985)—public elementary schools, 184,296; public secondary, 81,523; colleges and universities, 97,769. *Public school expenditures* (1985–86), $824,000,000 ($3,285 per pupil).

Despite some criticism of her senatorial appointment, newly elected Gov. Kay Orr—who is Nebraska's first woman governor and the first Republican woman elected governor of any U.S. state—was generally praised for her leadership in tax reform. For the first time since its enactment 20 years earlier, the state's income tax system was overhauled by the legislature. The new system bases the individual tax on federally adjusted gross income rather than, as in the past, on a percentage of federal tax liability as the state tax figure.

Governor Orr also urged enactment of a series of tax incentives for business. Within a few months of passage of her measures, supporters were claiming that the new incentives had already brought substantial increases in investment and jobs. The state gasoline tax, long the nation's highest, fell from 19 cents to 17.6 cents per gallon, taking Nebraska out of top place.

The state's economy showed some signs of improvement after the farm crises of the previous years. Bank profits were up and bank failures were down dramatically. The decline in value of farmland slowed to about half what it had been in 1984-85. In September, the farm problem drew national attention when singer Willie Nelson brought the third annual Farm Aid concert to Lincoln to raise money and public concern for the plight of agriculture. Farm Aid III was held in Memorial Stadium, briefly displacing interest in the Cornhuskers, the University of Nebraska's football team.

Interest in football reached its usual intensity as the Huskers enjoyed a successful season and were headed for the Fiesta Bowl on January 1. Hopes for an undefeated season were dashed on November 21 when the No. 1 ranked Huskers lost to the No. 2 ranked Oklahoma Sooners, 17-7.

WILLIAM E. CHRISTENSEN
Midland Lutheran College

NETHERLANDS, THE

For the Netherlands the year 1987 was marked by a continuing effort to reinvigorate the economy without totally abandoning the welfare system for which the country had become noted since the 1960s.

Political Developments. The government remained in the hands of the center-right coalition of the Christian Democratic (CDA) and Liberal (economically conservative and socially progressive) parties. The personal popularity of Premier Rudolf (Ruud) F. M. Lubbers, a Christian Democrat, remained high, although tension grew between the coalition partners over such issues as euthanasia, abortion, and foreign policy. National policy toward euthanasia, which drew attention abroad, remained ambiguous; in principle euthanasia continued to be against the law, usually permitted in practice. The principal opposition party, the Labor Party (PvdA), maintained its position as the largest single party in the elections for provincial legislatures on March 19. The party, however, found itself caught between a passionate left wing marked by hostility to the North Atlantic Treaty Organization (NATO) and commitment to the welfare state and socialist doctrines, and a pragmatic leadership that was ready to make concessions to possible coalition partners in order to return to government. The budget presented to the States-General (Parliament) on September 15 was designed to achieve a modest decrease in the national unemployment rate of more than 13% (about 700,000 persons), through a reduction of taxes and social insurance premiums. The income of government employees, pensioners, and persons on welfare would be reduced by 1–2%.

Exposures of fraud and corruption embarrassed the government. There was a major parliamentary investigation of bribery in housing investment by the semipublic pension fund for government workers, and the ministry of fisheries was revealed to have permitted Dutch fishermen to exceed with impunity their quotas under European Community regulations. There was angry debate over the continuation of pension payments to the widow of a wartime Dutch Nazi, Rost van Tonningen. In Amsterdam the new combined City Hall and Opera House was opened, amid revelations of immense cost overruns of about $47 million.

The economic position of the country improved slowly. Its dependence upon foreign trade, particularly with West Germany, remained overwhelming, limiting the effective range of the government's economic policies. Labor relations remained in general quiescent, although longshoremen in Rotterdam engaged in a strike against plans to increase use of containers. At the other end of the economic scale, medical specialists also went on strike briefly to protest efforts of government and insurance funds to cut their incomes sharply. Street battles were fought in The Hague and Amsterdam between squatters and police. The interlinked problems of drug addiction, prostitution, and the spread of the disease of AIDS continued to trouble the big cities, in particular Amsterdam. Vandalism by supporters of Dutch football ("soccer") teams caused trouble in Amsterdam and on trains. Measures were taken to limit the entry of refugees from Asia, especially Tamils and Kurds after they had been involved in violent rioting at reception centers.

Religion. The Dutch Roman Catholic Church remained riven by the conflict between conservative prelates, particularly Cardinal Adrianus Simonis, and opponents who sought to adapt church doctrine and practice to new demands. A call upon Catholics by Bishop H. Bomers of Haarlem not to vote either for the Liberal or Labor parties because of their acceptance of the practice of abortion was denounced by these parties and the Christian Democrats. Although mainline and conservative Protestants in general worked together in the umbrella Reformed (Calvinist) Church, right-wing Protestant fundamentalists with links to like-minded groups in the United States drew criticism for anti-Semitic agitation.

International Relations. In international affairs the country continued to play as big a role as its small size permitted. It was a committed member of the European Community, with its high-efficiency farmers benefiting from the otherwise burdensome program of agricultural subsidies. At the same time it was a restless member of NATO, hoping that détente and arms agreements between the United States and the Soviet Union would enable it to decrease its commitment especially to nuclear weapons and bases. With Rotterdam the most important port for incoming oil for Europe, it sent two minesweepers to the Persian Gulf in an effort to maintain its petroleum supplies despite the Iraq-Iran war.

HERBERT H. ROWEN, *Rutgers University*

NETHERLANDS • Information Highlights

Official Name: Kingdom of the Netherlands.
Location: Northwestern Europe.
Area: 14,405 sq mi (37 310 km²).
Population (mid-1987 est.): 14,600,000.
Chief Cities (Jan. 1, 1986 est.): Amsterdam, the capital, 679,140; Rotterdam, 571,372; The Hague, the seat of government, 443,961.
Government: *Head of state,* Beatrix, queen (acceded April 30, 1980). *Head of government,* Ruud Lubbers, prime minister (took office Nov. 1982). *Legislature*—States General: First Chamber and Second Chamber.
Monetary Unit: Guilder (1.9112 guilders equal U.S.$1, Nov. 17, 1987).
Economic Index (1986): *Consumer Prices* (1980 = 100), all items, 122.9; food, 117.0. *Industrial Production* (1980 = 100), 106.
Foreign Trade (1986 U.S.$): *Imports,* $75,580,000,000; *exports,* $80,555,000,000.

NEVADA

A rebounding economy, the longest legislative session in state history, a dispute over the creation of a new county, and Paul Laxalt's decision to bow out of the presidential race were news highlights in Nevada in 1987.

The Legislature and Taxes. Despite a public-opinion poll that showed that most Nevadans would support an increase in certain taxes to provide more funds for education, Gov. Richard Bryan chose to hold the line in his budget request to the 1987 legislature to avoid a general tax increase. The governor had given his blessing to a modest increase in the tax on gross-gambling winnings offered by the large casinos in order to prevent an initiative-petition drive for a larger increase.

The governor recommended no salary increases for the 1987-89 biennium for state employees, school teachers, and university professors in the light of sluggish revenues in the first quarter of the 1987 fiscal year. However, a much brighter revenue picture in the middle of the session allowed the governor and the legislature to agree on a 3% salary increase for public employees. In order to raise the appropriations for higher education, prisons, and welfare over the governor's original request, the legislature increased the cigarette tax by five cents, passed a modest increase in the property tax, and negotiated advance-tax payments from the mining industry. An interim committee was set up to study the state's "patchwork" tax system.

Other Legislation. The legislature enacted a controversial hospital-cost-containment plan, a compulsory seat-belt law, a ban on smoking in grocery stores, an increase in the state minimum wage, an increase of 14% in aid for dependent children, and a state holiday to honor Martin Luther King, Jr. However, campaign-reform legislation did not get out of committee.

On the last day of the record-breaking 151-day session, the legislature created the state's 18th county—Bullfrog—which just happens to include a proposed site for the nation's first high-level nuclear-waste dump. The new county was carved out of existing Nye County and has zero population; the reason for its creation was solely to take advantage of potential grants in lieu of taxes from the federal government if the site is selected for the dump. The Nye County Commissioners filed a lawsuit challenging the constitutionality of the act establishing the new county.

The Economy. The efforts of Governor Bryan and the Commission on Economic Development to diversify the state's economy continued to have some success, but the old standbys, gambling and tourism, fueled a remarkable economic rebound. Casinos experienced a 10.2% gain in gross-gambling revenues in fiscal 1987 over the previous year, with the Las Vegas area leading the way with a 12% increase. Sales-tax revenues increased 11.3% over fiscal 1986. Mining activity continued to be strong, especially in northern Nevada.

Laxalt's Withdrawal. After announcing in April that he planned to seek the 1988 Republican presidential nomination, former U.S. Sen. Paul Laxalt announced in August that he was withdrawing from the race because of inability to raise the needed campaign funds. Governor Bryan set up an exploratory committee to assist him in determining whether or not to run for the U.S. Senate in 1988 against incumbent Chic Hecht, (R).

DON W. DRIGGS
University of Nevada-Reno

NEVADA • Information Highlights

Area: 110,561 sq mi (286 352 km²).
Population (July 1, 1986): 963,000.
Chief Cities (July 1, 1986 est.): Carson City, the capital (1980 census), 32,022; Las Vegas, 193,240; Reno, 111,420.
Government (1987): *Chief Officers*—governor, Richard H. Bryan (D); lt. gov., Robert J. Miller (D). *Legislature*—Senate, 21 members; Assembly, 42 members.
State Finances (fiscal year 1986): *Revenue,* $2,391,000,000; *expenditure,* $1,917,000,000.
Personal Income (1986): $14,870,000,000; per capita, $15,437.
Labor Force (June 1987): *Civilian labor force,* 566,300; *unemployed,* 32,600 (5.7% of total force).
Education: *Enrollment* (fall 1985)—public elementary schools, 107,070; public secondary, 47,878; colleges and universities, 43,656. *Public school expenditures* (1985–86), $440,000,000 ($3,142 per pupil).

NEW BRUNSWICK

The province elected its first Liberal government in 17 years when voters turned massively against the ruling Conservatives.

Politics. A political era came to an end Oct. 13, 1987, when the Conservative government of Premier Richard Hatfield was crushingly defeated after ruling the province since 1970. The Liberals under 39-year-old Frank McKenna swept all 58 seats in the provincial legislature, leaving it without an official opposition. McKenna's new 21-member cabinet included a woman, Aldea Landry, as second in order of precedence. Mrs. Landry was named president of the executive council and minister responsible for federal-provincial relations.

Hatfield, 57, who lost his own seat in the Liberal rampage, was the principal issue in the election, as voters appeared to render their verdict on his personal behavior and judgment. In 1985 the premier was acquitted of possessing drugs after a quantity of marijuana was found in his luggage. Later that year, two students accused him of giving them cocaine at a party in 1981. Hatfield denied these allegations and no charges were laid, but the whispers they

NEW BRUNSWICK • Information Highlights

Area: 28,355 sq mi (73 440 km^2).
Population (1986 census): 710,422.
Chief Cities (1986 census): Fredericton, the capital, 44,352; Saint John, 76,381; Moncton, 55,468.
Government (1987): *Chief Officers*—lt. gov., Gilbert Finn; premier, Frank McKenna (Liberal). *Legislature*—Legislative Assembly, 58 members.
Provincial Finances (1987–88 fiscal year budget): *Revenues*, $2,878,000,000; *expenditures*, $3,300,000,000.
Personal Income (average weekly earnings, July 1987): $404.60.
Labor Force (September 1987, seasonally adjusted): *Employed* workers, 15 years of age and over, 319,000; *Unemployed*, 41,000 (12.9%).
Education (1987–88): *Enrollment*—elementary and secondary schools, 139,400 pupils; postsecondary—universities, 15,050; community colleges, 2,300.
(All monetary figures are in Canadian dollars.)

generated undoubtedly contributed to his and the Tories' shattering defeat.

Fiscal. The Tories' last budget, tabled in the legislature April 29 by Finance Minister John Baxter, brought the news that New Brunswick had lost the battle to balance its books. Baxter forecast a 1987-88 deficit of $97.4 million, compared with the $7 million deficit foreseen in the budget one year earlier.

In unveiling the earlier budget, Baxter had pledged eventually to erase the province's operating deficit altogether. A budget report made public July 12, 1987, showed that the deficit for 1986–87 was actually $72.4 million—ten times what had been predicted.

Vice-Regal. A prominent Acadian businessman, Gilbert Finn of Dieppe, was named lieutenant governor of New Brunswick August 14, by Prime Minister Brian Mulroney. Finn, 69, took up his appointment September 1, on the retirement of George Stanley.

Medical. The federal government announced June 5 that it was returning $353,000 to New Brunswick in response to the province's action in eliminating extra billing by doctors under shared-cost, the New Brunswick medical-care insurance plan. The money had been withheld from federal contributions until the province complied with federal legislation requiring an end to billing by doctors beyond the fee schedule.

Government Agreements. Agriculture Minister Hank Myers announced in Fredericton on April 16 that New Brunswick and the federal government had signed a shared-cost $13 million agreement aimed at making the province self-sufficient in feed-grain output by the year 2000. At present, 60% of the province's feed grains is imported.

The federal government would provide $100 million and New Brunswick $45 million for road construction in the province under a five-year agreement signed June 29.

JOHN BEST, *"Canada World News"*

NEWFOUNDLAND

Political winds blew gustily around provincial and federal Conservatives in Newfoundland in 1987. In December 1986, the New Democratic Party (NDP) had won a seat in a provincial by-election; then, in July, the Conservatives lost to the NDP in a federal by-election. Voters seemed to be expressing dissatisfaction with the Tory Party and the economy.

The Liberals did not fare much better. In March the provincial caucus, by a vote of 13-1, called for a leadership convention in order to resolve complaints about the autocratic style of leader Leo Barry. Only months before, Barry had been confirmed in office by a 97% vote of the party membership. In April when Clyde Wells announced his candidacy, Barry withdrew and the Liberals had a new leader.

Fishing Controversies. Leadership was the issue for the 23,000-member Newfoundland Fishermen's Union in 1987. In March the president of the union, Richard Cashin, and the executive decided to dissolve their affiliation with the international United Food and Commercial Workers and to form instead a new union (the Newfoundland Fishermen, Food and Allied Workers), affiliated with the Canadian Auto Workers. The Canadian Labour Congress refused to act on charges of union raiding. The legal battles that ensued remained unresolved at year's end. Because the price of fish remained high, however, fishermen seemed content. The province's largest fish processing firm, Fishery Products International, was privatized in March and raised more than $150 million in bond sales.

The international fishery produced headlines in 1987. Canada disputed the French claim to a 200-mile (322-km) limit around the tiny French islands of St. Pierre and Miquelon. Unwilling to take the matter to arbitration, the French continued to overfish, taking five times their cod allocation in the waters within the dis-

NEWFOUNDLAND • Information Highlights

Area: 156,649 sq mi (405 720 km^2).
Population (1986 census): 568,349.
Chief Cities (1986 census): St. John's, the capital, 96,216; Corner Brook, 22,719.
Government (1987): *Chief Officers*—lt. gov., James A. McGrath; premier, A. Brian Peckford (Progressive Conservative). *Legislature*—Legislative Assembly, 52 members.
Provincial Finances (1987–88 fiscal year budget): *Revenues*, $2,424,000,000; *expenditures*, $2,800,000,000.
Personal Income (average weekly earnings, July 1987): $418.28.
Labor Force (September 1987, seasonally adjusted: *Employed* workers, 15 years of age and over, 229,000; *Unemployed*, 40,000 (17.5%).
Education (1987–88): *Enrollment*—elementary and secondary schools, 136,000 pupils; postsecondary—universities, 11,610; community colleges, 3,000.
(All monetary figures are in Canadian dollars.)

puted zone off southern Newfoundland. When the federal government secretly signed a treaty giving the French a fish quota in Newfoundland waters, in exchange for an agreement to go to arbitration, Newfoundland Premier A. Brian Peckford objected: the province had not been consulted about the gift of its fish resources. Ottawa, by way of apology, closed Canadian ports to French vessels, while awaiting the results of negotiations.

Economy. When the Newfoundland House of Assembly opened in February, the government pledged to implement many of the recommendations of the Royal Commission on Employment and Unemployment. Unemployment rates topped those of any other province, and—although personal income taxes and the 12% sales tax are the highest in Canada—the provincial budget produced a record $173 million deficit.

The promise of oil development remained unfulfilled for another year, although Petro-Canada plans to develop the Terra Nova oil field off Newfoundland beginning in 1989. In the meantime, oil-related federal spending of more than $40 million gave some help to the Marystown shipyard and to postsecondary education in petroleum technology.

The provincial government was largely supportive of federal initiatives on two important national issues: the Meech-Lake revisions to the Constitution and the agreement with the United States on the issue of free trade.

SUSAN MCCORQUODALE
Memorial University of Newfoundland

NEW HAMPSHIRE

Throughout 1987 economic conditions in New Hampshire demonstrated the adage that prosperity can create its own problems. This was evident throughout the state as the jobless rate dipped to 2.1% for August. What would cause envy in many regions of the country was causing anguish in New Hampshire. The reason was unfilled jobs.

Economy. Despite entry-level jobs paying at least $4.00 to $5.00 per hour, *Help Wanted* signs continued to be displayed even after the summer tourists had departed. With essentially full employment, the sustained boom made it difficult for many firms in the state to expand and forced others to reconsider locating there. Throughout the year, New Hampshire sustained the lowest unemployment rate in the nation. Gains in personal income and the highest population growth in New England suggested the pervasive impact of the boom.

Another indication of changing times was the *Money* magazine ranking of Nashua, once an ordinary textile-manufacturing center, as the best among 329 cities in the country in which to live.

NEW HAMPSHIRE • Information Highlights

Area: 9,279 sq mi (24 032 km²).
Population (July 1, 1986): 1,027,000.
Chief Cities (1980 census): Concord, the capital, 30,400; Manchester, 90,936; Nashua, 67,865.
Government (1987): *Chief Officer*—governor, John H. Sununu (R). *General Court*—Senate, 24 members; House of Representatives, 400 members.
State Finances (fiscal year 1986): *Revenue,* $1,548,000,000; *expenditure,* $1,348,000,000.
Personal Income (1986): $16,339,000,000; per capita, $15,911.
Labor Force (June 1987): *Civilian labor force,* 601,200; *unemployed,* 14,800 (2.5% of total force).
Education: *Enrollment* (fall 1985)—public elementary schools, 106,912; public secondary, 54,062; colleges and universities, 52,283. *Public school expenditures* (1985–86), $454,000,000 ($3,115 per pupil).

Prosperity brought record revenues into the state treasury. At the end of the fiscal year in June, tax revenues were $537.7 million, $87.3 million higher than the amount projected. The surplus made it possible for the legislature to pass a record $2.7 billion biennial budget and approve tax reductions.

Conservation. A unique public-private effort enacted by the General Court was the $20 million appropriation for the Trust for New Hampshire Lands, a nonprofit organization that seeks to buy and protect as much as 100,000 acres (40 469 ha) of prime recreation land. Using state funds and private donations, the trust will attempt to preserve key parcels throughout the state, especially in areas endangered by rapid development.

Nuclear-Power Problems. The year had its disturbing features, none more so than the continuing saga of the Seabrook nuclear-power plant. The inability to develop an approved emergency evacuation plan, primarily due to disagreement with state officials in Massachusetts, plagued the owners. The absence of a plan meant that the $5 billion facility could not begin generating power even though construction of unit 1 was complete and ready to go on line. As a result, Public Service Company, Seabrook's principal investor, has been pushed to the brink of bankruptcy. In mid-October the company defaulted on $37 million in debt-interest payments. Unable to charge customers for its Seabrook investment until the plant generates power, Public Service seemed likely to file for voluntary bankruptcy soon. Still uncertain was the question of how much Seabrook power would raise electric rates. Should rates rise dramatically, most agreed that the state's economic health would be jeopardized.

During the spring the state experienced serious floods which caused extensive damage in several regions including the Merrimack Valley and the Ossippee region. Estimates of damage throughout the state totaled $10.7 million.

WILLIAM L. TAYLOR
Plymouth State College

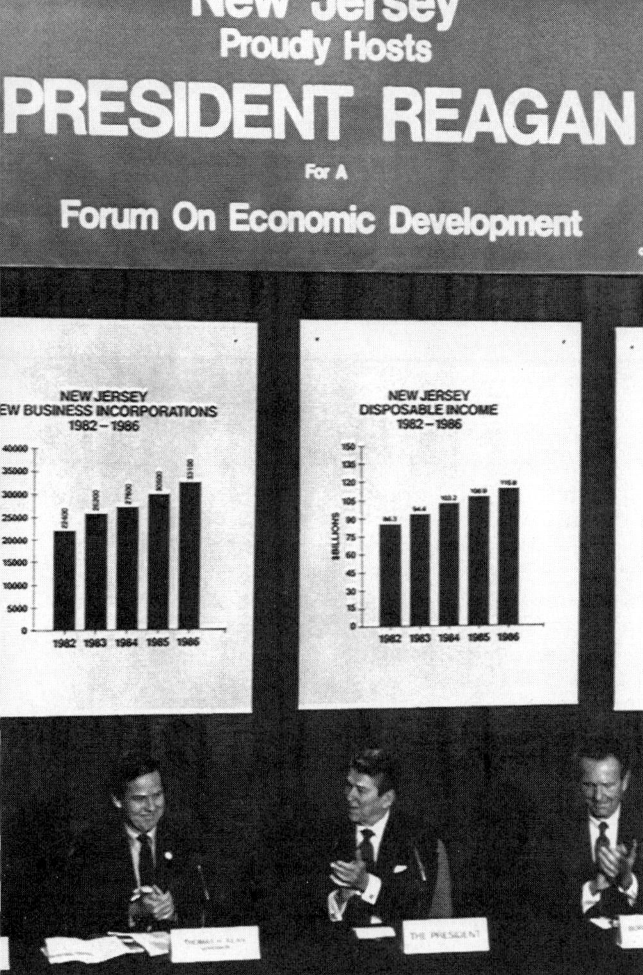

AP/Wide World

New Jersey Gov. Thomas Kean (left) *welcomed President Reagan in October for a forum on economic issues. The state's cities suffered from declining federal aid.*

NEW JERSEY

State aid to cities and environmental issues were the dominant concerns in New Jersey during 1987.

State Aid to Cities. In the midst of a booming state economy, New Jersey's major cities suffered from the cancellation of the federal revenue-sharing program that had gone into effect in 1986. A dispute between Gov. Thomas H. Kean (R) and city mayors arose when the governor refused to provide for state funds to take up the slack. Kean's $10.1 billion budget made no mention of urban relief, and the prevailing view in the executive department was that city governments must place more emphasis on forming partnerships with the private sector in order to achieve financial stability. However, negotiations between the governor and several mayors produced a $206 million aid package that would be paid for by repeal of the state homeowners' property tax deduction. But repeal was unacceptable to the Democratic leadership of the Senate and the Republican-controlled Assembly, who were afraid of voter reaction in a year when both houses of the legislature were up for reelection. After lengthy discussions between the governor, legislators, and municipal lobbyists, a $50 million compromise emerged, providing for state aid on a selective basis.

Tension between state and local authorities was also seen in the field of education, with particular agitation over the state's authority to control local school districts that do not meet standards of quality. A bill that would have expanded the state's power to dismiss officials in districts that had not complied with orders to improve standards failed passage in the legislature, but its supporters vowed to continue the fight.

Environment. The long-standing conflict between development and environmental protection appeared in New Jersey in a number of forms in 1987. The New Jersey Planning Commission pointed out that much of the state's economic growth was taking place in a haphazard manner that would lead to undesirable results by the year 2000. This was particularly true for the revitalization of the declining communities on the west bank of the Hudson River, where office buildings and high-priced residential units were going up with little regard for coordination of sewers or mass-transit systems. Similar concerns were voiced for the area along Route 1 connecting Princeton and New Brunswick, where a farming economy had abruptly given way to high-tech sprawl and traffic gridlock.

More immediate notice was given to the Jersey Shore over the summer. Several of the most widely used beaches had to be closed on account of water pollution and debris that was thought to have come from careless practices at a waste treatment plant in New York City.

NEW JERSEY • Information Highlights

Area: 7,787 sq mi (20 169 km^2).
Population (July 1, 1986): 7,620,000.
Chief Cities (July 1, 1984 est.): Trenton, the capital (1980 census), 92,124; Newark, 316,300; Jersey City, 219,480; Paterson, 139,160; Elizabeth, 106,560.
Government (1987): *Chief Officer*—governor, Thomas H. Kean (R). *Legislature*—Senate, 40 members; General Assembly, 80 members.
State Finances (fiscal year 1986): *Revenue,* $17,558,000,000; *expenditure,* $16,043,000,000.
Personal Income (1986): $141,919,000,000; per capita, $18,626.
Labor Force (June 1987): *Civilian labor force,* 4,028,800; *unemployed,* 166,800 (4.1% of total force).
Education: *Enrollment* (fall 1985)—public elementary schools, 740,497; public secondary, 375,697; colleges and universities, 297,658. *Public school expenditures* (1985–86), $5,722,000,000 ($5,544 per pupil).

Seeking long-term protection for the coastline, Governor Kean proposed a New Jersey Coastal Commission, modeled after similar bodies in California and Oregon. The commission would have jurisdiction over licensing of development schemes and spending of federal and state monies in four designated locations. Adoption of the plan was uncertain.

Other. Attention was focused early in the year on the custody fight in New Jersey Superior Court between Mary Beth Whitehead and Mr. and Mrs. William Stern over "Baby M." Mrs. Whitehead, who had carried and given birth to the child under a surrogate-motherhood contract, refused to turn the baby over to Mr. Stern, the natural father. After a lengthy trial, Judge Harvey R. Sorkow declared the surrogacy contract valid and awarded custody of the child to the Sterns. (*See also* feature article, page 55.)

Although no statewide elections were held, the entire legislature of 40 senators and 80 assemblymen was up for reelection. The Democrats and the Republicans retained control of the Senate and Assembly, respectively. However, the GOP's margin in the Assembly was reduced from 50R-30D to 42R-38D. Voters rejected a bond issue to build a baseball stadium in the Meadowlands.

HERMANN K. PLATT, *St. Peter's College*

NEW MEXICO

Slowly improving economic conditions and continued problems in the prison system received wide attention in New Mexico in 1987.

Economy. An unexpected $42 million surplus in the state treasury at the end of the 1987 fiscal year on June 30 was an indication of an economic upswing. Higher prices for natural gas and crude oil contributed to the surplus. The percentage of state revenues derived from these sources continued lower than in the past, however, with only 11.4% of revenues coming from gas and oil leasing and severance taxes in fiscal 1987, as compared with 34.4% in fiscal 1982.

Technical industries and services, such as Sandia Laboratories and Los Alamos National Laboratories, remained a significant factor in the state's economy, employing more than 60,000 people. To bolster this segment of the economy, state legislators and politicians made a bid to have New Mexico designated as the site of the federal government's new super collider atom smasher (*see* PHYSICS). Gov. Garrey Carruthers convened a special session of the state legislature in July which appropriated $10 million for the purchase of land on which to build the super collider.

Prisons. On July 4, seven prisoners escaped from the maximum security unit of the state prison in Santa Fe. The escapees included two men serving life sentences for murder. All were eventually captured, some up to several weeks later in California. The escape highlighted continuing problems in the state's prison system, which has had 10 administrators in 18 years and spends more per prisoner than all but one other state. Chief difficulties include overcrowding, understaffing, and violence among prison gangs.

Tourism. On May 8, President Reagan signed legislation designating the Santa Fe Trail as a national historic trail. In the 19th century the Santa Fe Trail linked Hispanic New Mexico with Independence, MO, a western commercial outpost of the United States. The trail enters New Mexico on its northern border, passes various historical points such as Fort Union (1851–91), near Las Vegas, NM, and terminates on the Plaza in Santa Fe.

Other. On April 2, Governor Carruthers signed legislation increasing the speed limit on interstate roads in rural areas to 65 mph (105 km/h).

Although Pope John Paul II did not stop in New Mexico on his 1987 visit to the United States, he did broadcast a personal message to the state's numerous, predominantly Hispanic and Indian, Catholic population. He urged these Catholics to hold fast to the 400-year tradition of Catholicism in New Mexico.

King Juan Carlos and Queen Sophia of Spain toured Santa Fe, once a remote provincial capital of the Spanish Empire, on September 29–30. Center of activities for the royal visit, the first ever by a Spanish monarch to New Mexico, was the Palace of the Governors, the original Spanish capitol building in Santa Fe and presently the oldest public building in the United States.

The New Mexico Museum of Indian Arts and Culture opened in Santa Fe on July 11. The state-owned museum planned to exhibit examples of 10,000 years of Indian tools and art.

MICHAEL L. OLSEN
New Mexico Highlands University

NEW MEXICO • Information Highlights

Area: 121,593 sq mi (314 925 km^2).
Population (July 1, 1986): 1,479,000.
Chief Cities (1980 census): Santa Fe, the capital, 48,953; Albuquerque (July 1, 1986 est.): 366,750; Las Cruces, 45,086.
Government (1987–88): *Chief Officers*—governor, Garrey Carruthers (R); lt. gov., Jack L. Stahl (R). *Legislature*—Senate, 42 members; House of Representatives, 70 members.
State Finances (fiscal year 1986): *Revenue,* $3,925,000,000; *expenditure,* $3,300,000,000.
Personal Income (1986): $16,894,000,000; per capita, $11,422.
Labor Force (June 1987): *Civilian labor force,* 681,200; *unemployed,* 60,400 (8.9% of total force).
Education: *Enrollment* (fall 1985)—public elementary schools, 187,479; public secondary, 90,072; colleges and universities, 68,295. *Public school expenditures* (1985–86), $849,000,000 ($3,374 per pupil).

NEW YORK

Public corruption—from prosecutions of elected officials to debates over the proper role of partisan politics in government—dominated the news in New York in 1987. The scandals that erupted in New York City in 1986 spilled over into state government in 1987. By year's end, several prominent political figures were facing trial, imprisonment, or fines.

Ethics and Corruption. Gov. Mario Cuomo (D), beginning his second four-year term after being reelected by the largest margin in New York State history, set the ethics agenda by challenging the state legislature early in the year to adopt stricter rules of conduct for itself, including limits on legislators' appearances before state agencies and broader financial-disclosure requirements. Newly elected Assembly Speaker Mel Miller, however, eager to demonstrate independence from fellow Democrat Cuomo, instead joined with the Republican-dominated Senate to pass a less stringent measure. Cuomo's veto of that bill touched off a months-long fight between the legislature and the popular governor, who was backed by newspaper editorial boards statewide. The battle ended when Miller and Senate Majority Leader Warren M. Anderson (R-Binghamton) accepted a tough code of ethics and legislation providing for stronger controls and audits on all state agencies, including the legislature.

Governor Cuomo during the year also created a Commission on Integrity in Government, which hired a sizable staff and launched public hearings during the fall on issues ranging from campaign financing to government contracting practices.

In September, as debate continued over the proper role of partisan politics in government, a Manhattan grand jury indicted State Senate Minority Leader Manfred Ohrenstein (D-Manhattan), three other current or former Democratic senators, and a key Ohrenstein aide, charging that they used the Senate staff for election campaign work. Legislative leaders claimed that the staff of a part-time legislature like New York's should be free to do political work part-time. Probes of the Assembly Democratic majority also were under way.

The debate over ethics only served to enhance the reputation of Cuomo, who was evaluating a race for the White House as 1987 began. Although he announced in mid-February that he would not run for president, speculation continued that he would enter the race after the first Democratic primaries in 1988. The governor's stepped-up speaking schedule and a visit to the Soviet Union in September did little to quell such talk, despite Cuomo's repeated disavowals of candidacy.

Other Legislation. In addition to the ethics bills, the six-month legislative session produced the largest state tax cut in New York history: a $4.4 billion personal income-tax-cut program and a corporate-tax-revision package that reduced the top corporate-tax rate from 10% to 9% for most businesses and 8% for small businesses. Legislators also enacted a five-year, $8.6 billion capital plan to begin rebuilding the facilities of New York City's Metropolitan Transportation Authority, and approved bills to ease state prison crowding by adding 4,800 beds. Under terms of legislation enacted in 1986, the state also moved toward a public takeover of the financially troubled Long

AP/Wide World

Mario Cuomo, New York's popular Democratic governor, maintained a heavy speaking schedule across the country but insisted that he would not run for president in 1988.

NEW YORK • Information Highlights

Area: 49,108 sq mi (127 190 km²).
Population (July 1, 1986): 17,772,000.
Chief Cities (July 1, 1986 est.): Albany, the capital, 101,727 (1980 census); New York, 7,262,700; Buffalo, 324,820; Rochester, 235,970; Yonkers, 186,080; Syracuse, 160,750.
Government (1987): *Chief Officers*—governor, Mario M. Cuomo (D); lt. gov., Stan Lundine (D). *Legislature*—Senate, 61 members; Assembly, 150 members.
State Finances (fiscal year 1986): *Revenue,* $50,909,000,000; *expenditure,* $43,139,000,000.
Personal Income (1986): $304,095,000,000; per capita, $17,111.
Labor Force (June 1987): *Civilian labor force,* 8,554,100; *unemployed,* 392,000 (4.6% of total force).
Education: *Enrollment* (fall 1985)—public elementary schools, 1,703,430; public secondary, 917,948; colleges and universities, 1,000,098; *Public school expenditures* (1985–86), $13,000,000,000 ($5,616 per pupil).

Island Lighting Company, with an eye toward mothballing the unlicensed and unpopular Shoreham nuclear power plant on Long Island.

The state also launched a program of rebuilding state roads and bridges, the need for which was spotlighted in April when a New York State Thruway bridge collapsed into rain-swollen Schoharie Creek, killing ten persons as cars and trucks plunged into the rushing waters. (*See* ENGINEERING, CIVIL.)

REX SMITH
Albany Bureau Chief, "Newsday"

NEW YORK CITY

Corruption scandals involving politicians and public officials, the fight against AIDS (acquired immune deficiency syndrome), and simmering racial tensions that sometimes turned violent dominated the 1987 headlines in New York City. Long-term urban problems—drugs, growing numbers of homeless people, crime, and commuting hardships—also made news.

The economic news was good most of the year. Wall Street, shrugging off an insider trading scandal, soared to new highs before crashing in the autumn (*see* STOCKS AND BONDS). The city economy was robust, tourism brushed record levels, thousands of jobs were created despite the departure of some major corporations, and the city ended its fiscal year with a $666 million surplus.

Corruption. As 1987 began, Mayor Edward I. Koch said the city was healing after a year of the worst corruption scandals in a generation. "The scalpel of the law is making us well again," he said. Stanley M. Friedman, former Bronx Democratic leader, was sentenced to 12 years in jail for racketeering, and the scandal-ridden Parking Violations Bureau had a new team and improved morale.

Despite the mayor's upbeat assessment, the scandals were not over. U.S. Rep. Mario Biaggi (D) of the Bronx and Meade H. Esposito, the former Brooklyn Democratic leader, were convicted of unlawful gratuities charges but were acquitted of more serious bribery and conspiracy charges. Former Transportation Commissioner Anthony Ameruso was found guilty of lying under oath. State Supreme Court Justice Francis X. Smith of Queens was convicted of perjury and sentenced to a year in jail in a case involving cable television franchises. In a related case, John A. Zaccaro, the husband of the 1984 Democratic vice-presidential candidate, was acquitted of trying to extort a bribe from a cable TV company. And former Cultural Affairs Commissioner Bess Myerson was indicted in October on charges of seeking to influence a judge who was presiding over her companion's divorce case.

Race Relations and Crime. Race relations in New York, exacerbated by disparities in jobs,

AP/Wide World

Bernhard Goetz, New York City's "subway gunman," was acquitted of murder in a highly publicized 1984 shooting but was sentenced to six months in jail for gun possession.

education, housing, and income, were deeply troubled. The police said race-related incidents rose sharply, and Mayor Koch and leaders of black and Hispanic communities called racism pervasive. Three white youths were found guilty of manslaughter in a December 1986 attack in Howard Beach, Queens, in which a black man was killed by a car as he fled from white youths. A fourth defendant was acquitted of all charges. The case drew national attention and heightened racial tensions in the city.

In other trials, Bernhard Goetz was acquitted of attempted murder and other serious charges, but was sentenced to six months in jail for illegal gun possession in the shooting of four black teenagers who asked him for money on a subway in 1984; former U.S. Labor Secretary Raymond J. Donovan was found not guilty of larceny in a subway construction fraud case, and 17 people were convicted of drug charges in the "pizza connection" case (*see* CRIME).

Crack, the smokable cocaine derivative, played havoc with hundreds of lives. Led by a nearly 15% jump in murders, serious crimes in New York City rose 5% during 1986, and the police said much of it was due to crack.

AIDS. As cases of AIDS continued to rise, the city and private groups pressed for education programs and carried the fight to the streets to help intravenous drug users, homosexuals, and other AIDS victims, who faced ostracism, loss of jobs, and other problems.

Other. The city sheltered a record number of homeless people during the winter and, under a new Koch administration policy, hospitalized those deemed incapable of caring for themselves.

An 11-day strike in January disrupted Long Island Rail Road commuters. Higher taxicab fares and bridge-and-tunnel tolls took effect. And $8.6 billion was earmarked to rebuild the city subway system.

With the Statue of Liberty having reopened in 1986, restoration efforts turned to Ellis Island, were 12 million immigrants entered the United States between 1892 and 1943. Across New York Harbor, another sight—the infamous garbage barge from Long Island—reappeared after an eight-week, four-nation odyssey in a vain search for a dump site; the stuff was finally burned at a Brooklyn incinerator (*see* special report, page 225).

Mayor Koch suffered a slight stroke in August, but after 72 hours in the hospital and a few days rest at home he was back at City Hall. Mario Merola, the Bronx district attorney for 15 years, died suddenly in October.

Schools Chancellor Nathan Quinones, under pressure because of failures in the school system, announced that he would retire at the end of the year, and the search for a new top school official was begun.

ROBERT D. MCFADDEN
"The New York Times"

NEW ZEALAND

In the general election on August 15, the voters of New Zealand returned a Labour government to office for the first time in 49 years. Prime Minister David Lange began his second three-year term with a 19-seat Labour majority in the 97-seat Parliament (expanded from 95).

Election. Polls earlier in the year had given Labour substantial leads in popular support, with the June figure of 57% being the highest ever received by any party. When Prime Minister Lange called the election on June 30, his party held a 26-point lead in the polls. Labour took a deliberately low-key (some said overconfident) approach to the campaign, and the opposition National Party, led by Jim Bolger, greatly reduced Labour's lead. Domestic economic issues dominated the campaign, and the election essentially amounted to a referendum on "Rogernomics"—the free-market approach of Finance Minister Roger Douglas.

The final tally showed both major parties increasing their vote total from the previous election in 1984. Labour won nearly 48% of the popular vote (up from 42%), and the National Party took 45% (up from 35%). The minor parties all lost ground. Translated into parliamentary representation, Labour secured 58 seats and National 39. Labour's 19-seat majority was four more than it held previously. The Democrats (formerly the Social Credit Party) lost their only two seats, leaving only the two principal parties with representation in the legislature. Labour held onto its Wairarapa seat by a single vote, the smallest margin in the country's electoral history.

NEW ZEALAND • Information Highlights

Official Name: New Zealand.
Location: Southwest Pacific Ocean.
Area: 103,737 sq mi (268 680 km²).
Population (mid-1987 est.): 3,300,000.
Chief Cities (1986 census): Wellington, the capital, 352,035; Auckland 889,225; Christchurch, 333,191; Hamilton, 167,711.
Government: *Head of state,* Elizabeth II, queen, represented by Archbishop Sir Paul Reeves, governor-general (took office Nov. 1985). *Head of government,* David Lange, prime minister (took office July 26, 1984). *Legislature* (unicameral)—House of Representatives.
Monetary Unit: New Zealand dollar (1.6155 N.Z. dollars equal U.S.$1, Nov. 17, 1987).
Gross Domestic Product (year ending March 1985): $21,700,000,000.
Economic Index (1986): *Consumer Prices* (1980 = 100), all items, 199.6; food, 184.6.
Foreign Trade (1986 U.S.$): *Imports,* $6,135,000,000; *exports,* $5,944,000,000.

Administration and Opposition. Prime Minister Lange's cabinet, announced August 19, was expanded to 20 members, including two women, two Maoris, and 16 ministers who had served in the previous government. In a surprise move, Lange relinquished his foreign-affairs portfolio to Russell Marshall and became minister of education.

In the wake of National's election defeat, George Gair surrendered his position as deputy party leader, and Ruth Richardson, a vigorous free-market advocate, became the party's finance spokesman.

Economy and Budget. The inflation rate of 18.2% during calendar-year 1986 was not a good omen, and the chief economic indicators continued in a similar vein in 1987. Unemployment rates rose from 5.9% of the work force in January to 6.8% (including those on subsidized work schemes) in July; the latter was the highest recorded figure since the Great Depression of the 1930s. Public concern was reflected in opinion polls, where unemployment was invariably cited as the single most important problem confronting the nation. By contrast, law, social, and racial issues were the prime concerns of less than one in five respondents.

The midyear budget confirmed the promise of Finance Minister Douglas that it would contain no election-year handouts. The budget, covering the year ending March 31, 1988, addressed the rising public debt by proposing the sale of government assets. It provided modest relief for low-income families and foreshadowed a revision of the taxation structure, by which 50% of revenues would come from individual taxpayers. Spending was projected to rise by only 10.5%, with the relatively small increase contributing to a forecast surplus of $379 million in government accounts; Douglas said that the surplus also would be used to start paying back the debt. A crackdown on overseas tax havens was threatened, but otherwise the budget adhered to a consistent free-market line.

Other Developments. As part of a radical restructuring of the New Zealand public service, nine government agencies were reorganized into state-owned corporations on April 1. On June 4, Parliament passed the Nuclear-Free Zone, Disarmament and Arms Control Bill; the hotly debated measure bans nuclear weapons and bars port visits to New Zealand by nuclear-powered vessels.

GRAHAM BUSH
University of Auckland

NIGERIA

The announcement by the military government of Gen. Ibrahim Babangida of a detailed plan for the return to civilian rule was the key political development in Nigeria during 1987. Violence broke out between Christians and Muslims. The economy showed improvement.

Domestic Affairs. In a white paper issued July 1, General Babangida unveiled detailed plans for a return to civilian government, pushing back the date two years from the promised 1990 target. The five-year transition would result in a government based largely on the 1979 Constitution. Nonparty local council elections were held in December 1987; a Constituent Assembly would convene in 1988; political parties would be allowed in 1989; state elections would be held in 1990; a census would be taken in 1991; and federal executive and legislative elections would be held in 1992.

Earlier in the year, on March 6, the endemic hatred between Christians and Muslims in northern Nigeria flared into open violence. The rioting began in Kaduna state, where Christians are a majority. Radical students, fearing that Muslim law would be extended throughout the nation, attacked and burned three mosques and killed seven Muslim teachers. Muslims quickly retaliated, attacking Christian homes, businesses, and churches in several northern cities. Before the army could restore order a week later, 15 persons had been killed; more than 1,000 persons were detained. General Babangida subsequently banned all social and religious organizations at the nation's universities.

The government also continued to have problems with the media. Two newspaper editors in Plateau state were arrested, and the popular magazine *Newswatch* was banned for six months.

Economic Development. The stringent economic measures begun by the government during 1986 continued to produce results. Inflation was checked, and spending by both the federal and state governments was reduced. The corrupt import licensing system was abolished, as were the commodity boards which had held down prices for agricultural produce. The various measures were part of a movement toward a free-market economy.

In an effort to reschedule its $20 billion foreign debt, Nigeria in late 1986 had negotiated agreements with commercial creditor banks and Western lender governments. There followed a $450 million loan from the World Bank and, in February 1987, an $825 million loan from the International Monetary Fund. The latter was the key element in Babangida's plan to revitalize the economy.

Petroleum production, which provides 90% of Nigeria's export earnings, continued to increase, and the improvement in the world market price for Nigeria's "sweet crude" provided the government with extra capital. The attempt to diversify was having mixed results, but the revitalized rubber industry was operating at 60% capacity and employing more than 25,000 persons. Palm oil production still did not reach pre-Biafran War (mid-1960s) levels, but output continued to grow. Despite making agricultural development a high priority, Nigeria still spent an inordinate amount of money on imported food. The government continued its experiments in counter-trade agreements as a short-term expedient.

Foreign Affairs. The major foreign policy aim of General Babangida's government was to convince its European and U.S. creditors that the necessary steps were being taken to make Nigeria solvent. The government maintained its support within the Organization of African Unity (OAU) for the Habré regime in Chad and for a hard line against South Africa. Differences with the United States over South Africa were eased by the visit to Lagos in January of U.S. Secretary of State George Shultz.

HARRY A. GAILEY
San Jose State University

NIGERIA • Information Highlights

Official Name: Federal Republic of Nigeria.
Location: West Africa.
Area: 356,668 sq mi (923 770 km²).
Population (mid-1987 est.): 108,600,000.
Chief City (1983 est.): Lagos, the capital, 1,097,000.
Government: *Head of state and government,* Maj. Gen. Ibrahim Babangida, president, federal military government (took office Aug. 27, 1985). *Legislature*—Armed Forces Ruling Council; National Council of Ministers and National Council of States.
Monetary Unit: Naira (3.899 naira equals U.S.$1, July 1987).
Economic Index (1985): *Consumer Prices* (1980 = 100), all items, 236,2; food, 251.6.
Foreign Trade (1985 U.S.$): *Imports,* $6,205,000,000; *exports,* $13,134,000,000.

NORTH CAROLINA

Jockeying for position in preparation for the 1988 elections was a favorite pastime of North Carolina politicians in 1987.

General Assembly. A record 135-day legislative session featured both intraparty bickering between Senate and House Democrats and partisan finger pointing between Republican Jim Martin—the nation's only governor without the veto—and the Democrat-controlled General Assembly. Despite the squabbles, a record $19.6 billion biennial budget was passed, including more than $500 million in new money for education, much of it to continue implementation of the Basic Education Program designed to provide a "floor" of support for each of the 141 school districts. An increase in the state corporate income tax, offset partially by repeal of local property taxes on business inventories, provided additional funds for school buildings and upgraded facilities. Bipartisan support for increased spending was accompanied by demands for stricter accountability on the part of the educational bureaucracy, with a correlation between additional appropriations and higher educational standards. Merit pay continued to be opposed by teachers' organizations.

"Pork barrel" appropriations, by which legislative leaders in the past sought to keep members in line, were made fairer by apportionment among more delegates. English was made the official language of the state, and consumers applauded a "lemon law" governing the sale of defective automobiles.

The Economy. General Fund collections for the fiscal year ending June 30 were up more than 10%, and unemployment remained above 4%. The state's native Piedmont Airlines, which won a prolonged contest to provide direct service to London from Charlotte, was purchased by USAir Group for $1.59 billion.

American Airlines opened a hub at Raleigh-Durham Airport and at year's end was servicing more than a hundred flights a day. The decision of the huge RJR Nabisco Corporation to move its headquarters from Winston-Salem to Atlanta was more a blow to the state's pride than to its economy.

Tourism, the fastest growing industry, brought in more than $5 billion, three quarters of it from out of state. The motion-picture industry continued its expansion. Meanwhile, with the eradication of the boll weevil, cotton made a comeback, 1987's crop reaching 100,000 acres (40 486 ha).

Politics and Religion. Republicans continued gaining proportionately in registration, although Democrats still held a 2.5-to-1 edge. The trend toward injection of religion into politics intensified. The widening split among Baptists resulted in the resignation of W. Randall Lolley, president of the Southeastern Baptist Theological Seminary. The Charlotte area in particular was caught up in the controversy surrounding Jim Bakker and the PTL Club, whose theme park is located just across the border in South Carolina.

H. G. JONES
University of North Carolina at Chapel Hill

NORTH CAROLINA • Information Highlights

Area: 52,669 sq mi (136 413 km²).
Population (July 1, 1986): 6,331,000.
Chief Cities (July 1, 1986 est.): Raleigh, the capital, 180,430; Charlotte, 352,070; Greensboro, 176,650; Winston-Salem, 148,080; Durham, 113,890.
Government (1987): *Chief Officers*—governor, James G. Martin (R); lt. gov., Robert B. Jordan (D). *General Assembly*—Senate, 50 members; House of Representatives, 120 members.
State Finances (fiscal year 1986): *Revenue,* $10,081,000,000; *expenditure,* $9,369,000,000.
Personal Income (1986): $78,763,000,000; per capita, $12,438.
Labor Force (June 1987): *Civilian labor force,* 3,316,200; *unemployed,* 161,500 (4.9% of total force).
Education: *Enrollment* (fall 1985)—public elementary schools, 749,451; public secondary, 336,714; colleges and universities, 327,288. *Public school expenditures* (1985–86), $3,416,000,000 ($3,366 per pupil).

NORTH DAKOTA

State legislators raised taxes in a near-record session in 1987, a longtime North Dakota officeholder opened a controversial bid for reelection, and the state lost its lieutenant governor to cancer.

Legislature. Meeting in emergency session in December 1986, state lawmakers increased the state sales tax 1% and raised the tax rate on personal income by almost 40%. Legislators returned to the Capitol again in January to launch a 73-day regular session—the third longest in state history—in which the sales tax was increased by another 0.5% and a one-year surcharge was slapped onto the income tax. Angry taxpayers filed petitions to refer the income tax-rate increase, but voters reaffirmed it in a March special election.

Cable-TV operators completed a petition drive to refer a bill that would tax cable service. Backers of a state lottery also filed petitions to give voters, who rejected a lottery in 1986, another chance to establish one. Both measures will be on the ballot in 1988.

Politics. Lt. Gov. Ruth Meiers, the first woman to hold that post in state history, died of cancer March 19 at age 61. Gov. George Sinner appointed Lloyd Omdahl to succeed her.

U.S. Sen. Quentin Burdick (D), a 27-year Senate veteran, announced that he would run for reelection in 1988 even though he will be 86 years old at the end of another six-year term. A group of Democratic legislators and local

NORTH DAKOTA • Information Highlights

Area: 70,702 sq mi (183 119 km²).
Population (July 1, 1986): 679,000.
Chief Cities (1980 census): Bismarck, the capital, 44,485; Fargo, 61,383; Grand Forks, 43,765; Minot, 32,843.
Government (1987): *Chief Officers*—governor, George A. Sinner (D); lt. gov., Lloyd Omadhl (D). *Legislative Assembly*—Senate, 53 members; House of Representatives, 106 members.
State Finances (fiscal year 1986): *Revenue*, $1,565,000,000; *expenditure*, $1,537,000,000.
Personal Income (1986): $8,470,000,000; per capita, $12,472.
Labor Force (June 1987): *Civilian labor force*, 341,200; *unemployed*, 14,400 (4.2% of total force).
Education: *Enrollment* (fall 1985)—public elementary schools, 83,702; public secondary, 34,868; colleges and universities, 37,939. *Public school expenditures* (1985–86), $343,000,000 ($3,059 per pupil).

party officials sent an open letter asking Burdick to step aside for a younger candidate, and Rep. Byron Dorgan (D) considered and then abandoned a challenge for the party's Senate endorsement. Burdick, chairman of the Senate's Environment and Public Works Committee and of the Appropriations Committee's subcommittee on agriculture, rural development, and related agencies, said he would be a traitor to his state if he stepped down after attaining a position of influence.

Republican Party officials suggested that Agriculture Commissioner Kent Jones (R) not seek reelection after an investigation found that was duped in a botched potato exporting deal that may cost the state $404,000.

Agriculture. Grain production was expected to decline by 8% in 1987. Production of durum, spring, and winter wheat was projected at a total 277.4 million bushels, compared with 289.9 million bushels in 1986. Barley production was expected to be 21% lower and corn 16% lower than the year before. Sugar-beet production, however, was up by 1%, and production of soybeans was expected to reach an all-time high, at 18.4 million bushels.

Economy. The state experienced its first bank failure in seven years when the Farmers State Bank of Maddock was closed by examiners May 8. A second bank, Citizens State Bank of Ray, was declared insolvent May 15.

Richard Rayl, director of the state office of management and budget, predicted a flat state economy for 1988. But Tax Commissioner Heidi Heitkamp reported that taxable sales were up for the first time in three years.

Crime. The murder and assault convictions of 11 men accused of the death on the Fort Totten Indian Reservation of a former policeman from nearby Devil's Lake were overturned by a three-judge appeals panel, on the ground that all the defendants could not be tried together.

JIM NEUMANN, *"The Forum," Fargo*

NORTHWEST TERRITORIES

A general election for the 24-member Legislative Assembly was held in the Northwest Territories (NWT) in October 1987. There was a large voter turnout of 71%.

New Government. The new assembly chose Dennis Patterson of Iqaluit (formerly Frobisher Bay) as the government leader. Patterson is the first person from the eastern Arctic to hold that position, which is similar in function to a provincial premier. It also selected an eight-member Executive Council (cabinet), including two Inuit (Eskimo), one Dene (Indian), and two Metis ministers. For the first time, native people make up the majority of the council.

Meech Lake Accord. A major concern of the government of the NWT and residents across the territory was the constitutional accord reached by the federal government and the ten provinces in June, without participation from the NWT or the Yukon. The accord specifies that all provinces and the federal government must agree before new provinces can be created, practically crushing the aspirations of people from either territory to become full partners in the Canadian system. It also allows for provinces to extend their boundaries into the territories. There were strong protests, and the government leaders of each territory filed court challenges to the accord.

Economy. Economic conditions continued to be depressed. Oil and gas exploration activity was low, although there was some renewed interest by Gulf Canada in Beaufort Sea resource potential. Pine Point Mines (lead and zinc), the largest mine in the NWT, substantially geared down as it moved toward complete closure by the fall of 1988. A new three-year economic development agreement with the federal government would provide $39 million for critical areas of the economy.

Papal Visit. On September 20, Pope John Paul II visited the native community of Fort Simpson on an island in the Mackenzie River.

ROSS M. HARVEY
Government of the Northwest Territories

NORTHWEST TERRITORIES • Information Highlights

Area: 1,304,903 sq mi (3 379 700 km²).
Population (1986 census): 52,238.
Chief Cities (1986 census): Yellowknife, the capital, 11,753; Inuvik, 3,389; Hay River, 2,964.
Government (1987): *Chief Officers*—commissioner, John H. Parker; government leader, Dennis Patterson. *Legislature*—Legislative Assembly, 24 elected members.
Public Finances (1986–87 fiscal year): *Revenues*, $694,077,000; *expenditures*, $693,011,000.
Personal Income (average weekly earnings, August 1987): $650.
Education (1987–88): *Enrollment*—public and secondary schools, 13,100 pupils. *Public school expenditures* (1986–87), $124,058,000.
(All monetary figures in Canadian dollars.)

NORWAY

The Norwegian government maintained that the economy was recovering in 1987 from the difficulties caused by the world oil price collapse in 1986. U.S.-Norwegian relations were strained because of illicit Norwegian sales of sensitive technology to the USSR.

Government. In June, the two members of the rightist Progress Party in the Storting (parliament) saved Prime Minister Gro Harlem Brundtland's Labor government by refusing to support the nonsocialists' attempt to take over the reins. In the September municipal elections this party raised its share of the vote from 5.9% in 1985 to 12.1% (19% in Oslo and Bergen) at the expense of both Labor and the Conservatives. The election was seen as a protest (also demonstrated by the relatively low turnout) against high taxes and interest rates, queues for hospital operations, and too liberal reception of asylum seekers. (It was estimated that, because of more restrictive policies elsewhere in Europe, the number of asylum seekers arriving in Norway would be 8,000 in 1987, compared with 2,700 in 1986 and 800 in 1985.)

In March, Thorwald Stoltenberg became foreign minister upon the death of Knut Frydenlund. In September, Norway mourned the death of the Labor Party's grand old man, 90-year-old Einar Gerhardsen, a founder of the welfare state and prime minister from 1945 to 1951 and again from 1955 to 1965.

Economy. The overheated economy continued in 1987, with an average of only 2% unemployment and bank-loan rates of up to 18%, despite efforts to adjust the disequilibrium caused by the sharp drop in oil prices in 1986. The Labor government claimed, however, that the tighter economic policies pursued since May 1986 have yielded results in terms of decline of private consumption and of the inflation rate and a lower-than-anticipated trade deficit. The main problem remains the low competitive ability of the traditional export industries. Nevertheless, the krone has shown great stability since the 1986 devaluation.

Kongsberg Vaapenfabrikk (KV). In general, political relations between Norway and the United States improved markedly after Norway lent strong support to the U.S. approach to disarmament. There had been strains, however, early in 1987 when it became public knowledge that Norway's state-owned Kongsberg Vaapenfabrikk (arms factory) had been cooperating since 1979 with Japan's Toshiba Machine Co. in enabling the USSR to produce quieter submarine propellers that cannot be detected by North Atlantic Treaty Organization (NATO) devices. This was in direct contravention of NATO/Japanese rules controlling the export of sensitive technology to the Soviet bloc; as of late in 1987 it was not known what action, if any, the U.S. Congress would take on a proposed embargo on imports from KV. An investigation was under way in Norway to determine the extent of the damage done and the assigning of responsibility.

NORWAY • Information Highlights

Official Name: Kingdom of Norway.
Location: Northern Europe.
Area: 125,182 sq mi (324 220 km²).
Population (mid-1987 est.): 4,200,000.
Chief Cities (Jan. 1, 1987): Oslo, the capital, 449,220; Bergen, 208,915; Trondheim, 134,654.
Government: *Head of state,* Olav V, king (acceded Sept. 1957). *Head of government,* Gro Harlem Brundtland, prime minister (took office May 2, 1986). *Legislature*—Storting: Lagting and Odelsting.
Monetary Unit: Krone (6.5325 kroner equal U.S.$1, Oct. 27, 1987).
Gross National Product (1986 U.S.$): $69,733,-000,000.
Economic Indexes (1986): *Consumer Prices* (1980 = 100), all items, 165.4; food, 179.3. *Industrial Production* (1980 = 100), 126.
Foreign Trade (1986 U.S.$): *Imports,* $20,306,-000,000; *exports,* $18,097,000,000.

State-Owned Companies. The dismal economic results experienced by KV in recent years refueled the general debate concerning the principle of state-owned firms, which often have shown great losses (although several were set up with no purpose of profit). Even Norway's highly profitable oil producer, Statoil, grossly underestimated its cost calculations in connection with the huge refinery at Mongstad.

Social Problems. On Jan. 1, 1987, a shortened work week of 37½ hours went into effect, contributing to already critical shortages of workers in the health sector, schools, and the building trades. The main problem in health and social affairs is the aging of the population. The number of elderly, both in absolute and relative terms, will continue to rise rapidly until the mid-1990s, at which time it will level off for ten years because of the low birthrates in the 1930s. Then it will increase dramatically when the baby boomers retire. Although long foreseen, this problem is now a political topic.

ELLEN NORBOM
Free-lance Writer

NOVA SCOTIA

The highlights of 1987 for Nova Scotia included the achievement of a secured future for the Sydney Steel Corporation (SYSCO). There was modest overall economic growth.

Legislation and Government. The government of Premier John Buchanan enacted 83 laws, including the Nova Scotia Savings Plan Act, which enables Nova Scotians investing in Nova Scotian companies to save up to $3,000 a year in provincial tax, and the Pension Benefit Act, which regulates the establishment and the administration of all provincial pension plans.

Canapress Photo Service

W.J. "Billy Joe" MacLean, right, made the political comeback of the year, when he won back his seat (as an independent) in the Nova Scotia legislature in a March by-election. MacLean, 50, had been expelled from that body in October 1986 after pleading guilty to fraud charges.

The government played a key role in securing an agreement between SYSCO and the Canadian National Railways (CNR) that commits CNR to buying approximately 80% of its rail requirements from SYSCO. The province used this as leverage for persuading the federal government to launch a $157 million modernization plan for SYSCO. The plan is expected to improve the competitiveness of SYSCO and to provide job security for its 1,100 employees.

To ensure proper administration of law and justice, the government also established a Royal Commission for investigating the conviction of Donald Marshall, who spent 11 years in prison for a murder he did not commit. Finally, the government announced various construction projects, including a $7.7 million communication centre for Mount Saint Vincent University and new schools. Such announcements sparked rumors about the timing of the forthcoming provincial election.

NOVA SCOTIA • Information Highlights

Area: 21,425 sq mi (55 491 km^2).
Population (1986 census): 873,199.
Chief cities (1986 census): Halifax, the capital, 113,577; Dartmouth, 65,243; Sydney, 27,754.
Government (1987): *Chief Officers*—lt. gov., Alan R. Abraham; premier, John Buchanan (Progressive Conservative). *Legislature*—Legislative Assembly, 52 members.
Provincial Finances (1987–88 fiscal year budget): *Revenues,* $2,911,600,000; *expenditures,* $3,180,000,000.
Personal Income (average weekly earnings, June 1987): $402.51.
Labor Force (September 1987, seasonally adjusted: *Employed* workers, 15 years of age and over, 360,000; *Unemployed,* 47,000 (11.5%).
Education (1987–88): *Enrollment*—elementary and secondary schools, 171,800 pupils; postsecondary—universities, 27,300; community colleges, 2,500.
(All monetary figures are in Canadian dollars.)

An embarrassment for Premier Buchanan was the return to the Legislative Assembly in March of Billy Joe MacLean, a former cabinet minister who was expelled from the legislature in October 1986 after being convicted of fraud. MacLean had won as an independent in a by-election and thus regained his seat.

Economy. Despite the sluggish residential housing sector and still depressed offshore energy sector, Nova Scotia experienced reasonable growth in the most productive parts of its economy. In manufacturing, Nova Scotia moved a step closer to becoming a regional aerospace center when Pratt & Whitney of Canada shipped the first engine parts from its new $125 million Halifax plant. IMP, another local company, won a part of the contract to replace the Navy's Sea King helicopters. Sydney-based Micronav sold microwave landing systems both in Canada and abroad.

Other sectors, such as construction, farming, forestry, fishing, and trade, also recorded growth. A number of residential and condominium projects were completed in Halifax, including the $15 million Waterfront Place. Farm cash receipts during the first nine months of 1987 were up by 6%, while pulpwood production and foreign exports increased by 4% and 19.6%, respectively.

The value of fish landings shot up by 5.6% during the first quarter of the year. Retail trade and the sale of automobiles remained brisk during the year's first four months. All this contributed to a lower jobless rate for Nova Scotia, down to 11.5% in September from 13.7% a year earlier. Overall, the province's real gross domestic product was expected to grow by 2.5% in 1987, slightly faster during the previous years.

R.P. SETH
Mount Saint Vincent University, Halifax

OBITUARIES

Culver Pictures

LIBERACE, Wladziu Valentino

American pianist: b. West Allis, WI, May 16, 1919; d. Palm Springs, CA, Feb. 4, 1987.

Wladziu Valentino Liberace was a master showman, known as much for glittering excess as for his talents as a pianist. With his trademark giant candelabra, spangled costumes, and rhinestone-studded pianos, he cultivated a wide popularity and an income that averaged $5 million a year for more than 25 years. He was the recipient of two Emmy Awards and six gold records.

Liberace's programs were blatantly geared to popular taste, featuring a mix of hit tunes and what he called "Reader's Digest versions" of the classics—Chopin's "Minute Waltz" in 37 seconds; lengthy concertos pared to under four minutes by "cutting out the dull parts." A

Culver Pictures

KAYE, Danny

American entertainer: b. Brooklyn, NY, Jan. 18, 1913; d. Los Angeles, CA, March 3, 1987.

A multitalented performer, Danny Kaye brought a childlike enthusiasm to a broad variety of comic, musical, and dramatic roles. He charmed audiences with his performances on Broadway, in the movies, and on television. He had them rolling in the aisles as the zany guest conductor of some of the world's great orchestras. The entertainer delighted young people everywhere as ambassador-at-large for the United Nations Children's Fund (UNICEF).

Background. The son of Ukrainian immigrants, Danny Kaye was born David Daniel Kaminski. His childhood aspiration was to become a doctor, but at 17, with no money for

UPI/Bettmann Newsphotos

TAYLOR, Maxwell Davenport

U.S. Army general and diplomat: b. Keytesville, MO, Aug. 26, 1901; d. Washington, DC, April 19, 1987.

Gen. Maxwell D. Taylor had a profound influence on U.S. military strategy from World War II through the Vietnam era. As chief of staff of the U.S. Army (1955–59), General Taylor had opposed fruitlessly the dominant view that a policy of massive nuclear retaliation should subordinate the role of the infantry. Taylor advocated instead a policy of "flexible response" which involved various levels of readiness for different kinds of conflicts.

Sen. John F. Kennedy adopted some of the general's views during his 1960 campaign for the White House. As president, Kennedy asked Taylor to investigate the Central Intellitypical performance featured numerous costume changes, sentimental commentary, and snatches of song and tap dancing.

Background. Liberace began to play the piano at the age of four and studied the classics at Wisconsin College of Music. He often said he was guided and encouraged by the renowned Polish pianist Paderewski, and like Paderewski he used only his last name on stage. (His friends called him Lee.) He appeared as a soloist with the Chicago Symphony in 1936. At the same time, he was earning money playing popular tunes in movie houses and cocktail lounges, under the name Walter Busterkeys. Within a few years he had combined the two styles and come up with a formula for success.

In the 1940s, Liberace was increasingly in demand as a nightclub performer; in the 1950s, he headlined in Las Vegas, and his syndicated television show was carried by more stations than *I Love Lucy*. Meanwhile, he gradually developed his flamboyant stage image. Briefly, in 1958, he attempted a more conservative look; but when he found his audiences shrinking, he want back to glitter. From then on, his costumes were ever more elaborate—a jacket of 24-karat gold braid; a cape of Norwegian blue fox. The formula never failed; in 1986, he still drew sellout crowds to concerts at Radio City Music Hall.

Liberace's on-stage glitz extended into his private life. He accumulated 20 cars and five homes, sporting such luxuries as a piano-shaped swimming pool and a reproduction of the Sistine Chapel ceiling, with the pianist's face at the center. He also designed commercial interiors, relaxed by cooking and growing orchids, and patented an invention, a disappearing toilet.

ELAINE PASCOE

---

medical studies, he dropped out of high school to work as an entertainer in nightclubs, vaudeville, and the "Borsch Belt" resorts of New York's Catskill Mountains. He made his Broadway debut in 1939, but it was in *Lady in the Dark* two years later that he achieved instant stardom with the song "Tchaikovsky," in which he rattled off 57 multisyllabic Russian names in 38 seconds.

Among the best remembered of Kaye's 18 motion pictures are *The Inspector General* (1949), *Hans Christian Andersen* (1952), *Knock on Wood* (1954), and *White Christmas* (1954). In *The Secret Life of Walter Mitty* (1947), based on the James Thurber story, his portrayal of the daydreaming hero connected empathetically with the zany impulses everyone sometimes has toward life's absurdities. Kaye had his own television series from 1963 to 1967, and in 1981 he was acclaimed for one of his few dramatic roles, as a Holocaust survivor in the television movie *Skokie*.

Always a quick study, Kaye learned to conduct an orchestra without being able to read music. His performances with the New York Philharmonic and other internationally famous orchestras were classics of comic improvisation. His work for UNICEF began in the 1950s and took him all over the world to raise funds for the organization. "I think I get along so well with kids," he once said, "because I'm not afraid to be a child."

In 1982, Kaye was named the recipient of the Motion Picture Academy's Jean Hersholt Humanitarian Award for his charitable work, and in 1984 he was honored by the Kennedy Center for lifetime achievement in the arts. Kaye's wife since 1940 was the composer-lyricist Sylvia Fine; they had one daughter.

LINDA TRIEGEL

---

gence Agency's involvement in the Bay of Pigs disaster and serve as his special military adviser and later as chairman of the Joint Chiefs of Staff (1962–64). He was U.S. ambassador to South Vietnam (1964–65) and a special consultant to President Johnson (1965–69).

In 1984, General Taylor outlined three major lessons he believed the United States should have learned from the Vietnam struggle. One, before the United States allies itself with another country, it should ascertain to what extent the ally can exploit U.S. help. Two, the United States should declare war during such conflicts. Three, television should not be allowed on the battlefield.

Background. Maxwell Davenport Taylor was graduated fourth in his class from the U.S. Military Academy at West Point, NY, in 1922. He taught French and Spanish at the academy from 1927 to 1932, attended various military training centers from 1932 to 1935, and was an assistant military attaché in China in 1939.

His activities during World War II included a daring secret visit to German-occupied Rome to determine the odds for an Allied airborne landing nearby; parachuting into France on D-Day; and leading the 101st airborne division in its attacks against German forces in the Netherlands in 1944.

Following the war, he was the 37th superintendent at his alma mater, first commander of the U.S. government in the divided city of Berlin, and the Defense Department's deputy chief of staff for operations and administration. He then was named commander of the U.S. Eighth Army in Korea in February 1953 and appointed Army chief of staff in June 1955.

Maxwell Taylor and Lydia Gardner Happer were married in 1925. They had two sons.

ROBERT M. LAWRENCE

Photos Culver Pictures

SEGOVIA, Andrés

Spanish guitarist: b. Linares, Spain, Feb. 21, 1893; d. Madrid, Spain, June 2, 1987.

In a career that spanned eight decades, Andrés Segovia established a legacy as the master practitioner of the classical guitar. His performance virtuosity and lifelong crusade on behalf of the instrument elevated the guitar from the tavern to the concert hall. His transcription of works by Bach, Handel, and other major composers vastly expanded its classical repertory. His dedication to teaching inspired new generations of performers. And his tireless concert schedule brought his music and his instrument to the entire world.

If he did not invent the guitar—as some hyperbolized—Segovia did revolutionize the technique of playing it. Largely self-taught, he

ASTAIRE, Fred

American dancer, stage, and film star: b. Omaha, NE, May 10, 1899; d. Los Angeles, CA, June 22, 1987.

One of America's foremost film stars, Fred Astaire was recognized rightly as a great dancer. His signature image—top hat, cane, and tails—conveyed polish and elegance. Charm and a specifically American nonchalance contributed to his gift for transforming popular entertainment into an art form. Astaire was trained in ballet, tap, and ballroom dancing. His dance solos were dazzling. Yet it was as a singer and actor playing out a romance with his dance partners—notably Ginger Rogers—that he captured the public's imagination.

Among the 41 films in which Astaire appeared, the ten Rogers-Astaire movies did the

GLEASON, Jackie

American entertainer: b. Brooklyn, NY, Feb. 26, 1916; d. Fort Lauderdale, FL, June 24, 1987.

Emerging in the 1950s as one of America's most popular television stars, Jackie Gleason brought to his performances an exuberance, an appetite for life, and a sheer physical presence—he weighed up to 285 lbs (129 kg)—that earned him the nickname "the Great One." He is best known for his role as Ralph Kramden, the blustering but lovable bus driver in the classic television sitcom *The Honeymooners*. In a string of television variety shows during the 1950s and 60s, he created such other memorable characters as Joe the Bartender, Reginald Van Gleason 3d, and the Poor Soul. Gleason also appeared in 15 films, including *The* discovered that a richer, cleaner sound could be produced by plucking the strings rather than playing them in the traditional manner with the fingertips.

Background. Born in the Andalusian city of Linares and reared in Granada, Segovia was surrounded—and captivated—by the sound of flamenco guitar early in life. His father, a prominent lawyer, hoped he would follow him in the legal profession, but Segovia had fallen in love with the guitar. His parents and his teachers at the Granada Musical Institute—where he studied piano, violin, and cello—failed to divert him, and he set out on his own to explore the guitar's classical possibilities.

In 1909, at age 16, Segovia gave his first professional recital in Granada. Numerous concerts followed, and his dazzling skill made him known throughout Spain. His recognition soon spread outside the country, and in 1919 he made a critically acclaimed tour of South America. His eagerly awaited Paris debut in April 1924 created a sensation, both for his virtuosity and for the relative novelty of a classical guitar program. He made his U.S. debut in 1928 with a 40-city tour that firmly established his reputation.

Using a six-string Hauser guitar and refusing to employ amplifiers, Segovia gave about 100 performances a year for much of his career; even in his 90s he appeared on stage up to 60 times a year. His demonstrations of the guitar's tonal range inspired a number of 20th-century composers—including Heitor Villa-Lobos, Francis Poulenc, Joaquin Rodrigo, and many others—to write music for it. And his thousands of students and disciples included the Englishman Julian Bream and the Australian John Williams.

ROBERT COMMANDAY

---

most to establish the Astaire legend. The sight of Astaire winning Miss Rogers' heart in a ballroom duet amid luxurious surroundings provided a surefire formula for Depression-era audiences.

Background. Astaire's reputation as a perfectionist derived from his lifelong training as a professional. He was born Frederick Austerlitz, the son of an Austrian immigrant who worked in a brewery and who changed his name during World War I. Fred and his older sister, Adele, were enrolled in a New York school in 1904 by their ambitious mother. The brother-sister team entered vaudeville as child performers in 1905 and then moved on to stage musicals after appearing in the Shubert Broadway revue, *Over the Top* in 1917. The Astaires performed in musicals on Broadway and in London, starring in *Funny Face, Lady Be Good!, The Band Wagon,* and other shows. Although Adele was said to overshadow her brother, her marriage in England to Lord Cavendish and her retirement in 1932 did not end Astaire's career but spurred his transition to films.

After a screen test at RKO Pictures, he won a small part in *Dancing Lady* in 1933, followed by his first appearance with Miss Rogers in *Flying Down to Rio.* Their subsequent musicals, through 1939 included *Top Hat, Roberta, Follow the Fleet,* and *Swing Time.* In 1949 they were reunited in *The Barkleys of Broadway.* Rita Hayworth, Judy Garland, and Cyd Charisse were among Astaire's other dancing partners in films in the 1940s and 1950s. Astaire appeared in nondancing dramatic roles in such films as *On the Beach* (1959), *The Towering Inferno* (1974), and *Ghost Story* (1981), his last film.

ANNA KISSELGOFF

Hustler (1961), for which he won an Academy Award nomination, *Requiem for a Heavyweight* (1962), the *Smokey and the Bandit* trilogy, and *Nothing in Common* (1986). His occasional appearances in theater included the Broadway musical *Take Me Along* (1959), which won him a Tony Award. And when he was not performing on screen or stage, he was often composing music or conducting the Jackie Gleason Orchestra, which recorded 35 albums.

Background. He was born Herbert John Gleason and grew up in humble surroundings in Brooklyn, NY. His father, an insurance clerk, disappeared when he was eight. Gleason dropped out of high school and began working as an emcee in cabarets, theaters, and carnivals. After appearing as a Manhattan nightclub comedian, he traveled to Hollywood in the early 1940s and earned bit parts in movies.

Gleason got his big break in 1949, when he won the role of Chester Riley in the NBC television series *The Life of Riley.* After one season as Riley and another in the DuMont Network's *Cavalcade of Stars,* CBS gave him his own weekly variety show in 1952. It was in this hour-long program, the first *Jackie Gleason Show,* that he began portraying the characters that would make him famous, including Ralph Kramden. *The Honeymooners* ran for only one season, 1955-56, but the 39 episodes made Kramden a beloved character for generations of television viewers.

At his home in Inverrary, FL, where he spent most of his latter years, Gleason indulged —to legendary excess—his passions for eating, drinking, smoking, golf, and lavish spending. His outlook on life was summed up in the familiar exclamation, "How sweet it is!"

JEFFREY H. HACKER

Ford Motor Company

FORD 2d, Henry

U.S. automotive executive: b. Detroit, Sept. 4, 1917; d. Detroit, Sept. 29, 1987.

The "last tycoon" of American industry reluctantly assumed control of the floundering family business, Ford Motor Company, at the age of 28. Little was expected of the eldest grandson of company founder Henry Ford, but he determinedly led the company back to prosperity over an eventful 34-year career as chief executive. In the process, Henry Ford 2d became the best known and one of the most respected industrialists of his time.

What distinguished Ford, after he rescued the No. 2 automaker from near-bankruptcy in the aftermath of World War II, was his grasp of the need to streamline the company's products and organization. He staunchly supported

AP/Wide World

LUCE, Claire Boothe

American writer, politician, and diplomat: b. New York, NY, April 10, 1903; d. Washington, DC, Oct. 9, 1987.

At a time when relatively few women pursued careers, Clare Boothe Luce had several—magazine writer and editor, playwright, politician, ambassador. She also was the wife of one of the most influential figures of her day, *Time* magazine founder Henry Luce, and for many years was named to various "most admired" and "most glamorous" lists of prominent women. She was a staunch political conservative and opponent of Communism.

Background. Clare Boothe was the daughter of a violinist and a former chorus girl who separated when she was eight years old. She attended a finishing school and in 1923 married

© A. Duclos/Gamma-Liaison

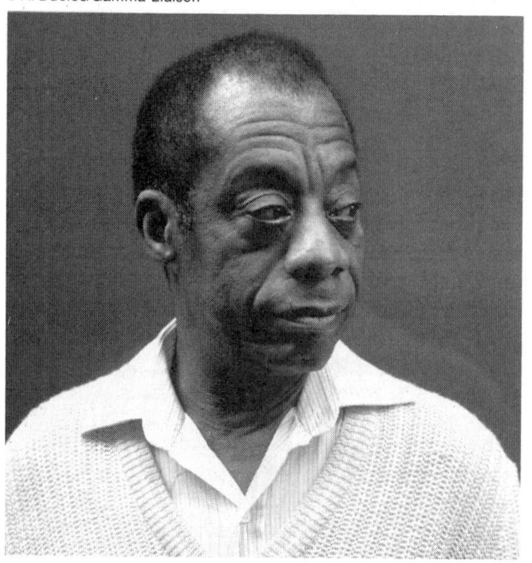

BALDWIN, James

U.S. writer: b. New York, NY, Aug. 2, 1924; d. St. Paul de Vence, France, Dec. 1, 1987.

James Baldwin, considered by some to be among America's great writers, saw himself as one who was to "bear witness to the truth." Through his powerful collections of essays, including *Notes of a Native Son* (1955), *Nobody Knows My Name* (1961), and *The Fire Next Time* (1963), he became an eloquent voice at the time of the American civil-rights movement of the 1960s. His words were especially foreboding when he said, "no society can smash the social contract and be exempt from the consequences. . . ." Although he saw himself primarily as a novelist, and in fact first gained fame with his novel, the partly autobiographiexecutives willing to take risks, resulting in such new-car successes as the Thunderbird, Mustang, and Taurus but also in such failures as the Edsel.

Ford was probably the most outspokenly unconventional leader of an American corporation. He publicly endorsed Democratic presidential candidates in the 1960s and was active in the civil-rights movement. Despite the Arab League boycott, he ordered a Ford sales presence in Israel and contributed substantial sums to Jewish philanthropies, recalling his grandfather's notoriety as a booster of anti-Semitic causes. He contributed significantly to the renovation of downtown Detroit by building the Renaissance Center. And he pioneered many worker benefits, such as pensions.

Background. Henry Ford 2d was the eldest son of Edsel Ford, the only offspring of the legendary Henry Ford. Young Henry's 21st birthday present was a seat on the company board, but he assumed a more active role in May 1943, when his father died and President Roosevelt ordered him to leave the U.S. Navy and help run the company.

Elected company president in 1945, "Henry the Deuce" set about a full-scale corporate reorganization to reverse losses of $9 million a month. His success can be measured by the fact that in 1987, Ford surpassed General Motors in net profits. Ford sales in 1946 totalled 900,000 vehicles and in 1986, 5.9 million; employment rose in the same years from 160,000 to 383,000. He was chairman of the company's finance committee at the time of his death.

Ford's survivors included his third wife, Kathleen; a son, Edsel 2d, and two daughters, Charlotte and Anne; his sister Josephine and his brother William.

MAYNARD M. GORDON

---

millionaire George Tuttle Brokaw. They were divorced six years later.

Through a friend, she became a caption writer with *Vogue* magazine. She quickly proved herself an able writer and joined the staff of *Vanity Fair,* rising to managing editor and celebrity status. Her satirical pieces were later collected in a book, *Stuffed Shirts*. In 1934 she left the magazine to devote herself to play writing. Soon thereafter she met and married Henry Luce. She is said to have given him the concept for *Life* magazine. Her first produced play, *Abide with Me* (1935), was a flop, but in 1936 she scored with *The Women*. In 1940 she went to Europe to cover the war for *Life* and to write *Europe in the Spring*.

In 1942, Luce ran for Congress as a Republican from Connecticut. Her campaign criticized the Roosevelt administration's war effort and New Deal policies, and she won election. She was reelected in 1944, but declined to run in 1946. Tragedy had struck in 1944 when her only child, Ann, was killed in a car crash; subsequently, Luce converted to Catholicism. In 1952 she made an unsuccessful bid for the Senate and campaigned for Dwight Eisenhower for president. He named her ambassador to Italy in 1953. She held that post until 1957, when she fell ill from arsenic poisoning (from paint dust from her villa ceiling). She was named ambassador to Brazil in 1959 but met Senate opposition, particularly from Oregon's Sen. Wayne Morse. After her confirmation, an idle remark by Luce created a furor that resulted in her resignation.

After the death of her husband in 1967, Luce moved to Hawaii. She returned to Washington in 1983, serving on President Ronald Reagan's Foreign Intelligence Advisory Board.

ELAINE PASCOE

---

cal *Go Tell It on the Mountain* (1953), many others considered the essays to be his outstanding contribution to literature.

His desire to escape what he saw as the racial bigotry in America led him to establish France as his residence. In his later years, however, he described himself as a "commuter," and spent much time in his native land.

Background. The son of a New Orleans clergyman, James Arthur Baldwin was born in New York City's Harlem and attended DeWitt Clinton High School in the Bronx. When he was 14 he became a preacher in a Pentecostal church in Harlem, gathering experiences which he would later utilize in *Go Tell It on the Mountain,* the book he said he "had to write if [he] was ever going to write anything else." By his early 20s he was writing for such prestigious publications as *The New Leader, The Nation, Commentary,* and *Partisan Review*.

A social activist, he not only struggled for racial progress but also was an early opponent of the U.S. involvement in Vietnam and in the early 1960s began to criticize discrimination against homosexuals. His open discussions of homosexuality in the novels *Giovanni's Room* (1956) and *Another Country* (1962) brought criticism from elements within the civil-rights movement and from others. Among Baldwin's other works are the novel *Tell Me How Long the Train's Been Gone* (1968), the play *Blues for Mister Charlie* (1964), the short-story collection *Going to Meet the Man* (1965), and the essay *The Evidence of Things Not Seen* (1985).

Baldwin's unique funeral service at New York's Cathedral of St. John the Divine, the first there since that of Duke Ellington in 1974, drew many mourners. They came, it would seem, to bear witness to Baldwin's truth.

SAUNDRA FRANCE MCMAHON

The following is a selected list of prominent persons who died during 1987. Articles on major figures appear in the preceding pages.

Abbott, Douglas (Charles) (87), Canada's finance minister (1946–54); was appointed to the Supreme Court of Canada in 1954, where he served until his retirement in 1973: d. Ottawa, Canada, March 17.

Abel, I. W. (78), president of the United Steelworkers (1965–77). A steelworker himself, in 1973 he made labor history when he signed the Experimental Negotiating Agreement with Big Steel, an agreement wherein the union agreed not to strike during the 1974 contract talks, and both sides agreed to submit to arbitration if necessary. He was the union's third president: d. Malvern, OH, Aug. 10.

Anghelis, Odysseus (75), leading member of the military junta that ruled Greece from 1967 to 1974: d. near Athens, Greece, March 22.

Anouilh, Jean (77), French playwright, who in his 50-year writing career wrote about 40 plays, many of them considered bleak. One of his most popular plays was *L'Invitation au Chateau* (1947). Other well known works are *Antigone, The Waltz of the Toreadors, The Lark,* and *Becket:* d. Lausanne, Switzerland, Oct. 3.

Astor, Mary (born Lucille Langhanke) (81), actress; entered the film industry during the silent movie era. She was probably best known for her performance in *The Maltese Falcon* (1941): d. Woodland Hills, CA, Sept. 24.

Bacon, Peggy (91), poet, author, artist, and illustrator of more than 60 books; in 1975 the National Collection of Fine Arts in Washington honored her with a year-long retrospective. She was author and illustrator of *Lion-Hearted Kitten:* d. Kennebunk, ME, Jan. 4.

Baird, Bil (William Britton) (82), puppeteer; performed in the theater, films, and on television, and trained other puppeteers, including Jim Henson, the Muppets' creator: d. New York City, March 18.

Baker, Carlos (77), professor and author. He wrote the authorized *Ernest Hemingway: A Life Story* (1969) and *Hemingway: The Writer as Artist* (1952), as well as literary criticism, fiction, and poetry: d. Princeton, NJ, April 18.

Baldrige, Malcolm (64), U.S. secretary of commerce during the Reagan administration (1981–87); was credited with guiding the administration in its shift toward a tougher trade policy with Japan and other trading partners: d. Walnut Creek, CA, July 25.

Barnett, Ross (89), governor of Mississippi (1960–64); known for his segregationist views, he attempted in 1962 to deny James Meredith, a 29-year-old black veteran, the right to enroll at the University of Mississippi: d. Jackson, MS, Nov. 6.

Barrow, Errol W. (67), prime minister of Barbados (1966–76; 1986–87): d. Bridgetown, Barbados, June 1.

Bender, Lauretta (88), child neuropsychiatrist; known for the development in 1923 of the Bender Gestalt Visual Motor Test: d. Annapolis, MD, Jan. 4.

Bennett, Michael (born Michael Bennett DiFiglia) (44), theater director and choreographer; the creator of *A Chorus Line,* Broadway's longest running show. Among his other Broadway productions were *Ballroom* (1978) and *Dreamgirls* (1981). Over the years he won a number of Tony Awards for choreography and directing: d. Tucson, AZ, July 2.

Bergman, Jules (57), science editor for ABC News from 1961: d. New York City, Feb. 12.

Bishop, Jim (James Alonzo) (79), newspaper columnist and author. Wrote 21 books, including the bestseller *The Day Lincoln Was Shot:* d. Delray Beach, FL, July 26.

Bloch, Herbert (79), German-born stamp-collecting expert: d. New York City, Sept. 7.

Bolger, Ray (83), actor of stage, screen, and television; he was a popular song and dance man best known for his role as the Scarecrow in the film *The Wizard of Oz* (1939). In 1948 he opened on Broadway in *Where's Charley?,* a vehicle that made him celebrated on the stage and out of which came his memorable singing number "Once in Love with Amy." His Hollywood career began in the 1930s: d. Los Angeles, CA, Jan. 15.

Brannum, Hugh (77), actor; portrayed Mr. Green Jeans on television's *Captain Kangaroo* (1955–84): d. East Stroudsburg, PA, April 19.

Brattain, Walter (85), physicist; shared the Nobel Prize in 1956 for invention of the transistor: d. Seattle, WA, Oct. 13.

Buchsbaum, Alan (51), architect; originator of the High Tech style: d. New York City, April 10.

Burke, Michael (70), chief executive of the New York Yankees baseball team (1966–73). He was also president of the Madison Square Garden sports arena between 1973 and 1981: d. Ireland, Feb. 5.

Burnham, James (82), founding editor of *The National Review.* He was a professor at New York University from 1929 to 1953 and worked briefly for the Central Intelligence Agency. His books include *The Managerial Revolution* (1941), *The Machiavellians* (1943), *The Struggle for the World* (1947), and *The Coming Defeat of Communism* (1950): d. Kent, CT, July 28.

Burns, Arthur F. (born Burnzeig) (83), U.S. economist; chairman of the Federal Reserve Board (1970–78). For 20 years, until 1953, he taught at Columbia University prior to heading President Dwight Eisenhower's Council of Economic Advisers for three years. He returned to academia as the president of the National Bureau of Economic Research (1957–67) and returned to government service in 1969 under President Richard Nixon. He also served as ambassador to West Germany (1981–85): d. Baltimore, MD, June 26.

Burton, Sala (61), U.S. representative (D-CA, 1983–87): d. Washington, DC, Feb. 1.

Caldwell, Erskine (83), author; particularly noted for his novels of the American South, including *Tobacco Road* (1932) and *God's Little Acre* (1933): d. Paradise Valley, AZ, April 11.

Campbell, Joseph (83), author of many books on mythology and folklore, including *The Hero with a Thousand Faces* (1949): d. Honolulu, HI, Oct. 30.

Carlson, Frank (94), Kansas Republican politician; he served two terms as governor, six terms as a member of the House of Representatives, and three terms in the U.S. Senate. He retired from the Senate in 1969: d. Concordia, KS, May 30.

Carroll, Madeleine (81), British-born actress; popular in the 1930s and 1940s. She starred in Alfred Hitchcock's *The 39 Steps* and *Secret Agent:* d. Marbella, Spain, Oct. 2.

Carter, Tim Lee (76), U.S. representative (R-KY, 1965–81): d. Glasgow, KY, March 27.

Casey, William (74), director of U.S. Central Intelligence during the Reagan administration. Recently, he was implicated in the Iran-contra affair under scrutiny by the U.S. Congress. Served as chairman of the Security and Exchange Commission (1971–73): d. Glen Cove, NY, May 6.

Chamoun, Camille Nimer (87), president of Lebanon (1952–58). At the time of his death, he was the minister of finance in Lebanon's caretaker cabinet: d. Beirut, Lebanon, Aug. 7.

Chouinard, Julien (58), Canadian jurist; a member of the Canadian Supreme Court (1979–87): d. Ottawa, Canada, Feb. 6.

Cochet, Henri (85), one of the "Four Musketeers," French tennis players who won France's first Davis Cup in 1927 and dominated world tennis for several years thereafter: d. near Paris, April 1.

I. W. Abel

Mary Astor

Ray Bolger

Arthur Burns

Photos, AP/Wide World

AP/Wide World
Sala Burton

AP/Wide World
William Casey

AP/Wide World
Camille Chamoun

Photo Trends
Lord Duncan-Sandys

Coco, James (56), actor; known for his comedic roles. He became a star in Neil Simon's *Last of the Red Hot Lovers:* d. New York City, Feb. 25.

Coe, Peter (59), British director; in 1961 he had three hits in London's West End theaters—*The Miracle Worker, The World of Suzie Wong,* and *Oliver!:* d. England, May 25.

Cohen, Wilbur Joseph (73), secretary of the U.S. Health, Education, and Welfare Department under President Lyndon Johnson. He helped design Medicare, Medicaid, and other social welfare legislation of the 1960s. As a young man he also helped create Social Security: d. Seoul, Korea, May 18.

Cole, W. Sterling (82), U.S. representative (R-NY, 1935–57). He also served as the first director general of the International Atomic Energy Agency: d. Washington, DC, March 15.

Collins, J. Lawton (91), Army general and Army chief of staff (1949–53). He was a combat leader in World War II and was selected to lead one of the two Army Corps that landed at Normandy on June 6, 1944: d. Washington, DC, Sept. 12.

Daugherty, (Hugh) Duffy (72), head football coach at Michigan State University (1954–72): d. Santa Barbara, CA, Sept. 25.

Daniels, Dominick V. (78), U.S. representative (D-NJ, 1959–77): d. Jersey City, NJ, July 17.

Davis, Edith Luckett (91), mother of U.S. first lady Nancy Reagan: d. Phoenix, AZ, Oct. 26.

de Broglie, Louis (94), French physicist; won the 1929 Nobel Prize for work in wave mechanics: d. Paris, March 19.

Delaney, James J. (86), U.S. representative; a Democrat from New York, he served 32 years in the House of Representatives and retired in 1979: d. Tenafly, NJ, May 24.

de Liagre, Alfred, Jr. (82), theater producer and director; his career spanned 50 years. He was perhaps most identified with the comedy *The Voice of the Turtle,* which he produced in 1943: d. New York City, March 5.

DeSillers, Ronnie (7), boy who received three unsuccessful organ transplants and the attention of President Reagan and the American public: d. Pittsburgh, PA, April 29.

Donner, Frederic (84), chairman and chief executive of the General Motors Corporation (1958–67). He also served as a company director for 32 years: d. Greenwich, CT, Feb. 28.

Draper, Charles (85), engineer; a developer of the navigation system that steered Americans to the moon and back: d. Cambridge, MA, July 25.

Duncan-Sandys, Lord (Duncan Edwin Sandys) (79), British politician and diplomat. As Britain's secretary for commonwealth relations (1960–64), he negotiated the independence of a number of British colonies and territories. He was a member of Parliament (1935–45; 1950–74). He became a peer in 1974: d. London, Nov. 26.

Du Plessis, Rev. David J. (81), Pentecostal minister; the only Pentecostal invited to the third session of the Second Vatican Council in 1964: d. Pasadena, CA, Feb. 2.

Eaker, Ira C. (91), U.S. Air Force general, commanded U.S. air forces in Europe during World War II and helped establish the Air Force as a separate military service. He set a world aviation record in 1929 when he stayed aloft for nearly a week. Later he made the first "blind" transcontinental flight entirely with instruments: d. Camp Springs, MD, Aug. 6.

Egan, Richard (65), motion-picture actor, known particularly for his roles in action films. Among his films are *The Damned Don't Cry, The Untamed, Violent Saturday, The View from Pompey's Head,* and *A Summer Place:* d. Santa Monica, CA, July 20.

Eisele, Donn F. (57), U.S. astronaut; one of three astronauts who in 1968 first flew the Apollo spacecraft that eventually took a man to the moon: d. Tokyo, Dec. 2.

Epton, Bernard E. (66), Chicago insurance lawyer and Illinois state politician; in 1983 he was the Republican candidate for mayor of Chicago: d. Ann Arbor, MI, Dec. 10.

Folsom, James E. (79), governor of Alabama (1947–51; 1955–59): d. Cullman, AL, Nov. 21.

Fosse, Robert Louis (Bob) (60), director and choreographer; noted for his choreography of the Broadway musicals *Pajama Game, Damn Yankees, Bells Are Ringing,* and *New Girl in Town.* In 1959 he directed his first Broadway musical, *Redhead,* followed by *How to Succeed in Business Without Really Trying, Sweet Charity, Pippin,* and *Chicago.* In films he choreographed *Pajama Game* and directed *Cabaret,* for which he won an Academy Award: d. Washington, DC, Sept. 23.

François, Jacques (78), the only civilian member of Haiti's three-man National Governing Council: d. Port-au-Prince, April 13.

Franju, Georges (75), French film director and cofounder of the Cinématheque Française, the French film archives founded in 1936: d. Paris, Nov. 5.

Fredericks, Carlton (76), longtime radio commentator and authority on nutrition and health: d. Yonkers, NY, July 28.

Freyre, Gilberto (87), Brazilian sociologist, teacher, and author; his most famous work was *The Masters and the Slaves,* written in 1933. He served as a federal congressman in Brazil from 1946 to 1951, helping to rewrite his country's constitution: d. Recife, Brazil, July 18.

Friend, Charlotte (65), medical microbiologist. In 1956 she discovered a virus (named the Friend virus) that causes leukemia in mice which has been an important tool in the study of cancer: d. New York City, Jan. 13.

Gerhardsen, Einar (90), prime minister of Norway (1945–51; 1955–65); played an important part in the establishment of the welfare state in Norway and in its pro-Western foreign policy after 1945: d. Lilleborg, Norway, Sept. 19.

Gimbel, Peter (59), filmmaker and underwater photojournalist; in 1956 he was the first person to scuba dive to the *Andrea Doria,* the sunken Italian liner. He produced two documentaries about the liner: d. New York City, July 12.

Gingold, Hermione (89), British-born comedienne and actress. She appeared often on television talk shows and was something of a regular on *The Jack Paar Show:* d. New York City, May 24.

Goodell, Charles E. (60), U.S. senator (R-NY, 1968–71). He also served in the House of Representatives for ten years: d. Washington, DC, Jan. 21.

Goodrich, Lloyd (89), director of New York City's Whitney Museum of American Art (1958–68) and a key figure in the art world for many years: d. New York City, March 27.

Green, Edith (77), U.S. representative (D-OR, 1955–75): d. Tualatin, OR, April 21.

Bob Fosse

Hermione Gingold
Photos, AP/Wide World

UPI-Bettmann Newsphotos
Edith Green

AP/Wide World
Woody Hayes

AP/Wide World
Woody Herman

Photo Trends
John Huston

Green, Freddie (75), jazz guitarist; played with the Count Basie orchestra for 50 years: d. Las Vegas, NV, March 1.

Greene, Lorne (72), Canadian-born actor, best known for his portrayal of Ben Cartwright on the television series *Bonanza* (1959–73): d. Santa Monica, CA, Sept. 11.

Greenwood, Joan (65), British actress; starred in many film comedies and stage plays in the 1940s and 1950s: d. London, Feb. 27.

Grigorenko, Petro G. (79), Russian general of the Soviet Army who became an outspoken critic of the Soviet government: d. New York City, Feb. 21.

Gross, H. R. (88), U.S. representative (R-IA, 1949–75): d. Washington, DC, Sept. 22.

Guldahl, Ralph (75), golfer; he dominated the professional game in the United States in the late 1930s: d. Sherman Oaks, CA, June 11.

Haley, Sir William J. (86), British journalist; headed *The Manchester Guardian* (1939–43) and its subsidiary *The Evening News, The Times* of London (1952–66), the British Broadcasting Corporation (1944–52), and for a brief time (1967–69) the *Encyclopaedia Britannica* in Chicago: d. Jersey Island, English Channel, Sept. 6.

Hammond, John (76), critic and record producer, a champion of racial equality, he loved jazz and blues and helped carry black music to a larger audience: d. New York City, July 10.

Harrison, William (91), U.S. Army lieutenant general; headed the United Nations armistice delegation in the Korean War: d. Bryn Mawr, PA, May 25.

Hawes, Emma (75), world bridge champion; in 1980 she became the fourth American woman to attain the rank of grand master: d. Fort Worth, TX, July 28.

Hayes, Woody (Wayne Woodrow) (74), football coach; served 28 years as coach at Ohio State University. In a career that spanned 33 years he became known as one of the greatest tacticians in football history. He became coach at Ohio State in 1951 and during his time there compiled a record of 205/61/10: d. Upper Arlington, OH, March 12.

Hayworth, Rita (born Margarita Carmen Cansino) (68), motion-picture actress; she gained international fame in the 1940s and 1950s. Her films include *Blood and Sand, Gilda, You Were Never Lovelier, Cover Girl, The Lady from Shanghai, Separate Tables,* and *They Came to Cordura.* Among her five husbands were the film actor and director Orson Welles and Prince Aly Khan: d. New York City, May 14.

Heifetz, Jascha (86), Russian-born violinist; a child prodigy who became known as perhaps the greatest violinist of his time, noted for his technical perfection and a careful regard for the composer's markings. As a child he was a pupil of the famed violin teacher Leopold Auer: d. Los Angeles, CA, Dec. 10.

Rita Hayworth
AP/Wide World

Jascha Heifetz
UPI-Bettmann Newsphotos

Hélion, Jean (83), French abstract and representational painter: d. Paris, Oct. 27.

Heller, Walter (71), economist; was chief economic adviser to Presidents Kennedy and Johnson in the 1960s, but spent most of his career as a professor of economics at the University of Minnesota. He was part of a group of liberal economists, associated with the Democrats, whose philosophy was based on tax-cutting and some deficit spending: d. Silverdale, WA, June 15.

Herman, Woody (74), musician and big-band conductor; he had a career that spanned 50 years. He had a series of bands, generally called the "Thundering Herd," which played popular music ranging from blues to bop and rock. Herman played clarinet and saxophone and sang: d. Los Angeles, CA, Oct. 29.

Hess, Rudolf (93), onetime deputy to Adolf Hitler and the last of Hitler's inner circle. He had been serving a life sentence in Spandau Prison in West Berlin since 1947: d. West Berlin, West Germany, Aug. 17.

Hitchcock, Henry-Russell (83), architectural historian and teacher; wrote or cowrote more than 20 books as well as many articles. He was associated with the Museum of Modern Art where his most famous exhibition was the 1932 International Style show done with the architect Philip Johnson: d. New York City, Feb. 19.

Holland, Charles (77), American-born tenor; he spent much of his life in Europe: d. Amsterdam, the Netherlands, Nov. 7.

Howser, Dick (51), baseball player and manager; skippered the New York Yankees in 1980, took over the Kansas City Royals in 1981, and led that team to a World Series championship in 1985. He had a 25-year career in the major leagues, starting in 1961 as a shortstop for the Kansas City Athletics. He also spent ten seasons as a coach for the Yankees: d. Kansas City, MO, June 17.

Ho Ying-chin (97), Nationalist Chinese leader, General Ho served briefly in 1949 as prime minister before the Communist takeover of mainland China. He was a long-time military associate of Chiang Kaishek, serving as the Chinese minister of war (1930–44). He later served as Taiwan's defense minister (1949–58): d. Taipei, Oct. 21.

Huston, John (81), film director; famed for such classics as *The Maltese Falcon; The Treasure of the Sierra Madre,* for which he won best writer and best director Academy Awards; *The Asphalt Jungle;* and *The African Queen.* He directed *Prizzi's Honor* (1985), a film for which his daughter won an Academy Award for acting. While in the armed forces during World War II, he directed and produced three films that are considered by film critics as among the finest made about World War II. The films are *Report from the Aleutians, The Battle of San Pietro,* and *Let There Be Light:* d. Middletown, RI, Aug. 28.

Iturbe Abásolo, Domingo (43), Spanish Basque military leader of the terrorist organization E.T.A.: d. Algeria, Feb. 27.

Jackson, Travis (83), baseball shortstop; played 15 years for the New York Giants from 1922 through the 1936 season. He was elected to the Hall of Fame in 1982: d. Waldo, AR, July 27.

Jochum, Eugen (84), German conductor; founder of the Bavarian Radio Symphony (1949–60); probably best known as a Bruckner specialist. In 1934 he became musical director of the Hamburg State Opera, and he founded and led the Hamburg Philharmonic from 1934 to 1949. He served as co-conductor of the Amsterdam Concertgebouw Orchestra (1961–64): d. Munich, West Germany, March 26.

Johnson, Eleanor M. (94), educator and longtime associate of *The Weekly Reader,* a children's periodical: d. Gaithersburg, MD, Oct. 8.

Johnson, Gus, Jr. (48), basketball player; star of the Baltimore Bullets (now Washington Bullets) (1963–72): d. Akron, OH, April 28.

Jonathan, Chief Leabua (72), prime minister of Lesotho (1966–86): d. Pretoria, South Africa, April 5.

Jutra, Claude (56), Canadian film director; best known for his film *My Uncle Antoine* (1971). Jutra's body was retrieved from the St. Lawrence River in April; he had disappeared in November 1986: d. Quebec (province), Canada, April 23 (reported).

Kabalevsky, Dmitri (82), Soviet composer; best known for his suite *The Comedians* and the Overture to his opera *Colas Breugnon:* d. USSR, Feb. 17 (reported).

Karami, Rashid (65), prime minister of Lebanon. A Sunni Muslim, over a period of 32 years he had held office ten times. He was assassinated when a bomb exploded in the helicopter in which he was traveling: d. Lebanon, June 1.

Kaye, Nora (born Nora Koreff) (67), American ballerina; she danced many classical roles but became known for creating a new contemporary look among dancers. She became a star in 1942 following her performance in the world premiere of Antony Tudor's *Pillar of Fire:* d. Santa Monica, CA, Feb. 28.

Kaye, Sammy (77), bandleader of the era of "swing" music; his career endured for some 50 years, and he had more than 100 hit records. Among the band's hit tunes were *The Old Lamplighter, Harbor Lights, The White Cliffs of Dover,* and *My Buddy:* d. Ridgewood, NJ, June 2.

Keyserling, Leon (79), chairman of the Council of Economic Advisers under President Harry Truman; he earlier served as an aide to Sen. Robert F. Wagner of New York, helping to draft the National Industrial Recovery Act of 1933, the Social Security Act of 1935, and the National Labor Relations Act (the Wagner Act): d. Washington, DC, Aug. 9.

King, Cecil (86), British newspaper leader: chairman of the International Publishing Corporation (1963–68): d. Dublin, Ireland, April 17.

Kishi, Nobusuke (90), prime minister of Japan (1957–60): d. Tokyo, Japan, Aug. 7.

Kolmogorov, Andrei N. (84), Soviet mathematician; the founder of modern probability theory: d. Moscow, Oct. 20.

Koruturk, Fahri (84), president of Turkey (1973–80): d. Istanbul, Oct. 12.

Labouisse, Henry R. (83), U.S. State Department and UN official. He was principal organizer of the Marshall Plan, the U.S. program to aid Europe after World War II, and directed the United Nations Children's Fund or UNICEF (1965–79): d. New York City, March 25.

Lamb, Edward (84), businessman, broadcaster, and lawyer; active in labor union and civil-rights causes. He gave up the practice of corporate law in the 1930s to handle labor-union cases. During the 1930s and 1940s he represented more than 75 unions. In 1946 he won a Supreme Court case enabling workers to collect pay "portal to portal": d. Maumee, OH, March 23.

Landon, Alfred M. (100), governor of Kansas (1933–37). A progressive Republican, he was that party's candidate for the presidency in 1936, losing the election in a landslide victory for Franklin Roosevelt: d. Topeka, KS, Oct. 12.

Lansdale, Edward G. (79), Air Force officer whose theories of counterinsurgent warfare were successful in the Philippines after World War II, but failed in South Vietnam: d. McLean, VA, Feb. 23.

Lash, Joseph P. (77), newspaperman-historian; he wrote many biographies, including a two-volume biography of Eleanor Roosevelt, which won him a Pulitzer Prize: d. Boston, Aug. 22.

Laurence, Margaret (60), Canadian novelist; well known for her novels and short stories set in the fictional town of Manawaka, Manitoba, including *A Jest of God* (1966) and *The Diviners* (1974): d. Lakefield, Ontario, Canada, Jan. 5.

Photos, AP/Wide World

Alf Landon *Margaret Laurence*

LeRoy, Mervyn (86), film director. In the late 1920s he began a directing career and went on to make some of Hollywood's outstanding films, including *Little Caesar* (1930) and *Mister Roberts* (1955): d. Beverly Hills, CA, Sept. 13.

Lescoulie, Jack (75), television personality; was a longtime co-host of the *Today* program, appearing between 1952 and 1961 and between 1962 and 1967: d. Memphis, TN, July 22.

Lévesque, René (65), provincial premier of Quebec (1976–85); he stepped down as premier after the Parti Québécois, the separatist party that he helped to found (in 1967) and led to power, suffered a fall in popularity. In 1959 he had joined the Liberal Party and held ministerial posts in the provincial government, but as he embraced the issue of a separate Quebec, he moved away from the Liberal Party and toward Parti Québécois: d. Montreal, Canada, Nov. 1.

Levi, Primo (67), Italian Jewish writer who trained as a chemist; wrote of his experiences during the Holocaust when he was imprisoned at Auschwitz. His books include *Survival in Auschwitz* and *The Periodic Table:* d. Turin, Italy, April 11.

Levine, Philip (87), medical researcher; discovered the Rh factor in human blood: d. New York City, Oct. 18.

Li Choh Hao (74), Chinese-born biochemist and a leading researcher in the function of the pituitary gland. He isolated and synthesized the human pituitary growth hormone in 1971 and in 1978 discovered beta-endorphin, a substance produced in the brain that is a pain killer: d. Berkeley, CA, Nov. 28.

List, Albert A. (86), industrialist and philanthropist: d. New York City, Sept. 11.

Locke, Bobby (Arthur D'Arcy) (69), South African golfer; was a world class golfer in the 1940s and the 1950s and was a four-time winner of the British Open (1949, 1950, 1952, 1957): d. Johannesburg, South Africa, March 9.

Ludlam, Charles (44), theater artist; established the Ridiculous Theatrical Company in New York City in 1967: d. New York City, May 28.

MacLean, Alistair (Stuart) (64), British author of the novels *The Guns of Navarone, Where Eagles Dare, Ice Station Zebra,* and others: d. Munich, West Germany, Feb. 2.

Madden, Ray John (95), U.S. representative (D-IN, 1943–77): d. Washington, DC, Sept. 28.

Malavasi, Ray (57), coach of the Los Angeles Rams football team (1977–82): d. Santa Ana, CA, Dec. 15.

Martin, Dean Paul (35), athlete, television performer, and musician, and the son of entertainer Dean Martin. A member of the Air National Guard, was killed in a plane crash: d. San Bernardino Mountains, CA, March 25 (crash discovered).

Nora Kaye

Culver Pictures

Sammy Kaye

AP/Wide World

Jack Lescoulie

AP/Wide World

René Lévesque

Photo Trends

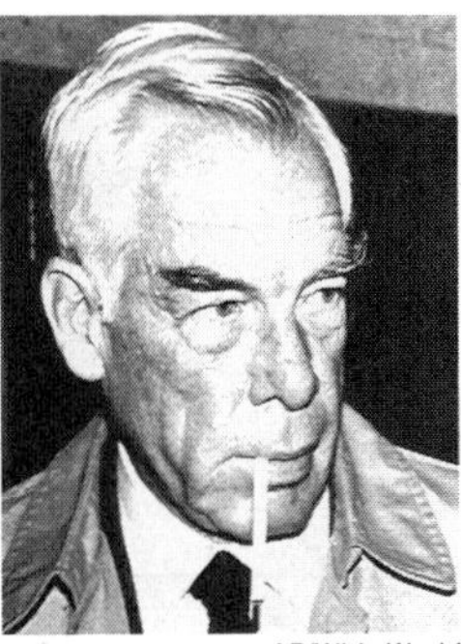
AP/Wide World
Lee Marvin

UPI-Bettmann Newsphotos
Gunnar Myrdal

Culver Pictures
Robert Preston

AP/Wide World
Bayard Rustin

Marvin, Lee (63), actor; played many "tough guy" roles in films and won an Academy Award in 1966 for his role in *Cat Ballou*. He also appeared on the stage and in many television dramas in the 1950s. Other films include *The Caine Mutiny* (1954), *The Dirty Dozen* (1967), and *Paint Your Wagon* (1969): d. Tucson, AZ, Aug. 29.

Masson, André (91), French painter. In the 1920s he was one of the early exponents of Surrealism. Among his best known works is the *Battle of Fishes:* d. Paris, Oct. 28.

McKee, William (80), Air Force four-star general. After his retirement from the military in 1964, he joined the National Aeronautics and Space Administration and under President Lyndon Johnson served as administrator in the Federal Aviation Administration: d. San Antonio, TX, Feb. 28.

McKinney, Stewart B. (56), U.S. representative (R-CT, 1971–87): d. Washington, DC, May 7.

McLaren, Norman (72), Scottish-born filmmaker, one of the most inventive figures in film animation; he became Canada's most admired film artist and for most of his career was associated with Canada's National Film Board. He developed the technique of pixillation—live action seen in staggered single frames: d. Montreal, Canada, Jan. 26.

Medawar, Sir Peter B. (72), British zoologist; who along with Sir Macfarlane Burnet won the Nobel Prize for Medicine in 1960 for work on the body's rejection of transplanted tissues: d. London, Oct. 2.

Menten, Pieter (88), convicted Nazi war criminal and art collector: d. Loosdrecht, the Netherlands, Nov. 14.

Minsky, Morton (85), one of four brothers who headed a burlesque family empire in the 1920s and 1930s: d. New York City, March 23.

Mitchell, Dale (65), baseball outfielder; played with the Cleveland Indians from 1946 until mid-1956 when he was traded to the Brooklyn Dodgers. He is probably best remembered for making the final out in Don Larsen's perfect game in the 1956 World Series: d. Jan. 5.

Mompou, Federico (94), Spanish composer; wrote more than 200 piano pieces; worked in a folklike idiom that was different from the trends of rational modernism: d. Barcelona, Spain, June 30.

Moore, Gerald (87), British classical pianist who as an accompanist became known in his own right. He retired in 1967 after a 50-year career: d. Buckinghamshire, England, March 13.

Moorhead, William S. (64), U.S. representative (D-PA, 1959–81): d. Baltimore, MD, Aug. 3.

Pola Negri

Geraldine Page
Photos, AP/Wide World

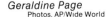

Murchison, Clinton William, Jr. (63), a member of a Texas wildcat oil family; he was involved in many business ventures, including the creation of the Dallas Cowboys football team in 1960. He sold the team in 1984: d. Dallas, TX, March 30.

Myrdal, Gunnar (88), Swedish Nobel Prize winning economist and social scientist; known for his book *An American Dilemma: The Negro Problem and Modern Democracy* (1944), which helped to destroy the "separate but equal" U.S. racial doctrine. He served in Sweden's Senate both before and after World War II. Between 1947 and 1957 he was secretary general of the United Nations Economic Commission for Europe in Geneva. Soon thereafter he went to India where his wife Alva was the Swedish ambassador. He began a ten-year study there that culminated in the three-volume *Asian Drama* (1968). In 1974 he shared the Nobel Prize in Economics. He also had presided over the Stockholm International Peace Research Institute: d. Stockholm, Sweden, May 17.

Negri, Pola (88), Polish-born silent screen actress; known as a vamp. Her off-screen life was well publicized. She popularized painted toenails in the 1920s, she married and divorced two noblemen, and was the fiancee of comedian Charles Chaplin: d. San Antonio, TX, Aug. 1.

Nix, Robert, Sr., (81), U.S. representative (D-PA, 1958–79): d. Philadelphia, PA, June 22.

Nixon, Edgar Daniel (87), civil-rights leader, prominent in the bus-boycott controversy after Rosa Parks refused to move to the back of the bus. In the 1920s, he helped organize the first successful black labor union, the Brotherhood of Sleeping Car Porters: d. Montgomery, AL, Feb. 25.

Nixon, F. Donald (72), California businessman and brother of former president Richard Nixon: d. Whittier, CA, June 27.

Northrop, John Howard (95), scientist; shared the 1946 Nobel Prize in chemistry: d. Wickenberg, AZ, May 27.

Nyiregyhazi, Erwin (84), Hungarian-born American classical pianist; enjoyed a career as a child prodigy in Europe and then as a young man in Germany and the United States in the 1920s. Later he retired from playing for decades prior to making a comeback in the 1970s: d. Los Angeles, CA, April 13.

O'Boyle, Cardinal Patrick (91), Roman Catholic archbishop of Washington, DC (1948–73). A champion of civil rights, he desegregated Washington churches and parochial schools three years before the 1954 U.S. Supreme Court ruling that outlawed school segregation: d. Washington, DC, Aug. 10.

O'Connor, Harvey (90), biographer and journalist; wrote *Mellon's Millions* (1933), *The Guggenheims* (1937), *The Astors* (1941), and several other books: d. Little Compton, RI, Aug. 29.

O'Konski, Alvin (83), U.S. representative (R-WI, 1943–73): Kewaunee, WI, July 8.

Page, Geraldine (62), actress; was a performer for more than 40 years and was long associated with the work of Tennessee Williams. Nominated several times for an Academy Award, she finally won an award for *The Trip to Bountiful* (1985): d. New York City, June 13.

Persichette, Vincent (72), American composer, educator, theorist, pianist, and conductor; he was associated with the Juilliard School for nearly 40 years: d. Philadelphia, PA, Aug. 14.

Poage, William Robert (87), U.S. representative (D-TX, 1937–79): d. Temple, TX, Jan. 3.

Preston, Robert (born Robert Preston Meservey) (68), actor of stage and films; particularly known for his role as the confidence man in *The Music Man* (stage, 1957; film, 1962): d. Santa Barbara, CA, March 21.

Rich, Buddy (69), jazz drummer; played with such leaders as Artie Shaw, Tommy Dorsey, and Harry James, and headed up his own bands as well. He opened his own New York club, Buddy's Place, in the 1970s: d. Los Angeles, CA, April 2.

Robison, Howard (71), U.S. representative (R-NY, 1958–75): d. Rehoboth, DE, Sept. 26.

Roca Calderio, Blas (born Francisco Calderio) (78), former member of Cuba's Communist Party Politburo and president of Cuba's National Assembly (1976–81): d. Havana, Cuba, April 25.

Rogers, Carl Ransom (85), psychotherapist and author; known for developing the client-centered approach to psychotherapy. He taught at Ohio State University, the University of Chicago, and the University of Wisconsin before founding the Center for Studies of the Person in La Jolla, CA. Among his best known books is *On Becoming a Person* (1961): d. La Jolla, CA, Feb. 4.

Rowan, Dan (65), comedian and cohost and coproducer of *Rowan and Martin's Laugh-In,* a popular weekly television series that ran from 1968 until 1973: d. Englewood, FL, Sept. 22.

Rustin, Bayard (75), a pacifist and civil-rights activist; was a chief organizer of the 1963 March on Washington and the 1964 New York school boycott. For a time he worked for the Congress of Racial Equality, for the War Resisters League, and for Dr. Martin Luther King, Jr.: d. New York City, Aug. 24.

Sabbe, Osman Saleh (55), Ethiopian rebel leader who for more than 20 years struggled to win independence for the province of Eritrea: d. Cairo, Egypt, April 4.

Salas, Rafael (58), executive director of the United Nations Fund for Population Activities (1969–87); he was a senior member of the Philippine government in the 1960s: d. Washington, DC, March 4.

Salt, Waldo (72), screenwriter; won an Oscar twice—for *Midnight Cowboy* and *Coming Home:* d. Los Angeles, CA, March 7.

Schidlof, Peter (65), Austrian-born violist of Britain's Amadeus Quartet: d. Cumbria, England, Aug. 16.

Schlumberger, Jean (80), French jewelry designer; set the famous Tiffany diamond in 1957: d. Paris, Aug. 29.

Scott, Randolph (89), film actor, best known for his work in Westerns: d. Los Angeles, CA, March 2.

Shawn, Dick (63), comedian and actor, known for his stand-up comic appearances and for his performance in the film *The Producers:* d: La Jolla, CA, April 17.

Sidarouss, Cardinal Stephanos (83), patriarch emeritus of the Coptic Catholic Church; was patriarch (1958–85) and was made a cardinal in 1965: d. Cairo, Egypt, Aug. 23.

Simpson, Joy (40), American opera singer: d. Cape Town, South Africa, March 25.

Sirk, Douglas (born Detlef Sierck) (86), film director; his more prominent films were *Magnificent Obsession, All I Desire,* and *Written on the Wind:* d. Lugano, Switzerland, Jan. 14.

Smith, Willi (39), fashion designer; known for trendy clothes and for his WilliWear sportswear: d. New York City, April 17.

Snedden, Sir Billy (Mackie) (60), former leader of Australia's Liberal Party: d. Sydney, Australia, June 27.

Lord Soames (Arthur Christopher John) (66), British statesman. The last colonial governor in Rhodesia (now Zimbabwe), he presided over its transition to majority rule in 1979. Lord Soames also was ambassador to France (1966–72) and held a seat in Parliament for 16 years, until 1966. He was a son-in-law of Sir Winston Churchill: d. Hampshire, England, Sept. 16.

Soyer, Raphael (87), Russian-born U.S. artist; was a social realist painter, who along with his two brothers achieved renown: d. New York City, Nov. 4.

Stanford-Tuck, Robert (Roland) (70) British World War II flying ace; became a highly decorated commander after fighting the German Luftwaffe in the Battle of Britain: d. London, May 5.

Susskind, David (66), producer and talk-show host; appeared on television for nearly 30 years. In addition he produced stage, film, and television shows: d. New York City, Feb. 22 (found dead).

Prince Takamatsu (82), prince of the Japanese royal family and brother of Emperor Hirohito: d. Tokyo, Japan, Feb. 3.

Randolph Scott *Earl Wilson*

Photos, AP/Wide World

Photos, AP/Wide World

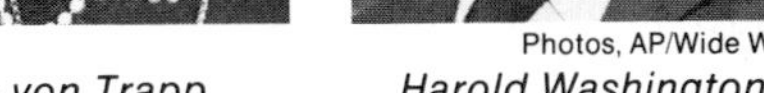

Maria von Trapp *Harold Washington*

Thomaz, Américo de Deus Rodrigues (92), former president of Portugal. A far rightist, he was handpicked to seek the presidency in 1958 by the dictator António Salazar and ousted in a leftist military coup in 1974. He then lived in exile in Brazil, returning to Portugal in 1978: d. Cascais, Portugal, Sept. 18.

Trifa, Valerian (72), archbishop; leader of the Rumanian Orthodox Episcopate based in Grass Lake, MI. He was accused of being a Nazi supporter who incited attacks on Jews and other civilians during World War II and was deported from the United States in 1984: d. Portugal, Jan. 28.

Tsatsos, Constantine (88), president of the Republic of Greece (1975–80): d. Athens, Oct. 8.

Tudor, Antony (born William Cook) (78 or 79), British-born ballet choreographer; widely considered the master of the psychological ballet. His greatest works include *Dark Elegies, Jardin aux Lilas, Romeo and Juliet, Pillar of Fire,* and *Undertow.* Tudor became associate artistic director of American Ballet Theater in 1974 and was named choreographer emeritus of that company in 1980: d. New York City, April 19.

Unruh, Jesse (64), California Democratic politician: d. Marina del Rey, CA, Aug. 4.

Vernon, Jackie (62), television and nightclub comedian: d. Hollywood, CA, Nov. 10.

Vitria, Emmanuel (67), Frenchman who was the world's longest surviving heart transplant patient. He lived for 18 years: d. Marseilles, France, May 11.

von Trapp, Baroness Maria (82), woman whose life was portrayed in the play and film *The Sound of Music:* d. Morrisville, VT, March 28.

Warhol, Andy *see* page 121.

Warriner, John (80), textbook author of a widely used series of English textbooks, called Warriner's *English Grammar and Composition,* published beginning in 1946: d. St. Croix, Virgin Islands, July 29.

Washington, Harold (65), mayor of Chicago (1983–87), the first black mayor of that city. He had earlier served as an Illinois state representative (1965–76) and state senator (1976–80). He was elected to the U.S. House of Representatives in 1980 and 1982 prior to becoming mayor: d. Chicago, IL, Nov. 25.

Wescott, Glenway (85), American expatriate novelist and essayist; lived in France in the 1920s and the 1930s. He achieved literary acclaim with his second novel, *The Grandmothers:* d. Rosemont, NJ, Feb. 22.

Wesley, Charles (95), educator and scholar; was a pioneer in the education of blacks. He wrote about a dozen books on black history including his doctoral dissertation published in 1925, *Negro Labor in the United States 1850 to 1925:* d. Washington, DC, Aug. 16.

Williams, Emlyn (81), Welsh actor, playwright, and director; his hit plays include *Night Must Fall* and *The Corn is Green,* both in which he also performed. In 1950 he began work on his one-man show in which he portrayed Charles Dickens; he subsequently toured the world with it: d. London, Sept. 25.

Wilson, Earl (79), syndicated columnist who chronicled show business and New York night life: d. Yonkers, NY, Jan. 16.

Wittig, Georg (90), German chemist; Nobel laureate in chemistry in 1979: d. Heidelberg, Germany, Aug. 26.

Wunder, George S. (75), cartoonist; wrote and drew the Terry and the Pirates comic strip for 26 years: d. New Milford, CT, Dec. 13.

Wydler, John W. (63), U.S. representative (R-NY, 1963–81): d. Washington, DC, Aug. 4.

Young, Dick (69), nationally syndicated sports columnist: New York City, Aug. 31.

Zorinsky, Edward (58), U.S. senator (D-NE, 1977–87); a maverick politician who switched from the Republican to the Democratic Party prior to his election to the Senate: d. Omaha, NE, March 6.

OCEANOGRAPHY

The U.S. National Science Foundation in 1987 began a major new initiative called the Global Geosciences Program, which consists of separate but related research efforts that treat the earth as an integrated system of global oceanic and atmospheric circulation systems and as a delicate, dynamic balance of biogeochemical fluxes that sustain life on the planet. A central goal is to establish major cause-and-effect relationships between the climate system, biogeochemical cycles, and tectonic activity which affect such major elements as carbon, nitrogen, oxygen, and sulfur. One component of the program is the Global Ocean Flux Study (GOFS), which will review satellite observations of ocean color to obtain data on plant pigment distribution and correlate this with direct observations of the upper ocean.

Much data already was available from application of the Coastal Zone Color Scanner (CZCS) satellite. Remotely-sensed pigment fields have shown variation in plankton biomass on scales of days to years for limited areas. A major new objective of CZCS was to produce global composites through the processing of some 65,000 individual two-minute satellite scans. The first satellite-derived views on an ocean-wide scale became available for the North Atlantic, detailing productive coastal upwelling areas (especially off northwest Africa); the outflows of the Amazon, Orinoco, and Mississippi rivers; and high productivity associated with the north wall of the Gulf Stream and with continental shelves, leaving a generally low concentration of phytoplankton in the central North Atlantic. The prototype CZCS instrument, launched in 1978 for a one-year feasibility study, was finally shut down in June 1986 because of a power failure. A new instrument capable of producing global maps of chlorophyll-like pigments for 75% of the surface of the planet remained a priority of the GOFS program and could be in orbit in 1990.

Manned spacecraft also provide a method for collecting previously unavailable data. Studies of photographs taken from past shuttle flights have shown such unexpected physical details as moderate-sized eddies in numerous regions of the world ocean, internal waves from the Strait of Gibraltar into the Mediterranean Sea, phytoplankton blooms, and the extent of river outflows. An expanded program was planned for future manned space missions.

The Tropical Ocean and Global Atmosphere program (TOGA), a major ten-year international effort, seeks to determine the extent to which regional climates are affected by changes such as the El Niño/Southern Oscillation (ENSO) and to predict such events. El Niño is a warming of the surface waters of the eastern Equatorial Pacific that occurs at irregular intervals of 2-7 years and lasts for 1-2 years; the Southern Oscillation is a shift in atmospheric pressures between the Indonesia/North Australia region and the southeast Pacific. TOGA seeks to develop a computer modeling capability to predict monthly and seasonal climate changes caused by such behaviors. The necessary field observations, using buoys and island stations in the western and central-tropical Pacific, are being done as a part of the World Climate Research Program (WCRP). Although data in December 1986 resembled those collected in an ENSO warming, the irregularities were weaker than those of the 1982-83 episode, the most recent full event.

Observations of ocean circulation made in 1987 by acoustic tomography—in which sonar pulses delineate the complex patterns within the water mass—were a prelude to the World Ocean Circulation Experiment (WOCE) planned for 1990-95. The array currently in operation in the Pacific Ocean north of Hawaii uses pulses transmitted between three buoys forming a triangle with sides 600 mi (970 km) long. Each buoy acts both as a transmitter of sonic pulses and as a receiver. From analysis of the multiple arrivals of pulses, it is possible to determine water conditions such as temperature at many depths and to map the ocean in three dimensions. WOCE will consider the formation mechanisms of the ocean's dominant water masses and their subsequent spread throughout the world ocean.

The first investigation by submersible of high-temperature hydrothermal vents in the Atlantic Ocean was made in 1986. The sites are about 1 km (.6 mi) deeper on the mid-Atlantic ridge than on more rapidly spreading oceanic ridges in the Pacific. However, ocean hot springs everywhere appear to be similar in terms of temperature (up to 350° C) and the mineral content of sulfates and silicates. Many similarities also exist worldwide in the specialized fauna of these sites, although examination in 1987 of vents in the Marianas trough did not reveal the rigid tube worms and giant clams typical of hot spring fields on the East Pacific rise and elsewhere.

Core samplings of the Ocean Drilling Program (ODP), taken near the Antarctic, revealed rapid temperature changes associated with plate tectonic movements. The ODP drill ship *Joides Resolution* moved on to investigate the time of the opening of the South Atlantic as South America moved away from Africa.

In the south-central Pacific, a research vessel associated with the Scripps Institution of Oceanography in California was rocked by an undersea volcanic eruption in mid-October. The research ship *Melville* was studying ocean currents in the area. Huge bubbles of steam and volcanic gas, also containing hot volcanic rocks, burst on the surface of the water.

David A. McGill
U.S. Coast Guard Academy

AP/Wide World

Ohio Gov. Richard Celeste (left) *and Honda Motor Company President Tadashi Kume announced in September that the automaker would build its second U.S. assembly plant near the existing one in Marysville.*

OHIO

Through much of 1987, the first year of his second term, Democratic Gov. Richard F. Celeste was the focus of considerable attention from Ohioans. As he was sworn in in January, there was lingering controversy over the awarding of numerous no-bid contracts late in 1986 for the installation of telephone systems in state offices. This came amid accusations of overcharging, resulting in gifts to the state Democratic treasury. In June, Governor Celeste, who was considering a run for the 1988 Democratic presidential nomination, saw his hopes evaporate as *The* (Cleveland) *Plain Dealer* reported that he had been "romantically linked" with at least three women other than his wife, one as recently as 1985. He announced in August that he would not run.

OHIO • Information Highlights

Area: 41,330 sq mi (107 044 km²).
Population (July 1, 1986 est.): 10,752,000.
Chief Cities (July 1, 1986 est.): Columbus, the capital, 556,030; Cleveland, 535,830; Cincinnati, 369,750; Toledo, 340,680; Akron, 220,060; Dayton, 178,920.
Government (1987): *Chief Officers*—governor, Richard F. Celeste (D); lt. gov., Paul R. Leonard (D). *General Assembly*—Senate, 33 members; House of Representatives, 99 members.
State Finances (fiscal year 1986): *Revenue,* $23,021,000,000; *expenditure,* $19,010,000,000.
Personal Income (1986): $149,807,000,000; per capita, $13,933.
Labor Force (June 1987): *Civilian labor force,* 5,293,400; *unemployed,* 384,400 (7.3% of total force).
Education: *Enrollment* (fall 1985)—public elementary schools, 1,206,138; public secondary, 587,637; colleges and universities, 514,745. *Public school expenditures* (1985–86), $5,900,000,000 ($3,547 per pupil).

Elections. Ohio voters on November 3 approved two state constitutional amendments. One ordered Ohio lottery profits to go directly into a fund for public schools instead of passing through the state's general fund. The second authorized $1.2 billion in general-obligation bonds to aid local bridge, waterworks, road, sewer, and solid-waste disposal projects.

Mayors in several major cities were reelected: Don Plusquellic in Akron; Sam Purses in Canton; Dana Rinehart in Columbus; Donna Owens in Toledo; and Patrick Ungaro in Youngstown. Cleveland Mayor George Voinovich, midway through his term, began a campaign for the 1988 Republican nomination for the U.S. Senate seat held by Democrat Howard Metzenbaum.

Economy and Industry. Numerous layoffs, especially in the state's steel and automobile facilities, were reported during the year. On the positive side, many small shops opened in or near manufacturing areas, and the Honda Motor Company announced plans to build a second assembly plant in the state.

British Petroleum, which had teamed with Cleveland-based Standard Oil in pumping oil from a major Alaskan field, increased its holdings in Standard Oil through a stock offer. Bids to take over rubber companies in Akron, however, were parried successfully.

Bullet Train. A plan approved by the 1986 state legislature for a $2 billion, high-speed passenger railroad linking major Ohio cities was derailed in mid-1987. The project was to have been financed by tax-exempt bonds, which collided with the new federal tax laws.

Crime. Donald Harvey, a 35-year-old former nurse's aide at hospitals in Cincinnati and in the state of Kentucky, admitted having poisoned or suffocated as many as 56 terminally ill patients from the early 1970s to 1987, when he was linked to one of the deaths. In August, Harvey pleaded guilty to murdering 24 people since 1983 and was sentenced to three consecutive life terms.

Urban Population. From 1984 to 1986, according to U.S. Census Bureau estimates, the seven most populous cities in Ohio—Columbus, Cleveland, Cincinnati, Toledo, Akron, Dayton, and Youngstown—experienced a combined population decline of some 25,200. All seven cities showed some loss, with Cleveland registering the largest (nearly 11,000).

JOHN F. HUTH, JR., *Former Reporter "The Plain Dealer," Cleveland*

OKLAHOMA

The Oklahoma legislature adjourned on July 17, 1987, after a 48-hour marathon session on the issue of reforming the state's Tax Commission. In a deadlock with the Democratic-controlled legislature, Republican Gov. Henry Bellmon—who took office in January—had vetoed a $40.2 million appropriation for the Tax Commission to deter the legislature from adjourning before reaching a compromise on proposed reforms. Under the final agreement, no more than two members of the same political party may serve on the commission, and an administrator would be appointed to centralize management.

When it convened in January, the legislature faced the task of cutting $200 million from the 1986–87 state budget, or else increasing revenues. It was able to achieve a $2.23 billion standstill budget, but only with tax increases of $275 million. The state sales tax, as well as taxes on gasoline, alcoholic beverages, and cigarettes were raised. Fees for tourism and recreation agencies, assessments on state-chartered banks, and university tuition were hiked.

Of the $2.23 billion budget appropriation, education received $1.1 billion for common schools, vocational-technical institutions, and higher education. Human services, agriculture, commerce, corrections, highways, and public safety all received increased appropriations. Funding for health services, veterans affairs, and tourism and recreation were cut back.

Economy and Economic Development. The state's economic growth continued to lag behind that of the nation as a whole. The Oklahoma Department of Commerce reported an upturn in the state's agricultural and oil industries, and oil prices and drilling activity increased. But Oklahoma's 29 bank failures in 1987 were second only to Texas.

Economic recovery was the main focus of the legislative session. Major economic-development measures created "Oklahoma Futures," a policy development board; the Center for the Advancement of Science and Technology, to concentrate on research; and the Capital Investment Board, to supervise a business-loan fund. Tax incentives were authorized for small businesses, inventors of new products, export trading companies, and oil recovery efforts. The state treasurer was authorized to lend $25 million annually to state banks for "below market value" loans to agribusinesses and distressed farms.

Legislation. Laws were passed to increase legislative oversight of administrative rule making by state agencies. The lawmakers failed to implement the governor's cabinet system, approved during the previous session. Benefits were increased in state retirement programs. The speed limit was increased to 65 miles per hour (105 km/h) on some highways, and a feasibility study on construction of new state turnpikes was ordered.

In the area of criminal justice, the controversial "make my day" bill was enacted, authorizing citizens to use deadly force in defending themselves against persons entering their homes whom they believe will harm them. Construction of privately operated juvenile detention centers, county jails, and prisons also was authorized.

Corruption Charges. Banking Commissioner Robert Empie was suspended by Governor Bellmon in March amid charges of insider trading, but he was reinstated the following month after being cleared of wrongdoing. In an agreement with the governor, whom he charged with a politically motivated attack, Empie stepped down June 30.

Chancellor of Higher Education Joe Leone resigned amid charges of filing duplicate travel claims, but a special district judge ruled that the state failed to prove its case.

JOHN W. WOOD, *University of Oklahoma*

OKLAHOMA • Information Highlights

Area: 69,956 sq mi (181 186 km²).
Population (July 1, 1986 est.): 3,305,000.
Chief Cities (July 1, 1986 est.): Oklahoma City, the capital, 446,120; Tulsa, 373,750; Lawton (1980 census), 80,054.
Government (1987): *Chief Officers*—governor, Henry Bellmon (R); lt. gov., Robert S. Kerr III (D). *Legislature*—Senate, 48 members; House of Representatives, 101 members.
State Finances (fiscal year 1986): *Revenue,* $5,905,000,000; *expenditure,* $5,629,000,000.
Personal Income (1986): $40,595,000,000; per capita, $12,283.
Labor Force (June 1987): *Civilian labor force,* 1,581,600; *unemployed;* 119,800 (7.6% of total force).
Education: *Enrollment* (fall 1985)—public elementary schools, 414,279; public secondary, 178,048; colleges and universities, 169,173. *Public school expenditures* (1985–86), $1,600,000,000 ($2,867 per pupil).

ONTARIO

For Ontario, Canada's most populous province, 1987 marked the second year of exceptional prosperity, with 9.4% growth in annual product. There was a 312,000 net gain in jobs, with a 3.5% increase in net product forecast for 1988. Despite the booming economy and falling unemployment, a federal free-trade treaty with the United States (*see* page 165) aroused fears in the province. Premier David Peterson and his Liberal Party—who generally opposed the free-trade measure—were returned to power in September elections.

Budget and Legislation. The good times were reflected in the speech from the throne in April and the budget in May. With revenues higher than anticipated, Treasurer Robert Nixon proposed to reduce the provincial deficit by C$331 million, to $980 million. Property and income-tax breaks were forthcoming for senior citizens, and medicare premiums were eliminated for 40,000 low-income earners. The handicapped would receive an additional $50 per month. More money was allocated for day care, $185 million, with $33 million over three years for capital expenditure on child care. Another $100 million was provided to upgrade the GO transit system in southern Ontario, and more than $290 million was to be spent over three years on highways.

Premier Peterson's Liberal government kept a 1985 election promise by introducing a bill requiring equal pay for work of equal value, despite opposition from business groups, objecting to the huge bureaucracy that would be required (they argued) to enforce it. In another victory for the premier, the Supreme Court of Canada in June upheld the act funding Catholic schools through grade 12.

High automobile-insurance premiums emerged as another lively issue. The New Democratic Party (NDP), falling behind in the polls, attempted to regain momentum by proposing a provincially run, no-fault auto-insurance system. The government countered with a proposal for privately run, no-fault insurance, and the insurance industry came up with plans of its own. In late April, legislation was tabled to freeze auto-insurance rates and in some cases to cut them. General oversight of the industry also was proposed to prevent companies from cross-subsidizing auto rates from other forms of insurance. The legislation died on the order paper (legislative calendar).

English-French tension erupted during the summer with a plan to extend bilingual services. Opposition was spearheaded by the Organization for the Preservation of the English language. Some townships in Eastern Ontario declared themselves unilingual English.

Elections. In late June, the two-year accord between the Liberals and NDP (which put the Liberals into office in exchange for a common legislative agenda) expired. Buoyed by the province's strong economic performance and his own rising popularity in the opinion polls, Premier Peterson called an election for September 10. The official opposition, the Progressive Conservatives led by Larry Grossman, tried to regain power by promising lower taxes and increased spending. They also sought to exploit the opposition to bilingualism and strongly supported the federal government's proposals for free trade with the United States. The NDP, vying to become the official opposition, came out strongly against free trade, and for a public auto-insurance system and better day care. The Liberals promised more money for education and to clean up the environment.

The result was a personal triumph for Premier Peterson, whose Liberals won 95 seats (up from 51) in the 130-seat legislature. Most commentators ascribed the victory to a public trust in the premier himself. The NDP won just 19 seats (down from 23) but became the official opposition, as the PCs won only 16 seats (down from 50). Larry Grossman lost his own seat and resigned as PC leader.

PETER J. KING, *Carleton University*

ONTARIO • Information Highlights

Area: 412,580 sq mi (1 068 580 km²).
Population (1986 census): 9,113,515.
Chief Cities (1986 census): Toronto, the provincial capital, 612,289; Ottawa, the federal capital, 300,763; Scarborough, 484,676; Mississauga, 374,005; Hamilton, 306,728; London, 269,140.
Government (1986): *Chief Officers*—lt. gov., Lincoln Alexander; premier, David Peterson (Liberal). *Legislature*—Legislative Assembly, 130 members.
Provincial Finances (1986–87 fiscal year budget): *Revenues,* $29,960,000,000; *expenditures,* $31,500,000,000.
Personal Income (average weekly earnings, July 1987): $454.13.
Labor Force (August 1987, seasonally adjusted: *Employed* workers, 15 years of age and over, 4,991,000; *Unemployed,* 290,000 (5.8%).
Education (1986–87): *Enrollment*—elementary and secondary schools, 1,852,300 pupils; postsecondary—universities, 183,200; community colleges, 91,900.
(All monetary figures are in Canadian dollars).

OREGON

The "Oregon Comeback," campaign slogan for new governor Neil Goldschmidt, seemed a statement of fact by midyear. Oregon's economy continued the upward trend it began in 1985 and the state's unemployment rate reached an eight year low—the first year in the 1980s that it was below the national average.

Oregon was expected to gain 34,000 new jobs in 1987, bringing the state's nonagricultural labor force to a historic high of 1.1 million jobs. The greatest employment increase was in manufacturing, with the service sector and

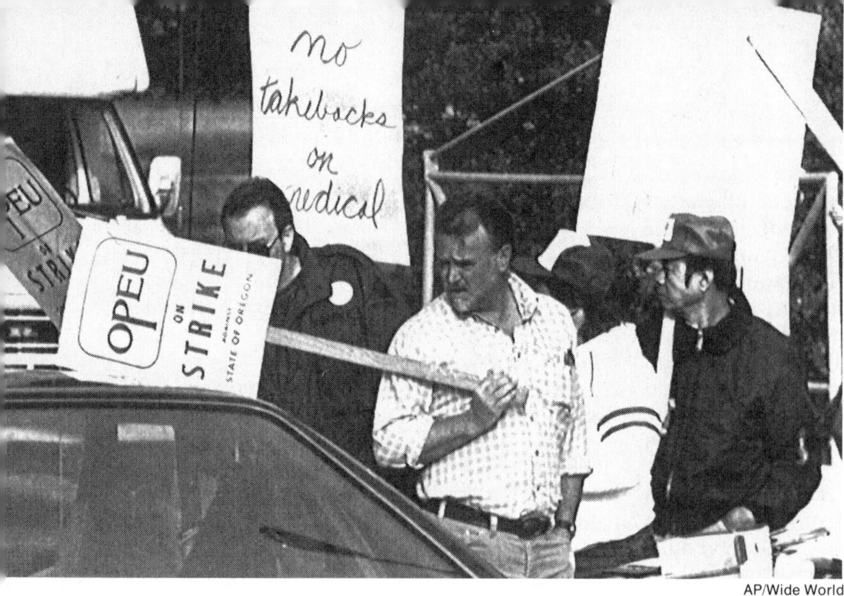

AP/Wide World

The Oregon Public Employees Union went on strike September 16 after contract talks broke down. The job action ended eight days later, when agreement on a new two-year pact—calling for 2% and 4% annual pay raises—was reached.

wholesale and retail trade sectors also posting significant gains. Farmers were plagued by labor shortages attributed to misunderstandings and uncertainty among migrant workers regarding the new federal immigration law. Particularly hurt were growers specializing in berries and other cannery.

Swearingen Engineering and Technology, Inc., an aircraft design firm based in Texas, may build an aircraft assembly plant in Salem. Such a plant would employ 2,000 to 3,000 people. No decision was made by year's end.

Forest fires destroyed more than 150,000 acres (60 700 ha) of timber in the state, most of it in the south. Costs of fighting fires in Oregon were estimated to surpass $50 million.

Legislation. Taxes, motor-vehicle legislation, and construction at state institutions were issues addressed by the legislature in 1987. The state income tax code was changed to incorporate many of the changes in the new federal code. The top rate was reduced from 10% to 9%, and it was estimated that the revision would cut the income taxes for 60% of Oregon households.

The state gasoline tax, currently 12 cents per gallon, would increase by 2 cents each year until it reaches 18 cents per gallon in 1990. Mandatory seat-belt legislation would take effect 90 days after adjournment; however, it would be submitted to the voters in November 1988 for final approval after a one-year trial. Another measure to be placed before the voters in the May 1988 primary election would require all motorcyclists to wear helmets. Current helmet law applies only to those younger than 18. The state's 55 miles per hour (89 km/h) speed limit was raised to 65 mph (105 km/h) on selected rural lengths of interstate highways.

A $32 million plan to ease prison overcrowding was submitted by Governor Goldschmidt. The plan, which won passage easily, would add more than 300 beds to the relatively new Eastern Oregon Correctional Institution at Pendleton. It further provides for construction of 1,000 new beds in correctional centers throughout the state. State prisoners may then be housed in a number of new sites, relieving Salem's prison population, and making family visitations less difficult.

For the first time in eight years, the State System of Higher Education received funding for capital construction projects. A total of $65 million would be spent on the eight state campuses and on several community colleges.

Other. In May, voters approved Governor Goldschmidt's "School Safety Net" plan. The plan permits school districts without tax bases (about one third of the state's districts) to fall back to the previous year's budget without voter approval when voters fail to approve a new levy. Forest Grove's schools closed three weeks early because of repeated failure of the property tax levy required to finance the district's ten schools for the entire year.

L. CARL AND JOANN BRANDHORST
Western Oregon State University

OREGON • Information Highlights

Area: 97,073 sq mi (251 419 km²).
Population (July 1, 1986): 2,698,000.
Chief Cities (July 1, 1984 est.): Salem, the capital (1980 census), 89,233; Portland, 387,870; Eugene, 105,410.
Government (1987–88): *Chief Officers*—governor, Neil Goldschmidt (D); secretary of state, Barbara Roberts (D); *Legislative Assembly*—Senate, 30 members; House of Representatives, 60 members.
State Finances (fiscal year 1986): *Revenue,* $5,524,000,000; *expenditure,* $4,925,000,000.
Personal Income (1986): $35,955,000,000, per capita, $13,328.
Labor Force (June 1987): *Civilian labor force,* 1,379,300; *unemployed,* 75,800 (5.5% of total force).
Education: *Enrollment* (fall 1985)—public elementary schools, 305,418; public secondary, 142,109; colleges and universities, 137,967. *Public school expenditures* (1985–86), $1,705,000,000 ($4,123 per pupil).

OTTAWA

Ottawa enjoyed a relatively quiet year in 1987, its citizens being mainly preoccupied with the perennial problems of traffic, urban renewal, and being a capital city.

A proposal by the National Capital Commission to create a "royal mile" by paving the ceremonial route linking Parliament and Government House pink was abandoned after a public outcry on grounds of expense. The city council also decided against a plan to demolish City Hall on Green Island to erect a bigger building. Although only 32 years old, it is considered a good example of modern (1950s) architecture, and Heritage groups objected. A subsequent decision to refurbish the existing structure produced a squabble over the choice of architect. More dramatically, the city and region agreed to partially reconstruct and open up the Rideau Street Mall, in the heart of the city, to regular traffic. Currently restricted to pedestrians and buses, it was a major item in the reconstruction of the downtown area several years ago and required major rerouting of traffic.

At the beginning of July, the province of Ontario began prosecution of the city for polluting the Rideau River by letting coal tar leak into it during transit way construction. Calls for a public inquiry into the Ottawa-Carleton transportation system and criticism of its C$400 million debt were stilled when it received the American Public Transportation Association's Outstanding Achievement award (the highest in North America) for being the most efficient transit system on the continent.

During the provincial election campaign, Premier David Peterson promised that the long delayed construction of highway 416 around the southwest of the city would begin in 1990.

The Ottawa Rough Riders of the Canadian Football League had their worst season in decades. Experiencing severe support problems, they were given by their owners for $1 to a group of local supporters, who are now running the club. Mayor Jim Durrell was working to attract the 1992 Commonwealth Games to Ottawa.

PETER J. KING, *Carleton University*

PAKISTAN

Both domestic violence and external security threats continued to plague Pakistan during 1987. The economy maintained its strong momentum, however, and the government of Prime Minister Mohammad Khan Junejo managed to survive despite increased political pressures from several quarters.

Politics. As Gen. Mohammad Zia ul-Haq completed a full decade in power, the last nine years as president, Pakistani political authority remained divided between civilian and military leadership, with gradual but cautious movement toward greater civilian control. In April the opposition in Parliament successfully called for constitutional amendments which would strengthen the office of prime minister and strip President Zia of his military authority. In general, the privileged role of the military in Pakistani politics and society came under increasing criticism from both politicians and the public. Sensitive to charges of corruption and inefficiency in his government, the prime minister reshuffled and expanded his cabinet.

Opposition political parties jockeyed for position in anticipation of the general elections promised for 1990. A conference of about a dozen opposition parties called for Zia's resignation and the establishment of an interim government, but this "all-parties" gathering failed to unite the opposition or even to get the participation of all of the major opposition players.

Benazir Bhutto's Pakistan People's Party (PPP) sought to improve its relations not only with the other parties in the Movement for the Restoration of Democracy (MRD), but also with such former opponents as the fundamentalist Jamaat-i-Islami. Benazir's personal popularity, as the charismatic daughter of the prime minister whom Zia overthrew in 1977 and executed in 1979, remained strong, but it was unclear whether her appeal could be translated into electoral victories for the PPP. In one test, the Mian Channu by-election in rural Punjab, the PPP candidate was soundly defeated by Junejo's Pakistan Muslim League (PML).

One major domestic problem was the high level of political violence in 1987. Ethnic factors, often a source of conflict in the past, have been intensified by the growing numbers of Pathans (Pushtuns) in Karachi and their uneasy relations with the Urdu-speaking Muhajir community there. In December 1986, a police crackdown on illicit drug traffic, largely Pathan-run, led to renewed Pathan-Muhajir rioting which reverberated well into 1987. A relatively new factor, in addition to the familiar patterns of ethnic violence, was the growing incidence of terrorist attacks, attributed by President Zia to *Wad,* the Afghan secret police. Bombings in a Karachi bazaar on July 14 killed more than 70 people. Critics of the government linked these acts of terrorist reprisal to Pakistan's involvement as a conduit for U.S. weapons assistance to the Afghan mujahidin (rebels).

The Economy. Pakistan's economy continued to grow impressively during 1987. Gross domestic product (GDP) grew 7%. Throughout the 1980s it has maintained a growth rate of better than 6%. Agriculture grew nearly 6% and manufacturing more than 7%. Exports were up 18% and imports down 2.5%, thereby helping to reduce Pakistan's trade deficit by more than 20%. Inflation was reduced to 3.5%,

Chinese Premier Zhao Ziyang, escorted by Pakistan Prime Minister Mohammad Khan Junejo, waves to young spectators at the start of his four-day official visit to Islamabad.

AP/Wide World

prompting the Asian Development Bank to note in its annual report that Pakistan was the only country in South Asia to bring inflation under control during the five-year period since 1982.

The government of Pakistan proposed an ambitious tax-reform package and a record budget, but ultimately retreated after heavy criticism from Parliament and public rioting in Karachi. Almost half of the 1987-88 development plan would be financed through foreign assistance. Debt servicing would constitute 26.4% of projected government current expenditures. Repayment of the principal on foreign loans is equivalent to one third of the country's annual export earnings.

Foreign Relations. Relations with India, Afghanistan, and the United States continued to dominate Pakistan's foreign-policy concerns. Despite serious attempts to improve their relations during the past decade, India and Pakistan came dangerously close to armed warfare in January, when both sides rapidly escalated troop concentrations on their long common border. Tensions were finally brought under control through diplomatic action.

More persistent were problems on the Afghan frontier. A Soviet-initiated cease-fire in January lasted only a few weeks, largely because of its rejection by the major mujahidin groups. Further sessions of the UN-sponsored Afghan-Pakistani proximity talks at Geneva similarly failed to resolve the major remaining issue—the timetable for Soviet troop withdrawal. Afghan incursions into Pakistani border areas continued, including intense and repeated bombing of refugee villages.

Pakistan's relations with the United States, including the prospects for renewal of American military support, were seriously undermined during 1987 because of the nuclear proliferation issue. In March an article by Indian journalist Kuldip Nayar in a British newspaper quoted Pakistani nuclear scientist Abdul Qadeer Khan as saying that Pakistan had a nuclear device. Despite subsequent denials from both Khan and the government of Pakistan, the alleged statement strengthened anti-Pakistan sentiment in the U.S. Congress. Then in July came the arrest in Philadelphia of a Pakistani national, Arshad Pervez, for attempting to export a special type of steel potentially destined for use in the manufacture of nuclear devices. Again, despite Pakistani official denials of any governmental involvement or prior knowledge, the event had strong political impact. Congress postponed until January 1988 action on the six-year $4.02 billion assistance package which both Pakistani and American officials earlier had expected to see pass without great difficulty.

WILLIAM L. RICHTER
Kansas State University

PAKISTAN • Information Highlights

Official Name: Islamic Republic of Pakistan.
Location: South Asia.
Area: 310,402 sq mi (803 940 km²).
Population (mid-1987 est.): 104,600,000.
Chief Cities (1981 census): Islamabad, the capital, 201,000; Karachi, 5,103,000.
Government: *Head of state,* Mohammad Zia ul-Haq, president (took power July 5, 1977). *Head of government,* Mohammad Khan Junejo, prime minister (installed April 10, 1985). *Legislature*—Parliament: Senate and National Assembly.
Monetary Unit: Rupee (17.36 rupees equal U.S.$1, Dec. 2, 1987).
Gross National Product (1986 fiscal year est. U.S.$): $32,000,000,000.
Economic Index (1985): *Consumer Prices* (1982 = 100), all items, 119.8; food, 119.3.
Foreign Trade (1986 U.S.$): *Imports,* $5,373,000,000; *exports,* $3,306,000,000.

PARAGUAY

Paraguayan President Alfredo Stroessner, 74, completed 33 years in power in May 1987, and the political machinery was in place for his election to an eighth term (1988–93).

Politics. In a bitter party election in August, the "militant" or hard-line wing of the ruling Colorado Party triumphed over the "traditionalists," placing Sabino Augusto Montanaro in the party presidency and capturing all 35 seats on the party's governing council. Montanaro, the interior minister, had been in Stroessner's cabinet since 1964. The internal elections underscored the splits within the dominant party. While the militants advocated a continuation of Stroessner's rule and the country's domination by the Colorados, the traditionalists emphasized the party record prior to Stroessner's emergence and favored a more open society, with less corruption and authoritarianism. The "ethical" wing abhorred corruption and wanted the party to select a civilian standard-bearer for 1988 to replace General Stroessner.

Dissent outside the official party also increased. The Roman Catholic Church continued a national dialogue that brought together opposition groups from labor, academic, journalistic, and church circles. A price for dissent was paid in January by Humberto Rubin, owner of the popular Radio Nandutí, when his station was forced off the air indefinitely. The government lifted a 40-year-old state of siege in April. Napoleón Ortigoza Gómez, a 55-year-old army captain who had been convicted of plotting against the Stroessner regime in 1962, was freed from jail in December.

Economy. Rebounding from a disastrous export record in 1986, when sales abroad reached only $232 million, total exports for 1987 were expected to reach $360 million. Practically all sales abroad were of agricultural products, and Brazil was the best customer. Paraguay expected to produce about one million tons of soybeans in 1987, or 100,000 tons more than usual. Exporting to the United States became more difficult. The U.S. government withheld preferential treatment of Paraguayan imports after January because of Paraguay's slow improvements in its human-rights record and its treatment of trade unions. A trade deficit of $240 million was expected in 1987.

Debt-service payments continued to absorb some $200 million, on a foreign debt of $2 billion. Although few new loans were available, the Inter-American Development Bank (IDB) Fund for Special Operations did lend $12 million for an agricultural education project that would improve facilities at five public and one private agriculture school. Agricultural activities accounted for about one third of the gross domestic product.

Foreign Affairs. Relations with the United States plummeted to new depths as the U.S. government protested censorship, welcomed opposition leaders at the U.S. embassy, and called for a transition to democracy. The wrath of Paraguay's leadership was channeled at U.S. Ambassador Clyde Taylor. In January, following the embassy's expression of "deep regret" over the closure of Radio Nandutí, Taylor was declared persona non grata by the ruling Colorado Party. In February, police lobbed tear gas at guests attending a reception in Taylor's honor given by a pro-democracy opposition group. A Mass attended by Ambassador Taylor in March was stopped by police, who detained Taylor briefly. The Mass had been called to mark the 1984 closure of *ABC Color,* the nation's largest daily newspaper.

LARRY L. PIPPIN, *University of the Pacific*

PARAGUAY • Information Highlights

Official Name: Republic of Paraguay.
Location: Central South America.
Area: 157,046 sq mi (406 750 km²).
Population (mid-1987 est.): 4,300,000.
Chief City (1982 census): Asunción, the capital, 455,517.
Government: *Head of state and government,* Gen. Alfredo Stroessner, president (took office 1954). *Legislature*—Congress: Senate and Chamber of Deputies.
Monetary Unit: Guaraní (550 guaraníes equal U.S.$1, August 1987).
Gross Domestic Product (1986 U.S.$): $3,800,-000,000.
Foreign Trade (1986 U.S.$): *Imports,* $746,000,000; *exports,* $275,000,000.

PENNSYLVANIA

No single focus dominated public concerns in Pennsylvania in 1987. With the exception of the hotly contested mayoral race in Philadelphia between incumbent Democrat W. Wilson Goode and former Republican mayor Frank L. Rizzo (*see* PHILADELPHIA), there were no major political races that caught the public's attention. It was not a year of public crises, but of less pressing issues.

The Budget. On January 20, Democrat Robert P. Casey was sworn in as governor. He succeeded Republican Gov. Richard L. Thornburgh, who had served eight years and was prohibited from seeking a third consecutive term by Pennsylvania's constitution. Thornburgh left Casey with a surplus in the treasury that enabled the new governor to sign budget legislation that both cut taxes and increased spending.

Despite the surplus, passage of the budget for the fiscal year beginning July 1 still was a difficult and contentious task. The Republican-controlled state Senate wanted to lower taxes sharply, while Governor Casey and the Democrat-controlled state House of Representatives stressed funding economic development programs and replacing funds cut from programs

PENNSYLVANIA • Information Highlights

Area: 45,308 sq mi (117 348 km²).
Population (July 1, 1986): 11,889,000.
Chief Cities (July 1, 1986 est.): Harrisburg, the capital (1980 census), 53,264; Philadelphia, 1,642,900; Pittsburgh, 387,490; Erie, 115,270; Allentown, 104,360.
Government (1987): *Chief Officers*—governor, Robert Casey (D); lt. gov., Mark Singel (D). *Legislature*—Senate, 50 members; House of Representatives, 203 members.
State Finances (fiscal year 1986): *Revenue,* $22,120,000,000; *expenditure,* $19,278,000,000.
Personal Income (1986): $169,392,000,000; per capita, $14,249.
Labor Force (June 1987): *Civilian labor force,* 5,713,300; *unemployed;* 354,200 (6.2% of total force).
Education: *Enrollment* (fall 1985)—public elementary schools, 1,092,558; public secondary, 590,663; colleges and universities, 533,198. *Public school expenditures* (1985–86), $6,490,000,000 ($4,235 per pupil).

during the recession of the early 1980s. After an all-night session in the legislature July 3, Governor Casey signed the compromise $10.5 billion budget. The legislation reduced the Capital Stock and Franchise Tax, a prime desire of the business community, and the Utility Gross Receipts Tax paid by utility customers. The biggest spending increase was an additional $214 million for the public schools. Although involving much less money, the most controversial provision of the budget was an increase of legislators' salaries by $12,000 to $47,000, the highest in the nation.

Donald Woomer and Linda Despot won a record $46 million in Pennsylvania's Super 7 lottery. After an initial payment, they would receive 25 annual checks of some $1.4 million.

AP/Wide World

Economy. By midyear, unemployment in Pennsylvania dropped briefly to 5%, slightly lower than the percentage for the rest of the United States. However, this figure did not indicate that all was well throughout the Commonwealth. In counties associated most heavily with Pennsylvania's traditional smokestack industries, unemployment still hovered around 10%. As the mix of jobs shifted to service providers, many workers struggled to maintain a standard of living that had been easily supported by industrial jobs at union wages. A slight decline in the size of the labor force was another troubling economic indicator. Nevertheless, despite some problems, the economy was growing—the reason Governor Casey faced the question of distributing a surplus rather than a less pleasant fiscal dilemma.

Steel Strike. On January 17 the United Steelworkers union reached an agreement with the USX Corporation (formerly US Steel) after a 170-day strike, the longest steel strike in American history. USX won wage concessions, while the union won a commitment by USX not to close certain plants. The union also agreed to accept the elimination of 1,346 jobs in return for USX's promise that for each job eliminated it would grant early retirement benefits to two workers and recall one laid-off worker.

Nuclear Power. As the cleanup continued at the nuclear reactor damaged in the 1979 accident at Three Mile Island, a scandal at the Peach Bottom nuclear plant in the northeastern part of the state again brought attention to problems with nuclear energy in Pennsylvania. The Nuclear Regulatory Commission ordered the Peach Bottom plant shut down because an investigation found that control-room operators were sleeping on duty. The plant was permitted to reopen only after management developed a detailed plan to assure that such problems would never recur.

Dwyer Suicide. Perhaps the most bizarre event of the year was the January 22 suicide of state Treasurer R. Budd Dwyer (R) during a televised press conference at his Harrisburg office. Dwyer had been convicted of accepting a $300,000 bribe for awarding a $4.6 million contract for computer services and was to have been sentenced the next day. Dwyer's family received $1.28 million in pension benefits, money they would not have gotten had he been sentenced. Pennsylvania law denies pension benefits to officials convicted of crimes while in office, but conviction legally does not occur until sentencing.

Lottery. The largest jackpot ever won in a North American lottery was claimed by a Pennsylvania couple in October. Donald S. Woomer and Linda K. Despot won the record-breaking $46 million pot in the Super 7 game, Pennsylvania's 15-year-old state lottery.

ROBERT E. O'CONNOR
The Pennsylvania State University

PERU

Amid verbal clashes and near fist fights, the Peruvian Chamber of Deputies approved legislation September 29 nationalizing ten banks, 17 insurance companies, and six other financial institutions. Foreign banks were not affected by the nationalization, which was considered Peru's most controversial domestic measure since the Valasco military regime instituted agrarian reform in 1969.

Bank Bill. President Alan García Pérez surprised even his own supporters by submitting the nationalization bill during July 28 Independence Day ceremonies. Passage through the Senate and Chamber of Deputies was assured by support not only from García's left-of-center American Popular Revolutionary Alliance Party (APRA), but also from the principal opposition party, the United Leftist coalition; organized labor; and Cardinal Juan Landazuri Rickets, the highest authority in Peru's Roman Catholic Church. However, Manuel Romero Caro, minister of industry, commerce, and tourism, resigned in August because of the proposed legislation.

New Cabinet. A new Cabinet headed by APRA Sen. Guillermo Larco Cox was sworn into office June 29. Luis Alva Castro, prime minister and minister of finance since García's July 1985 inauguration, resigned June 22, apparently to prepare for a presidential bid in 1990. (García had indicated earlier that he was not interested in running for reelection.) The new prime minister was a longtime García ally and vice-president of the Senate. Two of his Cabinet appointees, Minister of Health Ilda Urizar and Minister of Education Mercedes Cabanillas, were believed to be the first women named to Cabinet posts in Peruvian history.

Guerrilla War. The García government appeared no closer to controlling violence by Maoist guerrillas, despite the announced arrest of 462 presumed terrorists in 1986 and 63 in July-August 1987 alone. A new terrorist offensive that began January 15 included assassinations, sabotage of power lines, and bombings of cars, banks, and government offices. While García gained some popularity for lifting the curfew and state of emergency in Lima and Callao on July 28, both were reimposed September 15 because of a new wave of violence in the capital and interior.

University students organized protests in Lima in late February after 4,000 police officers conducted raids at three universities. More than 200 persons were detained for allegedly possessing subversive materials and weapons. Cardinal Landazuri said the police searches were "regrettable, but in response to a growing public clamor" for action against terrorism.

PERU • Information Highlights

Official Name: Republic of Peru.
Location: West Coast of South America.
Area: 496,224 sq mi (1 285 220 km²).
Population (mid-1987 est.): 20,700,000.
Chief Cities (mid-1985 est.): Lima, the capital, 5,008,400; Arequipa, 531,829; Callao, 515,200.
Government: *Head of state,* Alan García Pérez, president (took office July 28, 1985). *Head of government,* Luis Juan Alva Castro, prime minister (took office July 1985). *Legislature*—Congress: Senate and Chamber of Deputies.
Monetary Unit: inti (20.00 intis equal U.S.$1, official rate, Dec. 8, 1987).
Gross National Product (1985 U.S.$): $19,000,-000,000.
Economic Index (Lima, 1986): *Consumer Prices* (1980 = 100), all items, 5,991.1; food, 5,833.5.
Foreign Trade (1986 U.S.$): *Imports,* $2,160,000,000; *exports,* $2,467,000,000.

Economy. In February, Peru suffered a sharp drop in foreign-exchange reserves, to about $800 million. The drop was due mainly to a decline in the price of oil exports, as well as to an increase in imports brought about by the growth of the economy by 8.9% in 1986.

The inflation rate, which reached 26.3% for the first four months of 1987, was protested by workers with a general strike May 19. In an effort to curb popular unrest, García announced a 35% increase in the minimum wage in July. In addition, interest rates for borrowers were reduced to 32% from 40%, and monthly devaluations of the Inti were halted.

Great Britain's Midland Bank and First Interstate Bank of Los Angeles announced mid-September agreements with Peru to accept iron, copper, coffee, and other raw materials as payment of part of $200 million in debt due the banks. First National Bank of Chicago and Manufacturers Hanover Trust were reportedly investigating similar arrangements.

Petroperu President Haysuno Abramovich announced May 8 the discovery of a new oil field in the southeast jungles with reserves of an estimated 5 million barrels. The Ciriaco I wildcat well and four new wildcat gas wells led to discussions with foreign oil companies and governments over building a Trans-Andean pipeline to the Pacific Coast or a pipeline to Brazil.

Peru expected to earn $200 million in silver exports after temporarily suspending sales April 21. The move was coordinated with Mexico as a result of March talks between García and Mexican President Miguel de la Madrid. Silver prices stabilized at about $7.50–7.70 an ounce from August through October after having declined from $6.13 an ounce in August 1985 to $5.20 an ounce in August 1986.

NEALE J. PEARSON
Texas Tech University

PHILADELPHIA

In 1987, Philadelphia was at center stage as the United States celebrated the bicentennial of its Constitution. (*See feature article,* page 37.) Mayoral elections and governmental scandals also made news during the year.

Elections. In the Democratic mayoral primary campaign, former District Attorney Edward G. Rendell charged incumbent Mayor W. Wilson Goode with "ineptitude and mismanagement." The reputation of Mayor Goode, once considered one of the nation's most promising black politicians, had been tarnished by the 1985 MOVE incident. In an effort to dislodge members of MOVE, a small antiestablishment group, from their house, a police helicopter had dropped a bomb on the roof. Eleven MOVE members, including five children, died in the fire, and a two-block area of the city was destroyed. Rendell focused on the MOVE incident and other problems in the Goode administration, including frequent allegations of financial misconduct. Despite these charges, Mayor Goode won the Democratic nomination with 57% of the vote.

Mayor Goode's victory was aided by the switch of substantial numbers of whites to the Republican Party so that they could vote for former Police Commissioner and Mayor Frank L. Rizzo. A controversial law and order advocate who had changed parties, Rizzo won 58% of the vote in the Republican primary over moderate John J. Egan, Jr. In the general election in November, Mayor Goode was reelected with 51% of the vote.

Crime. Scandals in 1987 involved both the courts and the city council. The Pennsylvania Supreme Court ordered 15 judges to leave the bench because of charges involving cash gifts from the roofer's union. City Councilman Leland Beloff also left office because of his conviction for attempting to extort more than $1 million from developer William G. Rouse III.

In March police uncovered evidence of murder, sexual abuse, torture, and cannibalism at the home of Gary Heidnik, a self-proclaimed minister with a history of mental illness.

ROBERT E. O'CONNOR
The Pennsylvania State University

PHILIPPINES

AP/Wide World

Greater political stability and various economic and social reforms remained key objectives of Corazon Aquino during her second year as president of the Philippines.

Throughout the second year of Corazon Aquino's presidency, her ability to consolidate a centrist political position was tested by extremists on both the Left and the Right. Several factors contributed to her dilemma. Partyless herself, she had been elected by popular mandate and by a coalition of political organizations. Over the months, however, President Aquino's reform efforts were stymied by continuing political instability, and some of the Philippine people became impatient with her administration because of the absence of vital economic rehabilitation and social-restructuring programs. They grew concerned that elitist groups whose power had been usurped by former President Ferdinand Marcos would have that power restored.

Political Affairs. After taking power in 1986, President Aquino spurned the idea of ruling by decree and decided instead to wait for her constitutional convention to draft a new charter and let democratic processes recover lost momentum. That charter was approved by an overwhelming 76% in a plebiscite on Feb. 2, 1987, despite a coup attempt on January 28 and resistance both from the Left and from supporters of former Defense Minister Juan Ponce Enrile, who demanded still another presidential election. The results of the plebiscite gave a crucial vote of confidence to the Aquino government and confirmed her as president until June 20, 1992.

Further popular support came in May 11 elections for the new bicameral legislature. In a heavy voter turnout, candidates supported by President Aquino won 22 of 24 seats in the Senate and 80% of the House seats. Nevertheless, political rivalries within Congress kept the body in disarray after it was convened in late July. Aquino's coalition began to dissolve, and regional and local elections planned for November were postponed until January 1988.

As contentious national politics continued to distract President Aquino from implementing a popular agenda, her attempts at peacemaking and her aim to allow open, democratic debate left her vulnerable to attacks from radicals within the left-wing National Democratic Front (NDF), the political arm of the Communist insurgency called the New People's Army (NPA), and disaffected military forces.

The NDF had lost both prestige and momentum by boycotting the February 1986 presidential election which brought Aquino to power. But as a result of a presidential amnesty granted to 500 imprisoned members of the NPA and of government passivity, the NDF began to reassert itself. In January 1987, after Labor Minister Augusto Sanchez was forced to resign for having been too sympathetic toward the working class, the radicals declared their opposition to the draft constitution, demanding to be recognized as the de facto government in several provinces. On February 8, six days after the plebiscite and nine days after formally ending peace talks with the government, the NDF ended the cease-fire which had been in effect since December 1986. Partially as a result, no radical politician won a congressional seat in the May elections. This included Bernabe Buscayno, the founder of the NPA.

When the Communist Party subsequently was declared illegal, it began deploying "sparrow" units in Manila. By year's end, some 500 police and political figures had been killed by these "hit-and-run" terrorists. In late September the NPA severed southeast Bicol from the rest of Luzon by dynamiting bridges; they also hijacked trains and attacked constabulary headquarters. Meanwhile, former party head José Maria Sison traveled through Europe raising funds for the NPA.

The armed forces, already having developed a "garrison psychology" because of insufficient training and equipment, had been placed further on the defensive by the president's policy of "maximum tolerance." Consequently, they blamed Aquino for their growing casualties. They also argued that soldiers who had been charged with torture or murder under the Marcos regime or with participation in coup attempts against the Aquino government should be granted the same opportunity for amnesty as the NPA. After being replaced by Gen. Rafael Ileto as defense minister late in 1986, Enrile promoted his own presidential ambitions by appealing directly to the troops. As a result, during the February plebiscite the constitution was least favored near army camps. Later Enrile was elected on a national constituency basis to the last of the 24 Senate seats. Pressure from the growing number of military recalcitrants forced President Aquino to tolerate continuation of Marcos' 45,000-man Civilian Home Defense Forces despite its reputation for abuse and lack of discipline, as well as 260 vigilante groups which constituted virtual private armies in Cebu and Mindanao. She lost an ally on August 2 when Secretary of Local Government Jaime Ferrer, who had advised disarming the vigilantes and who had tried to remove the politics of greed from local appointments, became the first Philippine official of cabinet rank to be assassinated.

Factionalism in the armed forces betrayed its presence most prominently on August 28 in the fifth and bloodiest coup attempt against Malacañang (the presidential palace) since Aquino took office. The revolt was led by Col. Gregorio "Gringo" Honasan, Enrile's former chief security officer who had been placed on "floating status" after being involved in the July and November 1986 coups. Up to 1,500 dissident soldiers laid siege to the palace and government-controlled television stations and took over portions of three military bases. The coup was put down by loyalist forces within 24 hours, but 53 persons, including 22 civilians, were killed and hundreds wounded in the cross fire. More than 1,000 of the mutineers were captured, but Honasan himself escaped and was not captured until early December. At the Philippine Military Academy, 600 cadets held a three-day hunger strike in sympathy with the coup leader. Honasan's claim that the government was being too soft on Communism split even the Reform the Armed Forces Movement (RAM), which had helped to topple Marcos. Despite RAM's original aim of restoring professionalism in the army, some factions within the movement were prepared to put themselves above the constitution. Their cause was given implicit support on September 16, when Vice-President Salvador Laurel distanced himself from the Aquino regime by resigning his post as foreign secretary. The following day Executive Secretary Joker Arroyo, long identified as a defender of human rights against military abuse, resigned in the face of business and military opposition.

Despite the United States' unqualified public support of the Aquino government after each coup, it was alleged that Lt. Col. Victor Rafael, a military attaché at the American embassy in Manila, had tried to dissuade loyalist troops from attacking besieged rebel forces during the August coup. When Raul Manglapus gave up his Senate seat in October to replace Laurel as foreign secretary, he insisted on Rafael's removal. U.S. interference, as it was perceived, led Manglapus to argue for the early closing of U.S. naval and air bases on Luzon and "neutralization" of the islands according to the precedent set by Singapore.

Assessing her position between the revolutionary NPA and the coalition of army rebels and Marcos supporters, President Aquino declared, "Our country is threatened by totalitarian slavery on the Left and reversion to Fascist terror and corruption on the Right."

Land Reform and Labor Unrest. More and more clearly during 1987, the solution to the political conflict was seen to lie in genuine, massive land reform. Two thirds of the Philippine population still live in rural areas. Nearly seven million are landless, and several million more are impoverished tenants. If agricultural land were distributed more equitably, the NPA could rely less on the support of a dissident peasantry. In turn the armed forces would face a diminishing enemy and have no just complaint against the government's "failure of nerve." The allegations against Enrile as a longstanding accomplice of Marcos could be pursued in the courts. Meaningful "people power" would have been realized.

However, despite campaign pledges of "land to the tiller," little forward movement was seen. On March 3, after one year in office, the president announced a four-stage, five-year plan that would give title for more than 13 million arable acres (5 million ha) to the landless and to tenant farmers. First to be divided would be oversize rice and corn lands. The second step would be to divide idle or abandoned land, or land seized from Marcos "cronies." The third stage would involve sugar and coconut plantations. And the fourth would involve unused public lands. To finance payment to landlords for their property, a $2.5 billion fund was to be allocated over the duration of Aquino's six-year term. But the money was not raised and the program was not implemented while President Aquino waited for the newly constituted Congress to convene and to establish land-reform plans of its own.

A revolt by mutinous Philippine soldiers against the Aquino government began early August 28 and was put down within 24 hours. Fifty-three persons died in the fighting.

© Noli Yamsuan/Picture Group

PHILIPPINES • Information Highlights

Official Name: Republic of the Philippines.
Location: Southeast Asia.
Area: 115,830 sq mi (300 000 km²).
Population: (mid-1987 est.): 61,500,000.
Chief Cities (1980 census): Manila, the capital, 1,630,485; Quezon City, 1,165,865; Davao, 610,375; Cebu, 490,281.
Government: *Head of state and government,* Corazon C. Aquino, president (took office Feb. 25, 1986). *Legislature* (unicameral)—National Assembly.
Monetary Unit: Peso (20.95 pesos equal U.S. $1, Dec. 21, 1987).
Gross National Product (1986 est. U.S.$): $34,500,-000,000.
Economic Index (1986): *Consumer Prices* (1980 = 100), all items, 256.4; food, 248.8.
Foreign Trade (1986 U.S.$): *Imports,* $5,394,-000,000; *exports,* $4,842,000,000.

Because more than half of the new congressmen are landed elite, debate inevitably has bred delay. Aquino herself, though reluctantly willing to see Hacienda Luisita, her own family plantation in Tarlac, be divided, has wondered if profit sharing might not be preferable to land sharing. The preference in the countryside was demonstrated dramatically by the seizure of land by tenants down the entire length of the archipelago—in Isabela, Mindoro, Samar, Negros, and Bukidnon. In such instances, sugarcane usually has been replaced by more manageable and profitable crops (such as vegetables, cacao, ramie, and prawns) or by livestock. Hundreds of longstanding Basic Christian Communities, organized and directed by activist local priests, have worked peacefully for land reform. Despite denials by Bishop Antonio Fortich of Negros, the communities have been accused of Communist connections by hacenderos (landowners or proprietors) willing to use force to protect their land from subdivision. A tacit antireform alliance has developed between several provincial military commanders and some members of the traditional elite.

Similar unrest appeared in the nation's cities. On January 22 some 10,000 left-wing demonstrators approached Malacañang Palace. Despite a government policy of peaceful confrontation, security forces opened fire, killing 18 and wounding 96 laborers and farmers. Most of the Human Rights Commission resigned in protest. Four days later an even larger group marched on the palace and this time were embraced by the president and her cabinet. But on January 30, when liberal Labor Minister Sanchez was forced to resign, the May First Movement ended its support of Aquino. In August, when the government suddenly raised fuel prices—drastically increasing public transportation costs—the same union brought 6,000 demonstrators to the palace until the increases were amended. Still, on October 12, they organized strikes at 387 factories and businesses.

© Sandro Tucci/"Time" Magazine

Filipino workers prepare shrimp for export. Under President Aquino's program of free-market-oriented economic reforms, there is a new emphasis on improving export earnings. A national growth rate of about 6% was forecast for 1987.

Economy. Despite escalating disorder and political instability, the performance of the Philippine economy reflected the nation's potential. Reserves at the Central Bank tripled during the course of the year. The gross national product rose 5.5%, three times more than in 1986. (In the final year of the Marcos regime the GNP declined 4.39%.) Investments grew 23%; exports in electronics increased 58% and in garments 39%, as nontraditional products continued to gain on agriculture.

While world market conditions explained some of the increases, much was owed to a reduction in government corruption and the rest to a cautious resurgence of confidence with the end of monopolies. Inflation leveled off, and local interest rates fell from 28.6% to 11% before rising to 16–17% as the year drew to an end. Also at the local level, 310 Peoples' Economic Councils were established to identify investment and job opportunities.

Repayment of interest on the $28 billion national debt, still blamed largely on Marcos, represented 40% of total government expenditures. By year's end the Commission on Good Government had recovered less than $1 billion of the vast plunder taken from the country by the exiled Marcos, although 400 sequestered companies remained to be sold. Yet, there was much satisfaction when, on January 23, that debt was rescheduled at interest rates 40% lower than originally demanded.

The question remained, however, whether or not the financial recovery could reach in time that large majority of the population which lives below the poverty line. There was concern that the middle class might become prematurely complacent and, by withdrawing support from the broad popular front, abandon power to the hacenderos, the industrial oligarchs, and the most opportunistic among the military. The mood of cautious waiting turned somber when a typhoon killed 1,000 Bicolanos in November, and another 1,500–3,000 deaths resulted from the collision on December 20 of a tanker with a ferry off Mindoro.

Prospects. At the funeral of the slain Secretary Jaime Ferrer in August, President Aquino asked, "Can we have order without tyranny and peace without oppression?" A partial answer was expected from the regional and local elections in January 1988. But while all of Aquino's predecessors had risen to power as heads of strong political parties, the coalition that assisted her own rise has continued to unravel. The central ground on which President Aquino has taken her stand is more ill defined than firm. Her one hope for lasting order and peace was to stop the erosion of her personal popularity through programs for social reform, and thereby to consolidate and institutionalize a genuine party of the people.

LEONARD CASPER, *Boston College*
GRETCHEN CASPER, *Texas A&M University*

© Marie Cosindas, courtesy of Polaroid Corporation

Marie Cosindas' "William Powell Still Life" (1945) was part of the 40th anniversary exhibition of the Polaroid Collection, called "Legacy of Light."

PHOTOGRAPHY

The overwhelming market success of automated photographic equipment led to a fever pace of product introductions in both traditional camera and video hardware during 1987, while an astoundingly fast color film, Konica's SR-V 3200, marked the year's major breakthrough in software technology. Museums and publications remained busy arenas for the medium's most significant works, and 40- and 50-year anniversaries marked the longevity of some important manufacturing, publishing, and marketing aspects of the industry. All in all, 1987 saw the photography world—both the traditional silver halide side and emerging electronic imaging—in a healthy state.

Hardware and Software. The year 1987 saw the number of 35mm auto-focusing (AF) single-lens reflex cameras (SLRs)—with fully interchangeable lenses and many advanced forms of exposure control and automation—increase to ten, from six manufacturers. Especially notable were the Canon EOS models, which differ from the others in having circular electrical focusing motors in each interchangeable lens (instead of in the camera body) and a new electronic distance-detecting sensor called BASIS (base-stored image sensor), which instantly amplifies and stabilizes individual focusing signals.

Pentax's SF-1 represents another strikingly original approach to the design of an AF SLR camera system with its built-in pop-up flash. Other notable new SLR entries in 1987 were the Contax 167MT, Nikon N4004, Olympus OM77AF, and Yashica 230-AF SLR.

At the same time, the overwhelming popularity of AF compact 35mm cameras had created a demand for an ever-increasing variety of models, and in 1987 for the first time the compacts surpassed the SLR market in sales and new-product introductions. The most sophisticated new entry was the Ricoh TF-500, which offered a wider spread of focal lengths than its competitors.

The AF SLRs were creating enormous difficulties as well as opportunities for independent lens makers, who struggled to keep up with the proliferation of incompatible AF models. Upon the expiration of a restrictive licensing agreement with Minolta, five independent Japanese lens manufacturers—Cosina, Kabori, Tamron, Tokina, and Yake—were now free to sell Maxxum-compatible AF zoom lenses under their own—or other companies'—names and to incorporate Minolta's proprietary read-only-memory (ROM) chip in their own lenses in order to exchange auto-focusing information with the Maxxum body.

Advances in electronics also affected the more traditional types of photo equipment, such as medium- and large-format cameras, darkroom gear, and integrated flash, which continued to incorporate an ever-increasing degree of automation.

The pace of product innovation was equally fevered in video, with the introduction of hybrid photoelectronic still cameras and new camcorders. Kodak launched a very expensive still camera system that uses a floppy videodisc rather than traditional film; the system consists of seven new products, with the camera itself costing $3,000. And Minolta's new easy-to-use VHS-C3300 boasted an innovative auto-focus system.

Among the more unusual hardware introduced in 1987 was Polaroid's transparent-case Onyx and two inexpensive "disposable" film-with-lens cameras: Kodak's 110 Fling at $6.95 and Fuji's 35mm Quick Snap at $9.95. In both cases, the entire camera unit is turned over to a lab for processing and then discarded.

In software, film improved considerably, with new technology being used to improve the speed-grain relationship. Today, the films most capable of recording images in dim light are no longer black and white but color.

Japan's oldest film manufacturer, Konica, used a "core-shell" grain structure in its new color print film, with the astonishing speed of ISO 3200. The emulsion's higher-efficiency silver halide crystals and multilayer structure give the film its extra sensitivity and make its grain and sharpness as good as those of lower-speed films.

Kodak's VR-G 400 color print film became available in 1987. In 35mm transparencies, the improved crop included Scotch ISO 100 and 400 color slide films; Agfa's Agfachrome CT100, a more neutral, less warm-tone film; Fuji's ISO 64 tungsten film; and Polaroid's PolaBlue, the latest in the company's 35mm instant slide films.

In black and white, Fuji's Neopan ISO 400 was scheduled to arrive in the United States by late 1987. Also new on the market were Kodak's T-Max ISO 100 and 400 roll-and-sheet films; the technology uses tablet-form grains that yield more surface area, thereby enhancing light reception and processing efficiency without increasing grain size.

Exhibitions and Publications. The Museum of Modern Art (MoMA) in New York City sponsored a number of major retrospectives in 1987: "Panoramas of the Twenties," the work of Jacques-Henri Lartigue; Jan Groover's modern still lifes; Garry Winogrand's photographs since 1950, including some he never developed; and the early works of Henri Cartier-Bresson.

"Bunchberry flowers, Silver Lake, New Hampshire, June 5, 1953" was one of 120 prints in an Eliot Porter retrospective at the Amon Carter Museum in Fort Worth, TX.

At the International Center of Photography in New York, a retrospective of André Kertész's work appeared as "Diary of Light, 1912–1985," while Ralph Gibson's "Tropism" covered the period 1958–65. And at the Whitney Museum, also in New York, Cindy Sherman's show, covering ten years of work, represented the Post-Modernist style.

An exhibition called "Nam and the '60s: A Personal American View," selected from among 10,000 photos taken in the United States and Vietnam during that period, began a U.S. tour. And in Rochester, NY, the continued existence of the George Eastman House seemed more secure, as Kodak pledged money.

In book publishing, several personal journeys appeared in book form during 1987: in black and white, *Dreams and Schemes: Love and Marriage in Modern Times,* a study of weddings by Abigail Heyman; *A Time That Was: Irish Moments,* by Jill Freedman; and in color, the results of Joel Sternfeld's cross-country odyssey, *American Prospects.*

Two consumer magazines, *Popular Photography* and *Modern Photography,* celebrated their 50th anniversaries, as did the Polaroid Corporation. The well-known photo cooperative Magnum toasted its 40th birthday.

BARBARA L. LOBRON
Writer, Editor, Photographer

PHYSICS

The year 1987 in physics was highlighted by major advances in the field of superconductivity (*see* special report, page 427) and the proposed construction of a U.S. Superconducting Super Collider.

Neutrino Mass. According to the unified theory of weak and electromagnetic interactions, neutrinos have zero mass. Since these exotic particles interact extremely weakly with matter, however, the actual measurement of their physical properties is very difficult. If neutrinos should prove to have a mass, the consequences for astrophysics would be enormous. Since there are so many neutrinos, even a tiny mass for each one would be sufficient for neutrinos to dominate the mass of the universe. According to the "big bang" theory, the universe is open or closed depending on whether there is sufficient mass for the gravitational attraction to overcome the initial expansion.

There are three known types or "flavors" of neutrinos—electron, muon, and tau—each named after the charged particles associated with its formation or absorption. From the shape of the energy spectrum of the charged particles, physicists can infer the mass of the neutrino. Several years ago, a team of scientists in the Soviet Union announced the measurement of an electron neutrino mass of about 30 eV (electron volts). Their finding set off a number of experiments to examine the slope of the highest energy part (endpoint) of the energy spectrum of the electron emitted in radioactive beta decay. In 1986 a group of scientists in Switzerland concluded that the mass was less than 18 eV, while in 1987 a group at Los Alamos (NM) National Laboratory obtained an upper limit of 27 eV. Improvements in the Los Alamos measurement were expected to reduce the sensitivity estimate to about 10 eV.

A totally different and unplanned measurement was provided by neutrinos from the supernova SN1987A, first observed on Feb. 23, 1987 (*see also* ASTRONOMY). Neutrinos from the supernova were counted in the Japanese proton detector at Kamioka. According to the theory of relativity, if the neutrinos have zero mass they all must travel at the speed of light, while if the neutrinos do have a mass their velocity depends on both their mass and energy. If the neutrinos all are emitted at the same time, a measurement of the mass and energy of each event provides a direct determination of the neutrino mass. In the supernova research, a total of eight such events were recorded in a period of two seconds. W.D. Arnett and J.L. Rosner of the University of Chicago showed that if the neutrinos are emitted within a period of a few seconds, the upper limit for the neutrino mass is 12 eV.

Trapped Atoms. At room temperature, air molecules move at an average speed of about 500 m/sec (about 1100 mph). Each atom emits and absorbs only certain frequencies, which give it a unique signature. The observed spectrum is smeared by the thermal motion of the atoms. For the purpose of spectroscopic research, however, the ideal would be a group of atoms at rest. While methods do exist for trapping atomic beams, they work only for very low velocities. Thus, the crucial next step was to reduce the velocity of the atoms. Since reducing the velocity reduces the temperature (the kinetic energy is proportional to the absolute temperature), the process of slowing the atoms is called cooling.

Scientists have been able to slow atomic beams through the use of laser radiation pressure. The atom absorbs thousands of laser photons before reaching a typical required velocity of 33 ft/sec (10 m/sec). As the atoms slow, the frequency for resonance photon absorption changes. To compensate for the decreasing velocity, either the laser frequency or the magnetic field in which the atom is decelerating must be changed. Both methods have been successfully employed.

Once the atoms have been cooled by laser beams, they then can be trapped. One approach has been to use a "magnetic bottle": the neutral atom is trapped by a combination of magnetic and electric fields. Although the atom has no charge, it does have a small magnetic moment which interacts with the magnetic field. More recently, however, a group at Bell Laboratories has taken a different approach to trapping. After cooling a beam of neutral atoms, they trapped the atoms by use of laser light. Six laser beams were used to flood a container with radiation pressure, while a seventh laser beam (tuned to a different frequency) created a "light bottle" to trap the atoms. There is so much light that the atoms are said to be in "optical molasses." The Bell Labs group hopes to refine the technique so as to control a single atom.

Superconducting Super Collider. In January 1987, U.S. President Ronald Reagan endorsed a proposal for the Superconducting Super Collider (SSC), which would be the biggest and most expensive particle accelerator—or atom smasher—ever built. The design calls for two colliding beams of protons of 20 TeV each (1 TeV = 10^{12} eV). The circumference of the beam's orbit would be some 62 mi (100 km). The cost of SSC is estimated at $6 billion.

After the endorsement by President Reagan, the Department of Energy established a tentative timetable that called for construction to begin in 1989. Most scientists agree that it is the logical next step to explore the properties of the fundamental particles—quarks and leptons. Opposition focuses on the cost and the draining of resources from other areas.

GARY MITCHELL
North Carolina State University

High-Temperature Superconductors

A surprising new discovery in the field of physics has touched off a rush of activity among researchers worldwide and many signal a scientific and technological revolution. The startling breakthrough was the discovery of a whole new class of superconducting compounds. Superconductivity is the disappearance of electrical resistance in a substance at extremely low temperatures; the sudden loss of resistance enables the material to carry currents without losing energy. The technological advantages of transporting electricity without loss would be enormous. Until recently, however, applications have been limited to only a few specialized areas because of the extremely low temperatures—near absolute zero (0 Kelvin; -273° C; -460° F)—necessary to produce the phenomenon in known superconductors. But in 1986, at IBM's research labs in Zurich, Switzerland, physicists Karl Alexander Müller and Johannes Georg Bednorz found that a ceramic compound of lanthanum, barium, and copper oxide superconducts at temperatures above the previous record high of 23 K.

During the next several months, Müller's and Bednorz' results were confirmed, and researchers around the world used related ceramic compounds to produce superconductivity at higher and higher temperatures. In February 1987 at the University of Houston and the University of Alabama-Huntsville, a team of scientists led by Paul C. W. Chu, replaced the lanthanum with yttrium (another rare-earth element) and achieved superconductivity at above 90 K.

In October, Bednorz and Müller were awarded the Nobel Prize in Physics for their discovery. "Bednorz and Müller stand out clearly as the discoverers of this specific superconductivity," said the Swedish Academy in its statement. "They have inspired a great number of other scientists to work with related materials."

Applications Potential. While the scientific breakthrough has generated an unprecedented level of interest among physicists and materials researchers, it is the enormous applications potential that has fueled frantic industrial activity in the field of high-temperature superconductivity and has led to unique government involvement in the development of the new technology.

Possible applications of high-temperature superconductivity range from the exotic to the practical. Loss-free transmission of electricity is an appealing prospect. For example, nuclear reactors could be located in isolated areas for increased safety. Large-scale application of magnetic levitation may become possible, permitting trains to travel at high speeds without friction between wheels and tracks. Utility companies are intrigued by the idea of storing electrical power in giant superconductors—where the power would remain undiminished until needed. Initial uses may be less futuristic: applications which now use superconductors (such as magnets for nuclear accelerators or in magnetic resonance imaging devices) or new applications in the field of electronics. Superconducting switches and other elements will help to speed computing. With less heat to disperse, computers could be shrunk to smaller sizes, with a consequent increase in speed.

IBM Research

Superconductors repel magnetic fields, a phenomenon known as the Meissner effect. This can be demonstrated (and often is at scientific conferences) by the ability of a superconductor to levitate a magnet in midair. Large-scale application could, for example, allow trains to travel at high speeds several feet off the ground.

Background. Until early in this century, it was believed that electrical resistance would decrease to zero only at a temperature of absolute zero. In 1911 the Dutch physicist Heike Kamerlingh Onnes observed that when mercury was cooled below 4 K, its electrical resistance completely disappeared. Kamerlingh

Onnes had discovered the phenomenon of superconductivity: if an electrical current is set flowing in a superconducting ring, the current will still be flowing years later with no measurable loss. In the decades since Kamerlingh Onnes' discovery, low-temperature physicists have tried to raise the temperature at which a material becomes superconducting—the critical temperature, or T_c.

Efforts to raise T_c appeared to have reached a point of diminishing returns by 1973, when a high of 23.2 K was recorded. The so-called "holy grail" of low-temperature physics was 77 K, the boiling point of liquid nitrogen. If the large and complicated devices which keep liquid helium cold could be replaced by the smaller and simpler cooling systems required by liquid nitrogen, then the energy, expense, and complexity of producing superconductivity would be greatly reduced, and superconductivity could be applied in many practical situations.

Why the electrical resistance disappears remained unexplained until 1957, when J. Bardeen, L. N. Cooper, and J. R. Schrieffer (then at Bell Labs) produced an explanation—now called the BCS theory of superconductivity. According to this theory, conduction electrons combine to form pairs that move freely through the material. The attractive force that binds the electrons arises from the interaction of the electrons with the lattice (molecular structure); the whole system is involved. Most theorists believed that the BCS mechanism could not function for T_c much higher than 40 K. Thus, both experiment and theory suggested that T_c could not be raised significantly. This was the situation when Müller and Bednorz made their momentous discovery.

Many elements are superconductors, but none of the pure elements has a very high T_c. Thus, attention turned to compounds. The most successful results involved transition metal alloys and compounds, but that approach culminated in the 1973 T_c high of 23.2 K, for Nb_3Ge. During the 1970s, superconductivity also was discovered in some metallic oxides, but the values for T_c were not very high. Müller and Bednorz studied metallic oxides which were expected to have very strong electron-lattice interactions.

During the course of 1987 there were several reports of brief superconductivity or related effects at temperatures well exceeding 200 K. The superconducting properties of a particular material depend on the details of its structure, which reflect the method of preparation. However, fabrication techniques are not yet standardized. Often only part of the material is superconducting, and physical stresses may change or destroy the special properties. Nor are theorists in agreement as to the precise mechanism at work in the new oxide superconductors. Most believe that the BCS theory does not fully apply in high-temperature superconductivity. All agree that electron pairs are formed, but there is no consensus on what process replaces the electron-lattice interaction.

In the midst of the current rapid progress and uncertainty, what has been clearly established is the existence of superconductivity at temperatures above the boiling pont of liquid nitrogen. Less well established is the capacity to maintain high electrical currents in the presence of a strong magnetic field—a necessity for many large-scale applications of superconductivity. Superconducting materials change to normal when currents higher than some critical value are passed through them. At a given temperature, the critical current is lower when the material is placed in a magnetic field. Early results on the metallic oxides indicated that the critical currents were very small, which would hinder large-scale applications. However, research groups at IBM Yorktown and Stanford University have reported that thin films of yttrium barium copper oxide compounds carry currents considered sufficient for most applications.

Government Support and the Future. It has been predicted that high-temperature superconductivity will become an industry worth billions of dollars annually by the year 2000. The Japanese Ministry of International Trade and Industry (MITI) has designated superconductivity as its top priority. The U.S. federal government has initiated a unique effort to encourage industrial development of high-temperature superconductors. President Reagan in 1987 proposed a Superconductivity Initiative, which would support research through various government agencies and would require the Department of Defense to spend $150 million over the next three years on superconductivity research relevant to military needs. A key part of the initiative is the facilitation of information exchange between industrial and government laboratories, as well as technology transfer between industrial groups.

Whatever the future holds for commercial applications of high-temperature superconductors, the present is a singular time for the experimentalists attempting to understand the structure of these remarkable ceramics and for the theorists trying to explain the persistence of superconductivity to such high temperatures. The results could bring major change to almost every electrical product and process.

GARY MITCHELL

POLAND

Economic difficulties, prospects of far-reaching reforms, and struggle between government and opposition dominated the news in Poland during 1987.

Economy. According to data published in February, the consumer price index for 1986 was 18% above that of 1985, while personal incomes rose 20.3%. Less favorably for Poland, imports rose 6.9%, and exports rose only 6.1%. Early in February the government devalued the national currency, the zloty, by 16.7% against the dollar, making the rate 240 zlotys to the dollar instead of 200. The measure was intended to help Polish exports and negotiations for new credits from the International Monetary Fund (IMF). Poland's external debt reached a new high of $35.5 billion.

Unusually low winter temperatures, poor planning, and lack of sufficient power supplies caused severe hardships early in the year in Poland's major cities, especially in Warsaw. Many housing units were deprived of heat and lighting for long periods of time. At least 50 deaths were attributed to heating failures in the major cities in the first three months of the year, and at least 15% of elementary schools experienced some wintertime shutdowns.

At the end of March the government announced sweeping price increases—of 10% to 100%—for many items, including foodstuffs and energy. The Roman Catholic Church joined workers' organizations in criticizing the increases.

Reform Proposals. On October 10, the government disclosed plans for far-reaching economic reforms, designed in part to lessen the role of central planning and bureaucracy, reduce inflation, increase productivity, and make Polish goods more competitive on world markets. Austerity also was built into the government plans, inasmuch as wages would be tied to profitability of enterprises, and the prices of goods and services would be allowed to adjust to market demand without the artificial supports of government subsidies. Prices were expected to rise, at least in the short term as subsidies were phased out. Unprofitable plants would be allowed to close, thus creating the prospect of substantial unemployment.

Government sources maintained the reforms would cut inflation in Poland in half by 1990, the balance of payments would reach equilibrium by 1991, and the zloty would become an internationally convertible currency by the middle 1990s. Since the plan aroused fears for the fate of the less skilled and efficient workers, the government proposed a "safety net" in the form of direct assistance to the most disadvantaged.

Part of the reform package included breaking up the state banking monopoly and allowing competing commercial banks to operate. Citizens would have to pay more for the cost of health services, entertainment, and cultural

Poland's President and First Secretary Gen. Wojciech Jaruzelski (right) *traveled to Italy in January 1987, where he held talks with then Prime Minister Bettino Craxi* (left) *on trade and finance. It was Jaruzelski's first official visit to a Western nation in five years.*

events. Prime Minister Zbigniew Messner described these measures as necessary to allow Poland to receive financial help from the IMF and the World Bank.

The plan was approved by the Sejm (parliament), 387-0, on October 23, and the next day the government announced a nationwide popular referendum on its austerity program. Voters, facing price rises that the government pegged at more than 100% over three years, rejected the proposal in the November 29 balloting—the first time that the Communist leadership of an Eastern-bloc country was defeated in a popular referendum on a major government program. Another referendum question on the ballot, proposing a "Polish model of democratization," also was turned down. On December 15, the government announced that average consumer prices would be increased 27% in 1988, scaled back from the previously announced 40% because of the lack of support in the referendum.

Government Changes. Among important personnel changes associated with the new reform program, Deputy Prime Minister Zdzislaw Sadowski, a nonparty member and a known advocate of "market solutions and decentralized planning," was named to head the State Planning Commission in early October. Eighteen economy-related ministries were reduced to ten. And Jerzy Bilip was named minister of industry. In mid-December, party leader Gen. Wojciech Jaruzelski made several appointments to strengthen his control and fill positions with supporters of his economic reform program. Mieczyslaw Rakowski was named to the Politburo of the Polish United Workers Party (PZPR), and Gazeta Krakowska was named to head the propaganda section of the party's Central Committee.

Solidarity's Struggle. Members and sympathizers of the outlawed Solidarity movement continued their opposition activities throughout the year, frequently in the face of government repression. Forty-eight Solidarity activists were arrested and police made numerous house searches on the eve of the May Day (May 1) holiday. Solidarity supporters conducted demonstrations in several major cities in Poland on May Day. Police charged a crowd of several hundred in Warsaw, arresting at least eight persons and injuring others. At the beginning of June, police arrested a number of Solidarity activists in six Polish cities.

On October 26, two days after the government announcement of the referendum questions in parliament, Solidarity leaders called on the Polish people to boycott the referendum.

Church-State Relations. In June, Pope John Paul II conducted a week-long visit to his native Poland. It was the third such visit since his elevation to the papacy in 1978. The pope, who was outspoken in his praise of Solidarity, visited the grave of Father Jerzy Popieluszko, a Catholic priest and supporter of Solidarity who was murdered by the secret police in 1984, and conducted an outdoor mass in Gdansk, the birthplace of Solidarity. The mass was attended by an estimated one million people. Altogether, some ten million people, almost a third of the population, turned out to see the pope. In public appearances, the pope reminded Poland's rulers of the sanctity of human rights, and in his Warsaw speech on June 18 he warned his official hosts that "every violation or disrespect of human rights is a threat to peace." The regime responded to the pope's appearances, and the upsurge in pro-Solidarity demonstrations, by massive deployments of security forces, complete with roadblocks and armored vehicles.

Statements by leaders of both state and church during the year, and especially the speech by Pope John Paul II to the Polish bishops in Warsaw, in mid-June, indicated that mutual recognition and formal diplomatic relations between the Vatican and the Polish People's Republic had become part of the state-church agenda. The pope referred to such relations as "a normal and right thing," although he attached certain important conditions to it requiring "serious work" between the parties. These conditions appeared to involve a more conciliatory policy toward the church itself, greater democratization of Poland, and the accommodation of Solidarity's demands..

Foreign Affairs. General Jaruzelski went to Italy in January. He reportedly sought to establish regular diplomatic relations with the Vatican, and he invited the pope to visit Poland in June. Jaruzelski also conferred with Italian Prime Minister Bettino Craxi seeking more trade, credits, and investment from Italy. This was Jaruzelski's first official visit to a Western nation in five years. No major agreements were concluded. Later in January, Poland hosted, for the first time ever, a Japanese prime minister—Yasuhiro Nakasone—in Warsaw.

POLAND • Information Highlights

Official Name: Polish People's Republic.
Location: Eastern Europe.
Area: 120,725 sq mi (312 680 km²).
Population (mid-1987 est.): 37,800,000.
Chief Cities (Dec. 31, 1985): Warsaw, the capital, 1,659,400; Lodz, 847,900; Cracow, 740,100.
Government: *Head of state,* Gen. Wojciech Jaruzelski, chairman of the Council of National Defense and chairman of the Council of State (took office Nov. 6, 1985) and first secretary of the Polish United Workers' Party (took office Oct. 1981). *Head of government,* Zbigniew Messner, chairman of the Council of Ministers (took office Nov. 6, 1985). *Legislature* (unicameral)—Sejm.
Monetary Unit: Zloty (240 zlotys equal U.S.$1, 1987).
Gross National Product (1985 U.S.$): $240,600,000,000.
Economic Indexes (1986): *Consumer Prices* (1980 = 100), all items, 463.4; food, 519.0. *Industrial Production* (1980 = 100), 104.
Foreign Trade (1986 U.S.$): *Imports,* $11,107,000,000; *exports,* $11,884,000,000.

U.S. Deputy Secretary of State John C. Whitehead visited Warsaw in late January in what was widely reported as an attempt to improve U.S.-Polish relations. General Jaruzelski reportedly assured Whitehead that there would be no more political arrests in Poland; he allowed Whitehead to meet with Solidarity founder, Lech Walesa, and other opposition leaders. In mid-February, President Reagan announced the lifting of the remaining U.S. trade sanctions against Poland.

In April, Jaruzelski traveled to Moscow for talks with Soviet Communist Party leader Mikhail Gorbachev.

In late April, the Polish government announced that Albert Mueller, a second secretary in the political section of the U.S. Embassy in Warsaw, had been "caught red-handed" in espionage activities against Poland. Mueller was detained for 6½ hours after allegedly trying to deliver equipment, money, and instructions to a Polish contact. The government charged the United States with trying to worsen Polish-U.S. relations.

In late May, U.S. Sen. Edward Kennedy visited Poland and while there made a joint public appearance with Lech Walesa in Gdansk on Sunday, May 24, before thousands of Solidarity supporters.

In mid-June, a Polish warship fired accidentally on a West German naval supply ship, the *Neckar,* during Warsaw Pact exercises in the Baltic Sea. Three West German crewmen were injured. Poland offered a formal apology to the Bonn government.

U.S. Vice-President George Bush traveled to Poland in late September. He visited a number of places, including Warsaw, and was met by generally large and friendly crowds.

In mid-October it was announced in Tel Aviv that Poland and Israel had agreed to schedule direct flights between the two countries by Israel's El Al airline.

ALEXANDER J. GROTH
University of California, Davis

POLAR RESEARCH

Antarctic. In August 1987, six science teams, supported by the National Science Foundation (NSF), participated in the Second National Ozone Expedition (NOZE-2). The expedition is a cooperative effort of NSF, the National Aeronautics and Space Administration (NASA), and the National Oceanic and Atmospheric Administration (NOAA) with some support from the Chemical Manufacturers Association.

The expedition found that ozone at an altitude of about 11 mi (18 km) above Antarctica had been reduced about 50% below normal. Preliminary NOZE-2 data, collected between late August and mid-October, strongly supported the theory that special conditions of atmospheric circulation around Antarctica in winter speed chemical reactions that liberate chlorine that destroys ozone and creates the so-called ozone hole. The chlorine, most scientists believe, originates from the chlorofluorocarbon (CFC) compounds released into the stratosphere from spray cans, air-conditioning units, and industrial processes. Chlorine monoxide, an active form of chlorine that can destroy ozone, was found within the ozone hole in amounts more than 100 times above normal.

NASA participated in an airborne experiment conducted over the Antarctic Peninsula and the Weddell Sea in September that corroborated the 1986 and 1987 data collected by scientists at McMurdo, a U.S. research station in Antarctica. Besides satellite imagery, the NASA Airborne Antarctic Ozone Campaign involved 13 flights of an instrumented, medium-altitude DC-8 airplane and an adapted, high-altitude ER-2 airplane. NASA data support the theory that chemical and meteorological mechanisms in the atmosphere above Antarctica create conditions that deplete the ozone.

The ozone studies were among 69 Antarctic research projects that the NSF would support during the 1987-88 summer season. About 290 U.S. researchers would work in Antarctica between October and April at four U.S. stations —McMurdo, Amundsen-Scott South Pole, Siple, and Palmer—and aboard the research ships *Polar Duke* and *Polar Circle*. In other projects scientists would study how ozone depletion may affect marine life, gamma-ray emissions from Supernova 1987A, and the long-term climate record in ice cores.

On October 13, a 2,540 sq mi (6,579 km^2) iceberg broke away from the Ross Ice Shelf in west Antarctica. The iceberg, which is 98 mi (158 km) long and 25 mi (40 km) wide, presently does not threaten shipping.

In January 1987, geologists from four U.S. universities discovered fossils of a 6-ft (1.8 m) tall, flightless bird, the jaw of a large crocodile, and 50 fossil lobsters. The discoveries, made near the Antarctic Peninsula, support theories that Antarctica and South America were connected between 40 and 140 million years ago, and that modern marine organisms, now living in temperate waters, began in high latitudes.

Arctic. A team of scientists traveled to Greenland in July 1987 to make some of the most sensitive geophysical measurements ever made of the Newtonian gravitational constant and to test a new theory that a fifth, yet undiscovered force may exist in the universe. The experiment was designed to detect and measure through the ice possible variations in the constant over distances greater than 300 ft (91 m). Laboratory measurements of gravity generally are limited to lengths of a few inches.

WINIFRED REUNING
National Science Foundation

AP/Wide World

Portugal's Prime Minister Aníbal Cavaco Silva and his wife, Maria, celebrated the landslide victory of his Social Democratic Party in July 19 parliamentary elections.

PORTUGAL

Elections in July 1987 produced the first majority government since a 1974 revolution tumbled a half-century-old, right-wing dictatorship and thrust Portugal on the road to democracy.

Politics. Prime Minister Aníbal Cavaco Silva, who formed his country's 15th government in 11 years upon taking office in October 1985, encountered mounting resistance from opposition parties to attempts to streamline Portugal's inefficient economy. The minority status of his center-right Social Democratic Party (PSD) impeded initiatives, launched by the aloof, 48-year-old former finance minister, to curb featherbedding, to privatize elements of a sluggish public sector, and to stress market incentives in Western Europe's poorest economy, renowned for low output and paternalistic management practices.

Cavaco Silva resigned in April 1987 following his party's defeat over a parliamentary censure motion. Rather than invite the Left to form a coalition cabinet that would have included the nation's Moscow-oriented Communist Party (PCP), President Mário Soares called for legislative elections to be held on July 19.

Cavaco Silva's PSD scored a resounding victory in these contests, capturing not only a majority of the popular vote but control of the 250-seat parliament. Buoyed by both an improved economy and popular distaste for revolving-door governments, the electorate awarded the PSD 50.2% of the popular vote, up from 29.9% in 1985. This tally enabled Cavaco Silva's party to enlarge its number of seats from 88 to 146.

Meanwhile the Socialists (PS) headed by Vitor Constancio, who replaced Soares as party leader, firmly established themselves as the leading opposition group. The PS improved its performance from 20.8% of the vote in 1985 to 22.3% in July balloting, while boosting its seat totals from 57 to 59.

PSD and PS gains came at the expense of the Democratic Renewal Party (PRD), a Left-leaning political vehicle for former president Gen. Antonio Ramalho Eanes, which spearheaded the April fall of Cavaco Silva's government. This action alienated broad segments of the population, and the PRD's portion of the vote plummeted from 18% to 4.9%—with its parliamentary delegation cut from 45 to 7 seats. In the wake of the debacle, Eanes resigned as the PRD's chief.

Also losing ground were the Communists, whose vote share dipped from 15.5% to 12.2% as its legislative representation declined from 39 to 20 seats. The conservative Christian Democrats obtained only 4.3% of the vote and four seats compared with 10% and 22 seats two years before.

Economy. Cavaco Silva viewed the electoral outcome as a mandate for his economic philosophy; namely, opening up an economy burdened by decades of protectionism, bureaucratic impediments to private initiative, state subsidies, and widespread state intervention in economic affairs. Liberalizing reforms authored by then-Prime Minister Soares in the early 1980s set the stage for the impressive recovery. Also important was generous assis-

PORTUGAL • Information Highlights

Official Name: Portuguese Republic.
Location: Southwestern Europe.
Area: 35,552 sq mi (92 080 km²).
Population (mid-1987 est.): 10,300,000.
Chief Cities (1981 census): Lisbon, the capital, 807,937; Oporto, 327,368; Amadora, 95,518.
Government: *Head of state,* Alberto Mário Soares, president (took office March 1986). *Head of government,* Aníbal Cavaco Silva, prime minister (took office November 1985). *Legislature* (unicameral)—Assembly of the Republic.
Monetary Unit: Escudo (134.05 escudos equal U.S.$1, Dec. 24, 1987).
Gross National Product (1985 U.S.$): $20,700,000,000.
Economic Indexes (1986): *Consumer Prices* (1980 = 100), all items, 317.5; food (June 1987), 336.6. *Industrial Production* (1980 = 100), 123.
Foreign Trade (1986 U.S.$): *Imports,* $9,458,000,000; *exports,* $7,205,000,000.

tance from the European Community (EC), which Portugal joined on Jan. 1, 1986. The EC will provide at least $2 billion in additional aid for industrial modernization in the 1988–92 period.

Other factors—low oil prices, the cheap dollar, and an 83% jump in foreign investment in the first four months of 1987—helped brighten the economic picture. Economic growth exceeded the 4% figure registered in 1986, while inflation dropped 4 points to 8% amid favorable employment conditions and a current account surplus.

Foreign Affairs. In October, Gen. Vasco Rocha Vieira, Lisbon's chief representative on the Azores, voiced displeasure at the dwindling U.S. aid for the Lajes base in the mid-Atlantic islands. Four years earlier, Portugal had extended the 40-year-old treaty for the multipurpose air facility, which plays a vital role in NATO's defense strategy. Military aid reductions made by the U.S. Congress have reduced the flow, originally $200 million per year, to $147 million in 1987. "Controlling the Azores means control over most of the North Atlantic," said a U.S. military adviser concerned that Portugal might exercise its option to review the current seven-year base agreement in 1988.

GEORGE W. GRAYSON
College of William and Mary

POSTAL SERVICE

The public image of the United States Postal Service (USPS) has remained high during the 1980s, despite some criticism. A 1987 Roper poll showed that, among organizations people dealt with most, the USPS was second in popularity only to supermarkets. A 1983 poll had shown it to be the most popular government agency.

By the end of 1987 there was solid accomplishment to account for this rating. First-class postal rates were the lowest in the world, a position unlikely to change even with a proposed rate increase from 22 to 25 cents. Postal productivity was by far the highest in the world, outperforming the general economy in growth during the 1980s. Despite a probable operating deficit of $200 to $225 million for fiscal year (FY) 1987, ending Sept. 30, 1987, the USPS had been in the black five out of the last eight years.

Other developments during 1987 supported this favorable trend. Postmaster General (PMG) Preston R. Tisch, who succeeded Albert Casey in August 1986, pushed through a massive agency reorganization, begun by Casey, which stressed decentralization. In October 1986 the U.S. Postal Board of Governors approved an $11.7 billion plan to modernize facilities. Two thirds of the money would be used to renovate many of the 34,000 offices now in use and to construct a number of new facilities. Comer Coppie, senior assistant PMG for finance and planning, said that providing integrated retail terminals, window (service) automation, and self-service vending equipment would be emphasized. The other funds would mainly be used to support further automation of operations. This has become increasingly critical because of the recent huge expansion in mail volume. That jumped from 146 to 154 billion pieces in fiscal 1987. There have been many predictions that the rapid development of electronic communications would cause a drop in the volume of traditional mail, but this has not proved to be the case.

The Board of Governors unanimously adopted a new code of ethics in July 1987, in response to the October 1986 fining and sentencing of Peter C. Voss, former vice-chairman of the Board of Governors, for bribery and embezzlement. The service's $4 billion-a-year procurement service was then given a major overhaul which would be fully effective in January 1988. Important for short run fiscal stability was the conclusion during late August and September 1987 of new three-year collective bargaining agreements with the postal unions. The terms were generally viewed as favorable to the USPS. As a result most postal employees would receive pay increases of about 2% the first year, 1.3% the second, and 1.5% the third. Previous cost-of-living adjustments were continued. For the first time in more than a decade contracts were reached solely through negotiation.

Canada. The Canada Post Corporation (CPC), formed in 1981, closed its FY 1987 (ending March 31) with a deficit of C$129 million, in relation to a total expenditure of $3.1 billion. This deficit was less than one third of that for FY 1985. On April 1, first-class postage was raised from 34 to 36 cents with a further one-cent increase scheduled for Jan. 1, 1988. This was part of a new government plan to bring the CPC into the black by 1989.

The plan includes reductions in force of 10% or more, closing of many small post offices, use of a two-tiered wage system whereby newly hired employees would receive less starting salaries than present workers, and contracting out of some services through private-sector franchises. The latter proposal was especially instrumental in prompting a series of postal-work stoppages and strikes during the summer and fall of 1987. The last of these was ended only by legislation passed on October 17, ordering the striking members of the 23,500 strong Canadian Union of Postal Workers back to their jobs. There being heavy penalties for noncompliance, the union obeyed, and negotiations continued under mediation.

PAUL P. VAN RIPER
Texas A&M University

PRINCE EDWARD ISLAND

Prince Edward, youngest son of the queen of England, in 1987 paid his first visit to the Canadian island-province that bears his name. A cabinet minister was cleared of conflict-of-interest allegations, and potato marketing recorded its best year ever.

Royal Visit. Prince Edward paid a three-day visit to Prince Edward Island (P.E.I.) at the end of June. At a state dinner in Charlottetown the 23-year-old prince was officially welcomed by Environment Minister Tom McMillan, P.E.I.'s representative in the federal cabinet, who told him that the province was, "in every sense of the word, your island."

The prince visited a number of towns, mixed with the people in a series of walkabouts, took part in a youth festival, attended a performance of *Anne of Green Gables,* and even went for a ride on a lobster-fishing boat.

Legislature. The first session of the legislature under the Liberal government of Premier Joe Ghiz opened February 26 in Charlottetown and was prorogued May 14. Among the 77 bills passed was one requiring motorists to use seat belts, on pain of a maximum $100 fine. P.E.I. and Alberta were the last two provinces to legislate use of seat belts.

The legislature also approved laws to raise the drinking age from 18 to 19, give the Public Utilities Commission power to regulate gasoline and oil prices, and create an appeal division of the provincial Supreme Court. The provincial budget provided for expenditures of $566.9 million and a deficit of $9.7 million for 1987–88.

Minister Cleared. Fisheries Minister Johnny Ross Young was cleared of conflict-of-interest allegations in an August 3 ruling by Supreme Court Judge Charles McQuaid. The issue was first raised in the legislature in March by Conservative opposition member Andy Walker after Young and his family took a trip to Australia at the expense of Australian sport fisherman Jeff Kazim. At the time of the trip, Kazim was setting up an international tuna sport fishing club in Eastern Kings, with Young as honorary chairman.

Sales Record. Prince Edward Island shipped the largest volume of potatoes in its history in the 1986–87 shipping season, according to John MacDonald, the chairman of marketing and licensing for the Potato Marketing Board. MacDonald reported September 16 at the board's annual meeting in Charlottetown that 10,400,765 hundredweight of potatoes were shipped, eclipsing the previous high of 10,283,841 hundredweight shipped in 1984–85. Sixty-five percent went to Canadian markets, 18% to the United States, and 17% to other countries. Reduced production in most potato-producing areas of eastern North America was a factor in the record-breaking performance.

PRINCE EDWARD ISLAND • Information Highlights

Area: 2,185 sq. mi (5 660 km^2).
Population (1986 census): 126,646.
Chief Cities (1986 census): Charlottetown, the capital, 15,776; Summerside, 8,020.
Government (1987): *Chief Officers*—lt. gov., Lloyd G. MacPhail; premier, Joe Ghiz (Liberal). *Legislature*—Legislative Assembly, 32 members.
Provincial Finances (1987–88 fiscal year budget): *Revenues,* $528,200,000; *expenditures,* $566,900,000.
Personal Income (average weekly earnings, July 1987): $357.27.
Labor Force (September 1987, seasonally adjusted): *Employed* workers, 15 years of age and over, 61,900; *Unemployed,* 8,000 (13.8%).
Education (1987–88): *Enrollment*—elementary and secondary schools, 24,650 pupils; postsecondary—universities, 2,000, community colleges, 950.
(All monetary figures are in Canadian dollars.)

Share Acquisition. Industry Minister Leonce Bernard confirmed October 2 that the P.E.I. Development Agency had acquired 42% of the shares of Advance Medical Technologies Inc. in an effort to ensure the continued operation of the Charlottetown firm. The $2.8 million that the government agency already had invested in the sometimes troubled company had been converted into shares, giving it a say at the board-of-directors level. The government also holds a $1.4 million mortgage on Advance Medical's building and equipment.

JOHN BEST
Chief, Canada World News

PRISONS

The constant increase in the U.S. prison population, which began in the early 1970s, relentlessly continued. Sharply rising costs for new prisons as well as court orders restricting overcrowding encouraged the exploration of alternatives to imprisonment.

A federal penitentiary in Atlanta and a federal detention center in Oakdale, LA, were taken over for 11 and 8 days, respectively, by Cuban inmates in late November and early December (*see* CUBA).

The Toll of Overcrowding. An increase in arrests, speedier trials, and a decade-long policy requiring longer prison sentences combined to severely tax an already overcrowded prison system. The prison population continued to grow at an annual rate of almost 5% and by June had reached 570,519 inmates, another all-time high. That did not include the thousands of prisoners held in local jails and other facilities because the prisons to which they had been sentenced had run out of room.

More than 29 states had prison populations well beyond their official capacity. By midyear, 40 state prison systems and many of the largest city and county jails were under court orders because of poor conditions and overcrowding. In a number of areas—Florida, Oklahoma, and Texas, for example—these court orders required the release of prisoners before completion of their sentences in order to make room for newly sentenced inmates.

Estimates of prison construction costs for 1987 approached $3 billion, compared with less than $500 million in 1980. Across the nation almost 1,000 new places were being added each week for incoming prisoners, yet the institutions could not keep up with the demand. Confrontations between overworked prison officers and tense inmates were reported from Rikers Island in New York to Folsom in California.

Alternatives. A handful of states, including Florida, Kentucky, and Tennessee, began to hire private companies to operate prison facilities for profit. A Justice Department study released in June concluded that private operations offer an attractive alternative for quickly obtaining new beds, but noted that "contracting does not necessarily save significant amounts of money." Proponents of privatization, in addition to citing the increased efficiency that the profit motive might stimulate, also predicted savings due to the exemption of private firms from civil-service rules, unions, and some state procedures. However, questions of legal responsibility were raised, and charges of physical abuse and substandard conditions soon began to enter the courts.

Beyond Prison Walls. Programs offering special supervision outside prison were moving beyond the experimentation stage. By midyear, 20 states were evaluating electronic monitoring systems designed to maintain surveillance on low-risk offenders. Various devices, some strapped to the ankle of the offender, others using random and frequent telephone calls, limit the offender's movement to a designated area, usually his or her home. Although police or other officials are called in to investigate signals of noncompliance, the costs are a fraction of those required for traditional incarceration.

Intensive probation supervision was also being tried in a number of states. In this program, frequent contact with a probation officer is combined with community service, attendance in a training or rehabilitation program, and increased surveillance. A report on a program in Georgia issued in January by the Justice Department's National Institute of Justice, found that the approach was "cost effective and poses less of a risk to public safety than does ordinary probation."

Within the Walls. The high costs of incarceration—as much as $90,000 a cell for construction and $30,000 a year maintenance for each prisoner—forced certain states to reexamine prison industries, by which inmates contribute to the cost of their incarceration. Several successful programs were reported, although a widespread reintroduction of the practice seemed unlikely. One hotel chain installed computer terminals in a women's prison in Arizona and employed inmates as reservation operators. The enterprise helped pay the costs of incarceration, and the parent company hired many of the participants upon their release.

© Ed Kashi

The Contra Costa Detention Facility in Martinez, CA, is one of a number of new "direct-supervision" prisons, in which officers maintain constant, direct contact with inmates.

The most important changes taking place in the nation's prison system proceeded slowly and were going on within the prison walls. Two changes that emerged during the year occurred at either end of the spectrum of institutions that make up the nation's prison system, the most violent and the least threatening. The U.S. penitentiary at Marion, IL, has become a prison for the most dangerous, incorrigible, and violent prisoners in the federal system. Its regimen is more severe than any other prison in the nation, and probably in the nation's history. Transferral to Marion has become the ultimate threat faced by incorrigible prisoners, and the facility has taken some of the pressure off other parts of the system. At the other end of the spectrum, some states began to realize that the expense of building maximum-security prisons is not only prohibitive, but in many ways unneeded. The realization sparked a move to build less expensive but more humane environments to house certain criminals.

DONALD GOODMAN
John Jay College of Criminal Justice

PRIZES AND AWARDS

NOBEL PRIZES

Chemistry ($340,000): Donald J. Cram, University of California at Los Angeles; Jean-Marie Lehn, Louis Pasteur University, Strasbourg; Charles J. Pederson, E. I. duPont de Nemours & Co., retired; for achievement in the development and use of molecules that can "recognize each other and choose with which other molecules they will form complexes."

Economics ($330,000): Robert M. Solow, Massachusetts Institute of Technology, "for seminal contributions to the theory of economic growth."

Literature ($330,000): Joseph Brodsky, exiled Soviet-born poet and essayist, for "an all-embracing authorship, imbued with clarity of thought and poetic intensity." (*See* page 328.)

Peace Prize ($340,000): Oscar Arias Sánchez, president of Costa Rica, for his "outstanding contribution to the possible return of stability and peace to a region long torn by strife and civil war." (*See* BIOGRAPHY.)

Physics ($340,000): J. Georg Bednorz and K. Alex Müller, I.B.M. Zurich Research Laboratory, "for pioneering work in superconductivity."

Physiology or Medicine ($340,000): Susumu Tonegawa, Massachusetts Institute of Technology, for his discovery of how the body can continually change its genes to make antibodies against disease agents it has never encountered previously.

ART

American Academy and Institute of Arts and Letters Awards
- Academy-Institute Awards ($5,000 ea.): art—William Beckman, Gretna Campbell, Charles Griffin Farr, Brian O'Leary, Kenneth Snelson; music—Hugh Aitken, Thomas E. Barker, Joel H. Hoffman, Dennis Riley
- Nathan and Lillian Berliawsky Award ($5,000): Composers Recordings Inc.
- Walter Hinrichson Award: Mark Gustavson
- Charles Ives Fellowship ($10,000): Russell F. Pinkston
- Charles Ives Scholarships ($5,000 ea.): Mark Barenboim, Sebastian Currier, David Karl Gompper, Christopher Lewis James, Gary Philo, Randall Woolf
- Goddard Lieberson Fellowship ($10,000 ea.): Robert Beaser, Lee Hyla

Richard and Hinda Rosenthal Foundation Award ($5,000): Chris Martin

Capezio Dance Award ($5,000 ea.): Fred Astaire, Rudolph Nureyev, Bob Fosse, Jac Venza

Glenn Gould Prize ($50,000, Canadian): R. Murray Schafer (composer)

Grawemeyer Award for Composition ($150,000): Harrison Birtwistle, *The Mask of Orpheus*

John F. Kennedy Center Honors for career achievement in the performing arts: Perry Como, Bette Davis, Sammy Davis, Jr., Nathan Milstein, Alwin Nikolais

Edward MacDowell Medal: Leonard Bernstein

National Academy of Recording Arts and Sciences Grammy Awards for excellence in phonograph records
- Album of the year: *Graceland,* Paul Simon
- Classical album: *Horowitz: The Studio Recordings, New York 1985,* Vladimir Horowitz, Thomas Frost (producer)
- Country music song: *Grandpa, (Tell Me 'Bout the Good Old Days),* Jamie O'Hara (songwriter)
- Jazz vocal performance: (female) *Timeless,* Diane Schurr; (male) *'Round Midnight* from *Soundtrack 'Round Midnight,* Bobby McFerrin
- New artist: Bruce Hornsby and the Range
- Record of the year: *Higher Love* (Steve Winwood, artist; Russ Titelman, Steve Winwood, producers)
- Song of the year: *That's What Friends Are For,* Burt Bacharach and Carole Bayer Sager (songwriters award)

National Medal of Arts: Romare Bearden, J. W. Fisher, Ella Fitzgerald, Armand Hammer, Sydney and Frances Lewis, Howard Nemerov, Alwin Nikolais, Isamu Noguchi, William Schuman, Robert Penn Warren

Pagurian Award for Excellence in the Arts ($25,000): Erik Bruhn (posthumous)

Pritzker Architecture Prize ($100,000): Kenzo Tange

Pulitzer Prize for Music: John Harbison, *The Flight Into Egypt*

Samuel H. Scripps American Dance Festival Award ($25,000): Alvin Ailey

Wolf Prizes (*See* also Science section)
- Arts ($100,000): Isaac Stern, New York; Krzysztof Penderecki, Krakow, Poland

JOURNALISM

Maria Moors Cabot Prizes ($1,000 ea.): Guillermo Cano Isaza (posthumously), director of *El Espectador,* Bógota, Colombia; Luís Roberto Camacho (posthumously), correspondent for *El Espectador,* Leticia, Colombia; Raúl Echavarria Barrientos (posthumously), sub-director of *Occidente,* Cali, Colombia; Guy Gugliotta, Latin America correspondent and writer, *The Miami Herald; Gazeta Mercantil,* São Paulo, Brazil, and its managing editor, Robert Muller, and its Washington correspondent, Paulo Sotero

National Magazine Awards
- Design: *Elle*
- Essays and criticism: *Outside*
- Fiction: *Esquire*
- General excellence: *New England Monthly, Common Cause, Elle, People*
- Personal service: *Consumer Reports*
- Photography: *National Geographic*
- Public-interest: *Money*
- Reporting: *Life*
- Single-topic issue: *The Bulletin of the Atomic Scientists*
- Special-interest: *Sports Afield*

Overseas Press Club Awards
- Book on foreign affairs: Tad Szulc, *Fidel: A Critical Portrait*
- Business or Economic news reporting from abroad: (magazines and books)—Suzanne Wittebort, Clair Makin, Beth McGoldrick, Fiametta Rocco, Peter Koenig, Michael Vermuellen, Frederic Dannen, Darrell Delamaide, Isabel Bass, Kevin Muehring, Wendy Cooper, *International Institutional Investor,* "Big Bang: The City Encounters its Future"; (newspapers and wire services)—Evelyn Richards, Lew Simons, *The Mercury News,* San Jose, CA, "Trade War: Why Japan is Winning"
- Cartoon on foreign affairs: Jefff MacNelly, *The Chicago Tribune*
- Daily newspaper or wire-service interpretation on foreign affairs: Juan Tamayo, *The Miami Herald,* "The Terror Network"
- Daily newspaper or wire-service reporting from abroad: Serge Schmemann, former Moscow bureau chief, *The New York Times*
- Magazine article on foreign affairs: Seweryn Bialer, Joan Afferica, *Foreign Affairs,* "The Genesis of Gorbachev"
- Magazine reporting from abroad: Robert Shaplen, *The New Yorker,* "From Marcos to Aquino"
- Photographic reporting from abroad: (magazines and books)—Steven A. McCurry, *National Geographic,* "Hope and Danger in the Philippines"; (newspapers and wire services)—Akira Suwa, *The Philadelphia Inquirer,* "Inside Qaddafi's Libya"
- Radio interpretation of foreign affairs: Sara Terry, Monitoradio, "Austria"
- Radio spot-news reporting from abroad: Fred Kennedy, Phillip Till, NBC Radio, "The Tripoli Tapes"
- Television interpretation or documentary on foreign affairs: Richard Threlkeld, Betsy Aaron, George Strait, John McWethy, Peter Jennings, ABC News, "Soviet Union: Inside the Other Side"
- Television spot-news reporting from abroad: staff, Cable News Network, "U.S. Military Strikes on Libya"
- Robert Capa Gold Medal (photographic reporting from abroad requiring exceptional courage and enterprise): James Nachtwey, *Time*
- Madeline Dane Ross Award (for foreign correspondent showing concern for the human condition): Tom Squitieri, *The Sun,* Lowell, MA, "No Refuge"
- President's Award: Lee Huebner, *The International Herald Tribune*

George Polk Memorial Awards
- Book: Richard Kluger, *The Paper*
- Career award: James Reston, *The New York Times*
- Environmental reporting: *High Country News* (Colorado)
- Financial reporting: Peter C. Gosselin, *The Boston Globe*
- Foreign reporting: "Terrorism: The Syrian Connection," *Newsweek*
- International television reporting: David Fanning, Martin Smith, "Who's Running This War," *Frontline* (PBS)

Local reporting: Sally Jacobs, *The News and Observer* (Raleigh, NC)
Local-television reporting: Lee Coppola, "A Lesson in Deceit," WKBW, Buffalo
National reporting: Andrew Wolfson, Daniel Rubin, *Louisville Courier-Journal*
National-television reporting: Bill Moyers, "The Vanishing Family," CBS News
Regional reporting: Alex Beasley, Rosemary Goudreau, *The Orlando Sentinel* (FL)
Science reporting: "Science Times," *The New York Times*

Pulitzer Prizes
Commentary: Charles Krauthammer, The Washington Post Writers Group
Criticism: Richard Eder, *The Los Angeles Times*
Editorial cartooning: Berke Breathed, The Washington Post Writers Group
Editorial writing: Jonathan Freedman, *The San Diego Tribune*
Explanatory journalism: Jeffrey R. Lyon, Peter Gorner, *The Chicago Tribune*
Feature photography: David Peterson, *The Des Moines Register* (IA)
Feature writing: Steve Twomey, *The Philadelphia Inquirer*
General-news reporting: *The Akron Beacon Journal* (OH)
International reporting: Michael Parks, *The Los Angeles Times*
Investigative reporting: Daniel R. Biddle, H.G. Bissinger, Fredric N. Tulsky, John Woestendiek, *The Philadelphia Inquirer*
National reporting (two awards): *The Miami Herald, The New York Times*
Public service: Andrew Schneider, Matthew Brelis, *The Pittsburgh Press*
Specialized reporting: Alex S. Jones, *The New York Times*
Spot news photography: Kim Komenich, *The San Francisco Examiner*

LITERATURE

American Academy and Institute of Arts and Letters Awards
Academy-Institute Awards ($5,000 ea.): Evan S. Connell, Ernest J. Gaines, Ralph Manheim, Sandra McPherson, Steven Millhauser, Robert Phillips, Roger Shattuck
The American Academy in Rome Fellowship in Literature: Padgett Powell
Award of Merit ($5,000): A. R. Gurney, Jr.
Witter Bynner Prize for Poetry ($1,500): Antler
Sue Kaufman Prize for First Fiction ($2,500): Jeannette Haien, *The All of It*
Richard and Hinda Rosenthal Foundation Award ($5,000): Norman Rush, *Whites*
Jean Stein Award ($5,000): Wendell Berry
Harold D. Vursell Memorial Award ($5,000): Stephen Jay Gould
Morton Dauwen Zabel Award ($2,500)): Paul Metcalf

Bancroft Prizes ($4,000 ea.): Thomas M. Doerflinger, *A Vigorous Spirit of Enterprise: Merchants and Economic Development in Revolutionary Philadelphia;* Roger Lane, *Roots of Violence in Black Philadelphia 1860–1900*
Bollingen Prize in Poetry ($5,000): Stanley Kunitz
Canada's Governor-General Literary Awards ($5,000 ea.):
English-language awards
Drama—Sharon Pollock, *Doc*
Fiction—Alice Munro, *The Progress of Love*
Nonfiction—Northrop Frye, *Northrop Frye on Shakespeare*
Poetry—Al Purdy, *The Collected Poems of Al Purdy*
French-language awards
Drama—Anne Legault, *La visite des sauvages*
Fiction—Yvon Rivard, *Les Silences du corbeau*
Nonfiction—Régine Robin, *Le réalisme socialiste: une esthétique impossible*
Poetry—Cécile Cloutier, *L'Ecouté*
Jerusalem Prize ($5,000): J. M. Coetzee
Ruth Lilly Poetry Prize ($25,000): Philip Levine
National Book Awards ($10,000 ea.)
Fiction: Larry Heinemann, *Paco's Story*
Nonfiction: Richard Rhodes, *The Making of the Atomic Bomb*
National Book Critics Circle Awards
Biography/autobiography: Theodore Rosengarten, *Tombee: Portrait of a Cotton Planter*
Criticism: Joseph Brodsky, *Less Than One*
Fiction: Reynolds Price, Kate Vaiden
Nonfiction: John W. Dower, *War Without Mercy: Race and Power in the Pacific War*
Poetry: Edward Hirsch, *Wild Gratitude*
PEN/Faulkner Award ($5,000): Richard Wiley, *Soldiers in Hiding*
Pulitzer Prizes
Biography: David J. Garrow, *Bearing the Cross: Martin Luther King Jr. and the Southern Christian Leadership Conference*
Fiction: Peter Taylor, *A Summons to Memphis*
General nonfiction: David K. Shipler, *Arab and Jew: Wounded Spirits in a Promised Land*
History: Bernard Bailyn, *Voyagers to the West: A Passage in the Peopling of America on the Eve of the Revolution*
Poetry: Rita Dove, *Thomas and Beulah*
Ritz-Hemingway Award ($50,000): Peter Taylor, *A Summons to Memphis*

MOTION PICTURES

Academy of Motion Picture Arts and Sciences ("Oscar") Awards
Actor—leading: Paul Newman, *The Color of Money*
Actor—supporting: Michael Caine, *Hannah and Her Sisters*
Actress—leading: Marlee Matlin, *Children of a Lesser God*
Actress—supporting: Dianne Wiest, *Hannah and Her Sisters*
Cinematography: Chris Menges, *The Mission*
Costume design: Jenny Beavan, John Bright, *A Room With a View*
Director: Oliver Stone, *Platoon*
Film: *Platoon*
Foreign-language film: *The Assault* (the Netherlands)
Music—original score: Herbie Hancock, *'Round Midnight*
Music—song: Giorgio Moroder (music), Tom Whitlock (lyric); *Take My Breath Away* (from *Top Gun*)
Screenplay—original: Woody Allen, *Hannah and Her Sisters*
Screenplay—adaptation: Ruth Prawer Jhabvala, *A Room With a View*
Irving G. Thalberg Memorial Award: Steven Spielberg
Honorary Awards: Ralph Bellamy, E.M. (Al) Lewis
American Film Institute's Life Achievement Award: Barbara Stanwyck
Cannes Film Festival Awards
Golden Palm Award (best film): Maurice Pialat, *Under Satan's Sun* (France)
Best actor: Marcello Mastroianni, *Dark Eyes*
Best actress: Barbara Hershey, *Shy People*
Best director: Wim Wenders, *Wings of Desire*

PUBLIC SERVICE

American Institute for Public Service Jefferson Awards
National Awards ($5,000 ea.): William J. Brennan, Jr., Irving Brown, Ginetta Sagan, Steven Jobs
Local awards ($1,000 ea.): Joan W. Bailey, Elizabeth Brown, Fred Doescher, Howard Jones, Jim Knocke
Franklin D. Roosevelt Freedom Medals: Herbert Block, George F. Kennan, Mary W. Lasker, Thomas P. O'Neill, Jr., Rev. Leon H. Sullivan
Templeton Prize for Progress in Religion ($330,000): Rev. Stanley L. Jaki, Benedictine monk and distinguished professor, Seton Hall University
Harry S Truman Public Service Award: Sen. John Glenn
U.S. Presidential Medal of Freedom (awarded by President Ronald Reagan on June 23, 1987): Anne L. Armstrong, Justin W. Dart, Sr. (posthumously), Danny Kaye (posthumously), Lyman L. Lemnitzer, John A. McCone, Frederick D. Patterson, Nathan Perlmutter, Mstislav Rostropovich, William B. Walsh, Meredith Willson (posthumously); (awarded by President Reagan on Oct. 7): Warren E. Burger, Irving R. Kaufman; (awarded by President Reagan on Nov. 17): Caspar Weinberger

SCIENCE

Bristol-Myers Award for distinguished achievement in cancer research ($50,000): Donald Metcalf, Walter and Eliza Hall Institute, Melbourne, Australia
General Motors Cancer Research Foundation Awards ($130,000 ea.): R. Palmer Beasley, University of California, San Francisco, and University of Washington's medical

research unit in Taiwan; Jesse W. Summers, Institute for Cancer Research, Philadelphia; Basil I. Hirschowitz, University of Alabama, Birmingham; Robert A. Weinberg, Whitehead Institute for Biomedical Research and Massachusetts Institute of Technology, Cambridge

Louisa Gross Horwitz Prize for research in biology or biochemistry ($22,000): Günter Blobel, Rockefeller University

Albert Lasker Medical Research Awards

Basic medical research award ($15,000 shared): Leroy Hood, California Institute of Technology; Philip Leder, Harvard Medical School; Susumu Tonegawa, Massachusetts Institute of Technology

Clinical medical research award ($15,000): Mogens Schou, Aarhus University Psychiatric Institute (Denmark)

National Medal of Science (presented by President Ronald Reagan on June 25, 1987): Philip H. Abelson, Anne Anastasi, Robert Bird, Raoul Bott, Michael DeBakey, Theodor Diener, Harry Eagle, Walter Elsasser, Michael Freedman, William Johnson, Har Gobind Khorana, Paul C. Lauterbur, Rita Levi-Montalcini, George Pake, H. Bolton Seed, George J. Stigler, Walter H. Stockmayer, Max Tishler, James Van Allen, and Ernst Weber

National Medal of Technology (presented by President Ronald Reagan on June 25, 1987): Joseph Charyk, W. Edwards Deming, John Franz, and Robert N. Noyce

Tyler Prize for outstanding research in environmental science ($150,000 shared): Richard Evans Schultes, Gilbert F. White

Wolf Prizes (*See* also Art section):

Agriculture ($100,000): Theodor O. Diener, U.S. Department of Agriculture's Plant Protection Institute

Chemistry ($100,000): Sir David C. Phillips, Oxford University; David M. Blow, Imperial College of Science and Technology, London

Mathematics ($100,000): Kiyoshi Ito, Kyoto University, Japan; Peter D. Lax, New York University

Medicine ($100,000): Pedro Cuatrecasas, Glaxo, Inc., Research Triangle Park, NC; Meir Wilcheck, Weizmann Institute, Rehovot, Israel

Physics ($100,000): Herbert Friedman, Naval Research Laboratory, Washington, DC; Bruno B. Rossi, Massachusetts Institute of Technology, Cambridge, MA; Riccardo Giacconi, Space Telescope Science Institute, Baltimore, MD

TELEVISION AND RADIO

Academy of Television Arts and Sciences ("Emmy") Awards

Actor—comedy series: Michael J. Fox, *Family Ties* (NBC)

Actor—drama series: Bruce Willis, *Moonlighting* (ABC)

Actor—miniseries or a special: James Woods, *Promise* (CBS)

Actress—comedy series: Rue McClanahan, *The Golden Girls* (NBC)

Actress—drama series: Sharon Gless, *Cagney & Lacey* (CBS)

Actress—miniseries or a special: Gena Rowlands, *The Betty Ford Story* (ABC)

Animated program: *Cathy* (CBS)

Cinematography—miniseries or a special: Philip Lathrop, *Christmas Snow* (CBS)

Comedy series: *The Golden Girls* (NBC)

Directing—comedy series: Terry Hughes, "Isn't It Romantic?", *The Golden Girls* (NBC)

Directing—drama series: Gregory Hoblit, pilot episode, *L.A. Law* (NBC)

Directing—miniseries or a special: Glenn Jordan, *Promise* (CBS)

Directing—variety or music program: Don Mischer, *The Kennedy Center Honors: A Celebration of the Performing Arts* (CBS)

Drama series: *L.A. Law* (NBC)

Drama/comedy special: "Promise," *Hallmark Hall of Fame* (CBS)

Miniseries: *A Year in the Life* (NBC)

Supporting actor—comedy series: John Larroquette, *Night Court* (NBC)

Supporting actor—drama series: John Hillerman, *Magnum, P.I.* (CBS)

Supporting actor—miniseries or a special: Dabney Coleman, *Sworn to Silence* (ABC)

Supporting actress—comedy series: Jackee Harry, *227* (NBC)

Supporting actress—drama series: Bonnie Bartlett, *St. Elsewhere* (NBC)

Supporting actress—miniseries or a special: Piper Laurie, *Promise* (CBS)

Variety, music, or comedy program: *The 1987 Tony Awards* (CBS)

Humanitas Prizes

Long-form category (($25,000): Kenneth Blackwell, Tennyson Flowers, and Richard Friedenberg, *Promise*

One-hour category ($15,000): Alan Uger and Gary David Goldberg, episode of *Family Ties*

One-half-hour category ($10,000): Bob Randall, episode of *Kate and Allie*

Children's animation category ($10,000): John Loy and Alan Burnett, episode of *Smurfs*

Children's live-action category ($10,000): Melvin Van Peebles, *The Day They Came to Arrest the Book* (CBS Schoolbreak Special)

George Foster Peabody Awards

Radio: Canadian Broadcasting Corporation, *Paris: From Oscar Wilde to Jim Morrison;* Connecticut Public Radio, *One on One;* CBS News, *Newsmark: Where in the World Are We?;* Fine Arts Society, Indianapolis; NBC Radio News, for coverage of the attack on Tripoli, Libya; WHAS Radio, Louisville, *A Disaster Called Schizophrenia*

Television: ABC News, *This Week with David Brinkley;* Dorothy Stimson Bullitt, King Broadcasting, Seattle, "in appreciation for the continuation of her exemplary family-owned broadcast enterprise"; CBS Entertainment, Garner-Duchow Productions, *Promise;* CBS News, *CBS Reports: The Vanishing Family—Crisis in Black America;* CBS News, *Sunday Morning: Vladimir Horowitz;* Churchill Films, ABC Entertainment. *The Mouse and the Motorcycle;* Jim Henson, The Muppets, "for thirty years of good, clean fun and outstanding television entertainment"; John F. Kennedy Center for the Performing Arts, CBS Entertainment, *1986 Kennedy Center Honors: A Celebration of the Performing Arts;* KPIX-TV, San Francisco, *AIDS Lifeline;* MacNeil/Lehrer Productions, British Broadcasting Corporation, *The Story of English;* NBC Entertainment, *The Cosby Show;* Thames Television International, D.L. Taffner, Ltd., *Unknown Chaplin;* Thames Television International and WGBH-TV, Boston, *Paradise Postponed;* WCCO Television, Minneapolis, *Project Lifesaver;* WCVB-TV, Boston, *A World of Difference;* WFAA-TV, Dallas, *S.M.U. Investigation;* WQED/Pittsburgh, *Anne of Green Gables;* WQED/Pittsburgh, The National Geographic Society, *The National Geographic Specials;* WSB-TV, Atlanta, *The Boy King;* WTMJ-TV, Milwaukee, *Who's Behind the Wheel?*

THEATER

New York Drama Critics Circle Awards

Best new play ($1,000): *Fences,* by August Wilson

Best foreign play: *Les Liaisons Dangereuses,* by Christopher Hampton

Best musical: *Les Misérables,* by Alain Boublil, Claude-Michel Schönberg, Herbert Kretzmer, based on the novel by Victor Hugo

Antoinette Perry ("Tony") Awards

Actor—play: James Earl Jones, *Fences*

Actor—musical: Robert Lindsay, *Me and My Girl*

Actress—play: Linda Lavin, *Broadway Bound*

Actress—musical: Maryann Plunkett, *Me and My Girl*

Choreography: Gillian Gregory, *Me and My Girl*

Director—play: Lloyd Richards, *Fences*

Director—musical: Trevor Nunn and John Caird, *Les Misérables*

Featured actor—play: John Randolph, *Broadway Bound*

Featured actor—musical: Michael Maguire, *Les Misérables*

Featured actress—play: Mary Alice, *Fences*

Featured actress—musical: Frances Ruffelle, *Les Misérables*

Musical: *Les Misérables*

Musical—book: Alain Boublil and Claude-Michel Schönberg, *Les Misérables*

Musical—score: Claude-Michel Schönberg, Herbert Kretzmer, and Alain Boublil, *Les Misérables*

Play: *Fences* by August Wilson

Reproduction of a play or musical: *All My Sons*

Special award: San Francisco Mime Troupe

Pulitzer Prize for Drama: August Wilson, *Fences*

PUBLISHING

Guarded optimism in the U.S. publishing industry seemed justified through the first half of 1987, as sales and profits edged above the lackluster finish that characterized the closing quarter of 1986. Estimates for the second half of 1987 were even more optimistic.

But that optimism was tempered by concerns over the quickening pace of corporate takeovers and mergers in all areas. It was tempered, too, by projections that some segments were unlikely to fare much better than the general economy over the next five years.

The pace of technological investments quickened. One study found that 20% of all workers in the publishing industry (books, magazines, and newspapers) were using personal computers on the job while another 14% predicted that they would begin using one during 1987. Taken together, mergers and technological innovations were rapidly restructuring parts of U.S. publishing.

Books. In the U.S. book-publishing industry, the trend toward international publishing and corporate merger continued unabated during 1987. In March, the Australian communications magnate Rupert Murdoch, who already owned a number of newspaper, television, and film companies in the United States, announced plans to buy Harper & Row. In May, Random House announced a takeover of the British publishing enterprise of Chatto, Virago, Bodley Head and Jonathan Cape (CVBC); this gave Random House power in negotiating English-language rights with firms in Australia, Canada, New Zealand, Britain, and the United States. Later that month, British publishing tycoon Robert Maxwell offered $1.7 billion for Harcourt Brace Jovanovich (HBJ), by far the largest amount ever offered for a publishing company. But HBJ Chairman William Jovanovich called the $44-per-share offer "preposterous" and successfully fought off the hostile bid.

Concerns about these and smaller mergers centered on the bottom-line orientations of publishing conglomerates. Critics maintained that larger companies concentrate on popular, profitable fiction works and on educational, professional, and juvenile profit centers, while quality fiction and less popular works are neglected. These concerns were offset somewhat by changes in smaller, more specialized commercial presses and university presses. University presses broadened their effort to acquire mid-range books. Press runs of academic books declined, and new technologies were expected to make academic information available in new formats.

The impact of technology on the publishing industry was seen also in the continued development of new product lines. Publishers increased their efforts to sell audio and video products in 1987. One survey found that two thirds of the retailers canvassed were selling audio titles in 1987 and almost all planned to expand their inventory. Almost one third were selling video cassettes by the summer of 1987. New technologies also changed book printing with new computer systems for page makeup without a layout design and more sophisticated paperback covers for quality fiction. A few companies tried covers containing "holograms" or three-dimensional pictures.

Among booksellers, 1987 was promoted as "The Year of the Reader," a project begun by the Library of Congress and sanctioned by a congressional resolution. But the year was plagued by dissension in the American Booksellers Association (ABA). One of the largest U.S. booksellers, Waldenbooks, pulled out of the ABA and held a convention of its own.

Overall, 1987 was expected to be a good year for the U.S. book-publishing industry. The Department of Commerce predicted sales of $11.7 billion for the industry, a 4.5% increase. The sharp increases in sales of children's books continued, as did exports of U.S. books. The Association of American Publishers' monthly reports reflected vigorous first-quarter sales, with revenues up 12.4% over 1986 and unit sales up 4.8%. Professional books led the surge, and mass-market paperbacks trailed. In August, bookstores reported a 10% increase in the first half of 1987 compared with the first half of 1986.

School textbooks remained a source of controversy among religious and educational groups, as well as a subject of litigation in the court system. (*See* special report, page 214.)

Newspapers. Mergers and "group ownership" continued to dominate the U.S. newspaper publishing industry in 1987. Year-end figures for 1986 revealed a total of 103 newspaper sales, more than double the annual average from 1977 through 1985. Twenty-six more newspapers were sold during the first half of 1987, with the number expected to accelerate during the second half. Meanwhile, at the beginning of 1987, 73% (1,217) of all U.S. dailies were owned by newspaper groups (31 more than in 1986), accounting for 80% of all U.S. daily newspaper circulation. By midyear, the number of group-owned newspapers had climbed to 74% of all dailies, accounting for 81% of total daily circulation.

As the pace of acquisitions accelerated, the cost of newspaper properties soared. For example, the Hearst Corporation paid $400 million for the *Houston Chronicle,* the highest price ever paid for a single newspaper in the United States. U.S. newspapers were selling for 10–50 times their annual earnings, compared with 1–8 times annual earnings for British newspapers.

As domestic buyers bid up the prices of the remaining independents, foreign investment in

U.S. newspapers slowed. It was estimated that at least 150 U.S. daily newspapers were owned by foreign companies in 1987. Murdoch, probably the most visible foreign owner, was attempting to sell the *New York Post* and *The Boston Herald.*

Newspaper groups become more cautious in their investments in 1987. The trend of the prior several years toward diversification of holdings was reversed. Many newspaper companies sold "peripheral non-media holdings," including cellular-telephone companies, videotex services, and even cable-television holdings.

Growth in the U.S. newspaper industry was expected to be steady but not spectacular in 1987. Advertising revenues were projected to grow at about 7% for the year. The U.S. Commerce Department estimated that total revenues (in constant dollars) would rise about 2.2% in 1987 and 1.5–2.0% annually for the next five years.

Daily newspaper circulation was predicted to rise only 1% in 1987, after dropping nearly .5% in 1986, to 62.49 million. The average price per copy climbed 4%. As 1987 opened, 64.5% of the nation's daily newspapers cost 25 cents, down from 70.9% the previous year.

The number of daily newspapers published in the United States dropped by 19 to 1,657. Evening newspapers continued to outnumber morning newspapers two-to-one (1,187 to 500). During the first half of 1987, another ten afternoon papers were lost.

The battle for suburban readers heated up in 1987. One study found that all 168 U.S. dailies with circulations of more than 100,000 had tried some kind of content change designed to better reach suburbanites.

New technologies occupied much of the attention of newspaper publishers in the United States. Weekly newspaper publishing was revolutionized by "desktop publishing systems" that permit typesetting and some page design on personal computers and plain-paper, laser printers. One study estimated that three fourths of all U.S. and Canadian newspapers use at least one personal computer somewhere in their operation.

At least 40 states mounted campaigns in 1987 to tax newspapers and other services in an effort to raise revenues. The taxes took several forms, but most sought to tax circulation or advertising revenues.

The "credibility issue" lingered. Studies found that more newspapers ran corrections columns and ran them more prominently in 1987 than in previous years. Editors also began holding meetings with readers and running columns about the operation of the newspaper. One international study showed that 69% of Americans expressed confidence in their media, compared with only 47% in Spain and France, and only 40% in Great Britain and West Germany. But there were complaints.

As the campaigns of 1988 presidential candidates heated up, so did complaints about news coverage. Democratic candidate Gary Hart withdrew from the race following a *Miami Herald* report that he had spent the night with model Donna Rice. He charged that the news media had invaded his private life. Democrat Joseph Biden pulled out of the race after *The New York Times* revealed that he had been disciplined in law school for plagiarism and other media reported that he had borrowed heavily in his speeches from the words and phrases of others without attribution.

Peter O'Sullivan, right, *editor-in-chief of "The Houston Post," tells his staff that the paper has been sold to the Media News Group, an operating company that owns the "Dallas Times Herald." Scores of newspapers changed hands in 1987.*

AP/Wide World

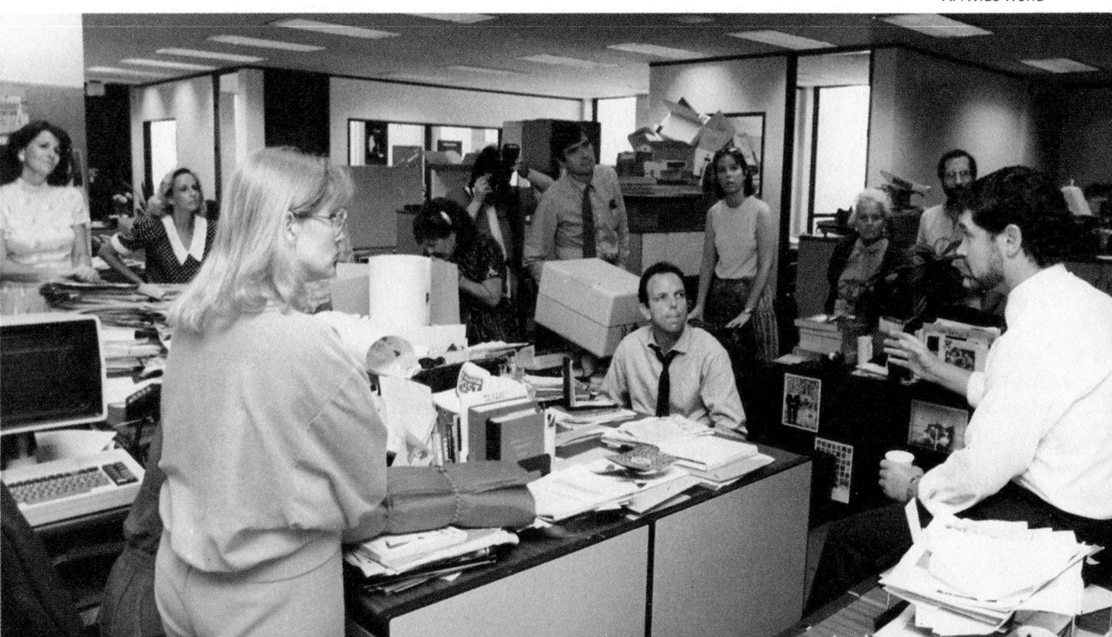

Magazines. There was little optimism in the U.S. magazine industry. After two years of decline in number of advertising pages and widespread estimates of decline in both newsstand and subscription sales for 1986, magazine industry observers were guarded about prospects for 1987.

Total magazine revenues at the beginning of 1987 were up only 1% in constant dollars over a year earlier, according to the U.S. Commerce Department. Only a 1.6% increase in total revenues was expected by midyear. The growth of magazine advertising revenues in 1987 was expected to be little better than the 4% overall gain in 1986. The number of advertising pages was projected actually to decline.

Circulation estimates were no better. The Council for Periodical Distributors Associations reported that, while newsstand dollar sales were up 3.2% in 1986, the number of magazines sold dropped 2.8%. Only a 6.6% increase in cover prices propped up sales revenues. Overall, magazine circulation was static. One study found that 52.6% of the magazines reporting showed some circulation gains in 1986 while the rest showed declines. The declines were attributed to increased video use by potential readers, busy life-styles, and declining numbers of outlets selling magazines.

Still, the U.S. Commerce Department estimated that circulation would hold steady or increase slightly in 1987, despite continued declines in single-copy sales. Foreign sales of U.S. magazines were expected to jump 36% in 1987, with the weakening U.S. dollar yielding lower cover prices for foreign buyers.

The air of uncertainty produced a number of industry innovations during 1987. Several publishers entered into joint agreements designed to reduce production costs. *Sail* magazine produced an insert for *Esquire* in February. *American Health* coproduced an insert for *Working Woman,* and *Success* produced one for *Good Housekeeping*. Time, Inc. joined Working Woman, Inc. in purchasing McCalls Publishing Company. And Murdoch Magazines and Hachette Publications entered a joint venture to produce a magazine for U.S. movie fans called *Premiere* (which was well-established in France). Time Incorporated's Time Distributing Services and The New York Times Company's Retail Magazine Marketing Company formed a partnership for distribution of titles owned by the parent companies.

Other changes seen in 1987 included the growth of "polly bagging"—inserting promotions and inserts wrapped in a plastic bag; more regional advertising programs, especially among magazines with less than 1 million circulation; and advertising networks, which permit an advertiser to get a larger specialized audience by buying advertising from a group of specialized publications. Magazines also began yielding to pressure to negotiate advertising rates, which had been fixed for many years. And the use of premiums spread in 1987, too.

The economic situation has made magazine properties cheaper and encouraged foreign companies to buy U.S. magazines. Since 1983 approximately 70% of sales of U.S. trade magazine groups have been to foreign buyers. But domestic concerns have also been active in buying U.S. magazines. In July, Peter Diamandis and a group of senior CBS editors purchased the company's magazine division in a leveraged buyout with money borrowed from Prudential Insurance Company and two of its subsidiaries. The price was $650 million, one of the highest ever paid for a magazine property. *Esquire* was bought by the Hearst group early in the year. In May, Affiliated Publications, which owns *The Boston Globe* newspaper, bought Billboard Publications. And Cahners Publishing Company purchased *Variety* during the summer.

As of 1987 there were about 3,200 magazine companies in the United States. Four of them accounted for 25% of total industry revenues, and the largest 20 brought in nearly half of all revenues. The *Capelle Circulation Report* said that 60% of all industry newsstand sales went to the 20 biggest titles.

U.S. magazines expanded their product lines in 1987 with a new interest in ancillary products, such as books, videos, and even trade shows. Consumer magazines were joined by business publications in marketing video products.

The year also saw a number of technological innovations. Holograms were used on magazine covers following several earlier successes in attracting advertisers. The Hearst organization began offering advertising rates on diskette. Lasers were introduced to provide better control in engraving gravure cylinders. And satellite access was spreading throughout the industry.

But overall the trend in technology was toward shifting publishing production systems out of the hands of craftsmen and into the hands of the creators of print content. The use of word processing, desktop publishing, personal computers, illustrator workstations, and cheaper digital color image assembly systems spread. The result was that editorial staffs gained more control over the printing process. Desktop publishing moved especially rapidly in 1987 as improvements in hardware and software accelerated.

Robert Gottlieb, editor and president of the book publisher Alfred A. Knopf, Inc., took the helm of *The New Yorker* in March, replacing William Shawn, the legendary editor of the publication for 35 years. Gottlieb became only the third editor in the magazine's 62-year history.

CHARLES C. SELF
The University of Alabama

PUERTO RICO

As Puerto Rico grieved over the deaths of 97 persons in the New Year's Eve 1986 fire at the Dupont Plaza Hotel, more shocking news was learned. A few weeks after the tragic fire, three hotel employees were arrested and charged with murder and arson. Hector Escudero Aponte, a maintenance worker, was charged with igniting the blaze with a can of Sterno cooking fuel. He was helped by Armando Jiménez Rivera, a busboy, who fetched the fuel, and by José Francisco Rivera, a bartender, who helped shield Escudero from view while he began the fire. The three pleaded guilty and are serving sentences ranging from 75 to 99 years.

The fire apparently spread quickly as it ignited a stack of new furniture wrapped in plastic and stored in the hotel ballroom. While the events leading to the tragic fire unfolded, so did the need for improvements in fire prevention and safety laws. Gov. Rafael Hernández Colón appointed a blue-ribbon fire-safety commission to recommend improvements. The commission's work led to a new law that requires sprinklers and other safety precautions in hotels and high-rise buildings. Also related to the Dupont fire, the amount of pending lawsuits resulting from the blaze reached an unprecedented $3 billion in local courts.

The U.S. Immigration and Naturalization Service opened a border patrol on Puerto Rico's west coast, the first outside the continental United States. The move brought to light the growing illegal traffic of immigrants from neighboring Dominican Republic. Shortly after the move, a boat load of 100 illegal refugees sank off the northeast town of Nagua as it set off for Puerto Rico. More than 50 persons were believed to have drowned.

The Commonwealth government clashed with federal authorities in the courts several times in 1987. The Corrections Administration was slapped with $1 million in fines for failing to reduce overcrowding in island prisons. Also, the Aqueduct and Sewer Authority had to face $32 million in court-ordered fines for failing to keep a timetable to improve waste-water treatment plants in an agreement with the U.S. Environmental Protection Agency.

The Puerto Rican legislature approved a tax-reform package in 1987. It simplifies the island's income tax code by reducing the number of brackets from 15 to 4, and by lowering the rate in the top bracket from 50% to 33%.

King Juan Carlos and Queen Sofia of Spain arrived in San Juan in May. The visit marked the first time a Spanish monarch had touched the soil of the former Spanish colony. (Puerto Rico was acquired by the United States in 1898.) King Juan Carlos opened the fifth Iberoamerican Conference of the National Commissions for the Celebration of the 500th Anniversary of the Discovery of America. Representatives of some 27 countries, including Cuba and Nicaragua, attended the conference.

A 17th century astrolabe, a primitive navigational instrument, and rare today, was discovered in a sunken galleon off the western coast of Rincón. The Puerto Rican Institute of Culture claimed custody of the astrolabe, setting off a debate about its ownership with the salvagers of the sunken ship.

DEBORAH RAMIREZ, *"The San Juan Star"*

PUERTO RICO • Information Highlights

Area: 3,515 sq mi (9 104 km²).
Population (mid-1986 est.): 3,300,000
Chief Cities (1980 census): San Juan, the capital, 434,849; Bayamon, 196,206; Ponce, 189,046.
Government (1987): *Chief Officer*—governor, Rafael Hernández Colón (Popular Democratic Party). *Legislature*—Senate, 27 members; House of Representatives, 51 members.

QUEBEC

The process of constitutional reconciliation between Quebec and the rest of Canada took a giant step forward in 1987.

The Meech Lake Accord. Prime Minister Brian Mulroney, Premier Robert Bourassa, and the other nine provincial premiers reached a historic agreement on April 30 at Meech Lake, outside Ottawa, providing for Quebec's return to the Canadian constitutional fold. On June 20, the Quebec legislature overwhelmingly passed a resolution endorsing the accord. Saskatchewan and the federal Parliament later followed suit. The ratification process was not expected to be completed until mid-1990.

The Meech Lake agreement ended an estrangement that began when Quebec rejected the new Constitution drawn up in 1981. The 1987 changes to that Constitution recognize Quebec as a "distinct society" within Canada, and give the provincial governments a voice in Supreme Court appointments, on immigration, and on the establishment of federal programs that affect the province.

Following the Liberal-dominated legislature's 95 to 18 vote for ratification, Premier Bourassa hailed the accord as the "greatest political victory" for Quebec in 200 years.

Parti Quebeçois Opposition Leader Pierre Marc Johnson accused Bourassa of "abject cowardice" for not obtaining stronger protections for Quebec's French-language rights under the Constitution. Meanwhile, outside Quebec, Prime Minister Mulroney was criticized widely for agreeing to recognize Quebec as a distinct society and, it was claimed, for hobbling constitutional evolution by extending veto power to the provinces (*see* CANADA).

As 1987 ended, the debate was far from over. However, Prime Minister Mulroney had

© M. Paquin/Publiphoto/Alpha Diffusion

During an October visit to Quebec, Queen Elizabeth II declared that "the constitutional accord of 1987 recognizes that Quebec constitutes a distinct society." It was the queen's first trip to the province since 1964.

the support of both the Liberal and New Democratic Party opposition parties in Parliament—though not all their members—as well as all or nearly all the provinces. The queen, on a tour of Quebec, also gave the agreement her blessing. Barring unforeseen political upheavals in the next two years, an end to Quebec's constitutional isolation seemed assured.

Royal Visit. From October 21 to October 24, Queen Elizabeth II made her first official visit to Quebec since 1964. Rounding off a 15-day Canadian tour built around her attendance at the Commonwealth summit in Vancouver, B.C., she was greeted by small but enthusiastic crowds in Quebec City and communities on the lower St. Lawrence south shore. The atmosphere was altogether warmer than it had been 23 years earlier, when truncheon-wielding police clashed with separatist demonstrators protesting her presence in Quebec City.

Hydro Rebuffed. Hydro-Quebec, the giant government owned electrical utility, suffered a humiliating defeat June 18 when Canada's National Energy Board refused to grant it a license to export C$3 billion worth of electrical power to New England beginning in 1990.

The board's decision immediately raised the questions of who controls Hydro-Quebec and whether the utility should be made more answerable to the government. Energy Minister Charles Caccia rebuked the corporation for challenging the board's right to demand proof that the power was surplus to Canadian requirements. Electrical utilities in Ontario, Newfoundland, and New Brunswick had filed objections to the plan. Provincial officials sought to assure New England customers that the power would be delivered in the end, following resubmission of the export application.

Cabinet Shuffle. Solicitor-General Gerard Latulippe resigned June 29, shortly after a Montreal newspaper confronted him with allegations of conflict of interest—his awarding of a contract to a friend and former colleague, lawyer Diane Fortier. After accepting Latulippe's resignation, Premier Bourassa carried out a limited cabinet shuffle involving six relatively junior ministers. Justice Minister Herbert Marx took over as interim solicitor-general.

René Lévesque and the Parti Quebeçois. René Lévesque, founder of the Parti Quebeçois (PQ), leader for many years of the Quebec separatist movement, and premier of the province from 1976 to 1985, died on November 1. Both he and his party had lost public support in the early 1980s, and the 1985 election that brought in the Liberals represented a massive repudiation of the PQ. Nevertheless, the thousands who gathered to pay a last tribute to the 65-year-old leader were proof that the idea of independence for Quebec is still a live issue. In fact, Pierre Marc Johnson was forced to resign as PQ leader a week after Lévesque's death, when party militants rejected his decision to put off the question of independence until new Quebec elections are held. Guy Chevrette was named interim leader, pending party elections.

JOHN BEST, *"Canada World News"*

QUEBEC • Information Highlights

Area: 594,857 sq mi (1 540 680 km²).
Population (1986 census): 6,540,276.
Chief Cities (1986 census): Quebec, the capital, 164,580; Montreal, 1,015,420; Laval, 284,164.
Government (1987): *Chief Officers*—lt. gov., Gilles Lamontagne; premier, Robert Bourassa (Liberal). *Legislature*—National Assembly, 122 members.
Provincial Finances (1987–88 fiscal year budget): *Revenues,* $27,250,000,000; *expenditures,* $30,150,000,000.
Personal Income (average weekly earnings, July 1987): $432.84.
Labor Force (September 1987, seasonally adjusted: *Employed* workers, 15 years of age and over, 3,319,000; *Unemployed,* 336,000 (10.1%).
Education (1987–88): *Enrollment*—elementary and secondary schools, 1,154,720 pupils; postsecondary—universities, 116,200; community colleges, 162,600.
(All monetary figures are in Canadian dollars.)

RECORDINGS

Two related topics animated the music recordings business in 1987: the skyrocketing popularity of compact discs (CDs) and the industry's reluctance to embrace digital audio tape, better known by the initials DAT. By year's end, as the record industry continued to lobby the U.S. Congress about its concern over DAT technology, Japanese manufacturers introduced the machine in Europe.

In the video industry, the pirating of prerecorded cassettes remained a serious and growing problem for movie-production companies. Video piracy—the illegal copying and distribution of copyrighted tapes—was estimated to cost the movie industry $1 billion.

Compact Discs. The popularity of compact-disc players has changed the recorded music market in much the same way as did the introduction of portable cassette players. The vinyl LP (long-playing record) has been a victim of both trends. Just as the spread of Walkman-like cassette machines quickly pushed prerecorded cassette-tapes ahead of LPs in terms of unit sales, now CDs have already overtaken LPs, in revenue if not units. According to a survey sponsored by the National Association of Record Merchandisers, market shares in terms of dollar volume broke down as follows: cassettes 56%, CDs 19%, LPs 18%, and 7-inch and 12-inch singles 7%. In a last-ditch attempt to save the single, some companies experimented with marketing them in a cassette format.

Worldwide sales of CDs were expected to top 150 million in 1987, with approximately 100 million in the United States. Some retailers predicted that within five years, CDs will dominate the mass market and LPs will begin to be phased out by the major labels and retailers.

Digital Audio Tape. DAT has created a furor throughout the industry, with some analysts predicting that its introduction to the marketplace could stop the CD market in its tracks. Digital audio tape records music using the same digital technology used to encode CDs. The record industry, which has long complained that it loses significant revenue to home taping, claims that these machines will enable pirates to make state-of-the-art copies of copyrighted materials. Further, they argue, the technology for economic manufacture of prerecorded DAT tapes is not yet available, leaving copied materials as the machines' only play-back fare.

The fight landed in Congress in 1987. Emphasis was put on a bill that would require manufacturers to include a "spoiler chip" in the tape machines. This chip, along with a supposedly inaudible encoded signal mixed into the recordings, would conspire to impede the recording process. But the plan touched off a controversy regarding the encoded signal, which some claim would ultimately damage the artist's work.

Courtesy of Toshiba America, Inc.

With the compact disc (CD) industry already booming, new hardware began competing with Walkman-type cassette players. Toshiba's new portable CD player and AM/FM tuner is only slightly larger than a standard-size disc.

Another proposed solution (rejected by Congress in 1982 when the record industry complained about home taping) is to impose a tax on both the tape machines and the blank tapes. The money would then be divided among copyright holders.

The argument against such restrictions is that there has been no conclusive proof that home taping diminishes sales of prerecorded music. Most home tapers, it is said, record favorite albums for use in the car or on a portable stereo, or tape compilations of favorite album tracks. This, the argument goes, only whets the consumer's appetite for more new music.

The debate may turn out to be moot. While the "spoiler chip" and encoded signal were being tested, Japanese manufacturers were readying the first DAT machines for U.S. shipment. The price—about $2,000 for the machines and $15 for a blank tape—is expected to limit initial demand. Still, many feel that once the technology is on the market, the DAT cat will be out of the bag.

CD Video. One new format that record companies are eager to exploit is CD video, or CD-V, which combines digital sound and video images. Much of the software will come in the form of 5-inch discs that will offer five minutes of music-video visuals and up to 20 minutes of audio. Some machines also will be equipped to accept 8- and 12-inch laser discs, as well as audio-only CDs. With CD-V discs expected to cost around $8, the record industry is hoping finally to profit from the investment it made in producing promotional music videos.

See also MUSIC.

JOHN MILWARD
Free-lance Writer and Critic

© Michael Creagan

More than 170 illegal Indian immigrants were detained by Canadian officials after landing in lifeboats on the shore of Nova Scotia in mid-July. The incident led Parliament to pass tougher restrictions on immigrants claiming refugee status.

REFUGEES AND IMMIGRATION

During 1987 controversy arose in the United States over the implementation of a sweeping immigration law passed late the previous year, as well as over U.S. refugee and asylum policy. The year also was notable for the continuing deterioration of international protection for refugees.

The most publicized events, however, were the takeovers of a Louisiana prison and a federal penitentiary in Atlanta, GA, by Cuban detainees who were to be repatriated under an agreement between Washington and Havana. The inmates rioted in protest and took prison guards and others hostage. The Louisiana takeover ended after eight days on November 29, and the Atlanta standoff was resolved after 11 days on December 3, upon agreement by the U.S. State Department to postpone the deportations pending individual case reassessments. (*See also* CUBA.)

Immigration. In October 1986, after nearly a decade of national debate, the U.S. Congress passed legislation reforming the nation's immigration laws. The 1986 Immigration Reform and Control Act addressed the issues of undocumented migration and the United States' historical dependence on often undocumented Mexican agricultural labor. The law offered legal status or amnesty to illegal aliens who entered the country before Jan. 1, 1982, and have lived in it continuously since that time; established sanctions against employers who hire illegal aliens; and allowed foreign farm workers who were employed for a least 90 days between May 1985 and May 1986 to qualify for temporary legal status, then permanent resident status, and eventually citizenship. The new law also includes civil-rights guarantees for Hispanic legal residents, increased funding for enforcement by the U.S. Immigration and Naturalization Service (INS), and established a program that allows U.S. growers to employ foreign farm workers on a temporary basis. Beginning on May 5, 1987, undocumented residents were given one year to apply for legalization.

The implementation of the act by the INS was sharply criticized by Hispanic groups and volunteer agencies. Concerns were raised that the application fees for legalization ($185 for individuals and $420 for families) were too high, that the legalization requirements were too strict, and that the amnesty regulations and procedures were too complicated, especially for immigrants who do not speak English. Stringent residence requirements which threatened to divide families of applicants who arrived at different times were a particular focus of criticism by religious organizations.

During the year, the Reagan administration took actions to deal with some of these criticisms. In early October it liberalized the rules for illegal aliens seeking amnesty, predicting that at least 100,000 would benefit from the change. While there was no reliable estimate of how many people would apply for amnesty under the new law, some groups suggested that the rules were liberalized because officials were disappointed with the number of applicants. The federal government also provided assistance to help such heavy-influx states as California, Texas, and Florida cope with the added financial strain on health and welfare systems. These new measures were expected to help stem the flow of illegal aliens every year. During 1987, the INS noted a significant reduction in the number of apprehensions at the border; however, Hispanic organizations disputed the figures.

U.S. Asylum Policy. One of the many important issues that the 1986 immigration law sidestepped was the fate of the many undocumented Central Americans who arrived in the United States after Jan. 1, 1982. Many human-rights organizations and religious institutions contended that these people had fled violence and persecution in their homelands and should be offered refuge in the United States. Although Nicaraguans benefited from a ruling by Attorney General Edwin Meese which allowed them to stay in the country indefinitely, Salvadorans and Guatemalans were portrayed by the administration as "illegal aliens."

Legislation introduced by U.S. Rep. Joseph Moakley (D-MA) and Sen. Dennis DeConcini (D-AZ) providing for temporary suspension of deportation for these Central Americans gained widespread support in 1987. And the U.S. Supreme Court ruled that the government had imposed too rigid a standard for deciding whether people were eligible for asylum. The landmark decision, *Immigration and Naturalization Service v. Cordoza-Fonseca,* specifically concerned the denial of political asylum to a Nicaraguan woman, but it applied equally to thousands of Salvadorans and Nicaraguans in a similar situation.

Despite this ruling, foreign policy and ideological factors continued to color the implementation of U.S. refugee and asylum policy, particularly in the emphasis on Southeast Asian refugees and the adjudication of asylum claims by Central Americans already in the United States. The U.S. admission quota for refugees worldwide in 1987 was 70,000 and, as in the past, admissions policies discriminated in favor of those fleeing Communist regimes. Most refugees admitted during the year came from Vietnam, Cambodia, and Laos, followed by several Eastern European countries, Iran, Afghanistan, Ethiopia, and Cuba. Refugees from Africa and Latin America constituted only a small fraction of the total allocations. A dominant characteristic of U.S. refugee policy became one of deterring asylum-seekers through long-term detention in prison-like facilities and the continued interdiction of Haitians at sea. At the same time, the United States again led the world in contributions to international refugee assistance and resettlement.

International Refugee Protection. The year 1987 was a bad one for most of the world's estimated 12 million refugees. The international protection of refugees deteriorated as the United States and Western Europe, traditionally the principal diplomatic supporters for the international refugee system, passed restrictive laws and tightened regulations to keep asylum-seekers out. After 173 Indian Sikhs arrived suddenly on the shore of Nova Scotia in July—recalling a similar incident in 1986—and fearing a flood of Central American asylum-seekers from the United States as a result of the 1986 Immigration Reform and Control Act, Canada suddenly shifted its open-door policy of immediate entry for refugees fleeing war and repression.

The deterioration in protection standards for refugees was having critical impacts in other parts of the world. Thailand's removal of Cambodian refugees from a secure refugee camp inside the country to dangerous border areas and the forcible repatriation of asylum-seekers from Laos were examples of the erosion of protection principles which took place in 1987. Elsewhere, the fate of Mozambican refugees grew worse as hundreds of thousands of persons were displaced or forced to flee to neighboring countries as a result of atrocities committed by South African--sponsored Mozambican resistance forces inside the country. Mozambican refugees were reported to have been forcibly repatriated from Malawi during the year, and in order to stem the influx of refugees into their country, South Africa erected an electrified fence along part of its border with Mozambique. In Botswana, Zambia, and Zimbabwe, South Africa's military attacked refugee camps and settlements. In Lebanon, the tragedy of Palestinian refugees also remained one of unending violence. The conflicts in Afghanistan, Sri Lanka, Central America, and Iran and Iraq, all major producers of refugees, remained virtually unresolved. Longstanding refugee populations along disputed borders—such as the Cambodian or the Afghan—continued to receive military as well as economic support for their armed struggles. Despite the peace plan proposed by President Oscar Arias of Costa Rica in August 1987, civil and armed conflict continued to disrupt the political and economic fabric of Central American societies and make life difficult for the millions of displaced persons and refugees in the region. Most of the more than 10,000 Vietnamese boat people living in crowded camps behind barbed wire in Hong Kong received no assurance that they ever would be resettled overseas.

Although some refugees were able to return home in Central America and Africa, most of these repatriations were controversial and occurred in less than ideal conditions. Many refugees returned to areas where conflicts still raged and were unable to reclaim the lands which they had abandoned several years before. There was a widespread feeling that the Office of the United Nations High Commissioner for Refugees was not capable of dealing effectively with contemporary refugee problems and that governments were not willing to demonstrate sufficient political will to achieve solutions to refugee situations worldwide.

GIL LOESCHER
University of Notre Dame

RELIGION

Overview

New ground was broken in Catholic-Jewish relations in 1987. Sharp differences had arisen between the two faiths over Pope John Paul II's beatification of Edith Stein, a Jewish-born nun who was killed at Auschwitz during World War II, and his granting of an audience to Austrian President Kurt Waldheim, who had allegedly been involved with Nazi killings during the war. The pope and Vatican officials met with American Jewish leaders in the late summer and announced plans to prepare an official Catholic document on the Holocaust and anti-Semitism and set up a mechanism for regular contacts with Jewish groups. On other interfaith fronts, the U.S. Catholic bishops established an office to promote relationships with religious leaders not in the Judeo-Christian tradition.

The Vatican also confronted dissent in the U.S. Catholic Church during the year. In a compromise worked out by three American bishops, the Holy See restored full powers to Seattle Archbishop Raymond Hunthausen, who had been disciplined for alleged laxity in failing to enforce official church teachings. In September, on his second visit to the United States, the pope was told by leading prelates that the church faced major problems in trying to enforce its standards in the face of dissent from lay people, a theme that was also discussed at the Synod of Bishops in October.

Disputes occurred between American Jews and Israel over whether Israel should take part in an international peace conference. Ultra-Orthodox and secular Jews clashed in violent confrontations in Israel over the question of Sabbath observance.

The merger of three U.S.-based denominations to form the 5.3-million-member Evangelical Lutheran Church in America was one of the major events in Protestantism. But perhaps the most publicized religious development of 1987 was the so-called "holy war" among television preachers, which raised questions of both theological and financial integrity.

Television Evangelism in Turmoil.

At the beginning of the year, evangelist Oral Roberts said he had been warned in a vision that God might take his life if he could not raise $8 million for scholarships for Third World medical students at his university in Tulsa, OK. He gave a deadline of March 31, and announced before that date that a donation by a Florida dog-track owner had put him over the top.

This controversial fund-raising method and the fact that his evangelistic association makes no public accounting of its income and spending made Roberts a target of criticism in the media and the religious community. However, the issue was soon eclipsed by an even bigger development.

The Bakker Scandal. In mid-March the Rev. Jim Bakker, one of the most popular television evangelists, announced that he was resigning

AP/Wide World

After resigning his PTL television ministry in March over a highly publicized scandal, the Rev. Jim Bakker and wife Tammy (left) *fought to regain control later in the year.*

his ministry because he was being blackmailed over a 1980 sexual encounter. He turned over the leadership of his PTL (People That Love or Praise the Lord) television network to the Rev. Jerry Falwell.

Shortly after, a lawyer for Bakker suggested that the Rev. Jimmy Swaggart, another television preacher, had been threatening a "hostile takeover" of PTL. Still another electronic evangelist, the Rev. John Ankerberg, then went public with charges of bisexuality against Bakker. The PTL founder's failure to appear before church committees to respond to those accusations as well as charges of improper use of PTL funds led to his defrocking by the Assemblies of God. The Pentecostal denomination also defrocked his second-in-command, Richard Dortch, for allegedly taking part in a cover-up of financial improprieties at PTL.

Soon Bakker and his wife, Tammy Faye, were charging that Jerry Falwell had "stolen" PTL from them. Bakker supporters rallied to the cause and pointed out that Falwell's fundamentalist Baptist theology seemed incompatible with the charismatic-Pentecostal approach that had characterized PTL since its founding in the early 1970s.

Under the Bakkers, PTL reflected a style of evangelism that was high on entertainment and low on theology. For example, the PTL empire includes Heritage USA, a "Christian theme park" in South Carolina. This style had been criticized not only by fundamentalists like Falwell, but also by more traditional Pentecostalists like Swaggart, who declared that "the gospel is not entertainment. It is very sober. It has no place for amusement parks."

Following the change of management at PTL, Falwell brought in a new board and announced that Bakker would not be allowed to return because of his alleged financial mismanagement. The board found that the Bakkers had received nearly $1.6 million in salary and bonuses for 1986. Fallwell said he did not think "any reasonable person could believe these salaries are acceptable." He said he received $100,000 a year with no perks.

Under the new board, the ministry filed for bankruptcy and submitted a reorganization plan that would sharply curtail the privileges of thousands of PTL "partners" who had been promised annual free vacations at Heritage USA in exchange for donations of $1,000 or more. But the bankruptcy court judge ruled that the PTL plan was unacceptable. He told creditors of the ministry to submit their own plan to have PTL pay off more than $60 million in debts. Falwell and the board than resigned in protest, charging that the alternative plan would pave the way for the Bakkers' return.

Background. The developments of 1987 brought new attention to the $2-billion-a-year "televangelist" industry, which encompasses 221 Christian television stations and 60 syndicated programs. Some of the organizations are the largest businesses in their home cities, such as those of Falwell in Lynchburg, VA, and Swaggart in Baton Rouge, LA.

For long-time observers of television ministries the scandal was a time bomb that had been ticking for years. The Charlotte (NC) *Observer* had been reporting on the Bakkers' luxurious life-style and controversial fund-raising tactics for more than a decade. Such reports had prompted an inconclusive Federal Communications Commission probe in the late 1970s of claims that PTL had diverted money raised for overseas mission projects.

The name-calling among broadcast preachers should not have come as a surprise, according to University of Chicago church historian Martin E. Marty. "Reporters knew that there was intense rivalry among evangelists," he said. "Onstage they would say they were brothers in Christ; offstage they would call them the competition. Because the market wasn't growing and expenses and dreams were growing, they had to become more sensational and push to the edge, a necessarily precarious position."

Regulatory Measures. The necessity of regulating the "teleministries" had been recognized even before the PTL affair, and a number of new efforts were generated by the scandal. The Evangelical Council for Financial Accountability (ECFA) had been organized in 1979 to set standards for evangelical organizations, but fewer than 400 of the more than 2,000 para-church ministries are members. Of the most famous evangelists only the Rev. Billy Graham, who was one of its founders, is a member.

In early March, just before the PTL scandal broke, officials of more than 350 evangelical organizations met in Kansas City and signed a statement committing their agencies to high standards of financial disclosure and integrity in fund-raising. Evangelical theologian Carl F.H. Henry told the gathering that "unfortunately, evangelical fund-raising practices are sometimes more shoddy than those of nonreligious agencies."

The board of National Religious Broadcasters (NRB), which encompasses 1,300 electronic ministries, voted during the year to establish a set of standards and an Ethics and Financial Integrity Commission to police them. Among other things, adherents to the NRB standards will be required to disclose every source of income and every expenditure, including salaries. However, the standards will not apply to such NRB nonmembers as Oral Roberts.

The U.S. Congress got involved in the issue in early October at a day-long hearing of a House Ways and Means subcommittee chaired by Rep. J. J. Pickle (D-TX). The subcommittee, which called the hearing to examine whether tax-exempt broadcast ministries were complying with the federal tax code, heard testimony from Jerry Falwell and Oral Roberts, among others.

Television evangelists differed about the propriety of Congress investigating their operations. The Rev. D. James Kennedy, head of the Florida-based Coral Ridge Ministries, told the subcommittee he thought the hearings set an "extremely dangerous precedent" that raised "a danger of the federal government controlling the church." But Jimmy Swaggart, who did not testify, said he and his fellow preachers "are, after all, stewards, and unless trying to evangelize the world is a crime, we have nothing to fear from scrutiny." The Bakkers did not appear before the subcommittee, ostensibly because they wanted to avoid a confrontation with Falwell.

Internal Revenue Service (IRS) Commissioner Lawrence R. Gibbs testified that his agency had 25 ongoing audits of evangelical organizations. But his predecessor, Donald Alexander, said the agency has difficulty monitoring religious agencies that are not required to file information with the IRS. "It is very hard to distinguish between mainstream and charlatan," Alexander said.

One problem with current government scrutiny of religious fund-raisers is the ambiguity of tax law, such as a requirement that employees of tax-exempt groups should be paid "reasonable" compensation. O. Donaldson Chapoton, the Treasury Department's assistant secretary for tax policy, suggested that Congress might consider setting a dollar limit for such employee compensation.

Impact. The flaps over PTL and Oral Roberts had an effect on giving to all major television evangelists. In June, Marion Gordon (Pat) Robertson cited a $12 million drop in donations to his Christian Broadcasting Network (CBN) in announcing a $25 million cutback in the operations of his network, including the dismissal of 470 employees. A $5.3 million drop in donations to Falwell's "Old-Time Gospel Hour" prompted it to drop 50 television stations.

The overall impact of the year's controversies indicated that broadcast ministries would have to recover more than their financial support in the future. A Gallup survey released in May found that 63% of the respondents thought television evangelists were not "trustworthy with money," and 53% thought they were dishonest. According to the Princeton Religion Research Center, which published the findings, the figures showed that "the sexual and financial scandals that have rocked the electronic church in recent months . . . have cast a long shadow over many of the nation's most popular television evangelists and the evangelical movement in general."

DARRELL J. TURNER
Religious News Service

Far Eastern

The Chinese government sent armed troops to Tibet after Buddhist monks staged independence rallies outside the Johkang temple in Lhasa, the region's most sacred religious site. Several police officers and civilians were killed in the demonstrations protesting Chinese rule over the Himalayan kingdom, which was taken over in 1950. The protests erupted at the end of a ten-day visit to the United States by the Dalai Lama, Tibet's political and religious leader, who has lived in exile in India since 1959. During the Chinese Cultural Revolution of the 1960s, all but a dozen of Tibet's estimated 3,500 temples and monasteries were destroyed. (*See* page 187.)

Chogyam Trungpa Rinpoche, a lama who left Tibet in 1959 and established the Naropa Institute in Boulder, CO, in the early 1970s, died of a heart attack in April at the age of 47. He was cremated at his movement's study center near Barnet, VT, in an ancient rite attended by more than 2,000 students and friends.

Osel Hita, a two-year-old Spaniard, was invested as the world's youngest lama at a ceremony in Dharmsala, India, in March. Hita is the fifth child of a Spanish couple who operate a Buddhist center near Granada, and he is believed to be the reincarnation of his parents' teacher.

In the United States, representatives of about 45 Buddhist groups met in Los Angeles in November to establish the American Buddhist Congress. Among other things, they pledged to seek agreement on a common date for the commemoration of the Vesak festival (marking the birth, death, and enlightenment of Shakyamuni Buddha) and petitioned the World Fellowship of Buddhists to elect a U.S. vice-president to represent the 3-5 million Buddhists in the country.

The ancient Hindu ceremony of sati, or immolation by a widow, took place in the Indian village of Deorala in September. Roop Kunwar, the young widow of a man from a prominent local family, became a saint and her cremation site was declared a shrine after she died on the funeral pyre. Sati has been illegal in India since 1829, but it occurs once or twice every decade.

Scholars from around the world assembled in Qufu, China, the hometown of Confucius, for a conference on the relevance of the religious philosopher's thought for today. It was the first open symposium on Confucius held in China since 1962. The gathering was sponsored jointly by the Confucius Foundation of China and the Institute of East Asian Philosophies in Singapore, and attracted scholars from Singapore, Japan, South Korea, Australia, and the United States.

DARRELL J. TURNER
Religious News Service

Islam

Calls by Muslim activists for the establishment of Islamic governments continued to cause alarm in many states with primarily Muslim populations, while in several countries with both Muslim and non-Muslim citizens, sectarian disputes sparked serious confrontations.

Leaders of the 41 states and 28 international agencies affiliated with the Organization of the Islamic Conference, representing 1 billion Muslims throughout the world, considered these and other common concerns in their annual summit meeting, held in Kuwait in January. Although an attempt to end the fighting between two Conference members, Iran and Iraq, was high on the agenda, the leaders were unable to bring the warring parties to the negotiating table.

In March, Tunisian authorities alleged that Iran was encouraging antigovernment activities in their country and among Tunisians living abroad. A few months later, bombs exploded at several Tunisian resort hotels where vacationers' drinking and sunbathing offended conservative Muslims. Officials reacted by cracking down on religious activists, arresting more than 90 persons. Many of those arrested belonged to the Islamic Tendency Movement, including its leader, Rashid Ghannouchi. Ghannouchi had advocated the peaceful establishment of an Islamic state in Tunisia, and he and his followers denied any involvement in the bombings. But the government, claiming that the Movement had collaborated with Iranian agents and had sent adherents to Iran for training, sought stiff penalties. In September, seven were sentenced to death and 56 others given jail terms; Ghannouchi was sentenced to life in prison. The outcome of the trials revealed the depth of official Tunisian concern about religiously based organizations.

Disturbances during the *hajj,* the annual Muslim pilgrimage to Mecca, also were linked to Iran. On July 31 near the Grand Mosque in Mecca, Saudi police clashed with Iranian pilgrims who were protesting the kingdom's close ties with the United States. More than 400 people died and many more were injured. Iran's leaders, suspected of encouraging if not ordering the demonstrations, launched scalding criticisms against the Saudi royal family. Specifically, they questioned their commitment to Islam and called them unfit to serve as guardians of Islam's holy places.

Conflict between Muslims and Christians erupted in Nigeria in March. Muslim demands that Islamic law be extended beyond the heavily Muslim northern regions, along with Nigeria's troubled economy and long-standing tribal rivalries, created a tense situation in which taunts from both sides triggered serious rioting.

Muslims and Coptic Christians also clashed in several Egyptian towns during the spring and through the autumn. Although President Hosni Mubarak warned that such militancy would not be tolerated, national elections in April saw the emergence of an opposition coalition in parliament which included the Muslim Brotherhood, an organization previously linked to similar disorders.

In the United States, leaders of the Presbyterian Church expressed concern that media publicity about the political activism of certain Muslim countries might be translated into negative attitudes about the Islamic faith itself. Stressing Islam's strong links to the Judeo-Christian tradition, the church's annual convention resolved to identify, expose, and counteract bigotry and prejudice against Islam in whatever ways it could.

Kenneth J. Perkins
University of South Carolina

Judaism

The most dramatic developments of 1987 for world Jewry were the release of several noted Jewish prisoners by the Soviet Union and revelations of a growing Jewish spiritual renaissance in that country. Best known among the freed prisoners were Ida Nudel and Iosif Z. Begun, whose years-long campaign for Jewish religious freedom had earned them several prison terms and a position of honor among refuseniks. The news of widespread spiritual resistance, especially on the part of women, found empathy in the West. On International Women's Day in March, 60 Jewish women went on a hunger strike in the USSR, and a demonstration of solidarity was held outside the Soviet mission to the UN in New York.

Some believed that the policy of *glasnost,* or openness, initiated by Soviet leader Mikhail Gorbachev presaged a new era of freedom and open borders in the Soviet Union; others feared that the much-publicized release of famous prisoners was a cover for continued restrictive policies and bode ill for the half million Soviet Jews who desire to emigrate.

Religious Issues. In Israel the issue of religious pluralism and recognition of branches of Judaism other than Orthodox continued to stir controversy. Early in the year it resulted in the resignation of the minister of interior, Rabbi Yitzhak Peretz. During the summer, open clashes erupted in Jerusalem between secularist groups who, in opposition to a municipal ordinance, organized film screenings in public movie houses on the Sabbath, and ultra-Orthodox elements protesting the violation of the Sabbath.

In a historic break with tradition, the Jewish Theological Seminary of America ordained two women cantors. The move pitted traditionalist groups against liberal elements within the Conservative movement.

© M. Milner/Sygma

In Jerusalem, Israel, ultra-Orthodox Jews protested the violation by secular groups of an ordinance banning public entertainment and other activities on the Sabbath. Clashes between the two elements sometimes turned violent.

Jewish-Christian Relations. In June, Pope John Paul II offended Jewish sensibilities by granting an audience to Austria's President Kurt Waldheim, accused of participating in Nazi war crimes. To defuse tensions in advance of his visit to the United States in September, the pontiff received a group of U.S. Jewish leaders at his summer residence outside Rome. The pope expressed sorrow over the "terrifying experience" of the Holocaust and blessed all those who "foster relationships of mutual esteem" with the Jews. On the second day of his U.S. tour, at a meeting in Miami, FL, attended by 196 Jewish leaders and 50 Catholic prelates, the pontiff defended Israel as a Jewish homeland but fell short of declaring official Vatican recognition of the state of Israel. He also called for renewed efforts to combat anti-Semitism.

At its annual General Assembly in June, the Presbyterian Church (U.S.A.) adopted a set of seven affirmations "for a new and better relationship under God between Christians and Jews." The document—downgraded from a "policy statement" to a "study document"—included an acknowledgment that Jews have a valid covenant with God.

Later that month the United Church of Christ, at its convention in Cleveland, went even further by issuing a formal policy statement affirming the validity of the Jewish faith and declaring that Judaism had not been "superseded" by Christianity. It was the first such formal policy statement from a major Protestant denomination in the United States.

Other. Awareness of the Holocaust—which West Germany's Chancellor Helmut Kohl termed a crime "unprecedented in history"—was reinforced by the highly publicized trials of accused Nazi war criminals Klaus Barbie in Lyons, France (found guilty and sentenced to life in prison in July) and John Demjanjuk in Jerusalem (still underway as 1987 ended), and by the execution of Feodor Federenko in the Soviet Union in July.

The Anti-Defamation League of B'nai B'rith reported a 7% decline in acts of anti-Semitic vandalism against Jews and Jewish property in the United States in 1986. Worldwide, however, 1987 saw the publication of openly anti-Semitic books and articles from Europe to Asia to South America.

World Jewry was heartened by renewed cultural contacts between Israel and several Communist bloc countries, hoping that it implied greater religious freedom for Jews in those nations.

The new $14 million Jewish Historical Museum was inaugurated in Amsterdam, the Netherlands.

LIVIA E. BITTON-JACKSON
Herbert H. Lehman College, CUNY

Orthodox Eastern

Dimitrios I of Constantinople visited the Moscow Patriarchate of the Russian Orthodox Church, Pope John Paul II, the Most Rev. Robert Runcie, the archbishop of Canterbury, and the headquarters of the World Council of Churches in Geneva during 1987. The visits, the first such travel by an ecumenical patriarch since 1589, offered church leaders an opportunity to discuss church matters, including inter-Orthodox problems. Church life in North America where the Orthodox remain divided along ethnic and political lines was part of the discussions. The pilgrimages indicated a greater toleration by the Turkish government of the patriarch's role in the predominantly Muslim nation. Recently the Turkish government has granted permission for certain confiscated church properties in Istanbul to be returned to the church.

The Russian Orthodox Church continued to prepare for celebrations marking the 1000th anniversary of Christianity in Russian lands in 1988. As part of the Soviet government's policies of "openness" *(glasnost)* and "restructuring" *(perestroika),* prominent Orthodox dissidents, including the Rev. Gleb Yakunin, the poet Irina Ratushinskaya, and religious activists Vladimir Poresh and Alexander Ogorod-

© Tass from Sovfoto

Dimitrios I of Constantinople (carrying staff), *the spiritual leader of the world's 150 million Orthodox Eastern Christians, became the first ecumenical patriarch since 1589 to visit the Russian Orthodox Patriarchate in Moscow.*

nikov, were released from prison in late 1986 and 1987. Sections of the ancient monasteries in Solovki and Optina were being returned to church control. Holy places in Kiev, such as Sophia Cathedral and the Caves Monastery, however, remained under government control. No major millennial celebrations were to be held in the Ukraine.

On April 3, 1987, the Greek Parliament passed legislation authorizing the government to assume control of land held by the Greek Orthodox Church and give it to farm cooperatives. The Greek church, which opposed the legislation, had said it would relinquish some 350,000 acres (140,000 ha) near its monasteries but sought to retain control of its distribution.

Several administrative changes occured in world orthodoxy. Patriarch Parthenios III, formerly the Metropolitan of Carthage, became the new primate of the Church of Alexandria. The Romanian Orthodox Church elected the elderly Metropolitan Theoktist of Moldavia as its new patriarch. The Church of Constantinople elevated John Zizioulas, the famous theologian and ecumenist, from the lay state to Metropolitan of Pergamos. The Church of Finland elected Metropolitan John of Helsinki as primate, replacing Archbishop Paul, who resigned because of poor health.

North America. The Antiochian Orthodox Archdiocese, headed by Metropolitan Philip (Saliba), received the former Evangelical Orthodox Church as a member. Now called the Antiochian Evangelical Orthodox Mission, the group of several thousands, led by the Very Rev. Peter Gillquist and others, was connected previously with the Campus Crusade for Christ and the "Jesus Movement" of the 1960s and 1970s. Its mission is to foster Orthodox evangelism in the United States and Canada.

The Orthodox Church in America (OCA), headed by Metropolitan Theodosius, the archbishop of Washington, added two bishops, both converts, to its synod: Bishop Tikhon (Fitzgerald) of Los Angeles and Bishop Seraphim (Storheim) of Edmonton, Alberta. Thousands of people visited St. Nicholas Albanian Orthodox Church in Chicago, where the main icon of the Virgin Mary on the altar screen was venerated as miraculously "weeping."

THOMAS HOPKO
St. Vladimir's Seminary, Crestwood, NY

Protestantism

Scandal and controversy in the television evangelism movement (*see* page 447), a major merger among the Lutherans, and significant action by the Presbyterian Church and the United Church of Christ to improve Christian-Jewish relations were among the items that made the headlines in Protestantism during 1987.

The fourth largest Protestant denomination in the United States was officially constituted on April 30, 1987, when representatives of the American Lutheran Church (ALC), the Association of Evangelical Lutheran Churches (AELC), and the Lutheran Church in America (LCA) met in Columbus, OH, to form the Evangelical Lutheran Church in America. Herbert Chilstrom, 55-year-old head of the LCA's Minnesota Synod, was elected bishop of the new denomination, which has 5.3 million members and would open headquarters in Chicago in 1988. Conservative dissidents from the ALC who opposed the merger formed the American Association of Lutheran Congregations, comprising 22 congregations and fellowship groups.

Conservatives consolidated their control over the Southern Baptists as the Rev. Adrian Rogers of Memphis was reelected president at the 14.6-million-member denomination's annual meeting in St. Louis in June. A report urging Southern Baptist agencies to promote strict biblical views also was approved.

For United Methodists, 1987 was a year of controversies over several members of the clergy and a major university. In August a church court in New Hampshire suspended the Rev. Rose Mary Denman from the ministry because she was a self-avowed practicing homosexual. In April the church's Judicial Council had upheld the 1985 conviction of the Rev. John P. Carter on sex harassment charges but reduced his term of suspension from three to two years. The Rev. Walker Railey was put on leave of absence from the pastorate of First United Methodist Church of Dallas and surrendered his clergy credentials during a police investigation of the near-fatal attack on his wife in April. The denomination took steps to maintain greater control over Southern Methodist University in Dallas, where a football scandal prompted the National Collegiate Athletic Association to cancel the school's 1987 season.

Members of the Assemblies of God joined with 35,000 other Christians involved in the charismatic movement for the North American Congress on the Holy Spirit and world Evangelization in New Orleans in July.

The Rev. Patricia McClurg, an executive of the Presbyterian Church (U.S.A) was installed as president of the National Council of Churches (NCC), the first clergywoman to hold the post. Chosen as president-elect, to take office in 1989, was the Rev. Leonid Kishkovsky, the first Orthodox leader named to the NCC presidency.

Ecumenism. The Presbyterian Church (U.S.A.) and the United Church of Christ (UCC) undertook significant initiatives in

Representatives of three U.S. Lutheran churches pour water into a baptismal font as a symbol of their unification into the Evangelical Lutheran Church in America.

AP/Wide World

Christian-Jewish relations and in relocating their headquarters in 1987. National conventions of both bodies adopted statements affirming that Christianity has not superseded God's convenant with the Jewish people. The 3.1-million-member PCUSA decided to relocate offices from New York, Philadelphia, and Atlanta to a new headquarters in Louisville, KY. The 1.7-million-member UCC, based in New York, narrowed the choice of a headquarters city to New York, St. Louis, and Cleveland but postponed a final decision until 1988.

More than two dozen Protestant and Orthodox leaders met and held an ecumenical worship service with Pope John Paul II in Columbia, SC, during his visit to the United States in September. The Second Anglican-Roman Catholic International Commission issued a joint statement saying that the two churches no longer have any substantial disagreement on how personal salvation is achieved. A set of guidelines on intermarriage was released by leaders of the Anglican and Roman Catholic churches in Canada, marking the first time such a joint document was issued at the national level. In an action against ecumenism, a coalition of Italian Protestant bodies proposed a one-year moratorium on official dialogues with the Roman Catholic Church because of its declaration of a year of emphasis on the Virgin Mary (Marian Year) "without preliminary ecumenical consultation."

Court Cases and Newsmakers. Two federal appeals panels overturned lower court rulings that had upheld the objections of fundamentalist parents to public school textbooks.

U.S. Surgeon General C. Everett Koop, an evangelical Presbyterian, found himself at odds with some of his long-time allies in the evangelical community for promoting sex education and the use of condoms as ways of fighting AIDS (*see* BIOGRAPHY). While the debate over U.S. policies in Central America continued in the churches, President Reagan held a White House meeting with Presbyterian leaders who disputed claims by his administration that there is religious persecution in Nicaragua.

Two prominent clergymen left their ministry positions in 1987. Marion G. "Pat" Robertson, founder of the Christian Broadcasting Network, resigned as a Southern Baptist minister to avoid the appearance of favoring one church as he launched his campaign for the 1988 Republican presidential nomination. The Rev. William Sloane Coffin, a Presbyterian, resigned as senior minister of Riverside Church in New York to head SANE/FREEZE, a peace and justice advocacy group.

Four Protestant missionaries were released by Sudanese rebels who had held them captive for seven weeks, and several evangelical workers were released by Mozambican rebels three months after they were abducted.

DARRELL J. TURNER, *Religious News Service*

Roman Catholicism

For the worldwide Roman Catholic Church the year 1987 was highlighted by several key papal trips and a synod of bishops that explored the roles of lay Catholics.

Pope John Paul II's trip to the United States in September culminated a series of trips that included visits to the Latin American nations of Argentina, Chile, and Uruguay and his native Poland. All of the pope's travels were spiced by tensions both political and religious. The October month-long synod brought into clear focus many of the differences in the universal church over the place of women and lay movements in the future of the church's ministerial work. While no specific conclusions were reached, the issues, particularly the outreach by the laity to the marketplace and workplace, were exposed, and the process for refinement of lay roles was initiated.

The Virgin Mary. Large crowds continued to flock to the Yugoslavian farming village of Medjugorje where four girls and two boys reportedly have seen visions of the Blessed Virgin Mary. The local bishop has denied the validity of the apparitions, which are said to have first occurred in 1981, but others in the Yugoslav church remained divided over them. Meanwhile the Vatican began marking a 14-month Marian Year in June. Earlier, Pope John Paul issued an encyclical stressing the role of Mary in the church. The document pointed to her as a source of unity among Christians because she is the "common mother."

Curran, Hunthausen, Waldheim. In the United States, dissent played a key role in continuing debates over 1986 Vatican actions against two well-known U.S. church figures, Father Charles Curran and Seattle Archbishop Raymond Hunthausen. Curran, ordered by Rome to stop teaching as a Catholic theologian because of his views on sexual morality, was later suspended by the Catholic University of America in Washington. He then challenged the suspension in civil court.

Hunthausen, who in 1986 was stripped of some of his episcopal authority by the Vatican because of alleged lack of discipline and control in his archdiocese, had his full authority restored in May 1987. In an unprecedented compromise worked out by a group of bishops and the Vatican, Bishop Thomas Murphy of Great Falls-Billings, MT, was named coadjutor archbishop of Seattle to assist and eventually succeed Hunthausen.

A dispute that drew worldwide attention began when Pope John Paul agreed to meet Austrian President Kurt Waldheim despite protestations by the worldwide Jewish community. Jewish groups had accused Waldheim of engaging in war crimes as a German officer during World War II. Waldheim and his supporters denied the charges. The pope met Waldheim as a head of state at the Vatican, and the Jewish community strongly criticized the pope, eventually forcing two unprecedented meetings between Jewish leaders and the pope to iron out differences.

The Vatican and the Pope. In March the Vatican issued a document rejecting virtually all forms of artificial fertilization and generation of human life outside the body, including in vitro fertilization, surrogate motherhood, and embryo experimentation.

Archbishop Paul Marcinkus, a Cicero, IL, native who heads the Vatican Bank, was sought on warrants issued by Italian courts in connection with fraudulent bankruptcy charges. The charges later were dropped.

Pope John Paul also had to deal with a variety of political situations that affected church life. He voiced strong support for opposition to the apartheid regime in South Africa; backed calls by U.S. and Central American bishops for an end to civil strife in Nicaragua, El Salvador, Guatemala, and Honduras; and made strong pleas for religious freedom in his native Poland and other areas of Eastern Europe.

During his U.S. trip, the pope stressed the need for unity in the worldwide church. He was pastoral but uncompromising in declaring that the church in all parts of the world must be linked to the Vatican and adhere to the central teaching authority of the Holy See.

Dissident Archbishop Marcel Lefebvre, suspended by Pope Paul VI in 1976 for refusing to recognize the teachings of Vatican Council II, reportedly was seeking reconciliation with Rome. The pope appointed Cardinal Edward Gagnon, a Canadian prelate assigned to Rome, to study the situation. The pope also named Bishop Anthony J. Bevilacqua of Pittsburgh to succeed Cardinal John Krol as archbishop of Philadelphia. Cardinal Krol, 77, announced his retirement, effective Feb. 11, 1988.

Regional Matters. Church ministries to victims of AIDS (Acquired Immune Deficiency Syndrome) were increased, especially in the United States. Several local churches, including some in San Francisco, New York, and Chicago, set up special counseling and medical outreaches to those suffering from AIDS and their families. Cardinal John J. O'Connor of New York was appointed a member of President Reagan's panel on the disease.

In the United States, pastoral plans for both black and Hispanic Catholics were developed at national meetings in Washington and later approved by the U.S. bishop's conference.

In Central America, late in the year, many Catholic bishops, especially Cardinal Miguel Obando y Bravo, the archbishop of Managua, were given significant roles in helping to implement a broad peace plan proposed by Costa Rican President Oscar Arias.

ROBERT L. JOHNSTON
Editor, *"The Chicago Catholic"*

RETAILING

U.S. retailing, following the big mergers of 1986, witnessed in 1987 a sweeping divestiture of Allied Stores Corporation, a bid for Dayton-Hudson Corporation, several chain spin-offs, and a general race for market share among existing players.

With Allied's new owners, Campeau Corporation of Toronto, eager to repay more than $1 billion in debt created by their purchase, 16 store divisions were sold by Allied to other companies. One, Bonwit Teller, was acquired by Hooker Corporation of Australia, which later also bought Parisian, Inc., a well-known Southern fashion chain. Other Allied stores were bought by Dillard Department Stores, Hess's Department Stores, and Raleigh Haberdashers.

The merger mill continued to churn, as Dart Group Corporation offered $68 a share for Dayton-Hudson; Woodward & Lothrop bought the John Wanamaker chain; Dee Corporation of London acquired Herman's Sporting Goods; and the McCrory Corporation purchased K Mart Corporation's remaining S.S. Kresge and Jupiter variety stores.

Why so much turning over of ownership in the store business? "The industry has large assets that are underproductive," said Stuart M. Robbins, a vice-president of Donaldson, Lufkin & Jenrette Securities. "Retailing's overall returns on investment and growth potential are better than the corporate averages. And breakup values are generally well in excess of current market prices."

The year's sales, however, were choppy, especially among the great, mass chains catering to lower-income shoppers. Sears Roebuck reported sluggish sales during much of the year, while discounters such as Zayre Corporation said that their blue-collar customers were hard hit by industrial cutbacks. During the fall season, apparel volume among such chains as The Gap turned sluggish, pushing that company and its rivals into heavy price-cutting and, consequently, lower profits.

But stores catering to the affluent—such as Bloomingdale's, Saks Fifth Avenue, and Lord & Taylor—did well. The performance of specialty stores created a desire among some giant chains to enter that field. Sears set up a specialty-store division, acquired a retail optical chain, and announced plans to build a $1 billion company of varied, smaller stores. R. H. Macy, meanwhile, said it would open a series of specialty-shop chains to augment its 100 department stores.

Translating into bright market values, the specialty-store trend took a somewhat different turn for other large retailers. Carter Hawley Hale Stores, for example, spun off a portion of its ownership in its Neiman Marcus, Bergdorf Goodman, and Contempo Casual stores, cashing in on a public issue. Similarly, Zayre divested some of its ownership in T. J. Maxx and Hit or Miss stores and received more than $90 million in proceeds.

If swelling real-estate values were a key spur to mergers—and they were—they also prompted J. C. Penney Company to decide to move its national headquarters from New York City to the Dallas area. Subletting its Manhattan offices for an expected large profit proved controversial, however, with city officials complaining and many Penney regulars refusing to desert New York for Texas. Other retailers were making similar moves, although on a smaller scale.

In the food field, A & P moved to recover much of its former glory by buying the Shopwell and Waldbaum supermarkets.

See also THE CONVENIENCE BOOM, page 63.

ISADORE BARMASH
"The New York Times"

© Michelle Begali/courtesy of Benetton

Specialty store chains such as Benetton, left, were doing a lively business that hurt some of the giant department stores. In the apparel industry, specialty chains were expected to reach $50 billion in sales by the 1990s, up from $30 billion in 1986.

RHODE ISLAND

Economic news was a dominant theme during 1987. Paced by growth in the service and high-tech sectors, Rhode Island's and New England's economies boomed.

U.S. Commerce Department figures available in August showed that the region ranked as the wealthiest in the nation. The state's unemployment rate remained one of the lowest nationally, dropping to 3.5%, the lowest level in 18 years, and well below the (also declining) national rate of 5.9%.

Business reported a growing labor shortage, labeled near critical by Gov. Edward D. DiPrete. Electric Boat, the submarine manufacturer, had 500 unfilled jobs at the beginning of the year at its Rhode Island plant. By late spring, the company was forced to shift work from Rhode Island to South Carolina as a result.

Tokyo-based Toray Industries, which decided in January to build a plastics plant in the state, faced serious difficulties in finding the 350 employees it would require.

The real-estate market shared the state's boom. In the first six months of the year the median price of single-family homes soared 42%. A late summer announcement revealed that home prices had been rising faster in Providence than in any other city in the country. Despite high mortgage rates, single-family house construction was up 3% over 1986.

State Budget. This prosperity brought both opportunities and headaches to Rhode Island's political leaders. The end of fiscal 1987 on June 30 showed a state budget surplus of $107.7 million. This was $10 million above what the governor and legislators had counted on when they adopted the fiscal 1988 budget.

In February the proposed state budget called for spending of $1.193 billion, up $77 million over fiscal 1987. This 6.9% increase was to be financed out of growing revenues. The projected surplus was then pegged at $45.4 million. Almost weekly, it seemed, the governor would up the surplus estimate. By June, when final spending decisions were due, the projection was for at least $93 million. Each higher figure had provoked a flurry of new proposals for spending the windfall. By adjournment in late June, a budget totaling $1.245 billion had been enacted, $127.5 million (11.4%) over 1986–87's. Prominent among numerous program increases and some new initiatives was relief for local communities and property taxpayers.

Legislative Record. A $65 million bond issue was authorized by the General Assembly for voter approval to fund the purchase of open-space land and preserve it. A new program was voted to attack the 25% school dropout rate, and substantial added resources approved for the University of Rhode Island. The Assembly's overall record earned praise for the cooperative efforts of the Democratic leadership and the Republican governor.

Acquired Immune Deficiency Syndrome (AIDS). Growing public concern brought a legislative mandate for one of the nation's first AIDS education programs for public-school children, to be inaugurated during 1987–88.

Politics. More than a year before November 1988, it became evident that Democratic Lt. Gov. Richard A. Licht would challenge Republican Sen. John H. Chafee, and candidates began eyeing the office Licht would be vacating. Meanwhile the governor held fund-raisers, presumably for a third term run.

ELMER E. CORNWELL, JR., *Brown University*

RHODE ISLAND • Information Highlights

Area: 1,212 sq mi (3 140 km²).
Population (July 1, 1986): 975,000.
Chief Cities (1980 census): Providence, the capital (July 1, 1986 est.): 157,200; Warwick, 87,123.
Government (1987): *Chief Officers*—governor, Edward D. DiPrete (R); lt. gov., Richard A. Licht (D). *General Assembly*—Senate, 50 members; House of Representatives, 100 members.
State Finances (fiscal year 1986): *Revenue*, $2,362,000,000; *expenditure*, $2,167,000,000.
Personal Income (1986): $14,213,000,000; per capita, $14,579.
Labor Force (June 1987): *Civilian labor force*, 518,400; *unemployed*, 20,000 (3.9% of total force).
Education: *Enrollment* (fall 1985)—public elementary schools, 89,958; public secondary, 43,484; colleges and universities, 69,927. *Public school expenditures* (1985–86), $567,000,000 ($4,669 per pupil).

ROMANIA

In 1987, Romania struggled on under the unyielding dictatorship of President and Communist Party leader, Nicolae Ceauşescu.

The Economy. In February, Romania's Seventh Five-Year Plan (1981–85) was declared fulfilled, but the impressive figures released by the government were counterbalanced by continuing serious shortages of energy, food, and consumer goods and the obvious hardships under which most Romanians have to live. Strict energy and gas rationing was reintroduced in February for factories, schools, theaters, shops, offices, and homes. The use of all private cars was banned, except in Bucharest. Romanians continued to suffer the lowest standard of living within the Soviet bloc. Meat and dairy products had almost disappeared from stores, and there were daylong queues for allotments of bread, flour, sugar, and cooking oil. The Eighth Five-Year Plan (1986–90) predicted average annual increases of 7.5 to 8.3% in industrial production, 6.1 to 6.7% in agriculture, and an overall increase of 52.7% in the volume of foreign trade. Romania's foreign debt due for repayment in 1986–87, totaling $880 million, was rescheduled for 1989–92.

AP/Wide World

Seeking stronger relations, Soviet leader Mikhail Gorbachev visited Romania, May 25–27, to outline his domestic reform policies. Romania's powerful party leader, Nicolae Ceaușescu (right), *was Eastern Europe's most vocal critic of that program.*

Politics. The government continued its determined campaign to force Romanian women to have more children. Practically all abortions continued to be illegal, and schoolgirls allegedly were encouraged to have children out of wedlock. Also continuing was the grandiose project to raze the entire center of Bucharest, destroying many historic houses, churches, and synagogues, to construct a vast avenue and government complex of new buildings and apartments.

A number of party and government officials exchanged positions. Miu Dobrescu became chair of the Central Council of the General Union of Trade Unions, and was replaced as chair of the Party Central Collegium by Nicolae Constantin. Constantin was replaced as deputy prime minister by Neculai Ibanescu. There were veiled signs of the emergence of several illegal, clandestine groups opposed to Ceaușescu and in favor of a multiparty democracy, including Romanian Democratic Action and the Romanian Association for the Defense of Human Rights.

Ceaușescu's greatest triumph had come on Sunday, Nov. 23, 1986. Almost 18 million Romanians aged 14 years or older voted in a nationwide referendum on Ceaușescu's proposal to reduce the country's military spending and manpower by 5%. Allegedly all but 228 eligible voters cast their ballots, all in favor of the proposal. Ceaușescu called the result "a vigorous expression of the deeply democratic character of our society" and called upon U.S. President Ronald Reagan and Soviet General Secretary Mikhail Gorbachev "to act to stop the irrational arms race."

Foreign Affairs. In foreign relations, there was marked intensification of Romania's long-standing dispute with Hungary over alleged Romanian mistreatment of the ethnic Hungarian minority in Transylvania. Both Hungarian Communist Party leader János Kádár and Secretary of State for Foreign Affairs Gyula Horn denounced Romania publicly, and there were reports of Hungarian strikes, pamphleteering, and clashes with the police in the region. Yugoslavia charged Romania with misuse of the jointly owned hydroelectric power station at the Iron Gates on the Danube.

In December 1986, President Hosni Mubarak of Egypt met with Ceaușescu. The two pledged increased cooperation, and Ceaușescu committed Romania to active participation in the search for a political settlement in the Middle East. In March 1987, Ceaușescu led a high-level delegation to Angola. In May, Soviet leader Gorbachev visited Romania and outlined his domestic reform policies. Earlier, in February, Ceaușescu had publicly criticized some of those policies as "a betrayal of socialism."

JOSEPH FREDERICK ZACEK
State University of New York at Albany

ROMANIA • Information Highlights

Official Name: Socialist Republic of Romania.
Location: Southeastern Europe.
Area: 91,699 sq mi (237 500 km²).
Population (mid-1987 est.): 22,900,000.
Chief Cities (July 1, 1986 est.): Bucharest, the capital, 1,989,823; Brașov, 351,493; Constanta, 327,676.
Government: *Head of state,* Nicolae Ceaușescu, president (took office 1967) and secretary-general of the Communist Party (1965). *Head of government,* Constantin Dăscălescu, prime minister (took office May 1982). *Legislature* (unicameral)—Grand National Assembly.
Monetary Unit: Leu (14.750 lei equal U.S.$1, July 1987).
Gross National Product (1985 U.S.$): $123,700,000,000.
Foreign Trade (1985 U.S.$): *Imports,* $10,400,000,000; *exports,* $12,200,000,000.

SASKATCHEWAN

The year 1987 appeared to mark a turning point for Saskatchewan. Politics became more polarized, and the province's resource economy harder to protect.

Restraint. The Progressive Conservative (PC) government of Premier Grant Devine enunciated a severe restraint policy in March in its 1987 *Saskatchewan Economic and Financial Report*. It forecast a C$1.5 billion deficit in 1987-88 unless actions were taken, and set out a basic strategy which was subsequently elaborated by several ministerial restraint announcements. Government employment dropped by 2,000 and third-party grant levels were frozen. The province eliminated the Public Utilities Review Commission which had been formed in 1982 and had saved taxpayers $200 million by regulating utility rates.

Privatization. Ministers hinted at the impending privatization of The Potash Corporation of Saskatchewan (PCS), the Saskatchewan Mining and Development Corporation (SMDC), and the commercial operations of Saskatchewan Government Insurance (SGI). Finally, in October, the government announced that it was planning to sell shares in SGI's insurance business but to have SGI retain the automobile-insurance business. More modest privatizations proceeded.

Politics. New Democratic Party (NDP) leader Allan Blakeney resigned, and a party leadership convention was scheduled for November 6-8. Roy Romanow, member of the Legislative Assembly for Riverdale, took over as party head when all serious leadership contenders failed to declare themselves.

The Legislature. The PCs did not call the normal spring session of the legislature and did not present a budget until June 17, contrary to recent Saskatchewan and Canadian budgetary practice. The government introduced and later made use of legislation allowing the cabinet, rather than the legislature as in the past, to make changes in the organization of the executive government.

Fiscal and Economic Issues. The $3.78 billion budget was heralded as a victory for the restraint program; the 1987-88 projected deficit now was only $577 million, down 60% from the March projection. Opponents suggested the original figures had been inflated. The accumulated deficit increased to $3.3 billion. Finance Minister Gary Lane announced tax increases of $265 million and reductions in projected spending amounting to $738 million. The provincial sales tax increased from 5% to 7%. Two weeks earlier, Lane had announced an increase in the provincial surtax on net income from 1 to 1.5%.

Resources. Resource problems were intense, especially in potash, where declining demand and burgeoning surpluses occurred. The government decided to write off an $810 million debt owed by PCS to the province. Then in August the U.S. Department of Commerce, alleging dumping, imposed preliminary duties ranging from 9% to 85% on Canadian potash producers, a serious turn since 60% of Saskatchewan potash is exported to the United States. Saskatchewan reacted to the U.S. action by passing the Potash Resources Act, allowing the cabinet to set the total volume of potash produced and to set production limits for each mine. Many hoped for a negotiated political settlement between Canada and the United States.

To counter world subsidies, Premier Devine called for another federal agricultural deficiency payment of between $1.6 billion and $3 billion. A U.S. appeals court in Denver upheld a decision banning enrichment of foreign uranium in the United States, but SMDC made strides, signing a ten-year agreement to sell 750,000 lbs. (340,200 kg) of uranium a year to South Korea. Natural-gas policy saw a two-phase deregulation of prices and sales procedures.

CHRISTOPHER DUNN
Formerly, University of Saskatchewan

SASKATCHEWAN • Information Highlights

Area: 251,865 sq mi (652 330 km²).
Population (1986 census): 1,010,198.
Chief Cities (1986 census): Regina, the capital, 175,064; Saskatoon, 177,641; Moose Jaw, 35,073.
Government (1987): *Chief Officers*—lt. gov., F. W. Johnson; premier, Grant Devine (Progressive Conservative). *Legislature*—Legislative Assembly, 64 members.
Provincial Finances (1987–88 fiscal year budget): *Revenues,* $3,200,000,000; *expenditures,* $3,779,-000,000.
Personal Income (average weekly earnings, July 1987): $402.03.
Labor Force (September 1987, seasonally adjusted: *Employed* workers, 15 years of age and over, 497,000; *Unemployed,* 34,000 (6.8%).
Education (1987–88): *Enrollment*—elementary and secondary schools, 215,400 pupils; postsecondary—universities, 21,470, community colleges, 3,700.
(All monetary figures are in Canadian dollars.)

SAUDI ARABIA

In its eighth year, the war between Iran and Iraq involved Saudi Arabia more directly in 1987 than ever before. Other major developments during the year included revelations that the Saudis had been involved in the U.S. Iran-contra affair and a large-scale riot in the holy city of Mecca.

Military. While officially neutral in the Persian-Gulf war, Saudi Arabia continued to support Iraq financially and diplomatically in 1987. And, as the war escalated, the Saudis also became increasingly involved militarily. On May 17, Saudi airplanes detected the approach of an Iraqi jet toward the U.S. Navy vessel *Stark,* which was struck by missiles from the Iraqi plane, killing 37 seamen; the local Saudi commander lacked the authority to comply with the U.S. request to force down the Iraqi plane. The following month, the Saudi government agreed to use its AWACS (Airborne Warning and Control System) surveillance planes to supply information to reflagged, U.S.-escorted Kuwaiti oil tankers; the AWACS planes would be protected by Saudi F-15 jet fighters. During the summer, Saudi minesweepers and frogmen helped detect mines floating in the Gulf, especially around the approaches to Kuwait; U.S. forces then destroyed the mines. Nevertheless, the Saudis feared direct attacks by Iran, and so they refused to allow U.S. helicopters and other aircraft to be stationed on Saudi soil.

The Saudis also paid a price for their support of Iraq: Saudi-owned civilian and military shipping—including the super tanker "Petroship B"—was attacked several times by Iranian Revolutionary Guards; a gas liquification plant on the Persian-Gulf coast of Saudi Arabia was rocked by a huge explosion on August 15, apparently the work of Saudi Shiites with ties to Iran; and the movement of about 50 Iranian gunboats toward Saudi oil facilities in early October apparently was turned back by the Saudi Navy and Air Force.

In response, the U.S. government agreed to sell Saudi Arabia more armaments, even though some members of Congress objected on the grounds that the Saudis had not done enough to support the U.S. effort in the Gulf conflict. On October 8, President Reagan and key senators reached a compromise agreement on a $1 billion arms sale to the Saudis, to include 12 more F-15 C/D jet fighters, 93 artillery ammunition carriers, and equipment to enhance the capabilities of previously sold U.S. tanks and planes. Some 1,600 Maverick antitank missiles were removed from the package, but President Reagan announced that if Saudi Arabia were directly attacked he would send them on his own authority.

Foreign Affairs. As befits a rich country with a small population, Saudi diplomacy has emphasized peacemaking among its friends and quiet subsidies to the enemies of its enemies. King Fahd personally arranged and attended a meeting of the feuding leaders of Algeria and Morocco on May 4, and he helped set up a secret conference of the Iraqis and Syrians, held in Jordan in late April. In Jidda, Philippine Muslims signed an agreement of reconciliation with their government.

But Saudi quiet diplomacy was made embarrassingly public when the U.S. congressional investigation of the secret sale of weapons to Iran revealed a major role played by Saudi Arabia. In 1985, Adnan Khashoggi, a wealthy Saudi businessman with ties to the royal family, helped raise money used for the purchase of arms that later went to Iran. The Saudi government claimed that Khashoggi was acting on his own. (*See also,* feature article, page 26.)

Also during the year, *The Washington Post* and U.S. journalist Robert Woodward reported that since 1984 various persons in the U.S. administration, including President Reagan and former CIA Director William Casey, had asked King Fahd to provide money for the Nicaraguan contras, Chad, and anticommunist groups in Italy. The Saudi government officially denied sending this money, but Senate investigations seemed to show that as much as $47 million was pledged. Saudi money also went to the guerrilla resistance in Afghanistan and to rebels in Angola.

Mecca Incident. Since the Iranian revolution of 1979, Iranian Shiite Muslims who had made the annual pilgrimage to Mecca had frequently engaged in demonstrations that were suppressed by the Saudi authorities. On July 31, 1987, many of the 155,000 Iranians present in Mecca were carrying pictures of their leader, the Ayatollah Khomeini, and chanting slogans critical of the United States, the Soviet Union, and Israel. Saudi police intervened, and a riot ensued. In the panic, a total of 402 people were killed: 275 Iranians, mostly women; 85 Saudi policemen; and 42 other pilgrims. More than 600 others were injured. Information Minister Ali Hasan al-Shaer said that "not a single bullet was fired" by Saudi police, but independent witnesses saw some gunfire.

On August 1, revenge-minded Iranian mobs seized the Saudi embassy in Tehran, and later that month Khomeini and the speaker of the Iranian parliament called for the overthrow of the Saudi dynasty.

Oil and Finance. The only substantial change in the Saudi government was brought about by the king and the royal family, who, after the dramatic dismissal of Oil Minister Sheikh Ahmed Zaki Yamani in late October 1986, confirmed Hisham Nazir as his permanent replacement on December 24.

Saudi oil policy changed dramatically, primarily to bring about reduced production quotas for OPEC (Organization of the Petroleum

SAUDI ARABIA • Information Highlights

Official Name: Kingdom of Saudi Arabia.
Location: Arabian peninsula in southwest Asia.
Area: 829,996 sq mi (2 149 690 km²).
Population (mid-1987 est.): 14,800,000.
Capital (1981 est.): Riyadh, 1,000,000.
Government: *Head of state and government,* Fahd bin 'Abd al-'Aziz Al Sa'ud, king and prime minister (acceded June 1982).
Monetary Unit: Riyal (3.7485 riyals equal U.S.$1, Dec. 31, 1987).
Gross Domestic Product (fiscal year 1985 est. U.S.$): $133,600,000,000.
Economic Index (1986): *Consumer Prices* (1980 = 100), all items, 96.5; food, 101.9.
Foreign Trade (1985 U.S.$): *Imports,* $23,623,000,000; *exports,* $27,480,000,000.

Exporting Countries) and thereby secure fixed prices. At the OPEC meeting of December 1986, Saudi Arabia's quota was lowered from 4.3 to 4.1 million barrels per day, and prices were fixed at an average of $18 per barrel—figures which were observed through much of 1987. In early February, U.S. Secretary of the Treasury James Baker visited the kingdom and reportedly encouraged the Saudis to pursue their reduced-quota policy. The June 1987 meeting of OPEC ministers slightly raised the Saudi quota, but the basic system of agreements from December 1986 was kept intact. Although the Saudis in late 1987 were producing oil at about their quota level, other countries, especially Kuwait, produced more oil than they had been allotted, thus keeping pressure on prices to fall.

After the cancellation of the previous year's budget because of instability in the price of oil, a budget for 1987 was announced. It called for some $45.3 billion in expenditures but a deficit of some $14 billion.

WILLIAM OCHSENWALD
Virginia Polytechnic Institute

SINGAPORE

Amid improving economic conditions, the government of Prime Minister Lee Kuan Yew and his People's Action Party moved in 1987 to quell political instabilities that threatened the general prosperity.

Economy. Rebounding from the slump of 1985, when the gross national product (GDP) declined for the first time in the nation's history, the economy grew a modest 1.9% in 1986 and approximately 4% in 1987, with even stronger growth expected in 1988. The decisions in 1986 to freeze prices, reduce the mandatory business contributions to the national savings fund, and cut personal and corporate taxes succeeded in easing the high cost of doing business in Singapore and in reducing unemployment to less than 5%. The recovery has been led by the electronics and oil refinery industries, both important to the national economy.

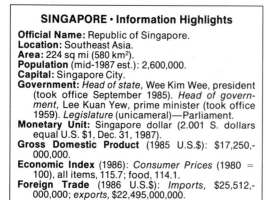

SINGAPORE • Information Highlights

Official Name: Republic of Singapore.
Location: Southeast Asia.
Area: 224 sq mi (580 km²).
Population (mid-1987 est.): 2,600,000.
Capital: Singapore City.
Government: *Head of state,* Wee Kim Wee, president (took office September 1985). *Head of government,* Lee Kuan Yew, prime minister (took office 1959). *Legislature* (unicameral)—Parliament.
Monetary Unit: Singapore dollar (2.001 S. dollars equal U.S. $1, Dec. 31, 1987).
Gross Domestic Product (1985 U.S.$): $17,250,000,000.
Economic Index (1986): *Consumer Prices* (1980 = 100), all items, 115.7; food, 114.1.
Foreign Trade (1986 U.S.$): *Imports,* $25,512,000,000; *exports,* $22,495,000,000.

Looking to tourism as another key to the economic future, the government in 1987 embarked on a five-year, $500 million program to attract visitors and increase tourism revenue. After the building boom of the early 1980s, hotel capacity far outstrips current demand. Occupancy rates were as low as 25% in 1986, with a 7% increase targeted for 1987.

After several months of testing, a 3.7-mi (5.9-km.) section of the Singapore Mass Rapid Transit System was opened in early November. The planned 42-mi (67-km) system was expected to be completed in the mid-1990s.

Political Affairs. In what the government described as a "Marxist conspiracy to subvert the existing social and political system," a total of 22 persons were arrested and jailed in police raids on May 21 and June 20. The ring allegedly had the goal of turning Singapore into a communist state through "manipulation of religious and other organizations." including the opposition Workers' Party and the Catholic Church. Vincent Cheng, a Catholic social activist, was described as the organizer of the plot, working under the direction of exiled political activist Tan Wah Piow, who fled the country in the late 1970s. By September, 14 of the detainees had been released, with the remainder held under one- or two-year detention orders. The government credited the 14 early releases to rapid rehabilitation.

In December the government announced that it was restricting the circulation in Singapore of the *Far Eastern Economic Review,* a weekly Asian newsmagazine published in Hong Kong. The government charged that it "had consistently published distorted articles on Singapore." Similar action had been taken earlier in the year against other publications, including *The Asian Wall Street Journal* and *Asiaweek* magazine. The government acted under a 1986 amendment to the Newspaper and Printing Presses Act, permitting it to cut a publication's revenue and visibility if its reporting is judged to be "slanted."

Foreign Affairs. Although its military force is relatively small, Singapore's weaponry remains the most sophisticated in the region. A major source of its military supplies through the years has been the Swedish arms industry. In mid-1987, however, the Swedish government imposed a ban on future arms sales to Singapore, when it was averred that missiles, explosives, radar, and other materiel had been sold to Persian Gulf states through a state-affiliated company in Singapore. The government denied any official involvement in the diversion.

Under a bilateral civil aviation agreement reached in September between Canada and Great Britain, Air Canada will continue to fly routes between London and Hong Kong, Singapore, and Bombay. The pact ended a longstanding dispute between the two countries on service to Asia.

AP/Wide World

With estimates of the number of homeless people in the United States ranging from 300,000 to 3 million, Congress passed and President Reagan signed legislation granting $1 billion in aid. State and local governments also took new action.

SOCIAL WELFARE

Nineteen hundred and eighty-seven may be remembered as the year that millions of American investors lost billions of dollars in the stock market. But it also was a year in which millions of other Americans continued to live in severely economically deprived conditions. The official poverty rate, announced by the U.S. Census Bureau on July 30, stood at 13.6% of the population. That figure was slightly lower than the percentage for the previous year (14%). Nevertheless, some 32.4 million Americans were found to fit the official definition of poverty, which is an annual cash income of less than $11,203 for a family of four. "There is nothing to be proud of in these statistics," said Rep. Thomas J. Downey (D-NY), acting chairman of the House Ways and Means Subcommittee on Public Assistance and Unemployment Compensation.

While the number of persons living below the poverty line declined since 1983, the number of poor families with children rose steadily —from 4.1 million in 1979 to 5.5 million in 1987, according to an analysis of Census Bureau statistics compiled by a private research group, the Center on Budget Policy Priorities. "Poor families are growing poorer and falling further below the poverty line," said the center's director Robert Greenstein.

The continuing problems for those mired in poverty came during a year in which the national civilian unemployment rate hit an eight-year low, falling to 5.9% in August—the lowest since November 1979. According to the U.S. Department of Labor, the number of adult Americans without jobs dropped from more than 8 million in 1986 to 7.1 million in September 1987.

Nevertheless, unemployment among teenagers remained high, more than 16%. For black teenagers the figure was around 30%, a nearly 10% decrease compared with 1986. Still, the government statistics do not include those unemployed persons who are not actively seeking work. Analysts estimate that there were some 6 million Americans who want to work, but were not actively looking.

One reason for the improved jobs picture was the addition in recent years of millions of jobs in the service sector—positions that pay significantly lower salaries and provide fewer benefits than most of the manufacturing jobs that were lost in the early 1980s. The number of service jobs increased from some 65 million in January 1981 to more than 75 million in mid-1987, according to the federal Bureau of Labor Statistics. Many of those jobs were retail trade positions, which pay an average hourly wage of just more than $6. The nearly 6 million Americans who worked full time in eating and drinking establishments received an average hourly wage of less than $4.50. Many of those full-time service-sector workers earned annual salaries that fit the definition of poverty.

Hunger. One result of the large number of unemployed and underemployed has been a serious hunger problem. For the second year in a row the Physicians' Task Force on Hunger in America estimated that some 20 million Americans—primarily infants, the elderly, and former blue-collar workers now employed in the service sector—suffer from "chronic inadequate nutritional intake." The task force, under the direction of Professor Larry Brown of the Harvard University School of Public Health, examined conditions in four areas of the country hard hit by economic and social dislocation: Texas and Louisiana; Minnesota and Iowa; Pennsylvania, Ohio, and West Virginia; and California's Silicon Valley.

"People obviously aren't dropping like flies," Brown said, "not like in the Third World where you go around and count bodies." But, he explained, "families miss meals, cut down, go without for a couple of days. The typical profile is one fairly well-rounded meal a day."

In the last few years scores of church groups, charitable organizations, and city and county officials have set up soup kitchens and food banks to help feed hungry Americans. Food banks—which gather and distribute surplus food to charitable organizations and to individuals—especially have grown widely in scope in cities and suburban areas. Second Harvest, the Chicago-based organization that works with some 200 food banks across the country, recently became the largest private, charitable feeding program in the nation. In 1986, Second Harvest food banks distributed 352 million lbs. (160 million kg) of food, representing $500 million in retail value, to some 38,000 different community feeding programs. Much of the food was donated directly by large food producers; nonfood businesses also made significant contributions to Second Harvest and other food banks and soup kitchens nationwide.

Homeless Persons. The biggest users of soup kitchens—which provide free meals on a regular basis—have been the homeless. Although exact numbers are impossible to ascertain, it was estimated that there were from 300,000 to 3 million homeless individuals in the United States in 1987. The problem is particularly acute in large cities. In Los Angeles, for example, the mayor's office estimated the homeless population at 30,000. In New York City, officials reported that some 11,000 persons and 5,100 families (including at least 13,000 children) used the city's shelter system in 1987. Overall, the experts estimated New York City's homeless population to be between 60,000 and 80,000.

Some suburban areas also had large numbers of homeless. Officials believed that New York City's surrounding suburbs—Long Island, Westchester County (NY), northern New Jersey, and Fairfield County (CT)—had between 30,000 and 54,000 homeless persons. That total had doubled since 1983. Homelessness was a problem even in affluent Santa Barbara, CA, where there were an estimated 1,500 homeless persons.

Congress for the first time in 1987 passed legislation authorizing the federal government to spend vast amounts of money to help the homeless. The legislation, which President Reagan signed into law in July, would provide the nation's homeless with as much as $1 billion in emergency and permanent housing, health care, food, education, job training, and other assistance in fiscal years 1987 and 1988. In the last two months of 1987 the Department of Housing and Urban Development distributed some $15 million in emergency housing-aid grants to local homeless organizations under provisions of the new law.

The mentally ill have been a very visible part of the homeless population since the early 1960s when large numbers of patients were released from mental institutions. Countless numbers of disheveled mentally ill persons have taken up residence in big city train stations, bus terminals, subways, street corners, and vacant lots. Many exhibit disruptive behavior: some mumble to themselves incessantly; some harangue passersby; some panhandle aggressively. Homeless advocates believe that about one fifth of all the homeless persons in the United States are former mental patients.

For the first time in 1987 several jurisdictions around the nation began efforts to rid the streets of the deinstitutionalized homeless. In Seattle, a tough new ordinance gave police wide new powers to stop panhandling. In New York City, Mayor Edward Koch put into effect a plan to hospitalize mentally ill homeless persons deemed to be "incapable of taking care of themselves." Under the plan, which was criticized by civil libertarians and advocates of the mentally ill when it went into effect in October, city workers forcibly picked up severely mentally ill homeless persons and placed them in city-run hospitals, such as the Bellevue Hospital Center.

In Los Angeles, police began strictly enforcing ordinances against sleeping on sidewalks. "It's not a specific spoken goal, but they want to get these cold, hungry people who aren't quite sane off their streets," Jennifer Wolch, an associate professor of urban planning at the University of Southern California, said of the crackdowns on the mentally ill homeless. "The homeless are increasingly being diverted to jails and to institutions. It's a very serious situation."

Welfare Reform. Meanwhile, in Washington, DC, debate continued over the role of the federal government in welfare. Since coming to office in 1981, President Ronald Reagan consistently advocated measures that would significantly cut back the federal role in welfare. Many Democrats in Congress, civil-rights groups, churches, and liberal groups, on the other hand, favored the continuance of government-backed programs aimed at helping deprived persons. Both sides strongly supported programs that encouraged welfare recipients to find employment and free themselves from the dependence on welfare programs.

Both the Reagan administration and its welfare critics agreed that such present multifaceted federal welfare programs as Aid to Families with Dependent Children (AFDC), food stamps, Medicaid, and Medicare needed to be overhauled. Sen. Daniel Patrick Moynihan (D-NY), chairman of the Senate Finance Subcommittee on Social Security and Family Policy, led the welfare-reform effort in Congress in 1987. In July he introduced a sweeping bill that, among other things, called for withholding child support from parents' wages, extending benefits to poor two-parent families, and setting up mandatory education, work, and training programs designed to help welfare recipients find jobs in the private sector.

In the House of Representatives, major welfare reform bills were introduced by both Democrats and Republicans. Both bills were similar in thrust to the Moynihan Senate measure. The Democrats' version, though—which was an amalgam of provisions adopted by four committees (Ways and Means, Education and Labor, Energy and Commerce, and Agriculture)—went further than the Republican plan. The Democrats' proposal, which was sponsored by Representative Downey, would, among other things, set up a mandatory state-run, federally-financed, work-training program for AFDC recipients. The Democratic bill also contained language that would increase some benefits and called for significantly more federal spending than the House GOP or Moynihan measures. President Reagan, who strongly criticized both the Moynihan and Democratic House proposals, endorsed the Republican plan. The 1987 congressional session adjourned without taking final action on the welfare-reform issue.

International

As serious as the social-welfare problems were in the United States, they paled in comparison with what was happening in many parts of the developing world. According to the United Nations World Food Council, hunger and malnutrition reached unprecedented proportions throughout the developing world in 1987. The council estimated that at least 512 million people, primarily in Asia and Africa, were seriously undernourished—compared with an estimated 475 million in 1980. "They are chronically deprived of the food needed to enjoy an active, healthy life," said Uwe Kracht, the council's chief of policy development. "Their lives are significantly impaired by poor diet."

The problem of hunger was most acute in the economically depressed nations of black Africa and the heavily populated countries of Asia, primarily India, Pakistan, and Bangladesh. But hunger was by no means confined to those areas of the world. Serious problems existed as well in Central and South America. The most alarming aspect of the problem was the effect of hunger and malnutrition on children. The World Food Council estimated that some 40,000 children died every day during 1987 due to hunger-related causes.

© Second Harvest

Food banks and soup kitchens have proliferated rapidly in U.S. cities and suburbs. Second Harvest of Chicago, above, is the nation's largest private charitable feeding program.

The nation most seriously affected in 1987 was Ethiopia, where Western officials reported that some 5 million people were threatened with famine. As was the case with Ethiopia's devastating famine of 1984–85, the severe lack of food in 1987 was due to a drought in the northern provinces of Eritrea and Tigre, compounded by the effects of an ongoing civil war between the Eritrean People's Liberation Front and the Marxist Ethiopian government of Lt. Col. Mengistu Haile Miriam. The food situation also was critical in the southeastern portion of the country, an area where peasants were forcibly resettled on state agricultural collectives. Efforts to deliver food to Ethiopia by the United Nations, Great Britain, the United States, and private relief agencies were severely hampered by the continued fighting.

Nothing approaching the problems of Ethiopia was evident in Western Europe. Nevertheless, sluggish economic conditions led to significant unemployment problems across the continent. In France and Italy unemployment rates approached 11%; in Great Britain more than 10% of the adult population was without jobs. Overall, there were nearly 16 million unemployed persons in Europe.

MARC LEEPSON
Contributing Editor
"American Politics" Magazine

© Sygma

South Africa's Minister of Home Affairs Stoffel Botha celebrates a strong victory by the ruling National Party in all-white parliamentary elections May 6. The overall results indicated a shift to the right among the nation's white voters.

SOUTH AFRICA

In response to increasing domestic and international pressure, white South Africa for several years has tried to convince the world that it is abandoning apartheid in favor of reform. Events in 1987 exposed this as simply part of South Africa's continuing campaign to win friends and influence people abroad while ensuring the maintenance of white power at home. Indeed, President Pieter W. Botha stated publicly in May that as long as he lived reform would take place only within the context of the protection of white South Africans. During parliamentary debates in October, for example, President Botha approved limited changes to the Group Areas Act, which would allow some communities to be integrated—but only with the residents' approval. At the same time, he rejected proposals to repeal laws segregating public facilities.

Whites-Only Election. Though it did not receive the overwhelming mandate it was seeking, the ruling National Party (NP) reaffirmed its dominance in white electoral politics by winning 127 of 178 seats in the May 6 election for the all-white House of Assembly. Significantly, the biggest gains were made by the far-right, whose policies called for a return to orthodox apartheid's rigid racial segregation and no compromise of white power. The NP's appeal to the right was thus preempted by the more reactionary Conservative Party (CP), which won 22 seats and replaced the Progressive Federal Party (PFP) as the official opposition; the PFP lost 8 of the 27 seats it held before the election. Andries Treurnicht of the CP replaced Colin Eglin of the PFP as the leader of the opposition and immediately attacked the National Party's proposed policy of power sharing as a further loss of white power. Continual pressure from the growing right wing, which won more than 500,000 of the 2 million total votes cast, was expected to push the government in a more conservative direction, especially on issues of security and the pace of change.

State of Emergency. On June 10, President Botha told Parliament that he was extending the state of emergency for another year and at the same time pledged that he would rather fight than hold talks with the banned African National Congress (ANC). The new emergency extended and bolstered some of the previous regulations. For example, it increased from 14 to 30 days the period for which individuals could be detained without written authorization. Bans on the media's reporting of unrest were reworded so as to circumvent an April Supreme Court ruling which declared the previous constraints invalid because of their "unreasonable vagueness." While repressive government measures temporarily imposed a superficial calm on South Africa, an increase in urban sabotage during 1987 was a reminder that widespread violence remains a constant reality.

Dakar Meeting. A historic meeting between 17 exiled leaders of the ANC and 61 predominantly Afrikaner business leaders, academics, and politicians was held in Dakar, Senegal, in July. Organized by the Institute for a Democratic Alternative in South Africa (IDASA) and its director, former PFP leader Frederik Van Zyl Slabbert, the meeting was an attempt to begin a dialogue on such issues as the structure of government and the economy in a liberated South Africa and the problems and strategies for transition. The significance of the meeting lay not in what was accomplished but rather in the fact that it took place at all. In addition, the ANC in particular exhibited a flexibility that suggested a willingness to compromise in future negotiations. It changed its position slightly with regard to nationalization, implying that it would accept limited steps in this direction within a predominantly free-enterprise economy. Notwithstanding the disagreement between the two sides on the ANC's commitment to the use of violence to overthrow the current regime, there was a jointly expressed preference for a negotiated settlement. At the same time, there also was a recognition that the "violence in the present white-dominated system" and "the attitudes of those in power" made a nonviolent solution unlikely. The ANC committed itself to maintaining a multiparty democracy in a post-apartheid South Africa and pledged that individual rights would be guaranteed by a bill of rights. IDASA made it clear that in recognizing the need to talk to the ANC it was not supporting the nationalist movement or its strategies. However, it also emphasized that the talks had shown that the South African government was wrong in its assessment that negotiation was not possible with the ANC. President Botha was quick to criticize the meeting and questioned the loyalties of those who attended.

SOUTH AFRICA • Information highlights

Official Name: Republic of South Africa.
Location: Southern tip of Africa.
Area: 471,444 sq mi (1 221 040 km^2).
Population (mid-1987 est.): 34,300,000.
Chief Cities (1985 census, city proper): Pretoria, the administrative capital, 443,059; Cape Town, the legislative capital, 776,617; Durban, 634,301; Johannesburg, 632,369.
Government: *Head of state and government,* Pieter Willem Botha, state president (took office Sept. 1984). *Legislature*—Parliament (tricameral): House of Assembly, House of Representatives (Coloured), and House of Delegates (Indians).
Monetary Unit: Rand (1.9417 rands equal U.S. $1, Dec. 21, 1987).
Gross Domestic Product (1985 U.S.$): $51,000,000,000.
Economic Index (1986): *Consumer Prices* (1980 = 100), all items, 228.3; food, 228.6.
Foreign Trade (1986 U.S.$): *Imports,* $11,980,000,000; *exports,* excluding exports of gold, $10,860,000,000.

Split in Dutch Reformed Church. Late in 1986, the General Synod of the Nederduitse Gereformeede Kerk (NGK), the largest Dutch Reformed Church in South Africa with an estimated membership of more than 1.6 million, issued a statement declaring that racism is a sin and that apartheid is an error. At that time the Synod also raised the possibility of opening the church to all races. In response, a group of 2,000 NGK members voted in June 1987 to break away and form a whites-only Afrikaner Gereformeerde Kerk under the leadership of Afrikaans theologian Willie Lubbe. Most Afrikaans newspapers reported limited support for the new church.

Proposed National Council. In September, Minister of Constitutional Development and Planning Chris Heunis introduced a bill in Parliament that would allow blacks to participate in a multi-racial National Council advisory body to draw up a new national constitution. A version of the bill had been introduced 16 months before but had been withdrawn because of black opposition. The new bill provided for 9 of the 30 members of the council to be elected by the 8–12 million blacks living in South African cities and rural areas, but it excluded those blacks in the so-called independent homelands. The majority of the remaining 21 members would be appointed by the state president, thus assuring white control. Not surprisingly, most black leaders again rejected the proposal. The ANC and United Democratic Front (UDF) both saw the bill as just another means to maintain white control. The UDF would be allowed to participate in the process should it choose to change its position, but the banned ANC would not.

Economic Uncertainty. The economic picture was mixed in 1987. On the one hand, disinvestment by such major multinational corporations as IBM, Ford, Citicorp, ITT, and Eastman Kodak continued, and the economic growth rate slowed somewhat. On the other hand, South Africa achieved a trade surplus, and the increase in the price of gold meant additional billions of dollars in foreign-exchange earnings. The Rev. Leon Sullivan, who had written a code of corporate conduct that had been adopted as a norm for U.S. corporations continuing to do business in South Africa, renounced those guidelines in June, urging a complete corporate pullout from South Africa and a near total embargo on trade. Perhaps more importantly, at least in long-term effects, were the impact of international sanctions and increasing black trade union militancy within the country. The U.S. Department of State estimated that sanctions cut South Africa's economic growth by approximately one third. By year's end the U.S. Congress seemed ready to consider even tougher sanctions.

On August 9, the National Union of Mine Workers (NUM), under the leadership of Cyril Ramaphosa, organized a legal strike of some 300,000 workers against coal and gold mines. The strike lasted three weeks and resulted in only minimal improvement for black mine workers, but it did demonstrate a developing ability of unions to sustain a strike against vital mining interests—which produce more than half of South Africa's foreign exchange. The strike was estimated to have cost the mines as much as $225 million in lost production. Nine workers were killed, 300 were wounded, and more than 400 imprisoned during the three weeks. The union had sought a 30% across-the-board wage increase, but the companies were unwilling to concede beyond a prestrike offer of 15–23%. However, the companies did increase some benefits and agreed to rehire all workers dismissed during the strike.

ANC Leader Released. Early in November, 77-year-old Govan A. Mbeki, one of the senior leaders of the ANC, was released from Robben Island maximum security prison, where he had been serving a life sentence for sabotage since 1964. Immediately upon his release, Mbeki flew to Pollsmoor prison near Cape Town, where he was allowed to talk with his close colleague, Nelson Mandela. The Pretoria government said that Mbeki had been set free because of his advancing age and ill health, which led to speculation that the way might be open for the release of Mandela as well. The existing emergency regulations made it a crime for newspapers to quote Mbeki, but the government temporarily lifted the ban in allowing a press conference after his release. Mbeki also was denied a passport to travel abroad.

Government Versus Universities. In October the government initiated an offensive against the nation's English-language universities, which it has long seen as centers of radical political activity. The new measures, introduced in parliament under the Universities Act by Minister of National Education F.W. De Klerk, would force university councils to police their campuses if they are to continue to receive substantial amounts of state financial support. Among other things, the universities would be forced to inform the government within 21 days of "disruptive incidents" on their campuses and would be required to take preventive or disciplinary action against students or staff found guilty of any disruptive act under the new measures. In rejecting the new restrictions, the vice-chancellor and the senate of the University of the Witwatersrand declared: "We are not a police force, policing and spying on the activities of our staff and students off campus and on campus. We do not see the policing of their political activities as part of our activities. We are concerned with the maintenance of discipline, not of a particular political outlook."

Political Resignations. Three members of the PFP—Peter Gastrow, Pierre Cronje, and Pieter Schoeman—resigned from the party in October. All three subsequently joined a newly formed political group called the National Democratic Movement (NDM). The NDM was led by Wynand Malan, who had been elected to parliament as an independent in the May balloting after defecting from the National Party. The three PFP members were part of the group that had met with the ANC in Dakar. While the PFP later sanctioned the visit, the three members had been reprimanded for attending the meeting without prior approval. The NDM called for an end to press restrictions and the state of emergency, and proposed a new political program that included a bill of rights, an end to racial segregation, and guarantees of equality of language, religion, and culture.

Military Involvement in Angola. The extent of South Africa's military support for the National Union for the Total Liberation of Angola (UNITA) became more evident in November. Since the beginning of the Angolan civil war in 1975, South Africa has consistently and publicly denied its support for UNITA. In 1987, however, Pretoria acknowledged its support for the rebel movement in order, according to some commentators, to prepare the South African public for a stepped-up military offensive. At the end of November, South Africa announced the loss of 23 soldiers in battles with Angolan troops and their Cuban allies over three previous weeks. Several South African newspapers and even some government supporters questioned the wisdom of escalating South Africa's presence in Angola, especially because of the military's central role in maintaining internal order.

Joint Executive Authority. Power sharing in one form or another has been discussed in South Africa for a number of years, but recommendations by various nongovernmental committees and commissions for some form of joint government between KwaZulu and Natal had been systematically rejected by the provincial or national governments for more than a decade. In late 1985, however, the provincial government of Natal entered into what appeared to be serious discussions with KwaZulu over joint administration of their adjoining territories. By February 1986, agreement to establish a Joint Executive Authority had been reached and submitted to the national government for approval. It languished there until November 1987, when the government adopted the new proposal and even conceded that a single legislature might be acceptable. The new structure is a loose confederation in which so-called joint authority will not compromise ultimate white power.

PATRICK O'MEARA
N. BRIAN WINCHESTER
Indiana University

SOUTH CAROLINA

Events relating to religion—Jim Bakker and the PTL ministry, a Billy Graham Crusade, and visits by Pope John Paul II and other religious leaders—highlighted the news in South Carolina in 1987.

Government. The adoption of a state budget was complicated by lengthy debate over funding and tax increases for such essential programs as public education, teachers' pay, and penal reform. Gov. Carroll A. Campbell, Jr., vetoed 272 appropriation items and tax increases amounting to $17 million. Time limitations prevented the legislature from a realistic consideration of the vetoes.

New laws reformed automobile insurance fees, increased the rural interstate speed limit to 65 miles per hour (105 km/hr), added 3 cents to the state gasoline tax, increased penalties for drunk driving, broadened pornography statutes, provided safeguards for health maintenance organizations, increased employers' job tax credits in the 16 poorest counties, and decreased estate taxes. Many exceptions to the state's Freedom of Information Act were removed, making it easier for citizens to use the law.

Black voters continued to push for single-member districts in local governments. Black parents maintained their demands for fairness in pupil assignments to schools.

Education. Despite funding cutbacks, the objectives of the Public Education Finance Act were on schedule. Overall test scores improved, although not in every district. Scholastic Aptitude Test (SAT) scores rose by 6 points over 1986, but were still the lowest among the states. New school accreditation standards were to take effect in 1988. The compulsory school-attendance age was raised to 17, and the dropout rate was the lowest since 1970. Most impaired schools removed deficiencies, although financing new school construction continued to be a major problem. Improved standards for teacher training in colleges resulted in the rejection of one quarter of those students who applied for teacher training programs in the state.

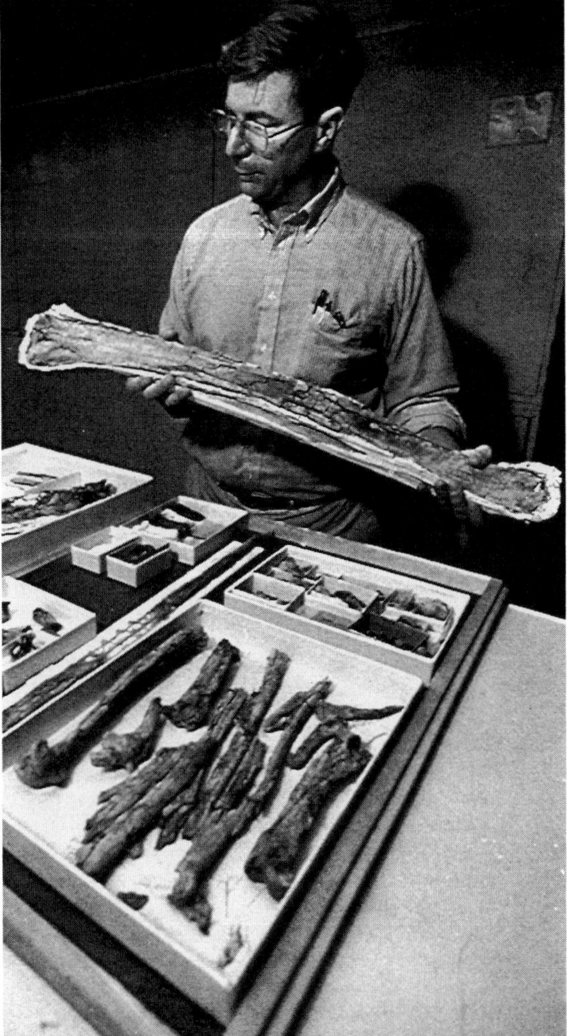

AP/Wide World

An anthropologist at the Smithsonian Institution examines the 30-million-year-old bones of a pseudodontorn, history's largest flying seabird, uncovered in South Carolina.

The University of South Carolina dedicated its new Swearingen Engineering Center, and the Higher Education Commission produced a plan to promote academic excellence and improved research in colleges and universities.

Economy. Unemployment dropped to 4.9% in August, an eight-year low. Investments in industrial expansion were substantially ahead of 1986, as was the growth in foreign investment. The textile industry, especially, prospered in 1987. Despite labor disagreements, the Mack Truck Company began production; as a result, ten truck-related industries have located in the state.

SOUTH CAROLINA • Information Highlights

Area: 31,113 sq mi (80 582 km²).
Population (July 1, 1986): 3,378,000.
Chief Cities (1980 census): Columbia, the capital (July 1, 1982 est.), 101,457; Charleston, 69,510; Greenville, 58,242.
Government (1987): *Chief Officers*—governor, Carroll A. Campbell, Jr. (R); lt. gov., Nick A. Theodore (D). *General Assembly*—Senate, 46 members; House of Representatives, 124 members.
State Finances (fiscal year 1986): *Revenue,* $6,362,000,000; *expenditure,* $5,641,000,000.
Personal Income (1986): $38,153,000,000; per capita, $11,299.
Labor Force (June 1987): *Civilian labor force,* 1,663,500; *unemployed,* 97,600 (5.9% of total force).
Education: *Enrollment* (fall 1985)—public elementary schools, 424,125; public secondary, 182,518; colleges and universities, 131,902. *Public school expenditures* (1985–86), $1,655,000,000 ($2,912 per pupil).

Agriculture rebounded from the 1986 drought. Tobacco and peach production were above normal, and tobacco outranked soybeans as the chief money crop. Cattle, milk, and broiler chickens were significant income sources. Although the rate of farm decline decreased, low prices and reduced federal allotments decreased planted acreage.

Religion. The complex issues relating to the bankruptcy of the PTL ministry continued to be litigated. A U.S. bankruptcy court in Columbia, SC, rejected the Rev. Jerry Falwell's bankruptcy reorganization plan. Falwell then resigned as chairman of the ministry, which he had taken over from Jim Bakker earlier in 1987. (*See* RELIGION—Overview.)

Pope John Paul II addressed an audience of 60,000 at the state university stadium and held an ecumenical conference at the university with 26 national church leaders. Billy Graham returned for a ten-day crusade.

ROBERT H. STOUDEMIRE
University of South Carolina

SOUTH DAKOTA

Economic conditions in South Dakota were fairly stable in 1987 in large degree because of federal support for agriculture and livestock production, the state's major industries. Revival of cultural commitments and tribal authority drew attention to South Dakota's Indians.

Legislature. In 1987, South Dakota became the first state since the 1974 imposition of a national 55 mile-per-hour (89 km/hr) speed limit to authorize a limit of 65 mph (105 km/hr) for rural interstate highway travel. The state also raised the minimum age for drinking alcoholic beverages to 21. At the same time it challenged a federal law linking a nationwide 21-year drinking age with the continuance of federal highway funding to states that did not comply. The U.S. Supreme Court decided against South Dakota, 7–2 *(South Dakota v. Dole).*

SOUTH DAKOTA • Information Highlights

Area: 77,116 sq mi (199 730 km²).
Population (July 1, 1986): 708,000.
Chief Cities (1980 census): Pierre, the capital, 11,973; Sioux Falls, 81,343; Rapid City, 46,492.
Government (1987): *Chief Officers*—governor, George S. Mickelson (R); lt. gov., Walter D. Miller (R). *Legislature*—Senate, 35 members; House of Representatives, 70 members.
State Finances (fiscal year 1986): *Revenue,* $1,241,000,000; *expenditure,* $1,074,000,000.
Personal Income (1986): $8,364,000,000; per capita, $11,814.
Labor Force (June 1987): *Civilian labor force,* 367,600; *unemployed,* 14,400 (3.9% of total force).
Education: *Enrollment* (fall 1985)—public elementary schools, 87,644; public secondary, 36,647; colleges and universities, 32,772. *Public school expenditures* (1985–86), $349,000,000 ($2,967 per pupil).

The legislature also established a special business development fund, which it hoped to support with a higher sales tax and a new state lottery system.

Economy. South Dakotans enjoyed an increase in average personal income over 1986 of 6.1% and a slight improvement in nonagricultural employment. Farmers and ranchers received fairly good prices for their grain and flax seed, and for livestock and wool. Tourism, the state's third largest industry after farming and ranching, remained profitable.

The economic mainstay, agriculture, seemed to have a stable future so long as it continued to receive federal supports. Participation in the federal Payment-in-Kind (PIK) plan required careful management but offered high returns. The farmer who chose to feed corn to livestock, rather than store it in the PIK program, earned still more. In addition, a "set-aside-acreage" conservation program paid the farmer not to grow corn on some acreage, and another program helped to improve highly erodable cropland. Most farmers agreed that only those who paid high interest for past loans on land and equipment were in financial difficulty. On the other hand, if federal support programs were curtailed and farm income were based solely on free market prices, farm collapse seemed likely.

Sheep and wool production, a "hard-times" industry, flourished. Ranchers with herds in western South Dakota produced calves, pigs, and lambs for sale to feeders in eastern counties who fattened them on PIK-supported corn for sale on rising markets.

Indian Affairs. Unemployment rates between 80 and 90% on reservations caused many Indians to seek urban jobs. Reservation populations continued to rise, however, along with a cultural renaissance indicated by increased interest in Indian-owned schools and colleges, religious activities, and the Sioux language. Tribal governance became increasingly important to all the people of South Dakota. "Tribal jurisdiction"—the capacity of elected Indian leaders to affect the activities of whites as well as Indians within the original boundaries of the reservations—remained controversial; and federal courts continued to waver on its legal dimensions.

Indians and whites worked together to resolve particular issues: the extent to which commercialism desecrates the Pipestone National Monument in nearby Minnesota; the affront to Indian culture that may result from weapons testing by Honeywell, Incorporated at a site near Hot Springs; and the possible consequences of a bill sponsored by Sen. Bill Bradley (D-NJ), which purports to return more than 1 million acres (400,000 ha) of federal land to Sioux people in the Black Hills.

HERBERT T. HOOVER
University of South Dakota

SPACE EXPLORATION

While the U.S. manned-space program remained grounded in 1987, the aftermath of the January 1986 *Challenger* accident in which seven astronauts were killed, the Soviet Union embarked on an intensive research program aboard the new Mir space station. The station was reoccupied, a large science module was added to the station complex, and a new manned-space endurance record of more than 300 days was established by cosmonaut Yuri Romanenko. The crisis in heavy-lift launch vehicles in the United States and Europe was eased with successful launches by the Titan and Ariane boosters and their return to operational status. The United States and the Soviet Union signed an accord on cooperation in space science, and several application and communication satellites were launched.

Man-in-Space. The Soviet Mir space station, which had been unoccupied since July 1986, was reoccupied on February 8 by cosmonauts Yuri Romanenko and Alexander Laveikin who had been launched aboard the Soyuz TM-2 spacecraft two days earlier. Following reactivation of the station, Romanenko and Laveikin initiated a program of oceanographic, meteorological, and hydrological observations and a series of experiments involving the processing of materials under zero-gravity conditions.

An unmanned astrophysics module, Kvant, was launched on March 31 but failed to dock with Mir when cloth debris became wedged in the docking mechanism. Romanenko and Laveikin performed an emergency space walk and, using the advantages of weightlessness, were able to pull the two station elements slightly apart and remove the debris. The docking was then successfully completed automatically by commands from ground controllers. The cosmonauts performed two more space walks in June and installed another solar array on the outside of Mir to provide electrical power for the science instruments aboard Kvant. X rays from the exploding supernova in the Large Magellanic Cloud were detected first by the Kvant instruments in August and provided the first intriguing glimpses into the core of a dying star.

On July 22, cosmonauts Alexander Viktorenko and Alexander Alexandrov and Syrian astronaut Mohammed Faris were launched aboard the Soyuz TM-3 spacecraft for a visit to Mir. Faris and Viktorenko returned to Earth on July 30 in the Soyuz TM-2 spacecraft along with cosmonaut Alexander Laveikin, who had been experiencing heart rhythm irregularities during his 174-day stay aboard Mir. Upon returning to Earth, Laveikin's condition was diagnosed as a normal variation.

On December 21, cosmonauts Vladimir Titov and Musa Manarov, accompanied by flight engineer Anatoly Levchenko, were launched aboard Soyuz TM-4 to replace the crew on board Mir. After a short orientation period for the new crew, Romanenko, who had spent 11 months in space, was returned to earth along with Levchenko and Alexandrov in the Soyuz TM-3 spacecraft, landing in Soviet Kazakhstan on December 29. Romanenko's 326 days in space surpassed the previous space endurance record of 237 days set by three Soviet cosmonauts in 1984. Titov and Manarov were expected to remain on board Mir through 1988.

© Tass from Sovfoto

Cmdr. Yuri Romanenko, 42, and Alexander Laveikin (top), *a 35-year-old civilian, were launched aboard Soyuz TM-2 February 6. The midnight launch was telecast live.*

Six unmanned Progress cargo vehicles were used in 1987 to resupply Mir at approximately two-month intervals, each carrying 4,000 lb (1 814 kg) of provisions. When their missions were completed, the Progress vehicles were sent on a destructive reentry path into the earth's atmosphere.

Space Shuttle. In 1987 no U.S. manned space-flight missions were conducted as the U.S. space shuttle fleet remained grounded in the aftermath of the *Challenger* accident. The focus of U.S. activities was on implementing the changes necessary to make the shuttle safe for re-flight. The redesign of the joint and seal between sections of the solid-rocket booster—identified by the Rogers Commission in 1986 as the cause of the *Challenger* accident—was completed and two full-scale and three subscale tests verified particular aspects of the joint redesign. However, during the last test, a failure was discovered in an unrelated booster nozzle component, further delaying the resumption of shuttle flights until 1988.

Development of the Soviet space shuttle, comparable in size and capability to the U.S. shuttle, continued in 1987. Takeoff and landing tests were conducted with a jet engine-powered version of the vehicle at the Baikonur Cosmodrome, in preparation for its initial orbital flight in 1988.

The Soviets also continued developments on a smaller space plane to be used for quick-reaction manned flights to the Mir space complex or other space activities. The fifth subscale test was conducted in 1987 and the first flight of the full-scale space plane is planned as early as 1990.

Space Station. The blueprints for the initial orbital configuration of the U.S./International space station were completed in 1987, and four industrial teams were selected to build the U.S. elements of the station. A mobile servicing unit will be provided by Canada, and Japan and the European Space Agency (ESA) will each contribute a manned-experiments module. Permanent manned operations of the U.S./International station are planned for 1996.

The European Space Agency uses an Ariane rocket to launch a TV Sat-1 communications satellite. The Ariane booster returned to operational status in 1987.

© Laurent Maous/Gamma-Liaison

Booster Development. The 18-month crisis in U.S. heavy-lift launch-vehicle capability was alleviated in 1987 with the return to service of the Titan booster. The European Ariane also returned to service after 16 months with two launches of communications satellites.

The Soviet Union's launch capability increased measurably in 1987 with the launch of the 170 million-horsepower *Energia* booster, capable of placing a 220,000 lb (100 metric ton) payload in orbit. This Saturn 5 class booster will be used as the launch vehicle for the Soviet shuttle and could help launch Soviet manned missions to the Moon and Mars. In 1987 the United States initiated studies of a new heavy-lift booster, the Advanced Launch System, which would be capable of orbiting 100,000 lb (45.4 metric ton) payloads beginning in 1994.

As a result of the decision to limit the launching of commercial satellites on the shuttle, U.S. industrial organizations announced plans to build Atlas-Centaur, Delta, and Titan-3 expendable boosters on a commercial basis to launch these satellites. The Soviet Union offered its Proton booster for launch of Western commercial satellites, but the U.S. government refused to grant a license to ship U.S.-built spacecraft to the Soviet Union for launch. China, taking advantage of the scarcity of Western launch vehicles, was successful in marketing its Long-March boosters to several U.S. industrial companies.

Science Missions. With access to space severely affected by the halt of the U.S. space shuttle program and the lack of expendable boosters for science missions, the U.S. space-sciences program remained grounded in 1987. Development of major space-science missions originally planned for launch during 1986-88—the Hubble Space Telescope, the Galileo mission to Jupiter, and the Magellan mission to Venus, as well as a number of Shuttle/Spacelab science flights—continued in preparation for launch once shuttle flights resume. In addition, the launch of the Mars Observer mission was delayed because of funding constraints. Other U.S. missions in peril of being postponed include: the entire U.S. surface exploration of Mars; the Comet Rendezvous Asteroid Fly-by; and the probe of Titan.

Japan launched an X-ray astronomy satellite, Ginga, in February from the Kagoshima Space Center, using a Nissan M-3S booster. The spacecraft also observed the X rays from the exploding supernova on August 15, shortly after they were detected by the instrumentation on board the Mir-Kvant complex.

In September a recoverable biological spacecraft, Biosat, carrying two monkeys and ten rats, was launched by the Soviet Union on a 13-day mission to assess the effects of weightlessness and space radiation on small animals. Upon recovery, U.S. investigators participated in the analysis of the tissues from the rats to compare the data with that obtained from the U.S. Spacelab-3 mission in 1985.

Two recoverable zero-gravity materials-processing missions were launched during the year. A Soviet materials-processing spacecraft was launched on April 24 and recovered two weeks later after performing sophisticated semiconductor and biological materials-processing experiments. China also launched a small recoverable satellite in August with a French supplied microgravity experimental package on a five-day mission to assess the utility of the spacecraft for materials processing.

Application Satellites. Launch of the GEOS-7 weather satellite on February 26 restored the U.S. two-spacecraft, geosynchronous-weather-monitoring system to full operational capability and eliminated the need to constantly shift the position of the single spacecraft back and forth to observe storms forming over either the Atlantic or the Pacific.

The Soviet Union orbited two Meteor-2 meteorological satellites in 1987 to join their low-altitude meteorological system. The satellites provide cloud-cover information and atmospheric data, along with multispectral imagery of selected land areas.

Three ocean/land remote-sensing missions were launched in 1987. Japan's space remote-sensing program was inaugurated in February with the launch of its Marine Observation Satellite (MOS-1). MOS-1 carries microwave, multispectral, and thermal infrared sensors to provide data for oceanographic, hydrologic, and land-resources applications. The largest civilian earth resources spacecraft ever launched, the 33,000 lb (15 metric ton) Cosmos 1870, was placed in orbit by the Soviet Union on July 25 to provide multidisciplinary remote-sensing data on the world's oceans, atmospheres, and land resources. A Soviet oceanographic satellite, Cosmos 1869, also was launched in July to join the Cosmos 1766 system in providing radar data on ocean conditions to support Soviet shipping activities. However, the Cosmos 1869 radar antenna failed to fully deploy, and the spacecraft is returning data only from the other sensors.

Three earth-resources satellites, the European SPOT-1 and the U.S. Landsat 4 and 5, continued to provide high-resolution multispectral imagery on a commercial basis to users worldwide for remote-sensing applications. The Soviet Union, in an attempt to capture part of the remote-sensing market, also offered to sell high-resolution imagery.

Communication Satellites. Of the 21 communication satellites launched in 1987, 16 were launched by the Soviet Union, 3 by ESA, 1 by the United States, and 1 by Japan. Palapa B-2 was launched for Indonesia by the United States; a European ECS-4, an Australian Aussat K-3, and a West German TVSat were launched by ESA Ariane boosters; and Japan launched an advanced communications technology demonstration spacecraft, the Engineering Test Satellite (ETS-5). All were placed in geosynchronous orbit.

The Soviet Union launched two replacement spacecraft for its low-orbit, global-communications systems; six small satellites for its low-orbit coplanar system; and a replacement Molniya spacecraft for its highly elliptical-orbit domestic communications network. Seven Soviet satellites were also placed in geosynchronous orbit in 1987—three Radugas, two Cosmos, one Ekran, and one Gorizont.

WILLIAM L. PIOTROWSKI

SPAIN

Civil and industrial unrest aimed at the government's economic policies mounted during 1987 and contributed to a decline in electoral support for the Socialist party (PSOE) of Prime Minister Felipe González.

Politics and Government. On June 10, two thirds of Spain's 28.5 million voters selected members for 8,004 local councils, 13 regional assemblies, and 60 seats in the European Parliament. Attempts by the opposition to turn this "triple election" into a referendum on the austerity program of the González administration failed. Despite its diminished totals, the PSOE easily preserved its position as the country's dominant party. Offsetting the Socialists' decline was the unimpressive showing of the conservative Popular Alliance (AP), the main opposition force.

The PSOE, which had garnered 44% of the ballots cast in the 1986 general election, captured just 37.2% in the June municipal contests and 40% in Spain's initial participation in elections for the European Parliament. AP candidates, who had secured 26% of the vote in 1986, saw their vote shares decline to 20% in the municipal elections and 23% in the balloting for the European Parliament.

Benefiting from the decline of the two largest parties were the Democratic and Social Center (CDS), a centrist party headed by former Prime Minister Adolfo Súarez; the Communist-dominated United Left; and several regional parties.

In obtaining 9.4% of the municipal vote, the CDS established itself as the country's third party. Behind it was the United Left whose 7% of the total marked a slight rise from 1986 but a decline from its showing in the 1983 local elections. Among the regional groupings that gained ground were the Aragonese party, which came in second to the PSOE in the region, and Herri Batasuna, the radical Basque

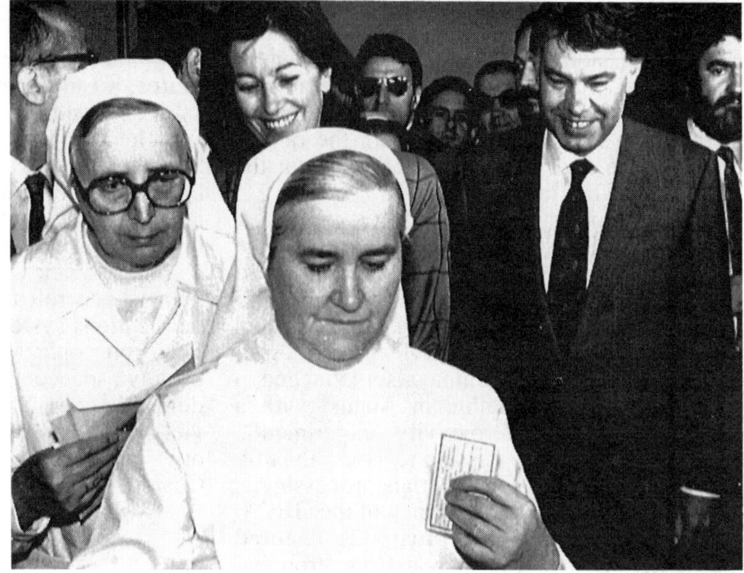

Two Catholic nuns precede Felipe González and his wife in casting their ballots in elections June 10. Although the prime minister's PSOE lost some strength, it remained Spain's dominant party.

AP/Wide World

nationalist party with links to the terrorist ETA.

Economy. The modest PSOE vote loss paled in comparison to a greater problem besetting the 45-year-old prime minister—namely, growing public discontent over economic policies deemed "antisocial" by organized labor. Upon coming to power in 1982, González trumpeted the message that wealth had to be created first before it could be redistributed. To that end, he limited government spending, curbed wage increases for public employees, encouraged private sector investment, reduced tariffs, and led Spain into the European Community.

These actions contributed to impressive economic growth, estimated at 4% in 1987 amid a projected 3% inflation rate. Moreover, large corporations reported impressive earnings.

However, to Nicolas Redondo, the seasoned leader of the Socialist General Union of Workers (UGT) who is known as "Nico," the pragmatic prime minister and his cabinet had fallen prey to an "aristocratic embrace" that persuaded them to promote private-sector profits rather than advance Socialism. After all, Redondo argued, González ran on a job-formation platform; yet, unemployment hovered at 2.8 million—approximately the number of jobs candidate González pledged to create. In his defense, the prime minister pointed out that his 1988 budget embraces major tax cuts for lower-income workers, while stipulating a 4% rise in public sector wages and pensions.

The modest size of the salary and pension adjustments prompted Nico to resign his parliamentary seat to avoid a "political confrontation" between the PSOE and its fraternal union. Still, the clash seemed inevitable as Nico's UGT joined forces with the Communist-led Workers' Commissions to launch demonstrations against the "unacceptable" budget ceilings. In Murcia, 60 UGT members turned in their Socialist party membership cards in an act of solidarity with their militant leader.

Foreign Affairs. Leftist criticism of economic policies sharpened Spanish demands for a sizable reduction in U.S. military forces in the country. In March 1986, Spanish voters approved continued membership in the North Atlantic Treaty Organization (NATO). In backing the referendum, González promised both that Spain would not enter NATO's integrated command and that the U.S.'s longstanding military presence would be diminished.

As a result, in mid-November Madrid formally notified Washington of its intention to abrogate, on May 14, 1988, the 34-year-old pact governing U.S. bases. While the accord covers a dozen installations, Spain's principal goal was removal of 72 F-16 warplanes stationed at Torrejon air base east of Madrid. At year's end, talks were under way for a new accord.

GEORGE W. GRAYSON
College of William and Mary

SPAIN • Information Highlights

Official Name: Spanish State.
Location: Iberian Peninsula in southwestern Europe.
Area: 194,884 sq mi (504 750 km^2).
Population (mid-1987 est.): 39,000,000.
Chief Cities (1982 est.): Madrid, the capital, 3,271,834; Barcelona, 1,720,998; Valencia, 770,277.
Government: *Head of state,* Juan Carlos I, king (took office Nov. 1975). *Head of government,* Felipe González Márquez, prime minister (took office Dec. 1982). *Legislature*—Cortés Generales: Senate and Congress of Deputies.
Monetary Unit: Peseta (111.9 pesetas equal U.S.$1, Dec. 2, 1987).
Gross National Product (1986 est. U.S.$): $187,600,000,000.
Economic Indexes (1986): *Consumer Prices* (1980 = 100), all items, 193.7; food, 197.2. *Industrial Production* (1980 = 100), 107.
Foreign Trade (1986 U.S.$): *Imports,* $35,022,000,000; *exports,* $27,158,000,000.

SPORTS

© Eric Bakke/Picture Group

Picketing Denver Bronco players explain their position outside Mile High Stadium during pro football's 24-day strike.

Overview

In a year that hardly lacked for drama, controversy, and sheer excitement, athletic competition during 1987 nonetheless seemed a simple matter of winning and losing. For, by often striking contrast, the *institutions* of sport—the leagues, owners, players' unions, television networks, and even the courts and voting public—repeatedly faced more complex issues of change, compromise, and long-term growth.

A "win at all costs" attitude was the downfall of the NFL Players' Association in its strike for free agency and other collective bargaining demands. Team owners offered modifications in the existing system, but the players insisted on complete free agency—only to return to competition 24 days later with no gain.

Major league baseball players, however, won a key round in their ongoing labor battles, as an arbitrator ruled that free agents in 1985 had been victims of collusion by team owners.

Nowhere was the need for change more glaring than in the coaching ranks and front offices of professional sports franchises. The NFL had no black coaches, major league baseball had no black managers. There were no black general managers and precious few blacks in executive positions. The issue came into the spotlight after a baseball vice-president commented on national television that blacks lack the "necessities" for front-office jobs. The show was to have been a tribute to the late Jackie Robinson, who 40 years earlier had broken major league baseball's color line.

The year's big scandal in collegiate sports involved Southern Methodist University (SMU), where football players were found to have been paid illegally by school officials. The NCAA imposed the harshest penalties ever on a college football team, including cancellation of the 1987 season.

By way of long-term entrenchment, the Miami Dolphins of the NFL inaugurated their new $106 million, 75,000-seat Joe Robbie Stadium. In Montreal, the dome on Olympic Stadium finally was completed, 11 years late. New domed stadiums were planned in a host of other cities, including Chicago, Atlanta, Toronto, St. Petersburg, FL, and Irwindale, CA. But in the interest of fiscal restraint, voters in San Francisco rejected a proposal to build an $80 million stadium as an alternative to Candlestick Park, and New Jersey voters turned down a referendum for a baseball stadium in the Meadowlands. In October, meanwhile, the Hubert H. Humphrey Metrodome in Minneapolis hosted the first indoor World Series games.

Other signs of growth and change: The NBA awarded four new franchises, to join the league by the 1989–90 season. . . . Former NBA great Bob Cousy and a group of promoters created the International Basketball Association for players no taller than 6′4″ (1.93 m). . . . The new American Soccer League, slated to begin operations in spring 1988, would return outdoor professional competition to the United States. . . . Calgary, Canada, and Seoul, South Korea, prepared for the 1988 Winter and Summer Olympics, respectively.

The Year in Sports

© Tony Duffy/Allsport

© Vandystadt/Allsport

© Paul Bereswill/"Sports Illustrated"

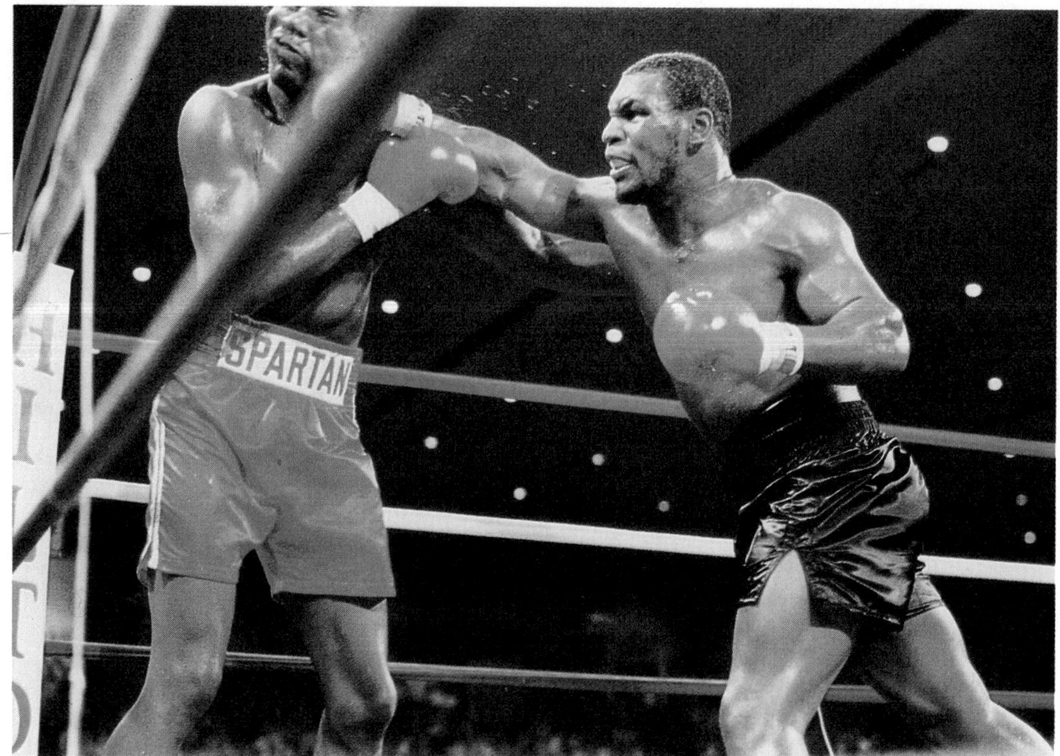

© Manny Millan/"Sports Illustrated"

AP/Wide World

Peak Performances: *The 1987 sports year saw several up-and-coming stars finally reach the top, while some of the established greats also rose to new heights. At the World Track and Field Championships in Rome, Ben Johnson of Canada* (opposite page, top left) *set a world record in the 100 meters. His astounding time of 9.83 seconds bettered Calvin Smith's four-year-old mark by .10 second. West Germany's Steffi Graf* (opposite page, top right) *was the top-ranked player on the women's professional tennis tour. At one point she had triumphed in seven straight tournaments, including the French Open a week short of her 18th birthday. Another young star who reached the pinnacle of his profession was 21-year-old Mike Tyson* (above, punching), *who earned a 12-round unanimous decision over Tony Tucker on August 1 to unify the heavyweight boxing title. The victory raised Tyson's pro record to 31-0, with 27 knockouts. And two great teams of the 1980s returned to championship form. In the National Hockey League, the Edmonton Oilers* (opposite page, bottom, in white) *defeated the Philadelphia Flyers in a seven-game final play-off series. For the Oilers—again led by Wayne Gretzky—the league's MVP for the eighth straight season—it was their third Stanley Cup in four years. In the National Basketball Association, the Los Angeles Lakers defeated the Boston Celtics, four games to two, to capture their fourth league championship of the 1980s. The Lakers were led by Earvin "Magic" Johnson* (right, shooting), *who was named MVP of both the regular season and the play-offs.*

AP/Wide World

Al Unser, Sr., who went to Indianapolis without a car, powered a Penske March-Coswoth to his fourth career victory in the 500, tying the record of A. J. Foyt. Only days short of his 48th birthday, Unser also became Indy's oldest winner.

Auto Racing

Nelson Piquet of Brazil won the Formula One world driving championship by a 12-point margin over Great Britain's Nigel Mansell. France's Alain Prost finished fourth, ending a four-year string in which he was either first or second in the standings. Piquet had three victories to Mansell's six, and backed into the championship when Mansell received heavy bruises and was ruled unable to drive in the season's last two races. Piquet became the fifth driver to win three world championships.

Al Unser, Sr., of Albuquerque, NM, pulled even with A. J. Foyt as the only four-time winners of the Indianapolis 500. Unser, who also won in 1970, 1971, and 1978, was without a car assignment until two weeks before the 1987 race when a crash left Danny Ongais physically unable to drive. Unser then stepped into Ongais' car and took the lead only after mechanical failure sidelined leader Mario Andretti and caused second-place finisher Roberto Guerrero to lose precious time during a pit stop.

Bobby Rahal of Dublin, OH, repeated his championship in the CART-PPG Indy Car series, outpointing runner-up Michael Andretti 188–158. Al Unser, Sr., Guerrero, and Rick Mears rounded the top five finishers. Michael Andretti and Rahal led the series with four victories, while Guerrero, Mario Andretti, and Emerson Fittipaldi were dual winners. Mario Andretti often had the dominant car, only to encounter mechanical failure during the races.

Dale Earnhardt of Mooresville, NC, dominated NASCAR's Winston Cup stock-car championship for the second consecutive year. Earnhardt collected 4,706 points to 4,207 for runner-up Bill Elliott, the Daytona 500 winner. The championship was the third for Earnhardt, who has won 24 races and earned $4,747,311 in the past five seasons.

STAN SUTTON, *"Louisville Courier-Journal"*

AUTO RACING

Major Race Winners, 1987

Indianapolis 500: Al Unser, Sr.
Marlboro 500: Michael Andretti
Quaker State 500: Rick Mears
Daytona 500: Bill Elliott

1987 Champions

Formula One: Nelson Piquet (Brazil)
CART: Bobby Rahal
NASCAR: Dale Earnhardt

Grand Prix for Formula One Cars, 1987

Brazilian: Alain Prost (France)
San Marino: Nigel Mansell (Great Britain)
Belgian: Prost
Monaco: Ayrton Senna (Brazil)
United States: Senna
French: Mansell
British: Mansell
West German: Nelson Piquet (Brazil)
Hungarian: Piquet
Austrian: Mansell
Italian: Piquet
Portuguese: Prost
Spanish: Mansell
Mexican: Mansell
Japanese: Gerhard Berger (Austria)
Australian: Berger

Baseball

The idea was noble: the 1987 baseball season would be dedicated to the late Jackie Robinson, the man who broke the notorious color line of the major leagues 40 years earlier. On April 6, however, with the season just two days old, player personnel director Al Campanis of the Los Angeles Dodgers told a television audience that blacks lacked "the necessities" to be field managers or general managers. After hearing about the remarks, Dodger President

Peter O'Malley fired the longtime executive. The incident sparked a furor that resulted in an affirmative-action plan endorsed by Baseball Commissioner Peter V. Ueberroth, who hired Dr. Harry Edwards, an associate professor of sociology at the University of California, Berkeley, as coordinator of the program.

For major league baseball, 1987 was also the year of the home run—itself a source of controversy. The American League (AL) and National League (NL) together produced a record 4,458 homers, 17% more than the previous high in 1986. The sharp increase led many to believe that the ball was livelier than in previous years and had pitchers and batters scrambling for new ways to outwit each other. During the season, two pitchers—Joe Niekro of the Minnesota Twins and Kevin Gross of the Philadelphia Phillies—were suspended for ten days after being discovered on the mound with illegal substances that could be used to scuff the ball, and one batter—Billy Hatcher of the Houston Astros—got the same penalty for using a cork-filled bat. There were many more accusations.

And in an ongoing battle off the field, players and owners awaited decisions by arbitrators reviewing two grievances over alleged collusion by management against free agents seeking to change teams. On September 21, arbitrator Tom Roberts ruled that the owners had conspired to restrict the movement of 63 players who became free agents after the 1985 season. He ordered players and management to negotiate terms of compensation or be subject to terms imposed by the arbitrator. A second grievance, filed on behalf of the 1986 free-agent class, was still pending as the year came to an end.

Play-Offs and World Series. For the third straight season, baseball had four new divisional winners. The San Francisco Giants won their first National League Western Division title since 1971. Pitching help acquired in midseason trades, coupled with a strong infield defense and a solid lineup, enabled the Giants to pass Cincinnati on August 15 and coast to a divisional title by a six-game margin. In the NL East, the St. Louis Cardinals edged the defending World Champion New York Mets, victims of a decimated pitching staff, by three games. St. Louis survived in September even though cleanup hitter Jack Clark was sidelined with a sprained ankle.

The races were closer in the American League, where the Minnesota Twins won the Western Division championship by two games over the Kansas City Royals, and the Detroit Tigers took the Eastern Division crown by two games over the Toronto Blue Jays.

The Twins won just 85 games but finished first because of an uncanny ability to win at home (where they compiled a 56–25 record), the power of four top sluggers, and the acquisition of ace reliever Jeff Reardon. The Tigers, who won 98 games during the regular season—the most in baseball, were heavily favored in the American League Championship Series (ALCS). But the well-rested Twins took advantage of the weary Tigers, who had had to sweep Toronto in the final weekend to assure a play-off berth. Seeking their first World-Series slot since 1965, the Minnesotans powered their way to a four-games-to-one triumph.

The Twins won the opener, 8-5, as eventual ALCS Most Valuable Player (MVP) Gary Gaetti homered in his first two at bats. The Twins took a 6–3 win the next day, as Detroit ace Jack Morris suffered the loss. Detroit rode a two-run homer by Pat Sheridan to a 7-6 win in Game 3 at Tiger Stadium. But the Twins took the final two contests, 5-3 and 9-5, behind their top pitchers, lefty Frank Viola and righty Bert Blyleven, respectively. The Minnesota bullpen performed especially well throughout the series.

In the National League Championship Series (NLCS), a record four home runs by San Francisco's Jeff Leonard, the MVP, were not enough to offset St. Louis' pitching, which held the Giants scoreless for the last 22 innings of the seven-game matchup.

Frank Viola of the Minnesota Twins was named World Series MVP for his victories in Games 1 and 7. The southpaw ace had a regular-season record of 17-10, with a 2.90 ERA.

AP/Wide World

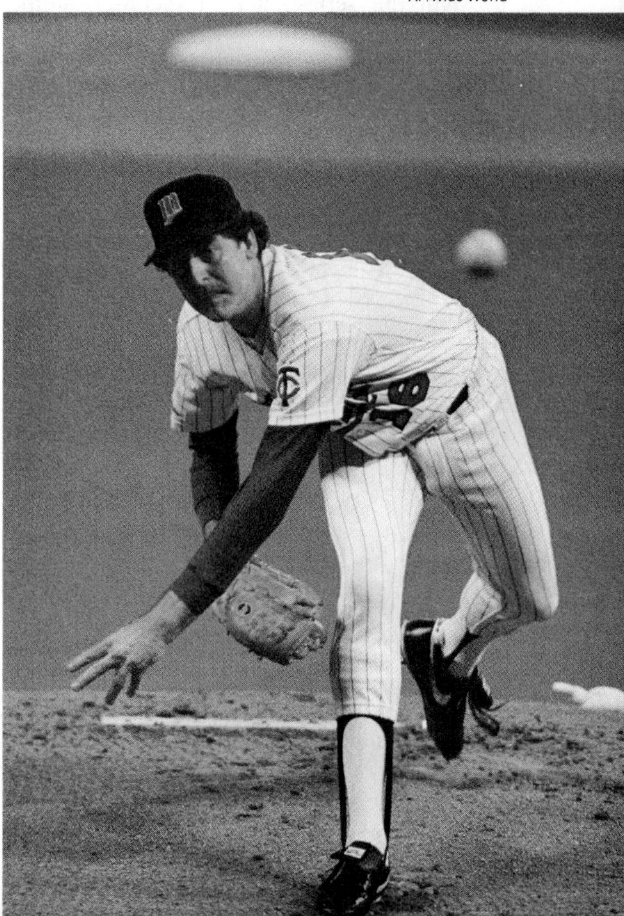

After the Cardinals won the opener, 5-3, Dave Dravecky's 5-0 two-hitter in Game 2 evened the series. Rookie Jim Lindeman drove in three runs in Game 3, sparking the Cards to a 6-5 win, but the Giants then scored successive 4-2 and 6-3 victories, sending the series back to St. Louis. John Tudor and two relievers blanked the Giants, 1-0, in Game 6, and Danny Cox followed with an eight-hit shutout the next night to give the Cards a 6-0 victory and their third World Series berth in six seasons. The big blow in the finale was a rare home run by José Oquendo with two men on base.

In the World Series, billed as a contrast between Minnesota's power and St. Louis' speed, the Twins used Dan Gladden's grand-slam—the first in the World Series since 1970—to give Viola a 10-1 victory in Game 1. Two other homers helped Blyleven to an 8-4 triumph in Game 2, also played at the Hubert H. Humphrey Metrodome in Minneapolis. These were the first World Series games ever played indoors.

Without the raucous support of their fans, however, the Twins fell silent when the series shifted to St. Louis. With just one home run in the three games at Busch Stadium, the Twins watched the Cardinals run wild, stealing five bases in the fifth game. Strong St. Louis relief enabled John Tudor, Bob Forsch, and Danny Cox to win 3-1, 7-2, and 4-2 decisions.

With the series back in the Metrodome, power again took precedence. Don Baylor's homer tied Game 6 in the fifth and Kent Hrbek's grand-slam iced the 11-5 Minnesota victory. Viola, the World Series MVP, pitched eight strong innings to win the finale, 4-2, making the Twins the tenth different world champion in as many years. Never before had the home team won every game in a World Series.

Regular Season. Hitters stole the baseball headlines throughout the 1987 campaign. Four players exceeded 40 home runs, and four teams topped 200, lending credence to the charges that the baseballs were "juiced up." After half a season of slugging that stamped him as an apparent threat to Roger Maris' single-season record of 61 home runs, Mark McGwire of the Oakland Athletics finished with 49 homers, 11 more than any previous rookie, to tie Andre Dawson of the Chicago Cubs for the major league lead. Dawson also led the majors with 137 runs batted in (RBIs) and became the first member of a last-place team to win the National League MVP award. George Bell of the Toronto Blue Jays hit 47 home runs and led the American League with 134 RBIs, figures that earned him AL MVP honors in a close race with Detroit shortstop Alan Trammell.

Both McGwire and San Diego's Benito Santiago, whose 34-game hitting streak from August 25 to October 3 was the longest ever by a first-year player, were unanimous selections as rookies of the year in the American and National Leagues, respectively.

AP/Wide World

Oakland first baseman Mark McGwire, whose 49 homers set a record for first-year players, was a unanimous selection as AL rookie of the year. He batted .289, with 118 RBIs.

After missing spring training in a salary dispute, Boston Red Sox pitcher Roger Clemens won the AL Cy Young Award for the second straight year after leading the league with 20 victories, 18 complete games, and 7 shutouts. Dave Stewart of the Oakland Athletics also won 20 games, two more than NL leader Rick Sutcliffe of the Chicago Cubs. A relief pitcher, Steve Bedrosian of the Philadelphia Phillies, edged Sutcliffe for the NL Cy Young Award after saving 40 games, including a record 13 in a row.

One of the most memorable performances of the season was turned in by Paul Molitor of the Milwaukee Brewers. On July 16, in his first game following reactivation from the disabled list, Molitor began a hitting streak that continued for 39 straight games, the seventh longest in baseball history. He compiled a .405 average during that stretch and finished the season at .353, ten points behind Boston's Wade Boggs, the league's batting champion for the fourth time in five years. Tony Gwynn of the San Diego Padres hit .370 to lead the majors; it was his second NL batting crown.

Former AL batting king Don Mattingly tied Dale Long's 1956 major-league mark by homering in eight straight games, July 8–18, and finished the season with a record six grand slams. Four players—Eric Davis of the Cincinnati Reds, Joe Carter of the Cleveland Indians, and Howard Johnson and Darryl Strawberry of the New York Mets—hit at least 30 home runs and stole as many bases, joining Dale Murphy as active members of the "30–30 club"; only five retired players had accomplished the feat. Vince Coleman of the Cardinals stole 109 bases to lead the majors, while Harold Reynolds of the Seattle Mariners swiped 60 to lead the American League.

Mike Schmidt of the Philadelphia Phillies became the 14th player to hit 500 home runs and finished the year with 35. It was the 13th time he hit at least 30; only Hank Aaron, with 15 seasons of 30 homers, did it more often. Schmidt was one of 15 players who hit three home runs in a 1987 game, but the best display of concentrated hitting was staged by Minnesota's Kirby Puckett on August 29–30. In consecutive nine-inning games, he produced ten hits, tying the major league mark, and hit two home runs in each. Puckett's 6-for-6 performance in the second game was the second of the month in the AL; Kansas City rookie Kevin Seitzer had done it on August 2.

While the hitters flourished, the pitchers suffered. Earned-run averages (ERAs) were up, complete games and saves were down. Houston's Nolan Ryan, at age 40, led the majors with a 2.76 ERA—tied with Toronto's Jimmy Key—and 270 strikeouts, including a season-high 16 on September 9, but he lost 16 of 24 decisions.

The season's only no-hitter was thrown by Milwaukee's Juan Nieves, whose 7–0 victory at Baltimore on April 15 was the first no-hit game in the 18-year history of the Brewers. The Nieves gem came during a 13-game Milwaukee winning streak that tied the record of the 1982 Atlanta Braves for the most consecutive wins at the start of a season.

Seattle's Mark Langston, who led the AL with 262 strikeouts, was one of 15 pitchers to work in the 58th All-Star Game, played in Oakland on July 14. The National League won, 2–0, when Montreal's Tim Raines—who had sat out the first weeks of the season in a salary dispute—singled in the go-ahead run in the 13th inning.

Raines' manager in Montreal, Buck Rodgers, was named NL manager of the year by the Baseball Writers Association of America (BBWAA). Sparky Anderson of Detroit won the AL award, while San Francisco's Roger Craig was named National League manager of the year by The Associated Press.

Three players—pitcher Jim (Catfish) Hunter, outfielder Billy Williams, and star Negro Leagues third baseman Ray Dandridge—were enshrined in the Baseball Hall of Fame.

DAN SCHLOSSBERG, *Baseball Writer*

BASEBALL

Professional—Major Leagues

Final Standings, 1987

AMERICAN LEAGUE

Eastern Division	W	L	Pct.	Western Division	W	L	Pct.
Detroit	98	64	.605	Minnesota	85	77	.525
Toronto	96	66	.593	Kansas City	83	79	.512
Milwaukee	91	71	.562	Oakland	81	81	.500
New York	89	73	.549	Seattle	78	84	.481
Boston	78	84	.481	Chicago	77	85	.475
Baltimore	67	95	.414	California	75	87	.463
Cleveland	61	101	.377	Texas	75	87	.463

NATIONAL LEAGUE

Eastern Division	W	L	Pct.	Western Division	W	L	Pct.
St. Louis	95	67	.586	San Francisco	90	72	.556
New York	92	70	.568	Cincinnati	84	78	.519
Montreal	91	71	.562	Houston	76	86	.469
Philadelphia	80	82	.494	Los Angeles	73	89	.451
Pittsburgh	80	82	.494	Atlanta	69	92	.429
Chicago	76	85	.472	San Diego	65	97	.401

Play-offs—American League: Minnesota defeated Detroit, 4 games to 1; National League: St. Louis defeated San Francisco, 4 games to 3.

World Series—Minnesota defeated St. Louis, 4 games to 3. First Game (Hubert H. Humphrey Metrodome, Minneapolis, Oct. 17, attendance 55,171): Minnesota 10, St. Louis 1; Second Game (Metrodome, Oct. 18, attendance 55,257): Minnesota 8, St. Louis 4; Third Game (Busch Stadium, St. Louis, Oct. 20, attendance 55,347): St. Louis 3, Minnesota 1; Fourth Game (Busch Stadium, Oct. 21, attendance 55,347): St. Louis 7, Minnesota 2; Fifth Game (Busch Stadium, Oct. 22, attendance 55,347): St. Louis 4, Minnesota 2; Sixth Game (Metrodome, Oct. 24, attendance 55,293): Minnesota 11, St. Louis 5; Seventh Game (Metrodome, Oct. 25, attendance 55,387): Minnesota 4, St. Louis 2.

All-Star Game (Oakland, CA, Coliseum, July 14, attendance 49,671): National League 2, American League 0 (13 innings).

Most Valuable Players—American League: George Bell, Toronto; National League: Andre Dawson, Chicago.

Cy Young Memorial Awards (outstanding pitchers)—American League: Roger Clemens, Boston; National League: Steve Bedrosian, Philadelphia.

Managers of the Year—American League: Sparky Anderson, Detroit; National League: Buck Rodgers, Montreal.

Rookies of the Year—American League: Mark McGwire, Oakland; National League: Benito Santiago, San Diego.

Leading Hitters—(Percentage) American League: Wade Boggs, Boston, .363; National League: Tony Gwynn, San Diego, .370. (Runs Batted In) American League: George Bell, Toronto, 134; National League: Andre Dawson, Chicago, 137. (Home Runs) American League: Mark McGwire, Oakland, 49; National League: Dawson, 49. (Hits) American League: tie, Kirby Puckett, Minnesota, and Kevin Seitzer, Kansas City, 207; National League: Gwynn, 218. (Runs) American League: Paul Molitor, Milwaukee, 114; National League: Tim Raines, Montreal, 123.

Leading Pitchers—(Earned Run Average) American League: Jimmy Key, Toronto, 2.76; National League: Nolan Ryan, Houston, 2.76. (Victories) American League: tie, Roger Clemens, Boston, and Dave Stewart, Oakland, 20; National League: Rick Sutcliffe, Chicago, 18. (Strikeouts) American League: Mike Langston, Seattle, 262; National League: Ryan, 270. (Shutouts) American League: Clemens, 7; National League: tie, Rick Reuschel, Pittsburgh and San Francisco, and Bob Welch, Los Angeles, 4. (Saves) American League: Tom Henke, Toronto, 34; National League: Steve Bedrosian, Philadelphia, 40.

Professional—Minor Leagues, Class AAA

American Association: Indianapolis
International League: Columbus
Pacific Coast League: Albuquerque

Amateur

NCAA: Stanford
Little League World Series: Hua Lin, Taiwan

AP/Wide World

Indiana's Keith Smart scores the winning bucket as the Hoosiers defeat Syracuse for the NCAA title.

Basketball

The Los Angeles Lakers defeated the defending champion Boston Celtics, four games to two, in the final round of the 1986–87 National Basketball Association (NBA) play-offs to recapture the league title after a one-year lapse. The Lakers had one of the best years in their history, compiling a 65-17 regular-season record and losing just three times in the play-offs.

In college ball, the University of Nevada-Las Vegas finished the regular season ranked as the No. 1 team, but the Runnin' Rebels were defeated by Indiana University in the semifinal round of the 49th National Collegiate Athletic Association (NCAA) tournament. The Hoosiers went on to the national championship by defeating Syracuse, 74-73, in the tournament final. The Southern Mississippi Golden Eagles won the National Invitation Tournament (NIT), and Tennessee captured the women's NCAA crown.

The Professional Season

Los Angeles had virtually the same team that was knocked out of the play-offs prematurely in 1985–86, but the Lakers parlayed superior play by guard Earvin "Magic" Johnson and superior depth to dominate the league from the very start of the season. Their total of 65 victories during the regular campaign was the highest in the team's history and the fifth highest in NBA history. Their arch rivals, the Celtics, were hampered by injuries throughout the final part of the season and won only 59 games, the first time in four years that they did not reach the 60 level. But Boston still won the Atlantic Division by 14 games over the Philadelphia '76ers. In the Central Division, three teams—the Atlanta Hawks, Detroit Pistons, and Milwaukee Bucks—all won at least 50 games, with Atlanta coming out on top. The Houston Rockets, who had reached the play-off finals in 1986, stumbled badly in the Midwest Division, losing the title to the Dallas Mavericks, who recorded a franchise-high 55 victories. Among the teams showing the greatest improvement were the Indiana Pacers, who won 15 more games than in 1985–86; the Golden State Warriors, who won 12 more games; the Chicago Bulls, who gained ten more victories; and the Portland Trail Blazers, who improved by nine.

The Lakers' Magic Johnson received his first league most valuable player (MVP) award —only the third time that a guard has captured the honor—and led the league in assists (12.2 per game). Johnson's greatest improvement came in scoring, as he averaged a career-high 23.9 points per game. The Bulls' Michael Jordan (*see* BIOGRAPHY) took the scoring title with a 37.1 average and became only the second player in NBA history to score more than 3,000 points in a season. (Wilt Chamberlain was the other.) Forward Charles Barkley of the '76ers led the league in rebounding (14.6), while center Mark Eaton of the Utah Jazz finished first in blocked shots (4.06). The Celtics' Larry Bird became the first player in NBA history to shoot 50% from the field and 90% from the foul line in the same season. Pacers' forward Chuck Person was named rookie of the year, narrowly beating out guard Ron Harper of the Cleveland Cavaliers. Among the other standout performers of the 1986–87 campaign were Kevin McHale of Boston (who led the league in field-goal percentage with .604), Dominique Wilkins of Atlanta (second in scoring at 29.0 per game), Tom Chambers of Seattle (MVP of the all-star game), Alvin Robertson of San Antonio (who led the league in steals with 3.21 per game), Isiah Thomas of Detroit, Akeem Olajuwon of Houston, Dale Ellis of Seattle, Alex English of Denver, and Moses Malone of Washington. Guard John Lucas of Milwaukee returned from drug problems to help give the Bucks another successful season.

In postseason play, the Lakers advanced to the finals with ease, while the Celtics had a much harder time of it. Los Angeles breezed through the first three play-off rounds, losing only one game in its series against Denver, Golden State, and Seattle. (The loss came against Golden State.) Boston, meanwhile, after beating Chicago in three straight, was pushed to seven games against both Milwaukee and Detroit; the Celts won both contests on their home floor. That set up the third final-round confrontation between Boston and Los Angeles in the last four years.

The well-rested, injury-free Lakers, who had the home-court advantage in the series, were heavily favored to win. They lived up to expectations in the first two games, both played in L.A. With their fast break in high gear, the Lakers rolled to a 13-point victory in Game 1, 126-113, and a 19-point romp in Game 2, 141-122. Forward James Worthy had 33 points, and Magic Johnson added 29 in the first contest; all five Laker starters had more than 20 points in the second. There was talk of a four-game sweep.

As they had been all year, however, the Celts were a different team on their home court. With Bird scoring 30 points and guard Dennis Johnson contributing 26, Boston took Game 3 by a 109-103 margin. That set up the pivotal game of the series, also played in the Boston Garden. The Celtics continued their strong play and led by as many as 16 in the second half, but the Lakers returned to their earlier form and rallied to pull out the victory, 107-106, on a driving hook shot by Magic with two seconds left. Now facing a three-games-to-one deficit, Boston battled back in Game 5 and kept their hopes alive with a 123-108 success. Dennis Johnson led the Celts with 33 points.

The series then moved back to Los Angeles, where the Lakers needed only one victory in two games to secure the title. With Magic dishing out 19 assists, the Lakers ran off with a 106-93 triumph in Game 6—and their fourth NBA championship in the 1980s. Johnson, who was brilliant in every game, was named the MVP of the play-offs. Kareem Abdul-Jabbar, the team's 40-year-old center and the league's all-time leading scorer, had 32 points in the final contest. He later agreed to a new two-year contract.

All in all, it was an upbeat season for the NBA. The Laker-Celtic matchup was a classic, registering the highest-ever television ratings for a final round of the play-offs. For the fourth year in a row, the league set a new attendance record. And the decision was made to add four new franchises—Charlotte, Minneapolis, Miami, and Orlando—by the end of the decade.

On the down side, however, drug problems continued to make headlines. Celtic draft pick Len Bias died of cocaine overdose prior to the start of the season; three current and two former Phoenix Suns players were indicted by a grand jury on charges of possessing or trafficking cocaine; and two Houston players—Lewis Lloyd and Mitchell Wiggins—were banned from the NBA, perhaps for life, for violating the league's drug policy.

Finally, basketball fans everywhere said good-bye to one of the game's most colorful and respected stars, Julius "Dr. J" Erving of the '76ers. The high-flying forward retired at the end of the season, after becoming only the third player to score more than 30,000 points in his professional career. On his final visit to each league city, Dr. J was saluted with special ceremonies and lengthy standing ovations.

The College Season

The most controversial figure of the 1986–87 college basketball season also wound up being the year's most successful coach. Bob Knight, the fiery veteran coach at Indiana University, guided the Hoosiers (24-4 during the regular season) to their third NCAA championship in his 16 years at the school. He was also the subject of a rare best-selling sports book, *A Season on the Brink,* by John Feinstein. Feinstein spent the 1985–86 season with Knight and the Hoosiers, and his intimate portrait of Knight's coaching habits caused a stir among followers of the game.

At the start of the 1986–87 season, Knight's Hoosiers were among a handful of teams considered good enough to win the NCAA title. Along with Indiana, such schools as Louisville, North Carolina, Nevada-Las Vegas, Purdue, Georgia Tech, Kentucky, and Kansas were regarded as the best in the nation. Louisville, the defending national champion, ended up having a mediocre season (17-14) and was not even invited to the NCAA tournament. Georgia Tech (16-12), Kentucky (18-10), and Kansas (23-10) all were relatively successful. And the others were outstanding. Nevada-Las Vegas (33-1) and North Carolina (28-3) topped the wire service polls for most of the season; Purdue (23-4) tied Indiana for the Big Ten championship. Other outstanding teams during the year included Alabama (26-4), Clemson (25-5), DePaul (26-2), Florida (21-10), Georgetown (26-4), Illinois (23-7), Iowa (27-4), Pittsburgh (24-7), Syracuse (26-6), and Temple (31-3). The Big Ten, Atlantic Coast, Southeastern, and Big East were widely regarded as the best conferences in the nation.

One of the highlights of the 1986–87 NCAA season was the addition of the controversial three-point shot. Under the new rule, three points were awarded for any shot made from outside a circle 18′ 8″ (5.69 m) from the basket. The three-point shot had a significant impact on the game throughout the season, including the NCAA tournament. A number of coaches and commentators voiced opposition to the new rule; many contended that the distance was simply too short. One of the opponents, ironically, was Indiana's Bob Knight, whose team reaped enormous benefits.

In part because of the three-point shot, the NCAA tournament saw a number of upsets. North Carolina, which entered the tourney ranked No. 2 in the nation behind Nevada-Las Vegas, lost in the East Regional final to Syracuse. Georgetown, the Big East champion and top seed in the Southeast Region, fell to another Big East entry, Providence, in the regional finals. Earlier, such powers as Temple,

PROFESSIONAL BASKETBALL

National Basketball Association
(Final Standings, 1986–87)

Eastern Conference

Atlantic Division	W	L	Pct.
*Boston	59	23	.720
*Philadelphia	45	37	.549
*Washington	42	40	.512
New Jersey	24	58	.293
New York	24	58	.293
Central Division			
*Atlanta	57	25	.695
*Detroit	52	30	.634
*Milwaukee	50	32	.610
*Indiana	41	41	.500
*Chicago	40	42	.488
Cleveland	31	51	.378

Western Conference

Midwest Division	W	L	Pct.
*Dallas	55	27	.671
*Utah	44	38	.537
*Houston	42	40	.512
*Denver	37	45	.451
Sacramento	29	53	.354
San Antonio	28	54	.341
Pacific Division			
*L.A. Lakers	65	17	.793
*Portland	49	33	.598
*Golden State	42	40	.512
*Seattle	39	43	.476
Phoenix	36	46	.439
L.A. Clippers	12	70	.146

*Made play-offs

Play-Offs

Eastern Conference

First Round	Atlanta	3 games	Indiana	1
	Boston	3 games	Chicago	0
	Detroit	3 games	Washington	0
	Milwaukee	3 games	Philadelphia	2
Second Round	Boston	4 games	Milwaukee	3
	Detroit	4 games	Atlanta	1
Finals	Boston	4 games	Detroit	3

Western Conference

First Round	Golden State	3 games	Utah	2
	Houston	3 games	Portland	1
	L.A. Lakers	3 games	Denver	0
	Seattle	3 games	Dallas	1
Second Round	L.A. Lakers	4 games	Golden State	1
	Seattle	4 games	Houston	2
Finals	L.A. Lakers	4 games	Seattle	0
Championship	L.A. Lakers	4 games	Boston	2
All-Star Game	West 154, East 149			

Individual Honors

Most Valuable Player: Earvin "Magic" Johnson, Los Angeles Lakers
Most Valuable Player (play-offs): Earvin "Magic" Johnson
Most Valuable Player (all-star game): Tom Chambers, Seattle
Rookie of the Year: Chuck Person, Indiana
Coach of the Year: Mike Schuler, Portland
Leading Scorer: Michael Jordan, Chicago, 37.1 points per game
Leader in Assists: Earvin "Magic" Johnson, 12.2 per game
Leading Rebounder: Charles Barkley, Philadelphia, 14.6 per game
Leader in Field Goal Percentage: Kevin McHale, Boston, .604

DePaul, Clemson, Purdue, and Illinois all were upset.

With so many favorites losing, the way was open for some upstart teams to make it to the Final Four. One of these was Providence, which finished fifth in the Big East during the regular season. Under second-year coach Rick Pitino and led by guard Billy Donovan, the Friars combined scrappy defense and great outside shooting, especially from three-point range, to defeat such heavyweights as Georgetown and Alabama on the road to the Final Four. Syracuse, another Big East team, was more highly regarded than Providence, but Jim Boeheim's Orangemen were still a long shot to reach the finals. Among their victims along the way were North Carolina and Duke. The two other Final Four teams, Nevada-Las Vegas and Indiana, both had entered the tournament as the top seeds in their regions. The Runnin' Rebels counted Iowa and Wyoming among their West Region victims, while the Hoosiers had defeated the likes of Louisiana State and Duke in the Midwest Region.

In the Final Four at New Orleans, Indiana and Nevada-Las Vegas were matched in one semifinal, while Syracuse and Providence played in the other. In the former, Indiana took a 14-point lead in the first half, but Nevada-Las Vegas stormed back to take the lead. The Hoosiers ultimately prevailed, 97-93, as All-America guard Steve Alford netted 33 points. In the other semifinal, Syracuse dominated the boards and took away Providence's three-point shooting, notching an easy 77-63 victory.

In the championship game, Syracuse led for most of the second half and seemed on the verge of a major upset. The underdog Orangemen took a 12-point lead with 12 minutes left to play and still led by three with only 38 seconds remaining. But the Hoosiers, led by Alford's backcourt mate, Keith Smart, engineered a stunning comeback and eked out a 74-73 victory. Smart, who scored 12 of his team's last 15 points, sank a 17-foot jump shot with five seconds on the clock to give the Hoosiers the championship. Alford scored 23 points in the contest—including seven three-pointers—but MVP honors for the Final Four went to Smart. The Syracuse attack was led by guard Sherman Douglas, who finished with 20 points; center Ron Seikaly had 19 points, and freshman forward Derrick Coleman hauled in 19 rebounds.

Indiana's Alford was one of five players selected unanimously for virtually every All-America team. Center David Robinson of Navy, who was among the nation's leaders in scoring, rebounding, field-goal percentage, and blocked shots, was everyone's choice as collegiate player of the year. He was also the first player picked in the NBA college draft. (Because of his commitment to the Navy, however, it would be at least two years before he could play professionally.) Joining Alford and Robinson as consensus All-Americas were guard Kenny Smith of North Carolina, forward Reggie Williams of Georgetown, and forward Danny Manning of Kansas. Among the year's other standout players were Armon Gilliam of Nevada-Las Vegas, Dennis Hopson of Ohio State, freshman J. R. Reid of North Carolina, Kevin Houston of Army (the nation's leading scorer), Jerome Lane of Pittsburgh (the nation's leading rebounder), Horace Grant of Clemson, Reggie Lewis of Northeastern, Reggie Miller of UCLA, Nate Blackwell of Temple, Dallas Comegys of DePaul, Ken Norman of Illinois, Christian Welp of Washington, and Mark Jackson of St. John's.

In other men's collegiate competition, Southern Mississippi defeated La Salle, 84-80, to win the 50th National Invitation Tournament (NIT). Southern Miss, which relied heavily on the three-pointer, was led by tournament MVP Randolph Keys.

In women's play, Tennessee upset Louisiana Tech, 67-44, to give coach Pat Head her first NCAA title after seven previous trips to the Final Four. Louisiana Tech had reached the title game by beating top-seeded Texas, the defending champion. Tennessee freshman guard Tonya Edwards won tournament MVP honors.

PAUL ATTNER
"The Sporting News"

COLLEGE BASKETBALL

Conference Champions*

Atlantic Coast: North Carolina State
Atlantic-10: Temple
Big East: Georgetown
Big Eight: Missouri
Big Sky: Idaho State
Big Ten: Indiana, Purdue (tied)
Colonial Athletic: Navy
East Coast: Bucknell
ECAC Metro: Marist
ECAC North: Northeastern
Ivy League: Pennsylvania
Metro: Memphis State
Metro Atlantic Athletic: Fairfield
Mid-American: Central Michigan
Mid-Continent: S.W. Missouri State
Mid-Eastern Athletic: North Carolina A&T
Midwestern Collegiate: Xavier
Missouri Valley: Wichita State
Ohio Valley: Austin Prep
Pacific Coast Athletic: Nevada-Las Vegas
Pacific-10: UCLA
Southeastern: Alabama
Southern: Marshall
Southland: Louisiana Tech
Southwest: Texas A&M
Southwestern Athletic: Southern U.
Sun Belt: Alabama-Birmingham
Trans America Athletic: Georgia Southern
West Coast Athletic: Santa Clara
Western Athletic: Wyoming

* Based on postseason conference tournaments, where applicable

Tournaments

NCAA: Indiana
NIT: Southern Mississippi
NCAA Div. II: Kentucky Wesleyan
NCAA Div. III: North Park College
NCIA: Washburn
NCAA (women's): Tennessee

Boxing

Among 1987's boxing highlights, the biggest attraction and one of the biggest upsets in the history of the sport came when Sugar Ray Leonard scored a split decision over Marvelous Marvin Hagler to take the middleweight title in a bout that generated more than $30 million in revenue.

Leonard was a 3–1 underdog and had not fought in three years. He had gone into retirement after suffering a detached retina, but the lure of a bout with the brawling Hagler, who had not lost a fight in 11 years, and an $11 million payday made him attempt the comeback. The risk of further damage to his eye added to the buildup for the bout.

Another highlight concerned Mike Tyson (*see* BIOGRAPHY), who in 1986 at 19 became the youngest battler to wear a heavyweight championship belt when he took the World Boxing Council (WBC) title. The 20-year-old Tyson unified the title by adding the World Boxing Association (WBA) and International Boxing Federation (IBF) crowns in 1987. Tyson established his undisputed status with two title fights in Las Vegas. Early in the year, he tacked on the WBA title with a unanimous decision over James (Bonecrusher) Smith in a 12-round bout. On August 1, Tyson took the IBF title away from Tony Tucker, who had captured the vacant crown two months earlier, with another 12-round unanimous decision. In June, between the two title fights, Tyson scored an impressive sixth-round knockout of Pinklon Thomas, a former champion.

On October 16 at Atlantic City in his first defense as undisputed champion, Tyson called on his storehouse of punching power against Tyrell Biggs, the 1984 Olympic champion. He scored a bruising seventh-round knockout and regained his reputation as a fearsome knockout specialist. Tyson's record was 32–0 as 1987 ended.

In December, Evander Holyfield knocked out Dwight Muhammad Qawi in the fourth round and retained his IBF and WBA cruiserweight titles. It was an impressive victory for the unbeaten Holyfield, now 17–0 with 13 knockouts, who has announced his intention of moving into the heavyweight division to seek a fight with undisputed champion Mike Tyson.

Thomas Hearns, who was among ten fighters who had won three different world titles, became the first to claim four when he stopped Juan Domingo Roldan of Argentina for the WBC middleweight title with a fourth-round knockout at Las Vegas in October. The championship had become vacant when Leonard had retired once again after beating Hagler April 6. Hearns previously held the WBA welterweight title, the WBC junior middleweight title, and the WBC light heavyweight crown.

Gerry Cooney, once a prime contender for the heavyweight crown, came out of a long layoff to lose to a talented Michael Spinks, who gave up the IBF heavyweight title he took from Larry Holmes, so he could fight Cooney. The unbeaten Spinks stopped Cooney, who weighed 238 pounds to Spinks' 208, in the fifth round on June 15 at Atlantic City. Spinks had bypassed the Home Box Office television "unification" series and a potential bout with Tyson to fight Cooney. Spinks earned $4 million, Cooney $2.5 million.

In February, Mark Breland, unbeaten in 17 bouts, became the first gold medalist from the 1984 U.S. Olympic team to win a world professional boxing title. Breland suffered a broken hand in the first round of his bout against Harold Volbrecht of South Africa, but was able to score a seventh-round knockout and win the then vacant WBA welterweight title at Atlantic City. Breland later lost the crown in an upset to Marlon Starling.

At Las Vegas Hilton's stadium in November, Julio Cesar Chavez completely demolished Edwin Rosario to take the WBA lightweight crown. The referee stopped the fight in the 11th round. Prior to the bout, Chavez had moved up five pounds from the super featherweight class. He had been the WBC champion in that division since September 1984.

GEORGE DEGREGORIO, *"The New York Times"*

World Boxing Champions*

Heavyweight: World Boxing Council (WBC)—Mike Tyson, United States, 1986; World Boxing Association (WBA)—Tyson, 1987; International Boxing Federation (IBF)—Tyson, 1987.

Cruiserweight: WBC—Carlos deLeon, Puerto Rico, 1986; WBA—Evander Holyfield, United States, 1986; IBF—Holyfield, 1987.

Light Heavyweight: WBC—Don La Londe, Canada, 1987; WBA—Virgil Hill, United States, 1987; IBF—Charles Williams, United States, 1987.

Middleweight: WBC—Thomas Hearns, United States, 1987; WBA—Sumbu Kalambay, Italy and Zaire, 1987; IBF—Frank Tate, United States, 1987.

Junior Middleweight (Super Welterweight): WBC—Gianfranco Rosi, Italy, 1987; WBA—Julian Jackson, Virgin Islands, 1987; IBF—Matthew Hilton, Canada, 1987.

Welterweight: WBC—Jorge Vaca, Mexico, 1987; WBA—Marlon Starling, United States, 1987; IBF—vacant.

Junior Welterweight: WBC—Roger Mayweather, United States, 1987; WBA—Juan Martin Coggi, Argentina, 1987; IBF—vacant.

Lightweight: WBC—José Luis Ramirez, Mexico, 1987; WBA—Julio Cesar Chavez, Mexico, 1987; IBF—Vincent Pazienza, United States, 1987.

Junior Lightweight (Super Featherweight): WBC—vacant. WBA—Brian Mitchell, South Africa, 1986; IBF—Rocky Lockridge, United States, 1987.

Featherweight: WBC—Azumah Nelson, Ghana, 1984; WBA—Antonio Esparragoza, Venezuela, 1987; IBF—Antonio Rivera, Puerto Rico, 1986.

Junior Featherweight (Super Bantamweight): WBC—Jeff Fenech, Australia, 1987; WBA—Julio Gervacio, Dominican Republic, 1987; IBF—Seung Hoon Lee, South Korea, 1987.

Bantamweight: WBC—Miguel Lora, Colombia, 1985; WBA—Wilfredo Vasquez, Puerto Rico, 1987; IBF—Kevin Seabrooks, United States, 1987.

Junior Bantamweight (Super Flyweight): WBC—Jesus (Sugar Baby) Rojas, Colombia, 1987; WBA—Khaosai Galaxy, Thailand, 1984; IBF—Elly Pical, Indonesia, 1985.

Flyweight: WBC—Sot Chitalada, Thailand, 1984; WBA—Fidel Bassa, Colombia, 1987; IBF—Chang Ho-Choi, South Korea, 1987.

Junior Flyweight: WBC—Chang Jung-Koo, South Korea, 1983; WBA—Yoo Myong-Woo, South Korea, 1985; IBF—Choi Jum Hwan, South Korea, 1986.

*As of Dec. 31, 1987; date indicates year title was won.

Football

In an unusual, strike-marred season that was a disappointment to many fans, the National Football League (NFL) crowned yet another new champion in 1987–88. With the regular season shortened from 16 to 15 games because of a players' union strike, and with the use of "replacement players" making three weeks of games about as predictable as a referee's coin-toss, the final standings underwent some surprising changes from previous years. The New York Giants, for one, fell from a record of 14-2 and a Super Bowl championship to a mark of 6-9 and a last-place finish in the National Conference's Eastern Division. When all was said and done, however, the battle for the NFL crown came down to two perennially powerful teams that had been strong contenders the previous year.

Super Bowl XXII, played on Jan. 31, 1988, at San Diego's Jack Murphy Stadium, pitted the American Football Conference (AFC) champion Denver Broncos, making their second straight Super Bowl appearance, and the National Football Conference (NFC) champion Washington Redskins, who had fallen to the Giants in the NFC title game the year before. After giving up ten points to the Broncos in the first quarter, the Redskins scored an incredible 35 points in the second quarter and went on to a 42–10 win. Redskins' quarterback Doug Williams was the game's most valuable player.

In collegiate competition, the unofficial national champion was determined for the second year in a row by the outcome of a major bowl game. The Miami Hurricanes (12-0) laid claim to the honors with a 20-14 victory over Oklahoma in the Orange Bowl on New Year's Day 1988. Tim Brown, Notre Dame's flashy wide receiver and kick-return specialist, won the Heisman Trophy.

The Canadian Football League (CFL) faced problems that stood in marked contrast to those in the NFL. With the league struggling to survive, CFL players accepted a 10% pay cut, and team owners agreed to a $3 million cap on expenses. The league got a boost, however, with a Grey Cup game—the CFL's version of the Super Bowl—that was as exciting as any in its 75-year history. The Edmonton Eskimos claimed the trophy with a 38-36 victory over the Toronto Argonauts on a 49-yard, last-minute field goal by Jerry Kauric. Played November 29 in Vancouver, the game featured a 115-yard touchdown run by Edmonton's Henry Williams on a return of a missed field goal attempt. (The field in CFL competition is 120 yards.) Eskimo quarterback Damon Allen was the game's most valuable offensive player.

The summer months witnessed the birth of the Arena Football League, with games played on a 50-yard indoor field with eight men on a team.

National Football League

The season began under a cloud, with the general contract between team owners and the NFL Players' Association (NFLPA) already having expired and the two sides having failed even to sit down at the bargaining table. Under the executive directorship of former player Gene Upshaw (*see* BIOGRAPHY), the union made good on its threats and called a strike on September 22, after the second week of games. The major sticking point was the union's demand for free agency, which would allow a player to entertain and choose freely among competitive bids from any and all teams once the contract with his current team has expired. Other issues included pension benefits, salary scales, drug testing, roster size, and protection for union representatives.

The walkout forced the cancellation of the following weekend's games, but the owners announced that the schedule then would be resumed with "replacement players" (called "scabs" by some) and the handful of the league's 1,585 players who refused to join the strike. The substitute games were marked by a clearly inferior level of play and meager stadium attendance, but the owners appeared to have less to lose than the players and stuck to their guns in opposition to free agency.

After the second week of replacement games, and with 15% of union players having crossed the picket lines, the NFLPA called off the strike on October 14. The final outrage for the union came when team owners refused to allow the striking players to compete in or be paid for the following weekend's games. The NFLPA filed a federal antitrust suit against the league and won a complaint with the National Labor Relations Board on the final missed games. The court ruling on free agency, however, was expected to take many months more.

With the replacement games counting in the standings and with some teams more affected by the layoff than others, the race for the playoffs took some unexpected turns. By the end of regular-season play, some unlikely teams had qualified for postseason play. In the AFC, the Indianapolis Colts (9-6) registered their first winning record in ten years and captured the Eastern Division title. The Houston Oilers (9-6) earned their first postseason appearance in seven years as a "wild-card" entry from the Central Division. The other AFC play-off qualifiers were not unexpected: the Broncos (10-4-1) and Cleveland Browns (10-5) repeated as champions of the Western and Central divisions, respectively, and the Seattle Seahawks (9-6) claimed the other wild-card berth.

The NFC play-off picture had some surprises, too. Most notably, the New Orleans Saints (12-3), who had never had a winning season or a postseason appearance in the 20 years of their existence, qualified for the play-offs as

© Jose R. Lopez/NYT Pictures

AP/Wide World

In the NFC championship game, left, *Washington's defense rose to the occasion, sealing a 17-10 victory over Minnesota. In the AFC title contest,* right, *Denver scored five touchdowns, as the Broncos defeated Cleveland, 38-33.*

a wild-card entry from the Western Division. The only team in the entire league with a better record was the San Francisco 49ers (13-2). The Redskins (11-4) supplanted the Giants as champions of the Eastern Division, and the Chicago Bears (11-4) finished atop the Central Division. The Minnesota Vikings (8-7), despite having lost all three of their replacement games, squeaked in as the other NFC wild-card entry.

The first week of the play-offs, pitting the wild-card teams in each conference, continued the string of surprises. In the AFC, the Oilers defeated the heavily favored Seahawks, 23-20, on an overtime field goal by Tony Zendejas. In the NFC contest, the underdog Vikings thoroughly dominated the Saints, 44-10.

The following weekends' games produced at least one result that could be counted as an upset. The "Cinderella" Vikings traveled to San Francisco to take on the powerful 49ers and dealt them an eyebrow-raising 36-24 defeat; Minnesota was led by Anthony Carter, who caught ten passes for 227 yards, the latter an NFL play-off record. In the other NFC contest, the Redskins took on the Bears at Chicago's frigid Soldier Field and rallied from a two-touchdown deficit to earn a 21-17 victory. In the AFC, the favored Browns had the home-field advantage against the Colts and rolled to a 38-21 victory. The Broncos, also playing at home, demolished Houston, 34-10.

Both conference championship games were close and exciting. The AFC matchup, between Denver and Cleveland, was a repeat of the previous year's contest, in which the Broncos came from behind and won on a field goal in overtime. This time, the home-field Broncos took a commanding 21-3 half-time lead but barely staved off a second-half Browns rally, winning 38-33. Denver thus became the first team since the Pittsburgh Steelers in 1979-80 to repeat as AFC champions. In the NFC championship contest, Washington and Minnesota played to a 7-7 standoff in the first half, but the 'Skins, playing in front of their home fans, proved more powerful in the end. Their 17-10 victory put them in the Super Bowl for the third time in the 1980s.

The NFL's rushing leader in 1987-88 was another of the year's surprises, as Charles White of the Los Angeles Rams ran for 1,374 yards (only four fewer than his six-year total entering the season). White took the place in the Rams' backfield of Eric Dickerson, who was traded to the Colts in midseason. Dickerson, who became the first player in league history to rush for more than 8,000 yards in his first five seasons, wound up leading the AFC with 1,288 yards. Another outstanding runner, rookie Bo Jackson of the Los Angeles Raiders, became one of only a handful of athletes in history to compete in two professional sports in the same year; he also played baseball for the Kansas City Royals. And as Jackson was beginning his pro football career, the NFL's all-time leading rusher, Chicago's Walter Payton, was bringing his to a close. After 13 years in the league, Payton totaled 16,726 rushing yards, 21,803 combined yards, and 492 pass receptions; the latter figure also represented a career record for NFL running backs.

Despite the prominence of running backs, the year's most consistently exciting performer was San Francisco wide receiver Jerry Rice, who set an NFL single-season record with 22 touchdown catches and was named player of the year. Other outstanding performers included St. Louis wide receiver J. T. Smith, who led the league in receptions with 91; quarterbacks Joe Montana of San Francisco and Bernie Kosar, the top-rated passers in the NFC and AFC, respectively; defensive lineman Reggie White of Philadelphia, who topped the league in sacks with 21; Washington's Barry Wilburn, who led all defensive backs with nine interceptions; and Buffalo linebacker Shane Conlan, who was named NFL rookie of the year.

Twelve-year veteran Steve Largent of Seattle caught 58 passes to surpass Charlie Joiner as the league's all-time leading receiver; he ended the season with 752 career catches. Largent also extended his own NFL records for consecutive games with a reception (to 152), most seasons with 50 or more receptions (10), and most seasons with 1,000 or more receiving yards (8).

On August 8, seven former stars were inducted into the Pro Football Hall of Fame in Canton, OH: Larry Csonka, Len Dawson, "Mean" Joe Greene, John Henry Johnson, Jim Langer, Don Maynard, and—taking time out from his role as head of the players' union—Gene Upshaw.

PROFESSIONAL FOOTBALL

National Football League

Final Standings

NATIONAL CONFERENCE

Eastern Division	W	L	T	Pct.	Points For	Points Against
Washington	11	4	0	.733	379	285
Dallas	7	8	0	.467	340	348
St. Louis	7	8	0	.467	362	368
Philadelphia	7	8	0	.467	337	380
N.Y. Giants	6	9	0	.400	280	312
Central Division						
Chicago	11	4	0	.733	356	282
Minnesota	8	7	0	.533	336	335
Green Bay	5	9	1	.367	255	300
Detroit	4	11	0	.267	269	384
Tampa Bay	4	11	0	.267	286	360
Western Division						
San Francisco	13	2	0	.867	459	253
New Orleans	12	3	0	.800	422	283
L.A. Rams	6	9	0	.400	317	361
Atlanta	3	12	0	.200	205	436

PLAY-OFFS

Minnesota 44, New Orleans 10
Minnesota 36, San Francisco 24
Washington 21, Chicago 17
Washington 17, Minnesota 10

AMERICAN CONFERENCE

Eastern Division	W	L	T	Pct.	Points For	Points Against
Indianapolis	9	6	0	.600	300	238
New England	8	7	0	.533	320	293
Miami	8	7	0	.533	362	335
Buffalo	7	8	0	.467	270	305
N.Y. Jets	6	9	0	.400	334	360
Central Division						
Cleveland	10	5	0	.667	390	239
Houston	9	6	0	.600	345	349
Pittsburgh	8	7	0	.533	285	299
Cincinnati	4	11	0	.267	285	370
Western Division						
Denver	10	4	1	.700	379	288
Seattle	9	6	0	.600	371	314
San Diego	8	7	0	.533	253	317
L.A. Raiders	5	10	0	.333	301	289
Kansas City	4	11	0	.267	273	388

PLAY-OFFS

Houston 23, Seattle 20
Cleveland 38, Indianapolis 21
Denver 34, Houston 10
Denver 38, Cleveland 33

SUPER BOWL XXII: Washington 42, Denver 10

The College Season

After a season in which they had risen to the number 1 ranking but lost the unofficial national championship to then-number 2 Penn State in a Fiesta Bowl upset, the Miami Hurricanes entered the 1987 season with one goal in mind: another chance. As it all turned out, the script went very much as they had hoped. After compiling an 11-0 record in the regular season, they entered the Orange Bowl as the second-ranked team in the country. Their opponents in that contest were the top-ranked Oklahoma Sooners, boasting their own 11-0 record as well as the nation's stingiest defense and most potent offense (averaging an amazing 499 yards and 43.5 points per game). And if a national championship were not incentive enough, the Sooners were seeking revenge of their own, having lost to Miami in their two previous meetings, in 1985 and 1986.

Miami began the scoring with a 65-yard opening drive that culminated in a 30-yard touchdown pass from quarterback Steve Walsh to fullback Melvin Bratton. Oklahoma's "wishbone" offense banged in the tying touchdown just before halftime, following an interception by all-America safety Rickey Dixon. Miami scored on its first two possessions in the third quarter—a 56-yard field goal by Greg Cox (the longest in Orange Bowl history) and a 23-yard TD pass from Walsh to Michael Irvin. Cox added a 48-yard field goal, and the Hurricanes blew to a 20-14 victory.

With Oklahoma falling to number 3 in the final wire-service polls, Florida State (11-1) laid claim to the number 2 ranking with a 31-28 victory over Nebraska (10-2) in the Fiesta Bowl, also played on New Year's Day. Nebraska, which had ranked first in the country before a 17-7 home-field loss to Big Eight rival Oklahoma in a classic late-November battle, finished sixth in the final polls.

AP/Wide World

Tim Brown, Notre Dame's flanker and kick returner, won the Heisman Trophy as the nation's top college player. He became the seventh Notre Dame player to win the award.

COLLEGE FOOTBALL

Conference Champions	Atlantic Coast—Clemson Big Eight—Oklahoma Big Ten—Michigan State Ivy League—Harvard Mid-American—Eastern Michigan Pacific Coast—San Jose State Pacific Ten—(tie) UCLA, USC Southeastern—Auburn Southland—Northeast Louisiana Southwest—Texas A&M Western Athletic—Wyoming
NCAA Champions	Division I-AA—Northeast Louisiana Division II—Troy State Division III—Wagner
NAIA Champions	Division I—Cameron (OK) Division II—(tie) Wisconsin-Stevens Point and Pacific Lutheran (WA)
Individual Honors	Heisman Trophy—Tim Brown, Notre Dame Lombardi Award—Chris Spielman, Ohio State Outland Trophy—Chad Hennings, Air Force

Major Bowl Games

All-American Bowl (Birmingham, AL, Dec. 22)—Virginia 22, Brigham Young 16
Aloha Bowl (Honolulu, HI, Dec. 25)—UCLA 20, Florida 16
Bluebonnet Bowl (Houston, Dec. 31)—Texas 32, Pittsburgh 27
California Bowl (Fresno, CA, Dec. 12)—Eastern Michigan 30, San Jose State 27
Cotton Bowl (Dallas, Jan. 1)—Texas A&M 35, Notre Dame 10
Fiesta Bowl (Tempe, AZ, Jan. 1)—Florida State 31, Nebraska 28
Florida Citrus Bowl (Orlando, Jan. 1)—Clemson 35, Penn State 10
Freedom Bowl (Anaheim, CA, Dec. 30)—Arizona State 33, Air Force 28
Gator Bowl (Jacksonville, FL, Dec. 31)—Louisiana State 30, South Carolina 13
Hall of Fame Bowl (Tampa, FL, Jan. 2)—Michigan 28, Alabama 24
Holiday Bowl (San Diego, CA, Dec. 30)—Iowa 20, Wyoming 19
Independence Bowl (Shreveport, LA, Dec. 19)—Washington 24, Tulane 12
Liberty Bowl (Memphis, TN, Dec. 29)—Georgia 20, Arkansas 17
Orange Bowl (Miami, Jan. 1)—Miami 20, Oklahoma 14
Peach Bowl (Atlanta, Jan. 2)—Tennessee 27, Indiana 22
Rose Bowl (Pasadena, CA, Jan. 1)—Michigan State 20, Southern California 17
Sugar Bowl (New Orleans, Jan. 1)—Syracuse 16, Auburn 16
Sun Bowl (El Paso, TX, Dec. 25)—Oklahoma State 35, West Virginia 33

The most controversial postseason contest was the Sugar Bowl matchup between Syracuse, which entered the game 11-0 on the strength of the passing and running of all-America quarterback Don McPherson, and Auburn, the champions of the Southeastern Conference. The controversy came with four seconds left, when Auburn, trailing 16-13 but on Syracuse's 13 yard line, opted for a tying field goal instead of a winning touchdown. The 16-16 deadlock gave Syracuse the number 4 spot in the final polls and Auburn (9-1-2) a number 7 ranking.

Louisiana State's 30-13 trouncing of South Carolina (8-4) in the Gator Bowl gave the Tigers (10-1-1) the fifth position in the polls. And Big Ten champion Michigan State (9-2-1) defeated Pac Ten co-champion Southern California (8-4) in the Rose Bowl, 20-17, for a final number 8 ranking.

In the Heisman balloting, Notre Dame's Tim Brown, who combined for 1,847 total yards in pass receptions, punt and kick returns, and rushing, finished well ahead of Syracuse's McPherson, the nation's top-rated quarterback. Brown became the seventh Notre Dame player to win the award and the first recipient since 1949 who was not a running back or quarterback. Finishing third in the balloting was sentimental favorite Gordie Lockbaum, a two-way (offensive and defensive) player for Division I-AA Holy Cross. Also receiving votes were Michigan State tailback Lorenzo White, who scampered for 1,459 yards, and Pittsburgh's junior tailback Craig Heyward, who powered for 1,655 yards.

The Outland Trophy for the nation's outstanding interior lineman was awarded to senior defensive tackle Chad Hennings of the Air Force Academy. The Lombardi Award for the best lineman or linebacker went to senior linebacker Chris Spielman of Ohio State, who made 78 solo tackles and 156 in all. Coach of the year honors went to Syracuse's Dick MacPherson (no relation to his star quarterback). And everyone's choice for freshman of the year was Florida running back Emmitt Smith, who rushed for a school-record 1,341 yards and became the first freshman ever to eclipse the 1,000-yard mark after his first seven games.

Other standout players throughout the season—and consensus all-Americas—included offensive linemen John McCormick of Nebraska, Mark Hutson of Oklahoma, Randall McDaniel of Arizona State, John Elliott of Michigan, and Dave Cadigan of Southern California; tight end Keith Jackson of Oklahoma; center Ignazio Albergamo of Louisiana State; defensive lineman Daniel Stubbs of Miami; linebacker Dante Jones of Oklahoma; defensive backs Bennie Blades of Miami and Deion Sanders of Florida State; and kicker David Treadwell of Clemson.

JEFFREY H. HACKER

Golf

The United States Professional Golfers' Association Tour was awash in the color of money in 1987, a year in which major winners were dispersed and the world of golf got bigger.

Curtis Strange won three tournaments and an incredible $925,941, breaking Greg Norman's year-old earnings record by almost $300,000. Strange and the other top players benefited from an infusion of commercial cash, Strange pocketing an extra $175,000 in official money by winning the season-long Nabisco Grand Prix. Paul Azinger, never before a winner on Tour, also won three times, earned $822,481, and was named the Professional Golfers' Association (PGA) Player of the Year. In 1987, 14 players won more than $500,000, including three who did not win a tournament. Dan Pohl won the PGA's Vardon Trophy for low scoring with a 70.25 average.

Japan's Ayako Okamoto won a race with Betsy King and Jane Geddes for honors on the Ladies Professional Golf Association (LPGA) Tour, winding up as the Rolex Player of the Year and the top money winner with $466,034. She also won the Mazda-LPGA Series, worth another $125,000. Geddes won five events, Okamoto and King four each.

UPI-Bettmann Newsphotos

Paul Azinger, who had never won a PGA tournament, took three—the Phoenix Open, Greater Hartford Open, and Las Vegas Invitational—and was named player of the year.

Golf

PGA 1987 Tournament Winners

MONY Tournament of Champions: Mac O'Grady (278)
Bob Hope Chrysler Classic: Corey Pavin (341)
Phoenix Open: Paul Azinger (268)
AT&T Pebble Beach Pro-Am: Johnny Miller (278)
Hawaiian Open: Corey Pavin (270)
Shearson Lehman Bros. Andy Williams Open: George Burns (266)
Los Angeles Open: Tze-Chung Chen (275)
Doral Ryder Open: Lanny Wadkins (277)
Honda Classic: Mark Calcavecchia (279)
Hertz Bay Hill Classic: Payne Stewart (264)
USF&G Classic: Ben Crenshaw (268)
Tournament Players Championship: Sandy Lyle (274)
Greater Greensboro Open: Scott Simpson (282)
The Masters: Larry Mize (285)
MCI Heritage Classic: Davis Love III (271)
Big "I" Houston Open: Jay Haas (276)
Panasonic Las Vegas Invitational: Paul Azinger (271)
Byron Nelson Golf Classic: Fred Couples (266)
Colonial National Invitational: Keith Clearwater (266)
The Memorial: Don Pooley (272)
The Kemper Open: Tom Kite (270)
Manufacturers Hanover Westchester Classic: J. C. Snead (276)
United States Open Championship: Scott Simpson (277)
Canon Sammy Davis Jr. Greater Hartford Open: Paul Azinger (269)
Canadian Open: Curtis Strange (276)
Anheuser-Busch Classic: Mark McCumber (267)
Hardee's Classic: Kenny Knox (265)
Buick Open: Robert Wrenn (262)
Federal Express St. Jude Classic: Curtis Strange (275)
PGA Championship: Larry Nelson (287)
The International: John Cook (11 points)
Beatrice Western Open: D. A. Weibring (207)
Provident Classic: John Inman (265)
NEC World Series of Golf: Curtis Strange (275)
B.C. Open: Joey Sindelar (266)
Bank of Boston Classic: Sam Randolph (199)
Greater Milwaukee Open: Gary Hallberg (269)
Southwest Golf Classic: Steve Pate (273)
Southern Open: Ken Brown (266)
Pensacola Open: Doug Tewell (269)
Walt Disney World/Oldsmobile Classic: Larry Nelson (268)
Seiko Tucson Open: Mike Reid (268)
Nabisco Championships of Golf: Tom Watson (268)

LPGA 1987 Tournament Winners

Mazda Classic: Kathy Postlewait (286)
Sarasota Classic: Nancy Lopez (281)
Tsumura Hawaiian Ladies Open: Cindy Rarick (207)
Women's Kemper Open: Jane Geddes (276)
GNA/Glendale Federal Classic: Jane Geddes (286)
Circle K Tucson Open: Betsy King (281)
Standard Register Turquoise Classic: Pat Bradley (286)
Nabisco Dinah Shore: Betsy King (283)
Kyocera Inamori Classic: Ayako Okamoto (275)
Santa Barbara Open: Jan Stephenson (215)
S&H Golf Classic: Cindy Hill (271)
United Virginia Bank Golf Classic: Jody Rosenthal (209)
Chrysler-Plymouth Classic: Ayako Okamoto (215)
Mazda LPGA Championship: Jane Geddes (275)
LPGA Corning Classic: Cindy Rarick (275)
McDonald's Championship: Betsy King (278)
Mayflower Classic: Colleen Walker (278)
Lady Keystone Open: Ayako Okamoto (208)
Rochester International: Deb Richard (280)
Jamie Farr Toledo Classic: Jane Geddes (280)
du Maurier Classic: Jody Rosenthal (272)
Boston Five Classic: Jane Geddes (277)
U.S. Women's Open: Laura Davies (285)
LPGA National Pro-Am: Chris Johnson (277)
Henredon Classic: Mary Beth Zimmerman (206)
Nestle World Championship of Women's Golf: Ayako Okamoto (282)
MasterCard International Pro-Am: Val Skinner (212)
Atlantic City LPGA Classic: Betsy King (207)
Rail Charity Classic: Rosie Jones (208)
Cellular One-Ping Golf Championship: Nancy Lopez (210)
Safeco Classic: Jan Stephenson (277)
Konica San Jose Classic: Jan Stephenson (205)
Mazda Japan Classic: Yuko Moriguchi (206)

Other Tournaments

British Open: Nick Faldo (279)
World Match Play: Ian Woosnam
U.S. Senior Open: Gary Player (270)
General Foods PGA Seniors Championship: Chi Chi Rodriguez (282)
Mazda Senior Tournament Players Championship: Gary Player (280)
U.S. Men's Amateur: Bill Mayfair
U.S. Women's Amateur: Kay Cockerill
U.S. Men's Public Links: Kevin Johnson
U.S. Women's Public Links: Tracy Kerdyk
U.S. Mid-Amateur: Jay Sigel
U.S. Women's Mid-Amateur: Cindy Scholefield
U.S. Senior Men's Amateur: John Richardson
U.S. Senior Women's Amateur: Anne Sanders
U.S. Junior Boys: Brett Quigley
U.S. Junior Girls: Michelle McGann
Ryder Cup: Europe 15, United States 13
Walker Cup: United States 16½, Great Britain-Ireland 7½
NCAA Men: Individual—Brian Watts; Team—Oklahoma State
NCAA Women: Individual—Caroline Keggi; Team—San Jose State

Nobody won more than one major championship on either Tour. Larry Mize chipped in on the second play-off hole to win the Masters. Scott Simpson outshot Tom Watson on the final nine to win the U.S. Open at The Olympic Club. Britain's Nick Faldo won the British Open at Muirfield. And Larry Nelson, emerging from a long slump, won his third major title at the PGA.

Britain's long-hitting Laura Davies defeated Okamoto and JoAnne Carner in a play-off for the U.S. Women's Open title. Geddes won the Mazda LPGA Championship, King won the Nabisco Dinah Shore, and Jody Rosenthal won the du Maurier Classic, the other women's majors.

As if Okamoto's sweep and Davies' Open victory were not enough, golf outside the United States got a significant boost when the Great Britain-Europe team defeated the United States, 15–13, with a brilliant shot-making display in the biennial Ryder Cup Matches at Muirfield Village in Dublin, OH. It was the first U.S. loss ever on home soil.

King won the Vare Trophy for the LPGA's low scoring with a 71.14 average. Tammi Green was named Rookie of the Year by the LPGA and Cindy Rarick, a two-time winner, won the Gatorade Most Improved Player Award.

On the Senior PGA Tour, Chi Chi Rodriguez won seven tournaments and a record $509,145. Gary Player won the U.S. Senior Open with a record score of 270 at Brooklawn Country Club. Al Geiberger was the season's hottest "rookie." He turned 50 on September 1 and won three of his first four tournaments, finishing with $264,798 in his abbreviated season.

LARRY DENNIS, *Free-lance Golf Writer*

Horse Racing

In the $3 million Breeders' Cup Classic at Inglewood, CA, in mid-November, the 1986 Kentucky Derby winner, Ferdinand, outdueled the 1987 Derby winner, Alysheba, down the stretch to win by a nose. It was the first meeting of Derby winners since Affirmed beat Spectacular Bid in the 1979 Jockey Club Gold Cup. Ferdinand ran the 1¼-mile race in 2:01 2/5 to beat 11 other horses, six of them million-dollar winners.

Alysheba followed his Kentucky Derby win with a victory in the second leg of the Triple Crown, the Preakness Stakes, but failed to win the third leg when Bet Twice captured the grueling 1½-mile Belmont in New York; Alysheba finished fourth in the race. By failing to win the Belmont, Alysheba missed out on the $1 million bonus for winning the Triple Crown, instituted in 1986. In September, however, Alysheba did win $600,000 in the Super Derby at Louisiana Downs.

Java Gold had an outstanding three-year-old season until sidelined in October with a bruised leg. Trained by Mack Miller, Java Gold had won six of his previous seven starts prior to finishing second to Creme Fraiche in the Gold Cup. Three-year-olds stood out in competition against older horses, as Java Gold, Gulch, and Polish Native all triumphed over veteran horses in major races.

Woody Stephens' two-year-old colt, Forty Niner, won five of six races, but Tejano and Success Express, both trained by D. Wayne Lukas, were the top money-winners among two-year-olds. Tejano won $1,177,189 while winning five of his ten starts, and Success Express earned $737,207 while winning four races.

Harness Racing. Mack Lobell, a three-year-old trotter, had 13 wins, 1 second-, and 1 third-place finish in 16 races, earning $1,204,233. Mack Lobell won two events in the Triple Crown of trotting—the Hambletonian and the Yonkers Trot—but lost to Napoletano in the Kentucky Futurity. Mack Lobell also set a world record of 1:52 1/5 in a one-mile race.

Jate Lobell earned $1,645,596 while winning 15 of 25 pacing events, and Frugal Gourmet captured 15 of 25 races, including the $902,500 Meadowlands Pace.

STAN SUTTON, *"Louisville Courier-Journal"*

HORSE RACING

Major North American Thoroughbred Races

Beldame Stakes: Personal Ensign, $303,500 (money distributed)
Belmont Stakes: Bet Twice, $548,600
Breeders' Cup Classic: Ferdinand, $3,000,000
Breeders' Cup Distaff: Sacahuista, $1,000,000
Breeders' Cup Juvenile: Success Express, $1,000,000
Breeders' Cup Juvenile Fillies: Epitome, $1,000,000
Breeders' Cup Mile: Miesque, $1,000,000
Breeders' Cup Sprint: Very Subtle, $1,000,000
Breeders' Cup Turf: Theatrical, $2,000,000
Budweiser-Arlington Million: Manila, $1,000,000
Florida Derby: Cryptoclearance, $500,000
Haskell Invitational Handicap: Bet Twice, $500,000
Hollywood Futurity: Tejano, $1,000,000
Hollywood Invitational: Rivlia, $300,000
Jockey Club Gold Cup: Creme Fraiche, $1,000,000
Kentucky Derby: Alysheba, $793,600
Man o' War Stakes: Theatrical, $351,000
Marlboro Cup: Java Gold, $750,000
Metropolitan Handicap: Gulch, $601,500
Mother Goose: Fiesta Gal, $250,000
Preakness: Alysheba, $543,600
Ruffian Handicap: Coup de Fusil, $249,600
Santa Anita Handicap: Broad Brush, $1,000,000
Suburban Handicap: Broad Brush, $387,100
Super Derby: Alysheba, $1,000,000
Travers: Java Gold, $1,123,000
Turf Classic: Theatrical, $600,000
Whitney Handicap: Java Gold, $288,500
Woodward: Polish Navy, $595,000

Major North American Harness Races

Breeders Crown: Call For Rain, $566,660
Cane Pace: Righteous Bucks, $581,540
Hambletonian: Mack Lobell, $1,046,300
Hambletonian Oaks: Armbro Fling, $338,780
Kentucky Futurity: Napoletano, $166,834
Kentucky Pacing Derby: Albert Albert, $572,340
Little Brown Jug: Jaguar Spur, $412,330
Meadowlands Pace: Frugal Gourmet, $902,500
Messenger: Righteous Bucks, $447,310
Merrie Annabelle: Stage Entrance, $437,500
Peter Haughton Memorial: Supergill, $600,750
Sweetheart Pace: So Cozy, $796,750
Woodrow Wilson Pace: Even Odds, $1,422,500

Ice Hockey

After a shocking fall from the throne the year before, the Edmonton Oilers regained the National Hockey League (NHL) championship in 1986–87. Unlike the 1985–86 play-offs, which were studded with upsets, postseason play in 1986–87 unfolded as it should have, with the league's two top teams battling it out for the Stanley Cup title. In the play-off finals, the Oilers defeated the Philadelphia Flyers, four games to three. It was the first time since 1971 that the championship series went to seven games.

Regular Season. The Oilers were the NHL's most successful team during the regular season, compiling a league-leading 106 points, scoring a league-leading 372 goals, and winning their sixth straight Smythe Division title. The Flyers (100 points) topped the Patrick Division for the third consecutive year. The Hartford Whalers (93) captured the Adams Division, and the St. Louis Blues (79) took the Norris Division.

In his eighth NHL season, Oiler center Wayne Gretzky failed in his quest for a fifth 200-point season but still won his seventh scoring title, with 183 points. Although it was Gretzky's lowest total since 1980–81, he still outdistanced the second-highest scorer, linemate Jari Kurri, by 75 points. Pittsburgh's Mario Lemieux and another Oiler center, Mark Messier, tied for third with 107 points each. Only seven players ended up with 100 points or more, down from 13 the year before.

Gretzky also led the league in goals, with 62 during the regular season. Only four other players scaled the 50-goal plateau: Philadelphia's Tim Kerr (58), Kurri (54), Lemieux (54), and Minnesota's Dino Ciccarelli (52). New York Islander winger Mike Bossy, who had a record nine straight 50-goal seasons, fell short with 38.

To the surprise of no one, "The Great Gretzky" captured his eighth straight Hart Trophy as the NHL's most valuable player. Boston's Ray Bourque, the league's top defenseman, finished a distant second in the voting. Gretzky's point total for the season moved him into fourth place on the all-time list (behind Gordie Howe, Marcel Dionne, and Phil Esposito) with 1,520.

Play-offs. After being bounced by the archrival Calgary Flames in the Smythe Division final in 1986, the Oilers easily won their division play-offs in 1987. After whipping the Los Angeles Kings in five games, they shot past the Winnipeg Jets—who had upset Calgary—in four straight.

In the Adams Division, the champion Hartford Whalers could not handle the fourth-place Quebec Nordiques, falling in the first round, four games to two. Meanwhile, the defending Cup champion Montreal Canadiens whipped the Boston Bruins in four straight. Then, in a hotly contested battle, Montreal squeaked past Quebec in seven games.

In the Norris Division, the Detroit Red Wings highlighted a comeback season by winning the play-off title. After whipping the Chicago Black Hawks in four straight, they rallied from a three-games-to-one deficit against the Toronto Maple Leafs (who had surprised St. Louis in the opening round) and won the next three straight.

The Patrick Division scramble was the most dramatic, as the Flyers avenged a 1986 loss to the New York Rangers, and the New York Islanders—battling back from a three-games-to-one deficit—ousted the Washington Capitals. The seventh game of the Isles-Caps series went into a fourth overtime period before New York center Pat LaFontaine ended the suspense. In the division final against Philadelphia, the Isles again stormed back from a 3–1 deficit, only to lose in Game 7.

In the conference finals, the high-scoring Oilers lost their first game to the defensive-minded Red Wings but won the next four straight to take the Campbell title. In the Wales Conference, the Flyers got past Montreal in six games, behind some splendid work by rookie goaltender Ron Hextall. The series was marred by a brawl before the start of Game 6; the NHL later handed out $24,000 in fines and suspended Philly's Ed Hospodar for the final series.

The final series was a dramatic roller-coaster ride—one of the most compelling in the last two decades. Not only did it match the two top teams, but it also matched the two top goalies—the Oilers' Grant Fuhr and the Flyers' Hextall. The Flyers were racked by injuries, but they refused to raise the white flag, even after Edmonton won the first two games. In Game 1, Gretzky scored one goal and assisted on Paul Coffey's winner, as the Oilers triumphed on home ice, 4–2. In Game 2, also played at Edmonton, Kurri beat Hextall in overtime for a 3–2 Oiler victory. The Oilers' Glenn Anderson had tied the game with a brilliant rush in the waning minutes of regulation play.

In Philadelphia for Game 3, the Oilers took a 3–0 lead in the second period but let it get away, as the Flyers rallied for a 5–3 victory. Rookie Scott Mellanby tied it in the third with a 30-footer against Fuhr, and Brad McCrimmon scored the winner. Gretzky took charge in Game 4, setting up three goals, and the Oilers skated to an impressive 4–1 triumph on Philadelphia ice.

The Flyers, down three-games-to-one, refused to go quietly. They rallied from a 3–1 deficit in Game 5 (at Edmonton), as Rick Tocchet jammed in the winner early in the third period. In Game 6 (at Philadelphia), they charged back from a 2–0 deficit, with defensemen J. J. Daigneault whistling a 50-footer past Fuhr for a 3–2 win.

ICE HOCKEY

National Hockey League
(Final Standings, 1986–87)

Wales Conference

Patrick Division	W	L	T	Pts.	Goals For	Goals Against
*Philadelphia	46	26	8	100	310	245
*Washington	38	32	10	86	285	278
*N.Y. Islanders	35	33	12	82	279	281
*N.Y. Rangers	34	38	8	76	307	323
Pittsburgh	30	38	12	72	297	290
New Jersey	29	45	6	64	293	368
Adams Division						
*Hartford	43	30	7	93	287	270
*Montreal	41	29	10	92	277	241
*Boston	39	34	7	85	301	276
*Quebec	31	39	10	72	267	276
Buffalo	28	44	8	64	280	308

Campbell Conference

Norris Division	W	L	T	Pts.	Goals For	Goals Against
*St. Louis	32	33	15	79	281	293
*Detroit	34	36	10	78	260	274
*Chicago	29	37	14	72	290	310
*Toronto	32	42	6	70	286	319
Minnesota	30	40	10	70	296	314
Smythe Division						
*Edmonton	50	24	6	106	372	284
*Calgary	46	31	3	95	318	289
*Winnipeg	40	32	8	88	279	271
*Los Angeles	31	41	8	70	318	341
Vancouver	29	43	8	66	302	314

*Made play-offs

Stanley Cup Play-Offs
Wales Conference

First Round	Montreal	4 games	Boston	0
	N.Y. Islanders	4 games	Washington	3
	Philadelphia	4 games	N.Y. Rangers	2
	Quebec	4 games	Hartford	2
Semifinals	Montreal	4 games	Quebec	3
	Philadelphia	4 games	N.Y. Islanders	3
Finals	Philadelphia	4 games	Montreal	2

Campbell Conference

First Round	Detroit	4 games	Chicago	0
	Edmonton	4 games	Los Angeles	1
	Toronto	4 games	St. Louis	2
	Winnipeg	4 games	Calgary	2
Semifinals	Detroit	4 games	Toronto	3
	Edmonton	4 games	Winnipeg	0
Finals	Edmonton	4 games	Detroit	1

Championship

Edmonton	4 games	Philadelphia	3

Individual Honors

Hart Trophy (most valuable player): Wayne Gretzky, Edmonton
Ross Trophy (leading scorer): Wayne Gretzky
Vezina Trophy (top goaltender): Ron Hextall, Philadelphia
Norris Trophy (best defenseman): Ray Bourque, Boston
Selke Award (best defense forward): Dave Poulin, Philadelphia
Calder Trophy (rookie of the year): Luc Robitaille, Los Angeles
Lady Byng Trophy (sportsmanship): Joe Mullen, Calgary
Conn Smythe Trophy (most valuable in play-offs): Ron Hextall
Adam Trophy (coach of the year): Jacques Demers, Detroit

NCAA: North Dakota

World Championship: Sweden

In Game 7, however, the Oilers wrapped up their third Stanley Cup on home ice with a suffocating defense and some splendid offense. The Flyers scored first, two minutes into the game, but Messier tied it later in the first period. Late in the second period, Kurri gave Edmonton the lead on a nifty pass from Gretzky. And with three minutes left in the third period, Anderson scored the Oilers' final—and clinching—goal.

Canada Cup. In the six-nation 1987 Canada Cup tournament, the host country defeated the Soviet Union in the three-game final series. All three games ended in a score of 6-5. The Soviets won the opener in overtime; the Canadians took Game 2 in overtime; and the Canadians won the clincher in regulation time.

JIM MATHESON
"Edmonton Journal"

Ice Skating

The two U.S. figure skaters who had won world singles titles in 1986 relinquished their crowns in 1987 to an East German and a Canadian. At the 1987 championships in Cincinnati, OH, 21-year-old Katarina Witt of East Germany, the 1984 and 1985 women's world champion (and the 1984 Olympic gold-medal winner), narrowly defeated the defending titleholder, 19-year-old Debi Thomas of the United States, with a spellbinding and nearly flawless performance in the free-skating finale. Caryn Kadavy of the United States and teammate Jill Trenary, the newly crowned U.S. champion, finished third and seventh, respectively.

In the men's competition, Brian Orser of Canada, a three-time runner-up in the world championships and the silver medalist in the 1984 Olympics, finally reached the top of the victory stand with his own riveting performance (including six triple jumps and an unprecedented three triple axels) in the long program. Flanking Orser on the podium were two former world champions: runner-up Brian Boitano of the United States, who had won the crown in 1986, and bronze medalist Alexander Fadeev of the Soviet Union, who had earned the title in 1985.

In the pairs competition, the Soviet team of Ekaterina Gordeeva and Sergei Krinkov successfully defended their crown. The 1984 Olympic gold medal team of Elena Valova and Oleg Vasiliev, also of the USSR, finished second. Jill Watson and Peter Oppegard of the United States took third.

Soviet skaters also dominated the ice dancing competition. Natalia Bestemianova and Andrei Bukin won the championship for the third year in a row, and countrymen Marina Klimova and Sergei Ponomarenko took the silver medal. Tracy Wilson and Rob McCall of Canada came in third.

In the U.S. championships, held at Tacoma, WA, the 23-year-old Boitano easily won his third straight men's title. Boitano's performance was highlighted by an unsuccessful attempt at the first quadruple jump in formal competition. Despite missing the jump, he easily out-pointed second-place finisher Christopher Bowman. Scott Williams took the bronze.

The women's competition was more hotly contested. Thomas, the defending champion, won the compulsory figures and short program but was bothered by sore heels in the long program and missed several jumps. That opened the way for the 18-year-old Trenary, who capped a remarkable comeback from a serious leg injury two years earlier. Trenary took the title from Thomas with a strong performance in the free-skating finale. Kadavy finished third in the long program and third overall.

GEORGE DE GREGORIO
"The New York Times"

AP/Wide World
East Germany's Katarina Witt, a 21-year-old Olympic gold medalist, captured the women's world figure skating crown.

Skiing

Swiss skiers were unquestionably the best in the world in 1987, winning 17 titles in World Cup and World Championship competition and placing among the top five a total of 39 times.

Pirmin Zurbriggen dominated the men's World Cup, making a virtual shambles of the race for the overall title. His 339 points were enough to dethrone easily reigning champion Marc Girardelli of Luxembourg, who finished second with 190. Markus Wasmaier of West Germany (174) was third, followed by Joel Gaspoz (153), another Swiss. Zurbriggen, who also had won the overall title in 1984, had a banner year, taking the top prize in three of the four disciplines. The 24-year-old Swiss captured the downhill crown with 125 points, beating out teammates Peter Mueller (105) and Franz Heinzer (90). In the giant slalom, Zurbriggen and Gaspoz both compiled 102 points, but Zurbriggen was awarded the title because he had more race victories. And in the super giant slalom, Zurbriggen outpointed Girardelli, 85–65. The only non-Swiss to capture a World Cup title was Bojan Krizaj of Yugoslavia, who outpointed Sweden's Ingemar Stenmark, 105–95, in the slalom.

In women's World Cup competition, defending overall champion Maria Walliser (269 points) led a 1–2–3–4–5 sweep by the Swiss. Vreni Schneider (262) finished a close second, followed by Brigitte Oertli (206), Erika Hess (169), and Michela Figini (162). Tamara McKinney turned in the top U.S performance, finishing sixth (127). In the individual disciplines, Figini nosed out Walliser, 93–90, for the downhill title. Another Swiss, Corrin Schmidhauser, won slalom honors, with McKinney finishing second. Schneider and Walliser tied for first (120 points) in the giant slalom. And Walliser added the super giant slalom crown, easily beating out Catherine Quittet of France, 82–57.

At the Alpine World Championships in Crans-Montana, Switzerland, the home team was simply awesome, winning eight of ten gold medals. On the men's side, Zurbriggen won the giant slalom and super giant slalom, and Mueller took the downhill. Only Frank Woerndl of West Germany in the slalom and Girardelli in the combined category were able to dent the Swiss dominance. In women's competition, Walliser won the downhill and super giant slalom; Hess finished in first position in the slalom and combined; and Schneider captured the giant slalom.

At the U.S. Alpine Championships, Tiger Shaw won the men's combined and super giant slalom; Doug Lewis took the downhill; Felix McGrath captured the giant slalom; and Bob Ormsby won the slalom. Among the women, Pam Fletcher was the outstanding performer, winning the downhill, super giant slalom, and combined. The slalom title went to McKinney, and the giant slalom crown went to Debbie Armstrong.

GEORGE DE GREGORIO

The X Pan American Games

With only 30 months in which to prepare, the city of Indianapolis, IN, threw itself into the task of hosting the X Pan American Games, Aug. 8–23, 1987, and pulled it off with flying colors. Indianapolis was only the second U.S. city (after Chicago in 1959) to stage the event, held every four years for athletes of the Western Hemisphere. Having promoted itself for nearly a decade as the "Amateur Sports Capital of the World," the city took its biggest stride toward proving that claim with a community-wide effort that kept logistics to a minimum. As is commonplace in modern times, however, controversies over politics and drugs again surfaced in the sports arenas.

The most notable of several political disturbances came at the boxing matches, where a group of Cuban fighters brawled with anti-Castro demonstrators in the crowd. And in the final week of the Games, six athletes from five countries were disqualified after having tested positive for the use of banned drugs.

In the competition itself, the United States won a record 369 medals (168 gold, 118 silver, 83 bronze). Cuba finished second with 175 (75 gold, 52 silver, 48 bronze). And Canada was third with 162 (30 gold, 57 silver, 75 bronze). However, the host country suffered defeat in at least three high-profile sports, and there were outstanding performers from a number of other nations.

The most stunning upset of the Games was Brazil's 120–115 victory over a U.S. men's basketball team that was expected to overwhelm all its opponents. The veteran Brazilian squad was led by Oscar Schmidt's 46 points and Marcel Souza's 31.

The baseball tournament provided the Americans with one of their most thrilling moments at well as one of their most disappointing defeats. A ninth-inning home run by Ty Griffin gave the United States a 6–4 early-round victory that ended Cuba's 33-game winning streak and touched off a frenzy similar to that triggered by the U.S. hockey team at the 1980 Winter Olympics. In a rematch a week later, however, the more experienced Cubans won their fifth straight Pan Am gold medal with a 13–9 come-from-behind victory.

The other major Cuban success—and U.S. disappointment—came in boxing, as Cuban fighters won the gold medal in 10 of 12 weight divisions.

U.S. swimmers dominated their competition with 27 gold medals in 32 events. But the individual star was 16-year-old Silvia Poll of Costa Rica, who won three gold, three silver, and two bronze medals. She became the first Costa Rican athlete ever to win a Pan Am gold.

© Richard Mackson/"Sports Illustrated"

Silvia Poll of Costa Rica, a freestyle and backstroke sprinter, won eight medals at the Pan Am Games. Her three golds tied a Pan Am record for women's swimming.

U.S. athletes also excelled in gymnastics and track and field. In gymnastics, the U.S. women won the team title and finished 1-2-3 in individual competition. Sabrina Mar earned five medals and the all-around championship. The U.S. men also won the team gold, with Scott Johnson—who collected four gold and four silver medals—taking the individual all-around title.

The highlight in track and field competition was the long jump of Jackie Joyner-Kersee, who tied the women's world record with a leap of 24′ 5½″ (7.45 m). An expected assault by Carl Lewis on Bob Beamon's 19-year-old men's world record (29′ 2½″, 8.90 m) failed to materialize, but Lewis still won the gold with the fourth-best jump of his career, 28′ 8½″ (8.75 m).

STAN SUTTON

SOCCER

In the post-World Cup year of 1987, international soccer looked back on a long history and faced up to some formidable contemporary problems. In Europe, the major competition came in league and club tournament play. In the United States, the Major Indoor Soccer League (MISL) continued to draw crowds.

World. The centennial of the English Football League, the world's oldest and largest professional soccer league, was marked by a year-long celebration. The festivities were kicked off in August with a match at London's Wembley Stadium between a select English League team and a squad of international all-stars led by Argentina's Diego Maradona. The English Selects won, 3–0.

Meanwhile, however, continuing fan violence and financial problems threatened the league's long-term future. Still on the minds of many was the rioting between British and Italian fans at the 1985 European-Cup final in Brussels, Belgium, in which 39 people were killed. In September 1987, 25 of the British fans were extradited to Belgium to face charges.

On the field, Porto of Portugal scored two late goals to defeat Bayern Munich of West Germany, 2–1, in the European-Cup final, held on May 27 in Vienna, Austria. I.F.K. Gothenburg of Sweden defeated Dundee United of Scotland in the two-game final series for the Union of European Football Association (UEFA) Cup. Coventry City defeated Tottenham Hotspur (led by Footballer of the Year Clive Allen), 3–2, for the English Football Association Cup. Everton won the English Football League's First Division title, while Naples (led by Maradona) won the Italian league title.

U.S. In the MISL, the underdog Dallas Sidekicks surprised the Tacoma Stars, four-games-to-three, in the final play-off series. Tacoma, led by six-time most valuable player (MVP) Steve Zungul, took a 2–0 lead, but Dallas won Games 3, 4, and 6 to set up the seventh-game showdown. Trailing 3–1 with less than three minutes to play, the Sidekicks rallied for a 4–3 overtime victory. The Dallas attack was spearheaded by a 25-year-old Brazilian named Tatu, the league's MVP and leading scorer.

A group of former U.S. soccer executives announced the formation of an outdoor regional soccer league that would begin operations in spring 1988. The new American Soccer League was to have five franchises.

In the NCAA tournament, Clemson defeated San Diego State, 2–0, in the championship match.

SWIMMING

World-class swimmers lowered world records at three major championships during 1987.

Janet Evans, a 15-year-old from Placentia, CA, emerged as the top American prospect for the 1988 Summer Olympics when she became the first woman since Tracy Caulkins in 1981 to win four titles at the U.S. Long-Course Championships, held in July in Clovis, CA. Evans broke two of swimming's oldest records, shattering the 800-m freestyle mark with a time of 8:22.44 and bettering the 1,500-m freestyle standard with a clocking of 16:00.73. Her two other victories came in the 400-m individual medley and the 400-m freestyle events. Also at the U.S. championships, Matt Biondi equaled his own world record of 22.33 seconds in the men's 50-m freestyle.

At the Pan Pacific Championships, held in Brisbane, Australia, in August, Tom Jager of the United States clipped .01 second off Biondi's record with a clocking of 22.32. And 18-year-old David Wharton, also of the United States, broke the 400-m individual medley record with a time of 4:16.12. U.S. swimmers dominated, winning 24 of 32 gold medals.

The European Championships, held in August in Strasbourg, France, produced six world records. Tamas Darnyi of Hungary claimed two records in the men's individual medley events. His clocking of 4:15.42 in the 400-m pushed Wharton out of the record book, and his time of 2:00.56 in the 200-m erased the three-year-old mark of Canada's Alex Baumann. The strong East German women, who won 14 of 16 events, were led by Anke Mohring, Silke Hoerner, and the 800-m freestyle relay team. Mohring clipped 2.91 seconds off Janet Evans' 800-m individual freestyle record with a clocking of 8:19.53. Hoerner captured the 100-m breaststroke in a world-record time of 1:07.91. In the relays, the East German women swam 7:55.47 to lower their mark in the 800-m by 3.86 seconds. And the West German men's 800-m freestyle relay team established a world standard of 7:13.10.

In diving, Greg Louganis of the United States, who had swept all three events in the U.S. Indoor Championships for five years in a row, was upset in all three events in 1987: in the one-meter by Doug Shaffer, in the three-meter springboard by Kent Ferguson, and in the ten-meter platform by Matt Scoggin. The three women's winners were Kim Fugett, Megan Neyer, and Michele Mitchell, respectively. In the U.S. Outdoor Championships, Louganis won the three-meter springboard and ten-meter platform competitions to lift his total number of national titles to 43; Shaffer took the one-meter event. On the women's side, the winners were Neyer (one meter), Kelley McCormick (springboard), and Mary Ellen Clark (platform). And at the World-Cup championships in the Netherlands, Louganis won the springboard crown, and the United States beat out China, 374–372, for the team title.

GEORGE DE GREGORIO

Tennis

An 18-year-old West German, Steffi Graf, and a 22-year-old Australian, Pat Cash, found places in the front rank of professional tennis for 1987, she winning the French Open and he winning Wimbledon. Yet the players they beat in those major meetings, Martina Navratilova and Ivan Lendl, appeared undiminished.

Graf, who defeated Navratilova twice in four tries—one the French final (6-4, 4-6, 8-6)—also won ten other tournaments to take over the 30-year-old American left-hander's long-held position of number 1 on the women's computer rankings. Navratilova, however, reaching all four major finals for the second time of her career, defeated Graf in the finals of two of them. She seized her eighth Wimbledon (7-5, 6-3) and fourth U.S. Open (7-6, 6-1) singles titles; earlier in the year she fell to Hana Mandlikova in the finals of the Australian Open (7-5, 7-6).

At the U.S. Open, Navratilova also won the doubles (with American Pam Shriver) and mixed doubles (with Spaniard Emilio Sanchez) titles, the first sweep of a Grand Slam event since Billie Jean King's 1973 Wimbledon. That booty strengthened Navratilova's all-time second place position in major titles with 48, behind Margaret Court's 66. At Wimbledon, Navratilova not only ended Graf's 45-match winning streak but also equaled Helen Wills Moody's record for singles titles in that event. In August, however, Graf interrupted Navratilova's five-year reign as number 1 by winning a Virginia Slims tournament in Los Angeles over Chris Evert (who had defeated Navratilova in the semis). The young West German ended the year with a triumph in the Virginia Slims championship at New York's Madison Square Garden, defeating the 17-year-old Argentine Gabriela Sabatini (4-6, 6-4, 6-0, 6-4). Also during the year, Graf led West Germany to its first Federation Cup. In the final, a 2-1 victory over the United States, she and Claudia Kohde-Kilsch beat Shriver and Evert in the decisive doubles match (1-6, 7-5, 6-4).

Martina Navratilova proudly displays her eighth Wimbledon singles trophy after defeating Steffi Graf in the finals. Graf, however, ended Navratilova's long reign as number 1.

AP/Wide World

Evert, despite not winning one of the four majors for the first time since 1974, led American women players with five tournament victories, raising her all-time record to 153. She has won at least one pro tournament for 18 successive years, also a record.

In men's competition, Lendl clearly was number 1 for the year despite being frustrated by 11th-ranked Cash in the Wimbledon final (7-6, 6-2, 7-5). The Czech-born U.S. resident kept his two other Grand Slam titles, both over Swede Mats Wilander—his third French Open (7-5, 6-2, 3-6, 7-6) and third straight U.S. Open (6-7, 6-0, 7-6, 6-4). The latter match lasted 4 hours, 47 minutes, a record for a major tournament final. Lendl totaled eight tournament victories during the year to take second place among all-time singles winners with 70, passing John McEnroe's 62 but well behind Jimmy Connors' 105. Lendl ended the year with his fourth Grand Prix Masters title at Madison Square Garden, again defeating Wilander in the final (6-2, 6-2, 6-3).

Another Swede, the number 2-ranked Stefan Edberg, won his second straight Australian Open (6-3, 6-4, 3-6, 5-7, 6-3), over the favorite son, Cash. The latter's affinity for grass was born out in a spectacular Wimbledon, where, as a long-shot, he lost only one set. There Cash got help from another Aussie, 70th-ranked Peter Doohan, who brought down the 1985 and 1986 champion, Boris Becker, in the upset of the year. Edberg won a total of six other tournaments and spearheaded Sweden's drive to a third Davis Cup in four years. The Swedes' victim in the final was India, which had ousted the defending-champion Aussies in the semifinals.

Tim Mayotte led the American men in tournament victories with five, while McEnroe failed to win a title for the first time in a decade as a pro. Abusive language during a U.S. Open match cost McEnroe a $17,500 fine and a two-month suspension. Although the 35-year-old Connors also did not win a tournament during the year, he was the leading American in the rankings, number 4.

BUD COLLINS, *"The Boston Globe"*

TENNIS

Davis Cup: Sweden
Federation Cup: West Germany
Wightman Cup: United States

Major Tournaments

Australian Open—men's singles: Stefan Edberg (Sweden); men's doubles: Stefan Edberg and Anders Jarryd (Sweden); women's singles: Hana Mandlikova (Czechoslovakia); women's doubles: Martina Navratilova and Pam Shriver; mixed doubles: Sherwood Stewart and Zina Garrison.
World Championship Tennis—Miloslav Mecir (Czechoslovakia).
Italian Open—men's singles: Mats Wilander (Sweden); men's doubles: Yannick Noah (France) and Guy Forget (France); women's singles: Steffi Graf (West Germany); women's doubles: Martina Navratilova and Gabriela Sabatini (Argentina).
French Open—men's singles: Ivan Lendl (Czechoslovakia); men's doubles: Anders Jarryd (Sweden) and Robert Seguso; women's singles: Steffi Graf (West Germany); women's doubles: Martina Navratilova and Pam Shriver; mixed doubles: Pam Shriver and Emilio Sanchez (Spain).
U.S. Clay Courts—Mats Wilander (Sweden).
Wimbledon—men's singles: Pat Cash (Australia); men's doubles: Ken Flach and Robert Seguso; women's singles: Martina Navratilova; women's doubles: Claudia Kohde-Kilsch (West Germany) and Helena Sukova (Czechoslovakia); mixed doubles: Jo Durie (Great Britain) and Jeremy Bates (Great Britain).
Canadian Open—men's singles: Ivan Lendl (Czechoslovakia); men's doubles: Pat Cash (Australia) and Stefan Edberg (Sweden); women's singles: Pam Shriver; women's doubles: Zina Garrison and Lori McNeil.
U.S. Open—men's singles: Ivan Lendl (Czechoslovakia); men's doubles: Stefan Edberg and Anders Jarryd (Sweden); women's singles: Martina Navratilova; women's doubles: Martina Navratilova and Pam Shriver; mixed doubles: Martina Navratilova and Emilio Sanchez (Spain); senior men's singles: Tom Gullikson; senior men's doubles: Tom Gullikson and Dick Stockton; senior women's doubles: Wendy Turnbull and Sharon Walsh-Pete; boys' junior singles: David Wheaton; girls' junior singles: Natalia Zvereva (Soviet Union).
Virginia Slims Championships—women's singles: Steffi Graf (West Germany); women's doubles: Martina Navratilova and Pam Shriver.
Grand Prix Masters—men's singles: Ivan Lendl (Czechoslovakia); men's doubles: Miloslav Mecir and Tomas Smid (Czechoslovakia).
NCAA (Division I)—men's singles: Andrew Burrow, Miami; men's team: Georgia; women's singles: Patty Fendick, Stanford; women's team: Stanford.

N.B. All players are from the United States unless otherwise noted.

Track and Field

One of track and field's most cherished records was among the marks that fell in 1987 when 25-year-old Ben Johnson of Canada lowered the 100-meter dash mark at the world track and field championships in Rome and became the world's "fastest human." In addition, Edwin Moses lost in the hurdles for the first time in 122 straight races, in Madrid.

Johnson's clocking of 9.83 seconds erased the record of 9.93 set on July 3, 1983, in Colorado Springs by Calvin Smith. Johnson set the new mark by beating Carl Lewis, his arch rival and the winner of four gold medals at the 1984 Olympics. Lewis had beaten Johnson nine times in 14 races since 1980, although Lewis had not beaten Johnson in the last two years. The victory by Johnson was his fifth straight over Lewis, and he became the first man not from the United States to hold the record in the 100 meters in 27 years.

Moses' record, the longest in the history of men's track and field, ended in the 400-meter hurdles at a meet in Spain on June 4. He was beaten by Danny Harris of Perris, CA, whose time of 47.56 seconds, his career best, edged Moses by 13 hundredths of a second at the finish. The loss was the first for Moses, the 1976 and 1984 Olympic gold medalist, since Aug. 26, 1977, when he was defeated by Harald Schmid of West Germany. The streak included victories in 107 finals. The longest winning streak in track and field is 180 victories in the women's high jump by Iolanda Balas from 1957–1967.

In Paris on July 16, 26-year-old Said Aouita of Morocco posted a record 4 minutes 50.81 seconds in the 2,000-meter run, breaking the 4:51.39 that Steve Cram of Britain set in 1985. A week later, Aouita, who also holds the world 1,500-meter record, bettered his 1985 mark in the 5,000-meter run in Rome on July 22. His 12:58.39 erased the 13:00.40 he had done in Oslo two years earlier. In May, he had set a mark of 8:13.45 in the two-mile run.

In the men's field events, 22-year-old Patrik Sjoberg of Sweden raised the high-jump mark set by Igor Paklin of the Soviet Union on Sept. 4, 1985. Sjoberg jumped 7′ 11¼″ (2.42 m) in a meet at Stockholm, bettering the 7′ 10¾″ (2.41 m) Paklin turned in at Kobe, Japan.

Sergei Bubka of the Soviet Union, who has dominated the pole-vault scene, lifted his record to 19′ 9¼″ (6.03 m) on June 23, in a meet in Prague. Since 1984 the 23-year-old Bubka has improved his standard each year.

Another field-event athlete, Alessandro Andrei of Italy, a shot-putter, packed a successful season into one day, breaking the world mark three times on successive attempts in the same meet. He first improved on the mark of 74′ 3½″ (23.44 m), set in 1986 by Udo Beyer of East Germany, with a put of 74′ 6½″ (22.72 m) on August 12 in Viareggio, Italy. Then he followed up with puts of 74′ 11¼″ (22.84 m) and 75′ 2″ (22.91 m).

In women's competition, 29-year-old Ginka Zagorcheva of Bulgaria lowered the 100-meter hurdles record with 12.25 seconds, clipping the previous mark of 12.26 set by another Bulgarian, Yordanka Donkova, in 1986.

Other women who set or tied world records in 1987 were: Kerry Saxby of Australia, 5-kilometer walk (21:16.0 on a road not a track); Xu Yongjiu, China, 10-kilometer walk (44:26.5); Stefka Kostadinova, Bulgaria, high jump (6′ 10¼″ or 2.09 m); Jackie Joyner-Kersee, United States, long jump (equals 24′ 5½″ or 7.45 m); Li Huirong, China, triple jump (46′ 0¾″ or 14.04 m); Natalya Lisovskaya, Soviet Union, shot put (74′ 3″ or 22.63 m); Petra Felke, East Germany, javelin throw (258′ 10″ or 78.9 m).

The Boston Marathon was won by Toshihiko Seko of Japan and Rosa Mota of Portugal; Ibrahim Hussein, a Kenyan native who resides in Albuquerque, and Britain's Patricia Welch took the New York Marathon.

GEORGE DEGREGORIO

Yachting *see* page 76.

SPORTS SUMMARIES[1]

ARCHERY—U.S. Champions: men: Rich McKinney, Gilbert, AZ; women: Terry Quinn, Houston.

BADMINTON—U.S. Champions: men's singles: Tariq Wadood, Reseda, CA; women's singles: Joy Kitzmiller, Manhattan Beach, CA.

BIATHLON—U.S. Champions: men: 10 km: Lyle Nelson, Essex, VT; 20 km: D. Binning, Pinedale, WY; women: 5 km: Pam Nordheim, Bozeman, MT; 10 km: Anna Sonnerup, Hanover, NH.

BILLIARDS—World Champions (nine-ball classic): men: Mike Sigel, Towson, MD; women: Jean Balukas, Brooklyn, NY.

BOBSLEDDING—U.S. Champions: two-man: Brent Rushlaw, Saranac Lake, NY, and Hal Hoye, Malone, NY; four-man: Bob Horvath, Rob Dickerman, W. Jones, and Ron Horvath. **World Cup:** Nat Roy, James Herberich, Brian Schimer, and Scott Pladel.

BOWLING—Professional Bowlers Association: U.S. Open: Del Balllard, Jr., Richardson, TX; Firestone Tournament of Champions: Pete Weber, St. Louis; National Championship: Randy Pederson, Santa Maria, CA. **American Bowling Congress:** regular division: singles: Terry Taylor, Nashville, TN; doubles: Ray Betchkal and Dennis Schlichting, Racine, WI; all-events: Ryan Schafer, Elmira, NY; master's division: Rick Steelsmith, Wichita, KS; team: Sound Track, Salamanca, NY. **Women's International Bowling Congress:** singles: Regi Jonak, St. Peters, MO; doubles: Laura Grant, Norwalk, CT, and Robin Romeo, Van Nuys, CA; all-events: Leanne Barrette, Oklahoma City; team: Tool Warehouse, Hollywood, FL.

CANOEING—U.S. Champions (flatwater): men's kayak: 500 m: Norman Bellingham, Rockville, MD; 1,000 m: Greg Barton, Newport Beach, CA; women's kayak: 500 m: Traci Phillips, Newport Beach, CA; men's canoe: 500 m: Jim Terrell, Indianapolis; 1,000 m: Bruce Merritt, Indianapolis.

CHESS—World Championship: Gary Kasparov of the Soviet Union retained his world title in a tie (12–12) match with Soviet challenger Anatoly Karpov in Seville, Spain.

CROSS COUNTRY—World Champions: men: John Ngugi, Kenya; women: Annette Sergent, France. **U.S. Athletics Congress Champions:** men: Larry Olsen, Mills, MA; women: Anna Thorhill. **NCAA:** men: Joe Falcon, Arkansas; team: Arkansas; women: Kim Betz, Indiana; team: Oregon.

CYCLING—Tour de France: Stephen Roche, Ireland. **World Pro Champions:** men: road: Roche. **World Amateur Champions:** men: road: Richard Vivien, France; sprint: Lutz Hesslich, East Germany; women: road: Jeannine Longo, France; sprint: Erika Salymae, USSR; pursuit: Rebecca Twigg Whitehead, United States.

DOG SHOWS—Westminster: best-in-show: Ch. Covy Tucker, German shepherd owned by Shirlee Braunstein and Jane Firestone.

FENCING—U.S. Champions: men: foil: Michael Marx, Portland, OR; épée: Timothy Glass, Chicago; saber: Steve Mormando, New York City; women: foil: Caitlin Bilodeau, New York City; épée: Donna Stone, NJ. **U.S. Collegiate:** men: foil: William Mindel, Columbia; épée: James O'Neill, Harvard; saber: Michael Lofton, NYU; team: Columbia; women: individual: Bilodeau, Columbia-Barnard; team: Notre Dame.

GYMNASTICS—U.S. Champions: men's all-around: Scott Johnson, Lincoln, NE; women's all-around: Kristie Phillips, Houston; rhythmic: Marina Kunyavsky, Los Angeles. **NCAA:** men's team: UCLA; women's team: Georgia.

HANDBALL—U.S. Handball Association Champions (four-wall): men: Naty Alvarado, Hesperia, CA; collegiate team: Memphis State.

HORSE SHOWS—World Cup: Katherine Burdsall, Litchfield, CT, riding The Natural. **U.S. Equestrian Team:** dressage: Dianna Rankin, Delray Beach, FL, riding New Lady Killer; three-day event (spring and fall): Kerry Millikin, Glenmore, PA, riding The Pirate; show jumping, Anthony D'Ambrosio, Mt. Kisco, NY, riding Nimmedor.

JUDO—U.S. Champions: men: 60-kg: Fred Glock, Colorado Springs; 65-kg: James Martin, Colorado Springs; 71-kg: Michael Swain, San Jose; 78-kg: David Faulkner, Colorado Springs; 86-kg: Joe Wanag, Wilton, CT; 95-kg: Robert Berland, Wilmette, IL; over 95-kg: Steve Cohen, Palatine, IL; open: Damon Keeve, San Francisco; women: 48-kg: Darlene Anaya, Albuquerque, NM; 52-kg: Jo Ann Quiring, Colorado Springs; 56-kg: Eve Trivella, Hartsdale, NY; 61-kg: Lynn Roethke, Long Island, NY; 66-kg: Christine Penick, San Jose; 72-kg: Belinda Pinkley, Colorado Springs; over 72-kg: Corrine Shigemoto, San Jose; open: Shigemoto.

[1] Sports not covered separately in pages 473–497.

LACROSSE—NCAA: men: Division I: Johns Hopkins; Division III: Hobart; women: Division I: Penn State; Division III: Trenton State.

LUGE—U.S. Champions: men: Frank Masely, Newark, NJ; women: Bonny Warner, Mount Baldy, CA; doubles: Miroslav Zajonc and Tim Nardiello, Lake Placid, NY.

MODERN PENTATHLON—World Champions: men: Joel Bouzou, France; women: Irina Kisseleva, USSR. **U.S. Champions:** men: John Scott, Santa Cruz, CA; women: Kim Dunlop, Tallahassee, FL.

PADDLEBALL—U.S. Champions (four-wall): men's open: Marty Hogan, St. Louis; women's open: Caprice Behner, Winfield, IL.

POLO—World Cup: White Birch Farm, Greenwich, CT. **International Gold Cup:** White Birch Farm.

RACQUETBALL—U.S. Champions: men: singles: Jim Cascio, Lancaster, PA; doubles: Doug Ganim, Columbus, OH, and Dan Obremski, North Huntington, PA; women: singles: Diane Green, Altamonte Springs, FL; doubles: Mona Mook and Trina Rasmussan, Sacramento, CA. **U.S. Pro Champions:** men: Marty Yellen, Southfield, MI; women: Lynn Adams, Costa Mesa, AZ.

ROWING—World Open Champions: men: single sculls: East Germany; double sculls: Bulgaria; quadruple sculls: USSR; pair without coxswain: Great Britain; pair with coxswain: Italy; straight four: East Germany; four with coxswain: East Germany; eight: United States; women: single sculls: Bulgaria; double sculls: Bulgaria; quadruple sculls: East Germany; pair without coxswain: Romania; four with coxwain: Romania; eight: Romania. **U.S. Collegiate Champions:** men: Harvard; women: Washington.

SHOOTING—Olympic Style Champions: men: air rifle: Peter Durben, St. Paul, MN; small-bore rifle, three positions: Dan Durben, Colorado Springs; skeet: Matthew Dryke, Ft. Benning, GA; trap: Kenneth Blasi, Goddard, KS; free pistol: Erich Buljung, Ft. Benning; air pistol: Buljung; women: air rifle: Launi Meili, Colorado Springs; small-bore rifle, three positions: D. Wigger, Colorado Springs; skeet: Connie Fluker, Houston; trap: D. Morrison, Ft. Benning; sport pistol: Bettie Blocksome, Hartselle, AL; air pistol: Joan Gladwell, Florida.

SOFTBALL—U.S. Champions: men: major fast pitch: Pay and Pack, Bellevue, WA; class-A fast pitch: Jolly Molly, Lebanon, PA; major slow pitch: Starpath Systems, Lexington, KY; super division slow pitch: Steele's Sports, Grafton, OH; class-A slow pitch: Minneapolis Merchants; modified fast pitch: WTB Broadway, Spokane, WA; women: major fast pitch: Orange County (CA) Majestics; class-A fast pitch: Inland Cities Raiders, Cypress, CA; class-A slow pitch: Stompers, Richmond, Va.

SPEED SKATING—U.S. Champions: men: outdoor: Dave Pavlacic, Floristan, MO; indoor: Brian Arseneau, Chicago; women: outdoor: Laura Zuckerman, Whitefish Bay, WI; indoor: Tara Laszlo, St. Paul.

SQUASH RACQUETS—World Hardball Champions: men: Mark Talbott, RI; women: Nancy Gengler, New York City.

SURFING—World Champions: men: Tom Curren, Santa Barbara, CA; women: Freida Zamba, Flagler Beach, FL.

TABLE TENNIS—U.S. Champions: men: Chartchai Teekaveerakit, Vienna, VA; women: In Sook Bhusan, Aurora, CO.

VOLLEYBALL—U.S. Champions: men's open: Molten, Torrance, CA; women's open: Chrysler Californians, Pleasanton, CA. **NCAA:** men: UCLA; women: Hawaii.

WATER POLO—World Champions: men: Yugoslavia. **European Champions:** men: USSR. **U.S. Collegiate Champions:** men: California at Berkeley; women: California at Santa Barbara.

WEIGHTLIFTING—U.S. Weightlifting Federation: men: 52-kg: Ken Nishihara, Torrance, CA; 56-kg: Gene Gilsdorf, Onaga, KS; 60-kg: Brian Miyamoto, Waimanolo, HI; 67.5-kg: Cal Schake, Newport News, VA; 75-kg: Roberto Urritia, Hollywood, FL; 82.5-kg: Derrick Crass, Belleville, IL; 90-kg: Tommy Calandro, Baton Rouge, LA; 100-kg: Ken Clark, Pacifica, CA; 110-kg: Rich Schutz, Mt. Prospect, IL; over 110-kg: Mario Martinez, San Francisco; women: 44-kg: Sibby Harris, Carrollton, GA; 48-kg: Kathi Nichol, Cedarhurst, NY; 56-kg: Maro Bohakjran, Marietta, GA; 60-kg: Giselle Shepatin, San Francisco; 67.5-kg: Arlys Kovach, West Covina, CA; 75-kg: Glenda Ford, Long Beach, CA; 82.5-kg: Karyn Marshall, Pelham, NY; over 82.5-kg: Becky Levi, Tucson, AZ.

WRESTLING—NCAA (freestyle): Iowa State.

YACHTING—America's Cup: Stars and Stripes, United States, defeated Kookaburra III, Australia (*see* page 76). **U.S. Yacht Racing Union:** championship of champions: Paul Foerster, Austin, TX; **Mallory Cup:** Scott Young, Austin, TX.

SRI LANKA

Sri Lanka remained a troubled and divided land. Ethnic strife, which has claimed more than 6,000 lives since 1983, reached new heights of violence in 1987. In an attempt to end the conflict between the Sinhalese majority and Tamil minority, President Junius R. Jayewardene and India's Prime Minister Rajiv Gandhi signed a historic accord on July 29, but the pact was rejected by the Tamil and Sinhalese extremists, and prospects for full implementation became increasingly uncertain. India, as the guarantor of the accord, sent several thousand troops to the northern part of the island, where the majority of Tamils live, but these troops were unable to compel the Tamil militants to lay down their arms.

Escalating Violence and Indian Involvement. Tensions between the government and Tamil militants increased early in the year when the militants rejected government proposals for the devolution of power and greater autonomy in the Tamil areas of the north and east and when the Sri Lankan army undertook a large-scale operation—called "Giant Step"—against the Tamil extremists. During one week in April, Tamil guerrillas killed some 400 people, mostly Sinhalese, in attacks on buses and other vehicles in the Trincomalee district in the eastern province and in a bomb blast in the main bus station in Colombo, the country's capital city. In late April and May, government troops mounted another major offensive against Tamil guerrilla strongholds in the north and east.

Early in June, the government of India, which had been trying to mediate the civil war in Sri Lanka, dispatched 19 fishing boats with food and medical supplies for the people in the northern province. The boats turned back after a tense confrontation with Sri Lankan naval vessels in the Palk Strait. Prime Minister Gandhi then dispatched five transport planes, escorted by four jet fighters, to the same part of northern Sri Lanka to drop 25 tons of "humanitarian relief" supplies. Colombo protested these moves as "a naked violation of Sri Lanka's sovereignty and independence."

The Indo-Sri Lankan Accord. In early July, in spite of his resentment at Gandhi's actions, President Jayewardene accepted the Indian leader's suggestion of secret talks aimed at ending the prolonged civil war in Sri Lanka. The result of three weeks of negotiations was a remarkable accord, signed in Colombo on July 29. It included the following provisions: 1) the northern and eastern provinces of Sri Lanka would be merged into one unit, with a single provincial council whose members would be elected before the end of 1987; 2) the people of the eastern province would decide in a referendum before the end of 1988 whether they would remain linked with the northern province as one administrative unit or would revert to their separate status; 3) hostilities throughout the country would cease within 48 hours of the signing of the accord, militant groups would surrender their arms within 72 hours thereafter, and the emergency in the northern and eastern provinces would be lifted by August 15; 4) a general amnesty would be granted to political prisoners, and special efforts would be made "to rehabilitate militant youth"; 5) the government of India would "underwrite and guarantee" the accord, provide military assistance if requested, and abstain from activities "prejudicial to the unity, integrity, and security of Sri Lanka"; and 6) Tamil would be recognized as an official language, and the Tamils would be recognized as a distinct community.

After the Accord. While the agreement was hailed throughout the world, it was opposed by Tamil militants, who had had no part in the negotiations, by militant Buddhists, by Sinhalese nationalists, by the opposition parties, and even by some members of the Sri Lankan government, including Prime Minister Ranasinghe Premadasa. In the aftermath of the signing, rioting broke out in many Sinhalese-majority areas. On July 30, a Sinhalese sailor in a naval honor guard struck Prime Minister Gandhi with a rifle butt, inflicting only minor injury. On August 18, as the Sri Lankan Parliament was about to meet for the first time since the accord was signed, a grenade explosion in the Parliament house killed one legislator and injured 15 others, including six government ministers; President Jayewardene, who was present in the chamber, was unharmed.

Resistance and violence by Tamils in the northern and eastern provinces were even greater. The main militant group, the Liberation Tigers of Tamil Eelam (LTTE), with its charismatic leader, Vellupillai Prabakaran, as its main spokesman, rejected the accord and refused to cooperate with the Sri Lankan government or the Indian peacekeeping forces which landed in the Jaffna peninsula at the re-

SRI LANKA • Information Highlights

Official Name: Democratic Socialist Republic of Sri Lanka.
Location: South Asia.
Area: 25,332 sq mi (65 610 km^2).
Population (mid-1987 est.): 16,300,000.
Chief Cities (1984 est.): Colombo, the capital, 643,000; Dehiwala-Mount Lavinia, 184,000; Jaffna, 133,000; Kandy, 120,000.
Government: *Head of state,* J. R. Jayewardene, president (took office Feb. 1978). *Head of government,* R. Premadasa, prime minister (took office Feb. 1978). *Legislature* (unicameral)—Parliament.
Monetary Unit: Rupee (29.750 rupees equal U.S.$1, August 1987).
Gross Domestic Product (1985 U.S.$): $6,300,-000,000.
Economic Index (Colombo, 1986): *Consumer Prices* (1980 = 100), all items, 190.5; food, 188.8.
Foreign Trade (1986 U.S.$): *Imports,* $1,793,000,000; *exports,* $1,099,000,000.

quest of President Jayewardene. Originally numbering about 3,000, the Indian force grew to more than 15,000 within a few weeks and came to be regarded with increasing hostility. This was especially true after Prime Minister Gandhi, in response to a series of attacks in early October in which more than 160 persons were killed, ordered a massive offensive against the Tamil guerrillas. Hundreds of Tamil civilians as well as organized militants and scores of Indian troops were killed.

In early November, on the eve of a debate in parliament on implementing measures in the July 29 accord, a bomb explosion in Colombo killed at least 32 people and injured more than 75. By year's end it seemed unlikely that the terms of the peace accord could be implemented. Tensions between Sinhalese and Tamils, moderate and militant Tamils, various Tamil militants, Indian peacekeeping forces and Tamils, and the governments of India and Sri Lanka were increasing rather than subsiding. Prospects for the end of the tragic conflict seemed to be dimming.

Consequences. The continuing ethnic violence had an adverse effect on Sri Lanka's relations with India and on its standing in the international community, as well as on its economy and political stability. The government was forced to turn to India and other countries, as well as to international agencies, for massive economic assistance to sustain its lagging economy and meet its reconstruction costs. By the end of the year, about $600 million in foreign aid seemed to be assured. In December, Finance Minister Ronnie de Mel estimated that Sri Lanka would need $3 billion in new foreign assistance over the next three years. In September, Minister de Mel had headed a mission to India to seek its further assistance in reconstruction and to establish broader economic cooperation.

During the year President Jayewardene made frequent requests to other countries seeking military assistance to help to "suppress a revolt against the democratically elected government." Aside from India, most of the countries to which Jayewardene appealed, including the United States, Pakistan, and China, offered some "logistical support" but little or no direct military aid.

See also INDIA.

NORMAN D. PALMER
University of Pennsylvania

STAMPS AND STAMP COLLECTING

Patriotism highlighted U.S. stamps in 1987, the year heralding the 200th anniversary of the signing of the U.S. Constitution. Several states, including Delaware, New Jersey, and Pennsylvania, marked their bicentennial of statehood, and appropriate stamps were issued for the anniversaries.

Selected U.S. Commemorative Stamps, 1987

Subject	Denomination	Date
Tow Truck	8.5¢	Jan. 24
Michigan Statehood	22¢	Jan. 26
Pan Am Games	22¢	Jan. 29
Love	22¢	Jan. 30
Tractor	7.1¢	Feb. 6
Julia Ward Howe	14¢	Feb. 12
Jean B. Du Sable	22¢	Feb. 20
Enrico Caruso	22¢	Feb. 27
Mary Lyon	2¢	Feb. 28
Penalty Mail	22¢	March 2
Locomotive (coil)	2¢	March 6
Girl Scouts	22¢	March 12
Canal Boat	10¢	April 11
Special Occasions (booklet of 10)	22¢	April 20
United Way	22¢	April 28
Flag Fireworks	22¢	May 9
Steel Plow (card)	14¢	May 22
Flag Over Capitol	22¢	May 23
Constitutional Convention (card)	14¢	May 25
American Wildlife (50)	22¢	June 13
U.S. Flag (card)	14¢	June 14
Delaware Statehood	22¢	July 4
U.S./Morocco	22¢	July 17
William Faulkner	22¢	Aug. 3
Lacemaking (four)	22¢	Aug. 14
Red Cloud	10¢	Aug. 15
Bret Harte	$5.00	Aug. 25
Pennsylvania	22¢	Aug. 26
Preamble (booklet)	22¢	Aug. 28
Flag Reply Card	14¢	Sept. 1
New Jersey	22¢	Sept. 11
Signing the Constitution	22¢	Sept. 17
CPA	22¢	Sept. 21
Take Pride (card)	14¢	Sept. 22
Milk Wagon (coil)	5¢	Sept. 25
Race Car (coil)	17.5¢	Sept. 25
Timberline (card)	14¢	Sept. 28
Locomotives (booklet)	22¢	Oct. 1
Christmas (contemporary)	22¢	Oct. 23
Christmas (traditional)	22¢	Oct. 23

Philatelic items honoring the bicentennial of the Constitution included a 14¢ commemorative postal card, a Preamble to the Constitution booklet of 22¢ stamps, and a commemorative to hail the actual signing of the document.

U.S. flag stamps issued in 1987 were a 22-cent "Flag With Fireworks," a 22-cent coil "Flag Over The Capitol," a 14¢ U.S. flag postal card, and a flag reply postal card (cost 28¢). As part of the patriotic fervor, a 14¢ postal card promoted the theme "Take Pride in America." The card was part of a campaign to encourage recognition of the nation's natural and cultural resources.

A favorite for collectors in 1987 was the pane of 50 stamps featuring American wildlife. A block of four stamps dedicated to lacemaking was issued a year late because of engraving problems. A booklet of five designs in each of four panes depicts five locomotives. The first stamp issued in 1987 was an 8.5 cent tow-truck design in the transportation series (in coil form) on January 24.

In continuation of the Great Americans Series, 1987 honorees were Mary Lyon, Chief Red Cloud, Bret Harte, and Julia Ward Howe. Enrico Caruso was hailed in the Performing Arts Series, Jean Baptiste Du Sable in the Black Heritage Series, and William Faulkner in the Literary Arts Series. Receiving special postal recognition in 1987 were the Girl Scouts, United Way, Certified Public Accountants, and the Pan American Games. On the popular annual list, the U.S. Postal Service released another "Love" stamp for all special occasions and a pair of Christmas stamps.

A particularly intriguing stamp issuance was a 22¢ commemorative honoring the bicentennial of the Treaty of Peace and Friendship between the United States and the kingdom of Morocco. Both countries issued stamps of identical design featuring an arabesque from a painted door in the Dar Batha Palace in Fez. The coloring of both stamps was the same. This is not a new idea for the U.S. postal authorities. In 1986, the U.S. released a stamp-collecting booklet in joint issuance with Sweden; and the United States and France issued stamps of similar design to pay tribute to the centennial of the Statue of Liberty.

Due to the Constitution celebration additions, there were six more issues in 1987 than in 1986.

SYD KRONISH, *The Associated Press*

STOCKS AND BONDS

Wall Street's great bull market came to a violent end on "Black Monday," Oct. 19, 1987, with a crash felt around the world. In a single day, $500 billion in market value was wiped out in an avalanche of selling that came perilously close to overwhelming the entire system for trading stocks.

The Dow Jones average of 30 industrials, the oldest and best-known measure of trends in stock prices, fell 508.32 points that day, with some 604 million shares traded on the New York Stock Exchange (NYSE)—nearly twice as many as ever before. The 22.6% drop in the Dow was the largest on record, surpassing even the worst days of the storied collapse in 1929. Selling waves swept through other stock markets around the world, from Tokyo to London. For the month of October, an index of 18 world markets calculated by the firm of Morgan Stanley Capital International fell 17.4%.

The numbers, as dramatic as they were, only began to tell the story. In the midst of the collapse, Wall Street leaders and government officials worked feverishly to keep it from turning into a full-scale disaster. Their mission was to keep the machinery of the markets, on stock exchange trading floors and in the computer network of the over-the-counter market, from breaking down altogether.

The effort was successful, to the extent that the stock market subsequently stabilized and the global crisis of confidence eased. Still, the Crash of 1987 left an indelible imprint. Its potential echo effects, in particular its implications for the world economy, remained a major uncertainty as the year drew to a close. At least a half dozen inquiries, including one by a task force appointed by President Reagan, were undertaken to determine the causes of the crash and how the apparatus of the marketplace needed to be reinforced or rebuilt.

The Rise and Fall. The year began with no hint of the crunch to come. In fact, the bull market in stocks that traced its origins to August 1982 had some of its most spectacular moments in the first eight months of 1987. Over that span, the Dow Jones industrial average reached 55 new highs. On January 8, the average, which had closed out 1986 at 1,895.95, broke 2,000 for the first time. By July 17 it surpassed 2,500. And on August 25, when it peaked at 2,722.42, it sported a 43.6% gain for the year. From its low point five years earlier, the market had more than tripled, gaining $2.25 trillion in value as measured by Wilshire Associates' index of more than 5,000 stocks. The talk on Wall Street was that all this extravagance soon would be justified by impressive achievements in the underlying economy. Corporate profits were strong and gaining momentum, aided by widespread moves at many companies in the mid-1980s to "restructure," cut costs, and become more competitive.

But there were clouds on the horizon as well—clouds that would be recalled as painfully obvious portents of the impending storm. In early spring, the bond market went into a convulsive decline, sending interest rates higher as worries mounted over a falling dollar on the foreign exchange and a possible resurgence of an old nemesis, inflation. Professional traders at some of Wall Street's biggest firms suffered large losses in their bond and mortgage-backed investments. Countless small investors in bond mutual funds discovered to their dismay that their "conservative" investments could quickly sustain losses of 10–15%.

The bond market rallied thereafter, but not for long. The dollar continued to slump against leading foreign currencies, adding to persistent worries about the deficits in the federal government's budget and in the nation's international trade accounts. On September 4 the U.S. Federal Reserve, citing inflation concerns, raised its discount rate from 5½% to 6%, marking the first time it had increased its rate on loans to private financial institutions since the spring of 1984. The stock market began to show signs of faltering. On September 21 the Dow Jones av-

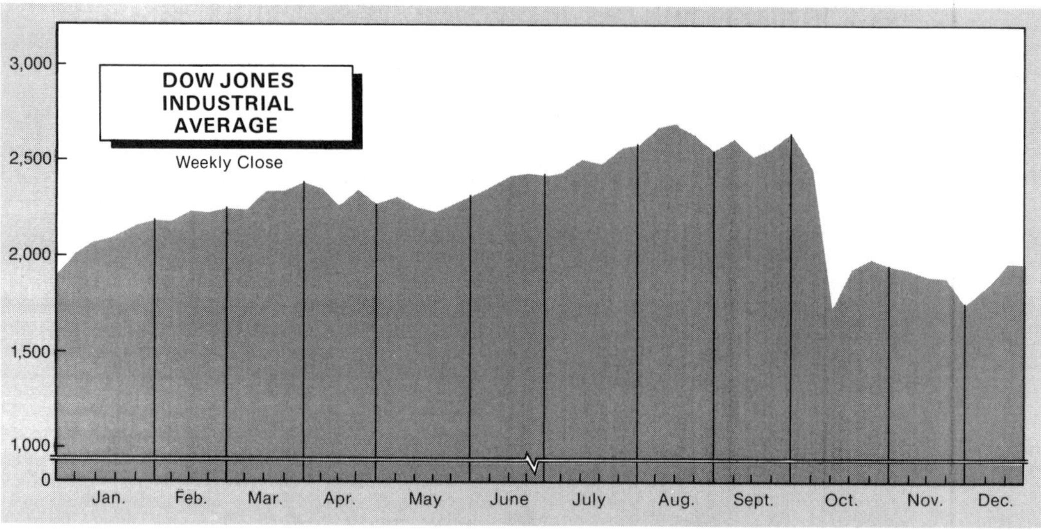

erage sank to 2,492.82, more than 200 points below its high of less than a month earlier. Yet many prominent forecasters remained unconcerned, arguing that the pullback actually was a healthy development—a long-overdue "correction" that would work off bull-market excesses and set the stage for further gains.

But the "correction" kept intensifying into October. On Wednesday, October 14, when market participants were confronted with another in a series of disappointing monthly reports on the trade deficit, the Dow fell 95.46 points. On Thursday it lost another 57.61, and on Friday the 16th it took its first 100-point drop ever, falling 108.35 to 2,246.74, with nearly all of the decline coming during the last few minutes of trading.

When brokers and money managers returned to work on Monday morning, the markets in Tokyo and London were slumping badly, and the crash was on. By the time the last sell order was executed in the U.S. markets that day, the Dow stood at 1,738.74. All the huge gains of earlier in the year had been obliterated, and no one knew where the bottom lay. The value of American stocks had contracted by $1 trillion in less than two months.

Tuesday, October 20 was equally, or even more, tumultuous. Specialists on the NYSE, who act as a meeting point for buy and sell orders and serve as buyers of last resort, had trouble keeping trading going in many stocks, including some of the big-name blue chips. Their capital reserves were eroding fast, banks were shying away from extending them additional credit, and the sell orders kept pouring in. Complaints were raised that some dealers in the over-the-counter market, who unlike specialists were free to handle orders in whatever stocks they chose, made themselves scarce rather than absorb any more losses. Defenders of these dealers contended that their telephone systems simply were overloaded. A similar phenomenon occurred at many brokerage firms, as numerous investors ran into a wall of busy signals or sat with their calls on hold while the value of their stocks gyrated wildly. There was talk that the markets would have to close.

The Fed, however, had taken an important first step toward coping with the crisis. On Tuesday morning it declared its readiness to provide liquidity, pumping whatever money was needed into the financial system to keep it from seizing up. Banks were persuaded that it was in their best interest to keep credit flowing to their Wall Street customers. Big Board volume on Tuesday reached 608,120,000 shares, surpassing Monday's total of 604,330,000. The battered blue chips rallied, producing a 102.27-point gain in the Dow average, although many smaller stocks kept tumbling.

Wednesday, October 21, brought a more substantial rise in stock prices, with the Dow climbing 186.84 to 2,027.85. Confidence spread that the shocks were subsiding. That allowed the financial community to turn its attention to another pressing concern, the mountain of order-processing and paperwork fast building up at both the exchanges and most brokerage firms. If the pace kept up, it was growing increasingly apparent that the work load might reach unmanageable proportions. On the other hand, authorities reasoned that to close the markets would deal a dangerous blow to confidence (though the Hong Kong stock exchange did decide to shut down for the rest of the week after Monday's debacle).

On Thursday afternoon John J. Phelan, Jr., the chairman of the NYSE, announced a compromise decision. The markets would continue to operate but the Big Board would close two hours earlier than usual for the next several days. Other exchanges and markets quickly adopted similar plans. That solution met with widespread approval and, except for an outburst of selling that sent the Dow down 157 points the following Monday, the worst of the crisis was past.

The Crash—Causes and Consequences. The fault-finding and bitterness, however, had just barely begun. In seeking explanations for the crash, many Wall Streeters described it as a kind of protest against an absence of decisive leadership in Washington and foreign capitals on international trade policy. If the United States and its key trading partners could not work together to resolve imbalances between their economies, investors seemed to be warning, the threat loomed of something like the Depression of the 1930s.

Not all the criticism could be deflected from Wall Street itself. In the eyes of some people, the crash was simply the inevitable consequence of an orgy of greed. Less moralistic observers focused their attention on the phenomenon known as "program trading" that had developed since the birth a few years before of markets for futures and options contracts based on stock-market indexes. In the most common form of program trading, called "index arbitrage," professionals operating with large amounts of capital and sophisticated computer programs seek to profit from temporary disparities between the levels of a stock-index futures contract and the index itself. If the futures contract in question is trading at a price significantly below where the index itself stands, for example, arbitragers would buy the contract and simultaneously sell a "basket" of stocks that closely resembles the makeup of the index. This kind of strategy in itself carries no high risk because it is hedged—that is, the two parts of the transaction offset each other to a great extent. But critics have long contended that program trading causes large and unpredictable swings in stock prices and destabilizes the stock market by linking it to the futures markets, where great risks can be taken with relatively small amounts of money.

For some time before the crash, Phelan of the NYSE had warned that the new methods of trading using such "derivative products" as index futures might cause a "meltdown" in the financial markets under the wrong circumstances. In the days immediately after Black Monday, he moved to restrain this type of activity by asking major brokerage firms not to use certain key exchange facilities for program trading. Once the market settled down in November, those sanctions were lifted.

Advocates of program trading protested that the criticism was unfair and that their computers were being used as a handy scapegoat for a problem that really was caused by greed, fear, and human error. Nevertheless, one primary question up for study in many post-crash inquiries was whether the rules governing program trading should be changed.

To some observers, neither Washington policy nor program trading was the main culprit in the crash. The problem, in their view, was simply that the bull market had gone, like so many others before it, to unwarranted extremes. At the peak in the summer, the typical big-name stock reached a price about 20 times the company's most recent 12-month earnings. By just about any historical standard, that kind of price-earnings (PE) ratio was dangerously high. In August the investment advisory service Market Logic caused something of a stir when it pointed out that the aggregate dividend yield of Standard & Poor's 500-stock composite index had fallen to a skimpy 2.65%, equaling a record low set in 1973 just before a severe bear market that lasted nearly two years. There were other warning signs as well. High-quality bonds were offering yields that exceeded those of stocks by as much as seven percentage points. That meant that bonds enjoyed an increasingly compelling allure as an alternative to stocks.

The trouble was, many investors were reluctant to heed those portents and sell stocks, since to do so meant the possibility of missing out on the bounties of a continuing bull market. A few analysts who had turned cautious as early as 1986 subsequently found themselves the object of scorn as prices continued to rise. Compared with price-earnings multiples of up to 60 in Japan, 20 in the United States did not seem so high. Besides, the bull's true believers argued, earnings were going to rise so fast that fat PEs might prove to be conservative.

Indeed, corporate profits were strong leading up to and during the crash. Other basic measures of the economy, including employment and production, were a picture of health.

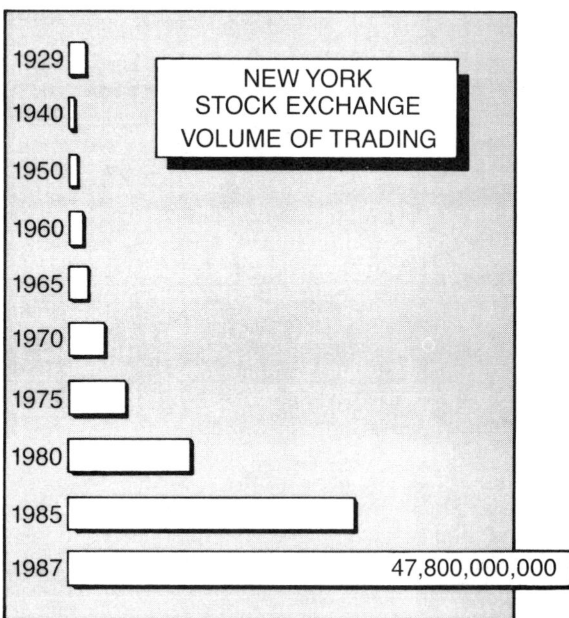

International Stock Exchanges

Indexes	1987 Open	Close	High	Low
Frankfurter's Allgemeine Zeitung	666.1	425.18	671.71	400.13
Hong Kong's Hang Seng	2,568.3	2,302.75	3,944.24	1,894.94
London's Financial Times 30-Stock	1,313.9	1,373.9	1,942.6	1,232.0
Paris' Compagnie des Agents de Change	397.8	280.7	460.4	280.7
Tokyo's Nikkei Average	18,701.3	21,564.0	26,643.43	18,544.05
Toronto's 300-stocks	3,066.18	3,160.05	4,118.94	2,783.25

Signs were emerging that the much-lamented decline of the dollar was serving the positive purpose of strengthening the position of U.S. manufacturers in the world marketplace. So the question of whether the debacle on Wall Street heralded equally bad times for Main Street had yet to be answered as 1987 ended. Some analysts argued that a $1 trillion reduction in wealth was bound to hurt many businesses, especially retailers. Economic forecasts for 1988 uniformly called for sluggish consumer spending at best. Though the stock market does not have a perfect record as a forecasting mechanism, pessimists pointed out that nearly all severe sell-offs in the past have been followed by recessions. A big drop in the market can frighten consumers into cutting back their plans for spending and investing.

On the other side of the debate, observers noted that the five-year boom on Wall Street had produced nothing of the same proportion in most other sectors of the economy. While growth did occur for many nuts-and-bolts businesses, it was often sluggish and spotty. Thus, the optimists said, if the general economy had not followed Wall Street on the way up, there was no compelling reason why it would be dragged down by the bull market's collapse. In the many comparisons between 1987 and 1929 that sprang up after Black Monday, it was noted widely that the crash in that former year did not by itself bring on the depression of the 1930s. The contraction in the economy had a series of causes, many students of the period say, including policy mistakes and misguided legislation on foreign trade, credit policies, and the federal budget.

Whatever the ultimate impact on the world at large, it was clear that Wall Street itself faced a period of pain and retrenchment. Even before the stock market nosedive, layoffs had begun in some areas of the securities business. The crash accelerated the pace of this trend. Several thousand people were expected to lose their jobs as a result of a single post-crash development—the acquisition of E.F. Hutton Group by another large investment firm, Shearson Lehman Brothers, plans for which were announced in early December.

One ironic, though coincidental, coda for the crash was sounded late in the year when financier Ivan Boesky was given a three-year prison sentence for his part in an insider-trading scandal. A Boesky-like character named Gordon Gekko was a central figure in the fictional movie *Wall Street* that opened just before year's end. The film, a morality tale on the evils of greed, was regarded by some as a kind of posthumous portrait, however unflattering, of the great bull market.

In real-life Wall Street, stocks staged a modest rally in December, and the Dow Jones average finished the year at 1,938.83, up 42.88 points, or 2.26%, from the end of 1986. Standard & Poor's 500-stock composite index closed at 247.08, up 4.91 points, or 2.03%. Other, broader indicators wound up with small to moderate losses. Thus, some future reader of the market statistics might conclude from a casual glance that 1987 was a "mixed" year of mostly small net changes for stocks. Nobody who took part in it will remember it that way.

CHET CURRIER, *The Associated Press*

SUDAN

Civil war and the refugee problems it created, government instability, and economic decay continued to confront Sudan in 1987.

The Government. The volatility of the coalition government formed after the 1986 election is closely tied to its Islamic structure, which is also the source of the ongoing civil war between the predominantly Muslim north and the Christian and animistic south.

The 1983 Constitution is based on Islamic law, known as the "September Laws." Although these laws were widely unpopular, armed resistance came mainly from the country's three southern provinces. The rebel Sudanese People's Liberation Army (SPLA), under Col. John Garang, sought to have the Islamic constitution replaced by a new, secular constitution. Government officials, however,

SUDAN • Information Highlights

Official Name: Republic of the Sudan.
Location: Northeast Africa.
Area: 967,494 sq mi (2 505 810 km²).
Population (mid-1987 est.): 23,500,000.
Chief Cities (1983 census): Khartoum, the capital, 476,218; Omdurman, 526,287; Khartoum North, 341,146.
Government: *Head of state,* Ahmad al-Mirghani, chairman, State Council (took over May 6, 1986). *Head of government,* Sadiq Siddiq al-Mahdi, prime minister (took over May 6, 1986). *Legislature* (unicameral)—National People's Assembly.
Monetary Unit: Pound (2.5 pounds equal U.S.$1, August 1987).
Foreign Trade (1985 U.S.$): *Imports,* $757,000,000; exports, $367,000,000.

were suspicious of the comparatively mild demands of the SPLA, since the rebel group maintained close ties with Marxist Ethiopia.

Rigidity characterized the debate within the government coalition concerning constitutional revision. Ideological clashes between liberal and conservative wings led to the collapse of the government on May 19, 1987, and again on August 23. Although Prime Minister Sadiq al-Mahdi formed new coalitions each time, traditional Islamic elements remained powerful within the government.

The fragile government was further weakened by riots in Khartoum in July involving students protesting the shortage of teachers and books. A total of 405 school children were arrested, and on July 23 the schools in Khartoum were closed indefinitely. On July 25, the government declared a one-year state of emergency because of strikes and social unrest throughout the Sudan. The civil strife was related directly to the government's inability to improve the nation's economy.

Economy. Sudan's foreign debt reached a staggering $10.6 billion in 1987. A rescheduling of debt repayments was arranged with the International Monetary Fund (IMF) and on July 28, Sudan paid a token $5 million to show the IMF that it was serious about repayments. Yet this gesture was made at some social cost, as 10,000 people marched through Khartoum on October 19 to protest moves agreed upon with the IMF to devalue the Sudanese pound by 44% and raise sugar and fuel prices.

Civil War. The bloodletting in Sudan's north-south civil war continued unabated. On March 26, several hundred Dinka tribesmen, the group from which rebels usually are recruited, were massacred in the town of Ed Da'ein by a government-armed Arab militia. On May 6, rebels claimed to have gunned down a civilian airplane near the town of Malakal, killing 13. On May 14, rebels shot down a government Hercules C-130 transport plane in the southern town of Wau. On July 7, the SPLA kidnapped a British nurse and three American aid workers. During the month of July, 75 government soldiers and 200 militiamen were killed in battle. Although the SPLA captured several southern towns, the war remained a stalemate.

Foreign Relations. Once-hostile Libya sent oil and aid to the Sudan in 1987. Ethiopia, however, continued to provide substantial financial and military support to the rebel SPLA. Relations between the Sudan and Egypt declined sharply after Jaafar al-Nemery's ouster in 1985, when Cairo granted political asylum to the deposed dictator. A "Brotherhood Charter" was signed by the two countries in February 1987; but continuing disputes about Sudanese relations with Egypt were a cause for the August government collapse.

JOHN P. ENTELIS and OMER ALPTEKIN
Fordham University

SURINAME

On November 25, a three-party opposition coalition swept to a convincing victory in the first elections held in Suriname since an army takeover in 1980.

The coalition Front for Democracy and Development captured 80% of the vote in balloting for a new 51-member legislature. The three parties, all with ethnic bases in Suriname's polyglot population, were the United Reform Party, supported by East Indians, the National Party of Suriname, which is strong among Creoles, and the Javanese Farmers' Party. All were active in Suriname's politics before the 1980 army coup, led by Lt. Col. Desi Bouterse, disbanded the parliament and installed a military-dominated government.

The new legislature will be less powerful than the old. Under Suriname's new constitution, approved in a popular referendum September 30, law-making power will reside in a State Council, which will include at least one representative from the army, probably Bouterse himself. The legislature will choose a president, who will be the government's chief executive.

During the previous seven years of military rule, Suriname had been plagued by severe economic problems and a guerrilla revolt that had driven 10,000 Surinamese refugees into neighboring French Guiana. All six parties in the campaign, including Lt. Col. Bouterse's recently formed National Democratic Party, had vowed to end the revolt and to rebuild the country's economy. A first step, coalition front leaders said, will be to reestablish friendly relations with the Netherlands, the former colonial power. The Netherlands suspended $110 million a year in aid after the military government executed 15 political dissidents in 1982.

The guerrilla war is essentially a tribal revolt by Maroons, or Bush Negroes, the descendants of African slaves who escaped from coastal plantations during colonial days and fled to Suriname's rugged interior. The Maroons resent Bouterse's attempt to exercise federal control over their tribal society.

Bouterse had pledged to respect the election results, but as the transition began it was not clear how much real power the military was willing to cede to a civilian government.

RICHARD C. SHROEDER
"Vision" Magazine

SURINAME • Information Highlights

Official Name: Republic of Suriname.
Location: Northeast coast of South America.
Area: 63,039 sq mi (163 270 km^2)
Population (mid-1987 est.): 400,000.
Capital: Paramaribo
Gross Domestic Product (1985 U.S.$): $1,100,-000,000.

SWEDEN

The triennial congress of the Social Democratic Party—Sweden's largest—took place in Stockholm Sept. 19–25, 1987, and, as expected, unanimously reelected Prime Minister Ingvar Carlsson as the party chairman. Carlsson voiced warm support of an agreement between the United States and the Soviet Union for the abolition of intermediate missiles in Europe. The 350-member congress passed a resolution in favor of 1% of Sweden's gross national product (GNP) to be the minimum level for future international development assistance and, in view of the recent unveiling of covert arms sales to India by the Bofors firm, demanded that an analysis be made of the Swedish defense industry's need for continuing arms exports.

The 1987–88 session of the Swedish Parliament (Riksdag) opened on October 6. In his statement on government policy, Prime Minister Carlsson pointed out that production and investments were increasing and the external deficit had been eliminated. Real incomes were rising, unemployment had been curbed, and measures to counteract air pollution and acidification were to be taken. With the other European Free Trade Association (EFTA) countries, Sweden would cooperate actively with the European Community (EC) nations in the removal of trade barriers within Europe. Also stressed were Sweden's policy of neutrality, efforts to establish a nuclear-free zone in Northern Europe, and support for the idea of creating a corridor free of battlefield nuclear weapons in Europe.

Economic Affairs. In the largest merger in Swedish industrial history, Sweden's ASEA group and BBC Brown Boveri of Switzerland agreed to combine their operations in a company to be named Asea Brown Boveri as of Jan. 1, 1988. The merger created a new worldwide industrial group which will be a leader in such fields as power generation, transmission and distribution, transportation equipment, electronics, automation, and industrial equipment. The company would have about 160,000 employees and annual sales of $15.5 billion.

SWEDEN • Information Highlights

Official Name: Kingdom of Sweden.
Location: Northern Europe.
Area: 173,730 sq mi (449 960 km²).
Population (mid-1987 est.): 8,400,000.
Chief Cities (Dec. 31, 1985 est.): Stockholm, the capital, 659,030; Göteborg, 425,495; Malmö, 229,936; Uppsala, 154,859.
Government: *Head of state,* Carl XVI Gustaf, king (acceded Sept. 1973). *Head of government,* Ingvar Carlsson, prime minister (elected March 12, 1986). *Legislature* (unicameral)—Riksdag.
Monetary Unit: Krona (6.04 kronor equal U.S.$1, Nov. 10, 1987).
Gross Domestic Product (1985 U.S.$): $99,000,000,000.
Economic Indexes (1986): *Consumer Prices* (1980 = 100), all items, 160.3; food, 185.3. *Industrial Production* (1980 = 100), 110.
Foreign Trade (1986 U.S.$): *Imports,* $32,508,000,000; *exports,* $37,221,000,000.

Sweden instituted a general price freeze on January 1. Certain modifications subsequently were announced to help alleviate difficulties encountered in various economic areas. Allowed to exceed with amounts corresponding to the increase in sales tax were price ceilings on cars as of June 15, and on agricultural products, oil, and gasoline as of July 1.

Assassination Unresolved. Almost two years after the assassination of Prime Minister Olof Palme the crime remained unresolved. On May 12 a special commission of jurists appointed to investigate the events following the assassination delivered its first report to Minister of Justice Sten Wickbom. The 193-page report criticized the police for some measures taken and others not taken and recommended

AP/Wide World

Signaling improved relations between two countries, Sweden's Prime Minister Ingvar Carlsson made a week-long visit to the United States in September. In Boston, *right, his itinerary included a tour of the U.S.S. "Constitution."*

that routines for emergency situations be revised.

Foreign Affairs. Prime Minister Carlsson had set for himself an extensive travel program during the year. On April 3–19 he visited China as head of a delegation of Swedish representatives of trade and industry. The prime minister had talks with Chinese leaders, including Deng Xiaoping, and took part in excursions outside the capital.

On September 9, Carlsson met with President Ronald Reagan in Washington. This was the first official visit of a Swedish prime minister to the U.S. capital since 1961 when Prime Minister Tage Erlander was received by President John Kennedy. At a press briefing prior to his trip, the prime minister said that U.S. and Swedish policies differ somewhat in the case of Nicaragua. Sweden fully supported the Central America peace proposal of Costa Rica's President Oscar Arias Sánchez.

From October 12 to 14, Prime Minister Carlsson made an official visit to Senegal. He had talks with President Abdo Diouf and attended a council meeting of the Socialist International at Dakar.

King Carl XVI Gustaf and Queen Silvia made a state visit to Iceland June 23–27 and were received by President Vigdis Finnbogadottir. The itinerary included a visit to Heimaey in the Westman Islands, which suffered a catastrophic volcanic eruption in 1973.

ERIK J. FRIIS
"The Scandinavian-American Bulletin"

SWITZERLAND

The environment, particularly the accidental spilling of toxic waste into the Rhine River, laws restricting refugee asylum, and national elections were major concerns in Switzerland in 1987. The role of Swiss banks in undercover U.S. arms sales to Iran and Nicaraguan contras also received much attention (*see* page 26).

SWITZERLAND • Information Highlights

Official Name: Swiss Confederation.
Location: Central Europe.
Area: 15,942 sq mi (41 290 km²).
Population (mid-1987 est.): 6,600,000.
Chief Cities (Jan. 1, 1986 est.): Bern, the capital, 138,574; Zurich, 351,545; Basel, 174,606.
Government: *Head of state,* Pierre Aubert, president (took office Jan. 1987). *Legislature*—Council of States and National Council.
Monetary Unit: Franc (1.3655 francs equal U.S.$1, Nov. 10, 1987).
Gross National Product (1985 U.S.$): $97,100,000,000.
Economic Indexes (1986): *Consumer Prices* (1980 = 100), all items, 124.2; food, 130.6. *Industrial Production* (1980 = 100), 108.
Foreign Trade (1986 U.S.$): *Imports,* $41,278,000,000; *exports,* $37,674,000,000.

Sandoz Disaster. On Nov. 1, 1986, a fire at the Sandoz chemical plant, located 3 mi (5 km) south of Basel, resulted in major mercury and phosphorus pollution of the Rhine River from water used to fight the fire. This was followed on November 7 by a further accidental Sandoz discharge of toxic wastes into the Rhine. The two waves of pollution rendered the Rhine devoid of fish and eels as far north as the Lorelei cliffs (approximately 217 mi, 350 km, from Basel) and destroyed crayfish, plant life, and microorganisms in the lower Rhine.

On Jan. 10, 1987, experts at the Swiss Polytechnical Institute forecast the possible regeneration of invertebrate microorganisms as early as the spring of 1987, and the rapid subsequent reappearance of fish and other life dependent on them. But a West German study predicted it would take 7–8 years to replace the eel population in the upper Rhine.

Pollution concerns again surfaced in April, with reports of increased radiation counts in winds coming from the east. A demonstration by 12,000 people in Berne on April 26, commemorating the anniversary of the 1986 Chernobyl nuclear catastrophe in the Soviet Union, became so violent that police dispersed the crowd with tear gas and rubber bullets.

Political Asylum. In a national referendum on April 4, voters approved by a 2–1 margin a government plan to limit the admission of refugees. The new legislation, which grants preference to refugees from "traditional countries," was seen by opponents as an attempt to limit refugees coming from Third World regions. It also allows the government to invoke emergency provisions restricting the number of admissions granted, should there be a sudden upsurge in arrivals.

The new law stipulates that all persons seeking asylum must register at border checkpoints as they enter Switzerland, rather than requesting asylum after arriving. It also permits detainment of those seeking asylum, in order to ensure expatriation if their applications are denied. Though vigorously opposed by the political left, the churches, and international human-rights organizations, the strong support registered for the bill may be seen as compatible with general Swiss restrictions on foreign workers that have been implemented in recent years.

Elections. In the national elections held October 18, Switzerland's center-right coalition of four parties retained the overwhelming parliamentary majority it has held since 1959. The parties won 158 of the 200 seats in the lower house and lost only one of their 43 seats in the 46-seat upper house. Two Green groups, whose primary concerns are environmental, gained eight seats in the lower house, for a total of 16, but failed again to gain a seat in the upper house.

PAUL C. HELMREICH, *Wheaton College, MA*

SYRIA

Syria in 1987 continued under the rule of Baath Party strongman President Hafiz al-Assad, who has governed the country since 1971 (*see* BIOGRAPHY). Even though Syria is of only moderate size and population (11 million), with relatively little oil and a weak economy, its policies in the Middle East are the subject of intense interest and concern. Syria has borders with Turkey, Iraq, Jordan, Israel, and Lebanon, and President Assad wields considerable influence among conflicting forces in the region. In response to various pressures and policy dilemmas, there were modifications in Syria's position during 1987, tactical if not basic. Although two fixed points remained—hostility to Israel and support (unique among Arab states) for Iran in its war with Iraq—even these positions were maintained less rigidly than in previous years.

Domestic Affairs. The Assad regime is always vigilant to protect its power against any threats, but its secretive nature usually makes it difficult to know just how serious the threats are. In May 1987, sources in Egypt reported that a group of Syrian Air Force officers stationed north of Damascus had attempted a coup. The rebellion reportedly was suppressed by government authorities, with 40 Air Force officers executed and 79 imprisoned. Syrian spokesmen, however, denied that any such attempt had taken place. On August 24, five Syrians were executed after being tried and convicted of bombing a train and a bus station in Damascus in April 1986, which had killed or wounded more than 400 people.

Syria's economic crisis, caused in part by heavy military spending and reduced assistance from Arab oil-producing countries, led to several cabinet changes during the year. On June 17 the National Assembly passed a vote of no confidence against Construction Minister Riyad Baghdadi—an action without any recent precedent—and on June 26, he and Agriculture Minister Mohammed al-Kurdi both resigned. Then in November, after the parliament censured four cabinet ministers for incompetence, President Assad made a wholesale reorganization of the cabinet, bringing in several technical experts and economic specialists. He also named Mahmoud Zubi to succeed Abdel-Raouf al-Kassem as prime minister. Earlier in the year, Gen. Mohammed Al-Khouli, the head of Air Force intelligence and a close friend of Assad, was dismissed following accusations from the West of Syrian involvement in terrorist attacks during 1985 and 1986.

Foreign Relations. The apparent motive in Syria's foreign policy changes was to ward off real or threatened isolation. Fairly clear proof of Syrian involvement in terrorist attacks in London, Paris, and West Berlin during 1985 and 1986 had led to the suspension of normal diplomatic relations with Great Britain, the withdrawal from Syria of the U.S. and other ambassadors, and a limited package of sanctions by the European Community and the World Bank. Early in 1987, however, these policies were largely reversed in response to what was perceived as increasing Syrian moderation and in the hope of evoking Syrian assistance in freeing Western hostages held in Lebanon. The changing Syrian policy was seen clearly in the closing-down on June 1 of the Damascus offices of the Palestinian terrorist group led by Abu Nidal and the expulsion from Syria of all non-Syrian members of the organization. From February through August, most Western sanctions against Syria were lifted and normal diplomatic links resumed.

Syria and Iran, though in one sense allies, remained rivals for influence in Lebanon, where each supports different factions. On February 22, about 7,000 Syrian troops entered West Beirut to restore order and took over offices and barracks of the Iranian-backed *Hizballah* (Shiite Party of God militia). This was one of several indications of cooling relations between Syria and Iran.

President Assad visited Moscow for three days in April and apparently was pressured by Soviet General Secretary Mikhail Gorbachev to moderate his policies. Immediately thereafter, Assad traveled to Jordan for talks (which came to little) with his archrival, President Saddam Hussein of Iraq. Similar pressures were exerted in the following months by Syria's fellow Arab states, whose attention was fixed on the Persian Gulf war rather than on the Palestinian issue. The effect of these pressures was seen surprisingly at the Arab League summit meeting in Jordan, November 8–10: Syria acceded to a resolution condemning Iran and to another authorizing the resumption by Arab states of diplomatic relations with Egypt.

See also MIDDLE EAST.

ARTHUR CAMPBELL TURNER
University of California, Riverside

SYRIA • Information Highlights

Official Name: Syrian Arab Republic.
Location: Southwest Asia.
Area: 71,498 sq mi (185 180 km²).
Population (mid-1987 est.): 11,300,000.
Chief Cities (Dec. 1982 est.): Damascus, the capital, (1983 est.) 1,202,000; Aleppo, 905,944; Homs, 414,401.
Government: *Head of state,* Gen. Hafiz al-Assad, president (took office officially March 1971). *Head of government,* Mahmoud Zubi, prime minister (took office Nov. 1987). *Legislature* (unicameral)—People's Council.
Monetary Unit: Pound (3.925 pounds equal U.S.$1, August 1987).
Gross Domestic Product (1985 U.S.$): $21,460,-000,000.
Economic Index (1986): *Consumer Prices* (1980 = 100), all items, 250.5; food, 256.1.
Foreign Trade (1986 U.S.$): *Imports,* $2,728,000,000; *exports,* $1,325,000,000.

TAIWAN

In June 1987, following up on initiatives begun in 1986, Taiwan's legislature passed a ten-article National Security Law allowing for the lifting of martial law, in effect on Taiwan for 37 years. Under the new legislation, the Taiwan Garrison Command no longer tries civilian cases, nor is it responsible for issuing permits to civilians allowing them to enter or leave the country. When the new law came into effect on July 15, 23 civilians convicted under the provisions of martial law were released and the 70 remaining in custody had their sentences reduced by half.

Some members of the opposition Democratic Progressive Party (DPP), formed just prior to the December 1986 elections, protested the fact that civilians who had been tried by military courts are not allowed by the new law to appeal their cases to civilian courts. Others called into question the new law itself, arguing that, in effect, it imposes the same restrictions under different authority.

The DPP had difficulty capitalizing on its December 1986 election success, in which it captured nearly one quarter of the vote from the ruling Kuomintang (KMT or Nationalist Party). A campaign to enroll 50,000 new members for the DPP succeeded in enlisting only 1,500, thereby barely doubling party membership. People seemed reluctant to join the party before a proposed Civic Organization Law, legalizing opposition parties, was enacted.

The opposition party also suffered from a lack of a strong leadership. In its absence, the opposition has tended to fragment. The new "May 19 Green Movement Headquarters" was formed by those who chose to take to the streets to express their opposition to the new National Security Law. Meanwhile, Wang Yi-hsiung, a successful DPP candidate in the 1986 legislative elections, announced plans to leave the DPP and form a new labor party that would be responsive to the needs of Taiwan's 1.7 million union members.

Within the KMT itself, moves toward political liberalization were the subject of intense debate. Some younger KMT members called for a reconstitution of the political system and new elections for the legislature, two thirds of the members of which were elected in 1948 prior to the defeat of the KMT in the civil war on the mainland. These "Young Turks" believe that the KMT should campaign on a reform platform, thereby defeating the DPP on its own ground. Meanwhile, KMT conservatives, uncomfortable with President Chiang Ching-kuo's reforms, formed two so-called Patriotic Fronts, which staged a joint anti-DPP rally in Taipei in mid-June.

Relations with the Mainland. Significant modifications occurred to the KMT's so-called "three-noes" policy of refusing to make contact, to trade, or to negotiate with the People's Republic of China. On October 14, the 38-year-old ban on travel by Taiwan citizens to the mainland provinces was lifted "for humanitarian reasons." The new rules permit travel to visit relatives "by blood or by marriage."

While the ban on direct trade between Taiwan and the mainland remains in effect, the

TAIWAN • Information Highlights

Official Name: Republic of China.
Location: Island off the southeastern coast of mainland China.
Area: 13,892 sq mi (35 980 km²).
Population (mid-1987 est.): 19,600,000.
Chief Cities (Dec. 31, 1985): Taipei, the capital, 2,507,620; Kaohsiung, 1,302,849; Taichung, 674,936; Tainan, 639,888.
Government: *Head of state,* Chiang Ching-kuo, president (installed May 1978). *Head of government* Yü Kuo-hua, president, executive yuan (premier) (took office, June 1984). *Legislature* (unicameral) —Legislative Yuan.
Monetary Unit: New Taiwan dollar (28.55 NT dollars equal U.S.$1, Dec. 31, 1987).
Gross National Product (1986 est. U.S.$): $72,600,-000,000.
Foreign Trade (1984 est. U.S.$): *Imports,* $21,600,000,000; *exports,* $30,400,000,000.

AP/Wide World

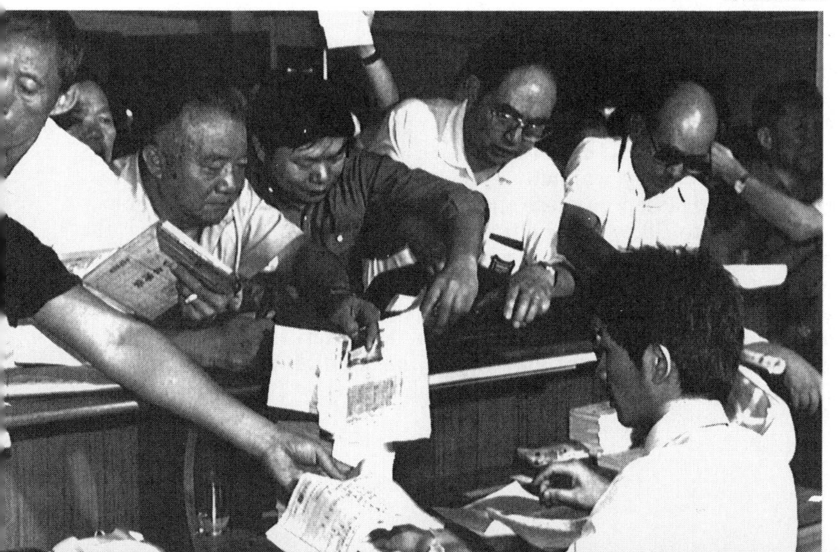

In mid-October the Taiwanese regime announced that, for the first time in 38 years, residents would be allowed to travel to mainland China to visit relatives. Applications poured in.

Editor's Note: Chiang Ching-kuo, president of Taiwan since May 1978, died Jan. 13, 1988.

current government policy calls for "no interference with transshipment trade." This trade, most of which is carried on through Hong Kong, may have reached as much as $2 billion in value in 1987.

Economy. Taiwan's "embarrassment of riches" grew during the course of 1987. Foreign-exchange reserves that totaled some $48 billion in mid-January were projected to exceed $70 billion by the end of December. In response, the government lifted controls on foreign exchange effective July 15. Under new regulations, any citizen can remit up to $5 million out of the country and bring $50,000 into the country annually.

Meanwhile, Taiwan continued to amass a substantial surplus in its balance of payments in trade with the United States. The U.S. government brought pressure to bear on Taipei to increase the value of the Taiwan dollar and to open its markets to American goods. Authorities on Taiwan responded by causing the currency to appreciate more than 25% against the U.S. dollar, but they argued that any further revaluation would cause major dislocations in Taiwan's industrial economy. Beyond that, the authorities noted that Taiwanese already were purchasing $200 worth of American goods per capita each year, whereas American per capita purchases of goods from Taiwan amounted to only about $10. American firms were accused of being insufficiently aggressive in selling goods on the Taiwan market.

Year-end projections called for an overall economic growth of 10.61% in 1987, down slightly from the 1986 figure of 11.64%. Per capital income in 1987 was projected at $4,952, up from $3,784 in 1986.

See also CHINA, PEOPLE'S REPUBLIC OF.

JOHN BRYAN STARR
Yale-China Association

TANZANIA

TANZANIA • Information Highlights

Official Name: United Republic of Tanzania.
Location: East coast of Africa.
Area: 364,900 sq mi (945 090 km²).
Population (mid-1987 est.): 23,500,000.
Chief City (1980 est.): Dar es Salaam, the capital, 900,000.
Government: *Head of state,* Ali Hassan Mwinyi, president (took office Nov. 1985). *Head of government,* Joseph S. Warioba, prime minister (took office Nov. 1985). *Legislature* (unicameral)—National Assembly, 233 members.
Monetary Unit: Tanzanian shilling (70.229 shillings equal U.S.$1, Sept. 1987).
Gross Domestic Product (1984 U.S.$): $4,200,000,000.
Economic Index (1984): *Consumer Prices* (1970 = 100), all items, 1,035.3; food, 1,222.2.
Foreign Trade (1986 U.S.$): *Imports,* $780,000,000; *exports,* $346,000,000.

In 1987 the Tanzanian economy showed some signs of improvement, and the influence of former President Julius Nyerere continued to be felt.

Economy. For the first time in a number of years there was cautious optimism about Tanzania's economic future. Positive, though modest, signs of economic growth appeared in 1987, the first year of the Economic Recovery Program of newly elected President Ali Hassan Mwinyi; inflation declined from 33% to 30% while export earnings and gross per capita income each rose slightly. Agricultural performance was mixed; sisal, cashews, and coffee production each continued to decline while cotton and maize production increased significantly. Indeed, for the first time in two years there was a maize surplus which was exported to neighboring countries.

Other positive factors include the discovery of new oil reserves near Pemba Island in July, a $100 million project to upgrade the port of Dar es Salaam, and the announcement that Tanzania's first coal mine at Kiwira would begin production in 1988. President Mwinyi negotiated an agreement with the International Monetary Fund (IMF) which made $200 million in standing credit available; there was $800 million in subsequent grants and loans from major international donor countries and a pledge of an additional $1.9 million from the Paris Club over the next two years. In July, donor nations agreed to refinance Tanzania's multibillion dollar foreign debt. The IMF agreement, which former President Nyerere had long resisted, carried with it rigid conditions, including currency devaluation, price controls, and reduced government spending.

Politics. Julius Nyerere was reelected as chair of the ruling Chama Cha Mapinduzi Party (CCM) in October. When he resigned as president in 1985, he had promised to quit the chair within two years so that his successor, Ali Hassan Mwinyi, could be both president and party chief as Nyerere had been, but the 65-year-old Nyerere is said to have pressured Mwinyi to renominate him. In 1985, Nyerere seemed to recognize that Tanzania's socialist policies and centralized political power had contributed to the country's economic problems. However, since then he has become increasingly critical of Mwinyi's acceptance of the IMF's stringent conditions for renewed aid and of policies aimed at changing Tanzania's socialist orientation in the direction of a free-market economy. In February, Nyerere publically warned the government against moving away from socialism, which he had introduced in 1967.

Finance Minister Cleopa Msuyua, an active advocate of a free-market economy, was dropped from the central committee of the party in November.

PATRICK O'MEARA AND
N. BRIAN WINCHESTER, *Indiana University*

TAXATION

Major tax-reform legislation the previous year, the mounting U.S. budget and trade deficits, the stock market crash in October (*see* STOCKS AND BONDS), and the breakdown in international coordination of economic policies led to further changes in U.S. tax laws in late 1987. The same factors, as well as the 1986 U.S. reforms themselves, also had an impact in other countries.

United States

Some 13 months after President Ronald Reagan signed into law the Tax Act of 1986, a reform that was to end all reforms, the budget accord reached on Nov. 20, 1987, between the White House and congressional leaders called for new changes in the tax laws for 1988. Such an outcome seemed to be precipitated by the loss of faith on the part of the securities markets and other countries in the ability or resolve of the U.S. leadership to reduce the budget deficit.

Whether or not the federal deficit was the main culprit behind such developments as the stock market crash and the decline of the dollar really was irrelevant. What was relevant was how the deficit was perceived. And, from the flurry of activities in October and November to reach a reduction accord before the end of the year, official Washington seemed to conclude that the size of the federal deficit does matter. On December 22, after extended congressional wrangling, President Reagan signed two compromise budget bills that funded the government through fiscal 1988 and fulfilled the deficit-reduction plan negotiated in November.

The two bills called for $33.4 billion in reductions from the projected federal deficit for fiscal 1988 and $42.7 billion in reductions for fiscal 1989. The omnibus spending bill reduced discretionary spending by $7.6 billion, of which $5 billion would come from defense. The second bill contained $17.6 billion in savings—including $9.1 billion in tax increases, $650 million in user fees, and reductions of $2.1 billion in the growth of Medicare and $1 billion in curbs on farm-subsidy increases—as well as an assumed savings of $1 billion in interest on the debt. The two bills also included $7.6 billion in receipts from sales of government assets and prepayment of U.S. loans.

The tax package would raise $23 billion in taxes over two years: $9 billion in 1988 and $14 billion in 1989. The burden of the increase was expected to fall mainly on contractors, corporations, and estates. Under the new law, long-term contractors—mostly defense contractors—are permitted to use the "completed contract" method of accounting to defer only 30% of their income; the law speeds up corporate estimated tax payments and prevents corporations from escaping taxes as they dispose of a company's assets during takeover. (The expected revenue gains from the speedup in tax payment was put at $800 million in fiscal 1988.) The tax bill freezes the existing estate tax rate at 55% for the next five years (it had been scheduled to fall to 50% in 1989) and extends the 3% telephone tax for the next three years. It also prohibits interest deductions on home equity loan amounts in excess of $100,000 and caps the amount of mortgage debt eligible for the deductions at $1 million. In addition, the bill ends the installment sales method of accounting used by large manufacturers and homebuilders that enabled them to defer taxes on sales made on credit until payments were received.

According to some analysts, the urgency to do something in 1987 about the deficit may have set U.S. tax and spending policy backward rather than forward. One feature that stands out in the new tax package is the absence of any serious initiative that would enhance the power of the federal tax system to generate adequate receipts over the long haul or to distribute the tax burden equitably or efficiently. Except for a few changes in accounting procedures, which may or may not yield the "expected" receipts, and the sale of government assets, a nonrecurrent form of revenue, the burden of enhancing the federal revenue system has fallen on two relatively minor sources—the telephone tax and the estate tax. Neither of these sources is elastic enough to generate the revenues needed to close the budget gap over the next 3 to 5 years.

In an environment where both friends and foes were calling on the United States to close the budget gap and trim the trade deficit, it seemed more than likely that in 1989, perhaps sooner, Congress once again would have to consider significant changes in the tax laws.

Problems and Prospects. During 1987, neither the White House nor congressional tax writers were willing to consider proposals that would have substantially altered the provisions of the 1986 Tax Reform Act, claiming that such a move would be damaging to the U.S. economy. However, there seemed to be a growing realization that such a position may not be sustainable in the future. Some critics of the 1986 legislation blamed it for the stock-market crash because it did away with provisions favorable to investment. Others contended that its revenue giveaway aggravated the deficit picture. Since some of the provisions of the 1986 legislation are staggered—the full effects will not be realized until 1990—there is ample room for change. If the economy in 1988 begins to falter, some of the provisions may be rescinded and other changes introduced. The capital-gains tax, for example, could be revised downward to 15%, and the investment tax credit could be reinstated. Alternatively, if the deficit outlook were to worsen, tax-rate cuts could be postponed and new tax increases legislated. Whether or not the 1986 act will undergo substantial revisions beyond those contained in the November 1987 tax/spending package, certain other problem areas were recognized: the "notch problem" associated with the two-bracket rate system; the overall progressivity of the federal tax system; and differences in the effect of the legislation on state and local governments.

The Notch Problem. When, in 1988, the two rate brackets replace the current 14-rate system, the income tax may have disincentive effects. The notch problem refers to the discontinuity in the schedule of rates which causes the first-bracket tax rate to jump in one step from 15% to 28% in lieu of graduating as income rises. This feature has the effect of doubling the marginal rate applicable to incomes in excess of that which is taxed at the 15% bracket level. To see how this jump in rates affects incentives, consider a married taxpayer filing jointly with $40,000 of taxable income. This taxpayer will pay 15 cents on every taxable dollar up to $29,750; between $29,750 and $40,000, the tax bite is 28 cents per dollar. For a single taxpayer with the same income, the jump is even worse. The first dollar of taxable income up to $17,850 is taxed at 15%, the remainder at 28%. The fact that the 1986 act has reduced average effective rates (taxes/taxable income) at both ends of the income scale puts the middle class at a disadvantage. Aside from this inequity, the notch problem also may have adverse effects on middle-class work effort, perhaps even tax compliance.

Progressivity. The cut in the top marginal rate from 50% to 28%, it is argued, was necessary to enhance the efficiency of the income-tax system—to stimulate risk-taking and incentives to save. The 1986 revision did indeed lower effective marginal personal income-tax rates, especially for married taxpayers filing jointly. On close inspection, however, this reduction may be illusory. Under the constraint of "revenue neutrality," the act reallocates the federal income-tax yield between the personal and the corporate income bases. The shortfall in the personal tax was recaptured from increases in the tax imposed on corporate income. Since owners of corporate capital are concentrated in the $75,000-and-over income classes, however, the overall effect on the top marginal personal income-tax rate at these levels of income may not be the one intended or desired. Preliminary estimates suggested that the top effective marginal rate for income levels of $100,000 and over rises under the 1986 act to 35%, compared with 27% if the equal-yield constraint was not met. Whether the degree of progression of the income-tax system as a whole has risen or fallen is an issue that remains to be clarified.

Federal-State-Local Relations. A significant yet overlooked consequence of the 1986 act is its impact on state and local governments. Some of the act's provisions raise the cost of municipal services, while others produce spillover gains to state treasuries. In an effort to cut abuses in the utilization of tax-exempt bonds at the state and local levels, the act sets volume limits on tax-exempt financing of private activities. These limits have raised the cost of state agencies that provide funding for single-family mortgages and multiple-family rental developments. Estimates of the impact of the volume limits on the 50 states point to a potential reduction in these agencies' activities in 1987 by about $31 billion, or 60%, compared with 1984. Since the act also places certain types of tax-exempt bonds, including mortgage-revenue bonds, among the preference items subject to the "alternative minimum tax," some state financing agencies have ceased altogether their rental development projects. Some states have been faced with the problem of how to provide affordable rental housing.

Not all states face such a fallout, however. Because the 1986 act has broadened the income-tax base, many states face the not altogether unpleasant problem of how to deal with windfall gains. Of the 40 states with broad-based income taxes, 30 are tied to federal taxable income or adjusted gross income. For these states the windfall will range from a rise of 2-3% in total state revenues for Ohio and Maryland, to 11% for Oregon. The wholesale cash-in of capital gains before the higher capital-gains tax takes effect has brought an "April revenue shower" to some wealthier states (e.g., Connecticut, New York, and California.)

IRS. In the aftermath of the 1986 reforms, the Internal Revenue Service (IRS) issued new rules for allocating total interest expenses. The ruling applies to passive activity loans and to credits, investment interest, and personal interest. The IRS also said that interest on loans to finance payments to individual retirement accounts qualifies as investment interest, but no ruling to that effect was yet forthcoming.

The W-4 withholding fiasco had a silver lining. Lack of clarity in the first issue of W-4 forms put taxpayers at risk of under-withholding, and thereby facing interest payments and/or penalties on taxes owed. A new provision would postpone for a year (until 1988) the increase from 80% to 90% of the share of tax liability that must be paid as estimated taxes mandated by the 1986 act. On the other hand, those taxpayers who reduced the number of withholding exemptions on the W-4 forms, hence increasing the federal tax take, could expect bigger refunds from state governments in those states that rely on federal withholding forms for withholding state taxes.

State and Local Taxes. Several states took action in 1987 to increase their revenues.

AP/Wide World

In March, Lawrence B. Gibbs, commissioner of the U.S. Internal Revenue Service, unveiled a new W-4A withholding form.

Twenty-three states collected a total of nearly $1 billion in delinquent taxes by wavering penalties for tax evasion. Other states were considering similar action. At the same time, several states were conducting well-designed advertising and promotional campaigns to discourage tax evasion.

Since Florida is prohibited by its constitution from enacting a personal income tax, the state legislature in April passed a 5% tax on most services in the state. The measure extended Florida's sales tax to all services performed within the state, excluding medical and some social services, stock brokerage, bank lending, and commissions on primary real-estate sales. In addition, out-of-state services would be taxed on the basis of the proportion of their business conducted in Florida. Following an extensive campaign against the measure by the advertising and media industries, the act was repealed late in the year, and a one-cent increase in the state sales tax was instituted instead. Unwilling to battle the powerful advertising and media lobby, other states that were considering similar service taxes now were reluctant to apply such a levy on advertising.

In anticipation of possible increases in federal taxes on such items as alcoholic beverages and tobacco, known as "sin taxes," some states moved to enact or increase such fees. Oklahoma, Utah, and Nevada were among the states that passed sin taxes. In other state actions, North Dakota increased its sales tax by 0.5% and added a one-year surcharge to its income tax; Nebraska overhauled its income-tax system, basing the individual state tax on federally adjusted gross income rather than on a percentage of federal tax liability, as it had been; and Idaho passed a permanent sales-tax increase to five cents as well as raised its income-tax rates.

International

Canada. The 1986 U.S. Tax Reform Act, particularly the reduction in the top marginal rates, has had a worldwide impact. The impact was greatest in Canada because of the close ties between the two economies. The Canadian tax package, in the form of a white paper unveiled on June 18, is designed to keep Canada's taxation system competitive with the United States'. Tax changes would be implemented in two stages. In the first stage, personal and corporate tax rates would be cut; in the second, the existing sales taxes would be replaced by a new, undetermined levy. A broader federal sales tax, a national value-added tax, and a federal tax on goods and services were among the latter options being considered. The year ended without final action on the plan.

West Germany. An agreement was reached in February by West Germany's coalition partners on the need for reforming the tax system effective Jan. 1, 1990. The main elements were: a reduction of the maximum personal income-tax rate from 56% to 53% and the lowest rate from 22% to 19%. Also proposed was a reduction in the rate for retained profits for corporations from 56% to 50%.

Austria. The government announced its intention to introduce a reform plan to take effect in 1989–1991. The main provisions were: a 6% reduction in personal income-tax rates, a cut in the number of tax brackets from 11 to 5, and simplification of the code.

Japan. The lower house of Japan's parliament passed a budget for the fiscal year that began April 1, 1987, after a controversial 5% sales tax was shelved. For all concerned the tax was dead. Legislation, proposed in late 1986 and enacted in 1987, cut personal income-tax rates by 1.54 trillion yen (about $10.2 billion). New tax increases also went into effect. The tax exemption of interest from personal savings was eliminated. A withholding tax of 20% was instituted. This measure was expected to raise 1.6 trillion yen (about $10.6 billion) in 1988. Also introduced was a residence tax (local tax) that was expected to raise 500 billion yen (about $3.3 billion).

ATTIAT F. OTT, *Clark University*

© Capital Cities/ABC, Inc.

© Gamma-Liaison

TELEVISION AND RADIO

In a newspaper column during 1987, the Roman Catholic priest and commentator Andrew Greeley wrote, "A modern version of the medieval morality play has slipped into prime-time television almost without anyone noticing it." He noted that, although they "rarely draw explicit moral conclusions for us," situation comedies including *Family Ties, Growing Pains, Mr. Belvedere, The Cosby Show,* and *My Sister Sam* were sensitively and candidly addressing such subjects as drugs, sex, ethics, and death. According to Father Greeley, "The shows hint lightly at the skills and traits that sustain love."

This was high praise for television, which had been criticized in recent years for pandering purely to the mentality of supermarket tabloids. Of course, the nighttime serials (*Dallas, Dynasty,* etc.) continued to glorify underhanded behavior in the bedroom and boardroom, and such miniseries as *Napoleon and Josephine: A Love Story* (starring Jacqueline Bisset) were said to reduce history to romance-novel story lines. The miniseries *Billionaire Boys Club,* based on the story of California financial whiz kids who committed murder, was seen as a typical case in slippery TV values, a wallow in glitzy excess disguised as a morality tale.

Still, Greeley noted a significant shift in the wind on the television landscape. Responding, apparently, to the AIDS (Acquired Immune Deficiency Syndrome) epidemic and resurgent monogamy in U.S. society at large, television found time for more than escapism and took a look at values. The hip, sensitive, contemporary realism which the National Broadcasting Company (NBC) had spearheaded since the beginning of the decade in *Hill Street Blues* (canceled in 1986), and in the superb hospital drama *St. Elsewhere* began to influence programs throughout the TV scene. For instance, *Frank's Place* (CBS) centered on a Harvard-educated black man who inherits a New Orleans restaurant; *Beauty and the Beast* (CBS) updated the fantasy tale with Ron Perlman as a hirsute champion of the urban homeless. *The New York Times* found Dabney Coleman's super-acerbic sportswriter *Slap Maxwell* to be "decidedly refreshing"; *A Year in the Life* (NBC) featured Richard Kiley as a father dealing with the thorny contemporary plights of his grown children; and *Thirtysomething* (ABC) felt for the pulse of baby boom couples tackling dual careers and parenthood.

New Network Programs. The Vietnam War program *Tour of Duty,* coming on the heels of the hit movie *Platoon,* was billed as television's most expensive series; the pilot alone cost $2 million. The show was seen by *The New York Times* as a surprising innovation for the faltering and usually conservative CBS, boldly scheduled opposite NBC's ratings champion, *The Cosby Show.* Home Box Office (HBO) offered its own three-part miniseries on the subject, *Vietnam War Story.*

The musical variety program, practically absent from the home screen since the 1970s,

ABC's seven-part miniseries "Amerika," far left, *hypothesized a Soviet occupation of the United States—and stirred controversy. NBC's Emmy-winning series "L.A. Law,"* left, *dramatizes the trials and tribulations of high-powered attorneys at the McKenzie, Brackman firm.*

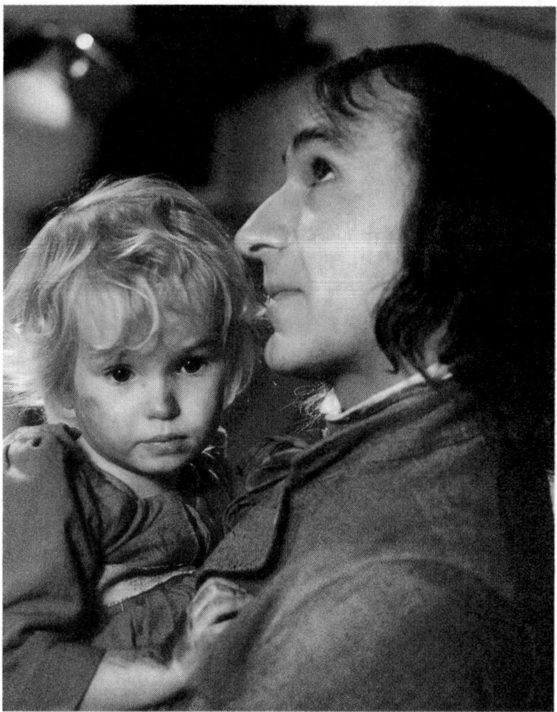

One of the highlights of the PBS season was a colorful adaptation of George Eliot's classic, "Silas Marner." Ben Kingsley (right) *starred.*

© Mobile Masterpiece Theatre

was revived by superstar Dolly Parton in her ABC series *Dolly*.

The most innovative of the season's law enforcement programs was *Private Eye* (NBC), a *film noir*-style sleuth series set in 1950s Los Angeles by trendsetter Anthony Yerkovich (writer for the hit *Miami Vice*). *Wise Guy* (CBS) was a graphic undercover-agent series in the mold of *Crime Story*.

Senior actors starred in more traditional action series as detectives and do-gooders. These included William Conrad *(Jake and the Fat Man),* Paul Sorvino *(The Oldest Rookie),* Dale Robertson *(J. J. Starbuck),* and Dennis Weaver (as a doctor in *Buck James*). George C. Scott played the title role in the Fox comedy *Mr. President,* though Fox's slow ratings start in its overall programming made it hard for some observers to see it as the bona fide "fourth network" it claimed to be.

Among the issues addressed in made-for-TV movies were illiteracy *(Bluffing It),* the Watergate scandal *(The Final Days),* and black poverty (*The Women of Brewster Place,* with Oprah Winfrey). After months of pre-broadcast controversy in 1986, *Amerika,* about a Soviet takeover of the United States, turned out to be a coolly received ratings bust.

Under the headline "Network TV Movie Legs Get Wobbly," *Variety* reported that because of declining ratings, theatrical movies "may be going the way of Westerns and musical-variety." At the end of the 1986–87 season, there were nine weekly slots for prime-time network movies, but only four as the 1987–88 season began, with cable channels taking away a growing chunk of new releases.

On the Public Broadcasting Service (PBS), the tradition of fine cultural and documentary series continued with *American Masters,* which profiled creative talents from Thomas Eakins to Buster Keaton; *The Ring of Truth,* on the history of science; *America by Design,* an architecture series; and *Tales from the Hollywood Hills,* taken from stories by such famous American writers as John O'Hara and F. Scott Fitzgerald.

News. Because of falling advertising revenues and a diminishing audience for the evening newscasts, the broadcast networks and Cable News Network (CNN) drastically cut costs and emphasized profits in their news departments, and *New York* magazine warned of "a news of lower expectations." The resignation of Roger Mudd, the respected senior NBC newsman, after the cancellation of yet another of his high-minded magazines, *1986,* symbolized the troubled times.

CBS Evening News anchor Dan Rather was the point man against the new bottom-line mentality, writing a newspaper editorial titled "From [Edward R.] Murrow to Mediocrity?" Rather made an even angrier gesture when his newscast was shortened by overtime coverage of the U.S. Open tennis tournament. In the unprecedented incident on September 11, he stormed off the set, and screens "went black" for six minutes. *Variety* crowed: "Rather in Lather Skips Blather." Oddly enough, Rather also was involved, as anchor, in one of the few

TELEVISION | 1987

Some Sample Programs

Amerika—A seven-part miniseries about what U.S. life might be like after a Soviet invasion. With Kris Kristofferson, Robert Urich, Sam Neill, Mariel Hemingway. ABC, Feb. 15.

Baby Girl Scott—TV movie exploring the plight of a couple whose severely premature infant can only be kept alive by drastic and costly medical means. With John Lithgow, Mary Beth Hurt. CBS, May 24.

The Battle for Afghanistan—*CBS Reports* documentary on Afghan resistance to the 1980 Soviet invasion. Narrated by Dan Rather. CBS, July 29.

The Beach Boys-25 Years Together—Musical celebration of the Beach Boys' 25th anniversary as a performing group, filmed on the beach at Waikiki, HI. ABC, March 13.

The Betty Ford Story—TV movie about the stresses that led the wife of President Gerald Ford to succumb to, then overcome, addiction to prescription drugs and alcohol. With Gena Rowlands, Josef Sommer. ABC, March 2.

The Bretts—An eight-part *Masterpiece Theatre* "comedy melodrama" about a 1920s British theatrical family. With Norman Rodway, Barbara Murray. PBS, Oct. 11.

The Comedy of Errors—*Live From Lincoln Center* broadcast of director Robert Woodruff's vaudeville-flavored version of Shakespeare's comedy. With Avner Eisenberg, The Flying Karamazov Brothers. PBS, June 24.

Daddy—TV movie about teenage pregnancy and parenthood and their effect on the life of the father. With Dermot Mulroney, Patricia Arquette. ABC, April 5.

Escape from Sobibor—TV movie based on the escape in World War II of hundreds of Jewish prisoners from a Nazi death camp in Poland. With Alan Arkin, Rutger Hauer, Joanna Pacula. CBS, April 12.

Eyes on the Prize—A six-part history of the antisegregation movement in the United States. PBS, Jan. 22.

The First Eden—A four-part series on the history of human life on earth. With David Attenborough. PBS, Nov. 2.

Gaudy Night, Have His Carcase, and **Strong Poison**—A ten-part adaptation on *Mystery!* of three novels by Dorothy L. Sayers in which amateur detective Lord Peter Wimsey and Harriet Vane solve the cases and their personal relationship. With Edward Petherbridge, Harriet Walter. PBS, Oct. 3.

God and Politics—A three-part examination of religion as a "determinant force in much of what shows up later in politics, economics, and upheaval." Host, Bill Moyers. PBS, Dec. 9.

Good-bye, Mr. Chips—A three-part *Masterpiece Theatre* adaptation of the James Hilton novel about a dedicated schoolmaster. With Roy Marsden. PBS, Jan. 4.

I'll Take Manhattan—A four-part miniseries adaptation of the glitzy Judith Krantz novel about a young woman's rise in the New York publishing scene. With Valerie Bertinelli, Perry King, Barry Bostwick, Jack Scalia, Francesca Annis. CBS, Mar. 1.

Inside the Persian Gulf—First in a projected series of *Jennings/Koppel Reports,* looking at the countries surrounding the Persian Gulf. With Peter Jennings, Ted Koppel. ABC, July 7.

In Love and War—TV movie based on the true story of Jim Stockdale, who was a prisoner of war in Vietnam for seven years, and his wife Sybil's crusade on behalf of all POWs. With James Woods, Jane Alexander. NBC, March 16.

It Ain't Over Till It's Over—Final episode of the *Hill Street Blues* series, in which the stationhouse is gutted by fire but the Blues fall in for roll call as they had for seven seasons. ABC, May 12.

Kojak: The Price of Justice—TV-movie mystery based on the character from the former TV detective series. With Telly Savalas, Kate Nelligan. CBS, Feb. 21.

LBJ: The Early Years—TV movie about the personal and political life of Lyndon Baines Johnson up to his becoming president in 1963. With Randy Quaid, Patti LuPone. NBC, Feb. 1.

Lena: My 100 Children—TV movie based on the life of Lena Kuchler-Silberman, who dedicated herself to leading Jewish refugee children to Palestine after World War II. With Linda Lavin. NBC, Nov. 23.

Life in the Fat Lane—An *NBC News Special* look at diet products, myths about weight control, and the problems faced by obese people. Narrated by Connie Chung. NBC, June 3.

A Little Princess—A three-part *Wonderworks* adaptation of Frances Hodgson Burnett's novel about a rich girl whose father dies suddenly, impoverished, forcing her to work as a servant. With Amelia Shankley, Nigel Havers, Maureen Lipman. PBS, Feb. 21.

The Long Journey Home—TV-movie thriller about a woman whose husband, reported missing in Vietnam, returns hotly pursued by an assassin. With Meredith Baxter Birney, David Birney. CBS, Nov. 29.

Monsignor Quixote—*Great Performances* adaptation of Graham Greene's political allegory about modern Spain. With Alec Guinness, Leo McKern. PBS, Feb. 13.

Not Your Average Russian (The Pozner File)—Profile of Vladimir Pozner, an influential and sometimes controversial Soviet spokesman considered a key figure in his country's efforts to change its image. PBS, June 17.

Nutcracker: Money, Madness, and Murder—A three-part miniseries based on the case of a young man who murdered his grandfather because his mentally ill socialite mother coerced him into the crime. With Lee Remick, Tate Donovan, John Glover, Elizabeth Wilson, Inga Swenson. NBC, March 22.

Our Planet Tonight—Spoof of TV-news magazine shows. With John Houseman, Morgan Fairchild. NBC, April 22.

Poor Little Rich Girl: The Barbara Hutton Story—A two-part TV movie about the life and seven marriages of Woolworth heiress Barbara Hutton. With Farah Fawcett, James Read, Kevin McCarthy. NBC, Nov. 16.

The Promise of the Land—*Smithsonian World* special about American farmers, their history and ideas, and soil conservation. Host, David McCullough. PBS, June 10.

The Ring of Truth—A six-part series examining the tools of the scientist's trade to see "how we know what we know." Host, physicist Philip Morrison. PBS, Oct. 20.

Rock Bottom—A two-part *Cagney and Lacey* episode dealing with detective Christine Cagney's brush with alcoholism after the death of her beloved father. With Sharon Gless, Tyne Daly. CBS, May 4.

Silas Marner—A two-hour *Masterpiece Theatre* adaptation of the classic George Eliot novel about a weaver who lives as a recluse until he takes in an orphan child. With Ben Kingsley. PBS, March 15.

South American Journey—An eight-part documentary about life in the countries of South America. Host, Jack Pizzey. PBS, July 5.

The Stone Fox—TV movie about a young orphan who saves his sick grandfather's farm by winning a dog-sled race. With Joey Cramer, Buddy Ebsen. NBC, March 30.

The Story of a Marriage—A five-part *American Playhouse* dramatization by Horton Foote of his story about his parents' marriage in rural Texas around World War I. With William Converse-Roberts, Hallie Foote, Matthew Broderick. PBS, April 6.

The Storyteller—Adaptation of a medieval story about a farmer's wife who wants a child and gets one that is half human and half hedgehog. With John Hurt and special effects by puppeteer Jim Henson. NBC, Jan. 31.

Sworn to Silence—TV movie based on fact about a small-town lawyer whose refusal to violate the confidentiality between him and his client leads to his ostracism for defending a murderer. With Peter Coyote, Dabney Coleman. ABC, April 6.

Tales from the Hollywood Hills—A three-part *Great Performances* series dramatizing three short stories (by Budd Schulberg, F. Scott Fitzgerald, and John O'Hara) set in Hollywood in the 1930s. PBS, Nov. 6.

The Ten-Year Lunch: The Wit and Legend of the Algonquin Round Table—An *American Masters* look at the 1920s New York literary circle. PBS, Sept. 28.

To Be a Teacher—*NBC White Paper* examining today's teachers. Host, Tom Brokaw. NBC, Jan. 5.

The Two Mrs. Grenvilles—A two-part TV movie adaptation of Dominick Dunne's novel about high society marriage and murder. With Claudette Colbert, Ann-Margret. NBC, Feb. 8.

War on Nicaragua—*Frontline* documentary examining U.S. policy in Nicaragua since 1981. PBS, April 21.

We the People—A four-part series about the U.S. Constitution and how it affects everyday American life. Host, Peter Jennings. PBS, Sept. 22.

positive new developments in TV news, *48 Hours,* a CBS series of so-called "instant documentaries" on current issues.

ABC anchor Barbara Walters sparked controversy over the role of the journalist when she acted as a courier of information from Iranian arms merchant Manucher Ghorbanifar, whom she had interviewed, directly to the White House.

Geraldo Rivera, as producer and host of the syndicated special: *American Vice: The Doping of a Nation,* created a media gaffe event by televising live, a police drug raid that turned up no drugs. Rivera was kidded mercilessly by such talk-show hosts as Johnny Carson and David Letterman, and *Time* magazine panned the show as "jugular journalism."

The bicentennial of the U.S. Constitution brought a host of programs saluting and analyzing the document, including ABC's *We the People* with Peter Jennings and PBS's *The Constitution in Crisis* with Bill Moyers. Moyers also won the highest honor, the golden baton, at the duPont/Columbus University broadcast journalism awards for his CBS documentary *The Vanishing Family: Crisis in Black America.*

Televised congressional hearings concerning the Iran-contra affair, about the covert sale of arms to Iran and diversion of the proceeds to Nicaraguan contras, drew unusually large daytime audiences for their blanket coverage, and made an instant media star out of National Security Council aide Col. Oliver North. (*See* feature article, page 26.)

Just prior to the December summit between President Reagan and Soviet General Secretary Mikhail Gorbachev and the signing of the arms reduction treaty in Washington, the two leaders brought their touted public-relations skills to bear in separate prime-time interviews with network news anchors.

Cable. The *Washington Journalism Review* reported that, by the end of 1987, nearly 50% of U.S. homes were hooked up to cable TV. The journal commented that "the strategy of advertising agencies to break the hegemony of the three broadcast networks" had allowed cable to increase its advertising revenue from a marginal $50 million in 1980 to $1 billion in 1988, while the networks' revenue had increased slowly—$5 billion to $8 billion—over the same period.

But the cable pioneer, Ted Turner, was so financially overextended that he had to call upon 14 cable-system operators for a $550 million bailout, and his personal share of Turner Broadcasting System (TBS) stock dropped from 81% to 50%. Nevertheless, pending approval by the TBS board of directors, Turner planned to market a new cable channel, Turner Network Television (TNT), that would compete with the three major networks by featuring popular sporting and awards events.

For the first time, a cable channel outbid the three networks to show some National Football League games. ESPN, cable's round-the-clock sports channel, paid the NFL $1.42 billion to televise 13 games, including the Pro Bowl, for each of three years beginning in the fall of 1987. But the NFL players' strike, which caused three weeks of games to be played with substitute players, was a ratings disaster for carriers of game telecasts on the networks and on cable.

Broadcast Rulings. The "Fairness Doctrine," the 38-year-old statute assuring equal time to opposing political opinions, was rescinded in the antiregulation movement of the Reagan administration's Federal Communications Commission (FCC). The broadcast industry hailed this as the removal of an unnecessarily burdensome rule, but public-interest spokesman Ralph Nader spearheaded extensive protests.

In one of the harshest penalties ever levied by the FCC, the RKO networks were stripped of licenses for two TV stations (including KHJ-TV in Los Angeles) and 12 radio stations because of an array of unethical deeds including advertiser overcharges. *Time* called it "a potential financial disaster" for RKO.

Radio. The FCC issued a formal warning to the radio industry that it would not, in the words of *The New York Times,* "turn a deaf ear" to the rising incidence of shock tactics by disc jockeys and talk-show hosts, including obscenity, innuendos, and ethnic and sexist slurs. Don Imus, the outrageous commentator on WNBC-AM in New York, retaliated by interviewing a mythical, profane "commissioner" from the FCC.

Radio newscasts faced the same twin travails—shrinking budgets and audiences—as their television counterparts. A study by the University of Missouri School of Journalism reported that radio newsrooms lost 2,000 employees in 1985–86, partly because of the FCC's elimination of some public-service programming requirements.

Garrison Keillor, the emcee whose gentle, homespun humor and tales of Lake Wobegon on National Public Radio's (NPR) *A Prairie Home Companion* had won him acclaim and a cult following since 1974, stunned fans by leaving the program to pursue his writing projects. NPR announced it would reshape the folk music-comedy show, heard on 300 stations, under a new name. But for the network's overall outlook, *Variety* reported "NPR Back in the Pink After Brush with Death," following the retirement of NPR's $7 million debt. NPR was able to launch the acclaimed morning newscast *Weekend Edition* and weekend versions of its afternoon magazine, *All Things Considered.*

See also PRIZES AND AWARDS.

DAN HULBERT
"Atlanta Journal & Constitution"

TENNESSEE

Ned Ray McWherter, pledging economy in government, was inaugurated in January 1987 as Tennessee's first Democratic governor in eight years. The speaker of the state House since 1973, McWherter proposed a status quo budget with no new programs or reforms requiring additional outlays. Teachers and public employees, limited to 4% salary increases, had expected more. Although Democrats controlled both houses of the legislature, Republicans exhibited strength in the Senate when they joined a minority of insurgent Democrats in retaining John Wilder as speaker over another candidate backed by most of the Democrats.

In a contest carefully watched across the state, U.S. Rep. William Boner (D) was chosen as Nashville's mayor. His resignation as congressman brought forth half a dozen candidates for the seat, including former gubernatorial hopefuls Jane Eskind and Bob Clement, and Phil Bredesen, whom Boner had narrowly defeated for mayor. Clement was elected to the seat in a special election in January 1988.

In a separate referendum, Davidson County voters rejected pari-mutuel betting on horse racing in a close contest in which church and other civic leaders played major roles. The legislature earlier in the year had given local governments the right to decide such matters by popular referendum.

Drought and unseasonably hot weather during July and August curtailed crop production. The central section of the state was hardest hit, but western cotton production also was down.

The state's economy continued to grow, while its unemployment continued to decline. Rates were lowest in the four urban areas and highest in rural western counties. Much of the growth came in the textile, apparel, and furniture and fixtures industries. BellSouth viewed Tennessee's economic outlook as "the brightest of all the South Central states." Foreign investments continued to grow, led by Japan's 50 diversified plants, employing 8,500 people.

Office of the Mayor

William H. Boner, 42-year-old five-term U.S. Congressman, was elected mayor of Nashville in September. His son Eric, 2, took part in the victory celebrations.

TENNESSEE • Information Highlights

Area: 42,144 sq mi (109 152 km²).
Population (July 1, 1986): 4,803,000.
Chief Cities (July 1, 1986 est.): Nashville-Davidson, the capital, 473,670; Memphis, 652,640; Knoxville, 173,210; Chattanooga, 162,170; Clarksville (1980 census), 54,777.
Government (1987): *Chief Officer*—governor, Ned McWherter (D); *General Assembly*—Senate, 33 members; House of Representatives, 99 members.
State Finances (fiscal year 1985): *Revenue*, $6,142,000,000; *expenditure*, $5,439,000,000.
Personal Income (1986): $57,645,000,000; per capita, $12,002.
Labor Force (June 1987): *Civilian labor force*, 2,335,100; *unemployed*, 158,400 (6.8% of total force).
Education: *Enrollment* (fall 1985)—public elementary schools, 574,517; public secondary, 239,236; colleges and universities, 194,845. *Public school expenditures* (1985–86), $1,937,000,000 ($2,533 per pupil).

People. Otis L. Floyd, Jr., was named president of Tennessee State University, a predominantly black institution, after two years of controversy over the selection of a head.

Former State Sen. Tommy Burnett returned from a brief term in federal prison, where he served for failure to file timely income tax returns. He was immediately elected to a seat in the legislature, where he played a leadership role in the 1987 session.

Knoxville banker C. H. Butcher was sentenced to federal prison on charges of loan and mail fraud. He joined his brother, former two-time gubernatorial candidate Jake Butcher, sentenced in 1986 for bank fraud and failure to report income taxes properly.

U.S. Rep. Harold E. Ford (D) of Memphis was indicted by a federal grand jury on 19 counts of fraud and conspiracy in an alleged scheme to trade political favors for loans from financial institutions controlled by the Butcher banks.

U.S. Sen. Albert Gore, Jr., surprised no one in announcing his candidacy for the Democratic nomination for president.

Marvin Runyon, the head of Nissan's massive automobile plant near Nashville, was named by President Ronald Reagan as chairman of the Tennessee Valley Authority (TVA) Board.

ROBERT E. CORLEW
Middle Tennessee State University

TERRORISM

Terrorism continued to plague governments and societies around the world in 1987. For the United States, the high-profile, dramatic terrorist incidents of previous years—such as the 1985 Trans World Airlines and *Achille Lauro* cruise ship highjackings—were replaced by less publicized, yet equally serious attacks against Americans abroad. Other countries also faced growing internal violence due to the acts of terrorist groups.

Europe. The Irish Republican Army (IRA) suffered its worst defeat in almost two decades of conflict in Northern Ireland on May 9. Eight IRA members were killed in a shoot-out with British security forces as they attempted to raid a police station in the town of Loughgall. The IRA struck back on November 8 when a 30-lb. (14-kg) bomb exploded during Remembrance Day in Northern Ireland—an annual ceremony to honor those who lost their lives in both World Wars. Eleven people were killed and 55 injured in the bombing. The IRA apologized for the high civilian casualties.

Another group that apologized for a terrorist incident was the Spanish Basque separatist group ETA. For years, ETA had primarily attacked Spanish government and military targets, but on June 19 a car bomb exploded in the underground garage of a crowded Barcelona department store. Seventeen people were killed in the incident, which led to an antiterrorism demonstration by more than 700,000 people in Barcelona.

Meanwhile, there were signs of increased cooperation between France and Spain in combating ETA. Several arrests of ETA members were made by both French and Spanish authorities, and Paris agreed to extradite ETA members to Spain. However, international cooperation in extraditing terrorists is not always guaranteed, as West Germany's refusal to extradite Mohammed Hamadei to the United States illustrates. Hamadei was wanted in the United States for the hijacking of TWA Flight 847 in Beirut in 1985 and the killing of an American Navy diver who was aboard the plane. He was arrested at Frankfurt airport on January 13 when liquid explosives were found in his luggage. One reason for Bonn's decision not to extradite Hamadei was that it would have put the lives of two West German hostages being held in Lebanon in danger.

American servicemen were the targets of terrorists in Greece on two separate occasions in 1987. In April and August, remote-controlled bombs exploded as buses carrying U.S. airmen passed by, injuring several people. In Italy, the Union of Fighting Communists—a faction of the Red Brigades terrorist group which had been very active in Italy in the 1970s—claimed responsibility for the assassination of Gen. Licio Giorgieri on March 20.

Middle East. Lebanon was once again the center of terrorism in the Middle East in 1987. Car bombings and kidnappings were regular occurrences in this war-torn country. The year began with several kidnappings of foreigners, including Americans. Also abducted was Anglican Church special envoy Terry Waite who was trying to gain the release of more than 20 foreign hostages being held by various pro-Iranian Shiite groups in Lebanon. One American

AP/Wide World

American journalist Charles Glass was reunited with his family in London after escaping from his Shiite Muslim kidnappers in south Beirut on August 18; he had been held for more than two m0nths. U.S. officials suggested that Glass had been allowed to escape in response to pressure from Syria and Iran.

hostage, journalist Charles Glass, escaped in August after two months of captivity. There was some speculation, however, that he might have been allowed to escape. Syria put pressure on terrorist groups in Lebanon to free all hostages.

On June 1, Lebanese Prime Minister Rashid Karami was killed when a bomb exploded aboard a helicopter in which he was traveling. On November 13, seven people were killed and 31 others injured when a bomb went off in Beirut's American University Hospital. A few days earlier, a bomb hidden in a briefcase exploded at Beirut airport, killing 6 people and wounding 73.

One of the more dramatic Palestinian terrorist attacks against Israel took place in 1987 when a member of the Popular Front for the Liberation of Palestine General Command, opened fire and tossed grenades at an Israeli army post near the border with Lebanon. The terrorist had used a motorized hang glider to enter Israel from Lebanon, and killed six Israeli soldiers and injured several others before being shot dead.

Among the other countries in the region experiencing terrorist incidents were Egypt and Kuwait. On May 26, two American diplomats were injured when members of the Revolution of Egypt—a group believed to have ties with the Palestinian terrorist group Abu Nidal—opened fire on their car as they were traveling to Cairo. In Kuwait, six Kuwaiti Shiites were sentenced to death for a series of terrorist incidents in January that were aimed at disrupting a meeting of Islamic nations.

Asia. The Philippines, India, Sri Lanka, and Pakistan all experienced mounting terrorism in 1987. In March a bombing occurred at the Philippine Military Academy a few days before President Corazon Aquino was to speak there. Four people were killed and 43 others injured in that attack. In August a member of Aquino's cabinet, Secretary of Local Government Jaime Ferrer, was assassinated on a street in a Manila suburb. And in October, two American servicemen were killed in separate attacks believed to be the work of the Communist New People's Army.

In India, terrorism associated with the Sikh campaign for a separate state in the Punjab claimed many lives. Among the more grisly incidents were massacres of bus passengers on roads in Punjab and the neighboring state of Haryana in July. More than 70 people, mostly Hindus, were killed in those attacks. Massacres also took place in Sri Lanka where Tamil rebels, who also have been fighting for a separate state, ambushed three buses and two trucks filled with civilians, killing more than 120 people. Meanwhile, a peace accord negotiated by India led to the introduction of Indian troops into Sri Lanka. Opposition to the accord by both Tamil guerrillas and Sinhalese extremists resulted in several terrorist incidents, including an August 18 assassination attempt against President J.R. Jayewardene during a session of Parliament. There was also a bombing during the rush hour in the capital city of Colombo in November that killed scores of people. A similar incident in April killed more than 100 people.

Other terrorist incidents in the region included a car bombing in July in a crowded market area in Karachi, Pakistan, which killed 72 people and injured 250 others. In Japan, Leftist radicals fired homemade rockets on the Imperial Palace in August, just as they had done during the 1986 Tokyo economic summit of major industrial democracies.

Latin America. While most attention focused on the guerrilla conflicts in Nicaragua and El Salvador, other countries in Latin America experienced significant terrorist incidents during 1987. Peru faced terrorist assaults from two groups—the Tupac Amarú Revolutionary Movement (MRTA) and Sendero Luminoso (Shining Path). The more serious threat has been posed by the Maoist Sendero Luminoso, whose attacks have included the bombings of power stations and railway lines, and the assassinations of government and military officials. The group also has terrorized peasant villages. In addition, American companies and diplomats have been the targets of terrorists in the country.

In Haiti, terrorists associated with the deposed regime of Jean-Claude Duvalier were responsible for several killings aimed at disrupting national elections originally scheduled for November. In Chile the Leftist Manuel Rodriguez Patriotic Front was responsible for several terrorist attacks, including the kidnapping of an army colonel. In Honduras, a pipebomb exploded in August at a restaurant frequented by U.S. servicemen, injuring six American soldiers and several Honduran civilians.

Africa and North America. There were bombings and assassinations throughout the year in South Africa as the conflict between the white-minority regime of Prime Minister P.W. Botha and the black majority population intensified in the racially segregated country. In Sudan and Mozambique, foreign workers were the victims of kidnappings by rebel groups, while in Burkina Faso, President Thomas Sankara was killed during a coup.

In the United States, Cuban inmates at the Atlanta Federal Penitentiary and at the Federal Detention Center in Oakdale, LA, seized several hostages in November to protest the planned deportation of 2,600 refugees to Cuba. Meanwhile, in Puerto Rico, five bombs exploded in different parts of the island on May 25, hours before King Juan Carlos of Spain was to appear in public.

JEFFREY D. SIMON, *The Rand Corporation*

TEXAS

A stagnant economy continued to be the dominant issue in Texas during 1987. Depressed oil and natural-gas prices as well as a downturn in the once-booming real-estate market spelled disaster for many Texans. The resulting lack of revenues prompted further belt-tightening measures by the state legislature, including reduced spending for welfare services and for higher education. Spectacular bankruptcy filings by former Gov. John Connally and the Hunt brothers—Nelson and Bunker, once reputed to be the world's richest men—served to spotlight the prevailing condition. Still, many believed that the downturn had bottomed out and that conditions would improve. Reflecting that mood of optimism, the George R. Brown Convention Center opened in Houston in September. Built under budget and completed ahead of time, the $105 million facility began sparking a revitalization of downtown Houston. In the city's political arena, Mayor Kathryn Whitmire was reelected.

Politics. The 1987 session of the state legislature was among the most controversial in the past decade. Gov. William Clements (R) took office on a pledge of no increase in taxes and a reduction of the budget through various economies. He particularly objected to a state income tax or corporation business tax of any kind. Citing the need to attract new business to Texas, and thereby reduce unemployment, he called for measures to restore a favorable economic climate. Deriding the opposition as the party of "tax and spend," he sought to forge an alliance between Republicans and conservative Democrats. After acrimonious debate and an additional legislative session, a compromise was reached. Plans for a personal or corporate income tax were scrapped, but an increase in the state sales tax was passed. Raising the sales tax from 5.25 to 6 cents per dollar gave Texans the dubious distinction of paying the third-highest state sales tax in the nation. Although he threatened a veto, Governor Clements ultimately signed the $38.3 billion budget bill, necessitating a record $5.7 billion increase in taxes. Opponents of a proposed lottery were able to kill the scheme in the legislature, but voters in November approved pari-mutuel horse racing. The latter question still had to be approved by county local-option vote.

Education. Despite tuition increases and reduced funding for state universities, enrollment continued to grow on Texas campuses. Texas A&M University and the University of Texas at Austin announced plans to limit enrollment to 40,000 students. This meant that only those graduating in the top 10% of their high-school class would be assured automatic acceptance. Despite cries of "elitism," administrators insisted that they would stick to their decision.

TEXAS • Information Highlights

Area: 266,807 sq mi (691 030 km²).
Population (July 1, 1986): 16,682,000.
Chief Cities (July 1, 1986 est.): Austin, the capital, 466,550; Houston, 1,728,910; Dallas, 1,003,520; San Antonio, 914,350; El Paso, 491,800; Fort Worth, 429,550; Corpus Christi, 263,900.
Government (1987): *Chief Officers*—governor, William Clements (R); lt. gov., William P. Hobby (D). *Legislature*—Senate, 31 members; House of Representatives, 150 members.
State Finances (fiscal year 1986): *Revenue,* $23,103,000,000; *expenditure,* $20,782,000,000.
Personal Income (1986): $224,877,000,000; per capita, $13,478.
Labor Force (June 1987): *Civilian labor force,* 8,483,000; *unemployed,* 815,800 (9.6% of total force).
Education: *Enrollment* (fall 1985)—public elementary schools, 2,260,679; public secondary, 871,026; colleges and universities, 769,692. *Public school expenditures* (1985–86), $10,043,000,000 ($3,384 per pupil).

The Texas Higher Education Coordinating Board was charged with the responsibility of developing a five-year plan for higher education in Texas. The board will investigate enrollment trends at Texas universities and attempt to develop a salary scale for faculty commensurate with the national average. As more and more professors leave the state for better-paying positions elsewhere, fears of a "brain drain" have been voiced.

Southern Methodist University (SMU) at Dallas, already on probation with the National Collegiate Athletic Association (NCAA), was found guilty of additional rules violations and forced to abandon football for two years. Allegations that members of the SMU Board of Regents, including Governor Clements, had knowledge of illegal payments to football players added to the gravity of the scandal. The University of Texas was cited for minor rules infractions but allowed to maintain its football program intact. Also, the University of Houston, having conducted an internal investigation, awaited an NCAA finding on charges of illegal financial assistance to student-athletes. On the positive side, efforts in the state legislature to water down the high school "no-pass, no-play" rule were unsuccessful.

Papal Visit. For many in Texas, the visit of Pope John Paul II to San Antonio on September 13 was the high point of the year. After an official welcome by Mayor Henry Cisneros, the pontiff celebrated Sunday Mass outdoors for some 300,000 worshipers.

Rescue. The eyes of the nation turned to the town of Midland in mid-October, when 18-month-old Jessica McClure fell into a narrow abandoned well and was trapped 22 ft (6.7 m) underground. After more than 58 hours, rescuers finally managed to dig a parallel shaft, unwedge the child, and hoist her to the surface.

STANLEY E. SIEGEL
University of Houston

THAILAND

The major event of 1987 in Thailand was King Bhumibol Adulyadej's 60th birthday. On the political front, the Royal Thai Army commander, Gen. Chaovalit Yongchaiyut, took several steps toward becoming a possible successor to Prime Minister Prem Tinsulanonda, who was expected to serve his full term until 1990.

The King's Birthday. King Bhumibol Adulyadej has reigned for 41 years, and his 60th birthday was marked with special festivities throughout the country. Cities and towns were ablaze with lights and decorated with flags for a week during December, and widespread parades, traditional dancing, and fireworks displays also occurred. In addition, areas around the country underwent environmental cleanup programs to show the nation's devotion to its monarch, and 30 doctors established a vasectomy clinic near the Grand Palace in Bangkok in December. More than 1,200 operations were performed at the clinic in ten hours. The clinic was intended to be a reminder that Thailand has been one of the most successful nations in Asia in controlling population growth.

Politics. General Chaovalit strengthened his base of political support in the military through his reorganization program and his handling of the September promotions list. As a result of these moves, there will be fewer generals and a leaner, more effective army. Many of the key commanders are now old friends and classmates of Chaovalit, who has said he will retire from the army in 1988. This will put him in a good position to seek the premiership when Prem retires, sometime between 1988 and 1990.

Early in 1987, Chaovalit expressed his determination to drive some well-entrenched Vietnamese forces out of the hills overlooking Chong Bok pass, near the Laotian-Cambodian border. After several months of fighting, the Thai were forced to withdraw and regroup after sustaining the largest number of casualties in any recent engagement with the Vietnamese.

THAILAND • Information Highlights

Official Name: Kingdom of Thailand (conventional); Prathet Thai (Thai).
Location: Southeast Asia.
Area: 198,456 sq mi (514 000 km^2).
Population (mid-1987 est.): 53,600,000.
Chief City (Dec. 1984 est.): Bangkok, the capital, 5,018,327.
Government: *Head of state,* Bhumibol Adulyadej, king (acceded June 1946). *Head of government,* Gen. Prem Tinsulanonda, prime minister (took office March 1980).
Monetary Unit: Baht (25.74 baht equal U.S.$1, August 1987).
Gross National Product (1985 U.S.$): $37,200,000,000.
Economic Index (Bangkok, 1986): *Consumer Prices* (1980 = 100), all items, 130.7; food, 116.6.
Foreign Trade (1986 U.S.$): *Imports,* $9,138,000,000; *exports,* $8,753,000,000.

Economics. The Thai economy continued to grow in 1987 but at a slower rate than in recent years, because the country has been plagued by drought, poor world prices for some of its exports, and a growing trend toward protectionism in the United States and other Western nations. The baht declined along with the U.S. dollar, to which it is linked, and the Thai stock market underwent a substantial correction, along with most other stock markets around the world.

The U.S. Congress passed legislation that would discourage Thai exports of palm oil and coconut products, and threatened to impose new limits on the amount of Thai textiles that could enter the United States. The United States also sought to persuade the Thai government to adopt legislation that would make it illegal to reprint books and other materials covered by American copyright without paying royalties to the author.

The long drought, which was particularly serious in northeast Thailand, called attention to the need to conserve water resources including the remaining watershed forests in the north and northeast. Thai forests, which once covered most of the country, have been decimated by years of illegal cutting combined with little reforestation. The government has launched an ambitious five-year program that will cost $500 million. It is aimed at doubling the forest cover and restoring water resources.

Foreign Relations. Foreign Minister Siddhi Savetsila—along with the other foreign ministers of the Association of Southeast Asian Nations (ASEAN)—continued to support the Cambodian resistance to Vietnam's occupation of that country. ASEAN tried to persuade Vietnam to negotiate a settlement of the Cambodia problem, but Vietnam sought to make the ASEAN nations deal directly with the regime it controls in Phnom Penh. The Cambodia question was reported to be a major topic of discussion between Thai leaders and Eduard Shevardnadze when the Soviet foreign minister visited Thailand in March.

Air Chief Marshal Siddhi became the first Thai foreign minister to visit the Soviet Union in May. A protocol establishing a Soviet-Thai commission on trade was signed during the visit. After leaving the USSR, Siddhi traveled to East Germany, Poland, and Czechoslovakia.

Despite the bruising caused by bitterly disputed trade issues, the United States provided increased military support in the form of an agreement to set up a joint war reserve stockpile in the kingdom.

In other diplomatic news, Thailand and Malaysia agreed to set up a joint ministerial-level commission on mutual cooperation, and Thailand established diplomatic relations with Suriname and Malawi.

PETER A. POOLE
Author, *"The Vietnamese in Thailand"*

© Michael Le Poer Trench

"Les Misérables," a musical adaptation of Victor Hugo's epic novel, opened on Broadway in March with record advance ticket sales of $11 million. The British import later captured eight Tony Awards, including best musical and score.

THEATER

It may have been only a small upward blip on the long downward slope of Broadway, but modest improvements in attendance and box office receipts during 1986–87 were enough to make *Variety* declare in a banner headline, "B'Way Legit Has Upbeat Season." Off-Broadway, nonprofit, and regional theaters continued in ascension with major new introductions and often inspired revivals. Signaling a major shift in the balance of the American theater scene, Actors Equity reported that in 1985–86 for the first time its members worked more hours in nonprofit theater—the resident companies off-Broadway and outside New York—than in the commercial sectors of Broadway and tour-booking houses.

Broadway. The total number of productions on the Great White Way jumped from 33 in 1985–86 to 40 in 1986–87 (measured from June 1 to May 31). Attendance increased 6.7% over the previous season to 6,968,277, reversing a five-year slide, while total box-office receipts climbed 8.7% to more than $207 million.

The gains were attributed to the so-called "British Invasion"—three new blockbuster musicals from England which joined the London-bred *Cats,* still purring along after five sell-out seasons on Broadway. Two of these new London transfers were also critical triumphs; The Royal Shakespeare Company's noble, thrilling production of *Les Misérables,* adapted from the 1862 Victor Hugo epic by the Anglo-French librettist team of Alain Boublil, Claude-Michel Schönberg (who also composed the pop-opera score), and Herbert Kretzmer; and *Me and My Girl,* a delightful British trifle of the 1930s rescued from obscurity by Richard Armitage, the producer and the son of the show's composer, Noel Gay. The show also launched Broadway's first new theater since the early 1970s, the Marquis in the lavish Marriott hotel.

Though *Les Misérables* won the showdown in the 1987 Tony Awards, with eight trophies to *Girl*'s three, perhaps the most significant winner in the musical category was best actor Robert Lindsay, a little-known British classics specialist whose acrobatic Cockney hero in *Girl* drew delirious comparison to such great clowns as Buster Keaton.

The other salvo in the British Invasion came from Andrew Lloyd Webber's *Starlight Express,* a family-oriented extravaganza in which the players wore roller skates and portrayed trains in a transcontinental race on a dizzying, dazzling track set. At $8 million, *Starlight* was the most expensive Broadway show ever and to some critics exemplified a troubling trend toward spectacle and sensory overkill. But it was a popular hit.

In the straight plays of Broadway's 1986–87 season, however, the well-made American family drama reestablished its durable appeal. August Wilson's *Fences,* which originated at Yale Repertory Theatre, won the 1987 Pulitzer

© Ron Scherl

James Earl Jones won a Tony as best actor and Mary Alice was judged best featured actress for their performances in August Wilson's Pulitzer-winning drama "Fences."

Prize and the Tony Award for best play, and provided the best actor role for James Earl Jones (*see* BIOGRAPHY) as an embittered former ballplayer jealous of his son's success in the changing racial environment of the 1950s. *Broadway Bound* completed Neil Simon's autobiographical trilogy. Though frequently heartwarming, it was the darkest and perhaps strongest work from a man formerly associated only with glib commercial comedies, and the role of the long-suffering mother earned Linda Lavin the Tony for best actress.

Tina Howe's *Coastal Disturbances* managed to transfer from off-Broadway's Second Stage and featured a stunning Broadway debut by Annette Bening as a New York "fast tracker" derailed by an old-fashioned summer romance.

In the British import plays, performances by Royal Shakespearians redeemed the arch sexual intrigues of pre-Revolutionary France in *Les Liaisons Dangereuses,* while an American replacement cast failed to support Ian McKellen in *Wild Honey,* an adaptation of a never-before-produced Chekhov comedy.

The Tony for best revival went to (the unfortunately short-lived) *All My Sons,* the 1947 Arthur Miller drama transferred from Connecticut's Long Wharf Theatre and starring Richard Kiley. Among best revival nominees, John Lithgow and Richard Thomas had a field day in the acclaimed Lincoln Center production of the newspaper comedy chestnut, *The Front Page;* and mixed notices could not keep crowds away from a London transfer of Shaw's *Pygmalion,* starring Amanda Plummer as Eliza Doolittle and a gaunt Peter O'Toole in his Broadway debut as Henry Higgins. Another Shaw play, the rarely performed *You Never Can Tell,* drew kudos for old pros Uta Hagen and Phillip Bosco.

Good actors who enrolled in weak new plays included Robert De Niro *(Cuba and his Teddy Bear)* and Mary Tyler Moore and Lynn Redgrave *(Sweet Sue).* Good actors in mixed revivals were Jean Stapleton and Tony Roberts *(Arsenic and Old Lace)* and the great Geraldine Page, who died during the brief run of Noel Coward's *Blithe Spirit* opposite Richard Chamberlain.

The irony of the British musical hits is that they succeeded with classically American ingredients: high-minded sentiment *(Les Misérables),* spectacle *(Starlight),* and cornball nostalgia *(Me and My Girl).* The miserably small selection of American musical entries, by contrast, failed in half-baked attempts to attack such viable issues as the struggle of Jewish immigrants *(Rags),* the warped values of beauty pageants *(Smile),* and even the authenticity of the Shroud of Turin *(Into the Light).* In other words, Britain was beating America at its own game. So the continuing plight of the American-made musical—underlined by the November closing of *La Cage aux Folles* after a smash run of more than four years—cast a shadow over the modest encouragements of the 1986–87 season on the Great White Way.

The first months of the 1987–88 season held some hope that the slow upward trend might continue, with a cluster of major openings far earlier (in mid-October) than in recent seasons. Lanford Wilson, a leading playwright absent from Broadway since early in the decade, made a strong homecoming with *Burn This,* a comedy/drama about a misfit romance set against the downtown art world, though critics were strongly split on the flamboyant performance of rising star John Malkovich. There were also some critical reservations about the 20th-anniversary revival of *Cabaret,* starring Joel Grey in his signature role of the Emcee, and about *Into the Woods,* the new Stephen Sondheim musical that irreverently rewrote Grimm's fairy tales and reunited the entire creative team, including librettist-director James Lapine, from his 1984 musical *Sunday in the Park with George.*

An unqualified smash, both critically and commercially, was Lincoln Center's revival of the 1934 shipboard romp, *Anything Goes,* featuring Patti Lupone and Cole Porter's efferves-

BROADWAY OPENINGS 1987

MUSICALS

Anything Goes (revival), music and lyrics by Cole Porter, original book by Guy Bolton, P. G. Wodehouse, Howard Lindsay, Russel Crouse, new book by Timothy Crouse, John Weidman; directed by Jerry Zaks; with Patti LuPone, Howard McGillin, Anthony Heald; Oct. 19–.

Cabaret (revival), music by John Kander, lyrics by Fred Ebb, book by Joe Masteroff, based on stories by Christopher Isherwood and the play *I am a Camera* by John van Druten; directed by Harold Prince; with Joel Grey, Alyson Reed, Regina Resnick; Oct. 22–.

Don't Get God Started, music and lyrics by Marvin Winans; written and directed by Ron Milner; with Vanessa Bell Armstrong, Chip Fields, Bebe Winans; Oct. 29–.

Dreamgirls (revival), music by Henry Krieger, book and lyrics by Tom Eyen; directed by Michael Bennett; production supervised by Bob Avian; with Susan Beaubian, Alisa Gyse, Arnetia Walker, Roy L. Jones; June 28–Dec. 13.

Into the Woods, music and lyrics by Stephen Sondheim; written and directed by James Lapine; with Bernadette Peters, Tom Aldredge, Joanna Gleason, Chip Zien, Robert Westenberg; Nov. 5–.

Late Nite Comic, music and lyrics by Brian Gari, book by Allan Knee; directed by Philip Rose; with Robert LuPone, Teresa Tracy; Oct. 15–17.

Les Misérables, music by Claude-Michel Schönberg, lyrics by Herbert Kretzmer, book by Alain Boublil and Claude-Michel Schönberg, based on the novel by Victor Hugo; adapted and directed by Trevor Nunn and John Caird; with Colm Wilkinson, Terrence Mann, Frances Rufelle, Randy Graff, Leo Burmester; March 12–.

The Mikado, music by Arthur Sullivan, words by W. S. Gilbert; directed by Brian Macdonald; with Richard McMillan, Arlene Meadows, Eric Donkin, Marie Baron, John Keane; April 2–May 3.

Rosa, music by Gilbert Bécaud, book and lyrics by Julian More, based on a novel by Romain Gary; directed by Harold Prince; with Georgia Brown, Bob Gunton; Oct. 1–11.

Stardust (The Mitchell Parish Musical), revue with music by Duke Ellington, Nat King Cole, Hoagy Carmichael, Benny Goodman, and others; lyrics by Mitchell Parish; conceived and directed by Albert Harris; with André DeShields, Michele Bautier; Feb. 19–May 17.

Starlight Express, music by Andrew Lloyd Webber, lyrics by Richard Stilgoe; directed by Trevor Nunn; with Greg Mowry, Robert Torti, Ken Ard; March 15–.

Teddy and Alice, music by John Philip Sousa, original music and adaptation of Mr. Sousa's music by Richard Kapp, lyrics by Hal Hackady, book by Jerome Alden; directed by John Driver; with Len Cariou, Nancy Hume, Ron Raines, Beth Fowler; Nov. 12–.

PLAYS

All My Sons (revival), by Arthur Miller; directed by Arvin Brown; with Richard Kiley, Jamey Sheridan, Joyce Ebert; April 22–May 17.

Asinamali, written and directed by Mbogeni Ngema; April 23–May 17.

Blithe Spirit (revival), by Noel Coward; directed by Brian Murray; with Richard Chamberlain, Blythe Danner, Judith Ivey, Geraldine Page; March 31–June 21.

Breaking the Code, by Hugh Whitemore; directed by Clifford Williams; with Derek Jacobi; Nov. 15–.

Broadway (revival), by Philip Dunning and George Abbott; directed by George Abbott; with Lonny Price, Richard Poe, Dorothy Stanley; June 25–27.

Burn This, by Lanford Wilson; directed by Marshall W. Mason; with John Malkovich, Joan Allen; Oct. 14–.

Coastal Disturbances, by Tina Howe; directed by Carole Rothman; with Annette Bening, Timothy Daly, Heather MacRae, Rosemary Murphy; March 4–.

The Comedy of Errors, by William Shakespeare; directed by Robert Woodruff; with Avner the Eccentric, the Flying Karamazov Brothers; May 31–July 26.

Death and the King's Horseman, written and directed by Wole Soyinka; with Earle Hyman, Eriq LaSalle, Alan Coates, Jill Larson; March 1–29.

Fences, by August Wilson; directed by Lloyd Richards; with James Earl Jones, Mary Alice; March 26–.

Les Liaisons Dangereuses, by Christopher Hampton, from the novel by Choderlos de Laclos; directed by Howard Davies; with Alan Rickman, Lindsay Duncan; April 30–Sept. 6.

A Month of Sundays, by Bob Larbey; directed by Gene Saks; with Jason Robards; April 16–18.

The Musical Comedy Murders of 1940, written and directed by John Bishop; April 6–Aug. 1.

The Nerd, by Larry Shue; directed by Charles Nelson Reilly; with Robert Joy, Peter Riegert, Mark Hamill; March 22–.

Pygmalion (revival), by George Bernard Shaw; directed by Val May; with Peter O'Toole, Amanda Plummer, John Mills; April 26–Aug. 2.

Safe Sex, by Harvey Fierstein; directed by Eric Concklin; with Harvey Fierstein, Wesley Ship, John Mulkeen, Anne De Salvo; April 5–12.

Sherlock's Last Case, by Charles Marowitz; directed by A. J. Antoon; with Frank Langella, Donal Donnelly; Aug. 20–Dec. 6.

Sleight of Hand, by John Pielmeier; directed by Walton Jones; with Harry Groener, Jeffrey DeMunn; May 3–9.

Stepping Out, by Richard Harris; directed by Tommy Tune; with Don Amendolia, Carole Shelley, Pamela Sousa, Victoria Boothby; Jan. 11–March 15.

Sweet Sue, by A. R. Gurney, Jr.; directed by John Tillinger; with Mary Tyler Moore, Lynn Redgrave; Jan. 8–May 31.

OTHER ENTERTAINMENT

Barbara Cook: A Concert for the Theatre, revue with music from *Carousel, The Music Man,* and other musicals, sung by Barbara Cook; April 15–26.

Penn and Teller, comedy-magic show, supervised by Art Wolff; with Penn Gillette and Teller; Dec. 1–.

Mort Sahl on Broadway, one-man show by comic Mort Sahl; Oct. 11–Nov. 1.

The Regard of Flight and **The Clown Bagatelles,** written and performed by Bill Irwin in collaboration with the company and Nancy Harrington; with M. C. O'Connor, Doug Skinner; April 12–26.

cent score. Popular success appeared more problematic for *Breaking the Code,* Hugh Whitemore's London drama based on the true story of the eccentric, homosexual mathematics professor who deciphered the Nazi U-boat code, though there was no question of the brilliant performance by the British classical actor Derek Jacobi.

The deaths of Michael Bennett and Bob Fosse, two of Broadway's greatest creative talents, decimated the top tier of director-choreographers.

Off-Broadway. Producer Joseph Papp, with typical impresarial bravado, announced his plan to produce all 36 of Shakespeare's plays over a six-year span, in his Public Theater complex and in Central Park under the umbrella of his New York Shakespeare Festival. He began with *A Midsummer Night's Dream,* starring Elizabeth McGovern and F. Murray Abraham and set in turn-of-the-century Brazil. Ever the risk taker, Papp also mounted one of the notable flops of 1986–87: *The Knife,* a musical study of sex-change operations by Britain's David Hare *(Plenty),* and starring Mandy Patinkin. But early in the 1987–88 season, Papp had better luck with another progressive British playwright, Caryl Churchill, whose *Serious Money* was a scathing satire of the ethics of high finance.

In *Driving Miss Daisy,* playwright Alfred Uhry crystallized 25 years of changes in the American racial environment through the complex relationship between a white Atlanta dowager and her black chauffeur. The play was one of the most acclaimed entries of 1986–87 and the exquisite Playwrights Horizons premiere featured Obie-winning performances by Dana Ivey and Morgan Freeman.

Playwright Horton Foote unveiled two more parts of his Texas family saga: *The Widow Claire,* starring Matthew Broderick, and *Lily Dale,* featuring starlet Molly Ringwald in her New York stage debut.

Playwright Terrence McNally ended a long critical dry spell thanks to smart stagings at Manhattan Theatre Club: *It's Only a Play,* a show business comedy, and *Frankie and Johnny at the Claire de Lune,* which drew high marks for Kathy Bates and Kenneth Welsh as misfit middle-aged lovers.

The 1987–88 season began with an acclaimed New York debut by Atlanta playwright Barbara Lebow, whose *A Shayna Maidel,* starring Melissa Gilbert, was a moving drama about Jewish sisters coming to terms with the memory of the Holocaust: and *Oil City Symphony,* another giddy, down-home musical revue with two of the writer-performers of *Pump Boys and Dinettes,* Deborah Monk and Mark Hardwick. The director Peter Brook brought *The Mahabarata,* his sprawling epic from Indian scripture, to the Brooklyn Academy of Music, but critics were split on whether it held up over its nine-hour length.

The departure of the Circle Repertory Company's founding artistic director Marshall Mason, after more than 20 years and several Tony Award-winning Broadway transfers, marked a major change of the guard in the American theater. Incoming director Tanya Berezin set about to pull Circle Rep out of its recent artistic doldrums.

Regional Theater. Theater Communications Group (TCG), the national information clearinghouse for the nonprofit theater, reported that in 1985–86, for the first time in five seasons, total income at 200 TCG member theaters grew faster than expenses, though deficits still remained at many theaters. Critics complained of a subtle "artistic deficit"—a tendency toward cautiousness or more crowd-pleasing fare. But the TCG magazine *American Theatre* projected that the growing percentage of contributed income (public, private, and corporate donations) might begin to relieve the financial pressure.

Yale Repertory Theatre (YRT), under the direction of Lloyd Richards, scored critical triumphs and introduced major new dramas to the American repertoire. *Joe Turner's Come and Gone,* another installment in August Wilson's cycle of black history plays, played at Boston's Huntington Theatre, Seattle Repertory Theatre, and Washington's Arena Stage; *A Walk in the Woods,* Lee Blessing's look at the human side of U.S.-Soviet arms talks, bowed at YRT and then was staged at La Jolla Playhouse near San Diego.

San Diego, in fact, was dubbed the most exciting new theater city by *Time* magazine and *The New York Times,* in much the same way Chicago was annointed in the mid-1980s. The city's flagship theater, Jack O'Brien's Old Globe, presented the initial tryouts of the Broadway-bound *Into the Woods* and successfully premiered *Another Antigone* by A.R. Gurney, featuring George Grizzard as a professor grappling with a coed's value system.

Farther up the coast in the emerging theatrical world of southern California, South Coast Repertory of Costa Mesa premiered *Three Postcards,* a Sondheimesque musical fantasy-comedy by Craig Lucas and Craig Carnelia about the dinner reunion of three Baby-Boom women. Hailed in some circles as one of the best American musicals of the season, it later fared poorly in the cramped scenic quarters of off-Broadway's Playwrights Horizons.

American Theatre magazine reported a resurgence in new interpretations of the classics, led by a "new wave" of young artistic directors including Robert Falls and Garland Wright, who served their first full season at the helms of the Goodman Theatre of Chicago and the Guthrie Theater of Minneapolis, respectively; Des McAnuff of La Jolla; and free-lance director Peter Sellars.

The Goodman recognized solo performance artists as one of the signature theatrical movements of the decade by offering three such artists on one bill: Avner the Eccentric, a mime/clown of the "New Vaudevillian" school; David Cale, the British monologuist; and Fred Curchack, who uses puppetry and magic to create a one-man version of Shakespeare's *The Tempest.* All three, along with monologuist Spalding Gray, toured the resident theaters extensively in 1987.

Senior directors known for revisionist classics also had solid seasons in 1986–87. Robert Brustein's challenging, critically praised calendar at American Repertory Theatre in Cambridge, MA, included an *Alcestis* from the controversial avant-garde director Robert Wilson. Adrian Hall premiered his epic adaptation of *All the King's Men* at his two theaters—the Dallas Theater Center and then at Trinity Square Repertory Company, in Providence, RI.

Soviet director Yuri Lyubimov, banned from producing in the USSR after more than 20 years of internationally acclaimed and controversial stagings, made a U.S. premiere at Washington's Arena Stage with his adaptation of *Crime and Punishment* that evoked the modern Soviet police state.

DAN HULBERT
"The Atlanta Journal and Constitution"

TRANSPORTATION

U.S. transportation activities experienced uneven growth among the various modes of transport during 1987, even though record production levels in terms of ton-miles and passenger-miles were attained. Production growth in 1987 in the domestic transportation industries closely coincided with overall increases in the net national product. For the first time since 1980, however, total freight expenditures expressed as a percentage of the gross national product (GNP) stabilized at approximately 8%. Because of anticipated shortages in physical supply, this expenditure category may well increase in 1988 due to shortages of drivers and capital attraction problems.

Although the sum total of carrier revenues reached record highs during 1987, net earnings were relatively flat due to fierce price competition among all transportation modes. Merger activity diminished somewhat in 1987, and intermodal acquisitions—purchases of truck and barge lines by railroads—diminished considerably. The Oct. 19, 1987, stock-market crash severely affected transportation stocks, which may well correct the excess capacity problem that has plagued the industry since 1980. The number of bankruptcies among general freight carriers diminished in the less-than-truckload (LTL) sector of trucking but increased in the truckload (TL) sector. Even Federal Express suffered declines in equity prices and earnings as competition with United Parcel Service (UPS) intensified. Restructuring of the overnight air-package industry increased in 1987, a process exacerbated by price competition.

Although domestic transportation activities remain cyclical in nature, some route stability became evident in air and rail systems during 1987. However, further restructuring could result if partial re-regulation laws are enacted.

Following four years of continuous service, Elizabeth Dole resigned as secretary of the U.S. Department of Transportation (DOT) on Oct. 1, 1987. During her tenure as secretary of the second largest executive agency in the government, Secretary Dole oversaw the privatization of Conrail and was responsible for administering the recovery of the Air Traffic Control System. James Burnley IV, a 39-year-old deputy secretary of the department, was appointed by President Reagan to succeed Mrs. Dole. After prolonged confirmation hearings in the Senate, he was sworn in on December 3.

Airlines. The year 1987 represented an extremely difficult one for the U.S. airline industry in terms of profits, customer service, and safety perceptions. A recent movement to reregulate segments of the industry expanded among members of Congress. The stock market's precipitous decline in October dramatically reduced carrier equity values across the board. The company hardest hit was Continental because of a heavy debt load incurred, resulting from purchasing Eastern and Peoples Express. Financial analysts' forecasts of earnings for the industry during the final quarter of 1987 and the first months of 1988 were flat at best and downward at worse. Carrier price discounting continues, and 72% of all tickets sold in 1987 were discounted—a harbinger of price instability.

Responding to a record number of consumer complaints about cancellations, delays, and lost luggage, both the Senate and House of Representatives pursued legislation requiring carriers to publish various service measures. The House of Representatives enacted a bill requiring issuance of free tickets when baggage is lost or delayed and when flights are cancelled. Several state attorneys general were attempting to enact consumer protection legislation designed specifically to curtail per-

In the competitive era of airline deregulation, U.S. carriers were scheduling too many flights at the most popular travel times —creating some huge runway jam-ups. Consumer complaints about airline service in general rose sharply in 1987.

© Kevin Horan/Picture Group

ceived or actual airline abuse of passengers, a move resisted by the Air Transportation Association, which is the carrier's trade association.

Responding to congressional and consumer complaints, the DOT through its rulemaking capability required airlines to provide monthly flight performance data for release to the public. The initial report for September 1987 was released by the DOT on Nov. 10, 1987, and the results were surprising to both passengers and airline management. A result of the report was that in terms of on-time performance, American experienced 84.5% of all domestic flights arriving on schedule, while USAir reported only 67.4% of its flights performing on schedule. Regarding the September flights that arrived late 70% of the time, Pan American was first with 6.1% of its flights delayed 15 minutes or more. United had the best record in that category with .06% of its flights late 70% of the time. Northwest Airlines received the largest number of consumer complaints in the category of mishandled baggage. Starting in December 1987, airline performance data were to be provided to travel agents who in turn can provide consumers with these performance measures. Late in the year, a House-Senate Conference Committee was reconciling consumer protection bills designed to resolve airline service problems. Congress did pass a ban on smoking on domestic flights scheduled to last two hours or less.

In the field of mergers and acquisitions, an administrative law judge with the DOT denied a proposed merger between USAir and Piedmont. American West, an upstart carrier based in Phoenix, AZ, objected to the proposed unification, citing economic concentration and very high prices for gates in the New York area as the principal reasons for contesting the merger. On appeal to the secretary of transportation, the adverse decision was reversed. While concentration remains high at certain airports, not all of the merged carriers benefited financially during 1987. Continental suffered large losses, and Northwest incurred losses while attempting to assimilate the former Republic Airline system.

Airline and aviation safety remained in the public spotlight during 1987 with numerous reports of near collisions. Delta was plagued with an unfortunate series of events ranging from aircraft flying off-course to landings at wrong airports. Several major crashes occurred in 1987. Northwest flight 255 bound from Detroit to Phoenix on August 16 constituted the second worst accident in U.S. aviation history. The flight crashed during takeoff, and 156 people perished. Continental Flight 1713 crashed on takeoff in Denver on November 15, killing 19. A South African jet crashed in the Indian Ocean in late November, killing some 160 persons. And PSA Flight 1771 crashed in December, killing 44.

During the first eight months of 1987, U.S. international carriers Pan American, TWA, United, and American, experienced an increase in the number of passengers on European routes as concerns regarding terrorism abated. However, the rapid decline of the U.S. dollar relative to the pound, mark, and yen late in the year could result in fewer U.S. citizens traveling abroad. Such a decline would have a serious impact on U.S. carriers.

Railroads. U.S. railroad industry earnings declined somewhat during 1987, and average returns on investment did not exceed 5%. The Interstate Commerce Commission (ICC) continued to declare the industry "revenue inadequate." A growing number of complaints against rail pricing activities intensified with the formation of shipper associations such as CURE, which seeks to re-regulate certain segments of the railroad industry. Congressional pressure to modify the Staggers Act, the railroad regulatory policy legislation of 1980, in the rate area increased during 1987.

The ICC again denied the merger of the Santa Fe and Southern Pacific Railroad and ordered divestiture. On appeal, the ICC affirmed its 1986 decision against the merger, and the railroad was in the process of being separated late in the year.

During 1987 rail carriers continued the trend toward "intermodalism" with numerous innovations such as Road Runner (a truck trailer with hydraulically interchangeable rail wheels) and double-breasting (creating nonunion affiliates of truckers' unions) that helped increase loading. Consequently, such developments are permitting railroads to attract high-value goods that normally move via truck routes.

In the area of legislation, Congress returned Conrail to the private sector. A successful equity offering was provided to the public, which resulted in the largest initial public stock offering in Wall Street history, more than $1 billion in new equity.

Ridership on Amtrak continued to increase in 1987. Continued upgrading of equipment has enabled the carrier to attract new riders in high-density travel corridors, but the long-term viability of the carrier was again questioned as the Reagan administration continued its efforts to end Amtrak's reliance on an annual federal subsidy. Meanwhile rail safety became an issue after 16 persons were killed and more than 170 were injured when an Amtrak passenger train and three Conrail diesel engines collided near Baltimore in January.

Truck acquisitions by railroads abated during 1987 even though track abandonments continued expanding. By the end of 1987, this phenomenon produced more than 350 new short-line railroads. These new carriers have brought continued rail service to various parts of the United States but produced controversy insofar as the ICC is concerned regarding labor protection provisions normally associated with asset transfers between carriers.

Major labor disputes continued regarding work rules in the industry, and Congress was seriously considering amending certain parts of the Railway Labor Act.

Trucking. In terms of earnings, the U.S. motor trucking industry remained relatively flat during the first two quarters of 1987, and then turned dramatically downward during the last two quarters. LTL and TL stocks were hard hit by the October stock-market decline.

Major companies such as Yellow Freight, Consolidated Freightways, and Roadway Express incurred drops in earnings even though production levels increased substantially. The level of concentration in the LTL sector of trucking continued to intensify, and a major antitrust case was filed in the Federal District Court in Greenville, SC, where allegations of predatory pricing have been levied against three major LTL carriers. Nevertheless, the number of new TL carriers continued to increase in 1987. Roadway Package Express continued to expand in its battle to enter the small package market.

Bankruptcies continued in trucking during 1987. Unemployment, in terms of numbers, expanded in the LTL segment of trucking by more than 25,000, and a major shakeout was occurring among the new truckload carriers that have entered the market since 1980. Because of heavy rate discounting, tonnage increased but earnings decreased. One major merger occurred during 1987—the merger of American Carriers with Smith Transfer. The number of carriers with Employee Stock Ownership Programs (ESOPs) was reduced by one when American Carriers acquired Smith from ARA Services, Inc.

During 1987, Congress passed, over President Reagan's veto, legislation permitting the states to raise the speed limits on rural sections of the interstate highways to 65 miles per hour (105 km/hr). Some LTL truckers opposed the measure, which was part of a $87.5 billion highway and mass-transit package, because of fuel conservation desires, while others supported the increased speed limits.

In the truckload area, a severe shortage of qualified drivers and the creation of the National Drivers Licensing and Registration process dramatically reduced the supply of drivers. Consequently, many companies did not enjoy the rapid expansion that they previously experienced. Insurance continued to be a major problem plaguing the trucking industry, and when available, insurance premiums reached record highs during 1987. Regulatory authorities continued to insist upon proof of insurance before issuing certificates, and insurance premiums were predicted to increase as the safety problem intensified.

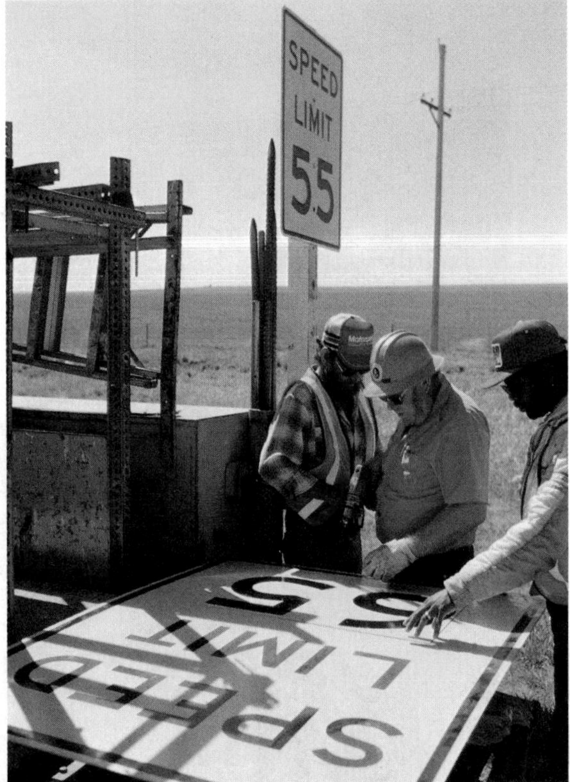

Several states raised the speed limit on rural interstate highways from 55 to 65 mph after federal legislation permitting such action was enacted over a presidential veto.

Safety in motor transportation continued to be enormously controversial, and numerous charges have been levied by all sectors of the industry concerning aging equipment, qualifications of drivers, and increasing accident rates. Congress began to address the problem, and legislation was to be introduced in 1988 to eliminate "commercial zone" exemptions.

Maritime Shipping. The maritime industry continued to be plagued by the dual problems of excess capacity and intense price competition in both domestic and international markets. International shipping continued declining in terms of bookings during 1987. Among inland water carriers, excess capacity, low-earning levels, and a record number of bankruptcies continued to depress this segment of transportation, although some upturns in tonnage were experienced during the year.

One bright segment of the maritime industry in 1987 was the expansion of cruise-ship traffic. This form of leisure transportation increased patronage for the fifth consecutive year (*see* TRAVEL). However, the wholesale freight segment of the maritime industry remained depressed because of excess capacity, low product demand, and intense competition from other modes of transport.

GRANT M. DAVIS, *University of Arkansas*

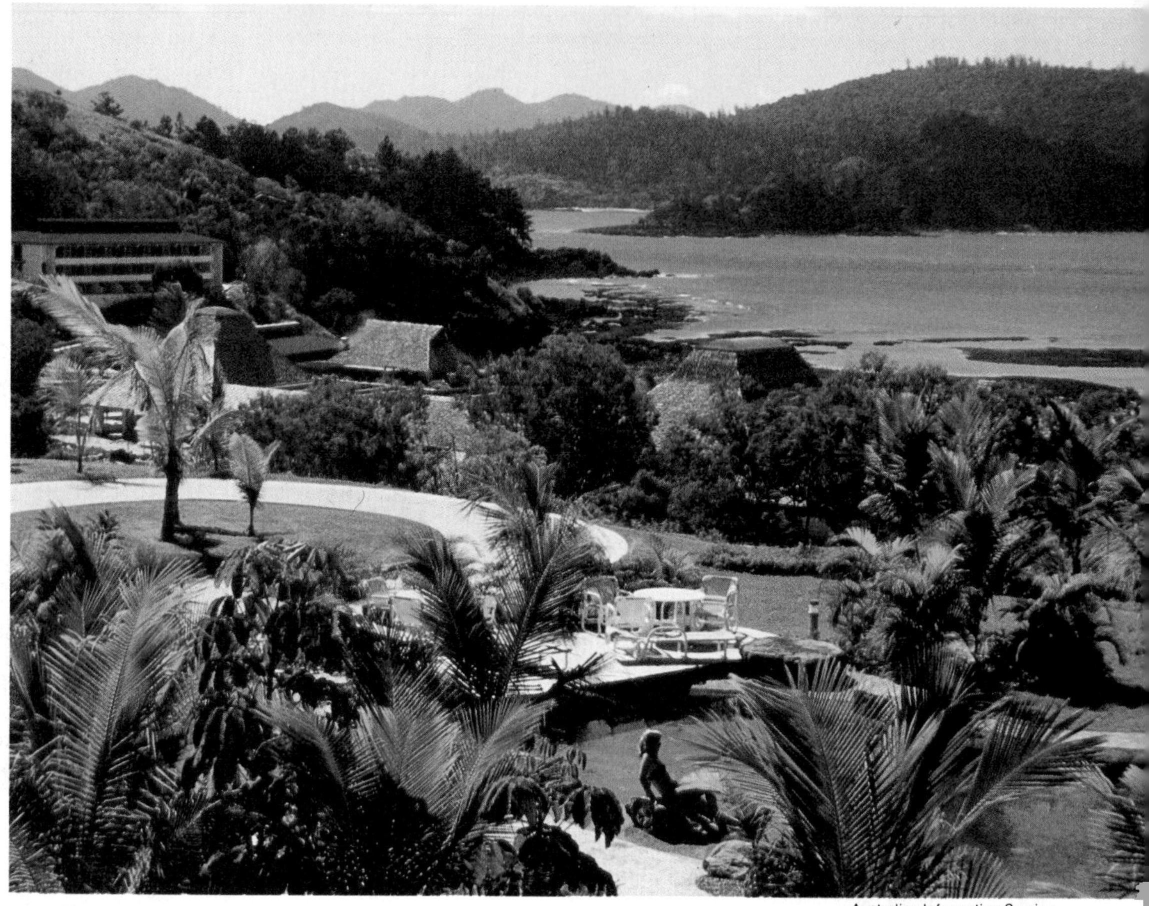

Australian Information Service

Vacation dreams of palm trees and Pacific breezes—as at Hamilton Island in Australia's Great Barrier Reef, above*—became a reality for an increasing number of Americans. U.S. travel to destinations in the Pacific was up during the year.*

TRAVEL

Following a year in which travel plans were shaped by the fear of international terrorism, it was back to normal for American travelers in 1987—and then some. Americans seemed to make travel, both overseas and at home, a priority in 1987. Travel in the United States by foreign visitors also was exceptionally strong.

Less-than-favorable dollar exchange rates did not deter Americans from traveling abroad. Reassured by the absence of terrorist incidents and a stable economy for most of the year, they responded to pent-up demand for travel following a stay-at-home year in 1986. It also appeared that part of the reason for the upward surge in overseas travel might just be the emergence of the first of the baby boomers into the age bracket that traditionally makes up the bulk of international travelers.

Life-styles were changing the way in which Americans traveled, too. As two-income families found it increasingly difficult to schedule vacation time, shorter vacations were replacing the traditional two-week (or longer) annual trips. Weekend jaunts and mini-vacations became increasingly popular for domestic travel. Even overseas travel showed a trend toward shorter trips, but more of them. No longer was a European tour a once-in-a-lifetime expectation for many Americans.

At Home. Americans took an estimated 1.1 billion "person trips"—a trip of 100 mi (160 km) or more from home—in their own country in 1987, according to U.S. Travel Data Center estimates. This was an increase of 4% over the previous record year. The American Automobile Association (AAA) also reported a record-breaking summer travel season and an overall 3% increase in leisure travel for the year. Though there was some indication that more people were choosing air travel for long-distance trips, vehicular travel still accounted for 85% of domestic leisure travel, according to the AAA.

Amtrak, too, had its busiest summer ever and estimated a healthy 12% increase in rider miles for the year along with a 15% rise in revenue. Rail passengers were finding they needed to make their plans further in advance; first-class space for train travel over the Christmas holidays was sold out three months ahead.

The year was particularly bright from the standpoint of international travel to the United States. Favorable exchange rates against the U.S. dollar helped account for an estimated 12% increase in foreign tourism to the United States. Total arrivals of 28.4 million included a record 10.5 million overseas visitors (up 18%) and a record 12.2 million from Canada (up 11%). Travel from Mexico rebounded somewhat after several downward years, with 5.8 million arrivals (up 4%).

Amtrak reported that rail travel by visiting foreigners was up a hefty 24%, led by residents of Great Britain, West Germany, Japan, and Australia/New Zealand. Overall, especially strong sources of foreign visitors to the United States were Japan (up 27%), Great Britain (up 20%), and West Germany (up 40%). Canada continued to make up the largest inbound segment, some 43% of the total. Mexico accounted for 20%, Europe 16%, and Asia 11%. Encouraged by the strong yen, Japanese travelers chose Hawaii in large enough numbers to offset flat arrival statistics from the mainland following the 1986 boom year.

Outward Bound. Fears for their personal safety calmed as the year proceeded without terrorist incidents directed at American travelers, some 13.5 million Americans headed overseas in 1987—up 13% from the previous year. Of the total, some 6.2 million chose Europe as their destination, a 20% rebound for the destination hardest hit by security fears in 1986. More and more flights out of more and more U.S. gateways were available to Europe, resulting in more promotional fares.

Closer to home, the United States sent another 13.5 million travelers to Mexico in 1987 to take advantage of the continued peso devaluation. That represented a big 18% increase over 1986. Travel to Canada, on the other hand, dropped 5%, to 13.4 million—not unexpected after the numbers that had opted for a Canada vacation the previous year because of Expo 1986, a world's fair in Vancouver, B.C.

With ever more Americans tracing their roots across the Pacific rather than the Atlantic, and with America's business ties to the Pacific becoming ever stronger, North American travel to the Pacific area continued its steady climb. A number of new trans-Pacific carriers contributed to an overall growth of 7%–8% for the year. Among especially strong destinations of growth for travel from the United States were Australia/New Zealand, Hong Kong, Thailand, and Singapore.

Cruising. Continuing the trend of the past several years, a record number of American passengers proved the popularity of cruising as a vacation style. An estimated 3.05 million North Americans sailed on cruise ships in 1987, some 9% more than the previous year. Shipboard demographics continued to reveal a younger cruise passenger; about one third of the year's total were under 35 years of age, another third in the 35-to-55 age group. Also notable in 1987 was the increased interest of single travelers in cruises—and the interest of the cruise lines in courting them as customers. Whereas singles traditionally have paid a hefty supplemental fare for the privilege of traveling solo, now a number of cruise lines offered attractive fares for them or guaranteed roommates to even out the cost differential.

Following a cruise-ship exodus from the Mediterranean in 1986 because of the fear of terrorism, 1987 saw the majority of cruise lines resume their Mediterranean programs. Still others were scheduled to do so in 1988—assuming continued calm waters. Alaska, which benefited in 1986 from the repositioning of ships from the Mediterranean as well as the regional draw of Canada's Expo, remained a strong cruise destination even without these incentives. The Caribbean showed no signs of diminishing in popularity or competitiveness.

The year saw the introduction of several new ships: Carnival Cruise Lines' 1,800-passenger *Celebration* and Regency Cruises' 960-passenger *Regent Star* in the Caribbean area, American Cruise Lines' 125-passenger *Charleston* along the East Coast, and Windstar Sail Cruises' 150-passenger *Wind Song* in French Polynesia.

Trend Setting. More and more Americans chose to travel by air in 1987—but they were not always happy about it. The year was marked by well publicized debate about air safety following a spate of air mishaps and near-mishaps. Passengers also expressed frustration over delayed flights and air congestion as airlines converged on hub airports in the United States and scheduled more departures at busy periods than airports could accommodate. In the latter part of the year, a federal regulation went into effect requiring airlines to report their on-time performance. Some carriers went so far as to acknowledge such problems in their advertising in an attempt to reassure passengers that all had been taken care of. Still, it seemed that it might be airport capacity itself that would turn out to be a limiting factor to travel within the country.

The travel industry in 1987 continued its love affair with electronic technology. Video cassettes, for example, became an increasingly popular way for travelers to preview tours and destinations. And late in the year a machine called the TickeTeller was demonstrated by TeleTix Company as a means of dispensing airline tickets and other documents directly to consumers. The company projected that travelers would soon be able to call a travel agent or airline to purchase a ticket, then pick it up from a TickeTeller machine at a hotel, airport, office, or even a nearby grocery store.

PHYLLIS ELVING
Free-lance Travel Writer

TUNISIA

The government's prosecution of Islamic activists and the end of the 31-year-old regime of President Habib Bourguiba were the major events of 1987 in Tunisia.

Trials of Muslim Fundamentalists. Opposition to the 84-year-old president's one-man rule developed during the year in all sectors of Tunisian society, but especially among Muslim fundamentalist groups. In September, 90 Muslim fundamentalists were tried on charges of exploding bombs at Tunisian resort hotels and attempting, with the alleged support of Iranian agents, to overthrow the government. The trial seemed destined to result in death sentences that would create new martyrs and further weaken Bourguiba's rule. Pressures from Western allies and fellow Arab states moderated the expected harsh sentences. Death threats from pro-Iranian sympathizers in Lebanon, along with a Tunisian group calling itself "Caravan of the Marchers," which threatened violence should death sentences be carried out, most likely also led to the milder sentences.

On September 27, the final verdict was announced: 7 of the 90 accused received death sentences and 69 others received long prison terms. Among those sentenced to prison was Rachid Ghannouchi, leader of the Islamic Tendency Movement (MTI), which has wide support among Tunisia's diverse social groups. It was thought that the death sentences would be commuted to life imprisonment following pressures from Amnesty International and French and U.S. diplomats in Tunis. Yet, on October 8, two Muslim fundamentalists were hanged at dawn after Bourguiba rejected appeals for a pardon and threats against Tunisian leaders.

The executions and the continued mass arrests of Muslim militants beginning in March and continuing through September involving nearly 2,000 people were intended to demonstrate the government's determination to curtail Islamic threats to the regime.

TUNISIA • Information Highlights

Official Name: Republic of Tunisia.
Location: North Africa.
Area: 63,170 sq mi (163 610 km^2).
Population (mid-1987 est.): 7,600,000.
Chief City (1987 est.): Tunis, the capital, 1,600,000, district population.
Government: *Head of state,* Zine El Abidine Ben Ali, president (took office Nov. 7, 1987). Hedi Baccouche, prime minister (took office Nov. 7, 1987). *Legislature* (Unicameral)—National Assembly.
Monetary Unit: Dinar (.841 dinar equals U.S.$1, August 1987).
Gross National Product (1986 est. U.S.$): $8,900,000,000.
Economic Indexes (1986): *Consumer Prices* (1980 = 100), all items, 123.8; food, 126.8. *Industrial Production* (1984, 1980 = 100), 112.
Foreign Trade (1986 U.S.$): *Imports,* $2,901,000,000; *exports,* $1,760,000,000.

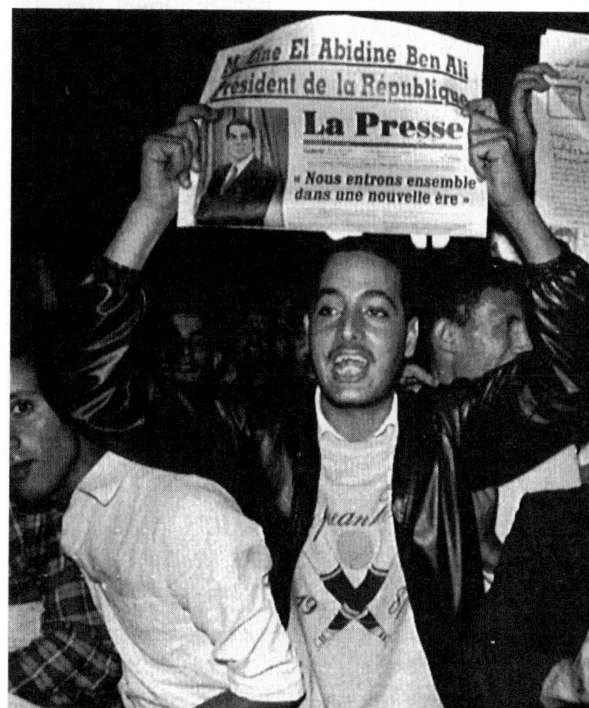

AP/Wide World

Tunisia's political opposition reacted jubilantly when Prime Minister Zine El Abidine Ben Ali ousted ailing President Habib Bourguiba, 84, in a bloodless coup November 7.

Succession Problem Settled. Following a year-long period of uncertainty about who would succeed the ailing Bourguiba, the president dismissed his premier, Rachid Sfar, on October 2 and replaced him with Gen. Zine El Abidine Ben Ali, whose most recent post was that of interior minister charged with clamping down on opposition groups on the right and the left. Ben Ali has been particularly active in suppressing Muslim-fundamentalist activity. The appointment cleared the way for him to succeed the aging president, and on November 7 he staged a bloodless coup, removing Bourguiba from office. A pro-Western officer trained in France and the United States, Ben Ali has shown himself capable of strong if not autocratic action in the past. In an address to the nation, he announced his intention of abolishing the post of president for life, held by Bourguiba.

The Economy. After a dismal performance in 1986, Tunisia's economy was beginning to show the mixed effects of the government's economic reform package. Exports have risen impressively; tourism has continued its strong rebound, although the bomb attacks on coastal resort cities in early August cast a new shadow over the tourist industry; and the argicultural harvest promised to be much higher in 1987 than in the previous year. Remittances from migrant workers abroad also were said to have gone up, and inflation has been held in check.

The development plan covering the period 1987–91, which was worked out in consultation with the International Monetary Fund (IMF) and the World Bank, was approved by Bourguiba on July 25. It gives priority to job creation, rural development, and stabilization of the balance of payments.

JOHN P. ENTELIS, *Fordham University*

TURKEY

Public attention in Turkey focused on two important ballots in 1987.

Internal Developments. On September 6, after vigorous controversy, a referendum took place on the question of repealing the constitutional ban on political activity by leaders of parties who had been held in large part responsible for difficulties leading to the military takeover of the government in 1980. It was approved by a margin of 50.19% to 49.81%. The closeness of the vote was attributed to the difficulty of balancing the desire for "full democracy" with the reluctance of reopening old political wounds.

Fears of the latter proved unfounded, however, in the general election held November 29, a year ahead of schedule. The voters returned the moderate right-wing Motherland Party of Prime Minister Turgut Ozal to power with 292 seats in the expanded 450-member Assembly. He received only 36% of the popular vote, however—a reflection of considerable dissatisfaction with inflation and social problems, and a result likely to cause new debate over the electoral system.

Finishing second with 25% and 99 seats was the moderate left Social Democratic Peoples Party led by Erdal Inonu, son of a former president. Of the parties led by pre-1980 leaders, the only one to receive the 10% needed for representation in the Assembly was the True Path Party led by former Prime Minister Suleyman Demirel (19%, 59 seats).

TURKEY • Information Highlights

Official Name: Republic of Turkey.
Location: Southeastern Europe and southwestern Asia.
Area: 301,382 sq mi (780 580 km²).
Population (mid-1987 est.): 51,400,000.
Chief Cities (1980 census): Ankara, the capital, 1,877,755; Istanbul, 2,772,708; Izmir, 757,854.
Government: *Head of state,* Gen. Kenan Evren, president (took office Nov. 10, 1982. *Head of government,* Turgut Özal, prime minister (took office Dec. 13, 1983). *Legislature*—Grand National Assembly.
Monetary Unit: Lira (1,010 liras equal U.S. $1, Dec. 31, 1987).
Gross National Product (1986 U.S.$): $52,900,000,000.
Economic Index (July 1987): *Consumer Prices* (1982 = 100), all items, 520.3; food, 501.8.
Foreign Trade (1986 U.S.$): *Imports,* $11,145,000,000; *exports,* $7,401,000,000.

Internal security continued to present problems. Kurdish insurgents increased their activities in the eastern provinces, and several serious clashes took place with Turkish armed forces. Despite this, the government decided that the general situation had improved sufficiently to allow in July the lifting of martial law, in effect since 1980, in the last four provinces affected.

The economy again was troubled by an inflation rate of about 35%. On the favorable side, Turkish exports continued strong, and a start was made in privatizing many State Economic Enterprises. Progress also continued on construction of a second Bosporus bridge and in the areas of energy development through several large dams. Favorable weather contributed to a good year for agriculture.

Foreign Affairs. In March, after protracted negotiations, Turkey and the United States signed a five-year renewal of the Defense and Cooperation Agreement (DECA) under which the United States leased military bases and Turkey received military aid. Turkey continued to be dissatisfied, however, about U.S. restrictions on the import of Turkish textiles and steel, and about congressional reductions in levels of military and economic aid that were requested by President Ronald Reagan's administration. Unresolved issues were reported to have been a contributing cause of the postponement of an official visit to the United States by President Kenan Evren.

In April, Turkey formally applied for admission to full membership in the European Community. Negotiations over the conditions and date of Turkish entry were expected to be difficult. In other matters of relations with Europe, Turkey was much angered when the European Parliament adopted a resolution upholding Armenian claims of a Turkish "massacre" in 1915. An attempt by some members of the U.S. Congress to pass a similar resolution was again defeated.

In August a second oil pipeline was opened from the Iraqi oil fields at Basra and Kirkuk to the Turkish Mediterranean port of Ceyhan. This was expected to increase the royalties that Turkey receives to about $300 million and to provide Turkey with increased oil security. Fees and customs revenues from oil shipped through Turkey by road generate about another $150 million. At the same time, Turkey sought to maintain good relations with Iran, although this was somewhat difficult in view of fears that Iranian fundamentalists were contributing to the resurgence of religious sentiments about which many Turks have expressed increasing concern in recent years. Turkish leaders again made known their willingness to help settle the Iran-Iraq war, including possible mediation.

Foreign visits by top Turkish officials included travel by President Evren to Morocco and to the Islamic Conference summit meeting in Kuwait. Prime Minister Ozal made an official visit to Syria, in a renewed attempt to ease strained relations with that country over border tensions that included smuggling and alleged Syrian toleration of Kurdish rebels operating from Syria.

There was little progress on the Cyprus situation nor on other outstanding issues with Greece, despite continued efforts by United Nations Secretary-General Javier Pérez de Cuéllar. Tensions with Bulgaria also continued high over the oppression of the Turkish minority there.

The 1987 Atatürk International Peace Prize was awarded to West German President Richard von Weizsäcker.

WALTER F. WEIKER
Rutgers University

UGANDA

When Yoweri Museveni seized power in Uganda early in 1986, he assumed control of a country beset by political anarchy and economic chaos where commerce had been undermined by illicit smuggling on a massive scale. Museveni's new ruling National Resistance Council has sought to reestablish some semblance of political and economic stability. In 1987 occasional fighting between government troops and antigovernment rebels occurred in remote areas of the north and east. Two alleged coup plots were uncovered in January.

Economy. In the August 1986 budget the government attempted, among other things, to reconcile the great disparity between the official and the unofficial exchange rates. Before the budget, government transactions, including the repayment of foreign debts, were set at 1,400 shillings to the U.S. dollar while all other transactions were set at 5,000 shillings. The new decree established both rates at 1,400 shillings which caused immediate chaos in the marketplace, and legal commerce virtually stopped. By mid-1987, while the official rate remained at 1,400 shillings, the unofficial rate soared to as high as 12,000 shillings causing severe dislocations. Prices for basic commodities multiplied, smuggling increased, and everyone suffered. Coffee farmers were the most adversely affected because the coffee marketing board initially changed the hard currency it paid to growers to the lower rate which meant that the farmers received less than one tenth of the world price. As a result some farmers refused to harvest their crops while others smuggled them into adjacent countries where they received substantially higher prices.

A major currency devaluation of 77.5% and a subsequent increase in prices paid to farmers as an incentive to increase agricultural production were measures that were taken in 1987. Even with new loans from the World Bank and the International Monetary Fund (IMF), significant economic recovery was constrained by major debt-repayment obligations and reduced coffee revenue which accounts for approximately 90% of Uganda's total exchange earnings. However, a rescheduling of debt repayments and a promise of more than $300 million in additional aid in 1988 should lead to significant improvement.

Internal Conflicts. Otema Allimadi, head of the Uganda People's Democratic Movement, joined two other exiled opposition leaders, William Omaria Lo-Arapia of the United National Front and Samuel Lowero of the Federal Democratic Movement in a "united front" to overthrow the Museveni government. Since 1986, Samuel Lowero's Federal Democratic Movement had been part of a coalition with Museveni's National Resistance Movement (NRM) but withdrew because it alleged that the government was violating basic human rights.

Opposition to Museveni's NRM also came from priestess Alice Lakwena's Holy Spirit Movement which challenged government troops. Thousands of "Lakwenas," despite their leader's promises of magical protection against bullets, were killed by the better-armed National Resistance army. In October government forces attacked the headquarters in the town of Butte killing more than 150 and capturing many more.

Disputes With Kenya. The border crisis between Kenya and Uganda had intensified since September of 1986 when Col. Muammar el-Qaddafi of Libya visited Uganda. Since then tensions between the two countries have affected trade and communications. Kenya was disturbed by reports that young Kenyan dissidents were receiving commando training in Libya and were then being returned to Uganda. On the other hand, Uganda claimed that rebels based in Kenya were killing civilians. Kenya also complained about the increase of Ugandan troops on the border. Relations worsened when Uganda's two senior diplomatic envoys were expelled from Kenya in December 1987.

PATRICK O'MEARA and
N. BRIAN WINCHESTER
Indiana University

UGANDA • Information Highlights

Official Name: Republic of Uganda.
Location: Interior of East Africa.
Area: 91,135 sq mi (236 040 km²).
Population: (mid-1987 est.): 15,900,000.
Chief Cities (1980 census): Kampala, the capital, 458,423; Jinja, 45,060.
Government: *Head of state,* Yoweri Museveni, president (Jan. 29, 1986). *Head of government,* Samson Kisekka, prime minister (Jan. 30, 1986). *Legislature* (unicameral)—National Assembly.
Monetary Unit: Uganda shilling (1,400 shillings equal U.S. $1, April 1987).
Foreign Trade (1985–86 est. U.S.$): *Imports,* $325,000,000; *exports,* $352,000,000.

© P. Piel/Gamma-Liaison

Believing that a more benign international environment is essential to his domestic reform program, Soviet General Secretary Mikhail Gorbachev and wife Raisa visited a number of Eastern-bloc and Western-alliance nations during 1987.

USSR

The affairs of the Soviet Union were dominated in 1987 by the consequences of the political succession that lifted Mikhail Gorbachev to power in March 1985. Domestic policy continued to take precedence over foreign policy, although Gorbachev registered a substantial success in the latter area at December's summit meeting with U.S. President Ronald Reagan. All told, the year was one of maturation for General Secretary Gorbachev, of painful choices for the Communist Party leadership that he heads, and of a growing awareness of the complexity of the internal problems that his reforms seek to remedy.

Domestic Affairs

Gorbachev's Agenda. Gorbachev's broad approach in 1987 was set largely by the rapid progress he already had made toward embracing *perestroika,* the "restructuring" or "rebuilding" of Soviet life.

The tone was set at the January 1987 plenary session of the party's Central Committee, which, Gorbachev disclosed, had been postponed three times because of the difficulty of reaching prior agreement. Gorbachev's address there may represent a watershed in Soviet politics no less then party leader Nikita Khrushchev's "secret speech" in 1956 about dictator Joseph Stalin's crimes. Gorbachev's main theme was how much he and his Kremlin colleagues had been educated by their two years in office. They had learned, he maintained, about the need to carry out changes in at least some underlying features of the Soviet system, and not merely the rather superficial changes in policy and style stressed only a year or two before: "The business of rebuilding has turned out to be more difficult, and the causes of the problems embedded in our society more profound, than we had imagined earlier."

For the first time, Gorbachev gave emphasis to confronting the country's Stalinist past, about which he had said very little in 1985 and 1986. During the long Stalin era, he now acknowledged, "authoritarian appraisals and opinions became irrefutable truths" in area after area, and these were shackling the population and the regime alike even decades after the tyrant's death. He broke more new ground by going beyond the economic issues that preoccupied him earlier to argue for what he called "democratization" of the Soviet political process. In particular, he recommended experimentation with multiple candidacies and genuinely secret ballots in elections for government and party posts. In both hierarchies, Soviet elections have long been stage-managed endorsements of a single, preselected candidate.

The January plenum, while noncommittal on the specifics of political change, did endorse Gorbachev's proposal that a special party conference be held in 1988 to discuss political and other reforms. The 19th Party Conference, the first since 1941, was subsequently scheduled to convene in Moscow June 28, 1988. More than the 27th Party Congress of 1986, held only one year into Gorbachev's term, it will provide a test of his seriousness and, as important, of his ability to deliver on his promises.

Political Leadership. Gorbachev in 1987 very nearly completed the eviction from the top leadership of favorites of the late Leonid Brezhnev, general secretary from 1964 to 1982. Two veteran members of the party Politburo were retired: Dinmukhammed Kunayev (age 75), the party boss in Kazakhstan and a personal protégé of Brezhnev; and Geidar Aliev (64), the senior of the USSR's deputy prime ministers. Three new men, meantime, were added to the Politburo, all of them members of the national party Secretariat and closely identified with Gorbachev's policies. Viktor Nikonov (58) is the secretary in charge of Soviet agriculture, Nikolai Slyunkov (58) of economic coordination and reform, and Aleksandr Yakovlev (64) of party propaganda and cultural affairs.

By year's end, only 2 of the Politburo's 13 voting members (besides Gorbachev himself) were holdovers from Brezhnev's leadership. Two had earned their seats under Yuri Andropov in 1983, but 8 of the 13, a large majority, had been promoted during Gorbachev's brief tenure as general secretary.

Gorbachev also continued to build a political machine at intermediate and lower levels. By the end of 1987, 19 of the 20 department heads in the Central Committee Secretariat had been appointed under Gorbachev. In the Council of Ministers, the headquarters of the government bureaucracy, the most decisive change was the dismissal in May of Defense Minister Marshal Sergei Sokolov and his replacement by his most junior deputy, Gen. Dmitri Yazov. This was punishment for the military's embarrassing inability to prevent the landing in central Moscow of a Cessna airplane piloted by a West German teenager, Mathias Rust. At the June plenum of the Central Committee, Yazov supplanted Sokolov as a candidate (nonvoting) member of the Politburo. Shortly afterward he announced that new blood would have to be injected into the officer corps and the forces brought into line with the spirit of the times.

Late 1987 brought a significant variation from the established pattern of replacement of political personnel. Gorbachev's previous targets had been mostly the elderly conservatives blamed for the stagnation of the 1970s. Now, however, he for the first time parted ways with a prominent member of his own reformist coalition: Boris Yeltsin, a candidate member of the Politburo and since 1985 the energetic party leader of the city of Moscow. Yeltsin precipitated the crisis by making an emotional outburst about the slow pace of actual reforms before the Central Committee in October 1987. Although he is said to have criticized the general secretary only indirectly, Gorbachev seems to have interpreted the attack as one on his authority as leader. In November, Yeltsin was removed from the fishbowl Moscow position in favor of a more reliable member of the inner party leadership, Lev Zaikov.

Economy. Compared to the early phases of the Gorbachev administration, in which woolly talk about "radical reform" far outstripped action, 1987 brought more definite and more ambitious steps toward economic reform.

Some of the reform was implementation of modest changes previously announced. On May 1, for instance, there came into effect a new law, enacted the previous autumn, that legalizes individual and family enterprise in 29 areas of consumer goods and services. Hitherto, such activity had existed only in the illegal "second economy."

Far more noteworthy was the surge of new thinking about comprehensive economic change and the creation of a legislative framework, albeit an unwieldy one, for putting such change into effect. The most candid economic debate in decades erupted in the Soviet press in the spring and summer of 1987. An especially remarkable contribution was the article "Debts and Advances," by the economist Nikolai Shmelev, which appeared in the June 1987 issue of the literary journal *Novi Mir*. Shmelev mercilessly attacked Soviet economic failures, saying they were discrediting socialism and guaranteeing "equal poverty for all." He demanded both a greater tolerance of private ownership and much more reliance on economic coordination by the market rather than by strictly centralized state planning.

Equally remarkable, Gorbachev publicly praised Shmelev's diagnosis, while disputing some of his prescriptions. In a marathon speech to the Central Committee on June 25, Gorbachev also made his first forthright admission of the need to achieve "the systematic mastery and management of the market, with due regard for its laws." This placed the Soviets considerably closer to the position of Communist marketizers, such as Deng Xiaoping of China and János Kádár of Hungary, than might have been thought possible even a few months earlier. Gorbachev told the plenum, moreover, that lower rates of growth might have to be accepted in order to achieve higher economic quality.

Several days later, the Supreme Soviet adopted the first major piece of reform legislation, a "Law on the Socialist Enterprise." Enabling regulations and decrees came out in a flood over the rest of the year.

The USSR's "new management mechanism," as it is labeled, is to be put into effect gradually through 1988–90. It restricts central planners to deciding on national economic strategy and new investment. Mandatory physical plans for firms are to be superseded by negotiated "state orders," which will buy up only part of the firm's production capacity. Output above this level will be distributed in a regulated market, and most profits will be retained by enterprise management. Unprofitable firms may be forced into bankruptcy and their workers retrained. The state will still set prices for land, energy, and most raw materials, but most consumer prices eventually will reflect the balance of supply and demand.

Important elements of the reform remained unrevealed. It was not clear, for example, how high a proportion of most firms' output would be covered by the "state orders," or how many prices would float with market tides. Under the best circumstances, technical work on the mechanics of the scheme will inevitably grind on for years to come.

As Gorbachev and his fellow leaders have said time and again, economic reform is potentially explosive in social terms. Most of its benefits are promised for the future, whereas the costs come immediately. Blue-collar workers, in particular, will fear and may even resist productivity-related wages, closings of antiquated plants, and an end to state subsidies on food and other consumer goods. Many white-collar bureaucrats also stand to lose status and, potentially, their jobs in the decentralization and reorganization of planning and management.

For all these reasons, Gorbachev seemed well aware as 1987 wore on of the political dynamics and hazards of economic reform. To build support, he made frequent appeals to patriotism, used his powers of patronage and appointment, and pressured the economic bureaucracy to work harder to provide prompt payoffs to the consumer. He seemed at times to be almost as concerned about containing the political side effects of economic reform as about nudging it forward.

Culture and Politics. Gorbachev's *glasnost* (publicity and openness), which has brought about the warmest thaw in Soviet culture and communications since Khrushchev, spread into new realms in 1987. While there were signs of concern among conservatives, there was no hint that key gains would be rolled back.

The most striking events were in literature and the cinema. Literary magazines, newspapers, and book publishers competed with one another to print long-suppressed works. Many of the best of them concerned what Gorbachev called the "forgotten names and blank spots" of Soviet history, notably the darkest years of Stalin's reign. Permission was finally granted, for example, for publication of Boris Pasternak's great novel about the Russian Revolution, *Doctor Zhivago,* three decades after its appearance in the West. Anatoly Rybakov's novel *Children of the Arbat* brings the terror of the 1930s to life. *Repentance,* Tengiz Abuladze's surrealistic antitotalitarian film, was given general release the opening day of the January 1987 plenum.

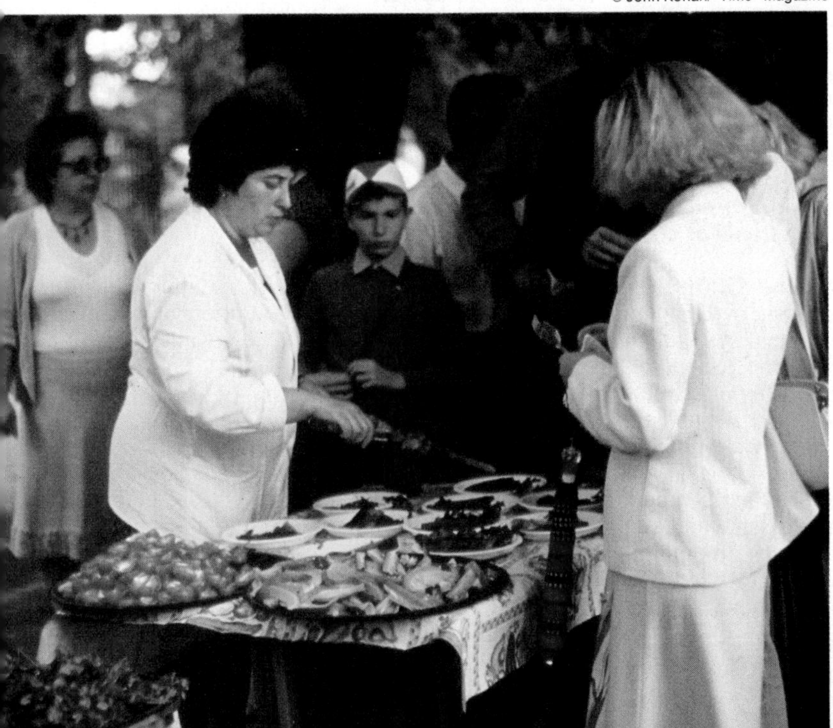

Visitors to Leningrad sample shish kebab from a cooperative-run outdoor café. New economic reforms are allowing entrepreneurial enterprise in specified consumer goods and services. By late 1987, some 650 cooperatives and 12,000 individuals were officially registered to conduct such business.

Denied permission to emigrate to Israel for 16 years—and exiled to Siberia from 1978 to 1982—Jewish dissident Ida Nudel (center) *was allowed to leave the Soviet Union in early October. She was greeted in Israel by Prime Minister Yitzhak Shamir* (right). *About 8,000 Jews were granted permission to leave the Soviet Union during 1987.*

Gorbachev's long-awaited speech in November on the 70th anniversary of the Bolshevik Revolution, although not going as far to attack Stalin as some wanted, gave further heart to anti-Stalinists. The October plenum of the Central Committee had formed a new commission to examine the cases of party members killed under Stalin. It will not be surprising if it rehabilitates Nikolai Bukharin, the outstanding moderate among Soviet leaders before Stalin's ascent. Bukharin, some of whose ideas find an echo in Gorbachev's today, was condemned at a show trial and shot in 1938.

Yegor Ligachev, the Politburo member who supervises ideology and culture at the highest level, inveighed several times in 1987 against critical "excesses" in the arts and the media. In fact, Gorbachev more tactfully made the same point, warning that "antisocialist" ideas had to be combated. Gorbachev worried, too, that many Soviets, once censorship had been loosened, did not have "the culture . . . to respect the point of view even of a friend or comrade."

One apparent motive of the Gorbachev thaw is to inhibit political dissent by drawing potential dissidents into the official system. In a related development in 1987, the regime released several hundred political prisoners, among them Jewish activists Iosif Begun and Ida Nudel. It also launched a wide-ranging study of the Soviet criminal code. One of the issues under consideration is whether to repeal or dilute clauses used to punish dissidents. And it somewhat liberalized restrictions on emigration, allowing about 8,000 Jews to leave (as against fewer than 1,000 in immediately preceding years).

Perhaps the most troubling outgrowth of *glasnost,* from the Kremlin's standpoint, is in the area of interethnic relations. Both ethnic Russians, who make up a bare majority of the Soviet population, and non-Russians have taken advantage of it to air grievances against one another. In several cases, complaints have been taken out onto the streets. In May, members of an ultraconservative Russian group called *Pamyat* (Memory) demonstrated in Moscow against neglect of the Russian historical heritage. Boris Yeltsin met with them, and there has been speculation that this may have hastened his downfall. Crimean Tatars held a large sit-in in Moscow later in the summer. In the three Baltic republics, local nationalists staged rallies to protest the forcible incorporation of their countries into the USSR and the primacy given the Russian language.

A crucial challenge for the new leaders will be to decide where to strike a balance between repression, which alienates the population, and permissiveness, which they fear will tear the Soviet system apart. Legal changes may prove to be part of the answer. Multicandidate elections, combined with the devolution of some decision-making to local and regional bodies, may prove to be another part.

Foreign Affairs

East-West Relations and Arms Control. Mikhail Gorbachev has insisted that a more benign international environment is essential to his internal reforms—reforms that, he hopes, will in the end make the USSR a stronger and more attractive player on the world stage. Vital to his strategy is an improvement in relations with the Western alliance and, above all, with the United States. In this respect, 1987 witnessed some progress.

Arms control was again the focus of the U.S.-Soviet dialogue, and it was the centerpiece of the third summit meeting between Gorbachev and President Reagan, held in Washington December 8–10. The summit gave Gorbachev his most direct exposure yet in the American media. He took advantage of the opportunity by bringing along a large team of consultants and publicists and, on one occasion, by plunging into a crowd to shake hands.

On substance, the two leaders signed a major arms-control agreement, committing the Soviet Union and the United States to destroy all existing stocks of INF (Intermediate Nuclear Forces) weapons, nuclear tipped missiles with approximate ranges of 300 to 3,400 mi (480–5 500 km). More than 1,500 deployed Soviet warheads, targeted on Western Europe, will be eliminated, whereas the United States will destroy more than 350. The Soviets also accepted a set of unprecedented verification procedures, among them the stationing of Soviet and U.S. inspectors on one another's territory for the 13-year life of the agreement and 20 short-notice inspection visits during the first three years of the treaty. Indeed, by the end of the INF negotiations the two sides had reversed their historic positions on verification, with the Soviets now taking the lead and the Americans resisting.

Josif Begun, another prominent Jewish dissident, was released from prison February 20, following a campaign by Western supporters and street demonstrations in Moscow calling for his freedom. Begun was jailed in 1983.

© F. Hibbon/Sygma

USSR • Information Highlights

Official Name: Union of Soviet Socialist Republics.
Location: Eastern Europe and northern Asia.
Area: 8,649,498 sq mi (22 402 200 km²).
Population (mid-1987 est.): 284,000,000.
Chief Cities (Jan. 1, 1986 est.): Moscow, the capital, 8,703,000; Leningrad, 4,901,000; Kiev, 2,495,000.
Government: *Head of state,* Andrei A. Gromyko, chairman of the Presidium of the Supreme Soviet, president (elected July 2, 1985). *Head of government,* Nikolai I. Ryzhkov, chairman of the USSR Council of Ministers (took office Sept. 1985). General secretary of the Communist Party, Mikhail S. Gorbachev (elected March 11, 1985). *Legislature*—Supreme Soviet: Soviet of the Union Soviet of Nationalities.
Monetary Unit: Ruble (0.642 ruble equals U.S.$1, August 1987—noncommercial rate).
Gross National Product (1985, U.S.$): $2,062,600,000.
Economic Indexes (1986): *Consumer Prices* (1980 = 100), all items, 104.1; *Industrial Production* (1985, 1980 = 100), 126.
Foreign Trade (1985 U.S.$): *Imports,* $88,873,000,000; *exports,* $97,330,000,000.

In addition, the Washington summit confirmed the superpowers' commitment to effect deep cuts in strategic nuclear weapons. Accord was reached on a compromise sublimit of 4,900 warheads on land- and sea-launched missiles, within a limit of 6,000 warheads, and on verification procedures more intrusive than those in the INF treaty. It was decided that the issue be discussed further at a fourth Gorbachev-Reagan summit in Moscow in 1988.

The summit, however, did not resolve the thorny issue of President Reagan's Strategic Defense Initiative (SDI, or "Star Wars"), which may preclude a future treaty on strategic arms. Nor was much progress made on regional conflicts, human rights, or trade.

With respect to Western Europe, Japan, and other allies of the United States, there was patient Soviet diplomacy in 1987 but no breakthroughs. A combination of persuasion and threats helped achieve West German cooperation in the INF treaty, which was the dominant issue in relations with Western Europe. Gorbachev voiced a willingness to discuss conventional force reductions in Europe and ordered a reassessment of Soviet military doctrine, whose traditional offense-oriented approach has helped justify Soviet conventional superiority in the European theater. These initiatives will require time to ripen.

A planned visit by Gorbachev to Tokyo was postponed indefinitely when the two countries could not agree on an agenda. As in the past, the territorial dispute over the Japanese "northern territories," annexed by the USSR after 1945, kept them from a rapprochement.

International Groupings. Gorbachev continued in 1987 to stress the affinity of the USSR for both the European community and the Asia-Pacific region. In a speech in Murmansk in September, he added the Arctic to the list, suggesting northern cooperation with Canada, the Scandinavian countries, and others. Yet, as with Europe and the Asia Pacific, rhetoric was not soon followed up by workable suggestions on how to execute his design.

One area in which Gorbachev may be prepared to make some tangible changes is that of international trade and commerce. He accepts more than previous leaders that participation in the "international division of labor" will help modernize the Soviet economy. In January 1987 Moscow issued new guidelines on joint ventures with non-Soviet firms. Although the new rules are more receptive to foreign investment than the old, Western and Japanese businessmen criticized some of their features. Greater flexibility with respect to supply arrangements, access to Soviet markets, and repatriation of profits may have to be introduced before much investment results.

An interesting change in 1987 was the new Soviet emphasis on international organizations. In September, Gorbachev issued a major statement on the United Nations and other international bodies, indicating a greater Soviet willingness to contribute to them and to abide by their decisions. Shortly thereafter, the Soviets cleared up much of their financial arrears at the UN.

A West German teenager, Mathias Rust, embarrassed the Soviet air-defense system by flying a small plane 400 miles over Soviet territory and landing in Red Square, May 29.

© Sygma

Third World and Regional Conflicts. On Third World issues, Gorbachev and the Politburo seemed more and more inclined to the view of those in the Soviet establishment who warn against further military and political entanglements at this point in Asia, Africa, and Latin America. Such individuals advanced their position with greater candor in the Soviet press in 1987, stressing that many developing countries might prefer to take the "capitalist path" for the indefinite future and that, without successful economic reform, the USSR could not hope to win influential new friends in the Third World.

At the same time, there was no evident lowering of the level of Soviet support for radical allies of long standing in Asia, Africa, and Latin America. The most costly involvement remained the military intervention in Afghanistan, which, by the end of 1987, had lasted twice as long as the Soviets' war with Nazi Germany in the 1940s. Equipment of the antigovernment forces with U.S. Stinger missiles sharply curbed the effectiveness of Soviet air power, and efforts by the pro-Soviet Afghan regime to coopt neutral and rebel groups made little headway.

Eastern Europe. Among the Soviets' East European clients, 1987 was a year of growing conviction that Gorbachev means business as a reformer and of growing consternation about the appropriate response. Gorbachev encouraged the local regimes to search out their own responses to economic and other problems and was especially positive toward the efforts of the Polish regime to do so. Moscow praised the decision of the Czechoslovak leader, Gustáv Husák, to transfer power in December 1987 to a somewhat younger and less hidebound leader. Soviet impatience with the antireform intransigence of Romanian President Nicolae Ceauşescu was stated frankly.

On the other hand, the Soviets continued to frown on "nonsocialist" alternatives to Soviet-type Communism, yet without categorically defining the boundary. The danger is that, as in the 1950s and 1960s, East European leaders, given initial encouragement by Soviet tolerance, will overstep the bounds and occasion Soviet retaliation. Should Soviet intervention in Eastern Europe take the form of military invasion, it may then profoundly and negatively affect the process of liberalization and reform within the USSR itself. It is noteworthy that, when Gorbachev visited Czechoslovakia in 1987, he made no apology for the Soviet invasion of August 1968. Of all the nightmares Gorbachev may have, that of having to choose between his reforms and his country's empire is surely one of the worst.

TIMOTHY J. COLTON, *University of Toronto*

AP/Wide World

Representatives of all 15 nations on the UN Security Council raise their hands in support of a July 20 resolution calling for a cease-fire "on land, at sea, and in the air" in the Persian Gulf. Iraq accepted the resolution; Iran ignored it.

UNITED NATIONS

For the United Nations, 1987 was seen as an institutional turning point. The organization came within days of bankruptcy in December. And yet it began a political resurgence as a forum used by the major powers to deal with significant issues, ranging from famine, AIDS (Acquired Immune Deficiency Syndrome), and the preservation of the ozone layer, to military struggles in the Persian Gulf, Central America, and Afghanistan.

The financial crisis was largely the result of politically motivated withholding by the United States, which owed a cumulative total of $314 million at year's end. But the American contribution to the UN's then $848 million budget for 1987, while less than the $212 million the United States was legally obliged to pay, was expected to be about $160 million. That would be far more than had been anticipated and more than enough to meet the payrolls. The crisis also forced the institution to trim excess fat from the staff through a hiring freeze, and to reorganize operations in a more efficient manner. While the problem was not resolved, a compromise agreement still held on budgetary reforms, giving major donors more of a say on how much the UN spends and what it is spent on. There were signs that anti-UN sentiment in the U.S. Congress was waning. And the Soviet Union, the major UN debtor for the organization's first 40 years, paid its dues in full in 1987 and announced that it would pay what it owed on peacekeeping assessments dating back to the Congo and Sinai operations of the 1950s and 1960s.

The Soviet fiscal turnabout was just one symptom of a larger policy change toward the organization by Kremlin leader Mikhail Gorbachev, who in a September article envisioned a larger UN role in resolving a wide range of political disputes involving the two superpowers. The Soviet-American convergence needed before the UN can deal with regional issues effectively was aided by the December summit between Gorbachev and President Reagan.

The most tangible expression of the shift toward UN centrality in world affairs began in January, after Secretary-General Javier Pérez de Cuéllar urged the major powers to take a more active role in dealing with the seven-year-long war between Iran and Iraq. For the first time in history, the Security Council's five permanent members convened in private and negotiated a resolution, adopted unanimously on July 20 by the full 15-member Council, demanding a cease-fire in the Persian Gulf and various other measures. Iraq accepted the resolution, but Iran did not, and in December the Council announced its joint "determination" to impose sanctions, such as an arms embargo, should Iran's recalcitrance continue.

In his annual report for 1987, issued in September, Pérez de Cuéllar noted evidence of "a greater solidarity among nations" in dealing with problems through the UN, which he called the "commonality factor." It was, he said, "as if the sails of the small boat in which all the people of the earth are gathered had caught again, in the midst of a perilous sea, a light but favorable wind."

U.S. Ambassador Vernon Walters was more cautious in his year-end assessment, saying that as vintages go, 1987 was "a good year but not a great year" for the UN. He conceded that the mood, previously dominated by tones of anti-Americanism and Third World radicalism, had mellowed to "a relatively moderate atmosphere."

Another major boon to the UN's public image was Pérez de Cuéllar's decision to open to public scrutiny the archives of the UN War Crimes Commission, a 17-nation body that disbanded in 1948 after compiling dossiers on suspected German and Japanese war criminals. One of the files, it was revealed, dealt with former UN Secretary-General Kurt Waldheim, the current president of Austria.

General Assembly. The 42nd regular session opened September 15, elected East German Deputy Foreign Minister Peter Florin as its president, and suspended work on December 21 after dealing with most of the 143 items on its agenda.

Despite its new policy of support for the UN, the Soviet Union remained on the losing end of overwhelming votes demanding its withdrawal from Afghanistan and the withdrawal of its ally, Vietnam, from Cambodia. A new Soviet proposal for transforming the UN was coolly received by both the West and the Third World. Washington came in for criticism as well, as the Assembly denounced congressional legislation intended to force the closing of the Palestine Liberation Organization observer mission at the UN.

Because of American withholdings, U.S. complaints about the lack of safeguards against UN budget increases went unheeded. The Assembly approved a budget of about $850 million for 1988, with only Israel opposed and the United States, Japan, and Australia abstaining. The "real" spending level was about the same as the 1987 budget, but unfavorable currency fluctuations raised the total sum.

Other signs of moderation in the Assembly included a larger proportion of resolutions adopted by consensus and a less strident tone toward Israel, especially on its dealings with South Africa. Also, lack of support forced Syria to withdraw its attempt to exempt acts by liberation movements from UN strictures against terrorism.

There were 62 disarmament resolutions adopted, including one calling a conference to consider a comprehensive ban on nuclear tests.

Security Council. The most significant action taken by the Council was the resolution on the Persian Gulf war, which marked a rare return to the concept of the framers of the UN Charter: joint action by the five big powers intended to end a breach of the peace. By December, all five had recognized that Iran's rejection of a cease-fire could not be modified by negotiation alone, and they began the process of drafting mandatory sanctions, with the support of other Council members.

The Council also dealt with southern Africa and the Arab-Israel dispute during the year, and issued a statement in January bolstering its earlier condemnation of hostage-taking.

Two long debates, one in February on repression in South Africa, the other in April on Pretoria's refusal to grant independence to the territory of Namibia, produced similar results: resolutions imposing sanctions on South Africa identical to those set by the U.S. Congress were vetoed by the United States and Britain. West Germany also voted against the measures, while France and Japan abstained.

In October, however, the Council reaffirmed its demand for Namibian independence. In November and again in December, it adopted resolutions demanding that South Africa withdraw its troops from Angola.

There was no Council action on the Arab-Israeli dispute until December 22, when a resolution was adopted deeply deploring Israeli actions to stamp out riots in the occupied West Bank and Gaza Strip, criticizing in particular the excessive use of force, which resulted in at least 22 deaths.

Secretariat. The secretary-general was preoccupied for most of the year by two issues —the UN's financial crisis and the drive to end the Persian Gulf war. He also actively pursued mediation efforts on Afghanistan, the Arab-Israeli dispute, Cambodia, and Western Sahara. In Central America, he accepted a role on a commission to monitor compliance with the peace accord initiated by Costa Rica and signed by four other regional countries. Pérez de Cuéllar offered to send UN observers to the area, and full access was offered by four of the nations. But by year's end, Honduran objections continued to delay deployment.

Many of the proposals he made to prod the Security Council into action on the Gulf were later incorporated into its July resolution, which called on the secretary-general to arrange for a cease-fire. He visited Baghdad and Tehran in September, and met emissaries from both nations at the UN. He reported a final deadlock on December 10.

A team of UN experts reported in May that both Iraqi and Iranian troops had been victims of poison gas, but there were indications that the Iraqis had been hit by one of their own shells. The Security Council expressed its "deep dismay" at the report, and demanded an end to the use of chemical weapons.

Undersecretary Diego Cordovez held two rounds of talks on Afghanistan in Geneva, and reported that the last obstacles to a pact on the withdrawal of Soviet troops from the country were a short timetable for the pullout and signs of progress toward a coalition government acceptable to both sides. The differences on a timetable were narrowed as Moscow offered 12 months and Pakistan asked all Soviet troops to leave within 8 months.

In May the secretary-general reported indications of "greater flexibility" on the convening of a Middle East peace conference, with all major powers now accepting the principle of such a meeting, although "very deep differences remain."

ORGANIZATION OF THE UNITED NATIONS

THE SECRETARIAT

Secretary-General: Javier Pérez de Cuéllar (until Dec. 31, 1991)

THE GENERAL ASSEMBLY (1987)

President: Peter Florin, German Democratic Republic
The 159 member nations were as follows:

Afghanistan
Albania
Algeria
Angola
Antigua and Barbuda
Argentina
Australia
Austria
Bahamas
Bahrain
Bangladesh
Barbados
Belgium
Belize
Belorussian SSR
Benin
Bhutan
Bolivia
Botswana
Brazil
Brunei Darussalam
Bulgaria
Burkina Faso
Burma
Burundi
Cambodia
Cameroon
Canada
Cape Verde
Central African Republic
Chad
Chile
China, People's Republic of
Colombia
Comoros
Congo
Costa Rica
Cuba
Cyprus
Czechoslovakia
Denmark
Djibouti
Dominica
Dominican Republic
Ecuador
Egypt
El Salvador
Equatorial Guinea
Ethiopia
Fiji
Finland
France
Gabon
Gambia
German Democratic Republic
Germany, Federal Republic of
Ghana
Greece
Grenada
Guatemala
Guinea
Guinea-Bissau
Guyana
Haiti
Honduras
Hungary
Iceland
India
Indonesia
Iran
Iraq
Ireland
Israel
Italy
Ivory Coast
Jamaica
Japan
Jordan
Kenya
Kuwait
Laos
Lebanon
Lesotho
Liberia
Libya
Luxembourg
Madagascar
Malawi
Malaysia
Maldives
Mali
Malta
Mauritania
Mauritius
Mexico
Mongolia
Morocco
Mozambique
Nepal
Netherlands
New Zealand
Nicaragua
Niger
Nigeria
Norway
Oman
Pakistan
Panama
Papua New Guinea
Paraguay
Peru
Philippines
Poland
Portugal
Qatar
Romania
Rwanda
Saint Christopher and Nevis
Saint Lucia
Saint Vincent and The Grenadines
São Tomé and Principe
Saudi Arabia
Senegal
Seychelles
Sierra Leone
Singapore
Solomon Islands
Somalia
South Africa
Spain
Sri Lanka
Sudan
Suriname
Swaziland
Sweden
Syria
Tanzania
Thailand
Togo
Trinidad and Tobago
Tunisia
Turkey
Uganda
Ukrainian SSR
USSR
United Arab Emirates
United Kingdom
United States
Uruguay
Vanuatu
Venezuela
Vietnam
Western Samoa
Yemen
Yemen, Democratic
Yugoslavia
Zaire
Zambia
Zimbabwe

COMMITTEES

General. Composed of 29 members as follows: The General Assembly president; the 21 General Assembly vice-presidents (heads of delegations or their deputies of Botswana, Cameroon, China, Comoros, France, Jordan, Mauritania, Mongolia, the Netherlands, Nicaragua, Paraguay, Portugal, Saint Vincent and the Grenadines, Singapore, Sri Lanka, Syrian Arab Republic, Togo, Tunisia, the Union of Soviet Socialist Republics, the United Kingdom of Great Britain and Northern Ireland, the United States of America); and the chairmen of the following main committees, which are composed of all 159 member countries.

First (Political and Security): Bagbeni Adeito Nzengeya (Zaire)
Special Political: Hamad Abdelaziz Al-Kawari (Qatar)
Second (Economic and Financial): Guennadi I. Oudovenko (Ukrainian Soviet Socialist Republic)
Third (Social, Humanitarian and Cultural): Jorge E. Ritter (Panama)
Fourth (Decolonization): Constantine Moushoutas (Cyprus)
Fifth (Administrative and Budgetary): Henrik Amneus (Sweden)
Sixth (Legal): Rajab A. Azzarouk (Libyan Arab Jamahiriya)

THE SECURITY COUNCIL

Membership ends on December 31 of the year noted; asterisks indicate permanent membership.

Algeria (1989)
Argentina (1988)
Brazil (1989)
China*
France*
Germany, Federal Republic of (1988)
Italy (1988)
Japan (1988)
Nepal (1989)
Senegal (1989)
USSR*
United Kingdom*
United States*
Yugoslavia (1989)
Zambia (1988)

THE ECONOMIC AND SOCIAL COUNCIL

President: Eugeniusz Noworyta (Poland)
Membership ends on December 31 of the year noted.

Australia (1988)
Belgium (1988)
Belize (1989)
Bolivia (1989)
Bulgaria (1989)
Belorussian Soviet Socialist Republic (1988)
Canada (1989)
China (1989)
Colombia (1990)
Cuba (1990)
Denmark (1989)
Djibouti (1988)
Egypt (1988)
France (1990)
Gabon (1988)
German Democratic Republic (1988)
Germany, Federal Republic of (1990)
Ghana (1990)
Greece (1990)
Guinea (1990)
India (1990)
Iran (1989)
Iraq (1988)
Ireland (1990)
Italy (1988)
Jamaica (1988)
Japan (1990)
Lesotho (1990)
Liberia (1990)
Libyan Arab Jamahiriya (1990)
Mozambique (1988)
Norway (1989)
Oman (1989)
Pakistan (1988)
Panama (1988)
Peru (1988)
Philippines (1988)
Poland (1989)
Portugal (1990)
Rwanda (1989)
Saudi Arabia (1990)
Sierra Leone (1988)
Somalia (1989)
Sri Lanka (1989)
Sudan (1989)
Syrian Arab Republic (1988)
Trinidad and Tobago (1990)
USSR (1989)
United Kingdom (1989)
United States (1988)
Uruguay (1989)
Venezuela (1990)
Yugoslavia (1990)
Zaire (1989)

THE TRUSTEESHIP COUNCIL

President: John A. Birch (United Kingdom)

China[2] France[2] USSR[2] United Kingdom[2] United States[1]

[1] Administers Trust Territory. [2] Permanent member of Security Council not administering Trust Territory.

THE INTERNATIONAL COURT OF JUSTICE

Membership ends on February 5 of the year noted.

President: Nagendra Singh (India, 1991)
Vice-President: Kéba Mbaye (Senegal, 1991)

Roberto Ago (Italy, 1997)
Mohammed Bedjaoui (Algeria, 1997)
Taslim O. Elias (Nigeria, 1994)
Jens Evensen (Norway, 1994)
Gilbert Guillaume (France, 1991)
Robert Y. Jennings (United Kingdom, 1991)
Manfred Lachs (Poland, 1994)
Kéba Mbaye (Senegal, 1991)
Ni Zhengyu (China, 1994)
Shigeru Oda (Japan, 1994)
José María Ruda (Argentina, 1991)
Stephen Schwebel (United States, 1997)
Mohamed Shahabuddeen (Guyana, 1997)
Nikolai Konstantinovich Tarassov (USSR, 1997)

INTERGOVERNMENTAL AGENCIES

Food and Agricultural Organization (FAO); General Agreement on Tariffs and Trade (GATT); International Atomic Energy Agency (IAEA); International Bank for Reconstruction and Development (World Bank); International Civil Aviation Organization (ICAO); International Fund for Agricultural Development (IFAD); International Labor Organization (ILO); International Maritime Organization (IMO); International Monetary Fund (IMF); International Telecommunication Union (ITU); United Nations Educational, Scientific and Cultural Organization (UNESCO); United Nations Industrial Development Organization (UNIDO); Universal Postal Union (UPU); World Health Organization (WHO); World Intellectual Property Organization (WIPO); World Meteorological Organization (WMO).

As part of the drive to cut costs and improve UN efficiency, several Secretariat divisions dealing with political matters were consolidated, and the top-heavy ranks of UN undersecretaries-general were trimmed by 15%.

Pérez de Cuéllar attended a ceremony at a hospital maternity ward in Zagreb, Yugoslavia, on July 11, marking the symbolic arrival of the 5 billionth human on earth, a baby boy named Matej Gaspar.

Specialized Agencies. The World Health Organization (WHO) announced an intensified campaign to promote global awareness of the drive against Acquired Immune Deficiency Syndrome (AIDS). The program director, Dr. Jonathan Mann, warned that 5 million to 10 million people already were infected with the deadly virus. In a gesture recognizing the health hazards of tobacco, the WHO banned smoking at its Rome headquarters.

The UN Children's Fund (UNICEF) announced in April that UN efforts had helped reduce child mortality in the world from 70,000 a day in 1950 to 38,000 daily by 1985. Much of the improvement came from a WHO immunization program which had reached 50% of the world's children in 1987, compared with 5% ten years before.

The Food and Agriculture Organization (FAO) warned that the massive African famine relief effort coordinated by the UN in 1984–86 could be dwarfed by a similar shortfall in food supplies that began at the end of 1987 and loomed even larger in 1988. The new disaster was caused by bad weather and civil strife in some nations.

In a related development, a UN report warned that most African nations faced economic disaster, as export earnings declined, the cost of imports rose, debt burdens increased, and both aid and credit were drying up. All this was taking place, the report noted, at a time when most African nations were complying with donor demands that they strengthen agricultural production and impose unpopular and harsh "reforms" of their economies, such as raising food prices.

On a more positive note, negotiations among some 30 nations in Vienna, under the auspices of the UN Environment Program, resulted in the first global agreement to limit manmade damage to the earth's ozone layer, which serves as a vital shield from solar radiation. Representatives of 24 nations signed the pact in September.

A UN conference, held in Vienna in June, endorsed a wide range of national and global measures to stamp out drug abuse and trafficking in illegal substances. Among them were agreements to smooth extradition of suspects and seize assets of traffickers.

The UN Center for Human Settlements supervised some 360 special projects in 1987 to meet the needs of homeless people around the world, as part of the International Year of Shelter for the Homeless.

AP/Wide World

Frederico Mayor Zaragoza of Spain, a 53-year-old biochemist, became director of UNESCO on November 16. His first act was to impose a hiring and promotions freeze.

By a one-vote margin, the United States failed in March to get the UN Human Rights Commission to take action on violations by Cuba. For the first time, the commission called on all parties involved in the civil strife in Sri Lanka to observe humanitarian rules. It also dispatched an envoy to Suriname to investigate charges of arbitrary executions.

The secretary-general warned that he may be forced to phase out operations of the UN Institute for Training and Research (UNITAR) if the voluntary funding it depends on continues to dry up.

The Paris-based UN Educational, Scientific and Cultural Organization (UNESCO) elected biochemist Frederico Mayor of Spain as its new director, after the controversial Amadou M'Bow of Senegal lost a bid for reelection. On the same day, November 9, FAO's director, Edouard Saouma of Lebanon, won a third term in Rome.

Rafael Salas of the Philippines, the executive director of the UN Fund for Population Activities, died in March and was replaced the following month by Dr. Nafis Sadik of Pakistan.

After observing votes in the Pacific territory of Palau in June and August, the UN Trusteeship Council voted in December to endorse the residents' decision to enter a "Compact of Free Association" with the United States. Palau is part of Micronesia, the last UN trust territory.

MICHAEL J. BERLIN
"The Washington Post"

© Peter Turnley/Black Star

In welcoming ceremonies at the White House, December 8, Soviet General Secretary Mikhail Gorbachev called the U.S.-Soviet treaty eliminating intermediate-range nuclear forces—signed that afternoon—"a giant step into the future."

UNITED STATES

In the peroration to his State of the Union address on Jan. 27, 1987, Ronald Reagan quoted Benjamin Franklin, who had declared two centuries earlier that he could see "a rising and not a setting sun" in the nation's future. "Well you can bet it's rising," the president asserted. ". . . America isn't finished yet, her best days have just begun."

The characteristic buoyancy reflected in those words helped sustain President Reagan throughout 1987. His credibility was undermined by the revelations of lengthy congressional hearings into the Iran-contra affair. (*See* feature article, page 26.) The economic growth and prosperity which were his proudest accomplishments were threatened by the calamitous stock market crash of Black Monday, October 19. Despite these setbacks, by year's end, in the glow of public approbation generated by his successful Washington summit with Soviet leader Mikhail Gorbachev, it was hard to convince Reagan's admirers that the president's own political sun was not again on the rise.

Domestic Affairs

The Reagan Administration. Still, 1987 was a year filled with travail. Along with vexing controversies over his stewardship of the nation's affairs, the 76-year-old chief executive, the oldest person ever to hold the office, had to begin the year with surgery, required to correct the obstruction of his urinary tract by an enlarged prostate. The good news from his stay at Bethesda Naval Hospital was that doctors found no further sign of the intestinal cancer for which the president had been treated in 1985.

Much of the public-policy arguments confronting Reagan in 1987 came from one of the long time bugbears of his presidency, the budget deficit. The perennial debate was touched off again on January 5 when the president sent to Congress the fiscal 1988 budget calling for $1.024 trillion in expenditures, the first trillion dollar budget ever submitted. It projected a reduction in the deficit to $108 billion. But some critics challenged the economic assumptions on which this forecast was based. Some also complained about the president's priorities, specifically his call for a 3% increase in defense spending after inflation, his cuts in various domestic programs, and his steadfast resistance to any substantial hike in taxes. Democratic Sen. Lawton Chiles of Florida, chairman of the Senate budget committee, called on the administration to meet with congressional leaders at what amounted to a budget summit to deal with what Chiles believed was the need for increased revenues.

Frank M. Carlucci, who had served as national security adviser since December 1986, was sworn in as secretary of defense on November 23. He succeeded Caspar Weinberger, who had held the post since the beginning of the Reagan presidency.

© J.L. Atlan/Sygma

That demand was brushed aside by the White House, until a 508-point drop in the Dow Jones stock average on October 19, echoed by similar price crashes in financial markets around the world. Many people attributed the decline to the size of the federal budget deficit. These events appeared to force the president to change his tactics. In an October 22 press conference, Reagan announced that he would begin high-level talks with the Congress over the budget deficit, and that except for cuts in Social Security benefits he was prepared to negotiate about "everything."

Another preoccupation of the administration during the year was the need to replace some of the president's senior advisers, a problem reflecting the attrition natural to a second-term presidency but compounded in this case by the deaths of two cabinet-level officials, William Casey, director of the Central Intelligence Agency (CIA), and Malcolm Baldrige, secretary of commerce.

Casey had resigned January 29, three months before his death at age 73 from the effects of a cancerous brain tumor. The process of replacing him was complicated by the Iran-contra case and the CIA's involvement in it. President Reagan's first choice, Robert M. Gates, who had been Casey's deputy, withdrew from consideration when it appeared that congressional questions about his role in the affair would delay his confirmation. In his place, the president named William H. Webster, director of the Federal Bureau of Investigation (FBI), who soon was approved by the Senate, and he picked Federal Judge William S. Sessions to take over the FBI.

The 64-year-old Baldrige, a champion rodeo rider, died July 25 after a horse reared and fell on him while he was preparing for a calf-roping competition. He was replaced by C. William Verity, 70, retired chairman of the steel company Armco, Inc.

Among other cabinet-level departures were Defense Secretary Caspar Weinberger, who resigned because of personal reasons and was replaced by White House National Security Adviser Frank M. Carlucci; and William Brock, labor secretary, who left to head the presidential campaign of Kansas Sen. Robert Dole and was replaced by Ann Dore McLaughlin, former undersecretary of transportation. McLaughlin became the only woman in the cabinet because Elizabeth Hanford Dole resigned as transportation secretary to aid her husband's presidential campaign. She was replaced by her former deputy, James H. Burnley, who at 39 became the youngest member of the Reagan cabinet. Earlier in the year the president had named former Tennessee Sen. Howard H. Baker, Jr., to take over as chief of staff at the White House. He succeeded Donald Regan, who had resigned in the midst of criticism for mishandling the way the president dealt with Iran-contra revelations.

In the economic policy area, one of the administration's most influential figures, Paul A. Volcker, resigned as chairman of the Federal Reserve Board after two terms to enter the private sector. He was replaced by Alan Greenspan, who had been chairman of the Council of Economic Advisers under President Ford. (*See also* BIOGRAPHY section, page 137.)

The administration encountered an unexpected problem as a result of the announcement on November 20 of an agreement with the Cuban government to repatriate 2,500 criminals and mentally ill refugees who had come to the United States in the 1980 Mariel boat lift. This news set off protest rioting at federal detention centers in Oakdale, LA, and Atlanta, GA, by Cuban inmates fearful of being sent back to the country they had fled. The prisoners overpowered guards and seized hostages, and it took nearly two weeks of negotiations before order could be restored. As part of their bargain with the prisoners, federal officials declared a moratorium on the return of Cubans to Cuba pending a review of their status. (*See* CUBA.)

Congress. With the Democrats controlling the Senate for the first time in the Reagan presidency as a result of the 1986 elections, as well as the House of Representatives, the stage was set for partisan conflict between the 100th Congress and the Republican White House. And as the year unfolded, nearly every significant action by the Congress seemed to lead to a bitter dispute with the executive branch. In January, Congress passed by huge margins a $20 billion Clean Water Act identical to a measure the president had pocket-vetoed after Congress adjourned in 1986. The bill, which provided funding for sewer development and for cleaning up polluted trouble spots around the country, had widespread support. But the president vetoed the measure, charging it was "loaded with waste and larded with pork." Congress easily overrode the veto, the seventh time it had overridden a Reagan veto.

A similar struggle, with much the same result, took place over an $87.5 billion highway and mass-transit bill, adopted by the House and Senate in March. Enhancing the appeal of the measure, especially in the West, was a provision permitting states to raise the speed limit on rural interstate highways to 65 miles per hour (105 km/hr). The president vetoed the bill, calling it an example of "pork-barrel politics," and waged an all-out fight on the issue in the Senate, but lost there by a 67 to 33 vote.

In a few cases Congress and the president did manage to reach compromise agreements, such as a comprehensive banking bill that allowed the insolvent Federal Savings and Loan Insurance Corporation to raise $10.8 billion by issuing long-term bonds. This provision was sought by troubled thrift institutions in the Midwest and Southwest. Reagan also signed into law bills reauthorizing the appointment of independent counsels to investigate charges of misconduct against high-ranking federal officials and providing $1 billion to feed and shelter homeless citizens for two years.

Nevertheless conflict with the president remained the dominant reality on Capitol Hill. The bitter and ultimately unsuccessful effort to confirm Judge Robert Bork to the Supreme Court (*see* LAW) exacerbated the friction. But the main battle throughout the year was over the budget deficit and fiscal policy. The Congress responded to the president's $1 trillion January budget proposal by adopting in June a $1 trillion budget resolution embodying its own goals and priorities. The resolution did not need the president's signature. But as congressional leaders crafted the revenue and appropriation measures to carry out the budget resolution they had to reckon with the threat of Reagan vetoes.

In September, Congress sought to force the president into softening his resistance to tax increases and his support for defense increases by passing a new enforcement mechanism for cutting federal budget deficits. The measure was intended as a substitute for the 1985 Gramm-Rudman Act, which had empowered the congressional General Accounting Office to determine what budget cuts should be made to meet the law's ceilings, a procedure found un-

Following the stock market crash, White House officials—including Treasury Secretary James Baker (second from right) *and Budget Director James Miller* (far left)*—and congressional negotiators agreed on a plan to reduce the budget deficit.*
© Arnie Sachs/Sygma

constitutional by the Supreme Court. The new law gave the budget cutting authority to the White House's Office of Management and Budget. President Reagan agreed on September 26 to sign the new approach into law, but warned that he would use his veto power to curb tax increases and cuts in defense spending.

Concerned about the psychology of consumers and investors after the October 19 stock market crash, congressional and executive-branch officials sought to find a way to avoid further confrontations over fiscal policy. On November 20, after nearly a month of hard bargaining, negotiators for both sides announced bipartisan agreement on a plan to reduce the projected federal deficit by $30 billion in fiscal 1988 and $46 billion in fiscal 1989, superseding the $23 billion in automatic cuts contemplated by the budget balancing law. Translating this agreement into specific legislation proved to be a difficult task, complicated by the desire of legislators to adjourn for the Christmas holidays, and by presidential insistence that the measure include support for the contra guerrillas fighting against the Sandinista government of Nicaragua.

Acting in the face of threats by the president to veto their proposals and to shut down the government if they failed to act in time, the lawmakers on December 22 finally reached agreement with the White House on a twofold deficit reduction package: A $604 billion catch-all spending bill reduced spending by $15.6 billion, including $5 billion in military spending. And a reconciliation bill included a $9.1 billion tax increase and other measures which trimmed an additional $17.6 billion from the deficit. The grand total of deficit reduction for fiscal 1988 amounted to $33.3 billion, well over the $30 billion goal set by White House and congressional negotiators. To gain presidential agreement, Congress approved $8.1 million in aid to the contras through the end of February. But the lawmakers also provided for a congressional vote early in February on any proposals for future military aid to the guerrilla forces.

In its closing hours Congress also passed legislation providing for $30 billion in federal funding for housing and community development over two years. But put off for the future was final action on a number of significant issues, including proposals to toughen trade laws, provide insurance against the costs of catastrophic illness, and to overhaul the welfare system.

Politics. Falling as it did between the midterm elections of 1986 and the 1988 presidential election, 1987 was what politicians in the past have called an "off-year." But as a result of the pressures of the modern political era, such was not the case. Instead, the year was packed with politics as both parties geared up for the struggle for the White House. The declining influence of political parties in the past 25 years and the consequent need for individual White House aspirants to forage on their own for support have been steadily speeding up the presidential selection process from one quadrennial to the next. This trend was accelerated even more in anticipation of the 1988 campaign because it was known that with President Reagan constitutionally barred from running again, for the first time since 1968 no incumbent would be on the ticket for either party.

Indeed, on the Republican side, the first official declaration of candidacy came from former Delaware Gov. Pierre S. duPont IV in June 1986. But in 1987 most of the action—and most of the turbulence—was in the Democratic competition as that party struggled to regroup after two successive defeats in presidential elections. Initially the Democratic front-runner was former Colorado Sen. Gary Hart who had made a strong bid for the nomination in 1984. But Hart was forced out of the race in May, soon after he announced his candidacy, when the *Miami Herald* reported that he apparently had spent a weekend in his Washington town house with a Miami model named Donna Rice.

Hart's misadventure emphasized the importance of the character issue in the campaign, and that concern also claimed another victim among Democratic candidates in Delaware Sen. Joseph Biden. He quit the race in September after it became known that he had used speech rhetoric from British Labour Party leader Neil Kinnock without crediting Kinnock, and also had misrepresented his law-school academic record.

These two episodes left the Democrats with only one well-known candidate, black leader Jesse Jackson, and he was given little chance of gaining the nomination because of his race. The other five contenders, all relatively obscure, made various appeals for support. Former Arizona Gov. Bruce Babbitt proposed a national sales tax to help cut the federal budget deficit. Massachusetts Gov. Michael Dukakis stressed the economic prosperity in his state. Missouri Rep. Richard Gephardt called for tougher trade policies. Tennessee Sen. Albert Gore claimed to be tougher on defense than his

UNITED STATES • Information Highlights

Official Name: United States of America.
Location: Central North America.
Area: 3,618,770 sq mi (9 372 614 km²).
Population (1986): 241,000,000.
Chief Cities (July 1, 1986 est.): Washington, DC, the capital, 626,000; New York, 7,262,700; Los Angeles, 3,259,300; Chicago, 3,009,530; Houston, 1,728,910; Philadelphia, 1,642,900; Detroit, 1,086,220.
Government: *Head of state and government,* Ronald Reagan, president (took office for second term, Jan. 20, 1985). *Legislature*—Congress: Senate and House of Representatives.
Monetary Unit: Dollar.

The Presidential Candidates

The Republicans

The 1988 presidential elections will mark the first time in 20 years that an incumbent chief executive is not on the ballot. By the end of 1987, six Republicans and seven Democrats were seeking their party nominations. The Democratic nominating convention was scheduled for July 18–21, 1988, in Atlanta; the GOP event was set for August 15–18 in New Orleans. The 13 candidates ranged in age from 39 to 64. Four hail from the East, four from the West, three from the Midwest, and two from the South. Eight have law degrees, and eight have served in the U.S. Congress.

Vice-President **George Bush,** *63, officially began his second bid for the White House in Houston, October 12. Although loyal to President Reagan, who defeated him for the GOP nomination but named him his running-mate in 1980, he took leave of the administration on some issues. A Yale graduate and World War II veteran, the former Texas oilman was a U.S. congressman (1967–71) and held various positions in the Nixon and Ford administrations.*

Robert Dole, *64, a U.S. congressman (1961–69) and senator (1969–), declared his candidacy in his hometown of Russell, KS, November 9. Dole, the Republican Party's 1976 vice-presidential nominee, promised to "tackle the runaway federal budget head on." A graduate of Washburn University (B.A. and LL.B.), he was wounded seriously while serving in World War II. It is the minority leader's second try for the top spot. Like Vice-President Bush, he is a former GOP national chairman.*

While even the supporters of **Pierre du Pont IV** *admit that his candidacy is a long shot, the former Delaware governor (1977–85) hopes to do well in the initial primaries and become a "top tier" contender. A member of the family that founded E. I. du Pont de Nemours & Co., the former three-term U.S. congressman (1971–77), 52, has called for mandatory drug testing for teenagers and work programs to replace welfare. He is a graduate of Harvard Law School.*

Offering "leadership for America," **Alexander M. Haig, Jr.,** *62, threw his "helmet into the [presidential] ring" on March 24. The former four-star general, who spent some 31 years in the military and was awarded the Distinguished Service Cross, pledged fiscal restraint and continued aid for the contras in Nicaragua. A 1947 graduate of the U.S. Military Academy, he was White House chief of staff (1973–74), commander of NATO forces (1974–78), and secretary of state (1981–82).*

Jack R. Kemp, *51, a nine-term U.S. congressman from Buffalo, NY, urged a continuation of the Reagan "revolution" but promised to "correct its mistakes." In declaring his candidacy, the former pro-football player reiterated his supply-side economic policy of lower taxes, lower interest rates, and less government spending. A graduate of Occidental College and an Army veteran, the conservative legislator is a supporter of the Strategic Defense Initiative.*

Photos, AP/Wide World

Pat Robertson, *57, former president of the Christian Broadcasting Network and host of "The 700 Club," emphasized economic renewal and a return of family values in beginning his presidential quest on October 2. The ordained Baptist minister had received the support of 3.3 million persons in a petition drive. A graduate of Washington and Lee, Yale Law School, and New York Theological Seminary, he is the son of the late U.S. Sen. A. Willis Robertson, (D-VA).*

The Presidential Candidates

The Democrats

"The next president must dare to be different," said 48-year-old **Bruce E. Babbitt** *in announcing his candidacy March 10. A Harvard-educated lawyer, Babbitt worked as a civil-rights attorney before serving as Arizona attorney general (1975–78) and governor (1978–87). He once described himself as at the "radical center" of the Democratic Party. Key campaign themes include social justice, efficient government, and effective national defense.*

A third-term governor of Massachusetts, **Michael S. Dukakis,** *53, announced his presidential candidacy March 16. A self-described "son of Greek immigrants," he attended Swarthmore College and Harvard Law School before serving in the Massachusetts legislature (1962–70). His years as governor (1973–79, 1983–) have been marked by an economic boom, a fact he cites often on the presidential campaign trail. His political ideology is regarded as liberal.*

U.S. Rep. **Richard A. Gephardt** *of Missouri became the first major Democrat to announce his candidacy, on February 23. With degrees from Northwestern University and the University of Michigan Law School, he entered local politics in his native St. Louis and was elected to Congress in 1976. He has represented the state's 3rd District ever since. The 46-year-old moderate was an early cosponsor of a bill that formed the basis of the Tax Reform Act of 1986.*

The youngest of the presidential hopefuls, 39-year-old **Sen. Albert Gore, Jr.,** *declared himself a candidate from "the New South" on June 24. The son of a former congressman and senator, Gore attended Harvard University, Vanderbilt Divinity School, and Vanderbilt School of Law. A Vietnam veteran, he worked as a newspaper reporter, homebuilder, and farmer before being elected to Congress in 1976. After three more terms, he was elected senator in 1984.*

Photos, AP/Wide World

Former U.S. Sen. **Gary Hart** *of Colorado entered the race April 13, withdrew May 8, and returned December 15. The 50-year-old Kansas native was graduated from Bethany Nazarene College (1958) and Yale Law School (1964). In 1967 he moved to Denver to practice law. He was the national presidential campaign manager for George McGovern in 1972 and served in the Senate from 1975 to 1987. He made a strong bid for the party's presidential nomination in 1984.*

The **Rev. Jesse Jackson,** *the 46-year-old Baptist Minister and longtime civil-rights activist, was perhaps the best-known of the Democratic candidates when he entered the race October 10. He had sought the party nod in 1984, aggressively promoting black voter registration. Jackson earned a B.A. from North Carolina A&T University and attended the Chicago Theological Seminary. His political organization is called the National Rainbow Coalition, based in Washington, DC.*

The oldest of the Democratic candidates, 58-year-old Sen. **Paul Simon** *of Illinois threw his hat in the ring May 18. A native of Oregon, he withdrew from college at 19 to publish a newspaper. He served in the Illinois legislature (1955–69), as lieutenant governor (1969–73), and in the U.S. Congress (1975–85) before entering the Senate in 1985. In addition to his bow ties, he is known for his support of jobs programs, civil rights, and arms control.*

rivals. And Illinois Sen. Paul Simon stressed his sincerity and commitment to traditional Democratic beliefs. Their efforts to establish their political identities appeared to have been set back on December 15, when Hart shocked the political world by announcing that he would reenter the race. "I have the power of ideas and I can govern this country," he declared. But some of the other candidates and party leaders criticized Hart for suggesting that the other Democratic contenders were not addressing the issues, and party National Chairman Paul Kirk said that by resuming his candidacy Hart had put his own interests above the good of his party.

On the Republican side the candidates were better known and the campaign was more orderly. Vice-President George Bush, helped by his ties to the still popular Reagan, was the leader in the polls, with his strongest challenge coming from Kansas Sen. Robert Dole, who relied on his experience on Capitol Hill. Three other long-shot candidates—New York Rep. Jack Kemp, a long-time advocate of supply-side economics; duPont, who urged significant changes in social security, welfare, and farm policy; and television evangelist Pat Robertson, with strong backing from the evangelic movement—all competed for support of the party's conservative wing. A fourth dark horse, Alexander Haig, stressed his background as secretary of state under Reagan and White House chief of staff under President Nixon. (*See* also pages 549–50).

In the midst of these presidential campaign preparations, voters went to the polls November 3 to pick candidates for state and local office. Democrats won the only two governorships at stake, electing Wallace Wilkinson, a wealthy businessman, in Kentucky and state auditor Ray Mabus in Mississippi. Democrats also won most of the big mayoralty contests, reelecting W. Wilson Goode, Philadelphia's first black mayor, Kathy Whitmire in Houston, and Raymond L. Flynn in Boston. They also chose Maryland State Attorney Kurt Schmoke as the first black mayor of Baltimore. On the Republican side, Mayor William Hudnut won a fourth term in Indianapolis. In Miami incumbent Mayor Xavier Suarez easily defeated former Mayor Maurice Ferre in a November 10 runoff.

Another mayoral vacancy developed in Chicago with the death of Harold Washington, the city's first black mayor, on November 25. The city's board of aldermen chose one of their members, another black, Eugene Sawyer, to replace him.

Ethics and Values. Teenage suicides and teenage pregnancies soared in number. The threat of AIDS (Acquired Immune Deficiency Syndrome) increased, bringing with it vexing dilemmas about the rights of victims of the plague. No wonder then to many Americans in 1987 their society appeared to be undergoing a period of moral upheaval and change. The sense of uneasiness was aggravated by allegations of misbehavior against prominent persons and institutions in several major areas of national life, including business, religion, politics, and government.

© Falk/Gamma-Liaison

W. Wilson Goode (D), Philadelphia's first black mayor, won reelection in November. Democrats won most of the nation's major mayoralty races during the course of the year.

Acting on information provided by Ivan Boesky, a confessed major figure in the 1986 insider trading scandals on Wall Street, the federal government arrested three investment bankers on February 12. They were accused of involvement in a plan to trade information between two leading financial firms, Kidder, Peabody & Co. and Goldman Sachs & Co., about plans of their clients for corporate takeovers in order to profit from investments in the targets of such takeovers. On April 23, Boesky himself pleaded guilty to conspiring to file false documents with the federal government. Despite his helping law enforcement officers by providing leads to investigations of "dozens" of other miscreants in the securities industry, Federal District Judge Morris Lasker said Boesky's crime was too serious "merely to forgive and forget." On December 18, Lasker sentenced Boesky to three years in prison.

Another blow to the prestige of the business community was the federal indictment brought against the Chrysler Corporation on June 24 on charges of tinkering with the odometers of 60,000 autos that already had been driven by company executives so the cars could be sold as new. On December 14 the automaker

Photos, AP/Wide World

Illegal or unethical behavior by prominent public figures made news repeatedly during 1987. Arbitrageur Ivan Boesky, left, *was convicted of insider stock trading; former White House aide Michael Deaver,* right, *was found guilty of perjury.*

pleaded no contest to the charges, and also agreed to pay $16 million to settle civil actions brought on behalf of consumers who purchased the cars.

The taint of scandal extended even to the pulpit. Television evangelist Rev. Jim Bakker resigned his ministry March 19, after admitting to engaging in extramarital sex seven years earlier. Bakker claimed that he had been betrayed into the encounter "by treacherous former friends" who then conspired to blackmail him in an effort to gain control of his PTL enterprise. In 1987 the latter included an amusement park, a hotel, and a satellite television system in addition to the television ministry. The damage from this disclosure was compounded by revelations that Bakker's wife, Tammy, cohost with him of a daily television talk program, was undergoing treatment for drug dependency. Another well-known television evangelist, Jerry Falwell, took over PTL at Bakker's request but soon became involved in a bitter controversy when Bakker accused Falwell of trying to take over his ministry. On October 8, Falwell resigned his PTL post. (*See* RELIGION—Overview.)

In the arena of government and politics, public cynicism and disillusionment was increased by revelations of misbehavior which forced the withdrawal of two Democratic presidential candidates from the campaign and by the findings of the congressional inquiry into the Iran-contra affair. In addition, there were a number of investigations of alleged criminal wrongdoing on the part of government officials. At the request of Attorney General Edwin Meese III, an independent counsel, James C. McKay, was assigned to investigate Meese's connection to Wedtech Corporation, a New York defense contractor whose efforts to gain business for itself had made it the subject of a number of other federal and state probes. On December 22, E. Robert Wallach, a lawyer and close friend of Meese, was indicted on federal charges of racketeering and conspiracy. McKay said there was "insufficient evidence as of this date" to bring criminal charges against Meese, but added that his inquiries into Meese's activities would continue.

Other federal investigations of Wedtech led to the indictment June 3 of Democratic Rep. Mario Biaggi of New York along with six other men on charges of taking bribes and extorting payments from the contractor. On September 22, Biaggi was convicted of having accepted a gratuity—a Florida vacation—for lobbying on behalf of a Brooklyn-based ship-repair firm. He was acquitted on more serious charges of bribery and conspiracy.

Meanwhile, independent counsel McKay's probe led to the indictment July 16 of former White House aide Lyn Nofziger on charges that he had lobbied Meese and other federal officials to help Wedtech in violation of the federal law banning lobbying by high public officials for at least a year after they leave government. Another former Reagan White House aide, Michael K. Deaver, was indicted for perjury on March 18 on charges of lying to a federal grand jury and to Congress investigating his lobbying activities. On December 16 a federal court jury found him guilty on three counts of lying under oath. Following the verdict, Whitney North Seymour, Jr., the same special prosecutor who had convicted Deaver, accused the Reagan administration of condoning "influence peddling" by former government officials. He specifically criticized Secretary of State George Shultz who testified to Deaver's integrity during the trial.

ROBERT SHOGAN
Washington Bureau, "Los Angeles Times"

The Economy

The U.S. economy teetered on wobbly scaffolding throughout most of 1987. Its underpinnings were weakened by many loose bolts, including volatile exchange rates, trade imbalances, and budget deficits. Although it was a good year for most Americans and, in fact, for most of the developed world, a sense of imminent danger prevailed throughout. It was a fear that something could let go at any moment. One of the bolts did snap. To the shock of America's 45 million shareholders, the Dow Jones industrial average plunged more than 500 points in a few chaotic hours on October 19, erasing in one swipe some $500 billion of equity values.

Never, not even in 1929, had a crash of such suddenness occurred. As it fell, the machinery snagged big and small, professional and amateur, foreign and domestic investors. Almost nobody was spared; some of the most successful practitioners of the investment arts suffered the greatest losses, not just to their portfolios but to their reputations, too. In a few hours, investors' soaring dreams of wealth were reduced to frantic concern about financing the moment. After dazed Americans had assimilated the shock, newspapers were filled with speculation about the potential consequences. Most economists quickly pared their forecasts for 1988. There would be a recession, many people said. Consumers would stop buying; business would cease spending.

But almost mysteriously, the thunderous impact of Wall Street's debacle seemed not to be felt on Main Street. The National Federation of Independent Business surveyed its members before and after the crash and found little difference in attitudes: bullish in both instances. The National Association of Purchasing Management in mid-November found its members "extremely optimistic." And an early December report from Federal Reserve district banks indicated little damage to economic growth to that point. Retail sales and housing held firm, automakers generally held to their production schedules, and surveys showed that while another dose of caution had been added to consumer confidence, it still remained fairly strong.

As if to contradict the evidence once more, almost everyone, nevertheless, continued to feel that the economy, strong as it was, was badly out of balance and subject to more stress fractures. There was so much to be done, and it was well known that the needed adjustments would be slow in coming.

The trade value of the dollar fell throughout the year. The imbalance of transactions between the United States and its trading partners continued. The federal budget deficit resisted attempts at control. More than 200 banks failed during the year, and others finally were realizing that multibillion dollar loans to less developed countries might not be collectible. And, as if there was not enough wrong with it, the stock market became host to some of the most enormous white-collar crimes of the century. Big traders, acting on confidential information—"inside" information not available to the general trading public—made easy profits. The crimes, said federal prosecutors, were not just on the periphery of the investment community; they were right in the center and had to be excised. Ivan Boesky, one of the most highly publicized and successful speculators, was among those destined to go to jail. More, undoubtedly, would follow.

In spite of all its problems and fears, the economy escaped recession. In fact, it grew at a remarkably steady pace throughout the year. Gross national product rose to $3.8 trillion, seasonally adjusted, from $3.7 trillion, a gain of 2.9%. And most economists looked for growth of at least 2% in 1988. The White House said it anticipated a 2.4% gain over 1987, a downward revision from its forecast of 3.5% issued during the summer.

The administration's revision was not necessarily a consequence of the great stock market crash, and it did not disappoint many people. In fact, there was a widespread belief that, incredibly, the crash had saved the day! Had it not brought expectations back to earth, so went the theory, the economy would have heated up, produced inflation and higher interest rates—and recession.

"Who would have predicted it on October 20th?" asked *Fortune* magazine. "The crash has not only failed to make a recession more likely before mid-1989; it has made one less likely." It explained that the economic pot was about to boil over; consumers were spending too much, Washington was stalling on cutting the budget deficit, and interest rates were moving higher. The crash changed the scenario: Under its new chairman, Alan Greenspan (*see*

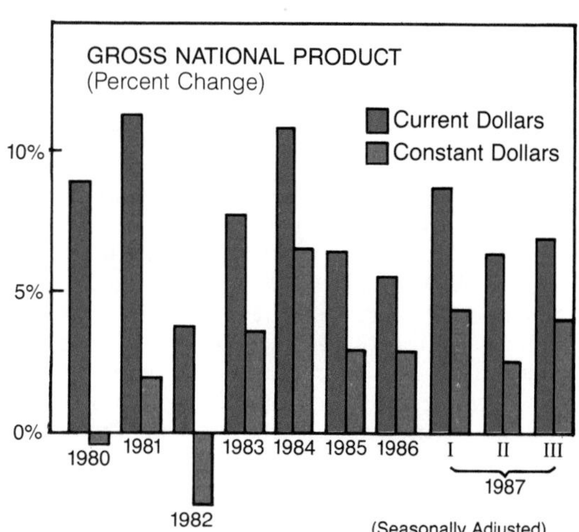

U.S. Department of Commerce, Bureau of Economic Analysis

AP/WIDE WORLD

With Christmas sales mixed, 1987 retail sales neared $126 billion; inflation was at 4.4%.

RETAIL SALES

1982
$89,107,000,000

1983
$97,599,000,000

1984
$107,448,000,000

1985
$114,968,000,000

1986
$121,201,000,000

1987
$125,900,000,000

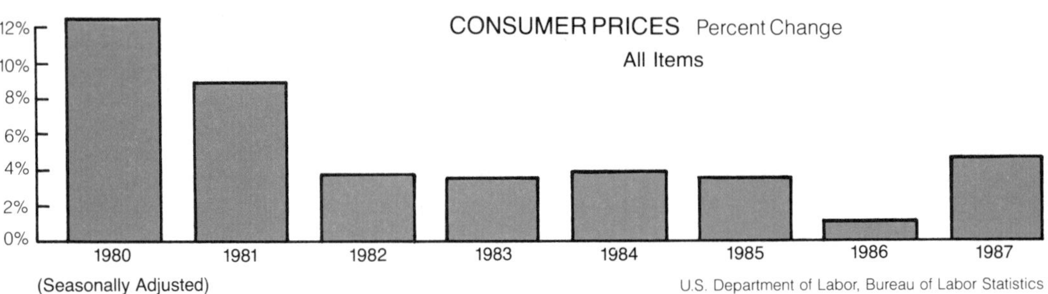

BIOGRAPHY), the Federal Reserve, which had been raising interest rates, reversed itself and flooded the post-crash economy with money to avert a collapse. Congress acted to reduce the deficit by $33 billion in fiscal year 1988. Consumers decided to rebuild savings. Business indicated it would spend, but very judiciously.

Even as they read such headlines, many Americans had a sense that something more might be in the offing. It was a continuation of the relentless foreboding that had been with them all year, a feeling that if there were dangers before the crash there certainly were even more afterward. It was, so to speak, as if there were an impact yet to be felt, of a sputtering fuse that nobody could see.

Still, there were emerging strengths in the economy. After almost two decades of recession or near-recession, the American manufacturing sector came alive, made more competitive abroad not just by the falling dollar but because programs to become lean, mean, and more productive finally were paying off. In November factories, utilities, and mines operated at 81.7% of capacity, the highest level in more than three years. Late in the year, the operating rate among producers of iron, steel, and other primary metals soared to an astonishing 87.9% from 71.9% a year earlier. Nonfarm productivity gained momentum throughout the year, achieving a 3.6% annual rate in the third quarter, a rate reminiscent of the 1950s.

There was hope for the farm belt, too. After six years of decline, farmland values rose. The Department of Agriculture reported that farm investors had regained sufficient confidence to bid up land prices between 8 and 10% during 1987 in such states as Illinois, Iowa, Kansas, and Nebraska. The department conceded that the increases might not persist and that there was still a long way to go before regaining the $300 billion decline in land values since 1981, but it suggested there was at least grounds for hope in farm areas that had been in their own private depression throughout the five-year economic expansion.

The expansion had brought good times to much of the nation, but especially to the Northeast, where help-wanted signs were as prominently displayed as menu boards at fast-food outlets. The Sunbelt, especially regions dependent on oil and mining, did not do as well, but they, too, showed signs of recovering. And much of the so-called rust belt, or Midwest manufac-

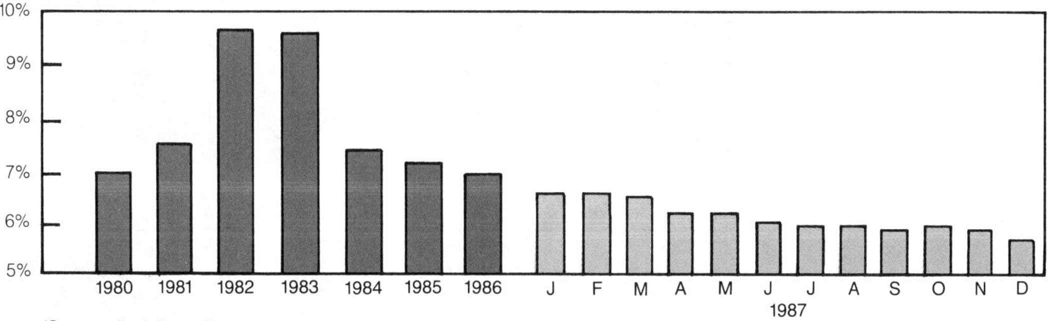

turing strip, had put its bad days behind it. While regions differed, the overall statistics were impressive.

Employment numbers were especially healthy. In December, Dr. Janet L. Norwood, commissioner of the Bureau of Labor Statistics, reported that the November jobless rate had fallen to 5.9%, the lowest since 1979, and that the number of people employed had risen by 3 million for the year to more than 113 million. The number of unemployed, 7.1 million in November, was more than one million below the level of a year earlier. Adult women accounted for 1.6 million of the 3 million new jobs, and adult men 1.3 million. Of special significance, one of the most rapidly strengthening areas of employment was in manufacturing. From June through November, factory jobs grew by 300,000, with 7 of 10 manufacturing industries adding workers. The commissioner said the average factory workweek of more than 41 hours was the longest in 21 years.

The economic problems remained; everyone was aware of them and fearful that they could produce further shocks. The budget deficit, down from a record $220 billion in fiscal 1986, still was an unhealthy $148 billion for fiscal 1987. The trade deficit, though improving, reached a record $170 billion for 1986. Inflation, as measured by the Consumer Price Index, was likely to come in at just under 5% for 1987, compared with 1.1% a year earlier.

The Declining U.S. Dollar

	W. German Deutsche Marks Per U.S. Dollar	British Pound Per U.S. Dollar	Japanese Yen Per U.S. Dollar
1982	2.376	.619	235
1983	2.724	.689	232.2
1984	3.148	.865	251.1
1985	2.461	.692	200.5
1986	1.941	.678	159.1
1987			
Jan.	1.808	.654	152.5
June	1.830	.621	147.0
Sept.	1.838	.614	146.3
Dec.	1.568	.530	121.0

UN Monthly Bulletin of Statistics

And the dollar resisted central bank efforts at stabilization.

The dollar's tumble against the yen and the German mark made a mockery of the so-called Louvre accord, reached by the world's leading industrial democracies at Paris in February. Signing of the accord pledged the United States, Japan, West Germany, Great Britain, France, and Canada to coordinate efforts to keep fluctuations within limits. They failed.

As the year ended, the future of the dollar —and, of course, the future of trading among the world's nations—remained in doubt. The White House said it hoped the dollar would fall no lower than it was—1.568 against the German mark and 121 in relation to the Japanese yen. The world's central banks also were intervening in the market, buying dollars. But nobody, not even the world's most powerful monetary figures, could dictate to a market that seemed intent on finding its own level.

It was but one of the question marks, one of the great challenges facing the world's economies in 1988. It hardly could have been clearer that the entire world economy was in transition and that it had a long way to go. Great imbalances remained: To balance world trade it was widely believed that the United States needed to export more, while the Japanese and West Germans expanded their economies, the better to accommodate those exports. But expansion could mean inflation too, and West Germany was especially wary of that possibility.

Potentially, an even greater imbalance remained—the financial condition of the Third World countries versus the big industrial powers. If the poorer nations were to expand their economies and thus become trading partners with other nations, they would first have to pay off their enormous debts. Lenders were accepting the notion that not all the debts could be repaid—to attempt doing so would be dangerous to lenders as well as to borrowers—and they were seeking a solution as the year ended. It would be a primary objective in 1988.

JOHN CUNNIFF, *The Associated Press*

Following the signing of the U.S.-USSR treaty on intermediate nuclear forces, Secretary of State George Shultz traveled to Europe to brief U.S. allies, including Britain's Foreign Secretary Sir Geoffrey Howe, left.

© I. Versele/Gamma-Liaison

Foreign Affairs

Amid the turmoil of 1987, as Ronald Reagan approached his last year in office, the president found some stability in U.S. foreign policy and managed several specific accomplishments. Most prominent among the results was the December summit meeting in Washington, DC, with Soviet General Secretary Mikhail Gorbachev. The summit had symbolic value but also was marked by concrete achievement: the leaders of the two superpowers signed a treaty eliminating intermediate-range nuclear weapons in Europe. It was President Reagan's first arms-control agreement, and it probably will be considered one of the major foreign-policy successes of his administration. Considering Reagan's longstanding ambivalence about arms control and relations with the Soviet Union, it also had an element of irony.

The summit presented an upbeat close to what was in many ways a disappointing year for the administration. For most of 1987, Reagan and the nation were mired in the Iran-contra affair, which raised old and new questions about Reagan's management of foreign policy. When attention was diverted from those revelations, it rested on other unsettling events, such as the Persian Gulf crisis, in which U.S. naval forces became embroiled in the Iran-Iraq war, or the confused diplomatic situation in Central America, where peace seemed always just over the horizon. In the Philippines, peace seemed much further away, despite U.S. support for President Corazon Aquino. And it was certainly no closer in South Africa, where U.S. economic sanctions, enacted in 1986, appeared to have little impact on the reform process.

A common thread running through many of these issues was the long-running struggle between Congress and the executive branch for control of U.S. foreign policy. It was, for example, a major factor in the Iran-contra affair. It was a dominant element in debates over Persian Gulf and Central American policy. It affected arms-control negotiations and was a factor in U.S. policy toward South Africa. It even affected the State Department's budget.

Turmoil also was evident at the National Security Council (NSC) during 1987: In November, National Security Adviser Frank Carlucci, who had been in that post only since December 1986, was named to replace Caspar Weinberger—who retired—as secretary of defense. Carlucci's replacement was his deputy, Lt. Col. Colin Powell, who became Reagan's sixth national security adviser.

Arms Control In contrast to other areas of foreign policy, arms control seemed to be going Reagan's way during 1987. If nothing else, the beleaguered Reagan could take some satisfaction in being the first U.S. president since Richard Nixon to host a visiting Soviet leader. Nor was the arms-control treaty that he and General Secretary Gorbachev signed on December 8 anything to scoff at. If ratified by the Senate, as was considered likely, the accord will require the United States to destroy 859 medium- and shorter-range missiles, including 429 already deployed in Western Europe; while the Soviet Union would be required to destroy 1,752, including 470 SS-20s and SS-4s based in the USSR and targeted on Western Europe and Asia.

The treaty may prove more important for two other reasons. It increased expectations and generated important momentum for possible agreement on the far more crucial area of reductions in strategic—i.e., long-range—nuclear weapons, the subject of another set of negotiations under way in Geneva. Second, it reaffirmed the validity of the arms-control process for the next U.S. president, so that Reagan's successor could pick up where he left off.

The central question at the end of 1987 was whether disagreement over Reagan's Strategic Defense Initiative (SDI, or "Star Wars") would block progress on a strategic weapons treaty in 1988. Soviet opposition to Reagan's SDI program was what led to the failure of the Reykjavik summit in October 1986, and it was an issue on which Congress had become a player in arms-control negotiations. Sentiment in the Democratic-controlled Congress was opposed to anything more than a limited SDI research program. There also was a strong belief that the 1972 ABM (Anti-Ballistic Missile) Treaty placed severe restrictions on testing and deployment. In its deliberations on defense legislation in 1987, Congress sought to give that narrow interpretation the force of law.

The administration made SDI one of the central elements in its defense and arms-control strategy, and argued that the treaty did not apply. Despite this apparent stalemate, there were efforts at the end of 1987 to find a compromise that would satisfy the president, the Congress, and the Soviets. It was even possible that the strategic-arms treaty could be negotiated—at least in principle—before Reagan leaves office in January 1989. At a minimum much of the foundation for such an agreement would be ready for Reagan's successor.

Progress on arms control suggested that the end of Reagan's second term may be coinciding with the beginnings of a new era in U.S.-Soviet relations. Gorbachev was the first truly modern Soviet leader and seemed interested in improved relations with the West as well as far-reaching economic reforms inside the Soviet Union. He appeared ready to make concessions on arms control and other issues of importance to the United States, including human rights and the withdrawal of Soviet troops from Afghanistan. *See also* ARMS CONTROL; MILITARY AFFAIRS.

Iran-Contra Affair. The U.S.-Soviet relationship was one of the few areas of Reagan's foreign policy—and of U.S. diplomacy—not hampered by the persistent conflict between Reagan and Congress. The Iran-contra investigation, the other major foreign-policy issue of 1987, was, for example, both a cause and effect of that conflict. That is, it happened in part because of the environment of conflict between the executive and Congress over foreign policy, and it was sure to contribute to future instances of conflict.

White House aides, particularly Marine Lt. Col. Oliver L. North and Vice Adm. John Poindexter of the NSC, appeared to have become convinced that congressional restrictions on covert actions were contrary to the national interest. In pursuing two specific policies for President Reagan—establishing ties with Iran while gaining the release of U.S. hostages in Lebanon, and extending support for the Nicaraguan contras—they felt justified in evading the congressional strictures. As noted in the majority report of the investigating committees, "Key participants in the Iran-contra affair had serious misconceptions about the role of the Congress and the president in making foreign policy."

The revelations resulting from the scandal —of deception, covert policies, and possible misappropriation of government funds—would probably only heighten the mistrust and conflict between the two branches. The minority report of the House and Senate committees, for example, called the conflict between the two branches "an underlying and festering institutional wound." *See* feature article, page 26.

Persian Gulf War. Even as the Iran-contra drama was unfolding at the hearings in the spring and summer of 1987, the Congress and the White House were tangling over the administration's stepped up military activity in the Persian Gulf. This began in the spring, when the U.S. Navy was ordered to increase its presence there, and continued during the summer, when a number of Kuwaiti and other foreign oil tankers were allowed to sail under U.S. flags and to receive U.S. military protection.

The administration viewed its increased military presence in the Gulf as necessary to show U.S. resolve and its ability to meet its international commitments. But many members of Congress were concerned that the activity would lead to open clashes with Iran and even a full-scale armed conflict with the Islamic republic. Its fears that this was another Lebanon waiting to explode were heightened by the apparently accidental attack by Iraq on the U.S.S. *Stark* in May, in which 37 U.S. sailors died. Other skirmishes encountered by U.S. forces throughout the year also heightened the fears.

Congress, however, proved unable or unwilling to pursue a different policy. At midyear, some members attempted to delay the reflagging but failed to get the necessary legislation

Speaker Jim Wright, left, *who played a major part in U.S. relations with Central America, and other congressmen listen as Costa Rica's President Arias explains his peace plan.*

© Dennis Brack/Black Star

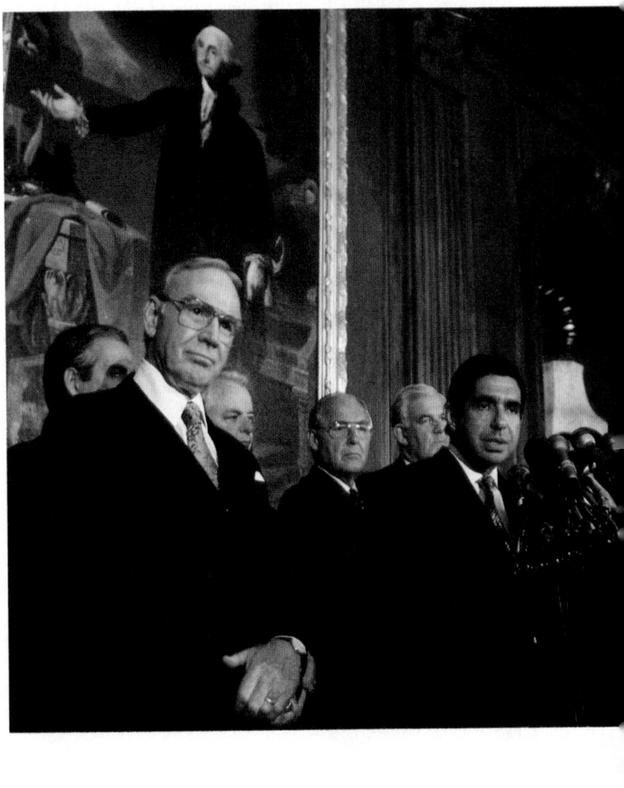

passed. Next, lawmakers sought to invoke the 1973 War Powers Act, which would have required the reflagging to end in 60 days unless Congress specifically authorized it. But this failed also. By the end of 1987, Congress had no choice but to yield to the executive branch's policy. Many members seemed unhappy with this sideline role. *See also* MIDDLE EAST.

Central America. On Central American policy, another area of major conflict between the two branches, it was the administration's turn to be frustrated bystanders during 1987. By the middle of the year, Congress, with both houses controlled by the Democrats, had usurped much of the administration's leverage, which was already limited. President Reagan was forced to abandon, at least for the immediate future, the policy of providing military aid to the contras fighting the Sandinista government in Nicaragua and was reduced to merely waiting for the results of a high-risk peace plan approved in Guatemala City by five Central American presidents in August. *See also* CENTRAL AMERICA.

AP/Wide World

Colin L. Powell, 50, became White House national security adviser late in the year. The lieutenant general had been serving as deputy to his predecessor, Frank C. Carlucci.

Reagan had been outmaneuvered, to a large extent, by House Speaker Jim Wright, who gave Central American officials assurances that Congress wanted to give the peace process a chance and would delay further contra aid as a means of showing support for the negotiations. The Reagan administration complained that Wright's activities, which included some mediation between the contras and Nicaragua's Sandinista regime, undercut the executive branch's role of implementing U.S. policy. But in an era of conflict and competition between the two branches, such complaints were hardly noticed. Nor would Regan's protests alone enable him to regain the initiative.

Budget Issues. Another major area of conflict between Congress and the White House in recent years has been foreign-aid levels, and that was still the case in 1987. The category of foreign-affairs spending dropped to $17 billion during the year, compared with $22 billion in 1985. In the face of administration protests that the cuts hampered the conduct of foreign policy, congressional appropriators countered that the administration would have to find new sources of revenue—taxes—if it wanted to increase spending on foreign aid.

The issue took on a further twist when the State Department announced that it would have to begin cutbacks in the foreign service because of an $84 million shortfall in its budget (part of the $17 billion international-affairs appropriation). The threatened cutbacks caused immediate morale problems in the elite diplomatic corps, but they also gave rise to skepticism in Congress. Some members suggested that the State Department cut back its expensive embassy security construction program, budgeted at more than $400 million annually, and use the money to pay foreign-service salaries. As the year drew to a close, it appeared that severe cutbacks would be avoided—but only until next year's budget. Beyond the immediate financial crunch, however, the budget restrictions posed broader issues: Can the United States maintain its power and prestige around the world as it cuts its foreign-aid budget year after year? Will the best and the brightest be attracted to a diplomatic corps always under siege from Congress?

Personnel. Another trend of President Reagan's second term that continued in 1987 was the gradual departure of the administration's most conservative top officials. A foreign-policy team that began in 1981 with Alexander Haig as secretary of state, Caspar Weinberger as secretary of defense, and Richard Allen as national security adviser was far different from the team as of late 1987: George Shultz at the State Department, Carlucci at the Defense Department, Powell at NSC, and, behind the scenes, Howard Baker as White House chief of staff.

The changes were bound to bring some calm. All four of the latter officials could, of course, be considered conservatives, but they were not martyrs to the cause. They gravitated less toward the ideological causes fought by their predecessors and more toward compromise. As the Reagan administration entered its final year, a central question would be how the president's team of advisers would handle the key issues on which the administration could still have an impact—chiefly, the negotiations with the Soviet Union involving strategic nuclear weapons and SDI, the Persian Gulf, and the Central American peace talks.

CHRISTOPHER MADISON
Staff Correspondent, "National Journal"

URUGUAY

A confrontation between the fledgling democracy and its military and police leadership was averted with the passage in December 1986 of a bill granting amnesty to officers accused of human-rights violations during the era of military rule (1973–85). President Julio María Sanguinetti had defended the measure, stating that amnesty was an "acceptable cost" for civilian, rather than military, rule. Congressional approval of the amnesty, however, provoked a petition drive for a plebiscite that could annul the law. By October 1987 the plebiscite campaign—headed by the widows of Congressmen Zelmar Michelini and Héctor González Ruiz, both of whom were assassinated during the 12-year military rule—had collected more than 550,000 signatures. Validation of the signatures was expected to take up to 90 days. If the law is annulled, civilian courts could pursue 360 charges of murder, torture, and other abuses filed by survivors and their families against 160 army and police officers.

An investigation by a congressional committee into the 1976 murders of former Congressmen Michelini and González Ruiz resumed in April. Its proceedings were hampered by the committee's inability to order army officers to testify.

In August, at the conclusion of an official inquiry into the deaths of three Communist Party activists between 1974 and 1983, the government announced that the military had not been responsible. President Sanguinetti was criticized for having named a military investigator to head the probe.

Economy. The economy continued its improvement in 1987, although its growth was expected to be closer to 2% than the 6% recorded the previous year. An inflation rate of 50% was forecast, down by 20% over 1986. Imports increased sharply, while exports were 20% higher than the previous year. Cereal production improved considerably. A 1987–89 economic plan was unveiled in September. Businessmen were encouraged over a goal of 4% annual economic growth, but labor was displeased with real wage increases that were said to be only 2% for 1987.

With the military budget estimated at only \$124 million in 1987 (by contrast, it was nearly \$400 million in 1982), reductions in outlays for the armed forces have become an important source of savings for the civilian regime. Armed forces personnel have been cut by one third, to 21,000, since restoration of civil rule in 1985.

New loans of \$80 million and \$45 million were obtained from the World Bank in June and October. The foreign debt surpassed \$5 billion, and the government announced in September that debt repayments would not exceed 8% of export earnings. Uruguay signed its first debt-for-equity swap in August. The deal, with Intercontinental Hotels, amounted to \$35 million. Tripartite trade arrangements with Brazil and Argentina were discussed in May.

Foreign Relations. A one-day summit was hosted in Montevideo on May 27 by President Sanguinetti, who was joined by Presidents José Sarney of Brazil and Raúl Alfonsín of Argentina. Foremost on the agenda was the formulation of a response to an increase in interest payments on the foreign debt, as the U.S. prime rate, on which loan interest was based, rose from 6.5% in December 1986 to 8.25% in May. The chief executives also discussed tense military-civil relations in the three Latin countries.

Soviet Foreign Minister Eduard Shevardnadze arrived in Montevideo on October 5 for a three-day official visit, marking the first time in the 61 years since diplomatic ties were established between the two countries that a Soviet minister had visited Uruguay.

On November 27, the presidents of eight Latin American countries (Uruguay, Argentina, Brazil, Peru, Mexico, Colombia, Panama, and Venezuela) met in Acapulco, Mexico, for a four-day discussion primarily of two central issues: the region's increasing debt load, and the problems of Central America, which President Sanguinetti had visited before arriving in Mexico.

LARRY L. PIPPIN
University of the Pacific

URUGUAY • Information Highlights

Official Name: Oriental Republic of Uruguay.
Location: Southeastern coast of South America.
Area: 68,039 sq mi (176 220 km²).
Population (mid-1987 est.): 3,100,000.
Capital (1980): Montevideo, 1,260,573.
Government: *Head of state,* Julio María Sanguinetti, president (took office March 2, 1985). *Legislature*—National Congress: Senate and House of Deputies.
Monetary Unit: Peso (267.50 pesos equal U.S.\$1, Dec. 2, 1987).
Gross Domestic Product (1986 U.S.\$): \$5,200,000,000.
Foreign Trade (1986 U.S.\$): *Imports,* \$820,000,000; *exports,* \$1,087,000,000.

UTAH

Criminal cases, higher taxes, and a flood-control project were major news in Utah in 1987.

Crime. One of the most bizarre criminal cases in Utah history ended on Jan. 23, 1987, when Third District Judge Kenneth Rigtrup sentenced Mark Hofmann with the recommendation "that you spend the rest of your natural life at the Utah State Prison." Hofmann had pleaded guilty to two counts of second degree murder for the 1985 bombing deaths of Ste-

A delegation from the Soviet Union visited Tooele, UT, in November for a tour of the U.S. Army's Chemical Agents Munitions Disposal System (CAMDS). The group studied U.S. methods of disposing of chemical weapons.

AP/Wide World

ven Christensen and Kathleen Sheets and to two counts of felony theft by deception—including a charge alleging he forged the Mormon "White Salamander" letter and his sale of the "McClellin Collection" to a Salt Lake City coin dealer. These forged documents raised questions about the early history of the Church of Jesus Christ of Latter-day Saints (Mormons). These guilty pleas were part of a controversial plea bargain arrangement after Hofmann had been charged with two counts of first degree murder, which carries a mandatory death sentence, and 28 counts of theft by deception and fraud. The plea arrangement included a promise by Hofmann to cooperate with authorities through a series of interviews in which he would acknowledge that all of the documents, which had been sold for more than $2 million, were fake.

UTAH • Information Highlights

Area 84,899 sq mi (219 889 km²).
Population (July 1, 1986): 1,665,000.
Chief Cities (1980 census): Salt Lake City, the capital (July 1, 1986 est.), 158,440; Provo, 74,108; Ogden, 64,407.
Government (1987): *Chief Officers*—governor, Norman H. Bangerter (R); lt. gov., W. Val Oveson (R). *Legislature*—Senate, 29 members; House of Representatives, 75 members.
State Finances (fiscal year 1986): *Revenue,* $3,311,000,000; *expenditure,* $3,071,000,000.
Personal Income (1986): $18,288,000,000; per capita, $10,981.
Labor Force (June 1987): *Civilian labor force,* 763,500; *unemployed,* 49,700 (6.5% of total force).
Education: *Enrollment* (fall 1985)—public elementary schools, 298,760; public secondary, 104,635; colleges and universities, 103,994. *Public school expenditures* (1985–86), $870,000,000 ($2,297 per pupil).

The lethal injection of Pierre Dale Selby on August 28 ended a 13-year saga of legal appeals up to the U.S. Supreme Court. Selby was the first person to be executed in Utah since Gary Gilmore was shot ten years earlier. Selby had been convicted and sentenced to death for the 1974 torture murders of three people during a robbery of the Ogden Hi-Fi Shop. The three murder victims and two survivors were held four hours in the shop basement when Selby and an accomplice forced them to drink liquid drain cleaner before he shot each of them in the head.

Selby's execution brought out about 150 death-penalty opponents who held a peaceful protest vigil outside the Utah State Prison. A few yards away a smaller group counted down the final seconds and praised the event as "long overdue."

Taxes. In 1987 the Utah Legislature was faced with considerable strain on state finances due to slow growth in the economy and disappointing revenue collections. The largest tax increase in Utah's history was enacted to increase the sales tax, the cigarette tax, the motor-fuel tax, and the local property tax by more than $150 million.

Flood Control. In a unique attempt to control flooding around the Great Salt Lake, Gov. Norman Bangerter initiated and the state legislature approved a $60 million project to lower the level of the lake. The lake had risen 12 ft (3.7 m) to a historic high and threatened major highways, railroads, sewage treatment plants, farms, and homes.

The flood control project included three large pumps at the western edge of the lake. These can pump 2 million acre-feet of water per year into a 500 mi^2 (1 295 km^2) lake that is 2–2.5 ft (.6–.8 m) deep. Pumping and a dry season reduced the level of the Great Salt Lake by about four feet in 1987.

LORENZO K. KIMBALL
University of Utah

VENEZUELA

President Jaime Lusinchi's ability to govern was hampered by demonstrations and strikes in March and April as well as by the efforts of former President Carlos Andres Pérez to become the 1988 presidential candidate of Venezuela's ruling Democratic Action (AD) party.

Pérez Nomination. In October, at its national convention, the left-of-center AD party nominated Pérez, president from 1974 to 1979 and Venezuela's most controversial politician, as its next presidential candidate. Elections would be held in December 1988. In March the powerful Venezuelan Labor Confederation had named Pérez as its choice for the AD nomination against the wishes of President Lusinchi, who supported former Interior Minister Octavio Lepage. The Christian Democratic-oriented COPEI, Venezuela's second most popular party, was unable to rally public support despite the nation's continuing economic and political problems or to decide on a presidential candidate.

Student Protests. Some 25,000 students and opposition-party members marched through the streets of Caracas March 26 in the biggest anti-government demonstration in recent years. The demonstration followed two days of disturbances in several cities, in which 160 people were injured and 300 detained. The protests, which caused $3 million in damages, started after a university student was shot by a well-known lawyer with police connections.

A second round of protests broke out in late April after the government raised public transportation fares. The 30–200% increases were said to be necessary to improve bus transportation and raise the wages of 150,000 transportation workers.

Apparently fearing further political tension, the government canceled a visit by U.S. President Ronald Reagan scheduled for early May.

Cuban Exile Released. Orlando Bosch, considered the most important anti-Castro activist in Miami's large Cuban colony, was released from a Caracas prison August 7. A Superior Court acquitted him of charges of helping to plant a bomb that caused a Cuban passenger jet to crash off Barbados in 1976. All 73 passengers were killed in the crash. Two Venezuelan codefendants were sentenced to 20-year prison terms. The court's decision to free Bosch on bond after 11 years in prison was expected to further cool Cuban-Venezuelan relations, which had improved slightly in 1986. A Venezuelan military court had found the 60-year-old Bosch innocent in 1980.

VENEZUELA • Information Highlights

Official Name: Republic of Venezuela.
Location: Northern coast of South America.
Area: 352,143 sq mi (912 050 km^2).
Population (mid-1987 est.): 18,300,000.
Chief Cities (1981 est.): Caracas, the capital, 2,299,700; Maracaibo, 929,000; Valencia, 523,000.
Government: *Head of state and government,* Jaime Lusinchi, president (took office Feb. 2, 1984). *Legislature*—National Congress: Senate and Chamber of Deputies.
Monetary Unit: Bolívar (30.8700 bolívars equal U.S.$1, Dec. 2, 1987).
Gross Domestic Product (1986 est. U.S.$): $57,000,-000,000.
Economic Index (Caracas, 1986): *Consumer Prices* (1984 = 100), all items, 124.3; food, (Oct. 1986) 152.9.
Foreign Trade (1986 U.S.$): *Imports,* $8,600,000,000; *exports,* $10,151,000,000.

Economy. Venezuela increased the average price of crude oil by 70 cents a barrel July 16, becoming the first OPEC member to do so since a common export price of $17.62 was established in December 1986. The slowly increasing price of world oil was expected to increase oil revenues to a level higher than the $7.2 billion earned in 1986 when the average export price was $12.90.

The government's desire to limit foreign exchange for imports led to a greater demand by the private sector that raised the exchange rate from 21.6 Bolivares per dollar to 33.5 in mid-October.

The slowly improving economy caused the government to predict in June that real growth in 1987 would be 1%, up from an earlier forecast of zero growth, assuming inflation was no higher than 28%.

A set of refinancing agreements with major private creditors was approved September 21, which lengthened payment on $20.34 billion in foreign debt to 14 years and reduced the amount to be paid in 1987 from $1.06 billion to $250 million and from $1.12 billion to $400 million in 1988.

Tensions With Colombia. Colombian guerrillas of the pro-Castro Army of National Liberation (ELN) killed nine border police in a predawn June 12–13 raid on a border post in the Perija Mountains. Amid a wave of rising nationalism, Venezuela delivered a strong protest after the Colombian warship *Caldas* sailed into disputed territorial waters in the Gulf of Venezuela August 9. The border with Colombia also was closed in several places in September because of the smuggling of drugs and undocumented aliens. Venezuela rejected Colombian proposals in September that Pope John Paul II mediate the territorial-waters dispute. Venezuela also rejected another proposal August 22 that the Organization of American States mediate the dispute.

NEALE J. PEARSON, *Texas Tech University*

Vermont Gov. Madeleine Kunin (right) *shares a light moment with counterparts Michael Dukakis of Massachusetts* (center) *and Garrey Carruthers of New Mexico* (left) *at the National Governors Conference in July. Kunin was reelected by the state legislature in January, after failing to win a required majority in November 1986 balloting.*

AP/Wide World

VERMONT

The 1987–88 legislature convened in January with the constitutional task of electing Vermont's next governor. Madeleine M. Kunin (D) had fallen just short of the required majority in her November 1986 bid for reelection because of the independent candidacy of Burlington's Socialist Mayor Bernard Sanders. Governor Kunin was overwhelmingly confirmed. Democratic majorities organized both houses of the legislature.

The Legislature. The legislative session, the longest since 1965, was judged by Governor Kunin to be "one of the most productive sessions for the people of the state." She made a drastic increase in state aid to education her main priority, and eventually secured legislative approval of it. Also passed were laws restricting drug testing and smoking in the workplace, raising the speed limit to 65 miles per hour (105 km/hr), and permitting interstate banking. Problems with a newly enacted solid-waste disposal formula aroused a post-session controversy. Republicans vainly called for a special session.

Economy and Politics. Thanks to an unexpectedly good economy, particularly in tourism and electronics, as well as to the new federal tax code (to which Vermont's income tax is "piggy-backed"), Vermont had a record $60 million budget surplus when the fiscal year ended June 30. Much of this windfall was allocated to support the boost in education aid, retire debts, create a fund to guard against future deficits, and provide for a legislative pay raise.

In the March local elections, Burlington's Mayor Sanders easily won election to a fourth two-year term. Referenda were held in 19 towns on the death penalty, and majorities in 11 favored it. In June, Burlington raised a tax issue with national implications when it billed the Medical Center Hospital of Vermont for property taxes on the grounds that it was a business rather than a charity. The hospital appealed to the courts, and in September a Superior Court ruling held that "charitable" institutions included nonprofit entities even though they collected fees for the bulk of their services. The city has appealed to the State Supreme Court.

The Judiciary. A case of alleged judicial impropriety dragged on through the year. Criminal charges were lodged against a former assistant judge, and misconduct charges were brought against three sitting Supreme Court judges by the state's judicial conduct board, setting off wide controversy. The board subsequently dropped its charges against one of the

VERMONT • Information Highlights

Area: 9,614 sq mi (24 900 km^2).
Population (July 1, 1986): 541,000.
Chief Cities (1980 census): Montpelier, the capital, 8,241; Burlington, 37,712; Rutland, 18,436.
Government (1987): *Chief Officers*—governor, Madeleine M. Kunin (D); lt. gov., Howard Dean (D). *General Assembly*—Senate, 30 members; House of Representatives, 150 members.
State Finances (fiscal year 1986): *Revenue,* $1,185,000,000; *expenditure,* $1,095,000,000.
Personal Income (1986): $7,220,000,000; per capita, $13,348.
Labor Force (June 1987): *Civilian labor force,* 293,700; *unemployed,* 9,800 (3.3% of total force).
Education: *Enrollment* (fall 1985)—public elementary schools, 62,703; public secondary, 27,454; colleges and universities, 31,416. *Public school expenditures* (1985–86), $295,000,000 ($3,554 per pupil).

judges who was reconfirmed in office and against another who had died. Charges against the third jurist, who left office upon reaching the mandatory retirement age, were pending in late 1987. To fill the two vacancies, Governor Kunin appointed her secretary of administration (a former Legal-Aid official) and a district judge known as a strong civil libertarian.

Controversy among Vermont's Abenaki Indians was sparked by a three-vote victory in a September election for chief by an insurgent leader, a militant former chief, over the interim chief. The secretary of state's office was unofficially brought in to supervise a recount, even though Vermont does not legally recognize tribal rights. The insurgents blocked the recount by padlocking tribal headquarters, and by late 1987 the Abenakis were divided into fiercely feuding factions.

ROBERT V. DANIELS AND SAMUEL B. HAND
University of Vermont

VIETNAM

The sixth congress of the Vietnamese Communist Party in December 1986 set in motion a series of leadership changes that continued during 1987. The party congress also expressed strong support for a process of economic reform and for continued Vietnamese domination of Cambodia.

Politics. The sixth party congress saw the unprecedented resignation of three veteran leaders—Truong Chinh, Pham Van Dong, and Le Duc Tho—who had guided the Vietnamese party and government for decades. Nguyen Van Linh, a 71-year-old reformer, was named secretary general of the party, but events during 1987 suggested that the old Stalinist approach to economic policy—involving tight centralized control and a ban on private initiatives—still had many supporters; and Linh might prove to be only a transitional leader.

Ailing former Interior Minister Pham Hung, 75, was chosen as premier, and Vo Chi Cong, the 74-year-old former agricultural minister, was named president. Both men are senior politburo members, but because of their age and health, the country actually is being run by the nine vice-premiers. These include Vo Van Kiet, the head of state planning, and Foreign Minister Nguyen Co Thach. Both are considered reformers and may be being groomed for top positions.

Economics. The Vietnamese economy has been in chaos since the 1985 currency reform introduced runaway inflation (estimated at 700% in 1987), and undermined confidence in the party's ability to manage economic affairs. Foreign debt has mushroomed, hard currency reserves are almost nonexistent, and, at $180 per capita, income is among the lowest in the world.

Increasing exports is a major priority of the current five-year plan. Exports and imports, each running at about $1 billion per year, are low by comparison with most Asian countries, but show a marked increase over the past few years.

Foreign investment appeared to be on the rise in 1987, however, with 500 foreign business delegations visiting the country in the first half of the year, compared with 700 delegations in all of 1986. Despite the economic boycott of Vietnam by most non-Communist nations since the 1979 invasion of Cambodia, many businessmen are attracted by the country's highly skilled and low-paid work force. Japanese and Korean firms are beginning to set up plants in Vietnam to assemble television sets, motorcycles, and cassette recorders.

In 1987, Japanese companies bought Vietnam's first shipment of crude oil. A Japanese consortium planned to build a five-story office building in Hanoi. Australia completed a satellite communications station in Ho Chi Minh City in 1987, and Japanese companies were negotiating to build a similar station in Hanoi. The Association of Southeast Asian Nations (ASEAN) has protested these violations of the boycott of Vietnam, but Singapore, an ASEAN member, had $210 million in trade with Vietnam in 1986, almost as much as Japan.

In late December the regime announced a broad new economic policy that effectively abandons central planning in favor of managerial decision-making at the factory level. The reform, which took effect Jan. 1, 1988, also introduces wage scales tied to productivity and other worker incentives, shareholding, and an expanded banking industry.

Foreign Relations. The stalemate over Vietnam's occupation of Cambodia continued in 1987. Vietnam and the Soviet Union tried to encourage direct negotiations between the Cambodian resistance groups and the Vietnamese-supported government in Phnom Penh. In December, however, Cambodia's Prime Minister Hun Sen traveled to France for three days of talks with former Cambodian leader Prince Norodom Sihanouk. The two announced that they would seek a peaceful solution to Cam-

VIETNAM • Information Highlights

Official Name: Socialist Republic of Vietnam.
Location: Southeast Asia.
Area: 127,243 sq mi (329 560 km²).
Population (mid-1987 est.): 62,200,000.
Chief Cities (1985 est.): Hanoi, the capital, 2,000,000; Ho Chi Minh City (1986 est.), 4,000,000.
Government: Communist Party secretary, Nguyen Van Linh.
Monetary Unit: Dong (15.000 dongs equal U.S.$1, August 1987).
Gross National Product (1984 U.S.$): $18,100,000,000.
Foreign Trade(1984 U.S.$): *Imports,* $1,823,000,000; *exports,* $763,000,000.

Air Vietnam, which relies on Soviet-built planes, announced plans in October to increase overseas flights to expand tourism and increase Vietnam's ties with the non-Communist world.

AP/Wide World

bodia's political problems and planned more talks in 1988. During 1987, Vietnam—hoping to discourage support of the resistance groups by China, Thailand, Singapore, and the United States—repeated its pledge to withdraw its troops from Cambodia by 1990. There was little progress, however, in easing tensions between Vietnam and China, one of the main supporters of the Cambodian resistance.

PETER A. POOLE
Author, "Eight Presidents and Indochina"

VIRGINIA

Once again in 1987, Virginians did something that would have been unthinkable in the state just a few years earlier. They voted to create a state lottery.

Elections. As they had in electing a black and a woman to top statewide offices in 1986, Virginians bucked their conservative image and the state's old guard political leaders by voting in favor of the lottery. Lottery proposals had failed for years in the state legislature, but Gov. Gerald L. Baliles said the people ought to have a chance to vote on the question. The legislature called for a referendum, and despite the announcements of Baliles and three former governors that they would vote no, 57% of state voters said yes to the proposal.

On the ballot along with the lottery were all 140 seats in the General Assembly. Though the heavily Democratic makeup of both the Senate and the House of Delegates remained essentially unchanged, the Republican Party appeared to have found an instant star in Edwina P. "Eddy" Dalton, widow of former Gov. John Dalton. Her defeat of a powerful, veteran state senator immediately cast the 51-year-old Mrs. Dalton, whose husband was governor from 1978–1982, as a leading candidate to run for lieutenant governor in 1989.

Virginians were stunned when U.S. Sen. Paul S. Trible, who had raised $1.4 million for his reelection, announced he would not run in 1988. He cited frustrations of office and a desire to spend more time with his family; many political observers suggested another motive was the prospect of facing former Gov. Charles S. Robb, probably the most popular politician in the state, for the seat.

The Legislature. Support by the popular Baliles was generally given credit for the General Assembly's passage of a number of bills. Among them were a ban on phosphates in detergents, a mandatory seat-belt law, and an overhaul of the state's income-tax structure.

The state Senate also made history by censuring a member, Peter K. Babalas of Norfolk, for ethical misconduct in voting to kill a bill that would hurt a corporate client. The two houses then passed a toughened conflict-of-interest bill.

Environment. The phosphate ban passed by the legislature is a measure designed to help

VIRGINIA • Information Highlights

Area: 40,767 sq mi (105 586 km²).
Population (July 1, 1986): 5,787,000.
Chief Cities (July 1, 1986 est.): Richmond, the capital, 217,700; Virginia Beach, 333,400; Norfolk, 274,800; Newport News, 161,700; Chesapeake, 134,400.
Government (1987): *Chief Officers*—governor, Gerald L. Baliles (D); lt. gov., L. Douglas Wilder (D). *General Assembly*—Senate, 40 members; House of Delegates, 100 members.
State Finances (fiscal year 1986): *Revenue,* $9,964,000,000; *expenditure,* $8,873,000,000.
Personal Income (1986): $89,169,000,000; per capita, $15,408.
Labor Force (June 1987): *Civilian labor force,* 3,017,400; *unemployed,* 138,900 (4.6% of total force).
Education: *Enrollment* (fall 1985)—public elementary schools, 665,151; public secondary, 302,953; colleges and universities, 292,416. *Public school expenditures* (1985–86), $2,903,000,000 ($3,210 per pupil).

clean up the environmentally distressed Chesapeake Bay. The cleanup effort got a major boost later in the year when Virginia, Maryland, Pennsylvania, and the District of Columbia signed a history-making pact to cut the flow of polluting nutrients into the economically important estuary. On a much less positive note, Virginia in 1987 suffered through another summer of drought, with farm losses pegged at more than $100 million.

Trials. In Virginia Beach, Michael and Karen Diehl were sentenced to 41 years and 31 years, respectively, in the beating death of a son. The Diehls, a fundamentalist Christian couple who had lived in a school bus with their 16 children, testified against themselves in the case.

In Bedford County, Elizabeth Haysom, a brilliant scholar born into wealth, was convicted and sentenced to 90 years for helping her boyfriend, Jens Soering, brutally kill her parents, Derek and Nancy Haysom. Soering, who faced capital murder charges in Virginia, was in jail in Great Britain and was challenging extradition to the United States as 1987 ended.

ED NEWLAND
"The Richmond Times-Dispatch"

WASHINGTON

In the state of Washington in 1987, trade issues and the cost of environmental cleanup and protection were prime concerns. The 50th state legislature met in regular and special sessions and approved a record 600 bills.

Trade and the Environment. In a state where international trade accounts for one of six jobs, Washington's congressional delegation worked to block passage of the omnibus trade bill and a bill that would mandate that growth in textile and clothing imports be limited to 1% annually above 1986 levels. (*See* INTERNATIONAL TRADE AND FINANCE.)

WASHINGTON • Information Highlights

Area: 68,139 sq mi (176 479 km²).
Population (July 1, 1986): 4,463,000.
Chief Cities (July 1, 1986 est.): Olympia, the capital (1980 census), 27,447; Seattle, 486,200; Spokane, 172,890; Tacoma, 158,950.
Government (1987): *Chief Officers*—governor, Booth Gardner (D); lt. gov., John A. Cherberg (D). *Legislature*—Senate, 49 members; House of Representatives, 98 members.
State Finances (fiscal year 1986): *Revenue*, $10,668,000,000; *expenditure*, $9,669,000,000.
Personal Income (1986): $66,978,000,000; per capita, $15,009.
Labor Force (June 1987): *Civilian labor force*, 2,246,600; *unemployed*, 163,700 (7.3% of total force).
Education: *Enrollment* (fall 1985)—public elementary schools, 506,890; public secondary, 242,816; colleges and universities, 231,553. *Public school expenditures* (1985–86), $2,580,000,000 ($3,705 per pupil).

On the environmental front, the state identified 600 toxic-waste sites, 90% of which were contaminated by five aluminum, aerospace, and electronic firms, and the larger military bases. The $204 million cleanup would be shared by the polluting firms, the federal government, a recently enacted tax on the substances, and the state's general fund.

The Hanford Reactor, 23 years old and designed for only 20 years of use, remained closed, affecting 6,300 jobs. Tests of wells and farm products that may be contaminated by radioactive groundwater were urged.

Legislature. Included among bills passed by the legislature in 1987 were measures to stop a hostile takeover of the Boeing Company by T. Boone Pickens and to give a tax break to large businesses after the Supreme Court ruled against the state's business and occupation tax. Gov. Booth Gardner continued to work toward reform of a tax structure that includes high sales taxes and a tax on gross business revenues regardless of net income, but no personal income tax.

Economy. It was a banner year for the state's forest products, due to increased productivity, world pulp and paper prices, and the weaker U.S. dollar.

The warmest, driest summer in 68 years led to lost revenue from lower electricity sales to California, outdoor water restrictions in Seattle, and early ripening of fruit crops. Apples rather than dairy products became the state's top cash crop for the first time.

Todd Shipyards, the last major shipbuilder in Seattle, filed for bankruptcy. The state lottery supplied a net of more than $76 million to the general fund. Washington, in competition with several other states, submitted a proposal to the U.S. Department of Energy to locate the Superconductor Super Collider in Lincoln County.

Archbishop Hunthausen. Acting upon the recommendations of a special three-member panel, Pope John Paul II restored Archbishop Raymond Hunthausen to full authority over the archdiocese of Seattle. A special Vatican investigation had judged the archbishop lax in overseeing certain church policies, and Auxiliary Bishop Donald Wuerl had been named to share his authority.

Crime. Terrence Peter Jackon (Silas Trim Bissell), who was labeled by the Federal Bureau of Investigation as the nation's most wanted fugitive terrorist, was arrested and later sentenced to two years in prison for his attempt in 1970 to bomb the Reserve Officers Training Corps building at the University of Washington.

Darren Creekmore, 25, was sentenced to 60 years in prison for killing his three-year-old son by abuse. The case sparked severe criticism of the state's Child Protective Services.

BARBARA HOLZ SULLIVAN, *Seattle*

© Carol M. Highsmith

Pennsylvania Avenue's Newest Attraction: The U.S. Navy Memorial, including Stanley Bleifeld's 7-foot (2m) bronze statue of a World War II sailor on a 100-foot circular granite plaza, was dedicated during an October ceremony.

WASHINGTON, DC

The statehood movement received a boost when the House of Representative's District of Columbia Committee voted 6 to 5 on June 3, 1987, to approve a bill to establish the state of New Columbia. Sponsors had hoped that the bill, tied to the bicentennial celebration of the U.S. Constitution, would speed through Congress. A tough legislative battle was expected in the House, but by year's end the bill had not reached the full membership.

The admission process began in 1980 with voter approval to call a constitutional convention. A constitution was finalized on May 29, 1982, and then adopted by the District voters on Nov. 2, 1982. Bills for statehood were introduced in each subsequent Congress and only successfully passed committee action in 1987.

Proponents of statehood are seeking to replace "second-class citizenship" with full voting rights in Congress for the District's nearly 630,000 residents (a population larger than those of four states). Currently the voters can elect a mayor and a 13-member council, but can send only one nonvoting delegate to the House of Representatives. Under home rule, granted by Congress in 1973, local legislation and budgets are subject to congressional veto.

Opponents of statehood argue that the district is authorized by the U.S. Constitution, which created a federal territory under the exclusive control of Congress. They argue that other cities with large populations do not have statehood privileges. They state that the proposed state constitution was too radical in guaranteeing a job or income for all, granting abortion rights, and banning discrimination based on sexual orientation. They point to recent inefficiency, waste, and corruption in the local government. Supporters accuse them of fearing that the city is too urban, poor, black, liberal, and Democratic.

A previous effort to have full congressional representation failed when only 16 of the required 38 states ratified a proposed constitutional amendment before the approval period expired in 1985.

Voter Actions. A voter initiative requiring deposits on beer and soft-drink containers failed, after an intensive campaign by retailers and the beverage industry. The opponents feared loss of sales, sanitation problems, and the inconvenience of handling and storing returnable bottles and cans.

A second initiative was passed ensuring that funding for the public school system would have "the highest priority" in the city's budget considerations. The initiative also required the school board, mayor, and council to hold public hearings on the annual education budget.

New Attractions. The U.S. Navy Memorial was dedicated in the downtown area. It contains a 7-foot (2-m) bronze "Lone Sailor" statue standing in a 100-foot (30-m) circular granite plaza, with an inlaid map of the world, surrounded by fountains, an amphitheater, and two 75-foot (23-m) flag-draped ship's masts.

The Arthur M. Sackler Gallery of Asian and Near Eastern Art and the National Museum of African Art opened as the ninth and tenth museums of the Smithsonian Institution on the Mall. The museums are located on three underground levels, beneath a 4.2-acre (1.7-ha) Victorian garden. The National Museum of Women in the Arts opened in a restored beaux arts Masonic temple in the downtown area. (*See also* page 118.)

MORRIS J. LEVITT
Howard University

WEST VIRGINIA

The economy became the primary concern of individual citizens and of the executive and legislative branches of state government throughout the year. The state had been beset over a period of several years by drastic slumps in the bituminous coal and steel industries and by accompanying population losses and decreasing tax revenues. By 1987 many West Virginians felt in their paychecks and insurance or retirement programs the impact of an economic downturn that the state government had been wrestling with for almost a decade.

Economic Woes. As the year neared its end, a controversy over the legitimacy of the 1987–88 fiscal budget was in the hands of the State Supreme Court, Legitimate or not, the budget passed by the Democratic-controlled legislature and opposed by Republican Gov. Arch A. Moore, Jr., already had been involved in several unusual scenarios. It scarcely had been placed in effect by the beginning of the fiscal year July 1 when a gubernatorial edict imposed a cut in expenditures for all state departments. In response, some departments announced plans to spend their year's allotment of funds before June 30, 1988, in an effort to force legislative action on supplemental funding.

Public school teachers and other state employees protested inadequate funding, citing external surveys that placed their salary scales from 15% to 30% below those of comparably sized states.

Income-tax refunds were in many cases delayed for several months. Vendors complained that their reimbursement for sales to state agencies often were 90 days or more in arrears. And the state's hospitals, faced with delays of as much as four or more months in payments from the State Employees Insurance Program, were considering several forms of alternative admissions policies.

Steps Toward Recovery. Some positive signs could be found. The unemployment rate dropped to a single-digit level for the first time in several years. West Virginia University was awarded a major U.S. Department of Energy contract aimed at the development of clean-burning use of high-sulfur coal. And the northern part of the state experienced an encouraging growth in computer-related industries.

The 1988 legislative session promised to be a most challenging one, with virtually all the major economic issues of the past two years still unresolved, if not growing worse. A right-to-work lobby was expecting firm opposition in a state long associated with strong union sentiment. Public employees' insistence on realistic and dependable funding of insurance, hospitalization, and retirement programs was anticipated to be unrelenting and well organized. And an election-year legislature faced an almost certain need to raise taxes, always an unpopular move when voters are getting ready to express their feelings at the polls.

A special one-day session of the legislature on December 8 authorized the governor to borrow $50 million from the state's consolidated investment funds, to be used only for education, public employees' health benefits, and Medicaid. The sum would have to be paid back by the end of fiscal year 1988. Officials at the same time estimated the state's unpaid bills at approximately $150 million, and the governor vetoed the authorization.

DONOVAN H. BOND
West Virginia University

WEST VIRGINIA • Information Highlights

Area: 24,232 sq mi (62 760 km²).
Population (July 1, 1986): 1,919,000.
Chief Cities (1980 census): Charleston, the capital, 63,968; Huntington, 63,684; Wheeling, 43,070.
Government (1987): *Chief Officers*—governor, Arch A. Moore, Jr. (R); secy. of state, Ken Hechler (D). *Legislature*—Senate, 34 members; House of Delegates, 100 members.
State Finances (fiscal year 1986): *Revenue,* $3,822,000,000; *expenditure,* $3,621,000,000.
Personal Income (1986): $20,289,000,000; per capita, $10,576.
Labor Force (June 1987): *Civilian labor force,* 745,100; *unemployed,* 67,400 (9.1% of total force).
Education: *Enrollment* (fall 1985)—public elementary schools, 249,034; public secondary, 108,889; colleges and universities, 76,659. *Public school expenditures* (1985–86), $942,000,000 ($2,821 per pupil).

WISCONSIN

With a governor and a legislature of different parties, Wisconsin's government experienced political repercussions throughout the year.

State Budget. One of the earliest points of contention occurred during debate over the state budget when Republican Gov. Tommy Thompson proposed a 6% cut in payments under Aid to Families with Dependent Children (AFDC). The Democratic-controlled legislature agreed to only a 1% cut. By vetoing digits in the budget bill, Thompson put the cut back at 6%. He pointed out that food stamp benefits

During a four-day, autumn visit to Seoul, South Korea, Wisconsin's newly inaugurated governor, Tommy G. Thompson, (left), *discussed economic matters with Ryu Ki-jung* (right), *president of the Korea Federation of Small Business.*

AP/Wide World

were increased, making the overall cut to those receiving AFDC 3.5%.

The welfare veto was an example of the governor's use of executive power. Although he incurred the wrath of the legislature with a record 290 vetoes in the budget, he ultimately won the gamble. Democrats did not have enough votes to override the vetoes, which allowed the governor to extend a 60% income-tax exclusion on capital gains on property held a year or more, to keep the minimum wage at its present level, and to withhold some restrictions on nursing homes.

Business Development. Thompson had campaigned on a program to boost the state's economy, and businesses were pleased with his initial efforts. Among budget provisions that affected businesses were increased spending for the Department of Development, the Division of Tourism, and Forward Wisconsin, a partnership between the state and private businesses. The budget also provided money to promote trade with Japan and to establish a state film office.

The governor's initiative was clearest, however, in dealing with two major state industries. When the Chrysler Corporation announced that it would buy out American Motors Corporation, Thompson offered financial support to keep production at AMC's Kenosha plant. The state would provide $6 million in job-training funds, and Chrysler would build Omnis and Horizons at the AMC plant, saving 1,500 existing jobs and adding 1,800 workers. When Australian financier Alan Bond threatened to buy out the G. Heileman Brewing Company of LaCrosse at $38 a share, Thompson called on the legislature to enact an antitakeover law. After the bill was passed, Bond increased the offer to $40.75 a share—a total of $1.25 billion —and Heileman accepted. The governor said the action turned a hostile takeover into a friendly merger, and the result was good for the state.

Other Actions. Also in the legislative session, bills were passed to require the use of automobile seat belts, increase the faculty at the University of Wisconsin to reduce class size, and establish a state lottery. The lottery had been approved, 65% to 35%, by voters in a referendum in April.

Milwaukee Fires. Two fires in Milwaukee's Inner City within 15 days focused attention on families crowded in poor housing. Twelve persons, including ten children, died on September 30, six children on October 15. The fires prompted a local ordinance requiring landlords to install smoke detectors, calls for better fire-prevention training, and investigations into housing conditions.

Economy. The Wisconsin economy continued to maintain growth, with total nonfarm employment expected to increase 2.3%, translating into 46,500 additional jobs. While nonmanufacturing sectors continued to be the source of most new jobs, 15% of the new job growth was in manufacturing. Personal income was expected to expand by 4.3% and wages and salaries to gain by 4.7%. Farm income, however, was expected to decline 8.3% from 1986.

PAUL SALSINI, *"The Milwaukee Journal"*

WISCONSIN • Information Highlights

Area: 56,153 sq mi (145 436 km²).
Population (July 1, 1986): 4,785,000.
Chief Cities (July 1, 1986 est.): Madison, the capital, 175,850; Milwaukee, 605,090; Green Bay (1980 census), 87,899.
Government (1987): *Chief Officers*—governor, Tommy G. Thompson (R); lt. gov., Scott McCallum (R). *Legislature*—Senate, 33 members; Assembly, 99 members.
State Finances (fiscal year 1986): *Revenue,* $10,886,000,000; *expenditure,* $9,125,000,000.
Personal Income (1986): $66,549,000,000; per capita, $13,909.
Labor Force (June 1987): *Civilian labor force,* 2,531,000; *unemployed,* 139,900 (5.5% of total force).
Education: *Enrollment* (fall 1985)—public elementary schools, 501,402; public secondary, 266,832; colleges and universities, 275,069. *Public school expenditures* (1985–86), $2,930,000,000 ($4,168 per pupil).

As a result of a May 1987 U.S. Supreme Court ruling, all-male public-service clubs, such as Rotary International in Duarte, CA, right, *may be required to admit women as members.*

© Bart Bartholomew/Black Star

WOMEN

With gains reported in salaries and professional advancement, and with three favorable U.S. Supreme Court decisions, 1987 was a year that saw some notable progress on women's issues in the United States. Other concerns, including abortion and the question of surrogate motherhood, received attention.

Careers. Two reports released in 1987 showed some advancement for women in business and the professions, although both indicated that large gaps remained between male and female earning power. A book-length report prepared for the Congressional Caucus on Women's Issues, titled *The American Woman 1987–1988,* showed that the average female college graduate earned only slightly more than the average male high-school dropout. Overall, women earned about 68 cents to the dollar earned by men, the report said.

Census Bureau figures released in September showed slightly higher earnings for women who worked full time; 70% of the earnings for men in 1986, up from 62% in 1979. Census officials said that more than half the pay gap could be explained by differences in education and experience and by the fact that women were more than three times as likely as men to have interrupted their careers at some point. However, the bureau's figures showed that even women with continuous work histories earned, on the average, just 69% of what men did. The study also pointed to a degree of segregation in occupations, with traditionally female fields offering lower salaries.

Three 1987 Supreme Court decisions were expected to affect the situation. In *Johnson v. Transportation Agency of Santa Clara County,* the court upheld, 6–3, a voluntary affirmative action program that had led to the promotion of a woman over a man who had scored slightly higher in a qualifying interview. In *Rotary International v. Rotary of Duarte,* the justices ruled unanimously that all-male public-service clubs could be required to admit women under state civil-rights acts. (Bars to such clubs and the networking opportunities they provide have often been cited by women as roadblocks to career advancement.) In the third case, *California Federal v. Guerra,* the court upheld a California law requiring employers to offer disability leave for pregnancy and childbirth. The decisions were hailed by women's groups, but critics charged that they opened the door for discrimination against white males.

Politics. Analyses of the 1986 elections showed that voting by women had a significant impact, apparently tipping the balance toward the Democratic Party in seven states and helping that party regain a majority in the Senate. Meanwhile, several reports showed steady increases in the numbers of women in state and local offices. Women made up 15.5% of state legislators in 1987, compared with 4% in 1969.

With census figures indicating that about 56% of people who actually vote are women, the female vote was expected to have even more impact on the 1988 presidential election. Pat Schroeder, a seven-term Democratic congresswoman from Colorado, tested the waters in 1987 for a possible presidential bid and received enthusiastic support from the National Organization for Women (NOW). But Schroeder withdrew in September. Jeane Kirkpatrick, former U.S. ambassador to the United Nations who had been mentioned as a possible presidential candidate, said that she would not run.

Other Concerns. NOW President Eleanor Smeal stepped down in 1987 and was replaced by Molly Yard, the group's political director (*see* BIOGRAPHY). Yard promised to continue the activist course begun by her predecessor. Among the group's immediate concerns was a campaign to block the confirmation of Supreme Court nominee Robert Bork, on the ground that his views would lead to a setback for women's rights.

Abortion continued to be debated hotly during the year. The government announced two new sets of rules, one that would bar federal grants for family-planning organizations that provide any type of support to foreign programs that advise on abortion, and one that would cut off funding for U.S. family-planning clinics that offer abortion counseling or refer clients to abortion services. The Planned Parenthood Federation and other groups campaigned vigorously against the new regulations.

Surrogate motherhood was also an issue, with feminist groups charging that the practice would lead to the exploitation of women. (*See* feature article, page 55.)

A NOW report found continuing discrimination against women in education and blamed the 1984 Supreme Court decision in *Grove City College v. Bell,* which had the effect of narrowing federal antidiscrimination laws. And studies in New York and several other states pointed to courtroom biases against women, including stereotypes that affected jury selection, attitudes toward female attorneys and judges, and the degree of credibility placed in statements by female witnesses.

ELAINE PASCOE, *Free-lance Writer*

WYOMING • Information Highlights

Area: 97,809 sq mi (253 326 km²).
Population (July 1, 1986): 507,000.
Chief Cities (1980 census): Cheyenne, the capital, 47,283; Casper, 51,016; Laramie, 24,410.
Government (1987): *Chief Officers*—governor, Mike Sullivan (D); secretary of state, Kathy Karpan (D). *Legislature*—Senate, 30 members; House of Representatives, 64 members.
State Finances (fiscal year 1986): *Revenue,* $2,004,000,000; *expenditure,* $1,633,000,000.
Personal Income (1986): $6,485,000,000; per capita, $12,781.
Labor Force (June 1987): *Civilian labor force,* 253,400; *unemployed,* 18,600 (7.3% of total force).
Education: *Enrollment* (fall 1985)—public elementary schools, 73,988; public secondary, 28,791; colleges and universities, 24,204. *Public school expenditures* (1985–86), $528,000,000 ($5,479 per pupil).

WYOMING

Soft markets for oil, gas, and coal were inescapably the year's major story in Wyoming during 1987. For the first time in memory, revenue shortfalls in the state's general operating budget dictated both substantial cuts and use of reserve funds that had been set aside in the early 1980s. As Gov. Mike Sullivan (D) took office in January, he set as an objective a 5% cutback in the total number of state employees. In August he requested a reduction in state agency budgets of 7%, a contingency for the next biennium.

Legislature. At its general session in February, the state legislature appropriated a total of $641.3 million, down from $771.6 million in 1986. Overall school funding was reduced by 3.5%. To balance the budget—a constitutional requirement in Wyoming—lawmakers transferred a total of $161 million from various reserve accounts to cover current operating deficits. Aiming at economic development initiatives, the legislature created an enterprise loan fund of $10 million under Amendment 4 (adopted in 1986) and set aside $30 million from the mineral trust fund for loans to Wyoming firms working on clean-coal and coal-enhancement projects. Additional legislation in this category included severance tax breaks for marginal oil, gas, and coal producers in the state. A bill to raise the legal drinking age from 18 to 21 failed; without this change, however, federal law stipulated forfeiture of 10% of the state's federal highway allocation. The issue reappeared in a special session of the legislature called by Governor Sullivan in May. Meeting for four days, lawmakers quickly raised the state speed limit to 65 miles per hour (105 km/h) in accordance with new federal guidelines, and then debated but again failed to raise the legal drinking age.

Economy. There was some indication that Wyoming's oil and uranium industries had bottomed out. Given a slight rise in the price of their product, the three companies producing uranium in the state marginally increased their operations. Oil-drilling activity in the state crept upward with a drilling rig count of about 60 in September, up by about half since 1986. The unemployment rate hovered at about 6.5% in late summer, also an improvement over 1986. But Wyoming's labor force was about 2% smaller than in 1986, reflecting in part an out-migration of workers. Higher agricultural prices and an 18% increase in tourism were two other positive signs.

Other Developments. In July state officials ordered the evacuation of some 200 homes in the Rawhide Village subdivision near Gillette following the identification of toxic gas seepage from coal seams beneath the area. The subdivision, which is adjacent to a major coal-mining operation, may finally prove uninhabitable; displaced residents were qualified to receive emergency federal aid. Litigation against the coal company followed, as homeowners found their property virtually worthless.

On a happier note, the captive population of 18 black-footed ferrets housed in a state-run breeding facility near Laramie produced eight youngsters (of which one died). This small colony was presumed by wildlife authorities to contain all that is left of one of North America's most endangered species.

H. R. DIETERICH, *University of Wyoming*

YUGOSLAVIA

In 1987, Yugoslavia faced a worsening economic crisis and rising ethnic tensions, a daunting challenge to a country without a strong central political authority to handle it.

Economy. In a deepening slump since the late 1970s, Yugoslavia's economy seemed saddled with insoluble problems—a foreign debt of about $20 billion, an annual inflation rate of almost 100%, and 14% of its work force unemployed. The government launched a new "economic stabilization program" to deal with the desperate situation. In February it announced that it did not intend to suspend interest payments on the country's foreign debt. A rash of wage increases for many high officials provoked strikes among workers and miners early in the year. Reacting to the high rate of inflation, the government in March ordered a three-month reduction in the prices of foodstuffs and consumer goods to January 1 levels.

A new wave of mass protests occurred throughout the country in July, following a general wage freeze. At midyear, all state enterprises were required to prepare a comprehensive financial accounting of their performance. Under tough new legislation, the government was obliged to stop subsidizing unproductive plants and declare them bankrupt. It was estimated that almost 7,000 enterprises had lost nearly $1.5 billion in the first quarter of 1987, with another 1,000 still carrying heavy losses from 1986. Demands for such stringent measures had come from the more prosperous northern republics (Slovenia, Croatia, Serbia), which also complained about the heavy drain of resources to their underdeveloped southern partners (the republics of Montenegro, Bosnia-Herzegovina, and Macedonia, and Kosovo province) and called for fewer state restrictions upon free market operations.

YUGOSLAVIA • Information Highlights

Official Name: Socialist Federal Republic of Yugoslavia.
Location: Southeastern Europe.
Area: 98,764 sq mi (255 800 km^2).
Population (mid-1987 est.): 23,400,000.
Chief Cities (1981 census): Belgrade, the capital, 1,470,073; Osijek, 867,646; Zagreb, 768,700.
Government: *Head of state,* collective state presidency, Lazar Mojsov, president (took office May 1987). *Head of government,* Branko Mikulić, president of the Federal Executive Council (took office May 1986). *Legislature*—Federal Assembly: Federal Chamber and Chamber of Republics and Provinces.
Monetary Unit: Dinar (952.5 dinars equal U.S.$1, Nov. 30, 1987).
Gross National Product (1985 U.S.$): $129,400,-000,000.
Economic Indexes (1986): *Consumer Prices* (1980 = 100), all items, 1,312; food, 1,369.8. *Industrial Production* (1980 = 100), 119.
Foreign Trade (1986 U.S.$): *Imports,* $12,164,-000,000; *exports,* $10,641,000,000.

Ethnic Strife. While the grave economic situation was met with sober discussion and planning, continuing ethnic tensions in the incendiary autonomous province of Kosovo released passion and violence. Since 1981, some 20,000 members of the Serbian minority have left the province, in response to harassment by the ethnic Albanian majority, numbering almost 80% of the total population of 1.8 million. In April, a crowd of 10–15,000 Serbs and Montenegrins clashed with police in the city of Kosovo Polje, while 300 of their number voiced their complaints to the leader of the Serbian Communist Party, Slobodan Milosevic.

During the night of September 1–2, a 20-year-old ethnic Albanian conscript went berserk with an automatic weapon in a barracks in Paracin in southern Serbia, killing four and wounding five, all non-Albanians. More than 10,000 people attended the funeral for the victims in Belgrade, shouting anti-Albanian slogans. Elsewhere in Serbia, Serbs vandalized Albanian-owned shops.

Government Vacillation. The federal government, suffering from a continuous lack of political authority since the death of Marshal Tito more than seven years ago, vacillated between repression and concessions. Peter Ivezaj, an ethnic Albanian with dual U.S.-Yugoslav citizenship convicted in 1986 of anti-Yugoslav activities in the United States and sentenced to seven years in a Yugoslav prison, was released and returned to the United States, and Milovan Djilas, Yugoslavia's most prominent dissident, prohibited from traveling abroad since 1969, was granted a passport. On the other hand, Miodrag Markovic, an elementary school teacher in Bosnia-Herzegovina, was sentenced to prison for dissemination of "hostile propaganda," defaming Tito and the Yugoslav Communist Party.

The execution of Andrija Artukovic, a convicted Croatian war criminal who was extradited by the United States, was postponed indefinitely because of his poor health.

Political Changes. In May, Lazar Mojsov, a Macedonian, succeeded Sinan Hasani as president of the collective state presidency for a one-year term. Hamdija Pozderac, from Bosnia-Herzegovina, was elected vice-president, but resigned in September because of his involvement in a national financial scandal over the state-run Agrokomerc food-processing conglomerate, which had issued some $233 million in worthless promissory notes; Pozderac was replaced in November by another Bosnian, former Foreign Minister Raif Dizdarević.

Other. In April, Yugoslavia and Oman agreed to establish a committee for economic cooperation, and in October, Yugoslavia and Turkey held discussions on bilateral economic relations and improving Balkan cooperation.

JOSEPH FREDERICK ZACEK
State University of New York, Albany

YUKON

Yukon's economic resurgence of 1986 not only continued in the first half of 1987 but did so at a significantly faster pace. The reopening of Faro's Curragh Resources mine in early 1986 helped stabilize Yukon's economy, and along with a healthy gold market, activity in the mining industry was heading for record highs. At the same time, tourism, Yukon's second-highest money earner, topped C$100 million in 1987, up $9 million from 1986.

Total mineral production in 1986 skyrocketed to $175 million, up from the $57 million for 1985. Gold production was up by $23 million to $66 million, silver rose marginally to $17 million, while lead produced $24 million. Zinc was at $67 million.

Government. In 1987 the ruling New Democratic Party (NDP) scored a by-election victory in the riding of Tatchun (Carmacks-Ross River), a constituency formerly held by Liberal leader Roger Coles. Coles was convicted in 1986 and served a jail term for selling cocaine.

The by-election gave the NDP government a majority in the 16-member legislature: nine New Democrats, six Conservatives, and one Liberal. Meanwhile, the NDP added to its national base by sweeping three Canadian by-elections, one of which was to replace Erik Nielsen, a Progressive Conservative Member of Parliament for 19 years.

Indian Land Claims. Land-claims talks remained stalled. Negotiators for both sides, the federal government and the Council for Yukon Indians, carried out a series of informal talks aimed at determining where they might start when formal negotiations begin again.

Meech Lake Challenge. In May, Yukon government leader Tony Penikett announced his opposition to the Meech-Lake agreement, a federal pact worked out during a conference of Prime Minister Brian Mulroney and the provincial premiers at Meech Lake, Que., in April. Yukon challenged the constitutionality of the agreement in the courts, arguing that it violates the rights of the territories. (*See* CANADA.)

DON SAWATSKY, *Whitehorse*

YUKON • Information Highlights

Area: 186,660 sq mi (483 450 km²).
Population (1986 census): 23,504.
Chief cities (1986 census): Whitehorse, the capital, 15,199.
Government (1987): *Chief Officers*—commissioner, J. Kenneth McKinnon; government leader, Tony Penikett (New Democratic Party). *Legislature*—16-member Legislative Assembly.
Public Finance (1987–88 fiscal year budget est.): *Revenues,* C$279,495,000; *expenditures,* C$291,-051,000.
Personal Income (average weekly earnings, July 1987): C$514.78.
Education (1987–88) *Enrollment*—elementary and secondary schools, 4,900 pupils.

ZAIRE

Relative economic stability achieved by adherence to International Monetary Fund (IMF) guidelines underscored Zaire's improved economy in 1987 and strengthened President Mobutu Sese Seko's control of the state.

Domestic Affairs. A new party, the Workers and Peasants Party (POP), was founded to contest with Mobutu's *Mouvement populaire de la révolution,* but it was no serious threat to MPR. Violence that had been endemic in Shaba and Equatorial provinces was at a minimum. Mobutu even granted amnesty to some former political opponents whom he had imprisoned.

Two major tragedies highlighted the dangers of travel in Zaire. On July 2 a train and truck crash killed 128 persons. Three days later a barge crossing the rain-swollen Luapula River capsized and more than 450 people died. But far more devastating than even such tragedies was the spread of AIDS. Approximately 7% of Kinshasha's 2.5 million population was infected with the virus.

Economic Development. Mobutu continued to operate within the guidelines of the IMF and thus was assured of its continued support. Although some consumer goods remained scarce, inflation was high, and the price of fuel increased by 40%, the economy did improve. One example was the agreement with Nigeria that would bring into Muanda refinery 300,000 tons of crude, enabling it to quadruple its previous production.

Foreign Policy. Mobutu paid a number of visits to foreign states, including the United States, to buttress the good relations with his chief benefactor. A joint military exercise with two battalions of U.S. special-forces troops was conducted in Shaba Province. Mobutu denied that Zairian airfields had been used to funnel U.S. supplies to UNITA rebel forces in Angola. He was a vocal critic of Libya, castigating the Organization of African Unity (OAU) for leniency in dealing with Libya's invasion of Chad. Visiting Chad in April, he admitted that Zaire had trained 2,000 Chadian commandos and that Zairian pilots flew Chadian transports in the war zone.

HARRY A. GAILEY, *San Jose State University*

ZAIRE • Information Highlights

Official Name: Republic of Zaire.
Location: Central equatorial Africa.
Area: 905, 564 sq mi (2 345 410 km²).
Population (mid-1987 est.): 31,800,000.
Chief City (1987 est.): Kinshasa, the capital, 2,500,000.
Government: *Head of state,* Mobutu Sese Seko, president (took office 1965). *Legislature* (unicameral)—National Legislative Council.
Monetary Unit: Zaire (120.75 zaires equal U.S.$1, June 1987).
Foreign Trade (1986 U.S.$): *Imports,* $884,000,000; *exports,* $1,092,000,000.

ZIMBABWE

The year saw the beginning of constitutional changes that would radically alter the nature of politics in Zimbabwe. When the president of Zimbabwe, Canaan Banana, opened the new session of parliament in June, he formally announced that the government planned to introduce constitutional amendments to abolish the white seats in the House of Assembly and in the Senate. Under the terms of the 1980 Lancaster House agreement, whites, now estimated at less than 100,000 out of a total population of 9 million, held 20 of the 100 seats in the House of Assembly and 10 of the 40 Senate seats. Under the terms of Zimbabwe's independence constitution, white seats could be abolished from 1987 onward if 70 of the 100-member Assembly supported a resolution to do so.

In August, black and white members of the House voted to abolish the reserved white seats. While the white Conservative Alliance supported the reform, it abstained in the final vote. Four white independents voted in favor of the change. With the approval of the Senate and the signature of the president, the bill became law in September.

Until the next general election in 1990, the vacancies caused by the abolition of the white seats in the House of Assembly would be filled by candidates elected by the remaining 80 members. Since the ruling Zimbabwe African National Union-Patriotic Front (ZANU-PF) controlled 68 of these seats, their candidates were ensured appointments. Prime Minister Robert Mugabe emphasized his intent to maintain the multiracial character of the House; hence, some whites were likely to be appointed.

A bill was passed in the fall providing for an executive president elected for a six-year term. The existing offices of prime minister and president (the latter ceremonial) thus were abolished. On December 31, Mugabe was sworn in as the first executive president, marking Zimbabwe's transition from a parliamentary democracy to a one-party state.

Unity Talks. Talks of a merger between ZANU-PF and opposition leader Joshua Nkomo's Zimbabwe African People's Union (ZAPU) ended in April after 18 months of discussion. Prime Minister Mugabe terminated the talks because he felt that they had become deadlocked. However, unity talks reopened in August, spurred by the abolition of the white seats and the desire of the government to move toward a one-party state. A major breakthrough came in December, when the two parties reached a "unity agreement," expected to reduce the often violent political and ethnic divisions in the country. At Mugabe's inauguration as executive president on December 31, Nkomo was sworn in as vice-president.

Smith Suspended. In April former Prime Minister Ian Smith was suspended from the Zimbabwean parliament for a year because he had told white South Africans at a Johannesburg meeting that international sanctions against their country would fail if they were united in their support for their government. Government officials in Harare saw this statement as a direct criticism of Prime Minister Mugabe's call for sanctions against South Africa.

As a consequence of his dismissal from parliament, Smith resigned as leader of the Conservative Alliance Party in May. He was replaced by Mark Partridge, who emphasized that special seats for whites ought to be retained in the Zimbabwean parliament for at least 10 to 20 years more.

Mozambique Relations. Since November 1986, Zimbabwean troops had been actively involved in aiding Mozambique in its military campaign against the rebel Mozambique National Resistance (Renamo) forces, which were said to be backed by South Africa. The combined Mozambique-Zimbabwe military offensive in the central provinces of Mozambique had prevented Renamo from gaining a foothold in that part of the country. Over the course of the year, Zimbabwean troops were able to improve the security of the 190-mile (306-km) Beira corridor, the important area between the Zimbabwean city of Mutare and the Mozambican port of Beira. The corridor is of vital importance for Zimbabwe and for the region. For Zimbabwe it is the shortest route to the sea, and for many of the landlocked countries of the region it represents an alternative to using the dominant South African transportation network.

In September, Renamo guerrillas carried out raids in Zimbabwe, reportedly killing several farmers and other civilians. Renamo had launched an offensive inside Zimbabwe in mid-June.

Patrick O'Meara
Indiana University

ZIMBABWE • Information Highlights

Official Name: Republic of Zimbabwe.
Location: Southern Africa.
Area: 150,803 sq mi (390 580 km²).
Population (mid-1987 est.): 9,400,000.
Chief Cities (provisional census, Aug. 1982): Harare (formerly Salisbury), the capital, 656,000; Bulawayo, 413,800; Chitungwiza, 172,600.
Government: *Head of state and government,* Robert Mugabe, executive president (sworn in Dec. 31, 1987). *Legislature*—Parliament: Senate and House of Assembly.
Monetary Unit: Zimbabwe dollar (1.692 Z dollars equal U.S.$1, July 1987).
Economic Indexes (1986): *Consumer Prices* (1980 = 100), all items, 229.7; food, 240.1. *Industrial Production* (1980 = 100), 112.
Foreign Trade (1986 U.S.$): *Imports,* $985,000,000; *exports,* $1,019,000,000.

Photo by LuRay Parker, © 1987, Wyoming Game & Fish Department

As a result of a major conservation effort to save the black-footed ferret, perhaps North America's most endangered species, two females gave birth to litters in Laramie, WY, during 1987.

ZOOS AND ZOOLOGY

According to Chinese scholars, 1987 was the Year of the Rabbit, but for zoologists and animal lovers generally it might have been called the Year of the Giant Panda. One of the world's rarest animals and probably the most adored, the roly-poly, black-and-white panda now numbers about 700 in the wild. To call attention to the species' plight and to raise money for panda conservation and captive-breeding, the People's Republic of China initiated a unique loan program. Under this plan, giant pandas are loaned to foreign zoos for three to six months; monies collected from visitors to the special exhibitions go directly to panda conservation in China.

In May two giant pandas arrived for a six-month stay at the New York Zoological Park (Bronx Zoo) and later traveled to Busch Gardens in Tampa, FL, for a three-month stay. Another two pandas went on display at the San Diego Zoo in August. Only pandas considered unsuitable for breeding programs—because of age or incompatibility—are loaned out. The only giant pandas permanently residing in the United States are Hsing-Hsing and Ling-Ling—gifts from China in 1972—at the National Zoological Park (NZP) in Washington, DC. The birth of a cub to Ling-Ling in June drew national attention, but the cub died four days after it was born. Ling-Ling, who was about 18 years old in 1987, may soon pass the breeding age for giant pandas.

Other Programs to Fight Extinction. Helping to protect wild animals from extinction is one of the most important objectives of zoos today. During 1987 there were breakthroughs in the efforts to save the black-footed ferret—perhaps North America's most endangered mammal. Eighteen ferrets—the only known ones left—were captured between 1984 and early 1987 near Meeteetse, WY, and set up in a state-operated breeding program in Laramie.

At the request of the Bronz Zoo, the Moscow Zoo in the USSR sent six Siberian ferrets on loan to Wyoming. By studying the reproductive behavior and needs of the still abundant Siberian species—thought to be the closest relative of the black-footed variety—zoologists hope to learn techniques helpful in breeding the endangered blackfoots. Meanwhile, researchers at the National Zoo (NZP) were investigating the feasibility of using artificial insemination to improve ferret reproduction. In January two litters were born to European ferret females that had been artificially inseminated. NZP scientists hope to adapt their procedure to the black-footed ferrets in the 1988 breeding season. Much to everyone's delight, the ferrets bred naturally in Laramie and two females gave birth to eight young (one died), bringing the number of black-footed ferrets in the world to 25. Wildlife officials plan to release ferrets into the wild when the number of breeding pairs reaches 200.

There are an estimated 20,000 Asian elephants remaining in the wild, scattered in pockets of forests; but their numbers are dwindling because of habitat destruction and hunting. Due to the long gestation period of elephants (20 to 22 months) and the difficulty of handling male elephants, few attempts have been made at breeding these mammoths. Besides, until recently, there were plenty of wild elephants. Two North American zoos—Washington Park in Portland, OR, and Busch Gardens in Tampa —have established propagation programs for Asian elephants. In 1987 one baby was born in Portland and two in Tampa. In addition, the zoos are working with scientists to use artificial insemination for breeding Asian elephants.

Researchers at the Cincinnati Wildlife Research Federation—staffed by people from the Cincinnati Zoo, Kings Island Wild Animal Habitat, and University of Cincinnati College of Medicine—also are studying artificial insemination and other reproductive techniques, particularly cryo-preservation of embryos. In 1987 they produced five litters of domestic kittens from frozen/thawed embryos—the first time this has been employed in cats. It is highly probable that scientists will be able to store indefinitely embryos from rare felids such as jaguars and mountain lions as a means of ensuring genetic diversity among these cats.

In May a female Sumatran rhinoceros at the Melaka Zoo in Malaysia gave birth—the first captive birth of this species in more than 100 years. Also called the hairy rhino, the Sumatran species is extremely shy and very rare. There are no reliable figures for numbers left in the wild, and only five reside in captivity. The Malaysian government is building a breeding facility, and British and North American zoos are cooperating in a similar effort in Indonesia.

A Tragedy. In addition to conserving species, zoos educate the public about the needs and behavior of wild animals. Sometimes people forget that the lions, tigers, and bears in zoos are not pets. Nothing pointed out that fact more vividly than the death of an 11-year-old boy at Prospect Park in Brooklyn, NY, in May. The child and two companions broke into the zoo after its closing and threw rocks at two polar bears to chase them into their caves so that they could get into the exhibit and swim in the moat. One of the bears grabbed and mauled the boy. Police officers shot the bears, but the child was already dead. The zoo at Prospect Park is more than 50 years old and slated for major renovation, which will provide better and more secure enclosures for animals. After reconstruction, the zoo will be operated by the New York Zoological Society, which manages the Bronx Zoo and the Central Park Zoo.

DEBORAH A. BEHLER
"Animal Kingdom" Magazine

© M. Austerman/Animals Animals

The California Condor

On April 19, 1987, scientists from the Condor Research Center in Ventura, CA, netted the last wild California condor. Known as Ivan or AC-9 (Adult Condor-9), the seven-year-old male was taken to the San Diego Wild Animal Park, which together with the Los Angeles Zoo is caring for all 27 living California condors (13 males and 14 females).

By far the largest of North America's land birds, the California condor has a wingspread of about 9 ft (2.7 m). Soaring on thermal updrafts, it can cover 150 mi (241 km) in a day at speeds approaching 80 mi (129 km) per hour.

The California condor once ranged over much of the West coast and the southernmost states, but its numbers declined drastically over the past 100 years—mostly due to poisoning, shooting, pesticides, collisions with high-tension wires, and habitat destruction. In 1985 the bird's numbers plunged to 15, with one nesting pair. Fearing that the genetic pool of California condors was too small for the species to recover, the U.S. Fish and Wildlife Service ordered all of the wild birds to be captured.

The Condor Recovery Team—experts from zoos, government agencies, and private conservation organizations—is monitoring the captive birds and is being very careful to pair up unrelated individuals. Most of the birds are still juveniles; it takes about six years for the condor to reach maturity. One adult pair at the San Diego Zoo has been courting, and zoo officials hope to have an egg in the spring of 1988. Meanwhile the recovery team is developing a plan to reintroduce the condor into the open skies, but experts caution that that event could be at least 40 years away.

DEBORAH A. BEHLER

Statistical and Tabular Data

Table of Contents

NATIONS OF THE WORLD

A Profile and Synopsis of Major 1987 Developments

Nation, Region	Population in millions	Capital	Area Sq mi (km²)	Head of State/Government
Angola, S.W. Africa	8.0	Luanda	481,351 (1 246 700)	José Eduardo dos Santos, president
	The fiercest fighting in a decade between rebels and government troops broke out in October in remote Cuando-Cubango Province. The UNITA rebels, under Jonas Savimbi, were aided by South African troops, and about 3,000 South African troops were reported to have remained in Angola when the fighting died down in November. The United States continued to provide aid to the rebels, who had been fighting Angola's Marxist government for 12 years. Government forces were aided by at least 35,000 Cuban troops and 1,000 Soviet advisers. Gross Domestic Product (GDP) (1986 est. US$): $3 billion. Foreign Trade (1986): Imports, $1.4 billion; exports, $1.2 billion.			
Antigua and Barbuda, Caribbean	0.1	St. John's	107 (440)	Sir Wilfred E. Jacobs, governor-general Vere C. Bird, prime minister
	Along with the six other members of the Organization of Eastern Caribbean States, Antigua and Barbuda voted May 31 to form a single nation. (The plan required approval in national referendums.) Meanwhile, with tourism on the increase, the country's economic picture brightened in 1987. A dozen hotels and condominium projects were under construction, and plans were made to dredge the harbor in St. John's and build a new pier to accommodate more cruise ships. GDP (1984): $158 million. Foreign Trade (1984): Imports, $134 million; exports, $41 million.			
Bahamas, Caribbean	0.2	Nassau	5,382 (13 940)	Sir Gerald C. Cash, governor-general Lynden O. Pindling, prime minister
	Prime Minister Lynden Pindling won a sixth term in general elections June 19, overcoming allegations that his government had become a tool of drug traffickers. Pindling dismissed questions about his finances and reports that members of his cabinet had taken bribes from drug smugglers, and he campaigned on a platform that stressed nationalism, black pride, and opposition to American domination. The opposition party charged that the election was tainted by vote fraud. GDP (1986): $2.1 billion. Foreign Trade (1985): Imports, $3.28 billion; exports, $2.70 billion.			
Bahrain, W. Asia	0.4	Manama	239 (620)	Isa bin Sulman Al Khalifa, emir Khalifa bin Salman Al Khalita, prime minister
	As the site of the only American naval facility in the Persian Gulf, Bahrain served as a staging point for U.S. minesweeping operations and also received the damaged frigate Stark *for repair after it was attacked by an Iraqi warplane in the gulf May 17. During the year, Bahrain issued statements supporting Iraq in its conflict with Iran but also said it wished to avoid a confrontation with Iran. GDP (1984 est.): $4.6 billion. Foreign Trade (1985): Imports, $3.11 billion; exports, $2.78 billion.*			
Barbados, Caribbean	0.3	Bridgetown	166 (430)	Sir Hugh Springer, governor-general Erskine Sandiford, prime minister
	Prime Minister Errol W. Barrow, 67, died June 1 and was succeeded by Erskine Sandiford, who had been minister of education and leader of the House of Assembly. Before Barbados won independence in 1966, Barrow led a home-rule administration, and he served as prime minister from 1966 to 1976 and from 1986 until his death. GDP (1984): $1.15 billion. Foreign Trade (1986): Imports, $587 million; exports, $275 million.			
Benin, W. Africa	4.3	Porto Novo	43,483 (112 620)	Mathieu Kérékou, president
	Benin's cabinet was shuffled in February in an effort to deal with a growing economic crisis. In August, the parliament passed a law calling for heavy penalties for the practice of sorcery, including transactions involving human bones and practices claiming to disturb the rain cycle. Gross National Product (GNP) (1984 est.): $974.2 million. Foreign Trade (1984): Imports, $225.4 million; exports. $172.5 million.			
Bhutan, S. Asia	1.5	Thimphu	18,147 (47 000)	Jigme Singe Wangchuck, king
	Bhutan held border talks with China in June and scheduled more talks for early in 1988. GDP (fiscal year 1984-85): $300 million. Foreign Trade (fiscal year 1984-85): Imports, $69.4 million; exports, $15.1 million.			
Botswana, S. Africa	1.2	Gaborone	231,803 (600 370)	Quett Masire, president
	Leaders of nine southern African countries met in Gaborone in March, seeking ways to loosen economic bonds with South Africa, which threatened to halt traffic on a vital rail line leading through Botswana to its coast. South African troops seeking guerrillas of the African National Congress staged a raid in Botswana January 1, and a car bomb killed three people in a Gaborone suburb April 9. Botswana was among 15 African nations facing food emergencies in 1987. GDP (fiscal year 1983-84): $905 million. Foreign Trade (1985): Imports, $535 million; exports, $653 million.			

<table>
<tr><th>Nation, Region</th><th>Population in millions</th><th>Capital</th><th>Area Sq mi (km²)</th><th>Head of State/Government</th></tr>
<tr><td>Brunei, S.E. Asia</td><td>0.2</td><td>Bandar Seri Begawan</td><td>2,228 (5 770)</td><td>Sir Muda Hassanal Bolkiah, sultan and prime minister</td></tr>
<tr><td></td><td colspan="4">GDP (1985): $3.42 billion. Foreign Trade (1985): Imports: $640 million; exports, $3.1 billion.</td></tr>
<tr><td>Burkina Faso, W. Africa</td><td>7.3</td><td>Ouagadougou</td><td>105,869 (274 200)</td><td>Blaise Compaoré, president</td></tr>
<tr><td></td><td colspan="4">President Thomas Sankara, an ardent preacher of revolution who took power in a coup in 1983, was overthrown October 15 by Blaise Compaoré, an army captain who had been one of his close associates. Sankara was shot by Compaoré's supporters, allegedly while resisting arrest. GDP (1983): $1.1 billion. Foreign Trade (1984): Imports, $207 million; exports, $79 million.</td></tr>
<tr><td>Burundi, E. Africa</td><td>5.0</td><td>Bujumbura</td><td>10,745 (27 830)</td><td>Pierre Buyoya, president</td></tr>
<tr><td></td><td colspan="4">President Jean-Baptiste Bagaza was overthrown in a military coup September 4, and Maj. Pierre Buyoya was named the country's new leader. He promised to lift restrictions on religion that had been imposed by the former regime. Bagaza, who was attending a meeting in Canada when the coup took place, sought political asylum in Uganda. GDP (1984 est.): $963 million. Foreign Trade (1986): Imports, $205 million; exports, $169 million.</td></tr>
<tr><td>Cameroon, Cen. Africa</td><td>10.3</td><td>Yaounde</td><td>183,568 (475 440)</td><td>Paul Biya, president</td></tr>
<tr><td></td><td colspan="4">Faced with a fiscal crisis and a decline in national oil production, President Biya cut the national budget by 30% and took steps to end bureaucratic waste. GDP (1983-84): $7.3 billion. Foreign Trade (1986): Imports, $1.70 billion; exports, $784 millon.</td></tr>
<tr><td>Cape Verde, W. Africa</td><td>0.3</td><td>Praia</td><td>1,560 (4 030)</td><td>Aristides Pereira, president
Pedro Pires, prime minister</td></tr>
<tr><td></td><td colspan="4">The U.S. decision to suspend air services between the United States and South Africa cut into an important source of Cape Verde's income, the granting of landing rights to South African Airways. The country continued to suffer from drought and erosion and to receive almost 60% of its GNP in foreign aid. GNP (1983): $110 million. Foreign Trade (1983): Imports, $68 million; exports, $1.6 million.</td></tr>
<tr><td>Central African Republic, Cen. Africa</td><td>2.7</td><td>Bangui</td><td>240,533 (622 980)</td><td>André-Dieudonné Kolingba, president of the Military Committee for National Recovery</td></tr>
<tr><td></td><td colspan="4">Former self-proclaimed emperor Jean-Bedel Bokassa, who returned from exile in France in 1986 and promptly was arrested, was convicted in June and condemned to death for at least 20 murders committed during his reign. In February, the inaugural congress of the new ruling party, the Rassemblement démocratique centrafricain (RDC), was held in Bangui. GDP (1984): $764 million. Foreign Trade (1985): Imports, $109 million; exports, $88 million.</td></tr>
<tr><td>Comoros, E. Africa</td><td>0.4</td><td>Moroni</td><td>838 (2 170)</td><td>Ahmed Abdallah Abderemane, president</td></tr>
<tr><td></td><td colspan="4">Parliamentary elections March 22 were marked by charges of irregularities and harassment of opposition candidates; all candidates supported by the president were elected. As part of independence day celebrations July 6, members of the opposition were restored to civil posts from which they had been dismissed. GNP (1985 est.): $114 million. Foreign Trade (1985): Imports, $25 million; exports, $15 million.</td></tr>
<tr><td>Congo, Cen. Africa</td><td>2.1</td><td>Brazzaville</td><td>132,046 (342 000)</td><td>Denis Sassou-Nguesso, president
Ange Edouard Poungui, prime minister</td></tr>
<tr><td></td><td colspan="4">Three army leaders were arrested and charged with plotting a coup early in the year, and 20 more officers were reported to have been arrested in July. In August former President Joachim Yhombi-Opango was arrested following an uprising. A rebel movement based in the north of the country was reported to continue to trouble the government. At least three persons were killed in a border clash with Zaire in mid-January. GDP (1984): $1.8 billion. Foreign Trade (1985): Imports, $751 million; exports, $1.08 billion.</td></tr>
<tr><td>Djibouti, E. Africa</td><td>0.3</td><td>Djibouti</td><td>8,494 (22 000)</td><td>Hassan Gouled Aptidon, president
Barkat Gourad Hamadou, premier</td></tr>
<tr><td></td><td colspan="4">As a staging area for French and other forces operating in and around the Persian Gulf, Djibouti saw increased prosperity in 1987. The country also was named headquarters of the Intergovernmental Authority for Drought and Development, a regional group formed to develop river basins. Eleven persons, including two French soldiers, were killed in a terrorist incident in March, in which a bomb exploded at a cafe. GDP (1986 est.): $344 million. Foreign Trade (1986): Imports, $197 million; exports, $96 million.</td></tr>
<tr><td>Dominica, Caribbean</td><td>0.1</td><td>Roseau</td><td>290 (750)</td><td>Clarence A. Seignoret, president
Mary Eugenia Charles, prime minister</td></tr>
<tr><td></td><td colspan="4">Dominica was among seven Caribbean countries that voted May 31 to form a single nation. The union was to be formed if approved in national referendums. GDP (1984 est.): $85.4 million. Foreign Trade (1985): Imports, $57 million; exports, $28.7 million.</td></tr>
<tr><td>Dominican Republic, Caribbean</td><td>6.5</td><td>Santo Domingo</td><td>18,815 (48 730)</td><td>Joaquin Belaguer, president</td></tr>
<tr><td></td><td colspan="4">Former president Salvador Jorge Blanco sought asylum in Venezuela after a warrant was issued for his arrest April 29 on charges of corruption. Labor strikes in July and August led to street violence in which two persons died, and President Joaquin Belaguer shuffled his cabinet in mid-August. GDP (1986 est.): $14.9 billion. Foreign Trade (1986): Imports, $1.43 billion; exports, $718 million.</td></tr>
<tr><td>Equatorial Guinea, Cen. Africa</td><td>0.3</td><td>Malabo</td><td>10,830 (28 050)</td><td>Teodoro Obiang Nguema Mbasogo, president
Cristino Seriche Bioko, premier</td></tr>
<tr><td></td><td colspan="4">Marking the eighth anniversary of his seizure of power, President Nguema announced the formation of a new political party and indicated that other parties might be recognized in the future. In a cost-cutting move, the United States announced that it would close its embassy in Malabo. GNP (1983): $75 million. Foreign Trade (1982): Imports, $41.5 million; exports, $16.9 million.</td></tr>
<tr><td>Gabon, Cen. Africa</td><td>1.2</td><td>Libreville</td><td>103,348 (267 670)</td><td>El Hadj Omar Bongo, president
Léon Mébiame, premier</td></tr>
<tr><td></td><td colspan="4">Gabon marked the 20th anniversary of President Bongo's accession to power while undertaking various budget cuts to help counter a decline in oil exports. Bongo visited the United States in August. GDP (1985): $3.3 billion. Foreign Trade (1985): Imports, $976 million; exports, $1.92 billion.</td></tr>
</table>

<table>
<tr><th>Nation, Region</th><th>Population in millions</th><th>Capital</th><th>Area Sq mi (km^2)</th><th>Head of State/Government</th></tr>
<tr><td>Gambia, W. Africa</td><td>0.8</td><td>Banjul</td><td>4,363 (11 300)</td><td>Sir Dawda Kairaba Jawara, president</td></tr>
<tr><td colspan="5">In elections in March, President Jawara was reelected in a landslide, and his People's Progressive Party increased its representation from 27 to 31 seats in the 36-seat parliament. GDP (1984): $125 million. Foreign Trade (1985): Imports, $93 million; exports, $43 million.</td></tr>
<tr><td>Ghana, W. Africa</td><td>13.9</td><td>Accra</td><td>92,100 (238 540)</td><td>Jerry Rawlings, chairman of the Provisional National Defense Council (PNDC)</td></tr>
<tr><td colspan="5">Ghanians celebrated 30 years of independence on March 6. In June, after unrest at the University of Ghana, several prominent government critics were arrested. Two other universities were closed because of unrest later in the year. GNP (1982): $10.5 billion. Foreign Trade (1985): Imports, $731 million; exports, $617 million.</td></tr>
<tr><td>Grenada, Caribbean</td><td>0.1</td><td>St. George's</td><td>131 (340)</td><td>Sir Paul Scoon, governor-general
Herbert A. Blaize, prime minister</td></tr>
<tr><td colspan="5">Grenada was among seven Caribbean island countries that voted May 31 to form a single nation. The union had yet to be approved in national referendums. GDP (1986 est.): $86.8 million. Foreign Trade (1985): Imports, $62.6 million; exports, $22.1 million.</td></tr>
<tr><td>Guinea, W. Africa</td><td>6.4</td><td>Conakry</td><td>94,927 (245 860)</td><td>Lansana Conté, president</td></tr>
<tr><td colspan="5">Nine former cabinet ministers and more than 50 other people were sentenced to death May 6 after secret political trials. All had been supporters of former President Ahmed Sékou Touré, whose government was overthrown in 1984. As one of Africa's poorest nations, Guinea was earmarked for a special aid package developed by Western nations, the World Bank, and the International Monetary Fund. GNP (1984): $1.6 billion. Foreign Trade (1984 est.): Imports, $403 million; exports, $537 million.</td></tr>
<tr><td>Guinea-Bissau, W. Africa</td><td>0.9</td><td>Bissau</td><td>13,946 (36 120)</td><td>João Bernardo Vieira, president</td></tr>
<tr><td colspan="5">President Vieira reshuffled his government in February. A new minister of justice was appointed and two new state secretariats, justice and foreign affairs, were created. GDP (fiscal year 1983): $154 million. Foreign Trade (1983): Imports, $57.1 million; exports, $8.6 million.</td></tr>
<tr><td>Guyana, N.E. South America</td><td>0.8</td><td>Georgetown</td><td>83,000 (214 970)</td><td>Hugh Desmond Hoyte, president
Hamilton Green, prime minister</td></tr>
<tr><td colspan="5">In January, Guyana devalued its dollar by 56% in an effort to halt a growing black market in currency and increase the competitiveness of its exports. Income from exports of bauxite, sugar, and rice had fallen substantially. Also in January, it was reported that a new political party, the United Republican Party, had been formed. GNP (1984 est.): $480 million. Foreign Trade (1985): Imports, $255 million; exports, $207 million.</td></tr>
<tr><td>Haiti, Caribbean</td><td>6.2</td><td>Port-au-Prince</td><td>10,714 (27 750)</td><td>Henri Namphy, head of governing council</td></tr>
<tr><td colspan="5">Haitians approved a new constitution in March and began a campaign for presidential elections that was marked by increasing violence. The military government, which had replaced the dictatorship of Jean-Claude Duvalier in 1986, did little to halt attacks on candidates and election officials by former Duvalier supporters. On election day, November 29, armed bands attacked Haitian voters and killed 34 persons, and the election was postponed until January 1988. Government soldiers were accused of complicity in the killings, and the United States cancelled military and some economic aid. See also page 173. GDP (1986 est.): $1.8 billion. Foreign Trade (1985): Imports, $442 million; exports, $174 million.</td></tr>
<tr><td>Ivory Coast, W. Africa</td><td>10.8</td><td>Yamoussoukro</td><td>124,502 (322 460)</td><td>Félix Houphouët-Boigny, president</td></tr>
<tr><td colspan="5">A Brazilian jetliner crashed 12 mi (19 km) east of Abidjan January 3, killing 49 of the 51 people aboard. U.S. Secretary of State George P. Shultz visited the Ivory Coast later in the month and termed the performance of the country's capitalist economy the "success story of Africa." The national government announced a crackdown on crime in August, after the minister of public works and transport was kidnapped, setting off a nationwide hunt. The minister was returned unharmed within several days. GDP (1986): $8.0 billion. Foreign Trade (1985): Imports, $1.74 billion; exports, $2.94 billion.</td></tr>
<tr><td>Jamaica, Caribbean</td><td>2.5</td><td>Kingston</td><td>4,243 (10 990)</td><td>Florizel Glasspole, governor-general
Edward Seaga, prime minister</td></tr>
<tr><td colspan="5">After agreeing to take steps to curb inflation and relax trade restrictions, Jamaica reached an agreement in January with the International Monetary Fund for a $132.8 million standby loan. In March it reached agreement with the "Paris Club" group of creditor nations to reschedule $125.5 billion of its official foreign debt. In April the government announced its support for a $2.6 billion U.S.-funded program to eradicate marijuana trading. The island country marked the 25th anniversary of its independence with celebrations and a visit from British Prime Minister Margaret Thatcher on July 17. GNP (1986 est.): $2 billion. Foreign Trade (1986): Imports, $981 million; exports, $596 million.</td></tr>
<tr><td>Kiribati, Oceania</td><td>0.06</td><td>Tarawa</td><td>274 (710)</td><td>Ieremia Tabai, president</td></tr>
<tr><td colspan="5">In elections in March, President Tabai won 50.1% of the popular vote and retained his position. GDP (1985 est.): $20 million. Foreign Trade (1986): Imports, $22 million; exports, $2.7 million.</td></tr>
<tr><td>Kuwait, W. Asia</td><td>1.9</td><td>Kuwait</td><td>6,880 (17 820)</td><td>Jabir al-Ahmad Al Sabah, emir
Saad al-Abdallah Al Sabah, prime minister</td></tr>
<tr><td colspan="5">Kuwait found itself being drawn deeper into the Persian Gulf conflict between Iran and Iraq in 1987. To protect its oil exports, the country arranged in July to have a number of its oil tankers registered under the U.S. flag and escorted through the gulf by the U.S. Navy; an agreement for Soviet escorts also was reported. Terrorists attacked Kuwaiti oil and gas installations in January and May, and Kuwait's embassy in Teheran was attacked by a mob on August 1. Iranian missiles struck a U.S.-owned tanker in Kuwaiti waters October 15 and hit Kuwait's main offshore oil terminal October 22. Earlier in the year, in January, Kuwait was host to a summit conference of 44 Islamic nations, members of the Islamic Conference Organization. See also MIDDLE EAST. GDP (1985): $19.7 billion. Foreign Trade (1986): Imports, $7.0 billion; exports, $8 billion.</td></tr>
<tr><td>Lesotho, S. Africa</td><td>1.6</td><td>Maseru</td><td>11,718 (30 350)</td><td>Moshoeshoe II, king
Justinus Lekhanya, chairman, military council</td></tr>
<tr><td colspan="5">Former Prime Minister Leabua Jonathan, who was ousted in a military coup in 1986 after 20 years of rule, died April 7 in Pretoria at the age of 73. In June, Charles Moteli, leader of the opposition United Democratic Party, was arrested after calling for a return to democratic government. GDP (1984): $325 million. Foreign Trade (1985): Imports, $326 million; exports, $300 million, including remittances of Lesotho workers in South Africa.</td></tr>
</table>

Nation, Region	Population in millions	Capital	Area Sq mi (km²)	Head of State/Government
Liberia, W. Africa	2.4	Monrovia	43,000 (111 370)	Samuel K. Doe, president

U.S. Secretary of State Shultz visited Liberia in January and remarked on what he termed progress in human rights; however, international rights organizations took issue with his statement and said that rights abuses continued under President Doe. A report released in February showed that millions of dollars in U.S. aid had been diverted to top Liberian government officials, and an agreement was worked out whereby U.S. financial experts would be hired to run key government ministries. In October, Doe announced the arrest of a group of army officers he said had plotted to overthrow the government. GDP (1984): $1.14 billion. Foreign Trade (1986): Imports, $235 million; exports, $404 million.

Nation, Region	Population in millions	Capital	Area Sq mi (km²)	Head of State/Government
Liechtenstein, Cen. Europe	0.03	Vaduz	62 (160)	Franz Josef II, prince Hans Brunhart, prime minister

GNP (1984 est.): $15,000 per capita. Foreign Trade (1984): exports, $440 million.

Nation, Region	Population in millions	Capital	Area Sq mi (km²)	Head of State/Government
Luxembourg, W. Europe	0.4	Luxembourg	998 (2 586)	Jean, grand duke Jaques Santer, prime minister

Luxembourg hosted a meeting of foreign and defense ministers of the Western European Union April 28 that led to a collective statement of concern over the proposed elimination of nuclear missiles in Europe. The Luxembourg franc was revalued January 12 along with other currencies of the European monetary system. GNP (1984): $3.2 billion. (Luxembourg's foreign trade is recorded with Belgium.)

Nation, Region	Population in millions	Capital	Area Sq mi (km²)	Head of State/Government
Madagascar, E. Africa	10.6	Antananarivo	226,656 (587 040)	Didier Ratsiraka, head of government Desire Rakotoarijaona, premier

The International Monetary Fund (IMF) classed Madagascar as a "debt-distressed" country and included it in a special aid package worked out late in the year with the World Bank and Western countries. Leftist political parties were increasingly outspoken during the course of the year regarding the country's economic problems and staged a May Day rally calling for a change in government. GDP (1984) $2.4 billion. Foreign Trade (1985): Imports, $402 million; exports, $274 million.

Nation, Region	Population in millions	Capital	Area Sq mi (km²)	Head of State/Government
Malawi, E. Africa	7.4	Lilongwe	45,745 (118 480)	Hastings Kamuzu Banda, president

In May, in Malawi's first election since 1983, members of President Banda's Malawi Congress Party ran unopposed and thus won all seats in parliament. The new cabinet, announced the following month, included two new members. Earlier in the year members of a fledgling rebel movement in the remote north raided a police station, killing three policemen and capturing a stock of weapons and ammunition. GDP (1982): $1.11 billion. Foreign Trade (1986): Imports, $252 million; exports, $243 million.

Nation, Region	Population in millions	Capital	Area Sq mi (km²)	Head of State/Government
Maldives, S. Asia	0.2	Male	116 (300)	Maumoon Abdul Gayoom, president

A severe storm in April caused an estimated $12 million in damage, but no deaths or injuries were reported. The United States and Britain provided emergency aid. GDP (1984) $76.7 million. Foreign Trade (1985): Imports, $52 million; exports, $22.8 million.

Nation, Region	Population in millions	Capital	Area Sq mi (km²)	Head of State/Government
Mali, W. Africa	8.4	Bamako	478,764 (1 240 000)	Moussa Traoré, president

Canadian Prime Minister Brian Mulroney met with President Traoré in late January and promised aid to Mali. As one of Africa's poorest countries, Mali also was slated to receive financial assistance under a World Bank-International Monetary Fund agreement worked out late in the year. GDP (1983) $1.1 billion. Foreign Trade (1986): Imports, $438 million; exports, $192 million.

Nation, Region	Population in millions	Capital	Area Sq mi (km²)	Head of State/Government
Malta, S. Europe	0.4	Valletta	124 (320)	Paul Xuereb, president Eddie Fenech Adami, prime minister

In hotly contested elections May 9, the conservative Nationalist Party won a narrow majority in parliament, ending 16 years of socialist rule. Eddie Fenech Adami succeeded Karmenu Mifsud Bonnici as prime minister. He promised to loosen the country's ties with Libya and increase links with Western Europe, if possible joining the European Community. Agatha Barbara stepped down as president in February. She was succeeded by Paul Xuereb. GDP (1985): $1.4 billion. Foreign Trade (1986): Imports, $887 million; exports, $497 million.

Nation, Region	Population in millions	Capital	Area Sq mi (km²)	Head of State/Government
Mauritania, W. Africa	2.0	Nouakchott	397,954 (1 030 700)	Maaouiya Ould Sid Ahmed Taya, president and prime minister

Mauritania broke diplomatic ties with Iran in 1987 over Iran's continued involvement in war with Iraq. In border talks with Mali, the two nations agreed to abide by frontiers demarcated in a 1963 treaty. GNP (1985 est.) $800 million. Foreign Trade (1986): Imports, $221 million; exports, $349 million.

Nation, Region	Population in millions	Capital	Area Sq mi (km²)	Head of State/Government
Mauritius, E. Africa	1.1	Port Louis	718 (1 860)	Sir Veerasamy Ringadoo, governor-general Aneerood Jugnauth, prime minister

Faced with a scandal that implicated some members of the government in drug trafficking, Prime Minister Jugnauth moved up elections that had been set for 1988 to Aug. 30, 1987. His coalition, helped by the country's recent economic success, won 39 of the 60 seats in parliament, and he retained his post. GDP (1985–86 est.): $1 billion. Foreign Trade (1985): Imports, $675 million; exports, $675 million.

Nation, Region	Population in millions	Capital	Area Sq mi (km²)	Head of State/Government
Monaco, S. Europe	0.03	Monaco-Ville	0.7 (1.9)	Ranier III, prince M. Jean Ausseil, minister of state
Mongolia, E. Asia	2.0	Ulan Bator	604,247 (1 565 000)	Jambyn Batmonh, chairman of the Presidium Dumaagiyn Sodnom, chairman, Council of Ministers

In January, the Soviet Union confirmed plans to withdraw some troops from Mongolia. The presence of the Soviet troops had been cited as a roadblock to improved Sino-Soviet relations. Mongolia and the United States agreed to establish diplomatic relations. GDP (1985 est.): $1.67 billion. Foreign Trade (1981): Imports, $655 million; exports, $436 million.

Nation, Region	Population in millions	Capital	Area Sq mi (km²)	Head of State/Government
Nauru, Oceania	0.008	Nauru	8 (20)	Hammer DeRoburt, president

After a series of elections in late 1986 and early 1987 that resulted in hung parliaments, President DeRoburt succeeded in retaining his position. With the island's supply of phosphate, its major export, expected to run out in seven years, the government appealed to the United Nations for help in replacing topsoil that had been removed during 50 years of mining by Britain, Australia, and New Zealand before Nauru gained independence in 1968. GNP (1984): $160 million. Foreign Trade: Imports, $14 million (1982); exports, $93 million (1984).

<table>
<tr><th>Nation, Region</th><th>Population in millions</th><th>Capital</th><th>Area Sq mi (km²)</th><th>Head of State/Government</th></tr>
<tr><td>Nepal, S. Asia</td><td>17.8</td><td>Katmandu</td><td>54,363 (140 800)</td><td>Birendra Bir Bikram, king
Marich Man Singh Shrestha, prime minister</td></tr>
<tr><td></td><td colspan="4">GDP (fiscal year 1985–86): $2.4 billion. Foreign Trade (fiscal year 1985–86): Imports, $460 million; exports, $162 million.</td></tr>
<tr><td>Niger, W. Africa</td><td>7.0</td><td>Niamey</td><td>489,189 (1 267 000)</td><td>Ali Seybou, president
Hamid Algabid, prime minister</td></tr>
<tr><td></td><td colspan="4">President Seyni Kountché died of a brain tumor November 10 after 13 years in office. Col. Ali Seybou, the army chief of staff, was named interim president hours before his death, and the appointment was confirmed November 14. GDP (1985 est.): $1.2 billion. Foreign Trade (1985): Imports, $309.4 million; exports, $250.6 million.</td></tr>
<tr><td>Oman, W. Asia</td><td>1.3</td><td>Muscat</td><td>82,031 (212 460)</td><td>Qaboos bin Said, sultan and prime minister</td></tr>
<tr><td></td><td colspan="4">With conflict and terrorism increasing in the Persian Gulf region, the government announced in February that identity cards would be issued to all Omanis over the age of 18. The government also increased customs duties early in the year in an attempt to counter the effects of shrinking income from oil exports. GDP (1985 est.): $9 billion. Foreign Trade (1985): Imports, $3.15 billion; exports, $4.97 billion.</td></tr>
<tr><td>Papua New Guinea, Oceania</td><td>3.6</td><td>Port Moresby</td><td>178,259 (461 690)</td><td>Sir Kingsford Dibela, governor-general
Paias Wingti, prime minister</td></tr>
<tr><td></td><td colspan="4">A major earthquake centered off the coast of Papua New Guinea left at least 1,000 people homeless February 9. Damage was worst in Umboi, an island off the northern coast. GNP (1984): $2.2 billion. Foreign Trade (1985): Imports, $873 million; exports, $909 million.</td></tr>
<tr><td>Qatar</td><td>0.3</td><td>Doha</td><td>4,247 (11 000)</td><td>Khalifa bin Hamad Al Thani, emir and prime minister</td></tr>
<tr><td></td><td colspan="4">GNP (1984) $6.4 billion. Foreign Trade (1986): Imports, $1.1 billion; exports, $2.6 billion.</td></tr>
<tr><td>Rwanda, E. Africa</td><td>6.8</td><td>Kigali</td><td>10,170 (26 340)</td><td>Juvénal Habyarimana, president</td></tr>
<tr><td></td><td colspan="4">More than 4,000 prisoners were released in an amnesty declared in July as part of Rwanda's celebration of the 25th anniversary of its independence. GDP (1984 est.): $1.6 billion. Foreign Trade (1986): Imports, $352 million; exports, $118 million.</td></tr>
<tr><td>Saint Christopher and Nevis, Caribbean</td><td>0.05</td><td>Basseterre</td><td>139 (360)</td><td>Clement A. Arrindell, governor-general
Kennedy A. Simmonds, prime minister</td></tr>
<tr><td></td><td colspan="4">Saint Christopher and Nevis was among seven eastern Caribbean countries that voted May 30 to establish a single nation, pending approval of the plan in national referendums. GDP (1986 est.): $66.7 million. Foreign Trade (1983): Imports, $47.3 million; exports, $30.6 million.</td></tr>
<tr><td>Saint Lucia, Caribbean</td><td>0.15</td><td>Castries</td><td>239 (620)</td><td>Sir Vincent Floissac, governor-general
John Compton, prime minister</td></tr>
<tr><td></td><td colspan="4">The ruling United Workers' Party retained a parliamentary majority in elections April 6 and 30, and Prime Minister Compton retained his post. Governor-General Sir Allen Lewis retired and was succeeded on April 30 by Sir Vincent Floissac. St. Lucia also voted with other eastern Caribbean states to form a single country. GDP (1984): $148.1 million. Foreign trade (1983): Imports, $106.8 million; exports, $49.7 million.</td></tr>
<tr><td>Saint Vincent and the Grenadines, Caribbean</td><td>0.1</td><td>Kingstown</td><td>131 (340)</td><td>Joseph Lambert Eustace, governor-general
James F. Mitchell, prime minister</td></tr>
<tr><td></td><td colspan="4">With other members of the Organization of Eastern Caribbean States, St. Vincent and the Grenadines voted May 31 to form a single nation, pending approval in national referendums. GDP (1985): $103 million. Foreign Trade (1983): Imports, $64.9 million; exports, $42.0 million.</td></tr>
<tr><td>San Marino, S. Europe</td><td>0.023</td><td>San Marino</td><td>23 (60)</td><td>Co-regents appointed semiannually</td></tr>
<tr><td>São Tomé and Principe, W. Africa</td><td>0.1</td><td>São Tomé</td><td>371 (960)</td><td>Manuel Pinto da Costa, president</td></tr>
<tr><td></td><td colspan="4">Under terms finalized in February, Portugal agreed to provide military training and equipment to São Tomé and Principe. The ruling cabinet was reshuffled in January; 14 new ministries and 4 national directorates were created. An economic recovery plan got underway in July. GDP (1981 est.): $30 million. Foreign Trade (1981 est.): Imports, $20 million; exports, $8.8 million.</td></tr>
<tr><td>Senegal, W. Africa</td><td>7.1</td><td>Dakar</td><td>75,749 (196 190)</td><td>Abdou Diouf, president</td></tr>
<tr><td></td><td colspan="4">Senegal's police force was suspended following strikes and demonstrations in April; members were to be reinstated after individual review. The director of public security was dismissed in the incident and was found dead a few days later, a possible suicide. A group of white South Africans and members of the African National Congress, the banned black South African group, held a historic meeting in Dakar in July. GDP (1984): $2.3 billion. Foreign Trade (1985): Imports, $620 million; exports, $402 million.</td></tr>
<tr><td>Seychelles, E. Africa</td><td>0.1</td><td>Victoria</td><td>108 (280)</td><td>France Albert René, president</td></tr>
<tr><td></td><td colspan="4">GDP (1985): $175 million. Foreign Trade (1985): Imports, $90 million; exports, $4.5 million.</td></tr>
<tr><td>Sierra Leone, W. Africa</td><td>3.9</td><td>Freetown</td><td>27,699 (71,740)</td><td>Joseph Momoh, president</td></tr>
<tr><td></td><td colspan="4">The government suppressed a coup attempt in March and arrested several senior police officers. Francis M. Minah, the country's former vice-president, also was arrested and charged with helping to plan the coup. GDP (1983–84 est.): $1 billion. Foreign Trade (1986): Imports, $132 million; exports, $148 million.</td></tr>
<tr><td>Solomon Islands, Oceania</td><td>0.3</td><td>Honiara</td><td>10,985 (28 450)</td><td>Sir Baddeley Devesi, governor-general
Ezekiel Alebua, prime minister</td></tr>
<tr><td></td><td colspan="4">In September, the Solomon Islands joined other South Pacific nations in condemning a referendum held in New Caledonia, in which New Caledonians voted to retain their ties to France. Ezekiel Alebua had become prime minister in December 1986. GDP (1985): $137 million. Foreign Trade (1986): Imports, $63 million; exports, $67 million.</td></tr>
</table>

<table>
<tr><th>Nation, Region</th><th>Population in millions</th><th>Capital</th><th>Area Sq mi (km²)</th><th>Head of State/Government</th></tr>
<tr><td>Somalia, E. Africa</td><td>7.7</td><td>Mogadishu</td><td>246,200 (637 660)</td><td>Mohamed Siad Barre, president</td></tr>
<tr><td colspan="5">A report leaked to the Western press by Somali dissidents indicated that the government had begun a campaign to lay waste to an area along the northwest border, in an effort to wipe out rebels backed by Ethiopia. The fighting in the north and continuing drought raised new fears of famine. GDP (1982 est.): $1.4 billion. Foreign Trade (1986): Imports, $407 million; exports, $108 million.</td></tr>
<tr><td>Swaziland, S. Africa</td><td>0.7</td><td>Mbabane</td><td>6,703 (17 360)</td><td>Mswati III, king
Sotsha Dlamini, prime minister</td></tr>
<tr><td colspan="5">More than a dozen prominent Swazis were arrested in May in a continuing government power struggle. During the year at least 11 members of the African National Congress, the outlawed South African group, were killed in shootings by unidentified gunmen; South African agents were rumored to be behind the killings. GDP (1984): $478 million. Foreign Trade (1985): Imports, $322 million; exports, $174 million.</td></tr>
<tr><td>Togo, W. Africa</td><td>3.2</td><td>Lomé</td><td>21,927 (56 790)</td><td>Gnassingbé Eyadéma, president</td></tr>
<tr><td colspan="5">Local elections—the first in 20 years to be held under universal suffrage—were scheduled for July 5. Diplomatic relations with Israel, broken since 1973, were restored in June. GNP (1983 est.): $790 million. Foreign Trade (1984): Imports, $271 million; exports, $191 million.</td></tr>
<tr><td>Tonga, Oceania</td><td>0.1</td><td>Nuku'alofa</td><td>270 (700)</td><td>Taufa'ahau Tupou IV, king
Prince Fatafehi Tu'ipelehake, premier</td></tr>
<tr><td colspan="5">On October 6, Tonga was shaken by an earthquake measuring 7.3 on the Richter scale. GDP (1985): $100 million. Foreign Trade (1986): Imports, $38 million; exports, $5 million.</td></tr>
<tr><td>Trinidad and Tobago, Caribbean</td><td>1.3</td><td>Port-of-Spain</td><td>1,981 (5 130)</td><td>Noor Hassanali, president
Arthur Robinson, prime minister</td></tr>
<tr><td colspan="5">Prime Minister Robinson, who took office in mid-December 1986, authorized price increases of 30–50% and confirmed internal self-government for Tobago under the terms of a 1980 agreement. In February, Noor Hassanali was chosen president by an electoral college drawn from the legislature. He succeeded Ellis Clark, who had served two terms. A report released the same month implicated some members of the former government in drug trafficking. GDP (1986 est.): $7.8 billion. Foreign Trade (1986): Imports, $1.36 billion; exports, $1.38 billion.</td></tr>
<tr><td>Tuvalu, Oceania</td><td>0.008</td><td>Funafuti</td><td>10 (26)</td><td>Sir Tupua Leupena, governor-general
Tomasi Puapua, prime minister</td></tr>
<tr><td colspan="5">GNP (1984): $4 million. Foreign Trade (1983): Imports, $2.8 million; exports, $1 million.</td></tr>
<tr><td>United Arab Emirates, W. Asia</td><td>1.4</td><td>Abu Dhabi</td><td>32,278 (83 600)</td><td>Zayid bin Sultan Al Nuhayyan, president
Rashid bin Said Al Maktum, prime minister</td></tr>
<tr><td colspan="5">In June, Sheik Sultan bin Mohammed al-Qasimi, ruler of the emirate of Sharjah, was ousted briefly by his brother Sheik Abdel-Aziz, who accused Sultan of mismanagement and extravagance. Sultan was restored to power within four days following pressure from Dubai and other members of the UAE, and Abdel-Aziz was named crown prince. The UAE renewed diplomatic ties with Egypt in November. GDP (1986 est.): $24 billion. Foreign Trade (1985): Imports, $6.79 billion; exports, $13.12 billion.</td></tr>
<tr><td>Vanuatu, Oceania</td><td>0.2</td><td>Port-Vila</td><td>5,699 (14 760)</td><td>George Ati Sokomanu, president
Walter Lini, prime minister</td></tr>
<tr><td colspan="5">Vanuatu signed an agreement granting landing rights to Soviet fishermen in January and also increased contacts with Libya, although it turned away Libyans who arrived in May to open an embassy. A hurricane left some 10,000 people homeless on February 7, and the country appealed for international aid. GDP (1984): $79 million. Foreign Trade (1986): Imports, $57 million; exports, $17 million.</td></tr>
<tr><td>Vatican City, S. Europe</td><td>0.001</td><td>Vatican City</td><td>0.17 (0.438)</td><td>John Paul II, pope</td></tr>
<tr><td colspan="5">A five-year-old scandal involving the Vatican bank came to a head in February, when an Italian court issued warrants for the arrest of three officers of the bank. The officers included Archbishop Paul V. Marcinkus, an American who headed the bank. They were charged with fraud in connection with the failure in 1982 of Banco Ambrosiano, which folded when it was unable to collect on $1.3 billion in loans to ten companies controlled by the Vatican bank. However, the bank officials remained inside the Vatican, and Italy's highest court ruled in July that they could not be extradited. The issue strained relations between Italy and the Vatican.</td></tr>
<tr><td>Western Samoa, Oceania</td><td>0.2</td><td>Apia</td><td>1,104 (2 860)</td><td>Malietoa Tanumafili II, head of state
Vaai Kolone, prime minister</td></tr>
<tr><td colspan="5">The 18th meeting of the South Pacific Forum, held May 29–30 in Apia,, was dominated by concern over a recent coup in Fiji. A major earthquake centered 250 mi (402 km) south of Western Samoa shook the region on October 6. GDP (1985): $86.8 million. Foreign Trade (1986): Imports, $48 million; exports, $12 million.</td></tr>
<tr><td>Yemen, North, S. Asia</td><td>6.5</td><td>San'a</td><td>75,290 (195 000)</td><td>Ali Abdallah Salih, president
Abdel Aziz Abd al-Ghani, prime minister</td></tr>
<tr><td colspan="5">North Yemen joined other Arab countries in backing Saudi Arabia's handling of the July 31 riots in Mecca, in which some 400 people were killed during the annual Muslim pilgrimage (hajj). GDP (1984) $3.1 billion. Foreign Trade (1985): Imports, $1.29 billion; exports, $10 million.</td></tr>
<tr><td>Yemen, South, S. Asia</td><td>2.4</td><td>Aden</td><td>128,560 (332 970)</td><td>Haider Abu Bakr al-Attas, president</td></tr>
<tr><td colspan="5">More than 90 supporters of former President Ali Nasir Muhammad al-Hasani were put on trial in 1987, in an aftermath of factional fighting that had deposed the president in 1986 and left several thousand people dead. GNP (1985 est.): $1.1 billion. Foreign Trade (1985): Imports, $762 million; exports, $316 million.</td></tr>
<tr><td>Zambia, E. Africa</td><td>7.1</td><td>Lusaka</td><td>290,583 (752 610)</td><td>Kenneth David Kaunda, president
Kebby Musokotwane, prime minister</td></tr>
<tr><td colspan="5">With income from copper exports in decline, Zambia's economy continued to suffer. As a result of riots over price increases in December 1986, the government in May abandoned an International Monetary Fund plan to restructure the economy and limited payments on its foreign debt. GDP (1985): $2.3 billion. Foreign Trade (1986): Imports, $472 million; exports, $352 million.</td></tr>
</table>

WORLD MINERAL AND METAL PRODUCTION

ALUMINUM, primary smelter (thousand metric tons)	1985	1986
United States	3,500	3,037
USSR[e]	2,200	2,300
Canada	1,282	1,355
Australia	851	882
West Germany	745	764
Brazil	550	762
Norway	712	729
Venezuela	396	424
China[e]	410	410
Spain	370	355
France	293	322
United Kingdom	275	276
Yugoslavia	271	273
Netherlands	251	268
Other countries[a]	3,246	3,185
Total	15,352	15,342

ANTIMONY, mine[b] (metric tons)	1985	1986
China[e]	15,000	15,000
Bolivia	8,925	10,243
USSR[e]	9,400	9,500
South Africa	7,390	7,024
Canada	1,075	3,900
Mexico	4,266	3,337
Turkey	1,478	1,990
Guatemala	1,060	1,649
Thailand	1,240	1,486
Australia	1,458	1,064
Czechoslovakia[e]	1,000	1,000
Morocco	750	928
Other countries[a]	3,414	3,935
Total	56,456	61,056

ASBESTOS[c] (thousand metric tons)	1985	1986
USSR[e]	2,900	2,900
Canada	750	640
Brazil	172	175[e]
Zimbabwe	174	174[e]
China[e]	150	150
South Africa	164	140[e]
Italy	136	115
Other countries[a]	232	228
Total	4,678	4,522

BARITE[c] (thousand metric tons)	1985	1986
China[e]	1,000	1,000
USSR[e]	540	540
Mexico	468	375[e]
India	580	350[e]
United States	670	269
Ireland	214	210
Thailand	231	200[e]
Other countries[a]	2,282	1,958
Total	5,985	4,902

BAUXITE[d] (thousand metric tons)	1985	1986
Australia	31,839	32,431
Guinea	13,100	12,130
Jamaica	5,975	6,964
Brazil	6,251	6,224
USSR[e]	5,175	5,175
Suriname	3,000[e]	3,847
Yugoslavia	3,538	3,459
Hungary	2,815	3,022
India	2,121	2,338
Greece	2,453	2,225
China[e]	1,650	1,650
Guyana	1,675	1,466
France	1,530	1,379
Other countries[a]	4,051	4,155
Total	85,173	86,465

CEMENT[c] (thousand metric tons)	1985	1986
China	142,500	161,560
USSR	130,722	135,108
United States	71,540	72,499
Japan	72,857	71,246
Italy	36,677	35,340
India	33,050	33,200
West Germany	25,758	26,500
Brazil	20,612	25,297
Spain	24,197	24,000
France	23,546	23,500
South Korea	20,424	23,403
Mexico	21,347	20,650
Turkey	17,581	20,000[e]
Other countries[a]	317,146	326,855
Total	957,957	999,158

CHROMITE[c] (thousand metric tons)	1985	1986
South Africa	3,699	3,480
USSR[e]	2,940	2,950
Albania[e]	825	850
India	560	620[e]
Turkey[e]	600	600
Zimbabwe	536	540
Finland[e]	450	450
Brazil[e]	275	285
Philippines	272	183
Other countries[a]	392	368
Total	10,549	10,326

COAL, anthracite and bituminous[c] (million metric tons)	1985	1986
China	872	870
United States	741	714
USSR	569	592
Poland	192	192
South Africa	174	177
Australia	158	170
India	149	163
United Kingdom	94	108
West Germany	82	80
Canada	60	58
North Korea[e]	36	36
Other countries[a]	178	180
Total	3,305	3,340

COAL, lignite[c f] (million metric tons)	1985	1986
East Germany	312	311
USSR	157	159
West Germany	121	114
Czechoslovakia	102	103
Poland	58	67
United States	63	63
Yugoslavia	57	57
Australia	37	38
Other countries[a]	215	218
Total	1,122	1,130

COPPER, mine[b] (thousand metric tons)	1985	1986
Chile	1,356	1,386
United States	1,106	1,147
Canada	739	768
USSR[e]	600	620
Zaire	563	503
Zambia	459	450
Poland	431	435
Peru	391	397
Australia	260	249
Philippines	222	223
China[e]	185	185
South Africa	195	184
Papua New Guinea	175	174
Mexico	179	182
Other countries[a]	1,128	1,104
Total	7,989	8,007

COPPER, refined, primary and secondary (thousand metric tons)	1985	1986
United States	1,435	1,479
USSR[e]	953	965
Japan	936	943
Chile	884	942
Canada	534	493
Zambia	479	460
West Germany	414	422
Belgium	456	414
China[e]	400	400
Poland	387	388
Peru	230	226
Zaire	227	218
Australia	199	198
South Africa	164	158
Spain	152	158
Other countries[a]	1,555	1,618
Total	9,405	9,482

DIAMOND, natural (thousand carats)	1985	1986
Australia	7,070	29,211
Zaire	20,159	23,304
Botswana	12,635	13,110
USSR[e]	10,800	10,800
South Africa	10,202	10,300[e]
China[e]	1,000	1,000
Namibia	910	950[e]
Ghana	560	600
Other countries[a]	2,859	2,558
Total	66,195	91,833

FLUORSPAR[g] (thousand metric tons)	1985	1986
Mexico	729	767
Mongolia[e]	740	740
China[e]	650	650
USSR[e]	560	560
South Africa	349	340[e]
Spain	306	300[e]
Thailand	299	255[e]
France	232	235[e]
Other countries[a]	1,009	1,022
Total	4,874	4,869

GAS, natural[h] (billion cubic feet)	1985	1986
USSR	22,700	24,200
United States	17,198	16,809
Netherlands	2,851	2,800[e]
Canada	2,831	2,696
United Kingdom	1,517	1,600
Algeria	1,370	1,320[e]
Mexico	1,145	1,130[e]
Indonesia	1,149	1,113
Romania	960	945
Other countries[a]	9,931	10,102
Total	61,652	62,715

GOLD, mine[b] (thousand troy ounces)	1985	1986
South Africa	21,565	20,514
USSR[e]	8,700	8,850
United States	2,427	3,733
Canada	2,815	3,365
Australia	1,881	2,479
China[e]	1,950	2,100
Brazil[e]	2,000	2,000
Colombia	1,143	1,400[e]
Philippines	1,063	1,295
Other countries[a]	5,128	5,201
Total	48,672	50,937

GYPSUM[c] (thousand metric tons)	1985	1986
United States	13,359	14,324
Canada	8,447	8,546
China[e]	5,700	6,500
Japan[e]	6,260	6,350
Spain	5,525	5,500
France[e]	5,400	5,400
Iran[e]	5,000	5,000
USSR[e]	4,900	5,000
Mexico	4,603	4,500[e]
United Kingdom	3,189	3,200[e]
West Germany	2,367	1,900[e]
Poland[e]	1,700	1,800
Australia	1,538	1,600[e]
Romania[e]	1,550	1,550
Other countries[a]	15,591	16,424
Total	85,129	87,594

IRON ORE[c] (thousand metric tons)	1985	1986
USSR	247,639	250,000[e]
Brazil	123,000	132,000[e]
Australia	92,867	92,262
China	80,268	90,000[e]
India	44,546	47,800
United States	49,533	39,448
Canada	39,502	37,308
South Africa	24,414	24,483
Sweden	20,454	20,489
Venezuela	16,228	19,100[e]
Liberia	15,318	15,295
France	14,447	12,436
Other countries[a]	85,129	83,001
Total	853,345	863,622

IRON, steel ingots (thousand metric tons)	1985	1986
USSR	154,668	161,000[e]
Japan	105,279	98,275
United States	80,067	73,001
China	46,716	52,056
West Germany	40,497	37,134
Italy	23,744	22,872
Brazil	20,456	21,234
France	18,832	17,868
Poland	16,100	17,148
Czechoslovakia	15,036	15,108
United Kingdom	15,722	14,811
Canada	14,640	14,088
Romania	13,795	14,000
South Korea	13,539	13,500[e]
Spain	14,235	11,976
India	11,054	11,892
Belgium	10,683	9,744
South Africa	8,582	9,144
East Germany	7,853	7,968
Mexico	7,367	7,170
Other countries[a]	78,003	79,407
Total	716,868	709,396

LEAD, mine[b] (thousand metric tons)	1985	1986
USSR[e]	440	440
Australia	498	435
United States	424	353
Canada	268	304
Mexico	198	200[e]
Peru	202	194
China[e]	160	160
North Korea[e]	110	110
Yugoslavia	110	110[e]
Other countries[a]	980	934
Total	3,390	3,240

LEAD, refined, primary and secondary[i] (thousand metric tons)	1985	1986
United States	1,103	981
USSR[e]	765	770
West Germany	356	367
Japan	267	362
United Kingdom	327	307
Canada	240	265
France	224	230
Mexico	224	219
China[e]	195	195
Australia	216	168
Spain	156	133
Italy	126	131
Other countries[a]	1,416	1,273
Total	5,615	5,401

	1985	1986
MAGNESIUM, primary (thousand metric tons)		
United States	127	126
USSR	87	89
Norway	55	57
France	14	13
Italy	8	7
Canada[e]	7	7
China[e]	7	7
Other countries[a]	15	16
Total	320	322
MANGANESE ORE[c] (thousand metric tons)		
USSR	9,900	9,700
South Africa	3,601	3,719
Brazil[e]	2,700	2,700
Gabon	2,340	2,513
Australia	2,003	1,649
China[e]	1,600	1,600
India	1,236	1,213
Other countries[a]	1,045	1,052
Total	24,425	24,146
MERCURY (76-pound flasks)		
USSR[e]	65,000	66,000
Spain	45,042	46,239
China[e]	20,000	20,000
United States	16,530	14,000[e]
Mexico	11,430	10,008
Other countries[a]	37,821	37,000
Total	195,823	193,247
MOLYBDENUM, mine[b] (metric tons)		
United States	49,174	40,680
Chile	18,389	16,316
Canada	7,852	12,900
USSR[e]	11,300	11,400
Mexico	3,761	3,502
Peru	4,036	3,484
Other countries[a]	3,629	3,299
Total	98,141	91,581
NATURAL GAS LIQUIDS (million barrels)		
United States	587	581[e]
USSR[e]	175	187
Saudi Arabia	123	150
Algeria	122	122[e]
Canada	125	120
Mexico	96	90[e]
Other countries[a]	279	281
Total	1,507	1,531
NICKEL, mine[b] (thousand metric tons)		
USSR[e]	180	185
Canada	170	181
Australia	86	78
New Caledonia	72	71
Indonesia	41	44
Cuba	34	35
South Africa	25	29
China	25	26
Other countries[a]	171	155
Total	804	804
NITROGEN, content of ammonia (thousand metric tons)		
USSR[e]	16,700	17,200
China[e]	15,000	15,500
United States	12,009	10,432
India	4,324	4,800[e]
Canada	3,620	3,500[e]
Romania	2,880	2,900
Indonesia	2,055	2,100[e]
Netherlands	2,386	2,065
France[e]	2,010	2,000
Mexico	1,859	1,900
Other countries[a]	25,188	24,657
Total	88,031	87,054
PETROLEUM, crude (million barrels)		
USSR	4,380	4,520
United States	3,274	3,168
Saudi Arabia	1,237	1,841
China	912	954
United Kingdom	894	884
Mexico	960	746
Iran	809	664
Venezuela	614	654
Iraq	521	607
Nigeria	537	535
Canada	538	534

	1985	1986
PETROLEUM, crude (cont'd)		
United Arab Emirates	439	498
Kuwait	358	488
Indonesia	484	459
Libya	387	376
Other countries[a]	3,140	3,148
Total	19,484	20,076
PHOSPHATE ROCK[c] (thousand metric tons)		
United States	50,835	37,870
USSR[e]	32,200	32,500
Morocco	20,737	21,178
China[e]	6,970	6,700
Jordan	6,067	6,249
Tunisia	4,530	5,951
Brazil	4,214	4,509
Israel	4,076	3,673
South Africa	2,433	2,920
Togo	2,452	2,314
Other countries[a]	12,150	12,359
Total	146,664	136,223
POTASH, K_2O equivalent basis (thousand metric tons)		
USSR	10,367	9,600[e]
Canada	6,661	6,969
East Germany	3,465	3,450
West Germany	2,583	2,165
France	1,750	1,617
Israel	1,100	1,255
United States	1,296	1,202
Other countries[a]	1,829	1,990
Total	29,051	28,248
SALT[c] (thousand metric tons)		
United States	36,380	33,296
China	14,446	17,300
USSR	16,100	16,057
West Germany	13,070	11,158
Canada	10,085	11,088
India	9,878	9,983
France	7,113	7,083
United Kingdom	7,146	7,076
Mexico	6,467	6,532
Australia	6,169	6,200[e]
Poland	4,865	4,900[e]
Romania	5,019	4,900[e]
Italy	3,746	4,032
East Germany	3,138	3,133
Other countries[a]	30,163	31,644
Total	173,785	174,382
SILVER, mine[b] (thousand troy ounces)		
Mexico	73,167	75,200
Peru	58,230	61,920
USSR[e]	47,900	48,200
Canada	38,484	39,190
Australia	34,912	35,044
United States	39,433	34,220
Poland	26,717	27,000[e]
Chile	16,633	16,110
Japan	10,915	11,307
South Africa	6,721	7,145
Sweden	6,102	6,300[e]
Yugoslavia	5,015	5,000
Other countries[a]	56,745	53,189
Total	420,974	419,825
SULFUR, all forms[j] (thousand metric tons)		
United States	11,609	11,087
USSR[e]	9,725	9,825
Canada	6,670	6,516
Poland	5,096	5,120
China[e]	2,900	3,100
Japan	2,498	2,361
Mexico	2,180	2,165
West Germany	1,569	1,575[e]
Spain	1,355	1,310[e]
France	1,723	1,306
Other countries[a]	9,236	9,770
Total	54,561	54,135
TIN, mine[b] (thousand metric tons)		
Malaysia	36,884	28,072
Brazil	26,514	27,400[e]
USSR[e]	23,000	23,500
Indonesia	21,759	22,102
Thailand	16,864	16,800[e]
China[e]	15,000	15,000

	1985	1986
TIN, mine (cont'd)		
Bolivia	16,136	11,900[e]
Other countries[a]	32,496	35,463
Total	188,653	180,237
TITANIUM MINERALS[c k] (thousand metric tons)		
ILMENITE		
Australia	1,442	1,308
Norway	736	802
USSR[e]	445	450
Malaysia	247	398
China[e]	140	145
India	143	140
Other countries[a]	288	159
Total	3,441	3,402
RUTILE		
Australia	212	220
Sierra Leone	81	97
South Africa[e]	55	55
Other countries[a]	28	26
Total	376	398
TITANIFEROUS SLAG		
Canada	845	850[e]
South Africa[e]	435	435
Total	1,280	1,285
TUNGSTEN, mine[b] (metric tons)		
China[e]	15,000	15,000
USSR[e]	9,200	9,200
South Korea	2,579	2,500[e]
Portugal	1,755	1,637
Mongolia[e]	1,500	1,500
Austria	1,481	1,500[e]
Australia	1,970	1,486
Canada	3,197	1,416
Bolivia	1,643	1,095
North Korea[e]	1,000	1,000
France	735	982
Brazil	1,090	817
United States	996	780
Other countries[a]	4,389	3,699
Total	46,535	42,612
URANIUM OXIDE (U_3O_8)[l] (metric tons)		
Canada	12,831	13,789
United States	5,080	5,800
South Africa	5,788	5,371
Australia	3,836	4,800[e]
Namibia[e]	4,400	4,400
Niger	3,946	3,900[e]
France	3,774	3,800[e]
Other countries[a]	1,966	1,928
Total	41,621	43,788
ZINC, mine[b] (thousand metric tons)		
Canada	1,172	1,294
USSR[e]	810	810
Australia	759	662
Peru	589	598
Mexico	292	285
Spain	235	223
Japan	253	222
United States	252	216
Sweden	216	214
China[e]	200	200
Poland	191	184
Ireland	192	182
Other countries[a]	1,597	1,560
Total	6,758	6,650
ZINC, smelter, primary and secondary (thousand metric tons)		
USSR[e]	1,000	1,005
Japan	740	708
Canada	692	572
West Germany	368	371
United States	334	316
Australia	293	310
Belgium	290	290[e]
France	286	290
Italy	216	229
China[e]	215	215
Spain	213	214
Netherlands	202	195[e]
Poland	180	179
Mexico	175	174
Other countries[a]	1,590	1,595
Total	6,794	6,663

[a] Estimated in part. [b] Content of concentrates. [c] Gross weight. [d] Includes calculated bauxite equivalent of estimated output of aluminum ores other than bauxite (nepheline concentrate and alunite ore). [e] Estimate. [f] Includes coal classified in some countries as brown coal. [g] Gross weight of marketable product. [h] Marketed production (includes gas sold or used by producers; excludes gas reinjected to reservoirs for pressure maintenance and that flared or vented to the atmosphere which is not used as fuel or industrial raw material, and which thus has no economic value). [i] Excludes bullion produced for refining elsewhere. [j] Includes (1) Frasch process sulfur, (2) elemental sulfur mined by conventional means, (3) by-product recovered elemental sulfur, and (4) elemental sulfur equivalent obtained from pyrite and other materials. [k] Excludes output in the United States, which cannot be disclosed because it is company proprietary information. [l] Excludes output (if any) by Albania, Bulgaria, China, Czechoslovakia, East Germany, Hungary, North Korea, Mongolia, Poland, Romania, and Vietnam.

Compiled by Charles L. Kimbell primarily from data collected by the U.S. Bureau of Mines, but with some modifications from other sources.

THE UNITED STATES GOVERNMENT*

President: Ronald Reagan

Vice-President: George Bush

Executive Office of the President

The White House

Chief of Staff to the President: Howard H. Baker, Jr.
Deputy Chief of Staff: Kenneth M. Duberstein
Assistant to the President for Legislative Affairs: William L. Ball III
Assistant to the President for Policy Development: Gary L. Bauer
Assistant to the President and Press Secretary: James S. Brady
Assistant to the President for National Security Affairs: Colin L. Powell
Assistant to the President for Domestic Affairs: T. Kenneth Cribb, Jr.
Counsel to the President: Arthur B. Culvahouse, Jr.
Assistant to the President for Operation: Rhett B. Dawson
Assistant to the President for Political and Intergovernmental Affairs: Frank J. Donatelli
Assistant to the President for Press Relations: M. Marlin Fitzwater
Assistant to the President for Communications and Planning: Thomas Griscom
Assistant to the President: Charles Hobbs
Cabinet Secretary and Assistant to the President: Nancy J. Risque
Office of Management and Budget, Director: James C. Miller III
Council of Economic Advisers, Chairman: Beryl W. Sprinkel
Office of United States Trade Representative, U.S. Trade Representative: Clayton Yeutter
Council of Environmental Quality, Chairman: A. Alan Hill
Office of Science and Technology Policy, Director: William R. Graham

The Cabinet

Secretary of Agriculture: Richard Lyng
Secretary of Commerce: C. William Verity, Jr.
Secretary of Defense: Frank C. Carlucci
- Joint Chiefs of Staff, Chairman: Adm. William J. Crowe, Jr.
- Secretary of the Air Force: Edward C. Aldridge, Jr.
- Secretary of the Army: John O. Marsh, Jr.
- Secretary of the Navy: James H. Webb, Jr.

Secretary of Education: William J. Bennett
Secretary of Energy: John S. Herrington
Secretary of Health and Human Services: Otis R. Bowen
- National Institutes of Health, Director: James B. Wyngaarden
- Surgeon General: C. Everett Koop
- Commissioner of Food and Drugs: Frank E. Young
- Social Security Administration, Commissioner: Dorcas R. Hardy

Secretary of Housing and Urban Development: Samuel R. Pierce, Jr.
Secretary of the Interior: Donald Paul Hodel
Department of Justice, Attorney General: Edwin Meese III
- Federal Bureau of Investigation, Director: William S. Sessions

Secretary of Labor: Ann D. McLaughlin
- Women's Bureau, Director: Shirley M. Dennis
- Commissioner of Labor Statistics: Janet L. Norwood

Secretary of State: George P. Shultz
Secretary of Transportation: James H. Burnley IV
Secretary of the Treasury: James A. Baker III
- Internal Revenue Service, Commissioner: Lawrence B. Gibbs

Independent Agencies

ACTION, Director: Donna M. Alvarado
Central Intelligence Agency, Director: William H. Webster
Commission on Civil Rights, Chairman: Clarence M. Pendleton, Jr.
Commission of Fine Arts, Chairman: J. Carter Brown
Consumer Product Safety Commission, Chairman: Terrence M. Scanlon
Environmental Protection Agency, Administrator: Lee M. Thomas
Equal Employment Opportunity Commission, Chairman: Clarence Thomas
Export-Import Bank, President and Chairman: John A. Bohn, Jr.
Farm Credit Administration, Chairman: Frank W. Naylor
Federal Communications Commission, Chairman: Dennis R. Patrick
Federal Deposit Insurance Corporation, Chairman: L. William Seidman
Federal Election Commission, Chairman: Thomas J. Josefiak
Federal Emergency Management Agency, Director: Julius W. Becton, Jr.
Federal Home Loan Bank Board, Chairman: M. Danny Wall
Federal Labor Relations Authority, Chairman: Jerry L. Calhoun
Federal Maritime Commission, Chairman: Vacant
Federal Reserve System, Chairman: Alan Greenspan
Federal Trade Commission, Chairman: Daniel Oliver
General Services Administrator: Terence C. Golden
Interstate Commerce Commission, Chairman: Heather J. Gradison
National Aeronautics and Space Administration, Administrator: James C. Fletcher
National Foundation on the Arts and Humanities
- National Endowment for the Arts, Chairman: Francis S. M. Hodsoll; National Endowment for the Humanities, Chairman: Lynne V. Cheney

National Labor Relations Board, Chairman: James Stephens
National Science Foundation, Chairman: Roland W. Schmitt
National Transportation Safety Board, Chairman: James E. Burnett
Nuclear Regulatory Commission, Chairman: Lando W. Zech, Jr.
Peace Corps, Director: Loret M. Ruppe
Postal Rate Commission, Chairman: Janet D. Steiger
Securities and Exchange Commission, Chairman: David S. Ruder
Selective Service System, Director: Samuel K. Lessey, Jr.
Small Business Administration, Administrator: James Abdnor
Tennessee Valley Authority, Chairman: C. H. Dean, Jr.
U.S. Arms Control and Disarmament Agency, Director: William Burns[2]
U.S. Information Agency, Director: Charles Z. Wick
U.S. International Trade Commission, Chairman: Susan W. Liebeler
U.S. Postmaster General: Preston R. Tisch[1]
Veterans Administrator: Thomas K. Turnage

The Supreme Court

Chief Justice, William H. Rehnquist

William J. Brennan, Jr.	Byron R. White	Thurgood Marshall	Harry A. Blackmun
John Paul Stevens	Sandra Day O'Connor	Antonin Scalia	Arthur M. Kennedy[2]

[1] Resignation announced. [2] Nominated but not confirmed.

* Selected listing, as of Jan. 15, 1988.

UNITED STATES: 100th CONGRESS
Second Session

SENATE MEMBERSHIP

(As of January 1988: 54 Democrats, 46 Republicans) Letters after senators' names refer to party affiliation—D for Democrat, R for Republican. Single asterisk (*) denotes term expiring in January 1989; double asterisk (**), term expiring in January 1991; triple asterisk (***), term expiring in January 1993. [1]Appointed in 1987 to fill vacancy.

Alabama
** H. Heflin, D
*** R. C. Shelby, D

Alaska
** T. Stevens, R
*** F. H. Murkowski, R

Arizona
* D. DeConcini, D
*** J. McCain III, R

Arkansas
*** D. Bumpers, D
** D. H. Pryor, D

California
*** A. Cranston, D
* P. Wilson, R

Colorado
** W. L. Armstrong, R
*** T. E. Wirth, D

Connecticut
* L. P. Weicker, Jr., R
*** C. J. Dodd, D

Delaware
* W. V. Roth, Jr., R
** J. R. Biden, Jr., D

Florida
* L. Chiles, Jr., D
*** B. Graham, D

Georgia
** S. Nunn, D
*** W. Fowler, Jr., D

Hawaii
*** D. K. Inouye, D
* S. M. Matsunaga, D

Idaho
** J. A. McClure, R
*** S. Symms, R

Illinois
*** A. J. Dixon, D
** P. Simon, D

Indiana
* R. G. Lugar, R
*** D. Quayle, R

Iowa
*** C. E. Grassley, R
** T. R. Harkin, D

Kansas
*** R. J. Dole, R
** N. L. Kassebaum, R

Kentucky
*** W. H. Ford, D
** M. McConnell, R

Louisiana
** J. B. Johnston, D
*** J. B. Breaux, D

Maine
** W. Cohen, R
* G. J. Mitchell, D

Maryland
* P. S. Sarbanes, D
*** B. A. Mikulski, D

Massachusetts
* E. M. Kennedy, D
** J. F. Kerry, D

Michigan
* D. W. Riegle, Jr., D
** C. Levin, D

Minnesota
* D. F. Durenberger, R
** R. Boschwitz, R

Mississippi
* J. C. Stennis, D
** T. Cochran, R

Missouri
* J. C. Danforth, R
*** C. S. Bond, R

Montana
* J. Melcher, D
** M. Baucus, D

Nebraska
** J. J. Exon, Jr., D
* D. K. Karnes (R) [1]

Nevada
* C. Hecht, R
*** H. Reid, D

New Hampshire
** G. J. Humphrey, R
*** W. B. Rudman, R

New Jersey
** B. Bradley, D
* F. R. Lautenberg, D

New Mexico
** P. V. Domenici, R
* J. Bingaman, D

New York
* D. P. Moynihan, D
*** A. D'Amato, R

North Carolina
** J. Helms, R
*** T. Sanford, D

North Dakota
* Q. N. Burdick, D
*** K. Conrad, D

Ohio
*** J. H. Glenn, Jr., D
* H. M. Metzenbaum, D

Oklahoma
** D. L. Boren, D
*** D. L. Nickles, R

Oregon
** M. O. Hatfield, R
*** B. Packwood, R

Pennsylvania
* J. Heinz, R
*** A. Specter, R

Rhode Island
** C. Pell, D
* J. H. Chafee, R

South Carolina
** S. Thurmond, R
*** E. F. Hollings, D

South Dakota
** L. Pressler, R
*** T. A. Daschle, D

Tennessee
* J. R. Sasser, D
** A. Gore, Jr., D

Texas
* L. Bentsen, D
** W. P. Gramm, R

Utah
*** E. J. Garn, R
* O. G. Hatch, R

Vermont
* R. T. Stafford, R
*** P. J. Leahy, D

Virginia
** J. W. Warner, R
* P. S. Trible, Jr., R

Washington
* D. J. Evans, R
*** B. Adams, D

West Virginia
* R. C. Byrd, D
** J. D. Rockefeller IV, D

Wisconsin
* W. Proxmire, D
*** R. W. Kasten, Jr., R

Wyoming
* M. Wallop, R
** A. K. Simpson, R

HOUSE MEMBERSHIP

(As of January 1988, 257 Democrats, 177 Republicans, 1 vacant) "At-L." in place of congressional district number means "representative at large." * Indicates elected special 1987 election. ** Will resign seat to be inaugurated governor of Louisiana in March 1988.

Alabama
1. H. L. Callahan, R
2. W. L. Dickinson, R
3. W. Nichols, D
4. T. Bevill, D
5. R. G. Flippo, D
6. B. Erdreich, D
7. C. Harris, Jr., D

Alaska
At-L. D. Young, R

Arizona
1. J. J. Rhodes, III, R
2. M. K. Udall, D
3. B. Stump, R
4. J. L. Kyl, R
5. J. Kolbe, R

Arkansas
1. W. V. Alexander, Jr., D
2. T. F. Robinson, D
3. J. P. Hammerschmidt, R
4. B. F. Anthony, Jr., D

California
1. D. H. Bosco, D
2. W. W. Herger, R
3. R. T. Matsui, D
4. V. Fazio, D
5. *N. Pelosi, D
6. B. Boxer, D
7. G. Miller, D
8. R. V. Dellums, D
9. F. H. Stark, Jr., D
10. D. Edwards, D
11. T. P. Lantos, D
12. E. L. Konnyu, R
13. N. Y. Mineta, D
14. N. D. Shumway, R
15. T. Coelho, D
16. L. E. Panetta, D
17. C. J. Pashayan, Jr., R
18. R. H. Lehman, D
19. R. J. Lagomarsino, R
20. W. M. Thomas, R
21. E. W. Gallegly, R
22. C. J. Moorhead, R
23. A. C. Beilenson, D
24. H. A. Waxman, D
25. E. R. Roybal, D
26. H. L. Berman, D
27. M. Levine, D
28. J. C. Dixon, D
29. A. F. Hawkins, D
30. M. G. Martinez, Jr., D
31. M. W. Dymally, D
32. G. M. Anderson, D
33. D. Dreier, R
34. E. E. Torres, D
35. J. Lewis, R
36. G. E. Brown, Jr., D
37. A. A. McCandless, R
38. R. K. Dornan, R
39. W. E. Dannemeyer, R
40. R. E. Badham, R
41. W. D. Lowery, R
42. D. E. Lungren, R
43. R. Packard, R
44. J. Bates, D
45. D. L. Hunter, R

Colorado
1. P. Schroeder, D
2. D. Skaggs, D
3. B. N. Campbell, D
4. H. Brown, R
5. J. M. Hefley, R
6. D. Schaefer, R

Connecticut
1. B. B. Kennelly, D
2. S. Gejdenson, D
3. B. A. Morrison, D
4. *C. Shays, R
5. J. G. Rowland, R
6. N. L. Johnson, R

Delaware
At-L. T. R. Carper, D

Florida
1. E. Hutto, D
2. B. Grant, D
3. C. E. Bennett, D
4. W. V. Chappell, Jr., D
5. B. McCollum, Jr., R
6. B. MacKay, D
7. S. M. Gibbons, D
8. C. W. Young, R
9. M. Bilirakis, R
10. A. Ireland, R
11. B. Nelson, D
12. T. Lewis, R
13. C. Mack, R
14. D. A. Mica, D
15. E. C. Shaw, Jr., R
16. L. J. Smith, D
17. W. Lehman, D
18. C. D. Pepper, D
19. D. B. Fascell, D

Georgia
1. R. L. Thomas, D
2. C. F. Hatcher, D
3. R. B. Ray, D
4. P. L. Swindall, R
5. J. R. Lewis, D
6. N. Gingrich, R
7. G. Darden, D
8. R. Rowland, D
9. E. L. Jenkins, D
10. D. Barnard, Jr., D

Hawaii
1. P. F. Saiki, R
2. D. K. Akaka, D

Idaho
1. L. Craig, R
2. R. H. Stallings, D

Illinois
1. C. A. Hayes, D
2. G. Savage, D
3. M. Russo, D
4. J. Davis, R
5. W. O. Lipinski, D
6. H. J. Hyde, R
7. C. Collins, D
8. D. Rostenkowski, D
9. S. R. Yates, D
10. J. E. Porter, R
11. F. Annunzio, D
12. P. M. Crane, R
13. H. W. Fawell, R
14. J. D. Hastert, R
15. E. R. Madigan, R
16. L. M. Martin, R
17. L. Evans, D

18. R. H. Michel, R
19. T. L. Bruce, D
20. R. Durbin, D
21. C. M. Price, D
22. K. J. Gray, D

Indiana
1. P. J. Visclosky, D
2. P. R. Sharp, D
3. J. P. Hiler, R
4. D. R. Coats, R
5. J. P. Jontz, D
6. D. L. Burton, R
7. J. T. Myers, R
8. F. McCloskey, D
9. L. H. Hamilton, D
10. A. Jacobs, Jr., D

Iowa
1. J. Leach, R
2. T. T. Tauke, R
3. D. R. Nagle, D
4. N. Smith, D
5. J. R. Lightfoot, R
6. F. L. Grandy, R

Kansas
1. C. P. Roberts, R
2. J. C. Slattery, D
3. J. Meyers, R
4. D. Glickman, D
5. B. Whittaker, R

Kentucky
1. C. Hubbard, Jr., D
2. W. H. Natcher, D
3. R. L. Mazzoli, D
4. J. Bunning, R
5. H. D. Rogers, R
6. L. J. Hopkins, R
7. C. C. Perkins, D

Louisiana
1. R. L. Livingston, Jr., R
2. C. C. Boggs, D
3. W. J. Tauzin, D
4. **C. E. Roemer III, D
5. T. J. Huckaby, D
6. R. H. Baker, R
7. J. A. Hayes, D
8. C. C. Holloway, R

Maine
1. J. E. Brennan, D
2. O. J. Snowe, R

Maryland
1. R. P. Dyson, D
2. H. D. Bentley, R
3. B. L. Cardin, D
4. C. T. McMillen, D
5. S. H. Hoyer, D
6. B. B. Byron, D
7. K. Mfume, D
8. C. A. Morella, R

Massachusetts
1. S. O. Conte, R
2. E. P. Boland, D
3. J. D. Early, D
4. B. Frank, D
5. C. G. Atkins, D
6. N. Mavroules, D
7. E. J. Markey, D
8. J. P. Kennedy II, D
9. J. J. Moakley, D
10. G. E. Studds, D
11. B. J. Donnelly, D

Michigan
1. J. Conyers, Jr., D
2. C. D. Pursell, R
3. H. E. Wolpe, D
4. F. S. Upton, R
5. P. B. Henry, R
6. B. Carr, D
7. D. E. Kildee, D
8. B. Traxler, D
9. G. Vander Jagt, R
10. B. Schuette, R
11. R. W. Davis, R
12. D. E. Bonior, D
13. G. W. Crockett, Jr., D
14. D. M. Hertel, D
15. W. D. Ford, D
16. J. D. Dingell, D
17. S. M. Levin, D
18. W. S. Broomfield, R

Minnesota
1. T. J. Penny, D
2. V. Weber, R
3. B. Frenzel, R
4. B. F. Vento, D
5. M. O. Sabo, D
6. G. Sikorski, D
7. A. Stangeland, R
8. J. L. Oberstar, D

Mississippi
1. J. L. Whitten, D
2. M. Espy, D
3. G. V. Montgomery, D
4. W. Dowdy, D
5. T. Lott, R

Missouri
1. W. L. Clay, D
2. J. W. Buechner, R
3. R. A. Gephardt, D
4. I. Skelton, D
5. A. D. Wheat, D
6. E. T. Coleman, R
7. G. Taylor, R
8. W. Emerson, R
9. H. L. Volkmer, D

Montana
1. P. Williams, D
2. R. C. Marlenee, R

Nebraska
1. D. Bereuter, R
2. H. Daub, R
3. V. Smith, R

Nevada
1. J. H. Bilbray, D
2. B. F. Vucanovich, R

New Hampshire
1. R. C. Smith, R
2. J. Gregg, R

New Jersey
1. J. J. Florio, D
2. W. J. Hughes, D
3. J. J. Howard, D
4. C. H. Smith, R
5. M. S. Roukema, R
6. B. J. Dwyer, D
7. M. J. Rinaldo, R
8. R. A. Roe, D
9. R. G. Torricelli, D
10. P. W. Rodino, Jr., D
11. D. A. Gallo, R
12. J. Courter, R
13. H. J. Saxton, R
14. F. J. Guarini, D

New Mexico
1. M. Lujan, Jr., R
2. J. R. Skeen, R
3. W. B. Richardson, D

New York
1. G. J. Hochbrueckner, D
2. T. J. Downey, D
3. R. J. Mrazek, D
4. N. F. Lent, R
5. R. J. McGrath, R
6. F. H. Flake, D
7. G. L. Ackerman, D
8. J. H. Scheuer, D
9. T. J. Manton, D
10. C. E. Schumer, D
11. E. Towns, D
12. M. R. Owens, D
13. S. J. Solarz, D
14. G. V. Molinari, R
15. B. Green, R
16. C. B. Rangel, D
17. T. Weiss, D
18. R. Garcia, D
19. M. Biaggi, D
20. J. J. DioGuardi, R
21. H. Fish, Jr., R
22. B. A. Gilman, R
23. S. S. Stratton, D
24. G. B. Solomon, R
25. S. L. Boehlert, R
26. D. Martin, R
27. G. C. Wortley, R
28. M. F. McHugh, D
29. F. Horton, R
30. L. M. Slaughter, D
31. J. Kemp, R
32. J. J. LaFalce, D
33. H. J. Nowak, D
34. A. Houghton, R

North Carolina
1. W. B. Jones, D
2. T. Valentine, D
3. H. M. Lancaster, D
4. D. E. Price, D
5. S. L. Neal, D
6. H. Coble, R
7. C. Rose, D
8. W. G. Hefner, D
9. J. A. McMillan, R
10. C. Ballenger, R
11. J. McC. Clarke, D

North Dakota
At-L. B. L. Dorgan, D

Ohio
1. T. A. Luken, D
2. W. D. Gradison, Jr., R
3. T. P. Hall, D
4. M. G. Oxley, R
5. D. L. Latta, R
6. B. McEwen, R
7. M. DeWine, R
8. D. E. Lukens, R
9. M. C. Kaptur, D
10. C. E. Miller, R
11. D. E. Eckart, D
12. J. R. Kasich, R
13. D. J. Pease, D
14. T. C. Sawyer, D
15. C. P. Wylie, R
16. R. Regula, R
17. J. A. Traficant, Jr., D
18. D. Applegate, D
19. E. F. Feighan, D
20. M. R. Oakar, D
21. L. Stokes, D

Oklahoma
1. J. M. Inhofe, R
2. M. Synar, D
3. W. W. Watkins, D
4. D. McCurdy, D
5. M. Edwards, R
6. G. English, D

Oregon
1. L. AuCoin, D
2. R. F. Smith, R
3. R. Wyden, D
4. P. A. DeFazio, D
5. D. Smith, R

Pennsylvania
1. T. M. Foglietta, D
2. W. H. Gray, III, D
3. R. A. Borski, Jr., D
4. J. P. Kolter, D
5. R. T. Schulze, R
6. G. Yatron, D
7. W. C. Weldon, R
8. P. H. Kostmayer, D
9. B. Shuster, R
10. J. M. McDade, R
11. P. E. Kanjorski, D
12. J. P. Murtha, D
13. L. Coughlin, R
14. W. Coyne, D
15. D. L. Ritter, R
16. R. S. Walker, R
17. G. W. Gekas, R
18. D. Walgren, D
19. W. F. Goodling, R
20. J. M. Gaydos, D
21. T. J. Ridge, R
22. A. J. Murphy, D
23. W. E. Clinger, Jr., R

Rhode Island
1. F. J. St Germain, D
2. C. Schneider, R

South Carolina
1. A. Ravenel, Jr., R
2. F. D. Spence, R
3. B. C. Derrick, Jr., D
4. E. J. Patterson, D
5. J. M. Spratt, Jr., D
6. R. M. Tallon, Jr., D

South Dakota
At-L. T. Johnson, D

Tennessee
1. J. H. Quillen, R
2. J. J. Duncan, R
3. M. Lloyd, D
4. J. Cooper, D
5. vacant
6. B. J. Gordon, D
7. D. K. Sundquist, R
8. E. Jones, D
9. H. E. Ford, D

Texas
1. J. Chapman, D
2. C. Wilson, D
3. S. Bartlett, R
4. R. M. Hall, D
5. J. W. Bryant, D
6. J. L. Barton, R
7. B. Archer, R
8. J. M. Fields, R
9. J. Brooks, D
10. J. J. Pickle, D
11. J. M. Leath, D
12. J. C. Wright, Jr., D
13. B. Boulter, R
14. D. M. Sweeney, R
15. E. de la Garza, D
16. R. D. Coleman, D
17. C. W. Stenholm, D
18. M. Leland, D
19. L. E. Combest, R
20. H. B. Gonzalez, D
21. L. S. Smith, R
22. T. D. DeLay, R
23. A. G. Bustamante, D
24. M. Frost, D
25. M. A. Andrews, D
26. R. K. Armey, R
27. S. P. Ortiz, D

Utah
1. J. V. Hansen, R
2. D. W. Owens, D
3. H. C. Nielson, R

Vermont
At-L. J. M. Jeffords, R

Virginia
1. H. H. Bateman, R
2. O. B. Pickett, D
3. T. J. Bliley, Jr., R
4. N. Sisisky, D
5. D. Daniel, D
6. J. R. Olin, D
7. D. F. Slaughter, Jr., R
8. S. Parris, R
9. F. C. Boucher, D
10. F. R. Wolf, R

Washington
1. J. R. Miller, R
2. A. Swift, D
3. D. L. Bonker, D
4. S. W. Morrison, R
5. T. S. Foley, D
6. N. D. Dicks, D
7. M. Lowry, D
8. R. Chandler, R

West Virginia
1. A. B. Mollohan, D
2. H. O. Staggers, Jr., D
3. R. E. Wise, Jr., D
4. N. J. Rahall, II, D

Wisconsin
1. L. Aspin, D
2. R. W. Kastenmeier, D
3. S. C. Gunderson, R
4. G. D. Kleczka, D
5. J. Moody, D
6. T. E. Petri, R
7. D. R. Obey, D
8. T. Roth, R
9. F. J. Sensenbrenner, Jr., R

Wyoming
At-L. D. Cheney, R

AMERICAN SAMOA
Delegate, Fofō Sunia, D

DISTRICT OF COLUMBIA
Delegate, W. E. Fauntroy, D

GUAM
Delegate, Ben Blaz, R

PUERTO RICO
Resident Commissioner
J. B. Fuster, D

VIRGIN ISLANDS
Delegate, Ron de Lugo, D

UNITED STATES: Major Legislation Enacted During the First Session of the 100th Congress

SUBJECT	PURPOSE
Clean Water	Authorizes $20 billion over nine years for measures to control water pollution. Presidential veto was overriden on February 4. Public Law 100-4.
America's Cup	Congratulates the crew of the *Stars and Stripes* on winning the America's Cup. Signed February 11. Public Law 100-5.
Homeless Aid	Appropriates $50 million for emergency aid for the nation's homeless by transferring funds within the Federal Emergency Management Agency. Signed February 12. Public Law 100-6.
Highway-Mass Transit	Reauthorizes highway and mass transit programs through fiscal year 1991; authorizes states to increase the speed limit on rural sections of interstate highways to 65 miles per hour (105 km/hr). Presidential veto was overridden on April 2. Public Law 100-17.
Veterans	Makes permanent a program of higher education benefits for veterans that was enacted on an experimental basis in 1984. Signed June 1. Public Law 100-48.
Marshall Plan	Commemorates the 40th anniversary of the Marshall Plan. Signed June 1. Public Law 100-49.
Statue of Liberty	Prohibits the imposition of an entrance fee at the Statue of Liberty National Monument. Signed June 19. Public Law 100-55.
Aid for the Homeless	Authorizes $443 million for fiscal 1987 and $616 million for fiscal 1988 for emergency shelter, health care, nutrition aid, and job and literacy training for the nation's homeless. Signed July 23. Public Law 100-77.
Banking	Provides $10.8 billion to bolster the Federal Savings and Loan Insurance Corporation through a complex borrowing scheme. Restricts creation of non-banks and nontraditional businesses by banks. Signed August 10. Public Law 100-86.
Iran-Iraq War	Demonstrates support for a cease-fire in the Iran-Iraq war and a negotiated solution to the conflict. Signed August 18. Public Law 100-96.
Quality Improvement	Establishes the Malcolm Baldrige National Quality Improvement Awards to recognize companies demonstrating high achievement in improving the quality of their goods or services. Signed August 20. Public Law 100-107.
Washington, DC	Authorizes the completion of the Federal Triangle in the District of Columbia and the construction of a public building to provide office space for an international cultural and trade center. Signed August 21. Public Law 100-113.
Debt Limit	Extends the government's borrowing authority to $2.8 trillion. Modifies the Gramm-Rudman-Hollings balanced budget law to give the executive branch authority to impose mandatory spending cuts, and relaxes the act's annual deficit targets. Signed September 29. Public Law 100-119.
Aviation Safety	Stiffens criminal penalty for airlines that do not comply with Federal Aviation Administration safety reporting requirements. Signed September 30. Public Law 100-121.
Older Americans	Provides nutrition and support services for elderly persons for an additional four years. Signed November 29. Public Law 100-175.
Independent Counsel	Renews the law permitting the establishment of an independent counsel to investigate alleged wrongdoing by government officials. Signed December 21. Public Law 100-191.
Veterans' Home Loans	Revises the Veterans Administration's home-loan guaranty program, including increasing the limits on home loans for veterans. Signed December 21. Public Law 100-198.
Government Funding	Appropriates $603.9 billion for government funding for fiscal 1988. Includes more than $14 million for aid and transportation expenses for the contras in Nicaragua. Bans smoking on domestic airline flights of two hours or less. Signed December 22. Public Law 100-202.
Budget Deficit	Reduces the budget by $17.6 billion in fiscal 1988 and $22 billion in fiscal 1989. Includes $9.1 billion in new taxes the first year and $14.1 billion in the second. Signed December 22. Public Law 100-203.
Jimmy Carter	Establishes the Jimmy Carter National Historic Site and Preservation District in the state of Georgia. Signed December 23. Public Law 100-206.
Mary Lasker	Provides for a special gold medal to be presented to Mary Lasker for her humanitarianism. Signed December 24. Public Law 100-210.
U.S.-Japan Fishery Agreement	Approves a two-year extension of the U.S.-Japanese fishing agreement. Bans dumping of plastics at sea. Reauthorizes for three years the Sea Grant College Program. Signed December 29. Public Law 100-220.
Soviet Emigration	Calls upon the Soviet Union to immediately grant permission to emigrate to all those who wish to join spouses or fiances in the United States. Signed December 29. Public Law 100-222.
Airports	Authorizes funding increases for Federal Aviation Administration grants to airports for expansion projects and for purchases of equipment to upgrade the air-traffic control system. Extends through 1990 various taxes flowing into the Airport and Airway Trust Fund to pay for aviation programs. Signed December 30. Public Law 100-223.
Veterans	Provides a 4.2% cost-of-living increase in benefits for disabled veterans and their dependents. Signed December 31. Public Law 100-227.
Farm Credit	Provides up to $4 billion for the Farm Credit System's lending system. Signed Jan. 6, 1988. Public Law 100-233.

SOCIETIES AND ORGANIZATIONS

This listing includes some of the most noteworthy associations, societies, foundations, and trusts of the United States and Canada. The information was verified by the organization concerned.

Academy of Motion Picture Arts & Sciences. Membership: 5,000. Executive director, James M. Roberts. Headquarters: 8949 Wilshire Blvd., Beverly Hills, CA 90211.

Alcoholics Anonymous (The General Service Board of A.A., Inc.). Membership: more than 1,000,000 in more than 73,192 groups worldwide in 115 countries. Chairman, Gordon Patrick. Headquarters: 468 Park Ave. S., New York, NY. Mailing address: Box 459, Grand Central Station, New York, NY 10163.

American Academy and Institute of Arts and Letters. Membership: 250. Executive director, Margaret M. Mills. Headquarters: 633 W. 155th St., New York, NY 10032.

American Academy of Political and Social Science. Membership: 10,500, including 5,500 libraries. President, Marvin E. Wolfgang. Headquarters: 3937 Chestnut St., Philadelphia, PA 19104.

American Anthropological Association. Membership: 10,529. Executive director, Eugene Sterud. Headquarters: 1703 New Hampshire Ave. NW, Washington, DC 20009.

American Association for the Advancement of Science. Membership: 132,000 and 285 affiliated scientific and engineering societies and academies of science. Meeting: Boston, Feb. 11–15, 1988. President: Sheila E. Widnall; executive officer, Alvin W. Trivelpiece. Headquarters: 1333 H. Street NW, Washington, DC 20005.

American Association of Museums. Membership: 10,000. Meeting: Pittsburgh, PA, June 3–7, 1988. Director: Edward H. Able. Headquarters: 1225 Eye St. NW, Suite 200, Washington, DC 20005.

American Association of Retired Persons. Membership: 25,000,000. Biennial convention: May 10–12, 1988, Detroit, MI. Executive director, Cyril F. Brickfield. Headquarters: 1909 K St. NW, Washington, DC 20049.

American Association of University Professors. Membership: 53,000. President, Julius G. Getman. Headquarters: 1012 14th St. NW, Washington, DC 20005.

American Association of University Women. Membership: 175,000. President, Sarah Harder. Headquarters: 2401 Virginia Ave. NW, Washington, DC 20037.

American Astronomical Society. Membership: 4,300. Meetings: Austin, TX, Jan. 10–14, 1988; Kansas City, MO, June 5–9, 1988. Executive officer, Peter B. Boyce. Headquarters: 2000 Florida Ave. NW, Suite 300, Washington, DC 20009.

American Automobile Association. Membership: 27,500,000 in 161 affiliated clubs. President, James B. Creal. Headquarters: 8111 Gatehouse Rd., Falls Church, VA 22047.

American Bankers Association (ABA). Membership: nearly 13,000. President, Charles H. Pistor. Annual convention: Honolulu, HI, Oct. 8–12, 1988. Headquarters: 1120 Connecticut Ave. NW, Washington, DC 20036.

American Bar Association. Membership: 316,400. Annual meeting: Toronto, Aug. 4–11, 1988; Midyear meeting: Philadelphia, PA, Feb. 3–10, 1988. President, Robert MacCrate; president-elect, Robert D. Raven; executive director and chief operating officer, Thomas H. Gonser. Headquarters: 750 N. Lake Shore Drive, Chicago, IL 60611.

American Bible Society. Distribution: U.S. 100,142,313; overseas, 188,983,320. Annual meeting: New York City, May 12, 1988. President, James Wood; general officers, Alice E. Ball, John D. Erickson, Daniel K. Scarberry. Headquarters: 1865 Broadway, New York, NY 10023.

American Booksellers Association, Inc. Membership: 6,106. Convention: Anaheim, CA, May 28–31, 1988. President, Rhett Jackson; executive director, Bernard Rath. Headquarters: 122 E. 42nd St., New York, NY 10168.

American Cancer Society, Inc. Membership: 124 voting members; 58 chartered divisions. Executive vice-president, G. Robert Gadberry. Headquarters: 90 Park Avenue, New York, NY 10016.

American Chemical Society. Membership: 137,000. National meetings, 1988: Toronto, June 5–11; Los Angeles, Sept. 25–30. President, Mary L. Good. Headquarters: 1155 16th St. NW, Washington, DC 20036.

American Civil Liberties Union. Membership: 250,000. President, Norman Dorsen; executive director, Ira Glasser. Headquarters: 132 W. 43rd St., New York, NY 10036.

American Correctional Association. Membership: 21,000. Executive director, Anthony P. Travisono. Headquarters: 4321 Hartwick Rd., College Park, MD 20740.

American Council on Education. Membership: 1,418 institutional members, 90 associated organizations, 59 constituent organizations, 38 affiliates, 24 international affiliates, and 15 associates. Annual meeting: Washington, DC, January 1988. President, Robert H. Atwell. Headquarters: One Dupont Circle NW, Washington, DC 20036.

American Council of Learned Societies. Membership: 45 professional societies concerned with the humanities and the humanistic aspects of the social sciences. President, Stanley N. Katz. Headquarters: 228 East 45th St., New York, NY 10017.

American Dental Association. Membership: 146,000. Annual session: Washington, DC, Oct. 8–11, 1988. President, Joseph A. Devine, D.D.S.; executive director, Thomas J. Ginley, Ph.D. Headquarters: 211 E. Chicago Ave., Chicago, IL 60611.

American Economic Association. Membership: 20,000 and 6,000 subscribers. President, Gary S. Becker. Headquarters: 1313 21st Avenue South, Nashville, TN 37212.

American Farm Bureau Federation. Membership: 3,503,835 families. President, Dean R. Kleckner. Headquarters: 225 Touhy Ave., Park Ridge, IL 60068.

American Geographical Society. Fellows and subscribers: 8,500. President, John E. Gould; director, Mary Lynne Bird. Headquarters: 156 Fifth Ave., Suite 600, New York, NY 10010.

American Geophysical Union. Membership: about 20,000 individuals. Meetings: spring—Baltimore, MD, May 16–20, 1988; fall—San Francisco, CA, Dec. 5–9, 1988. President, Peter S. Eagleson. Headquarters: 2000 Florida Ave. NW, Washington, DC 20009.

American Heart Association. Membership: 2,000,000 medical and lay volunteers in 55 affiliates and more than 1,750 local divisions. 1987–88 president, Howard E. Morgan, M.D. Headquarters: 7320 Greenville Ave., Dallas, TX 75231.

American Historical Association. Membership: 13,000. Annual meeting: Cincinnati, OH, Dec. 27–30, 1988. President, Natalie Zemon Davis; executive director, Samuel Gammon. Headquarters: 400 A St. SE, Washington, DC 20003.

American Horticultural Society. Membership: 40,000. Annual meeting: Atlanta, GA, April 1988. President, Everitt L. Miller. Headquarters: River Farm, Box 0105, Mount Vernon, NY 22121.

American Hospital Association. Membership: 43,451 persons; 5,986 institutions. Annual meeting: Washington, DC, Jan. 31–Feb. 3, 1988. Convention: New Orleans, LA, Aug. 8–10, 1988. Chairman of the board, Donald C. Wegmiller. Headquarters: 840 North Lake Shore Drive, Chicago, IL 60611.

American Hotel & Motel Association. Membership: 8,900. Annual convention: Dallas, TX, April 15–18, 1988. Executive vice-president, Kenneth F. Hine. Headquarters: 888 Seventh Ave., New York, NY 10106.

American Institute of Aeronautics and Astronautics. Membership: 31,030 plus 7,595 student members. Annual meeting: Crystal City, VA, May 3–5, 1988. Executive director, James J. Harford. Headquarters: 1633 Broadway, New York, NY 10019.

American Institute of Architects. Membership: 52,000. Convention: New York City, May 8–11, 1988. President, Donald J. Hackl, FAIA. Headquarters: 1735 New York Avenue NW, Washington, DC 20006.

American Institute of Biological Sciences. Membership: 8,000 with 35 societies and 6 affiliate organizations. Annual meeting: University of California at Davis, Aug. 14–18, 1988. President, H. Edward Kennedy. Headquarters: 730 11th St. NW, Washington, DC 20001.

American Institute of Certified Public Accountants. Membership: 250,000. Annual meeting: Los Angeles, CA, Oct. 2–5, 1988. Chairman, J. Michael Cook; president, Philip B. Chenok. Headquarters: 1211 Avenue of the Americas, New York, NY 10036–8775.

American Institute of Chemical Engineers. Membership: 60,000. President, S.I. Proctor. Headquarters: 345 E. 47th Street, New York, NY 10017.

American Institute of Graphic Arts. Membership: 5,000. President, Bruce Blackburn; executive director, Caroline Hightower. Headquarters: 1059 Third Ave., New York, NY 10021.

American Institute of Mining, Metallurgical and Petroleum Engineers, Inc. 4 member societies: Society of Mining Engineers, The Metallurgical Society, Iron & Steel Society, Society of Petroleum Engineers. Annual meeting: Phoenix, AZ, Jan. 25–29, 1988. President, Thomas V. Falkie. Headquarters: 345 E. 47th Street, New York, NY 10017.

American Institute of Nutrition. Membership: 2,250. Annual meeting: Las Vegas, NV, May 1–6, 1988. Executive officer, R.G Allison, Ph.D. Headquarters: 9650 Rockville Pike, Bethesda, MD 20814.

American Legion, The. Membership: 2,700,000. National Executive Committee is chief administrative body between national conventions. National convention: Louisville, KY, Sept. 2–8, 1988. Headquarters: 700 N. Pennsylvania St., Indianapolis, IN 46204.

American Library Association. Membership: 42,000. Meetings, 1988: Midwinter—San Antonio, TX, Jan. 9–14; Annual conference—New Orleans, LA, July 9–14. Executive director, Thomas J. Galvin. Headquarters: 50 E. Huron, Chicago, IL 60611.

American Lung Association. Membership: 138 affiliated groups. Annual meeting: Las Vegas, NV, May 8–11, 1988. President, Lois T. Ellison, M.D. Headquarters: 1740 Broadway, New York, NY 10019–4374.

American Management Association. Membership: 80,000. Chairman of the board, James R. Martin; president, Thomas R. Horton. Headquarters: 135 W. 50th St., New York, NY 10020.

American Mathematical Society. Membership: 21,516. President, George D. Mostow; Headquarters: P.O. Box 6248, Providence, RI 02940.

American Medical Association. Membership: 279,614. President, John J. Coury, Jr., M.D.; president-elect, William S. Hotchkiss, M.D. Headquarters: 535 N. Dearborn St., Chicago, IL 60610.

American Meteorological Society. Membership: 10,000 including 128 corporate members. Executive director, Dr. Kenneth C. Spengler. Headquarters: 45 Beacon St., Boston, MA 02108.

American Newspaper Publishers Association. Membership: 1,390. Annual convention: Honolulu, HI, April 25–27, 1988. Chairman and president, George W. Wilson, *Concord* (N.H.) *Monitor*. Executive offices: The Newspaper Center, 11600 Sunrise Valley Dr., Reston, VA 22091. Mailing Address: The Newspaper Center, Box 17407, Dulles International Airport, Washington, DC 20041.

American Nurses' Association. Membership: 188,000 in 53 state and territorial associations. National convention: Louisville, KY, June 11–15, 1988. President, Margretta M. Styles. Headquarters: 2420 Pershing Road, Kansas City, MO 64108.

American Physical Society. Membership: 38,000 American and foreign. President, Val L. Fitch; executive secretary, W.W. Havens, Jr. Headquarters: 335 E. 45th St., New York, NY 10017.

American Psychiatric Association. Membership: 33,293. Annual meeting: Montreal, May 7–13, 1988. President, Robert O. Pasnau, M.D. Headquarters: 1400 K Street NW, Washington, DC 20005.

American Psychological Association. Membership: 65,144. Annual meeting: Atlanta, GA, Aug. 12–16, 1988. President, Bonnie R. Strickland. Headquarters: 1200 17th Street NW, Washington, DC 20036.

American Red Cross. Chapters: 2,889. National convention: Cincinnati, OH, May 22–25, 1988. Chairman, George F. Moody; president, Richard F. Schubert. Headquarters: 17th and D Sts. NW, Washington, DC 20006.

American Society of Civil Engineers. Membership: 100,000. Executive director, Edward O. Pfrang. Headquarters: 345 E. 47th St., New York, NY 10017–2398

American Society of Composers, Authors, and Publishers. Membership: 25,934 writer members; 1,645 associate members; 9,892 publisher members. President, Morton Gould; secretary, Marilyn Bergman. Headquarters: One Lincoln Plaza, New York, NY 10023.

American Society of Mechanical Engineers. Membership: 117,000. President, L.S. Fletcher. Headquarters: 345 E. 47th St., New York, NY 10017.

American Sociological Association. Membership: 13,000. Meeting: Atlanta, GA, Aug. 24–28, 1988. President, Herbert Gans. Executive office: 1722 N St. NW, Washington, DC 20036.

American Statistical Association. Membership: 15,500. President, Robert V. Hogg. Meeting: New Orleans, LA, Aug. 22–25, 1988. Headquarters: 1429 Duke Street, Alexandria, VA 22314.

American Youth Hostels, Inc. Membership: 100,000; 39 councils in the United States. Executive director, Robert Johnson. Headquarters: P.O. Box 37613, Washington, DC 20013–7613.

Archaeological Institute of America. Membership: 8,000. President, James R. Wiseman; director, Joan C. Bowlen. Annual meeting: Baltimore, MD, Jan. 5–9, 1989. Headquarters: P.O. Box 1901, Kenmore Station, Boston, MA 02215.

Arthritis Foundation. Membership: 72 chapters. Annual scientific meeting: Houston, TX, May 23–28, 1988. Chairman, Betsey B. Case; president, Clifford M. Clarke. Headquarters: 1314 Spring St. NW, Atlanta, GA 30309.

Association of American Publishers. Membership: approximately 350. Annual meeting: Palm Beach, FL, March 20–23, 1988. Chairman of the board, Jeremiah Kaplan; president, Ambassador Veliotes; vice-president, Thomas McKee. Addresses: 220 E. 23rd St., New York, NY 10010; and 2005 Massachusetts Ave. NW, Washington, DC 20036.

Association of Junior Leagues, Inc. Membership: 269 member leagues in U.S., Canada, Mexico, and the United Kingdom. Annual conference: Chicago, IL, April 28–May 1, 1988. President, Virginia T. Austin. Headquarters: 825 Third Ave., New York, NY 10022.

Association of Operating Room Nurses, Inc. Membership: 37,100 with 349 local chapters. Convention: Dallas, TX, March 6–11, 1988. President: Alicia C. Arvidson; executive director, Clifford H. Jordan. Headquarters: 10170 E. Mississippi Ave., Denver, CO 80231.

Benevolent and Protective Order of Elks. Membership: 1,560,385 in 2,300 lodges. Convention: Las Vegas, NV, July 17–21, 1988. Grand exalted ruler, Frank O. Garland; grand secretary, S.F. Kocur. Headquarters: 2750 Lake View Ave., Chicago, IL 60614.

Bide-A-Wee Home Association, Inc. Executive director, Ursula Goetz. Headquarters: 424 W. 53rd St., New York, NY 10019.

Big Brothers/Big Sisters of America. Membership: 460+ local affiliated agencies. National conference: Milwaukee, WI, June 20–24, 1988. President, Joyce Black. Headquarters: 230 North 13th St., Philadelphia, PA 19107.

B'nai B'rith International. Membership: 500,000 in approximately 3,000 men's, women's, and youth lodges, chapters, and units. President, Seymour D. Reich; executive vice-president, Daniel Thursz. Headquarters: 1640 Rhode Island Ave. NW, Washington, DC 20036.

Boat Owners Association of the United States. Membership: 225,000. President, Richard Schwartz. Headquarters: 880 S. Pickett St., Alexandria, VA 22304.

Boys Clubs of America. Youth served: 1,285,000 in 1,100 affiliated Boys Clubs and Boys and Girls Clubs. National conference: Orlando, FL, May 6–10, 1988. Chairman, John Burns; national director, William Bricker. Headquarters: 771 First Ave., New York, NY 10017.

Boy Scouts of America. Membership: total youth members and leaders, 5,170,979 in 410 local councils. Biennial meeting: San Diego, CA, May 18–20, 1988. President, Charles M. Piggott; chief scout executive, Ben H. Love. National office: 1325 Walnut Hill Lane, Irving, TX 75038–3096.

Camp Fire, Inc. Membership: 500,000 boys and girls in more than 35,000 communities. President, Margaret Preska. Headquarters: 4601 Madison Ave., Kansas City, MO 64112.

Canadian Library Association. Membership: 3,500 personal, 800 institutional, 4,300 total. 1988 annual conference: Halifax, N.S. Executive director, Jane Cooney. Headquarters: 200 Elgin Street, #602, Ottawa, Ont. K2P 1L5.

Canadian Medical Association. Membership: 44,000. Annual meeting: Vancouver, B.C., Aug. 21–25, 1988. Secretary general, Leo Paul Landry, M.D. Address: 1867 Alta Vista Drive, Ottawa, Ont. K1G 3Y6.

Chamber of Commerce, U.S. Membership: approximately 4,200 associations and state and local chambers, approximately 180,000 business members. Annual meeting: Washington, DC, April 24–26, 1988. President, Richard L. Lesher; chairman, Oliver Delchamps. Headquarters: 1615 H Street NW, Washington, DC 20062.

Common Cause. Membership: 280,000. Chairman, Archibald Cox. Headquarters: 2030 M St. NW, Washington, DC 20036.

Consumers Union of United States, Inc. Executive director, Rhoda H. Karpatkin. Headquarters: 256 Washington St., Mount Vernon, NY 10553.

Council of Better Business Bureaus. Membership: 2,000. Headquarters: 1515 Wilson Blvd., Suite 300, Arlington, VA 22209.

Council of Foreign Relations, Inc. Membership: 2,427. Annual meeting: New York City, fall 1988. President, Peter Tarnoff. Headquarters: 58 E. 68th St., New York, NY 10021.

Daughters of the American Revolution (National Society). Membership: 212,000 in 3,150 chapters. Continental congress: Washington, DC, April 18–22, 1988. President general, Mrs. Raymond Franklin Fleck. Headquarters: 1776 D St. NW, Washington, DC 20006.

Esperanto League for North America, Inc. Membership: 750. President, Kew Thompson. Headquarters: P.O. Box 1129, El Cerrito, CA 94530.

Foreign Policy Association. President, John W. Kiermaier. Headquarters: 729 Seventh Ave., New York, NY 10019.

Freemasonry, Ancient Accepted Scottish Rite of (Northern Masonic Jurisdiction): Supreme Council, 33°. Membership: 456,580 in 111 valleys. Sovereign grand commander, Francis G. Paul. Headquarters: 33 Marrett Rd., Lexington, MA 02173.

Freemasonry, Ancient and Accepted Scottish Rite of (Southern Jurisdiction): Supreme Council, 33°. Membership: 625,000 in 221 affiliated groups. Sovereign grand commander, Fred Kleinknecht. Headquarters: 1733 16th Street NW, Washington, DC 20009.

Future Farmers of America. Membership: 430,375 in 50 state associations. National FFA convention: Kansas City, MO, Nov. 10–12, 1988. Executive secretary, Coleman Harris. Headquarters: Box 15160, Alexandria, VA 22309.

Gamblers Anonymous. Membership: 15,000. Headquarters: 3255 Wilshire Blvd., Los Angeles, CA 90010.

Garden Club of America, The. Membership: 15,000 in 187 clubs. Annual meeting: Detroit, MI, May 23–26, 1988. President, Mrs. Charles G. Ward, Jr. Headquarters: 598 Madison Ave., New York, NY 10022.

General Federation of Women's Clubs. Membership: 500,000 in 11,000 U.S. clubs and 10,000,000 worldwide. International president, Phyllis V. Roberts. Headquarters: 1734 N St. NW, Washington, DC 20036.

Geological Society of America. Membership: 16,000. President, Jack E. Oliver; executive director, F. Michael Wahl. Headquarters: 3300 Penrose Place, P.O. Box 9140, Boulder, CO 80301.

Girl Scouts of the U.S.A. Membership: 2,917,000. National president, Betty F. Pilsbury; national executive director, Frances R. Hesselbein. Headquarters: 830 Third Ave., New York, NY 10022.

Humane Society of the United States. Membership: approximately 500,000. Annual convention: Washington, DC, October 1988. President, John A. Hoyt. Headquarters: 2100 L St. NW, Washington, DC 20037.

Institute of Electrical and Electronics Engineers, Inc. Membership: 282,700. President, Russell C. Drew. Headquarters: 345 E. 47th St., New York, NY 10017.

Jewish War Veterans of the U.S.A. Membership: 100,000 in 450 units. Annual national convention: Las Vegas, NV, July 24–31, 1988. National commander, Edwin Goldwasser; executive director, Steve Shaw. Headquarters: 1811 R. St. NW, Washington, DC 20009.

Kiwanis International. Membership: 315,000 in 8,200 clubs in U.S. and abroad. President, Anthony J. Kaiser. Headquarters: 3636 Woodview Trace, Indianapolis, IN 46268.

Knights of Columbus. Membership: 1,456,484. Supreme knight, Virgil C. Dechant. Headquarters: Columbus Plaza, New Haven, CT 06507.

Knights of Pythias, Supreme Lodge International. Membership: 98,000 in 1,029 subordinate lodges. Supreme chancellor of Montreal, Que.: Joseph Kramer. Office: 2785 East Desert Inn Rd., #150, Las Vegas, NV 89121.

League of Women Voters of the U.S. Membership: 105,000. President, Nancy M. Neuman. Headquarters: 1730 M Street NW, Washington, DC 20036.

Lions Clubs International. Membership: 1,360,000 in 38,000 clubs in 161 countries and areas. Annual convention: Denver, CO, June 29–July 2, 1988. President, Sten A. Akestam. Headquarters: 300 22nd St., Oak Brook, IL 60570.

March of Dimes Birth Defects Foundation. Membership: 190 chapters. President, Charles L. Massey. Headquarters: 1275 Mamaroneck Ave., White Plains, NY 10605.

Mental Health Association. Membership: 650 state and local organizations. Headquarters: 1021 Prince St., Alexandria, VA 22314–2971.

Modern Language Association of America. Membership: 27,000. Annual convention: New Orleans, LA, Dec. 27–30, 1988. President, Winfred P. Lehmann. Headquarters: 10 Astor Place, New York, NY 10003.

National Academy of Sciences. Membership: 1,600. Annual meeting: Washington, DC, April 1988. President, Frank Press. Headquarters: 2101 Constitution Ave. NW, Washington, DC 20418.

National Association for the Advancement of Colored People. Membership: 450,000 in 1,700 branches and 500 youth and college chapters. National convention: Washington, DC, July 17–21, 1988. President, Enolia McMillan; board chairman, William S. Gibson; executive director, Benjamin Hooks. Headquarters: 4805 Mt. Hope Dr., Baltimore, MD 21215–3297.

National Association of Manufacturers. Membership: 13,000. President, Alexander B. Trowbridge. Headquarters: 1331 Pennsylvania Ave. NW, Suite 1500 North Lobby, Washington, DC 20004–1703.

National Audubon Society. Membership: 550,000 in 500 local groups. President, Peter A.A. Berle. Headquarters: 950 Third Ave., New York, NY 10022.

National Committee for Prevention of Child Abuse. Executive director, Anne H. Cohn. Headquarters: 332 S. Michigan Ave., Suite 950, Chicago, IL 60604.

National Conference of Christians and Jews, Inc. Membership: 75 regional offices. President, Jacqueline G. Wexler. Headquarters: 71 Fifth Ave., Suite 1100, New York, NY 10003.

National Council on the Aging, Inc. Membership: 6,000. President, Jack Ossofsky. Annual conference: Washington, DC, April 14–17, 1988. Headquarters: 600 Maryland Ave. SW, West Wing 100, Washington, DC 20024.

National Council of the Churches of Christ in the U.S.A. Membership: 32 Protestant, Anglican, and Orthodox denominations. General secretary, Arie R. Brouwer. Headquarters: 75 Riverside Dr., New York, NY 10115.

National Easter Seal Society. Annual conference: Dallas, TX, Nov. 14–19, 1988. President, Mrs. J. Thomas Kershaw, Jr. Headquarters: 2023 West Odgen Ave., Chicago, IL 60612.

National Education Association of the U.S. Membership: 1,800,000. Annual convention: New Orleans, LA, July 2–7, 1988. President, Mary Hatwood Futrell. Headquarters: 1201 16th St. NW, Washington, DC 20036.

National Federation of Business and Professional Women's Clubs, Inc (BPW/USA). Membership: 130,000 in 3,400 clubs. President, Beth Wray. Headquarters: 2012 Massachusetts Ave. NW, Washington, DC 20036.

National Federation of Independent Business, Inc. Membership: 560,000. President, John Sloan, Jr. Administrative office: 150 W. 20th Ave., San Mateo, CA 94403. Legislative and research office: 600 Maryland Ave. SW, Suite 700, Washington, DC 20024.

National Federation of Music Clubs. Membership: 500,000 in 4,500 clubs and 12 national affiliates. President, Mrs. Glenn L. Brown. Headquarters: 1336 North Delaware St., Indianapolis, IN 46202.

National Fire Protection Association. Membership: 39,000. Annual meeting: Los Angeles, CA, May 16–19, 1988; fall meeting; Nashville, TN, Nov. 14–17, 1988. President, Robert W. Grant. Headquarters: Batterymarch Park, Quincy, MA 02269.

National Organization for Women. Membership: 150,000 in 800 local groups. President, Molly Yard. Headquarters: 1401 New York Ave. NW, Suite 800, Washington, DC 20005.

National PTA (National Parent-Teacher Association). Membership: 6,000,000 in 25,000 local units. National convention: Salt Lake City, UT, June 18–21, 1988. President, Manya Ungar. Headquarters: 700 N. Rush St., Chicago, IL 60611.

National Safety Council. Membership: 12,500. President, T.C. Gilchrest. Headquarters: 444 N. Michigan Ave., Chicago, IL 60611.

National Urban League, Inc. President, John E. Jacob. Annual conference: Detroit, MI, July 31–Aug. 3, 1988. Headquarters: 500 East 62nd St., New York, NY 10021.

National Woman's Christian Temperance Union. Membership: approximately 200,000 in 5,000 local unions. National convention: Anaheim, CA, August 1988. President, Mrs. Kermit S. Edgar. Headquarters: 1730 Chicago Ave., Evanston, IL 60201.

Parents Without Partners, Inc. International membership: 187,000. International convention: Atlanta, GA, July 3–9, 1988. Executive director, Maurine McKinley. International office: 8807 Colesville Rd., Silver Spring, MD 20910.

Phi Beta Kappa. Membership: 440,000. Secretary, Kenneth M. Greene. Headquarters: 1811 Q. St. NW, Washington, DC 20009.

Photographic Society of America. Membership: 14,000. President, Paul Luebke. Headquarters: 2005 Walnut St., Philadelphia, PA 19103.

Planned Parenthood Federation of America, Inc. (Planned Parenthood-World Population). Membership: 187 U.S. affiliates. President, Faye Wattleton; chairperson of the Federation, Anne Saunier. Headquarters: 810 Seventh Ave., New York, NY 10019.

Rotary International. Membership: 1,029,583 in 22,784 clubs functioning in 161 countries and geographical regions. International convention: Philadelphia, PA, May 22–25, 1988. General secretary, Philip H. Lindsey. Headquarters: 1600 Ridge Ave., Evanston, IL 60201.

Salvation Army, The. Membership: 432,893. National commander, Andrew S. Miller. National headquarters: 799 Bloomfield Ave., Verona, NJ 07044.

Special Libraries Association. Membership: 12,500. Annual conference: Denver, CO, June 11–16, 1988. President, H. Robert Malinowsky. Headquarters: 1700 18th St. NW, Washington, DC 20009.

United Dairy Industry Association Annual convention: Minneapolis, MN, Sept. 21–22, 1988. Chief executive officer, Edward A. Peterson. Headquarters: Dairy Center, 6300 N. River Rd., Rosemont, IL 60016.

United States Jaycees. Membership: 250,000 in 6,500 affiliated chapters. Annual meeting: Richmond, VA, June 15–18, 1988. President, Mike Alcorn. Headquarters: P.O. Box 7, Tulsa, OK 74121–0007.

U.S. Metric Association. Membership: 2,500. Executive director, Valeris Antoine. Headquarters: 10245 Andasol Ave., Northridge, CA 91325.

United Way of America. Service organization for more than 2,300 autonomous local United Ways. 1988 volunteer leaders conference: San Francisco, CA, March 12–14, 1988. Chairman of the board of governors, James D. Robinson III; chairman and chief executive officer, American Express Co. Address: 701 N. Fairfax St., Alexandria, VA 22314.

Veterans of Foreign Wars of the United States. Membership: VFW and Auxiliary 2,800,000. Commander-in-chief, Earl L. Stock. Headquarters: VFW Building, Broadway at 34th St., Kansas City, MO 64111.

World Council of Churches (U.S. Conference). Membership: 31 churches or denominations in U.S. Moderator, Dr. Sylvia Talbot. Headquarters: 150 route de Ferney, 1211 Geneva 20, Switzerland. New York office: 475 Riverside Dr., Room 1062, New York, NY 10115.

YMCA of the USA. Membership: 13,000,000 in some 2,000 associations. Board chairman, Sam Evans. Headquarters: 101 North Wacker Dr., Chicago, IL 60606.

YWCA of the USA. Members and participants: approximately 2,000,000. President, Glendora M. Putnam. Headquarters: 726 Broadway, New York, NY 10003.

Zionist Organization of America. Membership: 130,000 in 600 districts. President, Milton S. Shapiro; executive vice-president, Paul Flacks. National convention: Jerusalem, Israel, July 1988. Headquarters: ZOA House, 4 East 34th St., New York, NY 10016.

Contributors

ADRIAN, CHARLES R., Professor of Political Science, University of California at Riverside; Author, *A History of American City Government: The Emergence of the Metropolis, 1920–1945:* CALIFORNIA; LOS ANGELES
ALPTEKIN, OMER, Fordham University: Sudan
ALTER, STEWART, Editor, *Adweek:* ADVERTISING
AMBRE, AGO, Economist, Office of Economic Affairs, U.S. Department of Commerce: INDUSTRIAL PRODUCTION
ANASTAPLO, GEORGE, Professor of Law, Loyola University of Chicago; Author, *Commentary on the U.S. Constitution, The Constitutionalist: Notes on the First Amendment:* THE BICENTENNIAL OF THE U.S. CONSTITUTION
ARNOLD, ANTHONY, Visiting Scholar, Hoover Institution, Stanford, CA; Author, *Afghanistan: The Soviet Invasion in Perspective, Afghanistan's Two-Party Communism: Parrham and Khalq:* AFGHANISTAN
ATTNER, PAUL, National Correspondent, *The Sporting News:* BIOGRAPHY—*Michael Jordan;* SPORTS—*Basketball*
AXELGARD, FREDERICK W., Fellow in Middle East Studies, Center for Strategic and International Studies; Author, *Iraq, the Gulf War, and the Struggle for Legitimacy;* Editor, *Iraq in Transition:* IRAQ
BARMASH, ISADORE, Business-Financial Writer, *The New York Times;* Author, *Always Live Better Than Your Clients, More Than They Bargained For, The Chief Executives:* RETAILING
BATRA, PREM P., Professor of Biochemistry, Wright State University: BIOCHEMISTRY
BECK, KAY, School of Urban Life, Georgia State University: GEORGIA
BEHLER, DEBORAH A., Associate Editor, *Animal Kingdom* magazine: ZOOS AND ZOOLOGY; ZOOS AND ZOOLOGY—*The California Condor*
BERLIN, MICHAEL J., United Nations Correspondent, *The Washington Post;* LAW—*International;* UNITED NATIONS
BEST, JOHN, Chief, *Canada World News:* NEW BRUNSWICK; PRINCE EDWARD ISLAND; QUEBEC
BITTON-JACKSON, LIVIA E., Professor of Judaic and Hebraic Studies, Herbert H. Lehman College of City University of New York; Author, *Elli: Coming of Age in the Holocaust, Madonna or Courtesan: The Jewish Woman in Christian Literature:* RELIGION—*Judaism*
BOND, DONOVAN H., Professor Emeritus of Journalism, West Virginia University: WEST VIRGINIA
BOULAY, HARVEY, Systems Manager, Rogerson House; Author, *The Twilight Cities:* MASSACHUSETTS
BOWER, BRUCE, Behavioral Sciences Editor, *Science News:* ANTHROPOLOGY; ARCHAEOLOGY
BRAMMER, DANA B., Associate Director, Public Policy Center, University of Mississippi: MISSISSIPPI
BRANDHORST, L. CARL, and JoANN C., Western Oregon State College: OREGON
BROZE, VINCENT, *Sail* magazine; Author, *The Sailor's Edge;* Coauthor, *Newport to Perth* and *The Challenge:* AMERICA'S CUP 1987
BURANELLI, VINCENT, Free-lance Writer and Editor; Author, *The Trial of Peter Zenger, Louis XIV;* Coauthor, *Spy/Counterspy: An Encyclopedia of Espionage:* ESPIONAGE; ESPIONAGE—*Embassy Security*
BURKS, ARDATH W., Professor Emeritus Asian Studies, Rutgers University; Author, *Japan: A Postindustrial Power:* BIOGRAPHY—*Noburu Takeshita;* JAPAN
BUSH, GRAHAM W. A., Associate Professor of Political Studies, University of Auckland; Author, *Local Government & Politics in New Zealand;* Editor, *New Zealand—A Nation Divided?*: NEW ZEALAND
BUTTRY, STEPHEN, Assistant National/Mid-America Editor, *The Kansas City Times:* MISSOURI
CASPER, GRETCHEN, Department of Political Science, Texas A&M: PHILIPPINES
CASPER, LEONARD, Professor of English, Boston College; Past Recipient of Fulbright grants to lecture in the Philippines: PHILIPPINES
CASTAGNO, ANTHONY J., Free-lance Writer, Energy Specialist: ENERGY
CHALMERS, JOHN W., Historical Society of Alberta; Editor, *Alberta Diamond Jubilee* Anthology: ALBERTA
CHRISTENSEN, WILLIAM E., Professor of History, Midland Lutheran College; Author, *In Such Harmony: A History of the Federated Church of Columbus, Nebraska:* NEBRASKA

CLARKE, JAMES W., Professor of Political Science, University of Arizona: ARIZONA

COLE, JOHN N., Cofounder, *Maine Times;* Author, *In Maine, Striper, Salmon, House Building:* MAINE

COLLINS, BUD, Sports Columnist, *The Boston Globe:* SPORTS —*Tennis*

COLTON, KENT W., Executive Vice President and Chief Executive Officer, National Association of Home Builders, Washington, DC: HOUSING

COLTON, TIMOTHY J., Director, Centre for Russian and East European Studies, and Professor of Political Science, University of Toronto: USSR

COMMANDAY, ROBERT, Music Critic, *San Francisco Chronicle:* MUSIC—*Classical;* OBITUARIES—*Andrés Segovia*

CONRADT, DAVID P., Professor of Political Science, University of Florida; Author, *The German Polity, Comparative Politics, The German Voter 1949–1987:* GERMANY; GERMANY—*Berlin's 750th Anniversary*

COOPER, MARY H., Staff Writer, *Editorial Research Reports:* INSURANCE, LIABILITY; MEDICINE AND HEALTH—*Catastrophic Health Insurance*

CORLEW, ROBERT E., Dean, School of Liberal Arts, Middle Tennessee State University: TENNESSEE

CORNWELL, ELMER E., JR., Professor of Political Science, Brown University: RHODE ISLAND

COSSER, ANNE, Free-lance Writer: ICELAND

CUNNIFF, JOHN, Business News Analyst, The Associated Press; Author, *How to Stretch Your Dollar:* BANKING AND FINANCE—*The Home Equity Loan;* UNITED STATES—*The Economy*

CUNNINGHAM, PEGGY, *The Evening News,* Baltimore, MD: MARYLAND

CURRIER, CHET, Financial Writer, The Associated Press: Author, *The Investor's Encyclopedia, The 15-Minute Investor:* STOCKS AND BONDS

CURTIS, L. PERRY, JR., Professor of History, Brown University: IRELAND

DANIELS, ROBERT V., Professor of History, University of Vermont: VERMONT

DARBY, JOSEPH W., III, Reporter, *The Times-Picayune,* New Orleans: LOUISIANA

DAVIS, GRANT M., Distinguished Professor of Business Administration, University of Arkansas; Author, *Carrier Management, Physical Logistics Management, Motor Carrier Economics, Regulation Operation:* TRANSPORTATION

DeGREGORIO, GEORGE, Sports Department, *The New York Times;* Author, *Joe DiMaggio, An Informal Biography:* SPORTS—*Boxing, Ice Skating, Skiing, Swimming, Track and Field*

DELZELL, CHARLES F., Professor of History, Vanderbilt University; Author, *Italy in the Twentieth Century, Mediterranean Fascism, Mussolini's Enemies:* BIOGRAPHY—*Giovanni Goria;* ITALY

DENNIS, LARRY, Free-lance Golf Writer: SPORTS—*Golf*

DICKSON, LYNDA F., Department of Sociology, University of Colorado at Colorado Springs: ETHNIC GROUPS

DIETERICH, H. R., Professor of History, University of Wyoming: WYOMING

DRIGGS, DON W., Chairman, Department of Political Science, University of Nevada-Reno; Coauthor, *The Nevada Constitution: Its Origin and Growth:* NEVADA

DUFF, ERNEST A., Professor of Politics, Randolph-Macon Woman's College; Author, *Agrarian Reform in Colombia, Violence and Repression in Latin America, Leader and Party in Latin America:* COLOMBIA

DUIKER, WILLIAM J., Professor, Department of History, The Pennsylvania State University; Author, *The Communist Road to Power in Vietnam, Vietnam Since the Fall of Saigon, China and Vietnam: The Roots of Conflict:* ASIA

DUNN, CHRISTOPHER, Formerly, Department of Political Science, University of Saskatchewan: SASKATCHEWAN

EL-KHAZEN, FARID, Professor, The American University of Beirut: LEBANON

ELKINS, ANN M., Fashion Director, *Good Housekeeping Magazine:* FASHION; FASHION—*The Latest for Children*

ELVING, PHYLLIS, Free-lance Travel Writer: TRAVEL

ENSTAD, ROBERT H., Writer, *Chicago Tribune:* CHICAGO; ILLINOIS

ENTELIS, JOHN P., Professor, Department of Political Science, Fordham University: MOROCCO; SUDAN; TUNISIA

EWEGEN, ROBERT D., Editorial Writer, *The Denver Post:* COLORADO

FAGEN, MORTON D., AT&T Bell Laboratories (retired); Editor, *A History of Engineering and Science in the Bell System,* Vols. I and II: COMMUNICATION TECHNOLOGY

FISHER, JIM, Editorial Writer, *Lewiston Morning Tribune:* IDAHO

FRANCIS, DAVID R., Economic Columnist, *The Christian Science Monitor:* BIOGRAPHY—*Alan Greenspan;* INTERNATIONAL TRADE AND FINANCE

FRIIS, ERIK J., Editor and Publisher, *The Scandinavian-American Bulletin:* DENMARK; FINLAND; SWEDEN

GAILEY, HARRY A., Professor of History, San Jose University: CHAD; MOZAMBIQUE; NIGERIA; ZAIRE

GEIS, GILBERT, Professor, Program in Social Ecology, University of California, Irvine; Author, *On White Collar Crime:* CRIME

GIBSON, ROBERT C., Regional Editor, *The Billings Gazette:* MONTANA

GOODMAN, DONALD, Associate Professor of Sociology, John Jay College of Criminal Justice, City University of New York: PRISONS

GORDON, MAYNARD M., Editor, *Motor News Analysis;* Author, *The Iacocca Management Technique:* AUTOMOBILES; OBITUARIES—*Henry Ford II*

GRAYSON, GEORGE W., John Marshall Professor of Government and Citizenship, College of William and Mary; Author, *The Politics of Mexican Oil, The United States and Mexico: Patterns of Influence:* BRAZIL; PORTUGAL; SPAIN

GREEN, MAUREEN, Author-Journalist, London: GREAT BRITAIN —*The Arts;* LITERATURE—*English;* LONDON

GROTH, ALEXANDER J., Professor of Political Science, University of California, Davis; Author, *People's Poland;* Coauthor, *Contemporary Politics: Europe, Comparative Resource Allocation, Public Policy Across Nations:* POLAND

HACKER, JEFFREY H., Free-lance Writer and Editor: *The Convenience Boom;* SPORTS—Overview; Football

HADWIGER, DON F., Professor of Political Science, Iowa State University; Coeditor, *Global Food Interdependence:* AGRICULTURE; FOOD

HAND, SAMUEL B., Professor of History, University of Vermont: VERMONT

HART, MARION, *Civil Engineering Magazine:* CIVIL ENGINEERING —*Bridge Safety*

HARVEY, ROSS M., Assistant Deputy Minister of Culture and Communications, Government of the Northwest Territories: NORTHWEST TERRITORIES

HELMREICH, ERNST C., Professor Emeritus of History, Bowdoin College; Author, *The German Churches under Hitler: Background, Struggle, and Epilogue:* AUSTRIA

HELMREICH, J. E., Professor of History, Allegheny College; Author, *Belgium and Europe: A Study in Small Power Diplomacy, Gathering Rare Ores: The Diplomacy of Uranium Acquisition, 1943–54:* BELGIUM

HELMREICH, PAUL C., Professor of History, Wheaton College; Author, *From Paris to Sèvres: The Partition of the Ottoman Empire at the Peace Conference of 1919–1920:* SWITZERLAND

HINTON, HAROLD C., Professor of Political Science and International Affairs, The George Washington University; Author, *Korea under New Leadership: The Fifth Republic, Communist China in World Politics, The China Sea: The American Stake in Its Future:* KOREA

HOOVER, HERBERT T., Professor of History, University of South Dakota; Author, *To Be an Indian, The Chitimacha People, The Sioux, The Practice of Oral History:* SOUTH DAKOTA

HOPKO, THE REV. THOMAS, Assistant Professor, St. Vladimir's Orthodox Theological Seminary: RELIGION—*Orthodox Eastern*

HOYT, CHARLES K., Senior Editor, *Architectural Record;* Author, *More Places for People, Building for Commerce and Industry:* ARCHITECTURE

HUFFMAN, GEORGE J., Assistant Professor, Department of Meteorology, University of Maryland: METEOROLOGY

HULBERT, DAN, *Atlanta Journal & Constitution:* TELEVISION AND RADIO; THEATER

HUTH, JOHN F., JR., Reporter (retired), *The Plain Dealer,* Cleveland: OHIO

JEWELL, MALCOLM E., Professor of Political Science, University of Kentucky; Coauthor, *American State Political Parties and Elections, Kentucky Politics:* KENTUCKY

JOHNSTON, ROBERT L., Editor/Associate Publisher, *The Chicago Catholic:* RELIGION—*Roman Catholicism*

JONES, H. G., Curator, North Carolina Collection, University of North Carolina at Chapel Hill; Author, *North Carolina Illustrated, 1524–1984:* NORTH CAROLINA

JUDD, DENNIS R., Professor, Department of Political Science, University of Missouri at St. Louis; Author, *The Politics of American Cities: Private Power and Public Policy;* Coauthor, *The Politics of Urban Planning: The East St. Louis Experience, Restructuring the City: The Political Economy of Urban Redevelopment:* CITIES AND URBAN AFFAIRS

KARNES, THOMAS L., Professor of History Emeritus, Arizona State University; Author, *Latin American Policy of the United States, Failure of Union: Central America 1824–1960:* BIOGRAPHY—*Oscar Arías Sanchez;* CENTRAL AMERICA

KAUFMAN, GEORGE G., Professor of Finance and Economics, School of Business Administration, Loyola University of Chicago; Author, *The U.S. Financial System: Money, Markets, and Institutions;* Coeditor, *Deregulating Financial Services: Public Policy in Flux:* BANKING AND FINANCE

KIMBALL, LORENZO K., Professor of Political Science, University of Utah: UTAH

KIMBELL, CHARLES L., Senior Foreign Mineral Specialist, U.S. Bureau of Mines: STATISTICAL AND TABULAR DATA—Mineral and Metal Production

KING, PETER J., Professor of History, Carleton University, Ottawa; Author, *Utilitarian Jurisprudence in America:* ONTARIO; OTTAWA

KINNEAR, MICHAEL, Professor of History, University of Manitoba; Author, *The Fall of Lloyd George, The British Voter:* MANITOBA

KISSELGOFF, ANNA, Chief Dance Critic, *The New York Times:* DANCE; OBITUARIES—*Fred Astaire*

KRAUSE, AXEL, Corporate Editor, *International Herald Tribune,* Paris: FRANCE

KRONISH, SYD, Stamp Editor, The Associated Press: STAMPS AND STAMP COLLECTING

KRZYS, RICHARD, Director, International Library Information Center; Professor, University of Pittsburgh; Author, *World Librarianship, A History of Education for Librarianship in Colombia:* LIBRARIES

LAI, DAVID CHUENYAN, Associate Professor of Geography, University of Victoria, British Columbia: HONG KONG

LAWRENCE, ROBERT M., Professor of Political Science, Colorado State University; Author, *Strategic Defense Initiative: Bibliography and Research Guide:* ARMS CONTROL; MILITARY AFFAIRS; MILITARY AFFAIRS—*Today's Marine Corps;* OBITUARIES—*Maxwell Taylor*

LEE, STEWART M., Chairman, Department of Economics and Business Administration, Geneva College; Author, *Personal Finance for Consumers:* BUSINESS AND CORPORATE AFFAIRS; CONSUMER AFFAIRS

LEEPSON, MARC, Contributing Editor, *American Politics Magazine:* DRUGS AND ALCOHOL; SOCIAL WELFARE

LEVINE, LOUIS, Professor, Department of Biology, City College of New York; Author, *Biology of the Gene, Biology for a Modern Society:* BIOTECHNOLOGY; GENETICS; MICROBIOLOGY

LEVITT, MORRIS J., Professor, Department of Political Science, Howard University; Coauthor, *Of, By, and For the People: State and Local Government and Politics:* WASHINGTON, DC

LEWIS, JEROME R., Director for Public Administration, College of Urban Affairs and Public Policy, University of Delaware: DELAWARE

LOBRON, BARBARA L., Writer, Editor, Photographer: PHOTOGRAPHY

LOESCHER, GIL, Professor of International Relations, University of Notre Dame; Author, *Calculated Kindness: Refugees and America's Half-Open Door, The Global Refugee Problem: U.S. and World Response:* REFUGEES AND IMMIGRATION

MABRY, DONALD J., Professor of History, Mississippi State University; Author, *Mexico's Acción Nacional, The Mexican University and the State;* Coauthor, *Neighbors—Mexico and the United States:* MEXICO

MADISON, CHRISTOPHER, Staff Correspondent, *National Journal:* UNITED STATES—*Foreign Affairs*

MAMMANA, DENNIS L., Free-lance Science Writer/Photographer: MEDICINE AND HEALTH—*Smoking in Public Places*

MARCOPOULOS, GEORGE J., Associate Professor and Deputy Chair, Department of History, Tufts University: CYPRUS; GREECE

MATHESON, JIM, Sportswriter, *Edmonton Journal:* SPORTS—*Ice Hockey*

MATTHEWS, WILLIAM H., III, Professor of Geology, Lamar University; Author, *Fossils: An Introduction to Prehistoric Life, Exploring the World of Fossils:* GEOLOGY

MAYER, BARBARA, Home Furnishings Writer, The Associated Press; Author, *Contemporary American Craft Art: A Collectors' Guide:* INTERIOR DESIGN

McCORQUODALE, SUSAN, Professor of Political Science, Memorial University of Newfoundland: NEWFOUNDLAND

McFADDEN, ROBERT D., Reporter, *The New York Times;* Coauthor, *No Hiding Place;* Recipient, New York Press Club's Byline Award: NEW YORK CITY

McGILL, DAVID A., Professor of Marine Science, U.S. Coast Guard Academy: OCEANOGRAPHY

MELIKOV, GREG, State News Desk, *The Miami Herald:* FLORIDA

MICHAELIS, PATRICIA A., Curator of Manuscripts, Kansas State Historical Society: KANSAS

MICHIE, ARUNA NAYYAR, Associate Professor of Political Science and Director of South Asia Center, Kansas State University: BANGLADESH

MILWARD, JOHN, Free-lance Writer and Critic: MUSIC—*Popular;* RECORDINGS

MITCHELL, GARY, Professor of Physics, North Carolina State University: PHYSICS; PHYSICS—*High-Temperature Superconductors*

MORTIMER, ROBERT A., Professor, Department of Political Science, Haverford College; Author, *The Third World Coalition in International Politics:* ALGERIA

MORTON, DESMOND, Professor of History and Principal, Erindale College, University of Toronto; Author, *A Short History of Canada, Bloody Victory: Canadians and the D-Day Campaign, Working People: An Illustrated History of the Canadian Labour Movement, A Military History of Canada:* CANADA; CANADA—*U.S. Relations*

MULLINER, K., Assistant to Director of Libraries, Ohio University; Coeditor, *Malaysia Studies: Archaeology, Geography, and Bibliography, Southeast Asia: An Emerging Center of World Influence?:* MALAYSIA

MURPHY, ROBERT F., Reporter, *The Hartford Courant:* CONNECTICUT

NAFTALIN, ARTHUR, Professor Emeritus of Public Affairs, University of Minnesota: MINNESOTA

NEUMANN, JIM, *The Forum,* Fargo, ND: NORTH DAKOTA

NEWLAND, ED, Assistant State Editor, *Richmond Times-Dispatch:* VIRGINIA

NORBOM, ELLEN, Free-lance Journalist: NORWAY

OCHSENWALD, WILLIAM, Professor of History, Virginia Polytechnic Institute; Author, *The Hijaz Railroad, Religion, Society, and the State in Arabia:* SAUDI ARABIA

O'CONNOR, ROBERT E., Associate Professor of Political Science, The Pennsylvania State University; Author, *Politics and Structure: Essentials of American National Government:* PENNSYLVANIA; PHILADELPHIA

OLSEN, MICHAEL L., Professor, New Mexico Highlands University: NEW MEXICO

O'MEARA, PATRICK, Director, African Studies Program, Indiana University; Coeditor, *Africa, International Politics in Southern Africa, Southern Africa, The Continuing Crisis:* AFRICA; KENYA; SOUTH AFRICA; TANZANIA; UGANDA; ZIMBABWE

OTT, ATTIAT F., Department of Economics, Clark University; Editor, *Personal Income Taxation, Reforming the Federal Tax Structure;* Member of Advisory Board, National Committee on Tax Policy: TAXATION

PALMER, NORMAN D., Professor Emeritus of Political Science and South Asian Studies, University of Pennsylvania; Author, *The United States and India: The Dimensions of Influence, Elections and Political Development: The South Asian Experience:* INDIA; SRI LANKA

PARKER, FRANKLIN, Distinguished Visiting Professor, Center for Excellence in Education, Northern Arizona State University; Coauthor, *Education in the People's Republic of China, Past and Present: An Annotated Bibliography, U.S. Higher Education: A Guide to Information Sources:* EDUCATION; EDUCATION—*Textbooks Under Criticism*

PASCOE, ELAINE, Free-lance Writer and Editor; Author, *Racial Prejudice:* ART—*The New Museums;* ART—*Andy Warhol;* BIOGRAPHY—*James Earl Jones, Ted Koppel, Liza Minnelli, Oprah Winfrey, Molly Yard;* FAMILY; OBITUARIES—*Wladziu Valentino Liberace, Claire Booth Luce:* WOMEN

PEARSON, NEALE J., Professor of Political Science, Texas Tech University; Author, *Recent Spanish Foreign Policy Toward Central America:* CHILE; PERU; VENEZUELA

PENN, W. S., Michigan State University; Author, *The Absence of Angels:* LANGUAGE—*Preserving the English Language*

PERETZ, DON, Professor of Political Science, State University of New York at Binghamton; Author, *The West Bank—History, Politics, Society & Economy, Government and Politics of Israel, The Middle East Today:* EGYPT; ISRAEL

PERKINS, KENNETH J., Assistant Professor of History, University of South Carolina: LIBYA; RELIGION—*Islam*

PIOTROWSKI, WILLIAM L., National Aeronautics and Space Administration: SPACE EXPLORATION (article written independent of NASA)

PIPPIN, LARRY L., Professor of Political Science, University of the Pacific; Author, *The Remón Era:* ARGENTINA; PARAGUAY; URUGUAY

PLATT, HERMAN K., Professor of History, Saint Peter's College: NEW JERSEY

POOLE, PETER A., Author, *The Vietnamese in Thailand, Eight Presidents and Indochina:* CAMBODIA; LAOS; THAILAND; VIETNAM

RAGUSA, ISA, Research Art Historian, Department of Art and Archaeology, Princeton University: ART

RALOFF, JANET, Policy/Technology Editor, *Science News:* ENVIRONMENT

RAMIREZ, DEBORAH, Reporter, *San Juan Star:* PUERTO RICO

REBACK, MARILYN A., Assistant Editor, *The Numismatist:* COINS AND COIN COLLECTING

REUNING, WINIFRED, Writer, Polar Program, National Science Foundation: POLAR RESEARCH

RICHTER, LINDA K., Associate Professor, Department of Political Science, Kansas State University; Author, *Land Reform and Tourism Development: Policy-Making in the Philippines:* BURMA

RICHTER, WILLIAM L., Professor and Head, Department of Political Science, Kansas State University: PAKISTAN

RIGGAN, WILLIAM, Associate Editor, *World Literature Today,* University of Oklahoma; Author, *Picaros, Madmen, Naïfs, and Clowns, Comparative Literature and Literary Theory:* LITERATURE—*World*

ROBINSON, LEIF J., Editor, *Sky & Telescope:* ASTRONOMY

ROSS, RUSSELL M., Professor of Political Science, University of Iowa; Author, *State and Local Government and Administration, Iowa Government and Administration:* IOWA

ROWEN, HERBERT H., Professor, Rutgers University, New Brunswick; Author, *The Princes of Orange: The Stadholders in the Dutch Republic:* NETHERLANDS

RUBIN, JIM, Supreme Court Correspondent, The Associated Press: BIOGRAPHY—*Robert Bork;* LAW

RUFF, NORMAN J., Assistant Professor, University of Victoria, B.C.; Coauthor, *The Reins of Power: Governing British Columbia:* BRITISH COLUMBIA

RUTHERFORD, MALCOLM, Assistant Editor, *Financial Times;* Author, *Can We Save the Common Market?:* GREAT BRITAIN

SALSINI, PAUL, *The Milwaukee Journal:* WISCONSIN

SAVAGE, DAVID, Free-lance Writer: CANADA—*The Arts;* LITERATURE—*Canadian*

SAWATSKY, DON, Free-lance Writer/Broadcaster; Author, *Ghost Towns and Trails of the Yukon:* YUKON TERRITORY

SCHLOSSBERG, DAN, Author, *Baseball Stars 1987, Baseball-Laffs, The Baseball Book of Why:* SPORTS—*Baseball*

SCHROEDER, RICHARD, Washington Bureau Chief, *Visión;* Syndicated Writer, U.S. Newspapers: BOLIVIA; CARIBBEAN; CARIBBEAN—*Haiti;* ECUADOR; LATIN AMERICA; SURINAME

SCHWAB, PETER, Professor of Political Science, State University of New York at Purchase; Author, *Ethiopia: Politics, Economics, and Society:* ETHIOPIA

SEIDERS, DAVID F., Chief Economist and Senior Staff Vice President, National Association of Home Builders, Washington, DC: HOUSING

SELF, CHARLES C., School of Communication, University of Alabama: PUBLISHING

SENSER, ROBERT A., Free-lance Labor Writer, Washington, DC: INDUSTRIAL COMPETITIVENESS; LABOR

SETH, R. P., Professor of Economics, Mount Saint Vincent University, Halifax: CANADA—*The Economy;* NOVA SCOTIA

SEYBOLD, PAUL G., Professor, Department of Chemistry, Wright State University: CHEMISTRY

SHEPRO, CARL E., Professor, North Slope Higher Education Center, University of Alaska at Barrow: ALASKA

SHOGAN, ROBERT, National Political Correspondent, Washington Bureau, *Los Angeles Times;* Author, *A Question of Judgment, Promises to Keep:* THE IRAN-CONTRA AFFAIR; BIOGRAPHY—*Howard Baker, Frank Carlucci, Jim Wright;* UNITED STATES—*Domestic Affairs*

SIEGEL, STANLEY E., Professor of History, University of Houston; Author, *A Political History of the Texas Republic, 1836–1845, Houston: Portrait of the Supercity on Buffalo Bayou:* TEXAS

SIMON, JEFFREY D., The Rand Corporation, Santa Monica, CA: TERRORISM

SMALLOWITZ, HOWARD, Associate Editor, *Civil Engineering Magazine:* ENGINEERING, CIVIL

SMITH, REX, Albany Bureau Chief, *Newsday:* NEW YORK STATE

SNODSMITH, RALPH L., Ornamental Horticulturist; Author, *Ralph Snodsmith's Tips from the Garden Hotline, Garden Calendar and Record Keeper 1985–1988:* GARDENING AND HORTICULTURE

SPERA, DOMINIC, Professor of Music, Indiana University; Author, *The Prestige Series—16 Original Compositions for Jazz Band:* MUSIC—*Jazz*

STARR, JOHN BRYAN, Lecturer, Department of Political Science, Yale University; Executive Director, Yale-China Association; Author, *Continuing the Revolution: The Political Thought of Mao;* Editor, *The Future of U.S.-China Relations:* CHINA; CHINA—*Tibet;* TAIWAN

STERN, JEROME H., Associate Professor of English, Florida State University; Editor, *Studies in Popular Culture:* LITERATURE—*American*

STEWART, WILLIAM H., Associate Professor of Political Science, The University of Alabama; Author, *Concepts of Federalism, Government and Politics of Alabama:* ALABAMA

STOUDEMIRE, ROBERT H., Distinguished Professor Emeritus, University of South Carolina: SOUTH CAROLINA

SULLIVAN, BARBARA, Free-lance Writer, Seattle: WASHINGTON

SULLIVAN, FRANK J., Acting Director, National Institute of Mental Health: MEDICINE AND HEALTH—*Mental Health*

SUTTON, STAN, Sportswriter, *The Courier-Journal,* Louisville, KY: SPORTS—*Auto Racing, Horse Racing, The X Pan-Am Games*

SYLVESTER, LORNA LUTES, Associate Editor, *Indiana Magazine of History,* Indiana University: INDIANA; INDIANA—*Hoosier Hysteria*

TABORSKY, EDWARD, Professor of Government, University of Texas at Austin; Author, *Communism in Czechoslovakia, 1948–1960, Communist Penetration of the Third World:* CZECHOSLOVAKIA

TAYLOR, WILLIAM L., Professor of History, Plymouth State College: NEW HAMPSHIRE

TESAR, JENNY, Science and medicine writer; Author, *Parents as Teachers:* BABY CRAVING; BIOGRAPHY—*C. Everett Koop;* COMPUTERS; MEDICINE AND HEALTH

THEISEN, CHARLES W., Assistant News Editor, *The Detroit News:* MICHIGAN

TONGE, PETER, *The Christian Science Monitor:* ENVIRONMENT—*Waste Disposal*

TRIEGEL, LINDA, Free-lance Writer and Editor: BIOGRAPHY—*Paul Newman;* OBITUARIES—*Danny Kaye*

TURNER, ARTHUR CAMPBELL, Professor of Political Science, University of California, Riverside; Coauthor, *Power and Ideology in the Middle East:* BIOGRAPHY—*Hafiz al-Assad;* JORDAN; MIDDLE EAST; SYRIA

TURNER, CHARLES H., Free-lance Writer: BIOGRAPHY—*Daniel Inouye;* HAWAII

TURNER, DARRELL J., Associate Editor, Religious News Service: BIOGRAPHY—*Jerry Falwell;* RELIGION—*Overview, Far Eastern, Protestantism*

VAN RIPER, PAUL P., Professor Emeritus and Head, Department of Political Science, Texas A&M University: POSTAL SERVICE

VOLSKY, GEORGE, Center for Advanced International Studies, University of Miami: CUBA

WEIKER, WALTER F., Professor of Political Science, Rutgers University: TURKEY

WILLIAMS, C. FRED, Associate Vice Chancellor for Educational Programs, University of Arkansas at Little Rock; Author, *Arkansas: An Illustrated History of the Land of Opportunity, Arkansas: A Documentary History:* ARKANSAS

WILLIS, F. ROY, Professor of History, University of California, Davis; Author, *France, Germany and the New Europe, 1945–1968, Italy Chooses Europe, The French Paradox:* EUROPE

WILMS, DENISE MURCKO, Assistant Editor, Children's Books, *Booklist Magazine,* American Library Association: LITERATURE—*Children's*

WINCHESTER, N. BRIAN, Associate Director, African Studies Program, Indiana University: AFRICA: KENYA; TANZANIA; UGANDA

WINDER, DAVID, Assistant Managing Editor, Former, British Isles Correspondent, *The Christian Science Monitor:* GREAT BRITAIN—*Margaret Thatcher Wins a Third Term*

WOLF, WILLIAM, New York University; Author, *The Marx Brothers, The Landmark Films, The Cinema and Our Century:* HOLLYWOOD AT 100; MOTION PICTURES

WOOD, JOHN, Professor of Political Science, University of Oklahoma: OKLAHOMA

WRIGHT, ROBIN, Senior Associate, Carnegie Endowment for International Peace; Author, *Sacred Rage: The Wrath of Militant Islam:* IRAN

YOUNGER, R. M., Journalist and Author; Author, *Australia and the Australians, Australia! Australia! The Pioneer Years—March to Nationhood—Challenge and Achievement:* AUSTRALIA; FIJI

ZACEK, JOSEPH FREDERICK, Professor of History, State University of New York, Albany; Author, *Palacky: The Historian as Scholar and Nationalist:* ALBANIA; BULGARIA; HUNGARY; ROMANIA; YUGOSLAVIA

Index

Main article headings appear in this index as bold-faced capitals; subjects within articles appear as lower-case entries. Both the general references and the subentries should be consulted for maximum usefulness of this index. Illustrations are indexed herein. Cross references are to the entries in this index.

A

H

I

J

K

L

M

N

O

P

Q

R

S